Los Angeles & Southern California

Andrea Schulte-Peevers
Amy C Balfour, Andrew Bender

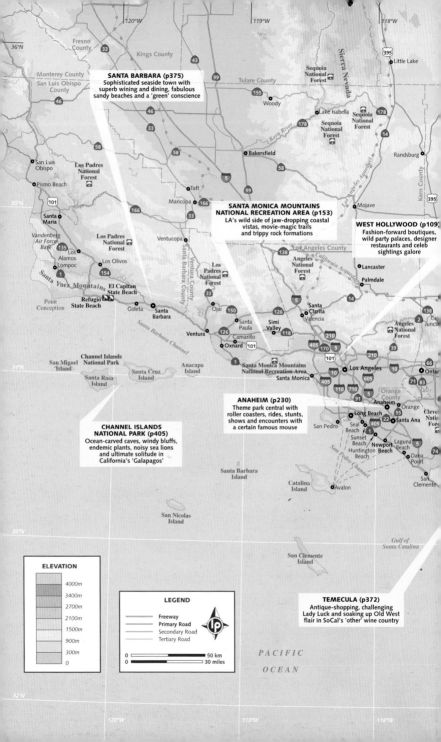

SANTA BARBARA (p375)
Sophisticated seaside town with superb wining and dining, fabulous sandy beaches and a 'green' conscience

SANTA MONICA MOUNTAINS NATIONAL RECREATION AREA (p153)
LA's wild side of jaw-dropping coastal vistas, movie-magic trails and trippy rock formations

WEST HOLLYWOOD (p109)
Fashion-forward boutiques, wild party palaces, designer restaurants and celeb sightings galore

CHANNEL ISLANDS NATIONAL PARK (p405)
Ocean-carved caves, windy bluffs, endemic plants, noisy sea lions and ultimate solitude in California's 'Galapagos'

ANAHEIM (p230)
Theme park central with roller coasters, rides, stunts, shows and encounters with a certain famous mouse

TEMECULA (p372)
Antique-shopping, challenging Lady Luck and soaking up Old West flair in SoCal's 'other' wine country

ELEVATION

	4000m
	3400m
	2700m
	2100m
	1500m
	900m
	300m
	0

LEGEND

Freeway
Primary Road
Secondary Road
Tertiary Road

0 ——— 50 km
0 ——— 30 miles

PACIFIC

OCEAN

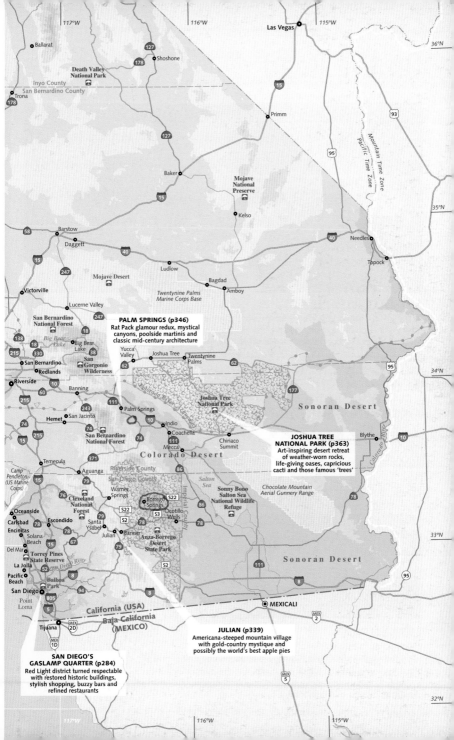

PALM SPRINGS (p346)
Rat Pack glamour redux, mystical canyons, poolside martinis and classic mid-century architecture

JOSHUA TREE NATIONAL PARK (p363)
Art-inspiring desert retreat of weather-worn rocks, life-giving oases, capricious cacti and those famous 'trees'

JULIAN (p339)
Americana-steeped mountain village with gold-country mystique and possibly the world's best apple pies

SAN DIEGO'S GASLAMP QUARTER (p284)
Red Light district turned respectable with restored historic buildings, stylish shopping, buzzy bars and refined restaurants

On the Road

ANDREA SCHULTE-PEEVERS Coordinating Author

All my life I'd dreamed about this moment, when the tidal surge brings teeming swarms of fish to reproduce in the sands of Southern California beaches. Here I had just added a little water to dry sand and watched, amazed, as tiny grunion hatchlings emerged and swam into life. Only in Southern California!

AMY C BALFOUR

What inspirational thought was I thinking after the one-mile hike to the top of gorgeous Cavern Point on Santa Cruz Island? 'I hope these Bono sunglasses don't look too stupid.' See the unfortunate answer for yourself in the above photo. Clearly an emergency purchase. And clearly a once-in-a-lifetime view.

ANDREW BENDER

After lunch in Thai Town, a friend and I browsed the bakeries, acupuncturists and other restaurants we now have to return to. Every visit to one of SoCal's ethnic neighborhoods brings a light-bulb moment, as I discover things I never knew existed – though they may have been there for years.

For full author biographies see p433

Los Angeles & Southern California Highlights

Hitting the waves on bedazzling beaches; glimpsing tabloid regulars in their favorite playgrounds; sampling Mozart in an architectural masterpiece; sliding down silky sand dunes or traipsing along palm-shaded desert canyons; feasting on boundary-pushing cuisine and washing it down with some of the best pinot you ever tasted. Sounds good – but why not let the experts speak for themselves? On these pages, a handful of readers, writers and staff reveal their favorite SoCal spots. Have we missed yours? Share them at lonelyplanet.com/bluelist.

HANAN ISACHAR

1 BEACHES

I'll never forget the exhilaration of catching my first bodyboarding wave. My insanely patient husband had tried for hours to teach me about spotting, timing and kicking but I just couldn't get it right. Then it came. My wave. I leapt up just so and off I went like a rocket, screaming at the top of my lungs all the way to the beach. What a ride! Finally, I felt like a true SoCal girl.

Andrea Schulte-Peevers, Lonely Planet author

DAVID PEEVER

SHOPPING AMONG CELEBRITIES

It usually goes down like this: 'Do I know that person?' Then the sneaky double-take: 'Oh my gawwwd, that's Ugly Betty.' Then the reality adjustment: 'She's short!' Then you see if she buys anything and immediately text all your friends, 'Ugly Betty just bought a scrunchie!' Even if you don't see stars during your visit, you can flip through the racks at It's a Wrap (p212) for clothes worn by actors and actresses during TV and movie shoots.

Amy C Balfour, Lonely Planet author

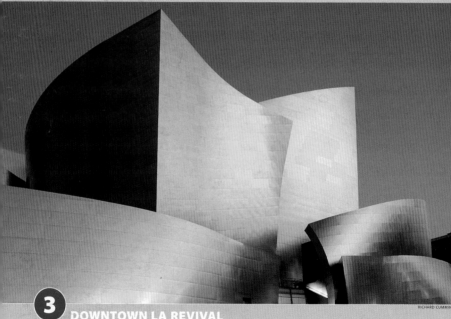

RICHARD CUMMIN

DOWNTOWN LA REVIVAL

When I first set foot in LA, it was in Downtown (p132) and I instantly fell in love. Yes: grimy, neglected, deserted-at-night Downtown! But past all that I saw a dynamic and intriguing area full of promise and potential. I've waited two decades, and Downtown LA is finally coming into its own. The warped and wonderful Walt Disney Concert Hall was only the beginning. Artists and attorneys now jockey for lofts in beautifully remodeled beaux-arts buildings. Café life spills out onto streets once teeming with the home-less, and megadevelopments are sprouting on former no-mans-land. And I couldn't be more excited!

Andrea Schulte-Peevers, Lonely Planet author

SAN DIEGO ZOO

I'll admit it. I melt over polar bears. The minute I saw the Polar Bear Plunge (p298), I reverted back to my four-year-old self.

**Andrew Bender,
Lonely Planet author**

MARK NEWMAN

4

LATINO LA

When I get back to my home town of LA, I'm greeted by an altogether different place. In the last 20 years the ethnic make-up has radically shifted. More Mexicans supposedly live in LA now than in any city in the world besides Mexico City. I feel like I'm on vacation when I go home, with lots of easy smiles and cowboy hats, Ranchero music on the radio and lilting laughter from south of the border. And, of course, lots of 4th and 5th generation Latinos who are more American than I am.

Steve Slattery, Lonely Planet staff, Oakland

RICHARD CUMMINS

OLIVER STREWE

6

SANTA BARBARA WINE COUNTRY

The film *Sideways* exposed Santa Ynez's highly underrated wineries (p396). Quaint boutiques are neatly tucked away in scenic rolling vineyards, owned often by ex-celebrities. Careful bringing up *Sideways* though – not everyone loves pinot noir.

marlonkobacker, Lonely Planet Bluelist contributor

COYOTES IN JOSHUA TREE NATIONAL PARK

Joshua Tree (p363) under a full moon is a magical place. Between the outlines of the famous trees and scrub brush, you can spy coyotes who will give an occasional yip or high-pitched howl. Any move towards these skittish creatures will send them scampering, but if you stand perfectly still and allow your eyes to adjust, you will be rewarded with a glimpse into the nocturnal life of the desert.

**Rana Freedman,
Lonely Planet staff, Oakland**

DAMON SCHELEL

8

JOHN ELK III

7

PALM SPRINGS

Compared to the foggy Bay Area, Palm Springs (p345) is a desert treat. I felt so happy walking next to a little creek in the Indian Canyons on a quiet weekday afternoon. Then I went back and floated in my tiki-themed motel pool, looking up at the stark rocky mountains and cloudless sky, thinking about this town's heyday when Elvis used to swim here.

Suki Gear, Lonely Planet staff, Oakland

Contents

On the Road 4

Los Angeles & Southern California Highlights 5

Destination Los Angeles & Southern California 12

Getting Started 14

Itineraries 19

History 27

The Culture 36

Food & Drink 52

Environment 57

Southern California Outdoors 63

Los Angeles & SoCal for Children 72
Are We There Yet? 72
Night-Night 73
Whining & Dining 74
Los Angeles 75
Orange County 75
San Diego County 76
Palm Springs & The Deserts 76
Santa Barbara 77

Los Angeles 78
Orientation 79
Information 100

Dangers & Annoyances 102
Sights 102
Activities 152
Walking Tour: Downtown LA 155
Courses 157
Los Angeles For Children 157
Tours 158
Festivals & Events 159
Sleeping 162
Eating 174
Drinking 190
Entertainment 195
Shopping 206
Getting There & Away 216
Getting Around 217
AROUND LOS ANGELES 220
Catalina Island 220
Six Flags Magic Mountain & Hurricane Harbor 221
Big Bear Lake 221
Death Valley National Park 223
Las Vegas 224

Orange County 227
Getting There & Around 229
DISNEYLAND & ANAHEIM 230
History 230
Information 230

SoCal Speaks 233
Sleeping 244
Eating 245
Drinking 247
Entertainment 247
Shopping 247
Getting There & Away 248
Getting Around 248
AROUND DISNEYLAND 249
Orange 250
ORANGE COUNTY BEACHES 252
Seal Beach 252
Sunset Beach 255
Huntington Beach 256
Newport Beach 261
Around Newport Beach 268
Laguna Beach 270
Around Laguna Beach 277

San Diego County 281

History	282
DOWNTOWN & AROUND	**282**
Orientation	282
Information	283
Tours	303
Festivals & Events	304
Sleeping	305
Eating	307
Drinking	311
Entertainment	313
Shopping	315
Getting There & Away	316
Getting Around	316
CORONADO & THE BEACHES	**317**
Information	318
Sights	318
Activities	321
Sleeping	322
Eating	325
Drinking & Entertainment	326
Shopping	327
Getting There & Around	327
LA JOLLA	**328**
Information	328
Sights	328
Activities	330
Sleeping	331
Eating	331
Drinking & Entertainment	333
Shopping	333
SAN DIEGO NORTH COAST	**333**
Del Mar	334
Solana Beach	335
Cardiff-By-The-Sea	335
Encinitas	336
Carlsbad	337
Oceanside	339
AROUND SAN DIEGO	**339**
Julian	339
Tijuana, Mexico	341

Palm Springs & the Deserts 345

PALM SPRINGS & COACHELLA VALLEY	**346**
History	346
Orientation	346
Sights	349

Activities	354
Tours	355
Festivals & Events	355
Sleeping	356
Eating	357
Drinking	359
Entertainment	359
Shopping	361
Getting There & Away	362
Getting Around	362
JOSHUA TREE NATIONAL PARK	**363**
Orientation	363
Information	363
Sights	363
Activities	364
Sleeping	365
Eating	367
Getting There & Away	368
ANZA-BORREGO DESERT STATE PARK	**368**
Orientation	368
Information	369
Sights	369
Activities	370
Sleeping	370
Eating	371
Getting There & Away	372
TEMECULA	**372**
Orientation	373
Information	373
Sights & Activities	373
Sleeping	373
Eating & Drinking	373
Entertainment	374
Getting There & Away	374

Santa Barbara County 375

History	376
SANTA BARBARA	**376**
Orientation	376
Information	376
Sights	378
Tours	385
Festivals & Events	385
Sleeping	386
Eating	388
Drinking	390
Entertainment	391
Shopping	391
Getting There & Away	392

Getting Around	392
AROUND SANTA BARBARA	**393**
Buellton	393
Solvang	393
Santa Barbara Wine Country	395
Along Highway 154	401
Ventura	402
Ojai	404
Summerland	405
Channel Islands National Park	405

Directory 408

Accommodations	408
Activities	411
Business Hours	411
Climate Charts	411
Discount Cards	413
Festivals & Events	413
Food	414
Gay & Lesbian Travelers	414
Holidays	414
Insurance	415
International Visitors	415
Internet Access	417
Legal Matters	417
Maps	418
Shopping	418
Solo Travelers	419
Tipping	419
Tourist Information	419
Tours	419
Travelers With Disabilities	419
Women Travelers	420

Transportation 421

GETTING THERE & AWAY	**421**
Air	421
Land	423
GETTING AROUND	**424**
Air	424
Bicycle	424
Bus	425
Car & Motorcycle	426
Hitchhiking	428
Local Transportation	428
Train	429

Health   **430**

BEFORE YOU GO   **430**
Insurance   430
Recommended
Vaccinations   430
Internet Resources   430
IN SOUTHERN CALIFORNIA **430**
Availability & Cost of
Health Care   430

Infectious Diseases   430
Environmental Hazards   431

The Authors   **433**

Behind the Scenes **434**

Index   **440**

World Time Zones **454**

Map Legend   **456**

Regional Map Contents

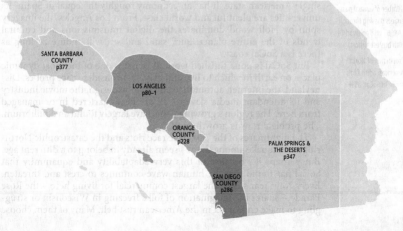

SANTA BARBARA
COUNTY
p377

LOS ANGELES
p80-1

ORANGE
COUNTY
p228

PALM SPRINGS &
THE DESERTS
p347

SAN DIEGO
COUNTY
p286

Destination Los Angeles & Southern California

You might have a great number of expectations about what you'll discover when you arrive in sunny Southern California. Surf, endless fun and sun, youth culture inventing itself before your eyes, and the legends of Hollywood and the 'Old West' surrounding you everywhere. And they are all here. But just for a moment, let us give you a slightly different take on the mythology of Los Angeles and Southern California.

There's a jutting outcrop of barren and heat-blasted rock high above Death Valley known as Aguereberry Point. The only way you can reach it is by taking the twisted and treacherous road wrenched and hewn in the 1930s by the eccentric prospector (Pete Aguereberry) after whom it is named. From here you can look out across 100 miles of one of the most desolate and forbidding landscapes on the planet and ask yourself, 'Why on earth would human beings ever risk their lives to cross this barren, hellish place?' To the east you'll spy the desolate mountains that pioneers just barely made it through; while to the west you will be able to make out towering mountains, their peaks covered with snow and the promise of life-giving water.

From this elevated viewpoint you can begin to imagine that even the slightest hope of what lay ahead was enough to keep early settlers alive for the last leg of their westward journey. If they did survive, their dreams would have been fulfilled. Among the wonders they found were alpine mountains soaring to over 10,000ft; coastal plains and beaches without equal; soil as rich as anywhere on earth, able to sustain livestock and produce wine, vast groves of fruit and fields of vegetables; and weather and sunlight that's the envy of all who live anywhere other than the Mediterranean. This was Southern California, the land of dreams and dreamers. And it is no less wondrous now.

Today's Southern California, or 'SoCal' as its new natives call it, is the culmination of the efforts of generations of such dreamers. Bear in mind that on the pages that follow we're talking about one half of a single American state. It has an economy roughly the equal of Spain. Its universities are plentiful and world class. From Los Angeles, the imagery spun by Hollywood dominates the digital transmissions and cultural trends of the entire planet. Surf, sand and sex will endure as long as there is a SoCal coast.

But SoCal is not a finished work. It remains one of the most dynamic places on earth in which to live and play. Just consider space probes, Disneyland, the internet, automotive and fashion design, the movie industry and its attendant media slaves – all are headquartered in or managed from here. The region's growing pains have largely found an equilibrium. The problem now is growth itself.

The nightmares of the '90s – the race riots and the catastrophic Northridge earthquake among them – seem already to belong to a different age. But perhaps it's because of this very adaptability and equanimity that SoCal has found that the human wave continues to crest and threaten. Every New Year's Day, the largest commercial for living here – the Rose Parade – snares the imagination of folks freezing in Wisconsin or struggling to make ends meet in the American rust belt. Many of them choose

FAST FACTS

SoCal geographical size: 42,383 sq miles

SoCal population: 21,586,200

LA unemployment 2007: 5.1%

Number of movie studios in LA: 30

Life expectancy: women 81.8 years, men 77.1 years (two years more than nationwide)

Median price for a single-family home LA County: $593,000

SoCal contribution to GDP in 2006: $793.1 billion

Average rush-hour speed on LA freeways: 17mph

Average per capita income in LA County: $34,426

Number of annual passengers passing through LAX: 61 million (world's fifth busiest airport)

Proportion of North American adult films made in SoCal: 85%

to move here. With this burgeoning humanity come the attendant problems of horrific traffic and skyrocketing costs of living and real estate. Public transport is woefully inadequate, so everyone hits the freeway where average 'rush hour' speed is a whopping 17mph. Sheer human impaction is a palpable force and begs the question that Rodney King so famously asked: 'Can't we all get along?'

The current mayor of Los Angeles – Antonio Villaraigosa, himself of Mexican descent – is a fellow with bold ideas about social initiatives and it's extremely difficult to envision a return to the infamous 'Zoot Suit Riots' of the '40s or the uproar that followed the 'all-white jury' verdict in the Rodney King beating case. You may be astonished to see the ethnic and racial mix of colleagues and friends walking along boulevards and beaches or gathering for meals together in SoCal's plethora of world cuisine restaurants. As we joke locally, 'Whatever happens in SoCal today will happen to the rest of the world a few years later.' We can only hope that, in terms of race and ethnic relations, this timetable speeds up enormously. Time and again, SoCal has proven itself to be resourceful, resilient, adaptive and innovative. With global warming threatening, you can bet the bank that Caltech, UCLA and other universities are directing their brains toward solving the issues.

The myths surrounding SoCal have somehow come true. You truly *can* surf in the morning in pleasant climes, spend the afternoon skiing down alpine slopes and end the day with alfresco dinner in the desert. Who wouldn't want to live here, even with the horrifying commuting times? Who wouldn't want to visit, or perhaps become a part of, one of the world's greatest and most successful natural and social experiments?

Getting Started

Southern California (SoCal) has excellent tourism infrastructure, and backpackers, families and urban nomads will all find their needs and expectations met. Room and travel reservations are a good idea between June and early September and around major holidays, but otherwise you can keep your advance planning to a minimum. Traffic in the heavily congested coastal areas can be a nightmare at times. Avoid traveling between 3pm and 7pm on weekdays or, in the spirit of slow travel, consider using alternative transportation – such as the train or bus – for at least part of your trip.

WHEN TO GO

See Climate Charts (p411) for more information.

SoCal's a great destination year-round, but most people visit in July and August when cloudless skies and high temperatures are pretty much guaranteed. This is the best time for frolicking on the beach, enjoying alfresco dinners and attending festivals and other open-air events. The mountains are gorgeous, especially if you're into hiking, biking or other outdoor pursuits. Summer is not ideal for exploring the desert, where the mercury can soar as high as 120°F. In all areas the desert lodging is scarce and costly during these months and you'll be jostling for space at major attractions. Note that in June thick clouds often blanket the beach towns, but by July the coast is usually clear, so to speak.

The shoulder seasons (March to May and September to November) bring smaller crowds, lower prices and more temperate weather. In spring wildflowers often brighten meadows, mountains and deserts, while in fall it can still be warm enough to swim in the Pacific.

Unless you're planning a beach vacation, winter (December to February) is a great time to visit, despite the greater chance of rain. It's ideal for exploring the desert, when temperatures are mild and pleasant. The mountains, meanwhile, have turned into a winter wonderland, drawing skiers and boarders to the slopes. City cultural calendars are in full swing, skies usually clear, temperatures still agreeable and lines as short as they'll ever be (except around holidays).

For information on holidays see p414, and for details of festivals and special events see p413.

COSTS & MONEY

SoCal ain't a bargain destination. Most people here make a pretty handsome living and appreciate the good life, which drives up the overall standard of living. What you spend depends largely on what kind of traveler you are,

---

DON'T LEAVE HOME WITHOUT...

- a cool playlist for road-tripping in style (p17)
- nerves of steel for driving on the freeways, especially in LA (p428)
- a sweater or light coat for those days when the sun is a no-show
- a set of smart clothes and shoes for hitting hot clubs, the opera or fancy restaurants
- checking the latest passport and visa requirements (p415)
- hotel or camping reservations for those places you really want to stay, especially in summer (p408)
- this book and a curious mind.

what experiences you wish to have and the season in which you're visiting. In summer and around holidays, renting a car, staying in midrange hotels, enjoying two sit-down meals a day and spending some money on sightseeing, activities and going to bars or clubs will cost between $200 and $300 per day (per person, traveling as an adult couple). Families can save by booking hotels that don't charge extra for children staying in the same room as their parents and by taking advantage of discounts at museums, theme parks and other sights. (See p72 for details.) Even to merely survive you probably won't be able to spend less than $70 per day, and this will have you sleeping in hostels, riding buses, preparing your own meals or eating fast-food, and limiting your entertainment. For ways to keep costs down, see p413.

Comfortable midrange accommodations starts at around $120 for a double room, although budget chains, especially along the freeways, may have lower rates. A two-course meal in an average restaurant, without alcoholic drinks, costs between $30 and $45, plus tax and tip. Museums charge anything up to $15 entry, while attractions such as Disneyland will set you back about $65 per person. Car rentals start at $20 per day, excluding tax and insurance.

TRAVEL LITERATURE

To get you in the mood for your trip, pick up some of these titles that paint vivid pictures of the land and society you're about to visit.

An engrossing tale that weaves together the fates of an environmental writer and an undocumented Mexican couple, *The Tortilla Curtain* (1996) by TC Boyle is an elegant novel about the clash of cultures and the elusiveness of the American dream.

Mike Davis' seminal work *City of Quartz: Excavating the Future in Los Angeles* (updated edition 2006) takes a razor-sharp look at LA's social history, power structures, absurdities and contradictions and examines how these realities will affect its future.

California Uncovered (2004), edited by Chitra Banerjee Divakaruni, is an insightful anthology of poems, profiles and essays – by seasoned and fresh voices – about California's many different faces and its complex, constantly evolving identity.

Hollywood Babylon (1958), Kenneth Anger's 'tell-all' book about the tawdry, sad and scandalous lives and times of Hollywood's Golden Era stars, is a classic, even if reportedly rooted more in rumor than reality.

Marc Reisner's must-read *Cadillac Desert: The American West and Its Disappearing Water* (1993) examines, in dynamic prose, the contentious, sometimes violent, water wars that gave rise to modern California.

In *Los Angeles: People, Places and the Castle on the Hill* (2002), AM Holmes checks into the legendary Chateau Marmont on the Sunset Strip to create this quick-witted and entertaining cultural dissection of the city and its people in all its surreal glory and glamour.

In *Where I Was From* (2003), Joan Didion's thoughts on California shatter palm-fringed fantasies as she skewers the stinking rich, the violence and shallowness as we accompany her pioneering family's own history on this warped shore.

My California: Journeys by Great Writers (2004) is an insightful collection of stories by such fine chroniclers as Pico Iyer, Patt Morrison and Carolyn See. Proceeds benefit the California Arts Council.

INTERNET RESOURCES

Hunt down bargain airfares, book hotels, check on weather conditions or chat with locals and other travelers about the best places to visit – or avoid – on the internet. Start with lonelyplanet.com, where you'll find travel news, links

HOW MUCH?

Dinner for 2 in Los Angeles: $60+

Motel room in San Diego: $80-120

Movie ticket to feature film: $11

Bottle of wine in Santa Barbara Wine Country: $20+

Cup of coffee at roadside diner: $1.50

Cup of coffee at fancy restaurant: $4

Valet parking: $3.50+

to useful resources, an accommodations booking engine and the interactive Thorn Tree forum. For more cool websites see p100.

California Department of Transportation (www.dot.ca.gov) Packed with tourist assistance, route planning, mapping assistance and highway and weather conditions.

California State Government (www.ca.gov) Links to general information, history, culture, doing business and environmental protection.

California State Parks (www.parks.ca.gov) Indispensable site for history, information and services at all state parks.

California Tourism (www.visitcalifornia.com) Links to all visitor bureaus throughout the state.

Roadside America (www.roadsideamerica.com) The 'online guide to offbeat attractions' covers lots of places they won't tell you about at the local tourist office.

Theme Park Insider (www.themeparkinsider.com) Visitors rate and evaluate rides and attractions at major theme parks in SoCal and elsewhere.

TRAVELING RESPONSIBLY

Since our inception in 1973, Lonely Planet has encouraged readers to tread lightly, travel responsibly and enjoy the magic of independent travel. Travel is growing at a jaw-dropping rate, and we still firmly believe in the benefits it can bring. But we also encourage you to consider the impact of your visit on both the global environment and local economies, cultures and ecosystems.

Traveling sustainably within congested Southern California is a challenge but there are some things you can do to lessen your impact. Build an itinerary around more than just Disneyland and other impacted hot spots. Get out of the car and onto a bike or hit the trail in gorgeous parks and wilderness. This book is full of ideas to get you off the beaten path. You might even want to put it away sometimes and just get lost. (Tell us if you find a great new place.)

For background on the wider environmental issues facing Southern California and how these are being tackled, see p61.

Getting There & Away

Flying has become second nature and few of us stop to consider using alternative travel methods. Yet, depending on where you're based, traveling to Southern California by land may be easier and more comfortable than you think. Amtrak operates three long-distance trains each day (p424) and Greyhound's bus network is extensive (p423). If you're driving, rent an efficient car – preferably a hybrid – rather than using your own vehicle, especially if it's an old gas-guzzler. And decline those 'free' upgrades – how big a car do you really need? Consider ride-sharing (p424). If you do choose to fly, offset your carbon emissions. See www.climatecare.org, www.terrapass.com or www.sustainabletravelinternational.org for details.

Slow Travel

Southern California is practically synonymous with car culture but, with time and patience, you can get around using public transportation. The trick is to focus your itinerary and do in-depth explorations of smaller areas rather than a sweeping loop. Even if you have a car, consider ditching it at least part of the time. Amtrak's *Pacific Surfliner* (p424) links all the coastal cities from San Diego to Santa Barbara, while inland destinations are served by Greyhound buses (p423). Cities and towns have local bus systems. Even in LA you'll be OK as long as you limit your ambition to seeing only one or two neighborhoods a day. Santa Barbara, Palm Springs and the Orange County beach towns are compact enough for exploring by bicycle. If you take an organized tour, make sure it operates on sustainable itineraries.

By the author of Pulitzer Prize-winning *Cadillac Desert: The American West and Its Disappearing Water*, Marc Reisner's *A Dangerous Place: California's Unsettling Fate* is a nightmare vision of California's impending 'big one' (earthquake).

TOP 10

California ● Las Vegas

PACIFIC
OCEAN   Los Angeles   Arizona

GREEN MEDALISTS

Southern California may not have a reputation for being leaders in the green movement, but the concept is definitely catching on.

1 Guided Tour – Sustainable Vine Wine Tour (p400)

2 Wildlife Viewing – Newport Bay Ecological Reserve (p264)

3 Getaway – Joshua Tree National Park (p363)

4 Alternative energy – Palm Springs Windmill Tours (p355)

5 Sustainable Winery – Alma Rosa Winery (p399)

6 Initiative – Santa Barbara's Car Free Project (p385)

7 Organization – Heal the Bay (p236)

8 Natural food store – Erewhon (p212)

9 Restaurant – Leaf Cuisine (p179)

10 Hotel – Ambrose (p169)

TOP READS

Great storytelling opens up a window on a destination's culture and people. Get ready for your trip by curling up with these works set in SoCal and penned by some of the finest local writers. For reviews, see p48.

1 *The Big Sleep* (1939) Raymond Chandler

2 *Day of the Locust* (1939) Nathanael West

3 *Post Office* (1970) Charles Bukowski

4 *Play it as it Lays* (1970) Joan Didion

5 *Less than Zero* (1985) Bret Easton Ellis

6 *Get Shorty* (1991) Elmore Leonard

7 *Floaters* (1996) Joseph Wambaugh

8 *Manhattan Beach Project* (2005) Peter Lefcourt

9 *There Will Never be Another You* (2006) Carolyn See

10 *Overlook* (2007) Michael Connolly

ROAD-TRIPPING TUNES

Create a SoCal playlist for your iPod, grab a convertible, crank up the volume and get drivin'. SoCal, so cool!

1 'California Dreaming' – The Mamas and the Papas

2 'Straight Outta Compton' – NWA

3 'Los Angeles' – X

4 'Hollywood Swingin' – Kool & the Gang

5 'Come a Long Way' – Michelle Shocked

6 'City of Angels' – Red Hot Chili Peppers

7 'Ventura Highway' – America

8 'California' – Phantom Planet

9 'All I Wanna Do' – Sheryl Crow

10 'Surfin' USA' – Beach Boys

Accommodations

Most hotel managers have thus far been reluctant to jump on the green bandwagon in Southern California and even such simple eco-initiatives as offering you the option of reusing your towels and sheets, switching to soap dispensers, replacing plastic or Styrofoam cups with glass and dropping prepackaged items from the breakfast buffet are still pretty rare. The more committed hotels recycle food and other waste, and some even put recycle baskets in guestrooms. Many now loan guests bicycles for free or a small fee. You can help raise awareness among hotel staff by thanking them for any ecofriendly programs they offer; if they don't have any, encourage them to do so and offer a few constructive hints.

Food

Fortunately, California cuisine is all about being local, organic and seasonal, so eating like a 'locavore' shouldn't be a tall order. Certified farmers markets abound (see www.farmernet.com for a complete list), as do organic food stores such as Whole Foods or Wild Oats. Choose restaurants that make use of organic produce whenever possible and only order fish, seafood or meat that's from sustainable sources. Bottled water shipped over from Fiji or France? No thank you, filtered tap will be fine (and cheaper). If carrying a bottle of water, refill it in restrooms or at water fountains. Take fast food off the menu.

For an exhaustive trove of advice on how to go green (including in triguing tips on how to green your sex life), check out www.treehugger .com/gogreen.php.

Responsible Travel Schemes

There are various organizations and accreditation programs that identify tourist facilities by a series of sustainable-travel criteria:

California Green Lodging Program (www.ciwmb.ca.gov/EPP/GreenLodging) List of state-certified green hotels throughout California.

Greenopia (www.greenopia.com/la) Urban dwellers guide to green living. Identifies green businesses in LA and provides a forum for exchange.

Green Hotels (www.greenhotels.com) Membership-based green hotels association with directory.

Worldwide Opportunities on Organic Farms (www.wwoofusa.org) Volunteering opportunities on organic farms, with about 10 farms in SoCal.

Itineraries
CLASSIC ROUTES

THE GRAND CIRCLE
Two to Three Weeks

Kick off in **Los Angeles** (p78), where top-notch sights, beautiful beaches and terrific food form a trifecta of treats. Follow up with a date with Mickey at **Disneyland** (p232) and a day of pleasure-filled downtime in **Laguna Beach** (p270) before heading south to **San Diego** (p281) for culture in Balboa Park and animal encounters at the zoo and SeaWorld. Escaping civilization, head to starkly beautiful **Anza-Borrego Desert State Park** (p368), the eerie **Salton Sea** (p372), which is a major migratory bird refuge, and to **Joshua Tree National Park** (p363) with its whimsical trees. Squeeze in a day of margarita-sipping and golfing in nearby **Palm Springs** (p346) before climbing from palms to pines en route to alpine **Big Bear Lake** (p221) for biking, hiking, fishing and skiing. From here it's west via the scenic Rim of the World Dr to **Ventura** (p402) for some great thrifting and an excursion to the **Channel Islands National Park** (p405). The final stop is **Santa Barbara** (p375), whose gorgeous Spanish-Mediterranean downtown has fun shopping and dining. Before heading back south to LA, stock up on fine pinots in **Santa Barbara Wine Country** (p395).

Southern California is a rich quilt of spirit-lifting coast, mystical deserts, bustling cities and impressive mountains, as you will discover on this 900-mile loop. Take your sweet time to fully immerse yourself in this banquet of treats, treasures and temptations.

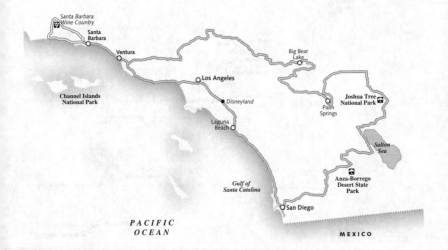

COASTAL DELIGHTS

One Week

Book-ended by San Diego and Santa Barbara, this route hugs the Pacific for most of its 240 miles. Before steering northward, admire fine art in **Balboa Park** (p297), leaping killer whales at **SeaWorld** (p320) and buff dudes in **Mission Beach** (p319), all in San Diego. **Legoland California** (p337) in Carlsbad gets a thumbs up from the preteen set while, further north, history buffs salivate over the beautifully restored **Mission San Juan Capistrano** (p277).

Our vote for prettiest OC town is artsy **Laguna Beach** (p270) whose secluded coves, craggy cliffs and azure waves create a Riviera-like feel. Want ritzy? Plow on to **Newport Beach** (p261), still reveling in its post-*The OC* glow, where bobbing yachts, the giant Fashion Island mall and dare-devil surfers are prevailing presences. Speaking of surfing, the official 'Surf City USA' – **Huntington Beach** (p256) – is just up the road and truly epitomizes the surf-sand-sex way of life. Still, to party big-city style, Huntingtonians head across the LA County border to Pine Ave in **Long Beach** (p130), while families find plenty of stimulus at the *Queen Mary* ocean liner and the state-of-the-art Aquarium of the Pacific.

Continue with a meander along surreally beautiful **Palos Verdes Dr** (p128) before plunging headlong into the South Bay towns of **Redondo Beach** (p128), **Hermosa Beach** (p127) and **Manhattan Beach** (p127). Their American-as-apple-pie vibe contrasts sharply with boho-chic (but wacky) **Venice** (p125). Increasingly sophisticated **Santa Monica** (p124) beckons with a lively pier, fun shopping and excellent restaurants. The busy but scenic Pacific Coast Hwy quickly takes you to celebrity haunt **Malibu** (p120), beautifully hemmed in by the ocean and mountains. Stop briefly in **Ventura** (p402) for a look at the mission and a bit of shopping before wrapping up in **Santa Barbara** (p375), a symphony of red-tile roofs, great architecture and restaurants.

Southern California's coast is a ribbon of myth and legend, immortalized in film, television, song and word. This 240-mile route reveals eye candy at every bend of the road. Resist the temptation to race through it: its true charms want to be savored.

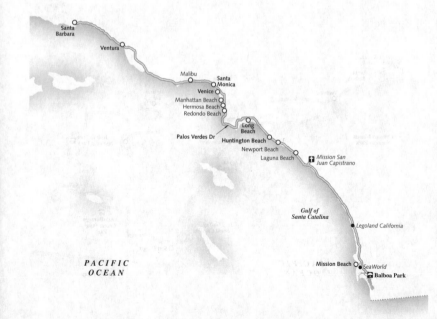

NO CAR? NO PROBLEM! Three Days

May we present: the logistics for three fun-filled carless days in LA, the city infamous for its traffic. **West Hollywood** (p109) makes a handy base of operation and puts you within walking distance – or short **DASH bus ride** (p219) – of the **Farmers Market/Grove** (p110), **Museum Row** (p110), hip restaurants and bars, and stylish shopping. Explore your immediate surroundings on day one, then the following morning catch the DASH bus north on La Cienega Blvd for **Hollywood Boulevard** (p103), perhaps stopping for a gut-filling breakfast at the **Griddle Café** (p176). Explore the legendary strip, then board the **Metro Rail** (p219) Red Line subway at Hollywood & Highland and head to **Union Station** (p133) in Downtown LA. Spend the afternoon following our walking tour on p155, making sure to return to Union Station before 5pm. Catch the Red Line to Pershing Sq, then take Metro Rapid Bus 720 from Broadway & 5th St West to Fairfax & Wilshire and catch the last DASH at 6pm.

On day three, pack a swimsuit because you're headed to the beach. But first, Beverly Hills. Board the DASH on La Cienega, transferring to the Metro Rapid 720 west bus at Fairfax & Wilshire. Get off at **Rodeo Drive** (p114) for a whiff of the lifestyles of the rich and famous and perhaps breakfast at **Nate 'n Al's** (p177). Then it's back on the bus and on to **Santa Monica** (p124). Spend a couple of hours in the sand, check out the Santa Monica Pier or squeeze in some quality shopping along Third St Promenade. Catch the Metro Rapid 720 east no later than 5pm, again changing to the last 6pm DASH at Wilshire & Fairfax.

Hollywood Sign. Walk of Fame. Walt Disney Concert Hall. Rodeo Dr. Beach. Yup, it can be done. LA without a car. You'll need patience, an open mind, a sense of direction and a couple of Metro day passes. Get an early start and plan on being back in the hotel at dinnertime.

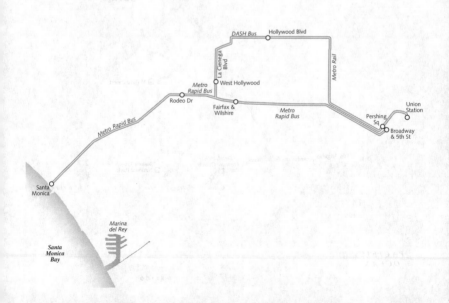

DESERT RAMBLINGS   One Week

Start your trip with a couple of days in dynamic **Los Angeles** (p78), then head east to retro-chic **Palm Springs** (p346), the hip-unhip-and-hip-again former hangout of Elvis and Sinatra. Budget some time for the **Desert Hills Premium Outlets** (p361) to snap up deals from Gap to Gucci, then spend the afternoon kicking back poolside with margaritas and planning the next day. Options: exploring palm-studded canyons, trading the heat for a pine-scented alpine wonderland, going Gumby with a massage – or all of the above.

Open roads, big skies and breathtaking scenery await on this 800-mile magical mystery tour through the SoCal desert and the glamour capitals of Los Angeles and Las Vegas. Pack a good camera, a keen eye and an open mind.

Then it's goodbye to civilization and off to near-mystical **Joshua Tree National Park** (p363), whose weathered boulders and whimsically twisted namesake trees have inspired many artists, most notably the band U2. Take time to linger, maybe joining a ranger-led walk to better engage with and understand this unique ecology. If you think this is stark beauty, turn your wheels north toward the starker-still Mojave Desert, a quiet pastiche of sand dunes, mountains, volcanic cinder cones and ghost towns.

By now, you're surely ready for a big-city fix. So step on it, and head northeast for **Vegas** (p224), baby. Sin City is exciting, seductive, outrageous and absolutely unique. Where else can you climb the Eiffel Tower, kiss your sweetie in a gondola and witness sexy sirens battle it out with pirates, all in a couple of hours? Before you gamble away your life savings, get back in the car for the drive west to **Death Valley National Park** (p223), where the desert puts on a truly spectacular show. Singing sand dunes, desert floor covered in saw-toothed miniature mountains, hills erupting in fireworks of color and mysteriously footloose boulders are just some of the amazing features awaiting you.

TAILORED TRIPS

IT'S KIDDIE TIME

It's no secret: kids love Southern California, with its glorious beaches, sunny skies and head-spinning trove of theme parks, outdoor adventures and cool museums. It will leave you thrilled and exhausted, but there's no question an audience with Mickey at **Disneyland** (p232) is an essential SoCal experience. To meet the adorable Peanuts, head to nearby **Knott's Berry Farm** (p249), America's oldest theme park, which pairs Old Western themes with futuristic roller-coasters and Camp Snoopy. Hard-core coaster freaks, though, will feel the g-force pull of **Six Flags Magic Mountain** (p221), with its fleet of stomach-wrenching brain-blasters. Lest your kids think SoCal is all about thrills, take them to such fabulous interactive museums as the **Discovery Science Center** (p250) in Orange County or the **Aquarium of the Pacific** (p130) in Long Beach. San Diego is also about animal magnetism: the famous **San Diego Zoo** (p298) has an entire Noah's Ark worth of critters, while at **SeaWorld** (p320) you'll enjoy the antics of Shamu, the killer whale, and his finned friends. And don't miss the **Wild Animal Park** (p341), where large mammals such as giraffes and zebras roam 'freely' in large enclosures.

SIDE-TRACKING SIDEWAYS

Following in the footsteps of Miles (Paul Giamatti) and Jack (Thomas Haden Church), the anti-heroes of the 2004 surprise hit movie *Sideways*, has become a popular diversion in the Santa Barbara Wine Country (p395). In Buellton, Miles and Jack stay at the otherwise unremarkable **Days Inn** and walk to the **Hitching Post II** (p393) and their meeting with Maya (Virginia Madsen). Nearby Solvang is where the two have breakfast at the **Solvang Restaurant** (p394). North of Buellton, Zaca Station Rd heads off Hwy 101 past the **Firestone Vineyard** (p397), where the two couples – Jack and Stephanie (Sandra Oh), Miles and Maya – share some romantic moments in the perfectly lit cask room. A bit further, Foxen Canyon Rd is a star in its own right. The **Fess Parker Winery** (p398) does almost too good a job posing as the pedestrian Frass Canyon Winery (you know they make a mean merlot). North, **Foxen Winery** (p398) also does a star turn (it's the tiny roadside place where Miles and Jack surreptitiously chug). In the south, Foxen Canyon Rd ends at Los Olivos where the couples have a romantic meal at **Los Olivos Café** (p400).

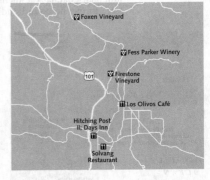

MAY THE SPIRIT MOVE YOU

Judging by the gossip rags, you might think SoCal is Sodom and Gomorrah reincarnate, but the region is actually among the most religiously diverse in the nation. After all, its recorded history begins with a string of Franciscan-founded missions, starting with **Mission San Diego de Alcalá** (p302) and moving north to **Mission San Juan Capistrano** (p277), **San Gabriel Mission** (p150), **Mission San Fernando Rey de España** (p151), **Mission San Buenaventura** (p402) and **Mission Santa Barbara** (p380). Beautifully restored, they provide a window on a time when SoCal was just a remote and dusty outpost. Jump two centuries ahead and you have some of the world's finest architects building

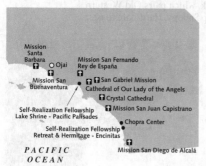

new houses of worship, most notably Rafael Moneo's boldly modern **Cathedral of Our Lady of the Angels** (p135) in LA and Philip Johnson's glass shrine, **Crystal Cathedral** (p250) in Orange County, the base of Robert Schuller, one of the first televangelists. In fact, the Southland is famous for spawning new religious movements, including Yogi Paramahansa Yogananda's **Self-Realization Fellowship Retreat & Hermitage** (p336), headquartered in Encinitas with another outpost in Pacific Palisades, LA (p123). In Carlsbad, Deepak Chopra is one of the leading New Agers with his **Chopra Center** (p338), and spiritualists are also drawn to the zen powers of the town of **Ojai** (p404).

MODERNIST MASTERPIECES

Being on the leading edge has been a SoCal characteristic since the early 20th century, and this is true of the field of architecture as well. As early as 1908, the brothers Charles and Henry Green created the seminal Craftsman bungalow, the **Gamble House** (p148) in Pasadena, whose terraces, sleeping porches and overhanging eaves extend the house into its natural environment. This principle was later expanded upon by Frank Lloyd Wright with his **Hollyhock House** (p108) in LA. Wright disciples Richard Neutra and Rudolph Schindler, both immigrants from Austria, took things even further by embracing the minimalist Bauhaus aesthetic from Europe. **Schindler House** (p110), the architect's former home and studio, offers essentially a primer on the modernist

elements that so greatly influenced midcentury California architecture, such as an open floor plan, flat roof and sliding glass doors. Nowhere was modernism embraced more than in Palm Springs, where architects such as **Albert Frey** (p350) built bungalows for Hollywood's elite. Louis Kahn's **Salk Institute** (p329) in San Diego is another fine example. Postmodern work is mostly concentrated in LA with Frank Gehry's **Walt Disney Concert Hall** (p134), Richard Meier's **Getty Center** (p117), Rafael Moneo's **Cathedral of Our Lady of the Angels** (p135) and Thom Mayne's **Caltrans District 7 Headquarters** (p155) – all of them Pritzker Architecture Prize winners and undisputed standouts.

THE GREAT OUTDOORS

On land, in the water and in the sky you'll find plenty of opportunities to get your heart pumping in Southern California – and we're not talking about spotting Jake Gyllenhaal or Leonardo DiCaprio in the flesh. Water babies can don a mask or strap on a tank for close-ups with garibaldi, sea anemones and other ocean creatures at either **La Jolla Underwater Park Ecological Reserve**(p330) in San Diego or **Casino Point Marine Park** (p220) on Catalina Island – both are protected ecoreserves. Catalina, with its craggy, coved coastline, provides perfect terrain for kayaking, especially for beginners, while saltier types may want to do battle with the waves at **Channel Islands National Park** (p405). The best mountain biking is at **Big Bear Lake** (p221), where a ski mountain morphs into a championship-level bike park during the summer. Rock climbers are spoiled for choice with a multitude of challenges on the desert-baked boulders of **Joshua Tree National Park** (p363), while golfers will enjoy smacking a Titleist down the fairway at one, or several, of more than 100 golf courses in nearby **Palm Springs** (p346). Bird-watchers will have a field day at **Malibu Lagoon State Beach** (p120) and especially in the **Newport Bay Ecological Reserve** (p264), while **Del Mar** (p334) is a prime area for hot air ballooning.

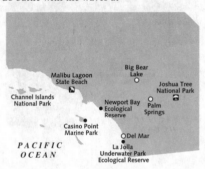

ROAD RAVES

In Southern California the road always beckons, so drop the convertible top, cue up 'California Dreaming' and step on it. One of our favorite drives delivers surreally beautiful ocean vistas along the **Pacific Coast Highway** through Malibu (p120). It's easily combined with a swing through the canyonland, undulating fields and bizarrely shaped buttes of the Santa Monica Mountains (turn inland on Topanga Canyon Rd, left on Mulholland Hwy and left again on Malibu Canyon Rd back to the Pacific Coast Hwy). Another evocative seaside route travels along **Palos Verdes Drive** (p128), while legendary **Mulholland Drive** (p106) will have you snapping close-ups of the Hollywood Sign and mammoth LA below. North of the city, **San Marcos Pass Road** (Hwy 154; p401) skirts Chumash rock art, thick forests and a placid lake en route to the Santa Barbara Wine Country. Mountain drives, meanwhile, are ideal for escaping the summer heat. The meandering **Angeles Crest Highway** (Hwy 2; p150) quickly delivers you to pine-scented heights, but the **Rim of the World Drive** (Hwy 18) to Big Bear Lake (p221) is actually more spectacular. The aptly named **Palms to Pines Highway** (Hwys 243 and 74), carved into the San Jacinto Mountains above Palm Springs, is another cool road and is also popular with motorcyclists.

GREEN GETAWAYS

Yes, it's crowded and congested, but there's also a 'wild' side to the Southland that most visitors never venture out to explore. Trust us, getting away from the high-velocity metro areas will feel like a mini-vacation, and you don't even have to travel far. If you're LA-based, head up Pacific Coast Hwy to the **Santa Monica Mountains National Recreation Area** (p153), the world's largest protected zone within an urban setting. Scramble along riverbeds, through shady canyons, past bizarrely formed pinnacles and visit famous movie sets. North of here, **Ojai** (p404) is a little inland Shangri-la with an artsy pedigree, stunning scenery, a spiritual vibe and otherworldly spa experiences. It's at the edge of the **Los Padres National Forest** (p401), an outdoor wonderland of rocks, creeks and waterfalls that's perfect for overnight camping. The same is true of **Big Bear Lake** (p221), a laid-back mountain town that morphs into SoCal's premier skiing area in winter. In summer, hikers and mountain bikers invade to escape the heat in the LA Basin. Another cool spot is **Julian** (p339), an old mining town in the hills east of San Diego, where you can pan for gold and gorge on scrumptious apple pie.

CAMP, KITSCH & CULTURE

We dare you count the number of times during your trip you'll be saying 'Only in Southern California!' The region is truly the capital of quirk and you'll encounter unique characters, places and experiences wherever you go. If aliens landed on LA's famous **Venice Boardwalk** (p125) they'd probably blend right in with the human zoo of chainsaw-jugglers, Speedo-clad snake-charmers and a roller-skating Sikh minstrel. Inland from here, the **Museum of Jurassic Technology** (p119) is a subversive repository of mind-twisting curiosities that'll bamboozle and astound you. The desert has always lured kooks, including George van Tassel who built a giant rejuvenation machine called the **Integratron** (p368) in the Mojave. Off the I-10, you'll do a double-take near Cabazon, where the **World's Biggest Dinosaurs** (p353) house exhibits on – of all things – creationism. In Palm Springs, octogenarian showgirls do the cancan in the **Palm Springs Follies** (p360), while at **Glen Ivy Hot Springs** (p251) you'll have fun making devil's horns on your head from sticky clay while wallowing in the mud pool. Cap the day at **Medieval Times** (p249) near Disneyland, where you can fancy yourself knight and damsel while watching jousting horsemen, eating chicken with your hands and wearing a paper crown. And then there's always **Las Vegas** (p224)…

History

Most people think of Southern California as being only recently settled by the Brady Bunch, but a lot happened before the suburban dream became the dominant cultural paradigm. This chapter provides a general overview of how the region has developed through the centuries. For city- or area-specific historical events, see the history sections in the destination chapters.

PREHISTORIC TIMES

Long before the first humans arrived in North America, mammoths, sloths, dire wolves, saber-toothed cats and other Ice Age animals prowled around the area we today call Southern California. Truckloads of fossils from these long-extinct critters have been pulled from LA's La Brea Tar Pits (p110), where they were trapped and killed in a gooey muck between 10,000 and 40,000 years ago. Roughly around the time the last of these animals vanished, the first humans began showing up in North America, having trekked from Siberia to Alaska via a long-gone land bridge across the Bering Strait. They weren't exactly speedy about moving south and, according to radiocarbon dating of artifacts such as shell middens (ancient refuse heaps), stone tools and arrowheads, it took descendants of these migrants some 2000 years to reach Southern California.

The most spectacular artifacts left behind by California's early inhabitants are their rock art, dating from 500 to 3000 years ago. Many sites are closed to the public in the interest of preservation, but you can visit Chumash Painted Cave State Historic Park (p401), near Santa Barbara.

NATIVE CALIFORNIANS

There's plenty of archaeological and anecdotal evidence from early European visitors and later research to puzzle together a clear picture of the day-to-day lives of native Californians. There were only about 150,000 to 300,000 early Californians, but even back then they were a diverse bunch, belonging to more than 20 language groups with about 100 dialects between them. They lived in small communities and often migrated with the seasons from the coast to the mountains. Dinner was mostly acorn meal supplemented by small game such as rabbits and deer, and fish and shellfish along the coast.

By all accounts, they were a crafty people, making earthenware pots, fish nets, bows, arrows and spears with chipped stone points, and developing a particular knack for basket weaving. These baskets were made from local grasses and plant fibers and decorated with attractive geometric designs. Some were so tightly woven they would hold water. You'll see some beautiful specimens at the Natural History Museum of LA County (p119) in LA

If you're wondering what happened to California's Native American population, find definitive answers in *Handbook of North American Indians*, edited by Robert Heizer.

The precise etymology of 'California' has never been established, but there is wide consensus that it is a derivation of 'Calafia,' the hero queen of a 16th-century Spanish novel, who ruled a race of gold-rich black Amazons.

TIMELINE

Around 13,000 BC	1542	1602
The first humans start crossing into North America via a land bridge. The bones of a woman found on Santa Rosa Island, one of the Channel Islands, date back 11,000 years.	The Spanish king dispatches an expedition to today's California after reading Garci Ordonez de Montalvo's novel *The Adventures of Esplandian*, which describes a mythical island filled with gold and ruled by Queen Calafia.	Sebastián Vizcaíno first sets foot on California soil on the feast day of San Diego de Alcalá. In honor of the saint, he names the spot San Diego.

and the Museum of Man (p299) in San Diego. Coastal and inland peoples traded but generally didn't interact much, partly because they spoke different languages. Conflict was almost nonexistent. Native Californians had neither a warrior class nor a tradition of warfare.

EUROPEAN DISCOVERY

The website of the Historical Society of Southern California (www.socalhistory.org) has biographies, information on the region's historical places and useful links to other websites on SoCal history.

Following the conquest of Mexico in the early 16th century, the Spanish turned their attention toward exploring the edges of their new empire, fueled by curiosity, lust for power and, above all, greed. Tales of a golden island to the west circulated widely, and in 1542 the Spanish crown sent Juan Rodríguez Cabrillo, a Portuguese explorer and retired conquistador, to find it. The fabled land, of course, proved elusive, but Cabrillo and his crew still made it into the history books as the first Europeans to step ashore in mainland California – in today's San Diego. He claimed the land for Spain, then sat out a storm in the harbor before sailing northward. Stopping over to check out the Channel Islands, he and his men got into a fight with the local Native Americans. Cabrillo broke a leg, fell ill, died and was buried on what is now the island of San Miguel. The Cabrillo National Monument (p319) in San Diego has some fascinating exhibits about the cantankerous explorer's journey and is the second-most visited monument in the US after the Statue of Liberty.

The Spanish left California for about 50 years until they decided they needed to secure some ports on the Pacific coast, and sent Sebastián Vizcaíno to find them. Vizcaíno's first expedition was a disaster that didn't get past Baja California but in his second attempt, in 1602, he rediscovered the harbor at San Diego and gave it its present name.

MISSION IMPROBABLE

To learn more about Southern California's missions, their cultural influence and their historical significance, log on to the California Missions website: www.californiamissions.com.

Everyone wanted a toehold on the west coast of the New World in the 18th century. Around the 1760s, as Russian ships sailed to California's coast in search of sea-otter pelts, and British trappers and explorers were spreading throughout the west, the Spanish king finally grew worried that his claim to the territory might be challenged. Conveniently for him the Catholic Church was anxious to start missionary work among the native peoples, so the Church and crown combined forces and established missions protected by presidios (military forts). The Native American converts were expected to live in the missions, learn trade and agricultural skills and ultimately establish pueblos, which would be like little Spanish towns. Or so the plan went.

The distance between California's missions equals a day's journey by horseback.

The first Spanish colonizing expedition, called the 'Sacred Expedition,' proved nearly disastrous. On July 1, 1769, a sorry lot of about 100 missionaries and soldiers, led by the Franciscan priest Junípero Serra and the military commander Gaspar de Portolá, limped ashore at San Diego Bay. They had just spent several weeks at sea sailing from Baja California; about half of their cohort had died en route and many of the survivors were sick or near

1769	1781	1821–1846
Gaspar de Portolá, at the behest of the Spanish king, leads the first European land expedition north from Baja California in order to establish a series of forts and missions in Alta California.	Mexican governor Felipe de Neve sets out from the Mission San Gabriel with a tiny band of settlers, trekking west for 9 miles and establishing the future Los Angeles.	During Mexico's rule over California, Spanish missionaries are kicked out and the missions are secularized and offered for sale. The governor's brother-in-law snaps up the Mission of San Juan Capistrano for $710.

death. It was an inauspicious beginning for the Mission San Diego de Alcalá (p302), the first of the chain of 21 California missions.

Lest you start feeling sorry for the Spanish, their suffering pales compared with the plight of the indigenous people. The colonizers virtually enslaved the Native Americans and made them construct the missions and presidios. Presidio soldiers, whose job was ostensibly to protect the missions and deter foreign intruders, actually passed much of their time raping and pillaging. Meanwhile, European diseases such as smallpox and syphilis further decimated the Native American population, as they had no immunity to them.

The missions did achieve modest success at farming, managing to just barely become self-sufficient, an essential achievement during the 1810–1821 Mexican war for independence from Spain when supplies from Mexico were cut off completely. As a way of colonizing California and converting the natives to Christianity, however, the mission period was an abject failure. The Spanish population remained small, the missions achieved little better than survival, foreign intruders were not greatly deterred and more Native Americans died than were converted.

Today, all of the SoCal missions in San Diego (the oldest; p302), San Juan Capistrano (the prettiest; p277), Ventura (p402) and Santa Barbara (p380), and Los Angeles (p150) have been restored and welcome visitors. The best preserved presidio is the one in Santa Barbara (p382).

An excellent resource for learning about early life in SoCal is *A World Transformed: Firsthand Accounts of California Before the Gold Rush*, edited by Joshua Paddison.

THE PATH TO STATEHOOD

Upon Mexican independence from Spain in 1821, many of the new nation's people looked to California to satisfy their thirst for private land. By the mid-1830s the missions had been secularized and their land divvied up into free land grants by Mexican governors. This process gave birth to the rancho system. The new landowners, called rancheros or Californios, prospered quickly and became the social, cultural and political fulcrums of California. The average rancho was a whopping 16,000 acres and largely given over to livestock to supply the trade in hide and tallow.

The first Los Angeles telephone book, issued in 1882, was only three pages long.

Meanwhile, American explorers, trappers, traders, whalers, settlers and opportunists increasingly showed interest in California. Some of the Americans who started businesses married locals and assimilated into Californio society. Impressed by California's untapped riches and imbued with Manifest Destiny (the doctrine to extend the US border from coast to coast), US president Andrew Jackson sent an emissary to offer the financially strapped Mexican government $500,000 for California. But the Mexicans were not interested in selling and soon a political storm was brewing.

In 1836 Texas seceded from Mexico and declared itself an independent republic. When the US annexed Texas in 1845, Mexico broke off diplomatic relations and ordered all foreigners without proper papers to be deported from California. In turn, the US declared war on Mexico and began an invasion. By July US naval units occupied every port on the California

1848	1850	1869
By signing the Treaty of Guadalupe Hidalgo on February 2, Mexico turns over one third of its territory, including California, New Mexico and parts of Arizona, to the US in exchange for $15 million.	On September 9, California becomes the 31st state of the US, entering the Union as a free (nonslavery) state. The first constitution is written in Spanish and English. Los Angeles is incorporated the same year.	Gold is discovered in Julian, near San Diego, which sparks another frenetic mining boom. Once the gold runs out San Diego goes back to being a sleepy little town of 2000 souls.

coast, but militarily California was a sideshow as the war was mostly fought in Mexico.

The capture of Mexico City by US troops in September 1847 put an end to the fighting and led to the signing of the Treaty of Guadalupe Hidalgo, in which the Mexican government ceded much of its northern territory to the US.

THE RISE OF A REGION

Many rancheros lost their land when the American government questioned their title under the 1851 Land Act. During this period of loose government, LA was a true Wild West town, filled with saloons, brothels and gambling dens. Added to the mix were thousands of Chinese immigrants who'd arrived for the gold rush and railroad work. These foreigners were viewed by many with suspicion and the state even enacted a special 'foreign miner's tax.'

The perception of LA and the rest of the region as a lawless backwater began to change with the arrival of the railroad. The transcontinental railroad had been completed in 1869 and shortened the trip from New York to San Francisco from two months to five days, instantly elevating the latter to California's metropolitan center. Southern California's parched climate, its distance from both fresh water and mining resources, and its relatively small population initially made it unattractive to the San Francisco railroad moguls. But eventually a bit of wheeling and dealing convinced the Southern Pacific Railroad to build a spur line to LA and Anaheim in Orange County in the mid-1870s. San Diego had to wait until 1884.

During the same period, agriculture diversified, with new crops, especially oranges, being grown in Southern California for markets on the East Coast and abroad. Unlike many fruits, oranges easily survive long-distance rail shipping. As California oranges found their way onto New York grocery shelves, a hard-sell advertising campaign began, and people from the Midwest and eastern US heeded the self-interested advice of crusading magazine and newspaper editor Horace Greeley to 'Go West, young man.' A population boom ensued, further driven by a steep drop in train fares after the Santa Fe Railroad Company (AT&SF) laid tracks linking LA with the East Coast across the Arizona Desert in 1887, thereby breaking the Southern Pacific monopoly. The lower fares spurred a major real estate boom lasting from 1886 to 1888. More than 120,000 migrants came to Southern California, settling in the 25 new towns laid out by AT&SF in the eastern part of Los Angeles County.

Much of the land granted to the railroads was sold in big lots to speculators who also acquired, with the help of corrupt politicians and administrators, much of the farmland that was released for new settlement. A major share of the state's agricultural land became consolidated into large holdings in the hands of a few city-based landlords, establishing the still-existing pattern of industrial-scale 'agribusiness' rather than small family farms.

Indian gaming brings some 8900 jobs to the Inland Empire, which comprises Riverside County and San Bernardino County.

Without the 1913 construction of the aqueduct from Owens Valley, LA would never have grown beyond 100,000 inhabitants.

1874	1892	1902
The US Department of Agriculture ships three seedless Brazilian navel orange trees to botanists in Riverside. By 1889 orange trees cover more than 13,000 acres, sending the previously woebegone local economy through the roof.	Oil is discovered in Downtown LA, sparking a major oil boom.	The first Rose Bowl football game takes place in Pasadena with the University of Michigan trouncing Stanford 49–0 before 7000 spectators. The next game isn't for another 11 years.

A BORDERLINE CASE

Southern California has always had a love-hate relationship with its immigrants but owes much of its success to its cultural diversity. Newcomers are typically welcomed in periods of rapid growth, only to be rejected when times get tough. Chinese railroad workers, for instance, were in great demand in the 1860s but ended up being victimized in the 1870s. The Webb Alien Land Law of 1913 prevented some Asian minorities from owning land. During WWII 120,000 people of Japanese heritage – many of them American citizens – were forcibly placed in internment camps. African Americans came to SoCal in large numbers to take jobs in the postwar boom, but found themselves unemployed when the economy slowed down.

It is estimated that more than three million undocumented immigrants are currently in California, despite continuing efforts to seal the notoriously porous border. Mexican and Latin American workers still do most of the farm labor and domestic work. In 1994, in the face of increasing unemployment and state government deficits, Californians voted in favor of Proposition 187, which denied illegal immigrants access to state government services, including schools and hospitals. Illegal immigration remains a volatile political topic, especially among conservatives who often employ migrants to tend their yards cheaply while also calling for their expulsion.

Never mind that there was no natural harbor or that the supply of fresh water was inadequate. Sharp minds and willing spirits would eventually overcome these obstacles. In 1899 LA's city fathers settled on San Pedro, 23 miles south of LA City Hall, as the site of the port of Los Angeles. It opened in 1907 and became the busiest harbor on the West Coast after the completion of the Panama Canal seven years later. Bringing water to town would be another major challenge. (For more on how this was achieved, see p62.)

MOVIES

The film industry – or simply the 'Industry,' as it's known in LA – has done much to promote California's image throughout the country and the world. As film, and later TV, became the predominant entertainment medium of the 20th century, California moved to center stage in the world of popular culture.

Entrepreneurial moviemakers – most of them European immigrants – began establishing studios in the first decade of the 20th century. German-born Carl Laemmle built Universal Studio in 1915, selling lunch to curious guests coming to watch the magic of moviemaking; Polish immigrant Samuel Goldwyn joined with Cecil B DeMille to form Paramount Studios; and Jack Warner and his brothers arrived a few years later. With the perpetually sunny weather, most outdoor locations could be easily shot, and moviemaking flourished. Fans loved early film stars like Charlie Chaplin and Harold Lloyd, and the first big Hollywood wedding occurred in 1920 when Douglas Fairbanks wed Mary Pickford. What's more, the proximity of the Mexican

Roman Polanski's *Chinatown* (1974) stars Jack Nicholson and Faye Dunaway in the story of Los Angeles' early-20th-century water wars. Robert Towne's brilliant screenplay deftly navigates the shrewd deceptions that made Los Angeles what it is today.

1913	1923	1925
The Los Angeles aqueduct, built under the direction of city engineer William Mulholland, starts supplying water to LA from the Owens Valley 350 miles to the north.	LA's famous landmark, the 45ft-tall Hollywood Sign, is built on Mount Lee to promote the Hollywoodland subdivision. The 'land' drops off in 1949 but the sign survives and becomes a historical monument in 1973.	At 6.44am on June 29, a 6.3-scale earthquake levels most of downtown Santa Barbara, killing 13 people and causing $8 million in property damage. The city is rebuilt in its distinctive Spanish colonial style.

border enabled filmmakers to rush their equipment to safety when challenged by the collection agents of patent holders such as Thomas Edison.

Although Hollywood became the cultural and financial hub of the movie industry, it's a myth that it was ever the center of movie production. There were studios in Culver City (MGM, now Sony Pictures) and Studio City (Universal Studios Hollywood), but moviemaking wasn't even limited to LA. American Film Company, founded in Santa Barbara in 1910, did box office for years and Balboa Studios in Long Beach was another major silent-era dream factory. And the first big movie palaces were not on Hollywood Blvd but on Broadway in Downtown LA.

For star gazers or movie buffs, LA is the equivalent of the holy grail. Experiences are infinite: you can tour major movie studios (p146), be part of a sitcom audience (p104), shop at Kitson (p209) and other boutiques favored by today's hottest stars, see where celebs live (p116), eat, drink and party, buy their old clothes (p212) or attend a film festival (p196). Other Southland communities are more low-key, but Santa Barbara, Newport Beach in Orange County and Palm Springs all have their own film festivals and are popular celebrity haunts.

MILITARY

Along with motion pictures, aviation became another major industry to have a significant impact on Southern California in the early 20th century. During and after WWI, the Lockheed brothers and Donald Douglas established aircraft manufacturing plants in LA, and Glenn H Curtiss set up shop in San Diego. Ryan Airlines built the *Spirit of St Louis* for Lindbergh's transatlantic flight in 1927, and Consolidated Aircraft opened its San Diego factory in 1931. At long last, San Diego had a raison d'être.

A few years later, the aviation industry – plumped up by billions of federal dollars for military contracts – helped lift Southern California out of the Great Depression. WWII had a huge impact on Southern California. After the 1941 bombing of Pearl Harbor, San Diego became (and remains to this day) home to the headquarters of the US Pacific Fleet, changing the city forever. Further north, Camp Pendleton, the huge Marine Corps base, was established in 1942. The Colorado Desert, near Palm Springs, temporarily became one of the biggest military training grounds in history. Aircraft manufacturing plants turned out planes by the thousands.

After the war, many service people settled in Southern California. The area's military-industrial complex continued to prosper during the Cold War, providing jobs in everything from avionics and missile manufacturing to helicopter and nuclear submarine maintenance. To this day, the Marine Corps trains recruits here and the navy holds advanced training for fighter pilots. There are submarine bases, aircraft testing facilities, air force bases and sprawling gunnery ranges.

1929	1943	1955
The first Academy Awards ceremony takes place in the Blossom Room of the Hollywood Roosevelt Hotel on Hollywood Blvd. About 250 people fork over $10 to be part of the crowd.	Tension between Americans and Mexicans reaches boiling point during the Zoot Suit Riots, which pit American sailors and soldiers against zoot suit–clad Mexican teens while police look on.	Disneyland opens in Anaheim on July 17 after a quick one-year construction period. Its 18 original attractions spread across five themed lands: Tomorrowland, Main Street USA, Adventureland, Frontierland and Fantasyland.

Military spending peaked in the 1980s under California governor and then president Ronald Reagan, but the end of the Cold War in 1990 spelled economic doom for this industry. Budget cutbacks closed numerous military bases, forcing defense contractors to move on or diversify. Workers who had grown accustomed to regular paychecks from McDonnell Douglas and other aerospace companies suddenly got laid off. However, September 11 and America's current 'war on terror' has in recent years sparked renewed interest in the armed forces and its related industries in the region.

Southern California's military history is most proudly nurtured in San Diego where destroyers, aircraft carriers and other steel-gray vessels can often be seen lying in port. To get a close-up look, scramble around the decommissioned aircraft carrier USS *Midway* (p296), now a museum. Old-timey planes – military and civilian – are on view at the Air & Space Museum (p301) in Balboa Park. Navy nuts also descend in droves in September for Fleet Week and the Miramar Air Show (p305). Military history and airplane buffs headed for the desert should check out the Palm Springs Air Museum (p353).

Los Angeles once had a wonderfully efficient system of streetcars, until General Motors allegedly conspired to destroy it (search Google for 'General Motors streetcar conspiracy' and make up your own mind).

SOCIAL CHANGE

Unconstrained by the burden of traditions, bankrolled by affluence and promoted by film and TV, California has always been a leader in new attitudes and social movements.

In the affluent 1950s, the emerging middle class moved to the suburbs, and no place in America better defined suburban life than Orange County. The Irvine Company, owner of more than 100,000 acres of agricultural land (the legacy of 19th-century Spanish land grants), built the first 'master-planned' communities. Strict rules governed their design – hence the county's uniform beige-box architecture. Everybody lived on a quiet street where children could safely play. Shopping centers and strip malls were kept separate, concentrated along wide, multilane boulevards. Everyone had a new freezer, a family sedan and a garage.

When the postwar baby boomers hit their late teens, many rejected their parents' values and heeded Tim Leary's counsel to 'turn on, tune in, drop out.' Though the hippie counterculture was an international phenomenon, Southern California was at the leading edge of its music, psychedelic art and new libertarianism. Sex, drugs and rock and roll ruled the day. Venice Beach was a major hub and hangout of Jim Morrison, Janis Joplin and other luminaries of that era.

In the late 1960s and early '70s, New Left politics, the anti-Vietnam War movement and Black Liberation forced their way into the political limelight, and flower power and give-peace-a-chance politics seemed instantly naive. The 1968 assassination of Robert Kennedy in LA, the sometimes violent repression of demonstrations, and the death of a spectator at a Rolling Stones

The 1970 documentary Gimme Shelter *was about the Rolling Stones concert at the Altamount Speedway where a Hells Angel security guard stomped and stabbed to death fan Meredith Hunter.*

In 1997 the Heaven's Gate cult brought unwanted publicity to the upscale San Diego suburb of Rancho Santa Fe, when leader Marshall Applewhite convinced 38 members to commit ritual suicide.

1965	**1968**	**1969**
It takes 20,000 National Guards to quell the six-day Watts Riots in south Los Angeles, which cause death, devastation and about $200 million in property damage. The same year, Rodney King is born.	Robert Kennedy is assassinated at the Ambassador Hotel in LA.	UCLA professor Len Kleinrock sends data from a computer in Los Angeles to another at Stanford, 360 miles away. He types in 'L', 'O' and 'G' before the system crashes. But the internet was born.

TROUBLE IN PARADISE

LA has a long history of racial strife, which reached its first explosive peak in 1965. The city was booming but not everyone was invited to the party. Entire neighborhoods, predominantly black South Central foremost among them, had for decades been suffering from institutional neglect and lack of opportunity. On a hot August day in 1965, frustration levels reached a boiling point. In the end, it was a relatively minor incident – a black motorist being pulled over on suspicion of drunk driving and then beaten – that caused the lid to blow. Six violent days later, when the so-called Watts Riots were over, 34 people were dead and more than 1000 were injured.

As the city began to lick its wounds, Governor Pat Brown appointed a commission to study the causes of the riots. Commissioners did a fine job identifying the problems – an unemployment rate double the LA average, overcrowded and underfunded classrooms, discriminatory housing laws etc – but lacked the vision, money or motivation to fix them. A generation later there would be a high price to pay for such indifference.

April 29, 1992: 'Not guilty.' The words cut through the stifling air of a hushed Simi Valley court-room, their gravity still unfathomed. More than a year earlier – in an eerie déjà vu of 1965 – four LAPD officers had stopped Rodney King, an African American, for appearing to be driving under the influence. When King initially resisted arrest, the cops allegedly started to kick, beat and shout at the man as he crouched on the sidewalk. A neighbor, infamously, caught the whole thing on videotape.

The cops' acquittal unleashed a replay of the Watts Riots on an even bigger scale, as rioting and looting spread through several neighborhoods. National Guards patrolled the streets with machine guns, businesses and schools were ordered to close and a dusk curfew was imposed. LA felt like a war zone. The shocking toll: 54 dead, 2000 injured, 12,000 arrested and $1 billion in property damage.

Police brutality has continued to stay in the headlines. In the late '90s, it became coupled with police corruption in the so-called 'Rampart scandal.' New police chief William Bratton, who arrived in 2002 from New York, was hired to clean up the LAPD's act and ease racial tensions. Although Bratton generally gets high marks, even he could not prevent another controversial incident. When demonstrators at a May 1 immigration rally started throwing bottles at officers, a melee ensued and the cops ended up being accused of using excessive force. With the abyss of distrust between the police and ethnic groups, it's anybody's guess what the future will hold.

concert at the hands of security guards (Hells Angels the Stones had hired for the occasion) stripped the era of its innocence.

What a difference a decade makes. In the 1980s and '90s, Southern California's new obsession became the healthy lifestyle, with a mood-altering array of aerobic classes and self-actualization workshops on offer. Leisure activities such as in-line skating, skateboarding, snowboarding and mountain biking all originated in California. Be careful what you laugh at. From pet rocks to soy burgers, Southern California's flavor of the month will probably be next year's world trend.

1984	**1992**	**1994**
Los Angeles hosts the Olympic summer games for the second time (the first time was in 1932). Russia didn't show up, leaving US athletes to win 83 gold medals, 63 more than runner-up Romania.	After a 25-year hiatus California resumes executions at San Quentin by snuffing Robert Alton Harris in the gas chamber for killing two teenagers in San Diego in 1978.	The Northridge earthquake (6.7 on the Richter scale) strikes at 4:30am on January 17, killing 72, injuring 11,846 and causing $12.5 billion in damages, making it among the costliest natural disasters in US history.

THE FUTURE IS NOW

No place in America was more affected by the year-2000 demise of the dotcoms and subsequent plunge of world markets than California, the nation's wealthiest state and the world's fifth-largest economy. To add insult to injury, the same year brought rolling blackouts to California's recently deregulated electricity market, forcing the state to buy its energy on the spot market, day by day, at ridiculously inflated prices. Consumers' bills doubled overnight. Governor Gray Davis, a Democrat, was forced into a corner and negotiated expensive long-term contracts that locked in very high rates for electricity but at least stabilized the market. After the contracts had been signed, allegations emerged that power generators, among them failed energy giant Enron, had created an artificial energy crisis by pulling electricity off the state's grid in a conspiracy to drive up prices. The companies went bust and the money vanished.

In November 2002 Governor Davis won a second four-year term, but Republican malcontents forced an October 2003 recall election on the grounds of 'malfeasance,' blaming the governor for the $40 billion budget deficit. Citizens were angry at Davis' habit of favoring big-money 'special interests,' and Republicans called for his ouster. The charisma-free Gray Davis was replaced with former bodybuilder, action hero and husband of Maria Shriver, Arnold Schwarzenegger, who ran as a moderate Republican.

Despite some early fumbles, the 'Governator' surprised just about everyone by distancing himself from the Bush administration and putting environmental issues, stem cell research and universal health insurance at the top of his agenda. In 2006 he was handily reelected and now enjoys enormous popularity.

Ballistic population growth, pollution, traffic and soaring real estate prices are among the problems that continue to cloud SoCal's sunny skies in the first decade of the new millennium. Meanwhile, the all-important high-tech sector struggles to regain its momentum, the need for public education reform builds, and the conundrum of immigration from Mexico which, though illegal, fills a critical cheap labor shortage for agriculture, continue to bedevil the state. But, with a strong economy, low unemployment and decreasing crime rate, overall morale remains high. And the sun still shines 300 days of the year.

Coyotes – a Journey Through the Secret World of America's Illegal Aliens (1987), Ted Conover's riveting account of his year posing as an illegal immigrant, reveals the hopes, fears and dangers of those hoping for a better life in the US.

In the book *Coast of Dreams* (2004) Kevin Starr, the former state librarian, collates in journalistic style California's recent history (1990 to 2003), during which unprecedented social upheaval forever changed the state's cultural direction.

2000	2003	2005
The population of LA County tops 10 million.	Arnold Schwarzenegger announces his candidacy for California governor on the August 6 edition of *The Tonight Show with Jay Leno*. During the October recall elections he gets 3.74 million votes, just enough to replace Gray Davis.	Antonio Villaraigosa elected mayor of LA, the first Latino since 1872. Born poor in East LA, he said in his victory speech, 'I will never forget where I came from.'

The Culture

Go ahead: mock. Bad-mouth, belittle, bemoan, besmirch, debase, decry, demean, disparage. Get it all out. Put down, reduce, ridicule, slam, sling mud, thrash, trash.

Now open wide and prepare to eat your words, because anyone who thinks that Southern California has no culture hasn't been paying attention.

REGIONAL IDENTITY

There's no city more American than Los Angeles, with all the good and all the bad. Its people are among the nation's richest and poorest, most established and newest arrivals, most refined and roughest, most beautiful and most plain, most erudite and most airheaded. Success here can be spectacular, failure equally so.

But what binds Angelenos is that they are seekers. Nearly everyone – or their forebears – arrived by choice. Whether from across the country or across the globe, they were drawn by a dream, be it fame on the silver screen or money to send back to the family. It's as if America's dreamers rushed west and stopped where the continent ran out of land.

They found plenty of company.

Stereotypes

Valley girls snap chewing gum in shopping malls, surfer boys shout 'Dude!' across San Diego beaches, new immigrants gather around street corners in search of day jobs, surgically enhanced babes sip margaritas poolside, gang-bangers flash hand-signals, harried soccer moms flip out in Orange County's rush-hour traffic and everyone works in 'the Industry.'

Reality

Certainly the stereotype exists, but if that's all you're expecting, you're in for a shock.

The first question you'll often hear from locals is 'What do you do for a living?' It's how people place each other and, unlike elsewhere in America, nobody here is surprised if the answer takes more than a minute; there's nothing unusual about holding down one or more jobs while working toward your ultimate goal.

Daily interaction tends to be pleasant, sometimes to the point that it can be hard to figure out what people really think. Saying someone has 'issues' is a polite way of implying that the person has problems. 'Let's get together' is often not to be taken literally; it can mean 'It was good talking with you, and now I have to go.'

Then, of course, there's the car you drive. There's an underlying truth to the common joke: the right car is to Angelenos what the right shoes are to Italians. Fancy imports, convertibles and muscle cars still turn heads, but the status symbol du jour is the ecofriendly Toyota Prius.

LA and the rest of SoCal have a symbiotic relationship; generally LA goes about its business and the rest of the region either depends on or resents it.

You can see this in politics, for starters. LA leans to the left – often there is no Republican candidate for mayor – and its politicians carry significant weight in Washington (eg Democratic Congress members Henry Waxman of West LA and Santa Monica, Jane Harman of the South Bay and Maxine Waters of South LA).

Few writers nail SoCal's culture as well as Joan Didion. In *Where I Was From* (2003), she contrasts California's mythology and reality.

A dozen SoCal colleges and universities are ranked in the top 50 nationally.

SoCal inventions include the Space Shuttle, Mickey Mouse, whitening toothpaste, the hula hoop (or at least the trademark), Barbie, skateboard and surfboard technology, the Cobb salad and the fortune cookie.

DAMN THAT TRAFFIC JAM!

Traffic is LA's great leveler. Outsiders often marvel that it's a city without a center; that's less true than it used to be thanks to Downtown LA development, but it's also more true in that business districts have dispersed in the last 10 years. And as home prices have risen near these new business districts, workers increasingly have to commute from further away. So while you could once count on traffic into Downtown in the morning and out of Downtown in the evening, now it could happen any time of day. The same could happen anywhere in SoCal. Or you might just as easily find the roads mysteriously clear.

Long-range regional plans call for extensions of subway and light rail lines, but for now our advice is to double the time you think it will take to get anywhere (triple at rush hour), take your cell phone, and should you get stuck in traffic, be Zen about it. Those waiting for you will understand.

However, the rest of SoCal tends to behave more like a 'red state.' We've heard progressive views met with 'Well, that's LA talking' in Orange County, a conservative stronghold with congressmen like Chris Cox and Dana Rohrabacher. However, things are changing even here, as Democrats like Loretta Sanchez win long-held Republican seats in Congress. Conservative politics extend to San Diego and the desert areas, largely because of the high numbers of military personnel and wealthy retirees who live there.

And then there's the rest of California. It's not unusual for Angelenos visiting San Francisco to be told point blank 'Ugh!', 'How can you live there?!?', 'That place is a hellhole!' and worse, and much of the interior of the state reviles LA for having 'stolen' its water. We wouldn't call this a rivalry, though, as it seems to be one-way. Angelenos generally seem to like the rest of the state, or are indifferent to it.

www.laobserved.com is a one-stop blog for media, news and media news.

LIFESTYLE

LA presents a microcosm of America's income disparities. Some of America's richest individuals live in SoCal communities like Montecito, Malibu, Bel Air, Palos Verdes, Newport Beach and Rancho Santa Fe, and their domestic help might commute 1½ hours by bus. But the vast majority here is middle class. After all, this is the birthplace of the planned community. In 2005, the latest year for which figures are available, the national median household income was $48,201, compared with an LA County median of $51,315 (while the percentage below the poverty line in LA was about 15.4%, compared with 12.3% nationally).

In outlying communities (little-visited by tourists) in the West San Fernando, Santa Clarita and San Gabriel Valleys, many people live out the American dream in quiet residential subdivisions. SoCal's poor are concentrated in certain inner-city neighborhoods and in towns in the inland valleys and deserts.

San Diego's carefree outward appearance belies a dark underbelly. Get the dirt in *Under the Perfect Sun: The San Diego Tourists Never See* by Mike Davis et al (2003).

All this means that the very rich and very poor rarely mix except in certain beach communities. Everyone, it seems, likes the weather.

Beach Life

Grab your flip-flops, blanket and umbrella, your bike or rollerblades. Beach culture offers a respite from city life, and it's so close. But which beach to choose? LA's Venice used to be the definitive hippie beach and despite rising real estate prices, some of that aesthetic remains on its boardwalk, a mile-and-a-half-long party with performers, merchants and graffiti artists. Neighboring Santa Monica, meanwhile, is great for kids, including the amusement park on its pier. For views, visit Malibu, La Jolla

---

LIFE AS AN ANGELENO Amy Balfour

Just who lives in LA? If you believe the stereotypes, they're a flaky bunch. Liberal. Self-absorbed. Greedy. Botoxed and blow-dried. Though these adjectives may have a hint of truth for certain subgroups, with 4 million people crammed into the city's 465 sq miles and 10 million jostling for space in sprawling LA County, no one label fits all.

How is LA's ethnic diversity playing out in the early 21st century? Simmering issues of distrust linger between various communities but day-to-day life isn't quite as bleak as portrayed in Paul Haggis' 2005 Oscar-winning *Crash*. The main problem? People are quick to demand respect but slow to give it out. The town also runs high on false friendliness and let's-do-lunch superficiality; there's a bit more 'I' and 'me' than 'we' and 'us.'

But Angelenos aren't all bad. Optimism, open-mindedness and outside-the-box thinking are the norm (studios execs excluded), and people tend to work hard. From illegal immigrants on the corner ready for a long day's work and downtown office workers earning overtime for ballooning mortgage payments to Hollywood assistants holding dreary day jobs while cramming free hours with indie projects, everybody's hustling. Griffith Park might be in flames, the Hollywood Hills crumbling and the ground shaking under our feet, but if it's not blocking traffic, get out of the way. Yes, our reach may sometimes exceed our grasp, but isn't that what LA's for?

---

or the innumerable Santa Barbara County beaches. For surf culture, try Orange County's Huntington Beach or San Diego's Encinitas, Mission or Pacific Beaches.

Gay & Lesbian SoCal

From shiny Palm Springs to San Diego's bohemian Hillcrest neighborhood, arty Laguna Beach and the booming LA enclaves of Silver Lake and West Hollywood, gay and lesbian SoCal is out and proud. High profile gay men and lesbians can be found at all levels of society, from government to business and the arts. The *Advocate* magazine, PFLAG (Parents and Friends of Lesbians and Gays), and America's first gay church and synagogue all started in Los Angeles. Although California does not have same-sex marriage or civil unions, both the state and cities around the region allows registered domestic partnerships.

Gay Pride marches take place throughout the Southland. The largest is in SoCal's gay capital, West Hollywood, with some 350,000 attendees. There are gay and lesbian groups for hiking, camping, swimming, volleyball, running, skiing and snowboarding, yoga and rodeo. Restaurants, coffee houses, bars, clubs, film festivals, houses of worship and theaters all cater to this burgeoning community.

Homelessness

Homelessness exists throughout the Southland (another local term for Southern California), in places you might expect (Downtown LA's Skid Row) and in places you wouldn't (Santa Monica's beachfront). Some homeless are working poor, bankrupt due to high medical care costs, for example. Others have become addicted to drugs or alcohol, or suffer from mental illnesses. Homeless people are more likely to be victimized than cause you harm. Whether you give them money or not is up to you, though a donation to a local charity may help more.

Mike Davis' *City of Quartz* (1990) is an excoriating history of LA and a glimpse into its possible future; in *Ecology of Fear*, he examines the decay of the natural environment in the LA Basin.

MULTICULTURALISM

There were different races even among the first settlers to LA in 1781, and today it is one of only two major metro areas in the nation without a majority ethnic group (the other is Honolulu). Across the region, immigrants from over 140 countries have put down roots, creating the largest populations of

Mexicans, Koreans, Armenians, Filipinos, Salvadorans, Guatemalans and Vietnamese outside their home countries, plus America's largest ethnic Cambodian, Japanese and Persian communities.

All this makes LA one of the most tolerant, cosmopolitan and open-minded societies anywhere. Although there are ethnic enclaves, it's not uncommon to interact with people of 10 races or more in a single day in any corner of the city. You might drop off your shirts with a Korean dry cleaner, have your nails done by a recent Vietnamese immigrant, pick up groceries from a Mexican grocer and a treat from the Cambodian-run doughnut shop. Dinner might just as easily be sushi, falafel, enchiladas or steak-frites, or maybe pad Thai while a Thai Elvis impersonator entertains. Interracial families barely raise an eyebrow.

Certainly, explosive race-related incidents have received high-profile exposure, as with the riots in 1965 in Watts and in 1992 in Los Angeles (p34), yet day-to-day civility between races is the norm. Animosity is hard to maintain when you encounter different races on a daily basis.

In his column ¡Ask a Mexican!, OC Weekly columnist Gustavo Arellano tackles such questions as why Mexicans swim with their clothes on, alongside weighty social issues involving immigrants' rights. See it at www .ocweekly.com or www .laweekly.com.

Latino SoCal

Forty percent of LA County's residents are Mexican by birth or ancestry, and by 2020 Latinos are projected to be the outright majority. Other groups from South and Central America continue to arrive, mostly because opportunities in their home countries are narrowing. Their collective influence is huge. From radio and TV stations to Spanish-language billboards, you'll see and hear Latino culture across the Southland. See p42 for more information.

Despite their numbers, Latinos had little say in leadership until fairly recently. Now LA's mayor, county sheriff, members of the city council and the powerful county board of supervisors are Latino, as well as many representatives in the California State Assembly and US Congress from across SoCal.

Spanish is the *lingua franca* of many SoCal restaurant kitchens, and there's a host of Latino products on grocery-store shelves. Even non-Latino Angelenos can expound on mole and corn versus flour tortillas.

On the music scene, Latino groups are top-sellers at Gibson Amphitheatre and Greek Theatre.

Barrios still exist, most notably in LA's 'gateway' community of Pico Union, where recent Mexican and Central American immigrants first get a toehold in the USA, but nowadays young Latino hipsters are joining their hipster brethren in neighborhoods like Venice, Silver Lake and Echo Park.

In *Once upon a Quinceañera* (2007), Julia Alvarez investigates the art, history and sociology of this ritual among Latinas turning 15 years old (an elaborate party akin to a Sweet Sixteen), infused with traditions from across Latin America.

SOCAL BY THE NUMBERS

Total regional population 21,185,000
Total population of Australia 20,266,000
Total population of California approx 36.5 million
LA County ethnic breakdown Latino 46.8%; Caucasian (non-Latino) 29.5%; Asian or Pacific Islander: 13.4%; African American: 9.7%
Cities in LA County 88
Area of LA County 4081 sq miles (10,571 sq km)
Area of Lebanon 4015 sq miles (10,400 sq km)
Rank of San Bernardino County in area among American counties One (20,105 sq miles)
Number of US states that would fit together into San Bernardino County Four – Rhode Island, Delaware, Connecticut and Massachusetts

For all this upward mobility, Latino workers still do most of the farm labor and domestic work, and many of them are without proper papers. Estimates put the numbers of undocumented/illegal immigrants at between 12 and 20 million nationwide, about one-quarter of whom live in California – the majority of those in SoCal. See p343 for a discussion of border issues.

Other Ethnic Groups

LA's – and SoCal's – vast space has allowed ethnic enclaves to thrive as in few other places. Neighborhoods throughout the region burst with ethnic cuisine, food, clothing and souvenir shops, and houses of worship. Many have community newspapers printed in the native language and social services agencies providing outreach.

LA's Koreatown is the largest, a vast swath between Hollywood and Downtown LA. Little Saigon, in the Orange County towns of Garden Grove and Westminster, has the largest population of ethnic Vietnamese outside Vietnam; many residents emigrated around the end of the Vietnam war, and the population here tends to be vocally opposed to the current Vietnamese regime. There are two Japanese neighborhoods (Downtown's Little Tokyo and around Sawtelle Blvd in West LA), America's first Thai Town, and enclaves from historic Filipinotown to Little Ethiopia. LA's Chinatown offers Chinese dim sum and Vietnamese *pho* (soup), and in the suburban San Gabriel Valley towns of Alhambra, Monterey Park and San Gabriel, Chinese signage is almost as prevalent as English. Venice Blvd in West LA bops with Brazilian cuisine and music, the mayor of Beverly Hills is Iranian-American, West Hollywood has a large Russian immigrant contingent, and it's not uncommon to see black-hatted Orthodox Jews walking to synagogue in the Fairfax and Pico-Robertson districts. Armenians form the largest ethnic group in Glendale, Signal Hill is home to a Cambodian community, and Cerritos and Artesia are the center of Indian activity.

ECONOMY

Even when the US economy is in recession, SoCal generally does all right. What LA lacks in large corporations (with fewer Fortune 500 headquarters than Richmond, VA or Charlotte, NC), it makes up for with diversity. Drivers of the SoCal economy include international trade (LA and Long Beach form the nation's largest port), technology, finance, film and TV production, health services, apparel design, furniture design and higher education.

SoCal's biggest industry, though, is tourism. Visitors are drawn by the weather, international connections at Los Angeles International Airport and the beaches, theme parks and, increasingly, culture. It's also a year-round destination for conventions, particularly big business in San Diego.

SPORTS

2008 marks 50 years since the Brooklyn Dodgers became the Los Angeles Dodgers, and New Yorkers have never quite forgiven LA. Angelenos, meanwhile, have made the Dodgers their own. Ringed by hills, Dodger Stadium is one of the most beautiful in baseball, while San Diego's new PETCO Park comes up a close second. Another team to keep an eye out for is the World Series 2002 winner and still-successful Los Angeles Angels of Anaheim.

Be sure to leave extra time to get downtown at the time of Dodger games and when the LA Lakers basketball team plays at Staples Center; for the latter you'll have to jostle for freeway space with famous fans including Jack Nicholson, Tobey Maguire and Snoop Dogg. The Lakers, in LA since 1967, have a storied history that includes players such as Kareem Abdul-

There are more ethnic Samoans in LA (approximately 60,000) than in American Samoa.

Metro LA has the world's third-largest Jewish population, after New York and Tel Aviv.

Fans of the Los Angeles Dodgers are (in)famous for leaving during the 8th inning in order to beat the traffic exiting Dodger Stadium.

RUNAWAY PRODUCTION

Film and TV production is big business in LA County, bringing in an estimated $31 billion in revenues and ranking third in employment (some 255,000 people) behind tourism and international trade. There's a critical mass of studios and talent, and locations around LA often stand in for other cities: Downtown for Midtown Manhattan, Pasadena for the Midwest, etc.

Other localities have caught on, though, and the high cost of filming in LA has sent location scouts looking elsewhere. States such as New Mexico, North Carolina, Louisiana and Connecticut have offered production credits, tax incentives, state-of-the-art facilities (particularly in New Mexico) and, in some cases, nonunionized workforces. And in Canada, film production is welcomed with open arms (and pocketbooks).

Jabbar, Magic Johnson, Shaquille O'Neal and Kobe Bryant. LA's other NBA team is the Clippers, typically also-rans in the standings as well as in the city's heart. The LA Sparks of the Women's National Basketball Association (WNBA) have been perennial league leaders, featuring their star player Lisa Leslie.

In a saga of money, politics and backroom dealing, LA has been without a National Football League (NFL) team since 1995 (and Angelenos don't seem to mind watching other cities shell out nearly $1 billion to the NFL for the next franchises). The San Diego Chargers, traditionally bottom-dwellers in the standings, have turned things around with a winning record in recent years. Angelenos, meanwhile, have made do quite nicely with two high-profile college football rivals: the UCLA Bruins and USC Trojans. Both are frequent contenders for league titles. NFL stars Matt Leinart and Reggie Bush played for USC.

SoCal has two National Hockey League (NHL) teams: the LA Kings and the Anaheim Ducks. The latter won the 2007 Stanley Cup.

LA's Major League Soccer (MLS) team, the Galaxy, got a boost with the 2007 arrival of soccer – er…football – icon David Beckham and his $250 million price tag. The Galaxy had a spirited Latino following BB (Before Beckham) but AB the team's games are selling out and making the league a household name. A 'Becks' jersey is the hottest ticket out there. Despite the arrival of Beckham, LA's other team, Chivas USA, provides strong competition.

Del Mar Thoroughbred Club in northern San Diego County is the ritziest of SoCal's horse-racing tracks, alongside Hollywood Park and Santa Anita Racetrack in LA County. The Toyota Grand Prix of Long Beach, a Formula 1 race, takes place every April, and California Speedway in Fontana is a mecca for NASCAR fans. In September San Diego hosts the Thunderboat Regatta (p304), in which superfast speed boats race on Mission Bay.

Surfing first hit the US mainland in 1929, when Hawaiian surf legend Duke Kahanamoku gave a demonstration in Huntington Beach (Orange County). It's been Surf City ever since, with numerous competitions every year including the US Open of Surfing each July. Other surf competitions take place in Carlsbad and Oceanside (northern San Diego County) and at San Onofre State Beach in southern Orange County.

Extreme sports in SoCal go back to the 1970s when the Santa Monica–Venice border neighborhood was nicknamed 'Dogtown' for the proliferation of skateboarders (chiefly the Z-boys – the 2005 film *Lords of Dogtown* chronicles their rise). Things have developed rapidly since then, and extreme sports deities Tony Hawk and Shawn White are both from the San Diego area. The Summer X-Games are held in and around Los Angeles in midsummer, at least until 2009; look for daredevil BMX, motocross, skateboarding and surfing competitions.

LA is one of only four cities to have hosted the summer Olympic Games twice, in 1932 and 1984. The others are Athens, London and Paris.

See www.avp.com for beach volleyball tournament schedules and locations.

READ ALL ABOUT IT!

For much of the last century, the *Los Angeles Times* was known as the finest newspaper in the west – a perennial winner of Pulitzer Prizes – but that reputation has been tarnished by ownership changes and in-house scandals.

In 1999 an inexperienced publisher made a revenue-sharing arrangement with the developer of Staples Center, unbeknown to staff who had compiled a special issue about the arena's opening. Staff revolted en masse over the breaking of the 'Chinese wall' between editorial and advertising. Not long after, the *Times'* parent company was purchased by Tribune Media of Chicago, and the paper was out of the hands of the Chandler family for the first time since it was founded in the 1880s. Under Tribune management, circulation continued to decline, and staff defections and firings increased.

In 2007 Tribune was put up for sale and, although several LA bigwigs bid, it went to Sam Zell, a Chicago real estate developer and financial engineer. Staffers expressed confusion and dismay all over again. The paper may yet be spun off to a local buyer if Zell parcels out the company. Stay tuned.

In Santa Barbara, meanwhile, the *News-Press* went through a shake-up of its own. In 2006 reporters at SoCal's oldest newspaper (founded in 1855) went into turmoil, accusing publisher Wendy McCaw of pressuring staff to change reporting. McCaw, for her part, accused staff of bias in reporting. Only two reporters from before the turmoil have not resigned or been fired.

MEDIA

LA is the city that popularized the high-speed car chase, the spectacular show trial and Paris Hilton, but its roots in the media are much deeper and broader.

LA radio stations are among the nation's most influential, particularly National Public Radio's KCRW (89.9FM) and the alt-rock KROQ (106.7FM). Both are famous for breaking new musicians on the American scene, from Blondie and Hole to Norah Jones and Coldplay. DJs such as Rodney Bingenheimer (KROQ) and Jason Bentley, Nic Harcourt and Tom Schnabel (KCRW) are local legends. The *New York Times* has called Harcourt 'the country's most important disc jockey.'

These days, the top-rated TV shows in the LA market tend to be Spanish-language broadcast on Spanish-language networks Univision, Telemundo, Telefutura and Azteca. The region's large Spanish-speaking population and the relative scarcity of channels explain this phenomenon. A watershed for Spanish-language media was the 2006 demonstrations for immigrants' rights; LA morning radio personality Eddie 'Piolín' Sotero (KSCA, 101.9FM) is credited with encouraging over 1 million marchers to fill LA's streets.

In the entertainment industry, reading the 'trades' (*Variety,* the *Hollywood Reporter* and *Backstage West,* the latter for actors) is an important everyday ritual.

In the LA market, four of the top 10 radio stations broadcast in Spanish. In San Diego, only one does.

In San Diego, radio stations whose call letters begin with X instead of the traditional K are broadcasting from Mexico.

RELIGION

LA is one of the world's most religiously diverse communities. It's the nation's largest Roman Catholic archdiocese, and Bahais, Buddhists, Hare Krishnas, Hindus, Jews, Muslims, Sikhs and members of every imaginable Christian denomination are well represented. LA is home to the world's second-largest Mormon temple, with another spectacular temple off the I-5 in San Diego.

Southern California has also long been famous for high-profile offshoots of mainstream traditions. The yogic Self-Realization Fellowship is headquartered in LA, with large centers in Pacific Palisades and the San Diego suburb Encinitas, and West LA's Kabbalah Center has seen many celebrity converts, most notably Madonna, Demi Moore and Ashton Kutcher.

ARTS

LA is the earth's undisputed entertainment capital. Few cities in the US can match its artistic diversity, and no other city can claim the cultural influence – both highbrow and low – that LA exerts worldwide.

It's no news that LA dominates mass media, but it also topped a recent survey of major American tourist destinations for the percentage of visitors to museums and concerts, from world-renowned venues like the Getty Center and Walt Disney Concert Hall to tiny galleries in Chinatown and 99-seat theaters in North Hollywood. Orange and San Diego Counties also have thriving art scenes.

Cinema & TV

Look back on your life and try to imagine a living in a world without Orson Welles whispering 'Rosebud,' Judy Garland clicking her heels together three times, John Travolta dancing in his white suit or the Terminator informing us that he'll 'be back.' LA is where these iconic images are hatched, nurtured and set to fly.

But it's more than the movies. It seems like every other car commercial is shot in Downtown LA, and fashion photographers are common on Santa Monica beach. The upshot: few people come to LA without seeing something or someone they recognize.

Volumes have been written about the films of Hollywood, so we're not going to attempt to cover them here. Instead, here's a sampling of movies that feature the city of Los Angeles, in some cases, almost as a character in itself.

CLASSICS

Perhaps the greatest LA film is Roman Polanski's *Chinatown* (1974), which is about early-20th-century water wars. Vincente Minelli's *The Bad and the Beautiful* (1952) takes a hard look at the film biz, with Lana Turner recalling the exploits of an aggressive, egotistic film producer played by Kirk Douglas. In David O Selznick's *A Star Is Born* (1937), Janet Gaynor plays a woman rising to stardom as her movie-star husband (Fredric March) declines in popularity. A 1954 remake starred Judy Garland; a 1976 remake starred Barbra Streisand.

The most memorable of James Dean's scenes in *Rebel Without a Cause* (1955) takes place above Los Angeles in Griffith Park. A violent world of deals, sexual betrayal and double-crossing drive both good and bad cops to hubristic destinies – and deaths – in the LA of the crime-ridden '50s in *LA Confidential* (Curtis Hanson, 1997). In *The Graduate* (1967), Dustin Hoffman and Anne Bancroft play a game of nihilism, floundering and sexual awakening in 1960s' Pasadena.

The world's first broadcast preacher, Aimee Semple McPherson, opened her own radio station to spread the word from LA's Angelus Temple back in 1924, pioneering the way for televangelists including the Schullers of Orange County's Crystal Cathedral (p250).

LA's San Fernando Valley is the capital of the adult film industry. Studio tours are not available…

SCIENTOLOGY

The LA-based Church of Scientology follows beliefs articulated by L Ron Hubbard in his book *Dianetics* (1950). Scientology's celebrity followers include Tom Cruise and Katie Holmes, Isaac Hayes, John Travolta, Beck and TV journalist Greta van Susteren.

According to the church's website, following the methods of Dianetics 'increases sanity, intelligence, confidence and well-being' and removes 'unwanted sensations, unpleasant emotions and psychosomatic ills that block one's life and happiness.' Church members famously oppose drug abuse and psychiatry. Many outside the church are deeply suspicious and consider Scientology a cult, or at best a commercial enterprise. Church members were convicted of fraud in French courts in 1999, and Germany does not accord it tax-exempt status as a religion.

MUST-SEE LA ACTION FILMS

■ *The Terminator* (1984) – starring the Governator.

■ *Die Hard* (1988) – amazing action scenes in Century City.

■ *The Bodyguard* (1992) – a diva (Whitney Houston) will always love her bodyguard (Kevin Costner) in this action-packed story.

■ *In the Line of Fire* (1993) – Clint has to save the Prez.

■ *Speed* (1994) – great premise: the bus will blow up if the speed falls below 50mph. Big caveat: since when do buses reach above 50mph?

CONTEMPORARY LA

Robert Altman's *Short Cuts* (1993) weaves together several stories by Raymond Carver, showing a sadly depraved Los Angeles and leaving no aspect of LA culture unexamined. Another multistory tale is told in Paul Haggis' Oscar-winning ensemble drama *Crash* (2005). In Joel Schumacher's *Falling Down* (1993), Michael Douglas plays an unemployed defense engineer for whom a traffic jam triggers a war with the world. Quentin Tarantino, in Chandleresque fashion, creates a surreal Los Angeles from the bottom up in *Pulp Fiction* (1994).

Stand and Deliver (Ramón Menéndez, 1988), based on a true story, stars Edward James Olmos as a take-no-prisoners LA high school teacher who whips a bunch of Latino gang members into shape by successfully teaching them college-level calculus. John Singleton's tragic *Boyz n the Hood* (1991), starring Cuba Gooding Jr, offers a major reality check on coming-of-age as a black teenager in the inner city. The small but filling *What's Cooking?* (2000) looks at LA from four different cultural perspectives (African American, Jewish, Latino and Vietnamese) as families gather to celebrate Thanksgiving in their own way. It's directed by Gurinder Chadha, who later directed *Bend It Like Beckham*. The 2007 film *Freedom Writers* (directed by Richard LaGravenese) stars Hilary Swank as a Long Beach high school teacher whose students work out their feelings about race and their own hardships through writing.

In David Lynch's surrealist *Mulholland Drive* (2001), an amnesiac woman tries to put her life back together through encounters with weird and terrifying people on various edges of dark LA mindscapes. *Laurel Canyon* (2002) shows another strange view of life in LA: a young med-school intern and his fiancée return to live with his pot-smoking mother (Frances McDormand), who's producing her latest boy toy's rock-and-roll record in the house.

Three of Paul Thomas Anderson's films have come to be called the 'Valley Trilogy' for their San Fernando Valley locations: *Boogie Nights* (1997) starred Mark Wahlberg as prodigiously endowed porn star Dirk Diggler; *Magnolia* (1999) brought together luminaries including Tom Cruise, Jason Robards and Philip Seymour Hoffman in a tale of interwoven families; and *Punch Drunk Love* (2002) saw Adam Sandler's character overcome serious anger management issues to win a woman's (Emily Watson) affections.

LA COMEDIES

Tony Richardson's outrageously sardonic commentary *The Loved One* (1965), based on an Evelyn Waugh novel about the funeral industry, features Sir John Gielgud and Liberace (as a huckstering mortician). Amy Heckerling and

Ridley Scott's sci-fi thriller *Blade Runner* (1982) projects modern LA way into the 21st century, with buildings reaching far into the sky and chaotic, neglected streets.

Cameron Crowe collaborated on *Fast Times at Ridgemont High* (1982), which launched the careers of Sean Penn, Jennifer Jason Leigh, Nicolas Cage and Forest Whitaker among others, as students at a fictional San Fernando Valley high school (emphasis on the 'high' in the case of Penn's Jeff Spicoli). *Bill & Ted's Excellent Adventure* (1989) featured Keanu Reeves and Alex Winter as time-traveling San Gabriel Valley teen slackers, and Julia Roberts became a screen queen for playing the definitive hooker with a heart of gold in Garry Marshall's *Pretty Woman* (1990). Steve Martin's *LA Story* (1991) hilariously parodies nearly every aspect of LA life, from lattes and colonics to earthquakes. He followed up with the wistful *Shopgirl* (2005), in which a lonely clerk (Claire Danes) selling gloves at Neiman-Marcus finds herself in a love triangle with a sophisticate (Martin) and a goofball (Jason Schwartzman).

The '90s offered some classic LA youth comedies. Heckerling returned to direct *Clueless* (1995) starring Alicia Silverstone as spoiled Beverly Hills teenager Cher Horowitz in an update of Jane Austen's *Emma*. *Swingers* (1996) was Vince Vaughn's breakout film as a Hollywood hipster, coining the word 'money' as the ultimate compliment, and bringing 'Vegas, baby, Vegas!' to the lexicon. And *Go* (1999), an ensemble piece about club kids and a drug deal gone bad, has a cast that reads like a *Fast Times* for the new generation: Katie Holmes, Sarah Polley, Taye Diggs, Timothy Olyphant, Scott Wolf and Jay Mohr.

HOLLYWOOD ON HOLLYWOOD

Hollywood likes nothing better than to make movies about itself. Self-indulgent? Maybe, but often very entertaining. To wit, our own subjective list of 10 Hollywood movies that every cinephile should know:

- *Sunset Boulevard* (1950) – The ultimate Hollywood story. Gloria Swanson plays Norma Desmond, a washed-up silent film star pining for her return, and William Holden plays the screenwriter she hires to make that happen.
- *Singin' in the Rain* (1952) – Exuberant musical fairytale about love in the time of talkies, starring Gene Kelly, Debbie Reynolds and Donald O'Connor.
- *What Ever Happened to Baby Jane?* (1962) – Filmdom's all-time classic catfight film. Bette Davis and Joan Crawford play sisters and former actresses undone after a disfiguring accident and the mind games between them.
- *Silent Movie* (1976) – Screwball comedy from Mel Brooks about a director trying to revive a movie studio by producing the first silent film in decades. *Silent Movie's* also a silent movie... except for one well placed word.
- *Postcards from the Edge* (1990) – Mike Nichols directs Shirley MacLaine and Meryl Streep as a mother-daughter pair dealing with stardom's seamy underbelly.
- *Barton Fink* (1991) – John Turturro and John Goodman have a battle of wits over how to write a screenplay in this dark comedy by the Coen Brothers.
- *The Player* (1992) – In arguably the most accessible film by legendary director Robert Altman, Tim Robbins plays a studio executive who takes his power too far and has to cover for it.
- *Ed Wood* (1994) – Tim Burton directs Johnny Depp as perhaps the worst director in Hollywood history, famous for wearing pink angora sweaters.
- *Swimming with Sharks* (1994) – Kevin Spacey plays a Hollywood agent with no soul. Is there any other kind?
- *Get Shorty* (1995) – In Barry Sonnenfeld's comedy based on the Elmore Leonard novel, John Travolta plays a mafioso who gets entangled in Hollywood and wonders which industry has fewer scruples.

BEYOND LA

In Jake Kasdan's *Orange County* (2002) a surfer desperately tries to get into Stanford University (in Palo Alto, CA) and escape his oddball family; in the meantime you get a humorous snapshot of culture in OC. Ask any oenophile about *Sideways* (2004), and you'll get an earful about Santa Barbara's wine country, Pinot Noir and Paul Giamatti. See p296 for films shot in San Diego.

TELEVISION

SoCal is a common setting for TV, from LA-based *Dragnet* (1950s), *The Beverly Hillbillies* (1960s), *The Brady Bunch* (1970s) and *LA Law* (1980s), through to teen dramedies *Beverly Hills 90210* (1990s), which made zip code into a status symbol, and *The OC* (2000s) set in Newport Beach. *Six Feet Under* gave a glimpse of modern LA through the eyes of a family running a funeral home. *Curb Your Enthusiasm* offers insights – if you can call them that – into Hollywood's smarmier side, while *Entourage* offers the highs, the lows and the intrigues through the eyes of a rising star and his posse. Newcomer *Californication* shows us with no holds barred what happens when a successful New York novelist goes Hollywood.

LA TV station KTLA was the first to use a news helicopter, in 1958.

Audience members come from across the nation for tapings of *The Tonight Show with Jay Leno* as well as innumerable sitcoms and game shows including *Jeopardy!* and *The Price is Right*.

ANIMATION

A young cartoonist named Walt Disney arrived in LA in 1923, and five years later he had his first breakout hit, *Steamboat Willie*, starring a mouse named Mickey. That film spawned the entire Disney empire, and dozens of other animation studios have followed with films, television programs and effects. Among the best known: Warner Bros (Bugs Bunny et al), Hanna Barbera (*The Flintstones*, *The Jetsons*, Yogi Bear and Scooby-Doo), Dreamworks (*Shrek*, *Madagascar*), Film Roman (the *Simpsons*, *King of the Hill*), Klasky Csupo (*Rugrats*), Nelvana (Babar, *Fairly Oddparents*). Even if much of the hands-on work takes place overseas (eg South Korea), concept and supervision is done in LA.

Music

LA's music biz and its attendant club scene arose out of the film industry and the massive post-WWII influx of classically trained European refugees and American jazz, and country music hopefuls. Today it's one of the world's music capitals, not least because so much of the recording industry is based here, and many local DJs end up producing film soundtracks.

SO YOU WANNA BE IN SHOWBIZ...

The following books are points of reference for anyone looking to make it in the Industry:

- *Adventures in the Screen Trade* by William Goldman – a great screenwriter holds court
- *The Art of War* by Sun Tsu – essential tactics for agents and other dealmakers
- *Hello, He Lied* by Lynda Obst – a producer's (and a woman's) perspective on this rough-and-tumble world
- *Story: Substance, Structure, Style and the Principles of Screenwriting* by Robert McKee – words of wisdom from a screenwriting guru
- *Where Did I Go Right?* by Bernie Brillstein – subtitle of this book from the legendary comedy producer: 'You're nobody in this Hollywood unless someone wants you dead'

CLASSICAL

First stop for fans of 'serious music' should be Downtown LA's Walt Disney Concert Hall, home of what's often called the world's greatest symphony orchestra, the LA Philharmonic. The dazzling conductor Esa-Pekka Salonen will pass the baton to young Venezuelan phenom Gustavo Dudamel in 2009. The LA Phil's summer home is the Hollywood Bowl, a favorite venue for classical, jazz and pop performances and even films accompanied by and orchestra.

Orange County boasts the Orange County Performing Arts Center (p270) in Costa Mesa, with two state-of-the-art concert halls, while the San Diego Symphony (p314) performs at Copley Symphony Hall and on Navy Pier in summer. At the time of writing Santa Barbara was looking forward to the March 2008 reopening of the historic Granada Theatre (p391), home to its own symphony. In Palm Springs, check the calendar at the Annenberg Theater at the Palm Springs Art Museum (p353).

The Los Angeles Opera (p202), under the direction of Placido Domingo, plays at Music Center in the Dorothy Chandler Pavilion.

www.losangeles .com/nightlife has extensive listings of local bands, with descriptions and links.

FILM & TV SCORES

LA-born film and TV music practically defines American culture. John Williams, a frequent collaborator with Steven Spielberg, is perhaps the best known of legions of film composers, having created music for *Jaws*, *Star Wars*, *E.T.*, *Raiders of the Lost Ark* and *Schindler's List*, to name just a few. The 1950s through 1980s were a golden age for film scoring, including works by Elmer Bernstein (*The Magnificent Seven*, *Airplane*, *Stripes*, *Ghostbusters*, etc), Bernard Herrmann (*Psycho*, *The Day the Earth Stood Still*, the *Twilight Zone* TV series) and Ennio Morricone (*The Good, the Bad & the Ugly*, *A Fistful of Dollars*).

Present-day composers include Williams, Randy Newman (*The Natural*, *Toy Story*, *Monsters Inc.*, *Cars*), Danny Elfman (*Pee-wee's Big Adventure*, *Edward Scissorhands*, *Men in Black*, *The Simpsons* theme) Lalo Schifrin (*Mission: Impossible*) for starters.

ROCK, PUNK & RAP

The history of LA rock acts reads like a history of American rock itself.

It's hard to say which Los Angeles band could be classed as the most emblematic of the 1960s. Cases could be made for The Doors and The Beach Boys, and The Mamas and the Papas, Joni Mitchell, The Byrds and Crosby, Stills and Nash are all essential LA music acts. The Sunset Strip and the legendary Whisky A-Go-Go were ground zero for the psychedelic rock scene.

The 1980s saw the rise of such punk bands as X, Black Flag, Bad Religion and Suicidal Tendencies, while the more mainstream Bangles, Go-Gos, Oingo Boingo, Jane's Addiction and Red Hot Chili Peppers took the world by a storm. Guns N' Roses was the '80s hard rock band of record. By the 1990s Beck and Weezer had gained national presence. Los Lobos was king of the Latino bands, an honor that has since passed to Ozomatli.

On the rap and hip-hop side of the scene, the '90s West Coast gangsta rap acts included Ice-T, Cypress Hill and NWA, whose *Straight Outta Compton* was a watermark for the genre. NWA's Dr Dre and Ice Cube went off to have their own solo careers, and Dr Dre fostered the careers of Snoop Dogg and Warren G, among others. Later, Korn, Limp Bizkit and Linkin Park combined hip-hop with metal and popularized nu metal. Another key '90s band was No Doubt of Orange County (which later launched the solo career of lead singer Gwen Stefani).

Important local acts since the turn of the millennium include alternative metal band System of a Down (on hiatus as we went to press), indie rockers

The cover image of the Eagles' album *Hotel California* is of the Beverly Hills Hotel, but the group remains unspecific as to which hotel inspired the title.

MUSIC FESTIVALS

A number of annual festivals host a mix of big-name and local acts. Buy tickets early for station-sponsored shows. Some highlights:

■ Coachella Valley Music & Arts Festival (p355) – sweat it in the desert with indie bands, up-and-comers, and occasional top-name talent

■ KROQ Acoustic Christmas – similar musicians; see also www.kroq.com

■ KROQ Weenie Roast – (see www.kroq.com) summer punk and modern rock event

■ Stagecoach Festival (p356) all things country and western, from Willie Nelson and Emmylou Harris to BBQ

■ Sunset Junction (p161) – late August festival where Sunset and Hollywood Blvds meet

---

Rilo Kiley, Latin-fusion sensations Ozomatli, singer-songwriter Gary Jules and the post-punk She Wants Revenge.

Literature

EARLY 20TH CENTURY

Los Angeles has sheltered many illustrious 20th-century writers, among them William Faulkner, F Scott Fitzgerald and Aldous Huxley. During WWII German writers Bertolt Brecht and Thomas Mann resided in LA, exiled from their war-torn homeland.

While much of the local writing talent always seems to be harnessed to the film industry – even Faulkner and Fitzgerald were in LA primarily to make a living by writing screenplays – LA provides an immense wealth of irresistible material to writers. Bookworms will find that novels about the city make for fascinating reading.

Los Angeles has been a favorite subject of novelists since the 1920s. Many have regarded LA in political terms, often viewing it unfavorably as the ultimate metaphor for capitalism. Classics in this vein include Upton Sinclair's *Oil!* (1927), a muckraking work of historical fiction with socialist overtones. Aldous Huxley's *After Many a Summer Dies the Swan* (1939) is a fine ironic work based on the life of publisher William Randolph Hearst (also an inspiration for Orson Welles' film *Citizen Kane*). F Scott Fitzgerald's final work, *The Last Tycoon* (1940), makes scathing observations about the early years of Hollywood by following the life of a 1930s movie producer who is slowly working himself to death.

LA literature is, rightly or wrongly, also associated with pulp fiction. Raymond Chandler is the genre's undisputed king. Start with *The Big Sleep* (1939) and after following Philip Marlowe, private eye, for one book, you may wind up reading all the others, too.

LATE 20TH CENTURY

Because of the great proliferation of SoCal-based authors, we're just highlighting titles that feature the region. LA fiction's banner year was in 1970. Terry Southern's *Blue Movie* concerned the decadent side of Hollywood. Joan Didion's *Play It as It Lays* looked at Angelenos with a dry, not-too-kind wit. *Post Office*, by poet-novelist Charles Bukowski, captured the down-and-out side of Downtown. (Bukowski himself worked at Downtown's Terminal Annex, p134.) *Chicano*, by Richard Vasquez, took a dramatic look at the Latino barrio of East LA.

The mid-1980s brought the startling revelations of Bret Easton Ellis' *Less Than Zero*, about the cocaine-addled lives of wealthy Beverly Hills teenagers. For a more comedic insight into LA during the go-go '80s, pick up Richard Rayner's *Los Angeles Without a Map* (1988), which follows a British man

---

One of the most cynical novels about Hollywood ever written, Nathanael West's *Day of the Locust* (1939) paints a noir picture of the savagery of Tinseltown.

Nobody could break down into simpler terms the psychology of SoCal's culture of fads better than Dr Seuss (Theodor Geisel) in his story *The Sneeches* (1961). Visit his library at the University of California, San Diego (p330).

who gets lost in his Hollywood fantasies while chasing a Playboy bunny. Kate Braverman's *Palm Latitudes* (1988) traces the intersecting lives of a flamboyant prostitute, a murderous housewife and a worn-out matriarch who maintain their strength and dignity against the backdrop of the violence and machismo of LA's Mexican barrio.

Literary pulp fiction made a comeback in the 1990s. Walter Mosley's famed *Devil in a Blue Dress* (1990), set in Watts, places its hero in impossible situations that test his desire to remain an honest man. Elmore Leonard's *Get Shorty* follows a Florida loan shark who moves to SoCal and gets mixed up in the film industry. Both stories – like many of the genre – translated brilliantly into film.

21ST CENTURY

The novels of Carolyn See, who teaches at UCLA, are well crafted and inspiring. In *The Handyman* (1999), a frustrated artist becomes a not-so-good handyman who winds up repairing the lives of his clients, while *There Will Never Be Another You* (2006) is an interwoven tale of death and fracturing relationships in post–September 11 LA. Tara Ison's *The List* (2007) is the darkly comic tale of a couple with a list of 10 things to do before they break up. T Coraghessan Boyle, who teaches at USC, is one of the region's most prolific authors of novels and short stories. *The Tortilla Curtain* (1995) is one of his notable SoCal tales. *Antonio's Gun and Delfino's Dream* (2007) is Sam Quinones' book of short stories of Mexican migration to the US. Peter Lefcourt is a former Hollywood type who now writes satirical novels about the Industry, including *The Deal* (2001) and *The Manhattan Beach Project* (2005). And the prolific Michael Connelly (a former crime writer for the *LA Times*) continues the city's pulp fiction tradition with novels about LAPD detective Hieronymus (Harry) Bosch, the latest being *The Overlook* (2007).

OUTSIDE LA

San Diego novelist Joseph Wambaugh draws on his own experience as a detective to craft crime-fiction novels such as *Floaters* (1996), which centers on the 1995 America's Cup race. Abigail Padgett, also from San Diego, writes engaging mysteries that weave together themes of Native American culture, mental illness and the SoCal desert. Sue Grafton, author of the Kinsey Millhone mystery series and the alphabet mystery series (*A is for Alibi*, et al) sets her novels in Santa Barbara, though in the books it's called Santa Theresa.

Visual Arts

In 2006 Paris' Pompidou Center hosted an exhibition that called Los Angeles an 'Artistic Capital,' a designation that may have surprised folks who haven't spent time here. New York may be the nation's largest art market, but much of the art in that market is made right here. Large art

Susan Sontag, the 'Dark Lady of American Letters,' spent her formative years in LA, although she lived much of her life in New York City; her much-sought-after papers were acquired by UCLA.

Douglas Coupland set the culture-defining *Generation X: Tales for an Accelerated Culture* (1991) in bungalows in Palm Springs. In it, he also coined the term McJob.

To learn more about LA's literary scene, read the *Los Angeles Times* book review or listen to 'Bookworm,' a weekly segment on radio station KCRW (www.kcrw.com).

OTHER IMPORTANT SOCAL AUTHORS

■ Aimee Bender – *Willful Creatures* (2006), *The Girl in the Flammable Skirt* (1988)

■ Ray Bradbury – *The Martian Chronicles* (1950), *Fahrenheit 451* (1953)

■ Jonathan Kirsch – *The Harlot by the Side of the Road* (1998), *A History of the End of the World* (2006)

■ Martin J Smith – *Straw Men* (2001), *Oops* (2006)

colonies have sprung up around Downtown LA, and there are burgeoning gallery scenes there and in LA's Chinatown, as well as in Santa Monica and Culver City.

California Institute of Arts (Cal Arts), in the northern LA county suburb of Valencia, is one of the art world's premier schools. Heavy hitters including Laurie Anderson, John Baldessari, Jonathan Borofsky, Judy Chicago and Roy Lichtenstein have taught there.

For museum-goers, SoCal offers a wealth of opportunities. In Los Angeles alone, the Getty Center, Los Angeles County Museum of Art (LACMA) and Museum of Contemporary Art are world-class venues that keep evolving; the Getty opened the Getty Villa in 2006 to showcase its classical collection, and at the time of writing LACMA planned to open the Broad Contemporary Art Museum in 2008, housing the renowned collection of local real estate magnate and philanthropist Eli Broad. Other unique venues include the Museum of Latin American Art in Long Beach (also recently expanded) and the Hammer Museum in the Westwood district of Los Angeles.

San Diego, too, has many fine museums, many within easy walking distance inside Balboa Park (p297). In Orange County, there's a growing art scene in Santa Ana, home of the Bowers Museum (p250), while in the longstanding artist colony of Laguna Beach, the Pageant of the Masters has just celebrated its 75th anniversary. Held each July and August as part of the city's Festival of the Arts (p274), it's got to be seen to be believed; local residents dress in costume to recreate famous paintings, with minutely detailed sets as their backdrop.

> To find galleries, museums, fine-art exhibition spaces and calendars of upcoming shows throughout SoCal, check out ArtScene at www.artscenecal.com.

Theater

SoCal has a large and active theater scene. The Ahmanson Theater and Mark Taper Forum at Downtown LA's Music Center (p135), Pasadena Playhouse (p203), South Coast Rep (p270), and San Diego's Old Globe Theaters (p314) and La Jolla Playhouse (p330) all have national reputations. Also well known is the Pantages Theater (p107) in Hollywood, which presents major Broadway-style touring productions.

Among actors, LA is known for 'equity waiver' theaters, whose capacity (under 99 seats) allows actors to appear outside of the rules of the stage-actors' union Actors' Equity. Often these small theaters are incubators for larger productions or showcases for up-and-coming actors, writers and directors. Check local listings.

> LA has the largest number of small theaters in the nation.

Architecture

SPANISH MISSION & VICTORIAN STYLES

The first Spanish missions were built around courtyards, using materials the native Californians and padres found on hand: adobe, limestone and grass. The missions crumbled into disrepair as the church's influence waned, but the style remained practical for the climate. It was later adapted as the rancho adobe style, as seen at El Pueblo de Los Angeles (p132), the Presidio (p303) in Santa Barbara and in San Diego's Old Town (p302).

During the late 19th century the upper class built grand mansions to keep up with East Coast fashion, which reflected popular design worldwide during the reign of the UK's Queen Victoria. One of the finest examples of Victorian whimsy is San Diego's Hotel del Coronado (p318). San Diego's Gaslamp Quarter (p284) is also filled with such buildings.

With its more simple, classical lines, Spanish Colonial architecture – or mission revival, as it's also called – rejected the frilly Victorian style and hearkened back to the California missions with arched doors and windows,

> Downtown LA's 73-story, 1018ft US Bank Tower (aka Library Tower) is the tallest building between Chicago and Taiwan.

long covered porches, fountains, courtyards, solid walls and red-tile roofs. The style's heyday lasted from 1890 to 1915. William Templeton Johnson and the young Irving Gill fortified this trend, especially in San Diego. The train depots in LA, San Juan Capistrano and San Diego were built in this style. San Diego's Balboa Park (p297) also showcases some outstanding examples.

CRAFTSMAN & ART DECO

Charles and Henry Greene and Julia Morgan ushered in the Arts and Crafts (Craftsman) movement of the early 20th century. Simplicity and harmony were key design principles in this movement, blending Asian, European and American influences. The movement's defining building is a one-story bungalow. Overhanging eaves, terraces and sleeping porches are transitions between, and extensions of, the house into its natural environment. Pasadena's Gamble House (p148) is one of the most beautiful examples of this.

By the early 1920s it became fashionable to copy earlier architectural periods. No style was off-limits: neoclassical, baroque, Moorish, Mayan, Aztec or Egyptian. Downtown LA's Richard Riordan Central Library (p136) and City Hall (p134) are prime examples.

Art deco also took off during the 1920s and '30s, with vertical lines and symmetry creating a soaring effect, often culminating in a stepped pattern toward the top. Heavy ornamentation, especially above doors and windows, featured floral motifs, sunbursts and zigzags. You can see it in the Eastern Columbia building (p138) in Downtown LA and the Sunset Tower Hotel (p165) in West Hollywood.

Streamline Moderne, a derivative of art deco, sought to incorporate the machine aesthetic, in particular the aerodynamic look of airplanes and ocean liners. Great examples of this style include the Coca-Cola Bottling Plant in Downtown LA (p140) and the Crossroads of the World (p108) building in Hollywood.

MODERNISM

Also called the 'International Style,' modernism was initiated in Europe by Bauhaus architects Walter Gropius, Ludwig Mies van der Rohe and Le Corbusier. Its characteristics include boxlike building shapes, open floor plans, plain facades, abundant glass and, for residences, easy access between indoor and outdoor spaces. Austrian-born Rudolph Schindler and Richard Neutra brought early modernism to LA and Palm Springs, where Swiss-born Albert Frey also worked. Both Neutra and Schindler were influenced by Frank Lloyd Wright, who designed LA's Hollyhock House (p108) in a style he fancifully called 'California Romanza.' Modernism has become the signature style of Palm Springs; see p350.

POSTMODERNISM

Postmodernism was partly a response to the starkness of the International Style, and sought to re-emphasize the structural form of the building and the space around it. Richard Meier perfected and transcended the postmodernist vision at West LA's Getty Center (p117). LA-based Frank Gehry is known for his deconstructivist buildings with almost sculptural forms and distinctive facade materials, such as at the high-profile Walt Disney Concert Hall (p134) in Downtown LA. Thom Mayne of LA's Morphosis firm has also made his mark with such avant-garde buildings as the Caltrans District 7 Headquarters (p157). Both Gehry and Mayne are winners of the Pritzker Prize, the Oscars of architecture.

The Irvine Company, a private real estate firm, controls much of southern Orange County's architectural design. The predominant style is Tuscan.

Palm Springs Weekend (2001) by Alan Hess and Andrew Danish is the definitive guide to midcentury modern architecture, with brilliant photographs.

www.lottaliving.com profiles modern architecture in LA.

Food & Drink

Southern California's culinary scene is one of the world's best and most diverse. Many trends began here, from the popularity of sushi and Mexican cuisine to really great salads and 'fusion' cooking (think Japanese-Italian and Chino-Latino). And California cuisine continues to redefine itself – and the way America eats.

STAPLES & SPECIALTIES

Southlanders are blessed with an abundance of choice. While LA is famous for chichi, high-end restaurants run by celebrity chefs, you needn't spend a fortune to eat well.

Jonathan Gold, restaurant critic for the *LA Weekly*, won the Pulitzer Prize for criticism in 2007, the first time a restaurant critic has won this award. Pick up the paper for free around town, or visit www.laweekly.com.

Ethnic Cuisines

No less than Ruth Reichl (editor of *Gourmet* magazine and former restaurant critic for the *Los Angeles Times*) has said that LA's real culinary treasure is its ethnic restaurants. With 140 nationalities in LA County alone, we can only scratch the surface, but this will get you started. For information on where to find ethnic restaurants, see p54.

MEXICAN

Mexican food is iconic here, and not just among people of Mexican heritage. Until you've tasted *carnitas* (braised pork) or fish tacos washed down with a cold beer or a margarita, you haven't experienced SoCal culture.

Virtually any Cal-Mex lunch or dinner starts with tortillas (flatbread made of wheat or corn flour). Small ones are wrapped around grilled or roasted meat, cheeses and vegetables and called tacos; larger, rolled versions are enchiladas (these are covered in sauce and baked), while burritos are huge tortillas, stuffed with the same sort of things, plus rice and beans. Rather than slushy sauce, local salsa is more likely a finely diced salad of tomatoes, onions, cilantro and jalapeño peppers.

The Cobb salad – lettuce, avocado, chicken breast, watercress, cheese, egg, chives and French dressing – was invented in 1937 by Bob Cobb, owner of the Brown Derby restaurant in Hollywood.

JAPANESE

Angelenos were chowing on sushi when vast stretches of America still considered spaghetti a foreign food, but SoCal's Japanese food scene goes far beyond raw piscine treats. Many a good meal starts with *edamame* (boiled soybeans in the pod) and continues with *kushiyaki* (grilled skewers of chicken or vegetables), tempura (lightly battered and fried vegetables or fish) or 'tofu steak' (tofu with egg and soy sauce, simmered on a hot iron plate).

CHINESE

Sure, you'll find *kung pao* this and General Tso's that but if you can, indulge in dim sum. A small army of servers stroll around cavernous rooms for up to 800 diners filled with circular tables, pushing carts loaded with dumplings like *har gao* (shrimp) and *shu mai* (pork). Regional cuisines of China, such as Hunan and Szechuan, are well represented.

SMALL BUT MIGHTY

One of the hottest trends these days is 'small plate' dining, in which diners order a number of diverse appetizer-sized dishes of food, allowing everyone at the table to share. It's not unlike Spanish tapas, but in SoCal you're just as likely to find small plates in Japanese or French restaurants.

KOREAN
The signature dish is beef ribs (*kalbi*), marinated in soy, sesame and garlic and grilled before you at the table – vents above each table whisk away the smoke. *Bibimbap* is a large bowl of mixed Korean vegetables and rice (meat optional) and hot chili sauce. All dishes are served with a variety of healthy side dishes including *kimchi* (spicy pickled cabbage).

VIETNAMESE
Vietnam's national dish is *pho* (pronounced 'fuh'), rice noodles in beef broth, topped with meat and served with a plate of bean sprouts and Vietnamese basil, which you add to the soup along with chili sauce or hoison sauce to taste. Also look for grilled meats and sausages over rice.

California Cuisine
The cardinal rule of California cuisine is that the ingredients should be extremely fresh, minimally processed and prepared so that the flavors speak for themselves. Locally grown and organic foods are increasingly used. Chefs generally rely on flavor-packed reduction sauces rather than fatty gravies. Apart from that, there are few rules, and influences may come from Europe, Asia or Latin America.

Fresh Fruits & Vegetables
Make all the jokes you want about Southern California being the land of fruits, nuts and flakes. It's true, and locals couldn't be prouder. Avocado, citrus, dates, berries and all manner of greens are just some of the crops grown between Santa Barbara County and the border.

In salads, forget iceberg lettuce (although that too is grown here): a SoCal salad is likely to include endive, radicchio, arugula and other greens that won't pass your spell checker. Other classics: the Cobb salad (invented in Hollywood), the Caesar salad (invented in Tijuana, Mexico) and the Chinese chicken salad – sliced Napa cabbage with slivered carrot, green onion and grilled chicken, with a sweet and tangy soy-based dressing.

Meat & Fish
People associate SoCal with vegetarianism, but locals love meat; new, trendy steakhouses are opening all the time. Many print on the menu the names of the farms that supply their produce, meats and cheeses.

With hundreds of miles of coastline, fishing is not only a huge industry, but a popular sport. As you travel between Santa Barbara and San Diego, spring through fall, you'll often see halibut and tuna on restaurant menus, some of it locally caught. Salmon is especially popular, though much of it comes from elsewhere.

DRINKS
California produces excellent wines up and down the state, with the largest SoCal growing regions in Santa Barbara County (known for pinot noirs and Rhône-style wines like Syrah, Morvedre and viognier) and Temecula, near San Diego. Many wineries have tasting rooms, and their wines are served at nearby restaurants, though 'local' does not always translate into 'inexpensive.'

Beer drinkers: seek out microbreweries listed in the destination chapters. They usually serve good pub grub as well.

The margarita (tequila, orange liqueur and lime juice) is the drink of choice with Mexican cuisine, and sake with Japanese – higher-grade tequilas and sakes will help avoid hangovers! The last decade has seen a big comeback

Some species of seafood are being overfished, causing environmental degradation. To find out what's safe to eat (and what's not), check out the Monterey Bay Aquarium's Seafood Watch List at www.mbayaq.org/cr /seafoodwatch.asp.

California produces more than 17 million gallons of wine annually.

Famed culinary writer MFK Fisher's post-humously published memoir, *To Begin Again: Stories and Memoirs 1908-1929* (1994), addresses the 'art of living well gastronomically.' It also describes Southern California before it was all built up.

of 1950s-style martini bars. The use of vodka instead of the traditional gin allows for such wacky deviations as lemon- and chocolate-flavored martinis that would make grandparents shiver. Palm Springs in particular embraces martini culture.

Some chichi joints in SoCal levy a tax on birthday-cake 'cuttage.' Well-wishers may be surprised to find they're being charged to cut the cake – even if it's already cut!

Expect strong coffee in SoCal's ubiquitous cafés, and tea drinkers can choose from dozens of varieties. In more casual restaurants, however, the brew will probably look like dirty dishwater. Virtually anything is available in decaf.

A special treat in Asian neighborhoods is boba tea, sweetened milk tea with black tapioca 'pearls' at the bottom, sipped through a thick straw.

Fruit smoothies are another SoCal staple: fruit blended with ice, yogurt, sorbet, 'vitamin boosters' or other goodies. These concoctions really hit the spot on a hot day.

CELEBRATIONS

Weddings, bar mitzvahs, movie premiers and such are often catered affairs designed to impress. Holidays like Thanksgiving and Christmas, meanwhile, tend to be home-based, with family and friends gathering 'round the roast turkey and TV. Most restaurants close on these holidays, except for Chinese restaurants.

A stunning exposé about food in America, *Food Politics: How the Food Industry Influences Nutrition and Health*, by Marion Nestle (2003), tracks the influence of big business on the American diet.

Barbecuing is the rule on warm-weather holidays like Independence Day and Labor Day: hot dogs, steaks and chicken, salmon and veggie burgers – if it fits on the grill, it goes.

Cinco de Mayo (May 5) is celebrated with gusto from Santa Barbara to San Diego. Look for wild revelers and copious tequila drinking at any Mexican restaurant.

WHERE TO EAT & DRINK

Dinner is usually the main meal of the day. Typical restaurant hours are 7am to 11am for breakfast, 11:30am to 2:30pm for lunch, and dinner between 5:30pm and 10pm. Most people start dinner between 6pm and 8pm. If a restaurant accepts reservations, book a table.

You'll find Mexican restaurants on virtually any block, as are Japanese places, though the latter are most concentrated in LA neighborhoods like Little Tokyo and Sawtelle Blvd in West LA. LA's Chinatown and communities to its east in the San Gabriel Valley are the epicenter of Chinese cooking. LA's Koreatown and Orange County's Little Saigon are both the largest respective expat communities outside their home countries. And San Diego has a thriving Little Italy. In LA, go to West Hollywood, Mid-City and Santa Monica for Californian cuisine.

For smoothies, look for outlets like Jamba Juice, and forget Starbucks for coffee; locals swear by LA-based chain Coffee Bean & Tea Leaf.

Some 90% of all dates grown in America are from the Coachella Valley, centered around the town of Indio. See p359 for more information.

Farmers Markets

Cities throughout the Southland have farmers markets on select days of the week, where farmers and small producers of foods such as honey and cheese come to sell their best, sometimes from hours away. Prices are usually sky-high but quality is excellent, and most vendors offer free samples. Keep an eye out for specialty produce that is available only for a week or two out of the year. Some farmers markets also provide activities and entertainment for the kids.

Many of the products at farmers markets are organic. Top chefs, whom you may well encounter at farmers markets, insist on organics, claiming that they're not only more environmentally friendly, they simply taste better, especially tomatoes and strawberries.

Supermarkets

In addition to traditional supermarkets such as Ralphs, Vons, Pavilions and Albertsons, the following specialty chains have faithful followings:

Bristol Farms (www.bristolfarms.com) Small chain of gourmet supermarkets. Attractive presentations, stellar selection and prices to match.

Gelson's (www.gelsons.com) Though rather pricey, this local chain excels at anything fresh – produce, meat, fish, flowers, baked goods etc – and is dependable in all other departments.

Trader Joe's (☎ 800-746-7857; www.traderjoes.com) Many Southlanders count this chain of small gourmet markets as one of life's essentials, alongside sunshine and the beach. TJ's, which began in the San Gabriel Valley, offers an amazing, budget-priced selection of great wines, cheeses and prepared foods.

Whole Foods Market (www.wholefoods.com) Excellent, comprehensive natural-foods store with fresh produce, meat and fish, plus shelves of vitamins.

Quick Eats

Virtually all grocery stores sell to-go food: sandwiches, freshly roasted chickens, sushi, salads, deli meats and cheeses. Sit-down restaurants can often accommodate you with quickly served meals if you let the staff know as soon as you arrive.

VEGETARIANS & VEGANS

SoCal is so vegetarian-friendly that it's almost a cliché. While strictly vegetarian restaurants are rare outside the bigger cities, virtually every restaurant offers at least some vegetarian options. Chinese and Indian restaurants are plentiful (people do astonishing things with tofu). In Western-style restaurants look for vegetarian pastas, grilled portobello mushrooms and more. Even many Mexican restaurants offer vegetarian dishes (unusual in Mexico) – just make sure they don't use lard in the beans.

HABITS & CUSTOMS

The dress code at Southern California restaurants is generally casual, or 'smart casual' at midpriced and top-end restaurants. For women this means a dress, nice pants or a skirt combined with a stylish top; men will do fine with a collared shirt or fashionable T-shirt (with maybe a sport coat), a nice pair of slacks or designer jeans, and presentable shoes. Fancier dress is expected only at receptions or old-line restaurants. If you're uncertain about what to wear, call ahead.

As at restaurants anywhere in the US, tips are a large part of servers' incomes, and not tipping or only giving a very small tip is a serious insult. Giving 15% to 20% of the bill is the norm. A simple rule of thumb is to double the tax as it appears on the bill. At bars, figure on $1 per drink. For particularly good service, you might tip even higher and/or offer a kind word to the manager. Tipping is not required at takeout or counter-service restaurants, though many of these have tip jars for you to leave some extra change and earn karma points.

By state law, smoking is illegal in restaurants and bars; the only exception is on outdoor patios, and many cities prohibit even that. Smokers who are guests in a private home should smoke outdoors unless your host indicates otherwise.

When invited to someone's home, it's polite to offer to bring something for the meal. Even when the host says no, many guests still bring chocolates, flowers or a bottle of wine. Do not bring food that requires preparation unless you've discussed it with the host, and do not expect the host to necessarily set out your gift that day.

See p74 for tips when traveling with children.

When Trader Joe's, the popular LA County-based grocery chain, opened its first store in New York City, it had to send employees from SoCal to give niceness training to local hires.

For informal gatherings, many Southlanders swear by 'Two-buck Chuck', nickname for Charles Shaw wines sold at Trader Joe's markets. These six varietal wines cost an unbelievably cheap $1.99 per bottle, but they've won numerous awards in wine competitions.

California grows more apples, pears, peaches, grapes, oranges and tomatoes than any other state in the US. Many of them end up at farmers markets throughout the Southland.

COOKING COURSES

If the proliferation of cooking shows on TV, fancy kitchen supply stores and gourmet food emporia is any indication, cooking at home is, well, hot. Immerse yourself in the local foodie scene and bring your SoCal trip back to your table at home by checking out any or all of these culinary schools.

California Sushi Academy (Map p97; ☎ 310-559-0777; www.sushi-academy.com; 2835 S Robertson Blvd, Mid-City, Los Angeles) You can study to be a professional sushi chef here, but most people just come for the 2½-hour basic seminars offered Saturdays for $80.

Chefmakers Cooking Academy (Map p94; ☎ 310-545-9111; www.chefmakers.com; 451 Manhattan Beach Blvd, Manhattan Beach, Los Angeles) In addition to more standard offerings, Chefmakers invites local celebrity chefs like Joe Miller of Joe's in Venice (p183) to teach classes ($125).

New School of Cooking (Map p97; ☎ 310-842-9702; www.newschoolofcooking.com; 8690 Washington Blvd, Culver City, Los Angeles) Seasoned instructors run multiweek courses or single-session three-hour classes ($75 to $95) built around a theme, technique, ingredient or dish (eg summer pies, wok, fish, paella).

Laguna Culinary Arts (Map p271; ☎ 949-494-4006; www.lagunaculinaryarts.com; 845 Laguna Canyon Rd, Laguna Beach, Orange County) Besides comprehensive home and professional chef courses, this outfit also offers three- and four-hour classes ($75 to $95) in which you learn how to prepare a particular specialty or full meal.

In *Spanglish* (2004), Adam Sandler plays a chef in a top LA restaurant, who learns a thing or two about life from Flor, the family maid, played by Paz Vega. Top chef Thomas Keller, of the French Laundry restaurant in Napa Valley, consulted on the food scenes.

Environment

THE LAND

When Cecil B DeMille and DW Griffith started making movies back in the early 20th century, they didn't set up their cameras in New York, Chicago or San Francisco. They came to Los Angeles. Why? The land, of course. Southern California packs more landscapes into its relatively small frame than most countries. The Santa Monica Mountains (p153) have stood in for Korea, Batman parked his car in Griffith Park's Bronson Caves (p144) and the Paramount Ranch (p153) has been passed off as the Indonesian island of Java.

For visitors, this is a pretty exciting prospect. It's no myth that you could greet the sunrise while surfing in Malibu, spend the afternoon skiing in Big Bear, then have dinner alfresco in Palm Springs (though nobody really does). With 250 miles of coastline, three peaks soaring over 10,000ft, fertile valleys where fine wines grow, pine forests, sand dunes, parched canyons and wildflower-draped hillsides, nature has been as creative in SoCal as Picasso in his prime.

We all know Southern California ends at the Mexican border, but ask 10 people where it starts and you'll get 10 different answers. Geographically speaking, though, it's pretty obvious. Looking at a map, you'll see a chain of east–west-trending mountains (no more than 5000ft high) just north of Santa Barbara, which divides the state in two. These are the so-called Transverse Ranges and include the lovely Santa Ynez Mountains.

South of here is the vast Los Angeles Basin, wedged between the Pacific and a bunch of north–south-running mountains that extend past San Diego into Mexico. On the other side of these mountains is the desert, well, two deserts to be precise. First there's the low-lying Sonoran or Colorado Desert, home to the Salton Sea (p372) and Anza-Borrego Desert State Park (p368). At Joshua Tree National Park (p363) it transitions into the higher elevated Mojave Desert, which also embraces Death Valley (p223). The infamous San Andreas Fault runs right through this area.

Los Angeles lies at the same latitude as Atlanta, Georgia; Beirut, Lebanon; and Osaka, Japan.

If you look at a map of the California coast, you can see the outline of a man's profile just north of Santa Barbara. Republicans call it Ronald Reagan; Democrats, Franklin Delano Roosevelt.

AN AUDIENCE WITH A MONARCH

Monarch butterflies are beautiful orange creatures that follow remarkable migration patterns and – like many Midwesterners and Canadians – prefer to spend the winter in California. Although most hang out on the state's Central Coast, the most intrepid make it all the way to Southern California. Walt Sakai, biology professor at Santa Monica College and a highly recognized authority on monarchs, shares with us his favorite local viewing spots:

■ The premier site in Southern California is Ellwood Main in Gaviota. From Hwy 101, take the Storke exit south, turn right on Hollister Ave and left on Coronado after the 7-Eleven. At the end of the road, walk into the gully and turn right towards a clearing. After Thanksgiving in late-November/early December is the best time to see the butterflies.

■ In Ventura (p402), a good spot is Camino Real Park in December and January. Monarchs can be found in the eucalyptus grove above the creek near the tennis courts, upstream and north of Telegraph Rd. Access is via the church parking lot and up the drainage. From Hwy 101, go north on Victoria Ave, left on Telegraph Rd, left on S Bryn Mawr and right on Aurora Dr.

■ Big Sycamore Canyon in Point Mugu State Park in the Santa Monica Mountains (p153) also plays host to the butterflies, especially in the sycamore trees by the Hike and Bike camping area. October is the best month to see them and they're often gone by mid-November.

LOS ANGELES RIVER: STRUGGLES OF A TORTURED STREAM

Obstreperous. Wimpy. Murderous. Unpredictable. And occasionally nonexistent. At a mere 52 miles in length, perhaps no other river on earth has experienced – or caused – more calamity per mile than the Los Angeles River. From its source near Calabasas it wends its way through the San Fernando Valley, then right through Downtown LA and finally empties into the Pacific at Long Beach, where the *Queen Mary* is the 'toothpick' in its mouth.

The LA River was the water source for the original pueblo settlers and has changed its course constantly. Sometimes its flow was completely halted by droughts. At other times it became a raging torrent, bringing death and destruction to nearby townships. It was this aspect of the river's 'Jekyll and Hyde' personality that inspired the Army Corps of Engineers to encase the 'off-and-on monster' in concrete in 1938.

Since that time the LA River has been many things: a movie set (*Terminator II, Chinatown, Transformers*); an eyesore, neglected and polluted; and a political battleground between developers, City Hall and green activists. Enter Friends of the Los Angles River (FoLAR; www.folar.org) in 1986. Spurred on by its founder, poet and journalist Lewis MacAdams, the river has become a cause célèbre for a vast coalition of environmental and political groups, including the Coastal Conservancy and the Trust for Public Land. Enormous effort is going into cleaning up its banks and marshes and protecting it from industrial runoff and toxic dumping. A master plan (http://ladpw .org/wmd/watershed/LA/LA_River_Plan.cfm) has been put in place that will create a sanctuary for 400 bird species and establish biking paths and parks along the river.

Where will the story of the Los Angeles River end? For now, all that's certain is that the river ends in Long Beach. Perhaps one day it will simply tire of its uneasy relationship with Los Angeles and just 'run off' – so to speak – with another city altogether.

So what about those earthquakes? Yup, we got 'em. Every day. Many of them. SoCal sits on one of the world's most active earthquake zones, right where the Pacific Plate and North American Plate butt heads. But don't worry, most are way too small to notice.

WILDLIFE

Animal encounters are probably not the main reason to come to Southern California (one particularly famous mouse notwithstanding). Still, keep your peepers open and you'll be surprised how many critters call the region home, as built up and congested as it is.

Animals

Take a virtual field trip courtesy of the myriad links put together by the California Geological Survey at www.conserva tion.ca.gov/cgs/geotour.

When it comes to animals in SoCal, think big. School-bus big. Sixteen-ton gray whale big. Although these fascinating creatures don't exactly have a permanent LA address, gray whales generally grace the region with their presence every year between December and April. That's when they migrate along the Pacific coast, traveling from their summer feeding grounds in the arctic Bering Sea, through to their southern breeding grounds off Baja California – and then all the way back again. You can watch them spout and breach from such shoreline viewing spots as the Cabrillo National Monument at Point Loma (p319) in San Diego or Point Vicente (p128) in Los Angeles. Better yet, it's well worth heading out to meet them on their turf by going on a whale-watching tour (p67).

Any time of year, you'll see pods of bottle-nosed dolphins and porpoises frolicking just offshore. If you're lucky, you may even get to swim along with these smiley mammals. To see pinnipeds such as clumsy seals, barking sea lions and playful sea otters in the wild rather than at SeaWorld, you'll probably have to travel to the Channel Islands National Park (p405). They're cute, they're worth it and kids love 'em.

Out on the boat, or just standing on the beach, you'll also spot plenty of winged creatures, including hefty pelicans darting for lunch like top gun pilots, and skinny sandpipers foraging for invertebrates in the wet sand. SoCal is also an essential stop on the migratory Pacific Flyway between Alaska and Mexico. Almost half the bird species in North America use local coastal and inland refuges for rest and refueling. Grab a pair of binoculars and scan the skies for avocets, green-winged teals and northern pintails at Malibu Lagoon State Beach (p121) in Los Angeles, Bolsa Chica State Ecological Reserve (p258) or Newport Bay Ecological Reserve (p264) in Orange County, or the Batiquitos Lagoon (p337) in San Diego.

Also keep an eye out for the regal bald eagle, which soared off the endangered species list in 2007. A bunch of them have regained a foothold on Catalina Island (p220) and some also like to spend winters at Big Bear Lake (p221), where actual bear encounters, while possible, are exceedingly rare.

And so, you might think, are animals in the desert. Wrong. The desert is far from deserted but most critters are too smart to hang out in the daytime heat. Roadrunners, those black-and-white mottled ground cuckoos with long tails and punk-style mohawks, can often be spotted on the side of the road. Other desert inhabitants include burrowing kit foxes, tree-climbing grey foxes, jackrabbits, kangaroo rats and a variety of snakes, lizards and spiders. Desert bighorn sheep and myriad birds flock to watering holes in palm oases.

> If you can't tell your green-winged teal from your white-tailed kite, pick up one of the excellent field guides published by the Audubon Society (www.audubon.org), which are small enough to carry in a purse or daypack.

Plants

You've seen them on film, you've seen them on TV. Those swaying palm trees with trunks as slender as a giraffe's neck that are so evocative of Southern California. Well, those guys are like most locals: they're not really from here. In fact, the only native SoCal palm tree is the fan palm, found naturally in such desert oases as the Indian Canyons (p350) of Palm Springs.

Oak trees are a different story. California has 20 native species of oak. Along the coast look for live, or evergreen, oaks with hollylike leaves and fuzzy acorns. You'll traipse past them in the Santa Monica Mountains and other coastal ranges. Other common plants include the aromatic California laurel, whose long slender leaves turn purple, and manzanita, treelike shrubs with intensely red bark and small berries.

The Torrey pine, on the other hand, is super-rare. This gnarly tree, which has adapted to sparse rainfall and sandy, stony soils, only grows

> Tree-huggers will thrill for *Oaks of California* by Bruce Pavlik et al (1991), which details the history and ecology of California's 20 indigenous species of oak, with gorgeous photographs and excellent locator maps.

GREENING UP LA

Cities in the US have lost 20% of their trees in the last decade alone. But if LA Mayor Anthony Villaraigosa has his way, that trend will soon be reversed in his city. Called the Million Trees Initiative (www.milliontreesla.org), the idea has caught on like – pardon the expression – wildfire. By enlisting the expertise and grassroots skills of groups like Tree People (www.treepeople.org) and the LA Department of Parks and Recreation (www.laparks.org), volunteers are being trained and directed in the task of planting hundreds of thousands of trees in the megalopolis over the next few years.

If people like Mayor Villaraigosa, Leonardo DiCaprio and Tree People founder Andy Lipkis have their way, the stereotypical images of Los Angeles will soon be harder to come by. Oh you'll still have the horrifying traffic, the relentless sprawl of development, and 747s roaring in and out of LAX. But there will be two gigantic differences: the air in which they exist will be far, far better and they'll be much harder to spot through the outreaching branches of all those new trees.

at Torrey Pines State Reserve (p330) near San Diego and on Santa Rosa Island (p405), part of Channel Islands National Park and home to dozens of endemic plant species. The same is true of Catalina Island, where you'll find the Catalina ironwood, Catalina mahogany, Catalina Manzanita and Catalina bedstraw at the Wrigley Memorial & Botanical Gardens (p220).

Except for the deserts and high mountain ranges, the hills of SoCal turn green in winter, not summer. As soon as the rains arrive, the dried-out brown grasses spring to life. As early as February, wildflowers pop up, most notably the bright orange California poppy, the state flower. Resist the temptation to pick one or risk facing a $500 fine. Along the coast little purple wild irises flower until June.

A colorful survey of California's wildflowers from desert to alpine can be found at www.calaca demy.org/research/botany/wildflow.

Nothing says desert more than a cactus. Cacti and other desert plants have adapted to the arid climate with thin, spiny leaves that resist moisture loss (and deter grazing animals), and seed and flowering mechanisms that kick into gear during brief rains. The sheer variety of cacti is astonishing. The cholla cactus, for instance, appears so furry that it's nicknamed 'teddy-bear cactus.' But beware, it's far from cuddly and instead will bury extremely sharp, barbed spines in your skin at the slightest touch. Ouch! If you're lucky enough to visit in spring, you'll get to see its bright-yellow flower.

Almost as widespread are prickly pears, flat cacti that produce showy flowers in shades of red, yellow and purple, and whose juice is still used medicinally in Mexico today. The smoke tree, a small, fine-leafed tree with a smoky blue color, is said to indicate the presence of underground water. Like figments from a Dr Seuss book, the whimsical Joshua trees are the largest type of yucca and are related to the lily. They were named by migrant Mormons, who saw them as Joshua welcoming them to the promised land. They grow throughout the Mojave but are, of course, most abundant in Joshua Tree National Park (p363).

For complete information about national parks, from activities to zoology, visit the National Park Service website at www.nps.gov.

Then there's the cactuslike creosote (actually a small bush with hard leaves and a distinctive smell) and the spiky ocotillo shrub, which grows up to 20ft tall and has canelike branches that produce blood-red flowers. And watch out for catclaw, nicknamed 'wait-a-minute bush' because its small, sharp, hooked spikes can snatch you as you brush past.

NATIONAL PARKS

Southern California has two federally protected parks. Joshua Tree National Park (p363), north of Palm Springs, straddles the transition zone between the Colorado Desert and the higher, cooler and moister Mojave Desert. It's home to the yuccalike Joshua tree, made famous by Irish rockers U2 who posed in the park on the cover of their 1987 *Joshua Tree* album. World-class rock climbers know 'J-Tree' as the best place to climb in California. Backpackers are less enthusiastic, as there is no natural water flow, but day hikers and campers enjoy the chance to scramble up, down and around the giant boulders and palm oases, while mountain bikers are hypnotized by desert vistas.

For a comprehensive list of all California State Parks, from beaches to mountains to historical parks, log on to www.parks.ca.gov.

The Channel Islands are an eight-island chain lying off the coast from Newport Beach to Santa Barbara. The four northern islands of San Miguel, Santa Rosa, Santa Cruz and Anacapa – along with tiny Santa Barbara island, 38 miles west of LA – comprise the Channel Islands National Park (p405). Remote and uninhabited, these islands support unique flora and fauna, including 150 endemic species, and extensive tide pools and kelp forests. Getting there requires a boat ride on often-choppy seas, which keeps visitor numbers refreshingly low.

SOUTHERN CALIFORNIA'S NATIONAL & STATE PARKS

Park	Features	Activities	Best time to visit
Anza-Borrego Desert State Park (p368)	badlands, canyons, fan-palm oases, caves, bighorn sheep, birds	4-wheel driving, stargazing, hiking, horseback riding hot springs: bighorn	Nov-Mar
Channel Islands National Park (p405)	rocky islands with steep cliffs, elephant seals, sea lions, otters, foxes	snorkeling, diving, kayaking, hiking, birding	year-round
Crystal Cove State Park (p264)	beach, woodland, marine park, coastal sage, sea anemones, cottontail rabbits, bobcats	hiking, biking, diving	year-round
Death Valley National Park (p223)	unique geology, sand dunes, canyons, volcanic craters, pickleweed, creosote bush, salt grasses, pines, coyotes, squirrels, bighorn sheep	hiking, 4-wheel driving, horseback riding	Oct-Apr
Joshua Tree National Park (p363)	rocky desert, fan-palm oases, Joshua trees, cacti, coyotes, sidewinders, stinkbugs	rock climbing, hiking, 4WD roads, mountain biking, birding	Sep-May
Mt San Jacinto Park (p350)	rugged alpine mountains, firs, oaks, deer, mountain lions, foxes	hiking, backbacking, cross-country skiing, snowshoeing	year-round
Newport Bay Wilderness State Ecological Reserve (p264)	estuary, beach, salt marsh, mud flats, dunes	bird watching, walking, kayaking	Aug-Apr
Santa Monica Recreation Area (p153)	tree-and chaparral-biking covered coastal range, maples, sycamores, ferns, milkweed, lizards, snakes, bobcats, hawks, falcons	hiking, mountain	year-round

The California condor is the largest flying bird in North America. In 1982 there were only two dozen or so left in the wild. Today, thanks to captive breeding programs, there are about 200.

The Surfrider Foundation (www.surfrider.org) is a grassroots, nonprofit, environmental organization with chapters throughout the US that works to protect our oceans and beaches.

ENVIRONMENTAL ISSUES

Southern California is a success story in many ways, but development and growth have taken a terrible toll on the environment. The creation of the Los Angeles Aqueduct made SoCal possible but also spelled doom to the Owens Valley. The pollution and destruction of wetlands threaten migratory birds on the Pacific Flyway. Each year more motor vehicles pollute the air, and open acres are swallowed up by giant subdivisions. Plus, there's overgrazing, logging, overfishing and oil spills.

QUENCHING SOCAL'S INSATIABLE THIRST

The growth of semi-arid Los Angeles into a megalopolis would not have been possible without water. When the city's population surged in the early 20th century, it became clear that groundwater levels would soon be inadequate to meet its needs, let alone sustain further growth. Water had to be imported and Fred Eaton, a former LA mayor, and William Mulholland, head of the LA Department of Water & Power (LADWP), knew just how and where to get it: by aqueduct from the Owens Valley, which receives enormous runoff from the Sierra Nevada.

The fact that the Owens Valley was settled by farmers who needed the water for irrigation purposes bothered neither the two men nor the federal government, which actively supported the city's less-than-ethical maneuvering in acquiring land and securing water rights in the area. Voters gave Mulholland the $24.5 million he needed to build the aqueduct and work began in 1908. An amazing feat of engineering – crossing barren desert floor as well as rugged mountain terrain for 233 miles – it opened to great fanfare on November 5, 1913. An extension to the Mono Basin in 1940 lengthened the aqueduct a further 105 miles.

The Owens Valley, though, would never be the same. With most of its inflows diverted, Owens Lake quickly shriveled up. A bitter feud between LA and Owens Valley farmers and ranchers grew violent when some opponents to the scheme tried to sabotage the aqueduct by blowing up a section of it. All to no avail. By 1928 LA owned 90% of the water in Owens Valley and agriculture was effectively dead. These early water wars formed the basis for the 1974 movie Chinatown. For the full story, pick up a copy of Cadillac Desert by Marc Reisner.

These days LA still gets about 50% of its water supply by aqueduct. The remainder is siphoned from the Sacramento and San Joaquin Rivers via the California Aqueduct and the Colorado River via the Colorado River Aqueduct; only about 15% comes from groundwater.

Water has always been a contentious issue. Global warming and droughts are threatening to decimate the Sierra Nevada snowpack, one of the major sources of water for the Southland. Because auto exhaust and industrial emissions contribute hugely to global warming, Governor Schwarzenegger and the California legislature are working in cahoots – and flying in the face of the Bush government – to reduce emissions by 25% by 2020. Hybrid cars have become the new status symbol, with Californians now owning more than 20% of all low-emission vehicles in the nation. Even the Gov switched to a hydrogen-powered Hummer.

A massive consumer of energy, California has also established full-scale alternative energy projects. The deserts offer not only abundant sunshine, but much wind and tremendous geothermal heat. There are thousands of windmills at locations such as the San Gorgonio Pass, north of Palm Springs. And starting in 2011, the world's largest solar farm is expected to supply energy for 21,000 homes from its Central Valley location near Fresno.

Southern California Outdoors

Weather forecasters in Southern California probably have the easiest job in the world. 'Today it's… sunny and mild. Tomorrow will be… sunny and mild. And our extended forecast is…' You get the picture. With its Mediterranean climate, SoCal is one of the great places to find yourself outdoors at any time of year. There are indeed changes with the seasons and in different regions but they are attenuated compared with other regions in the US. In what follows, we'll let you in on the ideal times and locations to get out and about, pump those legs and lungs and take in the wonders of one of the world's greatest natural playgrounds. The destination chapters have details about each of these activities.

The outstanding California Coastal Access Guide (2003; www.ucpress .edu) has comprehensive maps and breakdowns to every public beach, reef, harbor, overlook and coastal campground in the state.

SWIMMING

With miles and miles of wide, sandy beaches, you won't find it hard to get wet and wild in Southern California. Ocean temperatures become tolerable by about May and peak in August and September. Big waves, treacherous riptides (p412) and other aquatic occurrences do present dangers and it's not uncommon for lifeguards to perform up to 50 rescues on busy days. If unsure, talk with them before hitting the water and obey their commands if they're shouting instructions or waving their buoys at you from the shore. There are flags to distinguish between surfer-only sections, and sections for swimmers. After storms they put out flags for pollution warnings, and there are also flags displayed to indicate dangerous currents.

George Freeth, the father of California surf culture, was also the state's first lifeguard and earned a Congressional Medal of Honor for rescuing a boatload of stranded fishermen.

Family-friendly beaches with calm waters include Mothers Beach in Los Angeles (p126), Carpinteria State Beach (p384) near Santa Barbara, Silver Strand State Beach (p318) in San Diego and West Beach (p382) in Santa Barbara. Another method to keep kids' temperatures cool is by taking them to a water park, such as Hurricane Harbor (p221) north of Los Angeles or Knott's Soak City USA in both Anaheim (p249) and Palm Springs (p353). For our take on LA's top 10 beaches, see the boxed text on p154.

Pollution levels vary from beach to beach and day to day. Check the Beach Report Card issued by the nonprofit organization **Heal the Bay** (www.healthebay .com) for details. Stay out of the water for at least three days after a major rainstorm because of dangerously high levels of bacteria and pollutants that have been flushed straight out through the storm drains.

The Pacific waves may beckon but they're not as innocent as they look. Get the scoop on lurking underwater dangers from www.beachcalifornia .com/beach-safety-tips .html.

SURFING

Surf's up! Are you down? Even if you never set foot on a board – and we heartily recommend you do – there's no denying the influence of surfing on every aspect of California beach life, from clothing to lingo; it's an obsession up and down the coast, particularly in San Diego County and Orange County. Note that the Surf Sites map here has a few sites not mentioned in this book, but we've included them on the map as they're still good spots.

SoCal's 'big three' surfing spots are Rincon Point (p384) in Santa Barbara, a legendary right point-break that peels forever; Trestles near San Clemente/ San Onofre in Orange County (see p279), a premier summer spot with big but forgiving waves, a fast ride and both right and left breaks; and Surfrider Beach (p121) in Malibu, a clean right break that gets better with bigger waves.

SURF SITES

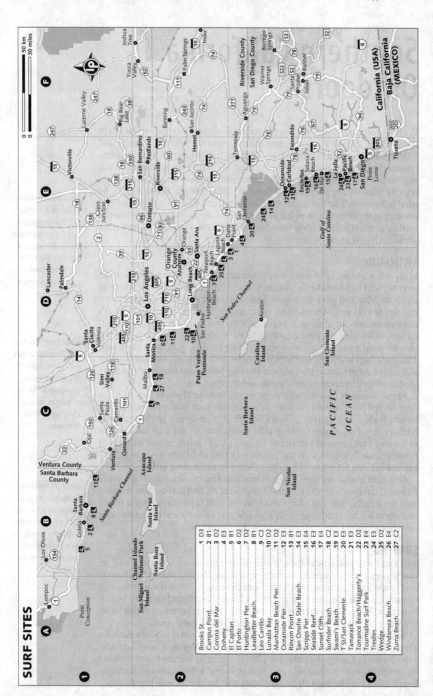

Brooks St.	1 D3
Campus Point.	2 B1
Corona del Mar.	3 D2
Doheny.	4 E3
El Capitan.	5 B1
El Porto.	6 D2
Huntington Pier.	7 D2
Leadbetter Beach.	8 B1
Leo Carrillo.	9 C2
Lunada Bay.	10 D2
Manhattan Beach Pier.	11 D2
Oceanside Pier.	12 E3
Rincon Point.	13 B1
San Onofre State Beach.	14 E3
Scripps Pier.	15 E4
Seaside Reef.	16 E3
Sunset Cliffs.	17 E4
Surfrider Beach.	18 C2
Swami's Beach.	19 E3
T St/San Clemente.	20 E3
Tamarack.	21 E3
Torrance Beach/Haggerty's.	22 D2
Tourmaline Surf Park.	23 E4
Trestles.	24 E3
Wedge.	25 D2
Windansea Beach.	26 E3
Zuma Beach.	27 C2

Swami's Beach (p336) in Encinitas in San Diego's North County, Huntington Beach (p256) in Orange County, and Zuma Beach (p154) and Lunada Bay (p154) in LA also get good marks.

The best spots to learn to surf are at beach breaks of long, shallow bays where waves are small and rolling. Leadbetter Beach (p384) in Santa Barbara and San Diego's Tourmaline Surf Park (p321) are especially good for catching your first wave. Huntington Beach (p256) is Orange County's surf mecca, with a surfing museum, surfing walk of fame and a pro-am surf series championship contest each September. There's also a surfing competition and nifty museum on the sport in Oceanside (p339) on San Diego's North Coast.

For the low-down on surf sites between Santa Barbara and San Diego, check out the comprehensive website and interactive database at www.surfline.com.

The most powerful swells arrive in late fall and winter, while May and June are generally the flattest months, although they do bring warmer water. Speaking of temperature, don't believe all those images of hot blonds surfing in skimpy swimsuits; without a wet suit, you'll likely freeze your butt off except during the height of summer.

Crowds can be a problem in many places, as can overly territorial surfers. Control your longboard or draw ire from agro dudes in Malibu, LA's Palos Verdes, San Diego's Windansea and Orange County's Huntington Beach. Tip: befriend a local surfer for an introduction – and protection.

Hey dude, if you're a kook, bone up on your surf-speak so the locals don't go agro and give you the stinkeye. (For translation, see www .riptionary.com.)

You'll find surfboard rentals on just about every patch of sand where surfing is possible. Expect to pay about $20 per half-day, with wet suit rental another $10 or so. Group lessons start at around $50 per person, while the going rate for private, two-hour instruction starts at $100. If you're ready to jump in the deep end, many surf schools offer weekend (around $150) and week-long camps ($350 and up).

Safety issues to watch out for include riptides, which are powerful currents of water that pull you away from the shore (p412).

Like cyclists, surfers can benefit from good sport-specific maps. Plan a coastal adventure using maps produced by the **Surf Report** (☎ 714-496-5922; www .surfmaps.net). The maps, which detail surf breaks and provide information on seasonal weather and water temperature, are sold county by county for $8 each or in a Southern California set for $35.

Enlightened surfers may also want to check out **Surfrider** (☎ 949-492-8170; www.surfrider.org), a nonprofit organization that strives to protect the coastal environment.

If you don't have the time or inclination to master the art of surfing, there are other ways to catch your 'dream wave' at just about any beach. Bodysurfing and bodyboarding (or boogie boarding) can extend your ride on the waves, sometimes as much as 100ft or more. Both activities benefit from the use of flippers to increase speed and control. If you're not sure how to do it, watch others or strike up a watery kinship and simply ask for pointers. But it's really quite easy and you'll be howling with glee when you catch that first wave.

Orange County-based *Surfer* magazine (www .surfermag.com) has travel reports, gear reviews and blogs, and also publishes the water-resistant *Guide to Southern California Surf Spots* ($20) with comprehensive reviews of some 250 surf spots.

Boarders and swimmers are both allowed in the same areas, but swimmers have the aquatic 'right of way' so be cautious.

Windsurfing & Kiteboarding

Experienced windsurfers tear up the waves along the coast, while new or 'mellower' surfers skim along calm bays and protected beaches. There's almost always a breeze, but the best winds blow in from March or April to the end of September. As always, wetsuits are a good idea any time of year.

Basically, any place that has good windsurfing also has good kiteboarding. Look for the people doing aerial acrobatics as their parachute-like kites yank them from the water. The best areas are wide-open spaces devoid of obstacles like piers and power lines. That way you and your sail-powered cohorts don't need to worry about unexpected flights that could slam you into concrete.

When in San Diego, beginners should check out Santa Clara Point in Mission Bay (p320). The winds are steady and most of the time blow toward the shore – perfect if you're a stranded first-timer. Santa Barbara's Leadbetter Beach (p384) is popular for all water sports and the area near Stearns Wharf in front of West Beach (p382) is a good starting spot. In LA, you'll see lots of action off Point Fermin (p129) and Cabrillo Beach in San Pedro.

The learning curve in windsurfing is steeper than other board sports – imagine balancing on a fast-moving plank through choppy waters while trying to read the wind and angle the sail just so. Lessons are available in most windsurfing hotspots for about $75 to $100 for a half-day beginner's lesson. Beginner kiteboarding lessons usually last a few days. The first day is spent learning kite control on the beach and the second day gets you into the water. Although it's harder to get started kiteboarding, experts say it's easier to advance quickly once the basics are down.

Most windsurfing businesses at least dabble in kiteboarding and many offer training in the $200 to $500 range for a full course (usually two or three lessons), including equipment hire. Shops usually won't rent kiteboarding gear to people who aren't taking lessons with them, but students often get a big discount on gear purchase.

Windsurfing gear rentals start at around $20 per hour for a beginner's board and $15 to $25 for a wet suit and harness for the day. Wind reports are available at www.iwindsurf.com (membership is required for detailed reports); for schools and shops check www.worldwindsurf.com.

BEACH VOLLEYBALL

You can find a pickup volleyball game on just about any SoCal beach, especially in Orange County and in LA's South Bay, and its popularity is increasing thanks to legendary local players like Kent Steffes and Karch Kiraly. Professional tournaments take place each summer, including in Huntington Beach, Long Beach, Hermosa Beach and Manhattan Beach.

KAYAKING

Few water-based sports are as accessible and fun for the whole gang as kayaking, and most people manage to get paddling along quickly and with minimal instruction. Sea kayaking is fabulous in the Channel Islands National Park (p405) off the Santa Barbara coast, and at Catalina Island (p220) off Los Angeles. Both deliver caves, bluffs and solitude and are also ideal overnight getaways for experienced paddlers. Day trips are equally rewarding, especially for beginners who can put in at Mission Bay (p320) in San Diego and enjoy the calm, protected waters. In La Jolla you can explore cliffs and caves and float above the San Diego–La Jolla Underwater Park's (p330) kelp forests and reefs. There's also decent kayaking in Gaviota (p384) near Santa Barbara, and in the craggy coves of Laguna Beach (p273) in Orange County.

Most outfitters offer a choice between sit-upon (open or ocean) kayaks and sit-in (closed-hull) ones, the latter usually requiring a few minutes of training before you head out. Both start at around $35 per person for the day. With both open and closed, you'll usually have a choice between single and tandem. Whatever kind of kayak you get, a reputable outfitter will make sure you're aware of the tide schedule and wind conditions of your proposed route.

For the complete low-down on surfing, pick up a copy of *Surfing California: A Complete Guide to the Best Breaks on the California Coast* by Raul Guisado and Jeff Class.

Kerri Walsh and Misty May, beach volleyball gold medalists at the 2004 Olympics, both live and play volleyball in Southern California.

Jerry Schad's *101 Hikes in Southern California: Experience Mountains, Seashore & Desert* (2005) gets you onto fantastic trails described in evocative detail and with plenty of insider tips on photography, water needs and other issues.

Many kayaking outfitters lead half-day ($55 to $75) or day-long (from around $110) trips. Some offer kayak/hike combos or oh-so-romantic full-moon paddles. There's nothing quite like seeing the reflection of the moon and stars glittering on the water and hearing the gentle splash of water on your kayak's hull. Small group tours led by guides with some local natural history knowledge are best.

California Kayak Friends (www.ckf.org) or **American Canoe Association** (www.acanet.org) provide extensive information on everything from safety and instruction to destinations and events for paddlesports aficionados.

For general resources log onto www.kayakonline.com/california.html.

SNORKELING & SCUBA DIVING

Southern California has some surprisingly excellent underwater playgrounds – from rock reefs to shipwrecks to kelp forests – suited for all skill and experience levels. As with any water sport, wet suits are recommended year-round.

Great places, especially for first-time divers, are the La Jolla Underwater Park (p330) in San Diego and Casino Point Marine Park (p220) at Catalina Island. Both are accessible right from the shore and boast fertile kelp beds teeming with critters close to the surface. More experienced divers might also want to steer towards Crystal Cove State Park (p264) just south of Newport Beach, Diver's Cove and Shaw's Cove in Laguna Beach (p273) and Mission Beach (p319) in San Diego (where you can explore a WWII military ship-wreck). Most of these places are also good for snorkeling.

Local dive shops are the best resources for equipment, guides, instructors and tours to nearby wrecks and islands. In order to explore California's deep waters, you must have an open-water certificate from the Professional Association of Dive Instructors (PADI), National Association for Underwater Instructors (NAUI) or another recognized organization such as the British Sub-Aqua Club (BSAC). Dive outfits (including one tank of oxygen) rent for $60 to $100 – it's wise to reserve at least a day in advance.

If you just want to dabble in diving, look for outfitters offering beginner courses that include basic instruction, followed by a shallow beach or boat dive, for about $100 to $150. If you're serious about learning and have the time and money, sign up for an open-water certificate course, which starts from around $350. The website www.ladiver.com maintains exhaustive listings of dive sites and shops, certification programs, safety resources and weather conditions for the Los Angeles area, with links to its sister sites in San Diego and Santa Barbara.

Snorkelers will find mask, snorkel and fin rentals widely available from concessionaires near the respective snorkeling sites (around $25 for the lot). Think you'll be taking the plunge more than twice? Buy your own set – it's cheaper. When heading out, don't go alone, don't touch anything and don't forget the sunblock!

WHALE-WATCHING

Every summer 15,000 gray whales feed in the arctic waters between Alaska and Siberia, and every October they start moving south down the Pacific Coast of Canada and the US to sheltered lagoons in the Gulf of California off Baja California. While there, the pregnant whales give birth to calves weighing up to 2500lb (who go on to live up to 50 years, grow to 50ft in length and weigh up to 45 tons). Around mid-March these whales turn around and head back to the Arctic. Luckily for us, during their 12,000-mile round-trip, the whales pass just off the California coast.

Lonely Planet's *Diving & Snorkeling Southern California & the Channel Islands* (2001) by David Krival is a hands-on guide to happy encounters with garibaldi, sheephead, calico bass and other offshore creatures in SoCal's waters.

Scuba Diving (www .scubadiving.com) and *Sport Diver* (www .sportdiver.com), published by PADI, are widely available magazines dedicated to underwater pursuits.

Yes, there is hiking in them thar hills. Just plough through www .etreking.com for ideas, trail descriptions and handy tips on exploring SoCal's mountains.

HIKING

Got wanderlust? With fabulous scenery throughout, Southern California is perfect for exploring on foot. This is true no matter whether you've got your heart set on peak-bagging 10,000-footers, trekking through cacti groves, hiking among fragrant pines or simply going for a walk on the beach accompanied by the booming surf. Wherever you go, expect encounters with an entire cast of furry, feathered and flippered friends. Keep an eye out for lizards darting among the rocks, porpoises pirou-etting offshore or eagles plummeting through the sky for prey. In spring and early summer, a painter's palette worth of wildflowers decorates leafy meadows, shaggy hillsides and damp forest floors.

The best trails are in the jaw-dropping scenery of national and state parks, national forests, wilderness areas and other public lands. You'll find the gamut of routes, from easy strolls negotiable by wheelchairs and baby strollers to more extreme, multiday backpacking routes through rugged wilderness.

There are bulletin boards showing trail maps and other information about the area at most major trailheads. Parks and national forests almost always have a visitor center or ranger station with clued-in staff happy to offer route suggestions and trail-specific tips. They also hand out or sell trail maps, which may be necessary depending on the length and difficulty of your hike. Look for contact information in the destination chapters throughout this book. For preliminary research, check out www.fs.fed.us/r5, the website of the United States Forest Service (USFS), Pacific Southwest Region.

Safety

Pick a hike that matches your time frame and the physical ability of the least-fit member in your group. Before heading out, seek local advice on trails, equipment and weather by calling or stop-ping at a ranger station, visitor center or local sports shop. Pay attention on the trail and be aware of potential dangers. Even a minor injury such as a twisted ankle can be life-threatening if you're alone. Always let someone know where you're going and how long you plan to be gone. Use the sign-in boards at trailheads or ranger stations. Carry a cell phone, but don't rely on it: service is spotty or nonexistent in many areas. Weather can be unpredictable, so carry adequate clothing and equipment. Afternoon summer thunderstorms, for instance, are quite common in the deserts. Always carry water, snack food and an extra layer of clothing and/or a raincoat.

Look out for western poison oak in forests throughout California, especially below 5000ft eleva-tion. It's a shrub most easily identified by its shiny triple-lobed reddish-green leaves, which turn crimson in the fall. Remember the following adage: 'Leaves of three, let it be.' If you brush against it, scrub the area with soap and water or an over-the-counter remedy such as Tecnu, a soap specially formulated to remove the oils from poison oak.

Encounters with mountain lions and bears are extremely rare but possible, and rattlesnakes and spiders also present potential dangers. See p412 and p431 for details.

Books & Maps

Pick up *Los Angeles Times* columnist John McKinney's excellent hiking guides, published by Olympic Press, among them *Day Hiker's Guide to Southern California* and *Day Hiker's Guide to California State Parks*. If you're visiting during wildflower season, carry a copy of the National Audubon Society's *Field Guide to Wildflowers: Western Region*, which is small enough to fit into a daypack.

For short, well-established hikes in national or state parks, the free and basic sketch maps handed out at ranger stations and visitor centers are usually sufficient. For longer trips into the backcountry, you ought to have a good topographic map such as those published by the **US Geological Survey** (USGS; www.store.usgs.gov). They can be ordered through the website or purchased at local ranger stations, outfitters and visitor centers.

And it's not only gray whales that make appearances. Blue, humpback and sperm whales, and tons of dolphins, can be seen frolicking offshore through the summer and fall, but these spottings are not to be as predictable as the grays.

The whales tend to stay closer to shore on their southbound leg, so your best chances of catching a glimpse are in December and January. You can try your

Fees

California state parks don't charge an admission fee but most levy a parking fee ranging from $5 to $15. There is no charge if you walk or bike into these parks. You'll need a National Forest Adventure Pass (NFAP) for visiting San Bernardino, Cleveland, Angeles or Los Padres national forests unless you're just driving through, or stopping at a ranger station or visitor center. If you are already paying another forest-use fee (eg camping or cabin fees) you don't need an NFAP. Passes cost $5 per day or $30 per year (seniors and disabled $15) and must be displayed on the windshield of your vehicle. The annual passes are good for one year from the month of purchase and are transferable. USFS ranger stations, selected sporting-goods stores and other vendors sell passes, or you can order one by phone (☎ 909-382-2622). For a full list of vendors, log on to www.fs.fed.us/r5/sanbernardino/ap.

The entrance fee to national parks varies from $10 to $20 per vehicle and is good for unlimited entries for seven consecutive days. If you're going to visit many national parks in California or elsewhere, consider getting the America the Beautiful Pass ($80; www.nps.org).

Hikes

No matter where you find yourself in Southern California, you're never far from a trail, even in the metropolitan areas. In Los Angeles you can hike for miles in America's largest urban park, Griffith Park (p143) and in the Santa Monica Mountains (p153) amid oak woodlands and other Mediterranean environs.

The rugged Santa Ynez Mountains lord over Santa Barbara, rising 4000ft from sea level within 10 miles of the ocean, an awesome sight. A 20-minute drive from town takes you to the Los Padres National Forest (p401), where you can pick up trailheads near San Marcos Pass. Rattlesnake Canyon, which runs past waterfalls, is especially scenic, albeit rather popular, and Red Rock Trail and Snyder Trail are other good choices. In Channel Islands National Park (p405), you can hike past frolicking sea lions and giant sprays of coreopsis flowers.

In San Diego the best hiking is along the coastal bluffs in Torrey Pines State Reserve (p330) at La Jolla's northern boundary, where you can see some of the last remaining stands of *Pinus torreyana* on the mainland. Further inland, a section of the legendary Pacific Crest Trail (PCT; a 2638-mile-long footpath from Mexico to Canada) passes through Anza-Borrego State Park. It also provides open-trail desert hiking, allowing you to choose your own path. However, hiking in this fashion is strenuous, requires good navigational skills and is definitely not recommended on hot days.

Instead, head to Palm Springs where you'll find relief in the cool pine forests of the Mt San Jacinto Wilderness State Park (p350), reached via the Palm Springs Aerial Tramway. Some 54 miles of trails await, including a tiring but nontechnical route up to the San Jacinto Peak (10,804ft). Palm Springs itself delivers fantastic hiking in winter among the palm groves of the Indian Canyons and Tahquitz Canyon. In the cooler months, hiking is also excellent in Joshua Tree National Park with its trippy lunar landscapes of trails skirting giant boulders, palm oases and the shaggy trees that seem to have leapt from a Dr Seuss book. Death Valley landscapes are harsh but surprisingly unhellish, ranging from rugged canyons to sand dunes, shady valleys to windswept mountain tops.

Though Orange County has been mostly developed, you can find good day-hiking in places such as Crystal Cove State Park (p264) in Newport Beach. If you're heading to Laguna Beach, check out the West Ridge Trail (p272), where you can enjoy gorgeous ocean views while trekking along a ridgeline high above the picturesque little town.

luck while staying shore-bound – it's free, but you're less likely to see them and you'll be rather removed from the action. Point San Vicente on the Palos Verdes Peninsula in LA, San Diego's Cabrillo National Monument and Cavern Point on Santa Cruz Island in Channel Islands National Park are famous viewing spots, but you could get just as lucky somewhere else.

Spotting a whale from a distance is fun but not comparable to the excitement of seeing one up close during a whale-watching trip. Half-day trips (from $20 to $35 per adult and $15 to $20 per child) range from 2½ to four hours, and all-day trips range from $75 to $100, with some including meals. Look for a tour that limits the number of people and has a trained naturalist on board. Don't forget binoculars.

Choppy seas can be nauseating for some landlubbers. To avoid seasickness, sit outside on the second level – not too close to the diesel fumes in back. Over-the-counter motion-sickness pills (eg Dramamine or Bonine) are effective but will make you drowsy. Acupressure wristbands work for some people, as does chewing ginger. Staring at the horizon, though, will likely give you little relief, no matter what you've heard.

> Since its introduction in 1997 the National Forest Adventure Pass has raised almost $25 million. The funds are used to improve facilities, trails and signs; increase public safety; clean up graffiti and litter; and other projects.

CYCLING & MOUNTAIN BIKING

Strap on your helmet! Southern California is superb cycling territory, no matter whether you're off on a leisurely spin along the beach, an adrenaline-fueled mountain exploration or a multiday bike-touring adventure. Avoid the mountains in winter and the desert in summer. Be aware of your skill and fitness level and plan accordingly.

Southland cities are not terribly bike-friendly, Santa Barbara and Palm Springs being exceptions. Mountain bikers will find fine destinations in the Santa Monica Mountains (p153) in Los Angeles as well as Crystal Cove State Park (p264) and Aliso & Woods Canyon Park (p273) in Laguna Beach. Speed freaks sing the praises of Snow Summit at Big Bear Lake (p221).

> For information on freeway access for bicyclists, a guide to bicycle touring in California and to download free maps, go to www.cabobike.org.

Fabulous paved beach trails include the South Bay Trail (p152) in Los Angeles, the path from Huntington State Beach to Bolsa Chica State Beach (p258) in Orange County, and the beachfront bike path along Cabrillo Blvd in Santa Barbara.

Bikes are usually not allowed in designated wilderness areas and are limited to paved roads in national parks. An exception is Death Valley National Park (p223), where Titus Canyon makes for an exciting off-road adventure past Indian petroglyphs and a ghost town. Do not attempt in summer! Joshua Tree National Park (p363) is another bike-friendly national park with miles of backcountry road.

State parks are a little more relaxed. Good 'chain-gang' destinations include Anza-Borrego Desert State Park (p368), east of San Diego. Most of the national forests and Bureau of Land Management (BLM) lands are also open to mountain bikers. Just be sure to stay on the tracks and not create new ones.

> For online reviews of dozens of mountain-bike trails, check out www.dirtworld.com. Product reviews can be found at www.mtbr.com.

Most towns have at least one bike rental place; many are listed throughout this book. Prices range from about $5 to $8 per hour and $15 to $30 per day (more for high-tech mountain bikes), depending on the type of bike and rental location. For short tours, staff at the local tourist offices can supply you with ideas, maps and advice. For the inside scoop on the local scene, check with the folks in the rental shops.

Other resources:

Adventure Cycling Association (☎ 800-775-2453; www.adventurecycling.org) Trip-planning resources such as the Cyclist's Yellow Pages.

Los Angeles Bicycle Coalition (☎ 213-629-2142; www.labike.org)

Santa Barbara Bicycle Coalition (www.sbbike.org) Includes downloadable tours of *Sideways* wine country.

GOLF

Most cities and regions of Southern California have public courses with reasonable greens fees, although many of the top-ranked courses are at

---

WANT MORE TO DO? SURE!

If none of the activities outlined in this chapter appeal, rest assured that there's plenty of other stuff going on in SoCal. Rock hounds can test their mettle on world-class climbs in Joshua Tree National Park (p363). Like to hook a tuna or sea bass? Fishing is free from municipal piers or get a license and go salty on a sport-fishing trip leaving year-round from such places as Balboa Island (p265) in Newport Beach, Fisherman's Village in Marina del Rey (p126) in Los Angeles and Mission Bay (p321) in San Diego. Trolling for trout? Head to Big Bear Lake (p221) in the mountains east of LA. If you'd like to explore the water under your own steam, rent a yacht, jet skis or paddle boat. Sheltered Mission Bay (p322) is a particularly fine spot for this kind of thrill. Del Mar (p334) in San Diego's North County, meanwhile, is the SoCal ballooning capital – is there anything more romantic than floating into the sunset? Or channel your inner John Wayne and head into the mountains on horseback. Some of the best rides are in, of all places, Los Angeles (p152). Indoors, yoga studios abound, especially in Los Angeles, where they keep inventing new spins on the downward dog. Try yoga for athletes, power yoga, Bikram yoga (in a heated room) or martial arts yoga. Classes cost about $15 to $20.

---

private golf clubs, where you have to be invited by a member to be allowed in, or get a referral from the pro at your home club (which doesn't always guarantee admission, depending on the exclusivity of the club). Semiprivate clubs are open to nonmembers, except at peak times, such as Saturday and Sunday mornings – check individual clubs for exact times. The Palm Springs and Coachella Valley area is the undisputed golfing mecca of SoCal with more than 100 courses; San Diego and surrounding areas have over 80.

Greens fees vary hugely, from $25 to $250 or more for 18 holes, depending on the course, season and day of the week, and that usually doesn't include the cart rental. Always book a tee time in advance or ask about walk-up policies. For information on golf courses throughout Southern California check out the following websites:

Coachella Valley (www.golfcoachellavalley.com)
Los Angeles (www.laparks.org/dos/sports/golf.htm)
Orange County (www.playocgolf.com)
Palm Springs (www.palmspringsteetimes.com)
San Diego (www.golfsd.com)
Santa Barbara (www.santabarbara.com/activities/golf)

Golfers can save money – sometimes by as much as 50% – by booking twilight play. For a public course directory go to www.golfsocal.com.

SPAS

If the road has left you feeling frazzled and achy, an hour or more at a day spa may be just what the doctor ordered. There are literally hundreds of spas throughout the Southland, from simple massage parlors to sumptuous luxury salons. Every place has its own 'treatment menu,' which usually includes a variety of massages such as Thai, shiatsu, deep-tissue, Swedish, tandem (for two people) and hot-stone. Beauty treatments range from facials to wraps, botanical baths, mud baths and such exotic procedures as mother-of-pearl enzyme facials, Moroccan-mint sugar scrubs and milk-and-honey baths. For a special treat visit the Glen Ivy Hot Springs (p251), which is famous for its red-clay mud pool but also has clear mineral-water tubs and a large swimming pool.

You'll usually find Thai massages for around $40 per hour, but other pummeling sessions can cost at least twice that. Smoothing your skin will likely set you back about $60. By the time you've added a 20% tip, the final tab may be high enough to put the frown right back on your forehead.

Learn how to minimize your impact on the environment while traipsing through the wilderness from the Leave No Trace Center (www.lnt.org).

Los Angeles & SoCal for Children

In *Tyler on Prime Time* (2003) by Steve Atinsky, a 12-year-old gets caught up in the world of TV production after he is sent to LA to live with his uncle, who works on a sit-com. Written by an actual TV writer.

(Tiny) hands down, Southern California has got to be one of the most child-friendly vacation spots on the planet. The kids will already be begging to go to Disneyland, Universal Studios, SeaWorld and Magic Mountain. Get those over with (you may well enjoy them too) and then introduce them to many other worlds.

SoCal's 'endless summer' of sunny skies and warm temperatures lends itself to outdoor activities too numerous to mention, but here's a start (big breath): swimming, bodysurfing, snorkeling, bicycling, kayaking, hiking (mountain or urban), horseback riding and walking. Many outfitters and tour operators have dedicated kids' tours.

Sometimes no organized activity is even needed. We've seen kids from Washington, DC, thrill at catching their first glimpse of a palm tree, and 11-year-olds with sophisticated palates in bliss over their first heirloom tomatoes at a farmers market or shrimp dumplings at a dim-sum palace.

The upshot: if the kids are having a good time, their parents are having a good time.

ARE WE THERE YET?
What to Bring

Sunscreen. Bring sunscreen.

And bringing sunscreen will remind you to bring hats, bathing suits, flip-flops and goggles. If you like beach umbrellas and sand chairs, pails and shovels, you'll probably want to bring or buy your own; all are readily available at local drugstores. At many beaches, you can rent bicycles of all stripes – check local listings for surf and other water gear.

Throughout this book, we've denoted kid-friendly establishments (sights, activities, hotels and restaurants especially) with the symbol (⛄), within the parentheses after each establishment's name.

For mountain outings, bring hiking shoes, plenty of food and water, and your own camping equipment. These can be purchased or rented from markets and outfitters near desert parks (see local listings), but remember that the best time to test out shoes, sleeping bags and such is before you take your trip. Murphy's Law dictates that wearing brand-new hiking shoes on a big hike results in blisters.

Whatever you bring, kids always seem to take more ownership of the process if they have their own minibackpacks to carry their own gear.

For short car trips, snacks, books and toys are always a good idea; for long trips, they're essential. From LA to all but the most remote destinations in our book, travel time should be within about two hours (plus traffic, of course). Drugstores everywhere sell inexpensive books and toys to constantly keep the kids amused. An MP3 player loaded with their favorite music will help control fidgeting. Some families travel with DVD players and many public libraries have extensive kids' collections; see regional chapters for library

---

TIP!

Don't pack your schedule too tightly. Traveling with kids always takes longer than expected, and in LA you'll want to build in time for distance, traffic and getting lost.

Also, kids are more likely to be engaged if they can help choose the activities. Offer them choices of sights and activities you think would be suitable.

JET LAG

Jet lag can be trying for adults, and that's multiplied with children. For example, if you're coming from the eastern US and your kids' bedtime is 8pm at home, that means 5pm in SoCal. To avoid meltdown, you'll probably dispense with dinner, baths, stories and 'Moooommyyyyyy…!' before most locals sit down for dinner. See p74 for info on babysitting services.

It may also mean waking up three hours earlier. If you're at a hotel, check the hours of nearby restaurants or prepare early-morning snacks – many hotels, particularly in outlying areas, have refrigerators just for this purpose.

---

listings and inquire directly as to lending requirements (some lend only to local residents).

Baby food, infant formulas, soy and cow's milk, disposable diapers (nappies) and other necessities are all widely available in drugstores and supermarkets. Breast-feeding in public is legal, although most women are discreet about it. Public toilets – in airports, stores, shopping malls, cinemas etc – usually have diaper-changing tables.

Important note: always check the weather before setting out. Winter (basically November to March) can be rainy and temperatures unpredictable. All but the heartiest, wet-suited surfers avoid the beach then. Desert winter nights can be near freezing, and even clear winter days won't necessarily be swimming weather.

Still bring the sunscreen though.

Flying

Airlines usually allow infants (up to the age of two) to fly for free, while older children requiring a seat of their own may qualify for reduced fares. You may want to bring your child's passport or birth certificate copy as proof of age. Generally good weather means good on-time performance at SoCal airports, but the same cannot necessarily be said for other airports on your route, so bring plenty of amusements and snacks. If traveling from overseas, order special kids' meals in advance.

Most airlines 'preboard' passengers traveling with small children. On Southwest Airlines (which has no assigned seating) you can snag seats together and other passengers tend to avoid sitting near the little ones.

Driving

California law requires all passengers in private cars to wear seat belts, and children under the age of six or weighing less than 60lbs must be restrained in a child-safety or booster seat. If you're not traveling with your own car seats, most car-rental firms rent them for about $5 per day, but it is essential that you book them in advance.

See What to Bring (opposite) for tips on keeping the kids amused while on the road. Rest stops on SoCal freeways are few and far between, and we wouldn't recommend gas-station rest rooms for bathroom breaks as maintenance tends to be shoddy. However, you're never very far from a shopping mall, which generally have well-kept rest rooms.

NIGHT-NIGHT

Hotels and motels commonly have rooms with two double beds or a double and a sofa bed. For families who prefer more space, many properties have 'adjoining' rooms (two rooms attached via an internal door). Alternatively, one- or two-bedroom suites may end up being more economical. Most places provide rollaway beds, usually for a small extra charge.

A good general resource is www.travelwith yourkids.com, which has advice on how to prepare for a trip and handle oneself on the road, although there's nothing specific to SoCal.

Having one parent travel in the back seat while the other drives can let you keep the kids amused with books and games and eliminate the 'He crossed the lii-i-i-ine!' dilemma.

The Traveling Baby Company (☎ 800-304-4866; www.traveling babyco.com) rents equipment, with delivery to Los Angeles, Ventura, Santa Barbara, Orange and San Diego Counties. Figure on $8/35 per day/week for a Pack 'n' Play or car seat; weekly multiequipment packages are available from $109.

Whichever room type you want, request it on booking. If you wait until you arrive, you might not get what you want.

Often larger chain hotels offer 'kids stay free' promotions; others include breakfast in the rates. Inquire about these promotions when booking. Some smaller B&Bs don't welcome children.

Some resort hotels, such as Loews Coronado Bay Resort and the Manchester Grand Hyatt in San Diego, offer activity programs for kids, particularly during summer. Fees can be cheaper than babysitting and everyone may enjoy the change of pace.

Babysitting

If you need a four-hour vacation from your kids and aren't lucky enough to have family or friends nearby in SoCal, here's a list of babysitting services in Los Angeles; if you're outside of LA, ask at your hotel for a recommendation. Rates may fluctuate based on factors such as the number of children and whether the kids have a cold or there's driving involved. Most services prefer at least 24 hours' advance notice.

Babysitters Agency of West LA (☎ 310-306-5437; per hr from $15; ☽ 9am-5pm Mon-Sat) In business for half a century (formerly Santa Monica Babysitters). Four-hour booking minimum Sunday to Friday, and a five-hour minimum Saturdays.

Babysitters Guild (☎ 310-837-1800; per hr $10-16, plus $6 transportation fee; ☽ 10:30am-4:30pm Mon-Fri) The oldest and largest agency in the city (since the 1940s). All sitters are screened, over 21 and fluent in English. Four-hour booking minimum (five hours on Saturdays).

Buckingham Nannies (☎ 310-247-1877, 800-393-4844; www.buckinghamnannies.com; per hr $12-25; ☽ 8:30am-5pm Mon-Fri) Uses fully qualified nannies with at least two years' experience. In addition to hourly fees, there's a $75/150 registration fee (valid three months/one year) and a $25 daily fee.

WHINING & DINING

Most SoCal restaurants – not just fast-food places – are easygoing with kids. A good measure is the noise level: the louder it is, the more kid-friendly it will be. Casual eateries in well-trafficked neighborhoods typically have high chairs available and many have specific children's menus, sometimes printed on a take-home coloring book or placemat – our favorite places provide crayons too. Even restaurants without kids' menus can usually whip up something your children will call yummy. Generally, earlier (before 6pm) is better for families with young ones.

If your server has gone to a lot of extra effort on your behalf, a generous tip is definitely in order (20% or more). This will also help endear you to the server for your next visit – get his or her name if you can, and even mention to the manager that they went above and beyond.

Theme parks have dozens of ways to get the kids hopped-up on sugar and salt at expensive prices, and many don't permit picnics or outside food to be brought in. One way to get around this: carry a cooler in the car and have a picnic in the parking lot (though be sure to get a hand-stamp for reentry).

One place kids are generally *un*welcome is high-end restaurants. Unless the children are exceptionally well behaved, properly dressed and old enough to appreciate the meal, neither the staff nor other diners are likely be charmed. Think of yourselves too: meals in such places last two hours or more – too long to expect all except the most remarkable little ones to sit without squirming or screaming, especially if it's late and especially if they're jet-lagged.

If all else fails, local supermarket chains like Trader Joe's and Gelson's have pleasing, wholesome takeout.

For information on everything from traveling with kids to how to store their artwork, www .peachheadfamilies.com is a highly regarded local discussion group website.

The website of *LA Parent* (http://losangeles .parenthood.com) includes a calendar of events and listings. The print version of this monthly magazine is distributed free in child-oriented places throughout town (the website lists locations).

LOS ANGELES

America's second-largest city has plenty to please its smaller visitors. This will get you started; see also p157 and neighborhoods listings for more information.

Kids old enough to appreciate movies will love Universal Studios Hollywood (p145); adjacent Universal CityWalk makes a colorful meal stop. Children also thrill at getting their picture taken beside the star of their favorite star on Hollywood Blvd; the hand-, foot- and wand-prints of the young stars of the Harry Potter movies were the latest additions to Grauman's Chinese Theater (p196) when we went to press. For an extra thrill (and no parking fees or traffic) reach both by LA's subway line.

Amusements in mountainous Griffith Park (p143) include the landmark Griffith Observatory, a merry-go-round and Travel Town for younger tykes. The zoo (p143) is popular, though it can't compare to San Diego's. Take more athletic kids hiking for fabulous views across the city and the Hollywood Sign.

Downtown's ethnic neighborhoods allow you to take little sophisticates 'overseas' with dramatic savings on airfares. In Chinatown's Central Plaza (p134), pick up touristy knickknacks or make a wish in a fountain. Stop nearby at Empress Pavilion (p185) for dim sum or a streetside shop for boba tea (with black 'pearls' of tapioca). Mexican-themed Olvera St (p133), LA's oldest street, mixes kitsch with quality. Little Tokyo (p138) makes for strolling and snacking; older kids can learn about the Japanese-American experience at the Japanese American National Museum.

In Exposition Park, the California Science Center (p120) is both great and free, and the Natural History Museum (p119) is, among other things, where Peter Parker (aka Spiderman) was first bitten. To see the cast of *Ice Age* (albeit in their former real-life selves), visit the Page Museum at the La Brea Tar Pits (p110). Parents also lavish praise on the nearby Zimmer Museum (p157) and the new Noah's Ark installation at the Skirball Cultural Center (p118).

For do-it-yourself fun, there are parks in cities around the county, but Pasadena and Santa Monica have some of the best. In Pasadena, start with Kidspace (p157), while Santa Monica Pier (p124) is justifiably famous. See local library listings for story hours and children's collections.

ORANGE COUNTY

By golly, they're right: it *is* a small world after all. There's more than just Disneyland (p230) to keep kids busy and engaged. Knott's Berry Farm (p249) is more homegrown and lower-key, where Charlie Brown and Lucy sub for Mickey and Minnie; it's a must for older kids during October's nighttime Halloween Haunt.

If your kids are shoppers, OC will tempt them. The Block at Orange (p250) is a contempo-cool mall with its own skateboard park, while in Costa Mesa, the Lab (p269) calls itself an 'antimall,' with vintage clothing and contemporary art exhibits. Kids with exotic tastes will enjoy the shopping and restaurants in Little Saigon (p251).

Hungry? Los Angeles Family (2006), edited by Jennifer Chang, steers you to the neighborhood restaurants throughout this vast metropolis - from bistros to dives - that won't torture grown-ups' sensibilities or palates.

For family listings in the *Los Angeles Times*, check out www.calendarlive.com/family. Events for children and families are also listed in the paper's Calendar section in the Thursday and (especially) Sunday editions.

Fun with the Family: Southern California (2007) by Laura Kath and Pamela Joy Brice features hundreds of ideas for day trips across the Southland.

GETTING IN

Children receive a wide range of discounts for everything from museum admissions to bus fares and motel stays. The definition of a 'child' varies – in some places anyone under 18 is eligible, while others put the cut-off at age six. Note that many amusement park rides have minimum height requirements.

And who doesn't love the beach? OC standouts include Huntington Beach (p256) for surf culture and Newport Beach (p261) for its piers, amusement park and upscale vibe, particularly on Balboa Island.

SAN DIEGO COUNTY

Do the zoo (p298). It's everything they say, and while you're there spend another day enjoying the rest of Balboa Park (p297), one of the nation's best collections of museums. The Reuben H Fleet Science Center (p300), the Model Railroad Museum (p300) and the Natural History Museum (p300) are all tailor-made for kids, and the plazas, fountains and gardens offer plenty of space for them to let off steam.

Kids elementary-school age and older will appreciate Old Town State Historic Park (p302) and the Mexican restaurants nearby.

Along the coast, SeaWorld (p320) is another national landmark (look for specials and combo tickets to keep costs down). Coronado is a calming getaway, featuring the Hotel del Coronado (p318) and the kid-friendly public library. Views from Cabrillo National Monument (p319) inspire awe, and its museum tells the story of the Spanish explorers who were central to local history.

Teens will be in their element among the surfers, bikers and bladers in Mission and Pacific Beaches (p319), while up the coast in La Jolla the Birch Aquarium (p329) entertains as it teaches. More active kids can go snorkeling (p330) off La Jolla Cove. The Wild Animal Park (p341) is North County's must-see.

PALM SPRINGS & THE DESERTS

Base yourself in Palm Springs, with its large assortment of casual restaurants and hotels in a range of prices, all within close proximity. Down Valley resorts are also fun for kids, with swimming, tennis and, for older kids, golf.

Kids of all ages love the Palm Springs Aerial Tramway (p349), whose cars rotate ever so slowly as they ascend nearly 6000 vertical feet up the San Jacinto Mountains. Temperatures at the top are up to 40°F lower than on the desert floor; in cooler months, bring warm clothing and snow gear (the latter can be rented).

Palm Desert's Living Desert Zoo (p353) is a fascinating desert museum. Older kids will enjoy hiking Indian and Tahquitz Canyon (p352), while Mane St in Pioneertown (p367) takes you back to the Old West (via an Old West movie set). At the center of it all is Joshua Tree National Park

On San Diego's buses and trolleys, each fare-paying adult can take up to two children (18 and under) aboard for free on Saturdays and Sundays.

When Bugs Bunny said that he knew he should have made a left turn at Albuquerque, he was trying to reach the carrot festival in the Coachella Valley. There is no carrot festival there these days.

TOP FIVE PIERS IN SOCAL FOR KIDS

- **Stearns Wharf, Santa Barbara** (p379) – the west coast's oldest continuously operating pier features the engaging Ty Warner Sea Center.

- **Santa Monica Pier** (p124) – the granddaddy of them all, built in 1908, has its own amusement park on top, an aquarium underneath and dance concerts on Thursdays in summer.

- **Balboa Island, Newport Beach** (p263) – it's not one but two piers, plus a reasonably priced amusement park made famous on TV's The OC.

- **Crystal Pier, Pacific Beach** (p320) – if you stay at the Crystal Pier Hotel (p324), the waves lapping beneath your bungalow on the pier are a natural sleep-aid.

- **Paradise Pier, Disneyland** (p243) – granted, it's not technically a pier (it's nowhere near the ocean), but who cares when the rides are so good?

(p363): the desert, clear and blue, makes for glorious hiking, light climbing and nature-watching.

Water-seekers should visit Knott's Soak City (p353) or your hotel swimming pool.

SANTA BARBARA

Pride of place belongs to Stearns Wharf (p379), the pier in central Santa Barbara, and nearby West Beach (p382) attracts many families. The city's lovely, Mission-style town center also boasts a low-key Museum of Natural History and Planetarium (p381), a zoo (p381) and, for young history lovers, El Presidio (p382), a historic Spanish fort which just celebrated its 225th anniversary. Cycling, roller-skating, boating and whale-watching (p383) abound.

Other family-friendly beaches worth seeking out include Carpinteria State Beach (p384), said to be the world's safest, and local favorite Arroyo Burro (p382).

Signature flavors of Santa Barbara County are the tacos at la Super Rica (p388) and the tiny doughnuts known as abelskiver, in the Danish-themed village of Solvang (p393). Mid-July's county fair (p386) lets you sample lots of local foods in one place.

Off the coast, Channel Islands National Park (p405) is a natural for families who like their vacations, well, natural: hiking, kayaking, camping, whale-watching and more.

Los Angeles

Buff, bronzed and beautiful, LA is a sly seductress tempting you with her beaches, bosoms and beemers. She's a bon vivant, passionately feasting on the smorgasbord of life, not taking anything too seriously. She's a beacon of hope for countless dreamers and daredevils. But she's also a cranky broad, a mistress of misery that'll chew up and spit out anyone who isn't quite A-list material.

Now is an exciting time to visit LA. Hollywood, Downtown and even humble Culver City are in the midst of an unstoppable urban renaissance. An open and experimental climate energizes the art, music and fashion scenes, and innovative chefs have ramped up local cuisine.

So if you think you've already figured out what LA is all about – smog, traffic, celebrity murders, Botox babes and Paris wannabes – think again. Explore the other LA: its truths aren't delivered through headlines or on a movie screen, but come to you at the local street, personal and experiential levels. There are superb art museums, some cutting-edge architecture, beautiful parks and gardens, and fun shopping. You can pick from an international smorgasbord of culinary experiences – Afghani to Zambian – then take in some world-class jazz or Beethoven. Explore and enjoy.

HIGHLIGHTS

- Watching the death-wish surfers face the towering waves at **Surfrider Beach** (p121) in Malibu, then throwing yourself into their tamer cousins on **Zuma Beach** (p154)

- Shopping like – and maybe spot – a star at **Fred Segal** (p210) or along **Robertson Blvd** (p207)

- Hot-rodding it along breathtaking **Palos Verdes Dr** (p128), then hunting for starfish and anemones in the tide pools of **Abalone Cove** (p128)

- Getting your freak on while milling with snake charmers, tarot readers and beefcakes on the **Venice Boardwalk** (p125)

- Feeling your spirits soar surrounded by the fantastic art, architecture, views and gardens of the **Getty Center** (p117)

- Joining the buff, the famous and their canine companions on a hike through **Runyon Canyon** (p153), preferably at sunset, for superb city views

- Hitting the bars of **Hollywood** (p191) for a night of tabloid-worthy decadence and debauchery

- Getting under the skin of LA by taking a guided tour with **Los Angeles Conservancy** (p159) or **Esotouric** (p159)

HISTORY

LA's human history begins with the Gabrielino and Chumash, who roamed the area as early as 6000 BC. Their hunter-gatherer existence ended in the late 18th century with the arrival of Spanish missionaries and Mexican settlers who founded the El Pueblo de la Reina de Los Angeles. This first civilian settlement became a thriving farming community but remained a far-flung outpost for decades.

During the Mexican–American War (1846–48), American soldiers encountered some resistance from General Andrés Pico and other Mexican commanders, but eventually LA came under US rule along with the rest of California. The city was incorporated on April 4, 1850.

A series of seminal events caused LA's population to swell to two million by 1930: the collapse of the northern-California gold rush in the 1850s, the arrival of the railroad in the 1870s, the birth of the citrus industry in the late 1800s, the discovery of oil in 1892, the launch of the harbor in San Pedro in 1907 and the opening of the LA aqueduct in 1913.

During WWI, the Lockheed brothers and Donald Douglas established aircraft manufacturing plants in LA. Two decades later, the aviation industry – helped along by billions of federal dollars for military contracts – was among the industries that contributed to a real-estate boom and sparked suburban sprawl. Another, of course, was the film industry, which took root here as early as 1908.

ORIENTATION

Los Angeles may be vast and amorphous, but the areas of interest to visitors are actually fairly well defined so it's easy to concentrate on particular areas. About 15 miles inland, Downtown LA finds itself fully in the grip of gentrification and combines high-brow culture with global-village pizzazz, a growing loft scene and an up-and-coming arts district. Pasadena, to the northeast, is a Euro-flavored mansion- and museum-packed enclave, while boho-chic Silver Lake and Los Feliz lie to the northwest. The latter borders the large urban playground of Griffith Park, home of the Hollywood Sign. Hip-again Hollywood itself is a bit further west of Griffith Park, but most TV and movie studios are actually north of the park in Burbank and Studio City in the San Fernando Valley.

FAST FACTS

- **Population LA County** 10.3 million (2007)
- **Population city of LA** 4.2 million (2007)
- **Average temps** Jan 47/66°F, July 62/82°F
- **LA to Disneyland** 26 miles
- **LA to San Diego** 120 miles
- **LA to Palm Springs** 110 miles
- **LA to Santa Barbara** 95 miles
- **LA to Las Vegas** 270 miles

Urban designer chic, raucous nightlife and lesbigays rule West Hollywood, an oddly shaped independent city that segues seamlessly into Mid-City where Museum Row is the main draw. Further west are ritzy Beverly Hills, Westwood with UCLA, estate-rich Bel-Air, burgeoning Culver City with the Sony Pictures, and upscale Brentwood with the hilltop Getty Center.

Santa Monica is the most tourist-friendly of the beach towns with fun beaches, shopping and dining. Others include swish-but-low-key Malibu, funky Venice, the purebred South Bay trio of Manhattan Beach, Hermosa Beach and Redondo Beach, and finally, hopping Long Beach.

Getting around is easiest by car, although public transport is usually adequate within specific neighborhoods. For information on traveling to and from Los Angeles International Airport (LAX), see p217.

Maps

Supermarkets, gas stations, tourist offices and convenience stores all sell maps, but the best are those published by the **American Automobile Association** (AAA; ☎ 800-874-7532; www.aaa.com), which has numerous branches around town, including one in **West LA** (off Map pp90-1; ☎ 310-914-8500; 1900 S Sepulveda Blvd; 🕑 9am-5pm Mon-Fri) and another in **Mid-City** (Map pp88-9; ☎ 323-525-0018; 5500 Wilshire Blvd; 🕑 9am-5pm Mon-Fri). AAA's *Central & Western Area* map is the single most useful map. Maps cost about $4 each but are free to members of AAA and its foreign affiliates.

(Continued on page 100)

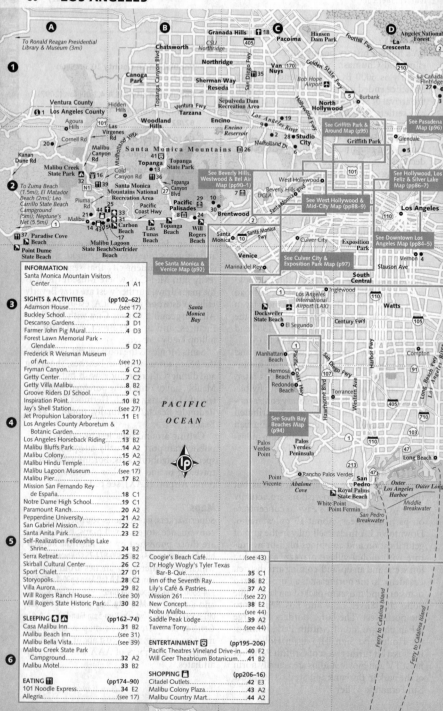

INFORMATION
Santa Monica Mountain Visitors
Center...1 A1

SIGHTS & ACTIVITIES (pp102–62)
Adamson House..........................(see 17)
Buckley School..............................2 C2
Descanso Gardens...........................3 D1
Farmer John Pig Mural......................4 D3
Forest Lawn Memorial Park -
Glendale.....................................5 D2
Frederick R Weisman Museum
of Art.....................................(see 21)
Fryman Canyon..............................6 C2
Getty Center................................7 C2
Getty Villa Malibu..........................8 B2
Groove Riders DJ School.....................9 C1
Inspiration Point..........................10 A2
Jay's Shell Station.......................(see 27)
Jet Propulsion Laboratory..................11 E1
Los Angeles County Arboretum &
Botanic Garden.............................12 E2
Los Angeles Horseback Riding..............13 B2
Malibu Bluffs Park.........................14 A2
Malibu Colony..............................15 A2
Malibu Hindu Temple........................16 A2
Malibu Lagoon Museum.....................(see 17)
Malibu Pier................................17 B2
Mission San Fernando Rey
de España..................................18 C1
Notre Dame High School.....................19 C1
Paramount Ranch............................20 A2
Pepperdine University......................21 A2
San Gabriel Mission........................22 E2
Santa Anita Park...........................23 E2
Self-Realization Fellowship Lake
Shrine.....................................24 B2
Serra Retreat..............................25 B2
Skirball Cultural Center...................26 C2
Sport Chalet...............................27 D1
Storyopolis................................28 C2
Villa Aurora...............................29 A2
Will Rogers Ranch House..................(see 30)
Will Rogers State Historic Park............30 B2

SLEEPING (pp162–74)
Casa Malibu Inn............................31 B2
Malibu Beach Inn.........................(see 31)
Malibu Bella Vista.......................(see 39)
Malibu Creek State Park
Campground.................................32 A2
Malibu Motel...............................33 B2

EATING (pp174–90)
101 Noodle Express.........................34 E2
Allegria.................................(see 17)

Coogie's Beach Café......................(see 43)
Dr Hogly Wogly's Tyler Texas
Bar-B-Que..................................35 C1
Inn of the Seventh Ray.....................36 B2
Lily's Café & Pastries.....................37 A2
Mission 261..............................(see 22)
New Concept................................38 E2
Nobu Malibu..............................(see 44)
Saddle Peak Lodge..........................39 A2
Taverna Tony.............................(see 44)

ENTERTAINMENT (pp195–206)
Pacific Theatres Vineland Drive-in.........40 F2
Will Geer Theatricum Botanicum.............41 B2

SHOPPING (pp206–16)
Citadel Outlets............................42 E3
Malibu Colony Plaza........................43 A2
Malibu Country Mart........................44 A2

0   10 km
0   6 miles

E   2   To Wrightwood (32mi)   F   G   H

Angeles Crest Hwy

San Gabriel Mountains

San Gabriel River

Red Box Rd

Cogswell Reservoir

Mt Wilson Observatory

Mt Wilson (5710ft)

San Gabriel Reservoir

Morris Reservoir

Angeles National Forest

Mt San Antonio (Old Baldy; 10,064ft)

11

Brookside Park

Altadena

San Antonio Heights

1

Pasadena

(134)

San Marino

Foothill Fwy

12   23   Arcadia

Monrovia

Azusa   Glendora

(210)

Rancho Cucamonga

(30)

Santa Fe Dam Recreation Area

(30)

Upland

66

San Gabriel

22

Temple City

Baldwin Park

(605)

Bonelli Regional County Park

Montclair

2

Ontario International Airport

Alhambra

34

Valley Blvd

El Monte

Covina

San Bernardino Fwy West Covina

Pomona

Ontario

Mission Blvd

Monterey Park

10

Atlantic Blvd

3B

Whittier Narrows Recreation Area

Valley Blvd

40

(10)

(57)

(71)

(60)

East Los Angeles

60

42

Industry   La Puente

Diamond Bar

Chino

Santa Ana Fwy

Pico Rivera

San Gabriel River Fwy

Pomona Fwy

Schabarum Regional Park

(60)

(57)

710

Whittier

Rowland Heights

142

Chino Hills State Park

83

3

La Habra Heights

Orange Fwy

Prado Flood Control Basin

Norco

See Southern Los Angeles Map (pp82–3)

Los Angeles County
Orange County

Cajbot Canyon Rd

Riverside County

Corona

5

Downey

La Habra

La Mirada

Richard Nixon Library

(71)

605

Imperial Hwy

Brea

39

Norwalk

Yorba Linda Blvd

Yorba Linda

Artesia Fwy

Buena Park

CSU Fullerton

Placentia

(90)

4

Paramount

Cerritos

Fullerton

Riverside Fwy

(91)

Irvine Regional Park

Lakewood

San Gabriel River Fwy

Knott's Berry Farm

(91)

(57)

Carson St

Lincoln Ave

Anaheim

(55)

Villa Park

Cleveland National Forest

Long Beach Airport

Cypress

39

Disneyland & Disney's California Adventure

(231)

E Willow St

Katella Ave

Stanton

Orange

605

CSU Long Beach

(22)

(22)

Santa Ana Mountains

Belmont Shore

Naples

Garden Grove Fwy

Garden Grove

5

Westminster

San Diego Fwy

Tustin

Beach Harbor

Seal Beach National Wildlife Refuge

Santa Ana

Eastern Transportation Corridor

Portola Hills

Long Beach Breakwater

Seal Beach Pier

Beach Blvd

405

Lake Forest

Bolsa Chica State Beach

Pacific Coast Hwy

Huntington Beach

Santa Ana River

Costa Mesa Fwy

John Wayne Airport (Orange County)

Irvine Center Dr

San Pedro Bay

Huntington Pier

1

Irvine

(231)

Huntington City Beach

Huntington State Beach

(55)

(73)

Mission Viejo

Costa Mesa

UC Irvine

Newport Beach

Newport Bay

Corona del Mar

Corona del Mar State Beach

Crystal Cove State Park

(73)

San Pedro Channel

(133)

Laguna Beach

Aliso Beach

(74)

6

Laguna Niguel

San Juan Capistrano

Ferry to Catalina Island

INFORMATION
Acres of Books.............................1 F1
Long Beach Tourist Information...2 F2

SIGHTS & ACTIVITIES (pp102–62)
Abalone Cove Shoreline Park.....3 B5
Aquarium of the Pacific.............4 F2
Banning Residence Museum.....5 D4
Bikestation................................6 F1
Cabrillo Marine Aquarium..........7 D5
Drum Barracks Civil War
  Museum..................................8 D4
Fort MacArthur Military Museum.9 C5
Gondola Getaway.....................10 F5
Green Hills Memorial Park.........11 C4
Korean Friendship Bell..............12 C5
Long Beach Museum of Art........13 F4
Los Angeles Maritime Museum...14 D5
Museum of Latin American Art...15 G1

Pike at Rainbow Harbor.............16 F2
Point Fermin Lighthouse............17 D5
Point Vicente Fishing Access......18 B5
Point Vicente Interpretive Center..19 B5
Point Vicente Lighthouse...........20 B5
Polytechnic High.......................21 E4
Ports O'Call Village....................22 D5
Queen Mary...............................23 F3
Scorpion....................................24 F3
South Coast Botanic Garden......25 C4
SS Lane Victory..........................26 D5
Sunken City................................27 D5
Terranea (under construction)....28 B5
Torrance High School.................29 C3
Walker Café...............................30 D5
Watts Labor Community Action
  Committee..............................31 D1
Watts Towers.............................32 D1
Wayfarers Chapel......................33 B5

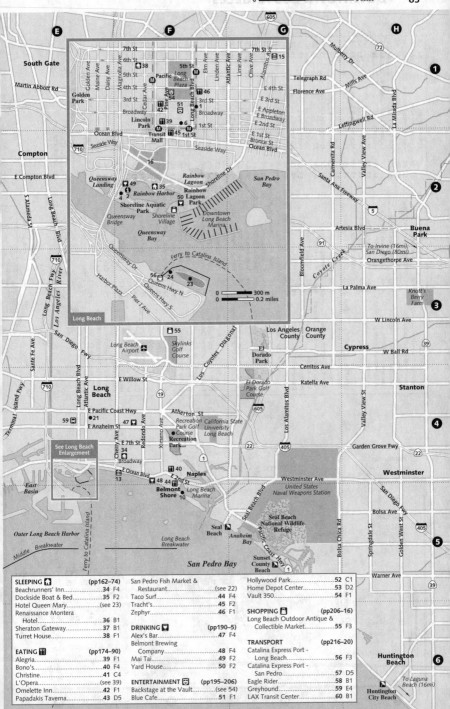

0 — 5 km
0 — 3 miles

SLEEPING (pp162–74)
Beachrunners' Inn....................34 F4
Dockside Boat & Bed................35 F2
Hotel Queen Mary...............(see 23)
Renaissance Montera
    Hotel.................................36 B1
Sheraton Gateway...................37 F1
Turret House...........................38 F1

EATING (pp174–90)
Alegria...................................39 F1
Bono's....................................40 F4
Christine.................................41 C4
L'Opera.............................(see 39)
Omelette Inn..........................42 F2
Papadakis Taverna...................43 D5

San Pedro Fish Market &
    Restaurant......................(see 22)
Taco Surf................................44 F4
Tracht's..................................45 F2
Zephyr....................................46 F1

DRINKING (pp190–5)
Alex's Bar...............................47 F4
Belmont Brewing
    Company............................48 F4
Mai Tai...................................49 F2
Yard House..............................50 F2

ENTERTAINMENT (pp195–206)
Backstage at the Vault........(see 54)
Blue Cafe................................51 F1

Hollywood Park.......................52 C1
Home Depot Center.................53 D2
Vault 350................................54 F1

SHOPPING (pp206–16)
Long Beach Outdoor Antique &
    Collectible Market..............55 F3

TRANSPORT (pp216–20)
Catalina Express Port -
    Long Beach.........................56 F3
Catalina Express Port -
    San Pedro..........................57 D5
Eagle Rider.............................58 B1
Greyhound..............................59 E4
LAX Transit Center...................60 B1

INFORMATION
Canadian Consulate..................................1 C6
Downtown Los Angeles Tourist
  Information......................................2 C6
El Pueblo Visitors Center......................3 B2
Japanese Consulate..............................4 C6
LA Chinatown Heritage & Visitors
  Center..5 E4
Little Tokyo Koban................................6 A4

SIGHTS & ACTIVITIES   (pp102–62)
African American Firefighter
  Museum...7 D8
America Tropical Mural....................(see 28)
Aratani/Japan America Theater........8 A4
Avila Adobe...9 B2
Bradbury Building................................10 D6
Brewery Art Complex............................11 F4
California Plaza....................................12 C6
Cathedral of Our Lady of the
  Angels..13 D5
Central Plaza.......................................14 E4
Chinese American Museum..................15 B3
City Hall..16 A3
Coca-Cola Bottling Plant......................17 D8
Colburn School of Performing
  Arts...18 C5
Dorothy Chandler Pavilion.............(see 39)
Eastern Columbia Building...................19 C7
Fashion Institute of Design &
  Merchandising...........................(see 25)
Flower Market.....................................20 C8
Geffen Contemporary
  at MOCA...21 B4
Globe Theater.....................................22 C7
Go for Broke Monument......................23 B4
Grand Central Market..........................24 D6
Grand Hope Park.................................25 B6
Grier Musser Museum..........................26 B5
Hollenbeck Youth Center.....................27 F6
Hop Louie....................................(see 14)
Italian Hall...28 B2
James Irvine Garden............................29 A4
Japanese American Cultural &
  Community Center...........................30 A4
Japanese American National
  Museum..31 B4
Koyasan Buddhist Temple....................32 A4
La Placita..33 B2
Los Angeles Theater............................34 C6
Los Angeles Times...............................35 D6
Mariachi Plaza....................................36 F6
Million Dollar Theater..........................37 D6
MOCA Grand Ave................................38 C6
Music Center.......................................39 D5
Old Plaza Firehouse.............................40 B3
Orpheum Theater................................41 C7
Palace Theater.....................................42 C6
Pantages Theatre................................43 C6
Pico House..44 B2
Richard Riordan
  Central Library.................................45 C6
St Vincent Court..................................46 C6
San Antonio Winery.....................(see 3)
Sepulveda House..................................47 C1
Southern California Institute of
  Architecture....................................48 E6
Staples Center.....................................49 B7
State Theater.......................................50 C6
Tower Theater.....................................51 C7
United Artists Theater..........................52 C7
US Bank Tower....................................53 C6
Walt Disney Concert Hall..............(see 39)
Wells Fargo Center..............................54 C6
Wells Fargo History Museum.......(see 54)

SLEEPING   (pp162–74)
Figueroa Hotel....................................55 B6
Inn at 657...56 A8
Millennium Biltmore Hotel...................57 C6
Omni Los Angeles Hotel.......................58 C6
Ritz Milner Hotel.................................59 B6
Standard Downtown LA........................60 C6
Stillwell Hotel......................................61 C7

EATING   (pp174–90)
Blue Velvet..62 B6
Café Metropol......................................63 E6
Ce Fiore..64 C6
Clifton's Cafeteria................................65 C6
Coloi Kitchen.......................................66 C6
Empress Pavilion..........................(see 14)
Grand Central Market....................24 D6
Haru Ulala...67 A4
Homegirl Café......................................68 F6
La Serenata de Garibaldi......................69 F6
Langer's..70 A5
Mama's Hot Tamales
  Café..71 A5
McCormick & Schmick's......................72 C6
Oomasa..73 A4
Patina...(see 53)
Pete's Café & Bar.................................74 D6
Philippe the Original............................75 B2
R23..76 E6
Tiara Café..77 C6
Water Grill...78 E6
Zip Fusion...79 C6

DRINKING   (pp190–5)
Ciudad...79 C6
Edison..80 D6
Gallery Bar...................................(see 57)
Golden Gopher....................................81 C6
Lost Souls Café....................................82 D6
Mountain Bar................................(see 14)
Rooftop Bar @ Standard
  Downtown LA...........................(see 60)
Seven Grand...83 C6

ENTERTAINMENT   (pp195–206)
Ahmanson Theatre.......................(see 39)
Bob Baker Marionette
  Theater...84 C5
Club Mayan..85 C7
Downtown Comedy
  Club...86 C6
East West Players.................................87 A4
La Cita..88 C6
Mark Taper Forum.......................(see 39)
Redcat...89 C5
Smell...90 D6
Walt Disney Concert
  Hall..(see 53)
Zipper Concert Hall......................(see 18)

0   1 km
0   0.5 miles

SHOPPING (pp206–16)
American Apparel Factory Store..91 D7
Bert Green Fine Art.................92 D6
Brewery Art Complex..............(see 11)
California Mart......................93 C7
Hive Gallery & Studios..............94 C6
Jewelry District.....................95 C6
LMAN Gallery......................(see 96)
Mary Goldman Gallery...............96 D4
Munky King........................(see 14)
New Mart...........................97 C7

TRANSPORT (pp216–20)
Greyhound..........................98 D8
LAX Flyaway Shuttle Stop............99 E5

Chinatown
Koreatown
Los Angeles River
Metrolink Station
Metro Gold Line
Little Tokyo
Arts District
Civic Center/Tom Bradley
Pershing Square
Financial District
7th St/Metro Center
South Park
Fashion District
Jewelry District
Los Angeles Convention Center
Los Angeles Trade-Technical College
MacArthur Park
Westlake/MacArthur Park
Mount St Mary's College
Metro Red Line
Metro Blue Line
Harbor Fwy
Santa Ana Fwy
Santa Monica Fwy

To LA County/USC Medical Center; Silver Lake; the Closet (0.4mi)
To East Los Angeles
To Self-Help Graphics & Art (2mi)
To El Mercado (1.1mi); Tamales Liliana's (1.25mi)
To Farmer John Pig Mural (1mi)
To Little Radio Warehouse (0.25mi)
To Dunbar Hotel (1.5mi); Watts Towers (6mi); Watts Labor Community Action Committee (6.5mi)
To Mercado La Paloma; Chichén Itzá (0.5mi)
To University of Southern California (USC); Exposition Park (0.75mi)
To Papa Cristo's (1mi); St Sophia Cathedral (1mi)
To Dong II Jang (1.2mi)
To Chosun Galbee (1.4mi); Mama's M Woods; M Hines (4.4mi)
To Prince (0.75mi)
To Korean American Museum (1mi)
To Bullocks Wilshire Building (0.25mi); Brass Monkey (0.75mi); AOC (1.3mi); Wiltern Theatre (1.5mi)

A   B   C   D

1

Universal Studios Hollywood

Hollywood Blvd

20

33

Hollywood Franklin Park   37   41

42   91   P

26   3   P   81   7

6   96   90   21   119   56   Hollywood/Vine   28

39   87   M   19   109   25   Hollywood Blvd   70   95   45

31   11   9   114   99   78   2

18   82   4   43   93   107

Selma Ave

2

Hollywood Reservoir Dam

Mulholland Dr   14

101

Dearborn Dr   10

Runyon Canyon Park   **Hollywood Hills**

92   13

Metro Red Line   Canyon Dr

3

Wattles Garden Park

16

Sycamore Ave   Scenic Gardens   38

36   40   Orchid Ave   Franklin Ave   34   102   23

Hollywood/Western

Hollywood Blvd   103   71

35   59   Harold Way

4

51   79   58   17   83   8   104   55   47   44   CBS Studios

W Sunset Ave   72   80

Delongpre Park   **Hollywood**

Fountain Ave   88

Hollywood Recreation Center

84   94   100

Santa Monica Blvd   85

74   15   98

5

Warner Hollywood Studios   **Poinsettia Recreation Center**

Beth Olam Memorial Park

105   22   29

62   Waring Ave   61

32   57

Melrose Ave

6

Pan Pacific Park

INFORMATION
Cyber Java...**1**	B4
Hollywood Library...............................**2**	C2
Hollywood Tourist Information........**3**	A2
LA Gay & Lesbian Center...................**4**	B2
Skylight Books....................................**5**	F4

SIGHTS & ACTIVITIES (pp102–62)
Alias Apartment Building...................**6**	A2
Capitol Records Tower........................**7**	C1
Crossroads of the World.....................**8**	B2
Egyptian Theatre.................................**9**	B2
Ford Amphitheatre............................**10**	B3

Guinness World of Records Museum..**11**	B2
Hollyhock House................................**12**	E4
Hollywood Bowl.........................(see 92)	
Hollywood Bowl Museum.................**13**	B3
Hollywood Bowl Overlook................**14**	B2
Hollywood Forever Cemetery...........**15**	C5
Hollywood Heritage Museum...........**16**	B3
Hollywood High School.....................**17**	B4
Hollywood Museum..........................**18**	B2
Hollywood Pro Bicycles....................**19**	B2
Hollywood Sign.................................**20**	C1
Hollywood Wax Museum..................**21**	B2
Hoopnotica..**22**	B5

Immaculate Heart High School........**23**	D3
John Marshall High School................**24**	G3
Joint...**25**	B2
Kodak Theatre...................................**26**	A1
Municipal Art Gallery..................(see 12)	
Musso & Frank Grill...........................**27**	B2
Pantages Theater...............................**28**	C2
Paramount Studios............................**29**	C5
Red Line Tours...................................**30**	B2
Ripley's Believe It or Not!.................**31**	B2
Shooters...**32**	B5
Sunset Ranch Hollywood..................**33**	D1

SLEEPING (pp162–74)

Best Western Hollywood Hills Hotel	34 C3
Elaine's Hollywood B&B	35 A4
Highland Gardens Hotel	36 B4
Hollywood Celebrity Hotel	37 A1
Hollywood Hills Hotel & Apartments	38 B3
Hollywood Roosevelt Hotel	39 A2
Magic Castle Hotel	40 B4
Orange Drive Manor Hostel	41 A4
Renaissance Hollywood Hotel	42 A1
USA Hostels Hollywood	43 C2
Villa delle Stelle	44 C4
W Hollywood (opens 2009)	45 C2

EATING (pp174–90)

Blair's	46 G3
Bowery	47 C4
Cafe Stella	48 F5
Café Tropical	49 G6
Casita Del Campo	50 G4
Cheebo	51 A4
El Cochinito	52 G5
El Conquistador	53 G5
Fred 62	54 F4
Hungry Cat	55 C4
Kung Pao Kitty	56 C2
Lucy's El Adobe	57 C5
Mashti Malone's	58 A4
Palms Thai	59 C4
Pho Café	60 G6
Providence	61 C4
Red Pearl Kitchen	62 B5
Sanamluang	63 E4
Scoops	64 E5
Tangier	65 F3
Vermont	66 F4
Yuca's	67 F3

DRINKING (pp190–5)

4100 Bar	68 F5
Akbar	69 F4
Beauty Bar	70 C2
Blu Monkey Lounge	71 D4
Cat & Fiddle	72 B4
Faultline	73 E6
Formosa Cafe	74 A5
Good Luck Bar	75 G4
Other Side	76 F4
Tiki Ti	77 F4
Velvet Margarita	78 C2
Woods	79 A4

ENTERTAINMENT (pp195–206)

American Cinematheque	(see 9)
ArcLight & Cinerama Dome	80 C4
Avalon	81 C1
Boardner's	82 B4
Catalina Bar & Grill	83 B4
Cinespace	(see 15)
Cinespia	(see 15)
Circus Disco	84 B5
Dragonfly	85 B5
Echo	86 H6
Echoplex	(see 86)
El Capitan Entertainment Center	(see 87)
El Capitan Theatre	87 A2
El Floridita	88 B4
Gabah	89 E6
Grauman's Chinese Theatre	90 A2
Highlands	91 A1
Hollywood Bowl	92 B3
Hotel Café	93 C2
Hudson Theatres	94 B5
Improv Olympic West	95 C2
Knitting Factory Hollywood	96 A2
Little Temple	97 F5
M Bar	(see 88)
MET Theatre	98 D5
Nacional	99 C2
Open Fist Theater	100 C5
Spaceland	101 G5
Upright Citizens Brigade	102 C3
Vanguard	103 C4

SHOPPING (pp206–16)

Amoeba Music	104 C4
Babeland	105 B5
Camille Hudson Shoes	106 F4
Farmers Market (Hollywood)	107 C2
Farmers Market (Silver Lake)	108 G5
Frederick's of Hollywood	109 A2
Kids are Alright	110 G6
La La Ling	111 F4
La Luz de Jesus	(see 118)
Luxe de Ville	112 H6
Matrushka	113 F5
Napoleon Perdis	114 B2
Panty Raid	115 H3
Rockaway Records	116 H4
Sirens & Sailors	117 H6
Wacko	118 F4

TRANSPORT (pp216–20)

Greyhound	119 C2

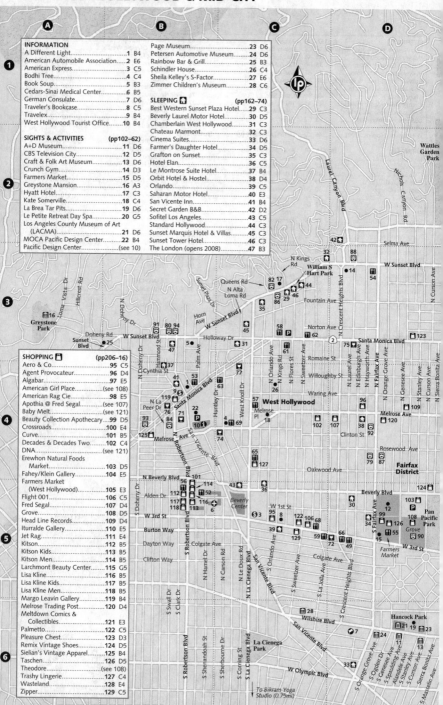

INFORMATION
A Different Light...........................1 B4
American Automobile Association...2 E6
American Express.........................3 C5
Bodhi Tree...................................4 C4
Book Soup....................................5 B3
Cedars-Sinai Medical Center.........6 B5
German Consulate.........................7 D6
Traveler's Bookcase......................8 C5
Travelex.......................................9 B4
West Hollywood Tourist Office.....10 B4

SIGHTS & ACTIVITIES   (pp102–62)
A+D Museum...............................11 D6
CBS Television City......................12 D5
Craft & Folk Art Museum.............13 D6
Crunch Gym.................................14 D3
Farmers Market...........................15 D5
Greystone Mansion......................16 A3
Hyatt Hotel.................................17 C3
Kate Somerville...........................18 C4
La Brea Tar Pits...........................19 D6
Le Petite Retreat Day Spa.............20 G5
Los Angeles County Museum of Art
(LACMA)...................................21 D6
MOCA Pacific Design Center.........22 B4
Pacific Design Center................(see 10)

Page Museum.............................23 D6
Petersen Automotive Museum.......24 D6
Rainbow Bar & Grill.....................25 B3
Schindler House...........................26 C4
Sheila Kelley's S-Factor...............27 E6
Zimmer Children's Museum..........28 C6

SLEEPING   (pp162–74)
Best Western Sunset Plaza Hotel....29 C3
Beverly Laurel Motor Hotel...........30 D5
Chamberlain West Hollywood........31 C3
Chateau Marmont.......................32 C3
Cinema Suites.............................33 D6
Farmer's Daughter Hotel..............34 D5
Grafton on Sunset........................35 C5
Hotel Elan...................................36 C5
Le Montrose Suite Hotel...............37 B4
Orbit Hotel & Hostel....................38 D4
Orlando......................................39 C5
Saharan Motor Hotel....................40 E3
San Vicente Inn...........................41 B4
Secret Garden B&B.......................42 D2
Sofitel Los Angeles......................43 C5
Standard Hollywood.....................44 C3
Sunset Marquis Hotel & Villas.......45 C3
Sunset Tower Hotel......................46 C3
The London (opens 2008)..............47 B3

SHOPPING   (pp206–16)
Aero & Co...................................95 C5
Agent Provocateur.......................96 C5
Algabar......................................97 E5
American Girl Place..................(see 108)
American Rag Cie.........................98 E5
Apothia @ Fred Segal...............(see 107)
Baby Melt..............................(see 121)
Beauty Collection Apothecary.......99 D5
Crossroads................................100 E4
Curve.......................................101 B5
Decades & Decades Two.............102 C4
DNA.....................................(see 121)
Erewhon Natural Foods
Market...................................103 D5
Fahey/Klein Gallery....................104 E5
Farmers Market
(West Hollywood)...................105 E3
Flight 001.................................106 C5
Fred Segal.................................107 D4
Grove.......................................108 D4
Head Line Records......................109 D4
Iturralde Gallery........................110 E4
Jet Rag.....................................111 E4
Kitson......................................112 B5
Kitson Kids................................113 B5
Kitson Men................................114 B5
Larchmont Beauty Center............115 G5
Lisa Kline..................................116 B5
Lisa Kline Kids...........................117 B5
Lisa Kline Men...........................118 B5
Margo Leavin Gallery..................119 D4
Melrose Trading Post...................120 D4
Meltdown Comics &
Collectibles............................121 E3
Palmetto...................................122 C5
Pleasure Chest...........................123 D3
Remix Vintage Shoes...................124 D5
Sielian's Vintage Apparel.............125 B4
Taschen....................................126 D5
Theodore.............................(see 108)
Trashy Lingerie..........................127 C4
Wasteland.................................128 E4
Zipper......................................129 C5

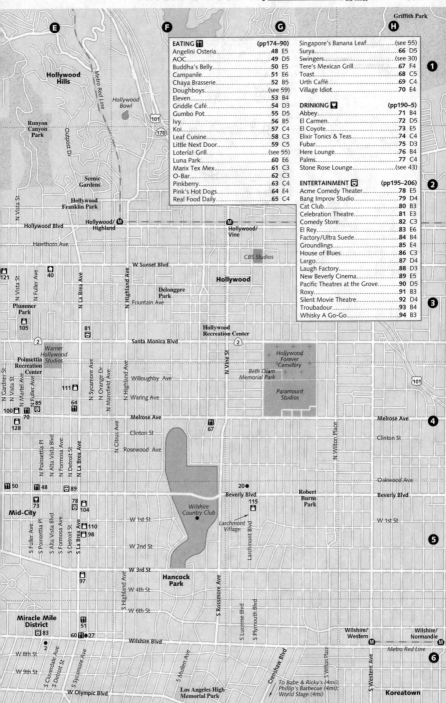

0 — 1 km
0 — 0.5 miles

EATING 🍴 (pp174–90)
Angelini Osteria..............................48 E5
AOC...49 D5
Buddha's Belly................................50 E5
Campanile.......................................51 E6
Chaya Brasserie...............................52 B5
Doughboys..............................(see 59)
Eleven..53 B4
Griddle Café....................................54 D3
Gumbo Pot......................................55 D5
Ivy..56 B5
Koi...57 C4
Leaf Cuisine....................................58 C3
Little Next Door...............................59 C5
Lotería! Grill............................(see 55)
Luna Park..60 E6
Marix Tex Mex.................................61 C3
O-Bar..62 C3
Pinkberry...63 C4
Pink's Hot Dogs...............................64 E4
Real Food Daily...............................65 C4
Singapore's Banana Leaf............(see 55)
Surya...66 D5
Swingers...................................(see 30)
Tere's Mexican Grill.........................67 F4
Toast...68 C5
Urth Caffé.......................................69 C4
Village Idiot....................................70 E4

DRINKING 🍷 (pp190–5)
Abbey...71 B4
El Carmen.......................................72 D5
El Coyote..73 E5
Elixir Tonics & Teas.........................74 C4
Fubar..75 D3
Here Lounge....................................76 B4
Palms..77 C4
Stone Rose Lounge.....................(see 43)

ENTERTAINMENT 🎭 (pp195–206)
Acme Comedy Theater......................78 B5
Bang Improv Studio..........................79 D4
Cat Club..80 B3
Celebration Theatre.........................81 E3
Comedy Store..................................82 C3
El Rey...83 E6
Factory/Ultra Suede.........................84 B4
Groundlings.....................................85 E4
House of Blues................................86 C3
Largo..87 D4
Laugh Factory.................................88 D3
New Beverly Cinema........................89 E5
Pacific Theatres at the Grove............90 D5
Roxy...91 B3
Silent Movie Theatre........................92 D4
Troubadour......................................93 B4
Whisky A Go-Go...............................94 B3

Downtown Beverly Hills

300 m
0.2 miles

W 3rd St
Burton Way
N Alpine Dr
N Crescent Dr
N Canon Dr
N Beverly Dr
N Rodeo Dr
N Camden Dr
N Bedford Dr
N Roxbury Dr
Foothill Dr
Dayton Way
N Rexford Dr
Clifton Way
Two Rodeo
Wilshire Blvd
S Spalding Dr
S Linden Dr
S McCarty Dr
S Roxbury Dr
S Bedford Dr
S Peck Dr
S Camden Dr
S Rodeo Dr
S El Camino Dr
S Beverly Dr
S Reeves Dr
S Carlon Dr
S Crescent Dr
S Santa Monica Blvd
Santa Monica Blvd
Brighton Way
Park Way
Canelita Ave
Beverly Gardens Park

Philbert Dr
Bella Dr
Cielo Dr
To Vibrato Grill & Jazz (2.5mi)
Benedict Canyon Dr
Green Acres Dr
Carolwood Dr
Baroda Dr

Bel Air
Chalon Rd
N Stone Canyon Rd
Bellagio Rd
Bel Air Country Club
Bel Air Rd
St Pierre Rd
St Cloud Rd
N Beverly Glen Blvd
Holmby Hills
Monovale Dr
Charing Cross Rd
Club View Dr
Mapleton Dr
Holmby Park
Comstock Ave
Los Angeles Country Club
S Beverly Glen Blvd

W Sunset Blvd
Reservoir
De Neve Dr
Charles E Young Dr W
Gayley Ave
Charles E Young Dr E
Royce Quad
University of California, Los Angeles (UCLA)
Charles E Young Dr S
Warner Ave
Wertholme Ave
Hilgard Ave
Malcolm Ave

To San Fernando Valley (5mi)
To Brentwood Inn (0.75mi)

Westwood Blvd
Veteran Ave
San Diego Fwy
Los Angeles National Cemetery
405
West Los Angeles Veterans Administration Center
Le Conte Ave
Broxton Ave
Kinross Ave
Weyburn Ave
Lindbrook Dr
Wilshire Blvd
Gayden Ave
Tiverton Ave
Westwood
Wellworth Ave
Selby Ave
Malcolm Ave
Ohio Ave
Santa Monica Blvd
S Santa Monica Blvd
2

Westwood Park
San Vicente Blvd
S Sepulveda Blvd

To British Consulate (0.1mi); Dutch Consulate (0.1mi); Liberati II (0.4mi); New Zealand Consulate (0.8mi)
To Sawtelle Kitchen (0.8mi); Hurry Curry (1mi); Yashima (1.1mi); Zip Fusion (1.1mi)
To Zankou Chicken (0.2mi); American Automobile Association (0.3mi); Odyssey Theatre (0.75mi)
To Landmark Theatres (0.8mi)
To Nuart Theatre (0.7mi)

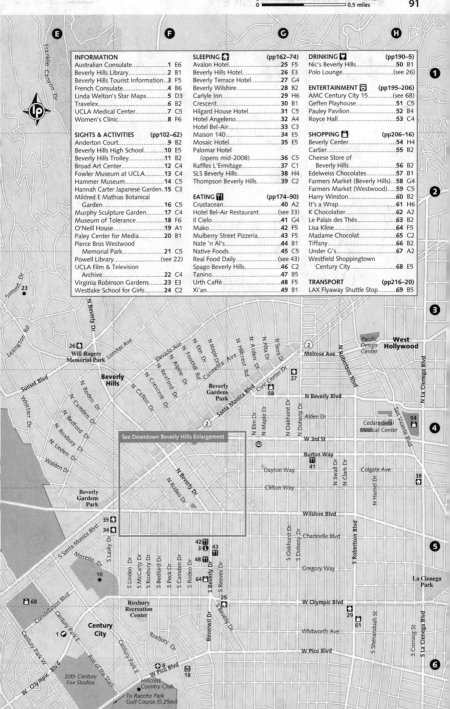

0 ━━━━ 1 km
0 ━━━━ 0.5 miles

INFORMATION
Australian Consulate..............................1 E6
Beverly Hills Library..............................2 B1
Beverly Hills Tourist Information..3 F5
French Consulate...................................4 B6
Linda Welton's Star Maps.................5 D3
Travelex...6 B2
UCLA Medical Center..........................7 C5
Women's Clinic......................................8 F6

SIGHTS & ACTIVITIES (pp102–62)
Anderton Court.......................................9 B2
Beverly Hills High School...................10 E5
Beverly Hills Trolley...........................11 B2
Broad Art Center...................................12 C4
Fowler Museum at UCLA..................13 C4
Hammer Museum...................................14 C5
Hannah Carter Japanese Garden.15 C3
Mildred E Mathias Botanical
    Garden..16 C5
Murphy Sculpture Garden................17 C4
Museum of Tolerance.........................18 F6
O'Neill House..19 A1
Paley Center for Media......................20 B1
Pierce Bros Westwood
    Memorial Park................................21 C5
Powell Library....................................(see 22)
UCLA Film & Television
    Archive..22 C5
Virginia Robinson Gardens................23 E3
Westlake School for Girls...................24 C2

SLEEPING (pp162–74)
Avalon Hotel..25 F5
Beverly Hills Hotel...............................26 E3
Beverly Terrace Hotel........................27 G4
Beverly Wilshire....................................28 B2
Carlyle Inn...29 H6
Crescent..30 B1
Hilgard House Hotel...........................31 C5
Hotel Angeleno....................................32 A4
Hotel Bel-Air...33 C3
Maison 140..34 E5
Mosaic Hotel...35 E5
Palomar Hotel
    (opens mid-2008)...........................36 C5
Raffles L'Ermitage.................................37 C1
SLS Beverly Hills....................................38 H4
Thompson Beverly Hills.....................39 B2

EATING (pp174–90)
Crustacean..40 A2
Hotel Bel-Air Restaurant.............(see 33)
Il Cielo..41 G4
Mako...42 F5
Mulberry Street Pizzeria....................43 F5
Nate 'n Al's..44 B1
Native Foods..45 C5
Real Food Daily..............................(see 43)
Spago Beverly Hills..............................46 C2
Tanino..47 B5
Urth Caffé..48 F5
Xi'an..49 B1

DRINKING (pp190–5)
Nic's Beverly Hills..................................50 B1
Polo Lounge......................................(see 26)

ENTERTAINMENT (pp195–206)
AMC Century City 15....................(see 68)
Geffen Playhouse..................................51 C5
Pauley Pavilion......................................52 B4
Royce Hall..53 C4

SHOPPING (pp206–16)
Beverly Center.......................................54 H4
Cartier..55 B2
Cheese Store of
    Beverly Hills.....................................56 B2
Edelweiss Chocolates..........................57 B1
Farmers Market (Beverly Hills)...58 G4
Farmers Market (Westwood).......59 C5
Harry Winston...60 B2
It's a Wrap..61 H6
K Chocolatier...62 A2
Le Palais des Thés................................63 B2
Lisa Kline...64 F5
Madame Chocolat.................................65 C2
Tiffany..66 B2
Under G's...67 A2
Westfield Shoppingtown
    Century City...................................68 E5

TRANSPORT (pp216–20)
LAX Flyaway Shuttle Stop..........69 B5

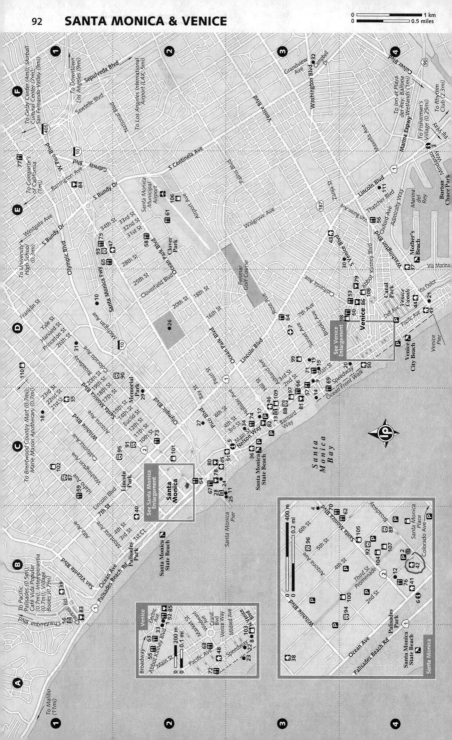

INFORMATION

Equator Books & Vinyl	1 B2
Interactive Café	2 B4
Marina del Rey Tourist Information	3 F4
Santa Monica Library	4 B3
Santa Monica Visitor Center	5 C3
Santa Monica Visitors Kiosk	6 B4
Venice Family Clinic	7 D3

SIGHTS & ACTIVITIES (pp102–62)

Abbot Kinney Mural	8 A3
Bailey House	(see 16)
Ballerina Clown	9 D3
Bergamot Station Arts Center	10 D1
Blazing Saddles	11 C3
Bryan Kest Power Yoga	12 B4
California Heritage Museum	13 C3
Chagall Returns to Venice Mural	14 C3
Chiat/Day Building	15 D3
Eames House & Studio	16 B1
Edgemar Center for the Arts	17 C3
Entenza House	(see 101)
Fred Segal Beauty	(see 101)
Gehry House	18 C1
Gold's Gym	19 D3
Homage to a Starry Night Mural	20 D4
Hoopnotica	21 D4
International Chess Park	(see 24)
Jim Morrison Mural	22 A3
Merry-Go-Round	(see 28)
Muscle Beach Venice	23 A3
Original Muscle Beach	24 C2
Pacific Park	25 C3
Santa Monica College	26 D2
Santa Monica High School	27 C2
Santa Monica Museum of Art	(see 10)
Santa Monica Pier Aquarium	28 C2
Santa Monica Skate Park	29 C2
Social & Public Art Resource Center	30 E4
Trúyoga	31 D1
Under the Sea	32 F3
Venice Reconstituted Mural	(see 48)
YAS	33 A2
Yoga Works	34 C3

SLEEPING (pp162–74)

Ambrose	35 C1
Bayside Hotel	36 C3
Best Western Jamaica Bay Inn	37 E4
Cal Mar Hotel Suites	38 A3
Channel Road Inn B&B	39 B1
Embassy Hotel Apartments	40 B2
Georgian Hotel	41 B4
HI-Los Angeles/Santa Monica	42 B4
Hostel California	43 E3
Inn at Venice Beach	44 D4
Loews Santa Monica Beach Hotel	45 C2
Sea Shore Motel	46 C3
Travelodge Santa Monica	47 E1
Venice Beach Cotel	48 A2
Venice Beach House	49 D4
Venice Beach Suites & Hotel	50 D4
Viceroy	51 C3

EATING (pp174–90)

3 Square Café & Bakery	52 B2
Abbot's Pizza	53 D4
Abode	54 C2
Axe	55 A2
Beechwood	56 E4
Caprice Fine French Pastries	(see 75)
Chaya Venice	57 D3
Counter	58 E2
Father's Office	59 C1
Hal's Bar & Grill	60 D4
Hump	61 E2
JiRaffe	62 B4
Joe's	63 A2
La Cabaña	64 D3
Lares	65 E1
Library Alehouse	66 C3
Lobster	67 C2
Mao's Kitchen	(see 88)
Omelette Parlor	68 A2
Piccolo	69 C3
Real Food Daily	70 B3
Rose Café	71 D3
Sidewalk Café	72 A2
Swingers	73 C2
Urth Caffé	74 C3
Violet	75 E1
Ye Olde King's Head	76 B4
Zip Fusion	77 E1

DRINKING (pp190–5)

Big Dean's	78 C2
Brig	79 D4
Chez Jay	80 C2
Circle Bar	81 C3
Hideout	82 C3
Liquid Kitty	83 B1
Otherroom	84 E1
Roosterfish	85 B2
	86 D4

ENTERTAINMENT (pp195–206)

American Cinematheque at Aero Theatre	87 C1
Bar Copa	88 C3
Edgemar Center for the Arts	(see 17)
Harvelle's	89 B4
Highways Performance Space & Gallery	90 D2
Madison Performing Arts Center (opens 2008)	91 C2
Magicopolis	92 B4
McCabe's Guitar Shop	93 E1
Puppet & Magic Center	94 B4
Santa Monica Drive-In at the Pier	(see 25)
Temple Bar	95 C2
Zanzibar	96 B3

SHOPPING (pp206–16)

Accents Jewelry	97 C3
ADHD	98 D4
Babystyle	(see 87)
Bergamot Station Arts Center	(see 10)
DNA	99 D3
Farmers Market (Santa Monica – Downtown)	100 B4
Farmers Market (Santa Monica – Main St)	(see 13)
Fred Segal	101 C2
Just Tantau	(see 60)
Kiehl's	102 C1
LA Louver Gallery	103 A3
Magellan's	(see 95)
Moondance Jewelry Gallery	(see 102)
Palmetto	(see 59)
Puzzle Zoo	104 B4
REI	105 B4
Santa Monica Outdoor Antique & Collectible Market	106 E2
Starbucks Hear Music	107 B4
Surfing Cowboys	108 D4
Undefeated	109 C3
Whimsic Alley	110 D1

TRANSPORT (pp216–20)

Route 66	111 E4

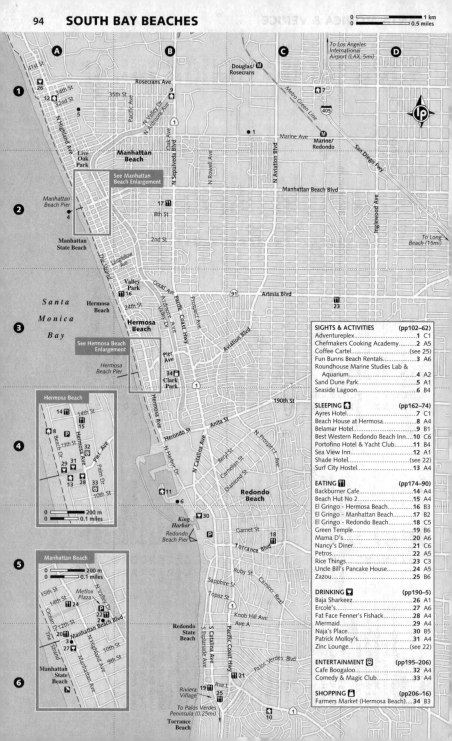

0 _____ 1 km
0 _____ 0.5 miles

A **B** **C** **D**

To Los Angeles
International
Airport (LAX, 5mi)

1

Douglas/
Rosecrans

Rosecrans Ave

35th Ave

Marine Ave

**Manhattan
Beach**

Live
Oak
Park

See Manhattan
Beach Enlargement

2

Manhattan
Beach Pier

Manhattan
State Beach

Manhattan Beach Blvd

To Long
Beach (15mi)

Santa

Valley
Park

Monica

Hermosa
Beach

Artesia Blvd

Bay

**Hermosa
Beach**

See Hermosa Beach
Enlargement

3

Hermosa
Beach Pier

Pier
Ave

190th St

Clark
Park

SIGHTS & ACTIVITIES (pp102–62)
Adventureplex..1 C1
Chefmakers Cooking Academy..........2 A5
Coffee Cartel....................................(see 25)
Fun Bunns Beach Rentals....................3 A6
Roundhouse Marine Studies Lab &
    Aquarium..4 A2
Sand Dune Park...................................5 A1
Seaside Lagoon....................................6 B4

Hermosa Beach

4

0 _____ 200 m
0 _____ 0.1 miles

Anita St

Herondo St

King
Harbor

Redondo
Beach Pier

**Redondo
Beach**

Garnet St

Torrance Blvd

SLEEPING (pp162–74)
Ayres Hotel...7 C1
Beach House at Hermosa....................8 A4
Belamar Hotel.....................................9 B1
Best Western Redondo Beach Inn....10 C6
Portofino Hotel & Yacht Club............11 B4
Sea View Inn.......................................12 A1
Shade Hotel...................................(see 22)
Surf City Hostel..................................13 A4

EATING (pp174–90)
Backburner Cafe.................................14 A4
Beach Hut No 2..................................15 A4
El Gringo - Hermosa Beach................16 B3
El Gringo - Manhattan Beach.............17 B2
El Gringo - Redondo Beach................18 C5
Green Temple......................................19 B6
Mama D's..20 A6
Nancy's Diner.....................................21 C6
Petros..22 A5
Rice Things...23 C3
Uncle Bill's Pancake House...............24 A5
Zazou..25 B6

5

Manhattan Beach

0 _____ 200 m
0 _____ 0.1 miles

Metlox
Plaza

Manhattan Beach Blvd

Ruby St

Sapphire St

Topaz St

Knob Hill Ave
Ave A

Redondo
State
Beach

DRINKING (pp190–5)
Baja Sharkeez......................................26 A1
Ercole's...27 A4
Fat Face Fenner's Fishack...................28 A4
Mermaid..29 A4
Naja's Place...30 A4
Patrick Molloy's..................................31 A4
Zinc Lounge...................................(see 22)

6

**Manhattan
State Beach**

Riviera
Village

To Palos Verdes
Peninsula (0.25mi)

**Torrance
Beach**

ENTERTAINMENT (pp195–206)
Cafe Boogaloo.....................................32 A4
Comedy & Magic Club.........................33 A4

SHOPPING (pp206–16)
Farmers Market (Hermosa Beach)......34 B3

0 _____ 1 km
0 _____ 0.5 miles

INFORMATION
Griffith Park Ranger Station....1 E3

SIGHTS & ACTIVITIES (pp102–62)
Bar S Stables.........................2 C1
Brady Bunch House.................3 A2
Bronson Caves.......................4 D3
Greek Theatre........................5 D4
Griffith Observatory................6 D4
Griffith Park Merry-Go-Round....7 E3
Griffith Park Southern Railroad..8 F4
Los Angeles Live Steamers........9 D2
Los Angeles Zoo & Botanical
 Gardens...............................10 E2
Museum of the American West..11 E2
NBC Studios..........................12 C2
New York Film Academy...........13 B2
Travel Town Museum................14 D2
Universal City Walk.................15 B3
Warner Bros Studios...............16 B2

SLEEPING (pp162–74)
Coast Anabelle Hotel...............17 C1
Graciela Inn..........................18 B1
Hilton Los Angeles/Universal
 City.....................................19 A3
Safari Inn..............................20 C1
Sheraton Universal Hotel..........21 A2

EATING (pp174–90)
Bob's Big Boy........................22 C1
Ca' del Sole..........................23 A2
Minibar.................................24 B3
Smoke House........................25 B2

ENTERTAINMENT (pp195–206)
Baked Potato.........................26 A3
BB King's Blues Club...............(see 15)
Big Free Outdoor
 Movie.................................(see 15)
Deaf West Theatre..................27 A1
Gibson Amphitheatre...............28 B3

SHOPPING (pp206–16)
It's a Wrap............................29 B1

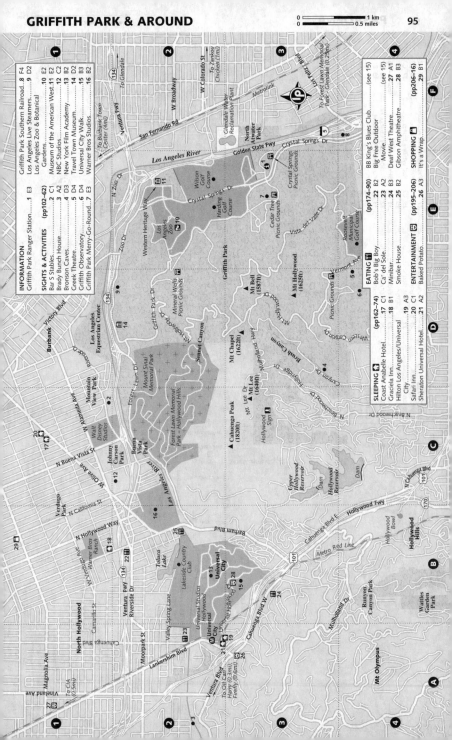

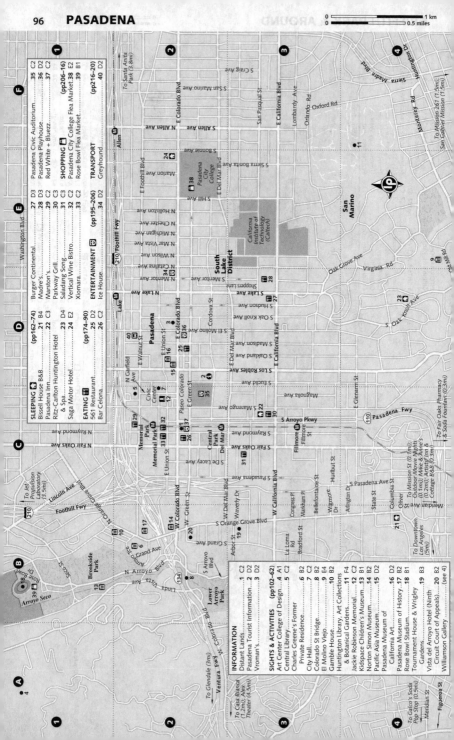

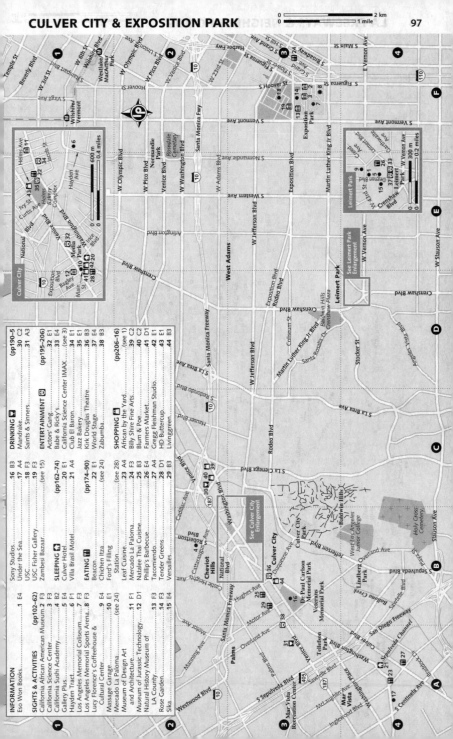

INFORMATION
Eso Won Books......................................1 E4

SIGHTS & ACTIVITIES (pp102–62)
California African American Museum....2 F3
California Science Center....................3 F4
California Sushi Academy....................4 B2
Gallery Plus..5 E4
Hayden Tract......................................6 F1
Los Angeles Memorial Coliseum..........7 F3
Los Angeles Memorial Sports Arena....8 F3
Lucy Florence's Coffeehouse &
   Cultural Center..............................9 E4
Massage Garage.................................10 E1
Mercado La Paloma...........................(see 24)
Museum of Design Art
   and Architecture............................11 F1
Museum of Jurassic Technology..........12 D1
Natural History Museum of
   LA County.....................................13 F3
Rose Garden......................................14 F3
Sika...15 E4

Sony Studios.......................................16 E4
Under the Sea.....................................17 A4
USC...18 F3
USC Fisher Gallery.............................19 F3
Zambezi Bazaar...............................(see 15)

SLEEPING 🛏 (pp162–74)
Culver Hotel.......................................20 E1
Villa Brasil Motel...............................21 A4

EATING 🍴 (pp174–90)
Beacon...22 E1
Chichen Itza....................................(see 24)
Ford's Filling
   Station...23 A4
Leaf Cuisine.......................................24 F3
Mercado La Paloma...........................25 B3
Natalee Thai Cuisine..........................26 E4
Phillip's Barbecue...............................27 A4
Tacomiendo.......................................28 D1
Tender Greens....................................29 B3

DRINKING 🍷 (pp190–5)
Mandrake...30 C2
Saints & Sinners.................................31 A3

ENTERTAINMENT 🎭 (pp195–206)
Actors' Gang......................................32 E1
Babe & Ricky's...................................33 E4
California Science Center IMAX.......(see 3)
Club El Baron....................................34 E1
Jazz Bakery..35 E1
Kirk Douglas Theatre..........................36 B3
World Stage.......................................37 E4
Zabumba..38 B3

SHOPPING 🛍 (pp206–16)
African by the Yard............................39 A4
Billy Shire Fine Arts............................40 C2
Blum & Poe..40 F3
Farmers Market..................................41 D1
Gregg Fleishman Studio......................42 E1
HD Buttercup.....................................43 E1
Livinggreen..44 B3

0 20 km
0 12 miles
Fontana
Riverside
Rubidoux
Lake Matthews
Rancho Cucamonga
San Antonio Heights
Upland
Montclair
Ontario
Chino
Norco
Corona
Prado Flood Control Basin
Cleveland National Forest
Portola Hills
Lake Forest
Mission Viejo
Pomona
Diamond Bar
Riverside County
Yorba Linda
Villa Park
Tustin
Irvine
Laguna Beach
Corona del Mar
Costa Mesa
Costa Mesa Fwy
Newport Beach
Glendora
Covina
Azusa
Baldwin Park
San Bernardino Fwy
West Covina
La Puente
Rowland Heights
Los Angeles County
Orange County
La Habra
Brea
Placentia
Orange Fwy
Anaheim
Orange
Santa Ana
Fullerton
Garden Grove
Garden Grove Fwy
Westminster
Stanton
Buena Park
Riverside Fwy
Huntington Beach
San Pedro Channel
San Pedro Bay
Angeles National Forest
Monrovia
Industry
Pomona Fwy
Whittier
La Habra Heights
La Mirada
Santa Ana Fwy
Cypress
Cerritos
Temple City
El Monte
Arcadia
Foothill Fwy
San Gabriel River Fwy
Monterey Park
Pico Rivera
Norwalk
Paramount
Artesia Fwy
Lakewood
Long Beach
Naples
Belmont Shore
Altadena
Pasadena
San Marino
San Gabriel
Alhambra
East Los Angeles
Downey
La Cañada Flintridge
Pasadena Fwy
Los Angeles
Vernon
Compton
Long Beach Fwy
Glendale
La Crescenta
Burbank
Watts
South Central
Harbor Fwy
San Pedro
Torrance
Inglewood
Century Fwy
San Diego Fwy
Foothill Fwy
Golden State Fwy
North Hollywood
Universal City
Studio City
Hollywood Fwy
Beverly Hills
West Hollywood
Culver City
El Segundo
Manhattan Beach
Hermosa Beach
Redondo Beach
Rancho Palos Verdes
Pacoima
Van Nuys
Santa Monica Fwy
Venice
Marina del Rey
Los Angeles International Airport (LAX)
Santa Monica Bay
PACIFIC OCEAN
Granada Hills
Northridge
Sherman Way
Reseda
Encino
Ventura Fwy
Brentwood
Santa Monica
Chatsworth
Tarzana
Pacific Palisades
Canoga Park
Hidden Hills
Woodland Hills
Topanga
Ventura County
Los Angeles County
Agoura Hills
Malibu
10
15
91
71
57
60
30
210
605
5
22
55
73
90
231
405
134
110
710
105
103
47
101
170

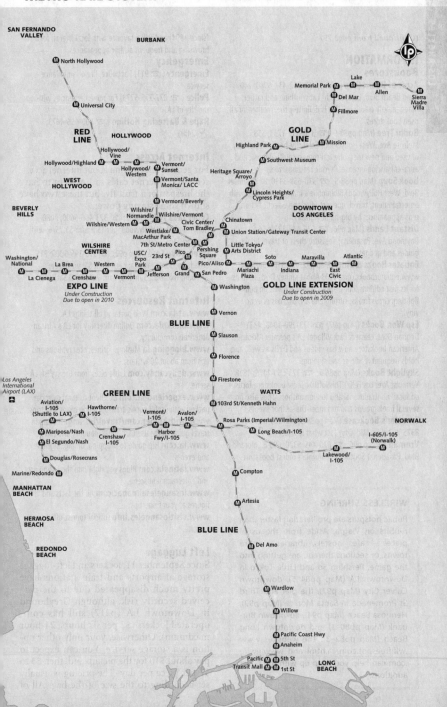

(Continued from page 79)

INFORMATION
Bookstores

Acres of Books (Map pp82-3; ☎ 562-437-6980; 240 Long Beach Blvd, Long Beach) Labyrinthine and rather maddeningly crammed, this is definitely the 'mother' of all used bookstores.

Bodhi Tree (Map pp88-9; ☎ 310-659-1733; 8585 Melrose Ave, West Hollywood) Celebrity-heavy dispensary of used and new metaphysical tomes, spiritual music and aura-enhancing incense. Psychic readings, too.

Book Soup (Map pp88-9; ☎ 310-659-3110; 8818 Sunset Blvd, West Hollywood) Bibliophile's indie gem packed with entertainment, travel, queer studies and eclectic fiction, plus appearances by big-name authors.

Distant Lands (Map p96; ☎ 626-449-3220; 56 S Raymond Ave, Pasadena) Treasure chest of travel books, guides and gadgets.

Equator Books & Vinyl (Map p92; ☎ 310-399-5544; www.equatorbooks.com; 1103 Abbot Kinney Blvd) Famous for its first editions, out-of-print and rare books on bull-fighting, circus freaks, surfing and art; also has eclectic vinyl.

Eso Won Books (Map p97; ☎ 323-290-1048; 4331 Degnan Blvd, Leimert Park Village) LA's premier African-American bookstore now has videos and DVDs as well, and holds frequent readings and signings.

Skylight Books (Map pp86-7; ☎ 323-660-1175; 1818 Vermont Ave, Los Feliz) This loftlike indie bookstore focuses on local, nontraditional and foreign authors. They also host several book groups and run meet-the-author events.

Traveler's Bookcase (Map pp88-9; ☎ 323-655-0575; 8375 W 3rd St, Mid-City) Just what it says.

Vroman's (Map p96; ☎ 626-449-5320; 695 E Colorado Blvd, Pasadena) Southern California's oldest bookstore (since 1894) and still a favorite with local literati for browsing and frequent author appearances.

Emergency

Emergency (☎ 911) For police, fire or ambulance service.

Police (☎ 877-275-5273) For nonemergencies within the city of LA.

Rape & Battering Hotline (☎ 800-656-4673; ☽ 24hr)

Internet Access

For general information about internet access, see p417. Internet cafés in LA seem to have the lifespan of a fruit fly, but these two have shown some staying power.

Cyber Java (Map pp86-7; ☎ 323-466-5600; 7080 Hollywood Blvd, Hollywood; per 15min/hr $1.75/6, wi-fi free; ☽ 7am-11:30pm)

Interactive Café (Map p92; ☎ 310-395-5009; 215 Broadway, Santa Monica; per 10min $1, wi-fi free; ☽ 6am-midnight Sun-Thu, 6am-2am Fri & Sat)

Internet Resources

www.at-la.com Web portal to all things LA.

www.blacknla.com Online directory for LA's African-American community.

www.blogging.la Musings, gripes, observations and tips from about 20 writers.

www.dailycandy.com Little bites from the stylish LA scene.

www.experiencela.com Excellent cultural calendar packed with useful public-transportation maps and trips.

www.gridskipper.com/travel/los-angeles Urban travel guide to the useful, offbeat, naughty and nice.

www.la.com Hip guide to shopping, dining, nightlife and events.

www.latinola.com Plugs you right into the Latino arts and entertainment scene.

www.losangelesalmanac.com All the facts and figures at your fingertips.

www.visitlosangeles.info Official tourist-office website.

Left Luggage

Since September 11, lockers and left-luggage storage at airports and train stations have pretty much disappeared due to the perceived security risk, although Greyhound in Downtown LA (p217) still has coin-operated lockers ($2 per six hours, 24-hour maximum). Otherwise, your only other option is a storage service. You can expect to pay about $10 for the pickup and then $3 to $7 per piece per day. The pricing is usually set according to the size of the bag. All of

---

WIRELESS SURFING

Public hotspots are proliferating faster than rabbits on Viagra. Aside from the usual places – cafés, hostels, libraries – entire towns, or sections thereof, are getting into the game: Pershing Sq and Little Tokyo in Downtown LA (Map pp84–5), downtown Culver City (Map p97), the pier and Third St Promenade in Santa Monica (Map p92), Hermosa Beach (Map p94), downtown Burbank (Map pp80–1) and downtown Long Beach (Map pp82–3). The websites www.wififreespot.com/ca.html and www.jiwire.com can help you keep up with the latest additions.

the services available are conveniently near LAX.

AeroEx (off Map pp82-3; ☎ 310-670-2834; 8639 Lincoln Blvd, Santa Monica)

MBI Enterprises (off Map pp82-3; ☎ 310-646-7460; 5551 W Manchester Blvd)

Libraries

There are public libraries everywhere, but the ones we've listed here are the largest and best. All of them offer free internet and wi-fi access, carry international periodicals, have special reading rooms for kids and host readings and cultural events.

Beverly Hills Library (Map pp90-1; ☎ 310-288-2244; www.bhpl.org; 444 N Rexford Dr, Beverly Hills; ⓨ 10am-9pm Mon-Thu, 10am-6pm Fri & Sat, noon-5pm Sun; ℗)

Hollywood Library (Map pp86-7; ☎ 323-856-8260; www.lapl.org; 1623 Ivar Ave, Hollywood; ⓨ 10am-8pm Mon-Thu, 10am-6pm Fri & Sat, 1-5pm Sun; ℗)

Richard Riordan Central Library (Map pp84-5; ☎ 213-228-7000; www.lapl.org; 630 W 5th St, Downtown; ⓨ 10am-8pm Mon-Thu, 10am-6pm Fri & Sat, 1-5pm Sun; ℗) Also see p136.

Santa Monica Library (Map p92; ☎ 310-458-8600; www.smpl.org; 601 Santa Monica Blvd, Santa Monica; ⓨ 10am-9pm Mon-Thu, 10am-5:30pm Fri & Sat, 1-5pm Sun; ℗)

Media

For cultural listings, see p42.

KCRW 89.9 fm (www.kcrw.org) National Public Radio (NPR); eclectic music, intelligent talk.

KPFK 90.7 fm (www.kpfk.org) Part of the Pacific radio network; news and talk.

La Opinión (www.laopinion.com) Spanish-language daily.

LA Weekly (www.laweekly.com) Free alternative news and listings magazine.

Los Angeles Magazine (www.losangelesmagazine .com) Glossy lifestyle monthly with a useful restaurant guide.

Los Angeles Sentinel (www.losangelessentinel.com) African-American weekly.

Los Angeles Times (www.latimes.com) Major daily newspaper.

Medical Services

Cedars-Sinai Medical Center (Map pp88-9; ☎ 310-423-3277; 8700 Beverly Blvd, West Hollywood; ⓨ 24hr emergency room; ℗)

LA County/USC Medical Center (off Map pp84-5; ☎ 323-226-2622; 1200 N State St, Downtown; ⓨ 24hr emergency room; ℗)

Rite-Aid pharmacies (☎ 800-748-3243) Call for the branch nearest you. Some are open 24 hours.

UCLA Medical Center (Map pp90-1; ☎ 310-825-9111; 10833 Le Conte Ave, Westwood; ⓨ 24hr emergency room; ℗)

Venice Family Clinic (Map p92; ☎ 310-392-8636; 604 Rose Ave, Venice) Good for general health concerns, with payment on a sliding scale according to your means.

Women's Clinic (Map pp90-1; ☎ 310-203-8899; 9911 W Pico Blvd, Suite 500, Century City; ℗) Fees are calculated on a sliding scale according to your capacity to pay.

Money

American Express (Map pp88-9; ☎ 310-659-1682; 8493 W 3rd St; ⓨ 9am-6pm Mon-Fri, 10am-3pm Sat)

Travelex Beverly Hills (Map pp90-1; ☎ 310-247-0892; 9595 Wilshire Blvd; ⓨ 9:30am-5:30pm Mon-Fri); West Hollywood (Map pp88-9; ☎ 310-659-6093; 8901 Santa Monica Blvd, inside US Bank; ⓨ 9:30am-5:30pm Mon-Fri, 9am-1pm Sat)

Post

Call ☎ 800-275-8777 for the nearest post office branch.

Tourist Information

Beverly Hills (Map pp90-1; ☎ 310-248-1015, 800-345-2210; www.lovebeverlyhills.org; 239 S Beverly Dr; ⓨ 8:30am-5pm Mon-Fri)

Downtown LA (Map pp84-5; ☎ 213-689-8822; www .visitlosangeles.info; 685 S Figueroa St; ⓨ 8:30am-5pm Mon-Fri)

Hollywood (Map pp86-7; ☎ 323-467-6412; Hollywood & Highland complex, 6801 Hollywood Blvd; ⓨ 10am-10pm Mon-Sat, 10am-7pm Sun) In the Kodak Theatre walkway.

Long Beach (Map pp82-3; ☎ 562-436-3645, 800-452-7829; www.visitlongbeach.com; 100 Aquarium Way; ⓨ 11am-7pm Sun-Thu, 11:30am-7:30pm Fri & Sat Jun-Sep, 10am-4pm Fri-Sun Oct-May)

Marina del Rey (Map p92; ☎ 310-305-9545; www .visitthemarina.com; 4701 Admiralty Way; ⓨ 10am-4pm)

Pasadena (Map p96; ☎ 626-795-9311, 800-307-7977; www.pasadenacal.com; 171 S Los Robles Ave; ⓨ 8am-5pm Mon-Fri, 10am-4pm Sat)

Santa Monica (☎ 800-544-5319; www.santamonica .com) Visitor Center (Map p92; ☎ 310-393-7593; 1920 Main St; ⓨ 9am-6pm) Information Kiosk (Map p92; ☎ 310-393-7593; 1400 Ocean Ave; ⓨ 9am-5pm Jun-Aug, 10am-4pm Sep-May)

West Hollywood (Map pp88-9; ☎ 310-289-2525, 800-368-6020; www.visitwesthollywood.com; Pacific Design Center, blue bldg, Suite M-38, 8687 Melrose Ave; ⓨ 8:30am-5:30pm Mon-Fri)

LOS ANGELES

LOS ANGELES IN...

Distances are ginormous in LA, so don't pack too much into a day, pad your travel time for traffic and confine your explorations to one or two neighborhoods.

One Day

Fuel up for the day at **Toast** (p176), then go star-searching on the **Walk of Fame** (opposite) along revitalized Hollywood Blvd. Up your chances of spotting actual celebs by hitting the fashion-forward boutiques on paparazzi-infested **Robertson Blvd** (p207) and having lunch at **Spago Beverly Hills** (p178). Take a digestive stroll along **Rodeo Dr** (p114) before heading to the lofty **Getty Center** (p117). Wrap up with dinner at Adobe or the Lobster, in **Santa Monica** (p182).

Two days

Keep a tab on rapidly evolving Downtown LA, starting with its roots at **El Pueblo de Los Angeles** (p132), catching up with the present at the dramatic **Walt Disney Concert Hall** (p134), then peek into the future over a latte at **Pete's Café & Bar** (p185) in the emerging gallery district. Check out the funky stores at **Sunset Junction** (p207), fuel up for the night ahead at **El Conquistador** (p175), then catch a band at the **Knitting Factory** (p198) or hit the **Velvet Margarita** (p192) for some raucous, silly boozing fun. Still feel like dancing? Hit the floor at **Avalon** (p201) and shake it till sunrise.

More days

If you can squeeze them in, here are some other favorites: **Venice Boardwalk** (p125), **Huntington Library, Art Collections & Botanical Gardens** (p147), **Surfrider Beach** (p121), **Abbot Kinney Blvd** (p126) and **Spaceland** (p198).

DANGERS & ANNOYANCES

Despite what the media would have you believe, LA is no worse than other major metropolitan cities when it comes to crime. Most violence is confined to areas where tourists rarely venture, such as areas with gang and drug activity in East LA, Compton and Watts; avoid these after dark. Homeless folk are prevalent but generally harmless, although medical and psychiatric problems may make them behave bizarrely. The toughest cases usually hang out on Skid Row in Downtown (roughly bounded by 3rd, Alameda, 7th and Los Angeles Sts), but homeless sightings are also quite likely in Santa Monica, Hollywood and along the Venice Boardwalk.

SIGHTS

Each of LA's neighborhoods has its own unique appeal and where you concentrate your sightseeing largely depends on your interests in the area. Classic sights such as museums and a whole range of great architecture are in Downtown, Mid-City, Pasadena and Hollywood. West Hollywood has the legendary Sunset Strip, some cool shopping and great bars, while the beach

towns are custom-made for travelers looking to soak up the laid-back SoCal vibe. Take your pick.

Hollywood

America loves a comeback, and Hollywood's is long overdue. For decades, the neighborhood had been riding on the coattails of its Golden Age glamour image, its very name synonymous with the entire movie industry. Never mind that the studios had left long ago for Burbank and Studio City and that the only 'stars' left were embedded in the sidewalk. Worse, you had to hopscotch around runaways and druggies to see them. No more.

Like the Terminator, you can't keep Hollywood down forever. As big bucks are being sunk into the area, shiny new clubs, trendy restaurants and luxe boutiques are supplanting tacky souvenir shops, tattoo parlors and stripper supply stores. It's all a faux Vegas-type glitz, to be sure, but most people are just happy to see life return to the streets. Even celebs are back, carousing at the hip-again Hollywood Roosevelt Hotel and embarrassing themselves at the clubs on Cahuenga. Box-office results aren't in, but a possible blockbuster awaits.

If you're relying on public transport, central Hollywood is a convenient base. The Metro Red Line whisks you to Los Feliz, Downtown and Universal Studios in minutes, and DASH buses provide easy links east along Hollywood Blvd and west to the Sunset Strip and fashionable Melrose Ave. Parking at Hollywood & Highland costs just $2 for four hours with validation from any merchant or the Hollywood visitors center (p101).

HOLLYWOOD SIGN

LA's most famous landmark first appeared in its hillside perch in 1923 as an advertising gimmick for a real-estate development called Hollywoodland. Each letter is 50ft tall and made of sheet metal. Once aglow with 4000 light bulbs, the sign even had its own caretaker who lived behind the 'L' until 1939. In 1932 a struggling young actress named Peggy Entwistle leapt her way into local lore from the letter 'H'.

The last four letters were lopped off in the '40s as the sign started to crumble along with the rest of Hollywood. In the late '70s, Alice Cooper and Hugh Hefner joined forces with fans and other celebs to save the famous symbol.

It's illegal to hike up to the sign, but good viewing spots are plentiful, including Hollywood & Highland (right), the top of Beachwood Dr and the Griffith Observatory (p143).

HOLLYWOOD WALK OF FAME

Big Bird, Bob Hope, Marilyn Monroe and Sting are among the stars being sought out, worshipped, photographed and stepped on day after day along the **Hollywood Walk of Fame**. Since 1960 more than 2000 performers – from legends to long-forgotten bit-part players – have been honored with a pink-marble sidewalk star. Follow this celestial gallery along Hollywood Blvd between La Brea Ave and Gower St, and along Vine St between Yucca St and Sunset Blvd. Check out www .hollywoodchamber.net for upcoming ceremonies, which are usually held once or twice a month.

GRAUMAN'S CHINESE THEATRE

Ever wondered what it's like to be in George Clooney's shoes? Just find his footprints in the forecourt of this world-famous **movie palace** (Map pp86-7; ☎ 323-463-9576; www.mann

theatres.com; 6925 Hollywood Blvd). The exotic pagoda theater – complete with temple bells and stone Heaven Dogs from China – has shown movies since 1927 when Cecil B DeMille's *The King of Kings* first flickered across the screen; it's still a studio favorite for star-studded premieres. To see the inside, buy a movie ticket or join a half-hour guided **tour** (adult/child & senior $12/8) offered throughout the day. Check in at the gift shop.

Most Tinseltown tourists are just content to find out how big Arnold's feet really are or to search for Jimmy Durante's nose, Betty Grable's legs or Whoopi Goldberg's braids. Douglas Fairbanks Sr, Mary Pickford (who both co-owned the theater with Grauman) and Norma Talmadge started the tradition back in 1927 and box-office superstars still get the nod today. Recent honorees have included Matt Damon, Brad Pitt and Daniel Radcliffe. Again, see www.hollywoodchamber.net for who's up next.

See also p196 for further information.

HOLLYWOOD & HIGHLAND

It's perhaps apropos that a Disneyfied shopping mall would be the spark plug for Hollywood Blvd's rebirth. A perfect marriage of kitsch and commerce, the main showpiece of **Hollywood & Highland** (Map pp86-7; ☎ 323-817-0200; www.hollywoodandhighland.com; 6801 Hollywood Blvd; admission free; ◷ 10am-10pm Mon-Sat, 10am-7pm Sun) is a triumphal arch inspired by DW Griffith's 1916 movie *Intolerance*. Guarded by giant elephants, it's as preposterous as it is impressive and frames some nice views of the Hollywood Sign. Next door, the Academy Awards are handed out at the **Kodak Theatre** (Map pp86-7; ☎ 323-308-6363; www.kodaktheatre.com; tours adult/child, senior & student $15/10; ◷ 10:30am-4pm Jun-Aug, 10:30am-2:30pm Sep-May), which also hosts other big events such as the American Idol finals, the Daytime Emmies, the ESPY awards and the Miss USA pageant. On the

---

TOURING HOLLYWOOD BLVD

Most of the sights described in this section line up neatly along a 1-mile stretch of Hollywood Blvd between La Brea Ave and Vine St. To learn more about major and minor landmarks, look for the red signs installed in front of them, or join a walking tour operated by Red Line Tours (p159).

YOUR 15 MINUTES OF FAME

Come on, haven't you always dreamed of seeing your silly mug on TV or in the movies? Well, LA has a way of making dreams come true, but you have to do your homework before coming to town. Here are some leads to get you started.

■ **Be in a Studio Audience** – Sitcoms and game shows usually tape between August and March before live audiences. To nab free tickets, check with **TV Tickets** (www.tvtix.com) or **Audiences Unlimited** (☎ 818-753-3470; www.tvtickets.com). The latter also has a booth in the Entertainment Center at Universal Studios Hollywood (p145). **CBS** (Map pp88-9; ☎ 323-575-2624; www.cbs.com; 7800 Beverly Blvd) handles its own ticketing; the office is off Fairfax past the open green gate and is open 9am to 5pm Monday to Friday (see p110 for further information). For tickets to the *Tonight Show* at **NBC** (Map p95; ☎ 818-840-3537; 3000 W Alameda Ave, Burbank), call or check www.nbc.com/nbc/footer/Tickets.shtml. Tickets to *Jimmy Kimmel Live*, which conveniently tapes at the **El Capitan Entertainment Center** (Map pp86-7; ☎ 800-866-5466 9849 or www.1iota .com; 6840 Hollywood Blvd). If you don't have tickets, you may still be able to sneak in just before the 6pm taping. Just ask one of the ushers outside the theater (if they don't ask you first!). Most shows have a minimum age of 18, but **Jam Packed TV Shows** (www.jampackedtvshows .com) usually has tickets to Nickelodeon tapings where kids as young as eight are accepted.

■ **Become a Seat Filler** – Savor the excitement of glitzy award shows like the Daytime Emmies, American Music Awards and People's Choice Awards. Empty seats don't look good on TV, so seat fillers get to put their butts in unclaimed chairs or to keep one warm while an audience member (possibly a star) takes a potty break. For the complete low down, see www.seatfiller .com or www.tvtickets.com/seatfillers.

■ **Become an Extra** – If you'd like to see yourself on screen, check with **Be In a Movie** (www .beinamovie.com) on how to become an extra in a big crowd scene at major film shoots. The company's supplied the masses for *Seabiscuit*, *The Doors* and *Anger Management*, to name a few. There's no money in it for you, but the behind-the-scenes experience and chance of seeing a big star live and in person should make you a hit back home at the office watercooler.

■ **Become a Game Show Contestant** – *Jeopardy* and *Wheel of Fortune* are among the game shows that tape in LA, but the chances of actually becoming a contestant are greatest on *The Price is Right*, now hosted by Drew Carey and taped at CBS. Check www.cbs.com/daytime /price for ticket details.

tour you get to sniff around the auditorium, admire a VIP room and see an Oscar statuette. Obtaining online discount coupons will help take some sting out of the rather steep admission price.

HOLLYWOOD ROOSEVELT HOTEL

Great architecture, rich history and delicious gossip rendezvous at this venerable **hotel** (Map pp86-7; ☎ 323-466-7000; www .hollywoodroosevelt.com; 7000 Hollywood Blvd; admission free; ☽ 24hr), where the first Academy Awards ceremony was held in 1929. Following a complete makeover, it's again firmly on the radar of tabloid regulars, who can often be spotted tucking into Kobe burgers at the insanely pricey Dakota steakhouse or misbehaving poolside at the velvet-rope Tropicana Bar. Back in her day, glamazon Marilyn Monroe shot her first print ad (for

suntan lotion) posing on the diving board of said pool, the bottom of which was later decorated with squiggles by artist David Hockney. And while we're name-dropping: actor Montgomery Clift, who stayed in room 928 while filming *From Here to Eternity*, apparently never checked out; his ghost can still be heard pacing and playing the bugle. The Roosevelt itself has made movie appearances aplenty, including in *Catch Me If You Can* and *Charlie's Angels*. See p163 for a review of the hotel.

EL CAPITAN THEATRE

Spanish Colonial meets East Indian at the flamboyant **El Capitan** (Map pp86-7; ☎ 323-467-7674; http://disney.go.com/disneypictures/el_capitan; 6838 Hollywood Blvd) movie palace built for live performances in 1926 and now run by Disney. The first flick to show here was *Citizen Kane* in 1941 and it's still a fine place to catch a movie. Before or after the show, peruse the museum-style exhibits in the lobby related to the current release. Kids love the colorful Disney Soda Fountain downstairs. See also p195.

EGYPTIAN THEATRE

The **Egyptian** (Map pp86–7; ☎ 323-466-3456; www.egyptiantheatre.com; 6712 Hollywood Blvd), the first of the grand movie palaces on Hollywood Blvd, premiered *Robin Hood* in 1922. The theater's lavish getup – complete with sunburst ceiling, hieroglyphs and sphinx heads – capitalized on the craze for all things Egyptian sparked by the discoveries of archaeologist Howard Carter. (Contrary to popular belief, though, the Egyptian actually opened *before* Carter stumbled upon King Tut's tomb). In its heyday, it had live caged monkeys and usherettes dressed like Cleopatra.

The Egyptian got a royal makeover in the late 1990s and became a shrine to serious cinema when the nonprofit American Cinematheque moved in (p195). Ask about upcoming tours (adult/child & senior $7/5).

HOLLYWOOD MUSEUM

The museums on Hollywood Blvd generally fall into the tourist-trap category, but we quite like the slightly musty **Hollywood Museum** (Map pp86–7; ☎ 323-464-7776; www.thehollywoodmuseum.com; 1660 N Highland Ave; adult/student & senior $15/12; 🕙 10am-5pm Wed-Sun). It's a convoluted temple to the stars, crammed with kitsch, posters, costumes and rotating props from both classic films and the latest smash hits. On our last visit Jake Gyllenhaal's shirt from the hit film *Brokeback Mountain* and Johnny Depp's pirate boots from *Pirates of the Carribean* captured everybody's attention. Hannibal Lecter's original jail cell is in the basement and can, rather oddly, even be rented for private parties. In fact, LAPD chief William Bratton has held two dinner parties there. Oh yes, but did he serve fava beans and chianti?

The museum is housed inside the handsome 1914 art deco Max Factor Building, where the make-up pioneer once worked his magic on such stars as Marilyn Monroe and Judy Garland. The make-up rooms, complete with custom lighting to complement the ladies' complexion and hair color, are still located on the ground floor, along with a wall of Factor's most glamorous clients

and the 1965 Silver Cloud Rolls Royce once owned by Cary Grant.

HOLLYWOOD BOWL & AROUND

Summers in LA just wouldn't be the same without this chill spot for symphonies under the stars, *Sound of Music* sing-a-longs and big-name rock, jazz and blues acts. A huge natural amphitheater, the **Hollywood Bowl** (Map pp86–7; ☎ 323-850-2000; www.hollywoodbowl.com; 2301 Highland Ave; 🕙 late Jun-Sep; ℗) has been around since 1922 and has great sound thanks to a new concert shell. Big projection screens give even the folks in the 'nosebleed' sections (tickets from $1 on many nights) close-ups of the performers. Come early to claim a table in the parklike grounds for a pre-show picnic (alcohol permitted, also during concerts). There are several concessions if you don't want to lug your own grub.

The bowl is the summer home of the LA Philharmonic (p202) and the Hollywood Bowl Orchestra. Sneak into free rehearsals usually held from 9am to noon on Tuesday, Wednesday and Friday during the season. The **Hollywood Bowl Museum** (Map pp86–7; ☎ 323-850-2058; www.hollywoodbowl.com/event/museum.cfm; admission free; 🕙 10am-showtime Mon-Sat & 4pm-showtime Sun late Jun–mid-Sep, 10am-4:30pm Tue-Fri mid-Sep–late Jun) relives such classic bowl moments as concerts by the Beatles, the Stones and Jimi Hendrix.

Parking is free during the day, but expensive and limited on performance nights. Save yourself the headache and take a shuttle, such as the one running from Hollywood & Highland, which costs $3 per person round-trip. The website has full details.

Another beloved outdoor venue, the **Ford Amphitheatre** (Map pp86–7; ☎ 323-461-3673; www.fordtheatres.org; 2580 Cahuenga Blvd E; tickets $5-45; 🕙 May-Oct; ♿) is just across Hwy 101. It presents an eclectic program of global music, dance and theater in a space where no seat is more than 96ft from the stage. Picnics are welcome.

Just south of the bowl is an unassuming little barn with a big history. Hollywood's first feature-length flick, Cecil B DeMille's *The Squaw Man*, was shot in this building in 1913–14, which was originally positioned at the corner of Selma and Vine Sts. DeMille went on to cofound Paramount and had the barn moved to the lot in the '20s. Now the **Hollywood Heritage Museum** (Map pp86–7; ☎ 323-874-4005; 2100 N Highland Ave; adult/child/senior $5/1/3; 🕙 11am-4pm Sat & Sun), it's filled with a great collection of costumes, projectors and cameras from the early days of movie-making, plus DeMille's recreated office.

MULHOLLAND DRIVE

If you found David Lynch's 2001 movie *Mulholland Drive* a tad bizarre, perhaps a drive along the road itself will clear things up. The legendary road winds and dips for 24 miles through the Santa Monica Mountains, skirting the mansions of the rich and famous (Jack Nicholson's is at No 12850, Warren Beatty's at No 13671) and delivering iconic views of Downtown, Hollywood and the San Fernando Valley at each road bend. Named for its creator, California aqueduct engineer William Mulholland, it's especially pretty just before sunset (go west to east, though, to avoid driving into the setting sun) and on clear winter days when the panorama opens up from the snow-capped San Gabriel Mountains to the shimmering expanse of the Pacific Ocean. Traffic is lightest on Sundays.

Driving the entire route takes about an hour, but even a shorter spin is worth it. At the very least, drive up to the **Hollywood Bowl Overlook** (Map pp86–7) for classic views of the Hollywood Sign and the beehive-shaped bowl below. Other pullouts offer hiking-trail access, for instance to Runyon Canyon (p153)

BEST FOR

- Bargains – Downtown (p207)
- Beach Scene - Hermosa Beach (p127)
- Nightlife - Hollywood (p191 and p195)
- Hot Dining - West Hollywood (p176)
- Families - Santa Monica (p124)
- Channeling your inner hippie - Venice (p125)
- History - Downtown (p132)
- Gardens - Pasadena & San Gabriel Valley (p147)
- Star Spotting - West Hollywood (p109)
- Glamour Shopping - West Hollywood (p207)
- Museums - Mid-City (p109)
- Architecture - Downtown (p132)
- Gays and Lesbian - West Hollywood (p112)

---

and Fryman Canyon (p153). Note that pulling over after sunset is *verboten* and may result in a traffic ticket.

Mulholland Dr runs from the US-101 Fwy (Hollywood Fwy; take the Cahuenga exit, then follow signs) to about 2 miles west of the I-405 (San Diego Fwy). About 8 miles of dirt road (closed to vehicles but not to hikers and cyclists) links it with Mulholland Hwy, which continues to serpentine through the mountains for another 23 miles as far as Leo Carrillo State Beach.

MUSSO & FRANK GRILL

Hollywood history hangs thickly in the air at **Musso & Frank Grill** (Map pp86-7; ☎ 323-467-7788; 6667 Hollywood Blvd), Tinseltown's oldest eatery (since 1919). Charlie Chaplin used to knock back vodka gimlets at the bar and Raymond Chandler penned scripts in the high-backed booths. Star-sightings are still possible today; Mick Jagger and Woody Allen are among fans of the noir ambience, gruff waiters and stiff martinis. Skip the food, except for the famous flannel cakes (thin pancakes).

RIPLEY'S BELIEVE IT OR NOT!

Life's pretty strange and it'll feel stranger still after you've visited **Ripley's** (Map pp86-7; ☎ 323-466-6335; www.ripleys.com; 6780 Hollywood Blvd; adult/child $13/9; ⊙ 10am-11pm Sun-Thu, 10am-midnight Fri & Sat), where exhibits range from the gross to the grotesque. If shrunken heads, a sculpture of Marilyn Monroe made from shredded $1 bills and a human-hair bikini capture your imagination, this is your place. It's in a pretty cool building: just look for the T-Rex bursting through the rooftop with a clock in its fangs whose hands run backwards.

GUINNESS WORLD OF RECORDS MUSEUM

You know the drill: the **Guinness** (Map pp86-7; ☎ 323-463-6433; www.guinnessattractions.com; 6764 Hollywood Blvd; adult/child/senior $16/7/14; ⊙ 10am-midnight; ♿) is all about the fastest, tallest, biggest, fattest and other superlatives. Combination tickets with the Hollywood Wax Museum (see following listing) are $18/9/16 per adult/child/senior.

HOLLYWOOD WAX MUSEUM

Starved for celeb sightings? Don't fret: at this **museum** (Map pp86-7; ☎ 323-462-5991; www.hollywoodwax.com; 6767 Hollywood Blvd; adult/child/senior $16/7/14; ⊙ 10am-midnight Sun-Thu, 10am-1am Fri & Sat;

FAMOUS ALUMNI

They may not be like the rest of us, but even celebs once studied math and French – well, sort of anyway. Our list shows you who went were.

Beverly Hills High School (Map pp90-1; 241 S Moreno Dr, Beverly Hills) Nicolas Cage, Jamie Lee Curtis, Angelina Jolie, Lenny Kravitz, Monica Lewinsky, Rob Reiner, David Schwimmer and Alicia Silverstone are among the celebs to hit the books at this public school.

Buckley School (Map pp80-1; 3900 Stansbury Ave, Sherman Oaks) This illustrious private school at the end of a cul-de-sac saw such 'A-list' students as Laura Dern, Sara Gilbert, Paris Hilton, Alyssa Milano, Matthew Perry and Nicole Richie.

Fairfax High (Map pp88-9; 7850 Melrose Ave, Mid-City) Home to a cool flea market at the weekend (see p209), this school taught algebra to David Arquette, Flea (of Red Hot Chili Peppers), James Elroy, Al Franken, Timothy Hutton, Demi Moore, Phil Spector and Slash (of Guns N' Roses).

Hollywood High School (Map pp86-7; 1521 N Highland Ave, Hollywood) Brandy, Carol Burnett, Laurence Fishburne, Judy Garland and Lana Turner are alumni depicted in the big mural on Highland Ave, but there are literally hundreds more, including James Garner and Sharon Tate.

Immaculate Heart High School (Map pp86-7; 5515 Franklin Ave, Hollywood) No boys are allowed at this Catholic school once attended by Tyra Banks, Natalie Cole and Mary Tyler Moore.

John Marshall High School (Map pp86-7; 3939 Tracy St, Silver Lake) Leonardo DiCaprio's alma mater doubled as Sunnydale High in the 1992 big-screen version of *Buffy the Vampire Slayer*.

Notre Dame High School (Map pp80-1; 13645 Riverside Dr, Sherman Oaks) Almost 100 percent of students at this co-ed Catholic school go on to college, including Rachel Bilson, Kirsten Dunst and Dave Navarro.

Polytechnic High (Map pp82-3; 1600 Atlantic Ave, Long Beach) Cameron Diaz, Snoop Doggy Dog, Marilyn Horne, Spike Lee.

Santa Monica College (Map p92; 1900 Pico Blvd, Santa Monica) Schwarzenegger studied English, and Dustin Hoffman honed his acting chops at this community college that also counts Buzz Aldrin, James Dean and Hillary Swank as alumni.

Santa Monica High School (Map p92; 601 Pico Blvd, Santa Monica) Robert Downey Jr, Rob Lowe, Sean Penn and Charlie Sheen undoubtedly caused trouble at this public school near the beach.

University High School (off Map p92; 11800 Texas Ave, near Santa Monica) Marilyn Monroe dropped out of Uni High; Jeff Bridges, James Brolin, Bridget Fonda, Nancy Sinatra, Elizabeth Taylor and Tone Loc were also taught here.

University of California, Los Angeles (UCLA; Map pp90-1; 405 Hilgard Ave, Westwood) Carol Burnett, James Dean, Francis Ford Coppola, Heather Locklear, Jim Morrison, Tim Robbins

University of Southern California (USC; Map p97; 3535 S Figueroa St, Downtown area) Neil Armstrong, Frank Gehry, Ron Howard, George Lucas, Tom Selleck, OJ Simpson, John Wayne, Robert Zemeckis

Westlake School for Girls (now Harvard-Westlake; Map pp90-1; 700 N Faring Rd, Bel Air) This posh enclave got Candice Bergen, Bridget Fonda, Sally Ride (first female astronaut) and Shirley Temple started on the path of life.

(⚘) Angelina Jolie, Halle Berry and other red-carpet royalty will stand still – very still – for you to snap their picture. This retro haven of kitsch and camp just celebrated its 40th anniversary Hollywood-style: with a facelift, that is. There are lots of new monsters in the horror exhibit, Matrix stars in the sci-fi room and even waxen miniatures of the Capitol Records Tower and other local landmarks. Combo tickets with the Guinness World of Records Museum (see previous listing) cost $18/9/16 per adult/child/senior.

HOLLYWOOD & VINE

If you turned on the radio in the 1920s and '30s, chances were you'd hear a broadcast 'brought to you from Hollywood & Vine'. Before long, though, the fabled intersection went from fab to drab to pathetic, just as the rest of Hollywood. But, if all goes to plan, by 2009 a new mega-development in its south-eastern corner with stores, lofts and a W hotel will once again train the world's spotlight on this famous hub.

Meanwhile, the splendidly restored **Pantages Theater** (Map pp86-7; ☎ 323-468-1770; www .pantages-theater.com; 6233 Hollywood Blvd) is an art deco survivor from the Golden Age and a fabulous place to catch a play or musical. Oscars were handed out here between 1949 and 1959 while Howard Hughes owned the building; his ghost reportedly still hangs around. The ubernoir Frolic Room bar next door was featured in *LA Confidential*.

On Vine, you'll quickly recognize the iconic circular 1956 **Capitol Records Tower** (Map pp86-7; 1750 N Vine St), one of LA's great Modern Era buildings. Designed by Welton Becket, it resembles a stack of records topped by a stylus blinking out 'Hollywood' in Morse code. Garth Brooks and John Lennon have their stars outside here.

CROSSROADS OF THE WORLD

One of the LA's first malls, Robert Derrah's 1936 Streamline Moderne **complex** (Map pp86-7; 6671 W Sunset Blvd) has an eye-catching nautical theme. The central structure is shaped like a ship, with its bow topped by a tower crowned with a rotating globe. The surrounding cottages, many in mock-Tudor style, house the offices of Taschen publishing (also see p216).

SOUTH HOLLYWOOD

Star Trek, *Indiana Jones* and *Shrek* are among the blockbusters that originated at **Paramount** (Map pp86-7; ☎ 323-956-1777; 5555 Melrose Ave), the only movie studio still in Hollywood proper. See p146 for tours.

Next to Paramount, **Hollywood Forever Cemetery** (Map pp86-7; ☎ 323-469-1181; www.holly woodforever.com; 6000 Santa Monica Blvd; ☻ 8am-6pm; ℗) boasts lavish landscaping, over-the-top tombstones, epic mausoleums and a roll call of dearly departed superstars. Residents include Douglas Fairbanks Sr and Jr, Cecil B DeMille, silent-era heartthrob Rudolph Valentino, mobster Bugsy Siegel, femme fatale Jayne Mansfield and punkrock icon Johnny Ramone. For a full list of residents, pick up a map ($5) at the flower shop (☻ 9am to 5pm).

The fact is, these hallowed grounds are anything but dead. The arrival of the summer months brings outdoor movie screenings (www.cinespia.com; p197) and theater (www.shakespeareinthecemetery.com), while in November the gates open for Día de los Muertos (Day of the Dead; p161).

LOS FELIZ & SILVER LAKE

These side-by-side communities on Hollywood's eastside (past the 101 Fwy) feel far removed from the artificial glam of Hollywood Blvd. Both attract a more boho-chic crowd of artists, writers, actors, fashion designers and

other creative types. Its cafés, bookstores and bars are often abuzz with late-night energy and liberal attitudes.

Los Feliz (loss *fee*-les) abuts Griffith Park and is the more grown-up of the two areas. Its main strip – cute and pedestrian-friendly Vermont Ave – has plenty of sidewalk cafés tempting you to keep tabs on passing hotties and hipsters over a cup of cap.

In the hills north of here is the spectacular **Ennis-Brown House** (off map pp86-7; ☎ 323-660-0607; www.ennishouse.org; 2607 Glendower Ave), one of Frank Lloyd Wright's four Mayan-inspired 'textile block' houses in LA. Unfortunately, it was deemed unsafe in 2004 and remains closed pending restoration. Wright influenced any number of architects, including Austrian immigrant Richard Neutra, whose nearby **Lovell House** (off map pp86-7; 4616 Dundee Dr) featured prominently in *LA Confidential*; it's not open to the public.

While the Ennis-Brown House sits crumbling, Wright's **Hollyhock House** (Map pp86-7; ☎ 323-644-6269; www.hollyhockhouse.net; 4800 Hollywood Blvd; tours adult/student/child $7/3/free; tours hourly ☻ 12:30pm-3:30pm Wed-Sun; ℗) sparkles in renewed splendor. It's a prime example of Wright's California Romanza style, typified by an easy flow between rooms, courtyard and gardens. Commissioned in 1919 by oil heiress and art nut Aline Barnsdall, its walls, carpets and furniture are awash in abstract hollyhocks, her favorite flower. Guided tours take you into the stunning living room with its moated fireplace and Japanese art.

Barnsdall envisioned her house to be part of a cutting-edge theater colony but, as eccentrics are prone to do, abruptly abandoned the idea in 1927. Instead, she donated the house and grounds to the city of LA with the proviso that they become a public art park. Today's **Barnsdall Art Park** is a lovely, quiet spot, with views of the Hollywood Sign, a theater, studios and the **Municipal Art Gallery** (Map pp86-7; ☎ 323-644-6269; adult/student/child $7/3/free; ☻ noon-5pm Tue-Sun; ℗), which presents mostly homegrown artists and also sells Hollyhock House tour tickets.

East of here, **Silver Lake** used to be grungy and edgy but it too is coming up in the world. Rising rents send bohemians packing, fancier restaurants are opening up, and dive bars are reborn as fancy cocktail lounges, but as yet it's all still a little unpolished and improvised. Sunset Junction (where Hollywood Blvd runs into Sunset) is still the epicenter of fun and funky shopping in indie boutiques with not a chain in sight.

West Hollywood & Mid-City

Rainbow flags fly proudly over Santa Monica Blvd, the epicenter of lesbigay life in LA. Celebs misbehaving on the fabled Sunset Strip provide ample fodder for the tabloids. Robertson Blvd and Melrose Ave are the main catwalks for style mavens. Welcome to unapologetically hip West Hollywood (WeHo), an independent city that packs more personality (some might say, frivolity) into its 1.9-sq-mile frame than most larger hoods.

To the south and east of WeHo is an amorphous area we have called Mid-City. It encompasses the Fairfax District with the Farmers Market, Miracle Mile with Museum Row and old-money Hancock Park with its grand mansions.

Street parking is heavily restricted in West Hollywood, but you'll find two hours of free parking at 8383 Santa Monica Blvd. Mid-City areas usually have plenty of street parking. DASH buses (p219) serve the area on the Fairfax Route and the Hollywood/West Hollywood Route.

SUNSET STRIP

A visual cacophony of billboards, giant ad banners and neon signs, the sinuous stretch of Sunset Blvd between Laurel Canyon and Doheny Dr has been nightlife central since the 1920s. Mobster Bugsy Siegel and his posse hung out at such clubs as Ciro's (now the Comedy Store; p205); Marilyn Monroe had her first date with Joe DiMaggio at the **Rainbow Bar & Grill** (Map pp88-9; 9015 Sunset Blvd); the Whisky A Go-Go (p199) gave birth to both the Doors and go-go dancing; and Led Zeppelin raced motorcycles in the **Hyatt Hotel** (Map pp88-9; 8401 Sunset Blvd), henceforth known as the

'Riot House'. Then, in the late '90s, the strip captured the limelight again with the House of Blues (HOB; p199), the ultraposh Skybar at the Mondrian Hotel and the sexy Standard Hollywood hotel (p164).

These days, though, it seems to be coasting on its fabled legacy. The young, hip and fickle have moved on to ghetto-glam Hollywood, leaving mostly buttoned-down and cashed-up suburbanites braving the velvet ropes, ordering $500 bottle service and listening to eardrum-friendly Stevie Wonder. Even the landmark Tower Records store is no more since the company went bankrupt in 2006. Like all aging divas, the strip is ripe for a makeover. Stay tuned.

PACIFIC DESIGN CENTER & AROUND

Design is big in WeHo, with around 130 trade-only showrooms at the **Pacific Design Center** (PDC; Map pp88-9; ☎ 310-657-0800; www.thepacificdesigncenter.com; 8687 Melrose Ave, West Hollywood; admission free; ☻ 9am-5pm Mon-Fri; P) alone and dozens more in the surrounding **Avenues of Art & Design** (Map pp88-9; Beverly Blvd, Robertson Blvd & Melrose Ave). PDC showrooms generally sell only to design pros, but sometimes you can get items at a mark-up through the Buying Program.

The PDC itself is an architectural landmark by Cesar Pelli of Petronas Twin Towers (Kuala Lumpur) fame. By 2009, a new racecar-red building will be joining the existing cobalt-blue one (nicknamed the Blue Whale) and another sheathed in forest green. The West Hollywood tourist office (p101) is on the mezzanine level of the blue building. At night, the fountains on the San Vicente Blvd side put on a colorful show.

Standing a bit forlorn amid the glassy behemoths is the **MOCA Pacific Design Center** (Map pp88-9; ☎ 213-289-5223; www.moca.org; admission free;

TICKETS TO SAVINGS

Besides the usual discounts (see p413 for an overview), there are a couple of other options to trim expenses in LA. One is the **Hollywood CityPass** (www.citypass.com; adult/child 3-11 $50/39), a voucher booklet valid for admission to a handful of Hollywood museums and tours. It's available online and at participating venues, which change periodically. Check the website for the latest scoop.

An alternative is the **Go Los Angeles Card** (www.golosangelescard.com; 1/2/3/5/7 days adult $49/79/149/161/179, child 3-12 $39/59/119/149/159), which gets you into as many of the 40 participating museums, tours and attractions (including Universal Studios Hollywood) as you can cram into its period of validity. It's sold online, and the website also has handy sample itineraries to help you determine what can be reasonably accomplished within a certain time frame.

🕑 11am-5pm Tue, Wed & Fri, 11am-8pm Thu, 11am-6pm Sat & Sun; **P**), a small satellite branch of Downtown's Museum of Contemporary Art (p135). Exhibits usually have an architectural or design theme.

SCHINDLER HOUSE

The former **home and studio** (Map pp88-9; ☎ 323-651-1510; www.makcenter.com; 835 N Kings Rd, West Hollywood; adult/senior & student $7/6, 4-6pm Fri free; 🕑 11am-6pm Wed-Sun) of Vienna-born architect Rudolph Schindler (1887–1953) offers a fine primer on the modernist elements that so greatly influenced mid-century California architecture. The open floor plan, a flat roof and glass sliding doors, while considered avant-garde back in the 1920s, all became design staples after WWII. Today, Schindler's old pad houses the **MAK Center for Art and Architecture**, which gives tours on weekends and hosts a slew of edgy exhibitions, lectures, performances and workshops.

FARMERS MARKET

Apples to zucchinis, cheeses to blinis – you'll find them at the landmark **Farmers Market** (Map pp88-9; ☎ 323-933-9211; www.farmersmarketla.com; 6333 W 3rd St, Fairfax District, Mid-City; admission free; 🕑 9am-9pm Mon-Fri, 9am-8pm Sat, 10am-7pm Sun; **P** 🚼), in business since 1934. Casual and kid-friendly, it's a fun place for a browse, snack or for people-watching. Next door, the **Grove** (Map pp88-9; ☎ 323-900-8080; www.thegrovela.com; 189 The Grove Dr) is a faux-European yet attractive outdoor shopping mall built around a central plaza with a musical fountain (nicest after dark, almost magical at Christmas time; also see p216).

North of here is **CBS Television City** (Map pp88-9; ☎ 323-575-2624; www.cbs.com; 7800 Beverly Blvd), where game shows, talk shows, soap operas and other programs are taped, often before a live audience (for tickets, see boxed text, p104).

LOS ANGELES COUNTY MUSEUM OF ART (LACMA)

LA's premier art museum, **LACMA** (Map pp88-9; ☎ 323-857-6000; www.lacma.org; 5901 Wilshire Blvd, Miracle Mile, Mid-City; adult/senior & student/child $9/5/free, after 5pm free; 🕑 noon-8pm Mon, Tue & Thu, noon-9pm Fri, 11am-8pm Sat & Sun) is an Aladdin's cave of paintings, sculpture and decorative arts stretching across the ages and borders. Yet, somehow, so far, it just hasn't quite got the respect it deserves. Sure, galleries are stuffed with all the major players – Rembrandt, Cé-

zanne, Magritte, Mary Cassat, Ansel Adams, to name a few – plus several millenia's worth of ceramics from China, woodblock prints from Japan, pre-Columbian art, and ancient sculpture from Greece, Rome, Egypt and lots of other treasures; the depth and wealth of the collection here is stunning. The way it's displayed – in dark galleries spread across a jumble of undistinguished buildings – is outdated and not particularly user-friendly. Even director Michael Govan calls the museum a 'sleeping giant'.

If all goes according to plan, this is about to change as LACMA is moving full steam ahead with a major revamp masterminded by Renzo Piano Phase 1. Opening in early 2008, it includes a new entry pavilion and the Broad Contemporary Art Museum. It will present part of the personal collection of developer Eli Broad, including seminal works by Jasper Johns, Roy Lichtenstein and Andy Warhol.

Some collections may be closed or moving during renovation, so check ahead if you're keen on seeing anything in particular.

LACMA also hosts headlining touring exhibits and frequent movie screenings, readings and other events, including a popular Friday-night jazz series. A café and a formal restaurant provide sustenance.

PAGE MUSEUM & LA BREA TAR PITS

Did you know that Manfred the mammoth, Sid the sloth and Diego the saber-toothed cat used to roam around LA in prehistoric times? Even if you're not a fan of the *Ice Age* animated film trilogy, you'll likely have a ball at the unique **Page Museum** (Map pp88-9; ☎ 323-934-7243; www.tarpits.org; 5801 Wilshire Blvd, Miracle Mile, Mid-City; adult/student & senior/child 5-12 $7/4.50/2; 🕑 9:30am-5pm Mon-Fri, 10am-5pm Sat & Sun; **P** 🚼), an archaeological trove of skulls and bones unearthed at **La Brea Tar Pits**, one of the world's most fecund and famous fossil sites. Thousands of ice-age critters met their maker between 40,000 and 10,000 years ago in gooey crude oil bubbling up from deep below Wilshire Blvd. Animals wading into the sticky muck became entrapped and were condemned to a slow death by starvation or suffocation. A life-size drama of a mammoth family outside the museum disturbingly dramatizes such a cruel fate. Parking costs $6.

Excavations continue every summer when you can watch paleontologists at work in **Pit 91** (admission free; ☼ 10am-4pm Wed-Sun Jul & Aug; ♿). At other times, they're fussing over bones in the glass-encased laboratory inside the museum itself, cleaning, identifying, cataloging and storing their discoveries.

PETERSEN AUTOMOTIVE MUSEUM

A four-story ode to the auto, the **Petersen Automotive Museum** (Map pp88-9; ☎ 323-930-2277; www.petersen.org; 6060 Wilshire Blvd, Miracle Mile, Mid-City; adult/child/senior & student $10/3/5; ☼ 10am-6pm Tue-Sun; **P** ♿) is a treat even to those who can't tell a piston from a carburetor. Start by ambling along a fun streetscape that reveals LA as the birthplace of gas stations, billboards, strip malls, drive-in restaurants and drive-in movie theaters. Then head upstairs where it's shiny cars galore, from vintage wheels to hot rods, movie cars to celebrity-owned rarities, presented in changing exhibits. Want to know how a combustion engine works? Find out one more floor up in the kid-oriented Discovery Center, where little ones also get to climb inside a 1910 Model T and pose as a motorcycle cop. Great photo-ops! Parking $6.

By the way, morbid trivia buffs might like to know that, in 1997, gangsta rapper Notorious B.I.G. was gunned down in his car outside the museum after leaving a Soul Train Music Awards party.

CRAFT & FOLK ART MUSEUM

Zulu ceramics, Japanese *katagami* paper art, Palestinian embroidery – cultural creativity has infinite ways of expression as you'll discover at this well-respected **museum** (Map pp88-9; ☎ 323-937-4230; www.cafam.org; 5814 Wilshire Blvd, Miracle Mile, Mid-City; adult/student & senior/child under 12 $5/3/free, 1st Wed of month free; ☼ 11am-5pm Tue, Wed & Fri, 11am-7pm Thu, noon-6pm Sat & Sun; ♿) where exhibits change every few months. Also check for upcoming kid-oriented workshops and storytelling sessions, usually held on Saturdays. The gift store is one of the best in town.

A+D MUSEUM

A + D = the **Architecture + Design Museum** (Map pp88-9; ☎ 323-932-9393; www.aplusd.org; 5900 Wilshire Blvd, Miracle Mile, Mid-City; adult/senior & students $5/2.50; ☼ 10am-6pm Tue-Fri, 10-6pm Sat & Sun), a small Getty-sponsored space that keeps the finger on the pulse of emerging trends, people and products in the design and architecture community, both locally and beyond.

HANCOCK PARK & LARCHMONT VILLAGE

LA has gorgeous homes galore, but there's nothing quite like the old-money mansions flanking the tree-lined streets of **Hancock Park**, a genteel neighborhood roughly bounded by Highland and Rossmore and Melrose and Wilshire. LA's founding families, including the Doheny's and Chandlers, hired famous architects to build their pads in the 1920s, and to this day low-profile celebrities such as Melanie Griffith, Antonio Banderas and Fred Savage make their homes here. It's a lovely area for a stroll or a drive-through, especially around Christmas when houses sparkle in a sea of twinkling lights.

Wrap up your visit here with a cappuccino and a browse through tiny **Larchmont Village** (Map pp88-9; Larchmont Blvd btwn Beverly Blvd & W 1st St; **P**), the neighborhood's small-town America-style commercial strip. Keep an eye out for celebs – Paramount Studios is just up the street.

Beverly Hills

Beverly Hills cuts through Los Angeles like the grand dame of royal cruise ships. Glittering streets, chic boutiques and posh restaurants all sparkle on her haughty decks with the security and charm befitting the securely monied. To tell the truth, though, the place feels like a deer park. It has no industry, no homeless people, an efficient police force, excellent schools, fancy hotels, more Ferraris per capita than anywhere else, 111 gardeners per sq mile and a median home value of $1.8 million.

Of course, Beverly Hills also has stars, mostly holed up in the hills and canyons north of Sunset Blvd. To find them, check out our tour in this book (p116), take a guided bus tour (p159) or buy a map to the stars' homes, for instance from **Linda Welton's Star Maps** (Map pp90-1) on the corner of Sunset Blvd and Baroda Dr.

These days, Beverly Hills' wealth is actually mostly new-money, brought here by immigrants from Iran who've been settling here since the fall of the Shah some 30 years ago. About 25% of the 35,000 residents are of Iranian descent, which has spawned the moniker 'Tehrangeles'. In March 2007, the city elected its first Iranian-born mayor, Jimmy Delshad.

In the downtown area, several city-owned garages offer two hours of free parking,

OUT & ABOUT IN LOS ANGELES *Andrew Bender*

LA is one of the country's gayest cities, with the rainbow flag flying especially proudly along Santa Monica Blvd in West Hollywood (WeHo). Dozens of high-energy bars, cafés, restaurants, gyms and clubs flank this strip. Most cater to gay men, although there's plenty for lesbians and mixed audiences. Thursday through Sunday nights are prime time.

Beauty reigns supreme among the buff, bronzed and styled of Boystown. Elsewhere, the scene is considerably more laid-back and less body-conscious. The crowd in Silver Lake runs from cute hipsters to leather-and-Levi's and an older contingent. Venice and Long Beach have the most relaxed, neighborly scenes.

Except for the hardcore places, LA's gay spots get their share of opposite-sex and straight patrons, drawn by gay friends, the fabulousness of the venues, abundant eye candy and, for women in gay bars, a non-threatening atmosphere. Within the gay community this new trend meets with – shall we say – diverse opinions.

If nightlife isn't your scene, there are plenty of other ways to meet, greet and engage. Outdoor activities include the **Frontrunners** (www.lafrontrunners.com) running club and the **Great Outdoors** (www.greatoutdoorsla.com) hiking club. For more ideas, check the freebie magazines (such as *Frontiers* and *IN Los Angeles*), which contain up-to-date listings and news about the community and gay-friendly establishments around town. The website www.westhollywood.com is another good source.

A Different Light (Map pp88-9; ☎ 310-854-6601; 8853 Santa Monica Blvd, West Hollywood) is LA's bastion of queer literature, nonfiction and magazines. The **LA Gay & Lesbian Center** (Map pp86-7; ☎ 323-993-7400; www.laglc.org; 1625 Schrader Blvd, Hollywood; ⊙ 9am-8pm Mon-Fri, 9am-1pm Sat) is a one-stop service and health agency.

The festival season kicks off in late May with the **Long Beach Pride Celebration** (☎ 562-987-9191; www.longbeachpride.com) and continues with the three-day **LA Pride** (www.lapride.org) in mid-June with a parade down Santa Monica Blvd. On **Halloween** (October 31; p161), the same street brings out 350,000 outrageously costumed revelers of all sexual persuasions. See p196 for the **Outfest** film festival.

There's gay theater all over town, but the **Celebration Theatre** (Map pp88-9; ☎ 323-957-1884; www.celebrationtheatre.com; 7051 Santa Monica Blvd, West Hollywood) ranks among the nation's leading stages for LGBT plays.

All WeHo hotels are de-facto gay-friendly, as are most hotels city-wide. **San Vicente Inn** (Map pp88-9; ☎ 310-854-6915, 800-577-6915; www.gayresort.com; 845 N San Vicente Blvd, West Hollywood; r $70-300; P ♿) is LA's men-only guesthouse. Rooms and cottages overlook a tropical garden, and the clothing-optional frolicking zones include a hot tub, sauna, pool and sundeck.

Eating & Drinking WeHo

Abbey (Map pp88-9; ☎ 310-289-8410; www.abbeyfoodandbar.com; 692 N Robertson Blvd; mains $9-13; ⊙ 8am-2am) From its beginnings as a humble coffee house, the Abbey has developed into WeHo's bar/club/restaurant of record. Always cool and fun. There are so many different flavored martinis that you'd think they were invented here, plus there's a full menu of pub grub and desserts. You can match your mood to the many different spaces, which range from outdoor patio to Goth lounge, chill room to your own private divan. On weekend nights, they're all busy. Breakfast is served until 2pm.

East West (Map pp88-9; ☎ 310-360-6186; www.eastwestlounge.com; 801 Larrabee St) Finally, WeHo has an intimate, mod lounge worthy of the deep-pocketed hotties who live here. Prices aren't exactly cheap but the drink menu is creative (lots of champagne cocktails), and bottle service is available. Lots of big windows and sidewalk seating to keep an eye on the busy street life cruising past outside.

Factory/Ultra Suede (Map pp88-9; ☎ 310-659-4551; www.factorynightclub.com; 652 La Peer Dr) This giant double club has an edgy New York feel, and sports different stripes every night. On Friday night, the Girl Bar (at Ultra Suede) is the preferred playground of fashion-forward femmes, while male hot bods strut their stuff on Saturdays. Music-wise, anything goes here as long as it's got a good beat.

Fubar (Map pp88-9; ☎ 323-654-0396; www.fubarla.com; 7994 Santa Monica Blvd) This unpretentious neighborhood-style bar offers a weekly lineup including karaoke, dance parties and, you know, sexier stuff. Check what's on before setting out.

Here Lounge (Map pp88-9; ☎ 310-360-8455; www.herelounge.com; 696 N Robertson Blvd) WeHo's premier venue for S&M (standing and modeling) is chic and angular, with lots of smooth surfaces – and that goes for both the crowd and the setting. Check the website for different club nights: gay, lesbian, even (sometimes) straight.

Palms (Map pp88-9; ☎ 310-652-6188; 8572 Santa Monica Blvd) This scene staple has been keeping lesbians happy for over three decades and even gets the occasional celebrity drop-in, as in Melissa Etheridge or Ellen DeGeneres. Beer is the beverage of choice and the Beer Bust Sundays are perfect for those who don't want the weekend to end.

Marix Tex Mex (Map pp88-9; ☎ 323-656-8800; 1108 N Flores St, West Hollywood; mains $8-16; ☯ 11:30am-11pm) It should be stamped on airline tickets: every gay or lesbian WeHo visitor has to go here at least once. Year-in year-out, the open-air Marix has patios for kick-ass margaritas and lots of meeting and greeting, plus great fish tacos, chipotle chicken sandwich and other Mexi faves.

Eleven (Map pp88-9; ☎ 310-855-0800; www.eleven.la; 8811 Santa Monica Blvd; mains $13-29; ☯ 6-10pm Tue-Sun, 11am-3pm Sat & Sun) Across the street from East West (see earlier listing), this glamour spot opened up in 2007. It's housed on two levels in a historic building. The New American cuisine here comes with prices as high as the acrobats who sometimes perform on tightropes above the foyer. Late at night, it turns into WeHo's chichi-est watering hole; check the website for club nights.

Beyond WeHo

Akbar (Map pp86-7; ☎ 323-665-6810; www.akbarsilverlake.com; 4356 W Sunset Blvd, Silver Lake) Best jukebox in town, Casbah-style atmosphere, and a great mix of people that's been known to change from hour to hour – gay, straight, on the fence or just hip, but not too-hip-for-you. Some nights, the back room turns into a dance floor; other nights you can watch comedy or do crafts. Check the website for details.

Casita Del Campo (Map pp86-7; ☎ 323-662-4255; www.casitadelcampo.com; 1920 Hyperion Ave, Silver Lake; mains lunch $8, dinner $14-17; ☯ 11am-11pm; Ⓟ) What's not to love about this Mexican cantina? It's cozy, it's fun, and if you go on the right night there's a tiny theater downstairs where you might catch a drag show.

Faultline (Map pp86-7; ☎ 323-660-0889; www.faultlinebar.com; 4216 Melrose Ave, Silver Lake; ☯ 5pm-2am Tue-Fri, 2pm-2am Sat & Sun) Indoor-outdoor venue that's party central for manly men, with nary a twink in sight. Take off your shirt and join the Sunday afternoon beer bust (it's an institution), but get there early or expect a long wait.

Oil Can Harry's (off Map p95; ☎ 818-760-9749; www.oilcanharrysla.com; 11502 Ventura Blvd, Studio City, San Fernando Valley; ☯ Tue & Thu-Sat) If you've never been country-and-western dancing, you'll be surprised at just how sexy it can be, and Oil Can's the place to do it, three nights a week, including lessons for the uninitiated. Saturday: retro disco.

Other Side (Map pp86-7; ☎ 323-661-0618; www.flyingleapcafe.com; 2538 Hyperion Ave, Silver Lake) Piano bar where the crowd skews older and you can actually hear yourself talk. On Friday nights, pianist James Lent swings it with a bevy of talented crooners. Prices are reasonable and the adjacent café does Cal cuisine.

Roosterfish (Map p92; ☎ 310-392-2123; www.roosterfishbar.com; 1302 Abbot Kinney Blvd, Venice; ☯ 11am-2am) The Westside's last gay bar standing is a friendly, been-there-forever kind of place that still manages to stay current and cool. It's dark and a little grungy, but never dangerous or skanky. Strike up new friendships while playing pool, shooting electronic darts or nursing your drink. Friday nights are busiest, drawing guys from all over town, or go for the neighborly Sunday afternoon barbecue.

including one at 9510 Brighton Way. For two hours of free valet parking, head to the garage underneath Two Rodeo (enter from Dayton Way). Narrated 40-minute tours aboard the **Beverly Hills Trolley** (Map pp90–1; ☎ 310-285-2438; cnr Rodeo Dr & Dayton Way; adult/child under 12 $5/1; ☼ 11am-4pm Tue-Sat Jul, Aug, Nov & Dec, Sat only otherwise) run hourly in dry weather.

RODEO DRIVE

It's pricey and pretentious, but no trip to LA would be complete without a saunter along **Rodeo Drive**, the famous three-block ribbon of style where sample-size fembots browse for Escada and Prada. The latter's flagship store at No 343 is a Rem Koolhaas-designed stunner lidded by a pitched glass roof. Most people gravitate to Euro-flavored **Two Rodeo** (Map pp90–1; cnr Rodeo Dr & Wilshire Blvd), a cobbled lane lined with outdoor cafés for primo people-watching. Tip: if Rodeo price tags make you gasp, head one block over to the more down-to-earth boutiques and chic chains (Lululemon to Jigsaw London) along Beverly Dr.

For Frank Lloyd Wright fans, there's the 1953 **Anderton Court** (322 N Rodeo Dr), a zany zigzag construction, although clearly not his best work. Also check out the 1988 **O'Neill House** (Map pp90–1; 507 N Rodeo Dr), a few blocks north. It doesn't have a famous architect, but the free-form art nouveau structure in the tradition of Catalán master Antonio Gaudí is definitely one of the more imaginative structures in Beverly Hills.

PALEY CENTER FOR MEDIA

Bye, bye Museum of TV & Radio and hello **Paley Center for Media** (MTR; Map pp90–1; ☎ 310-786-1000; www.mtr.org; 465 N Beverly Dr; suggested donation adult/child/student & senior $10/5/8; ☼ noon-5pm Wed-Sun). This Industry institution renamed itself in 2007, 'cause, well, this is the digital age after all, and who wants to sound like a fuddy-duddy? Behind the scenes, though, not much has changed. For visitors, the main lure is still the mind-boggling archive of TV and radio broadcasts going back to 1918. The Beatles' US debut on the *Ed Sullivan Show*? The moon landing? The *Ugly Betty* pilot? All here, docos to day soaps, cartoons to sitcoms, available for your listening and viewing pleasure at private consoles. Plus, two theaters for screenings, live broadcasts and discussions with the casts of *Desperate Housewives* and *Law & Order*. Getty

Center architect Richard Meier designed the crisp, gleaming white building. Pick up a schedule at the information desk or call ☎ 310-786-1025.

BEVERLY HILLS HOTEL

Affectionately known as the 'Pink Palace,' the **Beverly Hills Hotel** (Map pp90–1; ☎ 310-887-2887; 9641 Sunset Blvd) has served as unofficial hob-nobbing headquarters of the Industry elite since 1912.

In the 1930s, its Polo Lounge was a notori-ous postchukker hangout of Darryl F Zanuck, Spencer Tracy, Will Rogers and other lords of the polo crowd. Marlene Dietrich had her very own 7ft-by-8ft bed installed in Bungalow 11, and Howard Hughes, the billionaire rec-luse, went progressively off his nut during 30 years of delusional semiresidence. Elizabeth Taylor bedded six of her eight husbands in various bungalows. While filming *Let's Make Love,* Yves Montand and Marilyn Monroe were probably doing just that; Marilyn is also reported to have 'bungalowed' both JFK and RFK here as well.

Alas, by the '70s, the grande dame had lost her luster and the stars went elsewhere to frolic. It took 20 years for a 'knight in shining armor' to rescue her from oblivion. The Sultan of Brunei coughed up almost $300 million to make her regain her blush, lurid wink and ability to seduce the power players. Scripts are once again read and deals cut by the pool, in the Polo Lounge, the Fountain Coffee Shop and the hip new Bar Nineteen12. If you'd like to stay here, see p166 for details.

VIRGINIA ROBINSON GARDENS

Beverly Hills' ultimate 'secret' **garden** (Map pp90–1; ☎ 310-276-5367; www.robinson-gardens.com; 1008 Elden Way; tour adult/child 5-12/student & senior $10/3/5; ☼ 10am & 1pm Tue-Fri) is tucked among the manicured estates north of Sunset Blvd. Virginia Robinson, wife of department store mogul Harry Robinson, had a passion for plants and devoted much of her life to creat-ing this symphony of trees and flowers that can only be experienced on guided tours. You'll also get to peek inside the Robinsons' magnificent beaux arts mansion, where Fred Astaire, Ronald Reagan and other Hollywood royalty used to pop by for a game of bridge and a stiff whiskey. Make reservations at least two weeks in advance, and even further ahead in spring.

MY DATE WITH EMMY *Andrea Schulte-Peevers*

There were eight of us in a limo as long as Florida, dressed to kill, guzzling champagne and headed to the high-school prom. No, wait. I'd plucked three grey hairs earlier, my crimson gown was a tad (ahem!) snug and one of the other ladies was expecting her second child. Oh yeah. That's right. We were on our way to the Prime-Time Emmy Awards, but still as excited and goofy as kids expecting a cell-phone call from Mom reminding us to behave.

We queued in an interminable line of other limos and finally leapt out onto 100 yards of red carpet. Paparazzi flashes blitzed us into further insensibility. The fans gaped and twittered – but not for us. I turned around and stared right at Jim Brolin and 'Babs' Streisand (who was draped in a curtain-like frock possibly designed by Julie Andrews), smiling and waving to the cheering crowd.

'Oh my Gawd! He's so *handsome!*' gushed my friend as Tom Selleck cut a swath along the crimson like the bow of an aircraft carrier. And then there was adorable but wraith-like Teri Hatcher looking like she could really use a Big Mac. Zach Braff, James Spader, Felicity Huffman, Patricia Arquette… Oh! We were racking 'em up now alright! Then it was the plunge into the mothership of the Shrine where we sat in the 'nosebleed' balcony, next to that season's cast of *The Amazing Race*.

If sucking up were an art – and believe me, in Hollywood it *is* – the Emmies would be the Louvre. For four hours we were awash in tomorrow's headlines, gushing lists of 'thank yous' including swamis and pedicurists, and listening to the orchestra honking out their welcomes for the winners. We were swallowed by Hollywood's endless appetite for self-congratulations and ego-enhancement. But heck, if the excess be wretched, play on! My limo awaits!

MUSEUM OF TOLERANCE

Run by the Simon Wiesenthal Center, this **museum** (Map pp90-1; information ☎ 310-553-8403; www.museumoftolerance.com; 9786 W Pico Blvd; adult/child/student & senior $13/10/11; ⏰ 11am-6:30pm Mon-Thu, 11am-3:30pm Fri, 11am-7:30pm Sun; ℗) uses interactive technology to make visitors confront racism and bigotry, with particular focus given to the Holocaust. You can study various Nazi-era memorabilia, including letters by Anne Frank, a bunk bed from the Majdanek camp and Göring's dress-uniform cap. Lectures by Holocaust survivors take place several times a week.

A renovation in 2007 added a new history wall that celebrates diversity, exposes intolerance and champions rights in America. You can also cast your opinion on current issues in a poll booth with the results tabulated instantly for all to see. The 2nd floor has been converted into a creative space for interactive children's programs.

The last entry is 2½ hours before closing, and reservations (☎ 310-772-2505) are suggested.

A separate exhibit called **Finding Our Families, Finding Ourselves** (adult/child under 12 & student/senior $8/6/7; ⏰ same as main museum) examines the diversity of American society and what it means to be an American. It follows the personal histories of poet Maya Angelou, comedian Billy Crystal, musician Carlos Santana and baseball coach Joe Torre.

GREYSTONE MANSION & PARK

Gloomy and gothic, this 1928 castlelike **mansion** (Map pp88-9; ☎ 310-550-4654; www.greystone mansion.org; 905 Loma Vista Dr; park admission free; park ⏰ 10am-6pm Apr-Oct, 10am-5pm Nov-Mar; ℗) seems more suited for foggy Scottish moors than shiny Beverly Hills. In 1929 its owner, oil heir Ned Doheny, was found with a bullet in his head along with his male secretary in an alleged murder-suicide – an unsolved mystery to this day.

Nobody's lived here since but the mansion has appeared in countless movies and TV shows, including *Spider-Man III*, *Indecent Proposal* and *Alias*. It's empty and closed except for special events, but you're free to peer through the dusty windows and explore the surrounding park, which has an odd melancholic air about it. Views from the top are quite impressive (drive up to the parking lot).

Westwood, Bel Air & Brentwood

Westwood is practically synonym⸺
UCLA whose huge campus is b⸺
by Sunset Blvd and the Westv⸺
The village is pedestrian-frien⸺

LONELY PLANET GETS STAR-STRUCK: OUR GUIDE TO THE STARS' HOMES

Star-chasing isn't usually our style, but even we admit that visiting LA just wouldn't be the same without any celestial navigation. So here's our own gossipy tour of the stars' homes, custom-made just for you. Expect plenty of tall hedges and security cameras, and don't trespass. You can indulge your inner paparazzo in about 60 minutes, 90 minutes tops.

So rev up your engines and head to the Sunset Strip, then climb up Kings Rd to No 1467 and get ready to be a 'Paris-ite'. Yup, this is where everybody's favorite ex-jailbird, **Paris Hilton**, leads her 'simple life'. From the street at least, the house is indeed surprisingly modest and almost as beige and bland as the hotel chain she'll one day inherit.

Double-back down to Sunset, turn right and right again on Doheny Dr where **Halle Berry** is having a 'Monster's Ball' at No 1164, which was previously owned by *Malcolm in the Middle* star Frankie Muniz. All you can see through the tall Old Mexico gate are some parked cars and flowers. Berry's almost-next-door neighbor **Winona Ryder** hides behind a tall, thick hedge at No 1320, but hopefully some paparazzi have snipped a hole in the foliage so you can at least see her front yard.

Up, and up and up you continue on Doheny before hooking a right on Oriole Dr and a left on Oriole Way. From this hilltop perch **Leonardo DiCaprio** must feel quite literally like the king of the world at his modernist pad at No 9045. It's the one at the end of the cul-de-sac but only the top portion is visible. Leo also owns the adjacent lot but got sued in 2007 for allegedly infringing upon a neighbor's property when building a basketball court for himself.

Backtrack to Oriole Dr, then turn right on Thrasher Ave. On your right, at No 9000 just before the road veers to the left, is the 1962 concrete cube that DiCaprio buddy **Tobey McGuire** unloaded for a cool $10.8 million in May 2007, more than triple what he paid for it back in 2002. Nice move, Spidey! **Megan Mullally** (Karen on *Will & Grace*) lives right next door; **Keanu Reeves** is behind the metal fence and marble portal of No 9024; and **Courtney Love** used to live at No 8936.

Back down to Sunset you go, then its right on Doheny Rd. See that big white residential high-rise? That's the celeb-studded Sierra Towers (9255 Doheny Rd) where **Matthew Perry** owns a condo on the 22nd floor and **Elton John** shelled out about $2.5 million for his unit two floors below. Views from up there are also enjoyed by **Cher** but no longer by **Lindsay Lohan**, who sold hers in February 2007 for $2.3 million.

Turn right on Hillcrest Rd to catch a glimpse of **Jennifer Aniston**'s home at the end of the driveway at No 1004. We're not sure but we think it's one of those places up on the hill. We do know that it's a six-bedroom '70s house designed by modernist architect Hal Levitt, famous for gray-and-black marble floors, and that she snapped it up for a measly $13.5 million.

When Jen gets lonely, she has only a short walk to BFF **Courteney Cox** and her hubbie **David Arquette** who are at 1012 Wallace Ridge. You can get there by doubling back on Hillcrest, turning right on Drury Lane, right again on Loma Vista Dr and again right on Wallace Ridge. It's the first house on the right, with the velvety grass and the palm trees.

Turn around, go left on Doheny, right on Sierra Dr, right on Sunset and left on Hillcrest Rd where you can get a good look at **Larry King**'s house at No 707. From here it's right on Elevado Ave, right again on Palm Dr where America's most (in)famous Brit, Simon Cowell, paid $8 million to live at No 717. See those trees and the big hedge north across Sunset? Somewhere behind there is **Madonna**'s shack (9425 Sunset Blvd). The lady sure values her privacy.

And so do **Tom Cruise** and **Katie Holmes**, who forked over two-movie-salary's-worth ($30.5 million, to be exact) for a giant mansion at 1111 Calle Vista Dr. To get there, turn left on Sunset, right on Foothill Rd (which becomes Doheny Rd), then left on Calle Vista and it's the second house on your left. The house itself is at the end of a long driveway and there's just a black iron gate to gawk at. It's a 13,000-sq-ft mansion with seven bedrooms, nine bathrooms and a pool, so use your imagination. Then go back to Sunset, right and right again on Alpine Dr, where the Cruises used to make do with the mega-shack at No 918. Not much to see there either.

Ok, this is your last chance to snap pictures and it's a good one. You can see plenty of **Dr Phil**'s pretty Mediterranean-style villa at 1008 Lexington Rd. It has a tiled roof, lots of flowers, a Rapunzel tower and, at about 11,000 sq ft, is a lot bigger than it looks. That's it – show's over. Nothing to see here.

lonelyplanet.com

LOS

118 LOS ANGELES

LOS ANGELES

addition is
Richard
Center
the

enough but hardly a Latin Quarter despite the large student presence. A farmers market along Weyburn Ave livens things up on Thursday afternoons. Parking is expensive and at a premium, but you can snag an hour of free parking in the public garage at 1036 Broxton Ave.

North of Westwood, **Bel Air** is a favorite hideaway of stars whose sybaritic homes are generally well hidden behind security gates and dense foliage. **Brentwood**, west of the I-405 (San Diego Fwy), is only a little less exclusive and home to one of LA's big attractions, the hilltop Getty Center. Despite a high celeb quotient, it's pretty low-key and accessible. Marilyn Monroe died in her home at 12305 5th Helena Dr, but more recently Brentwood made headlines when Nicole Simpson and her friend Ron Goldman were murdered in her condo at 875 Bundy Dr. In the subsequent criminal trial, her husband OJ Simpson was (in)famously acquitted.

GETTY CENTER

In its billion-dollar in-the-clouds perch, high above the city grit and grime, the **Getty Center** (Map pp80-1 ☎ 310-440-7300; www.getty.edu; 1200 Getty Center Dr; admission free; ⏱ 10am-6pm Sun & Tue-Thu, 10am-9pm Fri & Sat; Ⓟ ♿) presents triple delights: a stellar art collection (Renaissance to David Hockney), Richard Meier's cutting-edge architecture, and the visual splendor of seasonally changing gardens. On clear days, you can add breathtaking views of the city and ocean to the list. A great time to visit is in the late afternoon after the crowds have thinned. Sunsets create a remarkable alchemy of light and shadow and are especially magical in winter, when the orange orb drops straight into the Pacific.

Even getting up to the 110-acre 'campus' aboard a driverless tram is fun. From the sprawling arrival plaza, a natural flow of walkways, stairs, fountains and courtyards encourages a leisurely wander between galleries, gardens and outdoor cafés. Five buildings hold collections of manuscripts, drawings, photographs, furniture and decorative arts and a strong assortment of pre-20th-century European paintings. Must-sees include Van Gogh's *Irises*, Monet's *Wheatstacks*, Rembrandt's *The Abduction of Europa* and Titian's *Venus and Adonis*. Don't miss the lovely Cactus Garden on the remote South Promontory for those amazing city views.

Tours, lectures ar
including audiogui
art accessible to all.
ily Tour, visit the i
borrow a kid-orien
the special kid boo
films and other cu
way they keep things dynamic for located
are free but some require reservations (or try standby).

Admission is free as well, but parking is $8; both Metro Bus 761 (p219) and the Big Blue Bus 14 (p219) stop at the Getty.

UNIVERSITY OF CALIFORNIA, LOS ANGELES (UCLA)

Founded in 1919, **UCLA** (Map pp90-1; ☎ 310-825-4321, tour reservations 310-825-8764; www.ucla.edu; 405 Hilgard Ave; free tours 10:30am & 1:30pm Mon-Fri, reservations required; Ⓟ) ranks among the nation's top universities, with five Nobel Prize winners on its faculty; four of its alumni are laureates as well. UCLA is also the alma mater of Jim Morrison, Ryan Dusick of Maroon 5, Brad Delson and Dave Farrell of Linkin Park, and LA mayor Antonio Villaraigosa.

The campus is vast; walking briskly from one end to the other takes at least 30 minutes. It would be mostly a lovely saunter, through landscaped grounds, profuse gardens and past replicas of Italian Renaissance churches on historic Royce Quad. One of them, the **Powell Library**, harbors the **UCLA Film and Television Archive** (☎ 310-206-5388; www.cinema.ucla.edu; admission free; ⏱ 9am-5pm Mon-Fri), the country's second-largest after the Library of Congress, with more than 220,000 movies and TV shows. It's only open to researchers, but regular screenings take place at the state-of-the-art Billy Wilder Theater in the Hammer Museum (p118).

Nearby, the **Fowler Museum at UCLA** (Map pp90-1; ☎ 310-825-4361; www.fowler.ucla.edu; admission free; ⏱ noon-5pm Wed-Sun, noon-8pm Thu) presents sometimes intriguing, sometimes baffling ethno-exhibits from non-Western cultures. A recent one featured stunningly intricate found-object art by El Anatsui, one of Africa's top sculptors. It's free, so why not pop in – you might be surprised.

Garden retreats include the **Murphy Sculpture Garden** northeast of Royce Quad, with more than 70 works by Rodin, Moore, Calder and other American and European artists set amid jacaranda and coral trees. The latest a ginormous torqued ellipse by ...erra in the plaza of the new **Broad Art** ...Designed by Richard Meier, it houses ...UCLA visual-arts programs and an MFA ...udent gallery.

In the campus' southeastern corner, the **Mildred E Mathias Botanical Garden** (Map pp90-1; ☎ 310-825-1260; www.botgard.ucla.edu/bg-home.htm; admission free; ✆ 8am-5pm Mon-Fri, 8am-4pm Sat & Sun) has more than 5000 native and exotic plants and flowers. Enter on Tiverton Ave. On winter weekdays, gates close an hour earlier.

It's only open by reservation, but the lovely **Hannah Carter Japanese Garden** (Map pp90-1; ☎ 310-794-0320; www.japanesegarden.ucla.edu; 10619 Bellagio Rd; admission free; ✆ 10am-3pm Tue, Wed & Fri; **P**) is well worth the trouble. Strolling through this spiritual gem inspired by the terraced gardens of Kyoto is an instant escape from city life. Sorry, no picnics. Call at least 10 days in advance. It's about one mile north of campus.

HAMMER MUSEUM
Originally a vanity project of the late oil tycoon Armand Hammer, his eponymous **museum** (Map pp90-1; ☎ 310-443-7000; www.hammer.ucla.edu; 10899 Wilshire Blvd; adult/senior/child under 17 $5/3/free; ✆ 11am-7pm Tue, Wed, Fri & Sat, 11am-9pm Thu, 11am-5pm Sun; **P**) has long since graduated to a widely respected art space. Selections from Hammer's personal collection include relatively minor works by Monet, Van Gogh, Mary Cassat and Honoré Daumier, but the museum really shines when it comes to cutting-edge contemporary exhibits featuring local, under-represented and controversial artists. As an intellectual forum, it presents incredibly diverse, high-caliber readings, lunchtime art talks, screenings, happenings, discussions, lectures and concerts, many of them free. Parking costs $3.

PIERCE BROS WESTWOOD MEMORIAL PARK
This little **cemetery** (Map pp90-1; ☎ 310-474-1570; 1218 Glendon Ave; admission free; ✆ 8am-dusk; **P**) packs more Old Hollywood star power per square foot than any other in town. Best of all, the staff is happy to have you here and will even help you locate your favorite six-foot-under resident. Lipstick prints usually decorate Marilyn Monroe's crypt next to one reserved for Hugh Hefner, and Natalie Wood, Burt Lancaster, Truman Capote and Jack Lemmon aren't far either. Rodney Dangerfield

is finally getting some respect in his spot on the park's south side. Enter via the driveway immediately to your left as you turn south on Glendon Ave.

SKIRBALL CULTURAL CENTER
Although it's the country's largest Jewish museum and cultural center, the **Skirball** (Map pp80-1; ☎ 310-440-4500; www.skirball.org; 2701 N Sepulveda Blvd; adult/student & senior/child 2-12 $10/7/5, free on Thu; ✆ noon-5pm Tue, Wed & Fri, noon-9pm Thu, 10am-5pm Sat & Sun; ♿) has something for people of any or no creed. The preschool set can board a gigantic wooden Noah's Ark (p157) while grown-ups gravitate to the permanent exhibit, an engagingly presented romp through 4000 years of history, traditions, trials and triumphs of the Jewish people. This includes displays explaining Jewish holidays, a replica mosaic floor from an ancient synagogue, and Hitler's racist rant *Mein Kampf*.

A busy events schedule features celebrities, Hollywood moguls and fine thinkers in panel discussions, lectures, readings and performances. Big crowds also turn out for the free outdoor world music summer concert series. Zeidler's Café (mains $6 to $10) serves tasty, kosher California fare.

Culver City
If you haven't been to Culver City lately (if ever), go! You won't recognize this once bleak, boring and run-down neighborhood that you could safely ignore as a local and definitely skip as a tourist. It's no-man's-land no more. Seemingly overnight Culver City has become a stylish yet unpretentious destination for fans of art, culture and food. Sony Pictures execs talk deals over Hefeweizen at Ford's Filling Station (p179), coiffed couples nibble a quick salad at Tender Greens (p179) before hurrying to a show at the Kirk Douglas Theatre (p203) and hipsters check out the latest homewares at HD Buttercup (p215). Even the venerable Culver Hotel (p167), where the Munchkins once slept, has been spruced up. It's been a miraculously speedy metamorphosis and, best of all, it's happened organically, not imagineered by some hot-shot developer or urban planning board. And the momentum will likely keep growing once the Expo light-rail line to Downtown LA starts running in 2010.

The buzz isn't limited to the downtown area where Washington and Culver Blvds meet. Continue east on Washington and you'll hit upon the fabulous **Helms Bakery Complex** (www.helmsfurniture.com; cnr Washington Blvd & Helms Ave), a giant former bakery turned furniture and design district. One of LA's best jazz venues, the Jazz Bakery (p200) has also found a home here, as have fabulous restaurants such as Beacon (p179).

The Helms complex also marks the beginning of Culver City's vital new **arts district**, which runs east along Washington to La Cienega and up one block to Venice Blvd. In 2003 art-world movers and shakers Blum & Poe (p208) relocated their gallery here from Santa Monica, drawn by cheap rents and airy, malleable spaces in old warehouses. Since then, more than three dozen galleries have piggybacked on their success, turning Culver City into LA's latest hub for contemporary and conceptual art. Also here is the **Museum of Design Art and Architecture** (Map p97; ☎ 310-558-0902; www.moodagallery.com; 8609 Washington Blvd; admission free; ☒ noon-6pm Mon-Fri), a starkly postmodern cube that also contains live-work lofts and an architecture firm. Architecture fans also gravitate to the **Hayden Tract** (Map p97; 3500 block of Hayden Ave), where Eric Owen Moss has turned a worn-out industrial compound into eye-poppingly deconstructivist office buildings.

Last but not least, Culver City has the **Museum of Jurassic Technology** (MJT; Map p97; ☎ 310-836-6131; www.mjt.org; 9341 Venice Blvd; adult/student & senior/child under 12 $5/3/free; ☒ 2-8pm Thu, noon-6pm Fri-Sun), LA's most intriguing exhibition space. Nope, it has nothing to do with dinosaurs and even less with technology. Instead, you'll find madness nibbling at your mind as you try to read meaning into displays about Cameroonian stink ants, a tribute to trailer parks and a sculpture of the Pope squished into the eye of a needle. It may all be a mind-bending spoof, an elaborate hoax or a complete exercise in ironic near-hysteria by founder David Wilson. Maybe. But one thing's certain: the MJT will challenge the way you look at museums. For an entertaining read about the place, pick up *Mr Wilson's Cabinet of Wonder* by ex–*New Yorker* staff writer Lawrence Weschler.

Exposition Park

A quick jaunt south of Downtown LA by DASH bus (p219), the family-friendly Exposition Park began as an agricultural fairground in 1872, then devolved into a magnet for the down-and-out, and finally emerged as a patch of public greenery in 1913. It contains three quality museums, a lovely **Rose Garden** (Map p97; admission free; ☒ 8:30am-sunset Apr-Dec) and the 1923 **Los Angeles Memorial Coliseum** (Map p97; ☎ 213-747-7111; www.lacoliseum.com; 3911 S Figueroa St). The last hosted the 1932 and 1984 Summer Olympic Games, the 1959 baseball World Series and two Super Bowls. The adjacent indoor **Los Angeles Memorial Sports Arena** (Map p97; ☎ 213-748-6136; 3939 S Figueroa St) dates from 1959 and is used for rock concerts, ice shows, the circus and even the occasional rodeo. Parking costs $6.

There are a few eateries in and near the park, but for a treat, head to nearby **Mercado La Paloma** (Map p97; ☎ 213-748-1963; 3655 S Grand Ave; admission free; ☒ 8am-6:30pm), an abandoned warehouse turned into a delightful Mexican marketplace with an art gallery, quality crafts stalls and numerous food stalls, including the excellent Chichen Itza (p187).

NATURAL HISTORY MUSEUM OF LA COUNTY

Dinos to diamonds, bears to beetles, hissing roaches to African elephants – this old-school **museum** (Map p97; ☎ 213-763-3466; www.nhm.org; 900 Exposition Blvd; adult/child/senior & student $9/2/6.50; ☒ 9:30am-5pm Mon-Fri, from 10am Sat & Sun; ☒) will take you around the world and back millions of years in time. It's all housed in a beautiful 1913 renaissance-style building that stood in for Columbia University in the first *Spider-Man* movie – yup, this was where Peter Parker was bitten by the radioactive arachnid.

The special exhibits usually draw the biggest crowds, but don't miss out on a spin around the permanent halls to see such trophy displays as a tyrannosaurus rex skull and a megamouth, one of the world's rarest and creepiest sharks. Historical exhibits include prized Navajo textiles, baskets and jewelry in the **Hall of Native American Cultures**. If diamonds are your best friend, head to the **Gem & Mineral Hall** with its walk-through gem tunnel and a Fort Knox–worthy gold collection. Summers see the opening of the **Pavilion of Wings** (separate admission adult/senior & student/child 5-12 $3/2/1; ☒ mid-Apr–early Sep) on the South Lawn, an enchanting landscape where some 30 species of butterflies roam freely.

Kids will have plenty of ooh and aah moments in the spruced-up **Discovery Center** where they can make friends with Cecil the iguana and Peace, a 9ft boa; dig for dinosaur fossils;

handle bones, antlers and minerals; and get close to tarantulas, scorpions and other creepy-crawlies.

For grown-ups, the museum turns up the volume during its First Fridays event series, which combines a lecture with guided tours and a party (with booze and live music) in the African mammal hall. Check the website for upcoming dates.

CALIFORNIA SCIENCE CENTER

A simulated earthquake, baby chicks hatching and a giant techno-doll named Tess bring out the kid in all of us at this multimedia **museum** (Map p97; ☎ 323-724-3623; www.californiasciencecenter .org; 700 State Dr; admission free; ☺ 10am-5pm; ♿) with plenty of buttons to push, lights to switch on and knobs to pull.

The enormous space is divided into three themed areas. Upstairs on the left, **World of Life** focuses mostly on the human body. You can 'hop on' a red blood cell for a computer fly-through of the circulatory system, ask Gertie how long your colon really is, watch open-heart surgery and learn about homeostasis from Tess, billed as '50ft of brains, beauty and biology.' Tots may have trouble understanding the science, but they *will* remember Tess.

On the right, **Creative World** is all about the ingenious ways humans have devised to communicate with each other, transport things and build structures. Meet a family of crash-test dummies, fly a virtual hovercraft and get all shook up during a fake earthquake.

Aircraft and space travel take center stage in the **Sketch Foundation Gallery**, in an adjacent Frank Gehry building (yes, he's everywhere). Spirits will soar at the sight of a pioneering 1902 Wright Glider, the original Gemini 11 capsule flown by US astronauts in 1996 and a replica Soviet Sputnik, the first human-made objects to orbit the earth in 1957.

It's all good educational fun but, we're sad to say, in this fast-moving tech-age some of the exhibits that were cutting-edge only years ago already seem oddly dated. That may change once the **World of Ecology** exhibit opens, supposedly in 2009. Currently under construction, the new pavilion will let you explore the natural world by studying animals in recreated habitats and features 175 new hands-on exhibits.

Already in business is the **IMAX** (p197), an ideal place for winding down after an action-filled day.

CALIFORNIA AFRICAN AMERICAN MUSEUM

This engaging **museum** (Map p97; ☎ 213-744-7432; www.caamuseum.org; 600 State Dr; admission free; ☺ 10am-4pm Wed-Sat) does an excellent job of showcasing African-American contributions to art and history. Using paintings, crafts, photographs and memorabilia, the permanent exhibit traces an entire people's journey from the African homeland into slavery and eventual freedom. An active lecture and performance schedule brings together the community and those wanting to gain a deeper understanding of what it means to be black in America.

UNIVERSITY OF SOUTHERN CALIFORNIA (USC)

George Lucas, John Wayne and Neil Armstrong are among the famous alumni of this well-respected **private university** (Map p97; ☎ 213-740-5371; www.usc.edu; 3535 S Figueroa St), founded in 1880 and just north of Exposition Park. Free 50-minute student-led **tours** (☎ 213-740-6605; tours@usc.edu; ☺ 10am-3pm Mon-Fri) touch on campus history, architecture and student life and leave on the hour from the Admissions Center. Reservations are strongly recommended.

Harris Hall is the home of **USC Fisher Gallery** (Map p97; ☎ 213-740-4561; www.fishergallery .org; 823 Exposition Blvd; admission free; ☺ noon-5pm Tue-Sat Sep-May), which presents changing selections from its ever-expanding collection of American landscapes, British portraits, French Barbizon School paintings and, perhaps surprisingly, Mexican modern masters such as Rufino Tamayo and Gronk (Glugio Nicandro).

Malibu

Malibu enjoys a near-mythical status as a 'Shangri-La on the Pacific' thanks to its large celebrity population, the incredible beauty of its shoreline and its legendary surfing beaches. Stretched out for 27 miles, it's a place with no discernible center, inhabited by people richer than God, and yet is far less glamorous than the tabloids make it sound.

Malibu has been celebrity central since the 1930s when money troubles forced landowner May Rindge to lease out property to her famous Hollywood buds. Clara Bow and Barbara Stanwyck were the first to stake out their turf in what would become the **Malibu Colony** (Map pp80–1). Privacy-seeking A-listers, including Leo, Britney, Jennifer and many others are or have been colonyites, owning or renting houses for as much as $25,000 per month. While it's impossible to get past the gate without a personal invitation from a resident, you could always join the paparazzi on the beach – just stay below the high-tide mark. For photogenic birds-eye views of the colony, head a little up the coast to **Malibu Bluffs Park**.

Meanwhile, the chances of spotting Leo by the wine racks or Brangelina in the toy store are greatest at the **Malibu Country Mart** (Map pp80-1; 3835 Cross Creek Rd), a villagelike outdoor mall, and the more utilitarian **Malibu Colony Plaza** (Map pp80-1; 23841 W Malibu Rd).

Despite its wealth and star quotient, the best way to appreciate Malibu is through its natural assets, so grab your sunscreen and a towel and head to the beach. Point Dume and Zuma are especially nice and teem with tight-bods on summer weekends. You may strike gold and find free parking on the Pacific Coast Hwy (PCH; check signs for restrictions), but otherwise parking lots charge between $6 to $10, depending on the time of year. On summer weekends, they often fill up by midday.

During the cooler months, hitting the trails of the Santa Monica Mountains National Recreation Area, including Malibu Creek State Park (p153) is a ticket to sanity for many locals. For access, consider using the ParkLINK Shuttle (see boxed text, below).

MALIBU PIER & AROUND

The vintage **pier** marks the beginning of Malibu's commercial heart. It's open for strolling

---

LINK TO NATURE

An eco-conscious way to explore the rugged Santa Monica Mountains rising behind Malibu is by hopping aboard the free **ParkLINK Shuttle** (888-734-2323; www.parklinkshuttle.com; 8am-8pm Jun-Aug, 8am-5pm Sep-May). Air-conditioned buses make stops near the Adamson House, Zuma and Point Dume beaches and major trailheads, including Malibu Creek State Park and the Paramount Ranch (p153). Or just stay aboard and complete the scenic loop in 1¾ hours. The website has a map, bus schedule and ideas for one-way hikes made easy by using the shuttle.

---

and fishing (no license required) and delivers fine views of the surf punks hooking gnarly waves off **Surfrider Beach**, one of the world's most famous surf spots. Malibu Creek meets the ocean here in what is officially known as **Malibu Lagoon State Beach** (Map pp80-1; 818-880-0350; www.parks.ca.gov; P wi-fi). The resulting saltwater marsh is a favorite with migratory birds and their human admirers. Bring a picnic and binoculars and grab a spot in the sand or at a picnic table near Malibu Creek Bridge. Unfortunately, the water quality is usually terrible, so swimmers should push on further north (never mind the surfers).

Up on a bluff overlooking Surfrider is the gorgeous Spanish-style **Adamson House** (Map pp80-1; 310-456-8432; www.adamsonhouse.org; 23200 PCH; adult/child $5/2; tours 11am-2pm Wed-Sat), which used to belong to the Rindge family and is awash in locally made, hand-painted tiles. Check out the 'Persian rug' in the entryway and the tiled dog bath outside. To learn more about Malibu's arc of history – Chumash to glamourtown – pop into the adjacent **Malibu Lagoon Museum** (Map pp80-1; 310-456-8432; admission free; 11am-3pm Wed-Sat).

Tile aficionados and hideaway fans should cross PCH and head up to the **Serra Retreat** (Map pp80-1; 310-456-6631; www.serraretreat.com; 3401 Serra Rd; admission free; 9am-4:30pm), another former Rindge home that is now a religious sanctuary. We recently spotted Martin Sheen, Malibu honorary mayor and a devout Catholic, chatting with one of the Franciscan friars in the lovely ocean-view gardens. You're free to walk around and enjoy the flowers and the views, but respect the tranquil, hushed ambience. The Serra Rd turn-off is about a quarter mile west of the Malibu Pier (look for the sign and tell the guard you're going to the retreat). The road winds through another celebrity enclave where Britney unloaded her home for a cool $12 million in 2007.

NORTHERN MALIBU

Self-assuredly holding court atop a grassy slope where deer graze at sundown, **Pepperdine University** (Map pp80-1; 310-456-4000; 24255 Pacific Coast Hwy) has views of the Pacific and the mountains and is easily one of the world's most beautiful campuses. Ken Starr, the independent investigator who revealed to the world where Bill Clinton put his cigars, teaches constitutional law at this private institution affiliated with the Church of Christ.

MALIBU BEACHES FOR ALL

Malibu's locals, famous for their love of privacy, don't want you to know this, but you're actually free to be on any beach as long as you stay below the high-tide line. That means you can walk, swim, beachcomb or whatever right on Carbon Beach, Broad Beach and wherever the famous like to frolic. You may get nasty looks from security guards, but there's nothing they can legally do to stop you from being there. Driving along PCH, keep an eye out for the brown Coastal Access signs. Locals have been known to take them down and put up 'Private Beach' or 'No Trespassing' signs; don't be deterred. For the full scoop and 'secret' access points, download the handy map and guide from www.laurbanrangers.org.

Art fans should check out the latest show at the university's **Frederick R Weisman Museum of Art** (Map pp80-1; ☎ 310-506-4851; www.pepperdine.edu /arts/museum; admission free; 🕑 11am-5pm Tue-Sun; **P**), which has some pretty edgy works created by American artists in the last 30 years.

One of the most beautiful drives through the Santa Monica Mountains starts right next to Pepperdine on **Malibu Canyon Rd**, which cuts through Malibu Creek State Park, bisects Mulholland Hwy (beyond which it's called Las Virgenes Rd) and joins with the 101 (Ventura Fwy) near Agoura Hills. Tucked behind some trees about 11 miles north of Pepperdine is the enchanting **Malibu Hindu Temple** (Map pp80-1; ☎ 818-880-5552; www.hindutemplemalibu.com; 1600 Las Virgenes Canyon Rd; admission free; 🕑 9am-noon & 5-8pm Mon-Fri, 9am-8pm Sat & Sun, closes 7pm Nov-Mar; **P**). Visitors are welcome, but should dress modestly. On weekends, the temple kitchen serves simple vegetarian meals ($5 donation) served from Styrofoam boxes.

Pacific Palisades

Pacific Palisades, founded by Methodists in the 1920s, is an upscale neighborhood with a small-town feel, high celebrity quotient and the Getty Villa blockbuster sight. Strolling along Sunset Blvd and its side streets you may well spot local residents Tom Hanks, Hillary Swank or Britney Spears picking up organic chocolates at **Intemperantia** (15324 Antioch St), a novel at the indie **Village Books** (1049 Swarthmore Ave) or a grilled veggie sandwich at **Café Vida Popular** (15317 Antioch St).

In the 1930s, the Palisades' gorgeous setting and Mediterranean charm lured numerous European exiles, including writers Thomas Mann and Lion Feuchtwanger. High up in the hills above Sunset Blvd, Feuchtwanger's old home, the **Villa Aurora** (Map pp80-1; ☎ 310-456-4231; www.villa-aurora.org; 520 Paseo Miramar), is now a German-American art and cultural center.

GETTY VILLA
Although self-described as the **Getty Villa Malibu** (Map pp80-1; ☎ 310-440-7300; www.getty.edu; 17985 Pacific Coast Hwy; admission free; **P**), this famous museum in a replica Roman villa is actually in Pacific Palisades. It's a stunning showcase for exquisite Greek, Roman and Etruscan antiquities amassed by oil tycoon J Paul Getty. When it reopened in 2006 after a seven-year renovation, the institution immediately found egg on its face when allegations of illegally obtained treasures surfaced (see boxed text, opposite). Although dozens of items have since been returned to Italy, there's plenty left, engagingly organized by themes such as 'Gods and Goddesses' and 'Monsters and Deities'. The TimeScape Room lends historical context to the various periods of artistic development. Kids can learn about life in ancient times at the Family Forum and encounter heroes, gods and giants on a special audio tour. Upstairs galleries house temporary exhibits. The upper balcony also has the best view of the lovely courtyard garden and reflecting pool.

Admission is by timed ticket, available by phone or online. No walk-ins unless you arrive by public bus and ask the driver to hole-punch your villa ticket. Parking costs $8.

WILL ROGERS STATE HISTORIC PARK
Rugged but small, this **park** (Map pp80-1; www .parks.ca.gov/default.asp?page_id=626; 🕑 8am-sunset; **P** wi-fi) sprawls across ranch land once owned by Will Rogers (1875–1935), an Oklahoma-born cowboy turned humorist, radio-show host and movie star. In the late '20s he traded his Beverly Hills manse for a 31-room **ranch house** (☎ 310-454-8212; admission free; tours 🕑 11am, 1pm & 2pm Tue-Sun) and lived here until his tragic 1935 death by plane crash. Following extensive renovations, guided tours allow you to again nose around the Western art and Native American rugs and baskets and marvel

at the porch swing right in the living room. Parking costs $7.

The park's chaparral-cloaked hills, where Rogers used to ride his horses, are lined with trails and offer an easy escape from the LA hubbub. The best time for a ramble is late in the day when the setting sun delivers golden views of the mountains, city and ocean from **Inspiration Point**, reached after an easy-to-moderate 1.5 miles trek. Trails continue along the Backbone Trail into Topanga State Park, if you're feeling ambitious.

A big polo fan, Rogers built his own field to yee-haw it with such famous buddies as Spencer Tracy, Gary Cooper and Walt Disney. The **Will Rogers Polo Club** (☎ 310-454-8212; www .willrogerspolo.org; admission free; ☷ 2pm Sat, 10am Sun late Apr-early Oct) still plays in the park on what is LA's only remaining polo field.

SELF-REALIZATION FELLOWSHIP LAKE SHRINE

No matter what your religious persuasion is, any negative vibes just seem to disappear while strolling these paradisiacal **grounds** (Map pp80-1; ☎ 310-454-4114; www.yogananda-srf.org /temples/lakeshrine; 17190 Sunset Blvd; admission free; ☷ 9am-4:30pm Tue-Sat, 12:30-4:30pm Sun; ℗). Paths meander around a spring-fed lake and past

clumps of flowers and swaying palms windmill-turned-chapel, where George F rison's memorial was held, and a shri containing some of the ashes of Mahatm. Ghandi. The fellowship was founded in 1920 by charismatic yogi Paramahansa Yogananda and blends traditions of Christian and Eastern religions. Overlooking the garden is the hilltop temple, crowned by a gilded lotus, where anyone can attend the lectures, meditations and services.

EAMES HOUSE & STUDIO

The striking **Eames House & Studio** (Map p92; ☎ 310-459-9663; www.eamesfoundation.org; 203 Chautauqua Blvd; suggested donation $5; ☷ 10am-4pm Mon-Fri, 10am-3pm Sat; ℗), built in 1949 by Charles and Ray Eames, resembles a Mondrian painting in 3-D. It's still used by the Eames family, but with at least 48-hour advance reservations you can study the exterior, walk around the garden and peek through the window into the kitchen and living room.

While here also have a look at the adjacent 1949 **Entenza House** (Map p92; 205 Chautauqua Blvd), a huge gleaming-white jumble by Charles Eames and Eero Saarinen; the best view is across the wall from the Eames House garden. Richard Neutra designed the nearby **Bailey**

GETTYGATE

It should have been a moment as triumphant and glorious as a Dionysian wedding depicted on a Grecian vase. Yet, the reopening of the Getty Villa in January 2006 had all the earmarks of a Greek tragedy. The world-famous institution found itself embroiled in an epic controversy about the true origin of dozens of its ancient treasures, including a famous statue of Aphrodite. Had some of them been looted from Italian archaeological digs and illegally spirited out of the country by shady art dealers? The Italian government seemed to think so and, in 2005, indicted Marion True, the Getty's former head of antiquities, alleging that she conspired with European art dealers and knowingly acquired stolen pieces. One of the dealers, Giacomo Medici, has already been sentenced to 10 years in prison and was fined €10 million. At press time, the Italian government had dropped civil charges against True and accused coconspirator Robert Hecht, but the criminal trial was still ongoing. Even if convicted, it's highly unlikely that either will serve jail time; True because she's an American citizen and Hecht because – at age 88 – he's considered too old.

Both maintain their innocence but, if anything, the case has firmly trained the spotlight on the 'don't-ask-don't-tell' practice that's long been commonplace in the art world. Although there are international laws in place against the illegal trafficking of cultural property, they are rarely enforced. That's why 'Gettygate' has made other museum curators quite nervous. The Italians have already come knocking on the doors of the Museum of Fine Arts in Boston and the Metropolitan Museum in New York, both of which will be returning several artifacts.

And so will the Getty. In August 2007, Getty director Michael Brand, agreed to send 40 of the 46 disputed pieces back to Italy, including Aphrodite (which will remain on display until 2010, however). The move will leave major holes in the collection, which the Italian government agreed to plug with long-term loans.

ts 123

LOS ANGELES

...nica

...onica is the belle by the beach, the ...t among LA's seaside cities, hemmed ...y luxe beachfront hotels and sprinkled with Kobe-burger restaurants and $100–T-shirt boutiques. It wasn't always so. A few years ago, that person talking to himself was probably an unhinged homeless guy, not some exec barking into his Bluetooth. Gentrification is everywhere. It's in the downtown area where condo-office-store combos are swallowing up every available open space. It's in the brand-new library with its stunning design and technology. And it's in the new **Madison Performing Arts Center** (www.smc.edu/Madison; 1310 11th St), a state-of-the-art midsize venue designed by Renzo Zecchetto; it's expected to open in 2008. Its chief fundraiser? Santa Monica College alumnus and two-time Oscar winner Dustin Hoffman.

Visitors love Santa Monica for its early-20th-century pier, excellent shopping and dining, and miles of sandy beaches wider than a football field is long. And if downtown with its retail chains feels too busy and vanilla, head to Montana Ave and Main St, which preserve small-town flair, albeit that of a very rich small town.

For visitors, Santa Monica is a central, safe and fun base for exploring LA. Parking is free for two hours at the four large public parking garages on 2nd and 4th Sts between Broadway and Wilshire Blvd. For Main St, the lot at Ocean and Hollister Ave has inexpensive metered parking. The electric Tide Shuttle (25¢ per ride) makes a loop from downtown to the beach, Main St and back every 15 minutes from noon to 8pm (to 10pm Friday and Saturday).

SANTA MONICA PIER

You'll instantly recognize it from film and TV: the neon-lit arch of the **Santa Monica Pier** (Map p92; ☎ 310-458-8900; www.santamonicapier.org; admission free; ⊙ 24hr; Ⓟ ⑤), which has entertained the plebs since 1908 and is the oldest amusement pier in California. Feel the ocean breeze as you stroll past snack shacks, a game arcade, entertainers and anglers to the far tip where the entire arc of the bay from Malibu to Palos Verdes unfolds before you. On summer nights, the pier comes alive with free concerts (Twilight Dance Series, p200) and movies (Santa Monica Drive-In, p197).

Kids get their kicks at **Pacific Park** (Map p92; ☎ 310-260-8744; www.pacpark.com; admission free; ⊙ 11am-11pm Sun-Thu, 11am-12:30am Fri & Sat Jun-Aug, shorter hr Sep-May; ⑤), a small amusement park with a solar-powered Ferris wheel, kiddy rides, midway games and food concessions. Rides cost between $1.50 and $4.50 each; a day of unlimited spins costs $20/11 (over/under 42in tall); check the website for discount coupons.

Near the pier entrance, nostalgic souls and their offspring can giddy up the beautifully hand-painted horses of the 1922 **merry-go-round** (Map p92; ☎ 310-395-4248; rides adult/child $1/0.50; ⊙ 11am-5pm Mon-Thu, 11am-7pm Fri-Sun, closed Tue & Wed Jan–mid-Mar) featured in the movie *The Sting*.

Peer under the pier – just below the carousel – for Heal the Bay's **Santa Monica Pier Aquarium** (Map p92; ☎ 310-393-6149; www.healthebay.org/smpa; admission by donation, suggested/minimum $5/2, child under 12 free; ⊙ 2-6pm Tue-Fri, 12:30-6pm Sat & Sun; ⑤). Sea stars, crabs, sea urchins and other critters and crustaceans scooped from the bay stand by to be petted – ever so gently, please – in their adopted touch tank homes.

South of the pier is the **Original Muscle Beach** (Map p92), where the Southern California exercise craze began in the mid-20th century, and new equipment now draws a new generation of fitness fanatics. Nearby, the search for the next Bobby Fischer is on at the **International Chess Park**. Anyone can join in. Following the **South Bay Bicycle Trail** (p152), a paved bike and walking path, south for about 1½ miles takes you straight to Venice Beach. Bike or in-line skate rentals are available on the pier and at beachside kiosks.

NOSMO KING IN SANTA MONICA

Smokers need to keep their cravings in check when visiting Santa Monica. In November 2006, the city put in one of the toughest anti-smoking laws in the country. Smoking is now prohibited in all outdoor restaurants and bars, on the beach, the Santa Monica Pier, Third Street Promenade, bus stops and within 20ft of any building open to the public. Violators risk getting a $250 fine.

THIRD STREET PROMENADE

Stretching for three long blocks between Broadway and Wilshire Blvd, **Third Street Promenade** is a case study on how to morph a dilapidated, dying main street into a dynamic and happening strip. It offers carefree and car-free strolling accompanied by the sound of flamenco guitar or hip-hop courtesy of street performers. You can grab a bite, catch a movie and browse the Gap or Zara. And every Wednesday and Saturday, hobby cooks and professional chefs jostle for the freshest foods at the farmers market (p209). It's a lively and dynamic zone except for Santa Monica Place, the shopping mall at the end of it, which is expected to be replaced by an open-plan mall before too long.

MAIN STREET

Retail therapy gets a fun twist along Main St, which is lined with owner-run boutiques and galleries that are light years from chainstore conformity. As you browse around, keep an eye out for Frank Gehry's playfully postmodern **Edgemar Center for the Arts** (p204), a former ice factory turned sculptural complex and cultural venue. For a trip back in time, check out the latest exhibit at the **California Heritage Museum** (Map p92; ☎ 310-392-8537; www .californiaheritagemuseum.org; 2612 Main St; adult/student & senior/child under 12 $5/3/free; ⏰ 11am-4pm Wed-Sun; P), housed in one of Santa Monica's few surviving grand Victorian mansions. Curators do a fine job presenting pottery, colorful tile, Craftsman furniture, folk art, vintage surfboards and other fine collectibles in as dynamic a fashion as possible. To see locals at play, come during the Sunday morning farmers market (p209) in the museum's parking lot.

SANTA MONICA MUSEUM OF ART

A saucy and irreverent home of edgy art and community events, this small **museum** (Map p92; ☎ 310-586-6488; www.smmoa.org; Bergamot Station, Bldg G1; suggested donation $5; ⏰ 11am-6pm Tue-Fri, 11am-8pm Sat; P) gives exposure to both local and national artists working with new and experimental media. Cool gift shop. It's part of the Bergamot Station Arts Center (p208), a cluster of galleries and arty shops.

GEHRY HOUSE

In his creative life before the Walt Disney Concert Hall, Frank Gehry was primarily known as that crazy guy who sculpted houses from chain-link fencing, plywood and corrugated aluminum. A great place to see the 'early Gehry' is his 1979 **private home** (Map p92; 1002 22nd St), a deconstructivist postmodern collage that architecture-critic Paul Heyer called a 'collision of parts.' Neighbors were none too pleased about it at first, but that was before Gehry had claimed his spot in the pantheon of contemporary architects.

Venice

If you weren't around in the hippie days, inhale an incense-scented whiff in Venice, a boho beach town and haven for artists, New Agers, homeless people and free spirits of all stripes. This is where Jim Morrison and the Doors lit their fire, where Arnold Schwarzenegger pumped himself to stardom and where Julia Roberts, Dennis Hopper and Angelica Huston make their homes today.

SoCal's quintessential bohemian playground is the legacy of Abbot Kinney (1850–1920). A tobacco mogul by trade and a dreamer at heart, Kinney dug canals and turned fetid swampland into a cultural and recreational resort he dubbed 'Venice of America'. For nearly two decades, crowds thronged to this 'Coney Island on the Pacific' to be poled around by imported gondoliers, walk among Renaissance-style arcaded buildings and listen to Benny Goodman tooting his horn in clubs. But time was not kind to Kinney's vision.

Most of the canals were filled and paved over in 1929 and Venice soon plunged into a steep decline until its cheap rents and mellow vibe drew first the beatniks, then hippies in the '50s and '60s. A few years later, Venice turned 'Dogtown' as modern skateboarding hit the big time. These days, there are pockets of gentrification, but overall it's still a low-key enclave with a strong sense of community. Think indie boutiques instead of cookie-cutter malls and not a Starbucks in sight. There's plenty of innovative architecture and public art but no traditional attractions as such, making the area great for independent exploring.

Abbot Kinney Blvd has street parking, while parking lots on and near the beach charge between $6 and $12 per entry.

VENICE BOARDWALK

Life in Venice moves to a different rhythm and nowhere more so than on the famous

Venice Boardwalk (btwn Venice Pier to Rose Ave; admission free; ☺ 24hr; ♿), officially known as Ocean Front Walk. It's a freak show, a human zoo and a wacky carnival, but as far as LA experiences go, it's a must. This is where to get your hair braided, your karma corrected or your back massaged qi gong–style. Encounters with budding Schwarzeneggers, hoop dreamers, a Speedo-clad snake charmer and a roller-skating Sikh minstrel are pretty much guaranteed, especially on hot summer days. The Sunday-afternoon drum circle draws hundreds of revelers for tribal playing and spontaneous dancing. If the noise doesn't show you the way there, just follow your nose towards whiffs of 'wacky tabaccy.' Alas, the boardwalk vibe gets a bit sketchy after dark.

VENICE CANALS

Even many Angelenos have no idea that just a couple of blocks away from the Boardwalk madness is an idyllic neighborhood that preserves 3 miles of Kinney's canals. The **Venice Canal Walk** threads past eclectic homes, bridges and waterways where ducks preen and locals lollygag in little row boats. It's best accessed from either Venice or Washington Blvds, near Dell Ave.

ABBOT KINNEY BLVD

Kinney would probably be delighted to find that one of Venice's most individualistic streets bears his name. Sort of a seaside Melrose with a Venetian flavor, the mile-long stretch of **Abbot Kinney Blvd** between Venice Blvd and Main St is chockablock with unique boutiques, galleries, vintage-clothing stores and interesting restaurants, including Axe (p182), Joe's (p183) and Abbot's Pizza (p182). In late September, the Abbot Kinney Festival (p161) draws thousands of revelers.

Marina del Rey

As the name suggests, Marina del Rey is really all about the water and has nearly as many boats as residents. Some 5300 vessels – funky live-aboards to sport-fishing crafts to experimental vessels – bob gaily in what is one of the largest artificial small-craft harbors in the country. Wrested from coastal wetlands in the '60s, the surrounding neighborhood consists mostly of generic concrete towers and has that disjointed, sterile feel typical of urban planning during the Modernist era. As an architectural case study, the Marina has its appeal, but the rest of us are really here to get active in what is truly an aquatic playground.

You could skim across the waves on jet skis, kayaks and surfboards or rent a yacht and sail away into the sunset. Feeling romantic? Tour the harbor on a leisurely dinner cruise. Adventurous? Head out to the open sea to hook sea bass or halibut. For swimming, there's the aptly named **Mother's Beach** (Map p92) perfect for relaxing while your wee ones play safely in the calm and shallow waters. And in winter,

---

VENICE ART WALK

Who needs galleries when you've got great outdoor art? Venice has plenty of both, so keep your eyes open as you stroll around town (and let us know your favorite finds!). A leisurely tour might start at the corner of Rose Ave and Main St where Jonathan Borofsky's 30ft tutu-clad **Ballerina Clown** (1989) offers up a surreal presence. One block south, Frank-Gehry's **Chiat/Day** office building is fronted by massive binoculars by Claes Oldenburg and Coosje van Bruggen.

But Venice's real strength is its murals. Fine specimens along the Venice Boardwalk include **Chagall Returns to Venice Beach** (1996; 201 Ocean Front Walk at Ozone Ave) by Christina Schlesinger, and **Venice Reconstituted** (1989; 25 Windward Ave) by Rip Cronk. The latter is a parody of Botticelli's *Venus in the Halfshell* and a cacophony of figures, many of them real Venetians. As you walk around, you'll find lots more Cronk murals. His **Homage to a Starry Night** (1990; Ocean Front Walk at Wavecrest Ave) was inspired by the Van Gogh original. The same artist also created the epic 30ft-high portraits of one-time Venice resident **Jim Morrison** (titled *Morning Shot*; 1991; 1881 Speedway) and of city-founder **Abbot Kinney** (2004; N Venice at Pacific Ave).

With such a strong mural tradition, it only makes sense that the nonprofit **Social & Public Art Resource Center** (SPARC; ☎ 310-822-9560; www.sparcmurals.org; 685 S Venice Blvd; admission free; ☺ 10am-6pm Mon-Fri), which promotes, preserves and produces public murals throughout LA, is based in Venice. Its gallery and bookstore are well worth a look if you're interested in this type of art.

you can come nose to nose with friendly grays on a whale-watching cruise. For specifics, see the Tours section starting on p158.

Most boats, including a daily ferry to Catalina Island (p220), leave from **Fisherman's Village** (off Map p92; ☎ 310-823-5411; 13755 Fiji Way), a cutesy strip of candy-colored Cape Cod–style cottages filled with tacky gift shops and forgettable restaurants. North of here, the small Burton Chace Park is a good spot for a picnic, flipping a Frisbee, flying a kite or watching the parade of boats sailing through the Main Channel. In July and August, there's a free concert series on Thursday and Saturday evenings (p200).

The same months also see the WaterBus in operation, a fun way to get around the Marina. It makes six strategic stops, including at Fisherman's Village and the park, and costs $1 per boarding or $5 for a day pass.

Just south of Marina del Rey, the **Ballona Wetlands** (off Map p92) are the last remaining wetlands in LA County and are home to hundreds of bird species, including the great blue heron. Their habitat, however, has shrunk significantly since construction began on Playa Vista, a custom-planned luxury community for about 11,000 residents.

There's free and metered street parking throughout the Marina.

South Bay Beaches

South of LAX, Santa Monica Bay is home to a trio of all-American beach towns – Manhattan Beach, Hermosa Beach and Redondo Beach – far removed from the grit and velocity of urban LA. Lovely if not lavish homes come down all the way to the gorgeous white beach, which is the prime attraction here. The beach is paralleled by the **South Bay Bicycle Trail** (p152).

Tourism has been filling local coffers since land baron and railroad tycoon Henry Huntington connected the beach towns to LA with his Pacific Electric Railway in 1905. Even today, attractions here are recreational rather than cultural.

MANHATTAN BEACH

The birthplace of surf music and beach volleyball, Manhattan Beach has gone chic, hip and happening. Its downtown area along Manhattan Beach Blvd has seen an explosion of trendy restaurants, boutiques and hotels. Many of them cluster in the new

Metlox Plaza (Manhattan Beach Blvd & Valley Dr), a small and upscale outdoor mall built on the site of a former pottery. Besides the Greek restaurant Petros (p184) and a True Religion premium denim flagship store, there's Shade (p171), the South Bay's first designer boutique hotel whose bar often spills over with starlets streaming in from the nearby Raleigh Studios where *Boston Legal* and *CSI Miami* are shot.

Still, even with this Hollywood-ification, Manhattan is still undeniably a seaside enclave with plenty of beach and surf action around the pier. Every August, thousands of babes in bikinis and hunks in trunks park themselves in the sacred sand to cheer on the pros during the **Manhattan Beach Open** (www.avp .com), the world's oldest and most prestigious volleyball tournament (played since 1960). Go to Marine Ave to see them practice year-round.

Family-fun awaits at the compact **Roundhouse Marine Studies Lab & Aquarium** (Map p94; ☎ 310-379-8117; www.roundhouseaquarium.org; suggested donation $2; ⏰ 3pm-sunset Mon-Fri, 10am-sunset Sat & Sun; 🚻) at the end of the 928ft-long pier. Pet a slimy sea cucumber, see Nemo the clownfish up close and check out the new deep-ocean tank with its sheephead, anemones and sunflower starfish. The upstairs Kids' Kelp Corner is stocked with games, books and playthings. Storytelling and crafts sessions are held at 11:30am on Sundays.

There's metered parking at the base of the pier for $1 per hour and a public parking garage on Valley Dr between Manhattan Beach Blvd and 13th St.

HERMOSA BEACH

Strolling down Hermosa Beach's **Pier Ave** on a summer weekend, you're immediately struck by two things: everybody's wearing flip-flops, tiny tees and a tan, and they all seem to be having way too much fun. The short, car-free strip is party central in a small town that's always lived the easy life. Once home to long-haired hippies and underground punk bands like Black Flag, it's now solidly ruled by hormone-crazed surfer dudes and the chicks that dig 'em. The beach is indeed *muy hermosa* (Spanish for beautiful) – long, flat and dotted with permanent volleyball nets. Go to 16th St to see local pros bump, set and spike in preparation for the **AVP Hermosa Open** (www .avp.com) in July.

LOS ANGELES

Hermosa is one of several towns claiming to be the birthplace of surfing and even has its own Surfers Walk of Fame, but in 2006 the official nod went to Huntington Beach (p256).

Every Memorial Day and Labor Day weekend (see p414 for dates), Hermosa's three-day **Fiesta Hermosa** (www.fiestahermosa.com), with music, food, kiddy rides and a huge arts-and-crafts fair, attracts large throngs of revelers.

REDONDO BEACH

Depending on your point of view, Redondo Beach is either depressingly grotty or refreshingly unglitzy. The action hub is the **Redondo Beach Pier** (www.redondopier.com), which arches from the bottom of Torrance Blvd all the way to **King Harbor**. The latter is an aesthetically challenged 1960s multilevel concrete construction but has a cool beer bar (Naja's Place, p193) and **Quality Seafood**, a fish and seafood shop where you can have your purchase cooked up, then sit at a picnic table to eat it.

From the same period is the **Seaside Lagoon** (Map p94; ☎ 310-318-0681; www.redondo.org/seaside lagoon; 200 Portofino Way at Harbor Dr; adult/child $4.50/3.25; ☆ 10am-5:45pm late May-early Sep; Ⓟ), a large, shallow saltwater outdoor pool with a slide and cascading fountain. It usually teems with an ethnic potpourri of families frolicking in the sand or picnicking in the grass. Alas, the lagoon's days may be numbered as the aging facility has difficulty meeting today's high water standards. Parking costs $4.25.

To see Redondo's more upscale side, you have to travel a couple of miles south to **Riviera Village** (www.rivieravillage.org; S Catalina Ave btwn Ave I & Elena Ave), at the foot of the Palos Verdes Peninsula. It's a lovely strip with indie boutiques, great restaurants like Zazou (p183) and Green Temple (p183) and the book-filled **Coffee Cartel** (1820 S Catalina Ave) for relaxed java-refueling sessions.

Palos Verdes Peninsula

The most absurdly beautiful coastal stretch in all of LA is not in Malibu or Santa Monica but on the little-known Palos Verdes Peninsula (PV in local jargon), a terraced promontory that captivates with equal drama and grace. Cruise along **Palos Verdes Dr** (Map pp82-3), especially at sunset, for awesome eyefuls of the shoreline. Steep cliffs tumble down to rocky shores and secluded coves as the roadway ribbons past rambling multi-

million-dollar mansions where horses graze lazily. Catalina Island looms hazily across the sparkling Pacific.

This is great kayaking, snorkeling, diving and surfing territory, but coastal access is a bit cumbersome and locals can be territorial. In fact, the only easily accessible beach is **Malaga Cove**, aka RAT (as in 'Right After Torrance') Beach (p154). This is also the famous Haggerty's surf spot mentioned in the Beach Boys' hit *Surfin' USA*. Turn right on Via Almar, drive to the free parking lot, then look for the trail down to the beach near the gazebo.

Further on, Palos Verdes Dr skirts the gleaming white 1926 **Point Vicente Lighthouse** (Map pp82-3; ☎ 310-541-0334; www.palosverdes.com /pvlight; Ⓟ), which was staffed until 1971. These days electronic sensors activate the fog horn; the ghostly hooting must drive nearby residents batty. You can peek inside from 11am to 3pm on the second Saturday of the month (free).

Captain Ahab is no match for the binocular-toting whale-watchers gathering at the adjacent **Point Vicente Interpretive Center** (Map pp82-3; ☎ 310-377-5370; 31501 Palos Verdes Dr W; admission free, donations appreciated; ☆ 10am-5pm; Ⓟ) between December and April. The revamped center has fun exhibits for boning up on the Pacific gray whale and its fascinating migration from Alaska to Mexico. Follow up your visit with a picnic beneath palm trees and a stroll along the blufftop trail.

Scenes from *Pirates of the Caribbean* and other movies were filmed just south of here at Long Point, a coastal terrace being turned into **Terranea** (Map pp82-3), a vast luxury resort of vacation villas and a golf academy. Eager buyers plunked down an average of 2.4 million per unit and the first 51 sold like hot cakes in just 2½ hours. A trail leads down to the pebbly beach from the free **Point Vicente Fishing Access** (Map pp82-3) parking lot. There's some tide-pooling here but the best place to hunt for starfish, anemones and other shoreline critters is at **Abalone Cove Shoreline Park** (Map pp82-3; ☆ 9am-4pm; Ⓟ), a rock-strewn eco-preserve one mile further on. The walk down to the beach gets pretty steep in some sections, so watch your footing. Parking costs $6.

Palos Verdes' most stunning non-natural attraction is the **Wayfarers Chapel** (Map pp82-3; ☎ 310-377-1650; www.wayfarerschapel.org; 5755 Palos

Verdes Dr S; admission free; 🕙 8am-5pm; P) across the road. Built by Lloyd Wright (son of Frank) in 1951, it's a glass church cradled by soaring redwood trees. Not surprisingly, this seaside sanctuary is an insanely popular spot to tie the knot, so avoid coming on weekends. During weddings you're still free to roam the grounds but you can't get inside the chapel.

Before leaving PV, floweristas should head inland to the **South Coast Botanic Garden** (Map pp82-3; ☎ 310-544-1948; www.southcoast botanicgarden.org; 26300 Crenshaw Blvd; adult/child 5-12/student $7/2.50/5; 🕙 9am-5pm; P), which has been reclaimed from a former landfill. So when you see all those fruit trees, redwoods, roses, dahlias and some other 2000 species, remember you're actually standing on a huge pile of trash. A tram operates on the weekends, and plant shows and sales take place year-round.

San Pedro

Amid the glitz and sprawl of Los Angeles, the port town of San Pedro (San *Pee*-dro) keeps it real. A slice of 1960s small-town America, its high street is devoid of chain-store clutter, down-to-earth locals ask how you're doing and actually mean it, and restored vintage cars time-warp you back to *American Graffiti* days. Despite some sprucing up, especially along 6th and 7th Sts in the historic downtown, an air of working-class grit remains, and so do many of the dive bars where Charles Bukowski probably ruined his liver. LA's late, great bad-boy poet now rests in **Green Hills Memorial Park** (Map pp82-3; 27501 S Western Ave; Ocean View plot 875; P).

'San Pedro is real quiet', Bukowski once observed. That's still true today, except for the distant clanging of containers being hoisted on and off gigantic cargo vessels at Worldport LA, the world's third-busiest container port after Singapore and Hong Kong. LA's own 'Golden Gate', the 1500ft-long suspended **Vincent Thomas Bridge** links San Pedro with Terminal Island.

Not surprisingly, most local attractions are situated along the waterfront, which is served by the **electric trolley** (all-day fare $1; 🕙 10am-6pm Fri-Mon). On the first Thursday of every month, historic downtown livens up during the **San Pedro Art Walk** (www.1stthursday .com; 🕙 6-9pm). Check the website for further details.

CABRILLO MARINE AQUARIUM

This city-owned **aquarium** (Map pp82-3; ☎ 310-548-7562; www.cabrilloaq.org; 3720 Stephen White Dr; suggested donation adult/child $5/1; 🕙 noon-5pm Tue-Fri, 10am-5pm Sat & Sun; P 🚻) is the smaller, older, less frantic and high-tech cousin of Long Beach's Aquarium of the Pacific (p131). It's also a lot lighter on your wallet and probably less overwhelming for small children. Spiky urchins, slippery sea cucumbers, magical jellyfish and other local denizens will bring smiles to even the most PlayStation-jaded youngster. Naturalists lead rambles around the rocky tide pools and salt marshes and organize all sorts of other educational programs, including the grunion-watches (April to July; see boxed text, p130).

LOS ANGELES MARITIME MUSEUM & AROUND

For a salty introduction to the area, visit this endearing but notoriously short-staffed **museum** (Map pp82-3; ☎ 310-548-7618; www.lamaritime museum.org; Berth 84; adult/child & senior $3/1; 🕙 10am-5pm Tue-Sat, noon-5pm Sun). Galleries set up in a historic ferry building tell the story of LA's relationship with the sea and display enough ship models (including an 18ft cutaway of the *Titanic*), figureheads and navigational equipment to keep your imagination afloat for an hour or two.

If you enjoy clambering around old ships, head a mile north to the **SS Lane Victory** (Map pp82-3; ☎ 310-519-9545; www.lanevictory.org; Berth 94; adult/child $3/1; 🕙 9am-3pm), a museum vessel that sailed the seven seas from 1945 to 1971. Self-guided tours take in the engine room and the cargo holds.

Further south, you'll be besieged by shrieking gulls and excited children at **Ports O'Call Village** (Map pp82-3; ☎ 310-732-7696; Berth 77; admission free; 🕙 from 11am-10pm). Skip the trinket stores and fill up on fresh fish and shrimp at the raucous San Pedro Fish Market & Restaurant (p184). Afterwards, hop on a port cruise or join a whale-watching trip (January to March; see p158 for details).

POINT FERMIN PARK & AROUND

Locals come to this grassy, blufftop community park to jog, picnic, watch windsurfers and kite-boarders or to enjoy jazzy tunes on balmy summer nights (see p200). Ostensibly the main visitor attraction is the restored 1874 wooden **Point Fermin Lighthouse** (Map pp82-3;

SEX ON THE BEACH

It's raw, primal, juicy and has thousands of participants. Drawn by the sexual tuggings of the full or new moon, countless writhing bodies hit the beaches of Southern California every summer, drawing gaping crowds of voyeurs. But lest you think this annual beachside orgy involves the gyrations of nubile teens, let it be known that we're talking about a phenomenon known as the 'running of the grunions'. These flagrant sexual champions are indeed – fish.

Grunions – like Mexicans, Germans and Oklahomans – are somehow mystically drawn to the warmth of Southern California, and for the very best of reasons. It's along these local beaches that 'scouts' from the endless offshore schools swim up to check out the conditions. If these are favorable, they send the 'all clear' signal whereupon the grunion minions begin to thrash upon the water's edge. The females half bury themselves tail-first in the sand and within moments have deposited their eggs. Then come multiple worthy male suitors to fertilize them to assure the next dynasty of grunion-hood.

The website www.grunion.org has information, dates and locations for where the grunions are expected to show up. First-timers should join the hugely popular grunion watches organized by the Cabrillo Marine Museum in San Pedro (p129). And no, they don't mind if you watch. All you need is a flashlight, bare feet and a sense of demure decency. Even fish deserve their 'private moments'.

☎ 310-241-0684; www.pointferminlighthouse.org; admission by donation; ☼ 1-4pm Tue-Sun), one of the oldest in the West, but we think the **Walker Café** (Map pp82-3; ☎ 310-833-3623; 700 Paseo del Mar; ☼ 10am-9pm) is way cooler. How many (friendly) biker bars embellished with porcelain figurines and framed posters of poker-playing dogs do you know? Bessie Walker started selling sandwiches in 1943 and the place has hardly changed a lick. Great Americana, greasy burgers, cold beers. And it's been featured in *Chinatown*, natch.

Just north of Point Fermin, in Angels Gate Park, are the **Korean Friendship Bell** (Map pp82-3), a gift from South Korea to the US government, and the **Fort MacArthur Military Museum** (Map pp82-3; ☎ 310-548-2631; www.ftmac.org; 3601 S Gaffey St; donations appreciated; ☼ noon-5pm Tue, Thu, Sat & Sun), an LA harbor defensive post until 1945. Unless you're a total pacifist, bring your kids to scale the gun batteries and search for secret tunnels, while you study up about yesteryear to the sound of toe-tapping big-band music.

WILMINGTON

Just north of San Pedro, in the small town of Wilmington, the 1864 Greek-Revival home of Phineas Banning (1830–85) – aka the 'father' of the port of LA – is now the **Banning Residence Museum** (Map pp82-3; ☎ 310-548-7777; www.banning museum.org; 401 East M St; suggested donation adult/child $5/1; ☼ hourly tours 12:30-2:30pm Tue-Thu, 12:30-3:30pm Sat & Sun; ⓟ). Packed with a trove of gorgeous antiques, it offers an intriguing glimpse into

the daily lives of well-heeled 19th-century Angelenos.

Two blocks south, the **Drum Barracks Civil War Museum** (Map pp82-3; ☎ 310-548-7509; www .drumbarracks.org; 1052 N Banning Blvd; suggested donation $5; ☼ tours hourly 10am-1pm Tue-Thu, 11:30am-2:30pm Sat & Sun; ⓟ) is the only surviving Civil War–era US Army structure in Southern California. It's filled with artifacts from the years 1861–6 when this was a training center and supply depot for battlegrounds in Southern California, Arizona and New Mexico.

Long Beach

If the glut of new lofts is any indication, Long Beach has come a long way since its working-class oil and navy days. Over the past decade or so, LA's southernmost seaside town has quietly reinvented its gritty downtown and made it an attractive place to live and party. On any Saturday night, the restaurants, clubs and bars along lower **Pine Ave** are abuzz with everyone from buttoned-down conventioneers to the testosterone-fuelled frat pack. Additional eateries line a new waterfront boardwalk linking the Aquarium of the Pacific with **Shoreline Village**, the departure point for boat cruises. The **Pike at Rainbow Harbor**, near the aquarium, is another new fun zone, complete with a small Ferris wheel.

Despite the name, the beach isn't such a big draw here. In fact, the water tends to be rather polluted thanks to the proximity of the giant Worldport LA. And those palm-studded mini-islands you see offshore? They're actually well-disguised oil-drilling rigs. If you want to hit the water locally, do it in **Belmont Shore**, about 2 miles east of downtown, right next to canal-laced Naples.

The stress-free way to get to Long Beach is by riding the air-conditioned Metro Rail Blue Line (p219). Once downtown you can walk or catch the red Passport buses, which swing by all the museums and other points of interest, including Belmont Shore (free within downtown; 90¢ otherwise, exact change required). From June to mid-September, the AquaBus links the aquarium and the Queen Mary, as does the high-speed AquaLink, which also goes out to Alamitos Bay (Naples). Bike rentals are available from **Bikestation** (Map pp82-3; ☎ 562-436-2453; 221 E 1st St; 🕑 7am-6pm Mon-Fri, 10am-5pm Sat & Sun) for $8 per hour or $32 for 24 hours.

AQUARIUM OF THE PACIFIC

Long Beach's most mesmerizing experience, the **Aquarium of the Pacific** (Map pp82-3; ☎ 562-590-3100; www.aquariumofpacific.org; 100 Aquarium Way; adult/child/senior $21/12/17; 🕑 9am-6pm; P) is a vast, high-tech indoor ocean where sharks dart, jellyfish dance and sea lions frolic. More than 12,000 creatures inhabit four recreated habitats: the bays and lagoons of Baja California, the frigid northern Pacific, the coral reefs of the tropics and local kelp forests. Parking costs $6.

Among the many not-to-be-missed exhibits is the **Shark Lagoon** where you can pet young sharks in a touch pool and go nose-to-nose – through a window – with their adult-sized cousins patrolling a larger tank. The teeth on the bull shark are the stuff that'll give you *Jaws*-style nightmares. The best time to be here is during the daily feeding sessions (check the schedule online or in the lobby).

Elsewhere, you'll be entertained by the antics of sea otters, spooked by football-sized crabs with spiny 3ft-long arms, and charmed by Seussian-looking sea dragons. It's a wondrous world that'll easily keep you enthralled for a couple of hours. On weekdays, avoid the field-trip frenzy by arriving around 2pm; on weekends beat the crowd by getting here as early as possible.

For an extra fee, the aquarium offers behind-the-scenes tours and, from late May to early September, ocean boat trips.

QUEEN MARY

Long Beach's 'flagship' attraction is the grand and supposedly haunted British luxury liner **Queen Mary** (Map pp82-3; ☎ 562-435-3511; www.queenmary.com; 1126 Queens Hwy; from adult/child/senior $23/12/20; 🕑 10am-6pm; P). Larger and more luxurious than even the *Titanic*, she transported royals, dignitaries, immigrants, WWII troops and vacationers between 1936 and 1964. Today, the sad air of a tourist trap hangs over her bow, but once you've studied the photos and memorabilia on display you might well be able to envision dapper gents escorting ladies in heels and gowns to the art deco lounge for cocktails or the sumptuous Grand Salon for dinner.

Basic admission includes the hokey 'Ghosts & Legends' special-effects tour which features strange apparitions in the 1st-class swimming pool and the boiler room. Various other tours and packages are also available and combination tickets with the aquarium cost $35/19 per adult/child. If you'd like to spend the night, see p171. On Saturdays, midnight screenings of *The Rocky Horror Picture Show* draw a rowdy party crowd. Parking costs $10, and opening hours can vary according to the season; check the website for times before you visit.

LAND'S END

If you've ever rolled tape in your head about California sliding into the sea, San Pedro's **Sunken City** is probably much like what you've imagined. In 1929 a tiny oceanfront neighborhood at the bottom of Pacific Ave began its spooky slide into the kelp beds offshore. What remains are weird up-thrusts of asphalt slathered with graffiti, dirt mounds punctuated with gopher holes and chasms preparing for their future as tide pools. It's 'land's end' à la Salvador Dali and a place that's drawn generations of teens looking to get high or make out. It's also a poignant reminder that nothing lasts forever, certainly not in California. It's fenced off but someone has conveniently snipped a hole in the chain-link and no one seems to mind people clambering around this post-apocalyptic playground.

...ar–era Soviet submarine **Scor-**
...on $11/10) is moored alongside
...you scramble around, imagine
how 78 crew members shared 27 bunks and
two bathrooms, often for months at a time.
Definitely not for the claustrophobic.

MUSEUM OF LATIN AMERICAN ART

This recently expanded gem of a **museum** (Map
pp82-3; ☎ 562-437-1689; www.molaa.org; 628 Alamitos Ave;
adult/student & senior/child under 12 $7.50/5/free, admission
free on Fri; ⏰ 11:30am-7pm Tue-Fri, 11am-7pm Sat, 11am-6pm
Sun) presents a rare survey of Latin American art
created since 1945. Cecilia Míguez' whimsical
bronze statuettes, Eduardo Kingman's wrench-
ing portraits of indigenous people and Arnaldo
Roche Rabel's intensely spiritual abstracts are
among the many outstanding pieces in the
permanent collection, selections of which rotate every six months. There are a few works
by Botero, Tamayo and Cuevas, but the focus
is really on artists who are megastars in their
home countries but haven't yet hit the big time
internationally. Some of the best pieces are in
the sculpture garden. Nice café, too.

LONG BEACH MUSEUM OF ART

The beachfront location is breathtaking, and
the restaurant in a nicely detailed 1912 Craftsman mansion serves tasty lunches, but **exhibits** (Map pp82-3; ☎ 562-439-2119; www.lbma.org; 2300
E Ocean Blvd; adult/student & senior/child under 12 $7/6/free;
⏰ 11am-5pm Tue-Sun) in the adjacent two-room
pavilion can be hit or miss. We've seen amazing
enamelware sharing exhibit space with ghastly
watercolors and sophomoric sculpture. Check
the schedule before forking over the admission
or come on free Fridays. Most of the art is by
contemporary regional artists.

BELMONT SHORE & NAPLES

If downtown Long Beach feels urban and corporate, Belmont Shore exudes quintessential
SoCal laidbackness. It has a fine beach with
a pier for fishing and sunsets, and keeps it
real along a buzzy four-block-long strip of
mostly nonchain boutiques, cafés filled with
surfers and students, and busy restaurants like
Bono's (p184).

Naples, just south of here, is Long Beach's
most exclusive neighborhood. It's a canal-
laced borough, not coincidentally created in
1903 by Arthur Parsons, a contemporary of
Venice's Abbot Kinney. It's best explored on
a gondola ride (p158).

Downtown Los Angeles

No matter what you've read or heard, Downtown is the most historical, multilayered and
fascinating part of Los Angeles. There's great
architecture from 19th-century beaux arts to
futuristic Frank Gehry. There's world-class
music at the Walt Disney Hall, top-notch art
at the Museum of Contemporary Art, superb
dining from tiny *taquerias* (taco shops) to
brassy gourmet restaurants. Downtown is a
power nexus with City Hall, the courts and
the hall of records. It's an ethnic mosaic with
Chinese, Japanese and Mexican enclaves. Yet,
despite its riches, Downtown just can't get no
respect – or visitors.

But if the ballet of cranes is any indication, that may be about to change. An entire
entertainment district is springing up around
the Staples Center, while on Grand Avenue,
Frank Gehry is masterminding a snazzy retail
and residential strip. But the real changes are
more subtle.

Once deserted as soon as the lawyers, execs
and cubicle slaves went home for the day, life
is returning to Downtown streets. Thousands
of young professionals, college kids and artists
are snapping up stylish lofts in gorgeously
rehabbed art deco buildings and modern new
developments. Bars, restaurants, a big supermarket and a movie theater have followed in
their wake. And the growing gallery district
along Main and Spring Sts draws scores to
its monthly art walks. Of course, things don't
change overnight, so don't expect Manhattan.
But the momentum is undeniably there, and
for adventurous urbanites, now is an exciting
time to be Downtown.

If you're open-minded and don't mind a little grit and grime here and there, Downtown
is your oyster. Thanks to its compactness, it's
also one of the few LA neighborhoods that's
best explored on foot. The walking tour on
p155 takes you on a journey of discovery of
main and hidden treasures. If you're arriving
by car, you can save by parking away from the
congested Financial District and Pershing Sq
areas. There are several lots in South Park and
Little Tokyo, for instance, charging only $4 or
$5 all day. An excellent way to get around is
by DASH shuttle (p219)

EL PUEBLO DE LOS ANGELES

Compact, colorful and car-free, this vibrant
historic district sits near the spot where LA's
first colonists settled in 1781. It preserves the

city's oldest buildings, some dating back to its days as a dusty, lawless outpost. More than anything, though, El Pueblo is a microcosm of LA's multi-ethnic heritage and the contributions made by immigrants from Mexico, France, Italy and China. To learn more about this fascinating legacy join a free guided tour leaving from the Old Plaza Firehouse (right) at 10am, 11am and noon Tuesday to Saturday.

If you're more the DIY type, you can also pick up a free self-guided tour pamphlet at the **El Pueblo Visitors Center** (Map pp84–5; ☎ 213-628-1274; Sepulveda House, 622 Olvera St; ☒ 10am-3pm). It's in a converted Victorian building right on **Olvera St** (Map pp84–5; www.calleolvera.com; ☒), a festively chaotic Mexican marketplace. Its gaudy decorations and souvenir stalls might scream 'tourist trap,' but there are actually some fairly authentic experiences to be had. You can shop for Chicano art, slurp thick Mexican-style hot chocolate or pick up handmade candles and candy. At lunchtime, construction workers and cubicle slaves swarm the little eateries for tacos, *tortas* (sandwiches) and burritos.

Even few Angelenos know that there would be no Olvera Street without civic champion Christine Sterling, who bullied and cajoled her famous friends – including LA *Times* publisher Harry Chandler – into saving LA's original business district from being razed for a railway station. With her vision, their money and free prison labor, Olvera St opened to great fanfare in 1930.

There's a small exhibit about Sterling, the 'mother of Olvera St,' in the **Avila Adobe** (Map pp84–5; ☎ 213-680-2525; E-10 Olvera St; admission free; ☒ 9am-3pm), the oldest surviving house in LA. Built in 1818 by a wealthy ranchero and one-time LA mayor, the ranch-style home was later used by the military, then became a boardinghouse and a restaurant. Restored and furnished in heavy oak, it's open for self-guided tours and provides a look at life in the early 19th century. Sterling herself lived here until her death in 1963.

A few doors down is the **Italian Hall** (Map pp84–5; 644-1/2 Main St), which sports a rare rooftop mural called *América Tropical* by David Alfaro Siqueiros, one of Mexico's great early-20th-century muralists. The 1932 work shows a crucified Native American in front of a Mayan pyramid and was so controversial back then that city fathers ordered it whitewashed immediately. The Getty Conservation Institute recently rehabilitated the mural and may possibly build a public viewing platform. Meanwhile, you can see a replica in East LA (p141).

Olvera St spills into the **Old Plaza**, El Pueblo's central square with a pretty wrought-iron bandstand. Sleepy during the week, it often turns into a full-blown fiesta zone on Saturday and Sundays, drawing crooning mariachis, costumed dancers, kissing couples and strolling families. The best time to be here is for one of the many Mexican festivals, like Cinco de Mayo (p160), Día de los Muertos (p161) or the endearing Blessing of the Animals (p160). Dotted around the plaza are statues of such key historical figures as Felipe de Neve, who led the first group of settlers, and King Carlos III of Spain, who financed the venture. The colonists' names are engraved on a nearby bronze plaque.

Across the street, the little 1822 church affectionately known as **La Placita** (Map pp84–5; ☎ 213-629-3101; 535 N Main St; admission free; ☒ 7am-7pm), meaning 'Little Plaza,' is a sentimental favorite with LA Latinos. On busy weekends priests go hoarse performing up to a dozen Spanish-language masses and dozens of baptisms. Peek inside for a look at the gold-festooned altar and painted ceiling.

South of the plaza are more historic buildings, including **Pico House** (Map pp84–5; 430 Main St), the 1870 home of California's last Mexican governor and later a glamorous hotel. Next door is the 1884 **Old Plaza Firehouse** (Map pp84–5; ☎ 213-625-3741; 134 Paseo de la Plaza; admission free; ☒ 10am-3pm Tue-Sun), the city's oldest fire station and now a one-room museum of dusty old fire-fighting equipment and photographs.

Follow the red lanterns to the small **Chinese American Museum** (Map pp84–5; ☎ 213-485-8567; www.camla.org; 425 N Los Angeles St; adult/student & senior $3/2; ☒ 10am-3pm Tue-Sun) in the 1890 Garnier Building, once the unofficial 'city hall' of LA's original Chinatown. Changing exhibits highlight various historical, cultural and artistic aspects of the Chinese American experience, usually with a local slant. It's a source of great pride for local Chinese, who donated many items on display.

UNION STATION

LA's original Chinatown sprawled where you'll now spot **Union Station** (Map pp84–5; 800 N Alameda St), which opened in 1939 as the last of America's grand rail stations. It's a glamorous exercise in Mission Revival with art deco accents. The marble-floored main hall with cathedral ceilings, original leather chairs and grand chandeliers is nothing but breathtaking and is often used in movies (eg *Guilty by Suspicion*, *Blade Runner* and *The Way We Were*).

The tiled twin domes north of the station belong to the **Terminal Annex**, once LA's central post office where Charles Bukowski worked for years, inspiring his 1971 novel *Post Office*.

CHINATOWN

As you walk north from El Pueblo, the aroma of chili and beans gradually gives way to soy and bok choy. Having been forced to make room for Union Station, the Chinese resettled a few blocks north along Hill St and Broadway. **Chinatown** (Map pp84-5; ☎ 213-680-0243; www .chinatownla.com) is still the community's traditional hub, even though most Chinese Americans now live in Rosemead, Monterey and other suburban communities in the San Gabriel Valley.

There are no essential sights here, but the area, a stop on Metro Gold Line, is fascinating and perfect for an aimless wander. Restaurants beckon with dim sum, *kung pao* and Peking duck, while shops overflow with curios, culinary oddities (live frogs anyone?), ancient herbal remedies and lucky bamboo.

Of late, parts of Chinatown have received an injection of hipness, no more so than at **Central Plaza** (Map pp84-5; 900 block of Broadway), conceived as an unabashedly kitschy walking mall. Outposts of contemporary cool like Munky King (p214) designer toys and the Mountain Bar (p194) mix it up with incense-scented import bazaars, an endearing wishing well and the kookily noir **Hop Louie** restaurant and bar in a five-tiered pagoda. Across Hill St, the galleries and studios (p206) along **Chung King Rd** bring out art students and aficionados in droves on opening nights.

If you want a bit of orientation, pick up a self-guided-tour brochure at the **LA Chinatown Heritage & Visitors Center** (Map pp84-5; ☎ 323-222-0856; www.chssc.org; 411 Bernard St; ☽ 11am-3pm Wed-Fri, noon-4:30pm Sun).

DODGER STADIUM

Baseball fans will be happy to learn that **Dodger Stadium** (off Map pp84-5; ☎ 866-363-4377; http://los angeles.dodgers.mlb.com/la/ballpark/tours.jsp; 1000 Elysian Park Ave; tours adult/child 4-14yr & senior \$15/10; ☽ 10am

& 1:30pm Tue & Thu; **P**) is now offering regular behind-the-scenes tours of the historic stadium. The 90-minute spins cover the press box, the Dodger dugout, the Dugout Club, the field and the Tommy LaSorda Training Center. Since tours are limited to 25 people, reservations are strongly advised. There are no tours on day-game days. For information about game tickets see p205.

CITY HALL

Until 1966 no LA building stood taller than the 1928 **City Hall** (Map pp84-5; ☎ 213-978-1995; 200 N Spring St; admission free; ☽ 8am-5pm Mon-Fri), which cameoed in the *Superman* TV series and 1953 sci-fi thriller *War of the Worlds*. On clear days, you'll have some cool views of the city, the mountains and several decades of Downtown growth from the observation deck. Also check out the grand domed rotunda on the 3rd level with a marble floor as intricate as those found in Italian cathedrals. Free guided tours run at 10am and 11am, Monday to Friday. The public entrance is on Main St.

LOS ANGELES TIMES

News junkies can get their fix on a free tour of the nearby **Los Angeles Times** (Map pp84-5; ☎ 213-237-5757; 202 W 1st St; ☽ tours 9:30am, 11am & 1:30pm Mon-Fri; **P**). The 45-minute tours usher you through the editorial offices, explaining the paper's history and the publishing process. Kids under 10 can't come and reservations must be made at least one week in advance.

GRAND AVENUE CULTURAL CORRIDOR

Grand Avenue, on the northern edge of the Civic Center area, is already a major cultural hub. It's also on the verge of what billionaire developer Eli Broad hopes will be LA's equivalent of Paris' Champs-Elysee or New York's Central Park. Ambitious talk or reality? We'll see.

The master plan, designed by Frank Gehry, calls for a large public park flanked by two soaring luxury condo towers buttressed by several smaller buildings containing high-end shops and the super-deluxe Mandarin Oriental Hotel. Phase One is expected to be completed in 2011 at a cost of \$2 billion.

Walt Disney Concert Hall

Frank Gehry pulled out all the stops for his iconic **concert venue** (Map pp84-5; ☎ 323-850-2000;

www.laphil.com; 111 S Grand Ave; tours $10-15; audio tours (Y) 10am-2pm most days; (P)) that's the home base of the Los Angeles Philharmonic (p202). The building is a gravity-defying sculpture of heaving and billowing stainless-steel walls that conjures visions of a ship adrift in a rough sea. The auditorium, meanwhile, feels like the inside of a finely crafted instrument, a cello perhaps, clad in walls of smooth Douglas fir. It's an imposing yet intimate hall with terraced 'vineyard' seating wrapped around a central stage. Even seats below the giant pipe organ offer excellent sightlines and still-decent acoustics. Tours reveal much about the history, architecture and acoustics of the place, but they won't let you see the auditorium. Self-guided audio tours and guided tours are available – call ahead for the guided-tour schedule. Parking costs $8.

Music Center

Disney hall is part of a cultural complex known as the **Music Center** (Map pp84-5; ☎ 213-972-7200, tours ☎ 213-972-7483; www.musiccenter.org; 135 N Grand Ave; admission free; (P)). Aside from the LA Phil's old home, the **Dorothy Chandler Pavilion**, which is now used for an expanded schedule by the LA Opera (p202), it encompasses the **Mark Taper Forum** (p203), the **Ahmanson Theatre** (p203) and a fountain plaza. Tours also make a brief stop in the Disney hall lobby. Free self-guided audio tours run from 10am to 2pm most days, while guided tours run from 10am to 1:30pm Tuesday to Friday, and 10am to noon on Saturday. Parking is $8.

Cathedral of Our Lady of the Angels

José Rafael Moneo mixed Gothic proportions with bold contemporary design for his 2002 **Cathedral of Our Lady of the Angels** (Map pp84-5; ☎ 213-680-5200; www.olacathedral.org; 555 W Temple St; admission free; (Y) 6am-6pm Mon-Fri, 9am-6pm Sat, 7am-6pm Sun, to 7pm during daylight savings; (P)), which exudes a calming serenity achieved by soft light filtering in through alabaster panes. Art abounds from the moment you step through Robert Graham's massive bronze doors guarded by a Madonna sculpture. Wall-sized tapestries as intricate and detailed as a Michelangelo fresco festoon the main nave. They depict 135 saints whose gaze is directed towards the main altar, a massive yet simple slab of red marble. Gregory Peck is buried in the beehive-like subterranean mausoleum.

Popular times to visit are for the 1pm weekday tours and the recitals at 12:45pm on Wednesday, both free.

Museum of Contemporary Art (MOCA)

A collection that spans the arc of artistic vision from the 1940s to the present and includes works by Mark Rothko, Dan Flavin, Joseph Cornell and other big-shot contemporary artists give **MOCA Grand Ave** (Map pp84-5; ☎ 213-626-6222; www.moca.org; 250 S Grand Ave; adult/student & senior/child under 12 $8/5/free, free 5-8pm Thu; (Y) 11am-5pm Mon & Fri, 11am-8pm Thu, 11am-6pm Sat & Sun; (P)) an edge in the art world. It's housed in a postmodern building by Arata Isozaki, a minimalist masterpiece that unifies pared-down geometric shapes behind by a red sandstone facade. Galleries are below ground, yet flooded with natural light via pyramidal skylights. Check it out during tours (free with admission) offered at noon, 1pm and 2pm and don't forget to swing by the bookstore gift shop, one of the best in town.

Tickets are also good for same-day admission at **Geffen Contemporary at MOCA** in Little Tokyo, a quick DASH bus ride away. Catch it at Grand Ave and 1st St.

The odd building next to MOCA, whose steeply pitched zinc roof makes it looks like an upside-down cake tin, is the **Colburn School of Performing Arts** (Map pp84-5; ☎ 213-621-2200; www.colburnschool.edu; 200 S Grand Ave). Sometimes called the 'Julliard of the West', it's a great place to keep tabs on tomorrow's talent during concerts, most of them free, held during the school year (September to May).

California Plaza & Angels Flight

MOCA is dwarfed by the soaring California Plaza office tower whose outdoor water-court amphitheatre hosts the **Grand Performances**, one of the best free summer performance series (p200) in the city. After a few breaks over the years, once again chugging down a steep incline to Hill St and **Grand Central Market** (p137) is **Angels Flight**, a historic funicular billed as the 'shortest railway in the world'. The little trains first started operating in 1901 when this neighborhood was called Bunker Hill and was populated by Victorians, but they were mothballed when the area was redeveloped in the '60s. Nostalgia revived them in the '90s but only until a fatal derailment occurred in 2001. With new safety measures in place, operations eventually resumed in late 2007.

Wells Fargo History Museum

Sponsored by California-based Wells Fargo Bank, this small but intriguing **museum** (Map pp84–5; ☎ 213-253-7166; www.wellsfargohistory.com /museums/lamuseum.html; 333 S Grand Ave; admission free; ☙ 9am-5pm Mon-Fri) chronicles the gold-rush era and the company's role in it. See an original Concord stagecoach, a 100oz gold nugget, an old bank office and all sorts of other artifacts, or ask the staff to start the 15-minute video.

The exhibits are on the ground floor of the **Wells Fargo Center**, another huge office tower that's filled with public art, including numerous nude sculptures by Robert Graham in the atrium and Jean Dubuffet's cartoonish *Le Dandy* in the Hope St entrance vestibule.

Richard Riordan Central Library

One of the coolest buildings in town, the Egyptian-flavored 1922 **central library** (Map pp84–5; ☎ 213-228-7000; www.lapl.org; 630 W 5th St; admission free; ☙ 10am-8pm Mon-Thu, 10am-6pm Fri & Sat, 1-5pm Sun, free tours at 12:30pm Mon-Fri, 11am & 2pm Sat, 2pm Sun) was designed by Bertram Goodhue and named for a former mayor. Sphinxes greet you at the 5th St entrance and a colorful 1933 mural showing milestones in LA history swathes a grand rotunda on the 2nd floor. Also duck into the adjacent children's section, which has a stunning painted ceiling and more murals.

In the modern Tom Bradley wing, escalators cascade down four glass-walled floors through a whimsically decorated glass atrium. Besides 2.1 million books, the library also holds a prized archive of historical photographs, art exhibits, a gift store and a restaurant and keeps a dynamic events schedule for both kids and grownups. One of the best programs is the **Aloud LA** (www.lfla.org/aloud) series of lectures, conversations and performances often featuring major movers and shakers in arts, literature and politics. It's free but hugely popular, so make online reservations early or join the stand-by line.

US BANK TOWER & BUNKER HILLS STEPS

The tallest of the many office towers in the heart of Downtown's financial district is the **US Bank Tower** (Map pp84–5; 655 W 5th St), at 1018ft the tallest building between Chicago and Taiwan. Film buffs might remember it being attacked by an alien spaceship in *Independence Day*.

The tower abuts the **Bunker Hill Steps**, an attractive staircase that links 5th St with the Wells Fargo Center and other hilltop office complexes. At the top is a small fountain featuring a female nude by Robert Graham. En route you pass McCormick & Schmick's, famous for its happy hour (p191).

PERSHING SQUARE & AROUND

The hub of Downtown's historic core, **Pershing Square** (Map pp84–5; www.laparks.org) was LA's first public park in 1866 and is now a postmodern concrete patch enlivened by public art, summer concerts, a holiday-season ice rink and the hulking 1923 **Millennium Biltmore Hotel** (Map pp84–5; ☎ 213-624-1011; www.thebiltmore .com; 506 S Grand Ave; ℗). LA's most illustrious defender of the grand-hotel tradition, it has hosted presidents, kings and celebrities, plus the 1960 Democratic National Convention and eight Academy Awards ceremonies. Its sumptuous interior boasts carved and gilded ceilings, marble floors, grand staircases and palatial ballrooms decorated by White House muralist Giovanni Smeraldi. Afternoon tea is served daily in the rococo-style Rendezvous Court. See p172 for details about staying at the hotel.

South of Pershing Sq, gold and diamonds are the main currency in the **Jewelry District** (Map pp84–5; ☎ 213-683-1956; www.lajd.net; Hill St btwn 6th & 8th Sts), the country's second largest after New York (p214). One of the marts occupies the historic **Pantages Theatre** (401-21 W 7th St), a hugely popular vaudeville venue in the 1920s. Nearby is one of Downtown's newest oddities, **St Vincent Court** (Map pp84–5; 7th St btwn Hill St & Broadway), a recently restored alleyway supposed to look like a quaint Parisian street, and lined with Middle Eastern cafés where clusters of men sip minty tea, and workers, shoppers and the occasional hipster chow down on gyro and kebabs.

BROADWAY

Now a cut-rate retail spine catering primarily to Latino shoppers, cacophonous Broadway started out in the early 20th century as a glamorous shopping and theater strip where megastars like Charlie Chaplin leapt from limos to attend premieres at lavish movie palaces. As LA grew more suburban, Broadway plunged into decline and over time most theaters were closed, even gutted and turned into churches or tawdry swap meets. But like the rest of Downtown, Broadway is changing. Several of the old theaters have been restored and again host screenings and parties, while other buildings are being converted into lofts, and even some hipster bars have sprung up.

There are parking garages all along Broadway and one-hour free parking at the Grand Central Market (see below; enter on Hill St) with purchase and validation.

Bradbury Building

This 1893 **building** (Map pp84–5; ☎ 213-626-1893; 304 S Broadway; admission free; ☯ 9am-6pm Mon-Fri, 9am-5pm Sat & Sun) is one of LA's undisputed architectural jewels. Its red-brick facade conceals a stunning galleried atrium with inky filigree grillwork, a rickety birdcage elevator and yellow brick walls that glisten golden in the afternoon light filtering through the tent-shaped glass roof. Location scouts love the place, whose star-turn came in the cult flick *Blade Runner*.

The building has a curious genesis. Mining mogul turned real-estate developer Lewis Bradbury picked not a famous architect but an unknown draftsman named George Wyman to come up with the design. Allegedly, Wyman consulted a Ouija board and accepted the gig after his dead brother told him it would be a success. The design was inspired by the popular 1887 Edward Bellamy novel, *Looking Back*, about a utopian civilization in the year 2000. The Bradbury was Wyman's only celebrated building. Security staff hand out a free pamphlet with more details and let you go up to the 1st-floor landing. LAPD Internal Affairs has its offices on the upper floors.

Grand Central Market

On the ground floor of a 1905 beaux arts building where architect Frank Lloyd Wright once kept an office, the historic **Grand Central Market** (Map pp84–5; ☎ 213-624-2378; 317 S Broadway; ☯ 9am-6pm) is perfect for sopping up Downtown's mélange of ethnicities, languages and cuisines. Stroll along the sawdust-sprinkled aisles beneath old-timey ceiling fans and neon signs, past stalls piled high with mangoes, peppers and jicamas and glass bins filled with dried chilies and nuts. There's even a small pastry factory and plenty of lunch counters for snacking on fish tacos, shwarma or chicken soup (see p135 for suggestions).

Broadway Theaters

Until eclipsed by Hollywood in the mid-1920s, Broadway was LA's entertainment hub with no fewer than a dozen theaters built in a riot of styles, from beaux arts to East Indian to Spanish Gothic. Their architectural and historic significance even earned them a spot on the National Register of Historic Places. Since they're usually closed to the public, the best way to see them is by joining one of the excellent tours offered by the LA Conservancy (p159), which also presents the Last Remaining Seats film series of Hollywood classics.

Million Dollar Theater (Map pp84–5; 307 S Broadway) was the first theater built by Sid Grauman of Chinese Theatre and Egyptian Theatre fame. Big bands played here in the '40s and, a decade later, it became the first Broadway venue to cater to Spanish speakers. Briefly a church, it's now under restoration.

Next up is the most ridiculously lavish movie palace on the strip, the 1931 **Los Angeles Theater** (Map pp84–5; 615 S Broadway). The soaring lobby is a sparkling hall of mirrors with a three-tiered fountain, crystal chandeliers and a grand central staircase leading to a lavish auditorium where Albert Einstein and other luminaries enjoyed the premiere of Charlie Chaplin's *City Lights*. Restored, it presents special events and screenings.

The exterior of the 1911 **Palace Theater** (Map pp84–5; 630 S Broadway), across the street, was inspired by a Florentine *palazzo* while the interior is French baroque fantasy filled with garland-draped columns and murals depicting pastoral scenes. It's an intimate space where no seat is further than 80ft from the stage.

Broadway's biggest entertainment complex is the 1921 **State Theater** (Map pp84–5; 703 S Broadway), which can seat 2500 people and has a flamboyant ceiling; it's now a Spanish-language church.

The 1913 **Globe Theater** (Map pp84–5; 744 S Broadway) started out as a live theater but, sadly, is now a swap meet. The world's first talkie, *The Jazz Singer* starring Al Jonson, premiered in 1927 at the **Tower Theater** (Map pp84–5; 802 S Broadway) whose lavish baroque interior is often used for location shoots.

Currently the busiest venue on Broadway is the 1926 **Orpheum Theater** (Map pp84–5; 842 S Broadway), which was built for vaudeville and has hosted such entertainers as Judy Garland, George Burns and Nat King Cole. Like the Los Angeles, it's a truly sumptuous place rivaling European opera houses with its silk tapestries, marble pilasters, gilded coffered ceiling and still-functioning Wurlitzer organ. Fully restored and upgraded, the venerable landmark now presents everything from American Idol auditions to The Shins concerts to film screenings.

Across the street, the 1929 **Eastern Columbia Building** (Map pp84-5; 849 S Broadway) is a strikingly turquoise art deco tower that originally housed a clothing store and was recently converted into luxury lofts by the Kor Group, which also operates Maison 140 and other fashionable hotels. Note the gilded sunburst pattern above the entrance and on the tower's clock face. One-bedroom apartments rent for $3000 a month; Johnny Depp allegedly bought the penthouse for a cool $2 million.

Finally, there's the 1927 Spanish Gothic **United Artists Theater** (Map pp84-5; ☎ 818-240-8151, 800-338-3030; www.drgenescott.com; 933 S Broadway) whose construction was bankrolled by Mary Pickford, Douglas Fairbanks Sr and Charlie Chaplin. It's long been the 'cathedral' of the late televangelist Dr Gene Scott (look for the 'Jesus Saves' sign on the rooftop), now run by his wife Melissa. The only way to get inside is by calling the 'voice of god' to ask for a free reservation for a Sunday service.

LITTLE TOKYO

Little Tokyo swirls with outdoor shopping malls, Buddhist temples, public art, traditional gardens and some of the most authentic sushi bars, *izakayas* (taverns) and *shabu shabu* parlors in town. The community can trace its roots back to the 1880s, but only a few historic buildings survive along E 1st St; in 1996, they were placed on the National Register of Historic Places. Stop by the **Little Tokyo Koban** (Map pp84-5; ☎ 213-613-1911; 307 E 1st St; 9am-6pm Mon-Sat) for maps and information. Parking is free for the first hour in the garage at 333 S Alameda St and there are inexpensive lots and metered street parking on 2nd St east of Central Ave. DASH bus A (DD on weekends) comes through here as well and so will the Gold Line extension when completed in 2009.

A great first stop on your Little Tokyo exploration is the **Japanese American National Museum** (JANM; Map pp84-5; ☎ 213-625-0414; www .janm.org; 369 E 1st St; adult/student/child under 6 $8/5/4/free; 11am-5pm Tue, Wed & Fri-Sun, to 8pm Thu), the country's first museum dedicated to the Japanese immigrant experience. You'll be moved by galleries dealing with the painful

chapter of the WWII internment camps and charmed by such exhibits as the *Star Trek* uniform of actor George Takei. Afterwards, relax in the tranquil garden, browse the well-stocked gift shop or grab a bite at the excellent café. Also ask about drumming workshops for kids and other fun events. Admission is free on Thursdays from 5pm to 8pm, and all day on the third Thursday of each month.

Arty types can pop next door to peruse the cutting-edge and often provocative exhibits at the **Geffen Contemporary at MOCA** (Map pp84-5; ☎ 213-626-6222; www.moca.org; 152 N Central Ave; adult/student & senior/child under 12 $8/5/free, free 5-8pm Thu; 11am-5pm Mon, 11am-8pm Thu, 11am-5pm Fri, 11am-6pm Sat & Sun). A branch of MOCA Grand Ave (p135), it presents mostly conceptual art and large-scale installations in a police garage converted by Frank Gehry. Tours (free with admission) run at noon, 1pm and 2pm.

The funny-looking tower across 1st St from the JANM is a *yagura*, a traditional fire lookout tower typically found in rural Japan. It's the gateway to the **Japanese Village Plaza** (Map pp84-5; ☎ 213-620-8861; btwn 1st & 2nd Sts), a modern outdoor mall with gift shops, restaurants and good people-watching. A few steps west, tucked into a hidden courtyard away from the street, is the **Koyasan Buddhist Temple** (Map pp84-5; ☎ 213-624-1267; 342 E 1st St).

Little Tokyo's main cultural hub is the **Japanese American Cultural & Community Center** (Map pp84-5; ☎ 213-628-2725; www.jaccc.org; 244 S San Pedro St; admission free; noon-5pm Tue-Fri, 11am-4pm Sat & Sun; P). The gallery spotlights local artists and there's also a library and a gift shop. With bamboo and a gurgling stream, the hidden **James Irvine Garden** (Map pp84-5; admission free; 9am-5pm) is great to chill in. Reach it by taking the elevator to the 'B' level and follow the signs.

Next door, at the **Aratani/Japan America Theater** (Map pp84-5; ☎ 213-680-3700) a handmade peacock-motif silk *doncho* (curtain) from Kyoto dramatically opens the stage for Kabuki, No (stylized dance-dramas), Bunraku (puppet shows) and Western-style performances.

ARTS DISTRICT

In the gritty, industrial section southeast of Little Tokyo an increasingly lively arts district has sprung up. It's drawn a young, adventurous and spirited crowd of people who live and work in makeshift studios above abandoned warehouses and small factories. There's enough of them here to support a growing number of cafés, restaurants and shops.

The area got a nod of respectability when the **Southern California Institute of Architecture** (Sci-Arc; Map pp84-5; ☎ 213-613-2200; www.sciarc.edu; 960 E 3rd St) moved into the former Santa Fe Freight Yard in 2001. It's a progressive laboratory whose faculty and students continually push the envelope in architectural design. You can see some of the results in the **gallery** (Map pp84-5; admission free; ☼ 10am-6pm) or attend a lecture or film screening; call or see the website for upcoming events.

Northeast, across LA's trickling 'river,' is the **Brewery Art Complex** (Map pp84-5; ☎ 323-342-0717; www.breweryart.org; 2100 N Main St; Ⓟ), LA's largest artist colony, in a former brewery. There are a few galleries, but studios are generally closed to the public except during the biannual Artwalks (usually in spring and fall; call or check the website for details), though you can wander around to examine the large installations – usually works in progress – scattered throughout.

Near the art complex is the **San Antonio Winery** (Map pp84-5; ☎ 323-223-1401; www.sanantoniowinery.com; 737 Lamar St; admission free; ☼ 8:30am-7pm Mon-Fri, 9am-7pm Sat & Sun; Ⓟ), LA's last remaining historic winery. It was founded in 1917 by Italian immigrant Santo Cambianica whose descendants still make buttery chardonnay, velvety cabernet sauvignon and other varietals. You can sample some of them for free in the tasting room, enjoy a meal at the Italian restaurant or learn more about the noble grape at a wine seminar. Free behind-the-scenes winery tours take place at noon, 1pm and 2pm from Monday to Friday, and on the hour from 11am to 4pm on Saturday and Sunday.

SOUTH PARK & FASHION DISTRICT

In the southwestern corner of Downtown, South Park isn't really a park at all but an emerging neighborhood bordering the Staples Center, LA Convention Center and what will soon be a new entertainment hub called **LA Live**. City planners and developers are betting the farm that this $1.7 billion dollar megaproject will pole vault Downtown LA onto the map of must-go destinations for both locals and visitors. At the time of writing, construction was progressing feverishly; the 7100-seat Nokia Theatre, which will host awards shows and major spectacles, should

already have opened. There will also be a huge live-music club, a megaplex movie theater, a dozen restaurants and a 54-story hotel tower shared by Marriott and the Ritz-Carlton.

The area got its first jolt in 1999 with the opening of the **Staples Center** (Map pp84-5; ☎ 213-742-7340; www.staplescenter.com; 1111 S Figueroa St; Ⓟ), a saucer-shaped sports and entertainment arena with all the high-tech trappings. It's home turf for the Los Angeles Lakers, Clippers and Sparks basketball teams, the Kings ice-hockey team and the Avengers indoor-football team. When major headliners – Bruce Springsteen to Justin Timberlake – are in town, they'll most likely perform at the Staples. Parking costs $20.

A few steps north of here is the small and peaceful **Grand Hope Park** (Map pp84-5; 9th St, btwn Grand Ave & Hope Sts). Designed by Lawrence Halprin, one of the country's foremost landscape architects, it was the first of South Park's beautification projects which began in the late '80s. It's often filled with students from the adjacent **Fashion Institute of Design & Merchandising** (FIDM; Map pp84-5; ☎ 213-624-1200; 919 S Grand Ave; ☼ 10am-4pm Tue-Sat), a private college with an international student body. The gallery has some interesting rotating exhibits, including costumes worn in Academy Award–nominated movies. Bargain hunters should check out the FIDM Scholarship Store, where you can get new but slightly

---

TOURS

- California Institute of Technology (Caltech) campus (Pasadena, p150)
- Cathedral of Our Lady of the Angels (Downtown, p135)
- Downtown LA Walks (p159)
- El Pueblo de Los Angeles & Olvera St (Downtown, p132)
- Getty Center (Brentwood, p117)
- *Los Angeles Times* (Downtown, p134)
- Metro Rail Art Tours (p159)
- San Antonio Winery (Downtown, left)
- Seabiscuit Tour at Santa Anita Park (San Gabriel Valley, p151)
- University of California, Los Angeles (UCLA) campus (Westwood, p117)

damaged contemporary clothing donated by department stores and chains like Forever 21 and Frederick's of Hollywood for just a few dollars.

FIDM graduates often go on to start their own companies in the nearby **Fashion District** (Map pp84-5; ☎ 213-488-1153; www.fashiondistrict.org). Bounded by Main and Wall Sts and 7th St and Pico Blvd, this 90-block area is nirvana for shopaholics but is rather chaotic. Prices are lowest in bazaarlike Santee Alley. For a primer on how to get around, see the boxed text LA's Fashion District Demystified on p213.

Cut flowers at cut-rate prices are the lure at the nearby **Flower Market** (Map pp84-5; ☎ 213-627-3696; www.laflowerdistrict.com; Wall St, btwn 7th & 8th Sts; admission Mon-Fri $2, Sat $1; ⊙ 8am-noon Mon, Wed & Fri, 6am-noon Tue, Thu & Sat), where a few dollars gets you armloads of Hawaiian ginger or sweet roses, a potted plant or elegant orchid. The market is busiest in the wee hours when florists stock up on posies by the truckload. Not to worry, though: there'll be plenty left when you get to go in. Bring cash.

Streamline Moderne doesn't get any sleeker than Robert Derrah's 1937 **Coca-Cola Bottling Plant** (Map pp84-5; 1334 S Central Ave), the design of which was inspired by classic ocean liners. See those portholes, catwalk, cargo doors and bridge? It's in the industrial no-man's-land southeast of the Fashion District but worth a quick detour if only to snap a picture of yourself and a giant Coke bottle.

Westlake & Koreatown

Until recently, historic **Westlake,** just west of Downtown, was the go-to zone for scoring rock cocaine or a fake drivers' license. Slowly but surely, though, the area is cleaning up its act and even toying with gentrification. Crime is down by 50% and families have returned to **MacArthur Park** (Map pp84-5; cnr Wilshire Blvd & Alvarado St) for picnics and paddling around a spring-fed lake. In 2007, world beats heated up the restored band shell during the inaugural summer concert series. (And yes, this is the park that 'melts in the dark' in the eponymous Jimmy Webb song made famous by Donna Summer.) Though still largely a working-class Latino neighborhood, artists, hipsters and young professionals are trickling into the neighborhood with bars, eateries and cultural spaces following in their tracks. Just get off at the Wilshire/MacArthur Park stop of the Red

Line subway and see for yourself, though for now you should stick to the daylight hours.

Fans of Victoriana will get their fill at the **Grier Musser Museum** (Map pp84-5; ☎ 213-413-1814; www.griermussermuseum.com; 403 S Bonnie Brae St; adult/student & senior/child $10/7/5; ⊙ noon-4pm Wed-Sat, reservations required) inside a beautiful Queen Anne home with intricate woodwork and luscious stained glass. It's stuffed with antiques and yesteryear's knickknacks, including a neat 1909 windup Victrola phonograph that still works. To keep things dynamic, the dedicated staff puts together monthly exhibits usually revolving around a holiday theme. The Christmas one is famous.

Westlake spills seamlessly into **Koreatown**, a vast, amorphous area that feels more like Seoul than LA. Korean immigrants began settling here in the 1960s and still form a very tight-knit community that is poorly assimilated into mainstream American life. Signs are mostly in Korean and many shopkeepers and servers speak only a few words of English. All this makes for an interesting experience, especially when it comes to food (see p186 for suggestions). Of late, Koreatown has also developed something like a nightlife scene. A good place for *soju* (similar to vodka) cocktails and Hite beer is the eccentric Prince (p194).

Wilshire Blvd is the most attractive thoroughfare and lined with historic churches and other buildings harkening back to the time when this area was a wealthy business and residential district known as Wilshire Center.

Coming from Downtown, first up is the 1929 art deco **Bullocks Wilshire** (off Map pp84-5; ☎ 213-738-8240; www.swlaw.edu/bullockswilshire; 3050 Wilshire Blvd), the country's first department store designed for shoppers arriving by car. Unfortunately, it closed in 1992 and is now a law school rarely open to the public.

These days, shopping around here is done at slick malls such as the new **Aroma Wilshire Center** (off Map pp84-5; ☎ 213-387-0111; 3680 Wilshire Blvd; Ⓟ) near the Metro Red Line Wilshire/Western station. Pick through Korean groceries, cosmetics, music, books, stationery and all sorts of fun imports, get a workout at the golf-driving range or work out the kinks at the fancy fitness center.

To connect with local Korean culture, pop into the free **Korean American Museum** (off Map pp84-5; ☎ 213-388-4229; www.kamuseum.org; 4th fl, 3727 W 6th St; admission free; ⊙ 11am-6pm Wed-Fri, 11am-3pm

Sat) which has changing art exhibits and cultural events.

A bit further east, the **Wiltern Theatre** (off Map pp84-5; ☎ 213-388-1400; www.wiltern.com; 3790 Wilshire Blvd), a 1931 theater turned concert venue, struts its stuff in a glorious turquoise mantle right at the intersection of Wilshire and Western Blvds (get it?). Sting, Fergie and Feist are among the artists who've played here.

East Los Angeles

The Los Angeles River is a bit like the US–Mexican border without the wall and the minutemen. Beyond the concrete gulch lies the oldest and largest Mexican community outside of Mexico. It's been the breeding ground for musicians like Los Lobos, athletes like boxer Oscar de la Hoya and actors like Anthony Quinn.

Life in the barrio is tough but lively. Stroller-pushing moms stop for *pan dulce* (sweet bread) and gossip at local *panaderías* (bakeries), pick up dinner at the *carnicería* (butchershop) and fresh tortillas straight from the factory. On summer nights, makeshift grills pop up at street corners, *taquerías* (taco shops) get packed with families, and laborers chill with a cold *cerveza* (beer) after another hard day's work.

There aren't any major stops on the tourist track out here, but even a quick drive or stroll and perhaps a bite in one of several excellent restaurants will deepen your understanding of this complex city. Access will be easier once the Metro Rail Gold Line extension is completed in 2009, but for now the best way to visit is by car via 1st St. Street parking is ubiquitous.

Just a tortilla toss east of the river is **Mariachi Plaza** (Map pp84-5; cnr Boyle Ave & 1st St), where traditional Mexican musicians in fanciful suits and wide-brimmed hats troll for work. Stop for coffee in the artsy Homegirl Café (p187)

or indulge in a classy meal at La Serenata de Garibaldi (p187).

East of here, a nondescript building houses the **Hollenbeck Youth Center** (Map pp84-5; 2015 E 1st St) where Oscar 'Golden Boy' de la Hoya punched himself into shape for the 1992 Olympic gold medal. Just past a giant cemetery is **El Mercado** (off Map pp84-5; 3425 E 1st St & Lorena), a colorful indoor market where locals come for homemade *mole* (sauce), *dulce de leche* (caramel), toys and tortilla presses. On weekends, it's a scene and a half in the two 3rd-floor restaurants where 'dueling' mariachi bands entertain families and kissing couples.

North of here, **Self-Help Graphics & Art** (off Map pp84-5; ☎ 323-881-6444; www.selfhelpgraphics.com; 3802 Cesar E Chavez Ave at Gage Ave; admission free) has been nurturing and promoting Latino art for the past three decades. Because of budget troubles, it's rarely open these days but the remaining staff still puts on the Southland's best and largest Día de Los Muertos (Day of the Day) celebration on November 1. The mural on the eastern wall (above Super Taco) is a recreation of David Alfaro Siqueros' controversial *América Tropical* on Olvera St (p133). Call for opening hours.

South Central

The area south of Exposition Park is traditionally referred to as South Central. Gangs, drugs, poverty, crime and drive-by shootings are just a few of the negative images – not entirely undeserved – associated with this district. Much of the area is bleak and foreboding, but there are also thriving pockets, such as the Leimert Park neighborhood, and world-class sights such as the Watts Towers.

WATTS TOWERS

South Central's beacon of pride, the fabulous **Watts Towers** (Map pp82-3; ☎ 213-847-4646; 1765 E 107th St; adult/teen & senior/child under 12 $7/3/free; tours

---

DETOUR: ST SOPHIA CATHEDRAL

This splendidly opulent **house of worship** (off Map pp84-5; ☎ 323-737-2424; www.stsophia.org; 1324 S Normandie Ave; admission free; 🕙 10am-4pm Tue-Fri, 10am-2pm Sat; 🅿) is the spiritual hub of the local Greek Orthodox community and is as rich and epic as a giant's treasure chest. It was financed by the Skouras brothers, Greek immigrants who made it big in Hollywood as studio heads. They hired set designers to swath every inch of wall space in the main nave with amazingly accomplished Biblical-themed murals. It's illuminated by muted light streaming through stained-glass windows and emanating from the Bohemian crystal chandelier. A visit here is easily combined with a plate of gyro at Papa Cristo's (p186).

(⏲ 11am–3pm Fri, 10:30am–3pm Sat, 12:30–3pm Sun) rank among the world's greatest monuments of folk art. In 1921 Italian immigrant Simon Rodia set out 'to make something big' and then spent 33 years cobbling together this whimsical free-form sculpture from a motley assortment of found objects – from green 7-Up bottles to sea shells, rocks to pottery. You can admire it any time, but to get inside you have to join a half-hour tour.

The adjacent **Watts Towers Art Center** (Map pp82–3; ☎ 213-847-4646; admission free; ⏲ 10am–4pm Tue-Sat, noon–4pm Sun) sponsors workshops, performances and classes for the community, hosts art exhibits and organizes the acclaimed **Watts Towers Day of the Drum and Jazz Festival** in September (p161).

CENTRAL AVENUE

From the 1920s to the 1950s, Central Ave was the lifeblood of LA's African-American community, not by choice but because segregation laws kept black people out of other neighborhoods. It was also a hotbed of jazz and R&B, a legacy commemorated every July with the **Central Avenue Jazz Festival** (p160) held outside the 1928 **Dunbar Hotel** (off Map pp84–5; 4225 S Central Ave). Duke Ellington once maintained a suite at what was LA's only 1st-class hotel for African Americans; it's now a low-income seniors center and, like much of the street, a rather drab sight.

North of here, towards Downtown, the **African American Firefighter Museum** (Map pp84–5; ☎ 213-744-1730; www.aaffmuseum.org; 1401 S Central Ave; admission free; ⏲ 10am–2pm Tue & Thu, 1–4pm Sun) has the usual assortment of vintage engines, uniforms and an 1890 hose wagon. It's in a restored 1913 fire station that, until 1955, was one of only two in town that employed black firefighters.

Further south, Central Ave takes you into **Watts**, the epicenter of the LA riots of 1965 and 1992 and still teeming with large numbers of kids growing up poor and angry. There are pockets of improvements thanks in part to such groups as the **Watts Labor Community Action Committee** (WLCAC; Map pp82–3; ☎ 323-563-5639; www.wlcac.org; 10950 S Central Ave; admission free; ⏲ daily), whose headquarters doubles as a cultural center. A huge bronze sculpture of a black woman called *Mother of Humanity* dominates the campus. Nearby, Mudtown Flats is a facade recreating iconic black LA historic sites and often used for movie shoots.

The most powerful exhibit, though, is the **Civil Rights Museum**, which takes you through the hull of a body-filled slave ship and along a Mississippi Delta dirt road to displays about Martin Luther King and the 1960s Civil Rights Movement.

LEIMERT PARK

The soft lilt of a saxophone purrs out from behind a storefront. Excited chatter streams from a coffeehouse. The intense aroma of fried chicken and collard greens wafts into the steamy noontime air. Welcome to **Leimert** (*luh-MERT*) **Park**, the old-school cultural hub of LA's African-American community. About 2½ miles west of Exposition Park, the mostly residential neighborhood was designed by the Olmsted brothers of New York Central Park fame and has been nicknamed 'the black Greenwich Village' by filmmaker and local resident John Singleton (*Boyz n the Hood*).

The action centers on Leimert Park Village – Degnan Blvd between 43rd St and the namesake park where bongo freaks gather for Sunday afternoon drum circles. Nearby, the World Stage (p200) is a destination for jazz aficionados, while blues brothers head around the corner to the historic Babe & Ricky's (p199). You can stock up on African fabrics at **African by the Yard** (Map p97; 4319 Degnan Blvd), paintings and sculpture at **Gallery Plus** (4333 Degnan Blvd), exotic shell and amber jewelry at **Sika** (4330 Degnan) and gifts and artifacts at **Zambezi Bazaar** (4334 Degnan Blvd).

Phillip's Barbecue (p188) has great ribs, while **Lucy Florence's Coffeehouse & Cultural Center** (Map p97; ☎ 323-293-2395; 3351 W 43rd St) serves up readings, music and theater alongside its

---

DETOUR: FARMER JOHN PIG MURAL

An unassuming factory building in the bleak industrial city of Vernon, about 4 miles east of Exposition Park, is brightened by a **mural** (Map pp80–1; 3049 E Vernon Ave, Vernon) that looks adorable but is really sick and twisted. Called *Hog Heaven*, it shows happy pigs romping around a bucolic countryside. Judging by their squeals, the truckloads of live pigs arriving here are not fooled: they seem to know they're headed not to heaven but to 'hog hell' and the only way out is as bacon or pork chops.

mocha and sweet-potato pie. The place that launched Macy Gray's career is owned by Ron and Richard Harris, also known the 'Swirl Twins' from *America's Next Top Model*.

Griffith Park

A gift to the city in 1896 by mining mogul Griffith J Griffith, **Griffith Park** (Map p95; ☎ 323-913-4688; admission free; ✆ 6am-10pm, trails close at dusk; P) is a wonderful playground with facilities for all age levels and interests. At five times the size of New York's Central Park, it is one of the country's largest urban green spaces and embraces an outdoor theater, the city zoo, an observatory, two museums, golf courses, tennis courts, playgrounds, bridle paths, 53 miles of hiking trails, Batman's caves and even the Hollywood Sign.

In May 2007, a devastating fire roared across its chaparral-cloaked hillsides, destroying about 850 acres – or one quarter – of the park and threatening structures and nearby residences. The burnt areas will remain closed long-term, but other hiking trails should be reopened by mid-2008. All facilities listed below are open. This includes the richly festooned 1926 **Griffith Park Merry-Go-Round** (Map p95; ☎ 323-665-3051; Park Center; rides $1; ✆ 11am-5pm daily May-Sep, Sat & Sun Oct-Apr) with beautifully carved and painted horses sporting real horse-hair tails.

Access to the park is easiest via the Griffith Park Dr or Zoo Dr exits off I-5 (Golden State Fwy). Parking is plentiful and free. For information and maps stop by the **Griffith Park Ranger Station** (Map p95; ☎ 323-665-5188; 4730 Crystal Springs Dr).

GRIFFITH OBSERVATORY

Billions and billions of stars for millions and millions of dollars. After four years and $93 million, this landmark 1935 **observatory** (Map p95; ☎ 213-473-0800; www.griffithobservatory.org; 2800 Observatory Rd; admission free, shuttle bus adult/child & senior $8/4, planetarium shows $7/5; ✆ noon-10pm Tue-Fri, 10am-10pm Sat & Sun;) again opens a window on the universe from its perch on the southern slopes of Mt Hollywood. Its revamped planetarium now boasts the world's most advanced star projector, and hollowing out the front lawn nearly doubled the original exhibit space, and added a store, a self-service café and a theater.

Apparently, all the fancy engineering (the historic structure had to be lifted up in order to perform excavations underneath it) left only relative chump change for the astronomical displays themselves, which often lack imagination, depth and clarity. The coolest gallery is in the basement, where you can admire the Big Picture – a floor-to-ceiling digital image of a sliver of the universe bursting with galaxies, stars and lurking dark matter. For more tangible thrills, weigh yourself on nine planetary scales (weight-watchers should go for Mercury), generate your own earthquake or head to the rooftop to peek through the refracting and solar telescopes housed in the smaller domes. The sweeping views of the Hollywood Hills, and the gleaming city below are just as spectacular, especially at sunset.

The observatory has starred in many movies, most famously *Rebel Without a Cause* with James Dean. Outside, have your picture snapped beside the actor's bust with the Hollywood Sign caught neatly in the background.

Admission to the observatory is by timed entry and shuttle-bus reservation only, although this may change. Call or check online for details.

LOS ANGELES ZOO & BOTANICAL GARDENS

The **Los Angeles Zoo** (Map p95; ☎ 323-644-4200; www.lazoo.org; 5333 Zoo Dr; adult/child/senior $10/5/7; ✆ 10am-5pm; P) with its 1200 finned, feathered and furry friends rarely fails to enthrall the little ones. What began in 1912 as a refuge for retired circus animals recently also won accreditation as a **botanical garden**. Still, it's definitely the zoo's animal magnetism that brings in over a million visitors each year.

Meerkats are the current squeezables of the Disney set, and one well-placed, big-eyed Timon wows kids entering the zoo. From there, undisputed crowd pleasers include swinging gibbons, frolicking sea lions, posturing chimpanzees, cuddling koalas, and, according to the zoo's director, anything currently defecating. Tots gravitate to **Adventure Island** with its petting zoo and hands-on play stations as well as the **Children's Discovery Center**.

The zoo also participates in the recovery program of the endangered condor; some 126 chicks have hatched here since the '80s.

MUSEUM OF THE AMERICAN WEST

Want to know how the West was really won? Then mosey over to this excellent **museum** (Map

00; www.autrynationalcenter.org; 4700
ay; adult/student & senior/child $9/5/3;
pm Tue-Sun, to 8pm Thu Jun-Aug; &) whose
hibits on the good, the bad and the ugly of
America's westward expansion rope in even
the most reluctant of cowpokes.

Start downstairs, where a soundscape
of music, hooves and whinnying leads
you through a frontier village to a nymph-
festooned saloon with some interesting cheat-
ing devices used in gambling. Nearby, the
Wyatt brothers take on their adversaries in
the infamous 1881 shoot-out at the OK Corral,
re-enacted here in an animated diorama. A
glass case holds the original gun used by Doc
Holliday, one of the fight's participants, and a
precious collection of Colt firearms, and Annie
Oakley's gold-plated pistols are also on display.
Other galleries test the romantic myths of the
Old West against its harsher realities, deal with
the clashes between conquerors and Native
Americans and examine the roles played by
successive waves of immigrants.

Kids can pan for gold, explore a stagecoach, watch themselves riding like Zorro on
TV or get a hands-on history lesson about
Chinese family life in 1930s LA. Year-round
gallery talks, symposia, film screenings and
other cultural events further spur the imagination. In summer, a popular music series is
held outside on Thursdays. Excellent café,
too.

TRAINS, TRAINS, TRAINS
The delightful outdoor **Travel Town Museum**
(Map p95; ☎ 323-662-4253; www.traveltown.org; 5200 W
Zoo Dr; admission free; ☒ 10am-4pm Mon-Fri, 10am-5pm
Sat & Sun, one hr longer during daylight savings; P &)
displays dozens of vintage railcars and loco-
motives, the oldest one from 1864. Kids are
all smiles imagining themselves as engineers,
clambering around the old-timey iron horses
or riding a miniature train ($2.50). A huge hall

holds historical fire engines and a model-train
network, which a dedicated local hobby club
operates, usually on weekends from 10am
to 4pm.

Just east of Travel Town, the **Los Angeles Live
Steamers** (Map p95; ☎ 323-662-8030; www.lals.org; 5202
Zoo Dr; ☒ 11am-3pm Sun; P &) is a group of local
folks with a passion for scale-model locomo-
tives. On Sunday afternoons, they offer free
rides on their one-eighth-size model trains.

And if that's not enough train stuff for you,
head to the **Griffith Park Southern Railroad** (Map p95;
☎ 323-664-6903; 4400 Crystal Springs Dr; adult & child/senior
$2/1.50; ☒ 10am-4:30pm Mon-Fri, 10am-5pm Sat & Sun;
P &), a small fleet of miniature trains that
has ferried generations of children around a
1-mile loop past pony rides, an old Western
town and a Native American village since 1948.

FOREST LAWN MEMORIAL PARK –
HOLLYWOOD HILLS
Pathos, art and patriotism rule at this humongous **cemetery** (Map p95; ☎ 323-254-3131; www
.forestlawn.com; 6300 Forest Lawn Dr; admission free; ☒ 8am-
5pm; P) next to Griffith Park. A fine catalog of
old-time celebrities – including Lucille Ball,
Bette Davis and Stan Laurel – rests within the
manicured grounds strewn with paeans to
early North American history. Look out for
the giant *The Birth of Liberty* mosaic, Boston's
re-created Old North Church and bronze statues of Washington, Jefferson and Lincoln
or watch a movie about the American Revo-
lution. Staff aren't helpful in locating stars'
graves but you can download guides from the
internet (try www.seeing-stars.com). More
dead stars are at the original Forest Lawn in
nearby Glendale (p146).

BRONSON CAVES
Scenes from *Batman, Star Trek, The Lone
Ranger* and many other TV shows and films
were shot in this former **quarry** in a remote

THE TRAGIC TALE OF GITA

In 2006, the LA Zoo's elephant program came under severe pressure and scrutiny after the
headline-making death of a much beloved 48-year-old Asian elephant named Gita. Elephants
traditionally don't do well in captivity because of a lack of space, exercise and stimulus, and
the LA Zoo has lost 11 pachyderms since 1975. To prevent further tragedy, Gita's 46-year-old
buddy Ruby was sent to a sanctuary in 2007. That brings the zoo's elephant herd down to one:
21-year-old Billy the bull. He'll be the first to move into the new $39 million Pachyderm Forest,
which is seven times bigger than the current enclosure and set to open in late 2009. Let's hope
Billy makes it until then.

corner of Griffith Park. It's well worth exploring for its steep cliffs, spooky caves and cool views of the Hollywood Sign. However, it's a bit tricky to find. Head north on Canyon Dr and park in the last lot before the locked gate at Hollywoodland Camp. Walk back south, then turn left and head past a gate and up a fire road for about a quarter-mile, then turn left when the trail forks and the caves will be right there. The trail continues on the other side of the caves.

GREEK THEATRE

A more intimate version of the Hollywood Bowl, this 5800-seat **outdoor amphitheater** (Map p95; ☎ 323-665-5857; tickets 213-480-3232; www .greektheatrela.com; 2700 N Vermont Ave; ⓨ May-Oct; Ⓟ) tucked into a woodsy hillside of Griffith Park is much beloved for its vibe and variety – Goo Goo Dolls to Joss Stone to Tony Bennett. Parking is stacked, so plan on a post-show wait.

San Fernando Valley

Despite being home to most of LA's major movie studios – including Warner Bros, Disney and Universal – much of the sprawling grid of suburbia known as 'the Valley' is an exercise in bleakness. It also has the dubious distinction of being the world capital of the porn-movie industry, memorably captured in Paul Thomas Anderson's 1997 *Boogie Nights*. Car culture was basically invented in the Valley, which also claims to have given birth to the mini-mall, the drive-in movie theater, the drive-in bank and the drive-in restaurant.

Attractions are few and scattered about; Burbank has the studios, and North Hollywood, west of here, is home to a growing arts scene. Studio City, west of Universal, has some decent nightlife and shopping along Ventura Blvd.

Note that temperatures here are usually 20°F higher – and pollution levels worse – than in areas further south. For studio tours, see the boxed text p146.

UNIVERSAL STUDIOS HOLLYWOOD & CITY WALK

One of the world's oldest continuously operating movie studios, **Universal** (Map p95; ☎ 818-622-3801; www.universalstudioshollywood.com; 100 Universal City Plaza; admission over/under 48in $61/51; annual pass $71; ⓨ vary by season; Ⓟ) presents an entertaining mix of fairly tame – and sometimes dated –

---

thrill rides, live action shows and a tram ride. It is a working studio, but the chances of seeing any action, let alone a star, are slim to none.

Try to budget a full day, especially in summer. To beat the crowds, get there before the gates open or invest in the Front of Line Pass ($120) or the deluxe guided VIP Experience ($200). Some rides have minimum height requirements. The Southern California City-Pass (see p413) and the Go Los Angeles Card (p109) are valid for general admission. Buying online tickets usually yields discounts and coupons.

First-timers should head straight for the 45-minute narrated Studio Tour aboard a rickety tram that drives around the soundstages in the front lot, then heads to the back lot past the crash site from *War of the Worlds*, vehicles from *Jurassic Park*, the spooky Bates Motel from *Psycho* and – with any luck – Wisteria Lane from *Desperate Housewives*. Also prepare to face down King Kong, brave a flash flood, and survive a shark attack, a spitting dino and an 8.3 magnitude earthquake. It's a bit hokey, but fun.

The best thrill ride is Jurassic Park, a gentle float through a prehistoric jungle with a rather 'raptor-ous' ending. Revenge of the Mummy is a short but satisfying indoor roller coaster romp through 'Imhotep's Tomb' that at one point has you going backwards. A new ride based on *The Simpsons* is set to open in 2008. Guests will be rocketed along with the Simpson family and experience a side of Springfield previously unexplored.

Of the live shows, Terminator 2: 3-D combines live-action stunts with digital imaging technology and stars the Governator himself. Spider-Man Rocks is a cutesy, fast-paced musical show with dance numbers and aerial acrobatics. The movie may have bombed, but

BEHIND THE CURTAIN: MOVIE MAGIC UNMASKED

Did you know it takes a week to shoot a half-hour sitcom? Or that you rarely see ceilings on shows because the space is filled with lights and lamps? You'll learn these and other fascinating nuggets of information about the make-believe world of film- and TV- making while touring a working studio. Star sighting potential is better than average except during 'hiatus' (May to August) when studios are pretty deserted. Unless noted, reservations are required and so is photo ID.

- **Warner Bros** (Map p95; ☎ 818-972-8687; www.wbstudiotour.com; 3400 Riverside Dr, Burbank; tours $45, minimum age 8; ⊗ 8:30am-4pm Mon-Fri, longer hr Mar-Sep; ⓟ) This tour offers the most fun yet authentic look behind the scenes of a major movie studio. The 2¼-hour romp kicks off with a video of WB's greatest film hits (*Rebel without a Cause, Harry Potter* etc) before a tram whisks you to sound stages, backlot sets and technical departments, including props, costumes and the paint shop. Tours conclude at the studio museum, a treasure trove of props and memorabilia, including Hogwarts' famous Sorting Hat. Tours leave roughly every half hour.

- **Sony** (Map p97; ☎ 323-520-8687; 10202 W Washington Blvd, Culver City; tour $25, minimum age 12; tours ⊗ 9:30am, 10:30am, 12:30pm, 1:30pm & 2:30pm Mon-Fri; ⓟ) Perhaps less entertaining than Warner Bros, but still quite good, this two-hour walking tour includes possible visits to the sound stages where *Men in Black, Spider-Man, Charlie's Angels* and other blockbusters were filmed. Munchkins hopped along the Yellow Brick Road in the *Wizard of Oz*, filmed when this was still the venerable MGM studio. You might even pop in on the set of *Jeopardy*.

- **Paramount** (Map pp86-7; ☎ 323-956-1777; 5555 Melrose Ave, Hollywood; tours $35, minimum age 12; ⊗ Mon-Fri; ⓟ) The only remaining studio in Hollywood proper runs two-hour tram tours of its historic lot that also incorporates the original Desilu and RKO Studios. Group size is limited to eight per tram, giving you ample opportunity to pepper your guide with questions. No two tours are alike as guides don't follow a set script and access to stages varies day by day. Visits to the sets of *Dr Phil* and *Nip/Tuck* are potentially on the cards.

- **NBC** (Map p95; ☎ 818-840-3537; 3000 W Alameda Ave, Burbank; adult/child/senior $8.50/5/7.50; ⊗ 9am-3pm Mon-Fri; ⓟ) This major TV studio offers tours that include a stop at the set of the *Tonight Show* with Jay Leno.

the WaterWorld show is a runaway hit with mind-boggling stunts that include giant fireballs and a crash-landing seaplane.

Snack food and drinks, including beer and margaritas, are available throughout the park, although you'll have more choices at the adjacent **Universal City Walk**, an unabashedly commercial fantasy promenade of restaurants, shops, bars and entertainment venues. Just make sure to get your hand stamped for re-entry. Parking costs $8.

Also here is the **Gibson Amphitheatre** (Map p95; ☎ 818-622-4440; www.hob.com; 100 Universal City Plaza), a big venue for headlining rock and pop acts.

FOREST LAWN MEMORIAL PARK – GLENDALE

This humungous **cemetery** (Map pp80-1; ☎ 818-241-4151; www.forestlawn.com; 1712 S Glendale Ave; admission free; ⊗ 9am-5pm; ⓟ) is the final home of such Golden Age superstars as Clara Bow, Humphrey Bogart and Jimmy Stewart. Alas, many of their graves are in mausoleums and off-limits to the public. It doesn't help that cemetery staff strongly discourage star seekers. You can download maps from the internet (for example www.seeing-stars.com), but be discreet or risk having them confiscated. The grounds are still worth a visit if only to marvel at the country-club feel of the place and oddly impressive art such as a stained-glass version of Leonardo da Vinci's *Last Supper*.

Highland Park & Mt Washington

Mt Washington and Highland Park wrap around the Arroyo Seco, a rocky riverbed running from the San Gabriel Mountains to Downtown LA. It was flooded with artists and architects in the early 20th century, but lost its idyllic setting with the arrival of I-110 (Pasadena Fwy) in 1940. Of late, though, there's been an artistic revival and the area is slowly becoming the go-to place for contemporary Latino art. About two dozen galleries now belong to the **Northeast Los Angeles Arts Organization** (NELAart; www.nelaart.com) and

DETOUR: RONALD REAGAN LIBRARY & MUSEUM

No matter how you feel about Ronnie Reagan (1911–2004), his **presidential library** (off Map pp80-1; ☎ 805-577-4000, 800-410-8354; www.reaganlibrary.com; 40 Presidential Dr; adult/teen/senior $12/3/9; ⌚ 10am-5pm; Ⓟ) is really quite fascinating. Galleries cover the arc of the man's life from his childhood in Dixon, Illinois, through his early days in radio and acting to his years as governor of California, although the focus is obviously on his stint as president (1980–88) in the waning years of the Cold War. The museum features re-creations of the Oval Office and the Cabinet Room, Reagan family memorabilia, gifts from heads of state, a nuclear cruise missile and even a graffiti-covered chunk of the Berlin Wall. His grave is on the grounds as well. The library is a bit of a drive, but worth the detour. Get there via the I-405 (San Diego Fwy) north to the 118 (Ronald Reagan Fwy) west; exit at Madera Rd South, turn right on Madera and continue straight for 3 miles to Presidential Dr.

keep their doors open late during Gallery Night every second Saturday of the month. Galleries are too scattered to be explored on foot, so plan on driving or hop on a bicycle for the free **Spoke(n) Art Tour** (http://bikeoven.com /spokenart).

Other area attractions spotlight a premetropolitan LA. Eight Victorian beauties saved from the wrecking ball were airlifted here to become the **Heritage Square Museum** (off Map pp84-5; ☎ 323-225-2700; www.heritagesquare.org; 3800 Homer St; adult/child 6-12/senior $10/5/8; ⌚ noon-5pm Fri-Sun), just off the Ave 43 exit of I-110 (Pasadena Fwy). You're free to walk around the grounds for close-ups of several impressive residences, including the way-cool Octagon House, a Methodist church and a carriage barn. The interiors can only be seen on tours offered on Saturday and Sunday on the hour from noon to 3pm (included in the admission price).

Another oldie is the 1910 **Lummis House** (off Map pp84-5; ☎ 323-222-0546; 200 E Ave 43 at Carlota Blvd; admission free; ⌚ noon-4pm Fri-Sun), the former home of writer, librarian and Arts & Craft pioneer Charles Lummis. It was built largely by hand using local boulders and old rails. Inside is a small exhibit on Lummis, who also founded LA's oldest museum, the nearby **Southwest Museum of the American Indian** (off Map pp84-5; ☎ 323-221-2164; www.southwestmuseum.org; 234 Museum Dr; Ⓟ ♿), which is undergoing massive restoration and only open on weekends for family-oriented activities.

Pasadena & San Gabriel Valley

The Rose Parade (p160) may have given Pasadena long-lasting fame, but it's the progressive spirit of this genteel city and its location beneath the lofty San Gabriel Mountains that make it a charming and attractive place year-

round. Its immaculate streets may conjure visions of Wisteria Lane (of *Desperate Housewives* fame), but there are also plenty of grand old Craftsman mansions, fine art museums, extraordinary gardens and a lively downtown to make it a lively happening place.

The main fun zone is **Old Pasadena**, a bustling 20-block shopping and entertainment district set up in successfully restored historic brick buildings along Colorado Blvd west of Arroyo Parkway. Other interesting strips, especially if you're into shopping, are **South Lake Ave**, about 1 mile east of here, and Mission St and Fair Oaks Ave in **South Pasadena**. The last is a stretch of Route 66 with a rare old-timey soda fountain (p189).

Pasadena is served by the Metro Rail Gold Line (p219) from Downtown LA. Pasadena ARTS buses (fare 50¢) plough around the city on seven different routes.

The surrounding communities of suburban San Gabriel Valley have large Asian populations and some excellent restaurants (p190). The northern town of La Cañada is the gateway to the Angeles Crest Hwy (p150).

HUNTINGTON LIBRARY, ART COLLECTIONS & BOTANICAL GARDENS

Unwind in the zenlike tranquility of the Japanese Garden? Study the jaunty pose of Thomas Gainsborough's *The Blue Boy*? Linger over the illuminated vellum of a 1455 Gutenberg Bible? It's hard to know where to start exploring this genteel **country estate** (Map p96; ☎ 626-405-2100; www.huntington.org; 1151 Oxford Rd; adult/child 5-11/student/senior $15/6/10/12; ⌚ 10:30am-4:30pm Tue-Sun Jun-Aug, noon-4:30pm Tue-Fri, 10:30am-4:30pm Sat & Sun Sep-May; Ⓟ), the legacy of railroad tycoon Henry Huntington and one of the most delightful and inspirational spots in LA. It's lovely year-round but best on a weekday in spring, as summers get very hot and weekends are busy.

Budget at least an hour to admire the 18th-century French and British paintings and rare and ancient books, then leave another hour or two for romping around the **Japanese Garden** with its sunken bridge and water-lily pond, the charming **Desert Garden** with Seussian-shaped organ-pipe cacti and giant blue agave, or the **Rose Garden**, which is at its redolent best from April to August. For little ones the interactive **Children's Garden** yields lots of tactile surprises.

Picnics are not allowed but, in any case, the classic way to cap off a visit to the Huntington is with afternoon tea in the **Rose Garden Tea Room** (Map p96; ☎ 626-683-8131; $15). It's hugely popular, so make advance reservations or else pick up some sandwiches in the adjacent self-service cafeteria.

While in the area, make a quick detour to **El Molino Viejo** (Old Mill; Map p96; ☎ 626-449-5458; www.oldmill.info; 1120 Old Mill Rd; admission free; ⊙ 1-4pm Tue-Sun; **P**), a brick and adobe structure that houses Southern California's first water-powered grist mill, built in 1816 for the San Gabriel Mission.

NORTON SIMON MUSEUM
Rodin's *The Thinker* is only a mind-teasing overture to the full symphony of art in store at this exquisite **museum** (Map p96; ☎ 626-449-6840; www.nortonsimon.org; 411 W Colorado Blvd; adult/senior/child under 18 & student $8/4/free; ⊙ noon-6pm Wed-Mon, to 9pm Fri; **P**). Norton Simon (1907–93) was an entrepreneur with a Midas touch and a passion for art who parlayed his millions into a respectable collection of Western art and Asian sculpture. The highly accessible, user-friendly galleries teem with choice works by Rembrandt, Renoir, Raphael, Van Gogh, Botticelli and Picasso, as well as an outstanding array of paintings and sculpture by Degas. Asian sculpture is in the basement, while Western sculpture graces the gorgeous garden inspired by Monet's at Giverny, France.

GAMBLE HOUSE
It's the exquisite attention to detail that impresses most at the **Gamble House** (Map p96; ☎ 626-793-3334; www.gamblehouse.org; 4 Westmoreland Pl; adult/student & senior/child $8/5/free; ⊙ noon-3pm Thu-Sun; **P**), a 1908 masterpiece of Craftsman architecture built by Charles and Henry Greene for Proctor & Gamble heir David Gamble. The entire home is a work of art, its foundation, furniture and fixtures all united by a common design and theme inspired by its Southern California environs. Note sleeping porches, iridescent stained glass and subtle appearances of the Gamble family crest's rose and crane pattern.

Other Greene & Greene homes, including **Charles Greene's former private residence** (368 Arroyo Tce), line nearby Arroyo Tce and Grand Ave. Pick up a self-guided walking-tour pamphlet at the Gamble House bookstore.

PASADENA CIVIC CENTER AREA
Pasadena's Civic Center, built in the 1920s, is a reflection of the great wealth and local pride that have governed the city since its early days. Highlights include the Spanish Renaissance–style **City Hall** (Map p96; 100 N Garfield Ave) and the **Central Library** (Map p96; 285 E Walnut St). Nearby, the **Jackie Robinson Memorial** (Map p96; cnr Garfield & Union Sts) honors the Pasadena-born athlete who, in 1945, became the first African American to be signed to a major-league baseball team, the Brooklyn (now LA) Dodgers.

A block east, a re-created Chinese palace that was once the home of local art dealer and Asia fan Grace Nicholson, is now the **Pacific Asia Museum** (Map p96; ☎ 626-449-2742; www.pacificasiamuseum.org; 46 N Los Robles Ave; adult/student & senior $7/5; ⊙ 10am-6pm Wed-Sun; **P**). Its nine galleries orbit an exotic courtyard and present changing selections of both ancient and contemporary art and artifacts from Asia and the Pacific Islands. From Himalayan Buddhas to Chinese porcelain and Japanese costumes, the quality and range of Nicholson's collection is stellar.

Just around the corner is the **Pasadena Museum of California Art** (Map p96; ☎ 626-568-3665; www.pmcaonline.org; 490 E Union St; adult/student & senior/child $6/4/free; ⊙ noon-5pm Wed-Sun; **P**), a progressive gallery dedicated to art, architecture and design created by California artists since 1850. Shows change every few months and have included masterpieces by Maynard Dixon, collages by Beatnik artist Jess, and vinyl toys by Gary Basemen, David Gonzales and other artists. Also swing by the Kosmic Kavern, a spray mural by Pop artist Kenny Scharf, in the garage.

DESCANSO GARDENS
Another set of lovely **gardens** (Map pp80-1; ☎ 818-949-4200; www.descanso.com; 1418 Descanso Dr; adult/child 5-

SMALL SCREEN LA   Ryan Ver Berkmoes

Since the 1950s most TV shows have been made in and around LA. The reasons are simple: studios are based here and union rules make it expensive to move crews very far from the sound stages. Although shows are often filmed in Canada (for tax reasons) or on location (eg New York and New Jersey for *The Sopranos),* Southern California is the location for series such as *CSI: Miami,* which is actually shot in and around Long Beach, possibly an insult to one or the other depending on where you live.

You may recognize the Venice Boardwalk from countless shows (eg the opening of *Three's Company*) but far more humdrum parts of the region are used most often. The number of car chases filmed in and around the workaday environs of Ventura Blvd and Burbank are incalculable, until you note the proximity of Universal Studios (p145) and Warner Bros (p146), two of the biggest TV-show producers.

Some LA locations have achieved their own fame through one or several shows. The websites www.tvacres.com and www.seeing-stars.com list oodles of locations in and around LA, but here are a few iconic places you can visit:

Brady Bunch House (Map p95; 11222 Dilling St, Studio City) The bland home of the classic 1970s sitcom family. Although it was prominent in the opening, nothing was actually shot here, leaving Bobby, Cindy and the rest to cavort on Astroturf on a Paramount sound stage. Note that the current owner has added a fence in front to keep warped fans from peeking in the windows in hopes of seeing Marcia in the shower or something.

Torrance High School (Map pp82-3; 2200 W Carson St, Torrance) Buffy Anne Summers (aka *Buffy the Vampire Slayer*) took on the evil subjects of algebra, calculus and chemistry during her day job as a student at Sunnydale High School, set here. The school also did a star turn as West Beverly High in *Beverly Hills 90210*.

Alias Apartment Building (Map pp86-7; 1731 N Sycamore Ave, Hollywood) Only on TV would a grad student live in a posh vintage Hollywood apartment like this. OK, it's Jennifer Garner and the student thing is only a cover for her role fighting evil-doers on the ABC series that ran from 2001 to 2006.

Shooters (Map pp86-7; 6810 Melrose Ave, Hollywood) Hangout for the ever-scheming, ever-copulating gang of *Melrose Place,* this real-life restaurant (named Fellini's) was used for exterior shots. The namesake courtyard apartment building at the center of the intrigue is at 4616 Greenwood Ave in Los Feliz.

Also worth checking out, and appearing elsewhere in the book:

- **LA City Hall** (p134) *Dragnet,* Daily Planet in the TV version of *Superman*
- **Bronson Caves** (p144) *Lone Ranger,* Bat Cave in the TV *Batman,* countless alien landscapes on *Star Trek* and bandit hideouts on *Bonanza*
- **Will Rogers State Beach** (p122) *Baywatch*
- **Paradise Cove** (p154) *Rockford Files*
- **Malibu Creek State Park** (p153) *M*A*S*H*

12/student & senior $7/2/5; ⏰ 9am-5pm; P), Descanso puts on a dazzling show all year, but especially so in January and February when some 34,000 camellias brighten the LA winter, some as tall as 20ft. In spring lilacs perfume the air, followed by roses in summer. It's easy to spend a whole day amid the greenery, waterways and bird sanctuary. The gardens are in La Cañada–Flintridge, about 6 miles northwest of Pasadena at the foot of the Angeles Crest Hwy (see boxed text, p150).

ART CENTER COLLEGE OF DESIGN
Overlooking the Arroyo Seco from its ridge-top perch is this world-renowned **arts campus** (Map p96; ☎ 626-396-2200, tour reservations 626-396-2373; www.artcenter.edu; 1700 Lida St). Free tours are offered during the school year at 2pm Monday to Friday; reservations are required. To see what students and alumni have been up to, check out the latest exhibit at the **Williamson Gallery** (www.artcenter.edu/Williamson; admission free; ⏰ noon-5pm Tue-Sun, to 9pm Fri).

CALIFORNIA INSTITUTE OF TECHNOLOGY (CALTECH)

With 31 Nobel laureates among its faculty and alumni, it's no surprise that **Caltech** (Map p96; ☎ 626-395-6327; www.caltech.edu; 551 S Hill Ave; P) is regarded with awe in academic circles. Earthquake studies were essentially pioneered here in the 1920s with the inventions of the seismograph and the Richter scale, and to this day Caltech scientists are usually the first experts to be consulted whenever a shaker strikes.

The hallowed campus is dotted with century-old buildings and shady old trees. Free student-led **tours** (☎ 626-395-6341; ☺ 11:15am year-round, 2:15pm Mar, Apr, Jul & Aug) depart from the Office of Undergraduate Admissions at 355 S Holliston. Alternatively, pick up a self-guided tour booklet at the office or download one from the website.

Caltech also operates the **Jet Propulsion Laboratory** (JPL; Map pp80-1; ☎ 818-354-0012; www.jpl.nasa.gov; 4800 Oak Grove Dr), NASA's main center for robotic exploration of the solar system, about 3.5 miles north of campus. It's possible to visit JPL during public lectures in the annual open house (usually in May) or by requesting a free tour well in advance (☎ 818-354-9314).

SAN GABRIEL MISSION

In 1781, a small group of settlers set out from this **mission** (Map pp80-1; ☎ 626-457-3035; www.sangabrielmission.org; 428 S Mission Dr; adult/child 6-17/senior $5/3/4; ☺ 9am-4:30pm; P) to found El Pueblo de Los Angeles in today's Downtown area. About 3 miles southeast of Pasadena in the city of San Gabriel, it's the fourth in the chain of 21 missions in California and one of the prettiest. Its church boasts Spanish Moorish flourishes, a copper baptismal font, carved statues of saints and a 1790 altar made in Mexico City. On the grounds you'll discover the cemetery, original soap-and-tallow vats and fountains. The small museum has historic Bibles, religious robes and Native American artifacts.

The mission surroundings are also well worth a quick stroll. Following Mission Dr takes you past the 1927 Civic Auditorium, the Civic Center, a historical museum and galleries.

DETOUR: ANGELES NATIONAL FOREST

The San Gabriel mountain range that hems in the northern edge of urban LA is part of the **Angeles National Forest** (Map pp80-1; ☎ 626-574-1613; www.fs.fed.us/r5/angeles) whose creeks, canyons and campgrounds provide quick city getaways year-round. It's particularly pretty during the spring wildflower season and even gets decent fall color. Traffic can be insane on busy weekends, especially in summer with people trying to escape the heat, and after decent snowfall in winter, which brings skiing in the higher elevations. Motorcyclists love the smooth and curvy road.

Access is via the two-lane **Angeles Crest Scenic Byway** (Hwy 2; www.byways.org/explore/byways/10245/travel.html), which treats you to fabulous views of big-shouldered mountains, the Mojave Desert and deep valleys on its 55-mile meander from La Cañada to the resort town of Wrightwood. The road skirts LA County's tallest mountain, officially called Mt San Antonio (10,064ft) but better known as **Old Baldy** for its treeless top. You'll pass ranger stations along the way, but the main **Chilao Visitor Center** (Map pp80-1; ☎ 626-796-5541; admission free; ☺ 8am-4pm Sat & Sun mid-Apr–mid-Oct) with natural exhibits and trails is about 27 miles from the turnoff.

By then, you will have passed the junction (after about 15 miles) to Red Box Rd which, 5 miles later, dead-ends at the **Mt Wilson Observatory** (Map pp80-1; ☎ 626-793-3100; www.mtwilson.edu; admission free; ☺ 10am-4pm Apr-Oct, weather permitting) atop 5715ft Mt Wilson. Operating since 1904, it was the world's top astronomical research facility in the early 20th century and is still in use today. You can walk around the grounds (download a handy self-guided tour from the website) and visit the museum. Free guided tours run at 1pm on Saturdays and Sundays. The website also has details on how to schedule a viewing session for the 1908 60-inch telescope (half-/full-night $650/1200 for groups of up to 25 people).

Note that visiting the Angeles National Forest requires a National Forest Adventure Pass (p69). Places to pick one up in La Cañada at the start of the drive are **Sport Chalet** (Map pp80-1; ☎ 818-790-9800; 920 Foothill Blvd) or **Jay's Shell Station** (Map pp80-1; ☎ 818-790-3836; 4530 Angeles Crest Hwy).

LOS ANGELES COUNTY ARBORETUM & BOTANIC GARDEN

It's easy to spend hours amid the global vegetation, waterfalls, spring-fed lake and historic buildings of this fantastic, rambling **park** (Map pp80-1; ☎ 626-821-3222; www.arboretum.org; 301 N Baldwin Ave; adult/student & senior/child 5-12 $7/5/2.50, 3rd Tue of month free; ⏰ 9am-5pm). Originally the private estate of real-estate tycoon Elias 'Lucky' Baldwin, it's so huge, there's even a tram to take around those who are foot-weary. The grounds are often used in filming, for instance standing in for the African jungle in *African Queen* and as Central Park in *End of Days*. It's in Arcadia, about 5 miles east of central Pasadena, right by the Santa Anita Park racetrack (see below).

SANTA ANITA PARK

Home of the legendary Seabiscuit, the art deco **thoroughbred racetrack** (Map pp80-1; ☎ 626-574-7223; www.santaanita.com; 285 W Huntington Dr, Arcadia; admission general $5, clubhouse $8.50, turf club $20, child under 17 free if accompanied by adult; racing season ⏰ Christmas–mid-Apr, late Sep–early Nov) is the oldest and one of the most prestigious in Southern California. Free **tram tours** (☎ 626-574-6677; ⏰ 8:30am & 9:45am Sat & Sun) taking you to Seabiscuit's barn, filming locations, the jockey's room and other sites are offered during racing seasons.

The track opened in 1934 and pioneered the use of the automated starting gate, the photo finish and the electrical timer. Stars who kept and raced their horses here have ranged from Bing Crosby and Errol Flynn to Mark McGrath (of Sugar Ray), Alex Trebek and Burt Bacharach. The only stain on its legacy happened during WWII when it served as a Japanese-American detention camp.

TOURNAMENT HOUSE & WRIGLEY GARDENS

Chewing-gum magnate William Wrigley spent his winters in the elegant Italian Renaissance-style **mansion** (Map p96; ☎ 626-449-4100; 391 S Orange Grove Blvd; admission free; tours ⏰ 2pm & 3pm Thu Feb-Aug) where the Tournament of Roses Association now masterminds the annual Rose Parade. When they're not busy, you can tour the rich interior and inspect Rose Queen crowns and related memorabilia. Feel free to nose around the rose garden any time.

ROSE BOWL STADIUM & BROOKSIDE PARK

One of LA's most venerable landmarks, the 1922 **Rose Bowl Stadium** (Map p96; ☎ 626-577-

3100; www.rosebowlstadium.com; 1001 Rose Bowl Dr) can seat up to 93,000 spectators and has its moment in the sun every New Year's Day when it hosts the famous Rose Bowl postseason college football game. At other times, it's sadly underused even though the UCLA Bruins football team play here and the occasional concert or special event also brings in the masses, as does a monthly flea market (p209). In 2006, *American Idol* held its Los Angeles auditions here.

The Rose Bowl is surrounded by **Brookside Park**, which is a nice spot for hiking, cycling and picnicking. Families should check out the excellent **Kidspace Children's Museum** (p157), and architecture nuts the gracefully arched 1913 **Colorado St Bridge** (Map p96) and the 1903 **Vista del Arroyo Hotel** (Map p96; ☎ 626-441-2797; 125 S Grand Ave), now home to the Ninth Circuit Court of Appeals.

PASADENA MUSEUM OF HISTORY

A palatial beaux arts mansion that once housed the Finnish consulate, this interesting **museum** (Map p96; ☎ 626-577-1660; www.pasadenahistory.org; 470 W Walnut St; suggested donation adult museum/house tour/combination $5/4/7, children free; ⏰ noon-5pm Wed-Sun, tours 1pm Wed-Fri, 1:30pm & 3pm Sat & Sun Oct-Jul; Ⓟ) now presents changing exhibits on some facets of the culture, history and art of Pasadena and its neighboring communities. If you want to see the precious antiques and furnishings of the house itself, you'll need to join a tour. The admission price also lets you sneak a peek inside a shed-like structure housing folk art from Finland.

ACTIVITIES

Cycling & Skating

Get a scenic exercise kick skating or riding along the paved **South Bay Bicycle Trail** that parallels the sand for most of the 22 miles between Will Rogers Beach near Santa Monica and Torrance Beach. Weekends get jammed and there are sections where you must push your bike – don't ignore the signs or risk getting fined.

Inland, the 8-mile Griffith Park trail passes by the zoo and museums. Another trip from Griffith Park travels along the LA River Bikeway, which parallels a surprisingly pleasant 5-mile stretch of the river from Atwater Village to Burbank. Have a look at www.labikepaths .com for lots of good information.

Mountain bikers will find the **Santa Monica Mountains** (opposite) a suitably challenging playground. The book *Mountain Biking in the Santa Monica Mountains* by Jim Hasenauer and Mark Langton is an excellent resource. Check www.corbamtb.com and www.social mtb.com for conditions.

You'll find numerous bike rental places throughout town, especially along the beaches. Rates vary but you should be able to get a decent bike from $30 a day.

Blazing Saddles (Map p92; ☎ 310-393-9778; Santa Monica Pier, Santa Monica) Also has several other outfits along Santa Monica and Venice beaches named Perry's Café. Also organizes bike tours (p159).

Fun Bunns Beach Rentals (Map p94; ☎ 310-372-8500; 1116 Manhattan Ave, Manhattan Beach)

Hollywood Pro Bicycles (Map pp86-7; ☎ 323-466-5890; 6731 Hollywood Blvd, Hollywood)

John Muir's 110-year-old Sierra Club lets nonmembers join their organized, very welcoming hikes and bike rides, geared to various fitness levels. See www.angeles.sierraclub.org to choose from hundreds. Their night hikes are especially cool.

Gyms

Many midrange and practically all top-end hotels have small fitness centers, but for edgier workouts try the following joints:

Crunch Gym (Map pp88-9; ☎ 323-654-4550; www .crunch.com; 8000 W Sunset Blvd, West Hollywood; per day $24; ☽ 5am-midnight Mon-Thu, 5am-10pm Fri, 7am-10pm Sat & Sun; ℗) Chisel your body into perfection at this high-tech gym famous for its innovative classes – cardio striptease to 'Ex-Factor,' a cathartic boxing class where you fasten a picture of your ex to the punching bag.

Gold's Gym (Map p92; ☎ 310-392-6004; www

.goldsgym.com; 360 Hampton Dr, Venice; per class/day/ week $10/20/70; ☽ 4am-midnight Mon-Fri, 5am-11pm Sat & Sun) Channel your inner Schwarzenegger at the hallowed original Gold's branch of Pumping Iron fame.

Hoopnotica (Map p92; ☎ 310-306-0300; www .hoopnotica.com; 2nd fl, 114 Washington Blvd, Marina del Rey; classes $19-38; call or check website for schedule; ℗) Twirl away your flabby abs with this high-energy workout using the old-school hula-hoop which, incidentally, was invented in LA in 1958. Pre-registration required; hoop rentals are $2. Also at 817 N Highland Ave in Hollywood (Map pp86-7).

Joint (Map pp86-7; ☎ 323-871-1504; www.thejoint fitness.com; 6531 Hollywood Blvd; per class $20; ☽ 6:30am-11pm; ℗) The tattooed instructors at this 'rock 'n' roll gym' will make sure you get 'the bod' with hardcore spinning and such radical classes as Budokon that mixes yoga and martial arts, and Mat Max, a muscle-shredding Pilates session. Two hours of free valet parking on Hudson Ave.

Muscle Beach Venice (Map p92; ☎ 310-399-2775; www.laparks.org/dos/reccenter/facility/veniceBeachRC .htm; 1800 Ocean Front Walk; per day $10; ☽ 8am-7pm May-Sep, 8am-6pm Oct-Apr) Gym rats with an exhibitionist streak can get a tan and a workout at this famous outdoor gym right on the Venice Boardwalk where Arnold and Franco Columbo once bulked up.

Sheila Kelley's S-Factor (Map pp88-9; ☎ 323-965-9685; http://sfactor.com; 5225 Wilshire Blvd, Mid-City; intro class $40) Release your inner sexpot while learning the stripper's strut, the cat walk and pole tricks at this strip aerobics center. A great workout you may get asked to repeat at home. Lindsay Lohan and Kate Hudson are fans.

Horseback Riding

Leave the rat race behind and hit the happy trails on horseback during guided rides led by experienced wranglers. A tip of about 20% is appropriate. Sorry, no kids under seven.

Bar S Stables (Map p95; ☎ 818-242-8443; 1850 Riverside Dr, Glendale; 1st hr $25, additional hr $15, cash only) Great for families, these rides explore the northern reaches of Griffith Park. Just show up and off you go.

Los Angeles Horseback Riding (Map pp80-1; ☎ 818-591-2032; www.losangeleshorsebackriding.com; 2623 Old Topanga Canyon Rd, Topanga Canyon; rides per hr $50, full moon rides $125; ℗) Sunset, day and full-moon rides along the Santa Monica Mountains Backbone Trail with fabulous views all around. Western-style only, group size limited to six people, reservations required.

Sunset Ranch Hollywood (Map pp86-7; ☎ 323-469-5450; www.sunsetranchhollywood.com; 3400 Beachwood Dr, Hollywood; 1/2hr rides $25/40; ℗) Rides through Griffith Park, plus famous Sunset Dinner Rides ($60, plus

HIKING IN THE SANTA MONICA MOUNTAINS

Hiking may not be an obvious activity to get your kicks in LA, but trust us: exploring the city's 'wild side' will feel like taking a micro-vacation from the mad bustle. Chumash Native Americans once roamed the hilly, tree- and chaparral-covered coastal range now protected as the **Santa Monica Mountains National Recreation Area** (www.nps.gov/samo). It extends from Griffith Park in Hollywood to Point Mugu across the Ventura county line. The 65-mile **Backbone Trail** covers its entire length, but there are lots of scenic shorter hikes, including those listed below. For more ideas, see Will Rogers State Historic Park (p122), drop by the **Visitors Center** (Map pp80–1; ☎ 805-370-2301; 401 W Hillcrest Dr, Thousands Oaks, take Lynn Rd exit off 101 Fwy; ☺ 9am-5pm) or consult www.lamountains.com.

■ **Malibu Creek State Park** (Map pp80–1) Nature puts on a magnificent show in this park, which has cameoed on film as Wales, the South Pacific and, most famously, Korea in M*A*S*H. Don't miss the lovely trail leading to the latter's main set, where an old Jeep and other relics rust serenely in the California sunshine. Stop by the visitors center (open weekends) to study stills from the shoots. The main parking lot ($8) is on Malibu Canyon Rd. Coming from Hwy 101 (Hollywood Fwy), take the Las Virgenes Rd exit. Another famous filming site in the park is the **Paramount Ranch** (Map pp80–1; ☎ 818-735-0896; Cornell Rd; ☺ 8am-sunset; **P**), a historic movie ranch. To get there, continue on Malibu Canyon Rd and turn west on Mulholland Hwy, then right on Cornell Rd. Both Malibu Creek and Paramount are stops on the ParkLINK Shuttle (see p121).

■ **Runyon Canyon Park** (Map pp86–7) Keep your celeb radar on high while exploring this gem of a park right above frenzied Hollywood Blvd. Paris Hilton has been spotted working her quads in sequins and on our last visit we quite literally bumped into British crooner Robbie Williams, jogging fresh out of rehab. Views of the city are stellar. Even if you're too short on time (or breath) for the full 3.5-mile loop, at least make it to Inspiration Point, reached in 15 minutes tops. Pooches are allowed to romp around off-leash. Mornings and late afternoon are best; weekends are the busiest. Catch the trail at Vista St or Fuller St in Hollywood or at the top on Mulholland Dr. For the full lowdown, see www.runyon-canyon.com.

■ **Fryman Canyon** (Map pp80–1) Sweeping views of the San Fernando Valley, deep forest canyons and year-round springs are among nature's gifts to hikers venturing along the 3.3-mile Betty B Dearing Trail, which continues through Wilacre Park. Most people start in Fryman Canyon Park at the Nancy Hoover Pohl Overlook off Mulholland Dr. To get to the trailhead, take Laurel Canyon Blvd to Mulholland Dr, turn right (west) and the parking lot will be on your right. This is one of the most heavily traveled trails around here, so avoid weekends if possible. You can also pick up the trail at Wilacre Park, on Fryman Rd, just off Laurel Canyon Blvd.

about $15 for food) to a Mexican restaurant in Burbank. Reservations nightly except on Friday when sign-up begins at 4:30pm. Lessons (Western or English riding) start at $40.
Wagon Wheel Ranch (☎ 310-567-3582; www.pv horses.com; Palos Verdes Peninsula; 1/2hr rides $60/100) Rides explore the wild side of posh Palos Verdes Peninsula delivering views of the ocean and the city. Moonlight rides available too. Riding is Western-style. Call ahead for reservations and directions.

Skateboarding

Skate rats should check out **Santa Monica Skate Park** (Map p92; ☎ 310-458-8228; cnr 14th St & Olympic Blvd, Memorial Park) with 20,000 sq feet of vert, street and tranny terrain.

Spas & Massages

Get your stressed-out self over to these pampering shrines where they'll work out the kinks and turn you into a glowing lump of tranquility.
Kate Somerville (Map pp88–9; ☎ 323-655-7546; www.katesomerville.com; 8428 Melrose Pl, West Hollywood; facials from $125) Facialist to the stars, Kate has made fans of Sandra Oh, Kirsten Dunst, Jessica Alba and other A-listers with her potent potions and customized treatments. A session at her posh but pleasant medi-spa will leave your skin quenched, radiant and ready for your own close-up.
Le Petite Retreat Day Spa (Map pp88–9; ☎ 323-466-1028; wwwlprdayspa.com; 331 N Larchmont Blvd,

TOP 10 LA BEACHES

Listed north to south. For access to Malibu's hidden beaches, see boxed text, p122.

- **Leo Carrillo** (off Map pp80–1) – Families love this summer-camp-style beach with enough stimulating tide pools, cliff caves, nature trails and great swimming and surfing to tire out even the most hyperactive kids.

- **El Matador** (off Map pp80–1) – This small, remote hideaway is a popular filming location thanks to super-scenic battered rock cliffs and giant boulders, but the surf is wild and clothing is optional (X-rated action has been observed).

- **Zuma** (off Map pp80–1) – Two miles of pearly sand with plenty of Halle Berry and Daniel Craig lookalikes emerging from the crystal-clear waves. Mellow swells make for perfect body surfing. Come early on weekends to snag parking.

- **Paradise Cove** (Map pp80–1) Brad and Angelina have been photographed strolling along the scenic sands of TV's *Rockford Files* fame (sorry, Jim's trailer is long gone). The water looks lovely but can be quite polluted. Eating at the beach café cuts the $25 parking fee down to $3. Walk-ins are $5.

- **Will Rogers** (Map pp80–1) – *Baywatch* stars Pamela Anderson and David Hasselhoff used to bounce along this sandy patch which is now a cruisey gay beach.

- **Santa Monica** (Map p92) – Wide slab of sand where beach-umbrella-toting families descend like butterfly swarms on weekends to escape the inland heat. Water quality is poor right by the pier but OK a few hundred yards away.

- **Venice Beach** (Map p92) – Get your freak on at LA's most hipsterific beach paralleled by the Venice Boardwalk. During Sunday's drum circle, the bongos reach crescendo and dancers turn to silhouettes as the sun dips into the ocean.

- **Manhattan Beach** (Map p94) – Brassy SoCal beach with a high flirt factor and hardcore surfers hanging by the pier for, like, totally epic waves. Families can check out marine life in the Roundhouse Marine Studies Lab & Aquarium (p127).

- **Hermosa Beach** (Map p94) – Possibly LA's most libidinous beach party with hormone-crazed tight-bods getting their game on over beach volleyball and in the raucous pubs along Pier Ave.

- **Malaga Cove** (Map pp82–3) – This crescent-shaped, cliff-backed shoreline is the only sandy Palos Verdes beach easily accessible by the hoi polloi. Blends into rocky tide pools and has excellent rolling waves for surfers (Haggerty's), but no lifeguards.

Mid-City) Petite but oh-la-la – this luxe spa is a soothing feng-shui zone that'll leave you feeling as limber as Gumby after a deep-tissue stone massage, as glowing as Brooke Shields after an enzyme facial and as sexy as Brangelina after a couples' massage in the outdoor cabaña.

Massage Garage (Map p97; ☎ 310-202-0082; www .themassagegarage.com; 3812 Main St, Culver City; massages 30/60/90 min $30/45/70, facials from $45; ◷ 10am-9pm) Feeling as run-down as your '89 Honda? Why not pull in for a 'test drive' (30 minutes), a 'tune-up' (60 minutes) or an 'overhaul' (90 minutes) at this industrial-flavored yet comfortable day spa? Choose from five massage treatments, including shiatsu and Swedish massage. For the complete detox, book a mud wrap ($80).

Pho Siam Thai Spa (off Map pp86-7; ☎ 213-484-8484; www.phosiam.com; 1525 Pizarro St, Silver Lake; mas-

sage 30/60/90/120 min $25/40/60/80, facials from $35; ◷ 9am-10:30pm; P) She may look tiny, but your Thai massage mistress will pull, stretch, push, knead and possibly walk on you until you feel like a marshmallow. The classy decor, soothing ambience and impeccable cleanliness make this place a steal.

Swimming & Surfing

Water temperatures become tolerable by late spring and are highest (about 70°F or 21°C) in August and September. Water quality varies; for updated conditions check the Beach Report Card at www.healthebay.org. See the boxed text Top 10 LA Beaches on above for tips on good swimming beaches.

The most legendary surfing spots are of course in Malibu. Surfrider gets tops marks, but Zuma and Carrillo also have their devotees. South of Santa Monica, you'll find mostly west-facing beach breaks. Venice Beach, Hermosa Beach and Manhattan Beach all have decent waves, but more experienced surfers head to Torrance Beach/Haggerty's and Lunada Bay in Palos Verdes. For the latest surfing and beach conditions, call ☎ 310-578-0478 or check http://beache s.co.la.ca.us.

If you want to learn surfing, expect to pay about $70 to $120 for a two-hour private lesson or $40 to $60 for a group lesson, including board and wet suit. Contact these schools for details.

Learn to Surf LA (☎ 310-663-2479; www.learntosurf la.com) Great for beginners, in Santa Monica; they guarantee you'll get up on the board on your first lesson.

Malibu Long Boards (☎ 310-467-6898; www.malibu longboards.com) Private lessons in Malibu by college-level surf instructor; email for free surf video.

Surf Academy (☎ 310-372-2790; www.surfacademy .org) Founded by a US surfing champion, they offer lessons up and down the coast.

Yoga

No matter whether you can twist yourself into a knot or are as stiff as a log, these studios will have you doing the downward dog and sun salutation in no time.

Bikram Yoga Studio Mid-City (off Map pp88-9; ☎ 310-854-5800; www.bikramyoga.com; 1862 S La Cienega Blvd; per class over/under 25 $20/10) International Bikram headquarters; Silver Lake (off Map pp86-7; ☎ 323-668-2500; www.bikramyogasilverlake.com; 3233 Glendale Blvd; per class $17) If you like it hot, try these rigorous 90-minute workouts in a studio heated up to between 95°F and 105° (bring a bath towel).

Bryan Kest Power Yoga (Map p92; ☎ 310-458-9510; www.poweryoga.com; 1410 2nd St, Santa Monica; class by donation; ⏰ 5:30am-10:45pm Mon-Thu, 8am-8pm Fri-Sun) You'll sweat, you'll tone, you'll meditate, you'll feel great after these ashtanga (power) yoga classes. The recommended donation is $12, but give what you can.

Trüyoga (Map p92; ☎ 310-829-2227; www .truyogala.com; 2425 Colorado Ave, Santa Monica; per class $16; ⏰ daily, call or check web for class schedule; P) Beginners to gurus, everyone will find a favorite class at this 'green' yoga studio built entirely from recycled and ecofriendly materials. No toxic fumes here. The entrance is next to Tully's Coffee inside the Yahoo Center complex.

YAS (Map p92; ☎ 310-396 6993; www.go2yas.com; 1101 Abbot Kinney Blvd, Venice; per class $15; ⏰ 7am-7.30pm Mon-Thu, 7am-6pm Fri, 8.30am-6pm Sat & Sun) This studio offers the yin and yang of workouts, combining 30 minutes of yoga and spinning each to put both your body and mind into a state of bliss. Also popular is their Yoga for Athletes classes. Weekends get busy, so preregister.

Yoga Works (Map p92; ☎ 310-664-6470; www.yoga works.com; 2215 main St; per class $18; ⏰ 7am-9pm) Dozens of classes per week for all levels of expertise, plus one- and two-day intro courses. Call about other branches.

WALKING TOUR: DOWNTOWN LA

Downtown LA is rapidly changing its stripes and is on the verge of becoming, once again, a dynamic and vital part of the city; this is a great time to take a closer look and witness history in the making. The area is reasonably compact and packed with trophy sights and countless hidden little gems. Along the way, you'll be treated to tremendous architecture, world-class museums, interesting nosh spots and plenty of places you might recognize from TV and the big screen.

Kick-off is at LA's major transportation hub, **Union Station** (**1**; p133), an elegant vestige from the era when the railroad was the main method of transportation. Crossing Alameda St plunges you straight into folkloric **El Pueblo de Los Angeles** (**2**; p132), the city's historic heart with buildings dating back to the Mexican period. Work your way south along Main St across the Hwy 101 overpass, from where you can already espy your next stop, the hulking **Cathedral of Our Lady of the Angels** (**3**; p135), a provocatively modernist house of worship on Temple St. Inside, it's quiet, cool and filled with original art.

Continue a block north, then turn left on Grand Ave, which takes you past the **Music Center** (**4**). This giant entertainment complex consists of two theaters and two concert halls, most famously the wonderfully contorted **Walt Disney Concert Hall** (**5**; p134), a Frank Gehry masterpiece and home of the world-renowned LA Phil. More culture awaits as you head south on Grand Ave passing first the **Colburn School of Performing Arts** (**6**; p135) and then **MOCA Grand Ave** (**7**; p135), Southern California's premier contemporary art museum.

WALK FACTS

Start & Finish Union Station
Distance 5 miles
Duration At least half a day, preferably a full day

MOCA sits at the edge of the Financial District with its mix of historic office buildings and modern monoliths. On your right is one such worker's beehive, the Wells Fargo Center, where the **Wells Fargo History Museum** (**8**; p136) offers a trip back to the stagecoach era. Head for the Hope St exit past the tropical indoor garden accented with nude sculptures, then turn left and walk to the top of the **Bunker Hill Steps** (**9**; p136) – anchored by another nude – which cascade down to 5th St past LA's tallest building, the **US Bank Tower** (**10**; p136), which is on your left. In front of you is the historic **Richard Riordan Central Library** (**11**; p136) and its modern addition, both worthy of a quick spin. From here head downhill on 5th St, past the grand **Millennium Biltmore Hotel** (**12**; p136) whose public hallways and ballrooms ooze with old-time glamour.

The hotel flanks **Pershing Square** (**13**; p136), the site of summertime concerts and a holiday-season ice rink. From here, head south on Hill St where you'll be looking at shimmering baubles in the **Jewelry District** (**14**; p136). Turn left on 7th St, then duck into Middle East–flavored **St Vincent Court** (**15**; p136) for a gyro and minty tea, saving room for dessert at the Depression-era **Clifton's Cafeteria** (**16**; p185). To get there, continue on 7th, turn left on Broadway and it'll be on your right. Still older than Clifton's are Broadway's many silent-era movie palaces, including the magnificent **Los Angeles Theater** (**17**; p137) across the street, which is used occasionally for screenings and special events.

For a quick spin around historic Downtown's emerging gallery district, walk right on 5th St to the corner of Spring St, which is dominated by the venerable **Alexandria Hotel** (**18**), which once bedded Bogart, Garbo and other Hollywood royalty, then became low-income housing and is now getting the loft-treatment. Charlie O's dive bar downstairs hosts a weekend comedy club (p205). Across the street, the **Red Dot Gallery** (**19**; ☎ 213-817-6002; 118 W 5th St; ⏱ 11am-8pm) is entered via Weenez hot-dog shop. Next up is **Bert Green Fine Art** (**20**; p207), whose owner basically invented Gallery Row and the Downtown Art Walk (p207). Check out what's up at **Pharmaka Gallery** (**21**; ☎ 213-689-7799; 101 W 5th St; ⏱ noon-6pm

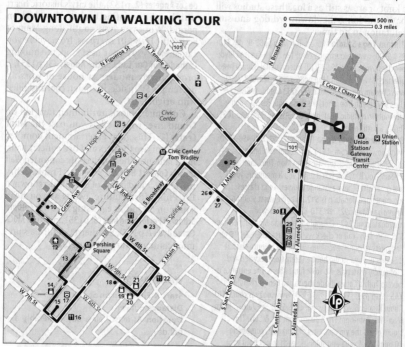

DOWNTOWN LA WALKING TOUR

0 .... 500 m
0 .... 0.3 miles

Wed-Sat) across the street, then turn left on Main St to walk past a slew of funky new businesses, including an indie bookstore, a fashion designer and several restaurants, including **Pete's Café & Bar** (**22**; p185).

Head back to Broadway via 4th St, turn right and get ready for the **Bradbury Building** (**23**; p137) whose lobby will take your breath away. Across the street, the lively **Grand Central Market** (**24**; p137) is a good spot to rest your feet and have a bite or a cuppa before continuing two more blocks on Broadway to 1st St. Turn right and look up at the magnificent **LA City Hall** (**25**; p134), whose observation tower is well worth it on clear days. Continue on 1st St past the **LA Times** (**26**; p134) on your right to the hulking **Caltrans District 7 Headquarters** (**27**; 100 S Main St), which has windows that open or close depending on the outside temperature and angle of the sun. Santa Monica–based architect Thom Mayne won the 2005 Pritzker Prize, the Oscar of architecture, for this futuristic design.

One block further and you're in Little Tokyo, home to great sushi parlors, the informative **Japanese American National Museum** (**28**; p138) and the edgy **Geffen Contemporary at MOCA** (**29**; p138). Just beyond, the **Go for Broke monument** (**30**; 160 N Central Ave) honors the Japanese-American soldiers fighting for America in WWII, even as their families were interned in camps.

Turn right on Temple St, left on Alameda St, walk past the snazzy new **Metropolitan Detention Center** (**31**; cnr Aliso & Alameda Sts), cross the freeway overpass and you're back at Union Station.

COURSES

Fred Segal Beauty (Map p92; ☎ 310-451-7260; www.fredsegalbeauty.com; 420 Broadway, Santa Monica; **P**) Intensive, pro-level workshops to get you up to speed with the latest tricks and trends in beauty, fashion and hair. Courses from $400.

Groove Riders DJ School (off Map pp80-1; ☎ 818-981-3366; www.grooveriders.com; 14566 Ventura Blvd, Sherman Oaks) Aspiring DJs can learn all about beat matching and beat juggling on turntables or CDs at this 'institute of mixology'. Courses start at $295.

New York Film Academy (Map p95; ☎ 818-733-2600; www.nyfa.com; 100 Universal City Plaza; **P**) NYFA's West Coast branch is located on the Universal Studios lot. Learn about acting, filmmaking, screenwriting, and music videos in full programs or workshops lasting from one to 12 weeks. Courses start at $1000.

Robert McKee's Story Seminar (☎ 888-676-2533; www.mckeestory.com) Even seasoned writers come to pick up tips and inspiration from McKee's three-day seminar featured in the movie *Adaptation*. Former students include the screenwriters of *A Beautiful Mind* and *Lord of the Rings*. Offered in LA several times a year for $545.

LOS ANGELES FOR CHILDREN

Looking around Rodeo Dr, the Sunset Strip and Grand Ave, you might think that LA's children have been banished to a gingerbread cottage in the woods. But the kids are here, trust me, you just gotta know where to look. Places listed in this section are specifically geared towards kids, but there's plenty more to do in town. Have a look at p75 for more family-friendly ideas. A listing of shops catering to kids is on p214.

Sights & Activities

Zimmer Children's Museum (Map pp88-9; ☎ 323-761-8989; www.zimmermuseum.org; 6505 Wilshire Blvd, Suite 100, Mid-City; adult/child 5-12 $8/5; ☼ 10am-5pm Tue, 12:30-5pm Wed, Thu & Sun, 10am-12:30pm Fri; **P** ☻) In the Jewish Federation Center, this charming museum brims with interactive exhibits that gently teach kids – Jewish or not – about tolerance, generosity, community spirit and other good values. Kids can 'fly' to exotic lands, fancy themselves an ambulance driver, work in a newsroom and take other fun journeys.

Kidspace Children's Museum (Map p96; ☎ 626-449-9144; www.kidspacemuseum.org; 480 N Arroyo Blvd, Pasadena; admission $8; ☼ 9:30am-5pm; **P** ☻) The single-digit set can get as creative, messy and interactive as they wish at this fun fantasy museum. They can build structures, dig up dino bones, even create an earthquake while their parents sip cappuccinos in the Wolfgang Puck-catered café. There's also a great garden space the kids can use for rock climbing, trike-riding and general romping. A separate center addresses the needs of children under four.

Noah's Ark at the Skirball Cultural Center (Map pp80-1; ☎ 310-440-4500; 2701 N Sepulveda Blvd; adult/student & senior/child 2-12 $10/7/5, Thu free; ☼ noon-5pm Tue, Wed & Fri, noon-9pm Thu, 10am-5pm Sat & Sun; ☻) Noah's Ark is an indoor playground like no other. Kids get to board a giant wooden ark where an entire menagerie of wondrously imaginative creatures waits for them. All are made from recycled materials – there's a

TOP 10 TOT-FRIENDLY EATERIES

- Bob's Big Boy (San Fernando Valley, p188)
- Cheebo (Hollywood, p175)
- Colori Kitchen (Downtown, p185)
- Coogie's Beach Café (Malibu, p180)
- Counter (Santa Monica, p180)
- Farmers Market (Mid-City, p176)
- Mama D's (Manhattan Beach, p183)
- San Pedro Fish Market & Restaurant (San Pedro, p184)
- Toast (Mid-City, p176)
- Uncle Bill's Pancake House (Manhattan Beach, p183)

pair of foam penguins, tortoises made from basketball hide and an elephant with car mats for ears. Kids get to explore, climb, build, and interact with each other and the animals while subtly learning that there's strength in diversity and that survival requires collaboration. See p118 for more about the Skirball Cultural Center.

Under the Sea (Map p97; ☎ 310-915-1133; www .undertheseaindoorplayground.com; 12211 W Washington Blvd, Suite 120, Culver City; adult/child 9 months–14yr free/$8; ☑ Mon-Fri; ☷) Ocean-themed indoor playground with a bounce house, climbing structures, a baby corner and other play stations. Call for specific opening hours. Check website for locations of the six other branches in town.

Adventureplex (Map p94; ☎ 310-546-7708; www .adventureplex.org; 1701 Marine Av, Manhattan Beach; admission for 1 adult & 1 child per 2hr from $10; ☑ 9am-7pm Mon-Fri, 10am-7pm Sat, 10am-6pm Sun; ☷) If romping around a four-story play structure straight out of *Blade Runner* and finding the perfect route on a rock wall won't tire out your tots, sign them up for one of the volleyball or dancing classes.

Sand Dune Park (Map p94; www.citymb.info; cnr 33rd & Bell Ave; admission free; ☑ 7:30am-9pm Apr-Oct, 6am-8pm Nov-Mar; ☒ ☷) If you want to tire 'em out, bring your kids to this unique park hidden on a residential block near Rosecrans and Highland. Hurling themselves down these 100ft-high sand dunes will be so much fun, they'll want to do it again, and again, and again…

Entertainment

Bob Baker Marionette Theater (Map pp84-5; ☎ 213-250-9995; www.bobbakermarionettes.com; 1345 W 1st St, near Downtown; tickets $12, reservations required; ☑ 10:30am Tue-Fri, 2:30pm Sat & Sun; ☒ ☷) Generations of Angelenos have been enthralled by Bob's adorable singing and dancing marionettes and stuffed animals that interact with their young audiences seated on a carpet. It's pure magic, and after the show everyone gets to enjoy some ice cream.

Magicopolis (Map p92; ☎ 310-451-2241; www .magicopolis.com; 1418 4th St, Santa Monica; tickets $22-27; ☑ 8pm Fri & Sat, 2pm Sat & Sun; ☷) Not only aspiring Harry Potters will enjoy the comedy-laced sleight-of-hand, levitation and other illusions performed by Steve Spills and cohorts in this intimate space. Escapes from reality last about 90 minutes, and there's even a small shop for all your wizard supplies.

Storyopolis (Map pp80-1; ☎ 818-509-5600; www.story opolis.com; 12348 Ventura Blvd, Studio City; ☑ 11am-5pm Tue-Sat, 11am-4pm Sun; ☒ ☷) A large and intelligent selection of children's books, family-friendly events (including free storytelling sessions at 11:30am Tuesday to Friday) and a gallery of original children's art make this place the best kids' bookstore in town.

Puppet & Magic Center (Map p92; ☎ 310-656-0483; 1255 2nd St, Santa Monica; admission $7.50; ☑ 1pm Wed, 1pm & 3pm Sat & Sun) Steve Meltzer's Puppetolio puppet show (suitable for ages three and up) has delighted audiences since 1998. All performances are followed by a tour 'behind the strings' and a visit to the puppet museum. Steve also runs puppet workshops.

TOURS
Boat

A lovely way to experience LA on a warm day is from the deck of a boat. **Hornblower Cruises** (☎ 310-301-6000; www.hornblower.com) and **Spirit Cruises** (☎ 310-548-8080; www.spiritdinnercruises.com) both run harbor tours, dinner cruises, champagne brunch cruises and whale-watching excursions (January to March). Boats depart from Marina del Rey, San Pedro and Long Beach.

Romantics should steer towards the one-hour **Gondola Getaway** (Map pp82-3; ☎ 562-433-9595; www.gondolagetawayinc.com; 5437 E Ocean Blvd, Long Beach; per couple $75, up to 4 additional persons per person $20; ☑ 11am-11pm) cruises. Aboard your private gondola you'll be piloted around canal-laced Naples in Long Beach by a real gondolier. Baguette, cheese, salami and an ice bucket are provided (you'll need to bring your own libations). Make reservations two to three weeks early, especially for the weekend sunset cruises.

Bus

Esotouric (☎ 323-223-2767; www.esotouric.com; walking/ bus tours $10/55) Discover LA's lurid and fascinating underbelly on these hip, offbeat, insightful and entertaining walking and bus tours themed around famous crime sites (Black Dahlia anyone?), literary lions (Chandler to Bukowski) and neglected neighborhoods (eg Downtown LA's Bunker Hill). Even the snack stops are unique: any takers for nicotine-flavored gelato?

Neon Cruise (☎ 213-489-9918; www.neonmona.org; tour $45; ☾ 6:45-10:30pm select Sat) From movie marquees to hotel signs, vintage neon is hot. Start by touring the fabulous Los Angeles Theater (p137), then see LA's best neon art from a genuine London double-decker bus. Call for tour dates and book early, tours always sell out.

Architecture Tours Los Angeles (☎ 323-464-7868; www.architecturetoursla.com; tour from $68; ☾ tours 9:30am & 1:30pm, reservation required) If you think LA architecture begins with Frank Lloyd Wright and ends with Frank Gehry, these van tours will broaden your horizon as you take in styles ranging from Tudor to utopian.

Dearly Departed (☎ 323-466-3696; www.dearly departedtours.com; tour $35; ☾ 1pm) Scott Michaels is LA's king of death and scandal and will clue you in on where celebs kicked the bucket, George Michael dropped his trousers, Hugh Grant received certain services and the Charles Manson gang murdered Sharon Tate & Co. Creepy, hilarious but not for kids or the prissy.

Urban Shopping Adventures (☎ 213-683-9715; www.urbanshoppingadventures.com; tour $36) Wanna dress like Beyoncé? Knockoff Gucci bags make you drool? Wonder where Kate Winslet gets her outfits? On these custom-guided shopping tours you'll get the inside scoop on bargain basements and tomorrow's fashions. Both walking and bus tours available.

Starline Tours (☎ 323-463-333, 800-959-3131; www .starlinetours.com; tour from $32) These standard narrated minibus sightseeing tours are predictably cheesy but not a bad way for first-timers to get oriented. Options include city tours, tours of the stars' homes, night tours and trips to theme parks. Buses leave from Hollywood Blvd.

Walking & Biking

Contact the tour company to find out times and departure points.

Los Angeles Conservancy (☎ 213-623-2489; www .laconservancy.org; tour $10, reservations required) Downtown LA's intriguing historical and architectural gems – from an art deco penthouse to a beaux arts ballroom and a dazzling silent-movie theater – are revealed on 2½-hour walking tours operated by this nonprofit group. Check the schedule and book tickets online or by phone.

Red Line Tours (☎ 323-402-1074; www.redlinetours .com; tour $22) Learn the secrets of Hollywood and Downtown on these 'edutaining' walking tours with nifty headsets to cut out traffic noise. Guides use a mix of anecdotes, fun facts, trivia and historical and architectural data to keep their charges entertained.

Downtown LA Walks (www.downtownlawalks.com) Get the nitty gritty on Downtown LA history, arts and culture or shopping with self-guided walking-tour podcasts ready to be downloaded for free to your MP3 player.

LA River Walks (☎ 323-223-0585; www.folar.org; suggested donation $5; ☾ 3rd Sun of month Jan-Nov) Discover the history, mystery and ecology of the LA River and find out why it's not just that ugly concrete channel you've been making jokes about. More extensive bus tours ($55) also run several times a year. Check the website for upcoming dates.

Metro Rail Art Tours (☎ 213-922-2738; www.metro .net; tour free; ☾ 10am 1st Sat & Sun of month) Some of LA's best contemporary art is not in a museum but in its metro stations. Discover edgy works by such artists as Jonathan Borowsky, Sam Erenberg and Gilbert 'Magu' Lujan on these two-hour tours leaving from the Hollywood/Highland station on Saturday and Union Station on Sunday.

Perry's Legends Beach Bike Tour (☎ 310-372-3138; tour $30; ☾ 11am May-Sep, reservation required) The mysteries of Muscle Beach, Jim Morrison's house and Skateboard Mamma all feature on this leisurely 90-minute bike tour of Santa Monica and Venice. Your guide communicates with you by headset. The tour charge includes water, a helmet and an additional 90-minute bike rental for self-exploring.

FESTIVALS & EVENTS

Banjos to bongos, film fests to book fairs, Day of the Dead to Doo Dah, the party never stops in LA. Basically, if you can't find something to do, you aren't looking. For a monthly listing of city-wide events see www.culturela.org. Art aficionados get their tips from www.artscenecal .com or check calendar listings in the *LA Times* or *LA Weekly*. Also see Out & About in Los Angeles (p112), Top Five Film Festivals (p196) and Free Sounds of Summer (p200).

January & February

Rose Parade (☎ 626-449-4100; www.tournamentof roses.com) This cavalcade of flower-festooned floats snakes through Pasadena on New Year's Day. Get close-ups of the stunning floats during postparade viewing at Victory Park. Avoid traffic and take the Metro Rail Gold Line to Memorial Park.

Chinese New Year (☎ 213-680-0243; www.lachinese chamber.org) Colorful celebrations in Chinatown mark the lunar new year, culminating with the Golden Dragon parade, food, floats, fashion and firecrackers. Occurs late January or early February.

Academy Awards (☎ 310-247-3000; www.oscars .org/bleachers) Ogle your favorite film stars from the Kodak Theatre's red-carpet adjacent bleachers. Apply in September for one of 600 lucky spots. Held in late February.

March

LA Marathon (☎ 310-444-5544; www.lamarathon .com) Rally the 25,000 runners and wheelchair racers, then wander performance stages and finish-line festivities. Held on the first Sunday in March, it's a 26.2-mile party through the city.

April

Toyota Grand Prix of Long Beach (☎ 888-827-7333; www.longbeachgp.com) World-class drivers and celebrities tear up city streets at this week-long racing spectacle by the sea in mid-April.

Blessing of the Animals (☎ 213-485-8372; www .cityofla.org/elp/) Chihuahuas to iguanas, all critters are welcome for a blessing from Cardinal Mahoney at this fun-loving Olvera St fest held on the Saturday before Easter.

Los Angeles Times Festival of Books (☎ 800-528-4637, ext 72665; www.latimes.com/festivalofbooks) It's a bookworm's paradise for one long weekend of reveling in readings, discussions and storytelling at UCLA. Late April.

Fiesta Broadway (☎ 310-914-8308; www.fiesta broadway.la; ☽ last Sun in Apr) One of the world's largest Cinco de Mayo parties brings out half a million folks to historic Downtown LA on the last Sunday of April. Dance, eat and sing along with chart-topping Latino performers.

Santa Clarita Cowboy Festival (☎ 661-286-4021; www.cowboyfestival.org) Yee-haw it with the best of them at this annual celebration of cowboy poetry, horseback

riding and country music at Gene Autry's old Melody Movie Ranch in Santa Clarita (near Six Flags Mountains). Late April.

May

Cinco de Mayo (☎ 213-625-5045; www.cityofla .org/elp) Celebrates the Mexican victory over the French at the Battle of Puebla (1862); free festivities around Olvera St in Downtown during early May.

Topanga Banjo Fiddle Contest & Folk Festival (☎ 818-382-4819; www.topangabanjofiddle.org) Toe-tappin' bluegrass and old-time tunes tear up the Paramount Ranch in the Santa Monica Mountains. Held in mid-May.

Fiesta Hermosa (☎ 310-376-0951; www.fiesta hermosa.com) Get in the mood for summer at this three-day festival where you can browse for arts and crafts, groove to surf music and feed your belly with a United Nations of food options. It's held on Memorial Day and again on Labor Day weekend.

Muscle Beach Body Building Competition (☎ 818-922-4626; www.musclebeachvenice.com) You're gonna get an eyeful of some buff dudes and babes flexing their quads and biceps at this thrice-annual testosterone-fest, the search for the next Arnold. Appropriately it's held at his old gym in the Venice Beach Recreation Center (p152). Held late May, July 4 and early September.

June

LA Pride (☎ 323-969-8302; www.lapride.org) Running since 1970, this three-day festival held in mid-June includes music, exhibitions, and a parade down Santa Monica Blvd.

Mariachi USA Festival (☎ 800-627-4224; www .mariachiusa.com) This four-hour fiesta held at the Holly-wood Bowl brings together the finest mariachi musicians and ballet-folklórico dancers and their fans on the third weekend in June.

Long Beach Bayou Festival (☎ 562-427-8834; www .longbeachfestival.com; tickets $30) A weekend of Cajun and Zydeco sounds and Creole food against the backdrop of the *Queen Mary*. Held in late June.

July

Independence Day (www.rosebowlstadium.com, www .hollywoodbowl.com, www.beaches.co.la.ca.us) Take a seat for official Fourth of July fireworks extravaganzas held at the Rose Bowl, the Hollywood Bowl or in Marina del Rey. Alternatively, drive up to any hilltop near Downtown and watch the skies explode.

Lotus Festival (☎ 213-485-1310; www.laparks.org /grifmet/lotus.htm) Celebrates Asian and Pacific Island culture with exotic foods, art, dragon-boat races, dancing, fireworks and other merriment. Held in mid-July.

Central Avenue Jazz Festival (☎ 213-485-2437; www.centralavenuejazzfestival.com) Big-name jazz players play for free during this weekend-long festival in late July, with music, food, arts and crafts, celebrating the pre-WWII era when Central Ave was a hotbed of West Coast jazz.

Blessing of the Cars (☎ 323-663-1265; www .blessingofthecars.com) This wacky festival is all about cars, rock and roll, hot-rod movies and a priest who will – if presumed upon – place holy water in your radiator. There are more tattoos on display than in the US Navy, and more nincompoops clambering for attention than in the US Senate.

August

Nisei Week Japanese Festival (☎ 213-687-7193; www.niseiweek.org) This free nine-day festival takes over Little Tokyo with parades, *taiko* drumming, tea ceremonies, karaoke, food, dancing and crafts. Held from early to mid-August.

Long Beach Jazz Festival (☎ 562-424-0013; www .longbeachjazzfestival.com) This three-day festival held in mid-August features top talents such as Barbara Morrison, Al Jarreau and Poncho Sanchez. Tickets often sell out, so book early.

Sunset Junction Street Fair (☎ 323-661-7771; www .sunsetjunction.org; admission $15) This multiblock street party with food, knickknacks and live music is held in mid-August.

LA Greek Fest (☎ 323-737-2424; www.lagreekfest .com) A weekend of ouzo, *sirtaki* (a Greek folk dance) and gyros right next to St Sophia Cathedral brings together the Greek community and friends in early September.

African Marketplace & Cultural Faire (☎ 213-293-1612; www.africanmarketplace.org) Series of festivals and events from late August to early September celebrating African culture with crafts, music and dancing.

September

LA County Fair (☎ 909-623-3111; www.lacountyfair .com) Eighteen days of monster trucks, rock 'n' roll, pie-eating contests, a Ferris wheel and cows at the fairgrounds in far-flung Pomona.

LA Triathlon (☎ 714-978-1528; www.latriathlon.com) It's swim, bike and run in an athletic tour de force that draws some top talent. Early September.

Oktoberfest (☎ 310-327-4384; www.alpinevillage .net/oktoberfest.htm) Largest Oktoberfest in SoCal with beer, sausages, oompah bands and chicken dancing at the Alpine Village in Torrance. Held in September and October.

Mexican Independence Festival (☎ 213-485-8372; www.cityofla.org/elp) On Olvera St, a free mid-September celebration of Mexico's independence from Spain with live performers, food, displays and celebrities from Mexico.

Abbot Kinney Festival (☎ 310-396-3772; www .abbotkinney.org) Soak up the groovy Venice vibe at this annual celebration of local arts, crafts, food and held in late September.

Watts Towers Drum & Jazz Festivals (☎ 213-847-4646; www.wattstowers.org) Two back-to-back events: multicultural beats on Saturday followed by a day of jazz, gospel and blues. Late September.

October

Catalina Island JazzTrax Festival (☎ 866-872-9849; www.jazztrax.com) The best and newest in smooth jazz brings fans from around the country to Catalina Island for the first three weekends in October.

West Hollywood Halloween Carnival (☎ 323-848-6400; www.visitwesthollywood.com) This free rambunctious street fair brings 350,000 revelers – many in over-the-top and/or X-rated costumes – out for a delicious day of dancing, dishing and dating on October 31. Kids are OK in the afternoon.

November

Día de los Muertos (Day of the Dead; ☎ 213-625-5045; www.olvera-street.com, www.ladayofthedead.com, www.selfhelpgraphics.org, www.festivaldelagente.org) Honor beloved ancestors with dance, face painting, decorated altars and candlelight processions on Olvera St, at Self-Help Graphics in East LA (p141), at Hollywood Forever Cemetery (p108) and with the Festival de la Gente along the 6th St Bridge in Downtown. Held around November 1.

Pasadena Doo Dah Parade (☎ 626-205-4029; www .pasadenadoodahparade.info) Embrace this wacky parody parade held on the Sunday before Thanksgiving. With its briefcase drill team, Royal Pains and Howdy Krishnas it's a tongue-in-cheek poke at Rose Parade perfection.

LADWP Light Festival (☎ 323-913-4688; www .dwplightfestival.com) Bright lights, no city in this mile-long stretch of enchanting holiday-themed light displays and music in Griffith Park. Walk, drive through slowly or take the shuttle leaving from the zoo on select dates. Runs from early November through until December 26.

Hollywood Christmas Parade (☎ 323-469-8311; www.hollywoodchamber.net) Celebs ring in the season by waving at fans from flash floats rolling down Hollywood Blvd. Easy access via the Metro Rail Red Line. Held the Sunday after Thanksgiving.

December

Marina del Rey Holiday Boat Parade (☎ 310-670-7130; www.mdrboatparade.org) Boats decked out in bright, blinking holiday cheer promenade for prizes in the marina. Check it out from Burton Chase Park. Mid-December.

LA County Holiday Celebration (☎ 213-972-3099; www.holidaycelebration.org) Celebrate Christmas Eve with free global music and dance at the Dorothy Chandler Pavilion (Map pp84-5).

Las Posadas (☎ 213-625-5045; www.cityofla.org/elp) Free candlelight processions that re-enact Mary and Joseph's journey to Bethlehem, followed by piñata-breaking and general merriment on Olvera St and around. From December 16 to 24.

SLEEPING

When picking a place to stay in sprawling Los Angeles, first try to decide on what type of experience you're most keen to have, whether it be beach, culture, urban edginess, stargazing, family activities, outdoors, studios, shopping, lifestyle or parties. Then choose a neighborhood that best reflects your expectations so you don't spend your holiday sitting in traffic.

Some bargains notwithstanding, hotel rates in LA are higher than the national average. During the peak summer season, even a $200 room will likely not be anything special. The lodging tax is 12% to 14% and is not included in rates listed below except where indicated. Unless noted, hotel parking is free. For general information about the types of accommodation available, see p408.

Hollywood

Hollywood is an excellent base of operation if you don't have your own wheels. You'll be close to landmark sights, hiking in Griffith Park and raucous nightlife, with easy access to efficient public transportation to Downtown, Universal Studios, Los Feliz and West Hollywood.

BUDGET

Orange Drive Manor Hostel (Map pp86-7; ☎ 323-850-0350; www.orangedrivehostel.com; 1764 N Orange Dr; incl tax dm $25-28, r $59-65; P ⬜ wi-fi) If you like your hostel with dash of quirk and history, this rambling old mansion should fit the bill. It's run more like a hotel, with rules and regulations and extra charges for parking and wi-fi. Security is good and cleanliness fairly consistent. Check-in is from 7am to 1am. Parking costs $5.

USA Hostels Hollywood (Map pp86-7; ☎ 323-462-3777, 800-524-6783; www.usahostels.com; 1624 Schrader Blvd; incl tax dm $27-29, r $64; ⬜ wi-fi) Not for introverts, this sociable hostel puts you within steps of the Hollywood party circuit. Dorms have attached bathrooms, and lockers for each guest. Making new friends is easy during staff-organized barbecues, comedy nights and tours or while microwaving your pizza

in the recently spruced-up kitchen. Freebies include a cook-your-own-pancake breakfast, all-day coffee/tea and wi-fi.

Elaine's Hollywood B&B (Map pp86-7; ☎ 323-850-0766; www.elaineshollywoodbedandbreakfast.com; 1616 N Sierra Bonita Ave; r $95-115, incl tax & breakfast) A great find if you're not the type in need of buckets of privacy, this B&B comprises just two rooms in a lovingly restored 1910 bungalow on a quiet street, yet it's smack-dab in Hollywood. Your outgoing hosts Avik and Elaine speak several languages, make a mean breakfast and will happily help you plan your day. Cash only.

MIDRANGE

Hollywood Celebrity Hotel (Map pp86-7; ☎ 323-850-6464, 800- 222-7017; www.hotelcelebrity.com; 1775 Orchid Ave; r incl breakfast $110-190; P ⬜ wi-fi) The art deco–style lobby is a sleek overture to this good-value property behind Hollywood & Highland. Rooms, while large and comfortable, can't quite carry the tune, but the bend-over-backwards-to-help staff, free breakfast and clean steam room still get our thumbs-up. No wheelchair access.

Highland Gardens Hotel (Map pp86-7; ☎ 323-850-0536, 800-404-5472; www.highlandgardenshotel.com; 7047 Franklin Ave; r $110-120, ste $140-330, child under 10 free; P ⬜ ⬜ ♿ wi-fi) This '50s residential-style motel is retro without even trying, but its heart-of-Hollywood location makes it quite a steal. Some rooms are still awaiting their date with a paint bucket, so if this matters have a look before checking in. All have a balcony or patio overlooking the courtyard with a groovy pool and tropical landscaping. And for all you trivia buffs: Janis Joplin overdosed in room 105.

Hollywood Hills Hotel & Apartments (Map pp86-7; ☎ 323-874-5089, 800-615-2224; www.hollywoodhillshotel .com; 1999 N Sycamore Ave; r incl breakfast $130-200, child free; P ⬜) Breathtaking city views, a curvy pool guarded by a pagoda, and roomy digs with balcony and kitchen are among the assets at this older but well-kept property. It's up in the hills yet still within walking distance of the Hollywood Blvd madness. Check-in is at the Magic Castle Hotel (opposite). Parking costs $9.

Best Western Hollywood Hills Hotel (Map pp86-7; ☎ 323-464-5181, 800-287-1700; www.bestwestern .com; 6141 Franklin Ave; r $150-225, child under 17yr free; P ⬜ wi-fi) Not all rooms are created equal at this family-run hotel with colorful retro touches; for more space and quiet get one in the back facing the sparkling tiled pool. Self-caterers will welcome the refrigerator and microwave, although the on-site coffee shop serves some pretty good comfort food and is open late; service, though, can be glacial. The hotel is pet-friendly.

Villa delle Stelle (Map pp86-7; ☎ 323-876-8100; www .villadellestelle.com; 6087 Harold Way; ste 150-210; **P** wi-fi) Designer-to-the-stars Brogan Lane has infused her quiet four-suite gem with effusive Golden Age glamour. You'll have plenty of space to stretch out in full-kitchen units with decor inspired by such icons as Humphrey Bogart, Grace Kelly and Lane's late husband Dudley Moore. Wine, cheese and a cheerful live-in manager greet your arrival. Pet-friendly.

Magic Castle Hotel (Map pp86-7; ☎ 323-851-0800, 800-741-4915; www.magiccastlehotel.com; 7025 Franklin Ave; r incl breakfast $160-330; **P** 🏊 🔥 wi-fi) Walls at this perennial pleaser are a bit thin (bring earplugs), but otherwise it's a charming base of operation with large, modern rooms (the full-kitchen suites sleep up to six), exceptional staff and a petite courtyard pool where days start with fresh pastries and gourmet coffee. Ask about access to the Magic Castle, a fabled members-only magic club in an adjacent Victorian mansion. (Say hi to the owl…). Parking costs $9.

TOP END

Hollywood Roosevelt Hotel (Map pp86-7; ☎ 323-466-7000, 800-950-7667; www.hollywoodroosevelt.com; 7000 Hollywood Blvd; r $200-400; **P** 🖥 🏊 wi-fi) Despite its uncanny resemblance to the Twilight Zone Tower of Terror at Disney's California Adventure (p243), the spooky-cool, revamped Roosevelt is again currying favor with Hollywood beauties. Staying here means you can hang with the kool kids but don't expect to be treated like one. Also see p104. Parking is $28.

Renaissance Hollywood Hotel (Map pp86-7; ☎ 323-856-1200, 888-236-2427; www.renaissancehollywood.com; 1755 N Highland Ave; r $270-400; **P** 🖥 🏊 wi-fi) Fancy sipping your mojito poolside with a view of the Hollywood Sign? Then this all-star behemoth behind Hollywood & Highland should do the trick. Gear up for a day of sightseeing in spacious, amenity-laden rooms (best views are above the 10th floor) with a mid-century vibe. Original art sets accents throughout; that abstract canvas in the lobby is by LA's own Charles Arnoldi. Parking costs $29.

West Hollywood & Mid-City

With its trendy nightlife, shopping and dining, West Hollywood is a perfect choice for the lifestyle crowd and urban explorers. Mid-City still puts you close to, but not in the middle of, the action but is excellent for easy access to Museum Row.

BUDGET

Orbit Hotel & Hostel (Map pp88-9; ☎ 323-655-1510, 877-672-4887; www.orbithotel.com; 7950 Melrose Ave; dm incl tax $20-22, r incl tax $60-100; **P** 🖥) Fun-seekers should thrive at this retro-styled hostel within staggering distance of hip shopping, boozing and dancing. Staff-organized movie nights, Sunday barbecues and club shuttles are ideal for meeting up with fellow-minded travelers. Dorms sleep six in full-size beds and have lockers, while private rooms come with TV; all rooms have a private bathroom.

Saharan Motor Hotel (Map pp88-9; ☎ 323-874-6700; www.saharanhollywood.com; 7212 W Sunset Blvd; r incl breakfast $85-95, child under 12 free; **P** 🏊 wi-fi) The cool neon sign should tip you off that this property is not exactly of recent vintage, but thanks to a makeover it's a value-for-money pick, at least if you're not too picky. It's reasonably close to nightlife and sights and across from a big supermarket, but the adjacent strip clubs probably don't make it ideal for families.

Beverly Laurel Motor Hotel (Map pp88-9; ☎ 323-651-2441, 800-962-3824; 8018 Beverly Blvd; r $95-120; **P** 🏊) Ride the retro wave on the cheap at this slicked up 1950s motel near the Farmers Market/Grove. Rooms wrap around a tiny pool and are just above basic, but framed photographs and diamond-patterned bedspreads add a stylish touch. The attached Swingers hipster diner (p176) makes colossal burgers and wicked Bloody Marys. Pet-friendly.

Cinema Suites (Map pp88-9; ☎ 323-931-0604; www .cinemasuites.biz; 925 S Fairfax Ave; s/d $100/120; **P**) It's not the fanciest B&B but the location is central, the price is right and you'll be sleeping in a wi-fi-enabled old Hollywood mansion where Greta Garbo used to buy her fur coats. The three rooms share a bathroom, and there's a kitchen where you can help yourself to a simple breakfast anytime. Check-out is at a hangover-friendly 2pm.

MIDRANGE

Grafton on Sunset (Map pp88-9; ☎ 323-654-4600, 800-821-3660; www.graftononsunset.com; 8462 W Sunset Blvd; r $120-280, ste $350-600, child under 18 free; **P** 🖥 🏊 wi-fi)

We like this charismatic boutique hotel for its feng shui aesthetic, enormous swimming pool, and rooms sporting such nifty touches as organic bath amenities, iPod docks and plush robes. Staying here puts you within a whisker of the strip's high-velocity club scene (ask the concierge about VIP access). Stargazers should scan the crowd at the hotel's Balboa bar and steak house. Parking is $24.

Secret Garden B&B (Map pp88–9; ☎ 323-656-3888, 877-732-4736; www.secretgardenbnb.com; 8039 Selma Ave; r incl breakfast $125-170; P 🖳 wi-fi) Near the Sunset Strip, this gay-friendly hideaway has a romantic Rapunzel tower tucked away in a dreamy garden and a charismatic owner-chef who whips up magical meals on an antique stove. All five rooms bulge with character and eclectic furnishings. For more privacy book the separate guesthouse with slate floor and a sleigh bed.

Standard Hollywood (Map pp88–9; ☎ 323-650-9090; www.standardhotel.com; 8300 W Sunset Blvd; r $150-275, ste $500; P 🖳 🏊) Kind of yesterday's news but still a good standby, this Sunset Strip haunt has you shacking up in shagadelic rooms with silver beanbag chairs, orange-tiled bathrooms and Warhol poppy print curtains. Its 'hidden' Purple Lounge (enter from Sweetzer) still sees some A-listers like James Blunt popping by for beers. Parking costs $24.

Farmer's Daughter Hotel (Map pp88–9; ☎ 323-937-3930, 800-334-1658; www.farmersdaughterhotel.com; 115 S Fairfax Ave; r $160-250; P 🖳 🏊 ♿) Denim bedspreads and rocking chairs give this flirty farmhouse, ah, motel, a contempo 'urban cowboy' vibe. It draws a mixed-age, mixed-interest crowd, from *The Price is Right* game-show hopefuls to style slaves headed for Melrose and the Grove to cost-conscious families. The adjacent restaurant, Tart, serves great Americana. Adventurous love birds should ask about the No Tell Room… Parking is $12.

Le Montrose Suite Hotel (Map pp88–9; ☎ 310-855-1115, 800-776-0666; www.lemontrose.com; 900 Hammond St; ste $165-450; P 🖳 🏊 wi-fi) It's a hop, skip and jump from anything that matters, yet this stylish hideaway still manages to feel like a cocoon of quiet and sophistication. The spruced-up suites are sheathed in an easy-on-the-eye palette of earth tones and lavender, and are popular with clued-in Industry folk. Bonus: the rooftop pool and tennis court. Parking costs $24.

Hotel Elan (Map pp88–9; ☎ 323-658-6663, 888-203-2212; www.elanhotel.com; 8435 Beverly Blvd; r $195-260; P wi-fi) Close to great restaurants and boutiques, the Elan flaunts an uncluttered urban feel and offers reliably good service and cloud-soft goose-down bedding. Standard rooms may be a bit too snug to fit tons of luggage, so opt for a junior lounge if space is an issue. Parking is $19.

Best Western Sunset Plaza Hotel (Map pp88–9; ☎ 323-654- 0750, 800-421-3652; www.bestwestern.com; 8400 W Sunset Blvd; r incl breakfast $200-300, child under 18 free; P 🏊 ♿ wi-fi) Granted, the name doesn't spell glamour, but the reasonable rates will take the sting out of paying $20 for that mojito at Skybar later that night. Even if you're not a party animal, you'll appreciate the central location, Melrose Place–like courtyard and handy freebies, including breakfast and local calls. Parking costs $12.

Orlando (Map pp88–9; ☎ 323-658-6600, 800-624-6835; www.theorlando.com; 8384 W 3rd St; $220-340; P 🖳 🏊 wi-fi) This fashionista favorite is smack-dab on boutique-lined W 3rd St and just a five-minute walk from the Beverly Center mall. Natural woods, earth-tones and votive candles provide a soothing antidote to an exhausting shopping spree, as do the heated saltwater pool and pocket-sized gym. Chic eateries abound, or stay at the hotel for top-rated Italian at La Terza. Parking is $24.

Chamberlain West Hollywood (Map pp88–9; ☎ 310-657-7400, 800-201-9637; www.chamberlainwesthollywood.com; 1000 Westmount Dr; r $260-290; P 🖳 🏊 wi-fi) This sassy lifestyle hotel scores points with trendy, design-minded travelers, even though it's not quite as edgy as other Kor Group outposts like the Avalon or Maison 140. The 112 gadget-filled studios and suites are draped in icy blues and dusky greys and come with gas fireplace, balcony and sumptuous bedding perfect after a night of cavorting on the nearby Sunset Strip. Nice rooftop pool, too. Parking costs $24.

TOP END

Sofitel Los Angeles (Map pp88–9; ☎ 310-278-5444, 800-521-7772; www.sofitella.com; 8555 Beverly Blvd; r $300-425, ste $575-1200; P 🖳 🏊 wi-fi) The Sofitel is the latest comeback kid among LA's luxe lodges, thanks to a $40 million cash infusion that created a place of sleek sophistication and unfussy ambience. Rooms have got ivory lacquered chests and premium beds, and the restaurant and Rande Gerber's slick Stone Rose Lounge (p192) have become the new darlings of the in-crowd. Rooms on the upper floors facing north have the best views. Parking costs $26.

Sunset Tower Hotel (Map pp88-9; ☎ 323-654-7100, 800-225-2637; www.sunsettowerhotel.com; 8358 W Sunset Blvd; r $345-375, ste $445-695; [P] [🖥] [🐾] wi-fi) Connect to the magic of yesterday when Errol Flynn, Truman Capote and Marilyn Monroe resided at this art deco marvel. Fully renovated, this classy boutique hotel with a historic pedigree spells romance in soothing rooms, a flirty bar (in Bugsy Siegel's former apartment) and a top-notch spa with Turkish *hammam* (steam bath). Expect famous faces but not of the Spears variety. Parking costs $28.

Chateau Marmont (Map pp88-9; ☎ 323-656-1010, 800-242-8328; www.chateaumarmont.com; 8221 W Sunset Blvd; r $350-785; [P] [🐾] wi-fi) Its French-flavored indulgence may look dated, but this faux-castle has long lured A-listers with its five-star mystique and legendary discretion. Howard Hughes used to spy on bikini beauties from the same balcony suite that today is Bono's favorite. The garden cottages are the most romantic, but the superstitious might want to steer clear of No 3 where John Belushi set his final speedball in 1982. Parking is $28.

Sunset Marquis Hotel & Villas (Map pp88-9; ☎ 310-657-1333, 800-858-9758; 1200 N Alta Loma Rd; www.sunsetmarquishotel.com; ste $360-615, villas $1000-3000; [P] [🖥] [🐾] wi-fi) 'Rock-and-roll retreat' may sound like an oxymoron, but not at this quiet and secluded tropical garden hideaway that often checks in visiting music royalty including Mick Jagger and Eric Clapton (there's even a recording studio on-site). The decor is surprisingly unshowy, with clear, modern lines and dark natural tones. Being a guest lets you hobnob at the ultraexclusive Whiskey Bar. Parking is $22.

Beverly Hills

Posh and sedate, Beverly Hills is among the safest areas in town and will likely impress your friends at the watercooler back home. It's reasonably central and close to UCLA and West Hollywood, but don't expect any bargains, hence the lack of budget listings in this section.

MIDRANGE

Beverly Terrace Hotel (Map pp90-1; ☎ 310-274-8141, 800-842-6401; www.beverlyterracehotel.com; 469 N Doheny Dr; r incl breakfast $160-230, child under 12 free; [P] [🐾] wi-fi) This older, Euro-style property dances on the border with West Hollywood and puts you close to the Santa Monica Blvd fun zone.

Rooms are cramped but contemporary and done up in soothing greens, crisp blues and bright reds. Locals often swamp the on-site Trattoria Amici for classic Italian served alfresco by the little pool.

Carlyle Inn (Map pp90-1; ☎ 310-275-4445, 800-322-7595; www.carlyle-inn.com; 1119 S Robertson Blvd; r incl breakfast $190-220; [P] [🖥] wi-fi) Forget about fancy. If you're into hip decor and Frette linens, don't bother with this 32-room Best Western on a nondescript section of Beverly Hills. Everyone else should be quite pleased with the handsome rooms, generous breakfast buffet and accommodating staff. Parking ($11), though, is a tight squeeze.

Maison 140 (Map pp90-1; ☎ 310-281-4000, 800-503-1395; www.maison140beverlyhills.com; 140 S Lasky Dr; r incl breakfast $240-270; [P] [🖥]) Parisian boudoir meets the Far East at this sensuous gem in the former home of silent-movie siren Lillian Gish. Enjoy the signature Lady Godiva cocktail in the intimate Bar Noir before retiring to rooms that skimp on size but have the wackiest wallpaper and cool furniture. Rates include pool privileges at the Avalon Hotel (below). Parking costs $21.

Crescent (Map pp90-1; ☎ 310-247-0505; www.crescentbh.com; 403 N Crescent Dr; s/d from $165/215; [P] [🖥] wi-fi) A mod hotspot with a buzzy fireside lounge and Dodd Mitchell–designed rooms, most of them on the small side. Parking costs $22.

TOP END

Avalon Hotel (Map pp90-1; ☎ 310-277-5221, 800-535-4715; www.avalonbeverlyhills.com; 9400 W Olympic Blvd; r $280-410; [P] [🖥] [🐾]) Mid-century modern gets a 21st-century spin at this fashion-crowd fave, which was Marilyn Monroe's old pad in its days as an apartment building. The beautiful, moneyed and metrosexual now vamp it up in the chic restaurant-bar overlooking a sexy hourglass-shaped pool. Rooms facing the other direction are quieter. Parking costs $28.

Mosaic Hotel (Map pp90-1; ☎ 310-278-0303, 800-463-4466; www.mosaichotel.com; 125 Spalding Dr; r $300-425, ste $600-800; [P] [🖥] [🐾] wi-fi) This 49-room boutique hotel splashed throughout with exotic fabrics offers soothing quarters after a day of power shopping, star-watching and joyous eating. Rooms exude a classic, timeless feel, while the Frette linens, Bulgari soaps and rainforest showerheads feed luxury cravings. Nice touch: free limo rides within town limits. Parking costs $25.

UPCOMING ATTRACTIONS

Given LA's near-mythical glamour factor, the relative dearth of hip boutique and lifestyle hotels is quite a shocker. Fortunately that's about to change as several old properties have made appointments with today's most inspired designers and will soon be satisfying scenesters' bottomless cravings for the next fab thing. Here's a quick preview of tomorrow's eagerly anticipated hotspots.

■ **Thompson Beverly Hills** (Map pp90-1; www.thompsonhotels.com; 9360 Wilshire Blvd, Beverly Hills) The old Beverly Pavilion is getting the Dodd Mitchell treatment complete with bi-level rooftop area with cabaña-lined pool, a bar and a glass-encased gym. So chic. Opened late 2007.

■ **The London** (Map pp88-9; www.thelondonla.com; 1020 N San Vicente Blvd, West Hollywood) British designer David Collins is putting a mod spin on the old Bel Age Hotel with Gordon Ramsey in 'hell's kitchen', a Golden Door spa on the rooftop and custom-made Waterworks baths. Bliss. Open early 2008.

■ **SLS Beverly Hills** (Map pp90-1; www.starwood.com; 465 S La Cienega Blvd, Beverly Hills) Under the stewardship of the folks behind the ultraswank Hyde and Area clubs, the old Meridien is being turned into a 'chic, bold and ultimately humane' space by none other than Philippe Starck. We'll see. Open mid-2008.

■ **Palomar Hotel** (Map pp90-1; www.kimptonhotels.com; 10740 Wilshire Blvd, Westwood) Once Cheryl Rowley is through with the ex-Doubletree, guests will be retiring to ecofriendly rooms decked out in black and red lacquer, faux snakeskin dresser tops and snakeskin patterned carpet. Open mid-2008.

■ **W Hollywood** (Map pp86-7; www.whotels.com; cnr Hollywood Blvd & Vine St) The most dramatic feature of this upcoming style pit at Hollywood & Vine will likely be the glass-encased bar that will hang over the building's edge, putting imbibers high above Hollywood Blvd. Vertigo sufferers, beware. Expected by 2009.

Beverly Wilshire (Map pp90-1; ☎ 310-275-5200, ☎ 800-819-5053; www.fourseasons.com/beverlywilshire; 9500 Wilshire Blvd; r $450-525, child free; P ❏ ☎ ❖) You can expect a red-carpet welcome at this quietly remodeled bastion of style, glamour and top-end anything, now under the aegis of the Four Seasons. It has corked Rodeo Drive since 1928, but the amenities are very much up-to-the-minute, both in the original Italian Renaissance wing and in the newer addition. And yes, this is the very hotel from which Julia Roberts first stumbled then strutted in *Pretty Woman*, and where Warren Beatty kept a suite for 10 years. Parking costs $32.

Beverly Hills Hotel (Map pp90-1; ☎ 310-276-2251, 800-283-8885; www.beverlyhillshotel.com; 9641 Sunset Blvd; r $450-600, ste & bungalows $950-6500; P ❏ ☎ ❖ wi-fi) If the walls of this belle hotel could talk, the tales would make you laugh, blush, cry and cringe. Staying here means dwelling in the utmost of luxury with a vibe that magically marries the historical with the contemporary. For historical background, see p114. Parking costs $29.

Raffles L'Ermitage (Map pp90-1; ☎ 310-278-3344, 800-800-2113; www.raffles-lermitagehotel.com; 9291 Burton Way; r $575-850, ste $1100-1400, child under 16 free; P ❏ ☎ wi-fi) A hushed, elegant Eurasian ambience embraces top-tier travelers at this luxe lair in a residential area of 90210. Everything is calculated to take the edge off travel: 24-hour check-in/check-out times, personalized business cards and letterhead, and a rooftop pool with 360° views and a megacool live-shark tank. The Writer's Bar is a Hollywood bigwig hangout. Parking is $31.

Westwood, Bel Air & Brentwood

These upscale areas put you right at the doorstep of UCLA and close to the hilltop Getty Center blockbuster attraction.

Brentwood Inn (off Map pp90-1; ☎ 310-476-9981, 800-840-3808; www.thebrentwood.com; 12200 W Sunset Blvd; r incl breakfast $160-240; P ❏) This 21-room gem feels more like bunking at a friend's place than at a motel yet doesn't lack in comfort. Rooms, though snug, get an airy feel thanks to cathedral ceilings. The hypoallergenic bedding, Aveda bath products and flatscreen TVs are top-notch. The stone-walled patio is perfect for enjoying the complimentary breakfast and organic afternoon tea.

Hilgard House Hotel (Map pp90-1; ☎ 310-208-3945, 800-826-3934; www.hilgardhouse.com; 927 Hilgard Ave, Westwood; r incl breakfast $170, ste incl breakfast $240-360; **P** wi-fi) There's something comfortably stuffy about this 55-room Euro-style hotel near UCLA. It's an unflashy, unpretentious abode with impeccable, smallish and traditional rooms popular with visiting parents and people with family at UCLA Medical Center. Breakfast is basic, but there are plenty of cafés mere steps away.

Hotel Angeleno (Map pp90-1; ☎ 310-476-6411, 866-2643-5361; www.hotelangeleno.com; 170 N Church Lane; r $210-250; **P** 🖥 🖴 wi-fi) Close to the Getty and UCLA (free shuttles provided), this circular landmark has rooms hued in chocolate and vanilla, which sport iPod nanos and 30" plasma TVs. Balcony views of the 405 Fwy right below are soooo LA surreal and the penthouse restaurant-bar is a romantic unwinding spot. Parking costs $18.

Hotel Bel-Air (Map pp90-1; ☎ 310-472-1211, 800-648-4097; www.hotelbelair.com; 701 N Stone Canyon Rd; r $395-625, ste $825-4000; **P** 🖥 🖴 wi-fi) An urge to splurge is well-directed towards this classy country estate where white swans preen in romantic gardens and rooms come with private entrances and classy French furnishings. The pool is solar-heated and vegetables are harvested from the on-site organic garden. Price tag too steep? Come for afternoon tea or drinks by the wood-burning fireplace. Parking is $28.

Culver City

Staying in this up-and-coming neighborhood, with its increasingly sizzling restaurant, art and design districts, will give you bragging rights about being on the cutting-edge of urban development in LA.

Villa Brasil Motel (Map p97; ☎ 310-636-0141; www.villabrasilmotel.com; 11740 Washington Blvd; r $75; **P**) Splashed in orange, blue and green, this little motel run by an amiable Brazilian family is quite literally a bright spot on otherwise drab Washington Blvd, not far from Sony Pictures. The tropical looks continue in the rooms, which are a tad twee but come with cable TV and ceiling fans; some have kitchenettes.

Culver Hotel (Map p97; ☎ 310-838-7963, 888-328-5837; www.culverhotel.com; 9400 Culver Blvd; r $150-325, child free; **P** 🖥 wi-fi) This 1924 heritage hotel sits smack-dab in newly hip and happening

---

TOP FIVE HOTEL BARS

- Industry – **Writer's Bar** (opposite) at Raffles L'Ermitage
- Luxurious – **Stone Rose Lounge** (p164), Sofitel hotel
- Romantic – **Bar Noir** (p165) at Maison 140
- Sexy – **Standard Rooftop Lounge** (p172)
- Trendy – **Zinc Lounge** (p171) at Shade Hotel

---

downtown Culver City, close to excellent eating, culture and galleries. It's loaded with movie history – the Munchkins stayed here while filming the *Wizard of Oz*. A mahogany-paneled lobby gives way to rooms with antique furnishings and marble bathrooms but surprisingly few amenities.

Malibu

Malibu makes for a nice city retreat and offers pretty camping, but it is rather remote from anything else.

Leo Carrillo State Park Campground (off Map pp80-1; ☎ 818-880-0350; reservations ☎ 800-444-7275; www.reserveamerica.com; 35000 W Pacific Coast Hwy; campsites $20-25; 🖴 wi-fi) This kid-friendly campground sits on a famous 1½-mile stretch of beach about 28 miles northwest of Santa Monica. Offshore kelp beds, caves, reefs, tide pools, plus the wilderness of the Santa Monica Mountains create a natural playground. There are 135 sycamore-shaded sites, flush toilets and coin-operated hot showers, so you won't have to rough it. Bookings for summer weekends should be made six months in advance.

Malibu Creek State Park Campground (Map pp80-1; ☎ 818-880-0367; reservations 800-444-7275; www.reserveamerica.com; campsites $20-25) Another beautiful spot in the Santa Monica Mountains, this park's movie credentials include *M*A*S*H* and *Planet of the Apes*. Laced by a creek, the hiking here is excellent with trails leading past craggy oak and stately sycamores. The park is about 5 miles north of the Pacific Coast Hwy via Malibu Canyon Rd.

Malibu Bella Vista (Map pp80-1; ☎ 818-591-9353; www.malibubellavista.com; 25786 Piuma Rd; r $85 & $125; **P** 🖴) Hosts Michael and Beth treat everyone staying at their lovely, if remote, ranch-style

B&B (also their home) like family. It's right in the Santa Monica Mountains, just behind the Saddle Peak Lodge gourmet restaurant (see p188) and framed by a vineyard. Choose from two rooms, one with a wood-burning fireplace and both with adjacent private bathrooms.

Malibu Motel (Map pp80-1; ☎ 310-456-6169; www .themalibumotel.com; 22541 Pacific Coast Hwy; r $120-220; **P** **⚲**) This 18-room motel has been redone in retro-on-the-cheap. Beds are comfy and draped in crisp linen but amenities are limited to a mini-fridge and small plasma TV. Come on, no alarm clock or coffeemaker? Light sleepers should gear up with ear plugs to combat PCH traffic noise. Still, not bad value for the area and the beach is just across the highway.

Casa Malibu Inn (Map pp80-1; ☎ 310-456-2219, 800-831-0858; casamalibu@earthlink.net; 22752 Pacific Coast Hwy; r $130-470; **P** wi-fi) This 'California Dreamin' beachfront getaway on exclusive Carbon Beach was just bought by Oracle boss Larry Ellison, so it's anybody's guess what'll happen to this (thus far) reasonably priced 21-room hotel where Lana Turner used to stay. For now, though, you can still let the crashing surf lull you to sleep.

Malibu Beach Inn (Map pp80-1; ☎ 310-456-6444; www.malibubeachinn.com; 22878 Pacific Coast Hwy; r from $325, ste from $725; **P** wi-fi) If you want to live like a billionaire, stay with one. Hollywood mogul David Geffen has plunked megabucks (chump change to him) into giving this intimate hacienda the deluxe treatment. It's right near his private house on Carbon Beach and has 47 superdeluxe ocean-facing rooms sheathed in soothing browns and outfitted with fireplaces, a handpicked wine selection and Dean & Deluca goodies.

Santa Monica

A great choice for first-timers, families, artsy and outdoorsy types, Santa Monica is central and gives you lots to do besides the beach. Smokers, though, might feel more comfortable elsewhere (see boxed text, p124).

BUDGET

HI-Los Angeles/Santa Monica (Map p92; ☎ 310-393-9913, 800-909-4776, ext 137; www.lahostels.org; 1436 2nd St; members/nonmembers dm $28/31, r without bathroom $70; **▯**) Near the beach and Third Street Promenade, this hostel has a location that's the envy of much fancier places but is low on character and charm. Its 200 beds in single-

sex dorms and bed-in-a-box doubles are clean and safe but gregarious types looking for a party vibe are probably better off in Venice or Hollywood.

Sea Shore Motel (Map p92; ☎ 310-392-2787; www .seashoremotel.com; 2637 Main St; r $100-140, ste 150-250; **P** wi-fi) These friendly, family-run lodgings put you just a Frisbee toss from the beach and right by the cafés and indie boutiques on happening Main St (expect some street noise). The tiled rooms are basic but attractive enough, and families can stretch out comfortably in the modern suites with kitchen and balcony in a nearby building.

Bayside Hotel (Map p92; ☎ 310-396-6000, 800-525-4447; www.baysidehotel.com; 2001 Ocean Ave; r $100-210, child under 10 free; **P** wi-fi) With a price tag this modest you know you're not getting the Ritz, but if you value location over luxury, it ain't a bad crash pad. Sure, rooms are basic and long in the tooth but who cares when you're watching the sunset, cold beer in hand, from your ocean-view room.

Travelodge Santa Monica (Map p92; ☎ 310-450-5766, 800-231-7679; www.travelodgesantamonica.com; 3102 W Pico Blvd; r incl breakfast $110-180, child free; **P** wi-fi) There's plenty to like about this chain entry next to a Trader Joe's supermarket and steps from restaurants and a funky coffee shop. Rooms are large and spotless (many have kitchenettes) and there's a courtyard with gas barbecue and picnic tables. The beach is about 2½ miles away, but the bus taking you there stops right outside.

MIDRANGE

Cal Mar Hotel Suites (Map p92; ☎ 310-395-5555, 800-776-6007; www.calmarhotel.com; 220 California Ave; ste $160-205, child under 10 free; **P** **⚲** wi-fi) The look of this place may be hopelessly stuck in the disco decade, but it's hard to complain if a moderate tariff buys you an apartment-style kitchen suite close to the beach and hopping Third Street Promenade. A fabulous choice for families and space-lovers, even if noise insulation isn't the greatest (request an upper-floor unit). Parking costs $10.

Embassy Hotel Apartments (Map p92; ☎ 310-394-1279; www.embassyhotelapts.com; 1001 3rd St; r $170-385) This hushed hideaway is embraced by gardens and delivers 1920s charm by the bucket. A rickety elevator takes you to light-flooded units oozing old-world flair. There's no aircon but rooms are equipped with modern kitchens. The relative paucity of hotel services makes this place better suited for do-it-your-selfers.

Channel Road Inn B&B (Map p92; ☎ 310-459-1920; www.channelroadinn.com; 219 W Channel Rd; r incl breakfast $195-450, child under 14 free; P ⬜ ⑂ wi-fi) This frilly family home in a leafy canyon mixes Cape Cod colonial with West Coast Craftsman and has romantic rooms facing the ocean or the lovely garden. Breakfast is a gourmet affair (especially when the apple French toast is served). There are also convivial afternoon teas and evening wine reception get-togethers with fellow guests. Free bike rentals.

Ambrose (Map p92; ☎ 310-315-1555, 877-262-7673; www.ambrosehotel.com; 1255 20th St; r incl breakfast $220-270; P ⬜ wi-fi) This sustainable boutique hotel beautifully blends Craftsman and Asian aesthetics and goes the extra mile when it comes to being green. Standard amenities in the spick-and-span rooms – some with balconies and fireplaces – include recycling containers alongside the gamut of electronic gadgets. Breakfast is an organic gourmet affair.

Georgian Hotel (Map p92; ☎ 310-395-9945, 800-538-8147; www.georgianhotel.com; 1415 Ocean Ave; r $230-300, ste $295-530; P ⬜ wi-fi) This eye-catching art deco landmark with its snug veranda for breakfast and sunset lounging has decor so *Great Gatsby*-esque that wearing a straw boater wouldn't feel out of place. The rooms, in soothing earth tones, are surprisingly modern. Cute factor: the rubber duckie in the tub. Parking costs $21.

TOP END

Viceroy (Map p92; ☎ 310-260-7500, 800-622-8711; www.viceroysantamonica.com; 1819 Ocean Ave; r $390-475; P ⬜ ⟲) Behind the hulking exterior, Hollywood glamour meets the seaside at this hip, urban outpost with a campy British Colonial design theme and a color palette from dolphin-gray to mamba-green. All the usual hot-spot trappings are here as well, from poolside cabanas to Italian designer linens, plus a bar and restaurant bustling with socialites. Parking is $20.

Loews Santa Monica Beach Hotel (Map p92; ☎ 310-458-6700, 800-235-6397; www.loewshotels.com; 1700 Ocean Ave; r $210-480, ste $610-2650; P ⬜ ⟲ ⑂) This fine hotel does everything to put you in the mood for a beach vacation, from the palm tree–lined lobby and fireside lounge to the glass-covered indoor–outdoor pool and sunny rooms decked out in classy, contemporary

style. Kids love the Fisher-Price welcome gift, making new friends during supervised activities and raiding the DVD and Game Boy closet. Parking costs $28.

Venice & Marina del Rey

Venice is funkyville and Marina del Rey is all about the yacht harbor. You can have the time of your life in either, and they're pretty close to LAX to boot.

BUDGET

Hostel California (Map p92; ☎ 310-305-0250; www.hostelcalifornia.us; 2221 Lincoln Blvd; 6-/30-bed dm $21/17, d without bathroom $50; P ⬜ wi-fi) Social types from around the world give high marks to this converted winery for its friendly staff, although standards of cleanliness seem to fluctuate. It's well linked by bus to LAX and the beach. The budget-challenged can shack up in the 30-bed dorm and boil their ramen in the communal kitchen. Passport/out-of-state ID and onward airline ticket required at check-in.

Venice Beach Cotel (Map p92; ☎ 310-399-7649; www.venicebeachcotel.com; 25 Windward Ave; dm $25-30, r with/without bathroom $80/60; ⬜ wi-fi) Among LA hostels, this pert little number does the best job in combining amenities with location. Just half a block from the Venice Boardwalk and the beach, it's a top-rated, friendly, safe and clean jumping-off base drawing a United Nations of travelers (passport required). Free coffee and boogie boards are nice perks but internet access costs about $4 per hour.

MIDRANGE

Venice Beach Suites & Hotel (Map p92; ☎ 310-396-4559; www.venicebeachsuites.com; 1305 Ocean Front Walk, Venice; r $120-280; P wi-fi) Everything's just beachy at this good-value place that scores big for its bend-over-backwards-to-help staff, the free bottle of wine at check-in and bevy of beach toys for rent. It's an older place, so if you don't like historic charm, ask for a newly remodeled room. Kitchen suites are big enough for dinner parties. Parking costs $20.

Best Western Jamaica Bay Inn (Map p92; ☎ 310-823-5333, 888-823-5333; www.bestwestern-jamaicabay.com; 4175 Admiralty Way, Marina del Rey; r $160-250; P ⟲ ⑂ wi-fi) Fronting sheltered Mother's Beach, this 42-room motel is great for families and even has its own playground. Palm trees add a tropical touch and the rooms have cheerful bedspreads, framed art and private balconies or patio (ask for one with ocean views). You can walk to restaurants and Venice Beach. Parking is $5.

Inn at Playa del Rey B&B (off Map p92; ☎ 310-574-1920; www.innatplayadelrey.com; 435 Culver Blvd, Playa del Rey; incl breakfast r $175-285, ste $305-425; P 🖳 👙 wi-fi) A gorgeous rambling cottage, this quiet and impeccably run inn has clean rooms with a contemporary feel (some with balcony or fireplace) and overlooks a bird sanctuary. You're close to the beach and marina, so ditch the car and hop on a free bicycle, then brag about your day's adventures at the evening wine reception. Sensational breakfasts, too.

Inn at Venice Beach (Map p92; ☎ 310-821-2557, 800-828-0688; www.innatvenicebeach.com; 327 Washington Blvd, Venice; r incl breakfast $180-260; P wi-fi) Close to the beach, the Venice canals and bars and restaurants, this value-conscious motel sports brightly hued rooms with a good range of amenities. All wrap around a central courtyard perfect for munching your free muffins in the morning. Parking costs $4.

Venice Beach House (Map p92; ☎ 310-823-1966; www.venicebeachhouse.com; 15 30th Ave, Venice; r without bathroom $145, with bathroom $195-225; P) This ivy-draped B&B in a 1911 Craftsman bungalow is a genteel retreat from the Venice Boardwalk hubbub, which is a mere block away. If early-20th-century vintage living appeals, you won't mind the slightly faded elegance of the nine rooms, some with shared bathrooms. Romantics should snatch the James Peasgood room with twin Jacuzzi. Parking costs $12.

South Bay Beaches

Those not used to the frenetic energy and multicultural hodgepodge of big cities may feel less overwhelmed in the clean, quiet and affluent communities of Manhattan Beach, Hermosa Beach and, to a lesser extent, Redondo Beach. Manhattan Beach is also quite close to LAX.

BUDGET

Surf City Hostel (Map p94; ☎ 310-798-2323, 800-305-2901; www.surfcityhostel.ws; 26 Pier Ave, Hermosa Beach; incl breakfast dm $25, d $60; 🖳 wi-fi) Steps from the sand, this convivial hostel puts the 'fun' in funky. Halls, dorms and rooms are splashed with cool murals, but clean freaks won't be too impressed. We do like the kitchen and long list of freebies (tea, coffee, linen, wi-fi, bodyboards, storage).

If you're looking to spend your days beaching and your nights partying, this is your place.

MIDRANGE

Best Western Redondo Beach Inn (Map p94; ☎ 310-540-3700, 800-780-7234; www.bestwestern.com; 1850 S Pacific Coast Hwy, Redondo Beach; r $100-195; P 🖳 🐕 wi-fi) This well-kept Med-style property is a fine choice for wallet-watching nomads. Room decor is typical motel-issue (think flowery bedspreads and draped windows) but you won't miss any of the basic comforts and amenities. The beach is about a half-mile away – be there in minutes by renting a hotel bicycle.

Sea View Inn (Map p94; ☎ 310-545-1504; www.seaview-inn.com; 3400 N Highland Ave, Manhattan Beach; r $125-265; P 🐕 👙 wi-fi) Rooms are nothing special and the four-block steepish trek to the beach is a calf-stretching workout, but otherwise this friendly, rambling property has a lot going for it, including free bikes and beach chairs and boogie-board rentals. The nicest rooms have ocean-facing balconies; the quietest ones face the alley.

Portofino Hotel & Yacht Club (Map p94; ☎ 310-379-8481, 800-468-4292; www.hotelportofino.com; 260 Portofino Way, Redondo Beach; r $170-320; P 🖳 🖳 wi-fi) This '60s oceanfront property next to the Redondo Pier recently went from drab to fab and now blends urban sophistication with nautical lightheartedness. Definitely get an ocean-view room with a balcony for watching the sunset and an adorable (if noisy) sea-lion colony. Marina-facing views overlook not only boats but also a power plant, partly hidden behind a Wyland whale mural. Parking is $15.

Belamar Hotel (Map p94; ☎ 310-750-0300, 888-235-2627; www.belamar.com; 3501 Sepulveda Blvd, Manhattan Beach; r $190-220, ste 300-780, child under 12 free; P 🐕 wi-fi) If it were in Hollywood, this designer hotel would be hipster central. But, alas, it's kinda in the middle of nowhere, 2 miles from happening downtown Manhattan Beach and opposite a cookie-cutter shopping mall. Still, a decent rate buys stylish digs, superb beds and easy access to a nature trail down to the beach for jogging off your jet lag.

TOP END

Beach House at Hermosa (Map p94; ☎ 310-374-3001, 888-895-4559; www.beach-house.com; 1300 The Strand, Hermosa Beach; r incl breakfast $290-460, child free; P 🖳 wi-fi) Whatever you've heard about California's laid-back lifestyle, this sparkling beachfront inn epitomizes it. Open up the balcony door of your lofty ocean-view suite to let in the ocean breezes or fall asleep to the soft crackling of a wood-burning fireplace. The paved bikeway is right outside and restaurants and nightlife are a quick stroll away. Parking will cost you $22.

ourpick **Shade Hotel** (Map p94; ☎ 310-546-4995, 866-987-4233; 1221 N Valley Dr, Manhattan Beach; r $300-400, ste $445-1000; P ⌨ wi-fi) Manhattan Beach goes Hollywood – with all the sass but *sans* attitude – at this mod luxury boutique hotel where rooms are jammed with lifestyle essentials (iPod docking stations, margarita blender) and even have color-therapy spa tubs big enough for two. The service is inspired, the beach is just three blocks away and the Zinc Lounge bar is buzzy with cool sea urchin chandeliers (see p193).

Long Beach

Long Beach is a handy for those planning on devoting equal amounts of time to both LA and Orange County. Home to the *Queen Mary* ocean liner and family-friendly Aquarium of the Pacific, it also has plenty to recommend it by itself.

Turret House (Map pp82-3; ☎ 562-624-1991, 888-488-7738; www.turrethouse.com; 556 Chestnut Ave; r incl breakfast $80-120; P ⌨ wi-fi) Owners Brian and Jeff (and their adorable dogs) have poured their hearts and cash into turning their butter-yellow B&B into an oasis of charm. The stately Victorian home has five cozy rooms, each with a fireplace, a TV and a bathroom complete with a clawfoot tub. Rates include passes to a nearby gym, and there's a hot tub on the premises, too. Pet-friendly.

Hotel Queen Mary (Map pp82-3; ☎ 562-435-3511, 800-437-2934; www.queenmary.com; 1126 Queens Hwy; r $110-220, ste $450-650, child under 17 free; P ⌨ wi-fi) There's an irresistible romance to ocean liners like the *Queen Mary*, a nostalgic retreat that time-warps you back to a long-gone, slower-paced era. The 1st-class staterooms are nicely refurbished and brim with original art deco details, but they're rather small and not for amenity hounds. Avoid the cheapest cabins on the inside – claustrophobic! Staying overnight gives you the full run of the ship and a self-guided tour. Parking costs $19. Also see p131.

Dockside Boat & Bed (Map pp82-3; ☎ 562-436-3111, 800-436-2574; www.boatandbed.com; Rainbow Harbor, Dock

---

BEDDING DOWN BEFORE TAKE-OFF

If you get into LAX late or have to catch an early flight, you'll probably want to stay near the airport. But how to avoid generic, beige-box–blandness? We've cased the area and found these stylish shut-eye zones. All have free shuttle buses to the airport.

■ **Custom Hotel** (off Map pp82-3; ☎ 310-645-0400; www.customhotel.com; 8639 Lincoln Blvd; r $120-390; P ⌨ ⚲ wi-fi) This hip new kid in town occupies a mid-century tower by Welton Beckett (who also drafted the crafty Capital Records Tower in Hollywood). The streamlined design scheme and poolside tapas bar might just radiate enough urban poshness to appeal to the style patrol. Just like plane tickets, the cheapest rates must be booked 21 days in advance. Parking costs $20.

■ **Renaissance Montura Hotel** (Map pp82-3; ☎ 310-337-2800, 800-228-9290; www.marriott.com; 9620 Airport Blvd; r $120-260; P ⌨ ⚲) European sophistication combines with American amenities at this recently overhauled haven whose soothing, art-filled design, ultracomfy bedding and smiling staff may just be the perfect jet-lag antidote. Parking is $18.

■ **Sheraton Gateway** (Map pp82-3; ☎ 310-642-1111, 800-325-3535; www.sheratonlosangeles.com; 6101 W Century Blvd; r $140-290; P ⌨ wi-fi) Almost like a self-contained resort, this chain stands out for its eye-candy design, intimate, boutique-style service and above-average eateries, including a sushi bar. Parking costs $24.

■ **Ayres Hotel** (Map p94; ☎ 310-536-0400, 800-675-3550; 14400 Hindry Ave, Manhattan Beach; r $150-200, ste 210-290; P ⌨ wi-fi) With its repro tapestries, crystal chandeliers and baroque furniture, this 173-room property pulls off Disneyfied old-European charm quite well, despite sitting right next to the 405 Fwy (windows are soundproofed). It's completely smoke-free and rates include a generous breakfast.

5, 316 E Shoreline Dr; r incl tax & breakfast $210-300, extra person $25; (P) wi-fi) Salty types with a sense of romance love this floating hostelry. Let yourself be rocked to sleep by the waves aboard your own private yacht with retro '70s charm, galley kitchens and high-tech entertainment centers. Boats are moored right along the newly expanded waterfront fun zone in downtown Long Beach, so expect some noise. Breakfast is delivered to your vessel. Parking is $12.

Beachrunners' Inn (Map pp82-3; ☎ 562-856-0202, 866-221-0001; www.beacherunnersinn.com; 231 Kennebec Ave; r $100-130; (P) (□) (♿)) With easy access to the beach, Downtown and Belmont Shore, this 1913 Craftsman B&B makes a great base of operation. Rooms won't fit a ton of luggage but the bold colors and uncluttered furnishing make a refreshing departure from Victorian frilliness. Wind down at the end of the day with a dip in the Jacuzzi or a drink and a chat with the caring owners in the garden.

Downtown Los Angeles

Culture vultures, ethno-fans and urban adventurers will be in heaven in Downtown LA, whose face is changing at lightning speed. Streets are still quite deserted and sketchy after dark, so don't expect to be walking to dinner.

BUDGET

Stillwell Hotel (Map pp84-5; ☎ 213-627-1151, 800-553-4774; www.stillwellhotel.com; 838 S Grand Ave; r $50-90, child under 11 free; (P) wi-fi) OK, OK, so this place is not for everybody. It's old, smells funny (partly because of age, partly because of the Indian restaurant downstairs) and may not be the cleanest, but come on, at these prices, what do you expect? It's close to LA Live and Staples Center and the cool noir bar serves cold beers. Parking costs $6.

Ritz Milner Hotel (Map pp84-5; ☎ 213-627-6981, 800-827-0411; www.milner-hotels.com; 813 S Flower St; r incl breakfast $80-130; (P)) 'A bed and a bath for a buck and a half' was the advertising slogan of this mini-chain, family-owned since 1918. The tab still ain't steep, but neither do you get the 'Ritz'. Still, the entire place has had a fairly recent date with a paint bucket and a designer, so it's definitely a solid, central and safe cheapie choice with a cool retro pub downstairs. Parking costs $9.

MIDRANGE

Inn at 657 (Map pp84-5; ☎ 213-741-2200, 800-347-7512; www.patsysinn657.com; 657 W 23rd St; r incl breakfast $125-200; (P) (□) wi-fi) Eclectic, well-tended gardens embrace this heritage inn run by the personable Patsy, who's famous for her scrumptious breakfasts that'll easily tide you through to the afternoon. Rooms are uncluttered and comfortable and the neighborhood is dotted with classic old Craftsmen mansions. Alas, the nearby freeway and paucity of restaurants within walking-distance puts a damper on the location.

our pick **Figueroa Hotel** (Map pp84-5; ☎ 213-627-8971, 800-421-9092; www.figueroahotel.com; 939 S Figueroa St; r $134-174, ste $195-245; (P) (□) (☎)) It's hard not to be charmed by this rambling oasis a mere basketball toss from LA Live and the Staples Center. A Spanish-style lobby segues smoothly to a bougainvillea- and cactus-laden poolside garden where guests and locals mingle at the Veranda Bar. The Moroccan-themed rooms make you feel like a pasha but vary in size and configuration and are pretty skimpy in the amenities department. Parking costs $8.

Standard Downtown LA (Map pp84-5; ☎ 213-892-8080; www.standardhotel.com; 550 S Flower St; r from $140; (P) (□) (☎)) This design-savvy hotel in a converted oil-company building appeals to a young, hip and shag-happy crowd, so don't come here with kids or to get a solid night's sleep (the upper floors are quieter). Rooms are mod and minimalist, but the platform beds and peek-through showers are no longer as racy as they used to be. Hit the rooftop bar for fab views and a sexy crowd (p194). Parking costs $25.

Omni Los Angeles Hotel (Map pp84-5; ☎ 213-617-3300, 800-843-6664; www.omnihotels.com; 25 S Olive St; r $170-290, ste $320-1000; (P) (□) (☎) (♿) wi-fi) Omni is all buttoned-up business during the week but its lower weekend rates make it an attractive base choice for families and culture vultures. The best rooms overlook the Museum of Contemporary Art and the Walt Disney Concert Hall, both just steps away. If you've got little ones in tow, ask about the Omni Sensational Kids package. Parking costs $28.

TOP END

Millennium Biltmore Hotel (Map pp84-5; ☎ 213-624-1011, 800-245-8673; www.thebiltmore.com; 506 S Grand Ave; r $160-360, ste $460-3000; (P) (□) (☎) wi-fi) Drenched in tradition and gold-leaf, this palatial hotel has bedded stars, presidents and royalty in modestly sized but gold-and-blue-hued rooms with all the trappings. The gorgeous art deco health club takes the work out of workout. Wi-fi is free but only works in the lobby. Parking costs $32. Also see p136.

San Fernando Valley

Most of the major studios, including Warner Bros and Universal, are based in the Valley north of the Hollywood Hills.

Safari Inn (Map p95; ☎ 818-845-8586, 800-782-4373; www.safariburbank.com; 1911 W Olive Ave, Burbank; r $160-180, f $200; P 🐾 wi-fi) This 1950s motel boasts a vintage neon sign but has of late been spruced up nicely. Beds are draped in boldly colored patterned spreads, and framed poster art adds charm to rooms that are otherwise on the small and darkish side. The 'breakfast' of wimpy coffee and stale Danish is rather lacking, but the pool is nice and you'll be close to the studios.

Coast Anabelle Hotel (Map p95; ☎ 818-845-7800, 800-782-4373; www.coasthotels.com; 2011 W Olive Ave, Burbank; r $160-180, ste $230; P 🖥 🐾 wi-fi) The Safari's more grown-up sister hotel, the Annabelle, is right across the street. The rooms are larger and everything is a bit nicer here, from the airy lobby to the art, furniture and mattress. The Olive bistro does good business and gets high marks for its friendly staff. The pool is shared with the Safari Inn (above).

Graciela Inn (Map p95; ☎ 818-842-8887, 888-956-1900; www.thegraciela.com; 322 N Pass Ave, Burbank; r $200-365, ste $560-745; P 🖥 wi-fi) This business-savvy boutique hotel near Universal and Warner Bros is a breath of fresh air in the charm-challenged Valley. Rooms are draped in fresh vanilla tones and feature ultracomfy beds, while the marble baths have extra-big tubs. Enjoy great views from the rooftop sundeck with hot tub. Parking costs $24.

If Universal Studios is the focus of your visit, you won't get any closer to the gate than by staying at the **Sheraton Universal Hotel** (Map p95; ☎ 818-980-1212, 800-325-3535; www.starwood.com/Sheraton; 333 Universal Hollywood Dr, Universal City; r $180-260, ste $330-1000, child under 18 free; P 🖥 🐾) or the **Hilton Los Angeles/Universal City** (☎ 818-506-2500, 800-445-8667; www.hilton.com; 555 Universal Hollywood Dr, Universal City; r $160-340, child under 18 free; P 🖥 🐾). Both of these monolithic glass towers have nicely appointed rooms with great city views from the upper floors, and shuttle service to the theme-park entrance. The Sheraton has special dog beds for Fido, and parking costs $16. Parking at the Hilton costs $15 to $20.

Pasadena

Pasadena is clean, quiet and blessed with excellent museums, stunning Craftsman architecture, bountiful gardens and a happening after-dark strip, but it gets hotter than hell in summer.

BUDGET

Saga Motor Hotel (Map p96; ☎ 626-795-0431, 800-793-7242; www.thesagamotorhotel.com; 1633 E Colorado Blvd; r $77-130; P 🐾 wi-fi) This well-kept '60s vintage inn puts you right on historic Route 66 without taking too big a bite out of your wallet. Rooms are dated but spotless and clean. The nicest face the well-proportioned pool with plenty of chaises and chairs for kicking back. Families should ask about the extra-large units.

MIDRANGE

Pasadena Inn (Map p96; ☎ 626-795-8401, 800-577-5690; www.pasadena-inn.com; 400 S Arroyo Parkway; r $100-330; P 🖥 🐾 wi-fi) This older property won't be featured on the pages of House Beautiful, but at least it'll give you some shut-eye at a modest tariff. In the morning you can drag your coffee and Danish out to the pool area, while at night the adjacent Thai restaurant make some decent curry if you don't feel like hoofing it to the Old Pasadena, about a 15-minute walk away.

Artists' Inn & Cottage B&B (off Map p96; ☎ 626-799-5668, 888-799-5668; www.artistsinns.com; 1038 Magnolia St; r incl tax & breakfast $135-225; P) Just three blocks from a Metro Gold Line station, this lovely Victorian farmhouse has 10 artist-inspired rooms and suites, some with fireplaces and canopy beds. If you don't like frilly Laura Ashley, ask for the Van Gogh or Expressionists rooms. Smoking is *verboten* but drinking is not: rates include postdinner port enjoyed in the privacy of your room. Check-in is from 3pm to 6pm.

Bissell House B&B (Map p96; ☎ 626-441-3535, 800-441-3530; www.bissellhouse.com; 201 S Orange Grove Blvd; r incl breakfast $195-350; P 🐾 wi-fi) Antiques, hardwood floors and a crackling fireplace make this secluded Victorian B&B on 'Millionaire's Row' a bastion of warmth and romance. The hedge-framed garden feels like a sanctuary, and there's a big pool for cooling off on hot summer days. Except for the boldly striped Prince Albert room, the decor is pretty frilly-flowery. The Garden Room has a double Jacuzzi.

TOP END

Ritz-Carlton Huntington Hotel & Spa (Map p96; ☎ 626-568-3900, 800-241-3333; www.ritzcarlton.com/hotels /hunting ton; 1401 S Oak Knoll Ave; r from $260, child under 18 free; P 🖥 wi-fi) Take away the palm trees and this dignified hostelry could be a French country estate complete with rambling gardens, giant swimming pool and covered picture bridge. Rooms are daubed in regal reds or blues, but the heavy drapery and patrician furniture collide with the flat-screen TVs and other 21st-century touches. The Sunday brunch ($55) is a pricey but memorable treat. Parking costs $25.

EATING

With great produce, innovative chefs and beautiful locales, LA's cuisine scene is as exciting, varied, fun and adventurous as the city itself. The best of California cooking makes creative use of local, seasonal and fresh ingredients and flirts with foreign influences, be they Mexican spices, Asian cooking techniques or Mediterranean flavor pairings. Other trends come and go; right now small plates, Kobe beef and spicy tuna are hot meal tickets, but LA's fickle eaters may well have moved on to something else in a few months' time. Some of the most exciting food comes courtesy of LA's huge immigrant populations – from Ethiopian *watt* (stew) to Mexican *pozole* (stew) and Vietnamese *pho* (soup), you'll find it here.

When choosing a restaurant, don't let decor be the deciding factor. Yes, some of the best-designed LA restaurants offer exquisite cuisine – Crustacean, O-Bar and Koi – but some of the tastiest meals can come from blink-and-you-miss-'em lairs like Yuca's, Sanamluang, Zankou Chicken and Tacomiendo.

Reservations are definitely a good idea at dinnertime. To score a table at the trendiest places, either call several days ahead to book or opt for an early or late-ish slot on a weekday, which may also fit well around seeing a show.

Restaurants with good selections for vegetarians are denoted with V. For more choices, check out www.vegparadise.com. For more of the lowdown on the cuisine scene, see p52.

Hollywood, Los Feliz & Silver Lake
BUDGET

Yuca's (Map pp86-7; ☎ 323-662-1214; 2056 Hillhurst Ave, Los Feliz; mains $1.40-4; 11am-6pm Mon-Sat; P) Lo-cation, location, location…is definitely not what lures people to this parking-lot snack shack. It's the tacos, stupid! And the *tortas*, burritos and other Mexi faves that earned the Herrera family the coveted James Beard Award in 2005. Grab a cold one at the liquor store next door and dig in.

Café Tropical (Map p86-7; ☎ 323-661-8391; 2900 Sunset Blvd, Silver Lake; sandwiches $3.50-5.50; 6am-10pm Mon-Fri, 7am-10pm Sat & Sun; wi-fi) Che would feel right at home in this Cuban bakery and coffee shop where an entire wall is swathed in photographs of the revolutionary heart-throb. Stop by for their flaky guava-cheese pie, pressed pork sandwiches and *muy macho café con leche* (very strong coffee with milk).

Sanamluang (Map p86-7; ☎ 323-660-8006; 5176 Hollywood Blvd, Hollywood; mains $5-10; 9am-4am; P) In the wee hours, this strip-mall joint gets howling with night owls hoping to restore balance to the brain. The poison of choice seems to be a steamy bowl of garlicky General's noodle soup, although anything with duck also gets a lots of takers. It's cash only and no alcohol.

El Cochinito (Map pp86-7; ☎ 323-668-0737; 3508 W Sunset Blvd, Silver Lake; dishes $8-13; 11am-8:30pm Mon-Wed & Sun, 11am-9pm Thu-Sat) This 12-table hole-in-the-wall 'little pig' is family run, neighborhood adored and serves traditional 'pre-Castro' Cuban at its finest. The *tostones* are thin and crispy and the roasted pork is melt-in-your-mouth tender, but really, you can't order wrong.

Other pitstops on a budget:

Fred 62 (Map pp86-7; ☎ 323-667-0062; 1850 N Vermont Ave, Los Feliz; mains $5-14; 24hr; 🖥) Polyethnic sandwiches, salads and noodles for young guns on small budgets.

Pho Café (Map pp86-7; ☎ 213-413-0888; 2841 W Sunset Blvd, Silver Lake; mains $6-8; 11am-midnight) *Pho*-nomenal Vietnamese soups at signless hipster hangout.

MIDRANGE

Palms Thai (Map pp86-7; ☎ 323-462-5073; 5900 Hollywood Blvd, Hollywood; mains $6-19; 11am-2am) It's in a new location but the food's as sharp as ever if the steady stream of Thai families, tattooed scenesters and cops is anything to go by. All the expected classics are accounted for, but adventurous eaters might like to try the wild-boar curry or the garlic-pepper frog. It ain't easy bein' green…

Red Pearl Kitchen (Map pp86-7; ☎ 323-525-1415; 6703 Melrose Ave, Hollywood; dishes $8-19; ⏰ 5:30pm-10pm Sun-Thu, to 11pm Fri & Sat, bar to 2am; **P**) Dark and draped in crimson red and bold gold, this Asian eatery is as sensuous, mysterious and kitschy as a 1940s Shanghai noir thriller. Sip a vodka-and-champagne-based Red Pearl while casually scanning the happy crowd and anticipating platters of such flavor bombs as wok-tossed Kobe beef and perky Thai green curry.

Lucy's El Adobe (Map pp86-7; ☎ 323-462-9421; 5536 Melrose Ave, Hollywood; mains $8-25; ⏰ 11:30am-11pm Mon-Fri, noon-11pm Sat; **P**) The Mexican food is only so-so but the Old Hollywood vibe is priceless. It was in these dark booths where Raymond Chandler made movie deals, the Eagles got hammered and Jerry Brown trysted with Linda Ronstadt. With Paramount across the street and other studios nearby, it still often feels like a commissary.

Bowery (Map pp86-7; ☎ 323-465-3400; 6268 Sunset Blvd, Hollywood; mains $8.50-18.50; ⏰ noon-2am Mon-Fri, 6pm-2am Sat & Sun; **P**) It's often standing-room only at this New York-ish gastropub with black-and-white subway tiles, a tin ceiling and a crowd that's like a two-inch heel – chic but tasty. There's Chimay ale on tap and sensible food on the menu. The roast chicken French dip sandwich puts an interesting twist on an old stand-by.

Hungry Cat (Map pp86-7; ☎ 323-462-2155; 1535 Vine St, Hollywood; dishes $9-27; ⏰ 11:30am-2:30pm Tue-Fri, 5:30pm-midnight Mon-Sat, 11am-3pm & 5-10pm Sun; **P**) This kitty is small and sleek and hides out near the ArcLight cinemas, making it a handy pre- or post-show stop. It fancies fresh seafood and will have you purring for hunky lobster roll, portly crab cakes and savory fish-*du-jour* specials. The Pug Burger – slathered with avocado, bacon and blue cheese – is a worthy meaty alternative.

Kung Pao Kitty (Map pp86-7; ☎ 323-465-0110; 6445 Hollywood Blvd, Hollywood; mains $10-14.50; ⏰ noon-10pm Sun-Thu, noon-2am Fri & Sat) This funky Asian cantina gets busiest late at night when scenesters on a bar hop descend here for generous helpings of coconut curry, Mongolian beef, *mu shu* pork and other standards. If you still need to get a buzz on, go for the Black Kat, a blonde-and-black marriage of Belgian Chimay and Guinness.

El Conquistador (Map pp86-7; ☎ 323-666-5136; 3701 W Sunset Blvd, Silver Lake; mains $10-17; ⏰ 11am-10pm Sun-Thu, 11am-11pm Fri & Sat) Halloween meets Margaritaville at this campy cantina that's a perfect launchpad for a night on the razzle. One cocktail may be all it takes to drown your sorrows, so be sure to load up on those yummy nachos, quesadillas and other above-average classics. The spinach and mushroom enchilada is a great meat-free choice.

Cheebo (Map pp86-7; ☎ 323-850-7070; 7533 W Sunset Blvd, Hollywood; mains breakfast/lunch $7-16, dinner $10-23; ⏰ 8am-11:30pm; **P** wi-fi) Cheap and cheerful, this joint makes heaping salads, bulging sandwiches and organic pizzas with pizzazz. Think lots of mouthwatering toppings, including the divine sausage and fennel combo. Kids love the free paper and crayons and special menu in the afternoons. The name, by the way, is a play on the Italian word for food, spelled *cibo*.

Blair's (Map pp86-7; ☎ 323-660-1882; 2903 Rowena Ave, Silver Lake; mains $14-28; ⏰ 7am-10pm Mon-Thu, 7am-11pm Sat & Sun; **P**) Despite haphazard service and a too-dark interior, Blair's upscale comfort food – crab cakes to short ribs – has vaulted this low-key corner restaurant to the top of many a local's fave list. Water Grill (p186) graduate Marshall Blair is at the helm.

Vermont (Map pp86-7; ☎ 323-661-6163; 1714 N Vermont Ave, Los Feliz; mains lunch $10-18, dinner $15-28; ⏰ 11:30am-3pm Mon-Fri, 5:30-11pm, bar to 1am; **P**) This is a smart, grown-up spot with a dining room punctuated by pillars and palmetto palms. The American contemporary food is smart and satisfying and reminds you of the simple goodness of slow-cooked pork, seared halibut or braised duck. The bar is a lively meet-and-greet zone.

More great bites:

Village Idiot (Map pp88-9; ☎ 323-655-3331; 7383 Melrose Ave, Hollywood; mains $10-16; ⏰ 11:30am-midnight Sun-Thu, 11pm-1am Fri & Sat) New falutin' gastropub with great fish and chips and other comfort food for a smart crowd.

Cafe Stella (Map pp86-7; ☎ 323-666-0265; 3932 W Sunset Blvd, Silver Lake; mains $16-33; ⏰ 6-11pm Tue-Sat; **P**) Courtyard-cloistered charmer serves classic French bistro fare to artsy locals.

TOP END

Providence (Map pp86-7; ☎ 323-460-4170; 5955 Melrose Ave, Hollywood; mains lunch $25-38, dinner $35-48; ⏰ noon-2.30pm Fri, 6pm-10pm Mon-Fri, 5.30-10pm Sat, 5.30-9pm Sun; **P**) Michael Cimarusti's gourmet creations will definitely take your tastebuds on a wild ride. Foie-gras parfait? Sea urchin with

---

TOP FIVE BREAKFAST SPOTS

- 3 Square Café & Bakery (Venice, p182)
- Marston's (Pasadena, p189)
- Nate 'n Al's (Beverly Hills, opposite)
- Toast (Mid-City, below)
- Uncle Bill's Pancake House (Manhattan Beach, p183)

---

truffles? To truly sample the master's talents, sign up for the nine-course tasting menu ($105, with wine $150).

West Hollywood & Mid-City

BUDGET

Little Next Door (Map pp88-9; ☎ 323-951-1010; 8142 W 3rd St; pastries, salads, sandwiches $3-12; ⏰ 9am-9pm; **P**) Bistro tables, staff in sailor outfits and an all-organic menu of homemade croissants, terrines and quiches make this cute café so cliché French, you half expect to see the Eiffel Tower around the corner.

Doughboys (Map pp88-9; ☎ 323-651-4202; 8136 W 3rd St. ⏰ 7am-midnight) Cream cheese–frosted cupcakes are among the naughty delights served up quickly at this boho-artist redoubt, which also has more sensible soups and sandwiches. Portions are huge.

Swingers (Map pp88-9; ☎ 323-653-5858; 8020 Beverly Blvd; dishes $4-10; ⏰ 6:30am-4am; **P**) Americana with a dollop of Hollywood is the ammo of this genuine retro diner where booths are red and servers wear fishnet stockings. Join the kool kids combating hunger pangs or hangovers with juicy burgers, awesome fries and other all-American faves while Little Richard heats up the juke box.

Griddle Café (Map pp88-9; ☎ 323-874-0377; 7916 W Sunset Blvd; dishes $6-9; ⏰ 7am-4pm Mon-Fri, 8am-4pm Sat & Sun) If you've greeted the day with bloodshot eyes, get back in gear at this tasty breakfast joint favored by Hollywood's young and tousled. The high-octane coffee, wagonwheel-sized pancakes and energy-restoring egg dishes might just do the trick.

Toast (Map pp88-9; ☎ 323-655-5018; 8221 W 3rd St; mains $9-13; ⏰ 7:30am-10pm; **V** ♿) From sitcom stars to dolly grips, the Hollywood crowd loves its Toast. Not to mention its tasty egg scrambles, luscious sandwiches, crunchy salads and frothy lattes. Avoid the crush on weekend mornings.

The original **Farmers Market** (Map pp88-9; 6333 W 3rd St; ⏰ 9am-9pm Mon-Thu, 9am-9:30pm Fri & Sat, 9am-7:30pm Sun; **P V** ♿) is a great spot for a casual meal any time of day, especially if the rug rats are tagging along. Favorite belly-filling stations include the following:

Lotería! Grill (☎ 323-930-2211; dishes $3-10) Handmade, back-to-basics Mexican.

Gumbo Pot (☎ 323-933-0358; mains $4-9) Southern food so finger-lickin' good, Blanche Dubois would approve.

Singapore's Banana Leaf (☎ 323-933-4627; mains $5-8) Southeast Asian perfumed with peanut, mango, tamarind and other exotic flavors.

Other fine budget options:

Pink's Hot Dogs (Map pp88-9; ☎ 323-931-4223; 709 N La Brea Ave; snacks $2.85-6.35; ⏰ 9:30am-2am Sun-Thu, 9:30am-3am Fri & Sat) Landmark doggeria with glacially moving lines. Chili-cheese dog worth the wait? Probably not.

Tere's Mexican Grill (Map pp88-9; ☎ 323-468-9345; 5870 Melrose Ave; dishes $3-8; ⏰ 9am-9pm Mon-Sat) No-frills, authentic Mexican grub near Paramount Studios.

Leaf Cuisine (Map pp88-9; ☎ 310-301-4982; 8365 Santa Monica Blvd, West Hollywood; mains $6.50-11; ⏰ 9am-9pm) The sibling of Culver City's original rawfood emporium (p179).

MIDRANGE

Urth Caffé (Map pp88-9; ☎ 310-659-0628; 8565 Melrose Ave; mains $7-13; ⏰ 9am-11pm Sun-Thu, 9am-midnight Fri & Sat; **P V**) They make some of the best lattes in town but you're here for a jolt of celeb-gawking, so park yourself on the patio, nibble on a scrumptious fruit tart and scan the crowd for tabloid regulars – discreetly, please. Yummy salads and sandwiches, too. Also in Santa Monica (p181) and Beverly Hills (p178).

Real Food Daily (Map pp88-9; ☎ 310-289-9910; 414 N La Cienega Blvd; mains $7-15; ⏰ 11:30am-2pm Mon-Fri, 5-9pm Sun-Thu, 5-10pm Fri & Sat; **V**) No need to drive to Santa Monica to enjoy Ann Gentry's famous vegan cuisine. See p181 for full review.

Buddha's Belly (Map pp88-9; ☎ 323-931-8588; 7475 Beverly Blvd; mains $8.50-16; ⏰ noon-10pm Mon-Thu, noon-11pm Fri & Sat, 3pm-10pm Sun; **P**) This place is always busy as a beehive and for good reason: light, inventive and fresh, the pan-Asian menu here has few false notes. Standouts include the mixed seaweed appetizer and the Singapore Seafood bonanza cuddling up with black squid-ink noodles. The bamboo-fringed patio delivers relief if the main dining room is too noisy.

Pizzeria Mozza (Map pp88-9; ☎ 323-297-0101; 641 N Highland; pizza $9-17; ✆ noon-midnight; **V**) 'At the table, one never gets old,' is the motto on the menu here. How true. Old age comes trying to score a reservation at this booked-weeks-ahead posh pizzeria from Nancy Silverton and Mario Batali. Fennel sausage, prosciutto, and salami are indicative of the high fat, high taste toppings gourmands and groupies demand. No reservation? Come early for a seat at the bar.

AOC (Map pp88-9; ☎ 323-653-6359; 8022 W 3rd St; plates $9-18; ✆ 6-11pm; **P**) At this jewel of a wine bar, Suzanne Goin feeds a feistily flavored small-plate menu to friends, lovebirds and trendy families. Over 50 wines can be ordered by the glass, all the better to find the perfect match for the artesanal cheeses, homemade terrines, braised lamb cheeks and other richly nuanced morsels. Reservations essential.

Surya (Map pp88-9; ☎ 323-653-5151; 8048 W 3rd St; mains $9-20; ✆ 11:30am-2pm Mon-Fri, 5:30-8:45pm Sun & Mon, 5:30-10pm Tue-Sat; **P**) Curries here are second to naan (pardon the pun) at this saffron-colored Indian restaurant dedicated to Surya, the Hindu god of the sun. Everything tastes genuine, fresh and inflected with an authentic medley of spices. Make sure your bill includes an order of something – anything – cooked in the tandoor (clay oven).

Chaya Brasserie (Map pp88-9; ☎ 310-859-8833; 8741 Alden Dr, West Hollywood; mains lunch $10-17, dinner $10-35; ✆ 11:30am-2:30pm Mon-Fri, 6-10:30pm daily; **P**) Shigefumi Tachibe's classy joint is an anomaly in this fast-lived city. For more than 20 years his sophisticated Franco-Asian creations – miso-marinated sea bass to filet mignon with potato-filled *soba* crêpes – have wowed discriminating power palates. Savvy shoppers flock here from Robertson Blvd for happy-hour deals on sushi and martinis.

Angelini Osteria (Map pp88-9; ☎ 323-297-0070; 7313 Beverly Blvd; lunch mains $10-24 dinner $10-38; ✆ noon-2:30pm Tue-Fri, 5:30-10:30pm Tue-Sun; **P**) Conversation flows as freely as the wine at this convivial eatery whose eclectic clientele shares a passion for Gino Angelini's soulful risottos, pungent pastas and rustic trattoria classics à la roasted veal shank and grilled quail.

O-Bar (Map pp88-9; ☎ 323-822-3300; 8279 Santa Monica Blvd, West Hollywood; mains $13-29; ✆ 6pm-midnight Sun & Mon, 6pm-1am Tue & Wed, 6pm-2am Thu-Sat; **P**) Boystown's swankiest eatery is a modernist design feast of stone pillars, dramatic lighting, fireplaces and rippling fountains. Dinner is contempo comfort food – mac 'n' cheese to short ribs – and the bar scene goes on and on and on.

TOP END

Koi (Map pp88-9; ☎ 310-659-9449; 730 N La Cienega Blvd, West Hollywood; mains $18-28; ✆ 6-11pm Sun-Thu, 6pm-midnight Fri & Sat; **P**) With its bamboo-fortified patios, bubbly fireside lounge and sexy crowd that may include Owen Wilson or Avril Lavigne, this high-octane spot is packed with so much eye candy, it's hard to focus on the food. Which is a shame, because the Asian nibbles (try the spicy tuna on crispy rice) are actually surprisingly good.

Ivy (Map pp88-9; ☎ 310-274-8303; 113 N Robertson Blvd, West Hollywood; mains $20-38; ✆ 11:30am-11pm Mon-Fri, 11am-11pm Sat, 10am-11pm Sun; **P**) The picket-fenced patio and rustic cottage may not look posh but never mind – the Ivy is *the* power lunch spot in town. The chances of catching A-lister babes choking on a carrot stick or studio execs discussing sequels over the lobster omelette are excellent if you're willing to put up with servers we found rather snooty and the steep bill. Desserts are outstanding.

Campanile (Map pp88-9; ☎ 323-938-1447; 624 S La Brea Ave, Miracle Mile, Mid-City; mains brunch $10-18, lunch $18-24, dinner $28-48; ✆ brunch Sat & Sun, lunch Mon-Fri, dinner Mon-Sat; **P**) In a gorgeous building commissioned by Charlie Chaplin, owner-chef Mark Peel has been turning market-fresh ingredients into beautiful dishes for over 15 years. Loyal locals practically mob the place on Mondays for $40 three-course dinners and on Thursdays for Grilled Cheese Night.

Beverly Hills
BUDGET & MIDRANGE

Mulberry Street Pizzeria (Map pp90-1; ☎ 310-247-8100; 240 S Beverly Dr; slices $3-4, pies $18-27; ♿) Cathy Moriarty's place (credits include *Raging Bull*, *Kindergarten Cop*) often crawls with East Coast transplants, which is no surprise because the New York–style pizza is about as authentic as it gets west of the Hudson. The crust is crispy, the tomato sauce tangy just so and the toppings classic – aah, little slices of heaven.

Nate 'n Al's (Map pp90-1; ☎ 310-274-0101; 414 N Beverly Dr; dishes $6-17; ✆ 7am-9pm; ♿) Dapper seniors, chatty girlfriends, busy execs and even Larry King have kept this New York–style nosh spot busy since 1945. The huge

LOS ANGELES

TOP FIVE CELEBRITY-SPOTTING RESTAURANTS

■ AOC (Mid-City, p177)

■ Ivy (West Hollywood, p177)

■ Koi (West Hollywood, p177)

■ Nobu Malibu (Malibu, p180)

■ Spago Beverly Hills (Beverly Hills, right)

---

menu brims with pastrami, lox and other old-school favorites, but we're partial to the corned beef or the roast beef, both made fresh on-site. If you hate long lines, avoid weekend breakfasts.

Urth Caffé (Map pp90-1; ☎ 310-205-9311; 267 S Beverly Dr; mains $7-13; ⏲ 7am-11pm; Ⓥ) Same great organic coffee and food but lower celebrity factor than the Melrose Ave original (p176).

Mako (Map pp90-1; ☎ 310-288-8338; 225 S Beverly Dr; small plates $7-23; ⏲ noon-2pm Wed-Fri, 6-10pm Mon-Sat; Ⓟ) Champion chef Makoto Tanaka trained with Wolfgang Puck and now supplies the faithful at his own minimalist-chic restaurant. The small-plate menu is ideal for sampling flavors and textures, from snow-crab tempura to wok-sautéed baby halibut or the excellent *yuzu* meringue tart. At lunch most people order the 'Bento Box' filled with whatever treats inspire Makoto that day.

Xi'an (Map pp90-1; ☎ 310-275-3345; 362 N Cañon Dr, Beverly Hills; mains $9-16; ⏲ 11:30am-10pm Mon-Fri, noon-11pm Sat, 5-10pm Sun; Ⓟ) Upbeat and noisy, Xi'an serves modern MSG-free Chinese fare calibrated to health- and waist-watchers but without sacrificing a lick to the taste gods. Swoon-worthy dishes include the black peppercorn chicken, and cod in black-bean sauce. It's popular with Beverly Hills belles, off-duty power-suits and chatty families.

TOP END

Il Cielo (Map pp90-1; ☎ 310-276-9990; 9018 Burton Way; mains $18-38; ⏲ 11:30am-3pm & 6-11pm Mon-Sat; Ⓟ) Candles, Chianti and a table for two in an enchanted garden are the hallmarks of a romantic night out. If your date doesn't make you swoon, then the rustic Northern Italian food should still ensure an unforgettable evening. That scene in *Legally Blonde* where Reese Witherspoon is dumped by her boyfriend was shot here.

Crustacean (Map pp90-1; ☎ 310-205-8990; 9646 S Santa Monica Blvd; mains lunch $11-34, dinner $19-35; ⏲ 11:30am-2:30pm Mon-Fri, 5:30-10:30pm Mon-Thu, 5:30-11:30pm Fri & Sat; Ⓟ) At this celeb-heavy Euro-Vietnamese restaurant, you can literally walk on water – on top of a floor-sunken koi stream, that is. The menu here is as intriguing as the sultry French Colonial decor, with top honors going to the whole roasted Dungeness crab and the garlic noodles, both bathed in owner-chef Elizabeth An's 'secret spices.' Reservations essential.

Spago Beverly Hills (Map pp90-1; ☎ 310-385-0880; 176 N Cañon Dr; mains lunch $19-48, dinner $32-66; ⏲ 11:30am-2:15pm Mon-Sat, 5:30-10:30pm daily; Ⓟ) Spago has long been an essential California kitchen, the one that pioneered the designer pizza and made Wolfgang Puck a household name. Book early if you want to scan the power-crowd for famous faces while noshing on the legendary smoked-salmon pizza ($24) or other frightfully pricey fusion fare.

Westwood, Bel Air & Brentwood

BUDGET

Zankou Chicken (off Map pp90-1; ☎ 310-444-0550; 1716 S Sepulveda Blvd; mains $3.70-8.50; ⏲ 10am-11pm; Ⓟ ♿) Fabulous chicken sent through the rotisserie for that light and crispy tan and served with addictive garlic sauce. See p188 for the full review.

Yashima (off Map pp90-1; ☎ 310-473-5297; 11301 W Olympic Blvd; mains $6-15; ⏲ 11:30am-10pm; Ⓟ Ⓥ) Upstairs in the Olympic Collection, Yashima serves fresh and authentic Japanese food, but no sushi. Instead, feast on big bowls of soba and udon noodles, rice bowls and tasty plates like *gomaee* (vegetables in sesame dressing) and salmon-skin salad.

Native Foods (Map pp90-1; ☎ 310-209-1055; 1110-1/2 Gayley Ave, Westwood; dishes $7-14; ⏲ 11am-10pm; Ⓥ) Pizzas, burgers, sandwiches, salads – the menu reads like those at your typical California café with one notable difference: no animal products will ever find their way into this vegan haven. Don't come for ambience but do try the Bali surf burger with fries.

Hurry Curry (off Map pp90-1; ☎ 310-473-1640; 2131 Sawtelle Blvd; mains $7.50-10.40; ⏲ 11am-10pm Sun-Thu, 11am-11pm Fri & Sat; Ⓟ) Curry rice is a Japanese staple food. It's basically a plate of rice on one side and a thick curry sauce on the other which contains beef, chicken, potato croquettes or tofu, plus veggies. Spice: mild to wild.

MIDRANGE

Sawtelle Kitchen (off Map pp90-1; ☎ 310-473-2222; 2024 Sawtelle Blvd; mains $7-16; ⏱ noon-2:30pm & 6-10pm Mon-Sat) This contempo dining room gives standard Western dishes an eccentric Japanese twist, mostly with success. Pasta is paired with Pollock caviar and daikon sprouts, the pork chops are drizzled with olive-ginger sauce and the yams deep-fried and served with plum-mayo. They don't have a liquor license but you're free to BYOB.

Zip Fusion (off Map p92; ☎ 310-575-3636; 11301 W Olympic Blvd; mains $10-17; ⏱ 11:30am-2:30pm Mon-Fri, 5-11:30pm Sun-Wed, 5-1:30am Thu-Sat; Ⓟ) Skip the sushi and instead focus on Jason Ha's boundary-pushing pan-Asian creations that appeal both to lunchtime collars and dinnertime heels. Order the Zip Alba-Cado and a *soju* cocktail and you'll know why. It's downstairs in the Olympic Collection minimall. The original branch is in Downtown (p186).

Tanino (Map pp90-1; ☎ 310-208-0444; 1043 Westwood Blvd, Westwood; mains lunch $11-28, dinner $13-32; ⏱ 11:30am-3pm Mon-Fri, 5:30pm-11:30pm Mon-Sat, 5:30pm-10pm Sun; Ⓟ) At Tanino, the decor, menu and service blend together as perfectly as a rich stew from Sicily where the eponymous chef hails from. The island's feisty cuisine provides the inspiration for such wonderful dishes as duck ravioli in mushroom sauce and fresh blueberries, and spaghetti with sautéed sea urchin, garlic and red chili.

Literati II (off Map pp90-1; ☎ 310-479-3400; 12081 Wilshire Blvd; mains lunch $12-19, dinner $14-36; ⏱ 11:30am-2:30pm & 5:30-11pm) Chris Kidder, formerly of Campanile (p177), is a stickler for fresh, organic, sustainable provisions and has built relationships with local farmers to ensure that only the best and freshest ingredients land on your plate. And trust us, you'll taste it: dishes are as sophisticated as a Joyce novel, as sensuous as a sonnet, as exciting as a spy thriller and as playful as a limerick.

TOP END

Hotel Bel-Air Restaurant (Map pp90-1; ☎ 310-472-5234; 701 N Stone Canyon Rd, Bel Air; breakfast $25, mains lunch $18-28, dinner $26-48; ⏱ 11-12:30am Sun-Thu, 11-1:30am Fri & Sat; Ⓟ) This classy hideaway scores a perfect 10 on the romance meter. Even getting there has that fairy-tale feel as you sashay along flowery paths, past preening swans and a crackling fireplace. Impeccable service, a superb farm-fresh Cal-French menu and a fanatical dedication to quality ensure that

you'll remember your meal long after paying the – significant – bill.

Culver City

BUDGET

Tacomiendo (Map p97; ☎ 310-915-0426; 4502 Inglewood Blvd; dishes $2-8; ⏱ 9:30am-10pm; Ⓟ ♿) Cops, construction workers and clued-in hipsters flock to this unassuming Mexican pit stop to fortify themselves on ginormous *tortas*, tacos, burritos and other staples. Everything's freshly prepared in the smokey open kitchen, so it's not exactly fast food. While you wait, sip a refreshing melon *agua* (fresh fruit drink) and help yourself to three salsas, pinto beans and crunchy radishes from the excellent condiment counter.

Leaf Cuisine (Map p97; ☎ 310-390-6005; 11938 W Washington Blvd; mains $6.50-11; ⏱ 8am-9pm Mon-Sat, 10am-9pm Sun; Ⓟ Ⓥ) OK, the idea of veggie-seed croquettes, kale salad or kelp-noodle *pad thai* may not get you salivating, but trust us, the folks at Leaf are geniuses when it comes to coaxing flavor out of the vegetable kingdom. Everything's organic, raw, vegan and healthy, just like the yoga mammas, Sony grips and health nuts like it.

Tender Greens (Map p97; ☎ 310-842-8300; www .tendergreensfood.com; 9523 Culver Blvd; dishes $10; ⏱ 11:30am-9pm Sun-Thu, 11:30am-10pm Fri & Sat; Ⓥ ♿) Herbivore or meathead, no matter your persuasion, your tastebuds will be doing sommersaults when treated to this eatery's carefully composed salads, tossed up as you move down the (usually considerable) line. The ahi-tuna nicoise and grilled flatiron steak are fabulous, and the chicken soup soul-restoring.

MIDRANGE

Beacon (Map p97; ☎ 310-838-7500; 3280 Helms Ave; mains lunch $9-18, dinner $10-20; ⏱ 11:30am-2pm Mon-Sat, 5:30-10pm Tue-Sun) When Kazuto Matsusaka opened Beacon in 2004, it became the guiding light in Culver City's culinary renaissance. Fusion is what he does best, turning carefully edited ingredients into adventurous small and big plates that can easily hold their own against the new competition. Try the miso-braised short ribs or crispy ahi-tuna pizza and leave room for the green-tea cheesecake.

Ford's Filling Station (Map p97; ☎ 310-202-1470; www.fordsfillingstation.com; 9531 Culver Blvd; mains lunch $14-17, dinner $14-32; ⏱ lunch & dinner) The 'Ford' in question is Ben Ford (yup, son of Harrison) and he'll fill you up in his lively gastropub favored by a chatty, boozy crowd. Flatbreads are toasted to perfection, the fish and chips have the lightness of tempura and the vegetarian polenta cake is a symphony of textures and flavors. Only the noise level needs some fine-tuning.

Reliable stand-bys:

Natalee Thai Cuisine (Map p97; ☎ 310-202-7003; 10101 Venice Blvd; mains $6-10; Ⓟ Ⓚ) Stylish top Thai parlor with healthily prepared pad thai, curries and other staples, all wittily introduced on the long menu.

Versailles (Map p97; ☎ 310-558-3168; 10319 Venice Blvd; mains $6-11; Ⓟ Ⓚ) We'll always have a soft spot for the Cuban-style roast lemon chicken and succulent roast pork doled out to everyone from college kids to grizzled grips.

Malibu
BUDGET

Lily's Café & Pastries (Map pp80-1; ☎ 310-457-3745; 29211 Heathercliff Rd, Point Dume Plaza; dishes $2-6.50; Ⓥ 7am-6pm Mon-Fri, 7am-5pm Sat, 8am-4pm Sun) Surfers who've worked up an appetite in the early morning waves invade this beloved indie place to refuel on the biggest, meanest breakfast burrito under the sun. Beware the salsa unless you plan on auditioning as a fire eater. Great coffee and pastries, too.

Coogies Beach Café (Map pp80-1; ☎ 310-317-1444; 23755 Malibu Rd at Malibu Bluffs; mains $5-17; Ⓥ 7:30am-9pm Sun-Thu, 7:30am-10pm Fri & Sat; Ⓟ Ⓚ) Even size 0 locals can't resist Coogie's famous whole-wheat pancakes packed with fresh strawberries and bananas. A great place to hit before or after the beach, this mall-based yet upscale diner serves breakfast until 3pm, tasty sandwiches and salads for lunch and fresh fish for dinner.

Neptune's Net (off Map pp80-1; ☎ 310-457-3095; 42505 Pacific Coast Hwy; dishes $6-10; Ⓥ 10:30am-8pm Apr-Oct, 10:30am-7pm Nov-Mar; Ⓟ Ⓚ) If you've worked up an appetite driving up PCH in your convertible, stop by this landmark seafood shack and pit stop for surfers, Harley

riders and families. The seafood dishes are superb, fresh from the tank and cooked up any way you like it. Order a cold beer and kick back on the ocean-view patio. Great clam chowder, too.

MIDRANGE & TOP END

Allegria (Map pp80-1; ☎ 310-456-3132; 22821 Pacific Coast Hwy, cnr Sweetwater Cyn; mains lunch $10-17, dinner mains $12-26, pizza $12-16; Ⓥ 11:30am-2pm Mon-Fri, 5-Mon-Fri, 11:30am-10:30pm Sat & Sun; Ⓟ) This convivial trattoria near the Malibu Pier is often filled with patrons lusting after the pizzas tickled by wood fire just long enough to produce perfectly crispy thin crusts. Other dishes beckon too, including pretty pastas, tender osso buco and crispy fried calamari paired with a tomato sauce that's got some kick.

Taverna Tony (Map pp80-1; ☎ 310-317-9667; 23410 Civic Center Way, cnr Cross Creek Rd; mains $13-23; Ⓥ 11:30am-midnight Sun-Thu, 11:30-12:30am Fri & Sat; Ⓟ) This lively Greek spot fronted by a flowery terrace packs them in day after day with finger-lickin' fare that feeds both the soul and belly. For a serious indulgence, loosen your belt and order the Greek Feast ($33 per person; two-person minimum) with 15 different dishes. Reservations advised.

Nobu Malibu (Map pp80-1; ☎ 310-317-9140; Ste 18a, 3835 Cross Creek Rd; sushi $6-12, dishes $14-38; Ⓥ 6-10pm Sun-Thu, 6-11pm Fri & Sat; Ⓟ) Tucked in the Malibu Country Mart shopping center, Nobu coasts on its fame and famous clientele. Everyone else will still enjoy the creative Japanese fare but perhaps not the smallish portions, high prices, and the indifferent service we found here. Still, the stargazing, especially on the dimly lit patio, can't be beat. Don't dress up or you won't blend in.

Inn of the Seventh Ray (Map pp80-1; ☎ 310-455-1311; 128 Old Topanga Canyon Rd; mains lunch $12-20, dinner $22-34; Ⓥ 11:30am-3pm Mon-Fri, 10:30am-3pm Sat & Sun, 5:30-10pm daily; Ⓟ Ⓥ) If you've lived through the '60s, you might experience flashbacks at this New-Agey hideaway in an impossibly idyllic setting in Topanga Canyon. All of the food is organic, much is raw, most of it meatfree and some rather esoteric. The agave-glazed vegan duck ($23) is a perennial favorite.

Santa Monica
BUDGET

Counter (Map p92; ☎ 310-399-8383; 2901 Ocean Park Blvd; burgers from $6.50; Ⓥ 11am-10pm Mon-Thu, 11am-11pm

---

TOP FIVE VEGETARIAN PICKS

- Green Temple (Redondo Beach, p183)
- Inn of the Seventh Ray (Topanga Canyon, right)
- Leaf Cuisine (Culver City, p179)
- Real Food Daily (Santa Monica, opposite)
- Zephyr (Long Beach, p184)

Fri & Sat, noon-9pm Sun) Let your creativity fly at this crisp postmodern patty-and-bun joint where you build your own gourmet burger by mixing and matching your favorite bread, meat, cheese, topping and sauce. Apparently, this adds up to 312,120 burger combinations. Ponder that while munching on a bucket of tasty fries.

Real Food Daily (Map p92; ☎ 310-451-7544; 514 Santa Monica Blvd; mains $7-15; ⏰ 11:30am-10pm; **V**) New World vegan-cooking-guru Ann Gentry gives meat and dairy substitutes an interesting inflection, although some of the dishes sound better than they taste (keep the salt within reach). Still, the lentil-walnut pâté is a complex starter and classics like the Salisbury seitan (a wheat gluten-based dish) feed the body and soul.

Ye Olde King's Head (Map p92; ☎ 310-451-1402; 116 Santa Monica Blvd; mains $11-20; ⏰ 10am-10pm Mon-Thu, 10am-midnight Fri & Sat, 8am-10pm Sun; **P**) This is the unofficial HQ of Santa Monica's huge British expat population, and if you don't mind the fusty odor of over 30-years' worth of kitchen and Guinness fumes, you'll feel quite Piccadilly here. They do English breakfast and afternoon tea, but it's the King's fish and chips ($13 to $16) that truly deserves our royal respects.

Father's Office (Map p92; ☎ 310-393-2337; 1018 Montana Ave; tapas $3.50-5, burgers $12; ⏰ 5pm-1am Mon-Thu, 4pm-2am Fri, noon-2am Sat, noon-midnight Sun) This elbow-to-elbow gastropub is definitely a candidate for 'burger king' in town. Theirs is a dry-aged-beef number dressed in smoky bacon, sweet caramelized onion and an ingenious combo of Gruyère and blue cheese. Pair it with fries served in a mini shopping cart and a mug of handcrafted brew chosen from the three-dozen on tap.

For industrial-weight omelettes and sandwiches, head to the always popular **Omelette Parlor** (Map p92; ☎ 310-399-7892; 2732 Main St; dishes under $7; ⏰ 6am-2:30pm Mon-Fri, 6am-4pm Sat & Sun).

Santa Monica also has a branch of **Swingers** (Map p92; ☎ 310-393-9793; 802 Broadway), the happening diner near the Farmers Market (see p176 for a full review).

MIDRANGE
Violet (Map p92; ☎ 310-453-9113; 3221 Pico Blvd; small plates $5-16; ⏰ 11:30am-2pm Tue-Fri, 6-10pm Tue-Sun) With his skinny jeans, tattoos and jet-black hair, Jared Simons looks more like a rock star than LA's latest hot, young chef. His

smartly seductive – if incredibly noisy – neighborhood bistro is often packed to capacity. The draw is sophisticated farm-fresh spins of American and California favorites, served in grazer-friendly small portions. Before 7pm, you can pick from seven plates costing just $7.

Lares (Map pp92; ☎ 310-829-4559; 2909 Pico Blvd; mains $7-23; ⏰ 8am-1am; **P** 🦽) There's nothing trendy about this family-run Mexican neighborhood favorite whose subdued Spanish Colonial furnishings make it feel more festive than fiesta. The slow-cooked *carnitas* – juicy and fall-apart pork – are a specialty, as are the sizzling fajitas. Just don't OD on the smokey chipotle salsa. Good margaritas, too.

Hump (Map p92; ☎ 310-313-0977; 3221 Donald Douglas Lp S, 3rd fl; dishes $8-20; ⏰ noon-2pm Mon-Fri, 6-10pm daily; **P**) Romance runs high behind the bamboo-accented windows at this tiny but superb rooftop sushi bar with stellar views of private planes soaring off to the great unknown. It's at the Santa Monica airport and named for an aviator's nickname for the Himalayas.

Library Alehouse (Map p92; ☎ 310-314-4855; 2911 Main St; mains $9-23; ⏰ 11:30am-midnight) Locals gather for the food as much as the beer at this wood-paneled gastropub with a cozy outdoor patio in the back. Angus burgers, fish tacos and hearty salads sate the 30-something postwork regulars while 29 hand-crafted microbrews keep 'em hanging around till midnight.

Lobster (Map p92; ☎ 310-458-9294; 1602 Ocean Ave; mains $12-38; ⏰ 11:30am-10pm Sun-Thu, 11:30am-11pm Fri & Sat; **P**) The ocean views impress as much as the food at this lively seafood shrine. It's always packed to the gills thanks to dock-fresh ingredients and Allyson Thurber's flawlessly crafted plates. Impress your server with your local knowledge by ordering a side-serve of the off-menu truffle parmesan fries and make sure you order the rich chocolate banana-bread pudding or the beautifully feathery *panna cotta*.

More options:

Caprice Fine French Pastries (Map p92; ☎ 310-453-1932; 3213 Pico Blvd; ⏰ 7:30am-5:30pm Mon-Sat) For the most delectable and pretty cakes and desserts under the sun, ring the doorbell and buy 'em right off the bakery tray.

Urth Caffé (Map p92; ☎ 310-314-7040; 2327 Main St; mains $7-13; ⏰ 6am-11pm; **V**) Mini-chain famous for its organic coffees, teas and food. See p176 for details.

TOP END

JiRaffe (Map p92; ☎ 310-917-6671; 502 Santa Monica Blvd; mains $26-38; ☼ dinner; ℗) Raphael Lunetta knows his waves and his kitchen. The avid surfer who studied cooking in France is a wizard when it comes to Cal-French compositions: pork chops are caramelized and paired with cider sauce; glazed salmon comes with saffron lemon couscous and artichokes. It's elegant, complex and supremely satisfying.

Abode (Map p92; ☎ 310-394-3463; 1541 Ocean Ave; small plates $10-22, mains $26-39; ☼ 11:30am-2:30pm Mon-Fri, 10am-2pm Sat & Sun, 5:30-10pm daily; ℗) The latest to enter the pantheon of respected gourmet restaurants in Santa Monica, Abode will indeed make you feel right at home. With chocolate booths, tangerine chairs and walnut tables, its design is as tastefully composed as its contemporary American cuisine. Only organic, sustainable and artesanal ingredients find their destiny in such dishes as arctic char with truffle berry guacamole and vegetarian eggplant chorizo.

Venice

BUDGET

Abbot's Pizza (Map p92; ☎ 310-396-7334; 1407 Abbot Kinney Blvd; slices $2.50-3, pizzas $9.50-16; ☼ 11am-11pm; 🕹) Join the flip-flop crowd at this shoebox-sized pizza kitchen for habit-forming crispy-crust pies tastily decorated with tequila-lime chicken, Portobello mushrooms, goat cheese and other gourmet morsels served up at tummy-grumbling speed.

Mao's Kitchen (Map p92; ☎ 310-581-8305; 1512 Pacific Ave; lunch $7.50, mains $7-12; ☼ 11:30am-10:30pm Sun-Thu, to 3am Fri & Sat) Cheap and cheerful, Mao's feeds the local hipster proletariat with country-style Chinese prepared with SoCal flair (read: fresh ingredients, no MSG). Reliable menu picks include the orange-ginger chicken and the onion pancakes. Savvy eaters take advantage of the bargain lunches served until 5pm.

La Cabaña (Map p92; ☎ 310-392-6161; 738 Rose Ave; mains $7-14; ☼ 11am-3am) The party vibe is infectious at this late-night Mexican cottage with dark nooks for making out and a brick patio where smoking is allowed. Dishes are fresh and vividly spiced, a señora pounds out fresh tortillas and the margaritas kick butt. Best of all, they let you linger in peace until long after you've sopped up the last delicious drop.

Rose Café (Map p92; ☎ 310-399-0711; 220 Rose Ave; mains $8-11; ☼ café 8am-5:30pm, restaurant 8am-3pm; ℗ 🕹) Laptop-toting writers, pony-tailed artists and beefcakes from nearby Gold's Gym dig this Euro-style café-bakery with two hedge-framed patios to slurp your latte or scarf up rave-worthy salads and frittatas. Before leaving, browse for unique knickknacks in the little gift store.

MIDRANGE

Hal's Bar & Grill (Map p92; ☎ 310-396-3105; 1349 Abbot Kinney Blvd; mains lunch $9-16, dinner $13-34; ☼ 11:30-2am Mon-Fri, 10-2am Sat & Sun; ℗) The name may evoke brass and wood, but Hal's dining room is an all-cool industrial loft brightened by revolving art from local artists who treat the place like an extended living room. The menu, sourced from farm-fresh ingredients, changes seasonally but always features superbly executed staples such as grilled chicken ($18), Caesar salad ($7) and bread pudding with crème anglaise ($7). Free jazz on Sunday and Monday.

3 Square Café & Bakery (Map p92; ☎ 310-399-6504; 1121 Abbot Kinney Blvd; mains lunch $8-13, dinner $15-19; ☼ 8am-3pm Mon-Fri, 5-10pm Tue-Sat, 9am-4pm Sun; ℗) Hans Röckenwagner is back with a minimalist café where newbies and loyalists devour his famous pretzel burgers, gourmet sandwiches and apple pancakes. Next door, bakery shelves are piled high with rustic breads, fruity tarts and jam-oozing doughnuts called *Berliners*.

Beechwood (Map p92; ☎ 310-448-8884; 822 Washington Blvd; bar menu $4-15, mains $16-26; ☼ 6-11pm Tue-Sat, bar to 2am & 6pm-midnight Sun & Mon; ℗) With its woodsy details, cubic furniture and toasty fire-pit patio, this place is a luscious port of call for Modern American bistro fare. Singles and small groups gravitate to the lively bar to graze on richly flavored pork ribs or sweet-potato fries, while couples retreat to the dimly lit dining room for grilled barramundi, roast quail or other seasonal delights.

Sidewalk Café (Map p92; ☎ 310-399-5547; 1401 Ocean Front Walk, Venice; mains $9-14; ☼ 8am-11pm) For American staples with front-row seats of the Venice Boardwalk weirdness, there's no better place than this tried-and-true café.

TOP END

Axe (Map p92; ☎ 310-664-9787; 1009 Abbot Kinney Blvd; mains lunch $6-12, dinner $16-26; ☼ 11:30am-3pm Tue-Fri, 9am-3pm Sat & Sun, 6-10pm Tue-Sun; ℗) It's good vibes all around at this minimalist-chic space (pronounced 'a-*shay*') where eco-conscious patrons tuck into sharp-flavored dishes woven together from whatever is local, organic and in season. The flatbreads with a sampler of delicious spreads are a good overture for the sake-marinated beef or hearty Persian bean stew.

Joe's (Map p92; ☎ 310-399-5811; 1023 Abbot Kinney Blvd, Venice; mains lunch $13-15, dinner $27-29, ☽ noon-2:30pm Tue-Fri, 6-10pm Sun & Tue-Thu, 6-11pm Fri & Sat; ℗) Joe's was one of the first restaurants on Abbot Kinney's restaurant row and, like a fine wine, only seems to get better with age. It's a casual yet stylish neighborhood spot where the accent is on gimmick-free Cal-French food. The choicest tables are out on the patio by the waterfall fountain.

Piccolo (Map p92; ☎ 310-314-3222; 5 Dudley Ave; pasta $16-20, mains $27-36; ☽ 5:30-10pm Sun-Thu, 5:30-11pm Fri & Sat; ℗) This teensy spot, mere steps from the boardwalk, pays homage to the original Venice with vintage black-and-white photos and Carnevale masks. The food too is as authentic as it gets with beef carpaccio, Tuscan bean soup, pistachio-encrusted lamb loin and any of the homemade pastas getting big thumbs up from the grown-up bohemian crowd. No reservations.

South Bay Beaches
BUDGET

Uncle Bill's Pancake House (Map p94; ☎ 310-545-5177; 1305 N Highland Ave, Manhattan Beach; mains $3-12.50; ☽ 6am-3pm Mon-Fri, 7am-3pm Sat & Sun; �disabled) Grab a stool, a booth or better yet an ocean-view table at this greet-the-day South Bay institution. Sexy surfers, tottering toddlers and gabbing girlfriends – everybody's here for the famous pancakes and big fat omelettes (try the 'Istanbul' made with turkey). Put your name on the list – the wait's worth it.

Rice Things (Map p94; ☎ 310-214-9033; 2401 Artesia Blvd, Redondo Beach; meals $5-8; ☽ 11am-9pm; ℗) OK, so the ambience is zero and it ain't the best Japanese food you'll ever eat, but the prices are simply hard to beat. Order the combo meal, which comes with a side of sushi and a drink and you'll be outta there, tummy filled nicely, for about $6.

Nancy's Diner (Map p94; ☎ 310-316-7676; 1550 S Pacific Coast Hwy, Redondo Beach; mains $5-10; ☽ 24hr) It's old-school, divey and hard to find, but after a night of partying, there's nothing like Nancy's greasy home-cooking to restore balance to the brain. It's behind a row of stores, near Albertson's supermarket.

El Gringo (Map p94; mains $6-11; ☽ 11am-9pm; ☐) Hermosa Beach (☎ 310-376-1381; 2620 Hermosa Ave) Manhattan Beach (☎ 310-372-6080; 921 N Sepulveda Blvd; ℗) Redondo Beach (☎ 310-316-8032; 821 Torrance Blvd; ℗) Grotty-looking dives usually make the best Mexi-fare and this tri-city mini-chain definitely delivers. Authentic charm is doled out with as much abandon as the delish dishes. Skip the standards in favor of *machaca* (shredded beef) burritos, *pollo negro* (blackened chicken) salads and flavor-packed *xcholti* (pronounced 'soul-chee') soup.

Green Temple (Map p94; ☎ 310-944-4525; 1700 S Catalina Ave, Redondo Beach; mains $9-13; ☽ 11am-9pm Sun-Thu, 11am-10pm Fri & Sat; Ⓥ) Sit in the flowery courtyard or amid funky Asian artwork at this sanctuary where meat is a no-no and organic, local produce is plentiful. Salads, including the tasty Sproutada, come with a slice of delicious homemade bread and there's also an entire page of Mexican dishes. Waist-watchers can ask for the 'junior' portions.

In Hermosa Beach, a time-honored way to start the day is with pancakes, waffles or omelettes from the **Backburner Cafe** (Map p94; ☎ 310-372-6973; 87 14th St, Hermosa Beach; mains $2.25-7.25; ☽ 6am-2pm) or **Beach Hut No 2** (Map p94; ☎ 310-376-4252; 1342 Hermosa Ave, Hermosa Beach; mains $3-6; ☽ closes around 2pm).

MIDRANGE & TOP END

Mama D's (Map p94; ☎ 310-456-1492; 1125 Manhattan Ave, Manhattan Beach; mains lunch $5-8, dinner $9-22; ☽ 11:30am-10pm; ☐) This neighborhood Italian fits like a well-worn shoe and puts 'heap' into 'cheap'. The thin-crust pizzas, homemade ravioli, tangy cioppino and freshly baked bread, all served with a smile, keep regulars coming back for more. Expect a wait.

Christine (Map pp82-3; ☎ 310-373-1952; Hillside Village, 24530 Hawthorne Blvd, Torrance; mains lunch $10-17, dinner $16-26; ☽ 11:30am-2pm Mon-Fri, 5-10pm daily; ℗) This top pick in the South Bay is more about substance on the plate than chichi decor and clientele. Chef Christine finds inspiration in the feisty flavors of Provence, Tuscany and the Pacific Rim, all expertly woven together in such dishes as warm mushroom salad with gorgonzola or *char sui* glazed filet mignon.

Zazou (Map p94; ☎ 310-540-4884; 1810 S Catalina Ave, Redondo Beach; mains lunch $12-20, dinner $16-31; ☽ 11:30am-2:30pm Tue-Fri, 11:30am-3pm & 5:30-10pm Sat & Sun; ℗) Zazou is French for hip, but this South Bay foodie favorite in Riviera Village is all about substance, not smoke and mirrors. Dip into a pool of pleasurable dishes inspired by sunny climes of Italy and France. The rock-shrimp pasta and osso-buco lamb are both stand-outs.

Petros (Map p94; ☎ 310-545-4100; 451 Manhattan Beach Blvd, Manhattan Beach; mains lunch $12-16, dinner $20-36; ⏰ 11am-midnight Sun-Thu, 11am-1am Fri & Sat; ℗) Finally, a Greek restaurant for the 21st century, without the sirtaki and plate-smashing. Petros is all about class and substance as evidenced in such dishes as feta-encrusted rack of lamb or the smokey eggplant and walnut dip. Grab a seat on the people-watching patio or lose your baseball cap for a dress-code-worthy experience indoors.

San Pedro & Long Beach
BUDGET
Omelette Inn (Map pp82-3; ☎ 562-437-5625; 108 W 3rd St, Long Beach; mains $4-8; ⏰ 7am-2:30pm; ♿) From clerks to cops to city-council members, *every*body's got a soft spot for this unassuming joint where breakfasts and sandwiches are served in belt-loosening portions. Build up your own omelette from more than 40 ingredients or pick from tried-and-true menu favorites such as The Sicilian or Grecian Formula.

Zephyr (Map pp82-3; ☎ 562-435-7113; 340 E 4th St, Long Beach; dishes $5-8; ⏰ 11am-8pm Tue-Sat, 11am-4pm Sun; Ⓥ) All vegan, with several raw options, and mostly organic, relative newcomer Zephyr has become ground zero for Long Beach's health-conscious hipsters.

For tasty Mexi snacks, head to **Taco Surf** (Map pp82-3; ☎ 562-434-8646; 5316 E 2nd St, Long Beach; dishes $5-12, happy hour 2-5pm Mon-Fri), a Baja-style cantina with $1 tacos and beers during happy hour.

MIDRANGE
Papadakis Taverna (Map pp82-3; ☎ 310-548-1186; 301 W 6th St, San Pedro; mains $10-45; ⏰ 5:30-10pm; ℗)

TOP FIVE ROMANTIC SPOTS

- Ca' del Sole (San Fernando Valley, p188)
- Firefly (Studio City, p188)
- Il Cielo (Beverly Hills, p178)
- Inn of the Seventh Ray (Malibu, p180)
- L'Opera (Long Beach, right)

The gods have been smiling upon this award-winning Greek restaurant for decades, possibly because Tom and John are usually around to welcome old hands and newcomers with Hellenic charm. Or possibly because the food's just that good. Crisp salads, succulent lamb and creative pastas (try pasta Vassiliko with Greek sausage) all fill the tummy nicely. Opa!

Bono's (Map pp82-3; ☎ 562-434-9501; 4901 E 2nd St, Long Beach; mains $12-30; ⏰ 11:30am-9pm Sun-Thu, 11:30am-10:30pm Fri & Sat; ℗) Sonny Bono's daughter Christy presides over this upbeat, beachy lair right on Belmont Shore's buzzy 2nd St. The menu is strongest on light yet flavor-packed salads and sandwiches – the Lobster, Avocado & Papaya salad is a standout. Dinner mains like sesame-crusted ahi and honey-glazed salmon are well executed but lack imagination.

Alegria (Map pp82-3; ☎ 562-436-3388; 115 Pine Ave, Long Beach; tapas $7-11, mains $15-20; ⏰ 11:30am-11pm; ℗) The trippy, Technicolor mosaic floor, an eccentric art nouveau bar and trompe l'oeil murals form an appropriately spirited backdrop to Alegria's fresh and vivid Latino cuisine. The tapas menu is great for grazers and the paella a feast for both eyes and stomach. There's even live flamenco on some nights.

San Pedro Fish Market & Restaurant (Map pp82-3; ☎ 310-832-4251; 1190 Nagoya Way, San Pedro; meals $20-40; ⏰ 9am-8pm; ♿) Seafood feasts don't get any more decadent than at this family-run harbor-view institution. Pick from the day's catch, have it cooked to order, lug your tray to a picnic table, fold up your sleeves and devour meaty crabs, plump shrimp, slimy oysters and tender halibut.

TOP END
L'Opera (Map pp82-3; ☎ 562-491-0066; 101 Pine Ave, Long Beach; mains $11-32; ⏰ 11:30am-11pm; ℗) Even simple dishes like bruschetta and pesto gnocchi become feistily flavored culinary works of art at this elegant dining shrine. The waiters are old-school and the sommelier capable of dissecting each wine down to the molecular level. We were blown away by the *ravioli ai tartufo* (truffle ravioli) and the buttery filet mignon with wild mushrooms.

Tracht's (Map pp82-3; ☎ 562-499-2533; 111 E Ocean Blvd; mains $14-48; ⏰ noon-2pm & 5-10pm; ℗) Long Beach is not known for innovative cuisine, but that should change now that Suzanne Tracht has come to town. Her contempo-chic dining room at the revamped Renaissance Hotel serves the same upscale chophouse fare as her original restaurant Jar in West Hollywood. Regulars swear by the pot roast with carrots and caramelized onions. Great fire-pit patio, too.

Downtown Los Angeles
BUDGET

Grand Central Market (Map pp84-5; ☎ 213-624-2378; 317 S Broadway; meals $2-9.50; ☒ 9am-6pm; P ☺) This historic indoor market is packed with wonderful snack options. Maria's Pescado Frito (central aisle) has fabulous fish tacos, ceviche tostadas and fish soup; Kabab & More (right aisle) has finger-lickin' charbroiled kebabs served with tangy hummus; while the old-timey China Café (upper level, near Hill St) makes sinus-clearing chicken soup and heaping plates of chow mein. See also p137.

Philippe the Original (Map pp84-5; ☎ 213-628-3781; 1001 N Alameda St; sandwiches $5-6; ☒ 6am-10pm; P ☺) From LAPD hunks to smooching couples, everyone loves Philippe's, where the French-dip sandwich was invented a century ago. Order a crusty roll filled with meat (beef is best, insiders ask for 'double-dipped') along with some crunchy coleslaw and hunker down at communal tables on the sawdust-covered floor. Coffee is just 9¢ (and that's no misprint). Cash only.

Haru Ulala (Map pp84-5; ☎ 213-620-0977; 368 E 2nd St; sushi & dishes $2-10; ☒ 6pm-midnight Sun-Thu, 6pm-2am Fri & Sat) The Kirin flows as freely as the conversation at this Little Tokyo *izakaya* (tavern) where the best seats are at the bar with full view of the cooks and sushi meister in action. Choice picks from the crayon-scrawled menu are the green-tea noodles, the slow-cooked Kurobuta pork belly and the sake-marinated cod.

ourpick Colori Kitchen (Map pp84-5; ☎ 213-622-5950; 429 W 8th St; mains $6-10; ☒ 11am-3pm Mon-Sat, 6pm-10pm Fri & Sat; ☺) Everybody feels like family in this Euro-flavored eatery where owner-chef Luigi kicks Italian comfort food into high gear. It's a fab choice for anyone who doesn't believe in shelling out $20 for a plate of pasta that cost the restaurant $2 to make. Service is tops. BYOB or hit the Golden Gopher (p194) two doors down for postprandial libations.

Clifton's Cafeteria (Map pp84-5; ☎ 213-627-1673; 648 Broadway, Downtown; dishes $3-8; ☒ 6:30am-7pm; ☺) This eatery was founded in 1931 by a Salvation Army captain who doled out free grub to starving Angelenos during the Great Depression. They still serve 'grub' but it's the ultracampy enchanted forest setting, complete with fake trees, squirrels and deer, that makes it so special.

MIDRANGE

Café Metropol (Map pp84-5; ☎ 213-613-1537; 923 E 3rd St; dishes $7-15; ☒ 8:30am-10pm Mon-Sat, 9am-2pm Sun; P) This exposed-brick, high-ceilinged, art-studded bistro embodies the ways in which the Arts District is transforming Downtown. Metropol's a bit tricky to find, but the gourmet sandwiches and *panini*, organic salads and pizzas – all made with choice ingredients imported from Europe – make it worthwhile. There's live music on some nights (cover $5, plus $10 minimum).

Oomasa (Map pp84-5; ☎ 213-623-9048; 100 Japanese Village Plaza; mains lunch $9-13, dinner $10-20; ☒ 11:30am-12:30am Wed-Sun) Sushi purists rejoice: you won't find any truffle-oil-infused wasabi nonsense at this old-school Litte Tokyo joint. From dark-red tuna to marbled salmon, it's all superfresh, expertly cut, affordably priced and best enjoyed while snuggled into an old-timey booth.

Empress Pavilion (Map pp84-5; ☎ 213-617-9898; 3rd fl, Bamboo Plaza, 988 N Hill St; dim sum per plate $2-6, dinner $10-30; ☒ 10am-2:30pm & 5:30-9:30pm; P) Other Chinatown places do dim sum, but regulars swear by this Hong Kong–style banquet hall with seating for a small village (500 people, to be exact). Dumplings, wontons, pot stickers, barbecued pork and other delicacies just fly off the carts wheeled right to your table by a small army of servers.

Pete's Café & Bar (Map pp84-5; ☎ 213-617-1000; 400 S Main St; mains lunch $10-17, dinner $11-27; ☒ 11:30am-2am) *The* late-night hotspot in the Old Bank District, Pete's has a classic interior and is alive with loft dwellers, politicos, journos and artists. The menu is modern American feel-good food, including a mean burger doused in fontina and tomato aioli. Come on, be extra bad and get a side of killer blue-cheese fries. Food's served till closing time.

R23 (Map pp84-5; ☎ 213-687-7178; 923 E 2nd St; mains lunch $9-13, dinner $12-30; ☒ 11:30am-2pm Mon-Fri, 5:30-10pm Mon-Sat; P) In an unlikely spot deep in the industrial heart of the Arts District, R23 is an avant-garde sushi parlor housed in a former railroad loading dock with exposed brick walls, and is decorated with Frank

Gehry–designed cardboard chairs and over-sized paintings of nudes. Regulars rave about the lobster tempura, the Dungeness-crab salad and the scallion-stuffed duck breast.

Tiara Café (Map pp84-5; ☎ 213-623-3663; 127 E 9th St, Downtown; sandwiches $8-11, mains $14-16; ◷ 11:30am-3pm; Ⓟ Ⓥ) Pretty in pink and with a high ceiling, this Fashion District lunch spot feeds designers, sales clerks and frenzied bargain hunters with healthy, organic fare that can be calibrated to meet vegan and vegetarian needs. The salads are fresh and abundant and the sandwiches are custom-made. Carbophobes should try the rice paper–wrapped versions.

For a progressive spin on sushi and vibrant Asian fare, try **Zip Fusion** (Map pp84-5; ☎ 213-680-3770; 744 E 3rd St; mains $10-17; ◷ 11:30am-2:30pm Mon-Fri, 5-10:30pm Sun-Wed, 5-11:30pm Thu-Sat). See p179 for details.

TOP END

Water Grill (Map pp84-5; ☎ 213-891-0900; 544 S Grand Ave; mains $24-54, ◷ 11:30am-9:30pm Mon-Fri, 5-9:30pm Sat, 4:30-8:30pm Sun; Ⓟ) Only the brisk ocean breeze is missing from this classic seafood restaurant popular with Downtown power-suits and salt-and-pepper-haired couples grateful for the dim lighting. The quality is consistently high, the selection mind-boggling, the service impeccable and the preparation inspired. Start out with a fruit-of-the-sea platter, move on to the sumac-coated barramundi and definitely leave room for the signature chocolate bread pudding.

Patina (Map pp84-5; ☎ 213-972-3331; 141 S Grand Ave, Walt Disney Concert Hall; mains lunch $18-26, dinner $34-44; ◷ 11:30am-1:30pm Mon-Fri, 5-11pm daily, to 9:30pm on nonperformance days; Ⓟ) Chef Joachim Splichal is everywhere these days, but this handsome restaurant at the Walt Disney Concert Hall remains his flagship. The Euro-Cal fare – Berkshire pork, Scottish salmon, lamb rib eye – is a great fusion of substance and style without taking any unnecessary flights of fancy.

Westlake & Koreatown

Langer's (Map pp84-5; ☎ 213-483-8050; 704 S Alvarado St, Westlake; pastrami sandwiches $11, mains $5-20; ◷ 8am-4pm Mon-Sat; ♿) Generations of smoked-meat lovers have flocked to this old-school Jewish deli famous for its juicy hot pastrami sandwiches (No 19 with coleslaw and Swiss cheese is the best seller) and fresh chopped liver. The Metro Red Line subway station is right outside.

Mama's Hot Tamales Café (Map pp84-5; 13-487-4300; 2122 W 7th St, Westlake; tamales $2.75, mains $6-10; ◷ 11am-3.30pm Mon-Fri, 9am-3:30pm Sat & Sun; ♿) Tamales (a stuffed cornmeal patty) of the world unite at this cheerful nosh spot right by MacArthur Park. Try chicken-potato tamales from Oaxaca, spicy beef tamales from Acapulco or spinach-mushroom tamales from Peru. They're so good, you'll want to pick some up for later in the attached *mercado* (market).

Papa Cristo's (off Map pp84-5; ☎ 323-737-2970; 2771 W Pico Blvd; mains $6-16; ◷ 9am-8pm Tue-Sat, 9am-4pm Sun; ♿) You'll kick up your heels like Zorba himself after filling your tummy with Greek soul food at this frenzied bistro in the shadow of St Sophia Cathedral. The gyros are the real deal and the rack of lamb is a steal at $10. Gather your posse and come for the Big Fat Greek Thursday Night Dinner ($19) at 6:30pm, when tables bend with nibbles and belly dancers perform.

Dong Il Jang (off Map pp84-5; ☎ 213-383-5757; 3455 W 8th St; mains $9-24; ◷ 11am-10pm; Ⓟ) This is a wonderfully old-school Korean restaurant with chocolate-brown booths, waitresses in starched dresses and lots of traditional fare. If you go for the barbecue, be sure to order the *ros gui* (thin beef slices); if you have leftovers, they make *kim chee* fried rice for you to take home. Other tempting dishes: *duk mandoo* (dumpling soup) and *chap chae* (noodles with vegetables). Alas, service can be lackluster and English appears to be a foreign language here.

Manna (off Map pp84-5; ☎ 323-733-8516; 3377 Olympic Blvd; lunch $7; ◷ 11am-11pm Sun-Thu, 11am-midnight Fri & Sat; Ⓟ) This huge, bustling place is always packed with carnivores in the mood for a total pig out. The meat quality may not be off the charts, but the price is right and the ambience is raucous. The all-you-can-eat barbecue ($17) is great for large parties and families.

Chosun Galbee (off Map pp84-5; ☎ 323-734-3330; 3300 Olympic Blvd; mains $20-35; ◷ 11am-11pm; Ⓟ) If you're a Korean-food virgin, this is not a bad place to lose your innocence. Barbecue is why you're here, cooked at your table, which is preferably on the trendy-looking bamboo-accented concrete and metal patio. The *chosun galbee* (short rib cubes) and *bulgogi* (beef slices), both marinated in a tangy soy-based

FROZEN TREAT MANIA

Ever since the first storefront opened in Hollywood, Angelenos have been caught up in **Pinkberry** (Map pp88-9; ☎ 310-659-8285; 868 Huntley Dr, West Hollywood) mania. People brave rock-star-worthy lines to get their 'crackberry fix', a tangy, stiff frozen treat that comes only in two flavors: 'original' or 'green tea'. Although touted as low in calories (125 per 5oz serving), it can quickly become a full meal if you get a bigger size and top it off with nuts, berries or fruit. Neither is it especially healthy since it's not made with live yoghurt cultures. But that doesn't seem to bother the league of 'addicts'. Try it and see for yourself, then see how the competition measures up:

- **Scoops** (Map pp86-7; ☎ 323-906-2649; 712 N Heliotrope Dr, Hollywood; ⏱ noon-10pm Mon-Sat) This teensy ice-cream parlor scores one for location and 10 for originality. Owner Tai Kim is a flavor magician who keeps coming up with new, adventurous combos, which he's happy to let you sample. Pistachio orange, Guinness tiramisu and saffron date are all worth a mouthwatering detour.

- **Mashti Malone's** (Map pp86-7; ☎ 323-874-6168; 1525 N La Brea Ave, Hollywood; ⏱ 11am-11pm) When Pinkberry's inventor was still in diapers, Mashti Malone was already feeding exotic ice creams and sorbet to the slobbering hordes. Saffron, pistachio, rosewater and pomegranate are typical ingredients.

- **Ce Fiore** (Map pp84-5; ☎ 213-626-0806; 134 Japanese Village Plaza, Downtown; ⏱ 11am-10:30pm) Ce Fiore's mouthwatering nonfat frozen Italian yoghurt has the same calories as Pinkberry and is based on live cultures. Its green-tea flavor is made with real *matcha* and the raspberry and pomegranate is a powerful antioxidant fix.

sauce, and served with delicious *panchan* (side dishes) are excellent.

Blue Velvet (Map pp84-5; ☎ 213-239-0061; 750 S Garland Ave; mains lunch $9-19, dinner $24-32; ⏱ 11:30am-2:30pm & 5:30-10:30pm; P) David Lynch would likely approve of Blue Velvet's magical views, sleek poolside lounge, edgy yet ecofriendly decor and especially ex-Patina chef Kris Morningstar's market-driven menu. Compelling dinner options include slow-poached ocean trout and venison loin with bacon-onion puree. Wicked unisex bathrooms.

Highland Park & East LA

Tamales Liliana's (off Map pp84-5; ☎ 323-780-0829; 3448 E 1st St, East LA; dishes $1.35-10.50; ⏱ 9am-9pm Mon-Fri, 7am-9pm Sat & Sun; ♿) Across from El Mercado and a tortilla factory, Liliana's makes tamales the way they ought to be: light, yet tight and generously stuffed with spicy pork, chicken or beef. We also like the Zacateca-style *huaraches* – oval flatbreads topped with tasty meats, fresh salad and drizzled with *crema* (sour cream). Try them with the fire-roasted salsa.

Homegirl Café (Map pp84-5; ☎ 323-268-9353; 1818 E 1st St, East LA; dishes $2-8; ⏱ 8am-4pm) 'Jobs not Jail' is the motto of this artsy Eastside café run by young at-risk women and serving home-made and healthful Mexi-faves. Great choices

include the wicked jalapeño-pesto chicken sandwich, unbelievably complex *mole* and various vegetarian dishes. Wash it down with delicious spinach-mint lemonade. It's right on Mariachi Plaza.

La Abeja (off Map pp84-5; ☎ 323-221-0474; 3709 N Figueroa St, Highland Park; mains $3-7.50; ⏱ 8am-2pm Mon, 8am-4pm Wed-Sat, 8am-3pm Sun; ♿) The booths are torn, the decor silly and the air-con absent, but the food, oh, the food, is truly some of the best Mexican in town. Brave the drive and inevitable wait to taste their *enchilada verde* swimming in a tangy green sauce, the juicy *machaca* (shredded beef) and the spicy *carne adobada*.

La Serenata de Garibaldi (Map pp84-5; ☎ 323-265-2887; 1842 E 1st St, East LA; breakfast $7.50-9.50, mains lunch $10-16, dinner $12-25; ⏱ 11:30am-10:30pm Mon-Fri, 9am-10:30pm daily; P) In a pretty hacienda near Mariachi Plaza, La Serenata is a good choice for barrio first-timers and one of the few sophisticated sit-down restaurants in East LA. The accent is clearly on fresh fish and seafood, beautifully prepared in umpteen ways and served with cheer. The margaritas, though, need work.

Exposition Park & Leimert Park

Chichen Itza (Map p97; ☎ 213-741-1075; 3655 S Grand Ave; dishes $2-6; ⏱ 6:30am-8:30pm; ♿) Part of the Mercado La Paloma (p119), this casual eatery near

Exposition Park is the go-to place for excellent and authentic food from Mexico's Yucatán peninsula. Everything's delicious but don't miss *brazo de reina*, a banana-leaf-steamed tamale stuffed with spinach, ground roasted pumpkin seeds, egg and drenched in tomato sauce. Yum.

Phillip's Barbecue (Map p97; ☎ 323-292-7613; 4307 Leimert Blvd, Leimert Park Village, South Central; meals $5-12; P ✦) The pork and beef ribs are fall-off-the-bone tender and the sauce smokey at this soulful hole-in-the-wall, and we're not whistling Dixie. The latter comes with various degrees of heat, so go easy. The 7-Up cake makes for an unusual finish. Cash only.

San Fernando Valley
BUDGET
Bob's Big Boy (Map p95; ☎ 818-843-9334; 4211 Riverside Dr, Burbank; meals $6-9; ✹ 24hr; P ✦) Bob, that cheeky pompadoured kid in red-checkered bib pants, hasn't aged a lick since serving his first double-decker burger in 1936. This Wayne McAllister–designed Googie-style 1950s coffee shop is the oldest remaining Big Boy's in America. On Fridays hot-rods crank it up in the parking lot, while car-hop service brings in families and love doves on Saturdays.

Zankou Chicken (off Map p95; ☎ 818-244-2237; 1415 E Colorado St, Glendale; mains $3.70-8.50; ✹ 10am-11pm; P ✦) Wake up and smell the garlic after feasting on Zankou's lip-smacking rotisserie chicken slathered with vampire-repelling sauce. Half a bird costs just $6 and comes with creamy hummus, salad and pita bread. Cash only. Leonardo DiCaprio and Heather Graham are fans.

Dr Hogly Wogly's Tyler Texas Bar-B-Que (Map pp80-1; ☎ 818-780-6701; 8136 N Sepulveda Blvd, Van Nuys) Serves some of the best Texas-style barbecue this side of Dallas.

MIDRANGE & TOP END
Minibar (Map p95; ☎ 323-882-6965; 3413 Cahuenga Blvd W, Universal City; small plates $6-15; ✹ 5:30-10:30pm Sun-Thu, 5:30pm-1am Fri & Sat; P) The stylishly dressed seek out the mod tones and tasty morsels after a hard day in the studio mines – under somewhat disconcerting portraits of wide-eyed waifs. The menu, divided into This, That & The Other sections, offers a global piñata of flavors, from venison *mole* to salmon-brie strudel to gouda-stuffed yucca bread.

Ca' del Sole (Map p95; ☎ 818-985-4669; 4100 Cahuenga Blvd, Toluca Lake; mains $13-22; ✹ 11am-3pm Mon-Fri, 5-11pm Mon-Sat, 11am-9pm Sun; P) Bordering NBC/Universal's busy Gate 3, the 'house of the sun' keeps Industry power-brokers happy over tantalizing antipasti, *bigoli* (Venetian-style seafood spaghetti) and the unfortunately named *stinco di maiale* (roasted pork shank). Enjoy these and other delectable northern-Italian favorites basking in the glow of the fireplace or relaxing on the romantic patio.

Firefly (off Map p95; ☎ 818-762-1833; 11720 Ventura Blvd, Studio City; mains $16-24; ✹ 6pm-2am Mon-Sat) Start off with an aperitif in the sexy, bordello-red library lounge, then retreat to a muslin-curtained cabana where you'll soon be munching addictive crunchy fried olives. Reliable mains include the tangy lemon tagliatelle, pan-seared salmon and baked pork. It's unsigned, so look for an ivy-covered building with the valet stand.

Smoke House (Map p95; ☎ 818-845-3731; 4420 Lakeside Dr, Burbank; mains $20-35; ✹ 11:30am-10:30pm Mon-Thu, 11:30am-11pm Fri & Sat, 10am-9pm Sun; P) Surrender helplessly to your inner carnivore at this Industry hangout of the old-school variety. Bob Hope and Bing Crosby were early fans, and today George Clooney, Kevin Costner and other big wigs continue to enjoy potent Bloody Marys and yummy cuts of aged steaks and prime rib. Whatever you order, don't miss out on the legendary garlic bread. Famous Sunday brunch, too.

Saddle Peak Lodge (Map pp80-1; ☎ 818-222-3888; 419 Cold Canyon Rd, Calabasas; brunch $15-18, dinner mains $32-42; ✹ 11am-3pm Sat & Sun, 5-10pm Wed-Sun; P) As rustic as a Colorado mountain lodge, this rural oasis tucked into the Santa Monica Mountains serves up elk, venison, buffalo and other game in a setting watched over by mounted versions of the same. This is fine dining, so don't come here after a day on the trail. Reservations are recommended.

Pasadena
BUDGET
Casa Bianca (off Map p96; ☎ 323-256-9617; 1650 Colorado Blvd; mains $8-14.50, pizzas $5-20; ✹ 4pm-midnight Tue-Thu, 4pm-1am Fri & Sat; ✦) For over half a century, the Martorana family has plied Oxy students (from nearby Occidental College) and pizza punters of all stripes with habit-forming thin-crust pies. Their homemade lasagna and ravioli are also culinary excursions straight to

the Boot. Pass the inevitable wait with drinks at nearby Chalet.

Marston's (Map p96; ☎ 626-796-2459; 151 E Walnut St; mains breakfast & lunch $8-12, dinner $15-26; ☼ 7am-2:30pm Tue-Fri, 5:30-9:30pm Wed-Sat, 8am-2:30pm Sat & Sun; P ⅙) Marston's serves lunch and dinner, but it's the prospect of the scrumptious all-American breakfasts here that helps us get out of bed. But no matter when you get there, this diminutive cottage with its sunny porch is likely to be packed to the rafters.

Fair Oaks Pharmacy & Soda Fountain (off Map p96; ☎ 626-799-1414; 1526 Mission St; lunch $4-9; ☼ food 11am-6pm, soda fountain & store 9am-9pm Mon-Sat, 10am-7pm Sun) Get your kicks at this original 1915 soda fountain right on Route 66. Slurp an old-fashioned 'phosphate' (flavored syrup, soda water and 'secret potion') while waiting for a heaping sandwich or hamburger or stocking up on classic candy in the gift shops. It's touristy, sure, but fun nonetheless.

MIDRANGE

Burger Continental (Map p96; ☎ 626-792-6634; 535 S Lake Ave; breakfast/lunch buffet $5/9, Sunday brunch $15, dishes $8-16; ☼ 7am-11pm; P ⅙) What sounds like a patty-and-bun joint is in reality a high-energy Middle Eastern nosh spot that delivers a first-class culinary journey at economical prices. Breakfast and lunch are all-you-can-eat buffets and there are nightly specials as well. Live bands and belly dancers provide ear and eye candy from Wednesday to Sunday. Great patio.

Saladang Song (Map p96; ☎ 626-793-5200; 383 S Fair Oaks Ave; mains $8-20; ☼ 7:30am-9pm Sun-Thu, 7:30am-10pm Fri & Sat; P ⅙) Thai gets a contemporary twist at this pseudo-industrial outpost whose always-bustling patio is hemmed in by artsily rendered concrete walls. Even simple curries become culinary poetry here, but it's such dishes as the steamed fish cake and coconut-flecked salmon that make foodies take notice. The original Saladang next door has a more traditional menu.

Vertical Wine Bistro (Map p96; ☎ 626-795-3999; 70 N Raymond Ave; mains $12-24; ☼ 5-11pm Sun-Thu, 4pm-1am Fri & Sat; P) Although it's a sophisticated wine bar dressed in cocoa and candlelight, don't worry if you can't tell your pinot noir from your pinot grigio. Each dish, including such menu stars as pulled pork and harissa-grilled chicken, comes with its own wine recommendation. Sample several 2oz tastes or choose a bottle from the 400 options on the wine menu.

Mike & Anne's (off Map p96; ☎ 626-799-7199; 1040 Mission St; mains breakfast/lunch $7-11, dinner $13-21; ☼ 11:30am-2:30pm & 5:30-10pm Mon-Fri, 8:30am-10pm Sat & Sun) Right on darling Mission St in South Pasadena, Mike & Anne's is a sweet and unhurried jewel with mostly local patrons clamoring for the clever but unfussy food à la chorizo-stuffed calamari or boneless shortribs with potato mousseline. Sit inside below exposed wood beams or on the patio overlooking a miniature park.

Bar Celona (Map p96; ☎ 626-405-1000; 46 E Colorado Blvd; tapas $5-9, mains lunch $8-14, dinner $17-30; P) Rioja-tinted walls offer a fiery backdrop for the seafood paellas and wine-braised steaks streaming from the kitchen into the candle-lit dining room. Grazers can pick their way around the tapas menu, while sangria-sipping scenesters wind down the night in the adjacent lounge.

561 Restaurant (Map p96; ☎ 626-683-7319; 561 E Green St; mains $18-28; ☼ 11:30am-1:30pm & 5:30-8pm Mon-Fri; P) For a preview of what'll be cooking in tomorrow's kitchens, pop by this popular bistro run by Cordon Bleu–level students of the California School of Culinary Arts. Dishes are inspired (grilled ono with black thai coconut rice) and the service is impeccable. The adjacent **café** (mains $7-11; ☼ 6am-9pm Mon-Fri) serves more informal fare.

TOP END

Madre's (Map p96; ☎ 626-744-0900; 897 Granite Dr; mains $15-33; ☼ 5-10:30pm Tue-Sun; P) Jennifer Lopez obviously had a lot of fun decorating her restaurant in a style that might be termed girly shabby-chic – think flowers, chandeliers, etched mirrors and lacy tablecloths. Inspiration for the menu, which blends robust Cuban and Puerto Rican classics, came from her grandmother. Try tasty empanadas, grilled *churrasco* (flank steak) or J Lo's personal favorite, *ropa vieja* (slow-cooked, spicy beef).

Xiomara (Map p96; ☎ 626-796-2520; 69 N Raymond Ave; mains $17-32; ☼ 11:30am-3pm Mon-Fri, 9:30am-2:30pm Sun, 5-11:30pm daily; P) The restrained decor is the perfect foil for the flavor explosions arriving on your plate at this humming Nuevo Latino bistro. It's easy to dream of faraway places while nursing a signature mojito (here called a Mambo), but the food – spiced with attitude – will quickly give you a reality check. The poblano (mild chili pepper) risotto is a great meat-free choice.

Parkway Grill (Map p96; ☎ 626-795-1001; 510 S Arroyo Parkway; mains lunch $12-24, dinner $21-38; ⏰ 11:30am-2:30pm Mon-Fri, 5-10pm daily; Ⓟ) Meat-lovers will be in pig heaven at this very smart, grown-up restaurant in a historic brick building with a cool 1920s Chicago bar. Get an order of flatbread sprinkled with blue cheese, pears and walnuts while pondering the virtues of the mesquite-grilled filet mignon over the cedar-plank salmon with honey-truffle glaze. Hard to go wrong here.

DRINKING

From funky beach pubs to underground dives, snazzy hotel lounges to designer cocktail temples and historic watering holes where Bogie and Bacall used to knock 'em back, in LA you're rarely far from a good time. Hollywood Blvd and the Sunset Strip are classic bar-hopping grounds, but there's also plenty of good drinking in Santa Monica, Hermosa Beach, Downtown and Koreatown.

That said, LA is not really a boozeville city, in large part because of the dependence on the automobile. Drinking and driving just don't mix, cabs are expensive and finding a designated driver is not always possible.

Compared to other megacities, it's also an early town, with alcohol being served only until 2am. If you do decide to drive, you'll find that most of the swankier places have valet parking. The parking icon listed with each entry below, though, simply connotes that parking is available.

Beverly Hills

Nic's Beverly Hills (Map pp90-1; ☎ 310-550-5707; 453 N Canon Dr, Beverly Hills; ⏰ 6-10pm Mon-Fri, to 11pm Fri & Sat) Martinis for every palate lure the cocktail crowd to upscale but fun-loving Nic's, where the libations range from the colorful and sassy to the no-frills and classy. Reserve the chilled VodBox for flights of international vodka.

Polo Lounge (Map pp90-1; ☎ 310-276-2251; 9641 Sunset Blvd, Beverly Hills; ⏰ 7am-1:30am) With its mix of tennis whites, business suits, and chichi dresses, this swanky, wood-paneled watering hole has the feel of a Hollywood country club. Isaac Mizrahi to George Hamilton to David Arquette, you never know who you'll see murmuring in the perpetually reserved, dark booths. It's part of the Beverly Hills Hotel (see p114).

TO DIM OR NOT TO DIM SOME

Sinophiles tired of the *kung pao* school of Chinese cooking know that for the best Asian food they must travel to the far east – of LA that is. If you've ever driven through the suburbs of Monterey Park, Alhambra, Rosemead and San Gabriel, you won't find it hard to believe that LA County is home to the largest Asian population in the USA. Exotic signage abounds, supermarkets are more likely to sell bok choy than iceberg, and Eastside hipsters hang out in tea and boba shops. And then, of course, there are the restaurants, hundreds of them, from innocuous (and often excellent) strip-mall joints to bustling dim sum parlors and lavish banquet temples. Chefs are often recent immigrants, making the cooking as authentic as you'd find in the homeland. Here are some of our favorites:

Mission 261 (Map pp80-1; ☎ 626-588-1666; 261 S Mission Dr, San Gabriel; dim sum $2-8, dishes $11-40; ⏰ dim sum 10:30am-3pm Mon-Fri, 9am-3pm Sat & Sun, dinner daily; Ⓟ) Inside a century-old adobe near the San Gabriel Mission (p150), this is the holy grail of dim sum, many of them fashioned into artistic shapes. Order by filling out a form rather than selecting from passing carts. Dinner is for adventurers – think braised goose and sea-cucumber stew or obscene-looking geoduck clam.

101 Noodle Express (Map pp80-1; ☎ 626-300-8654; 1408 E Valley Blvd, Alhambra; dishes $3-8; ⏰ 11am-3pm & 5-10pm Mon-Fri, 11am-10pm Sat & Sun; Ⓟ ♿) Prosaic name, strip-mall setting, plain decor – why bother? Because of the divine dumplings – plump, handmade and bursting with such creative fillings as spinach shrimp and pumpkin pork. Another must is the beef or chicken roll: a thick Chinese pancake cradling hoisin-sweetened meat. You'll rarely see a table here without one.

New Concept (Map pp80-1; ☎ 626-282-6800; 700 S Atlantic Blvd, Monterey Park; mains $9-20; ⏰ 11am-10pm Mon-Fri, 8am-10pm Sat & Sun; Ⓟ) At this buzzy eatery – the only US branch of a chain based in Beijing – the dim sum is to-die-for and the chef whips up boundary-pushing Cantonese feasts, usually with delicious results, even if some sound like a *Survivor* challenge (snow-frog-fat soup anyone?).

TOP FIVE HAPPY HOURS

Sometimes, after a long day on the tourist track, all you want to do is wind down the day without eviscerating your wallet. Thank goodness someone invented Happy Hour. You find them everywhere in LA, but not all are created equal, so we've sussed out the finest lairs for bargain nibbles and drinks to get you happy in no time.

- **Ciudad** (Map pp84-5; ☎ 213-486-5171; 445 S Figueroa St, Downtown; 🕓 3-7pm Mon-Fri; **P**) Knock back $4 mojitos or piscoritas (made with potent Peruvian schnapps) while staying stable with quesadillas and fish tacos at this spunky Latin restaurant.
- **Chaya Venice** (Map p92; ☎ 310-396-1179; 110 Navy St, Venice; 🕓 5-7pm; **P**) This neighborhood haven is always packed, especially in the early evening when sushi rolls, fried calamari, miso soup, spicy tuna tartar and other delicious tastes cost just $3 or $4.
- **Luna Park** (Map pp88-9; ☎ 323-934-2110; 672 S La Brea Ave, Mid-City; 🕓 5:30-7pm Mon-Fri; **P**) Rub shoulders with investment bankers, n'er-do-wells and cultured types (it's just around the corner from Museum Row) while enjoying tasty $4.50 bites and $6 drinks at this comfy-chic local favorite.
- **McCormick & Schmick's** (Map pp84-5; ☎ 213-629-1929; 633 W 5th St, Downtown; 🕓 3:30-7pm & 9-11pm Mon-Thu, 3-11pm Fri) This serial fish house keeps you happy not once but twice daily. Drinks are full price but such belly-fillers as fish tacos, teriyaki-beef skewers and the incredible cheeseburger are just $1.95 each.
- **Tangier** (Map pp86-7; ☎ 323-666-8666; 2138 Hillhurst Ave, Los Feliz; 🕓 5:30-8pm; **P**) Fill your belly on the cheap with spinach salad to nachos with homemade tortillas, then wash it down with $3 beers or cosmos at this eclectic venue that presents bands, comedy, belly dancing and other performances later at night.

Hollywood, Los Feliz & Silver Lake

Bigfoot Lodge (off Map pp86-7; ☎ 323-662-9227; 3172 Los Feliz Blvd, Los Feliz; 🕓 5pm-2am) Smokey the Bear presides over this log-cabin alt-lounge perfect for camping out with a minty Girl Scout Cookie martini or two. After 10pm DJs hit the decks with Brit faves, rockabilly and surf punk. By then, the line usually snakes down the block.

Good Luck Bar (Map pp86-7; ☎ 323-666-3524; 1514 Hillhurst Ave, Los Feliz; 🕓 7pm-2am Mon-Fri, 8pm-2am Sat & Sun; **P**) The clientele is sexy, the music loud and the drinks strong at this red-velvet watering hole with all the lascivious seductiveness of a Chinese opium den. Order a baby-blue Yee Mee Loo, then make friends at the bar or while lolling on the oversized couches.

4100 Bar (Map pp86-7; ☎ 323-666-4460; 4100 W Sunset Blvd, Silver Lake; 🕓 7pm-2am; **P**) Past the bouncer and the thick velvet curtain awaits this good-looking bar with an unpretentious and omni-sexual crowd, a jukebox heavy on alt-rock, and bartenders who've been around the block once or twice.

Tiki Ti (Map pp86-7; ☎ 323-669-9381; 4427 W Sunset Blvd, Silver Lake; 🕓 6pm-1am Wed & Thu, 6pm-2am Fri & Sat) This garage-sized tropical tavern packs in showbiz folks from neighboring KCET TV station, grizzled old-timers and local scenesters for sweet and wickedly strong drinks (try a Rae's Mistake, named for the bar's founder). The under-the-sea decor is surreal. Cash only.

Cat & Fiddle (Map pp86-7; ☎ 323-468-3800; 6530 Sunset Blvd, Hollywood; 🕓 11:30am-2am; **P**) Morrissey to Frodo, you never know who might be popping by for Boddington or Sunday night jazz. Fortunately, this Brit pub staple with its leafy beer garden is more about friends and conversation than faux-hawks and working the deal.

Blu Monkey Lounge (Map pp86-7; ☎ 323-957-9000; 5521 Hollywood Blvd, Hollywood; 🕓 8pm-2am; **P**) Hollywood bars without attitude are about as rare as blue monkeys, so this is a refreshing find. DJs spin a head-bobbing mix of electronica, rock and world music as the crowd gets comfortable in plush sofas, at the shiny walnut bar or in the smoking patio amid feel-good Moroccan-themed decor. Drinks could be stronger, though.

Formosa Cafe (Map pp86-7; ☎ 323-850-9050; 7156 Santa Monica Blvd, Hollywood; 🕓 4pm-2am Mon-Fri, 6pm-2am Sat & Sun; **P**) Bogart and Gable used to knock 'em back at this bat cave of a watering hole so authentically noir that scenes from *LA Confidential* were filmed here. Skip the Chinese food and check out the Elvis collection.

Velvet Margarita (Map pp86-7; ☎ 323-469-2000; 1612 N Cahuenga Blvd, Hollywood; ☑ 11:30am-2am Mon-Thu, 11:30am-4am Fri; 6pm-4am Sat; 6pm-2am Sun; [P]) Sombreros, velvet Elvises, cheesy Mexican cult-movie projections and margarita-swilling scenesters – it's Cabo San Lucas meets Graceland at this dark palace of kitsch tailor-made for dedicated drink-a-thons. The margarita inside a pineapple is pricey ($15) but cool. *Ay caramba*!

Boardner's (Map pp86-7; ☎ 323-462-9621; 1652 N Cherokee Ave, Hollywood; ☑ 1pm-2am; [P]) Keeping barflies boozy since 1942, this dimly lit dive is hot again with young guns and the occasional celeb – Kiefer Sutherland, Heath Ledger and Vince Vaughn included. If the booze doesn't get you, maybe the nightclub in the back will where – depending on the night – you'll be kicking it with indie rockers, pop zombies or fetish fiends.

Beauty Bar (Map pp86-7; ☎ 323-468-3800; 1638 N Cahuenga Blvd, Hollywood; ☑ 9pm-2am Sun-Wed, 6pm-2am Thu-Sat) Still beautilicious after all these years, this pint-sized retro cocktail bar is the 'it' place for having your nails painted in lurid pink while catching up on gossip and getting liquefied on martinis, pinkie raised and all ($10, 6pm to 11pm Thursday to Saturday).

Woods (Map pp86-7; ☎ 323-876-6612; 1533 La Brea Ave, Hollywood; ☑ 8pm-2am; [P]) In the mood for a Hansel and Gretel moment? Then join the other 'lost kids' at this lounge with decor that feels like going camping but without the tent and the DEET. Drink your way through the menu sitting at tree-trunk cocktail tables under a twinkle sky and antler chandeliers.

West Hollywood & Mid-City

For gay and lesbian bars, see the boxed text on pp112-13.

Stone Rose Lounge (Map pp88-9; ☎ 310-228-6677; 8555 Beverly Blvd, Mid-City; ☑ 4pm-2am; [P]) With the glow of his Sky Bar slowly fading, bar baron Rande Gerber has dreamed up this glamour vixen at the hip-again Hotel Sofitel. Dressed in warm crimson and passionfruit, the lounge lures chatty sophisticates huddled in intense tête-à-têtes and grateful for the mellow lighting and low sound levels.

El Coyote (Map pp88-9; ☎ 323-939-2255; 7312 Beverly Blvd, Mid-City; ☑ 11am-10pm Sun-Thu, 11am-11pm

> **FREE BOOZE!**
>
> If you'd like to get knackered for cheap or free (and who doesn't?), check out http://la.myopenbar.com for a neat day-by-day list of wallet-friendly liquoring-up opportunities during booze promotions at clubs and bars, or during gallery openings (if you're actually interested in the art!). You can even sign up for their weekly 'boozeletter'. Cheers! (Oh yeah, and don't do a 'Paris Hilton'; that drinkin' and drivin' thing just ain't cool no more.)

Fri & Sat; [P]) It's always fiesta time at this red-boothed, been-there-forever cantina where the stiff margaritas pretty much guarantee a cheap buzz. Service is swift and sweet but the food plays only a supporting role. Celebrity trivia: Sharon Tate ate her last meal here before getting wacked by Charles Manson's mad posse.

El Carmen (Map pp88-9; ☎ 323-852-1552; 8138 W 3rd St, Mid-City; ☑ 5pm-2am Mon-Fri, 7pm-2am Sat & Sun; [P]) A pair of mounted bull heads and Lucha Libre (Mexican wrestling) masks create an over-the-top 'Tijuana North' look and pull in an Industry-heavy crowd at LA's ultimate tequila tavern (over a hundred to choose from).

Elixir Tonic & Teas (Map pp88-9; ☎ 310-657-9300; 8612 Melrose Ave; ☑ 8am-10pm Sun-Thu, 8am-midnight Fri & Sat) Get your Zen on sipping a blissful tonic (an ancient-Chinese-medicine-inspired fruit-and-herbal drink) at this roaringly peaceful bamboo garden sanctuary. For DIY recharging at home, pick up a bottle-to-go at the storefront that also hawks precious teas, fat Buddhas and astrology books.

Santa Monica & Venice

Hideout (Map p92; ☎ 310-429-1851; 112 W Channel Rd, Santa Monica; ☑ 7pm-2am; [P]) Will Rogers' favorite speakeasy turned gay bar turned Westside hotspot, the postage-stamp-sized Hideout has seen a lot in the past 80 years. It's still a comfy hangout for locals happy to trade their flip-flops for heels and spend $10 for cocktails in a plastic cup.

Otherroom (Map p92; ☎ 310-396-6230; 1201 Abbot Kinney Blvd, Venice; ☑ 5pm-2am) Dark, loud and industrial, this loftlike lounge screams 'Soho transplant' but is actually a laid-back lair for local lovelies, artists and professionals. Only beer and wine are served, but the selection is tops and handpicked. Hungry? Simply ask for take-out menus from nearby restaurants. Locals gets to skip the line, everyone else should expect a wait until after 10pm for entry to the bar.

Circle Bar (Map p92; ☎ 310-450-0508; 2926 Main St, Santa Monica; ☼ 9pm-2am) This former dive bar has been reincarnated as a sizzling 'meet' market packed with wrinkle-free hotties. Strong drinks, loud music and a seductive red-on-black decor further loosen inhibitions, but waiting in line to get past the bouncers can be a turnoff.

Brig (Map p92; ☎ 310-399-7537; 1515 Abbot Kinney Blvd, Venice; ☼ 6pm-2am; Ⓟ) Old-timers remember this place as a divey pool hall owned by ex-boxer Babe Brandelli (that's him and his wife smiling down from the outside mural). Now it's an up-to-the-minute-design den where a trendy mix of grown-up beach bums, arty professionals and professional artists come to carouse and sip apple martinis.

Big Dean's (Map p92; ☎ 310-393-2666; 1615 Ocean Front Walk, Santa Monica; ☼ 11am-9pm Mon-Thu, 10am-10pm Fri-Sun) On a hot Santa Monica afternoon, drag your flip-flops to this cheap and groovy beach patio bar where Muscle Beach beef-cakes used to hang out back in the '50s. These days you're more likely to share a pint with Skateboard Mama, an octogenarian character who gets around on a wind-powered skateboard.

Liquid Kitty (Map p92; ☎ 310-473-3707; 11780 Pico Blvd, West LA; ☼ 6pm-2am Mon-Fri, 8pm-2am Sat & Sun; Ⓟ) If you're in the mood for a purrrr-fect martini, hit this laid-back lounge bathed in bat-cave darkness, perhaps after fuelling up on cheap tacos at Don Antonio's across the street. Don't look for a name out front, just for the twinkling martini glass. Live music sometimes, cover never.

If you like bars with booze history, pop into **Chez Jay** (Map p92; ☎ 310-395-1741; 1657 Ocean Ave, Santa Monica) or the **Galley** (Map p92; ☎ 310-452-1934; 2442 Main St, Santa Monica), both low-key, classic watering holes with campy nautical themes.

Culver City

Saints & Sinners (Map p97; ☎ 310-842-8066; 10899 Venice Blvd; ☼ 5pm-2am) No, although the name suggest it this is not an S&M bar, although the velvet walls, fireplace and naughtily named cocktails have a certain '70s porn feel – but in a good way. DJs usually play a wicked mix

of indie, '80s and punk but on Tuesdays you get to bring in your own iPod for 20-minute guest-DJ stints.

Mandrake (Map p97; ☎ 310-837-3297; 2692 S La Cienega Blvd; ☼ 4pm-midnight Tue-Thu, 4pm-1am Fri, noon-1am Sat, 6pm-midnight Sun) Opened by an art-minded trio and the anchor of Culver City's new gallery row, this little bar is paneled like a sauna and just as hot. Belly up to the shiny blue bar or join tousled art-school grads for a smoke on the patio by way of a backroom where a DJ helms the decks.

South Bay

Ercole's (Map p94; ☎ 310-372-1997; 1101 Manhattan Ave, Manhattan Beach; ☼ 10am-2am) Check your attitude at the door when you come to scruffy but lovable Ercole's – the South Bay's favorite dive since 1927. Old salts, pub crawlers, volleyball stars, wobbly coeds – expect all to wander in. What's best? The $8 beer pitchers and Taco Tuesdays.

Zinc Lounge (Map p94; ☎ 310-546-4995; 1221 N Valley Dr, Manhattan Beach; ☼ 5-10pm Sun-Thu, 5-11pm Fri & Sat; Ⓟ) USC grads with money to burn bring their A-game – and long-legged dates – to this sleek lounge at the hip Shade Hotel. On weekends, the deep-blue space is often wall-to-wall by 9pm with more punters riding the velvet rope. By 11pm, though, the party's over to keep the hotel guests happy.

Naja's Place (Map p94; ☎ 310-376-9951; 154 International Boardwalk, Redondo Beach; ☼ 2pm-midnight Mon-Thu, noon-2am Fri & Sat, noon-10pm Sun) Hofbräuhaus move over – Naja's is a beer drinker's true nirvana. With a dizzying 77 brews on tap and hundreds more in bottles, you'll never run out of choices at this salty harborfront joint in King's Harbor. Best on Sunday afternoons.

Baja Sharkeez (Map p94; ☎ 310-545-6563; 3801 Highland Ave, Manhattan Beach) This 'Animal House by the sea' is a fine place to get into trouble. Buckets of beer and birdbath-sized margaritas plus an abundance of bare skin help fan the party. Don't say we didn't warn you.

Hermosa's pedestrian promenade, Pier Ave, is one big, loud pumping party on week-nights and all day on weekends. It's a rowdy, early-20s crowd releasing their hormones at such watering holes as **Patrick Malloy's** (Map p94; ☎ 310-798-9762; 50 Pier Ave) and **Fat Face Fenner's Fishack** (Map p94; ☎ 310-379-5550; 53 Pier Ave), which has a handy 2nd-floor balcony for babe- and dude-watching. If you're past college age, check out the legendary **Mermaid** (Map p94;

☎ 310-374-9344; 11 Pier Ave), a charmingly divey '50s flashback that serves some surprisingly good food to boot.

Long Beach

Alex's Bar (Map pp82-3; ☎ 562-434-8292; 2913 E Anaheim St; ☿ 3pm-2am Mon-Thu, noon-2am Fri-Sun; wi-fi) Local cool kids hang out at this punk hole where the drinks are cheap and strong, the bartenders are not aspiring actors and the music – both live and canned – kicks ass. Enter from the back. Scenes from the 2006 Jack Black comedy *Tenacious D: The Pick of Destiny* were filmed here.

Belmont Brewing Company (Map pp82-3; ☎ 562-433-3891; 25 39th Pl, Belmont Shore) This bustling gastropub has a great outdoor deck overlooking the Belmont Pier (perfect for watching sunsets), fresh and handcrafted brews (try the Long Beach Crude stout or Top Sail ale), and a well-priced menu that goes far beyond pub grub.

Yard House (Map pp82-3; ☎ 562-628-0455; 401 Shoreline Dr; ☿ 11am-midnight Sun-Thu, 11am-2am Fri & Sat) The jukebox plays Steeley Dan and other classic rock as rivers of suds flow freely at this spaceship helm of a pub. A mind-boggling 250 beers on tap are pumped up via miles of beer lines. Slap-happy frat brats guzzle their fill from 'beer bongs' – yard-long glasses. It's the original branch of a growing chain.

Mai Tai (Map pp82-3; ☎ 562-435-1200; 97 Aquarium Way; ☿ 4pm-1:30am Sun-Thu, noon-1:30am Fri & Sat) With two happy hours (4pm to 7pm and 8pm to 11pm), getting a cheap buzz is a no-brainer at this Hawaiian-themed bar next to the Aquarium of the Pacific. The crowd is cool and the signature drink just $4.

Downtown Los Angeles

Edison (Map pp84-5; ☎ 213-613-0000; 108 W 2nd St, off Harlem Alley; ☿ 5pm-2am Wed-Fri, 6pm-2am Sat; ℗) *Metropolis* meets *Blade Runner* at this industrial-chic basement boîte where you'll be sipping mojitos surrounded by turbines and other machinery back from its days as a boiler room. Don't worry, it's all tarted up nicely with cocoa leather couches and three cavernous bars. No athletic wear, flip-flops or baggy jeans.

Rooftop Bar @ Standard Downtown LA (Map pp84-5; ☎ 213-892-8080; 550 S Flower St; cover after 7pm Fri & Sat $20; ☿ noon-1:30am; ℗) Lawyers and execs mix it up with sorority sisters and cubicle hotties at this libidinous outdoor lounge swimming in

a sea of twinkling skyscrapers. Once you find your way to the top, you too can mark your turf among the space-pod cabanas, lounges, fireplace and pool for cooling off if it all gets too steamy.

Seven Grand (Map pp84-5; ☎ 213-614-0736; 515 W 7th St; ☿ 4pm-2am Mon-Fri, 8pm-2am Sat) For a glamour vibe without the velvet rope, beat a trail to this dusky whiskey bar with tongue-in-cheek hunting decor. There are 175 varieties of the amber stuff, so this is not a place for the indecisive. For non-whiskey-philes a slate of a dozen tap beers awaits. DJs and smoking patio, too.

Mountain Bar (Map pp84-5; ☎ 213-625-7500; 473 Gin Ling Way; ☿ 6pm-2am Tue-Sun) Loft dwellers and Eastside hipsters knock back beers at this high-ceilinged Chinatown bar after gallery-hopping on nearby Chung King Rd. After a few pints, the Kool-Aid-orange decor might make you feel like you're sitting inside a volcano.

Lost Souls Café (Map pp84-5; ☎ 213-617-7006; 124 W 4th St; ☿ 7am-10pm Sun-Thu, 7am-6pm Fri & Sat; wi-fi) A keen java radar is required to track down this coffeehouse-cum-community-lab down a dark alley off 4th St (don't worry, it only looks scary). Inside, it's a cool spot where local latterati hang out for a chat, to check their email or to listen to poets or bands.

Golden Gopher (Map pp84-5; ☎ 213-614-8001; 417 W 8th St; ☿ 5pm-2am Tue-Fri, 8pm-2am Sat-Mon) Campy gopher lamps give even pasty-faced hipsters a healthy glow at this dark drinking den with a smoking patio and in-store liquor store for postclosing revelries.

Gallery Bar (Map pp84-5; ☎ 213-624-1011; 506 S Grand Ave; ☿ 4pm-2am) Nostalgia lovers will love the five-star ambience at this classic noir bar in the Millennium Biltmore Hotel (p172). The signature drink is the Black Dahlia, named for the infamous 1947 murder victim, aspiring actress Elizabeth Short, last spotted alive in the hotel lobby. Her death remains a mystery.

Koreatown

Prince (off Map pp84-5; ☎ 213-389-2007; 3198 W 7th St, Koreatown; ☿ 4pm-midnight; ℗) In the movie *Chinatown*, Faye Dunaway meets with Jack Nicholson at this campy joint that defies any categorization. It's a former hotel lounge with colonial-era British-pub looks (check out the wacky soldier lamps) and *soju* and Hite beer on the menu. The crowd is a potpourri of ethnicities united by a penchant for stiff drinks at civilized prices.

Brass Monkey (off Map pp84-5; ☎ 213-381-7047; 3440 Wilshire Blvd; 2-drink minimum or cover $15; ☯ 10am-2am) You might need to knock back a couple of brewskis to loosen your nerves before belting out your best J Lo, Justin or Jackson Five at this 1930s bank vault turned kooky karaoke joint. All you *American Idol* wannabes can pick from 60,000 songs in six languages. Those in the know usually come early to stake out a good spot before the action starts at 9pm (4pm on Friday). Enter through the back.

ENTERTAINMENT

LA's party scene is lively, edgy and multi-faceted. You can hobnob with hipsters at a trendy Hollywood dance club, groove to experimental sounds in a Silver Lake music venue, or catch a concert on the pier, a movie in a cemetery or a multimedia event at an abandoned warehouse.

LA also has plenty in store for those in favour of more highbrow pursuits, including a world-class philharmonic orchestra and an opera led by Plácido Domingo, who makes up one third of the original Three Tenors. Mainstream, offbeat and fringe theater and performance art all thrive here, as do the comedy clubs. Seeing a movie, not surprisingly, has become a luxe event in this town with a new generation of stadium-style multiplex movie theaters offering giant screens, total surround-sound, and comfy tiered leather seats.

LISTINGS

These publications will help you plug into the local scene in no time:

ArtScene (www.artscenecal.com) Monthly freebie listing art-gallery shows.

Flavorpill (www.flavorpill.com) Online magazine spotlights offbeat happenings; sign up for its free weekly emails.

LA Alternative Press (www.laalternativepress.com) Biweekly with an Eastside focus.

LA City Beat & LA Valley Beat (www.lacitybeat .com) Not as comprehensive as the *LA Weekly* but steadily improving all the time; you can pick it up for free on Thursdays.

LA Magazine (www.lamagazine.com) A monthly glossy that features 'The Guide,' a highly selective what's-on section.

LA Weekly (www.laweekly.com) Awesome alt-mag is the single best source for what's happening in LA; free on Fridays.

Los Angeles Times (www.latimes.com) Has useful pullout Calendar section on Thursdays.

TICKETS

Tickets for most events are available from individual venues by phone, in person and sometimes also online. For information on half-price theater tickets, see p203. For hard-to-get tickets or 'sold-out' shows, try these:

Al Brooks Ticket Agency (☎ 213-626-5863)

Barry's Ticket Service (☎ 818-990-8499; www .barrystickets.com)

Ticketmaster (☎ 213-480-3232; www.ticketmaster .com)

Cinemas

Not surprisingly, LA celluloid fans are demanding beings and most movie theaters are now ultradeluxe, stadium-style and have ear-popping surround-sound. Ticket prices are sky-high, naturally, with Saturday night shows fetching as much as $15, although $11 ($7.50 for children or seniors) is more typical. You can save a buck or two during midweek and pre-6pm screenings. Tickets for most theaters can be prepurchased through **Moviefone** (from any LA area code ☎ 777-3456; www.moviefone.com) or at or www.movietickets.com.

ArcLight & Cinerama Dome (Map pp86-7; ☎ 323-464-4226; www.arclightcinemas.com; 6360 W Sunset Blvd, Hollywood; adult/child/senior from $11/7.75/9.75) Pre-assigned seats, a trendy in-house bar and exceptionally high star-sighting potential make this 14-screen multiplex one of the top flick magnets in town. Check out the awesome 1963 geodesic Cinerama Dome next door. Bonuses: age 21+ screenings where you can booze it up along with your popcorn, and Q&As with directors, writers and actors.

American Cinematheque (☎ 323-466-3456; www .americancinematheque.com; adult/senior & student $10/8) Hollywood (Map pp86-7; 6712 Hollywood Blvd); Santa Monica (Map p92; 1328 Montana Ave) If nonprofits make you yawn, we promise this one won't. Their tributes, retrospectives and foreign films are well curated and presented in two rescued Golden Age venues: the Egyptian Theatre and the Aero Theatre. Directors, screenwriters and actors often swing by for postshow Q&As. Also see p105.

El Capitan Theatre (Map pp86-7; ☎ 323-347-7674; http://disney.go.com/disneypictures/el_capitan; 6838 Hollywood Blvd, Hollywood; adult/child & senior from $14/11; ♿) Disney usually rolls out family-friendly blockbusters at this over-the-top movie palace,

LOS ANGELES

often with costumed characters putting on the Ritz in live preshow routines. The best seats are on the balcony in the middle of the front row. Also see p104.

Grauman's Chinese Theatre (Map pp86-7; ☎ 323-464-8111; www.manntheatres.com/chinese; 6925 Hollywood Blvd, Hollywood; adult/child/senior $11.25/8/8.50) Nowhere in the world are movie premiers as glitzy as at this Industry favorite, so you never know which famous behind may have graced the seat before you. Make sure you buy tickets for the glam historic theater, not the ho-hum Mann Chinese 6 multiplex next door. Also see p103.

New Beverly Cinema (Map pp88-9; ☎ 323-938-4038; www.newbevcinema.com; 7165 W Beverly Blvd, Mid-City; adult/child/senior $7/6/4) Serious filmophiles and megaplex foes put up with the worn seats and musty smell of this beloved double-feature revival house that started out as a vaudeville theater in the '20s and went porno in the '70s. In 2007, Quentin Tarantino held the world premier of *Grindhouse* here, shortly before the cinema's longtime owner passed away suddenly. His wife and son have promised to keep the reels rolling.

Pacific Theatres at the Grove (Map pp88-9; ☎ 323-692-0829; www.thegrovela.com; 189 The Grove Dr, Mid-City; adult/senior/child $11.50/7.75/8.25) This is a fancy all-stadium, 14-screen multiplex with comfy

reclining seats, wall-to-wall screens and superb sound. The Monday Morning Mommy Movies series (11am) gives the diaper-bag brigade a chance to catch a flick with their tot but without hostile stares from nonbreeding moviegoers.

Nuart Theatre (off Map pp90-1; ☎ 310-478-6379; www.landmarktheaters.com; 11272 Santa Monica Blvd, near Westwood; adult/senior & child $9.50/7.25) This hip art house presents the best in offbeat and cult flicks, including a highly interactive screening of *The Rocky Horror Picture Show* supported by an outrageous live cast at midnight on Saturdays. Bring glow sticks and toilet paper.

Landmark Theatres (off Map pp90-1; ☎ showtimes 310-281-8233, information 310-470-0492; www.landmarktheatres.com; 10850 W Pico Blvd, West LA; adult/child/senior $11/8/9) 'Art-house multiplex' may seem like an oxymoron, but the Landmark is betting the bank that it can fill its dozen deluxe stadium-style screening rooms with fans of indie and foreign films. The supremely comfortable leather chairs, gourmet snack menu, wine bar and free parking may just do the trick.

Silent Movie Theatre (Map pp88-9; ☎ 323-655-2520; www.silentmovietheatre.com; 611 N Fairfax Ave, Mid-City; tickets $10) 'Silents are golden' at this 1942 vintage theatre, which is the only one in the US

TOP FIVE FILM FESTIVALS

In SoCal, it's not love or money but movies that make the world go round. Besides churning out blockbuster productions, the region hosts dozens of film festivals, including such highly specialized ones as the Festival of Science Fiction, Fantasy & Horror and the Pan African Film & Art Festival. We've picked through the pile for our faves. Check the websites for lineups and ticket information.

AFI Fest (☎ 866-234-3378; www.afi.com) This LA festival, held in November, is one of the most influential in the country and presents top-notch films by newbies and masters from around the world. *Monster, The Cider House Rules* and other Academy Award winners premiered here.

Los Angeles Film Festival (☎ 866-345-6337; www.lafilmfest.com) Headquartered in Westwood, this June festival corrals the best in indie movies from around the world – shorts to music videos, documentaries to features. In 2006 it held the US premiere of *The Devil Wears Prada*.

Outfest (☎ 213-480-7088; www.outfest.org) The largest continuous film fest in SoCal, this GLBT celebration has been held every July in Los Angeles for over a quarter-century. It features more than 200 shorts, films and videos by and about the community.

Palm Springs International Film Festival (☎ 760-322-2930, 800-898-7256; www.psfilmfest.org) Founded in 1990 by Sonny Bono, this balmy January festival is getting more glam every year. It's an intimate yet star-studded affair with more than 200 films from dozens of countries.

Newport Beach Film Festival (☎ 949-253-2880; www.newportbeachfilmfest.org) The buzz surrounding this April competition has been increasing steadily since Oscar-winner *Crash* premiered here in 2005. It's still small enough to be bumping into filmmakers and actors attending screenings or workshops.

MOVIES UNDER THE STARS

Angelenos love their movies and their fine weather, so it's only logical to combine the two. Screenings under the stars have become a popular summer tradition with classic and contemporary flicks spooling off in various locations around town. Come early to stake out a good spot and bring pillows, blankets and snacks.

Cinespia (Map pp86-7; www.cemeteryscreenings.com; admission $10; ⏰ Sat May-Oct) has a 'to-die-for' location at Hollywood Forever Cemetery (p108), *the* place of perpetual slumber for a galaxy of old-time movie stars. Classics by Milos Forman, Robert Altman and Alfred Hitchcock are projected onto a mausoleum wall around 9pm, but the hipster crowd starts lining up long before gates open at 7:30pm for picnics and cocktails (yes, alcohol is allowed!) while a DJ spins smooth soundtracks.

If that's too morbid for you, catch the Pacific sea breeze while camping out on the Santa Monica Pier where the **Santa Monica Drive-In at the Pier** (Map p92; www.santamonicapier.org; admission free) presents populist faves every Tuesday in September. Despite the name, cars are not allowed. Tickets are free but must be picked up at the Santa Monica Visitors Center (p101). Donations benefiting nonprofit Arts Fighting Cancer are appreciated.

If a day at Universal Studios hasn't left you exhausted, stick around for the **Big Free Outdoor Movie** (Map p95; ☎ 818-622-1111; www.citywalkhollywood.com; Universal City Walk; admission free; ⏰ Thu Jul & Aug). The line-up focuses on old and new classics, produced by Universal of course, and presented on a giant screen right on the Universal City Walk.

Nearby Burbank also gets in on the act with its **Summer Nights at Burbank Town Center** (Map p95; ☎ 818-566-8617; www.burbanktowncenter.com; admission free; ⏰ Wed mid-Jul–mid-Aug) showing recent blockbusters in a block party setting around the intersection of San Fernando Blvd and Cypress St.

A more low-key event is **Outdoor Movie Nights** (off Map p96; www.sppreservation.org; 913 Meridian Ave; admission free; ⏰ dusk Sat Jul & Aug) in South Pasadena, where family-oriented flicks such as *Babe* and *The Wizard of Oz* are beamed onto a tarp hanging from the 1888 Meridian Iron Works. It's close to the Metro Gold Line's Mission St station.

devoted to the early films of Charlie Chaplin, Lillian Gish, Valentino and other stars of the silent age. Screenings are accompanied by live music and often preceded by cartoons or shorts. Check the website or listings magazines for upcoming shows.

AMC Century City 15 (Map pp90-1; ☎ 310-289-4262; www.amctheatres.com; Westfield Shoppingtown Century City, 10250 Santa Monica Blvd; adult/child/senior $11/8/9) Since being expanded and updated, this mall-based multiplex can now shower up to 3000 flick fans in 15 theatres with blockbuster movies on wall-to-wall screens, stadium-style 'loveseats' with lifting armrests and top-notch sound.

California Science Center IMAX (Map p97; ☎ 213-744-7400; www.californiasciencecenter.org/Imax/Features/Features.php; Exposition Park, 700 State Dr, near Downtown; adult/child/student & senior $8/4.50/5.75; ♿) It takes a 3-D projector the size of a Volkswagen to project the high-tech IMAX movies on a screen soaring seven stories tall and stretching 90ft wide. Most of the nature-themed films are family-friendly.

Pacific Theatres Vineland Drive-In (Map pp80-1; ☎ 626-961-9262; www.pacifictheatres.org; 443 N Vineland Ave, City of Industry; tickets $7) Nostalgia requires a long drive, but nowhere else in Southern California can you catch a first-run flick from the comfort of your Cadillac. There are four large screens with Dolby sound piped in directly to your FM radio.

Live Music

Big-name acts appear at several venues around town, including the Staples Center (p139), the Gibson Amphitheatre (p146) next to Universal Studios Hollywood, the historic Wiltern Theater (p141) near Downtown and, in summer, the Hollywood Bowl (p105) and the Greek Theatre (p145) in Griffith Park. For world music, check out what's playing at the Ford Amphitheatre (p105) in Hollywood.

The following are some of our favorite clubs for live music. Cover charges vary widely – some gigs are free, but most average between $5 and $10. Unless noted, venues are open nightly and only open to those aged 21 or older. Amoeba Music (p215) hosts free concerts. For free summer concerts, see the boxed text on p200.

ROCK & ALTERNATIVE

Spaceland (Map pp86-7; ☎ 323-661-4380; www.clubspaceland.com; 1717 Silver Lake Blvd, Silver Lake) Beck and the Eels played some early gigs at what is still LA's best place for indie and alt-sounds from noise pop to punk-folk to mash-ups. Big-name talent like Pink has been known to pop by and hit the mike for quick and dirty impromptu sets. Mondays are free and on Wednesdays the UK's NME presents the latest underground talent.

Troubadour (Map pp88-9; ☎ 310-276-6168; www.troubadour.com; 9081 Santa Monica Blvd, West Hollywood; ☺ Mon-Sat; Ⓟ) The celebrated 1957 rock hall launched a thousand careers, those of James Taylor and Tom Waits included. It's still a great spot for catching tomorrow's headliners and appeals to beer-drinking music aficionados that keep attitude to a minimum. Come early to snag a seat on the balcony or you'll be standing all the way. Mondays are free. No age limit.

Temple Bar (Map p92; ☎ 310-393-6611; www.templebarlive.com; 1026 Wilshire Blvd, Santa Monica; ☺ 8pm-2am; Ⓟ) This candlelit place scores high on the groove-meter for its unique Buddha-meets-beach decor and a crowd that defines the word eclectic. Same goes for the globe-spanning music, from edgy jazz to upbeat Latin and funky hip-hop.

Hotel Cafe (Map pp86-7; ☎ 323-461-2040; www.hotelcafe.com; 1623-½ N Cahuenga Blvd; Ⓟ) An anomaly in glittery Cahuenga Corridor, this recently enlarged but still intimate venue is the 'it' place for handmade music by message-minded singer-songwriters. Big names like Suzanne Vega and The Prom show up on occasion but most nights it's more of a stepping stone for newbie balladeers. Get there early and enter from the alley.

Knitting Factory Hollywood (Map pp86-7; ☎ 323-463-0204; 7021 Hollywood Blvd, Hollywood) The lineup at this bastion of indie bands isn't quite as out there as at the New York City mother club, but there's still plenty of cool sounds to be enjoyed. Depending on the night, you'll have long-haired hipsters, aging folkies or skinny-jean punks bopping their heads or thrashing to folk rock, goth funk or progressive jazz. Acoustics are it at the Alter-Knit Lounge. All ages.

Echo (Map pp86-7; ☎ 213-413-8200; www.attheecho.com; 1822 W Sunset Blvd, near Silver Lake; Ⓟ) Eastside hipsters hungry for an eclectic alchemy of sounds pack this funky-town dive that's basically a sweaty bar with a stage and a smoking patio. It books indie bands and also has regular club nights, like Dub Club (dancehall and reggae) on Wednesday and Part-Time Punks (post-punk, mutant disco) on Sunday. Down below is the garage-size Echoplex (enter through the alley), with a lineup of promising upwardly mobile bands on Check Yo' Ponytail nights.

Largo (Map pp88-9; ☎ 323-852-1073; www.largo-la.com; 432 N Fairfax Ave, Mid-City; ☺ closed Sun) This close-knit supper club is much beloved by acoustic musicians and their audiences and has a strict no-chattering policy. The cabaret-style performances by Jon Brion (now on select Fridays) are legendary and always sell out. The only way to ensure you get in is to make dinner reservations; too bad the food's mediocre. Also check for comedy nights. No age limit.

Vault 350 (Map pp82-3; ☎ 888-808-2858; www.vault350.com; 350 Pine Ave, Long Beach; Ⓟ) With venues like this, Long Beach is definitely moving up on the hipness scale. There ain't a bad seat in the house and the booking policy is ace (Cypress Hill to Rx Bandits) in this converted 1927 bank building. With a capacity of 1000, it's a fairly intimate space but usually gets seriously jammed.

Blue Cafe (Map pp82-3; ☎ 562-983-7111; www.thebluecafe.com; 210 The Promenade, Long Beach; ☺ closed Mon) Punk, country, hip-hop, indie-rock – this beer-soaked all-comer tavern with a lively sidewalk terrace is one of the few Long Beach hangouts that keeps it real. The crowd is just as diverse and unpretentious, with MySpace hotties sharing beers and a pool table with geeky goons and tattooed scenesters.

Cat Club (Map pp88-9; ☎ 310-657-0888; 8911 W Sunset Blvd, West Hollywood) Slim Jim Phantom, drummer for the 1980s rockabilly band Stray Cats, owns this teensy rock den with its cozy sofa loft and smoking patio. If you can, come on Thursday when the charmingly named Starfuckers (Slim Jim, ex–Guns N' Roses Dizzy Reed and a changing roster of their aging rockstar friends) get jamming around midnight.

Little Temple (Map pp86-7; ☎ 323-660-4540; www.littletemple.com; 4519 Santa Monica Blvd, Silver Lake; ☺ 9pm-2am Tue-Sun; Ⓟ) The Eastside cousin of Santa Monica's Temple Bar (opposite), this Asian-themed lounge with a red-lantern glow is perfect for anyone with a yen for Zen and soulful sounds. Afro-Cuban, deep house, hip-hop, and a side of salsa keep hipsters happy.

Smell (Map pp84-5; ☎ 213-625-4325; www.thesmell .org; 247 S Main St, Downtown) This aptly named underground club in the dark belly of Downtown books mostly try-hard Cali bands of the noise-rock and punk persuasion mixed with the occasional import from the UK or Japan. The all-ages policy means no liquor license, so expect lots of kiddies sneaking hooch in the alley.

Roxy (Map pp88-9; ☎ 310-276-2222; 9009 W Sunset Blvd, West Hollywood; P) A Sunset fixture since 1973, the Roxy has presented everyone from Bruce Springsteen to Frank Zappa and still occasionally manages to book music that matters today. It's a small venue, so you'll be up close and personal with the bands unless you join the cashed-up grown-ups on the raised platform for table service (minimum consumption, amount varies). All ages.

House of Blues (Map pp88-9; ☎ 323-848-5100; www .hob.com; 8430 W Sunset Blvd, West Hollywood; 5:30pm-2am Mon-Sat, 10-2am Sun; P) Frankly, there ain't much blues playing these days at this faux Mississippi Delta shack but at least its small size and imaginative decor make it a neat place to catch bands of all stripes, Zucchero to Johnny Vatos to Social Distortion. The Sunday gospel brunch (seatings at 10am and 1pm; adult/child $40.50/19) is an energetic affair with mediocre food, catchy songs and plenty of white folk swaying and clapping along.

Little Radio Warehouse (Map pp84-5; www.little radio.com; 1218 Long Beach Ave) Another Downtown underground club, this one even has its own internet radio station. It's still pretty improvised but you know they're onto something if bands like Sonic Youth stop by for on-the-QT concerts. Otherwise, it's the usual roster of hopeful garage rock bands. With cheap drinks and parties till sunrise, the place definitely feels more Berlin than LA.

El Rey (Map pp88-9; ☎ 323-936-6400; www.theelrey .com; 5515 Wilshire Blvd, Mid-City; P) This is one gorgeous venue, an old deco dance hall decked out in red velvet and chandeliers and flaunting an awesome sound system and excellent sightlines. Although it can hold 800 people, it feels quite small. Performance-wise, it's popular

with indie bands plus one-off headliners like Lucinda Williams and Billy Bob Thornton.

Whisky A Go-Go (Map pp88-9; ☎ 310-652-4202; www .whiskyagogo.com; 8901 W Sunset Blvd, West Hollywood; P) Like other aging Sunset Strip venues, the Whisky coasts more on its legend status than current relevance. Yup, this was where the Doors were the house band and go-go dancing was invented back in the '60s. These days the stage usually belongs to dedicated but never-gonna-make-it hard rockers. All ages.

BLUES

The monthly Bones & Blues concert series on the last Friday of the month brings some of the best homegrown talent to the Watts Labor Community Action Committee (p142). Past performers have included Linda Hopkins, Poncho Sanchez and Karen Briggs.

Babe & Ricky's (Map p97; ☎ 323-295-9112; www .bluesbar.com; 4339 Leimert Blvd, Leimert Park Village, South Central; Thu-Mon) This legendary blues joint is great any day but Mondays are cult: $8 buys the deep-throated vocals of octogenarian crooner Ms Mickey Champion and Mama Laura's late-night soul-food buffet.

Harvelle's (Map p92; ☎ 310-395-1676; www .harvelles.com; 1432 4th St, Santa Monica) The dark blues grotto has been packing 'em in since 1931 but somehow still manages to feel like a well-kept secret. There are no big-name acts here, but the quality is usually pretty high. Sunday's sexy Toledo Show mixes soul, jazz and cabaret and Monday's All-Star Pro Jam gets the coolest crowds.

McCabe's Guitar Shop (Map p92; ☎ 310-828-4403; 3101 Pico Blvd, Santa Monica) Sure, this mecca of musicianship sells guitars and other instruments, but you want to come for concerts in the postage-stamp-sized back room where the likes of Jackson Browne, Liz Phair and Phranc perform live and unplugged. Tomorrow's talents show up for open-mike nights on the last Sunday of the month.

Cafe Boogaloo (Map p94; ☎ 310-318-2324; www .cafeboogaloo.com; 1238 Hermosa Ave, Hermosa Beach; Tue-Sun) This relaxed joint offers up a mixed musical bag that might include zydeco one night, blues the next, followed by American Roots. A welcome escape from the usual Hermosa Beach frat-pack madness, Boogaloo also serves wicked cocktails, two dozen microbrews and a Cajun menu.

Other swinging hotspots:

Red White + Bluezz (Map p96; ☎ 626-792-4441; www.redwhitebluezz.com; 70 S Raymond Ave, Pasadena; P) Wine bar and restaurants bring in the best area talents on Thursday, Friday and Saturday nights.

BB King's Blues Club (Map p95; ☎ 818-622-5464; Universal City Walk, Universal City; P) Local and touring acts come to tourist-saturated Universal City Walk.

JAZZ

LA hosts a couple of California's top jazz parties: the Long Beach Jazz Festival (p161) in August and the Catalina Island JazzTrax Festival (p161) in October. From April to November, there's free jazz on Fridays at the Los Angeles County Museum of Art (p110). Clued-in jazz fiends also sign up for monthly jazz salons held in private homes. Check out **Jazz at the 'A' Frame** (www.aframejazz.com) and **Concerts at the Atelier** (www.davidandersenpianos.com). For upcoming events, check out www.lajazz.com.

Baked Potato (Map p95; ☎ 818-980-1615; www.thebakedpotato.com; 3787 Cahuenga Blvd; cover $10-25 plus 2 drinks; ⌚ 7pm-2am) Near Universal Studios a dancing spud beckons you to come inside this diminutive jazz and blues hall where the schedule mixes no-namers with big-timers, including Mike Landon and Kevin Eubanks from the *Tonight Show*. Drinks are stiff but baked potatoes (priced from $6.50 to $15) are optional.

Jazz Bakery (Map p97; ☎ 310-271-9039; www.jazzbakery.org; 3233 Helms Ave, Culver City; cover $15-30; P) Ruth Price's nonprofit jazz joint in the Helms Bakery regularly pulls in such headliners as Mark Murphy and Steve Lacy alongside top local talent. The audience is serious and respectful, so don't even think about whispering, eating or leaving your cell phone on. Two shows nightly at 8pm and 9:30pm. Students under 21 can grab tickets that are unsold at show time for half-price.

World Stage (Map p97; ☎ 323-293-2451; www.theworldstage.org; 4344 Degnan Blvd, Leimert Park Village, South Central; ⌚ varies) Cool cats of all ages come out to this no-nonsense space founded by the late jazz drummer Billy Higgins. There's no food or drink, just good music from some of the best emerging talents in the jazz scene. The Thursday jam session has people grooving until 2am.

FREE SOUNDS OF SUMMER

Summer is a great time to visit LA, not in the least because of the free concert series that are offered all over town. Most take place weekly. Check the websites listed here or the listings magazines (p195) for details.

Some of the biggest crowds come out for the **Twilight Dance Series** (www.twilightdance.org; ⌚ Thu), whose eclectic, multicultural lineup turns the Santa Monica Pier into a dance and party zone. In 2007, the stellar program included Los Lobos and Patti Smith.

In keeping with its overall renaissance, Downtown has become a hotspot for concerts. **Pershing Square** (www.laparks.org/pershingsquare/concerts.htm) gets into old-school swinging on Wednesday nights, while Thursday concerts – curated by Spaceland – have an alternative, hip-hop or world-beat bent. Cubicle slaves mix with power shoppers for the Tuesday and Thursday lunchtime concerts. In the Financial District, **Grand Performances** (www.grandperformances.org) brings international music, dance and theater acts – Ozomatli to Guangdong Modern Dance Company – to high-rise-flanked California Plaza several times weekly.

Along the coast, you can listen to jazz, cabaret and pop music against the backdrop of sailboats at the **Marina del Rey Summer Concerts** (www.visitthemarina.com; ⌚ Thu & Sat) in Burton Chace Park, or enjoy an ocean-view picnic during **Music by the Sea** (www.musicbythesea.org; ⌚ Sun) concerts in San Pedro's Point Fermin Park.

Museums also get into the music game. At LACMA, art and jazz prove an irresistible mix to culture vultures and desk jockeys alike during **Friday Night Jazz** (www.lacma.org/art/music/music.htm), which actually runs from April to November. The Hammer Museum presents just-about-to-get-big LA and UK bands in a double bill during **Also I Like to Rock** (www.hammer.org; ⌚ Thu). And the Skirball Cultural Center, near the Getty, brings quality world-music acts to a stage surrounded by a lily pond during **Sunset Concerts** (www.skirball.org; ⌚ Thu) at the beautiful Skirball Cultural Center.

Last but not least, Pasadena has the **One Colorado Summer Series** (www.onecolorado.net; ⌚ Sat) featuring jazz, salsa, blues and classical music.

Catalina Bar & Grill (Map pp86-7; ☎ 323-466-2210; www.catalinajazzclub.com; 6725 W Sunset Blvd, Hollywood; cover $10-18 plus dinner or 2 drinks; ⊗ closed Mon; **P**) LA's premier jazz club is now tucked in a ho-hum office building (enter through the garage), but once inside the spacious yet sultry room, all is forgiven. The booking policy is top-notch and brings in such top talent as Art Blakely and the Marsalis brothers, but up-and-comers are spotlighted too. Two shows nightly.

Vibrato Grill & Jazz (off Map pp90-1; ☎ 310-474-9400; www.vibratogrilljazz.com; 2930 Beverly Glen Circle, Bel Air) Trumpet-legend Herb Alpert is the man behind this posh Bel Air supper club, and he's got the pull to bring in Billy Childs, Toots Thielemans and other big-name acts. Bright abstract paintings, also by Alpert, adorn the walls, while bronze busts of Louis Armstrong & Co preside over the sleek wood and granite bar. There's usually no cover with dinner or a two-drink minimum; all ages.

For more cool tunes, check out **Backstage at the Vault** (Map pp82-3; ☎ 562-590-5566; www.backstagejazz .com; 330 Pine Ave, Long Beach), an intimate jazz and blues supper club out the back of Vault 350.

LATIN & WORLD

El Floridita (Map pp86-7; ☎ 323-871-8612; 1253 N Vine St, Hollywood; cover $10, free with dinner; ⊗ Mon, Wed, Fri & Sat) The original Floridita in Havana was Hemingway's favorite hangout and the Hollywood version is *the* place for grown-up *salseros* to go *cubano*. Order a mojito and watch the beautiful dancers do their thing (or join in if you feel you've got the moves). The Monday night jams are legendary; make reservations at least a week in advance (for any day, for that matter).

Club Mayan (Map pp84-5; ☎ 213-746-4674; www .clubmayan.com; 1038 S Hill St, Downtown; ⊗ 9pm-3am Fri & Sat; **P**) Kick up your heels during Saturday's Tropical Nights when a salsa band turns the heat up a few notches. Pull out your nattiest suit and slinkiest cocktail dress and start hitting the dance floor. Don't know how? Come early for lessons. On Fridays it's house and hip-hop.

Zabumba (Map p97; ☎ 310-841-6525; 10717 Venice Blvd, Culver City; cover $3-8; ⊗ closed Mon) See if you can keep your hips from moving when being doused with bossa nova, jazz, *axé*, samba and salsa at this Brazilian restaurant-bar-club right on LA's 'Little Rio' strip.

Club El Baron (Map p97; ☎ 818-231-2565; http://club tropical.tangoafficionado.com; 8641 Washington Blvd, Culver City; cover $10, with class $15; ⊗ Wed) Every Wednesday, tango mania grips this simple Salvadoran restaurant, where the Los Angeles Tango Trio gets nattily dressed couples sashaying across the floor. No experience necessary: just show up at 8pm for an expertly taught intro classes.

Nightclubs

So what about the hottest Hollywood clubs? Consider this: One, hotness is temporary. Two, bouncers can be aggressively unfriendly. Three, you'll be standing on the sidewalk all night while the celebutantes slip in the back. Still interested? Bring a blonde or be one, dress sharp, arrive early, and play it cool. Even making it onto the 'guest list' (for instance by signing up for it online) does not guarantee that you'll be spared a long wait, rejection, or both. Clubs in other parts of the city are considerably more laid-back, but most require you to be at least 21 (bring picture ID). Cover charges range from $5 to $20. Doors are usually open from 9pm to 2am.

Cinespace (Map pp86-7; ☎ 323-817-3456; www .cinespace.info; 6356 Hollywood Blvd, Hollywood; ⊗ 6pm-2am Thu-Sat, varies Sun-Wed) DJ-to-the-stars Steve Aoki has a Tuesday residency at this upstairs playground of skinny-jeansters who favored eyeliner long before certain pirates made it fashionable. The dinner-and-a-movie nights (Thursday to Saturday) are perfect if you're not into switching venues halfway through the evening.

Avalon (Map pp86-7; ☎ 323-462-8900; www.avalon hollywood.com; 1735 N Vine St; **P**) Booking superstar DJs for its Saturday night electronic 'Avaland,' the 1400-capacity former theater hopes to win the battle for hottest weekend dance club. It's the only club with an after-hours permit, so party kids are still spilling onto the sidewalk when the sun comes up. A-listers can get into

---

TOP FIVE LATE-NIGHT NOSH SPOTS

- Bowery (Hollywood, p175)
- La Cabaña (Venice, p182)
- Palms Thai (Hollywood, p174)
- Pete's Café & Bar (Downtown, p185)
- Swingers (Mid-City, p176)

the club-in-a-club Spider-Club. Check the website for hours.

La Cita (Map pp84-5; ☎ 213-687-7111; www.dance right.com; 336 S Hill St; ✆ 10pm-2am Thu) A Mexican dive bar turns into a hot 'n' heavy dance club for hipsters on 'Dance Right' Thursdays when DJs whip the crowd into a frenzy with hip-hop, soul, punk and whatever else gets people moving. RSVP online for free admission and come early for dollar Dewars and picture taking.

Highlands (Map pp86-7; ☎ 323-461-9800; 6801 Hollywood Blvd, 4th fl, Hollywood; ✆ 10pm-3am nightly) A clubber's nirvana, this sizzling club on the 4th floor of Hollywood & Highland has eight bars, a restaurant and four dance floors teeming with shiny happy and just-legal hotties. The multiple balconies are perfect for smoking, stargazing and breathtaking views of the LA skyline.

Nacional (Map pp86-7; ☎ 323-962-7712; 1645 Wilcox Ave, Hollywood; ℗) Another entry in Hollywood's growing cadre of club lounges, this one has a seductive prerevolution-Cuba theme with fiery mood lighting and clunky but comfy Bauhaus furniture. The door policy is picky on weekends when world-class guest DJs are often at the decks but relaxes for the Bud Brother's Monday Social (www.budbrothers .com), the city's longest-running house music club.

Bar Copa (Map p92; ☎ 310-452-2445; 2810 Main St, Santa Monica; cover Fri & Sat $5; ✆ 9pm-2am Tue-Sun) There's a tantalizing underground vibe at this pint-sized, signless dancing den where drinks are reasonable, the crowd attitude-free and DJs spin a 'Happy Feet'-inducing mix of dancehall, R&B, soul and hip-hop. Get there before 10pm to avoid the inevitable queue.

Circus Disco (Map pp86-7; ☎ 323-462-1291; www.circus disco.com; 6655 Santa Monica Blvd, Hollywood; ℗) It's quite literally a 'seven-ring circus' on Saturday nights when DJs spin mostly hip-hop and Latin in – count them – seven separate rooms in this ginormous warehouse. Strapping gay boyz sweat it out on the dancefloor on Tuesday and Friday nights, but there's always the patio for cooling off.

Zanzibar (Map p92; ☎ 310-451-2221; www.zanzibar live.com; 1301 5th St, Santa Monica; ✆ Tue-Sun) Beat freaks will be in heaven at this groovetastic boîte dressed in a sensuous Indian-African vibe with a shape-shifting global lineup that goes from Arabic to Latin to African depend-

ing on the night. The crowd is just as multi-culti. Show up early to avoid the inevitable line.

Vanguard (Map pp86-7; ☎ 322-463-3331; www .vanguardla.com; 6021 Hollywood Blvd, Hollywood; ℗) This warehouse of a club deals mostly in house and hip-hop, so expect plenty of b-boy posing. The pounding beats streaming from the enormous bass are so powerful, it feels as though God himself is speaking to you. If your eardrums need a rest, head to the plush patio.

Gabah (Map pp86-7; ☎ 323-664-8913; 4658 Melrose Ave, Hollywood; ✆ Wed-Sun) It's a *gabah* (jungle in Arabic) out there but you and your posse will be shaking your booties to the latest in hip-hop and R&B at this edgy club on a skanky stretch of Melrose Ave. Cash only.

Other places to live it up:

Rhythm Club (off Map p92; ☎ 310-606-5606; http:// rustyfrank.com/rhythmclub; 8025 W Manchester Blvd, Playa del Rey; ✆ 8-11:30pm; cover DJ/band $8/12; ℗) Jump jivin' weekly swing club with DJs and live bands in a former Elk's Club near LAX.

Dragonfly (Map pp86-7; ☎ 323-466-6111; 6510 Santa Monica Blvd, Hollywood) Hardcore party chamber with theme nights ranging from laid-back reggae to sexy sounds for the fetish set.

Classical Music & Opera

Los Angeles Philharmonic (☎ 323-850-2000; www .laphil.org; 111 S Grand Ave, Downtown; ℗) The world-class LA Phil performs classics and cutting-edge works at the Walt Disney Concert Hall (p134) from October to June and at the Hollywood Bowl (p105) in summer. In 2009, music director Esa-Pekka Salonen will be handing the baton to Venezuelan wunderkind Gustavo Dudamel. For some Disney concerts, 'choral bench' tickets behind the orchestra are available for $15. They are released at noon on the Tuesday two weeks before the concert and are available in person at the box office or by phone. Student and senior rush tickets for $10 go on sale two hours before showtime.

Los Angeles Opera (☎ 213-972-8001; www.laopera .com; 135 N Grand Ave, Downtown; ℗) Helmed by Plácido Domingo, this renowned opera ensemble plays it pretty safe with such sonic crowd-pleasers as *Carmen* and *Aida*, although lesser known works such as Leos Janácek's *Jenufa* also are part of the repertory. Performances take place at the Dorothy Chandler Pavilion (p135).

Los Angeles Master Chorale (☎ 800-787-5262, 213-972-7282; www.lamc.org) It may lack the glamour of the Phil or Opera, but this 120-voice choir gives consistently strong recitals infused with vigor and lyrical sensibility. Performances are from October to June at the Walt Disney Concert Hall (p134).

Los Angeles Chamber Orchestra (☎ 213-622-7001, ext 215; www.laco.org) LA's top chamber ensemble specializes in a wide repertory of music from the 17th century to the present. Performances take place at UCLA's **Royce Hall** (Map pp90–1; 405 Hilgard Ave, Westwood), the **Alex Theater** (off Map p96; 216 N Brand Blvd) in Glendale, west of Pasadena, and the **Zipper Concert Hall** (Map pp84–5) at the Colburn School of Performing Arts (p135).

Also recommended:

Da Camera Society (☎ 310-440-1351; www.da camera.org) Chamber music in historic venues around town. Check the website.

Pasadena Symphony (☎ 626-584-8833; www .pasadenasymphony.org; 300 E Green St, Pasadena; **P**) Concerts at the historic Pasadena Civic Auditorium (Map p96).

Theater

From glitzy Broadway shows to gritty one-act dramas, live theater is thriving in LA, thanks to a limitless talent pool and a willingness to push the creative envelope. On dozens of stages you can watch budding talent hamming it up or seasoned thespians such as Annette Bening or Richard Dreyfuss getting back to their roots.

Except for Highways Performance Space & Gallery and Redcat, venues listed below have resident ensembles. Touring musicals often set up at the Pantages Theatre (p107).

Many theaters now sell tickets through their websites. Half-price tickets to selected shows are available online through **LAStageTIX** (www .theatrela.org) or in person at the visitors centers in Hollywood and Downtown LA (p101). Tickets are released on Tuesdays for up to 100 shows during the remainder of the week.

In summer check the listings mags for performances by **Shakespeare Festival LA** (www .shakespearefestivalla.org) and **Shakespeare by the Sea** (www.shakespearebythesea.org), which present the best of the Bard in changing venues around town. Tickets are free with a canned-food donation for charity. See the websites for full details. Check out www.seatadvisor.com for seating charts and www.los-angeles-theatre .com for current shows.

LARGER STAGES

Mark Taper Forum (Map pp84–5; ☎ 213-628-2772; www.taperahmanson.com; Music Center, 135 N Grand Ave, Downtown; **P**) Part of the Music Center, the Mark Taper is one of the three venues used by the Center Theatre Group, SoCal's leading resident ensemble and producer of Tony-, Pulitzer- and Emmy-winning plays. It's an intimate space with only 14 rows of seats arranged around a thrust stage, so you can see every sweat pearl on the actors' faces. The theater has gone through a complete overhaul, finishing in summer 2008.

Ahmanson Theatre (Map pp84–5; ☎ 213-628-2772; www.taperahmanson.com; Music Center, 135 N Grand Ave, Downtown; **P**) Much larger than the Taper, this grand space is another Center Theatre Group venue in the Music Center. It's used primarily for big-time musicals on their way to or from Broadway.

Kirk Douglas Theatre (Map p97; ☎ 213-628-2772; www.taperahmanson.com; 9820 Washington Blvd, Culver City) An old-timey movie house has been recast as a 300-seat theater, thanks to a major cash infusion from the Douglas family. Since its opening in 2004, it's become an integral part of Culver City's growing arts scene. The Center Theatre Group (see above) uses it primarily as a showcase of new LA plays, and for theater by and for children.

East West Players (Map pp84–5; ☎ 213-625-7000; www.eastwestplayers.org; 120 N Judge John Aiso St, Little Tokyo, Downtown; **P**) Founded in 1965, this pioneering Asian-American ensemble seeks to build a bridge between Eastern and Western theatrical styles. Its repertory of Broadway to modern classics takes a backseat to acclaimed premiers by local playwrights. Alumni have gone on to win Tony, Emmy and Academy awards.

Pasadena Playhouse (Map p96; ☎ 626-356-7529; www.pasadenaplayhouse.org; 39 S El Molino Ave, Pasadena; **P**) In business since 1924, this venerable theater underwent a serious sprucing up in the '80s and has been thriving ever since. Shows are a mix of tried-and-true classics by Sondheim and Coward as well as new works by contemporary playwrights such as Scott Schwarz (of *Bat Boy: The Musical* fame).

Will Geer Theatricum Botanicum (Map pp80–1; ☎ 310-455-3723; www.theatricum.com; 1419 N Topanga Canyon Blvd, northwest of Santa Monica; **P**) TV's Grandpa Walton founded this beloved theater as a refuge for blacklisted actors like himself during the 1950s McCarthy years. The woodsy setting is a perfect backdrop for such classic crowd-pleasers as Shakespeare's *A Midsummer Night's Dream* and Bram Stoker's *Dracula*. The season runs from June to mid-October. To get there, head north on Pacific Coast Hwy, turn inland on Topanga Canyon Blvd and proceed for 6 miles; the theater will be on your left.

Geffen Playhouse (Map pp90-1; ☎ 310-208-5454; 10886 Le Conte Ave, Westwood) David Geffen forked over $17 million to get his Mediterranean-style playhouse back into shape and, boy, is it gorgeous. Just the perfect venue to show off his Hollywood clout. A recent lineup included the West Coast premiere of *Third* by Wendy Wasserstein and the US premiere of Joanna Murray-Smith's *Female of the Species* starring Annette Bening.

Redcat (Map pp84-5; ☎ 213-237-2800; www.redcat.org; 631 W 2nd St, Downtown; wi-fi), This is the city's finest venue for avant-garde and experimental theater, performance art, dance, readings, film and video. The large gallery showcases cutting-edge local and international talent (Tuesday to Sunday), and there's a sexy lounge for pre- or post-show drinks. The curious name, by the way, is an acronym for Roy and Edna Disney/Cal Arts Theater.

SMALLER STAGES

Actors' Gang (Map p97; ☎ 310-838-4264; www.theactorsgang.com; Ivy Substation, 9070 Venice Blvd, Culver City) The 'Gang' was founded in 1981 by Tim Robbins and other renegade UCLA acting-school grads. Its daring and offbeat reinterpretations of classics have a loyal following, although it's the bold new works pulled from ensemble workshops that make this socially mindful troupe one to watch.

Hudson Theatres (Map pp86-7; ☎ 323-856-4249; www.hudsontheatre.com; 6539 Santa Monica Blvd, Hollywood; P) This quartet of stages (plus a cute café) is a driving force on Hollywood's Theater Row and has catapulted a number of productions to Broadway, TV and the big screen, including *Reefer Madness* and *Sweet Deliverance*. Nia Vardalos' *My Big Fat Greek Wedding* had its world premier right here.

MET Theatre (Map pp86-7; ☎ 323-957-1152; www.themettheatre.com; 1089 N Oxford Ave, Hollywood; P) It never hurts to have friends in high places. Holly Hunter and Ed Harris have strutted their stuff on the MET's stage and other Hollywood bigwigs – from Dustin Hoffman to Angelina Jolie – have funneled in some

cash. The fare here runs from edgy to traditional and has included the premiere of Sam Shepard's *Curse of the Starving Class*.

Odyssey Theatre (off Map pp90-1; ☎ 310-477-2055; www.odysseytheatre.com; 2055 S Sepulveda Blvd, near Westwood; P) This well-respected ensemble presents new work, updates the classics and develops its own plays in a ho-hum space of three 99-seat theaters under one roof. Every few years, British enfant terrible Steven Berkoff makes audiences laugh and cringe with his latest provocative one-man play.

Open Fist Theater (Map pp86-7; ☎ 323-882-6912; www.openfist.org; 6209 Santa Monica Blvd, Hollywood) The name is supposed to reflect the ensemble's mission of keeping an open mind while pushing hard for social change. Sure. In any case, they're pretty good at finding relevance for today's mad mad world both in new plays and classics by such Euro writers as Brecht and Antoine de Saint-Exupéry.

Edgemar Center for the Arts (Map p92; ☎ 310-399-3666; www.edgemarcenter.org; 2437 Main St, Santa Monica) There are two stages and a gallery, but more than just being a passive venue, the Edgemar provides a platform for cross-over collaborations between playwrights, musicians, actors, dancers and performance artists and, through its acting school, also sees itself as a nurturing ground for the next generation of thespians.

Highways Performance Space & Gallery (Map p92; ☎ 310-315-1459; www.highwaysperformance.org; 1651 18th St, Santa Monica) Provocative and experimental performance art is what socially progressive artists cook up in this cutting-edge lab of creativity. This results in a multicultural, all-embracing mosaic of cabaret, music, readings, dance recitals, mixed-media shows and plays that continually push the envelope of expression.

Deaf West Theatre (Map p95; ☎ 818-762-2773; www.deafwest.org; 5112 Lankershim Blvd, North Hollywood) Deaf West, founded in 1991, was the first professional sign-language theater west of the Mississippi. Its three plays per season draw from the classics, adaptations and original works. All performances are in sign language with voice interpretation and/or supertitles.

Comedy

On any given night, famous and up-and-coming stand-up comics are polishing their chops in LA comedy clubs. The legendary clubs on the Sunset Strip still draw headliners but also command up to $20 for admission, plus dinner or a drink minimum. If that's not at all funny to you, you'll also find fine laughs at smaller, edgier and cheaper venues all over town. Largo (p198) also hosts comedy nights.

Upright Citizens Brigade (Map pp86-7; ☎ 323-908-8702; www.ucbtheatre.com; 5919 Franklin Ave, Hollywood; **P**) Quality comedy for free? Get outta here! Nope, it's true. Founded in New York by *Saturday Night Live* alumni Amy Poehler, Ian Roberts and others, this sketch-comedy group cloned itself in Hollywood in 2005 and now delivers an assembly line of yucks during several shows nightly. Most are $5 or $8 but Sunday's 'Asssscat' is freeeee.

Acme Comedy Theater (Map pp88-9; ☎ 323-525-0202; 135 N La Brea Ave, Mid-City; **P**) Three sketch-comedy and three improv companies magically spin everyday material into comedy gold at this recently renovated, high-tech space that counts Alex Borstein and Fred Goss among its alumni.

Comedy & Magic Club (Map p94; ☎ 310-372-1193; www.comedyandmagicclub.com; 1018 Hermosa Ave, Hermosa Beach; **P**) Carlin, Romano, Seinfeld – his puffy shirt is on display – have all paced the boards at this Hermosa Beach club. For big names, get here before 6pm to nab a good table and be ready to share your job or hometown to the ever-inquisitive opening acts. Always hot is Jay Leno, who tests out jokes most Sunday nights. Over 18s only.

Downtown Comedy Club (Map pp84-5; ☎ 213-514-5345; www.downtowncomedyclub.com; 501 S Spring St, Downtown; ☻ Fri & Sat) *Saturday Night Live* alumnus Garrett Morris is the man behind the curtain of this weekend club at the divey Charlie O's cocktail lounge in the Alexandria Hotel. Tickets come with a unique money-back guarantee: you don't laugh, you don't pay. Isn't that funny?

M Bar (Map pp86-7; ☎ 323-856-0036; www.mbarhollywood.com; 1253 N Vine St, Hollywood) LA's epicenter of alternative, offbeat und underground comedy, this minimall supper club has over-the-top decor, a casual vibe and crazy-funny nightly shows, including the unmissable *Uncabaret*, which is on every other Saturday.

Groundlings (Map pp88-9; ☎ 323-934-4747; www.groundlings.com; 7307 Melrose Ave, Hollywood; **P**) This improv school and company has launched Lisa Kudrow, Jon Lovitz, Will Ferrell and other top talent, although not in a while. Still, their sketch comedy and improv can be

belly-achingly funny, especially on Thursdays when the main company, alumni and surprise guests get to riff together. All ages welcome.

Ice House (Map p96; ☎ 626-577-1894; www.icehousecomedy.com; 24 N Mentor Ave, Pasadena; **P**) Dana Carvey, Lily Tomlin and Billy Crystal have honed their chops at this former ice warehouse. Today's lineup includes Latino funnyman Rudy Moreno and contestants from *Last Comic Standing*. Drinks are disappointing, the show – usually – not. Over 18s only.

Laugh Factory (Map pp88-9; ☎ 323-656-1336; www.laughfactory.com; 8001 W Sunset Blvd, West Hollywood; **P**) The Marx Brothers used to keep offices at this long-standing club with multicultural programming: Asian Thursdays, African-American Sundays and Latino Mondays. Over 18s.

More laughs:

Bang Improv Studio (Map pp88-9; ☎ 323-653-6886; www.bangstudio.com; 457 N Fairfax Ave, Mid-City; **P**) You'll get lots of bang – and laughs – for your buck at this pint-sized improv stage with attached school. All ages welcome.

Comedy Store (Map pp88-9; ☎ 323-656-6225; www.thecomedystore.com; 8433 W Sunset Blvd, West Hollywood; **P**) Yup, this is where 'Kramer' went off his racist rocker, which underscored that this once-legendary club has seen better days.

Improv Olympic West (Map pp86-7; ☎ 323-962-7560; www.iowest.com; 6366 Hollywood Blvd, Hollywood; **P**) Home of the 'Harold,' a 30-minute improv technique.

Sports

BASEBALL

Since moving here from Brooklyn in 1958, the **Los Angeles Dodgers** (☎ 866-363-4377; www.dodgers.com; tickets $10-225; **P**) have become synonymous with LA baseball. The Boys in Blue play from April to October at Dodger Stadium (p134). Tickets are usually available on game day. Parking costs $15.

BASKETBALL

They may have lost some of their hustle, but the **LA Lakers** (☎ 800-462-2849-7; www.nba.com/lakers; tickets $10-230) still pack all 19,000 seats at the **Staples Center** (Map pp84-5; ☎ 213-742-7340; www.staplescenter.com; 1111 S Figueroa St, Downtown; **P**). It's also home base for the city's other men's NBA team, the perennial underdogs **LA Clippers** (☎ 888-895-8662; www.nba.com/clippers; tickets $15-175), and the Lisa Leslie–led women's team, **LA Sparks** (☎ 877-447-7275-7; www.wnba.com/sparks; tickets $8.50-150). The WNBA season (late May to August) follows the regular men's NBA season

(October to April). Tickets are sold online, by phone and at the Staples Center box office. Lakers tickets are hardest to come by. Parking at the Staples Center costs $20.

You can also catch great hoop action with the **UCLA Bruins** (☎ 310-825-2946; www.uclabruins.com) at Pauley Pavilion (Map pp90–1) on the campus in Westwood.

FOOTBALL

Without a professional football team, LA fans make do with college teams competing in the Pacific 10 (Pac-10) Conference. The **UCLA Bruins** (tickets ☎ 310-825-2946; www.uclabruins.com; tickets $17-47) play at the Rose Bowl (p151), while the **USC Trojans** (☎ 213-740-4672; www.usctrojans.com; tickets $51) are based at the Los Angeles Memorial Coliseum (p119) in Exposition Park. The season runs from September to November.

Die-hard football fans can also feed their habit by watching the **Los Angeles Avengers** (tickets ☎ 213-742-7340; www.laavengers.com) of the Arena Football League (AFL) fight it out at the Staples Center (p139) from February to June.

HORSE RACING

LA County has two major thoroughbred racing tracks:

Santa Anita Park (Map pp80-1; ☎ 626-574-7223; www.santaanita.com; 285 W Huntington Dr, Arcadia; general/club house/turf club admission $5/8.50/20, child under 17 free if accompanied by adult; P) Horse-racing enthusiasts consider Seabiscuit's former haunt a top track in America, with seasons from Christmas to mid-April and late September to early November. See p151 for historical background.

Hollywood Park (Map pp82-3; ☎ 310-419-1500; www.hollywoodpark.com; 1050 S Prairie Ave, Inglewood; general/clubhouse/turf club admission $7/10/20; P) About 3 miles east of LAX, this track gets active from late April to mid-July and early November to Christmas.

ICE HOCKEY

The **Los Angeles Kings** (tickets ☎ 213-742-7340; www.la kings.com; tickets $25-115) play in the National Hockey League (NHL) whose regular season runs from October to April, followed by the play-offs. Despite an enthusiastic fan base, the team has never won the Stanley Cup in more than three decades of existence. Home games are played at the Staples Center (see p205).

SOCCER

The arrival of David Beckham in 2007 has trained the spotlight firmly on the **Los Angeles Galaxy** (www.lagalaxy.com) soccer team and, if the early games were any indication, has increased the popularity of the sport beyond its traditional Latino audiences. Men cheer whenever the British hunk kicks the ball, women when he takes off his shirt.

In 2005, the Galaxy was joined by a second Major League Soccer franchise, the **Club Deportivo Chivas USA** (http://chivas.usa.mlsnet.com/MLS/cdc). Local derbies usually sell out but otherwise home-game tickets at the **Home Depot Center** (Map pp82-3; 18400 Avalon Blvd; P), in the southern LA suburb of Carson (take the Avalon exit off I-405), should be available on game day. The season runs April to October.

SHOPPING

LA is a great place to shop, and we're not just talking malls and chains. The city's zest for life, envelope-pushing energy and entrepreneurial spirit also generate a cosmopolitan cocktail of indie boutiques. They're fun to nose around and are packed with clothes and stuff you won't find on the high street back home. For many Angelenos shopping is one of life's great pleasures, a benign diversion that's as much about visual and mental stimulus as it is about actually buying stuff. Whether you're a penny-pincher or a power-shopper, you'll find plenty of opportunities to drop some cash in the city's mosaic of neighborhoods. For bookstores, see p100.

Art

When you start hearing more buzz about gallery hopping in Culver City than club hopping on Hollywood Blvd, it's enough to make you put down your Godiva chocolate razzmatini. But it's true, LA's art scene is hot on the lips of hipsters and the hoi polloi. Long described as 'burgeoning,' it seems LA's artists and galleries have now fully arrived. For the latest, check www.artscenecal .com and www.calendarlive.com/galleriesand museums. For commentary and links see http://art.blogging.la.

DOWNTOWN LOS ANGELES

Still raw and experimental, Downtown has of late emerged as the most vibrant place for bleeding-edge art. Galleries cluster along **Chung King Rd** in Chinatown, in the **Brewery Art Complex** (Map pp84-5; ☎ 323-342-0717; www.breweryart .org; 2100 N Main St; P), a large artist colony in a former brewery, and especially so on **Gallery**

Row (Map pp84–5; www.galleryrow.com; Spring & Main Sts btwn 2nd & 8th). The last is at its liveliest during the Downtown Art Walk on the second Thursday of the month when galleries stay open until at least 9pm. The entire Brewery also turns into an art party, but only on two weekends a year, usually in spring and fall; check the website.

Bert Green Fine Art (Map pp84–5; ☎ 213-624-6212; www.bgfa.us; 102 W 5th St; ☺ noon-6pm Tue-Sat) The 'godfather' of Gallery Row likes art that's raw,

---

SHOPPING BY NEIGHBORHOOD

Hollywood

Despite gentrification, **Hollywood Blvd** is still good for picking up Oscar fridge magnets and 'I Love LA' T-shirts, while Amoeba on Sunset Blvd is one of the world's best music stores. Los Feliz's **Vermont Ave** and Silver Lake's **Sunset Junction** are shopping meccas for individualists. From innovative local fashions to wacky gifts, gourmet cheese to lowbrow art, you'll be in hipster heaven without a Gap in sight.

West Hollywood

WeHo is the Holy Grail for fashionistas wanting to dress like young Hollywood royalty. The main strip is paparazzi-lined **Robertson Blvd** where Kitson, Curve and Lisa Kline hold court. **Melrose Ave** west of Fairfax has Fred Segal, Marc Jacobs and other hot designers, plus gift and home stores. **West Third St** is another trendy drag.

Mid-City

Melrose Ave east of Fairfax is thrift-shop-chic central with lots of vintage and resale stores selling cool garb for people without a trust fund. Also in the mix are rocker and Goth supply dens and trashy boutiques. **La Brea Ave** between Santa Monica and Wilshire Blvds used to be mostly about furniture but is now attracting upscale indie boutiques, galleries and food stores. Small but fun, **Larchmont Village** also makes for a quick browsing break. The outdoor **Grove** is among LA's nicest malls.

Beverly Hills

Bring your money bags. **Rodeo Dr** is a catwalk for the Gucci and Prada brigade and **Wilshire Blvd** is department-store row with Barney's New York and Neiman-Marcus as well as a Niketown and the world's biggest Hugo Boss store. If price tags make you gasp, head to **Beverly Dr** for chic international chains like Lululemon to Jigsaw London.

Downtown

The **Fashion District** can yield great bargains if you're willing to brave the crowds and sensorial onslaught. Pick up ethnic gifts or strange food-stuffs on **Olvera St** or **El Mercado** in East LA, **Chinatown** and **Little Tokyo**. To keep tabs on the latest in LA art, check out the galleries on **Gallery Row** and along **Chung King Rd** in Chinatown.

Santa Monica

Santa Monica has the best shopping along the beach, in three distinct zones. Third St Promenade has Old Navy, Anthropologie, Zara and the usual high-street retail burgs. To unchain yourself, head to tony **Montana Ave** for well-edited specialty boutiques beloved by celebrity locals, or laid-back **Main St** where stores still reflect the vision, philosophy and taste of their owners.

Venice

Outlandish **Venice Boardwalk** is the place to go if you're after a spiked leather hat for your dog or maybe a spiked leather bikini for yourself. More classy shopping is found along **Abbot Kinney Blvd**, currently the most exciting and interesting shopping strip on the Westside, with a funky but fashionable mix of art, clothing and New Age emporiums.

provocative and not for sissies – expect naked bodies and 'porn' flowers.

Mary Goldman Gallery (Map pp84-5; ☎ 213-617-8217; 932 Chung King Rd; ☽ noon-6pm Wed-Sat) Specializes in established avant-garde artists from LA, New York and Europe in all types of media, including big-wigs Sanford Biggers and Rob Fisher.

Hive Gallery & Studios (Map pp84-5; ☎ 213-955-9051; www.thehivegallery.com; 729 S Spring St; ☽ 1-6pm Thu-Sat) Tunnel-shaped Gallery Row arts collective with a pop surreal focus and awesome show openings on the first Saturday of the month.

LMAN Gallery (Map pp84-5; ☎ 213-628-3883; www.lmangallery.com; 949 Chung King Rd; ☽ noon-6pm Wed-Sat) One of the few galleries on Chung King Rd to represent emerging and mid-career Asian and Asian-American artists.

CULVER CITY

Once a blank spot on LA's art map, Culver City has quietly emerged as a hotbed of savvy, edgy art with a string of galleries set up in warehouses along La Cienega Blvd between Venice and Washington Blvds and a few more west along Washington as far as the former Helms Bakery.

Blum & Poe (Map p97; ☎ 310-453-8311; www.blumandpoe.com; 2754 S La Cienega Blvd; ☽ 10am-6pm Tue-Sat) Major player and juggernaut of the Culver City arts district; reps such international stars as Takashi Murakami, Sam Durant and Sharon Lockhart.

Billy Shire Fine Arts (Map p97; ☎ 323-297-0600; www.billyshirefinearts.com; 5790 Washington Blvd; ☽ noon-6pm Tue-Sat) Champions raw, urban, lowbrow art by such emerging geniuses as Tony Fitzpatrick, Bari Kumar and Gary Baseman.

Gregg Fleishman Studio (Map p97; ☎ 310-202-6108; www.greggfleishman.com; 3850 Main St, Culver City; ☽ noon-6pm Wed-Sat) Like Eames on acid, Fleishman puts the 'fun' in functional with his ingenious bent furniture and modular playhouses.

SANTA MONICA & VENICE

A nexus of the Westside art scene is **Bergamot Station Arts Center** (Map p92; www.bergamotstation.com; 2525 Michigan Ave; ☽ 10am-6pm Mon-Fri, 11am-5:30pm Sat; **P**), a former trolley terminus turned art campus that draws moneyed folk to wander through nearly a dozen galleries. Don't miss the lowbrow art at **Copro Nason Gallery** (Map pp00-0; ☎ 310-829-2156; www.copronason.com), formal abstract paintings at **Ruth Bachofner Gallery** (Map p92; ☎ 310-829-3300; www.ruthbachofnergallery.com) and

modern ceramics at **Frank Lloyd Gallery** (Map p92; ☎ 310-264-3866; www.franklloyd.com).

Venice has plenty of artists and public art (p126) but no dedicated gallery district. The single most seminal gallery is **LA Louver** (Map p92; ☎ 310-822-4955; http://lalouver.com; 45 N Venice Blvd; ☽ 10am-6pm Tue-Sat), which gets a crowd picking out their next Tony Berlant, David Hockney or Ed Kienholz.

WEST HOLLYWOOD & MID-CITY

This is a well-established area with plenty of prestigious galleries along the Avenues of Art & Design (Beverly, Melrose and Robertson Blvds) around the Pacific Design Center and also along La Brea Blvd north of Wilshire.

Fahey/Klein Gallery (Map pp88-9; ☎ 323-934-2250; www.faheykleingallery.com; 148 S La Brea Ave, Mid-City; ☽ 10am-6pm Tue-Sat) The best in vintage and contemporary fine-art photography by the likes of Annie Leibovitz, Herb Ritts and William Claxton.

Margo Leavin Gallery (Map pp88-9; ☎ 310-273-0603; www.artnet.com/gallery/174240/margo-leavin-gallery.html; 812 N Robertson Blvd, West Hollywood; ☽ 11am-5pm Tue-Sat) Contemporary paintings, drawings and sculpture by John Baldessari, William Leavitt and other hot shots.

Iturralde Gallery (Map pp88-9; ☎ 323-937-4267; http://artscenecal.com/Iturralde.html; 2nd fl, 116 S La Brea Ave, Mid-City; ☽ 11am-5pm Tue-Fri) Contemporary art from Latin America, including Marcos Ramirez 'Erre' from Tijuana and sculpture by Brazil-born Valeska Soares.

Candy & Chocolates

If you can't give her Cartier, give her some fine chocolate. The best stores are in Beverly Hills.

Madame Chocolat (Map pp90-1; ☎ 310-247-9990; 212 N Cañon Dr, Beverly Hills; ☽ 10am-6pm Mon-Sat) Gold-leaf ceiling, marble counters, big chandelier – with its Louis XIV looks this chocolate boutique is truly fit for a king. Holding court is Madame herself, aka master chocolatier Hasty Khoei, who will tempt you with truffles, bonbons and chocolate-covered Cheerios.

Compartes of California (off Map p92; ☎ 310-826-3380; www.compartes.com; 912 S Barrington Ave, Brentwood; ☽ 10am-5:30pm Mon-Sat, 11am-5:30pm Sat) Compartes has supplied mouthwatering truffles, toffees and chocolates to Frank Sinatra, Nicole Kidman and other chocophiles for over half a century. Their specialty, though, is hand-dipped fruits – try the apricots drenched in rich dark chocolate.

K Chocolatier (Map pp90-1; ☎ 310-248-2626; 9606 S Santa Monica Blvd, Beverly Hills; ⌚ 10am-6pm Mon-Fri) Dark mints to Viennese marzipan, Diane Krön's chocolate creations are truly decadent. This goes especially for the K Sensuals line made with Chinese herbs that supposedly work like Viagra for women.

Edelweiss Chocolates (Map pp90-1; ☎ 310-275-0341; 444 N Cañon Dr, Beverly Hills) Presidents, princes and Paris have kept this exquisite chocolate emporium in business since 1942. Dipped fruit to moist marshmallows and nut clusters, each confection is an edible gem and is handmade fresh in the tiny on-site 'factory'.

Farmers Markets

Farmers markets are sprouting faster than weeds throughout Los Angeles. The best of them are certified, meaning that farmers can only sell their own seasonal fruit and veg. Some also offer flowers, nuts, honey and other natural products. For a full list see www .farmernet.com.

Beverly Hills (Map pp90-1; Civic Center Dr; ⌚ 9am-1pm Sun)

Culver City (Map p97; Main St; ⌚ 2-7pm Tue)

Hermosa Beach (Map p94; Valley Dr btwn 10th & 8th Sts; ⌚ noon-4pm Fri)

Hollywood (Map pp86-7; Ivar & Selma Aves btwn Sunset & Hollywood Blvds; ⌚ 8am-1pm Sun)

Santa Monica (Map p92) Downtown (Arizona Ave & 3rd St; ⌚ 9am-2pm Wed, 8:30am-1pm Sat); Main St (at California Heritage Museum; ⌚ 9:30am-1pm Sun)

West Hollywood (Map pp88-9; Plummer Park, 1200 N Vista St; ⌚ 9am-2pm Mon)

Westwood (Map pp90-1; Weyburn Ave; ⌚ 1-7pm Thu)

Fashions
DESIGNER

Keen on keeping tabs on what's humming on the sewing machines of LA's indie designers? Browse the racks of these boutiques for outfits with an urban, cheeky and fresh LA twist.

Kitson (Map pp88-9; ☎ 310-859-2652; 115 N Robertson Blvd, West Hollywood; ⌚ 10am-7:30pm Mon-Sat, noon-5pm

---

OUR FAVORITE FLEA MARKETS

Flea markets are like urban archaeology: you'll need plenty of patience and luck when sifting through other people's trash and detritus, but oh the thrill when finally unearthing a piece of treasure! We've rounded up the best of LA's many hunting grounds, so arrive early, bring small bills, wear those walking shoes and get ready to haggle.

- **Rose Bowl Flea Market** (Map p96; Rose Bowl, 1001 Rose Bowl Dr, Pasadena; admission $7-20; ⌚ 5am-4:30pm 2nd Sun of month) Some vintage junkies think this ginormous flea market is the cat's pajamas, but we think it's pretty overpriced and overrated. More than 2200 vendors vie for your dollars, so bring stamina, sunscreen and water. True pros show up at 5am (when admission is $20), flashlight in hand.

- **Pasadena City College Flea Market** (Map p96; 1570 E Colorado Blvd, Pasadena; admission free; ⌚ 8am-3pm 1st Sun of month) A favorite among thrifty trinket hunters, this monthly market is less overwhelming than the Rose Bowl, with about 450 vendors and a great music section. Proceeds help finance scholarships and student activities.

- **Melrose Trading Post** (Map pp88-9; 7850 Melrose Ave, Mid-City; admission $2; ⌚ 9am-5pm Sun; Ⓟ) Young Hollywood loves snapping up trendy retro threads, jewelry, homewares, art and offbeat stuff proffered at fair prices by about 100 hip purveyors. It's held in the parking lot of Fairfax High with admission proceeds going towards school programs.

- **Santa Monica Outdoor Antique & Collectible Market** (Map p92; Airport Ave, off Bundy Ave, Santa Monica; admission 6am-8am $7, 8am-3pm $5; ⌚ 6am-3pm 4th Sun of month; Ⓟ) Antique hounds on a mission will find enough Victorian armoires, porcelain chamber pots, antique vases and other stuff to fill an entire village of B&Bs. Quality is generally high, and so are the prices. It's at the Santa Monica Airport.

- **Long Beach Outdoor Antique & Collectible Market** (Map pp82-3; Veteran's Memorial Stadium, Conant St btwn Lakewood Blvd & Clark Ave; admission $5; ⌚ 6:30am-3pm 3rd Sun of month; Ⓟ) Bargains abound at this sprawling market with over 800 stalls hawking everything from vintage postcards to pottery, fur to furniture. Near Long Beach Airport.

Sun) High-energy tunes keep cover girls flipping fast through up-to-the-second hoodies, purses, shoes and jeans by Victoria Beckham. It's a routine stop for celebs before or after lunch at the Ivy (p177). Guys should check the goods at **Kitson Men** (Map pp88-9; 146 N Robertson Blvd).

Lisa Kline (Map pp88-9; ☎ 888-547-2554; 136 N Robertson Blvd, West Hollywood; ☯ 10am-7pm Mon-Sat, 11am-5pm Sun) Lisa Kline was a style-maker on Robertson long it became a fashion runway. She stocks plenty of denim plus all the hot labels you see on Lindsay, Cameron and Jessica (current faves include Project e, Crocs and Splendid Mills) and also does her own line. Women with real curves, alas, will find little selection. Lisa's growing emporium includes a **men's store** (143 S Robertson Blvd), a **kids' store** (123 S Robertson Blvd) and another **women's branch** (Map pp90-1; 315 S Beverly Dr, Beverly Hills).

Fred Segal (☯ 10am-7pm Mon-Sat, noon-6pm Sun) Santa Monica (Map p92; ☎ 310-458-8100; 500 Broadway; P); West Hollywood (Map pp88-9; ☎ 323-655-3734; 8100 Melrose Ave) Celebs and beautiful people circle for the latest from Jet, Jill Stewart and McQ at this warren of high-end boutiques under one impossibly chic but slightly snooty roof. It's even mentioned in Pink's 2006 hit *Stupid Girl*. The only time you'll see bargains (sort of) is during the two-week blowout sale in September.

DNA Venice (Map p92; ☎ 310-399-0341; 411 Rose Ave; ☯ 11am-8pm Mon-Fri, 10am-8pm Sat, 11am-7pm Sun; P) West Hollywood (Map pp88-9; ☎ 323-882-8464; 7519 Sunset Blvd; ☯ noon-9pm Mon-Fri, 11am-9pm Sat, 11am-7pm Sun) Tiny DNA is crammed with the same hip garb selling for much more at Barneys, Neiman Marcus and top-level boutiques around town. The reason? It's all overstock, available here at clearance prices. Labels vary but stylish stuff abounds.

Aero & Co (Map pp88-9; ☎ 323-651-1902; 8403 W 3rd St, Mid-City; P) Feminine Figmint, playful Ponderosa and arty Gabriella Artigas jewelry are among the edgy local designers getting a platform at Cynthia and Alisa's 'gallery of clothes.' Gwen Stefani and Maggie Gyllenhaal have been spotted browsing the racks.

Sirens & Sailors (off Map pp84-5; ☎ 213-483-5423; 1104 Mohawk St, Echo Park; ☯ noon-7pm Mon-Sat, noon-6pm Sun) The space is Lilliputian, but Jennifer Phillips' selection of trailblazing LA labels (Grey Ant, Rojas and Project 44 among them) has landed her firmly on the radar of cutting-edge kids and studio stylists.

Matrushka (Map pp86-7; ☎ 323-665-4513; 3822 W Sunset Blvd, Silver Lake; ☯ noon-7pm Mon-Fri, 11am-6pm Sat & Sun) Who says fashion has to be superficial? Not Lara Howe and Beth Ann Whitaker who infuse many of their handmade tees, dresses, pants and skirts with a lefty political touch. Everything's made from eye-catching fabrics, no two pieces are alike, it's OK to be size 12 and prices are comrade-friendly.

American Rag Cie (Map pp88-9; ☎ 323-935-3154; 150 S La Brea, Mid-City; ☯ 10am-9pm Mon-Sat, noon-7pm Sun; P) This industrial-flavored warehouse-sized space has kept trend-hungry stylistas looking good since 1985. Join them in their hunt for updated European vintage threads, deluxe tees, saucy shoes and top-tier denim by the Warhol Factory, J Brand and Levi's coveted Capital E line. You can even have your own pair custom-made for $350.

Curve (Map pp88-9; ☎ 310-360-8008; 154 N Robertson Blvd, West Hollywood; ☯ 11am-7pm Mon-Sat, noon-7pm Sun; P) Jennifer Aniston and Marisa Tomei are among the stars snapping up the sexy, sassy and sometimes even sensible international designer pieces at this edgy boutique with its neat glass ceiling. Don't even think about shopping here if you're size six or higher. Parking in back.

American Apparel Factory Store (Map pp84-5; ☎ 213-488-0266; 747 Warehouse St, Downtown; ☯ 9am-7pm Mon-Fri, 9am-2pm Sat; P) It's now an international chain, but deep in Downtown's industrial zone is the belly of the beast, the very place where all those rainbow-colored tees, dresses and shorts are cobbled together. Some items have small flaws but prices are at least 30% off retail. Check www.americanapparel.net for regular store locations throughout LA.

Another stylista haven is **Theodore** (Map pp88-9; ☎ 323-935-1636; 189 The Grove Dr, Grove Mall, Mid-City; ☯ 11am-7pm; P), which has far-out fashions from Ann Demeulemeester, Alexander McQueen, Roberto Cavalli, Great China Wall and other hot designers.

There are several other cool stores on Sunset Blvd near Sirens & Sailors, including **Kids are Alright** (Map pp84-5; ☎ 213-413-4014; 2201 Sunset Blvd) and **Luxe de Ville** (Map pp84-5; ☎ 213-353-0135; 2151 Sunset Blvd).

LINGERIE & EROTICA
Move over Victoria's Secret… Tacky to tasteful, in freewheeling LA there's no shortage of stores to get your nocturnal niceties.

Under G's (Map pp90–1; ☎ 310-273-9333; 417 N Bedford Dr, Beverly Hills; ⏰ 10am-6pm Mon-Sat, 11am-5pm Sun) This pretty store stocks tightly edited designer unmentionables – G-rated body slips to itsy-bitsy G-strings – from hot labels like La Perla, Eberjey, Cosabella and Ritratti. No matter whether you're tiny or titanic, the winsome sales ladies will help you find a flattering fit.

Trashy Lingerie (Map pp88–9; ☎ 310-652-4543; 402 N La Cienega Blvd, Mid-City; ⏰ 10am-7pm Mon-Sat, noon-5pm Sun) Those who worship at the altar of hedonism should check into this cluttered store, stocked with burlesque-inspired corsets, cat masks, school-girl outfits and whatever else girls and boys with imagination might need for a night of naughtiness. To keep out lookyloos, you must pay $5 for an 'annual membership' at the door.

Frederick's of Hollywood (Map pp86–7; ☎ 323-957-5953; 6751 Hollywood Blvd, Hollywood; ⏰ 10am-9pm Mon-Sat, 11am-7pm Sun) This famous purveyor gave us the cleavage-enhancing push-up bra and the G-string but, in 2005, competition forced it to abandon its original flagship store and move down the street to Hollywood & Highland. The new, smaller branch still sells everything from chemises to crotchless panties, all tastefully displayed with no need to blush.

Babeland (Map pp86–7; ☎ 323-634-9480; 7007 Melrose Ave, Mid-City; ⏰ noon-10pm Mon-Sat, noon-6pm Sun) This women-owned store quite literally puts 'babes in Toyland' but don't expect the PG variety. Neatly arranged between candy-colored walls are dildos, handcuffs, strap-ons, vibes and other tools to tickle your fancy – or whatever. All staff are 'sex educators' happy to advise on how to play.

Pleasure Chest (Map pp88–9; ☎ 323-650-1022; 7733 Santa Monica Blvd, West Hollywood; ⏰ 10am-midnight Sun-Wed, 10am-1am Thu, 10am-2am Fri & Sat) LA's kingdom of kinkiness is filled with sexual hardware catering to every conceivable fantasy and fetish, though more of the naughty than the nice kind.

Other sexy stores:

Agent Provocateur (Map pp88–9; ☎ 323-653-0229; 7961 Melrose Ave, Mid-City; ⏰ closed Sun) This British chain is one of the hottest tickets in hubba-hubba playwear.

Panty Raid (off Map pp86–7; ☎ 323-668-1888; 2738½ Glendale Blvd, Silver Lake; Ⓟ) This little indie panty parlor has all the cool labels – Hanky Panky to Hard Tail.

VINTAGE & RESALE

LA is a shopper's paradise for those with diva tastes but more pauperlike bank balances. Thanks to leagues of label hounds addicted to staying ahead of the fashion curve, there's plenty of great used clothing to be found across the city – and we're not talking musty thrift-store chic.

Decades & Decades Two (Map pp88–9; ☎ 323-655-0223, 323-655-1960; 8214 Melrose Ave, Mid-City; ⏰ 11:30am-6pm Mon-Sat, noon-5pm Sun) Industry stylists and celebs love Cameron Silver's knack for digging up rare '60s and '70s couture and accessories by such design legends as Pucci, Courrèges, Paco Rabanne and Chanel. His recently expanded style salon also includes Decades Two, where the focus is on barely worn contemporary styles that may include Jimmy Choo heels, Stella McCartney jackets, Prada totes and Marc Jacobs skirts.

Shareen Vintage (off Map pp84–5; ☎ 310-276-6226; 350 N Ave 21, Downtown; ⏰ 10am-5pm Wed & Sat, noon-6pm Sun; Ⓟ) You'll feel like the ultimate insider journeying down a grimy cul-de-sac to this signless warehouse where Shareen Mitchell wants you looking fab in yesteryear's fashions. If that mod mini is all wrong for you, she'll let you know. Most items sell for between $20 and $45 with some going for $1 to $5 during blowout sales every third Saturday of the month.

St Vincent de Paul Thrift Shop (off Map pp84–5; ☎ 323-224-6280; 210 N Ave 21, Downtown; ⏰ 9:30am-6pm; Ⓟ) This 'Pentagon-sized' thrift shop is the best in town, bar none. And it's just a few doors from Shareen Vintage.

Sielian's Vintage Apparel (Map pp88–9; ☎ 310-246-9595; 9013 Melrose Ave, West Hollywood; ⏰ 11-7pm Mon-Fri, noon-6pm Sat) Like Shareen (see above), Sielian used to sell her frocks on flea markets but now her fan base of artists, stylists and celebs like Lucy Liu can feed their fashion cravings in a neatly kept storefront with dressing rooms. Most items cost between $60 and $180.

Melrose between La Brea and Fairfax is resale city. At warehouse-sized **Wasteland** (Map pp88–9; ☎ 323-653-3028; 7428 Melrose Ave, Mid-City; ⏰ 11am-8pm Mon-Sat, 11am-7pm Sun) you could pocket an American Apparel tee along with a Prada bag and '70s polyester shirt for less than $50. Prices are lower and styles more contemporary across the street at **Crossroads** (Map pp88–9; ☎ 323-782-8100; 7409 Melrose Ave; ⏰ no

IT'S A WRAP

Dress like a movie star – in their actual clothes! Packed-to-the-rafters **It's a Wrap** (www.itsawraphollywood.com; ⏰ 10am-8pm Mon-Fri, 11am-6pm Sat & Sun) Beverly Hills (Map pp90-1; ☎ 310-246-9727; 1164 S Robertson Blvd) Burbank (Map p95; ☎ 818-567-7366; 3315 W Magnolia Ave) sells wardrobe castoffs from TV and film studios – mostly small-size designer duds – at steep discounts. We've seen stuff from *CSI Miami*, *Law & Order* and *Alias*. Tags are coded (there's a list at the check-out counter), so you'll know what to brag about.

8pm Mon-Sat, noon-7pm Sun), which has premium denim (Seven, True Religion) and coveted Calvin, BCBG and other labels. Around the corner is **Jet Rag** (Map pp88-9; ☎ 323-939-0528; 825 N La Brea Ave; ⏰ 11am-7:30pm), famous for its Sunday 'rag picker' parking-lot sale when each item sells for $1.

SHOES
Camille Hudson Shoes (Map pp86-7; ☎ 323-953-0377; 4685 Hollywood Blvd, Los Feliz; ⏰ noon-8pm Mon-Sat, noon-7pm Sun) Discerning footishistas regularly make the pilgrimage to this ubercool boutique for Camille's own line of patent-leather flats in vibrant colors (canary yellow to hot pink) and basic black. She also stocks a choice selection of Euro imports.

Remix Vintage Shoes (Map pp88-9; ☎ 323-936-6210; 7605 Beverly Blvd, Mid-City; ⏰ noon-7pm Mon-Sat, noon-6pm Sun) Feet feeling retro? Check out the never-worn vintage and repro trotters from the 1920s to the '70s. From wingtips to wedges, your feet will be trippin' the light fantastic.

Undefeated (Map p92; ☎ 310-399-4195; 2654B Main St, Santa Monica; ⏰ 10am-7pm Mon-Sat, 11am-6pm Sun) Get your kicks at this slammin' sneaker store specializing in vintage and limited editions, handselected from the manufacturer by the manager. Think Nike X Junya Watanabe and Dunk NL and Adidas Comptown. When new shipments arrive, expect sidewalk campouts.

Fine Foods & Drinks
Traveling gourmets should have no problem ... g some rare and exotic treats. For de-... ut LA's oldest winery, see San Anto-...ery (p139).

Cheese Store of Beverly Hills (Map pp90-1; ☎ 310-278-2855; 419 N Beverly Dr, Beverly Hills; ⏰ 10am-6pm Mon-Sat) Mimolette and Raclette are not characters in a French opera but just two of the hundreds of handcrafted bries, blues, goudas and other cheeses temptingly displayed at this delectable fromagerie along with the world's finest olive oils, wines, pâtés and pestos.

Le Palais des Thés (Map pp90-1; ☎ 310-271-7922; 401 N Cañon Dr, Beverly Hills; ⏰ 10am-6pm Mon-Sat, noon-5pm Sun) If you consider fine tea one of life's great pleasures, you'll find kindred spirits at this exquisite boutique. Friendly staff will gladly help you find a new favorite from among the 250 varieties of quality teas, each with its own distinctive character.

Galco's Soda Pop Stop (off Map pp84-5; ☎ 323-255-7155; 5702 York Blvd, Highland Park; ⏰ 9am-6:30pm Mon-Sat, 9am-4pm Sun; P) Nostalgia buffs go nuts at this little corner store stocked with a peerless selection of rare and old-time soda pops, from Boylan's root beer to Faygo's Rock & Rye Cola. If want your kids to know what junk food grandma used to love, check out the old-fashioned candy assortment.

Erewhon Natural Food Market (Map pp88-9; ☎ 323-937-0777; 7660 Beverly Blvd, Mid-City; ⏰ 8am-10pm Mon-Sat, 9am-9pm Sun; P) The 'mother' of all natural-food stores supplies organic, hormone-free and sustainable anything to a hyper-conscious crowd that includes a sizeable smattering of celebs. Vitamin-pill poppers comb through multiple aisles while deli dabblers enjoy healthy soups, wraps and salads.

Health & Beauty
If you're confused by Sephora and afraid of the gauntlet of perfume sprayers at Bloomingdales, try one of the following well-stocked indie stores where personal attention is key.

Palmetto Fairfax District (Map pp88-9; ☎ 323-653-2470; 8321 W 3rd St); Santa Monica (Map p92; ☎ 310-395-6687; 1034 Montana Ave) Jane Kennedy's all-natural beauty emporium lets you indulge all your femme pampering needs, from prettily packaged potions to Julie Hewitt's LA-based make-up line and Commando invisible underwear.

Napoleon Perdis (Map pp86-7; ☎ 323-462-7711; 6621 Hollywood Blvd, Hollywood) A judge on *Australia's Next Top Model*, Napoleon Perdis has brought his 'star powder' to Hollywood where he's adding extra luster to Teri

Hatcher, Paula Abdul and other famous faces. At his flagship store you can go color-crazy with samples displayed on mirrored tables or ask the nonsnooty sales girls for some advice. There's another branch in the Westfield Shoppingtown Century City mall (p216).

Beauty Collection Apothecary (Map pp88-9; ☎ 323-930-0300; 110 S Fairfax Ave, Mid-City; **P**) Glamazons and metrosexuals love the huge selection of brands – from Ahava to Z Bigatti – at this sleek Farmers Market–adjacent boutique. We especially like the products by local skincare gurus to the stars, including Murad, Ole Henriksen and Brave Soldier.

Apothia @ Fred Segal (Map pp88-9; ☎ 323-651-0239; www.apothia.com; 8118 Melrose Ave, Mid-City; **P**)

Beauty purveyor to the stars for a quarter century, Apothia has all the hottest, hard-to-find A-lister products that the glossies say you can't live without. Best sellers include Bella Bronze self-tanning cream and DuWop pink shimmer lip venom. It's inside the Fred Segal boutique.

Marie Mason Apothecary (off Map p92; ☎ 310-394-5710; 225 26th St, Santa Monica; ⏱ 10am-6pm Mon-Sat, noon-5pm Sun; **P**) The baby-blue walls, white shelves and antler chandeliers here exude the feel of an intimate beach bungalow and create a breezy setting for the exclusive beauty goods available at this Brentwood Country Mart boutique. Look for hard-to-find Trilogy from Australia and local Sage body lotions.

LA'S FASHION DISTRICT DEMYSTIFIED

Bargain hunters love this frantic 90-block warren of fashion in southwestern Downtown (also see p139). The deals can be amazing, but first-timers are often bewildered by the district's size and immense selection. For orientation, check out www.fashiondistrict.org, where you can download a free shopping-tour podcast or order a map guide to the area. Power-shoppers hungry for the latest inside scoop can book a custom-guided tour with **Urban Shopping Adventures** (☎ 213-683-9715; www.urbanshoppingadventures.com; tour $36).

Basically, the area is subdivided into several distinct retail areas:

- Women – Los Angeles St between Olympic and Pico Blvds; 11th St between Los Angeles and San Julian Sts
- Children – Wall St between 12th St and Pico Blvd
- Men & bridal – Los Angeles St between 7th & 9th Sts
- Textiles – 8th St between Santee and Wall Sts
- Jewelry & accessories – Santee St between Olympic Blvd and 11th St
- Designer knockoffs – Santee Alley and New Alley (enter on 11th St between Maple and Santee Aves)

Shops are generally open from 10am to 5pm daily, with Saturday being the busiest day by far because that's when many wholesalers open up to the public. Cash is king and haggling may get you 10% or 20% off, especially when buying multiple items. Refunds or exchanges are a no-no, so choose carefully and make sure items are in good condition. Most stores don't have dressing rooms.

Sample Sales

Every last Friday of the month, clued-in fashionistas descend upon the corner of 9th & Olympic armed with cash and attitude to catfight it out for designer clothes – Betsey Johnson to Calvin Klein to Von Dutch – priced below wholesale. Their destination: the showrooms at the **New Mart** (Map pp84-5; ☎ 213-627-0671; www.newmart.net/samplesales.htm; 127 E 9th St), which specializes in contemporary and young fashions, and the **California Mart** (Map pp84-5; ☎ 213-630-3600; 110 E 9th St), a huge mart across the street with a great fashion bookstore on the ground floor. Open from 9am to 3pm, this is the only time the general public is allowed in these trade-only buildings. Come early and – harsh but true – don't bother coming at all if you're wearing size 8 or higher. Also leave your modesty at home, as you'll either be trying things on in front of others or not at all. Check the websites for upcoming dates and participating showrooms.

Also recommended:

Kiehl's (Map p92; ☎ 310-255-0055; 1516 Montana Ave, Santa Monica; ☼ 10am-7pm Mon-Sat, noon-6pm Sun; Ⓟ) The entire body and skincare product palette in an old-time apothecary. Free samples.

Larchmont Beauty Center (Map pp88-9; ☎ 323-461-0162; 208 N Larchmont Blvd, Mid-City; ☼ 8:30am-8pm Mon-Sat, 11am-6pm Sun) Not as chic but well-edited and lower-priced with intelligent service.

Jewelry

Jewelry District (Map pp84-5; ☎ 213-683-1956; www .lajd.net; Hill St btwn 6th & 8th Sts, Downtown) For bargain bling head to this bustling Downtown district where you can snap up watches, gold, silver and gemstones at up to 70% off retail. The mostly traditional designs are unlikely to be seen on Paris or Angelina, but the selection is unquestionably huge. Quality varies, though, so buyer beware.

Just Tantau (Map p92; ☎ 310-392-9878; 1353 Abbot Kinney Blvd, Venice; ☼ 10am-9pm) Everything a gift store should be – fun, happy to see you and stocked with handpicked playful jewelry and other charming items. Perfect for guys hoping to gain points with a 'Just-because-I-wanted-to' gift for that special gal.

Moondance Jewelry Gallery (Map p92; ☎ 310-395-5516; 1530 Montana Ave, Santa Monica; ☼ 10am-6pm Mon-Sat, 11am-5pm Sun) You'll be over the moon with delight at this go-to place for the latest baubles by Me & Ro, Anthony Nak, Temple St Clair and other hot jewelry artists. Marcia Cross, Arnold and Reese Witherspoon are among loyal fans of this gorgeous, gallery-like store.

Accents Jewelry (Map p92; ☎ 310-396-2284; 2900 Main St, Santa Monica) Pretty baubles to adorn just about every body part from ears to toes fill the glass vitrines at this friendly little store on bustling Main St. Besides owner Steven Hanna's own creations, you'll be tempted by dozens of other lines, most of them in sterling silver and many designed by his former students.

You're guaranteed superior quality, with corresponding price tags, at any of the shops on Rodeo Dr in Beverly Hills. For those of us who failed to triple our net worth during the most recent bull run, even a pair of tiny diamond stud earrings may remain elusive at $4000. But, hey, there's no cost for oohing and aahing at the trio of treasure chests listed below.

Tiffany (Map pp90-1; ☎ 310-273-8880; 210 N Rodeo Dr)

Cartier (Map pp90-1; ☎ 310-275-4272; 370 N Rodeo Dr)

Harry Winston (Map pp90-1; ☎ 310-271-8554; 310 N Rodeo Dr) The ultimate diamond purveyor to the stars.

Kids' Stuff

Whimsic Alley (Map p92; ☎ 310-453-2370; 2717-1/2 Wilshire Blvd, Santa Monica; ☼ 11am-5pm Wed-Sun) Muggles love LA's own Diagon Alley, where Harry Potter and friends seem to wait just one portkey away. Flip through Hogwarts sweaters and capes at Haber & Dasher, find your favorite wand at Phoenix Wands, or poke around nooks overflowing with Harry Potter memorabilia and like-minded literature on piratology, dragons and wandmaking.

American Girl Place (Map pp88-9; ☎ 877-247-5223; 189 The Grove Dr, Grove Mall, Mid-City; ☼ 9am-9pm Mon-Sat, 9am-7pm Sun; Ⓟ) Little girls go ga-ga for this make-believe toyland where they can take their plastic friends to lunch or afternoon tea at the café or a revue-style show, get photographed for a mock American Girls magazine cover at the photo studio or give them a makeover in the doll hair salon. Make reservations early for the café and the show.

La La Ling (Map pp86-7; ☎ 323-664-4400; 1810 N Vermont Ave, Los Feliz; ☼ 10am-7pm Mon-Sat, 11am-4pm Sun) Hip babies and toddlers keen on making a fashion statement in kindergarten should drag their parents to this self-proclaimed 'baby lifestyle boutique' to stock up on camouflage pants, Darth Vader onesies and miniature Paper Denim & Cloth jeans. While you shop, your bambinos can take art, music and even language lessons to say *'merci beaucoup'* for their cool new stuff.

Puzzle Zoo (Map p92; ☎ 310-393-9201; 1413 Third St Promenade, Santa Monica; ☼ 10am-10pm Sun-Thu, 10am-midnight Fri & Sat) Those searching galaxy-wide for the caped Lando Calrissian action figure, look no more. Puzzle Zoo stocks every imaginable Star Wars figurine this side of Endor. Also crowding the floor-to-ceiling shelves: an encyclopedic selection of puzzles, board games and toys.

Munky King (Map pp84-5; ☎ 213-620-8787; 441 Gin Ling Way, Downtown; ☼ noon-7pm Sun-Thu, 11am-8pm Fri & Sat) How do you catch a unique Moofia mini? You 'nique up on it. Or head to this tiny toy temple in Chinatown where fanciful figurines – part toy, part art, part guilty pleasure – dot shelves like colorful candy confections.

Babystyle (Map p92; ☎ 310-434-9590; 1324 Montana Ave, Santa Monica; ☼ 10am-6pm Sun-Fri, 10am-7pm Sat) Style-conscious babies kick their strollers toward the bright colors and cool clothes and accessories perfect for every stage of mother and babyhood. The tees for tots – 'Preschool is cool' – are impossibly cute.

Kitson Kids (Map pp88-9; ☎ 310-246-3829; 108 S Robertson Blvd; ⏰ 10am-7pm) For fashion-forward kiddies.

Home & Hearth

ADHD (Map p92; ☎ 310-581-8579; 1337 Abbot Kinney Blvd, Venice; ⏰ 10am-6pm Wed-Sun) *Extreme Makeover* star Ty Pennington knows about style and now he's sharing it with the rest of us in his new furniture and home-accessories boutique. The name stands for Art Design Home Decor but is also a pun on Ty's attention-deficit hyperactive disorder about which he's been very outspoken.

Zipper (Map pp88-9; ☎ 323-951-0620; www.zippergifts .com; 8316 W 3rd St, Mid-City; ⏰ 11am-7pm Mon-Sat; P) Pottery Barn graduates with a mod penchant will love this pretty pad packed with hand-picked whimsies for the home. Even day-to-day items get a zany twist here, like that leaf-shaped teacup or tiger-striped cocktail shaker. Nice take-home gifts for your design-forward friends.

HD Buttercup (Map p97; ☎ 310-558-8900; 3225 Helms Ave, Culver City; ⏰ 10am-7pm Mon-Sat, 11am-6pm Sun; P) A home decorator's nirvana, this airy, super-sized showroom in the former art deco Helms Bakery unites innovative and top-quality items from dozens of manufacturers. Silky bed linens to vintage steel desks, Turkish rugs to postmodern coffeetables, you'll find them here, along with bath and body products, gift items and jewelry.

Livinggreen (Map p97; ☎ 310-838-8442; 10000 Culver Blvd, Culver City; ⏰ 10am-5pm Mon-Sat; P) 'It's not easy being green' opined Kermit, but after a trip to this eco-superstore we beg to differ. From natural-fiber rugs to Tassajara bamboo furniture to nontoxic paints and cleaners by Ed Begley, you'll find everything you need for your eco-lifestyle.

Algabar (Map pp88-9; ☎ 323-954-9720; 342 S La Brea Ave, Mid-City; ⏰ 11am-5pm Tue-Fri, noon-5pm Sat) Forget about mass brands, Gail Baral has hopscotched from India to Japan to France to source handmade tableware, linen, frames, vases and other inspired lifestyle enhancers. These share her lofty space with fine teas from Mariage Frères, waiting to be sampled at the in-house tasting bar along with gourmet olive oils, chocolate and other tasty treats.

Surfing Cowboys (Map p92; ☎ 310-450-4891; 1624 Abbot Kinney Blvd, Venice; ⏰ 11am-7pm Tue-Sat, 11am-6pm Sun) Mid-century modern gets a beachy twist in this loftlike warehouse where a recent visit turned up a motorized long board, trippy hula-girl lamps and a Scarpa glass coffeetable.

Music

LA's indie music stores have been dying off at an alarming rate and even the legendary Tower Records bit the dust in 2006. Here are some of the survivors:

Amoeba Music (Map pp86-7; ☎ 323-245-6400; 6400 W Sunset Blvd, Hollywood; ⏰ 10:30am-10pm Mon-Sat, 11am-9pm Sun; P) Click, click, click… is the sound of scores of customers flipping through half-a-million new and used CDs, DVDs, videos and vinyl at this granddaddy of music stores. Handy listening stations keep you from making buying faux pas. Call the store or check the *LA Weekly* for free in-store live performances by touring bands.

Rockaway Records (Map pp86-7; ☎ 323-664-3232; 2395 Glendale Blvd, Silver Lake; ⏰ 11am-7pm; P) Rockaway buys, sells and trades all types of great music. Used CDs are fairly priced and there are plenty of booths for prepurchase listening. Collectors can forage through the rare-music section or stock up on posters, magazines and memorabilia.

Starbucks Hear Music (Map p92; ☎ 310-319-9527; 1429 Third St Promenade, Santa Monica; ⏰ 9am-11pm Sun-Thu, 9am-midnight Fri & Sat) Starbucks' prototype music store is still pulling in throngs looking for handpicked jazz, blues, world, folk and electro. You can prelisten to each CD or burn your own compilation at the Listening Bar.

Head Line Records (Map pp88-9; ☎ 323-655-2125; 7706 Melrose Ave, Mid-City; ⏰ noon-8pm) This is one of the best places in town for indie punk and hardcore, both domestic and rare imports, including limited editions. Owner John is a good source for plugging into the scene.

Odds & Ends

Wacko (Map pp86-7; ☎ 323-663-0122; 4633 Hollywood Blvd, Los Feliz; ⏰ 11am-7pm Mon-Wed, 11am-9pm Thu-Sat, noon-6pm Sun) Billy Shire's giftorium of camp and kitsch has been a fun browse for over three decades. Pick up dashboard Jesuses, a Frida Kahlo mesh bag, an inflatable globe or other, well, wacky, stuff. In back is La Luz de Jesus (Map pp86–7), one of LA's top lowbrow art galleries.

Taschen (Map pp88-9; ☎ 323-933-9211; 6333 W 3rd St, Mid-City; ☼ 9am-9pm Mon-Fri, 9am-8pm Sat, 10am-7pm Sun; ℗) Benedikt Taschen publishes some of the hippest books under the sun but he loves vintage landmarks and swooped when the Farmer's Market Clock Tower became available. In keeping with the image, the interior, though, is all Philippe Starck postmodern.

Meltdown Comics & Collectibles (Map pp88-9; ☎ 323-851-7223; 7522 Sunset Blvd, West Hollywood; ☼ 11am-10pm) LA's coolest comics store beckons with indie and mainstream books, from Japanese manga to graphic novels by Daniel Clowes of *Ghost World* fame. Also here is the kid-oriented store-within-a-store called Baby Melt, with a great if smallish selection of off-beat books, clothing and toys. Look for Hello Kitty goods, Roman Dirge's mix-and-match Halfsies mini-figures, and reprints of Tin Tin in several languages.

Skeletons in the Closet (off Map pp84-5; ☎ 323-343-0760; 1104 N Mission Rd, Downtown; ☼ 8:30am-4:30pm Mon-Fri) This ghoulish gift shop, operated by the LA County Coroner's Office, is located two floors above the morgue. Best sellers include personalized toe-tags, body-outline beach towels, even travel garment 'body bags.' Proceeds benefit the Youthful Drunk Driving Visitation Program, an alternative sentencing program.

Outdoor & Travel

For travel-oriented bookstores, see Distant Lands and Traveler's Bookcase on p100.

REI (Map p92; ☎ 310-458-4370; 402 Santa Monica Blvd, Santa Monica; ☼ 10am-9pm Mon-Fri, 10am-9pm Sat, 11am-7pm Sun) This 'cathedral to outdoor gear' has finally moved to a central location, making it easier to stock up on everything from wool socks to speed-dry underwear, rolling backpacks to Everest-capable sleeping bags. The staff are friendly and knowledgeable. REI also rents camping equipment.

Flight 001 (Map pp88-9; ☎ 323-966-0001; 8235 W 3rd St, Mid-City; ☼ 11am-7pm Mon-Sat, 11am-6pm Sun) Get ready for take-off at this stylish store designed to look like an airplane cabin. All the predictables are there – luggage to locks to guidebooks – plus some fun but handy items like pill towels that inflate in water, single soap sheets and a cool lomo fish-eye camera.

Magellan's (Map p92; ☎ 310-394-9417; 1006 Wilshire Blvd, Santa Monica; ☼ 10am-7pm Mon-Sat, noon-5pm Sun; ℗) This brick-and-mortar version of the popular mail-order store has a huge assort-ment of clothing, accessories, books, maps, games and whatever else you need for a pleasant trip.

Shopping Malls

Grove (Map pp88-9; ☎ 323-900-8080; 189 The Grove Dr, Mid-City; ☼ 10am-9pm Mon-Thu, 10am-10pm Fri & Sat, 11am-8pm Sun; ℗) Power shoppers love this outdoor mall next to the Farmers Market, made to look like a European streetscape but really all-American marketing genius. Highlights include little-girl fave American Girl Place (p214) and big-girl boutique Theodore (p210).

Westfield Shoppingtown Century City (Map pp90-1; ☎ 310-277-3898; 10250 Santa Monica Blvd, Century City; ☼ 10am-9pm Mon-Sat, 11am-6pm Sun; ℗) A complete revamp has catapulted this Beverly Hills-adjacent alfresco mall into the 21st century, even though its labyrinth of lanes is as confusing as ever. Godiva, Kenneth Cole, and Abercrombie & Fitch are among more than 100 mostly high-end stores anchored by Bloomingdales and Macy's. LA's best food court is upstairs, next to the high-tech AMC Century City 15 movie theater (p197).

Beverly Center (Map pp88-9; ☎ 310-854-0071; 8500 Beverly Blvd, West Hollywood; ☼ 10am-9pm Mon-Fri, 10am-8pm Sat, 11am-6pm Sun) Despite the bunkerlike looks, this is LA's glamour mall, popular with Hollywood celebs in need of some one-stop shopping. Show your hotel key at guest services for discounts, then lose yourself in over 160 boutique shops, department stores, and restaurants.

Citadel Outlets (Map pp80-1; ☎ 323-888-1724; 5675 E Telegraph Rd, City of Commerce; ☼ 10am-8pm; ℗) For some great bargains, steer your chariot down the I-5 freeway to a Babylonian 'palace' reborn as LA's recently enlarged outlet mall. The fanciful facade now conceals about 80 brand-name retailers, including Guess, Tommy Hilfiger, Old Navy, Calvin Klein and Ann Taylor. It's about 9 miles south of Downtown off the Atlantic Blvd N exit.

GETTING THERE & AWAY
Air

The main LA gateway is **Los Angeles International Airport** (LAX; Map pp82-3; ☎ 310-646-5252; www.lawa .org), a U-shaped, bi-level complex with nine terminals linked by a free Shuttle A leaving from the lower (arrival) level. Cabs and hotel and car-rental shuttles stop here as well. A free minibus for disabled people can be ordered by calling ☎ 310-646-6402. Ticketing and check-in are on the upper (departure) level. The hub for most international airlines is the Tom Bradley International Terminal.

Domestic flights operated by Alaska, American, Southwest, United and other major US airlines also arrive at **Bob Hope/ Burbank Airport** (Map pp80-1; ☎ 818-840-8840, 800-835-9287; www.burbankairport.com) in Burbank in the San Fernando Valley, which is handy if you're headed for Hollywood, Downtown or Pasadena.

To the south, on the border with Orange County, the small **Long Beach Airport** (Map pp82-3; ☎ 562-570-2600; www.longbeach.gov/airport) is convenient for Disneyland and is served by Alaska, US Airways and Jet Blue.

Another option is mid-size **Ontario International Airport** (Map pp80-1; ☎ 909-937-2700; www.lawa.org/ont), about 35 miles east of Downtown LA. It handles flights by 11 airlines, including Alaska, American, Delta, Southwest and United.

Bus

The main bus terminal for **Greyhound** (Map pp84-5; ☎ 213-629-8401; 1716 E 7th St) is in a grimy part of Downtown, so try not to arrive after dark. Take bus 18 to the 7th St subway station or bus 66 to Pershing Square Station, then hop on the Metro Rail Red Line to Hollywood or Union Station with onward service around town. Some Greyhound buses go directly to the terminal in **Hollywood** (Map pp86-7; ☎ 323-466-6381; 1715 N Cahuenga Blvd) and a few also pass through **Pasadena** (Map p96; ☎ 626-792-5116; 645 E Walnut St) and **Long Beach** (Map pp82-3; ☎ 562-218-3011; 1498 Long Beach Blvd). For general information about traveling aboard Greyhound, including sample fares, see p423 and p425.

Car & Motorcycle

If you're driving into LA, there are several routes by which you might enter the metropolitan area.

From San Francisco and Northern California, the fastest route to LA is on I-5 through the San Joaquin Valley. Hwy 101 is slower but more picturesque, while the most scenic – and slowest – route is via Hwy 1 (Pacific Coast Hwy, or PCH).

From San Diego and other points south, I-5 is the obvious route. Near Irvine, I-405 branches off I-5 and takes a westerly route to Long Beach and Santa Monica, bypassing

Downtown LA entirely and rejoining I-5 near San Fernando.

From Las Vegas or the Grand Canyon, take I-15 south to I-10, then head west into LA. I-10 is the main east–west artery through LA and continues on to Santa Monica.

Train

Amtrak trains roll into Downtown's historic **Union Station** (Map pp84-5; ☎ 800-872-7245; 800 N Alameda St). Interstate trains stopping in LA are the *Coast Starlight* to Seattle, the *Southwest Chief* to Chicago and the *Sunset Limited* to Orlando. The *Pacific Surfliner* travels daily between San Diego and Santa Barbara via LA. See p424 for full details.

GETTING AROUND
To/From the Airports

We've provided an overview of options here. Another good source of information is www.toandfromtheairport.com/losangeles.

LAX

All services mentioned below leave from the lower terminal level. Practically all airport-area hotels have arrangements with shuttle companies for free or discounted pick-ups. Door-to-door shuttles, such as those operated by **Prime Time** (☎ 800-733-8267) and **Super Shuttle** (☎ 800-258-3826), charge $18, $23 and $14 for trips to Santa Monica, Hollywood or Downtown, respectively.

Curbside dispatchers will summon a taxi for you. The flat rate to Downtown LA is $44.50, while going to Santa Monica costs about $30, to Hollywood $42 and to Disneyland $90.

Public transportation has become a lot easier since the arrival of **LAX FlyAway** (☎ 866-435-9529; adult/child 2-12 $4/2; ☺ 5am-1am). These buses travel nonstop to Downtown's Union Station (Map pp84-5; 45 minutes) and Westwood Village near UCLA (Map pp90-1; 30 minutes). To get to Hollywood, connect to the Metro Red Line subway at Union Station ($5.25; 1¼ hours).

For Santa Monica or Venice, catch the free Shuttle C bus to the **LAX Transit Center** (Map pp82-3; 96th St & Sepulveda Blvd), then change to the Santa Monica Rapid 3 (75¢; one hour). The center is the hub for buses serving all of LA. If you're headed for Culver City, catch Culver City bus 6 (75¢; 20 minutes); for Manhattan Beach, Hermosa Beach and Redondo Beach, hop

LOS ANGELES

FREEWAY LOGIC

Angelenos live and die by their freeways and sooner or later you too will end up part of this metal cavalcade. It helps to know that most freeways have both a number and a name which corresponds to where they're headed. However, to add to the confusion, freeways passing through Downtown LA usually have two names. The I-10, for instance, is called the Santa Monica Fwy west of the central city and the San Bernardino Fwy east of it. The I-5 heading north is the Golden State Fwy, heading south it's the Santa Ana Fwy. And the I-110 is both the Pasadena Fwy and the Harbor Fwy. Generally, freeways going east–west have even numbers, those running north–south have odd numbers. See Map p98 for further information.

---

aboard Metro Bus 439. Trip-planning help is available at ☎ 800-266-6883 or www.metro .net. Also see Public Transportation, right.

The **Disneyland Resort Express** (☎ 714-978-8855; http://graylineanaheim.com/airport_info.cfm) travels hourly or half-hourly from LAX to the main Disneyland resorts for $19 one way or $28 round-trip for adults.

BOB HOPE/BURBANK AIRPORT

For door-to-door shuttle companies, see LAX (p217). Typical shuttle fares to Hollywood are $24, to Downtown $26 and to Pasadena $24. Cabs charge about $20, $30, $40, respectively. Metro Bus 163 South goes to Hollywood (30 minutes), while Downtown is served by Metro Bus 94 South (one hour).

LONG BEACH AIRPORT

Shuttle service (see LAX, p217) costs $30 to Disneyland, $37 to Downtown LA and $27 to Manhattan Beach. If you're using a cab, expect to pay $45, $65 and $40, respectively. By public transportation, the trip on Long Beach Transit bus 111 South to the Transit Mall in downtown Long Beach takes about 45 minutes. From here you can catch the Metro Blue Line to Downtown LA.

Bicycle

Most buses are equipped with bike racks, and bikes ride for free, although you must securely load and unload them yourself. Bicycles are also allowed on Metro Rail trains except during rush hour (6:30am to 8:30am and 4:30pm to 6:30pm Monday to Friday). See p424 for tips on where to hire a bike.

Car & Motorcycle

Unless time is no factor – or money is extremely tight – you're going to want to spend some time behind the wheel, although this means contending with some of the worst

traffic in the country. Avoid rush hour (7am to 9am and 3:30pm to 6pm).

Parking at motels and cheaper hotels is usually free, while fancier ones charge anywhere from $8 to $25 for the privilege. Valet parking at nicer restaurants and hotels is commonplace with rates ranging from $2.50 to $10.

For local parking suggestions, see the introductions to individual neighborhoods in the Sights section.

The usual international car-rental agencies have branches at LAX and throughout LA (see p427 for toll-free reservation numbers) and there are also a couple of companies renting ecofriendly vehicles (see boxed text, p427). If you don't have a prebooking, use the courtesy phones in the arrival areas at LAX. Offices and lots are outside the airport, but each company has free shuttles leaving from the lower level.

For Harley rentals, go to **Eagle Rider** (Map pp82-3; ☎ 310-536-6777, 888-900-9901; www.eaglerider .com; 11860 S La Cienega Blvd, Hawthorne; ☺ 9am-5pm), just south of LAX, or **Route 66** (Map p92; ☎ 310-578-0112, 888-434-4473; www.route66riders.com; 4161 Lincoln Blvd, Marina del Rey; ☺ 9am-6pm Tue-Sat, 10am-5pm Sun & Mon). Rates start at $155 per day, with discounts for longer rentals.

Public Transportation
METRO BUS & RAIL

Most public transportation is handled by **Metro** (☎ 800-266-6883; www.metro.net), which offers trip-planning help through its toll-free number and the website.

The regular base fare is $1.25 per boarding or $5 for a day pass with unlimited rides. Weekly passes are $17 and valid from Sunday to Saturday. Monthly passes are $62 and valid for one calendar month.

Single tickets and day passes are available from bus drivers and vending machines at each train station. Weekly and monthly passes must be bought at one of 650 locations around town, including Ralphs, Vons and Pavilions supermarkets (call or see the website for the one nearest you).

Metro Buses

Metro operates about 200 bus lines, most of them local routes stopping every few blocks. Metro Rapid buses stop less frequently and have special sensors that keep traffic lights green when a bus approaches. Commuter-oriented express buses connect communities with Downtown LA and other business districts and usually travel via the city's freeways.

Metro Rail

This is a network of four light-rail lines and one subway line, with four of them converging in Downtown (see Map p99). A fifth light-rail line, the Expo Line linking Downtown LA with Culver City, is expected to open in 2010.

Blue Line Downtown to Long Beach; connects with the Red Line at 7th St/Metro Center station and the Green Line at the Imperial/Wilmington stop.

Gold Line Downtown's Union Station to Pasadena via Chinatown, Mt Washington and Highland Park; connects with the Red Line at Union Station. Its East LA extension via Little Tokyo and Mariachi Plaza is expected to be completed by 2009. Another extension to Foothill in the eastern San Gabriel Valley is supposed to follow by 2010.

Green Line Norwalk to Redondo Beach; connects with the Blue Line at Imperial/Wilmington.

Purple Line Subway between Downtown LA and Koreatown; shares six stations with the Red Line.

Red Line The most useful for visitors! Subway going from Downtown's Union Station to North Hollywood (San Fernando Valley) via central Hollywood and Universal City; connects with the Blue Line at the 7th St/Metro Center station in Downtown and the Metro Orange Line express bus at North Hollywood.

MUNICIPAL BUSES

Santa Monica–based **Big Blue Bus** (BBB; ☎ 310-451-5444; www.bigbluebus.com) serves much of western LA, including Santa Monica, Venice, Westwood and LAX (75¢). Its express bus 10 runs from Santa Monica to Downtown ($1.75; one hour).

The **Culver CityBus** (☎ 310-253-6500; www.culvercity.org) provides service throughout Culver City and the Westside, including LAX (75¢). **Long Beach Transit** (☎ 562-591-2301; www.lbtransit.com) serves Long Beach and surrounding communities.

DASH BUSES

These small clean-fuel shuttle buses, run by the **LA Department of Transportation** (LADOT; ☎ your area code + 808-2273; www.ladottransit.com), operate along 30 routes serving local communities (25¢ per boarding), but only until 7pm and with limited services on weekends. Many lines connect with other DASH routes; see the website for details. Here are some of the most useful lines:

Beachwood Canyon Route (Mon-Sat) Useful for close-ups of the Hollywood Sign, runs from Hollywood Blvd & Vine St up Beachwood Dr.

Downtown Routes (daily) Six separate routes, actually, hitting all the hotspots, including Chinatown, City Hall, Little Tokyo, the Financial District and Exposition Park.

Fairfax Route (Mon-Sat) Makes a handy loop past the Beverly Center mall, the Pacific Design Center, western Melrose Ave, the Farmers Market/Grove and Museum Row.

Hollywood/West Hollywood Route (Mon-Sat) Connects Hollywood & Highland with the Sunset Strip, the shopping zone around the Pacific Design Center, western Melrose and the Beverly Center.

Hollywood Route (daily) Covers Hollywood east of Highland Ave and links with the Los Feliz Route (daily) at Franklin Ave & Vermont Ave.

Taxi

Because of LA's size and its traffic, getting around by cab will cost you a king's ransom. And forget about flagging one down: cabbies only respond to phone calls, although there are usually some lined up at airports, train stations, bus stations and major hotels. Fares are metered and cost $2.65 at flag fall plus $2.45 per mile. Cabs leaving from LAX charge a $2.50 airport fee. For details, check www .taxic absla.org.

Checker (☎ 800-300-5007)
Independent (☎ 800-521-8294)
Yellow Cab (☎ 877-733-3305)

AROUND LOS ANGELES

Hit the road, Jack, and leave behind LA's congestion, crowds and smog in no time. Get an early start to beat the commuter traffic (or catch a Greyhound bus) and point the compass across the ocean, up into the mountains or into the vast and imposing desert. Even Sin City, across the Nevada stateline, is only a few hours away.

CATALINA ISLAND

Mediterranean-flavored Catalina Island is a popular getaway for harried Angelenos, but sinks under the weight of day-trippers in summer. Stay overnight, though, and feel the ambience go from frantic to romantic. Catalina has a unique ecosystem and has gone through stints as a hangout for sea-otter poachers, smugglers and Union soldiers before it was snapped up by chewing-gum magnate William Wrigley Jr (1861–1932) in 1919. For years he sent his Chicago Cubs baseball team here for spring training. Today, most of it is owned by the Santa Catalina Island Conservancy, which ensures that it's kept development free. Commercial activity is concentrated in Avalon, which is small enough to be explored in an hour or two, so plan on spending the rest of the day hiking, taking to the water or heading out on a tour. The **tourist office** (☎ 310-510-1520; www.catalina.com; ◷ vary) is on the Green Pier. The only other settlement, even tinier than Avalon, is Two Harbors in the remote backcountry, which has only a general store, a dive and kayak center, a snack bar and a lodge. If you want to lose the crowds, head here.

Sights & Activities

It's a nice stroll along the waterfront to the 1929 art deco **Casino** (☎ 310-510-0179; 1 Casino Way), which has well-done murals, a movie theater with a twinkling ceiling and a fabulous up-

stairs ballroom; the last can only be seen on guided one-hour tours ($14.50). Tickets also include admission to the modest but insightful **Catalina Island Museum** (☎ 310-510-2414; www .catalinamuseum.org; adult/child/senior $4/1/3; ◷ 10am-4pm Apr-Dec, closed Thu Jan-Mar) in the same building. Continuing past the casino takes you to the privately owned **Descanso Beach**, where you can fork over $2 to lie in the grass or sand, get sloshed at the bar, or go snorkeling. There's good snorkeling at Lovers' Cove and at Casino Point Marine Park, an actual marine reserve that's also the best shore dive. Rent gear at any of these locations or on the Green Pier. Another way to escape the throngs is by kayaking to the quiet coves along Catalina's rocky coastline. Heading out from Descanso Beach (rental available) will get you there in no time.

To get into the nature-protected backcountry, hop on the **Airport Shuttle** (☎ 310-510-0143; round-trip $17; up to 6 times daily) or on the **Safari Bus** (☎ 310-510-4205; tickets $6.50-26; ◷ mid-Jun–early Sep). The Safari Bus goes all the way to Two Harbors. Both companies require advance reservations; you must also get a permit from the **Catalina Conservancy** (☎ 310-510-2595; www .catalinaconservancy.com; 125 Claressa St, Avalon; biking/ hiking $50/free) if you're going to be hiking or mountain biking. There's very little shade, so bring a hat, sunscreen and plenty of water.

Alternatively, you could just hop on an air-conditioned tour bus and let someone else show you around. Both **Catalina Adventure Tours** (☎ 310-510-2888; www.catalina adventuretours.com; adult/child from $33/19) and **Discovery Tours** (☎ 800-626-7270; www.visitcatalina.com; adult/child from $70/35) operate a variety of tours that'll treat you to memorable views of the rugged coast, deep canyons and sandy coves and possible encounters with eagles and a herd of bison, left behind after a 1924 movie shoot.

About 1.5 miles inland from Avalon harbor is the peaceful **Wrigley Memorial & Botanical Gardens** (☎ 310-510-2595; 1400 Avalon Canyon Rd; adult/child $5/free; ◷ 8am-5pm), where you'll enjoy sweeping garden views from a monument awash in colorful local tile. Nearby is Catalina's surprisingly challenging nine-hole public **golf course** (☎ 310-510-0530; www.visitcatalina.com; $31-36), which meanders along a long and narrow canyon. Wrap up the day with a luxuriant massage, facial or mud wrap at **A Touch of Heaven** (☎ 310-510-1633; www.atouchofheaven.com; Metropole Market Place). While you're getting worked on, your kids can play a round of skeeball, pinball or video games at the **arcade** in the same complex.

Sleeping & Eating

Rates soars on weekends and between May and September and at other times are about 30% to 60% lower than what's listed below. For camping information, see www.visitcatalina island.com/avalon/camping.php.

Hermosa Hotel & Cottages (☎ 310-510-1010, 877-453-1313; www.hermosahotel.com; 131 Metropole St; r without bathroom $45-75, cottage with bathroom $65-170) Central, clean, tidy – your only budget pick on the island.

La Paloma & Las Flores (☎ 310-510-0737, 800-310-1505; www.lapalomalasflores.com; 328 Sunny Ln; cottage $160-240, r $190-250; wi-fi) Choose from Old Catalina cottages or newer rooms with two-person spas and balconies.

Villa Portofino (☎ 310-510-0555, 888-510-0555; www.hotelvillaportofino.com; 111 Crescent Ave; r $140-390) Comfortable and elegant with gas fireplaces and bay-view sundeck.

Casino Dock Café (☎ 310-510-2755; 1 Casino Way; dishes $5-10; 7:30am-6pm Apr-Nov) Casual waterfront hangout, good for a beer and a simple meal.

Cottage (☎ 310-510-0726; 603 Crescent Ave; breakfast & lunch $6-13, dinner $10-23; 6am-10pm Sun-Thu, to 11pm Fri & Sat) Huge breakfasts, sandwiches and American, Italian and Mexican favorites are served here.

Catalina Country Club Restaurant (☎ 310-510-7404; 1 Country Club Dr; mains lunch $8-12, dinner $20-35) Fine dining on creative California fusion.

Getting There & Away

The following companies operate ferries to Avalon and Two Harbors. Reservations are recommended in summer.

Catalina Express (☎ 310-519-1212, 800-481-3470; www.catalinaexpress.com; adult/child round-trip $60/46) Ferries to Avalon from San Pedro, Long Beach and Dana Point in Orange County and to Two Harbors from San Pedro. It takes one to 1½ hours, with up to 30 ferries daily.

Catalina Marina del Rey Flyer (☎ 310-305-7250; www.catalinaferries.com; adult/child round-trip $69) Catamaran to Avalon and Two Harbors from Marina del Rey in LA (one to 1½ hours).

Catalina Passenger Service (☎ 949-673-5245; www .catalinainfo.com; adult/child round-trip $61/46) Catamaran to Avalon from Newport Beach in Orange County (1¼ hours, once daily).

SIX FLAGS MAGIC MOUNTAIN & HURRICANE HARBOR

About 30 miles north of LA, right off the I-5 (Golden State Fwy), velocity is king at **Six Flags Magic Mountain** (☎ 661-255-4111; www.sixflags.com /parks/magicmountain; 26101 Magic Mountain Pkwy, Valencia; adult/child under 4ft & seniors $60/30; 10am daily mid-Mar–Aug, Fri-Sun Sep & Oct, Sat & Sun Nov-Mar, closing times vary from 6pm-midnight;), a daredevil roller-coaster park that has had its own financial ups and downs lately and almost got sold off to land developers in 2006. Fortunately, operators decided to hang on to it, so for now you can still go up, down and inside out faster and in more baffling ways than anywhere else besides a space shuttle. Parking is $15.

Teens and college kids get their jollies on the 16 bone-chilling roller coasters, including the aptly named **Scream**, which goes through seven loops, including a zero-gravity roll and a dive loop, with you sitting in a floorless chair. If you've got a stomach of steel, don't miss **X**, where you ride in cars that spin 360° while hurtling forward and plummeting all at once. Note that many rides have height restrictions ranging from 36 to 58 inches. However, families need not worry as there are plenty of tamer rides for the elementary-school set and preteens, plus shows, parades and concerts to keep everyone entertained.

Still, on hot summer days, little ones might be more in their element next door at **Six Flags Hurricane Harbor** (☎ 661-255-4100; www.sixflags.com /parks/hurricaneharborla; 26101 Magic Mountain Parkway; adult/child under 4ft & senior $30/21; daily Jun-Aug, Sat & Sun only May & Sep, call for hr;). At this jungle-themed water park you can chill in a tropical lagoon, brave churning wave pools and plunge down wicked high-speed slides with names like Reptile Ridge and Taboo Tower.

Combination tickets to both parks are $70 regardless of age and can be used on the same day or on separate days (a good idea). Check the website for packages or discounts. If you don't have your own vehicle, look for organized tour flyers in your hotel.

BIG BEAR LAKE

Big Bear Lake is a low-key and family-friendly mountain resort (elevation 6750ft) about 110 miles northeast of LA. Snowy winters lure scores of ski bunnies and boarders to its two mountains, while summers bring hikers, mountain bikers and watersports enthusiasts wishing to escape the stifling heat down in the basin. Even getting there via the spectacular, curvy and panorama-filled Rim of the World Dr (Hwy 18) is a treat.

Orientation & Information

Big Bear Blvd (Hwy 18), the main road, runs south of the lake, skirting the pedestrian-friendly 'Village' with cutesy shops, galleries, restaurants and the **visitors center** (☎ 909-866-7000, 800-424-4232; www.bigbear.com; 630 Bartlett Rd; 🕓 8am-5pm Mon-Fri, 9am-5pm Sat & Sun). The ski resorts are east of the Village. Quiet N Shore Dr (Hwy 38) provides access to campgrounds and trails.

If you're driving, pick up a National Forest Adventure Pass (p69), available at the **Big Bear Discovery Center** (☎ 909-866-3437; www.bigbeardiscoverycenter.com; 40971 N Shore Dr, Fawnskin; 🕓 8am-6pm mid-May–mid-Sep, 8am-4:30pm mid-Sep–mid-May) on the North Shore.

Activities

Big Bear's two ski mountains are jointly managed by **Big Bear Mountain Resorts** (☎ 909-866-5766; www.bigbearmountainresorts.com; adult lift ticket Mon-Fri half-/full-day $39/49, Sat & Sun $50/62). The higher of the two, **Bear Mountain** (8805ft) is nirvana for freestyle freaks with 117 jumps, 57 jibs and two pipes, including a 580ft in-ground super-pipe. **Snow Summit** (8200ft) is more about traditional downhill and has trails for everyone, including at night. Altogether the mountains are served by 26 lifts and crisscrossed by over 55 runs, the longest being 1.5 miles. Ski and boot rentals are about $25. After a day on the slopes, prevent muscle fatigue with an expert massage by **Mountain Mobile Massage** (☎ 909-800-8103; 30/60min $55/85); best of all, a therapist will come to you.

In summer, Snow Summit issues its siren call to **mountain bikers**. Several pro and amateur races take place here each year. The 13-mile **Grandview Loop** is great for getting your feet in gear. The **Scenic Sky Chair** (one-way/day $10/20; 🕓 May-beginning of ski season) provides easy access to the top. Maps, tickets and bike rentals are available from **Bear Valley Bikes** (☎ 909-866-8000; 40298 Big Bear Blvd; bikes hr/day incl helmet from $9/25).

Hiking is another major summer activity, as are swimming, jet skiing, kayaking, boating and fishing. Boating rentals are available along the lakeshore.

To get off the beaten track, take your car for an off-road spin along the **Gold Fever Trail**, a 20-mile self-guided romp on a graded dirt road around an old gold-mining area. If you prefer to let someone else do the driving, contact **Big Bear Off-Road Adventures** (☎ 909-585-1036; www.offroadadventure.com) for its tour schedule.

Sleeping & Eating

Accommodation at Big Bear Lake runs the gamut from snug B&Bs and cabins to lodges, motels and hotels. Staff at the visitors center book accommodation for $10 per reservation. The following places are recommended.

Grey Squirrel Resort (☎ 909-866-4335, 800-381-5569; www.greysquirrel.com; 39372 Big Bear Blvd; cabins $94-240; P 🐾 wi-fi) Set amid the pines, this is a clump of delightful cabins, some with a fireplace, a sundeck and a Jacuzzi.

Knickerbocker Mansion Country Inn (☎ 909-878-9190, 877-423-1180; www.knickerbockermansion.com; 869 Knickerbocker Rd; r Mon-Thu $125-225, Fri-Sun $140-240; P 🖳) Classy and ornate B&B in a hand-built 1920s log home. Great breakfasts. Two-night minimum stay on weekends.

Adventure Hostel (☎ 909-866-8900, 866-866-5255; www.adventurehostel.com; 527 Knickerbocker Rd; dm $20-25, r from $49; P 🖳 wi-fi) Clean, recently remodeled and friendly hostel on the edge of the Village run by people happy to clue you in about the best trails, runs and other fun things.

Grizzly Manor Cafe (☎ 909-866-6226; 41268 Big Bear Blvd; dishes $5-8; 🕓 6am-2am; P 🚻) One-man grillmeister Jayme makes bear-sized breakfasts for quirky locals and the tourists who love them.

Kujo's (☎ 909-866-6659; 41799 Big Bear Blvd; quiches & sandwiches $7.50-11; 🕓 10:30am-4:30pm Sun-Thu, 8:30am-8:30pm Fri & Sat; P 🚻 wi-fi) Soul- and energy-restoring pit stop with 30 varieties of home-made quiches, ginormous sandwiches and a killer roquefort burger.

Old Country Inn (☎ 909-866-5600; 41126 Big Bear Blvd; mains lunch $8-13, dinner $14-22; 🕓 8am-9pm Mon-Fri, 7am-10pm Sat & Sun; P 🚻) Hearty German cooking at night; big salads, sandwiches and burgers at lunchtime.

Getting There & Away

Big Bear is on Hwy 18, an offshoot of Hwy 30 in San Bernardino. A quicker approach is via Hwy 330, which starts in Highland and intersects with Hwy 18 in Running Springs. If you don't like serpentine mountain roads, pick up Hwy 38 near Redlands, which is longer but easier on the queasy. **Mountain Area Regional Transit Authority** (Marta; ☎ 909-878-5200; www.marta .cc) buses connect Big Bear with the Greyhound and Metrolink stations in San Bernardino ($7, 1¼hr).

DEATH VALLEY NATIONAL PARK

The name itself evokes all that is harsh and hellish – a punishing, barren and lifeless place of Old Testament severity. Yet closer inspection reveals that nature is putting on a truly spectacular show in Death Valley, with water-fluted canyons, singing sand dunes, palm-shaded oases, scuttling rocks, sculpted mountains and plenty of endemic wildlife. It's truly a land of superlatives, holding the US records for hottest temperature (134°F, or 56°C, measured in 1913), lowest point (Badwater, 282ft below sea level) and being the largest national park outside Alaska (4687 sq miles). Peak tourist season is during the spring wildflower bloom.

Orientation & Information

Centrally located Furnace Creek has a general store, restaurants, lodging, post office, gas station, ATM and a **visitors center** (☎ 760-786-3200; www.nps.gov/deva; ☾ 8am-5pm) whose website is an excellent pretrip planning resource. Stovepipe Wells Village, about 24 miles northwest, has a store, gas station, ATM, motel-restaurant and ranger station. Gas and sustenance are also available at Scotty's Castle in the north, and Panamint Springs on the park's western edge. The entrance fee ($20 per vehicle, valid for seven days) must be paid at self-service pay stations located throughout the park. For a free map and newspaper present your receipt at the visitors center.

Sights & Activities

Start out early in the morning by driving up to **Zabriskie Point** for spectacular valley views across golden badlands eroded into waves, pleats and gullies. Escape the heat by continuing on to **Dante's View** at 5000ft, where you can simultaneously see the highest (Mt Whitney) and lowest (Badwater) points in the contiguous USA. The drive there takes about 1½ to two hours round-trip.

Badwater itself, a foreboding landscape of crinkly salt flats, is a 17-mile drive south of Furnace Creek. Along the way, you'll want to check out narrow **Golden Canyon**, easily explored on a 2-mile round-trip walk, and

Devil's Golf Course, where salt has piled up into saw-toothed miniature mountains. A 9-mile detour along **Artists Drive** is best done in the late afternoon when the hills erupt in fireworks of color.

Near Stovepipe Wells Village, north of Furnace Creek, you can scramble along the smooth marble walls of **Mosaic Canyon** or roll down powdered sugar at the undulating **Sand Dunes** (magical during a full moon). Another 36 miles north is the fantastical **Scotty's Castle** (☎ 760-786-2392; adult/child/senior $11/6/9; ☾ 9am-5pm), where costumed guides bring to life the strange tale of lovable con-man Death Valley Scotty. About 8 miles west of here, giant **Ubehebe Crater** is the result of a massive volcanic eruption. Hiking to the bottom and back takes about 30 minutes. It's slow going for another 27 miles on a tire-shredding dirt road (high clearance required) to reach the eerie **Racetrack**, where you can ponder the mystery of faint tracks that slow-moving rocks have etched into the dry lakebed.

The most spectacular backcountry adventure, though, is the 27-mile trip along unpaved **Titus Canyon Road**, which climbs, curves and plunges through the Grapevine Mountains past a ghost town, petroglyphs and dramatic canyon narrows. It's a one-way road accessible only from Hwy 374 near Beatty; the entrance is about 2 miles outside park boundaries.

Sleeping & Eating

During wildflower season accommodations are often booked solid and campgrounds are full by midmorning, especially on weekends. Campgrounds are first-come, first-served, except for Furnace Creek, which accepts reservations from October to April.

Furnace Creek Inn (☎ 760-786-2345; www.furnace creekresort.com; r $275-405, mains lunch $10-14, dinner $21-29; ☾ mid-Oct–mid-May; ☒) Elegant, Mission-style hotel with spring-fed pool and a restaurant that isn't quite as gourmet as advertised.

Furnace Creek Ranch (☎ 760-786-2345; www.furnace creekresort.com; r $116-193; ☒) is a rambling resort with 224 dated cabins and motel rooms. Its **Wrangler Restaurant** (breakfast buffet $10, lunch $10-12, mains dinner $19-29; ☾ 6am-9:30pm) serves belly-filling buffet breakfasts and turns into a pricey steakhouse at night.

Next door, **Forty-Niner Café** (mains $6-19; ☾ 7am-9pm) cooks up American standards, although the juiciest burgers are at the **19th Hole Bar & Grill** (burgers $10; ☽ lunch Oct-May).

Long in the tooth but still the most bang for the buck, **Stovepipe Wells Village** (☎ 760-786-2387; www.stovepipewells.com; r $91-111, mains breakfast & lunch $5-8, dinner $10-23; 🖳 🖭) also has a quirky restaurant that delivers above-par cowboy cooking.

Central camping options:

Furnace Creek (☎ 877-444-6777; www.recreation.gov; Furnace Creek area; campsites $12-18; ☽ year-round) Pleasant grounds, including some shady sites.

Sunset (Furnace Creek area; campsites $12; ☽ Oct-Apr) Huge and RV-oriented.

Stovepipe Wells (Stovepipe Wells Village; campsites $12; ☽ Oct-Apr) Parking-lot style, but close to the sand dunes.

Texas Spring (Furnace Creek area; campsites $14; ☽ Oct-Apr) Small and best for tents; nice hillside location.

Getting There & Away

There is no public transportation to Death Valley. Coming from LA, head north on the I-5 Fwy to CA-14 which turns into US-395 near Inyokern. Turn off onto CA-190 near Olancha and proceed into the park. Gas is expensive inside the park, so make sure you fill up beforehand.

LAS VEGAS

Vegas is the ultimate escape. A few frenzied sleepless nights here are more intoxicating than a weeklong bender anywhere else. Be as naughty as you want, pretend to be someone else entirely, and watch your most devilish fantasies become real. Sin City stands ready to give you an alibi: what happens in Vegas, stays in Vegas. Who can resist such outrageous temptation? Not you, not me. Sleep? Fuhgeddaboudit. In this city of fake Elvises, everybody lives like a king.

Orientation & Information

Las Vegas Blvd, aka the Strip, is the main north–south drag and lined with the most famous hotel-casinos. Downtown Las Vegas is the original town center with Fremont St as its main drag. For information, rooms or tickets, contact the **Las Vegas Visitor Information Center** (☎ 702-892-0711, 877-847-4858; www.visitlasvegas.com; 3150 Paradise Rd; ☽ 8am-5pm), which also offers internet access and free local calls.

Casinos & Sights

There's plenty to do besides gambling at the massive casino-resorts on and off the Strip. From volcanoes to roller coasters, lions to vixens, superb restaurants to hot dance clubs, you'll have no trouble being entertained 24/7. Of course there are entire books devoted to Vegas, but here's a peek at the best the city has to offer.

Wynn Las Vegas (☎ 702-770-7100, 888-320-9966; www.wynnlasvegas.com; 3131 Las Vegas Blvd; r weekday/weekend from $219/299; 🅿 🖳 🖭) The most expensive hotel-casino built to date exudes an air of secrecy – the entrance is obscured from the Strip by a $130-million man-made mountain. Check out Le Rêve, a water-themed show.

Bellagio (☎ 702-693-7111, 877-987-6667; www.bellagio.com; 3600 Las Vegas Blvd S; r weekday/weekend from $160/330; 🅿 🖳 🖭) Inspired by a lakeside Italian village this pleasure *palazzo* has a gasp-worthy lobby, dancing fountains in a huge lake, world-class restaurants and even a fine art gallery ($17).

Caesars Palace (☎ 702-731-7110, 800-634-6001; www.caesarspalace.com; 3570 Las Vegas Blvd S; ste weekday/weekend from $150/220; 🅿 🖳 🖭) This Greco-Roman fantasyland is as over-the-top Vegas as ever with marble reproductions of classical statuary, goddess-costumed waitresses and the swanky Forum Shops.

Venetian (☎ 702-414-4500, 888-283-6423; www.venetian.com; 3355 Las Vegas Blvd S; ste weekday/weekend from $150/220; 🅿 🖳 🖭) Hand-painted ceiling frescoes, roaming mimes and full-scale reproductions of famous Venice landmarks are found at this romantic if surreal casino where you can take a gondola ride or admire masterpieces at the Guggenheim Hermitage Museum (adult/child $19/12.50).

Mandalay Bay (☎ 720-632-7777, 877-632-7800; www.mandalaybay.com; 3950 Las Vegas Blvd S; r from $140; 🅿 🖳 🖭 wi-fi) The stand-out daytime attraction of this classy and tropically themed casino is an amazing walk-through aquarium (adult/child $16/11) where you pet pint-sized sharks.

TI (Treasure Island; ☎ 702-894-7111; www.treasureisland.com; 3300 Las Vegas Blvd S) TI has ditched the swashbuckling theme and put the 'sin' back in casino with its burlesque lounge, party-friendly hot tub and racy after-dark 'Sirens of TI' show where femme-fatale pirates dressed like lingerie models face renegade freebooters.

Mirage (☎ 702-791-7111, 800-627-6667; www.mirage.com; 3400 Las Vegas Blvd S; r weekday/weekend from $109/159; 🅿 🖳 🖭 wi-fi) This Polynesian-inspired creation comes replete with a rainforest atrium, saltwater aquariums, a royal white-tiger habitat and a fiery faux volcano that erupts nightly.

MGM Grand (☎ 702-891-7777, 800-929-1111; www .mgmgrand.com; 3799 Las Vegas Blvd S; r weekday/weekend from $90/200; P 🖳 🖳) The world's largest hotel is guarded by a giant lion while inside awaits a live lion habitat, flashy entertainment and gourmet restaurants.

Paris Las Vegas (☎ 702-946-7000, 877-796-2096; www.parislasvegas.com; 3655 Las Vegas Blvd S; r weekday/weekend from $100/150; P 🖳 🖳) This Gallic caricature strives to capture the essence of the City of Light with recreated landmarks, including the impressive ersatz Eiffel Tower (adult/child $12/10).

New York-New York (☎ 702-740-6969, 866-815-4365; www.nynyhotelcasino.com; 3790 Las Vegas Blvd S; r weekday/weekend from $80/160; P 🖳 🖳) This mini-metropolis has freshly remodeled rooms, scaled-down replicas of the Big Apple's skyline and a bumpy roller-coaster ride.

Luxor (☎ 702-262-4444, 888-777-0188; www.luxor .com; 3900 Las Vegas Blvd S; r weekday/weekend from $80/150; P 🖳 🖳 wi-fi) This 30-story black glass pyramid is stuffed with Egyptian statues and a stunning replica of the Great Temple of Ramses II, while the King Tut Museum ($10) features exquisite reproductions of ancient artifacts.

Fremont Street Experience (www.vegasexperience .com; Fremont St; ☽ hourly 7pm-midnight) Downtown's main attraction, this four-block pedestrian mall is topped by an arched steel canopy that every evening explodes into a free jaw-dropping light-and-sound show enhanced by 550,000 watts of wraparound sound.

Sleeping

With over 130,000 hotel rooms, from penthouse villas to fleabag motels, Vegas has accommodations for every budget. Rates rise and fall dramatically depending on demand, with rates generally lowest in July, August and January and highest on weekends and during conventions. Downtown hotels are generally less expensive than the Strip. Whatever you do, do *not* arrive without a reservation as there are times when every hotel is booked solid. For options and rates, see Casinos & Sights on opposite. People traveling on a budget should try **USA Hostels Las Vegas** (☎ 702-385-1150, 800-550-8958; www.usahostels.com /lasvegas; 1322 Fremont St; dm/r incl breakfast from $20/46;

🖳 🖳 wi-fi) or **Main Street Station** (☎ 702-387-1896, 800-713-8933; www.mainstreetcasino.com; 200 N Main St; r from $50; P).

Eating

All the major casinos have multiple restaurants to suit all price ranges. Most have buffets. Here are just a few choices.

Wichcraft (☎ 702-891-3199; MGM Grand, 3799 Las Vegas Blvd S; sandwiches $7-9; ☽ 10am-6pm) This design-y little sandwich shop can set you up with a breakfast bite on the fly. Or order a hot *panini* and lounge about in the acid-green chairs.

Mon Ami Gabi (☎ 702-944-4224; Paris Las Vegas, 3655 Las Vegas Blvd S; ☽ 11:30am-3pm & 5-11pm; V 🖳) Grab a sidewalk table below the Eiffel Tower, order steak-frites or quiche and watch the world on parade. Squint and it'll feel just like you're on the Champs Élysées.

Buffet at Bellagio (☎ 702-693-7111; casino level, Bellagio, 3600 Las Vegas Blvd S; breakfast $15, lunch $22, dinner $28-36; ☽ 8am-10pm Mon-Thu & Sun, 8am-11pm Fri & Sat) Vegas' best live-action buffet includes smoked salmon, sushi, Chinese, Italian and other crowd-pleasers.

Drinking & Entertainment

For listings, consult the free **Las Vegas Weekly** (www.lasvegasweekly.com) and **CityLife** (www.lvcitylife.com). Same-day discount tickets to shows are available from **Coca-Cola Tickets 2Nite** (☎ 888-484-9264; Showcase Mall, 3785 Las Vegas Blvd S; ☽ noon-9pm) in front of the giant Coca-Cola bottle.

Mix (☎ 702-632-9500; 64th fl, Mandalay Bay, 3950 Las Vegas Blvd S; admission after 10pm $20-25) Arrive before sunset and take a free glass-elevator ride up to this sky-high restaurant lounge with one of the most breathtaking views in Vegas.

Ghostbar (☎ 702-942-7777; Palms, 4321 W Flamingo Rd; admission $10-25) This pimped-out panorama bar at the top of the Palms draws a clubby crowd thick with celebs. Dress to kill.

Ice (☎ 702-699-9888; 200 E Harmon Ave; admission $5-20; ☽ Tue & Fri-Sun) Vegas' most stellar DJs spin house to hip-hop at this off-Strip jewel box.

O (☎ 702-796-9999; Bellagio, 3600 Las Vegas Blvd S; tickets $94-150; ☽ Wed-Sun) 'Eau' (French for 'water') is Cirque du Soleil's original epic venture into aquatic theatre and a spectacular feat of imagination and engineering.

Getting There & Away

McCarran International Airport (LAS; ☎ 702-261-4636; www.mccarran.com) has direct flights from LAX and smaller SoCal airports. Greyhound has regular buses to and from Los Angeles ($36, six hours) and San Diego ($36, eight hours).

Las Vegas is 270 miles northeast of LA and is reached in four to five hours by heading east on the I-10, then north on the I-15.

Getting Around

In town, the **Monorail** (www.lvmonorail.com; single/day pass $5/15) stops at major resort-hotels along the Strip. The **Deuce** (www.thedeucelasvegas.com; $2) is a 24-hour double-decker bus shuttling between the Strip and downtown.

Orange County

Never underestimate the power of a primetime soap. With the success of MTV's *Laguna Beach* and Fox's *The OC,* Orange County went from humdrum to hip in just five short years. In fact, glamorous teens, glistening beaches and high school catfights have forced King Mickey to share the Orange County spotlight at the start of the new millennium. But the mouse isn't worried. He knows today's trash-watching teens will soon grow up, get married and bring their kiddies to Disneyland. And he'll be ready with the latest in family-friendly attractions.

But Mickey and trendy teens are just a tiny part of the OC story. Three million people and 34 independent cities jostle for space in the county's 798 sq miles, a huge swath of real estate stretching south from LA to San Diego. And while there's a whiff of truth to stereotypical images of life behind 'The Orange Curtain' – big box mansions, nondescript neighborhoods, fortress-like shopping malls, blow-dried conservatives tossing Happy Meals from their humvees – there are deep pockets of individuality, beauty and open-mindedness keeping the OC 'real.' From Huntington Beach's surfers keeping seaside sparkle with monthly clean-ups and Laguna's city fathers promoting art festivals and gallery walks to Vietnamese and Latino immigrants seeking the American dream in Westminster and Santa Ana, there's a lot to admire.

So make the most of Mickey's hospitality, the 42 miles of shimmering coast and the world-class shopping malls, but take time to get off the beaten path to see what else makes Orange County thrive.

HIGHLIGHTS

- Waving at Mickey during the **Disneyland Parade of Dreams** (p242) then relaxing on a comfy couch in the stunning lobby of the **Grand Californian** (p245)

- Checking out sexy surfers while pedaling the beach **bike path** (p259) in Huntington Beach

- Slurping a frothy date shake at **Ruby's Crystal Cove Shake Shack** (p266) just off a gorgeous stretch of the Pacific Coast Hwy

- Fighting outrageous bed-hair inside the eye of a hurricane at the **Discovery Science Center** (p250) in Santa Ana

- Enjoying bluff-top views of pounding aquamarine surf from **Heisler Park** (p272) in Laguna Beach

- Camping on the beach at **Doheny State Beach** (p279) in Dana Point

Disneyland ★

★ Discovery Science Center

Huntington Beach ★

★ Ruby's Crystal Cove Shake Shack

★ Laguna Beach

★ Doheny State Beach

ORANGE COUNTY

HISTORY

Settlers began arriving en masse in Orange County after the Civil War, responding to the lure of cheap land and fertile fields. Rumor had it that almost anything could be grown in the rich soil, and many crops – such as oranges, apricots, corn, lemons, pumpkins, peaches and walnuts – did indeed thrive despite occasional irrigation and drought issues.

The Southern Pacific Railroad connected to Anaheim in 1875. When the Santa Fe Railroad reached Los Angeles in the mid-1880s, a rate war ensued and by 1886 travelers could reach the west coast from Kansas City on a $1 fare. Land deals were plentiful,

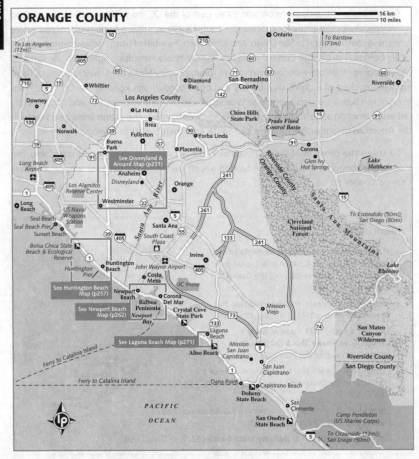

ORANGE COUNTY

and many of the sprawling cities we know today – Anaheim, Fullerton, Santa Ana – got their start at this time as farming communities. In 1886 land in Anaheim sold for about $175 per acre.

By the late 1880s citizens were ready to break free from Los Angeles County. In 1889 a state bill was introduced for the creation of the County of Orange, named after one of its most promising crops. LA wasn't quite as enthusiastic about the break and lawsuits ensued. By June that year, however, its creation was confirmed, and the new county celebrated with fireworks and parades. Oil had been discovered in the area at about the same time, and by the 1890s it had become a thriving local industry. It is still going strong today, as evidenced by active pumps dotting the landscape.

GETTING THERE & AROUND
Air
Coming from overseas, you'll change flights and clear US Customs at one of the major western gateway airports such as LA, San Francisco, Chicago or Dallas. Airlines serving Orange County include Alaska, Aloha, American, Continental, Delta, Frontier, Northwest, Southwest, United and US Airways/America West.

If you're heading to Disneyland or the Orange County beaches, you can avoid the always-busy Los Angeles International Airport (LAX) by flying into the easily navigated **John Wayne Airport** (SNA; ☎ 949-252-5200; www.ocair .com; 18601 Airport Way) in Santa Ana. If you want restaurants and duty-free shopping, stick to LAX, but for get-in, get-out domestic travel,

SNA is ideal. The airport is 8 miles inland from Newport Beach, via Hwy 55, near the junction of I-405 (San Diego Fwy).

Long Beach Airport (LGB; ☎ 562-570-2600; www .longbeach.gov/airport; 4100 Donald Douglas Dr), just across the northern county line, is a handy alternative.

See p248 for details of the Disneyland Resort Express Airport Bus from LAX to Disneyland.

Bus
If you want to get around by public transportation, the **Orange County Transportation Authority** (OCTA; ☎ 714-636-7433; www.octa.net; info line 5am-10pm Mon-Fri, 7am-7pm Sat & Sun) operates a fleet of buses serving towns and destinations throughout the county. The fare is $1.25 per ride or $3 for a day pass. Both types of tickets are sold onboard and you'll need exact change. Look for maps at train stations and online.

Car
The easiest way to get around is by car but avoid driving on the freeways during morning and afternoon rush hours (7am to 10am and 3pm to 7pm).

Train
Fullerton, Anaheim, Santa Ana, Irvine and San Juan Capistrano are all on Amtrak's *Pacific Surfliner* train route (p429). These cities, plus the City of Orange, are also linked by **Metrolink** (☎ 800-371-5465; www.metrolinktrains .com) commuter trains, which come from Downtown LA.

ORANGE COUNTY IN TWO DAYS

If you're saving Disneyland for another day, spend two days at the beach.

Day one, start in Seal Beach with a breakfast burrito at **Nick's Deli** (p254). Drive south to **Huntington City Beach** (p257) to soak in the beach rays and watch the surfers. Grab lunch downtown then wander the shops or rent a bike or surfboard and savor a full-blown beach day. Sip cocktails at **Duke's** (p260), then double back and enjoy top-notch seafood at **Walt's Wharf** (p254) in Seal Beach or hearty Italian at **Roman Cucina** (p256) in Sunset Beach.

Day two, stop by Huntington Beach's **Sugar Shack** (p260) for breakfast then continue south to Newport Beach, driving to the end of **Balboa Peninsula** (p263) to watch daredevils boogie-boarding the **Wedge** (p264). If it's a lazy day, ride the **ferry** (p263) to Balboa Island. Shoppers will want to head directly to Newport Beach's outdoor **Fashion Island** (p268) or Costa Mesa's sprawling **South Coast Plaza** (p269). Later, stop by **Ruby's Crystal Cove Shake Shack** (p266) for an afternoon shake and gorgeous ocean views. The art- and outdoor-minded should drive south to **Laguna** (p270) for an art stroll, seaside hike or mountain-bike ride. For dinner in Laguna, eat out-of-this-world rolls at **242 Café Fusion Sushi** (p276) or scrumptious noodle dishes at tiny **Thai Brothers** (p275).

DISNEYLAND & ANAHEIM

ORANGE COUNTY

pop 328,000

Mickey is one lucky mouse. Created by animator Walt Disney in 1928, this irrepressible rodent caught a ride on a multimedia juggernaut (film, TV, publishing, music, merchandising and theme parks) that rocketed him into a global stratosphere of recognition, money and influence. Plus, he lives in the Happiest Place on Earth, a slice of 'imagineered' hyper-reality where the streets are always clean, the employees – called cast members – are always upbeat and there's a parade every day of the year. It would be easy to hate the guy, but since opening his Disneyland home in 1955, he's been a pretty thoughtful host to millions of guests.

There are a few potholes on Main St – every ride seems to end in a gift store, prices are high and there are grumblings that management could do more to ensure affordable housing for employees – but even the most determined grouch should find something to warrant a grin, if nothing more than the beaming face of one breathless kiddy enjoying a magical day.

HISTORY

In the 1990s Anaheim, the city surrounding Disneyland, undertook a staggering $4.2 billion revamp and expansion, cleaning up run-down stretches where hookers once roamed and establishing the first police force in the US specifically to guard tourists (they call it 'tourist-oriented policing'). The cornerstone of the five-year effort was the addition of a second theme park in February 2001, Disney's California Adventure (DCA). Adjacent to the original park, it's designed to pay tribute to the state's most famous natural landmarks and cultural history. Also added was Downtown Disney, an outdoor pedestrian mall. The ensemble is called the Disneyland Resort. In Anaheim, access roads near the park have been widened, landscaped and given the lofty name The Anaheim Resort.

In 2007 Anaheim's city council dared nibble the hand that feeds it by initiating plans to build 1500 low-cost housing units on land zoned for resort development. Although the land wasn't owned by Disney, the mouse was not amused. Referenda and initiatives are still flying. Who's

right? It would be ideal for Disney employees to be able to afford housing close to work without long commutes, as is currently the case for many. On the other hand, Disney may build a third park across from the proposed housing spot and is probably envisioning higher-end surroundings. Stay tuned.

INFORMATION

Internet Access

Unless you're staying at a Disneyland hotel, there is no internet access in any of the parks. Most of the local hotels and inns provide internet access, usually for a daily fee.

Anaheim Visitor & Postal Center See Tourist Information (p232).

FedEx Kinko's (☎ 714-703-2250; 700 W Convention Way; per min $0.20-0.50 depending on computer; ☉ 7am-10pm Mon-Fri, 8am-5pm Sat & Sun) In the Anaheim Marriott at the convention center near the corner of Harbor Blvd and Katella Ave.

Lockers & Package Pick-Up

You can check items in lockers, which cost $7 to $12 per day depending on the locker's size. All have in-and-out privileges. There are lockers on Main St, but don't confuse these with the free package-check areas for purchases made at the park's shops. In Disneyland you can store packages at the Newsstand, at the south end of Main St. The same service is offered in DCA at Engine-Ears Toys. If you're staying at a Disneyland Resort hotel, request to have packages sent directly to your hotel.

Lost & Found

Lost & Found (☎ 714-817-2166) To the left of DCA's main entrance.

Medical Services

Western Medical Center Anaheim (☎ 714-533-6220; 1025 S Anaheim Blvd; ☉ 24hr) Emergency room available 24/7.

Money

In Disneyland, City Hall has foreign currency exchange and basic services. In DCA, head to the Guest Relations Lobby just inside the park or to the Guest Relations Window to the left of DCA's main entrance.

Bank of America (☎ 714-533-4470; 1818 S Euclid St) In Anaheim.

Travelex (☎ 714-502-0811; 1565 S Disneyland Dr; ☉ 10am-4pm Mon-Fri) In Downtown Disney; change foreign currency here.

Post

Holiday Station post office (☎ 714-533-8182; www.usps
.com; 1180 W Ball Rd; ⏰ 8:30am-5pm Mon-Fri) Mail
packages and letters at this full-service post
office.

Smoking

Most parts of the park are nonsmoking. Check
the maps for designated smoking areas.

Strollers & Wheelchairs

After passing through the turnstiles, look for
stroller and wheelchair rentals to your right
before entering Main St. Strollers cost $10 per
day and wheelchairs $10 for manual and $35
for an Electronic Conveniece Vehicle (ECV)
per day.

Tickets & Opening Hours

Both parks are open 365 days a year. You can
access the **current schedule** (☎ recorded info 714-781-
4565, live assistance 714-781-7290; www.disneyland.com) by
phone or online. Park hours vary, depending
on the marketing department's forecasted attendance numbers. During peak season (mid-
June to early September) Disneyland's hours

are usually 8am to midnight; the rest of the
year, 10am to 8pm or 10pm. DCA closes at
10pm in summer, earlier in the off-season.

One-day admission to *either* Disneyland or
DCA costs $63 for adults and $53 for children
aged three to nine. To visit *both* parks in one
day costs $83/73 per adult/child. Multi-Day
Park Hopper Tickets cost $122/102 for two
days, $159/129 for three days, $179/149 for
four days and $189/159 for five days of admis-
sion within a two week period. Ticket prices
increase annually; check the website for the
latest information or to buy tickets. An entry
ticket includes admission to the parks' individual attractions.

You can also purchase a Southern California CityPass for $235/189, which permits
three-day admission to Disneyland and DCA,
as well as one-day admission to other local
attractions.

FASTPASS & SINGLE RIDERS

With a bit of pre-planning, you can significantly
cut your wait time for popular attractions.
Walk up to a Fastpass ticket machine – located
near the entrance to the ride – and insert your

ORANGE COUNTY

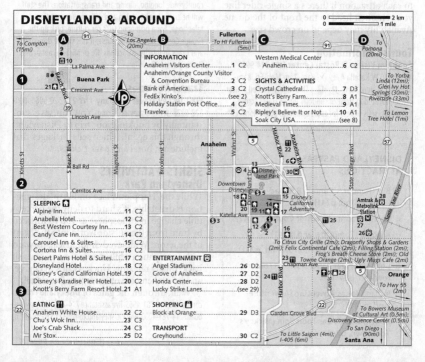

DISNEYLAND & AROUND

INFORMATION
Anaheim Visitors Center...........1 C2
Anaheim/Orange County Visitor
& Convention Bureau...........2 C2
Bank of America...........3 C2
FedEx Kinko's...........(see 2)
Holiday Station Post Office......4 C2
Travelex...........5 C2

Western Medical Center
Anaheim...........6 C2

SIGHTS & ACTIVITIES
Crystal Cathedral...........7 D3
Knott's Berry Farm...........8 A1
Medieval Times...........9 A1
Ripley's Believe It or Not...........10 A1
Soak City USA...........(see 8)

SLEEPING 🏠
Alpine Inn...........11 C2
Anabella Hotel...........12 C2
Best Western Courtesy Inn......13 C2
Candy Cane Inn...........14 C2
Carousel Inn & Suites...........15 C2
Cortona Inn & Suites...........16 C2
Desert Palms Hotel & Suites...17 C2
Disneyland Hotel...........18 C2
Disney's Grand Californian Hotel..19 C2
Disney's Paradise Pier Hotel......20 C2
Knott's Berry Farm Resort Hotel..21 A1

EATING 🍴
Anaheim White House...........22 C2
Chu's Wok Inn...........23 C3
Joe's Crab Shack...........24 C3
Mr Stox...........25 D2

ENTERTAINMENT 🎭
Angel Stadium...........26 D2
Grove of Anaheim...........27 D2
Honda Center...........28 D2
Lucky Strike Lanes...........(see 29)

SHOPPING 🛍
Block at Orange...........29 D3

TRANSPORT
Greyhound...........30 C2

ORANGE COUNTY

DOING DISNEY RIGHT

Here are some tips to help you make the most of your visit:

- Plan on at least one day for each park, more if you want to go on all the rides. Lines are longest during summer and around major holidays. Generally, midweek is better than Friday, Saturday or Sunday, and arriving early is best. If you really want to avoid crowds, come in spring or fall or right after Labor Day. Nobody's here in February. However, crowds reappear for the holiday decorations in December and the first week of January.

- In summer bring a hat, suntan lotion, patience and – if cutting costs is important – bottled water.

- Many rides have minimum age and height requirements; avoid tantrums by prepping the kids.

- When you arrive at the park, expect to have your bags searched before passing through the turnstiles (looking for bombs, knives, etc). You're allowed to bring in food.

- Plan your time carefully. As you enter, pick up a park map and a show schedule to help you prioritize.

---

ticket. You'll receive a slip of paper showing a window of time for boarding. Show up within the window of time printed on the ticket and join the Fastpass line. There's still a wait, but it's shorter. You can only get one Fastpass at a time. If you're alone, ask the greeter at the entrance to each attraction if there's a single-rider line; you can often head to the front of the queue. Availability may depend on crowd size.

Tourist Information
Anaheim Visitor & Postal Center (☎ 714-991-4636; 640 W Katella Ave; ⏰ 8am-7pm Mon-Fri, 8am-3pm Sat, 4-8pm Sun; P ⌨) This family-owned visitor center, located in front of the Jolly Roger Hotel across from DCA, sells tickets for tours and local attractions. Lots

---

DISNEYLAND FASTPASS ATTRACTIONS

- Big Thunder Mountain Railroad (Frontierland, p241)

- Splash Mountain (Critter Country, p242)

- Autopia (Tomorrowland, p241)

- Space Mountain (Tomorrowland, p241)

- Buzz Lightyear Astro Blasters (Tomorrowland, p241)

- Indiana Jones Adventure (Adventureland, p241)

- Roger Rabbit's Car Toon Spin (Mickey's Toontown, p241)

---

of brochures, maps, and tips for travel in Anaheim and surrounding areas. Internet access costs $0.25 per minute. **Anaheim Visitors Center** (☎ 714-765-8888; www.anaheimvisitorscenter.com; 800 W Katella Ave; ⏰ 8am-5pm Mon-Fri, 9am-6pm Sun; P) Just south of DCA at the Anaheim Convention Center, offers information on countywide lodging, dining and transportation. The staff will help you book lodging and will answer questions via telephone. For a primer on OC's car culture, pick up the *Orange County Area Driving Guide;* it has simple directions and maps to nearby attractions. No public internet access. Parking costs $9.

Travel Agencies
Walt Disney Travel Company (☎ 714-520-5060, 800-828-0228; www.disneytravel.com) You can save substantially by booking your trip to Disneyland through this agent, which sells packages that include air, hotel and park tickets.

SIGHTS & ACTIVITIES
Disneyland Park
While the 'Happiest Place on Earth' designation is debatable, it's hard to deny the perceptible change in atmosphere as you're whisked by tram from the outside world into the heart of the resort. Wide-eyed children lean forward with anticipation while stressed-out parents sit back, finally relaxing. Uncle Walt's in charge, and he's taken care of every possible detail.

Walk through the gates of **Disneyland** (☎ recorded info 714-781-4565, live assistance 714-781-7290, switchboard 714-781-4000; www.disneyland.com; 1313 S Harbor Blvd)

(Continued on page 241)

SoCal Speaks

As they say in Hollywood, it's all about the story: your name in lights, the greatest new car, the chicest jeans, fusion cuisine, fusion families, rock, punk, eternal salvation! If the story sticks in LA, it becomes a trend, and if it becomes a trend in LA, it won't be long before the rest of the world catches on.

This may sound like an awesome responsibility, but Angelenos take it in their stride, creating great stories simply by going about their business, and the rest of SoCal follows suit.

So read on, dudes and dudettes, as SoCal-ites tell their stories – and the stories of their communities. You'll find Antonio Villaraigosa, who journeyed from the barrio of East LA to the mayor's office of the nation's second largest city (and the cover of *Newsweek*). A restaurateur and club owner tells how she made San Diego her community, and a preservationist takes on those who seek to destroy Palm Springs' architectural heritage. A propmaster shares the secret to success in Hollywood, an environmentalist says that LA is actually getting cleaner, and a columnist of 46 years tells a Santa Barbara tale of haves and have-nots.

LA director Dennis Woodruff's next project shifts up a gear
DAVID PEEVERS

A Wealth of Culture

NAME	Antonio Villaraigosa
AGE	54
OCCUPATION	Mayor, City of Los Angeles
RESIDENCE	Los Angeles

'LA is filled with artists and inventors, cultural entrepreneurs and institutions. Angelenos are pushing the envelope in every art form'

Los Angeles began as a small town founded by 44 Mexican settlers on the site where Olvera Street is today, so the history of this city is deeply entwined with Mexico and Latin America. LA is also home to Little Tokyo, Koreatown, Thai Town, Little Armenia, Chinatown, Filipinotown and many other ethnic enclaves. The diversity of Los Angeles is its strength. Put simply, we have a wealth of culture.

Economists tell us that more than any other city in the nation, LA's economy is driven by its creative industries, to the tune of $140 billion annually. It's our creativity – movies, music, art, fashion, food and design – that forms an integral part of life here. Home to the world's entertainment industry, LA is filled with artists and inventors, cultural entrepreneurs and institutions. Angelenos are pushing the envelope in every art form – and the world is coming to LA to witness and participate in the electricity and excitement that comes from so much creative output.

AS RELATED TO ANDREW BENDER

Oscar gets cleaned up for the Academy Awards at LA's Kodak Theater

RICK GERHARTER

East LA has a fruitful art scene
DAVID PEEVERS

ESSENTIAL LA ETHNIC EATS

Chosun Galbee (p186) If you've never tried Korean barbecue, this contemporary, neat-as-a-pin spot is the place to start. Even Koreans are impressed.

Nobu Malibu (p180) Nobu Matsuhisa's innovative Japanese cooking style spawned the Nobu empire of restaurants, with outposts in all the world's culinary capitals.

La Serenata de Garibaldi (p187) Bye-bye burritos, hello gourmet Mexican: think the freshest seafood in creamy, piquant sauces.

Papa Cristos (p186) A staple of LA's Greek community and a classic for lunchtime takeout or Thursday dinner with dancing.

Versailles (p180) A temple to Cuban cooking: the roast chicken with garlic sauce is so popular you'd think it had its own blog.

Stall selling Mexican goods in Olvera street
KRZYSZTOF DYDYNSKI

Nature & Nurture

NAME	Karin Hall
AGE	46
OCCUPATION	Executive Director, Heal the Bay
RESIDENCE	Santa Monica

'the bay will heal itself if given the opportunity'

LA's infrastructure is unusual: the sewer and storm-drain systems are separate, and storm drains empty directly into the ocean. So our job is educating people about what they can individually do to help preserve it.

It isn't just about toxic chemicals: it's also about trash; it's about not overwatering lawns, not overfertilizing, picking up after pets, not throwing cigarette butts, not using helium balloons and letting them go free – when they pop, they end up in the ocean, and sea birds and animals think they're food.

Here's the amazing thing, though: the bay will heal itself if given the opportunity. Twenty years ago there were dead zones, there were fish with three eyes, and tide pools had disappeared. Now most of the beaches in Los Angeles County and Southern California are A-rated during dry weather. The message is that people can coexist with the ocean; we just have to be really aware of the impact we have.

AS RELATED TO ANDREW BENDER

GO GREEN IN SOCAL

Farmers Markets
Visit them in communities throughout SoCal. The one in **Santa Monica (p209)** is the granddaddy of them all.

La Jolla Cove (p329)
Snorkel your way through sea caves and reefs.

Sustainable Vine Wine Tour (p400) Tour organic vineyards in Santa Barbara's Wine Country, in a bio-diesel van.

Santa Monica Bay: it's got to be perfect
DAVID PEEVERS

Propping Up Hollywood

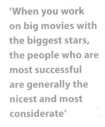

NAME	Will Grant
AGE	40
OCCUPATION	Propmaster
RESIDENCE	Venice

My interaction with actors comes while I'm doing props; I've worked with Adam Sandler, Jon Heder, Brad Pitt, Halle Berry, John Travolta, Hugh Jackman... You relate to them one worker to another, although they get a lot more fame for their work than I do. But they wouldn't be as well known as they are if the people around them weren't doing a good job, too. When you work on big movies with the biggest stars, the people who are most successful are generally the nicest and most considerate.

You work really closely with people for the duration of a movie. You almost form a little family, and then the family breaks up when the show ends. You may work with a few of the same people on your next job, but there are others you won't work with again for 10 years. I guess that contributes to LA being a city that's very 'in the moment' and not thinking so much about yesterday.

AS RELATED TO ANDREW BENDER

'When you work on big movies with the biggest stars, the people who are most successful are generally the nicest and most considerate'

HOT SPOTS FOR FILM & TV BUFFS

Paley Center for Media (p114) In this museum of TV and radio, you can view just about anything.

Studio Tours (p146) Warner Bros, Paramount, Sony and NBC all open their gates to guests on behind-the-scenes tours.

Outfest (p196) LA's gay & lesbian film festival is also its oldest and largest.

That's all, folks! Bugs Bunny calls it a wrap at Warner Brothers Studio
DAVID PEEVERS

Croce's Community

NAME	Ingrid Croce
AGE	60 years young
OCCUPATION	Owner, Croce's Restaurant and Jazz Bar
RESIDENCE	San Diego

'[San Diego] has a welcoming, open diversity that I've never found anywhere else'

GREAT LIVE MUSIC VENUES

Spaceland (p198) The likes of Beck and Pink have played and continue to play at this indie-rock palace.

Troubadour (p198) Iconic club from 1957 that launched the likes of James Taylor and Tom Waits, and continues to draw cutting-edge live acts.

Hollywood Bowl (p105) Summer home of the LA Philharmonic, and a dramatic venue for jazz, pop and film screenings.

I really believe in community.

When Jim [Ingrid's deceased husband, singer Jim Croce] and I were living in the Pennsylvania countryside, Arlo Guthrie, James Taylor and the Manhattan Transfer would all end up in our kitchen. While Jim played his guitar, I made frittatas [with ingredients] from our garden.

Then in 1973 we moved to San Diego, and immediately it felt like home. It has a welcoming, open diversity that I've never found anywhere else. On our last night together Jim and I visited the Gaslamp [Quarter], downtown. It was dilapidated and run-down, like *Deadwood*, but we wanted to build a restaurant and bar there and help build a new community. The next week Jim's plane crashed, and he was gone.

After I spent 12 years fighting legal battles for our royalties, a friend had dinner at our home and insisted, 'You should open a restaurant!' When a space came up for lease on the very same corner where Jim and I once stood, I opened Croce's Restaurant and Jazz Bar.

I've been lucky to watch the city grow from the ground up, and it's my dream fulfilled.

AS RELATED TO ANDREW BENDER

All things are bright and beautiful in the Gaslamp Quarter, downtown San Diego

RICHARD CUMMINS

When Buildings Go Bad

NAME	Tony Merchell
AGE	53
OCCUPATION	Member, Palm Springs Modern Committee; Founding VP, Palm Springs Preservation Commission
RESIDENCE	Desert Hot Springs

If a Spanish- or Mediterranean-style building deteriorates, it acquires a patina, whereas if a modern building deteriorates it really goes to hell pretty fast. When I came out to Palm Springs in the early 1990s, I was just stunned by the amazing quantity and quality of modern architecture, but it was all run-down and decrepit – the city was in a depression.

Then, in 1996, two important things happened: the *New Yorker* magazine ran an article about Palm Springs architecture; and I presented a paper about it at a conference in Slovakia. People began buying houses here, fixing them up and embracing that aesthetic: modern indoor-outdoor living, clean lines and exuberance. Palm Springs has really turned around over the last 10 years.

Now we're in a major battle to conserve commercial buildings. I think developers are intentionally letting their buildings go bad so that the general public doesn't care if they get bulldozed, and then the developers can put up four- or five-story condos.

AS RELATED TO ANDREW BENDER

'I was just stunned by the amazing quantity and quality of modern architecture'

SOCAL ARCHITECTURE MUST-SEES

Capitol Records Tower (p108) In a city of donut and hot dog stands shaped like donuts and hot dogs, this 1956 landmark sets the standard: shaped like a stack of 45s, at the heart of Hollywood.

Gamble House (p148) Touchstone of the California craftsman movement.

Downtown Santa Barbara (p378) The Spanish-Moorish architecture here is classic California.

Walt Disney Concert Hall (p134) LA's (and the 21st century's) signature building by LA's signature architect, Frank Gehry.

Tramway Gas Station (p350) Albert Frey's masterpiece is so iconic that Palm Springs made it the city's visitor center.

Architecture in Palm Springs is all shook up by the Elvis Honeymoon Hideaway

TONY MERCHELL

The Oprah Effect

NAME	Barney Brantingham
OCCUPATION	Columnist, Santa Barbara Independent
RESIDENCE	Santa Barbara

'the median home price in Santa Barbara is $1 million or more, and that's just for an ordinary house'

COMMUNITIES OF THE RICH & FAMOUS

Drive through these enclaves to get a feel for how the beautiful people live.

Montecito (p392) If it's good enough for Oprah... Good luck getting to see her house.

Bel Air (p115) It's hard to imagine not wanting to live in a mansion in Bel-Air's lush green hills.

Palm Desert (p361) Browse the El Paseo shopping street to rub elbows with well-dressed retirees and ladies who lunch.

Newport Beach (p261) It's no coincidence that TV's *The OC* was set here.

The view from the Santa Barbara County Courthouse tower would humble even the worst criminals

JOHN ELK III

In the early years of the 20th century, the rich of the Midwest and the East Coast [McCormicks, Peabodys, Fleischmanns et al] began coming here for the winter and building huge estates, some of which are still here. A lot of them were great philanthropists who helped build the community: art collections, stadiums, the harbor.

In more recent years came the 'new rich' – entertainment people, financial people – [buying] their second or third homes, and Oprah Winfrey with her $50 million home on 42 acres in Montecito in 2001. In part because of the 'Oprah effect', land value in Montecito shot up. People thought, 'If she's here, this must be a very special place to live.' Now the median home price in Santa Barbara is $1 million or more, and that's just for an ordinary house. In Montecito, the median is $2 million and there are homes in the $10-, $20- or $30-million range.

So you have Montecito millionaires, and then you have the Lower East Side of Santa Barbara. In some cases there are immigrants – legal or illegal – just scratching out a living, including families and young workers, squeezing five or 10 people into a house.

AS RELATED TO ANDREW BENDER

(Continued from page 232)

and along the red-brick path – suggestive of a red carpet – a stunning floral Mickey Mouse blooms before you. A sign above the nearby archway reads 'Here you leave today and enter the world of yesterday, tomorrow and fantasy' – an apt but slightly skewed greeting that's indicative of the upbeat, slightly skewed 'reality' of the park itself. A reality that's an undeniable delight to the millions of children who visit every year. This is their park, but adults who can willingly suspend disbelief and give in to the 'magic of Disney' will have just as much fun.

MAIN STREET USA

Fashioned after Walt's hometown of Marcelene, Missouri, bustling Main St, USA resembles the classic turn-of-the-20th-century all-American town. It's an idyllic, relentlessly upbeat representation complete with barbershop quartet, penny arcades, ice-cream shops and a steam train. The music playing in the background is from American musicals. There's a flag-retreat ceremony every afternoon.

If you're visiting on a special day and want to embrace the Disney experience wholemouse, stop by **City Hall** to pick up some ornamental flair in the form of over-sized buttons celebrating birthdays, anniversaries and the 'Just Married.' There's also an **Information Center** here. The **Disneyland Railroad**, a steam train that makes a loop around the park and rolls into four different stations, stops nearby. At the time of writing, **Great Moments with Mr Lincoln**, a 15-minute audio-animatronic presentation on Honest Abe, was expected to reopen in the not-too-distant future.

There's plenty of shopping, but wait until the end of the evening: Main St's stores remain open after the park's attractions close. Main St ends in the **Central Plaza**, the center of the park with five 'spokes' extending to the eight different lands (eg Frontierland and Tomorrowland). Lording over the plaza is **Sleeping Beauty Castle**, the castle featured on the Disney logo. Inside the iconic structure (which was fashioned after a real castle in southern Germany), dolls and big books tell the story of Sleeping Beauty.

Pay attention to the cool **optical illusion** along Main St. As you look from the entrance up the street toward Sleeping Beauty Castle, everything looks far away and big. When you're at the castle looking back, everything looks

closer and smaller – a technique known as forced perspective, a trick used on Hollywood sets where buildings are constructed at a decreasing scale to create an illusion of height or depth. Welcome to Disneyland.

TOMORROWLAND

How did 1950s imagineers envision the future? As a galaxy-minded community filled with monorails, rockets and Googie-style architecture, apparently. The retro-high-tech **Monorail** glides to a stop here, its rubber tires traveling a nine-minute, 2.5-mile round-trip route to Downtown Disney. Kiddies glide to a stop for the re-imagineered Submarine Voyage, debuting in 2007 as the new and improved – and more commercially attractive – **Finding Nemo Submarine Voyage**. Look for Nemo from within a refurbished submarine and rumble through an underwater volcanic eruption. On **Star Tours** you are clamped into a StarSpeeder vehicle piloted by a dysfunctional android on a wild and bumpy ride through a big-screen, slightly nauseating deep space. **Space Mountain**, one of the park's signature attractions and one of the best roller coasters in America, will take your head off as you hurtle into complete darkness at frightening speed.

FANTASYLAND

At the core of the park, behind Sleeping Beauty Castle, Fantasyland is filled with the characters of classic children's stories, such as Dumbo the Elephant and Peter Pan. Children like whirling around the **Mad Tea Party** teacup ride. Kids and ironic hipsters get a kick out of the un-Disneyesque, *Wind in the Willows*–inspired **Mr Toad's Wild Ride**, a loopy jaunt in an open-air jalopy through Mr Toad's mansion, underground London, Winky's pub and, sadly, the courthouse. If you only see one attraction in Fantasyland, visit **It's a Small World**, a boat ride past hundreds of animatronic children from all of the world's cultures singing the song of the same name in an astounding variety of languages. Young children go nuts for this musical voyage. Another classic, the **Matterhorn Bobsleds** is a steel-frame roller coaster that mimics a bobsled ride down a mountain. Smokers cluster in the smoking area behind the mountain.

FRONTIERLAND

Arrgh matey! In a bold nod to blatant commercialism, Captain Jack Sparrow and his pirate crew have hijacked an American classic. Frontierland's Tom Sawyer Island – the only attraction in the park personally designed by Uncle Walt – was recently re-imagined in wake of the successful *Pirates of the Caribbean* movies. Reopening in 2007 as **Pirate's Lair on Tom Sawyer Island**, the island now honors Tom in name only. After a raft ride to the island, wander among roving pirates, cannibal cages, ghostly apparitions and buried treasure. Somewhere, Injun Joe is smiling. The rest of Frontierland gives a nod to the rip-roarin' Old West.

ADVENTURELAND

Dedicated to exploration and adventure, Adventureland loosely derives its style from Southeast Asia and Africa. The hands-down highlight is the jungle-themed **Indiana Jones Adventure**. Enormous Humvee-type vehicles lurch and jerk through the wild for spine-tingling encounters with creepy crawlies and scary skulls in re-creations of stunts from the famous film series. (Look closely at Indie during the ride: is he real or animatronic?) Nearby, little ones love climbing the stairways of **Tarzan's Treehouse** and imagining what it would be like to live in the trees.

NEW ORLEANS SQUARE

Adjacent to Adventureland, New Orleans Square has all the charm of the French Quarter but none of the marauding drunks. New Orleans was Walt's and his wife Lilian's favorite city, and Walt paid tribute to it by building this stunning square. **Pirates of the Caribbean**, the longest ride in Disneyland (17 minutes) and 'inspiration' for the movies, opened in 1967 and was the first addition to the original park. You'll float through the subterranean haunts of tawdry pirates, where buccaneers' skeletons perch atop their mounds of booty. At the **Haunted Mansion** 999 'happy haunts' – spirits, goblins, shades and ghosts – appear and evanesce while you ride in a cocoonlike 'Doom Buggy' through web-covered graveyards of dancing skeletons.

CRITTER COUNTRY

Tucked behind the Haunted Mansion, Critter Country's main attraction is **Splash Mountain**, a flume ride which tranports you through the story of Brer Rabbit and Brer Bear, based on the controversial film *Song of the South*. Just past Splash Mountain, hop in a mobile beehive on **The Many Adventures of Winnie the Pooh**.

SHOWS & PARADES

Verify all shows and times once you arrive in the park; they are subject to change. See opposite for events at DCA.

In summer look for **fireworks** above the park, nightly around 9:30pm. (In winter, snow falls after the fireworks; check schedules for locations.) The **Parade of Dreams**, starring famous Disney characters, takes place twice daily in high season.

Fantasmic!, an outdoor extravaganza on Rivers of America across from New Orleans Square, may be the best show of all, using lasers, pyrotechnics (at one point the water catches fire), full-size ships and over-the-top production values. Arrive early to scope a spot – the best are down the front by the water – or splurge and reserve balcony seating upstairs in New Orleans Square. **Premium seating tickets** (☎ 714-781-4400; adult/child $59/49) can be reserved up to 30 days in advance. Ordinary seats are included in the price of park admission.

At the new **Princess Fantasy Faire** in Fantasyland, your little princesses and knights can join the Royal Court and meet some of the Disney Princesses.

Disney's California Adventure

Across the plaza from Disneyland's monument to fantasy and make-believe is Disney's California Adventure (DCA), an ode to California geography and history – or at least a sanitized version. DCA, which opened in 2001, covers more acres than Disneyland and feels less crowded, even on summer afternoons. If the other park leaves you feeling claustrophobic and jostled, you'll enjoy this one better, though it lacks the density of attractions and depth of imagination.

SUNSHINE PLAZA

The entrance to DCA was designed to look like an old-fashioned painted-collage postcard. As you pass through the turnstiles, note the gorgeous mosaics on either side of the entrance. One represents Northern California, the other Southern California. After passing under the Golden Gate Bridge, you'll arrive at Sunshine Plaza, where a 50ft-tall sun made of gold titanium 'shines' all the time (heliostats direct the rays of the real sun onto the Disney sun). A Michael Eisner–penned plaque here

---

DCA FASTPASS ATTRACTIONS

- Twilight Zone Tower of Terror (Hollywood Pictures Backlot, below)

- Rockin' California Screamin' (Paradise Pier, right)

- Mulholland Madness (Paradise Pier, right)

- Soarin' Over California (Golden State, right)

- Grizzly River Run (Golden State, right)

---

explains that the park celebrates the richness and diversity of California, its land, its people and 'the dreams that it continues to inspire.' For a personal moment of inspiration, close your eyes and stand in the plaza to hear – over the blaring beach music – the simulated sound of the surf as produced by the plaza's fountain. A neat trick.

HOLLYWOOD PICTURES BACKLOT

California's biggest factory of dreams is Tinseltown, presented here in the guise of Hollywood Pictures Backlot, complete with soundstages, movable props, and – of course – a studio store. If you're early, you'll have an unobstructed look at the forced-perspective **mural** at the end of the street, a sky-and-land backdrop that looks, at least in photographs, like the street keeps going. Very cool. The big attraction, though, is the 183ft-tall **Twilight Zone Tower of Terror**, a 13-story drop down an elevator chute in a haunted hotel – one eerily resembling the historic Hollywood Roosevelt Hotel in Los Angeles. From the upper floors of the tower, you'll have stellar views of the Santa Ana mountains, if only for a few heart-pounding seconds.

A BUG'S LAND

With its giant clovers, rideable insects, and oversized scraps of faux litter, A Bug's Land is understandably beloved by the 36-inches-and-under set. The attractions here were designed in conjunction with Pixar Studios after its film *A Bug's Life*. Little ones have a great time splashing in the 'irrigation systems' at **Bountiful Valley Farm**. (Come during the heat of the day so they don't get too cold afterward.) But the best attraction is the 3-D **It's Tough to Be a Bug**. Hilarious and oddly touching, it packs some unexpected tactile surprises.

GOLDEN STATE

Broken into sections that recognize California's cultural achievements, the Golden State has several distinct areas. **Condor Flats** recognizes the state's aerospace industry. Its main attraction, **Soarin' Over California**, is a virtual hang-gliding ride using IMAX technology; it's sure to give you 'bird-envy' as you float over the state's most beautiful landscapes and sights, including the Golden Gate Bridge, Yosemite Falls and, of course, Disneyland itself. Enjoy the light breeze as you soar, keeping your nostrils open for the smell of the sea, orange groves and pine forests blowing in the wind. **Grizzly River Run** takes you 'rafting' down a faux Sierra Nevada river; you *will* get wet so come when it's warm. Raise a glass to Napa at the **Golden Vine Winery**. Its wide, centrally located patio is a great place for relaxing and regrouping.

PARADISE PIER

If you like rides, you'll love Paradise Pier, which is supposed to look like a combination of all the beachside amusement piers in California. The state-of-the-art **Rockin' California Screamin'** roller coaster occupies 10 acres and resembles an old wooden coaster, but it's got a smooth-as-silk steel track: the beginning of the ride feels like you're being shot out of a cannon. Awesome. Want a bird's-eye view of the park? Head to the **Sun Wheel**, a giant Ferris wheel where gondolas pitch and yaw as the wheel makes its grand circuit. For 16-story views without the pitching and yawing, ask to be seated in one of the stationary gondolas.

SHOWS & PARADES

The premier show at DCA is **Aladdin**, a 40-minute one-act musical extravaganza, based

---

DCA SINGLE RIDER ATTRACTIONS

- Maliboomer (Paradise Pier, above)

- Mulholland Madness (Paradise Pier, above)

- Rockin' California Screamin' (Paradise Pier, above)

- Soarin' Over California (Golden State, above)

- Grizzly River Run (Golden State, above)

---

on the movie of the same name. It's in the Hyperion Theater on the Hollywood Studios Backlot. Arrive 30 to 60 minutes early to get good seats. Sit in the mezzanine for the best view of the flying carpet.

In the evening the **Electrical Parade** ends the day at DCA, with half a million tiny colored lights blinking on fabulous floats. If you're here in summer and have a park hopper ticket, first see the Electrical Parade, then head to Disneyland to watch the fireworks.

Downtown Disney

The 0.25-mile long pedestrian mall that is Downtown Disney feels longer than it is, mostly because it's packed with stores, restaurants, entertainment venues and, in summer, hordes of people. For specific recommendations on shopping, see p247.

On summer evenings musicians play outside. Short-term visitors to Downtown Disney can **self-park** at the lot just off Disneyland Dr; it's free for three hours. After that, rates jump to $6 for each additional hour, charged in 20-minute increments.

SLEEPING

Anaheim gets most hotel business from Disneyland tourism, but the city is also a year-round convention destination. Room rates spike accordingly, so the rates below may fluctuate. Most properties offer packages combining lodging with tickets to Disneyland or other local attractions. Some operate shuttles to the parks; inquire when you book. Many have family rooms that sleep up to six people.

For the full Disney experience, stay in one of the resort's three **hotels** (☎ reservations 714-956-6425, 800-225-2024; www.disneyland.com): Disney's Paradise Pier Hotel, Disneyland Hotel and Disney's Grand Californian Hotel. One-night stays are expensive, but rates fluctuate almost daily. Save money by booking multinight stays and vacation packages. Each hotel has at least two restaurants and two bars, plus a business center with computers where you can check your email. Wi-fi access at these hotels is included in your resort fee. Inquire at reception about wi-fi hotspots and access cards. High-speed internet access is available with a cable in rooms.

Budget

HI Fullerton (☎ 714-738-3721, 800-909-4776, ext 138; www .hiusa.org; 1700 N Harbor Blvd, Fullerton; dm members/non-

members $22/25; ☒ Jun-Sep; **P** wi-fi) About five miles north of Disneyland, this two-story Spanish-style cottage – formerly a damkeeper's house – has a kitchen, washer and dryer, screened-in porch, internet access and beds for 20 guests in three clean dorm rooms (male, female, mixed). The office closes at 11:30pm but 24-hour access is available. Staff are friendly. Bus 47 runs to the hostel from the Anaheim Greyhound station. From the Amtrak station, take bus 43. To/from Disneyland is a straight shot on bus 43. Open summer only.

our pick Lemon Tree Hotel (☎ 714-772-0200; 866-311-5595; www.hotelaaa.com; 1600 E Lincoln Ave; r $69-129; **P** 📧 🚇 wi-fi) It's hard to be hip in Anaheim, but Aussie-owned Lemon Tree gives it a shot with a funky, upbeat charm that will have you forgetting Fastpasses in no time. Rooms are decorated with faux-rustic, mission-style flair – wrought-iron lamps, paintings of senoritas, chunky wood furniture – and some have kitchens. It's 2.5 miles and two left turns to Disneyland. Extended stays available.

Knott's Berry Farm Resort Hotel (☎ 714-995-1111, 866-752-2444; www.knottshotel.com; 7675 Crescent Ave, Buena Park; r $69-189; **P** 📧 🚇 wi-fi) If you want a theme-park vacation for less money, this eight-story resort hotel at Knott's Berry Farm is a great alternative. Ask about the themed Camp Snoopy rooms, located in a separate section of the hotel, where your kids will be treated to *Peanuts* gang decor and goodnight visits from Snoopy himself. All for an extra $50. Complimentary shuttle to Disneyland. Wi-fi costs $12.

Best Western Courtesy Inn (☎ 714-772-2470, 800-233-8062; www.bestwestern.com/courtesyinn; 1070 W Ball Rd; r $89-129; **P** 📧 🚇 wi-fi) Refreshingly honest management will tell you there's nothing particularly special about this 37-room motel. That said, the rooms are clean and reasonably priced, and all have a microwave and fridge. Walk to Disneyland in 10 minutes.

Midrange

Desert Palms Hotel & Suites (☎ 714-535-1133, 888-788-0482; www.desertpalmshotel.com; 631 W Katella Ave; r $59-165, ste $185-449; **P** 📧 🚇 wi-fi) A five-story, 187 room hotel bordering DCA, the mazelike Desert Palms has rooms with microwaves and fridges; downstairs there's a bar, restaurant, fitness center, hot tub and continental breakfast in the morning. A little worn but that may be due to the rotating hordes of families. Wi-fi costs $10 per day.

Cortona Inn & Suites (☎ 714-971-5000, 800-416-6819; www.cortonainn.com; 2029 S Harbor Blvd; r $69-329; P ⊠ wi-fi) Formerly a Days Inn, this well-maintained two-story motel has fridges and microwaves in every room, plus on-site laundry facilities and small games room. Rates include continental breakfast. You can walk to Disneyland in 20 minutes. Wi-fi costs $10 per day.

Candy Cane Inn (☎ 714-774-5284, 800-345-7057; www.candycaneinn.net; 1747 S Harbor Blvd; r $99-189; P ⊠ wi-fi) You'll find more flower beds than candy canes at this oh-so-cute motel, known for welcoming grounds bursting with gorgeous blooms. Rooms have all mod-cons, plus down comforters and plantation shutters. The hotel is adjacent to the main gate to Disneyland. It's a top choice and booking a year out is strongly advised.

Anabella Hotel (☎ 714-905-1050, 800-863-4888; www.anabellahotel.com; 1030 W Katella Ave; r $119-189; P ☐ ⊠ wi-fi) Formerly three separate motels on adjacent lots, this sprawling, 7-acre complex has the feel of a laid-back country club, complete with trams carrying guests from the lobby to their buildings. Rooms are decorated in Spanish Colonial style, with extras such as granite bathroom counters, fridge and web TV. Grab a Tanganita at the on-site Tangerine Grill & Patio. Parking costs $10 per night, wi-fi $10 per day.

Carousel Inn & Suites (☎ 714-758-0444, 800-854-6767; www.carouselinnandsuites.com; 1530 S Harbor Blvd; r $140, ste $180-240; P ☐ ⊠ wi-fi) Just over the berm from Disneyland, this recently remodeled four-story motel makes an effort to look good, with upgraded furniture and pots of flowers hanging from its exterior corridors' wrought-iron railings. The rooftop pool has great views of Disneyland's fireworks. Suites sleep four to eight people. It's a sister property with Anabella Hotel. Wi-fi is $10 per day.

Alpine Inn (☎ 714-535-2186, 800-772-4422; www .alpineanaheim; 715 W Katella Ave; r $149-159; P ⊠) Connoisseurs of kitsch will hug their Hummels over this snow-covered chalet sporting an A-frame exterior and icicle-covered roofs. Right on the border of DCA, the inn also has views of the Ferris wheel. Rooms are on the older side, but clean. There are five family-friendly suites.

Disney's Paradise Pier Hotel (☎ 714-999-0990; 1717 S Disneyland Dr; r $225-255; P ☐ ⊠) Sunbursts, surfboards and a giant superslide are all on deck at the Paradise Pier Hotel, the cheapest, but most fun, of the Disney hotel trio. Kids will love the beachy decor, not to mention the 186ft waterslide and the tiny-tot video room filled with mini Adirondack chairs. Rooms are just as spotlessly kept as at the others and are decorated with colorful fabrics and custom furniture. The hotel connects directly to DCA. Request a room overlooking the park.

Top End

Disneyland Hotel (☎ 714-778-6600; 1150 Magic Way; r $285-325; P ☐ ⊠) Built in 1955, the year Disneyland opened, the park's original hotel seems in need of a dash of bibbidi-bobbidi-boo. Staff seem a little less 'happy' here, and the rooms – though good-sized – are a bit more tired than inspired. But this 990-room hotel hasn't turned into a pumpkin yet; it's redeemed by its great pool – the best of the three Disney hotels – and a 110ft waterslide. The monorail stops outside.

our pick Disney's Grand Californian Hotel (☎ 714-635-2300; 1600 S Disneyland Dr; r $380-705; P ☐ ⊠) Soaring timber beams rise majestically above the cathedral-like lobby of the six-story Grand Californian, a monument to the American Arts and Crafts movement and the top choice for lodging at Disneyland. Rooms have cushy amenities, such as triple-sheeted beds, down pillows and all-custom furnishings, from bedspreads to bathrobes. Outside there's a redwood waterslide into the pool. At night, kids wind down with bedtime stories by the lobby's giant stone hearth. But it's not all about the kids – for a little personal pampering, sip tea in the Tea Pavilion as you await your exotic coconut rub and milk ritual wrap at the plush Mandara Spa. Even if you're not staying here, a brief respite in the astounding lobby is a must (and totally acceptable). Enter from Downtown Disney or DCA.

EATING

For both parks, call **Disney Dining** (☎ 714-781-3463) if you have dietary restrictions, need to make dining reservations or want to inquire about character dining (meals during which Disney characters work the dining room and greet the kids). If you're here for a birthday, call and ask about decorate-your-own-cake parties and birthday meals (you'll need to order 48 hours ahead). Every restaurant at Disneyland Resort has a kids' menu. Park maps indicate restaurants and cafés where you can find healthy foods and vegetarian options; look for the red apple icon.

Disneyland Park

In the park itself, each 'land' has several places to eat. The following are some spots for sit-down dining. All can be reached at Disney Dining.

Carnation Cafe (Main St; mains under $11; ☯ 8am-9pm) Good sandwiches and hot main courses. Try the chicken pot pie or the steak melt.

River Belle Terrace (Frontierland; mains under $12; ☯ 10am-3pm Mon-Thu, 9am-9pm Fri-Sun) Kids love the Mickey Mouse pancakes served until 11:30am.

Blue Bayou (New Orleans Square; mains lunch $19-30, dinner $25-35) Surrounded by the 'bayou' inside Pirates of the Caribbean, this is the top choice for sit-down dining in Disneyland Park. Famous for its Monte Cristo sandwiches at lunch, and Creole and Cajun specialties at dinner. Make reservations or wait in line.

Disney's California Adventure

Trattoria at Golden Vine Winery (☎ 714-781-3463; mains $10-13; ☯ 11am-6pm) DCA's best place for a sit-down lunch serves surprisingly inexpensive and wonderfully tasty Italian pasta, salads and gourmet sandwiches.

Vineyard Room (☎ 714-781-3463; 3-course prix fixe $43, with wine $67; ☯ dinner Fri-Sun) DCA's white-tablecloth dining room serves contemporary Cal-Italian cuisine in three-course set menus, from polenta and portobello to prosciutto and veal. If you want to splurge but can't quite swing the Napa Rose, this is a fine backup.

There's a food court at Pacific Wharf.

Downtown Disney

Most of the restaurants in Downtown Disney are chains that can accommodate large crowds. Call ahead for priority seating or bookings.

Catal & Uva Bar (☎ 714-774-4442; mains breakfast $7.50-11, lunch $9-40, dinner $17-40; ☯ breakfast, lunch & dinner) The chef cooks up a fusion of Californian and Mediterranean cuisines (pappardelle pasta with braised lamb, whitefish with piquillo pepper sauce) at this airy two-story restaurant decorated in a sunny Mediterranean-Provençal style with exposed beams and lemon-colored walls. Sit on the balcony for downtown's best midrange dining.

La Brea Bakery (☎ 714-781-3463; mains breakfast $8-13, lunch & dinner $10-22; ☯ breakfast, lunch & dinner) For

a no-fuss, tasty meal, try the mouth-watering selection of stuffed *paninis* (sandwiches) and fresh salads at this breezy café best known for its breads and lighter fare. In a hurry? Grab a premade sandwich from the express line.

Naples Ristorante & Pizzeria (☎ 714-781-3463; $12-27; ☯ lunch & dinner) Resist the temptation to swipe a glistening slice of pepperoni from a passing table as you're led to your seat at this bustling pizza and pasta joint. If you just can't wait, there's an express line serving $4.50 slices to go.

our pick **Napa Rose** (☎ 714-300-7170; Grand Californian Hotel, 1600 S Disneyland Dr; mains $32-38, 4-course prix fixe $75; ☯ dinner) There are echoes of Frank Lloyd Wright in the stunning white-tablecloth dining room of the Grand Californian Hotel, where soaring windows, high-back Arts and Crafts–style chairs and towering ceilings befit Disney's – and possibly all of Orange County's – finest restaurant. On the plate, the contemporary 'California Wine Country' (read: Northern California) cuisine is as impeccably crafted and visually stunning as Sleeping Beauty Castle. Make reservations and bring your checkbook.

Outside Disneyland

Most restaurants on the streets surrounding Disneyland and DCA are chains. By driving just a mile or so away, variety improves.

Chu's Wok Inn (☎ 714-750-3511; 13053 Chapman Ave, Orange; dinner $7-15; ☯ 9:30am-9pm Sun-Thu, 9:30am-10pm Fri & Sat; Ⓟ) There's table service at this family-run, hole-in-the-wall Mandarin Chinese strip-mall restaurant near the Crystal Cathedral. It's just east of Harbor Blvd at Haster St.

Joe's Crab Shack (☎ 714-703-0505; 12011 Harbor Blvd, Garden Grove; mains $8.50-23; ☯ 11am-10pm Sun-Thu, 11am-11pm Fri & Sat) This dockside fish house, complete with a decorated corrugated-metal ceiling, has a decent selection of some pretty good food, especially for a chain seafood restaurant. Lots of customers digging into crabs and nibbling on mac and cheese.

Mr Stox (☎ 714-634-2994; 1105 E Katella Ave; mains lunch $12-19, dinner $20-40; ☯ lunch Mon-Fri, dinner daily) Mr Stox serves some of Anaheim's best Cal-American cooking in a clubby atmosphere with oval booths and thick carpeting. The chef bakes five different breads daily. Prime steaks. Great seafood. Pricey. Wear nice shoes and make reservations.

Anaheim White House (☎ 714-772-1381; 887 S Anaheim Blvd; mains lunch $13-22, dinner $27-39; ☯ lunch

Mon-Fri, brunch Sun, dinner daily) Fancy your dinner inside a wedding cake? With delicate white lights on the outside and ornate gold leaf on the inside, this unapologetically frou-frou restaurant is just one fancy spoon from over-the-top. But formality can be refreshing in laid-back SoCal, especially if backed by fine Franco-Italian cuisine. From prawn-garnished fettuccine to filet mignon with gorgonzola sauce, the choices are delectable. Great for special occasions. Make reservations and get gussied up.

DRINKING

You can't buy any alcohol in Disneyland Park, but you can at DCA and in Downtown Disney.

Uva Bar (☎ 714-774-4442; Downtown Disney) Named after the Italian word for grape, centrally situated Uva is the best outdoor spot in Downtown Disney to sip wine, nibble tapas and people-watch. There are 40 wines available by the glass.

ESPN Zone (☎ 714-300-3776; Downtown Disney) Come early and score a leather recliner with waitress service at this sports and drinking emporium with 175 TV monitors – there are even screens above the men's room urinals. Only dedicated sports fans will be able to tolerate the visual and aural onslaught.

Hook's Point (☎ 714-781-3463; Disneyland Hotel; ☾ closed Sun & Mon in winter) A great alternative to the frat-boy joints, this quiet wine bar in the Disneyland Hotel has good fruit-and-cheese platters and sparkling wine by the glass.

ENTERTAINMENT

Disney's cocoonlike atmosphere can lead one to forget there's a thriving city outside its walls. But without venturing too far from the magic, you can actually catch great live bands and major-league games. Too tired to venture far? No worries, Downtown Disney offers occasionally decent live music, a 12-screen cinema and hours of people-watching.

Downtown Disney

AMC Theatres (☎ 714-769-4262; ☾ 11am-11pm Sun-Thu, 10am-midnight Fri & Sat; **P**) Pick from 12 screens of current-release movies; every theater has stadium seating. Parking is free for up to five hours with movie validation.

Ralph Brennan's New Orleans Jazz Kitchen (☎ 714-776-5200; www.rbjazzkitchen.com; Downtown Disney; ☾ 11am-10pm Sun-Thu, 11am-11pm Fri & Sat) You can hear New Orleans jazz on the weekends and piano jazz weeknights at this bar and restaurant. The food quality is erratic but sometimes good.

House of Blues (☎ 714-778-2583; www.hob.com; Downtown Disney) The best place for rock and blues, HOB occasionally gets some heavy-hitters; call or check online for show times and tickets. Johnny Lang, Lindsey Buckingham and *American Idol*'s Elliott Yamin are a few recent names on the lineup. On Sunday there's a fun gospel brunch; make reservations. Come for the music, not the food.

Outside Disneyland

Grove of Anaheim (☎ 714-712-2700; www.thegroveofanaheim.com; 2200 E Katella Ave; **P**) At this moderately small venue, headliners range from Alice Cooper to UB40 to Shawn Colvin; call for current schedules. Sight lines are great. Parking costs $8.

Angel Stadium (☎ 714-940-2000, 888-796-4256; www.angelsbaseball.com; 2000 Gene Autry Way, Anaheim; tickets $9-60; **P**) The Los Angeles Angels of Anaheim play major-league baseball from May to October. Parking costs $8.

Honda Center (☎ 877-945-3946; www.mightyducks.com; 2695 E Katella Ave, Anaheim; **P**) 2007 Stanley Cup winners the Anaheim Ducks play hockey from September to May at this venue, formerly known as Arrowhead Pond. Parking costs $12.

SHOPPING

Each 'land' has its own shopping, appropriate to its theme.

Disneyland Park

Emporium (☎ 714-781-7290; Main St) The biggest store in Disneyland has the largest variety of souvenirs, clothing and Disneyana, from T-shirts to mouse ears.

China Closet (☎ 714-781-7290; Main St) This shop sells porcelain Disney figurines and snow globes.

Downtown Disney

Most shops in Downtown Disney open and close with the parks.

Compass Books & Cafe (☎ 714-502-9999) Decorated in the style of an old-school Explorers' Club, high adventure feels nigh at Compass Books. If it would just add a few comfy couches, the store would be perfect. In the meantime, peruse bestsellers, manga paperbacks and local travel tomes.

Island Charter (☎ 714-635-9499) Images of Earhart and Lindbergh come to mind wandering this travel-minded store complete with Tilly hats, bomber jackets, Tommy Bahama shirts and model planes.

Club Libby Lu (☎ 714-772-3793) Have daughters? If so, the sparkly, pop-infused charms of Club Libby Lu will throw off your schedule. From 'I love Troy' messenger bags and sassy bracelet charms to a style studio and minispa, it's all, like, totally cute – and precisely marketed to entrap your tweens. Resistance is futile.

Starabilias (☎ 714-284-0155) Autograph hounds, start here. From jeans signed by Jimi Hendrix to a poster from *The Graduate* signed by Dustin Hoffman and Anne Bancroft, there's an eclectic mix of stars and memorabilia plus trading cards and retro lunchboxes.

Vault 28 (☎ 714-300-7004) There's a chance this store is actually an illusion. From distressed T-shirts with edgy Cinderella prints to black tank tops patterned with white skulls, the hip inventory is disconcerting. There's even an artsy photo of a ruffled, morning-after Mickey looking to dash across the street in his cleanest dirty shirt. The store stocks a few familiar brands like Chip & Pepper, but it's the Disney lines – Kingdom Couture and Disney Vintage – that are most intriguing.

World of Disney (☎ 714-300-7919) Pirates and princesses are hot at this massive mecca of mouse-related merchandising. Grab last-minute must-haves here.

GETTING THERE & AWAY
Air

See p229 for information on air connections. **Southern California Gray Line/Coach America** (☎ 714-978-8855, 800-828-6699; www.graylineanaheim.com) runs the Disneyland Resort Express between LAX and Disneyland-area hotels at least hourly ($19/28 one way/round-trip to LAX, $14/24 to SNA).

Bus

Greyhound (☎ 714-999-1256; www.greyhound.com; 100 W Winston Rd) has frequent departures to/from Downtown Los Angeles ($9.50, 1½ hours) and San Diego ($17, 2¼ to 3 hours).

Car

The Anaheim Resort is just off I-5 on Harbor Blvd, about 30 miles south of Downtown LA.

The park is roughly bordered by Ball Rd, Disneyland Dr, Harbor Blvd and Katella Ave.

Arriving at Disneyland and DCA is like arriving at an airport. Giant easy-to-read overhead signs indicate which ramps you need to take for the theme parks, hotels or Anaheim's streets. The system is remarkably ordered.

PARKING

All-day parking costs $11, cash only. Enter the 'Mickey & Friends' parking structure from southbound Disneyland Dr at Ball Rd. (It's the largest car park in the world, with a capacity of 10,300 vehicles.) Follow the signs and take the tram to reach the parks. The lots stay open until two hours after the parks close.

The lots for Downtown Disney are reserved for shoppers and have a different rate structure: the first three hours are free, with an additional two more free hours if you have a validation from a table-service restaurant or the movie theater. After that you'll pay $6 per hour, up to $30 a day. Downtown Disney also has valet parking from 5pm to 2am for an additional $6 plus tip. Cash only.

Each of the three Disneyland Resort hotels has a parking area for guests.

Train

The depot next to Angels Stadium is where **Amtrak** (☎ 714-385-1448; www.amtrak.com; 2150 E Katella Ave) trains stop. Tickets to/from LA's Union Station are $12 (45 minutes), to San Diego $24 (two hours).

GETTING AROUND
Bus

The bus company **Anaheim Resort Transit** (ART; ☎ 714-563-5287, 888-364-2787; www.rideart.org) provides frequent service to/from Disneyland from hotels in the immediate area, saving headaches from parking and walking. An all-day pass costs $3 and must be bought before boarding at one of a dozen kiosks or online, otherwise it's $3 each trip. Children under nine travel free.

Many hotels and motels have free shuttles to Disneyland and other area attractions, so check at the reception.

Monorail

Take the monorail from Tomorrowland to the Disneyland Hotel, across from Downtown Disney, and save about 20 minutes of walking time. It's free if you've bought a park admission ticket.

AROUND DISNEYLAND

Disneyland's not the only game in town. Within five easy miles of the mouse house you'll find several sights and attractions worth a visit in their own right. Anaheim's streets are laid out in an easy-to-navigate grid, with most neighborhoods flowing seamlessly from one to the next. So get out, explore, expand your horizons. It is a small world, after all.

KNOTT'S BERRY FARM

They bring 'em in by the busloads to **Knott's** (☎ 714-220-5200; www.knotts.com; 8039 Beach Blvd, Buena Park; adult/3-11yr $50/19), the first theme park in America. Just 4 miles northwest of Anaheim off the I-5, Knott's is smaller and less frenetic than the Disneyland parks, but it can be fun, especially for roller-coaster fanatics, young teens and kids who love the *Peanuts* characters.

Opening hours vary seasonally, so call ahead. On days that the park is open past 6pm, special admission prices apply for entry after 4pm (adult/child $25/19). Check the website or call for the latest discounts – some can be substantial. Bring dry clothes and bathing suits for the kids. Parking costs $10. There's free three-hour parking for Knott's California Marketplace.

The park opened in 1932, when Mr Knott's boysenberries (a blackberry-raspberry hybrid) and Mrs Knott's fried-chicken dinners attracted crowds of local farmhands. Mr Knott built an imitation ghost town to keep them entertained, and eventually hired local carnival rides and charged admission. Mrs Knott kept frying the chicken but the rides and Old West buildings became the main attraction.

Today the park keeps the Old West theme alive with shows and demonstrations at **Ghost Town**, but it's the thrill rides that draw the crowds. The newest is 2007's spinning **Sierra Sidewinder**, a coaster that rips through banks and turns while rotating on its axis. Nearby, the suspended, inverted **Silver Bullet** screams through a corkscrew, a double spiral and an outside loop. From the ground, look up to see the dirty socks and bare feet of suspended riders who've removed their shoes. **Xcelerato** is a '50s-themed roller coaster that blasts you, as if from a cannon, from 0mph to 82mph in under 2½ seconds. There's a hair-raising twist at the top. **Camp Snoopy** is a kiddy wonderland populated by the *Peanuts* characters.

In October Knott's hosts what is regarded as SoCal's best and scariest Halloween party. On select dates from late September through to Halloween, the park closes at 5:30pm and reopens at 7pm as Knott's Scary Farm. Horror-minded thrills include creepy mazes including the Doll Factory and Killer Clowns, monster-themed shows, and horrific scare zones, not to mention 1000 restless monsters roaming the park.

There are plenty of eateries here but the classic meal is the button-busting fried chicken and mashed potato dinner at the nuthin'-fancy **Mrs Knott's Chicken Dinner Restaurant** (chicken dinner $14, mains $15-20). In a hurry? Grab a bucket from **Chicken-to-Go** next door. Both are in the California Marketplace, a shopping and dining mall outside the park's main gate.

Next to Knott's is the affiliated water park **Soak City USA** (☎ 714-220-5200; www.knotts.com; adult/3-11yr $28/17, after 3pm $17/17; ☾ May-Sep), with high-speed slides, tubes and flumes. You must have a bathing suit without rivets or metal pieces to go on some slides. Bring a towel.

MEDIEVAL TIMES DINNER & TOURNAMENT

Hear ye, hear ye! All those who have sired knights-to-be and future princesses, gather ye clans and proceed forthwith to **Medieval Times** (☎ 714-523-1100, 888-935-6878; www.medievaltimes.com; 7662 Beach Blvd; adult/under 12yr $53/36) for an evening-long medieval feast and performance. Yep, it's over-the-top but in a harmless, party-like-it's-1199 sort of way. Guests root for various knights as they joust, fence and show off their horsemanship (on real live Andalusian horses) to protect the honor of the kingdom and the beautiful princess. Dinner is OK – roast chicken and spare ribs that you eat with your hands – but the show's the thing. Make reservations and accept that you'll be wearing a cardboard crown for the evening.

RIPLEY'S BELIEVE IT OR NOT!

Cannibals, deformities and The Last Supper designed in toast: exactly what you'd expect from **Ripley's** (☎ 714-522-7045; www.ripleysbp.com; 7850 Beach Blvd; adult/4-11yr/senior $14/10/12; ☾ 10am-6pm Mon-Fri, 9am-7pm Sat & Sun), one block north of Knott's. For those unfamiliar with the museum and its founder, Robert L Ripley was

---

DETOUR: RICHARD NIXON LIBRARY

The bad boy of presidential libraries recently got a reality check. Long maligned because of inaccuracies in the Watergate exhibit room, the privately run **Richard Nixon Presidential Library & Birthplace** (☎ 714-993-5075; www.nixonlibrary.org; 18001 Yorba Linda Blvd, Yorba Linda; adult/7-11yr/student/senior $10/4/6/7; ☺ 10am-5pm Mon-Sat, 11am-5pm Sun) was transferred in 2007 to federal control with oversight by the National Archives. The old Watergate exhibit – which called the scandal a 'coup' instigated by Nixon's rivals and provided favorably edited White House tapes – was completely torn out; a bold move considering Nixon is buried just outside. In exchange, the library will receive 42 million pages of the president's papers and almost 4000 hours of tapes. The Watergate exhibit will be completely revamped. The museum offers a fascinating walk though America's modern history. Noteworthy exhibits include excerpts from the Nixon and Kennedy debates, the pistol given to Nixon by Elvis Presley, audiotapes of conversations with Apollo 11 astronauts while on the moon and access to the presidential helicopter, complete with wet bar and ash trays. The library is in Yorba Linda, in northeastern Orange County. To get there, exit east on Yorba Linda Blvd from Hwy 57 and continue straight to the library.

---

an adventurer, reporter and collector who traveled the globe in the 1920s and '30s in search of curiosities. His documentation of human oddities has provided twisted entertainment for years. Kids will rave or be scarred for life – know your child before entering. At this particular Ripley's there's a rather unfortunate tennis ball–sized exhibit on the left as you exit the jungle corridor. We can say no more: see for yourself and join us in suffering the unforgettable imagery.

BOWERS MUSEUM OF CULTURAL ART

Gliding under the radar like a stealth bomber, the small, generally unknown **Bowers Museum** (☎ 714-567-3600; www.bowers.org; 2002 N Main St; all exhibits adult/student & senior $17/12, prices may fluctuate depending on special exhibit; ☺ 11am-4pm Tue-Sun) explodes onto the scene every year or two with a remarkable special exhibit that reminds LA-centric museum-goers that the Bowers is a power player on the local and national scenes. At the time of writing, China's famed Terra Cotta Warriors were due to make their American debut from May 18 to October 12, 2008. The permanent exhibit is impressive too, with a rich collection of pre-Columbian, African, Oceanic and Native American art.

DISCOVERY SCIENCE CENTER

Heading south on the I-5, follow the giant 10-story cube – balanced on one of its points – to the doors of the hottest kiddie attraction in town, the **Discovery Science Center** (☎ 714-542-2823; www.discoverycube.org; 2500 N Main St; adult/child $13/10; ☺ 10am-6pm). More than 100 interactive displays await in exhibit areas named Dy-

namic Earth, The Body, Dino Quest and more. Step into the eye of a hurricane – your hair will get mussed – or grab a seat in the Shake Shack for a 6.9 quake. Warning: parents may be tempted to nudge their kids aside for a turn at many of the displays.

CRYSTAL CATHEDRAL

You needn't be an 'Hour of Power' fan to appreciate the architecture of the **Crystal Cathedral** (☎ 714-971-4000; www.crystalcathedral.org; 12141 Lewis St) in Garden Grove, about 2 miles southeast of Disneyland. The awe-inspiring cathedral is built in the shape of a four-pointed star and boasts 10,661 windows, seating for 3000 and a 16,000-pipe organ. Designed by the late Cleveland-born Philip Johnson, International Style architect turned postmodernist, the church anchors a vast campus of gardens, reflecting pools, fountains and sculpture. Explore on your own or take a free 30- to 45-minute tour (offered regularly from 9am to 3:30pm Monday to Saturday).

ORANGE

pop 127,000

The city of Orange, southeast of Disneyland, is home to the mega-sized mall **Block at Orange** (☎ 714-769-4000; www.theblockatorange.com; 20 City Blvd West), where you'll find all the latest OC chain-store fashion, plus restaurants, movie theaters and a skateboarding park. But there's more charm in the town's historic center, called **Old Towne Orange**. It was originally laid out by Alfred Chapman and Andrew Glassell who, in 1869, received the 1 sq mile piece of real estate in lieu of legal fees.

Shopping here surrounds a **plaza** (cnr Chapman & Glassell Sts) where you can find the best, most concentrated collection of antiques, collectibles and consignment shops in Orange County. Though it's fun to browse, real bargains are rare and some dealers may try to pass off replicas as antiques. Sprinkled among the antique shops are the **Dragonfly Shops & Gardens** (☎ 714-289-4689; 260 N Glassell St), a white-picketed cottage selling native Californian plants and garden-minded gifts, and **Frogs Breath Cheese Store** (☎ 714-744-1773; 143 N Glassell St) where wine and cheese tastings are held Thursday through Sunday among gourmet pastas, oils, chocolates and fancy fromages.

Try breakfast at the **Filling Station** (☎ 714-289-9714; 201 N Glassell St; mains under $10; ☺ breakfast & lunch), a former gas station now serving gourmet scrambles and pancake sandwiches instead of unleaded. For a quick cup of joe and a bagel, recharge at locally owned **Ugly Mugs Cafe** (☎ 714-997-5610; 261 N Glassell St). For lunch or dinner, scope a patio table at **Felix Continental Cafe** (☎ 714-633-5842; 36 Plaza Sq; mains lunch $5-14, dinner $9.50-14; ☺ breakfast, lunch & dinner). This Orange institution serves perfectly flavored Caribbean, Cuban and Spanish mains, most accompanied by several tasty sides. Cal-American **Citrus City Grille** (☎ 714-639-9600; 122 N Glassell St; mains lunch $9-22, dinner $14-35) is pricey and noisy, but the food's terrific.

For entertainment, try **Lucky Strike Lanes** (☎ 714-937-5263; Block at Orange, 20 City Blvd West; ☺ 11am-1am Mon-Thu, 11am-2am Fri & Sat), a stylin' bowling alley. On weekends call to reserve a table or lane. It costs $7 per game, plus $4 shoe rental.

LITTLE SAIGON

Ready for a break from big-eared mice, generic malls and boysenberry pie? Head to Little Saigon in nearby Westminster, southwest of Anaheim near the junction of I-405 and Hwy 22. Vietnamese immigrants began arriving here after the end of the Vietnam War in the 1970s, carving out their own vibrant commercial district around the intersection of Bolsa and Brookhurst Aves. At its heart is the **Asian Garden Mall** (☎ 714-894-8018; 9200 Bolsa Ave), a behemoth of a structure packed with 400 ethnic boutiques, including herbalists and jade jewelers. Across the street, the **New Saigon Mall Cultural Court** marries commercialism and spirituality with its impressive display of statues and murals.

One of the best reasons to visit is the food. Newbies can start at **Lee's Sandwiches** (☎ 714-903-8855; 9200 Bolsa Ave; www.leessandwiches.com; Asian sandwiches $2-3), a fast-growing Western chain serving budget-friendly Asian sandwiches alongside traditional American favorites. The traditional toppings on these belly-fillers provide a delish, not-too-spicy kick. Try the pork.

A great casual eatery at Asian Garden Mall is **Pho 79** (☎ 714-893-1883) which has a variety of noodle and vegetable dishes. The *pho ga* (chicken noodle soup) is superb. For a real treat (involving some fun navigational requirements) visit **Brodard** (☎ 714-530-1744; 9892 Westminster Ave; mains $5.95-11.95; ☺ 8am-9pm, closed Tue), known for its *nem nuong cuon* – rice paper wrapped tightly around spamlike pork paste and served with a delicious special sauce. It's oddly addictive. Here's the route: drive to the mall at the corner of Brookhurst Ave and Westminster Ave, continue to the

DETOUR: GLEN IVY HOT SPRINGS

Nicknamed 'Club Mud' for its popular red clay mud pool, this lovely **day spa** (☎ 888-258-2683; www.glenivy.com; 25000 Glen Ivy Rd; admission Mon-Thu $35, Fri-Sun & holidays $48; ☺ 9:30am-6pm Apr-Oct, 9:30am-5pm Nov-Mar) has 19 pools and spas filled with naturally heated mineral water, surrounded by 5 acres of landscaped grounds profuse with bougainvillea, eucalyptus and palm trees.

The spa is technically in Corona, just east of Orange County in Riverside County. To get there, exit I-15 at Temescal Canyon Rd, turn right and drive 1 mile to Glen Ivy Rd, then right again and go straight to the end. If traffic isn't too bad, it's about a 45-minute drive between the spa and Old Towne Orange. You can wallow in the water, lounge in the saunas or steam rooms, take an aqua aerobics class, treat yourself to a massage (for an extra fee) or swim laps in a larger swimming pool. Minimum age for entry is 16. It gets pretty busy in summer, so arrive early for a chair.

For lunch, try a heaping salad at the spa's **Café Sole**, or head back toward the freeway to stock up on produce at **Tom's Market** (☎ 951-277-4422, 888-444-1516; 23900 Temescal Canyon Rd, Corona) or try a cheap, tasty taco at **Senor Tom's** (☎ 951-277-1002).

back of the 99 Cent Store, turn right, drive past the dumpsters and park near the red awning–covered entrance.

Cheat sheet: *pho* is soup, *ga* is chicken, *tom* is shrimp and *bo* is beef. Enjoy.

ORANGE COUNTY BEACHES

While it's true you'll find gorgeous sunsets, prime surfing and just-off-the-boat seafood when traveling Orange County's sun-kissed coast, it's the unexpected discoveries you'll remember long after you've left the 42 miles of surf and sand behind. Whether it's watching kitesurfers skip across the waves in Seal Beach, playing Frisbee with your pooch in the surf at Huntington Dog Beach, wandering around eclectic art displays on a bluff-top trail in Laguna or just sacking out on the sand at a Doheny State Beach campsite – you'll discover that each beach town has its own brand of quirky charm. You just have to find which suits your personality best.

Starting southeast of Los Angeles County's Long Beach (p130), Seal Beach is the OC's northernmost beach town. From here, you can follow Route 1, also known as the Pacific Coast Hwy or simply PCH, south along the coast for more than 40 miles, passing through Sunset Beach, Huntington Beach, Newport Beach, Laguna Beach and Dana Point before reaching San Clemente, which borders San Diego County. From Seal Beach in the north to Laguna Beach in the south, the drive takes about 45 minutes to an hour.

Accommodations in summer get booked far in advance; prices rise and some properties impose minimum two- or three-night stays. You can stay in one town and take day trips to the others.

SEAL BEACH
pop 24,100

In the pageant for charming small towns, Seal Beach enjoys an unfair advantage over the competition: 1.5 miles of pristine beach glittering like an already-won crown. And that's without mentioning three-block Main St, a stoplight-free zone bustling with locally owned restaurants, mom-and-pop specialty shops and indie coffeehouses that are low on 'tude and high on charisma. But truth be told, Seal Beach's lasting small-town allure may owe a debt to the Scylla and Charybdis lurking beside the primary thoroughfare into town, Seal Beach Blvd: Leisure World ('Seizure World' to the non-PC) is a sprawling retirement community looming just west of Seal Beach Blvd, while the huge US Naval Weapons Station (look for grass-covered bunkers) crouches to the east. But thoughts of shuffleboard and apocalypse aside, Seal Beach is one of the last great Californian beach towns and a refreshing alternative to the more crowded coasts further south.

Information
Chamber of Commerce (☎ 562-799-0179; www.seal beachchamber.org; 201 8th St, Suite 120; ☺ noon-3pm Mon, Wed, Fri) Dispenses lodging and other information, but only about businesses that have joined the chamber.
Post Office (☎ 562-598-6915; 221 Main St; ☺ 9am-5pm Mon-Fri) Conveniently located on bustling Main St just two blocks from the beach.
Public Library (☎ 562-431-3584; www.ocpl.org; 707 Electric Ave; ☺ noon-8pm Mon & Tue, 10am-6pm Wed & Thu, 10am-5pm Sat, closed Fri & Sun) Internet access free for one hour with guest pass.

Sights
In the morning settle into a chair at one of the indie coffee joints on Main St and check out the laid-back local scene – barefoot surfers trotting toward the surf, friendly shopkeepers opening their doors and silver-haired Leisure World foxes scoping the way-too-young beach bunnies. All so enjoyable you might just trade beach time for a day-long coffee-crawl.

Once the java kicks in, resist temptation and follow Main St onto the **Seal Beach Pier**, which extends 1885ft over the ocean. The current pier, built in 1985, replaced the 1906 original, which fell victim to winter storms in the early 1980s, but it has been rebuilt with a wooden boardwalk. It's splintery in places, so wear shoes (no high heels!). Snap a picture of the playful bronze seal standing guard at the pier's eastern base – he may be the only one you see.

On the **beach**, which faces south here, families spread out on blankets, build sandcastles and play in the water. The gentle waves make it a great place to learn to surf. Surfers and boogie boarders are segregated; read the signs or ask a lifeguard. Newbie surfers should stick close to the pier. For surf conditions, look for the sign on the sand between the parking lots.

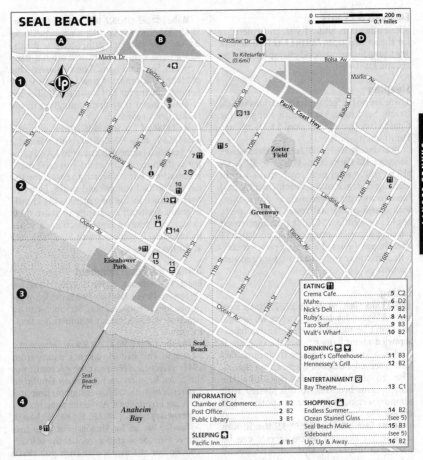

SEAL BEACH

ORANGE COUNTY

INFORMATION
Chamber of Commerce	1	B2
Post Office	2	B2
Public Library	3	B1

SLEEPING 🏠
Pacific Inn	4	B1

EATING 🍴
Crema Cafe	5	C2
Mahe	6	D2
Nick's Deli	7	B2
Ruby's	8	A4
Taco Surf	9	B3
Walt's Wharf	10	B2

DRINKING 🍺 🍸
Bogart's Coffeehouse	11	B3
Hennessey's Grill	12	B2

ENTERTAINMENT 🎭
Bay Theatre	13	C1

SHOPPING 🛍
Endless Summer	14	B2
Ocean Stained Glass	(see 5)	
Seal Beach Music	15	B3
Sideboard	(see 5)	
Up, Up & Away	16	B2

Though there's a hideous oil derrick just off shore, if you take off your glasses and focus on what's immediately in front of you, it's lovely. The ocean here is popular with round stingrays, attracted to the warm water flowing in with the San Gabriel River from the north. (Soak your foot in warm water if stung, and seek medical assistance if necessary.) On windy days, walk up the beach to 2nd and 4th Sts and watch kitesurfers skipping across the waves.

There's two-hour free parking along Main St but you may have a difficult time finding a spot in summer. You might have to park inland, or pay $3 per two hours or $6 for a day at the lots by the pier. The beach is open from 4:30am to 10pm.

Activities

Rent a bicycle at the **Pacific Inn** (p254), two blocks from Main St, for $15 per hour or $50 per day. Learn to surf with **M&M Surfing School** (☎ 714-846-7873; www.mmsurfingschool .com), which offers five-day long surf intensives for about $240; it also leads single-day instruction for $60 to $80, which includes rental of the board and wet suit. Or you can just rent a soft (foam) board for $25 per day. One fast-growing sport – due to the area's thermal winds – is kitesurfing. A two-day $440 introductory lesson from **Kitesurfari** (☎ 562-596-6451, 866-949-5483; www.kitesurfari.com; 452 Pacific Coast Hwy) should give you a sufficient taste of this great activity in the three hours each day.

Festivals & Events

Kite enthusiasts should visit in September for the annual **Japan America Kite Festival** (www.kiteclub.org) featuring world champion kite flyers and kite ballet.

Sleeping

There are no budget accommodations in Seal Beach; head inland and south along Pacific Coast Hwy (generally called PCH) toward Huntington Beach.

PacificInn (☎ 562-493-7501, 866-466-0300; www.pacific inn-sb.com; 600 Marina Dr; r $149-169; **P** □ ⚑ wi-fi) The only motel near town that's within walking distance of the beach (two blocks) has rooms with extras such as down comforters and comfy mattresses. The property could use a little TLC, but free high-speed wireless access, a sunny central pool and $1 draft happy hours at a nearby pub – there's a flyer in the room – make up for tired surroundings.

Eating

our pick **Nick's Deli** (☎ 562-598-5072; 223 Main St; mains under $6; ☽ 7am-7pm Mon-Fri, 7am-5pm Sat, 7am-4pm Sun) Don't be fooled by the extensive hand-scrawled menu hanging over the counter at Nick's, a local's joint where traditional deli fare is served alongside Mexican specialties. The crowds flock here for one thing: the scrumptious breakfast tortilla stuffed with scrambled eggs, chorizo, bacon, potatoes and cheese. Don't miss it.

Crema Cafe (☎ 562-493-2501; 322 Main St; mains under $9; ☽ 6:30am-4pm Tue-Sun) Service can be harried at this breezy, open-air café, but all is forgiven after a bite of their 'basic' French crepe covered with powdered sugar, whipped crème and caramel sauce. Add strawberries or bananas for an extra splash of flavor. For those in a hurry, the muffins are fab too.

Ruby's (☎ 562-431-7829; 900a Ocean Ave; most mains under $10; ☽ 7am-10pm, 7am-9pm winter; ♿) At the end of the pier, this red-and-white '50s-theme diner whips up pretty good burgers and shakes and a great clam chowder. The ocean views are fantastic too.

Taco Surf (☎ 562-594-0600; 115 Main St; mains under $10; ☽ 11am-9:30pm) There's sawdust on the floor, beach music on the speakers and hot sauce on the table at this Baja-style Mexican cantina that serves yummy fish tacos and homemade salsa. There's beer and wine margaritas, but no tequila.

Mahe (☎ 562-431-3022; 1400 Pacific Coast Hwy; mains $8-42; ☽ 5-10pm Mon-Sat, 4-10pm Sun, cocktail lounge until late) Raw-fish fans gather barside for the $25 all-you-can-eat sushi-fest offered daily between 5pm and 6pm. The surfboard-chic of Mahe's front room is great for beach-weary families looking for a sit-down meal, although scoping singles may prefer mingling in the rockin' back room.

Walt's Wharf (☎ 562-598-4433; 201 Main St; mains lunch $7.50-21, dinner $12-40) Everybody's favorite for fresh fish (some drive in from LA), Walt's packs them in on weekends. You can't make reservations but it's worth the wait for the oak fire–grilled seafood and steaks. Don't be overwhelmed by the long menu – the knowledgeable waitstaff are happy to share their expertise. There's a huge selection of wines by the glass. If you can't wait for a table, eat at the bar.

Drinking & Entertainment

Bogart's Coffeehouse (☎ 562-431-2226; 905 Ocean Ave; ☽ 6am-9pm Mon-Fri, 7am-10pm Sat & Sun; wi-fi) Sip espresso on the sofa and play Scrabble with an ocean view. On Saturday it sometimes hosts live music.

Bay Theatre (☎ 562-431-9988; www.baytheatre.com; 340 Main St) This historic cinema, dating from 1947, revives great films on the big screen, from the Marx Brothers and *American Graffiti* to *Lawrence of Arabia*. Movies start on time and there are no previews. Avoid the popcorn.

Hennessey's Grill (☎ 562-598-6456; 143 Main St; ☽ 7am-1am Mon-Sat, 7am-11pm Sun) For a no-fuss pint of Guinness, grab a stool at the smooth wooden bar at this popular Irish pub that's perfect for solos or small groups. The place is jam-packed for burgers on two-for-one Tuesdays.

Jazz, folk and bluegrass bands play Wednesday evenings in summer from 6pm to 8pm as part of **Summer Concerts in the Park** (☎ 562-799-0179; Eisenhower Park) by the pier at the foot of Main St.

Shopping

Be sure to walk the full three blocks of Main St to see all the little shops.

Endless Summer (☎ 562-430-9393; 124 Main St) Teenie Wahine, Roxy and Billabong jostle for attention at this bustling store for beach babes that's packed to the rafters with bikinis, beach bags, shades and sundresses.

Up, Up & Away (☎ 562-596-7661; 139½ Main St) In addition to kites of every color, you'll find decorative flags galore. Frogs, lighthouses, dogs with sunglasses – if you want it waving in front of your house, there's a flag for it here. Badass kites are up the back.

Ocean Stained Glass (☎ 562-596-6806; 322 Main St) Stained glass isn't just for churches anymore. From dichroic fused glass jewelry to bright window hangings and unique lamp covers, one-of-a-kind gifts are the draw here.

Sideboard (☎ 562-594-8159; 322 Main St) This place boasts everything from fancy pickles and Turkish olive oils to scone cookers and bamboo cutting boards. Cooking buffs beware: it's hard to leave this indie culinary shop empty-handed.

Seal Beach Music (☎ 562-430-0594; 118 Main St) Musicians will dig this great old-fashioned small-town musical instrument shop. The sign says their hours are 11am to 7pm unless they've gone fishing.

SUNSET BEACH

Tucked on a 1-mile strip of coastal real estate between charming Seal Beach and glossy Huntington Beach, this tiny community spits in the face of Orange County conformity. With a high concentration of dive bars, ratty motels and beach bum 'tude, it's a great place to surf, kayak and drink, but you might not want to, um, live there. There's no home mail delivery so locals pick

ORANGE COUNTY

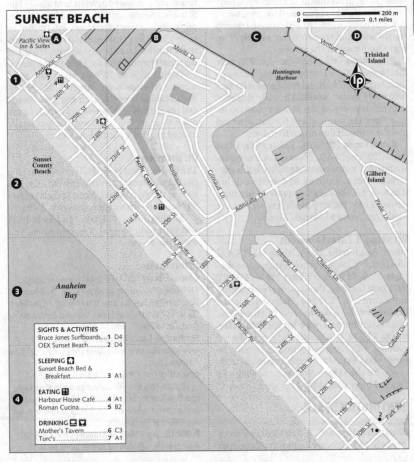

SUNSET BEACH

SIGHTS & ACTIVITIES	
Bruce Jones Surfboards....**1**	D4
OEX Sunset Beach..........**2**	D4

SLEEPING	
Sunset Beach Bed & Breakfast....................**3**	A1

EATING	
Harbour House Café......**4**	A1
Roman Cucina..............**5**	B2

DRINKING	
Mother's Tavern............**6**	C3
Turc's..........................**7**	A1

up their mail at the post office on PCH in the middle of town.

Activities

For an easy but scenic paddle, kayakers should check out adjacent Huntington Harbor. Stop by **OEX Sunset Beach** (☎ 562-592-0800; 16910 Pacific Coast Hwy; kayak rental 2hr/1 day $10/40) for rentals and transportation. Across the street, surfers can rent hard (fiberglass) and soft boards from **Bruce Jones Surfboards** (☎ 562-592-2314, 888-592-2314; 16927 Pacific Coast Hwy) at $20 per half day.

Sleeping & Eating

Sunset Beach Bed & Breakfast (☎ 562-592-1666; www .sunsetbeachbedandbreakfast.com; 16401 Pacific Coast Hwy; r $175-275; **P**) This two-story B&B is an oasis of floral charm in the middle of somewhat scruffy Sunset Beach. The rooms are decorated with a colonial flair that makes a pleasant backdrop for the wine and cheese offered nightly. Two night minimum in the summer.

Harbor House Café (☎ 562-592-5404; 16341 Pacific Coast Hwy; mains $7-19) Laptop-carrying businessmen, high school kids and middle-aged couples mix easily under ramshackle walls slathered with movie posters at this 24-hour classic roadside diner. The menu is long, the portions huge and the waitstaff downright friendly.

Roman Cucina (☎ 562-592-5552; 16595 Pacific Coast Hwy, cnr 20th St; mains $15-30; ☽ dinner) For hearty Italian fare, follow the twinkling lights to this trattoria, known as much for its delectable dishes (thick slices of bruschetta, savory salads, huge pastas) as for the ripped waiters serving the food. Don't miss $5 Martini Mondays.

Drinking & Entertainment

Sunset Beach is the unofficial capital of SoCal dive bars. For a wood-paneled, trapped-in-the-captain's-hold vibe, try **Turc's** (☎ 562-592-2311; 16321 Pacific Coast Hwy), the ivy-covered building at the corner of PCH and Anderson St in the shadows of the water tower–like house. Just south is tiny but raucous biker bar **Mother's Tavern** (☎ 562-592-2381; 16701 Pacific Coast Hwy), in the red building with Harleys out front, just past the barber shop. On a lazy Sunday, you might catch a rockabilly band here. Note, gals traveling solo may feel more comfortable bringing a friend.

HUNTINGTON BEACH

pop 190,000

Hawaiian-Irish surfing star George Freeth (brought to California by pioneer developer Henry Huntington) gave demonstrations in Huntington Beach (HB) in 1914, and the city has been a surf destination ever since. In recent years, its surfing image has been heavily marketed, city fathers even getting a bit aggressive in ensuring HB's exclusive rights to their now-trademarked nickname 'Surf City, USA.' The moniker originally came from the 1963 song by surf daddies Jan and Dean. But the city does have a reason to protect its surfing turf. The sport is big business, with buyers for major retailers coming here to see what surfers are wearing, then marketing the look.

At times the city can seem like a teenager with growing pains. Long considered a low-key, not-quite-fashionable beach community, recent and uninspired development along Main St has left downtown with a vaguely antiseptic, prefab feel – a vibe refreshingly interrupted by sidewalk surfing skate rats and hollering late-night barflies. Despite the changes, HB is still the quintessential spot to celebrate the coastal California lifestyle. With consistently good waves, surf shops, a surf museum, beach bonfires, a canine-friendly beach and lots of hotels and restaurants with awesome views, it's a fun place to enjoy sun and sand that's centrally located for exploring the SoCal coast.

Orientation

The Pacific Coast Hwy (PCH) runs along the coast; Main St runs perpendicular to PCH and ends at the pier. Inland, Main St ends at Hwy 39 (Beach Blvd), which connects to I-405.

Coming from I-405, take Hwy 39 to PCH and turn right (north). Once in town, you won't need a car.

Information

Central Library (☎ 714-842-4481; www.hbpl.org; 7111 Talbert Ave; internet access per hr $5; ☽ 1-9pm Mon, 9am-9pm Tue-Thu, 9am-5pm Fri & Sat, 1-5pm Sun; ▣ wi-fi) This is the main branch located in Huntington Beach Central Park.

Huntington Beach Hospital (☎ 714-842-1473; www.hbhospital.com; 17772 Beach Blvd) There's a 24-hour emergency room.

Post office (☎ 714-536-4973; 316 Olive Ave; ☽ 8:30am-5pm Mon-Fri) Buy stamps and mail packages near Main St at the Beach Center branch. There's a self-service stamp machine available 6:30am to 6pm weekdays, and 6:45am to 5pm Saturday.

Public Library – Main St Branch (☎ 714-375-5071; www.hbpl.org; 525 Main St; internet access per hr $3;

10am-7pm Tue-Fri, 9am-5pm Sat;) Smaller than the main branch but just five blocks from the beach.
Visitors Bureau (714-969-3492, 800-729-6232; www.surfcityusa.com; 301 Main St, Suite 208; noon-7pm Mon-Fri, 11am-7pm Sat & Sun) Hard-to-spot office is on the 2nd floor overlooking Main St. Provides maps and info.

Sights
Look for the **Surfing Walk of Fame** on the corner of PCH and Main St, which immortalizes local legends.

THE BEACH
One of SoCal's best beaches, the sand here gets packed on summer weekends with surfers, volleyball players, swimmers and families.

Huntington City Beach (714-536-5281; 5am-10pm;) surrounds the pier at the foot of Main St. Parking is $1.50 per hour or $12 for the day. Further south, **Huntington State Beach** (714-536-1454; 6am-10pm;) extends from Beach Blvd (Hwy 39) to the Santa Ana River and the Newport Beach boundary. Parking costs $12 a day.

If you forgot to pack beach gear, you can rent umbrellas, volleyballs, towels and even swim suits at **Zack's** (714-536-0215; www.beachfoodfun.com; Zack's Pier Plaza, cnr Pacific Coast Hwy & Main St) just north of the pier. Friendly **Dwight's** (714-536-8083; 201 Pacific Coast Hwy on The Strand), around since 1932, rents bikes, boogies boards, umbrellas and chairs south of the pier.

ORANGE COUNTY

HUNTINGTON BEACH

0 ————— 1 km
0 ————— 0.5 miles

To Bolsa Chica Ecological Reserve (entrance; 1.3mi);
Bolsa Chica State Beach Visitors Center (1.3mi);
Bolsa Chica Interpretive Center (1.8mi);
Huntington Harbor (1.8mi);
Pacific View Inn & Suites (3.7mi)

To Central Park (Equestrian Center 1.1mi; Frisbee Golf Course 1.1mi; Park Bench Cafe 1.3mi; Central Library 1.3mi)

Yorktown Av

To Beach Inn Motel (2.1mi); Hospital (2.5mi); Comfort Suites (4.7mi); Hotel HB (4.9mi)

Indianapolis Av

Atlanta Av

Huntington City Beach

Huntington Beach Pier

PACIFIC OCEAN

INFORMATION
Post Office 1 D1
Public Library - Main St Branch .. 2 C3
Visitors Bureau 3 D1

SIGHTS & ACTIVITIES
Bolsa Chica State Beach 4 A1
Dog Beach 5 A2
Dwight's 6 D2
HB Wahine 7 D1
Huntington Beach Surf & Sport .. 8 D2
Huntington City Beach 9 C3
Huntington State Beach 10 D4
International Surfing Museum ... 11 D1
Surfers' Hall of Fame .... (see 8)
Surfing Walk of Fame 12 C2
Zack's 13 C2

SLEEPING
Best Western Huntington
    Beach Inn 14 C3
Hilton Waterfront Beach
    Resort 15 D3
Huntington Surf Inn 16 C3
Hyatt Regency Huntington
    Beach Resort & Spa 17 D4
Sun 'N Sands Motel 18 C3

EATING
Avila's El Ranchito 19 D1
Duke's 20 C2
Red Pearl Kitchen 21 D1
Smokin' Moe's 22 D1
Spark Woodfire Grill 23 D2
Sugar Shack 24 D1

DRINKING
Huntington Beach Beer Co 25 D1
Hurricanes Bar & Grill 26 D1
Java Point Coffee .... (see 8)
Killarney Pub & Grill 27 D1

ENTERTAINMENT
Pierside Surf City 6 .... 28 D2

SHOPPING
American Vintage Clothing 29 D1
Carmen Parks Boutique .... (see 29)
Electric Chair 30 D1
Huntington Beach Surf & Sport.. (see 8)

See Enlargement

In the evening, volleyball games give way to beach bonfires. If you want to build one or have a barbecue, stake out one of the 1000 cement fire rings early in the day, especially on holiday weekends, when you should plan to arrive when the beach opens. To indicate that it's taken, surround the ring with your gear. You can get wood from concessionaires on the beach.

Bathrooms and showers are located north of the pier at the back of the snack-bar complex. The beach closes at 10pm and reopens at 5am; the pier closes at midnight. Parking lots by the beach – when you can get a spot – are 'pay and display'. Feed the ticket booths scattered across the parking lot – $1.50 per hour or $12 per day – then post the ticket in your windshield. Bring dollars and coins. Otherwise, park at the municipal lots along PCH or on the street further inland. The Promenade parking structure costs $9 per day while other municipal lots are $10 per day. Street meters are $1 for 40 minutes.

Dogs romp in the surf at **Dog Beach**, north of Goldenwest St, south of Seapoint Ave, between Huntington City and Bolsa Chica State Beaches. Nearly a mile long, it's a picture-perfect place to play with your pooch.

HUNTINGTON PIER

The 1853ft Huntington Pier has been here – in one form or another – since 1904. The mighty Pacific has damaged giant sections of it half a dozen times and completely demolished it twice since then. The current concrete structure was built in 1983. On the pier you can rent a fishing pole for $3 per hour at **Let's Go Fishin'** (☎ 714-960-1392) bait and tackle shop. About half way up the pier, there are two tiny stores in trailers: the **Surf City Store** (☎ 714-374-0277) is the only shop in town licensed to use the name 'Surf City' on its merchandise – pick up a T-shirt; across the way, consider buying a kite at the **Kite Connection** (☎ 714-536-3630).

INTERNATIONAL SURFING MUSEUM

One of the few of its kind in California, this small **museum** (☎ 714-960-3483; www.surfingmuseum .org; 411 Olive Ave; donation adult/child $2/1; ☻ noon-5pm Mon-Fri, 11am-6pm Sat & Sun May-Sep; noon-5pm Wed-Fri, 11am-6pm Sat & Sun Oct-Apr) off Main St is an entertaining stop for surf-culture enthusiasts. The less-enthused may need more detailed explanations. A potentially fascinating collection of vintage surfboards and skateboards lacks organization and details, while the Women of Surfing display is little more than a haphazard photo album backed by a photo-covered whiteboard. For the best historical tidbits, spend a minute chatting with the knowledgeable, friendly staff members. They're all volunteers and happy to share their expertise.

BOLSA CHICA STATE BEACH

Bolsa Chica State Beach (☎ 714-846-3460, reservations 800-444-7275; 17851 Pacific Coast Highway; P) is a 3-mile strip of sand stretching alongside the Pacific Coast Hwy between Sunset Beach to the north and Dog Beach to the south. Parking costs $10. It faces a monstrous oil rig half a mile off shore. You'll find picnic tables, fire-rings and hot showers, plus a bike path running north to Anderson Ave – home of Turc's (p256) – in Sunset Beach and south to Huntington State Beach. Favored by surfers, volleyball players and fishers, Bolsa Chica is mobbed on summer weekends. At the small **visitors center** (☎ 714-377-5691; www.parks.ca.gov; ☻ 9am-4pm; wi-fi) you can check out the views through telescopes pointed at the beach and **Bolsa Chica State Ecological Reserve** (☎ 714-846-1114; ☻ 6am-8pm; P), on the other side of PCH. The reserve looks rather desolate, but this restored salt marsh is an environmental success story that teems with bird life. Its 1700 acres have been saved by a band of determined locals from numerous development projects over the years. Sadly, it's also one of the last coastal wetlands in SoCal – 94% of them having succumbed to development. A 1.5-mile loop trail starts from the parking lot on PCH. A small **interpretative center** (3842 Warner Ave) sits just north.

Activities

SURFING

Surfing in HB is competitive. Control your longboard or draw ire from local dudes who pride themselves on being 'agro.' Surf north of the pier.

If you're a novice, it's a good idea to take lessons. You could try M&M Surfing School (p253) in nearby Seal Beach. The local Zack's at the beach offers one-hour instruction for $70 including board and wetsuit; if you just want to rent a board, it's $15 an hour or $30 for a day. There's also **HB Wahine** (☎ 714-969-9399; www.hbwahine.com; 301 Main St, Suite 201), a great women-only surf school. Private lessons are $50 an hour with a two-hour minimum.

For rentals only try **Huntington Beach Surf & Sport** (p261). This mega-store at the corner of PCH and Main St rents boards for $8 per hour or $25 a day. Wetsuits are $5 per hour and $15 a day.

CYCLING & SKATING

One of the best ways to explore the coast is by riding a bicycle or skating on the 8.5-mile **bike path** that runs from Huntington State Beach in the south to Bolsa Chica State Beach. Rent skates and bikes north of the pier on the beach at Zack's for $10 an hour or $30 a day. South of the pier, rent bikes at Dwight's for $8 an hour or $25 a day. Ask for a copy of the owner's hand-drawn map of the bike path with distances from Huntington Beach Pier.

FRISBEE

Throw a disc back and forth for hours on the beach or test your skills at the **Huntington Beach Disc Golf Course** (☎ 714-425-9931; Goldenwest St btwn Talbert Ave & Ellis Ave; Mon-Fri $1, Sat & Sun $2; **P**) at Huntington Central Park. Aim for baskets at this scenic 18-hole course. Newbies and seasoned players are welcome and there's a pro-shop on site.

KAYAKING

For an up-close look at ritzy homes and tricked-out yachts, kayak the calm waters of **Huntington Harbor** located in northern HB and east of Sunset Beach. Try Sunset Beach's OEX Sunset Beach (p256) for kayak rentals and transport.

Festivals & Events

Expect big crowds on the **4th of July** (www.hb4thofjuly.org) when the city closes sections of Main St and PCH for an Independence Day parade. The day-long celebration ends with evening fireworks over the pier.

If you can only make one event, consider the **US Open of Surfing** (www.usopenofsurfing.com) in late July. It's a six-star competition lasting several days and drawing more than 600 world-class surfers. Festivities include beach concerts, motocross shows and skateboard jams.

Surf chicks get their own festival in early September with the increasingly popular **Boardfest** (www.boardfest.com). If you're here for the Christmas holidays, don't miss the **Huntington Harbor Cruise of Lights** (www.cruiseoflights.org), an evening boat tour past harborside homes that enthusiastically twinkle with holiday lights. Ticket sales support projects initiated by the Orange County Philharmonic.

For a current list of events, contact the HB Visitors Bureau.

Sleeping

There aren't many budget options in HB, especially in summer when nothing-special motels hike their prices to ridiculous levels. If you want budget accomodation, head inland along Hwy 39 toward I-405 for average motels with midrange prices.

Beach Inn Motel (☎ 714-841-6606; 18112 Beach Blvd; r $99-110; **P**) This no-nonsense, no-frills motel is located on Route 39, a busy thoroughfare linking I-405 to the coast. The motel's not as close to the beach as its name implies, but it is clean and fairly quiet.

Comfort Suites (☎ 714-841-1812; 800-714-4040; www.comfortsuites.com/hotel/ca102; 16301 Beach Blvd (Hwy 39); r $99-119; **P** 🖳 💆 wi-fi) Hot breakfast items such as scrambled eggs and bacon or ham and cheese omelettes make this chain motel just a little bit more special than the competition. The rates are pretty reasonable too. Closer to Hwy 405 than to the beach.

GETTING AWAY FROM IT ALL: HUNTINGTON CENTRAL PARK

If you want a break from the beach scene but don't want to drive too far, the 354-acre **Huntington Central Park** (☎ 714-536-5486; www.ci.huntington-beach.ca.us; 8000 Goldenwest St; **P** 👫), just north of downtown, is a fantastic suburban retreat that boasts a Frisbee golf course, an equestrian center, a down-and-dirty adventure playground, lakes, shaded trails and two popular breakfast joints. Parking lots are on Goldenwest St, Gothard St and at the library on Talbert Ave. For a thoughtful examination of local flora and fauna, stop by the child-friendly **Shipley Nature Center** (☎ 714-842-4772; www.shipleynature.org; 17829 Goldenwest St; 🕙 9am-1pm Mon-Sat; **P** 👫) an 18-acre nature sanctuary within the park with exhibits on local animal habitats and conservation efforts as well as a self-guided nature trail.

Pacific View Inn & Suites (Map p255; ☎ 800-726-8586; www.pacificviewinnandsuites.com; 16220 Pacific Coast Hwy; r $100-120; ⓟ wi-fi) This three-story mustard and maroon motel won't win any beauty contests, but the staff are friendly and it's close to the beach – you just have to dash across PCH.

Hotel Huntington Beach (☎ 714-891-0123, 877-891-0123; www.hotelhb.com; 7667 Center Ave; r $100-150; ⓟ ⓓ wi-fi) This eight-story hotel, which looks like an office building, is decidedly sans personality and a bit worn, but the rooms are clean and perfect for get-up-and-go travelers. The hot tub is a perk.

Sun 'N Sands Motel (☎ 714-536-2543; www.sunnsands.com; 1102 Pacific Coast Hwy; r $120-230; ⓟ ⓓ wi-fi) Rates spike absurdly high in summer at this nothing-special, mom-and-pop motel, but its location across from the beach lets them get away with it. Potato chips, toothpaste, contact solution and other sundries are for sale in the lobby. It can get loud at night.

Huntington Surf Inn (☎ 714-536-2444; www.huntingtonsurfinn.com; 720 Pacific Coast Hwy; r $149-179; ⓟ) You're paying for location at this two-story motel located just south of Main St and across from the beach. The rooms are clean, if a bit worn, and there's a small common deck area with a beach view. Don't ask for a refund; you won't get it.

Best Western Huntington Beach Inn (☎ 714-536-7500; www.bestwestern.com; 800 Pacific Coast Hwy; r $199-309; ⓟ wi-fi) Don't be surprised to see an oil derrick pumping right outside your window at this Best Western. But then, derricks are standard issue for oil-rich HB. Otherwise, the cookie-cutter rooms are well kept and relatively quiet.

Hyatt Regency Huntington Beach Resort & Spa (☎ 714-698-1234, 800-233-1234; 21500 Pacific Coast Hwy; www.huntingtonbeach.hyatt.com; r $350-495; ⓟ ⓓ wi-fi) It looks like an ersatz Spanish-style condo complex on steroids, but the deluxe rooms are inviting and impeccably maintained; there's also a good spa. Parking costs $25 per day and wi-fi is $10.

Hilton Waterfront Beach Resort (☎ 714-845-8000, 800-445-8667; www.waterfrontbeachresort.hilton.com; 21100 Pacific Coast Hwy; r $439-509; ⓟ ⓓ wi-fi) The sprawling, lounge-filled poolside is reminiscent of Vegas, but then you see the backdrop: miles and miles of gorgeous deep-blue sea. The hotel's giant tower stands in blatant disregard of the town's low rooflines, but if you want an ocean view from up high, this is the

only place. Use of hotel boogie boards, beach chairs and volleyballs is free, but wireless access isn't ($10). Parking costs $22 per day.

Eating

our pick Sugar Shack (☎ 714-536-0355; 213 Main St; mains $4-6; ⓧ breakfast & lunch) Get here at 6am to see surfer dudes don their wet suits. Breakfast is served all day, either on the bustling Main St patio or inside where you can grab a spot at the counter or a two top. The $5 Breakfast Special offers two pancakes, an egg, and bacon or sausage. Expect a wait for this HB institution.

Avila's El Ranchito (☎ 714-960-9696; 318 Main St; mains $4-15) Fill up with a messy Mexican combo platter on El Ranchito's festive Main St patio. On the fence about ordering a margarita? Fall off and order up, these perfectly prepared babies are lip-smackin' good.

Duke's (☎ 714-374-6446; 317 Pacific Coast Hwy; mains lunch $5.50-13, dinner $19-27; ⓧ lunch & dinner) It may be touristy, but this Hawaiian-themed restaurant – named after surfing legend Duke Kahanamoku – is a kick. With unbeatable views of the beach, a long list of fresh fish and a healthy selection of sassy cocktails, it's a primo spot to relax and show off your tan. Don't miss the poke roll appetizer. For drinks and appetizers, step into the Barefoot Bar to the right as you enter.

Smokin' Mo's BBQ (☎ 714-374-3033; 301 Main St; mains under $7; ⓧ 11am-9pm) Southern-born food snobs who swear there's no good barbecue in California will change their mind at laidback Smokin' Mo's. This place gets it right. According to the story on the wall, Mo's owners drove cross-country to learn from the best, and it shows. From the tasty pile of minced pork and the messy coleslaw to the four unique sauces, it's all good at this concrete-floor joint. Check out the big pig on the surfboard overhead.

Park Bench Cafe (☎ 714-842-0775; 17732 Goldenwest St; mains $6-11; ⓧ 7:30am-2pm Tue-Fri, 7:30am-3pm Sat & Sun; ⓟ ⓕ) Sometimes Fido likes to order off the menu too. For an off-the-beaten-path meal in a dog-friendly setting, try this casual outdoor restaurant in Huntington Central Park (p259). Order an omelette or burger for yourself and a juicy Hound Dog Heaven patty for your pooch. Kids welcome too.

Red Pearl Kitchen (☎ 714-969-0224; 412 Walnut Ave; mains $10-22; ⓧ dinner) A pressed-tin ceiling and orange-and-red paper lanterns add style to this sexy industrial-chic Southeast Asian eatery off Main St, whose fiery, flavor-packed cooking draws inspiration from the cuisines of Thailand, Vietnam, Malaysia and Japan. Plan to share plates. Full bar available.

Spark Woodfire Grill (☎ 714-960-0996; 300 Pacific Coast Hwy; mains $18-36; ☽ dinner) Come before dark to this 2nd-floor Cal-Mediterranean restaurant and watch the sun set over the water while dining on hickory- and oak-fire-grilled steaks, chops and seafood, as well as crispy-thin pizza from the wood-fired oven. Try the grilled-chicken polenta with goat cheese.

Drinking

It's easy to find a bar in HB. Walk up Main St and you'll spot them all.

Huntington Beach Beer Co (☎ 714-960-5343; 201 Main St, 2nd fl; ☽ 11am-1am daily) This cavernous brew pub specializes in ales and has eight giant, stainless-steel kettles brewing all the time. There's also good pub grub. DJs and bands play on weekend nights.

Hurricanes Bar & Grill (☎ 714-374-0500; 200 Main St, 2nd fl; ☽ 11am-2am daily) Two words: meat market. But then again, any strip of beach bars worth its sea salt needs at least one. Beach Party Sundays, ocean-view patios, 32 beer taps and loads of special cocktails – if you're not slurping body shots by midnight, you have no one to blame but yourself.

Killarney Pub & Grill (☎ 714-536-7887; 209 Main St; ☽ 11am-1:30am Sun-Thu, 8am-1:30am Sat & Sun) It bills itself as an Irish pub, but the profusion of plasma TV screens makes it a sports bar with green-painted walls. Rollicking good fun for beer-drinking sports enthusiasts.

Java Point Coffee (☎ 714-374-9256; 300 Pacific Coast Hwy; ☽ 6am-8pm Sun-Thu, to 9pm Fri & Sat) It's not a bar, but after all that drinking, you'll need some coffee. Enter Huntington Surf & Sport off Main St, and you'll find the counter next to the rows of surfboards. Look down after ordering, you might be standing on the concrete handprints of a surfing legend. Opens at 6am.

Entertainment

Pierside Surf City 6 (☎ 714-969-3151; 300 Pacific Coast Hwy; admission $7) First-run movies at the corner of Main St.

Shopping

Most stores stay open until 8pm, some until 10pm on weekends.

American Vintage Clothing (☎ 714-969-9670; 201c Main St) Thrift and vintage hounds should check out this small but jam-packed store. Boots, Jim Morrison T-shirts, earrings and loads of dresses arranged by decade. Enter off Walnut Ave.

Carmen Parks Boutique (☎ 714-374-9100; 201d Main St) If you grow weary of surf fashion, stop by this helpful high-end women's boutique. Labels include Chip & Pepper, Tyler Malibu and Michael Stars.

Electric Chair (☎ 714-536-0784; 410 Main St) Get pierced at this subversive shop for f*@k-the-man accessories. You'll find skull and vampire couture, fetish fashion and one lonely 'I Love Elvis' tee.

Huntington Beach Surf & Sport (☎ 714-841-4000; www.hsssurf.com; 300 Pacific Coast Hwy) Towering behind the statue of surf hero Duke Kahanamoku at the corner of PCH and Main St, this massive store supports the Surf City vibe with vintage surf photos, concrete handprints of surf legends and lots of tiki-themed decor. You'll also find rows of surfboards, beachwear and surfing accessories. There's a coffee shop, Java Point in the back.

Also try HB Wahine (p258), a fun store for gals who surf and those who want to learn – ask about their lessons. You'll find Etni hoodies, Truth tanks, Emu boots, and sleek baby-blue surfboards stocked here. There's even an indoor sk8 ramp. The name is pronounced wah-hee-nee, the Hawaiian word for girl.

NEWPORT BEACH

pop 72,000

Primetime soap *The OC* may have lasted only four short seasons, but its impact on Newport Beach, home of the fictional Cohen family, will likely be felt for years. The adventures of its glamorous but angst-ridden teens lent a hipper, youthful sheen to the city's longstanding

---

BADDEST BEACH DIVE BARS

■ Turc's, Sunset Beach (p256) – Ivy-covered, dark and made for drinking. Gotta problem?

■ Mother's Tavern, Sunset Beach (p256) – If your mother's here, be worried.

■ Goat Hill Tavern, Costa Mesa (p270) – Ladies, avoid the bathrooms.

■ Marine Room Tavern, Laguna Beach (p276) – There are few marines, but lots of Harleys. Rockin'.

ORANGE COUNTY

ORANGE COUNTY

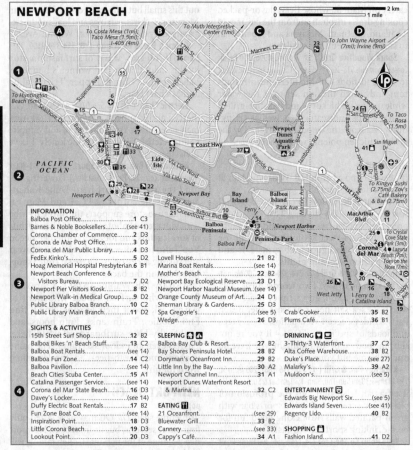

NEWPORT BEACH

0 — 2 km
0 — 1 mile

To Costa Mesa (1mi);
Taco Mesa (1.5mi);
I-405 (4mi)

To Muth Interpretive
Center (1mi)

Mariners Dr

To John Wayne Airport
(7mi); Irvine (9mi)

To Huntington
Beach (5mi)

PACIFIC
OCEAN

Newport Pier

E Coast Hwy

Newport
Dunes
Aquatic
Park

To Taco
Rosa
(1.5mi)

To Kingyo Sushi
(2.75mi); Zov's
Café Bakery
& Bar (2.75mi)

Newport Bay

Bay
Island

Balboa
Island

Balboa
Peninsula

Newport Harbor

Balboa
Pier

Peninsula Park

Corona
del Mar

To Crystal
Cove State
Park (3mi)
To Laguna
Beach (7mi);
Toes on the
Nose (7mi)

West Jetty

Ferry to
Catalina Island

INFORMATION	
Balboa Post Office	1 C3
Barnes & Noble Booksellers	(see 41)
Corona Chamber of Commerce	2 D3
Corona del Mar Post Office	3 D3
Corona del Mar Public Library	4 D3
FedEx Kinko's	5 D2
Hoag Memorial Hospital Presbyterian	6 B1
Newport Beach Conference &	
Visitors Bureau	7 D2
Newport Pier Visitors Kiosk	8 B2
Newport Walk-in Medical Group	9 D2
Public Library Balboa Branch	10 D2
Public Library Main Branch	11 D2

SIGHTS & ACTIVITIES	
15th Street Surf Shop	12 B2
Balboa Bikes 'n' Beach Stuff	13 C2
Balboa Boat Rentals	(see 14)
Balboa Fun Zone	14 C2
Balboa Pavilion	(see 14)
Beach Cities Scuba Center	15 A1
Catalina Passenger Service	(see 14)
Corona del Mar State Beach	16 D3
Davey's Locker	(see 14)
Duffy Electric Boat Rentals	17 B2
Fun Zone Boat Co	(see 14)
Inspiration Point	18 D3
Little Corona Beach	19 D3
Lookout Point	20 D3

Lovell House	21 B2
Marina Boat Rentals	(see 14)
Mother's Beach	22 B2
Newport Bay Ecological Reserve	23 D1
Newport Harbor Nautical Museum	(see 14)
Orange County Museum of Art	24 D1
Sherman Library & Gardens	25 D3
Spa Gregorie's	(see 5)
Wedge	26 D3

SLEEPING	
Balboa Bay Club & Resort	27 B2
Bay Shores Peninsula Hotel	28 B2
Doryman's Oceanfront Inn	29 B2
Little Inn by the Bay	30 A2
Newport Channel Inn	31 A1
Newport Dunes Waterfront Resort	
& Marina	32 C2

EATING	
21 Oceanfront	(see 29)
Bluewater Grill	33 B2
Cannery	(see 33)
Cappy's Café	34 A1
Crab Cooker	35 B2
Plums Café	36 B1

DRINKING	
3-Thirty-3 Waterfront	37 C2
Alta Coffee Warehouse	38 B2
Duke's Place	(see 27)
Malarky's	39 A2
Muldoon's	(see 5)

ENTERTAINMENT	
Edwards Big Newport Six	(see 5)
Edwards Island Seven	(see 41)
Regency Lido	40 B2

SHOPPING	
Fashion Island	41 D2

image as a paradise for wealthy yachtsmen and
their trophy wives. Pictures of the TV teens
still grace local travel guides and their quasi-
fictional haunts are still draws, although the
actors' once-ballyhooed concrete handprints
have been banished from the Newport Beach
Conference & Visitors Bureau and sent to
less glitzy digs at a neighboring (Recreational
Vehicle) RV park and campground.

Prime-time fame aside, the city's basics
haven't changed too much: seafood lovers still
flock to the harbor for just-off-the-boat seafood, boogie boarders still brave man-eating
waves at The Wedge and the ballet of yachts
in the harbor still captivates the imagination.
Retail shopping remains popular too, especially at Fashion Island, a posh outdoor mall

that continues to be one of the county's major
shopping centers.

Orientation

Hwy 55 (Newport Blvd) is the main access
road from I-405. It intersects with Pacific
Coast Hwy, then merges with Balboa Blvd
leading to the eastern tip of the Balboa Peninsula. Hwy 73 (Corona del Mar Fwy) also
connects I-405 with Newport Beach via
MacArthur Blvd before continuing as a toll
road to Laguna Beach and beyond.

PCH skirts the harbor on its route through
town; though the highway runs north–south
through the state, in Newport it cuts east–
west. In town PCH is called West Coast Hwy
and East Coast Hwy, depending on which side

of the bay it's on. South of PCH via Balboa Blvd, the Balboa Peninsula makes a natural 6-mile barrier between Newport Harbor and the ocean. Most tourist activity is centered here, including beaches and the Balboa Fun Zone. Six of the seven harbor islands are artificial, the result of dredging (Bay Island is natural and allows no vehicular traffic).

Balboa Island is the biggest, and has fun boutiques and eateries stretched out along Marine Ave. The remaining islands are exclusively residential. There's also more shopping north of PCH at Fashion Island.

Information
BOOKSTORES
There's a Barnes & Noble Booksellers at Fashion Island (p268) inside Atrium Court.

INTERNET ACCESS
FedEx Kinko's (☎ 949-760-1595; 230 Newport Center Dr; per hr $12; ⏱ 6am-11pm Mon-Fri, 8am-11pm Sat & Sun) On the southern end of the Newport Center Dr ring, near Anacapa Dr.

Public Library Balboa Branch (☎ 949-644-3076; www.city.newport-beach.ca.us/nbpl; 100 E Balboa Blvd; ⏱ 9am-9pm Mon & Wed, 9am-6pm Tue, Thu-Sat) Closer to the beach than the main branch. Ask for a two-hour internet guest pass.

Public Library Main Branch (☎ 949-717-3800; www.city.newport-beach.ca.us/nbpl; 1000 Avocado Ave; ⏱ 9am-9pm Mon-Thu, 9am-6pm Fri & Sat, noon-5pm Sun) The main branch is near Fashion Island. Again, ask for a two-hour internet guest pass.

MEDICAL SERVICES
Hoag Memorial Hospital Presbyterian (☎ 949-764-4624; www.hoaghospital.org; 1 Hoag Dr, cnr Hwys 1 & 55) Emergency room operating 24 hours. Follow Superior Ave north from PCH, turn right onto Hospital Rd and follow it to Hoag Dr.

Newport Walk-in Medical Group (☎ 949-760-9222; 360 San Miguel Dr; ⏱ 8am-8:30pm Mon-Fri, 9am-6pm Sat & Sun) For nonemergency care.

MONEY
Travelex (☎ 714-751-1203; South Coast Plaza, Costa Mesa; ⏱ 10am-9pm Mon-Fri, 10am-8pm Sat, 11:30am-6pm Sun) Change money at the giant mall in Costa Mesa (see p269), on the 1st floor near the carousel.

POST
Balboa Post Office (☎ 949-675-2469; 204 Main St, Balboa Peninsula; ⏱ 9am-4pm Mon-Fri) Conveniently close to the beach.

TOURIST INFORMATION
Newport Beach Conference & Visitors Bureau (☎ 949-719-6100, 800-942-6278, 24hr recorded info 949-729-4400; www.newportbeach-cvb.com; 110 Newport Center Dr, Suite 120; ⏱ 8am-5pm Mon-Fri) Located on the road that loops around Fashion Island, the bureau stocks good lodging and dining guides and a detailed town map.

Newport Pier Visitors Kiosk There's an unmanned kiosk between the parking lot and the pier with a large map of the area, a change machine and an ATM.

Sights
BALBOA PENINSULA & ISLAND
Six miles long and 0.25 miles wide, the Balboa Peninsula has a white-sand beach on its ocean side and countless stylish homes, including the 1926 **Lovell House** (1242 W Ocean Front). Designed by Rudolph Schindler, one of SoCal's most seminal modernist architects, it was built using site-cast concrete frames with wood. It's on the beach beside the bike path and across from a small playground.

Hotels, restaurants and bars cluster around the peninsula's two piers: **Newport Pier** near the western end and **Balboa Pier** at the eastern end. The oceanfront strip teems with beachgoers, and people-watching is great. Near Newport Pier, you'll find rental shops that carry umbrellas, beach chairs, boogie boards and other necessities. Meters range from $0.50 cents to $1 per hour. Free parking can be found on residential side streets just a block or two from the sand.

Opposite the Balboa Pier on the harbor side of the peninsula, the **Balboa Fun Zone** (☎ 949-673-0408; www.thebalboafunzone.com; ⏱ 11am-8pm Mon-Thu, 11am-9pm Fri, 11am-10pm Sat) has delighted locals and visitors since 1936. There's a small Ferris wheel (where Ryan and Marissa shared their first kiss on *The OC*), arcade games, touristy shops and restaurants as well as the Newport Harbor Nautical Museum, which at the time of writing was in the process of moving here from its former location on East Coast Hwy. Nearby is the landmark 1905 **Balboa Pavilion**, which is beautifully illuminated at night. The closest parking lot to the Fun Zone is the municipal lot beside the Balboa Pier. It costs $0.50 per 20 minutes or $8 max for the day.

The Fun Zone is also the place to catch a harbor cruise, fishing or whale-watching excursion (see p265), or the ferry to Balboa Island just across the channel. The **Balboa Island Ferry** (www.balboaislandferry.com; with/without car $1.50/.60) is tiny, holding just three cars packed single file between open-air seats. The distance covered is just 1000ft, and the trip lasts less than five minutes. The ferry lands at Agate Ave, about 11 blocks west of Marine Ave, the main drag lined with cute shops, cafés and restaurants. Ferries run about every 10 minutes from 6:30am to midnight Sunday to Thursday, and until 2am Friday and Saturday. For close-ups of the island's beautiful, well-maintained homes, take a stroll along its shoreline. It's about 1.5 miles around.

At the very tip of the peninsula, by the West Jetty, the **Wedge** is a bodysurfing and knee-boarding spot famous for its perfectly hollow waves that can get up to 30ft high. The waves are shore-breakers. They crest on the sand, not out to sea, so you can easily slam your head. There's usually a small crowd watching the action. This is *not* a good place for learning how to handle the currents; newcomers should head a few blocks west for calmer water. Park on Ocean Blvd or Channel Rd and walk through the tiny West Jetty Park.

MUSEUMS

Less than a mile from Fashion Island is the **Orange County Museum of Art** (☎ 949-759-1122; www.ocma.net; 850 San Clemente Dr; adult/under 12yr/student & senior $10/free/8, 3rd Thu free; ✆ 11am-5pm Tue-Sun, to 8pm Thu), an accessible starting point for cultural wanderings in the county. This engaging museum highlights Californian art and cutting-edge contemporary artists, with exhibits rotating through two large spaces every four to six months. At the time of writing, 'Art Since the 1960s: California Experiments' an installment in their *Collection Histories/Collective Memories* series, was due to open in 2008. On the third Thursday of the month, stop by for indie bands and DJs during $5 Orange Crush evenings. There's also a sculpture garden, eclectic gift shop and a theater screening classic, foreign and art-related films.

The **Newport Harbor Nautical Museum** (☎ 949-675-8915; www.nhnm.org; 600 E Bay Ave, Balboa Fun Zone; admission free; ✆ 10am-6pm, closed Tue) is setting up new digs in the Balboa Fun Zone. At the time of writing, the official grand opening was scheduled for 2009, but the museum is already open to visitors. Exhibits document the region's maritime heritage through old-time photographs, ship models, paintings and memorabilia. There's a kid-friendly touch tank and an awesome big-screen video of Laird Hamilton surfing monster waves.

CRYSTAL COVE STATE PARK

The 3.5 miles of open beach and 2000 acres of undeveloped woodland at this state **beach** (☎ 949-494-3539, 949-492-0802; www.parks.ca.gov; 8471 N Coast Hwy; **P**) let you forget you're in a crowded metropolitan area, at least once you get past the parking lots ($10) and stake out a place on the sand.

You can mountain bike and hike on the inland side while diving is a draw along the coast. Many visitors don't know it, but Crystal Cove is also an underwater park. Scuba enthusiasts can check out two historic anchors dating from the 1800s as well as the crash site of a Navy plane that went down in the 1940s.

You can rent your own discreet little **cottage** (www.crystalcovebeachcottages.org) on the beach but competition is extremely fierce for these historic and surprisingly cheap accommodations. To reserve cabins and inland campsites and check the cabin rates, contact **ReserveAmerica** (☎ 800-444-7275; www.reserveamerica.com; campsites $10-14).

NEWPORT BAY ECOLOGICAL RESERVE

Inland from the harbor, where run-off from the San Bernardino Mountains meets the sea, the brackish water of the Newport Bay Ecological Reserve supports more than 200 species of birds. This is one of the few estuaries in SoCal that has been preserved, and it's an important stopover on the Pacific Flyway (see the Environment chapter).

It's also under the flyway for planes taking off from SNA, but this annoyance doesn't overly detract from the awesome wildlife viewing. Stop by the **Muth Interpretive Center** (☎ 949-923-2290; 2301 University Dr; ✆ 10am-4pm Tue-Sun; **P** ✆) at the corner of Irvine Ave and N University Dr. Walk past the informational marker down a short hill to the center; it isn't visible from the parking lot. Inside, take a minute to wander. There's a tank-filled activity room crawling with mostly local snakes, spiders and other creatures, as well as a display about the building, which is made from sustainable and renewable materials. Before heading out, grab a trail map and information about the 752-acre reserve as well as guided walking and kayaking tours.

Activities

BOATING

The best thing about Newport Beach is its harbor and beaches. At least take a harbor tour (right), but, better yet, rent your own watercraft.

Kayak, sail or motor around the harbor with an outboard motorboat from **Marina Boat Rentals** (☎ 949-673-3372; 600 E Bay Ave) at the Fun Zone on Balboa Peninsula. Kayaks/sailboats cost $15/40 per hour and motorboats start at $60 per hour. Prices are about the same at **Balboa Boat Rentals** (☎ 949-673-7200; 510 E Edgewater), where kayaks cost $15 per hour, sailboats $45 per hour, and powerboats $65 per hour.

Rent a flat-bottomed electric boat that you pilot yourself, and take a cruise with up to 12 friends. No boating experience required. Boats have heat and closable canopies. Bring CDs, food and drinks for a fun evening outing. Maps provided. Reserve one with **Duffy Electric Boat Rentals** (☎ 949-645-6812; www .duffyboats.com; 2001 West Coast Hwy; per hr $95 with 1hr minimum). Advance reservations recommended. Marina Boat Rentals rents them for less ($80 per hour for an 18-footer), but they're not as cushy.

CYCLING & SKATING

For beach views, ride a bike along the **dedicated path** that runs the length of the Balboa Peninsula. Inland, there's an invigorating **scenic loop** on the paved road that encircles the Upper Newport Bay and Ecological Reserve (in the afternoon the reserve gets breezy and cool; carry a sweater). There are lots of places to rent bikes, skates and surreys (with the fringe on top) at the Newport and Balboa Piers. Near the Fun Zone, head to **Balboa Bikes 'n' Beach Stuff** (☎ 949-723-1516; 601 E Balboa Blvd; bikes per hr/day $9/20) on the corner of Palm. Prices may fluctuate, and shop hours are variable, so call ahead to check. Closed on rainy days. For bikes near Newport Pier, visit **15th Street Surf Shop** (☎ 949-673-5810; 103 E 15th St; bikes per hr/day $5/17).

DIVING

There's terrific diving just south of Newport Beach at the underwater park at Crystal Cove State Park (opposite). Divers can check out reefs, anchors and an old military plane crash site. For rentals and day trips, stop by **Beach Cities Scuba Center** (☎ 949-650-5440; www.beachcitiesscuba .com, 4537 W Coast Hwy). Full equipment rental is about $60 per day.

SPAS & MASSAGES

After power shopping at Fashion Island, indulge yourself at **Spa Gregorie's** (☎ 949-644-6672; www.spagregories.com; 200 Newport Center Dr, Suite 100) just south of the mall. A deep-tissue massage is $90 per hour and facials cost $90 to $100 per hour. Once rejuvenated, stroll a few doors down to Muldoon's for some Irish-style mingling and drinking.

SURFING & SWIMMING

Surfers flock to the breaks at the small jetties surrounding the Newport Pier between 18th and 56th streets. Built in the 1960s after a storm destroyed much of the beach, the jetties are so prized by local surfers that they successfully protested the city's attempt to fill the spaces between them in 2004. Word of warning: locals can be territorial. For lessons, try Toes on the Nose (p273) at nearby Laguna Beach.

As for swimming, families will find a more relaxed atmosphere and calmer waves at the Newport Harbor Beaches along the peninsula, particularly at 10th St and 18th St. The latter, also known as Mother's Beach, has a lifeguard as well as restrooms and a shower.

Tours

One of the best ways to see Newport Beach is on a boat. Several companies offer narrated harbor tours from near the Balboa Pavilion. Just to the east of the Ferris wheel, the **Fun Zone Boat Co** (☎ 949-673-0240) operates 45- or 90-minute trips ($12 and $15) from Balboa Peninsula near the Fun Zone. It's $7 for kids between the ages of five and 11. **Catalina Passenger Service** (☎ 949-673-5245; 400 Main St, Balboa Peninsula) has 45-minute (adult/child $12/7) and 90-minute (adult/child $15/3) cruises that leave hourly from Balboa Pavilion. Both run extra boats during the Christmas Boat Parade for about $20 per person. Make reservations.

Take a whale-watching trip from December 26 through to March; call **Davey's Locker** (☎ 949-673-1434; www.daveyslocker.com; 400 Main St, Balboa Peninsula), also at the Balboa Pavilion, which offers trips for $25/20 per adult/child. It also operates sport-fishing trips out to sea, including half-day ($33) and overnight ($120) excursions. You can also ride with them in the Christmas Boat Parade ($18/14 per adult/child).

Festivals & Events

For details on local events, contact the visitors bureau (p263).

The week before Christmas brings thousands of spectators to Newport Harbor to watch the nightly **Christmas Boat Parade**, a tradition that began in 1919. The 2 ½-hour parade of lighted and decorated boats begins at 6:30pm. You can watch it all for free from the Fun Zone or Balboa Island or on a harbor tour.

Sleeping

Rates listed are for high season. They drop by as much as 50% in winter.

ourpick **Newport Channel Inn** (☎ 949-642-3030, 800-255-8614; www.newportchannelinn.com; 6030 W Coast Hwy; r $119-289; **P** wi-fi) Cyclists love the proximity to the beach bike path – it's just across PCH from this spotless two-story motel. Other perks include large rooms, a big common sundeck and genuinely friendly owners. Enjoy a vacation-lodge vibe under the A-frame roof of Room 219, which sleeps up to seven. Close to Cappy's Café too. Top budget choice.

Newport Dunes Waterfront Resort & Marina (☎ 949-729-3800, 800-765-7661; www.newportdunes.com; 1131 Backbay Dr; r $185-365; **P** **□** wi-fi) Sometimes 'resort' means expensive campground, and this is one of those times. But RVs and tents aren't required for a stay here: two dozen tiny A-frame cottages are available, all within view of Newport Bay. Trails, rentable kayaks, a pool and a playground await. The scrappy lobby now houses the concrete handprints of several cast members from *The OC*, the memorial having been booted from its spot of honor at the Newport Beach Visitors Bureau after building management requested its removal.

Little Inn by the Bay (☎ 949-673-8800, 800-438-4466; www.littleinnbythebay.com; 2627 Newport Blvd; r $199-259; **P** **□** wi-fi) If you've ever dreamed of sleeping on an island for under $300, now's your chance. Just know it's a traffic island surrounded by two busy thoroughfares. But if you're not bothered by street noise, this easygoing 18-room motel is a good option, if steep in high season. You can walk to the beach, and bikes and boogie boards are available for rent. There's air-con in half the rooms.

Doryman's Oceanfront Inn (☎ 949-675-7300; www .dorymansinn.com; 2102 W Oceanfront; r $199-379; **P**) They leave your room door open until you

check in at this 2nd-floor oceanfront B&B, a welcoming tradition that also offers ample opportunity for snooping through the unique rooms decorated with Victorian country flair. Each room is unique, and six have an ocean view. Good for couples and antiques lovers, it's a great location right by the Newport Pier, although it can get a bit loud.

Bay Shores Peninsula Hotel (☎ 949-675-3463, 800-222-6675; www.thebestinn.com; 1800 W Balboa Blvd; r $244-290; **P** **□** **⊠** wi-fi) No longer affiliated with Best Western, this three-story, newly renovated motel is ready to flex some surf-themed muscle. From *Endless Summer* surfing murals and complimentary fresh-baked cookies to the shelves of free rental movies, Bay Shores is beachy, casual and customer-focused. It's also pretty close to the beach, which accounts for the price.

Balboa Bay Club & Resort (☎ 949-645-5000, 888-445-7153; www.balboabayclub.com; 1221 W Coast Hwy; r $365-595; **P** **□** **⊠**) Humphrey Bogart courted Lauren Bacall at this harborside, full-service luxury resort, back when it was still a private yacht club. Now there's a hotel attached to the historical building, and its discreet architecture complements the craftsmanship of the yachts moored outside. Rooms have topflight amenities – book one on the waterside. It's pricey, but perfect for a kiss-and-make-up splurge. Good restaurant, too. Parking costs $18 for 24 hours.

Eating

Don't be alarmed to find many of the best restaurants tucked into pre-fab strip malls. This is the OC after all.

Ruby's Crystal Cove Shake Shack (☎ 949-464-0100; 7703 E Coast Hwy; shakes $4.62 incl tax; ♥ 10am to sunset; **P**) South Carolina has South of the Border, South Dakota has Wall Drug and SoCal has Ruby's Shake Shack, formerly known as Crystal Cove Shake Shack. But this place is so good, tacky billboards simply aren't needed. Although this been-here-forever wooden shake stand, between Newport and Laguna, is now owned by the Ruby's Diner chain, the shakes and ocean view are as good as ever. Don't fear the date shake, it's delish. The Shake Shack is located just east of the Crystal Cove/Los Trancos entrance to Crystal Cove State Park Historic District.

Cappy's Café (☎ 949-646-4202; 5930 W Coast Hwy; mains $6-12; ♥ 6am-3pm Mon-Fri, 6am-4pm Sat & Sun; **P**) Around since 1958, this bright blue diner serves

YUMMIEST BEACH BREAKFAST JOINTS

- Nick's Deli, Seal Beach (p254) – Order the breakfast burrito. Change your life.

- Harbor House Café, Sunset Beach (p256) – Find large portions and friendly staff here.

- Sugar Shack, Huntington Beach (p260) – Enjoy tasty breakfast on the cheap.

- Cappy's Café, Newport Beach (opposite) – Don't hassle the steak and eggs.

- Plums Cafe, Costa Mesa (below) – Not really at the beach. But yummy.

tasty omelettes, country fried steak, stuffed French toast and numerous other cholesterol-heavy breakfasts, though egg substitutes are now available. They cook the bacon crispy.

Plums Cafe (☎ 949-722-7586; 369 E 17th St; mains $7-13; ☕ breakfast & lunch; P) Raise your breakfast game with a gourmet dish at this tasty bistro tucked in the corner of a cookie-cutter strip mall near Newport Beach. With its exposed brick walls and sleek designs, Plums will have you feeling oh-so-chic as you nibble hazelnut pancakes, Oregon pepper bacon and French-rolled omelettes.

Taco Rosa (☎ 949-720-0980; 2632 San Miguel Rd; most mains $8-25; P ⚤) Locals bring out-of-town guests to this festive, family-friendly Mexican restaurant (at the back of a strip mall) for thoughtfully prepared dishes a step above your everyday taco-beans-rice combos. The blackened chicken burrito is tops as is the chocolate fountain where kids hover for free samples. Beloved Taco Mesa (p269), in Costa Mesa, is run by the same family.

Kingyo Sushi (☎ 949-721-5883; 21135 Newport Coast Dr; mains $8-30) This tiny sushi joint just down from Zov's may be new on the scene but it's already drawing a loyal following. Efficient service, accessible sushi chefs and sinfully good rolls will have you joining the fan club. If you like it spicy, the Kingyo roll – with Cajun tuna *tataki* (seared on a hot flame), spicy tuna and chili sauce – is a must.

Zov's Café Bakery & Bar (☎ 949-760-9687; 21123 Newport Coast Dr, mains $8.50-17) Don't be put off by the strip mall setting. Bustling Zov's is the creation of passionate local chef and restaurateur Zov Karamardian, famous for her Mediterranean-style dishes prepared with Californian flair.

From Moroccan salmon salads and grilled lamb sandwiches to spinach and ricotta ravioli, it's all good. The desserts are excellent too. For chocoholics, the milk chocolate bomb should satisfy your cravings.

Bluewater Grill (☎ 949-675-3474; 630 Lido Park Dr; mains lunch $10-25.50, dinner $14-25.50; ☕ 11am-10pm Mon-Thu, 11am-11pm Fri & Sat, 10am-10pm Sun) Sit on the wooden deck and watch the boats at this polished harborside restaurant/oyster bar that serves incredibly fresh fish. Great for Bloody Marys and a leisurely seafood and coleslaw lunch.

Crab Cooker (☎ 949-673-0100; 2200 Newport Blvd; mains $11-29; ☕ 11am-9pm Sun-Thu, 11am-10pm Fri & Sat) Expect a wait at this always-busy fish joint, which serves great seafood and fresh crab on paper plates to an appreciative crowd wearing flip-flops and jeans. Don't miss the delicious chowder – it's loaded with clams. If you're in a hurry, saunter up to the fish market counter just inside and order your seafood to go.

21 Oceanfront (☎ 949-673-2100; 2100 W Oceanfront; most mains $25-49; ☕ dinner) Prime steaks and fresh seafood served in a dimly lit Victorian-style dining room make this refined oceanfront restaurant a favorite for birthdays and anniversaries. Don't forget your wallet.

Drinking

Alta Coffee Warehouse (☎ 949-675-0233; 506 31st St; ☕ 6am-11pm Mon-Thu, 6am-midnight Fri & Sat, 7am-11pm Sun) Hang your mug at this cozy coffee shop housed in an inviting beach bungalow that lures locals with a book exchange, art on the walls (for sale) and honest baristas who dish the lowdown on the day's desserts.

Malarky's (☎ 949-675-2340; 3011 Newport Blvd) Follow the laughing leprechaun to this beachy dive where hunky lifeguard bartenders pour tequila for sorority girls and their frat-boy suitors from USC. Bring ID – you *will* get carded.

Muldoon's (☎ 949-640-4110; 202 Newport Center Dr, Fashion Island; ☕ closed Mon) The SoCal Irish tradition continues at upbeat Muldoon's, anchoring a small strip mall across the street from Fashion Island. It's one of the only spots open past 11pm for the beyond-30 set. Ten beers on tap. Good, if pricey, Irish pub grub.

3-Thirty-3 Waterfront (☎ 949-673-8464; 333 Bayside Dr) Sip cocktails with Newport's most stylish up-and-comers at this upscale lounge where views of the yacht-filled harbor are superb. It's perfect for happy hour or just relaxing with friends. Save room for nibbling: the small plates here are excellent – try the not-so-tiny sliders with the delicious fries.

Duke's Place (☎ 949-645-5000; Balboa Bay Club & Resort, 1221 W Coast Hwy) Don white linen, valet the car and sip margaritas under a portrait of John Wayne while tapping your toe to piano jazz and watching the yachts at the high-style Balboa Bay Club & Resort bar and lounge.

Entertainment

Regency Lido (☎ 949-673-8350; 3459 Via Lido) Showing movies since 1938, the Lido now screens independent films. Glow-in-the-dark murals on the walls keep things funky. It's on the corner of Newport Blvd and Via Lido just as you drive over the bridge onto the peninsula.

See first-run mainstream films at either **Edwards Island Seven** (☎ 949-640-1971; 999 Newport Center Dr) or **Edwards Big Newport Six** (☎ 949-640-4600; 300 Newport Center Dr), both at Fashion Island. General admission is $10, children under 11 and seniors $7.50. For matinees (shows before 6pm), general admission is only $8.50 (children under 11 and seniors $7.50).

Shopping

Fashion Island (☎ 949-721-2000; 550 Newport Center Dr; ☺ 10am-9pm Mon-Fri, 10am-7pm Sat, 11am-6pm Sun) With nearly 200 stores, this is the place to shop in Newport Beach. A chic outdoor mall that opened in 1967, Fashion Island sits in the middle of a traffic loop known as Newport Center Dr. Anchored by Bloomingdales, Macy's and Neiman Marcus, the mall's breezy, Mediterranean-style walkways are lined with specialty stores, national chains, upscale kiosks, numerous restaurants and the occasional koi pond and burbling fountain. The old-fashioned carousel and a minitrain lure the kiddies while their mothers heed the call of 40 or so women's apparel and accessory stores including Juicy Couture, Betsey Johnson, Kate Spade and Nike Women. There's a small indoor section, Atrium Court, with a Barnes & Noble.

On Balboa Island, Marine Ave is lined with cute shops in a village atmosphere, a good place to pick up something for the kids.

AROUND NEWPORT BEACH

Two nearby communities that don't have Newport's name recognition but still draw crowds for their very specific charms are Corona del Mar and Costa Mesa.

Corona del Mar

Savor some of SoCal's most beloved ocean views from the bluffs of Corona del Mar, an upscale Newport community stretching along PCH and hugging the eastern flank of the Newport Channel. Although the city is governed by Newport Beach, it has its own separate post office, library, Chamber of Commerce and upscale chichi vibe. In addition to stellar views, you'll find numerous rocky coves and child-friendly tidepools.

INFORMATION

Chamber of Commerce (☎ 949-673-4050; 2855 East Coast Hwy, Suite 101; ☺ 9am-5pm Mon-Fri) Has brochures and information on local shops and businesses.
Public Library (☎ 949-644-3075; www.newport-beach.ca.us/nbpl; 420 Marigold Ave, ☺ 9am-6pm Tue-Sat)
US Post Office (☎ 949-673-2989; www.usps.com; 406 Orchid Ave; ☺ 8:30am-5pm Mon-Fri, 9am-3pm Sat) Mail letters and buy stamps. A stamp machine is available when the window's closed.

SIGHTS & ACTIVITIES

Corona del Mar State Beach (☎ 949-644-3151; ☺ 6am-10pm; **P**) lies at the foot of rocky cliffs. There are restrooms, fire rings (arrive early to snag one) and volleyball courts. Parking costs $8 on weekdays, $10 on weekends. Arrive by 9am on weekends to get a space. Enter off Ocean Blvd across from Jasmine Ave. If you're early or lucky, you may find free parking atop the cliffs behind the beach along Ocean Blvd.

Children love the tide pools at **Little Corona Beach** just to the east, but be aware that the pools are being loved to death. Don't yank anything from the rocks and tread lightly; light, oxygen and heavy footsteps can kill the critters. Because there's no parking lot, crowds may be lighter. Look for street parking on Ocean Blvd near Poppy Ave.

Lookout Point sits above the beach on Ocean Blvd near Heliotrope Ave. Conceal your chardonnay: technically you can't drink here, though many people do. In fact, some people practically throw cocktail parties here, mostly because of the fantastic views overlooking the mouth of the harbor.

Take the stairs to **Pirate's Cove**, a great waveless beach, which is good for families. Some of the scenes for *Gilligan's Island* were shot in the cove. A bit further east on Ocean Blvd, near the intersection with Orchid Ave, is **Inspiration Point**, where the views of surf, sand and sea are equally impressive. Make sure your camera batteries have juice before you get here.

Corona del Mar's prize attraction is the **Sherman Library & Gardens** (☎ 949-673-2261; www .slgardens.org; 2647 E Coast Hwy; adult/child $3/1, Mon free; ☯ gardens 10:30am-4pm daily, library 9am-4:30pm Tue-Thu, sometimes closes for lunch at 1pm). The gardens are manicured, lush and exploding with color. Profuse orchids, a rose garden, a koi pond and even a desert garden are just a few high points. The small, noncirculating research library holds a wealth of historical documents from California, Arizona, Nevada and Baja, as well as paintings by early Californian landscape artists. The California city directories here are a boon to detectives and genealogists; some date to the early 1800s and include a citizen's name, job, spouse, children and address.

Costa Mesa

If not for South Coast Plaza, a sprawling shopping complex boasting 300 luxury stores, Costa Mesa would likely be considered just another landlocked suburb transected by the I-405. But nearby Newport Beach and Anaheim won't be kicking sand in the face of Costa Mesa anytime soon, not as long as the mall – properly termed a 'shopping resort' – continues to attract 25 million visitors a year and report annual sales approaching $1.5 billion.

But Costa Mesa does have other things going for it beside shopping. Visitors will find Orange County's cultural heart here. The ambitious Orange County Performing Arts Center draws international performing-arts luminaries and Broadway road shows while the Tony Award–winning South Coast Repertory earns accolades for its commitment to original plays and playwrights.

From the beaches, Costa Mesa is the next city inland from Newport Beach via Hwy 55. To reach South Coast Plaza, take the Del Mar/Fair Dr exit and continue straight along Hwy 55, then turn left on Bristol and follow it to the mall.

INFORMATION
Public Library (☎ 949-646-8845; www.ocpl.org; 1855 Park Ave; ☯ 10am-9pm Mon-Thu, 10am-5pm Fri & Sat, noon-5pm Sun) Free internet access and wi-fi.

Travelex (☎ 714-751-1203; South Coast Plaza, Costa Mesa; ☯ 10am-9pm Mon-Fri, 10am-8pm Sat, 11:30am-8pm Sun) On the 1st floor near the carousel.

SIGHTS & ACTIVITIES
Like any self-respecting SoCal diva, **South Coast Plaza** (☎ 800-782-8888; www.southcoastplaza.com, 3333 Bristol St) is getting a facelift for her 40th birthday – too bad it's costing $155 million dollars. The money will cover a new 300,000 sq ft Bloomingdales, the county's first H&M and 150,000 sq ft of travertine flooring outside glamorous Jewel Court. The changes seem superfluous when added to the mall's already stellar statistics: 300 luxury stores, seven department stores, five valet stations and 12,750 parking spaces. First-time visitors should grab a map at one of the four concierge booths. Shops range from tried-and-true (Abercrombie & Fitch, Ann Taylor and Gap) to high end (Ferragamo, Armani and Hermes).

The **Lab** (☎ 714-966-6660; www.thelab.com; 2930 Bristol St; ☯ 10:30am-9pm Mon-Sat; 11am-6pm Sun), an ivy-covered, outdoor 'Anti-mall,' is a refreshing alternative to the South Coast Plaza. Indie-minded shoppers can sift through vintage clothing, unique sneakers and trendy duds. In-your-face contemporary art exhibits are displayed in the adjoining ARTery gallery.

Vegans, tree-huggers and rock climbers, lend me your ears. The **Camp** (☎ 714-444-4267; www.thecampsite.com, 2937 Bristol St; ☯ 10:30am-9pm Mon-Sat, 11am-6pm Sun) offers one-stop shopping for all your outdoor and natural-living needs. Adventure 16, Cyclewerks, Liburdi's Scuba and Native Foods are a few of the stores clustered around a cozy outdoor walkway dotted with inspirational quotes.

From South Coast Plaza, follow the Unity Bridge pedestrian walkway over Bristol St to the quiet indulgences of the ever-so-posh **Spa** (☎ 714-850-0050; www.thespaandfitnessclub.com; 695 Town Center Dr) . The South Coast Swedish Massage costs $105 for 50 minutes, while the Anti-Aging Facial costs $145 for 80 minutes – a price that may return one or two of those wrinkles.

EATING
Taco Mesa (☎ 948-642-0629; 647 W 19th St; mains under $10; ☯ lunch & dinner) Sister restaurant to Taco Rosa (p267), this inexpensive Mexican hotspot is consistently named a local favourite.

Native Foods (☎ 714-751-2151; 2937 Bristol St, The Camp; mains $7-15; ☯ 11am-10pm; **P** **V**) Lunch in a yurt? In Orange County? Them's the digs at Native Foods, an inviting vegetarian spot smack in the middle of the Camp (p269). Boasting a substantial non-meat menu – from organic salads to veggie burgers to rice bowls to six-topping pizzas – it'll take some time to order.

Habana (☎ 714-556-0176; 2930 Bristol St, The Lab; mains $14-36; ☺ lunch & dinner; P) With its flickering votive candles, ivy-covered courtyard and spicy Cuban specialties, this sultry cantina whispers rendezvous. Mains include paella, *ropa vieja* (steak in tomato sauce) and a delicious salmon *al parilla* (grilled) with spicy tomato sauce. Plantains and black beans available with most dishes. On weekends, the bar gets jumpin' late night.

DRINKING

Kitsch Bar (☎ 714-546-8580; 891 Baker St) You won't find pink flamingos or Elvis bobbleheads at this not-so-kitschy watering hole. Just a low-key, dimly lit lounge where the vibe is upscale and decidedly hip. Enter between not-so-hip State Farm Insurance and Costa Mesa Dentistry.

Goat Hill Tavern (☎ 949-548-8428; 1830 Newport Blvd) Seriously divey, but some dudes swear by it.

ENTERTAINMENT

Orange County Performing Arts Center (☎ 714-556-2787; www.ocpac.org; 600 Town Center Dr) The Arts Center includes the acoustically stunning 3000-seat Segerstrom Hall, the 2000-seat Segerstrom Concert Hall and the smaller multifunctional Samueli Theater. Wide-ranging calendar.

South Coast Repertory (☎ 714-708-5555; www.scr.org; 655 Town Center Dr) Started by a band of plucky theater grads in the 1960s, the South Coast Repertory has evolved into an award-winning company that's managed to hold true to its mission 'to explore the most urgent human and social issues of our time.' Stages its ground-breaking plays from fall through to spring.

LAGUNA BEACH

pop 25,000

It's easy to love Laguna: secluded coves, romantic cliffs, azure waves and waterfront parks imbue the city with a Riviera-like feel. But nature isn't the only draw. From public sculptures and artist-friendly festivals to walking tours and free summer shuttles, the city's taken thoughtful steps to promote culture and tourism while maintaining quality of life (though some may call support of MTV's racy reality show *Laguna Beach* a troubling exception).

One of the earliest incorporated cities in California, Laguna has a strong tradition in the arts, starting with the 'plein air' impressionists in the early 1900s, and is the home of several renowned festivals (see p274). There are several dozen galleries, a well-known art museum and a popular art walking tour on the first Thursday evening of the month. Laguna swells with tourists on summer weekends, but away from the downtown village (the central business district) and Main Beach (where the downtown village meets the shore), there's plenty of uncrowded sand and open water.

Bring quarters for the meters. Lots of quarters.

Orientation

Hwy 1 goes by several names in Laguna Beach. South of Broadway, downtown's main street, it's called South Coast Hwy; north of Broadway it's North Coast Hwy. And you'll hear locals call it both Pacific Coast Hwy and just PCH.

Laguna stretches for about 7 miles along PCH. Shops, restaurants and bars are concentrated along a 0.25-mile stretch in the Village, along three parallel streets: Broadway, Ocean Ave and Forest Ave.

Information

BOOKSTORES

Barnaby Rudge Bookseller (☎ 949-497-4079; www.barnabyrudge.com; 1445 Glenneyre St) Wonderful antiquarian book store. Sells maps and prints too.

Laguna Beach Books (☎ 949-494-4779; www.lagunabeachbooks.com; 1200 South Coast Hwy; P) Located in the Old Pottery Place minicomplex at Brooks St, this friendly shop stocks everything from chick lit and mysteries to surf culture. Good section on SoCal and local travel.

Latitude 33 (☎ 949-494-5403; 311 Ocean Ave) Good independent, generalist bookstore that's crammed floor-to-ceiling with books. There's a small but varied travel section and helpful staff. It's also a great camera-repair shop.

INTERNET ACCESS

Laguna Beach Library (☎ 949-497-1733; www.ocpl.org; 363 Glenneyre St; ☺ 10am-8pm Mon-Wed, 10am-6pm Thu, 10am-5pm Fri & Sat) A maximum of one hour's use per day; make a donation. It's at the corner of Park Ave, one block east of PCH.

Laguna Beach Visitors & Conference Bureau (☎ 949-497-9229, 800-877-1115; www.lagunabeachinfo.org; 252 Broadway; ☺ 10am-4pm Mon-Fri, 10am-2pm

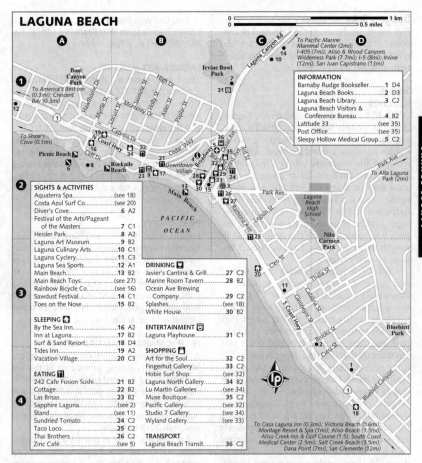

LAGUNA BEACH

INFORMATION
Barnaby Rudge Bookseller	**1** D4
Laguna Beach Books	**2** D3
Laguna Beach Library	**3** C2
Laguna Beach Visitors & Conference Bureau	**4** B2
Latitude 33	(see 35)
Post Office	(see 35)
Sleepy Hollow Medical Group	**5** C2

SIGHTS & ACTIVITIES
Aquaterra Spa	(see 18)
Costa Azul Surf Co	(see 20)
Diver's Cove	**6** A2
Festival of the Arts/Pageant of the Masters	**7** C1
Heisler Park	**8** A2
Laguna Art Museum	**9** B2
Laguna Culinary Arts	**10** C1
Laguna Cyclery	**11** C3
Laguna Sea Sports	**12** A1
Main Beach	**13** B2
Main Beach Toys	(see 27)
Rainbow Bicycle Co	(see 16)
Sawdust Festival	**14** C1
Toes on the Nose	**15** B2

SLEEPING
By the Sea Inn	**16** A2
Inn at Laguna	**17** B2
Surf & Sand Resort	**18** D4
Tides Inn	**19** A2
Vacation Village	**20** C3

EATING
242 Cafe Fusion Sushi	**21** B2
Cottage	**22** B2
Las Brisas	**23** B2
Sapphire Laguna	(see 2)
Stand	(see 11)
Sundried Tomato	**24** C2
Taco Loco	**25** C2
Thai Brothers	**26** C2
Zinc Café	(see 5)

DRINKING
Javier's Cantina & Grill	**27** C2
Marine Room Tavern	**28** B2
Ocean Ave Brewing Company	**29** C2
Splashes	(see 18)
White House	**30** B2

ENTERTAINMENT
Laguna Playhouse	**31** C1

SHOPPING
Art for the Soul	**32** C2
Fingerhut Gallery	**33** C2
Hobie Surf Shop	(see 32)
Laguna North Gallery	**34** B2
Lu Martin Galleries	(see 34)
Muse Boutique	**35** C2
Pacific Gallery	(see 32)
Studio 7 Gallery	(see 34)
Wyland Gallery	(see 33)

TRANSPORT
Laguna Beach Transit	**36** C2

ORANGE COUNTY

Sat, 10am-2pm Sun Jul & Aug, closed Sun Sep-Jun) You can check your email free for 15 minutes here.

MEDICAL SERVICES
Sleepy Hollow Medical Group (☎ 949-494-3740; 364 Ocean Ave; ☼ 8am-6pm Mon-Sat, 9am-1pm Sun) For nonemergency care.

South Coast Medical Center (☎ 949-499-1311; www.southcoastmedcenter.com; 31872 Coast Hwy) For a 24-hour hospital emergency room, head 4 miles south of the downtown village along Hwy 1 to this center. It's in South Laguna Beach at 7th Ave.

POST
Post office (☎ 949-362-8306, emergency 949-499-7193; 350 Forest Ave; ☼ 8:30am-5pm Mon-Fri) The Playa Branch sits near the corner of Beach St in the downtown village. There's also a self-service machine if the window's closed.

TOURIST INFORMATION
Laguna Beach Visitors & Conference Bureau (☎ 949-497-9229, 800-877-1115; www.lagunabeachinfo.org; 252 Broadway; ☼ 10am-4pm Mon-Fri, 10am-2pm Sat, 10am-2pm Sun Jul & Aug, closed Sun Sep-Jun) Helpful staff, bus schedules, local restaurant menus and pamphlets on everything from hiking trails to self-guided public-art walks are available here. For those smitten with *Laguna Beach*, ask for the fact sheet pointing out lots of show locales. The free weekly *Coastline Pilot* is a good source for local news and events. There's also free 15-minute internet access available.

Dangers & Annoyances

Fire is a particular danger in Laguna. The canyons act like chimneys and small grass fires quickly become infernos. Use extreme caution with matches and cigarette butts.

Sights

BEACHES

With 30 public beaches and coves, Laguna Beach is perfect for do-it-yourself exploring. There's always another stunning view or hidden cove just around the bend. Although many of the coves are blocked from street view by multimillion-dollar homes, a good local map or sharp eye will take you to the numerous stairways leading from PCH down to the beach. Just look for the 'beach access' signs, and be prepared to pass through people's backyards to reach the sand. Unlike its neighbors to the north, Laguna doesn't impose a beach curfew.

Centrally located **Main Beach** has volleyball and basketball courts as well as benches, tables, a playground and restrooms. It's the best beach for swimming. North of Main Beach, it's too rocky to surf; tidepooling is best. Pick up a tide table at the visitors bureau. (Tidepool etiquette: tread lightly and don't pick anything up that you find living in the rocks.) Just north of Main Beach, stroll the grassy, bluff-top **Heisler Park** for sweeping views of the craggy coves and deep-blue sea. Bring your camera – with its palm trees, bougainvillea-dotted bluffs and soaring flocks of pelicans, the scene is one for posterity. Drop down below the park to **Diver's Cove**, a deep, protected inlet popular with snorkelers and, of course, divers. A scenic walkway connects Heisler Park to Main Beach. North of town, **Crescent Bay** has big hollow waves good for bodysurfing, but parking is difficult; try the bluffs atop the beach.

About 1 mile south of the Downtown Village, **Victoria Beach** has volleyball courts and **La Tour**, a Rapunzel's-tower–like structure from 1926. Skimboarding (at the south end) and bodysurfing are also popular here. Take the stairs down Victoria Dr; there's limited parking on Pacific Coast Hwy. Just south, **Aliso Beach** has parking and is popular with surfers, boogie boarders and skimboarders. With its picnic tables, fire pits and play area, it's also good for families. Pay-and-display parking here is $1 per hour. For a free spot, drive south and park on PCH.

You can rent beach chairs, umbrellas and boogie boards from **Main Beach Toys** (☎ 949-494-8808; 150 Laguna Ave at Pacific Coast Hwy).

LAGUNA ART MUSEUM

This breezy **museum** (☎ 949-494-8971; www.laguna artmuseum.com; 307 Cliff Dr; adult/under 12yr/student & senior $10/free/8; 🕙 11am-5pm) has changing exhibits usually featuring one or two California artists, and a permanent collection heavy on California landscapes, vintage photographs and works by early Laguna artists. There are free docent tours at 2pm daily, and an interesting gift shop. Hours may be extended depending on the exhibit. Check the website for further information.

PUBLIC ART

Laguna is full of public art, from well-placed murals to free-standing sculptures in unlikely locations. Pick up the *Public Art Brochure* from the visitors bureau for a self-guided tour. It shows color photos of all 51 of Laguna's public art pieces, as well as a bulleted map to help you navigate. Stop by Heisler Park to see almost a dozen sculptures.

PACIFIC MARINE MAMMAL CENTER

A nonprofit organization dedicated to rescuing and rehabilitating injured or ill marine mammals, the **mammal center** (☎ 949-494-3050; www.pacificmmc.org; 20612 Laguna Canyon Rd; admission by donation; 🕙 10am-4pm) has a small staff and many volunteers who help nurse the ailing sea lions and seals back to health.

Located northeast of town, you can visit – there are several outside pools and holding pens – but remember, this is a rescue center, not SeaWorld. Still, it's educational and heartwarming. And you can buy a stuffed animal in the gift shop to benefit the center.

Activities

HIKING

Surrounded by a green belt – a rarity in SoCal – Laguna has some good areas preserved for hiking. Hikers who love panoramic views should take the short, scenic drive to **Alta Laguna Park**, a hidden park up-canyon from town. Few nonlocals ever visit. Inside the park, the moderate **Park Avenue Nature Trail**, a 1.25-mile one-way hike, takes you through fields of wildflowers in spring.

The 2.5-mile **West Ridge Trail** follows the ridgeline of the hills above Laguna for stunning ocean views. It's open to hikers and mountain bikers. The visitors bureau stocks a fold-out trail guide. Take Park Ave from town to its end at Alta Laguna Blvd then turn left to the park, where there are restrooms and telephones. Both trails are in-and-out trails, not loops.

KAYAKING

Take a guided kayaking tour of the craggy coves of the Laguna coast in an inflatable, self-bailing kayak with **North Laguna Float Company** (☎ 949-494-5910; 2hr guided floats $35), a good company with reasonable prices. Most trips are scheduled for weekdays. On weekends, consider a tour in a hard-plastic two-seater with **La Vida Laguna** (☎ 949-275-7544; www.lavida laguna.com; 2hr guided floats $75, under 11yr discounted). You might just see a colony of sea lions. Make reservations for both.

CYCLING

Laguna Beach isn't the greatest for road biking. Drivers along always-busy PCH are distracted by the view, so pay attention if you head out on that road. Conditions and traffic improve once you get out of town.

Up in the hills, you can have a blast mountain biking. Crystal Cove State Park (p264) and **Aliso & Woods Canyons Wildnerness Park** (28373 Alicia Pkwy, Laguna Niguel) are locally recommended. Rent a bike and get trail info at **Laguna Cyclery** (☎ 949-494-1522; lagunacyclery.net; 240 Thalia St; ⏰ 10am-6pm Mon-Fri, 10am-5pm Sat & Sun) The cost of 24-hour rental is about $35 to $100 for road bikes and $35 to $65 for mountain bikes. They'll also arrange to have your bike shipped from overseas, although this can be expensive. Just north of town, try **Rainbow Bicycle Co** (☎ 949-494-5806; www.teamrain .com; 485 N Coast Hwy; ⏰ 11am-6pm Mon, 10am-6pm Tue-Sat, noon-4pm Sun), which rents road bikes for $35 per day and mountain bikes for $45 per day.

DIVING

With its coves, reefs and rocky outcroppings, Laguna is one of the best beaches on the SoCal coast for scuba diving and snorkeling. One of the most famous spots is **Diver's Cove** just below Heisler Park. It's part of the Glenn E Vedder Ecological Reserve, an underwater park stretching to the northern border of Main Beach. Also popular is **Shaw's Cove** just to the north. Check conditions before heading out: since 1997, 23 divers have drowned off the Laguna coast.

The visitors bureau (p271) has tidal charts. For rentals or a place to rinse your gear, stop by **Laguna Sea Sports** (☎ 949-494-6965; www.laguna seasports.com; 925 N Coast Hwy) near Shaw's Cove. Check out its website for info about local dive spots and diving etiquette.

SPAS

Follow the giant flower pots from the Surf & Sand Resort lobby to the tranquil charms of **Aquaterra Spa** (☎ 949-376-2772; www .aquaterraspa.com; 1555 S Coast Hwy). The signature massage is $110 for 50 minutes.

Spa Montage (☎ 866-271-6953; www.spamontage .com; 30801 S Coast Hwy), at the luxurious Montage Resort, allows you to relax until your strings squeak in a 'Symphony in Massage', with two massage therapists pounding out your pain in tandem for $440 to $600. A 60-minute facial is $220.

SURFING

Because of the coves, the surfing here isn't as stellar as it is further north. If you must, try the beaches at Thalia St and Brooks St (beware of the rocks). Rent a board or get instruction from **Costa Azul Surf Co** (☎ 949-497-1423; www.costaazul.net; 689 S Coast Hwy). Rental boards cost $30, wet suits $20. Lessons include board rental and cost $95 per hour for one person or $75 each per hour for two to three people. Also consider classes with **Toes on the Nose** (☎ 949-494-4988; www.toesonthenose.com; 276 S Coast Hwy). They cost $100 each for two hours for one person and $90 for two hours for two to three people.

Tours

Stop by the visitors bureau to pick up brochures detailing self-guided tours. The *Heritage Walking Companion* is a tour of the town's architecture with an emphasis on Laguna's many bungalows and cottages, most dating from the 1920s and '30s. The *Self-Guided Tour Laguna by Bus* gives a more general overview. Each involves riding public transportation (which is a relief: if you tried to take the tours using your own car, you'd go nuts trying to find parking, especially on weekends).

On the first Thursday of the month, downtown gets festive during the popular **First Thursdays Gallery Art Walk** (☎ 949-683-6871; www .firstthursdaysartwalk.com). During this free event, make the rounds between 40 local galleries and the Laguna Art Museum from 6pm to

---

LAGUNA ART FESTIVALS

With a stunning 6-acre canyon as its backdrop, Laguna's **Festival of the Arts** (650 Laguna Canyon Rd; 10am-11:30pm Jul & Aug; adults/students/seniors $7/4/4) is a two-month celebration of original artwork in almost all its forms. The 140 exhibiting artists – all approved pursuant to a juried selection process – display artwork ranging from paintings and hand-crafted furniture to scrimshaw. Begun in 1932 by local artists who needed to drum up buyers, the festival now attracts patrons and tourists from around the world. In addition to the art, there are free daily artists' workshops, docent tours and live entertainment. Look for the slightly more indie-minded art show, the **Sawdust Festival** (949-494-3030; www.sawdustartfestival.org; 935 Laguna Canyon Rd; adult/child/senior $7/3/6; 10am-10pm Jul & Aug) across the street.

The most thrilling part of the main festival, a tremendous experience that will leave you rubbing your eyes in disbelief, is the **Pageant of the Masters** (949-497-6582, 800-487-3378; www.pageanttickets.com; admission $25-300), where human models are blended seamlessly into re-creations of famous paintings. It began in 1933 as a sideshow to the main festival. Tickets are hard to secure, unless you order weeks or months in advance – though you may be able to snag last-minute cancellations at the gate. Nightly performances begin at 8:30pm.

9pm. Free shuttles run from the Laguna Art Museum and the **Bluebird Center** (1590 S Coast Hwy) to various participating galleries between 6:15pm and 8:45pm.

Sleeping

Remember that lodging in Laguna is on busy PCH, so expect traffic noise. Bring earplugs or ask for a room away from the road if you're sensitive. There are no budget lodgings in Laguna in summer. Listed are summer rates; come fall, they drop significantly.

America's Best Inn (949-494-6464, 877-363-7229; www.lagunabeachamericasbestinn.com; 1404 N Coast Hwy; r $129-209; P wi-fi) About 1 mile northwest of the Village, this easygoing, better-than-average motel has good prices, at least for Laguna. Take the shuttle to downtown. Can accommodate big groups and is popular with on-the-cheap wedding parties in the fall.

Tides Inn (949-494-2494, 888-777-2107; www.tideslaguna.com; 460 N Coast Hwy; r $150-295; P wi-fi) Tides Inn is a bargain for Laguna, especially considering its convenient location three blocks north of the Village. Plush bedding, soothing tones and a clean, decorative style contribute to the inn's upscale vibe. As a fun touch, each room has its own inspirational quote – try to find yours painted somewhere inside. Pets are welcome in some rooms for an extra charge.

Vacation Village (949-494-8566, 800-843-6895; www.vacationvillage.com; 647 S Coast Hwy; r & ste $179-639; P) If you found *Cheaper by the Dozen* charming, you'll love this kid-friendly motel. Southeast of downtown and right on

the beach, this 130-unit complex has motel rooms in several satellite buildings. About half the rooms have kitchens. Many of the oceanfront rooms were recently remodeled and sport a slightly hipper vibe. Two pools and a Jacuzzi room round out the appeal. Group-friendly, too.

our pick By the Sea Inn (949-497-6645, 800-297-0007; www.bytheseainn.com; 475 N Coast Hwy; r $199-259; P wi-fi) Be it good feng shui, friendly staff or a close proximity to the beach, something just feels right at this recently renovated 36-room inn, where guests return year after year. From the big green pillows and flat screen TVs to the hardwood floors, the decor is new, comfy and clean. For a relaxing close to the day, settle into the outdoor Jacuzzi with a glass of wine and your honey as the sun drops over the ocean. Wi-fi available in some rooms and by the pool.

Aliso Creek Inn (949-499-2271; www.alisocreekinn.com; 31106 S Coast Hwy; r $220-324; P) It feels like summer camp at friendly Aliso Creek Inn where roaming deer, a rippling creek and rustic townhouses share sprawling grounds. This tranquil alternative to the bustling downtown motel scene is also home to a nine-hole golf course. Don't be surprised to see rabbits, raccoons or other canyon-loving critters. There's a restaurant and easy access to Aliso Beach.

Inn at Laguna (949-497-9722, 800-544-4479; www.innatlagunabeach.com; 211 N Coast Hwy; r $239-569; P wi-fi) This three-story white concrete hotel, at the north end of Main Beach, walks the fine line between hip and homey with personable finesse. All rooms have a fresh, clean look complete with French blinds and thick featherbeds. Some have balconies overlooking the water. Extras include VCRs, clock radios with CD player, bathrobes and a continental breakfast delivered to your room. Cookies and apple cider at 5pm. Parking costs $14 per day.

Casa Laguna Inn (☎ 949-494-2996, 800-233-0449; www.casalaguna.com; 2510 S Coast Hwy; r $300-490; P ⌨ ☏ wi-fi) Laguna's B&B gem is built around a historic 1920s mission revival house surrounded by lush gardens. Rooms are inside former artists' bungalows built in the 1930s and '40s. All have delicious beds and some have Jacuzzis. There's also full chef-prepared breakfast – which could include salmon cakes or gourmet French toast – as well as evening wine and cheese. Wonderful.

Surf & Sand Resort (☎ 949-497-4477, 800-524-8621; www.surfandsandresort.com; 1555 S Coast Hwy; r $335-565; P ⌨ ☏) Be lulled to sleep by the crashing of waves at this sparkling, great-for-a-splurge seaside resort where every room has an ocean view. Rooms boast ultra-comfy beds, flat-screen TVs, an iPod dock with speakers and a soothing natural color scheme. There's also a full-service spa (p273).

Montage Resort & Spa (☎ 949-715-6000, 866-271-6953; www.montagelagunabeach.com; 30801 S Coast Hwy; r $695-895; P ⌨ ☏ wi-fi) If you want to demonstrate your devotion to your lover, you'll find nowhere more indulgent on the coast than this over-the-top luxury resort. Even if you're not staying here, come for a spa treatment or a cocktail and check out the art in the lobby and the spectacular inlaid sunburst in the swimming pool. At the south end of the resort, there's underground public parking ($0.25 for 15 minutes) and a public-access walkway that loops around the grounds atop the bluffs overlooking the sea, and provides free entry to the sandy shore.

Eating

Laguna has a lot of good restaurants. Vegetarians and Mexican food aficionados will be particularly happy.

Taco Loco (☎ 949-497-1635; 640 S Coast Hwy; dishes $3-12; ☽ 11am-midnight Sun-Thu, 11am-2am Fri & Sat; V) Throw back Coronas with the surfers while watching the passersby on PCH at this fantastic traditional Mexican sidewalk café where taco options seem endless: blackened mahi,

pork, veggie and shrimp to name a few. Order at the counter.

Zinc Café (☎ 949-494-6302; 350 Ocean Ave; dishes $4-9; ☽ breakfast & lunch; V) Ground zero for Laguna's see-and-be-seen vegetarians, Zinc has a hedge-enclosed patio where you can munch on tasty veg meals (including options with eggs). If you've been hesitant to order oatmeal at a restaurant, resist no more. Zinc's fresh fruit–covered version is delish. Order at the counter.

Stand (☎ 949-494-8101; 238 Thalia St; mains under $10; ☽ 7am-7pm; V) With its friendly, indie-spirited vibe, this tiny tribute to vegetarian cuisine reflects what's best about Laguna living. Not to mention the food is actually tasty. From hummus and guac sandwiches and sunflower sprout salads to bean and rice burritos, the menu is varied and all of it tempting. For a snack, try a smoothie, an all-natural shake or the corn tortilla chips with salsa. Order at the counter next to Laguna Cyclery – they're both in the red mini-barn. Grab a patio table and a free yoga mag. Delightful.

Cottage (☎ 949-494-3023; 308 N Coast Hwy; mains breakfast & lunch $6-11, dinner $10-27; ☽ breakfast, lunch & dinner) It feels like grandma's house inside this cute bungalow where scrumptious cranberry-orange pancakes are served until 3pm in various rooms of the house. The patio's popular too. Dinner is served nightly but breakfast is the big reason to come.

Sundried Tomato (☎ 949-494-3312; 361 Forest Ave; mains lunch $7-16, dinner $13-30) White linens and buttoned-down staff make this upscale café the very model of a chichi beach bistro. But don't worry, just order the salad sampler – pan-Asian, chopped and roasted chicken – with a glass of sauvignon blanc and you'll fit right in. The sundried tomato butter is sinful.

Thai Brothers (☎ 949-376-9979; 238 Laguna Ave; mains $11-17; ☽ noon-late) Everyone's happy at this tiny Thai joint just off PCH. Maybe it's the warm *tom yum* soup, the spicy red curries or the heaping plates of noodles flavored just right. For those who like it hot, the Fire Eater – with sliced chicken and veggies in a spicy sauce – is lick-your-plate good. Locals love the place.

Sapphire Laguna (☎ 949-715-9888; 1200 S Coast Hwy; mains lunch $12.50-16.50, dinner $10.50-29.50; ☽ lunch & dinner) The current darling of Laguna's see-and-be-seen set, this purveyor of global cuisine serves succulent specialties ranging from chicken pot pie to pan-seared barramundi. For the best view, snag a seat on the patio. The home-fried sage and rosemary sea salt potato chips may be long-winded but they're also utterly addictive. Reservations a must. Come for dinner rather than lunch.

Las Brisas (☎ 949-497-5434; 361 Cliff Dr; mains lunch $15-23, dinner $15-30) Locals roll their eyes at the mere mention of this tourist-heavy spot, but out-of-towners flock here for a reason: the view. It's one of the best you'll ever have of Laguna. Though the Mexican-seafood menu is nothing memorable, you won't soon forget the image of crashing waves as you sip margaritas on the glassed-in patio on the bluff. Cocktail hour gets packed. Don't come if it's dark outside; do make reservations.

242 Cafe Fusion Sushi (☎ 949-494-2444; 242 N Coast Hwy; dinner $18-45; ☯ dinner Tue-Sun) One of the only female sushi chefs in Orange County slices and rolls Laguna's best sushi – and it's artfully presented too. The place seats maybe 20 people at a time, so expect a wait or come early. The yellowtail with spicy miso sauce and the Laguna Canyon Roll are life-enhancing.

Drinking

There may be as many bars in Downtown Village as there are art galleries. Most cluster along S Coast Hwy and Ocean Ave, making for an easy pub crawl.

Javier's Cantina & Grill (☎ 949-494-1239; 480 S Coast Hwy; ☯ 11:30am-10pm Mon-Thu, 11:30am-11pm Fri & Sat, 10am-10pm Sun) Coronas, Pacificos and margaritas are the libations of choice at this upscale Mexican cantina. Surrounded by art galleries, tiny Javier's barely contains the stylish crowds spilling out the door on First Thursdays Gallery Art Walk.

Marine Room Tavern (949-494-3027; 214 Ocean Ave; ☯ 11am-midnight Mon-Fri, 10am-midnight Sat) The party's always rockin' at this lively Village tavern where the Harley-loving crowd isn't afraid to whoop it up, sometimes on the sidewalk. Although you won't find food or many marines, there is a full bar. Live music most nights.

Ocean Ave Brewing Company (☎ 949-497-3381; 237 Ocean Ave; ☯ 10am-2am Tue-Sun) For pub grub and microbrews, this is the place. Kick back on the sidewalk-adjacent patio for primo people-watching.

Splashes (☎ 949-497-4477; Surf & Sand Resort, 1555 S Coast Hwy; ☯ 11:30am-10pm Sun-Thu, to 11pm Fri & Sat) Settle in by the window and enjoy your favorite daydream while sipping fancy cocktails as the sun sets over crashing waves at this Surf & Sands Resort (p275) lounge. Snooty bartenders aside, Splashes is a great place to spend happy hour. Try an $8 Splashes lemonade or one of the $10 martinis.

White House (☎ 949-494-8088; 340 S Coast Hwy; ☯ 8am-10pm Mon-Fri, 9am-10pm Sat & Sun, bar to 2am daily) Serves OK food early, but come for the nightly entertainment and drink until 2am. Great for groups ready for a night on the town. There's a patio if things get too crowded inside.

Entertainment

Laguna Playhouse (☎ 949-497-2787; www.lagunaplayhouse.com; 606 Laguna Canyon Rd) The oldest continuously operating theater on the West Coast stages lighter plays in summer, heavier works in winter.

Shopping
SHOPS

Laguna's Downtown Village is a shopper's paradise, with hidden courtyards and eclectic little shacks that beg exploration. Forest Ave downtown has the highest concentration of chic boutiques.

Art for the Soul (☎ 949-497-8700; 272 Forest Ave; ☯ 10am-6pm) Decorated in big, bold colors, this eclectic gallery is the place to fill your bags with funky frames, painted martini glasses and upbeat books.

Hobie Surf Shop (☎ 949-497-3304; 294 Forest Ave; ☯ Mon-Thu 9am-8pm, 9am-9pm Fri & Sat, to 10pm daily in summer) Hobart 'Hobie' Alter started his internationally known surf line in his parents' Laguna Beach garage more than 50 years ago. Today, this is one of only four Hobie retail store where you can stock up on beachwear and surf boards.

Muse Boutique (☎ 949-497-7026; 300 Forest Ave; ☯ 10am-8pm Sun-Thu, 10am-9pm Fri & Sat) Fans of MTV's *Laguna Beach* will recognize this upbeat gallery where beach-chic couture glitters under a sky-blue ceiling dotted with wispy clouds.

Pacific Gallery (☎ 949-494-8732; 228 Forest Ave; ☯ 11am-6pm) Here you'll find gifts that are whimsical, artistical and sometimes irresistible.

ART GALLERIES

Laguna has three distinct gallery districts: Gallery Row along N Coast Hwy in North Laguna, in Downtown Village along Forest

Ave and S Coast Hwy, and south on S Coast Hwy between Oak St and Bluebird Canyon. Pick up an art-walk map at the visitors bureau. **Laguna North Gallery** (☎ 949-494-4324; www.lagunanorthgallery.com; 376 N Coast Hwy; ☽ 11am-4:30pm) and **Studio 7 Gallery** (☎ 949-497-1080; www.studio7gallery.com; 384b N Coast Hwy; ☽ 11am-5pm) are cooperative galleries showcasing affordable plein air prints by local artists. On the same block, **Lu Martin Galleries** (☎ 949-494-8074; 372 N Coast Hwy) showcases eye-catching original oil paintings by regional and international artists. More galleries cluster along Forest Ave and S Coast Hwy in Downtown Village. These range from the high-end, high-cost paintings and sculptures at two-story **Fingerhut Gallery** (☎ 949-376-6410; www.fingerhutart.com; 210 Forest Ave) to the bright, DayGlo charms of the whales and sea creatures inhabiting the canvases at the **Wyland Gallery** (☎ 949-497-9494; www.wylandgalleries.com; 218 Forest Ave). Head south on PCH for another cluster of galleries in South Laguna.

Galleries participating in the First Thursdays Gallery Art Walk are typically open that night until 9pm.

Getting There & Away

To reach Laguna Beach from I-405, take Hwy 133 (Laguna Canyon Rd) southwest. Laguna is served by OCTA bus 1, which runs along the coast.

Getting Around

Laguna is hemmed in by steep canyons, and parking is a perpetual problem. Pack quarters to feed the meters. If you're spending the night, leave your car at the hotel and ride the local bus. Parking lots in the village charge $10 or more per entry and fill up early in the day in summer. Parking can be hard to find near the beaches on busy summer weekends. Arrive early and bring dollar bills and quarters. The coin-only meters cost $1 per hour and the pay-and-display lots cost $2 per hour. There's a change machine on Cliff Dr just past Heisler Park and a few scattered throughout downtown. Alternatively, park a few blocks away from downtown, in the free residential areas near the beach.

Through town, PCH moves slowly in summer, especially in the afternoon on weekends. If you can't find parking downtown, drive to the north end of town by the beach and ride the bus.

Laguna Beach Transit (☎ 949-497-0746; www.lagunabeachcity.net; 300 block of Broadway) has its central bus depot on Broadway, just north of the visitors bureau in the heart of the village. It operates three routes at hourly intervals (no service between 12:30pm and 1:30pm or on Sunday or holidays). Routes are color-coded and easy to follow but subject to change. For tourists, the most important route is the one that runs north–south along PCH. Pick up a brochure and schedule at your hotel or the visitors bureau. Rides cost $0.75.

To alleviate summer traffic, the city recently started a **free shuttle service** (☎ 949-497-0746) that travels between popular events such as the Sawdust Festival and the Pageant of the Masters between 9:30am and 11:30pm. Look for the big open trolley or transit buses with flags on top. Available between June 20 and the end of September.

AROUND LAGUNA BEACH
San Juan Capistrano

Famous for its swallows that fly back to town every year on March 19 (though sometimes they're just a bit early), San Juan Capistrano is also home to the 'jewel of the California missions.' It's a little town, about 10 miles south and inland of Laguna Beach, but there's enough history and charm here to make almost a day of it.

INFORMATION

Friends of San Juan Capistrano Library (☎ 949-493-2688; Public Library; ☽ 10am-8pm Mon-Wed, 10am-6pm Thu, 10am-5pm Sat, noon-5pm Sun) At the back of the main library complex. Here you'll find great deals on used books and magazines, and an eclectic travel section.
Information Kiosk (Verdugo St at the train tracks; ☽ 8:30am-3:30pm) Staffed by volunteers, this is a good stop for maps and brochures.
Public Library (☎ 949-493-1752; www.ocpl.org; 31495 El Camino Real; ☽ 10am-8pm Mon-Thu, 10am-5pm Sat) Free internet access.

SIGHTS & ACTIVITIES

Located at the corner of Camino Capistrano and Ortega Hwy, **Mission San Juan Capistrano** (☎ 949-234-1300; www.missionsjc.com; 26801 Ortega Hwy; adult/4-11yr/senior $7/5/6; ☽ 8:30am-5pm) draws visitors from around the world. The charming Serra Chapel – whitewashed and decorated with colorful symbols – is believed to be the oldest building in California. It's the only one

...g in which Father Junipero Serra
...ass. Serra founded the mission on No-
...mber 1, 1776, and tended it personally for
many years, confirming 213 people on one
particularly busy June day in 1783. Plan on
spending at least an hour poking around the
sprawling grounds – lush gardens, fountains,
courtyards and mission structures – including the padre's quarters, soldiers' barracks
and the cemetery. Particularly moving are
the towering remains of the Great Stone
Church, almost completely destroyed by a
powerful earthquake on December 8, 1812
that killed 42 Native Americans worshiping
inside.

San Juan Capistrano is also where the legendary swallows return each year to nest – on
March 19, the feast of Saint Joseph – after win-
tering in South America. Their flight covers
about 15,000 miles. The **Festival of the Swallows**
is the highlight of the mission's active year-
round events schedule.

One block west, next to the Capistrano
train depot, the **Los Rios Historic District** is a
cutesy assemblage of 31 historic cottages and
adobes that now mostly house cafés and gift
shops. To see furnishings and decor in an
1870s-era home as well as vintage photographs of the area, stop by the **O'Neill Museum**
(31831 Los Rios St). You can pick up a walking
tour guide of Historic Downtown San Juan
Capistrano at most of the stores in the downtown area.

EATING

There are a lot of restaurants within walking
distance of the mission. Most are pretty good,
but here are a few favorites.

Sarducci's Capistrano Depot (☎ 949-493-3593; 26701
Verdugo St; mains $10-16; ☺ 8am-9pm Sun-Thu, to 10pm Fri
& Sat) Watch the *Pacific Surfliner* glide into
town as you nosh on tasty salads, sandwiches
and pastas on a courtyard patio right beside
the train tracks at this one-time depot. Despite
its politically incorrect name, the Oriental
salad is delish.

Cedar Creek Inn (☎ 949-240-2229; 26860 Ortega
Hwy; mains lunch $11-18, mains dinner $11-30; ☺ lunch
& dinner) For floral-framed views of the mission, request a table on the brick-lined patio.
With its baskets of flowers, wooden terraces
and snazzy umbrellas, it makes for an inspiring setting. Heaping salads look to be most
popular at lunch. Monte Cristo sandwiches
are also served.

Ramos House Café (☎ 949-443-1342; 31752 Los Rios
St; mains $12-17; ☺ breakfast & lunch Tue-Sun) Famous
for earthy comfort food flavored with herbs
from the garden round back, Ramos House
is the best spot for breakfast or lunch near the
mission. To find it, walk across the railroad
tracks at the end of Verdugo St and turn right.
Burlap tablecloths, passing trains and dis-
concertingly enthusiastic waitresses ('Oh my
gosh, the duck hash is awesome!') add color.

ENTERTAINMENT

Believe it or not, there's more to this town
than missions and swallows.

Coach House (☎ 949-496-8930; www.thecoachhouse
.com; 33157 Camino Capistrano) This well-known entertainment venue features a roster of local
and regional rock and alternative bands; expect a cover of $10 to $35, depending on who's
playing. Recent performers include Little Feat,
The Subdudes, Suzanne Vega and The Marshall Tucker Band.

Camino Real Playhouse (☎ 949-489-8082; www
.caminorealplayhouse.org; 31776 El Camino Real) This small
but passionate playhouse has an eclectic annual schedule that includes the ShowOff! International Playwright Festival, Shakespeare
Under the Stars and the 1890s-style Western
Melodrama series where audience participa-
tion is encouraged.

GETTING THERE & AWAY

From Laguna Beach, take OCTA bus 1 south
to K-Mart Plaza, then connect to bus 191/A
in the direction of Mission Viejo, which drops
you near the mission ($2.50, one hour).

The Amtrak depot is one block south and
west of the mission; it would be perfectly reasonable to arrive by train from LA or San
Diego in time for lunch, visit the mission and
be back in the city for dinner.

Drivers should exit I-5 at Ortega Hwy and
head west for about 0.25 miles.

Dana Point

Dana Point was once called 'the only romantic
spot on the coast.' Too bad that quote dates
from seafarer Richard Dana's voyage here in
the 1830s. For the last few decades, Dana Point
has been stuck, never mustering the same recognition as its more charismatic neighbors to
the north. This situation may be partly due to
the fact that the city's prime beach frontage is
managed by outside entities including Orange
County and the state. But changes are afoot,

and the city's investigating ways to increase the inflow of tourists. Stay tuned, and in the meantime check-out the 7 miles of gorgeous coast before word gets out.

INFORMATION

Visitors Center (☎ 949-248-3500; www.danapoint .org; 33282 Golden Lantern; ☽ 9am-4pm Fri-Sun Jun-early Sep) Stop at this tiny booth across from Mariner's Village for brochures and maps. Gung-ho volunteers here love their city.

SIGHTS & ACTIVITIES

Most attractions cluster in and around man-made Dana Point Harbor.

The child-friendly **Ocean Institute** (☎ 949-496-2274; www.ocean-insitute.org; 24200 Dana Pt Harbor Dr; adult/3-12yr $6/4; ☽ 10am-3pm most week days; P ⎲), encompasses four separate ocean-centric 'adventures.' On Sundays, admission includes the opportunity to discover what life was like aboard an 1830s-era tallship by climbing aboard the **Brig Pilgrim** (☽ 10am-2pm Sun), a 130ft replica of the ship sailed by Richard Dana during his journey around Cape Horn to the California coast.

The **Ocean Education Center** (☽ 10am-3pm most weekends) is a school during the week, but on weekends families are welcome to enjoy interactive marine-focused exhibits. Board the **R/V Sea Explorer** (adult $35-78, child $22-78), a 70ft floating lab, for a research-focused trip or join a 'pyrate' adventure on a 118ft replica of a Revolutionary-era tallship, the **Spirit of Dana Point** (adult/child $33/17).

Just south of Laguna Beach is **Salt Creek Beach** (33333 S Pacific Coast Hwy, at Ritz Carlton Dr; www.ocparks .com; ☽ 5am-midnight; P), an 18-acre county-run park popular with surfers, boogie boarders, bodysurfers and tidepoolers. Families make the most of the park's picnic tables, grills, restrooms and showers – all within the shadows of the bluff-top Ritz Carlton. Parking is $1 per hour.

Adjacent to the southern border of Dana Point Harbor is **Doheny State Beach** (☎ 949-496-6172; 25300 Dana Pt Harbor Dr; www.dohenystatebeach.org; ☽ 6am-8pm, to 10pm in daylight savings time; P wi-fi). There are 170 picnic tables, 99 grills, volleyball courts and a butterfly exhibit at this 62-acre park sporting a mile-long beach. Great for swimmers, surfers, divers and tidepoolers. Parking costs $10. Stop by the **Visitor Center** (☎ 949-496-6172; ☽ 10am-4pm Sat & Sun, vary Mon-Fri) for aquariums, mounted birds and a

500-gallon simulated tidepool. Doheny also allows **beach camping** (☎ 800-444-7275, international callers 916-638-5883), the only park to do so in Orange County, perhaps explaining why it's regularly voted the county's 'Best Camping Site.'

Rent a bicycle at **Wheel Fun Rentals** (☎ 949-496-7433; beach cruiser per hr/day $8/28) just south of the picnic area at Doheny State Beach and pedal the **San Juan Creek Bikeway** which begins north of the park. Rent kayaks for harbor paddling from the satellite 'office' of **UP Sports** (☎ 949-443-5161; www.upsportsoc.com), a van in the parking lot just south of the Ocean Institute. It's $20 per hour or $65 for four hours. Find the main office at 34105 Pacific Coast Hwy. For scuba and surfing rentals, try **Beach Cities Scuba** (☎ 949-443-3858; www.beachcitiescuba.com; 34283 Pacific Coast Hwy).

Surfers should check out world-renowned **Trestles** (Map p64) just south of San Clemente at San Onofre State Beach. Known in the surfing community for its natural surf break – which consistently churns out perfect waves – Trestles has garnered unexpected headlines recently. Surfers and environmentalists are fighting the extension of a nearby toll road that could negatively affect the waves. Get there now or, better yet, get involved. See www.surfrider.org for more details.

TOURS

Dana Wharf, in Mariner's Village at Dana Point Harbor, is the starting point for most area ocean tours and trips to Catalina Island. For sportfishing, try **Dana Wharf Sportfishing** (☎ 949-496-5794; www.danawharf.com; 34675 Golden Lantern). Five-hour trips, which are best for beginners, cost about $35. Rod and reel rent for $12 a day. Their **whale watching** tours – which follow migrating grays – run from January to April and cost $25 for adults and $15 for children aged three to 12. If you prefer dolphin spotting, join **Capt Dave's Dolphin Safari** (☎ 949-488-2828; www.dolphinsafari.com; 34451 Ensenada Place) for a 2½-hour trip on a high-tech catamaran. Operating year-round, it's $49 per person for adults and $35 for kids three to 12.

Catalina Express (☎ 800-481-3470; www.catalina express.com; 34675 Golden Lantern; P) runs daily trips to Avalon on Catalina Island. Round-trip, it costs $61/47.50/55 for adults/children two to 11/seniors. One-way trips last approximately 1½ hours. Parking costs $9 per day.

ORANGE COUNTY

EATING

Traveling families, chattering businessmen and the occasional lonely pirate fill up on hearty diner-style dishes at the **Brig** (☎ 949-496-9046; 34461 Golden Lantern; mains $8-11; ⊙ breakfast, lunch & dinner; ♿). Those wanting straight-off-the-boat fresh fish can order as much as they can eat from the counter at pier-side **Jon's Restaurant** (☎ 949-496-2807; 34665 Golden Lantern; mains under $12; ⊙ 11am-7pm Sun-Thu, 11am-8pm Fri & Sat, longer hr Apr-Oct). After a long

day on the yacht, you should escort your *cherie amour* to bright and breezy **Gemmell's** (☎ 949-234-0063; 34471 Golden Lantern; mains lunch $8-19, dinner $17-29) for award-winning, French-inspired cuisine.

Catalina Island

If you're planning a trip to Catalina Island, you can pick up the ferry 8 miles south of Laguna Beach in Dana Point. For details, see (p221).

San Diego County

New York has its cabbie, Chicago its bluesman and Seattle its coffee-drinking boho. San Diego, meanwhile, has the valet guy in a polo shirt, khaki shorts and crisp new sneakers. With his perfectly tousled hair, great tan (of course) and gentle enthusiasm, he looks like he's on a perennial break from college, and when he wishes you welcome, he really means it.

This may sound pejorative, but our intention is quite the opposite. San Diego calls itself 'America's Finest City' and its breezy confidence and sunny countenance filter down even to folks you encounter every day on the street.

What's not to love? When much of the nation shivers under blankets of rain and snow, San Diegans picnic in the park and slice through waves on surfboards. Beaches or forests are rarely more than 10 minutes' drive away. It's America's eighth-largest city, yet we're hard-pressed to think of a place of any size that's more laid-back.

San Diego bursts with world-famous attractions for visitors, including the zoo, SeaWorld, Legoland and the museums of Balboa Park. The ritzy, picturesque enclave of La Jolla has pride of place on San Diego's coast. Conventions are big business too, and next to the convention center is the always-buzzing Gaslamp Quarter. San Diego's beach communities are great for hanging 10, dipping in the world's largest pool (aka the Pacific), listening to a live band or dancing 'til the wee hours, and there's a burgeoning culinary scene throughout the county. As corny as it sounds, San Diego indeed has something for everyone, from museums and naval ships to shopping and shell-collecting.

SAN DIEGO COUNTY

HIGHLIGHTS

- Museum-hopping in **Balboa Park** (p297)
- Swilling margaritas in **Old Town** (p309) and pub-crawling downtown's **Gaslamp Quarter** (p311)
- Marveling at the **Hotel del Coronado** (p318)
- Cooing at koalas and pandering to pandas at the **San Diego Zoo** (p298)
- Skating seaside in **Pacific Beach** (p319)
- Hang gliding, kayaking or giving your credit card a workout in **La Jolla** (p328)
- Sampling the next great exotic cuisine in **Hillcrest** (p310)
- Watching the sunset from a rooftop café in **Del Mar** (p334)

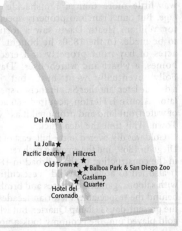

Del Mar ★
La Jolla ★
Pacific Beach ★   Hillcrest
Old Town ★ ★   ★ Balboa Park & San Diego Zoo
★ Gaslamp
Quarter
Hotel del
Coronado

SAN DIEGO COUNTY

FAST FACTS

- **Population San Diego County** 2.94 million

- **Population city of San Diego** 1.26 million

- **Average temps** Jan 45/65°F, July 63/75°F

- **Downtown San Diego to La Jolla** 13 miles

- **Downtown San Diego to Tijuana** 18 miles

- **San Diego to Julian** 62 miles

- **San Diego to Disneyland** 94 miles

- **San Diego to LA** 120 miles

HISTORY

Evidence of human habitation in the region goes back to at least 18,000 BC, in the form of middens (ancient refuse heaps). When Spanish explorer Juan Rodríguez Cabrillo became the first European to sail into San Diego Bay in 1542, the region was divided peaceably between the native Kumeyaay and Luiseño/Juaneño peoples. Their way of life continued undisturbed until Junípero Serra and Gaspar de Portolá arrived in 1769. They founded the first permanent European settlement in California – a mission and fort on the hill now known as the Presidio.

When the United States took California from Mexico in the 1840s, San Diego was little more than a ramshackle village. But San Francisco property speculator William Heath Davis saw a fortune to be made. In the 1850s he bought 160 acres of bay-front property and erected homes, a wharf and warehouses. 'Davis' Folly' eventually went bust, but just a decade later, another San Francisco speculator, Alonzo E Horton, acquired 960 acres of waterfront land and promoted it as 'New Town.' This time the idea stuck.

Gold was discovered in the hills east of San Diego in 1869, and the ensuing rush resulted in the construction of the railroad in 1884. It also led to a classic Wild West culture, with saloons, gambling houses and brothels behind the respectable Victorian facades of the present-day Gaslamp Quarter. But when gold played out, the economy took a nose-dive and the city's population plummeted by as much as 50%.

Spurred by San Francisco's international exhibition of 1914, San Diego's staged the Panama–California Exposition (1915–16), aiming to attract investment to the city with its deepwater port, railroad hub and perfect climate. Boosters built exhibition halls (see p297) in the romantic Spanish Colonial style that still defines much of the city today.

However it was the 1941 bombing of Pearl Harbor that permanently made San Diego. Top brass quickly chose San Diego, with its excellent, protected port, as home of the US Pacific Fleet. The military literally reshaped the city, dredging the harbor, building landfill islands, and constructing vast tracts of instant housing.

The opening of the University of California campus in the 1960s heralded a new era as students and faculty slowly drove a liberal wedge into the city's homogenous, flag-and-family culture. The university, especially strong in the sciences, has also become an incubator for the region's biotech sector.

DOWNTOWN & AROUND

The city of San Diego offers diverse museums and a world-class zoo, eye-popping architecture and toe-tapping music. The coastal communities, including Coronado, Ocean, Mission and Pacific Beaches, La Jolla and North County are covered in separate sections.

ORIENTATION

San Diego's downtown, a compact grid northeast of San Diego Bay, revolves around the historic Gaslamp Quarter, a beehive of restaurants, bars and boutiques; the convention center sits to its southwest along the water, and office towers rise to the north. Within the city center, north–south 'avenues' are numbered (First, Second etc), while east–west 'streets' are lettered (A, B, C etc) heading south and named after trees in alphabetical order (Ash, Beech etc) heading north.

The airport, train station and Greyhound bus terminal are all in or near downtown San Diego. I-5 is the main north–south freeway, connecting San Diego with Los Angeles, Orange County and Tijuana; I-8 runs east from Ocean Beach, up Mission Valley and eventually into Arizona. The Cabrillo

Fwy (CA163) heads north from downtown through Balboa Park.

Waterfront attractions along the Embarcadero lie just west of the downtown grid, and upscale Coronado is reached via a soaring bridge south of downtown. North of downtown are San Diego's Little Italy and museum-rich Balboa Park (home of the San Diego Zoo). The park segues into Hillcrest, the city's lesbigay hub, west of which is tourist-oriented Old Town.

INFORMATION
Bookstores

Every shopping mall in San Diego has at least one bookshop, usually of the large, chain variety. Bookhounds should peruse the offerings of bookstores on Fifth Ave between University and Robinson Aves in Hillcrest.

Le Travel Store (Map pp288-9; ☎ 619-544-0005; 745 4th Ave) has an excellent selection of maps, travel guides and accessories. Helpful staff.

Internet Access

All public libraries provide free internet access; no library card is required. You can make reservations one day in advance by calling the main library (p284). There are also 15-minute express terminals available if you don't have a reservation. You can also pay to log on at Kinko's copy stores throughout the city – check a telephone directory for the nearest location – or try the coffeehouses (p311).

Internet Resources

Access San Diego (www.accessandiego.com) Excellent source for barrier-free travel around San Diego.
Gaslamp.org (www.gaslamp.org) Everything you need to know about the bustling Gaslamp District, including parking secrets.
San Diego Convention & Visitors Bureau (www .sandiego.org) Search hotels, sights, dining, rental cars and more, and make reservations.
Sandiego.com (www.sandiego.com) Comprehensive ad-based portal to all things San Diegan, from fun stuff to serious business.

Left Luggage

Greyhound Station (Map pp288-9; ☎ 619-515-1100; 120 W Broadway) has lockers for $6 to $8 per day, and a storage counter for $8 per bag per day.

SAN DIEGO COUNTY

SAN DIEGO IN TWO DAYS

If your time is limited, here's a whirlwind itinerary of the essential San Diego. Things will go more smoothly if you've got access to a car, but public transportation can work if you plan ahead.

Day 1
Start off with breakfast and espresso at an outdoor café on Little Italy's **India Street** (p285) then take a walk past the Victorian mansions of **Bankers Hill** (p303) on your way to **Balboa Park** (p297). Pick a museum or two that interest you, and have lunch at one of the cafés or restaurants, detouring to the gardens along the way. Devote the afternoon to the **San Diego Zoo** (p298), which is among the world's best. For dinner and – if you're up for it – a night out on town, head to the **Gaslamp Quarter** (p307); many restaurants have terrace seating for people-watching, and the partying ranges from posh to raucous.

Day 2
Take the ferry to Coronado for a sea-view breakfast at the **Hotel del Coronado** (p318), before a drive up to **La Jolla** (p328). Explore **Torrey Pines State Reserve** (p330), **Birch Aquarium** (p329) or edgy **Black's Beach** (p329), kayak the **sea caves** (p331), try a **glider ride** (p331) or head to **La Jolla Village** (p328) to browse the 1920s Spanish-revival landmarks, the **Museum of Contemporary Art San Diego** (p328) or boutiques along Girard Ave – you'll have plenty of choice for lunch or a snack. As the sun begins its descent over the ocean, head to Del Mar, where you can cheer or snuggle from one of the cafés on the roof of **Del Mar Plaza** (p335) as the sky turns brilliant orange and fades to black.

If you have Days 3 and 4, include **SeaWorld** (p320) and a visit to **Julian** (p339), the **San Diego Wild Animal Park** (p341) or **Tijuana** (p341).

Libraries

Main library (Map pp288-9; ☎ 619-236-5800; www
.sannet.gov/public-library; 820 E St; ⊗ noon-8pm Mon
& Wed, 9:30am-5:30pm Tue & Thu-Sat, 1-5pm Sun; wi-fi)
About two blocks east of the Gaslamp Quarter. There are
smaller branch libraries.

Media

Gay & Lesbian Times (www.gaylesbiantimes.com) Free
weekly.

KPBS 89.5 FM (www.kpbs.org) National public radio
station.

San Diego Magazine (www.sandiegomagazine.com)
Glossy monthly.

San Diego Union-Tribune (www.signonsandiego.com)
The city's major daily.

The following free weekly tabloid-sized listings magazines cover the active music, art and
theater scenes. Find them in shops and cafés:
Citybeat (www.sdcitybeat.com)
San Diego Reader (www.sdreader.com)

Medical Services

Mission Bay Hospital (Map pp292-3; ☎ 858-274-
7721; 3030 Bunker Hill St, Mission Bay)

Rite-Aid pharmacies (☎ 800-748-3243) Call for the
branch nearest you.

Scripps Mercy Hospital (Map pp290-1; ☎ 619-294-
8111; 4077 5th Ave, Hillcrest; ⊗ 24hr emergency room)

Money

You'll find ATMs throughout San Diego.
Travelex (Map pp288-9; ☎ 619-235-0901; 177 Horton
Plaza; ⊗ 10am-6pm Mon-Fri, 10am-4pm Sat, 11am-4pm
Sun) For foreign-currency exchange.

Post

For post-office locations, call ☎ 800-275-
8777 or log on to www.usps.com.
Downtown Post Office (Map pp288-9; 815 E St;
⊗ 8:30am-5pm Mon-Fri)

Tourist Information

International Visitors Information Center (Map
pp288-9; ☎ 619-236-1212; 1040-1/3 W Broadway at
Harbor Dr; ⊗ 9am-5pm Mon-Sat, 10am-5pm Sun) The
on-site official visitors center for the city is located across
from Broadway Pier, along the Embarcadero.

Old Town State Historic Park Visitor Center (Map
pp290-1; ☎ 619-220-5422; www.parks.ca.gov; Old
Town Plaza; ⊗ 10am-5pm) For in-person information
about state parks in San Diego County, head to the
Robinson-Rose House at the end of the plaza in Old
Town.

SIGHTS
Downtown

San Diego's downtown is adjacent to the waterfront in the area first acquired, subdivided
and promoted by Alonzo Horton in 1867.
Most of the land on the waterside of the trolley line is landfill. Until the mid-1920s the
southern end of Fifth Ave was the main dock
for unloading cargo ships; and junkets and
fishing boats were once moored where the
San Diego Convention Center now rises like
sails over the bay.

Even if downtown generally lacks intense
urban energy, you wouldn't know it in the
Gaslamp Quarter, the primary hub for shopping, dining and entertainment. The addition
of PETCO Park baseball stadium has only
enhanced this atmosphere. The Embarcadero
is good for a harborside stroll.

In the northwestern corner of Downtown,
Little Italy is a vibrant neighborhood close to
the freeway, within walking distance of the
harbor, and full of good eats.

GASLAMP QUARTER

When Horton first established New Town San
Diego in 1867, Fifth Ave was its main street
and home to its principal industries – saloons,
gambling joints, bordellos and opium dens.
While more respectable businesses grew up
along Broadway, the Fifth Ave area became
known as the Stingaree, a notorious red-light
district. By the 1960s it had declined to a skid
row of flophouses and bars, but the seedy
atmosphere made it so unattractive to developers that many of its older buildings survived
when others around town were being razed.
In the early 1980s, when developers started
thinking about demolition and rebuilding,
local protests saved the area.

Wrought-iron street lamps, in the style of
19th-century gas lamps, were installed, along
with trees and brick sidewalks. Restored buildings (built between the 1870s and the 1920s)
now house restaurants, bars, galleries and
theaters. The 16-block area south of Broadway
between Fourth and Sixth Aves is designated a
National Historic District, and development is
strictly controlled. There's still a bit of sleaze
though, with a few 'adult entertainment' shops,
but we'll say they lend texture.

William Heath Davis House (Map pp288-9; ☎ 619-
233-4692; www.gaslampquarter.org; 410 Island Ave, cnr
4th Ave; admission $3; ⊗ 11am-6pm Tue-Sat, 11am-3pm
Sun) is one of nine prefabricated houses that

Davis brought from Maine in 1850. This one contains a small museum with 19th-century furnishings. From here, the Gaslamp Quarter Historical Foundation leads a weekly, two-hour **walking tour** (adult/senior & student $10/8; 🕑 11am Sat), but the tour's risqué topics and stop-and-go walking aren't appropriate for children.

Third Ave is the historic heart of San Diego's Chinese community. Immigrants were once taught English and religion in the Chinese Mission Building, built in the 1920s and designed by Louis J Gill (minimalist San Diego architect Irving Gill's nephew). Today it houses the **San Diego Chinese Historical Museum** (Map pp288-9; 🕿 619-338-9888; 404 3rd Ave; admission free; 🕑 10:30am-4pm Tue-Sun). The small, white stucco structure has red tiles decorating the roofline, hardwood floors, and an inviting backyard. Displays include Chinese-American artifacts and local art objects.

At the edge of the Gaslamp, **Westfield Horton Plaza Center** (Map pp288-9; 🕿 619-239-8180; 🕑 10am-9pm Mon-Fri, 10am-8pm Sat, 11am-7pm Sun; 🅿) is a five-story, seven-block shopping mall that was credited with bringing visitors back to Downtown. It's not very inviting from the outside; critics say it turns its back on Downtown (though when it was built in 1985 there wasn't much to welcome visitors). Inside, however, Los Angeles–based urban architect Jon Jerde – who also designed Universal CityWalk (p145) – created fanciful, toy-town arches and postmodernist balconies making it feel slightly like an MC Escher drawing. Parking is free for three hours with validation.

MUSEUM OF CONTEMPORARY ART SAN DIEGO

Adjacent to a San Diego Trolley stop, this **museum** (Map pp288-9; 🕿 858-454-3541; www.mcasd.org; 1001 & 1100 Kettner Blvd; adult/senior/25 & under $10/$5/free; 🕑 11am-6pm Sat-Tue, 11am-9pm Thu & Fri, guided tours 6pm Thu, 2pm Sat & Sun; 🅿) has brought contemporary artwork to San Diegans since the 1960s in the La Jolla branch (p328); check local listings for exhibits. The Downtown branch dates from 1986, and an additional pavilion opened across the street in 2007, a slick renovation of a section of San Diego's train station with permanent works by Jenny Holzer and Richard Serra. Tickets are valid for seven days in all locations and there is discounted parking (with validation) at 501 West C Street.

While here, stop at San Diego's **Union Station** (aka **Santa Fe Depot**) which looks a lot like a piece from a model railway, with Spanish-style tile work and a historic Santa Fe Railway sign on top. It was built in conjunction with the 1915 exposition (see p282) in the hopes that the Santa Fe Railway would make San Diego its terminus, although that designation eventually went to Los Angeles.

PETCO PARK

A quick stroll east of the Gaslamp, this **baseball park** (Map pp288-9; 🕿 619-795-5011; www.petcoparkevents.com; 100 Park Blvd; tours adult/child/senior $9/5/6; tours 🕑 10:30am, 12:30pm & 2:30pm Tue-Sun subject to game schedule) is Downtown's newest landmark, home of the San Diego Padres baseball team. It's an architecturally alluring venue incorporating some historic buildings. If you can't make it to a game (p315), take an 80-minute behind-the-scenes tour.

SAN DIEGO CHILDREN'S MUSEUM

This interactive children's **museum** (Museo de los Niños; Map pp288-9; 🕿 619-233-8792; www.sdchildrensmuseum.org; 200 West Island Ave) has been closed for reconstruction; it should be open again in spring 2008, with a theater, storytelling, music, activities and exhibits in a 'green' building with indoor–outdoor exhibition space.

US GRANT HOTEL

No hotel in town can compare to the Hotel del Coronado (p318) for history, but **US Grant** (Map pp288-9; 🕿 619-232-3121; 326 Broadway), built in 1910, comes close. It's on the National Register of Historic Places for a past including celebrity guests, magnificent ballrooms, a one-time Turkish bath and a speakeasy. It had a big-bucks makeover in 2006; visitors can take a free tour with advance reservation by calling the concierge desk. See also p306 for sleeping options here.

Little Italy

Bounded by Hawthorn and Ash Sts on the north and south, and Front St and the waterfront on the east and west, San Diego's Little Italy was settled in the mid-19th century by Italian immigrants, mostly fishermen and their families, who created a cohesive and thriving community. They enjoyed a booming

(Continued on page 296)

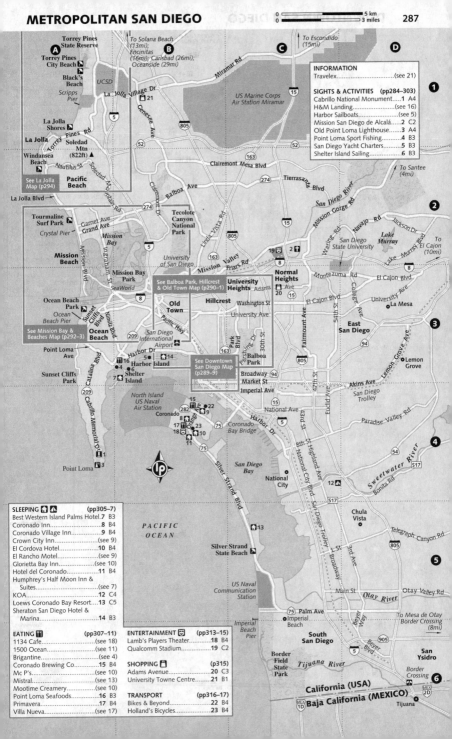

INFORMATION
Travelex.........................(see 21)

SIGHTS & ACTIVITIES (pp284–303)
Cabrillo National Monument.....1 A4
H&M Landing.......................(see 16)
Harbor Sailboats...................(see 5)
Mission San Diego de Alcalá....2 C2
Old Point Loma Lighthouse......3 A4
Point Loma Sport Fishing.........4 B3
San Diego Yacht Charters.........5 B3
Shelter Island Sailing.............6 B3

SLEEPING (pp305–7)
Best Western Island Palms Hotel.7 B3
Coronado Inn.........................8 B4
Coronado Village Inn.............9 B4
Crown City Inn.....................(see 9)
El Cordova Hotel..................10 B4
El Rancho Motel....................(see 9)
Glorietta Bay Inn...................(see 10)
Hotel del Coronado...............11 B4
Humphrey's Half Moon Inn &
  Suites.............................(see 7)
KOA..................................12 C4
Loews Coronado Bay Resort....13 C5
Sheraton San Diego Hotel &
  Marina.............................14 B3

EATING (pp307–11)
1134 Cafe..........................(see 18)
1500 Ocean........................(see 11)
Brigantine..........................(see 4)
Coronado Brewing Co...........15 B4
Mc P's...............................(see 10)
Mistral...............................(see 13)
Mootime Creamery...............(see 10)
Point Loma Seafoods.............16 B3
Primavera...........................17 B4
Villa Nueva.........................(see 17)

ENTERTAINMENT (pp313–15)
Lamb's Players Theater..........18 B4
Qualcomm Stadium...............19 C2

SHOPPING (p315)
Adams Avenue.....................20 C3
University Towne Centre..........21 B1

TRANSPORT (pp316–17)
Bikes & Beyond....................22 B4
Holland's Bicycles.................23 B4

To Airport Lounge
(0.15mi); Casbah
(0.5mi)

INFORMATION
Downtown Post Office..............1 F4
International Visitors
  Information Center................2 B4
Le Travel Store........................3 H5
Main Library.............................4 F4
San Diego Convention &
  Visitors Bureau...................(see 2)
Travelex..................................5 G5

SIGHTS & ACTIVITIES   (pp284–303)
Firehouse Museum....................6 C2
Maritime Museum......................7 B3
Museum of Contemporary Art
  San Diego.............................8 C4
Museum of Contemporary Art
  San Diego Annex...................9 C3
Our Lady of the Rosary Catholic
  Church................................10 C2
PETCO Park.........................(see 70)
San Diego Aircraft Carrier
  Museum..............................11 A4
San Diego Children's Museum...12 D5
San Diego Chinese Historical
  Museum..............................13 D5
San Diego Convention Center...14 D6
US Grant Hotel.....................(see 28)
USS Midway........................(see 11)
Westfield Horton Plaza............15 G5
William Heath Davis House.......16 E5

San Diego Bay

Little Italy

County Center/
Little Italy

Cruise Ship Terminal

Santa Fe
Depot

Santa Fe Depot

San Diego Trolley
American Plaza Terminal

Broadway

Broadway Pier

Navy Pier

US Naval
Supply
Center

Pantoja
Park

Tuna Lane

Tuna
Harbor

Seaport Village

Market St

Westfield
Horton Plaza

Downtown

Island Ave

Seaport Village

San Diego Trolley

Harbor Dr

Convention
Center West

Embarcadero
Marina Park

San Diego
Convention
Center

Civic
Center

See Enlargement

0   500 m
0   0.3 miles

Middletown

Balboa Park

(163)

SLEEPING (pp305–7)
500 West Hotel....................17 C4
Bristol Hotel.......................18 G4
HI San Diego Downtown Hostel.19 H6
Horton Grand Hotel..............20 E5
Hotel Occidental..................21 E1
Hotel Solamar.....................22 E5
Ivy....................................23 H5
J Street Inn.........................24 D5
La Pensione Hotel.................25 C2
Manchester Grand Hyatt........26 C5
Sofia Hotel.........................27 F4
US Grant Hotel....................28 G4
USA Hostels San Diego..........29 H5
W Hotel.............................30 C3
Westgate Hotel....................31 G4

EATING (pp307–11)
Anthony's Fish Grotto & Fishette.32 B3
Bandar..............................33 H5
Bondi................................34 E6
Buon Appetito.....................35 C2
Café 222............................36 D5
Cafe Lulu...........................37 H5
Café Sevilla........................38 H6
Café Zucchero.....................39 C2
Cheese Shop.......................40 H6
Chi Chocolat.......................41 C1
Croce's Restaurant &
    Jazz Bar.....................(see 64)
Dick's Last Resort.................42 E6

Filippi's Pizza Grotto.............43 C1
Fish Market.........................44 A5
Gaslamp Strip Club...............45 E6
Ghirardelli Soda Fountain &
    Chocolate Shop..............46 H6
Indigo Grill........................47 C2
Mimmo's Italian Village.........48 C1
Mona Lisa..........................49 C1
Oceanaire..........................50 E5
Red Pearl Kitchen.................51 E5
Solunto Baking Co & Honey Bee..52 C2

DRINKING (pp311–13)
Bitter End..........................53 H5
Cafe Lulu......................(see 37)
Caffe Italia.........................54 C2
Karl Strauss Brewery & Grill....55 C3
Moose McGillycuddy's...........56 H5
Onyx Room & Thin...............57 H5
Red Circle Bar.....................58 H5
Star Bar........................(see 58)
W Hotel........................(see 30)
Waterfront.........................59 B1

ENTERTAINMENT (pp313–15)
4th & B..............................60 E3
Anthology..........................61 C3
Arts Tix.............................62 G4
Copley Symphony Hall...........63 G4
Croce's Restaurant & Jazz Bar..64 H5
Croce's Top Hat Bar & Grille....65 H5

Horton Grand Theatre............66 E5
House of Blues.....................67 H4
On Broadway.......................68 E4
Pacific Gaslamp 15................69 H5
PETCO Park.........................70 F6
Regal United Artists Horton
    Plaza 14.......................71 H5
San Diego Opera...................72 D3
San Diego Repertory
    Theater........................73 G5
San Diego Symphony.........(see 63)
Shout House.......................74 H6
Spreckels Theater.................75 G4
Stingaree...........................76 E5

SHOPPING (p315)
Gallery 5+5.........................77 E5
Horton Plaza..................(see 15)
Michael J Wolf Fine Arts.........78 E6
Surf & Skatewear Shops..........79 E5

TRANSPORT (pp316–17)
6th & K Parkade...................80 E6
California Rent a Car..............81 B1
Coronado Ferry....................82 B4
Greyhound Station................83 G4
Hornblower Cruises...............84 B3
Park it on Market..................85 E5
San Diego Harbor Excursion....86 B4
Transit Store.......................87 G4
West Coast Rent a Car............88 C1

San Diego City College

B St

Fifth Avenue

San Diego Trolley

City College

C St

Broadway

E St

F St

G St

Westfield Horton Plaza

E St

F St

G St

J St

K St

PETCO Park

Gaslamp Quarter

Market St

12th & Imperial Transfer Station

0   200 m
0   0.1 miles

A B C D

1

82

Friars Rd

Morena
Linda
Vista

Morena Blvd

Friars Rd

San Diego River

Riverwalk
Golf Course

40

46

Hotel Circle Pl

Hotel Circle N

2

5

Taylor St

Presidio
Park

8 Mission Valley Fwy

41

Hotel Circle S

48

209

Heritage
Park

Rosecrans St

Pacific Hwy

Taylor St

Juan St

Congress St

See Old Town Enlargement

Lewis St

Fort Stockton Dr

Washington Pl

Washington St

Falcon St

Eagle St

Lewis St

Albatross St

76

Washington St

3

Jefferson St

Moore St

Old Town Ave

Hortensia St

52

California St

43

Old Town

University Ave

Hawk St

Goldfinch St

Hillcrest

Front St

1st Ave

Midway Dr

San Diego Trolley

Hancock St

Washington St

Bush St

Sutter St

Kite St

San Diego Fwy

Barnett Ave

Pacific Hwy

US Marine Corps
Recruit Depot

77

Jackdaw St

Winder St

Brant St

Reynard Way

Dove St

Curlew St

Mission Hills

55
63
53

Chalmers St

Walnut St

Vine St

Upas St

Thorn Ave

Ind St

Union St

Kettner Blvd

California St

Horton Ave

Reynard Way

32

4

8

Gamet St

Whitman St

Jackson St

Presidio
Park

29

Rosecrans St

Sunset St

Taylor St

Juan St

22

Hillcrest

0 _____ 200 m
0 _____ 0.1 miles

Middletown

Washington St

45

5

Calhoun St

Wallace St

Old Town
Transit Center

21
Old Town
San Diego
State Historic
Park

8

Mason St

Sunset St

Jackson St

Presidio Dr

57

50

78

6th Ave

34

15

San Diego Trolley

3

Old Town
Plaza

Flagpole

9

88

P

P

Heritage Park Row

75

49

62

5th Ave

58

13

85

83

86

81

32

4th Ave

47

3rd Ave

University Ave

Brant St

Front St

6

Congress St

P

P

Mason St

Twiggs St

Church of the
Immaculate
Conception

38

Heritage
Park

Conde St

Robinson Ave

51

67

Junipero
Serra Hall

72

70

37

73

59

54

64

68

42

Pennsylvania Ave

State St

Front St

1st Ave

5

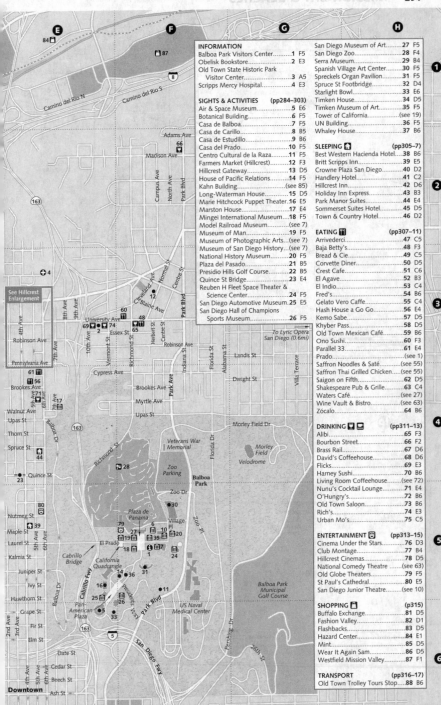

INFORMATION

Balboa Park Visitors Center	1 F5
Obelisk Bookstore	2 E3
Old Town State Historic Park Visitor Center	3 A5
Scripps Mercy Hospital	4 E3

SIGHTS & ACTIVITIES (pp284–303)

Air & Space Museum	5 E6
Botanical Building	6 F5
Casa de Balboa	7 F5
Casa de Carillo	8 B5
Casa de Estudillo	9 B6
Casa del Prado	10 F5
Centro Cultural de la Raza	11 F5
Farmers Market (Hillcrest)	12 F3
Hillcrest Gateway	13 D5
House of Pacific Relations	14 F5
Kahn Building	(see 85)
Long-Waterman House	15 D5
Marie Hitchcock Puppet Theater	16 E5
Marston House	17 E4
Mingei International Museum	18 F5
Model Railroad Museum	(see 7)
Museum of Man	19 F5
Museum of Photographic Arts	(see 7)
Museum of San Diego History	(see 7)
National History Museum	20 F5
Plaza del Pasado	21 B5
Presidio Hills Golf Course	22 B5
Quince St Bridge	23 E4
Reuben H Fleet Space Theater & Science Center	24 F5
San Diego Automotive Museum	25 E5
San Diego Hall of Champions Sports Museum	26 F5
San Diego Museum of Art	27 F5
San Diego Zoo	28 F4
Serra Museum	29 B4
Spanish Village Art Center	30 F5
Spreckels Organ Pavilion	31 F5
Spruce St Footbridge	32 D4
Starlight Bowl	33 E6
Timken House	34 D5
Timken Museum of Art	35 F5
Tower of California	(see 19)
UN Building	36 F5
Whaley House	37 B6

SLEEPING (pp305–7)

Best Western Hacienda Hotel	38 B6
Britt Scripps Inn	39 E5
Crowne Plaza San Diego	40 D2
Handlery Hotel	41 C2
Hillcrest Inn	42 D6
Holiday Inn Express	43 B3
Park Manor Suites	44 E4
Sommerset Suites Hotel	45 D5
Town & Country Hotel	46 D2

EATING (pp307–11)

Arrivederci	47 C5
Baja Betty's	48 F3
Bread & Cie	49 C5
Corvette Diner	50 D5
Crest Cafe	51 C6
El Agave	52 B3
El Indio	53 C4
Fred's	54 B6
Gelato Vero Caffe	55 C4
Hash House a Go Go	56 E4
Kemo Sabe	57 D5
Khyber Pass	58 D5
Old Town Mexican Café	59 B6
Ono Sushi	60 F3
Parallel 33	61 E4
Prado	(see 1)
Saffron Noodles & Saté	(see 55)
Saffron Thai Grilled Chicken	(see 55)
Saigon on Fifth	62 D5
Shakespeare Pub & Grille	63 C4
Waters Café	(see 27)
Wine Vault & Bistro	(see 63)
Zócalo	64 B6

DRINKING (pp311–13)

Alibi	65 F3
Bourbon Street	66 F2
Brass Rail	67 D6
David's Coffeehouse	68 D6
Flicks	69 E3
Harney Sushi	70 B6
Living Room Coffeehouse	(see 72)
Nunu's Cocktail Lounge	71 E4
O'Hungry's	72 B6
Old Town Saloon	73 B6
Rich's	74 E3
Urban Mo's	75 C5

ENTERTAINMENT (pp313–15)

Cinema Under the Stars	76 D3
Club Montage	77 B4
Hillcrest Cinemas	78 D5
National Comedy Theatre	(see 63)
Old Globe Theaters	79 F5
St Paul's Cathedral	80 E5
San Diego Junior Theatre	(see 10)

SHOPPING (p315)

Buffalo Exchange	81 D5
Fashion Valley	82 D1
Flashbacks	83 D5
Hazard Center	84 E1
Mint	85 D5
Wear It Again Sam	86 D5
Westfield Mission Valley	87 F1

TRANSPORT (pp316–17)

Old Town Trolley Tours Stop	88 B6

0 _____ 1 km
0 _____ 0.5 miles

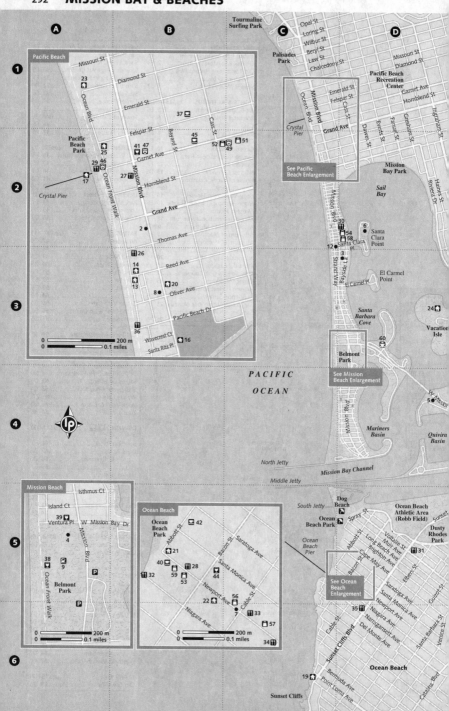

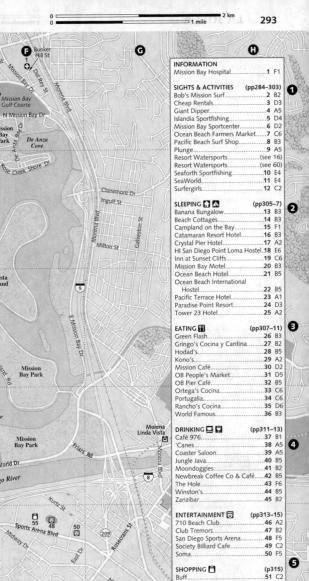

INFORMATION
Mission Bay Hospital.....................1 F1

SIGHTS & ACTIVITIES (pp284–303)
Bob's Mission Surf..........................2 B2
Cheap Rentals...............................3 D3
Giant Dipper..................................4 A5
Islandia Sportfishing......................5 D4
Mission Bay Sportcenter................6 D2
Ocean Beach Farmers Market.....7 C6
Pacific Beach Surf Shop.................8 B3
Plunge..9 A5
Resort Watersports.................(see 16)
Resort Watersports.................(see 60)
Seaforth Sportfishing...................10 E4
SeaWorld.....................................11 E4
Surfergirls....................................12 C2

SLEEPING (pp305–7)
Banana Bungalow.......................13 B3
Beach Cottages............................14 B3
Campland on the Bay..................15 F1
Catamaran Resort Hotel..............16 B3
Crystal Pier Hotel........................17 A2
HI San Diego Point Loma Hostel.18 E6
Inn at Sunset Cliffs......................19 C6
Mission Bay Motel.......................20 B3
Ocean Beach Hotel......................21 B5
Ocean Beach International
  Hostel......................................22 B5
Pacific Terrace Hotel...................23 A1
Paradise Point Resort..................24 D3
Tower 23 Hotel...........................25 A2

EATING (pp307–11)
Green Flash.................................26 B3
Gringo's Cocina y Cantina...........27 B2
Hodad's......................................28 B5
Kono's...29 A2
Mission Café...............................30 D2
OB People's Market....................31 D5
OB Pier Café...............................32 B5
Ortega's Cocina..........................33 C6
Portugalia...................................34 C6
Rancho's Cocina.........................35 D6
World Famous.............................36 B3

DRINKING (pp311–13)
Café 976.....................................37 B1
'Canes...38 A5
Coaster Saloon............................39 A5
Jungle Java..................................40 B5
Moondoggies..............................41 B2
Newbreak Coffee Co & Café.......42 B5
The Hole......................................43 F6
Winston's....................................44 B5
Zanzibar......................................45 B2

ENTERTAINMENT (pp313–15)
710 Beach Club...........................46 A2
Club Tremors...............................47 B2
San Diego Sports Arena...............48 F5
Society Billiard Cafe....................49 C2
Soma...50 F5

SHOPPING (p315)
Buff...51 C2
Buffalo Exchange.........................52 B2
Cow...53 B5
Gone Bananas.............................54 D2
Kobey's Swap Meet.....................55 F5
Mallory's.....................................56 C5
Newport Avenue Antique
  Center......................................57 C6
Pilar's Beachwear........................58 D2
South Coast Longboards..............59 B5
South Coast Wahines..............(see 29)

TRANSPORT (pp316–17)
Bahia Belle..................................60 D3
Cheap Rentals.........................(see 3)

0 _____ 2 km
0 _____ 1 mile

INFORMATION
DG Wills...1 D6
La Jolla Visitor Center.....................2 D5
Post Office......................................3 D5
UCSD Bookstore.............................4 D2
UCSD Information Center................5 C1
Warwick's..6 D5

SIGHTS & ACTIVITIES (pp284–303)
Athenaeum Music & Arts Library....7 D5
Birch Aquarium...............................8 C3
Bishop's School..............................9 C6
Cave Store....................................10 D5
Children's Pool..............................11 D5
Geisel Library................................12 D2
La Jolla Historical Society...............13 D5
La Jolla Woman's Club...................14 D6
Museum of Contemporary Art.......15 C6
OEX...16 B4
Salk Institute.................................17 C2
Scripps Institution of
   Oceanography...........................18 C3
Surf Diva..............................(see 16)
Torrey Pines Gliderport..................19 C1
Torrey Pines Golf Course...............20 C1

SLEEPING (pp305–7)
Estancia La Jolla Hotel & Spa........21 C2
Grande Colonial............................22 D5
Hotel Parisi...................................23 D5
La Jolla Village Lodge....................24 D5
La Valencia...................................25 D5
Lodge at Torrey Pines...................26 C1
Scripps Inn...................................27 C6

PACIFIC
OCEAN

Black's
Beach

Torrey Pines
City Beach

Torrey
Pines
State
Reserve

Genesee Ave

Torrey Pines
Scenic Dr

Old Miramar Rd

University of California,
San Diego (UCSD)

Gilman Dr

La Jolla Village Dr

To Travelex (2mi);
University Towne
Centre (2mi)

La Jolla
Village
Square

Scripps Pier

Expedition
Way

Scripps
Research
Institute

Torrey Pines Rd

Gilman Dr

La Jolla Scenic Dr N

Nobel Dr

Villa La Jolla Dr

Kellogg
City Park

La Jolla
Shores

Spindrift
Golf Course

El Paseo Grande

La Jolla Shores Dr

Av de la Playa

San Diego–La Jolla
Underwater Park
Ecological Reserve

Pas Dorado

Point
La Jolla

La Jolla
Cove

Ardath Rd

Via Capri

See Enlargement

La Jolla
Community
Park

Torrey Pines Rd

Downtown

Pearl St

La Jolla
Natural Park

Soledad
Mountain
Park

Girard Ave

La Jolla
Country Club

Windansea
Beach

La Jolla Blvd

Genter St

Draper Ave

Nautilus St

Nautilus St

Bonair St

Palomar Ave

Neptune Pl

La Jolla Blvd

Virginia Way

La Electric Ave

EATING (pp307–11)
George's at the Cove....................28 D5
Girard Gourmet............................29 D5
Harry's Coffee Shop.....................30 D6
Jack's...31 D5
Marine Room...............................32 B4
My Place......................................33 D6

Nine-Ten.............................(see 22)
Porkyland....................................34 D6
Roppongi.....................................35 D5
Tapénade.....................................36 D6
The Cottage.................................37 D6
Trattoria Acqua...........................38 D5

DRINKING (pp311–313)
Cendio...39 D5
Karl Strauss Brewery....................40 D5
La Jolla Brewhouse.......................41 D6
La Sala.................................(see 25)
Living Room Coffeehouse............42 D5
Pannikin......................................43 D6

ENTERTAINMENT (pp313–15)
Comedy Store..............................44 D6
La Jolla Playhouse........................45 C3
Mandeville Auditorium.................46 D2

SHOPPING (p315)
Art & Design Building...................47 D6

Ellen
Browning
Scripps
Park

Coast Blvd

Boomer
Beach

Coast
Boulevard
Park

Jenner St

Prospect St

Herschel Ave

Ivanhoe Ave

Eads Ave

Fay Ave

Silverado St

Kline St

Girard Ave

Cuvier St

Pearl St

La Jolla
Community
Park

Prospect St

Draper Ave

Silverado St

Eads Ave

Herschel Ave

Drury Ave

Torrey Pines Rd

0 _____ 500 m
0 _____ 0.3 miles

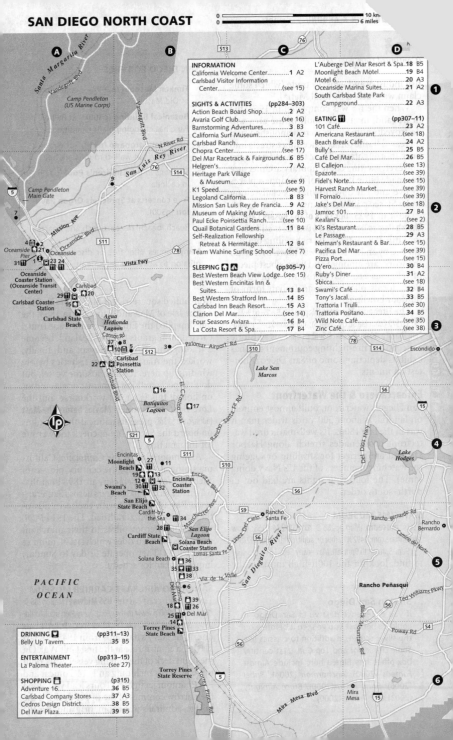

SAN DIEGO NORTH COAST

0 ——— 10 km
0 ——— 6 miles

INFORMATION
California Welcome Center...........1 A2
Carlsbad Visitor Information
   Center............................(see 15)

SIGHTS & ACTIVITIES (pp284–303)
Action Beach Board Shop............2 A2
Avaria Golf Club.....................(see 16)
Barnstorming Adventures............3 B3
California Surf Museum................4 A2
Carlsbad Ranch.........................5 B3
Chopra Center.........................(see 17)
Del Mar Racetrack & Fairgrounds....6 A2
Helgren's...............................7 A2
Heritage Park Village
   & Museum..........................(see 9)
K1 Speed................................(see 5)
Legoland California....................8 B3
Mission San Luis Rey de Francia.....9 A2
Museum of Making Music...........10 B3
Paul Ecke Poinsettia Ranch........(see 10)
Quail Botanical Gardens............11 B4
Self-Realization Fellowship
   Retreat & Hermitage.............12 B4
Team Wahine Surfing School......(see 7)

SLEEPING (pp305–7)
Best Western Beach View Lodge..(see 15)
Best Western Encinitas Inn &
   Suites.............................13 B5
Best Western Stratford Inn........14 B5
Carlsbad Inn Beach Resort........15 A3
Clarion Del Mar......................(see 14)
Four Seasons Aviara................16 B4
La Costa Resort & Spa..............17 B4

L'Auberge Del Mar Resort & Spa..18 B5
Moonlight Beach Motel..............19 B4
Motel 6..................................20 A3
Oceanside Marina Suites...........21 A2
South Carlsbad State Park
   Campground.......................22 A3

EATING (pp307–11)
101 Café................................23 A2
Americana Restaurant..............(see 18)
Beach Break Café....................24 A2
Bully's..................................25 B5
Café Del Mar.........................26 B5
El Callejon............................(see 13)
Epazote................................(see 39)
Fidel's Norte..........................(see 15)
Harvest Ranch Market..............(see 39)
Il Fornaio.............................(see 39)
Jake's Del Mar.......................(see 18)
Jamroc 101...........................27 B4
Kealani's..............................(see 2)
Ki's Restaurant.......................28 B5
Le Passage.............................29 A3
Neiman's Restaurant & Bar.......(see 15)
Pacifica Del Mar.....................(see 39)
Pizza Port.............................(see 15)
Q'ero...................................30 B4
Ruby's Diner.........................31 A2
Sbicca..................................(see 18)
Swami's Café..........................32 B5
Tony's Jacal..........................33 B5
Trattoria I Trulli.....................(see 30)
Trattoria Positano...................34 B5
Wild Note Café.......................(see 35)
Zinc Café..............................(see 38)

DRINKING (pp311–13)
Belly Up Tavern......................35 B5

ENTERTAINMENT (pp313–15)
La Paloma Theater...................(see 27)

SHOPPING (p315)
Adventure 16..........................36 B5
Carlsbad Company Stores..........37 A3
Cedros Design District..............38 B5
Del Mar Plaza.........................39 B5

(...rom page 285)

...ry and whiskey trade (which some claim was backed by local Mafia).

When the I-5 was completed in 1962, the heart (and, many say, soul) of the area was destroyed; entire blocks were demolished, and increased traffic turned once-quiet streets into busy thoroughfares. Over the last few years, however, exciting contemporary architecture has made Little Italy one of the hippest places to live and eat downtown, especially along India St; see p308 for listings.

Built in 1925, **Our Lady of the Rosary Catholic Church** (Map pp288-9; cnr State & Date Sts) is still a hub for Little Italy activity. Its rich ceiling murals, painted by an Italian who was flown over to do the work, are among San Diego's best pieces of religious art. Across the street in Amici Park, locals play bocce, an Italian form of outdoor bowling.

The **Firehouse Museum** (Map pp288-9; ☎ 619-232-3473; 1572 Columbia St, cnr Cedar St; admission $2; ☻ 10am-2pm Thu & Fri, 10am-4pm Sat & Sun) preserves a historic collection of fire-fighting equipment and has exhibits depicting some of San Diego's 'hottest' moments.

Embarcadero & the Waterfront

San Diego's waterfront, built almost entirely on landfill, is about 500 yards wider than it was in the late 1800s. Its well-manicured waterfront promenades stretch along Harbor Dr, and are perfect for strolling or jogging (or watching members of the US Navy doing same). The following sights are laid out in north–south order.

MARITIME MUSEUM

This **museum** (Map pp288-9; ☎ 619-234-9153; www .sdmaritime.com; 1492 N Harbor Dr; adult/child/senior $12/8/9; ☻ 9am-8pm, until 9pm late May–early Sep; ☻) is easy to find: look for the 100ft-high masts of the

---

SAN DIEGO FOR FREE

- **Timken Museum** (p299) – a collection of Old Masters
- **Botanical Building** (p300) – at Balboa Park; has changing plant exhibitions
- **Hotel del Coronado** (p318) – the rooms are pricey, but walk-throughs are free
- Sea lions at the **Children's Pool** (p329) in La Jolla.
- Free concerts at **Spreckels Organ Pavilion** (p300).
- Beach, beach, beach, beach and beach.

Many venues offer free or discounted admission to active military members.

---

iron-hulled square-rigger *Star of India*. Built on the Isle of Man and launched in 1863, the tall ship plied the England–India trade route, carried immigrants to New Zealand, became a trading ship based in Hawaii and, finally, worked the Alaskan salmon fisheries before winding up here. It's a handsome vessel, but don't expect anything romantic or glamorous on board: this is an old workhorse, not the *Love Boat*. In summer, **Movies before the Mast** (adult/child $13/8) presents nautical-themed films on board the *Star of India*; check the website for information.

Also moored here: the *California*, California's official tall ship; the century-old steam yacht *Medea*; the *Berkeley*, an 1898 boat that originally ferried passengers across San Francisco Bay to connect with the terminus of the transcontinental railroad. The 1914 *Pilot*, which took harbor pilots to their merchant ships, has narrated rides which last 30 minutes and cost $3. They operate Friday to Sunday; inquire ahead for schedules.

SAN DIEGO AIRCRAFT CARRIER MUSEUM

The giant aircraft carrier **USS Midway** (Map pp288-9; ☎ 619-544-9600; www.midway.org; Navy Pier; adult/child/senior & student $15/8/10; ☻ 10am-5pm; P ☻) was one of the Navy's flagships from 1945–91, last playing a combat role in the first Gulf War. On the flight deck of the hulking vessel, walk right up to aircrafts including an F-14 Tomcat and F-4 Phantom jet fighter. Tours lead you along the narrow confines of the upper decks to the bridge, admiral's war room, brig and 'pri-fly'

Shot in San Diego

If you experience déjà vu in San Diego, it could be because you've seen it before...on the silver screen. In addition to classics like *Some Like it Hot* and *Top Gun*, 21st-century box-office hits filmed here include *Almost Famous* (2000), *Anchorman* (2004), *Babel* (2006), *Bring it On* (2000), *Bruce Almighty* (2003) and *Traffic* (2000).

(primary flight control, the carrier's equivalent of a control tower), but lines can be long. If crowds are thin when you arrive, see the upper decks first. There are also three flight simulators (phone for rates and reservations). Some inside areas get stuffy on warm summer days: come early to avoid midday heat and crowds. Allow enough time to spend two to four hours on board. Parking from $5.

SEAPORT VILLAGE & AROUND
South of the USS *Midway,* you can stroll along **Tuna Harbor** for a long view of the aircraft carrier en route to **Seaport Village** (Map pp288-9; ☎ 619-235-4014; www.seaportvillage.com; ⊙ 10am-10pm; ℗ ♿). Neither seaport nor village, this collection of novelty shops and restaurants has an unconvincing faux–New England theme. It's touristy and twee but good for souvenir shopping and casual eats.

Wrapping southeast along the **Embarcadero Marina Park** – where there's a public fishing pier and an open-air amphitheater with free summer concerts – you'll see the 'sails' of the **San Diego Convention Center** (Map pp288-9; ☎ 619-525-5000; www.sdccc.org; Harbor Dr). This structure, stretching for half a mile, was designed by Canadian avant-garde architect Arthur Erickson and opened in 1989. It books out five years in advance with close to a million visitors annually. Two hours free parking with validation.

Balboa Park
With its museums, gardens and world-famous zoo, Balboa Park tops the list of sights in the downtown area. Its name honors the Spanish conquistador believed to be the first European to sight the Pacific Ocean.

Maps from 1868 show that Alonzo Horton's plans for San Diego included a 1400-acre City Park at the northeastern corner of what was to become Downtown. Ever the businessman, Horton enhanced the value of the land by restricting development here, although at the time it was all bare hilltops, chaparral and steep-sided arroyos (water-carved gullies).

Enter Kate O Sessions, a UC Berkeley botany graduate who in 1892 started a nursery on the site to landscape fashionable gardens for the city's emerging elite. The city granted her 30 acres of land in return for planting 100 trees a year in the park and donating 300 more for placement throughout the city. By the early 20th century, Balboa Park had become a well-loved part of San Diego.

In 1915–16, San Diego hosted the Panama–California Exposition (see p282), much of which took place in Balboa Park. New Yorkers Bertram Goodhue and Carlton Winslow designed the expo's pavilions in a romantic, Spanish Colonial style with beaux-arts and baroque flourishes. The pavilions were meant to be temporary – constructed largely of stucco, chicken wire, plaster, hemp and horsehair – but they proved so popular that many were later replaced with durable concrete structures in the same style. These buildings now house the museums along **El Prado**, the main pedestrian thoroughfare in the park.

Another expo, the 1935 Pacific–California Exposition, brought new buildings southwest of El Prado around the Pan-American Plaza. The Spanish Colonial architectural theme was expanded to include the whole New World, from indigenous styles (some of the buildings had Pueblo Indian and Mayan influences) through to the 20th century.

The San Diego Zoo (p298) occupies 100 acres in the north of Balboa Park.

ORIENTATION & INFORMATION
You can stroll around Balboa Park any time, but use common sense after dark. To visit all the museums and attractions would take days so plan carefully. Start at the **Balboa Park Visitors Center** (Map pp290-1; ☎ 619-239-0512; www.balboapark.org; 1549 El Prado; ⊙ 9:30am-4:30pm), in the House of Hospitality, where you can pick up a good park map (suggested donation $1) and buy admission passes; among them are the **Passport to Balboa Park** (good for one-time entry to the park's 13 museums within one week of purchase adult/child $35/19) and the **Combo Pass** (Passport plus zoo admission adult/child $59/33). Some museums occasionally have free Tuesday admission, though that's often restricted to local residents.

Balboa Park is easily reached from Downtown on bus 7, 7A or 7B along Park Blvd. By car, Park Blvd provides easy access to free parking areas near most of the exhibits, but the most scenic approach is over the Cabrillo Bridge from the west. El Prado is an extension of Laurel St, which crosses Cabrillo Bridge with the Cabrillo Fwy (CA163) 120ft below. Make a point of driving this stretch of freeway: the steep roadsides, lush with hanging greenery, look like a rain-forest gorge.

The free Balboa Park Tram bus stops at various points on a continuous loop through the main areas of the park. However, it's easiest and most enjoyable to walk.

SAN DIEGO ZOO

This justifiably famous zoo is one of SoCal's biggest attractions, showing more than 3000 animals, representing over 800 species in a beautifully landscaped setting, typically in enclosures that replicate their natural habitats.

The zoo originated with the Panama–California Exposition of 1915–16, which featured an assortment of animals in cages along Park Blvd. Local legend has it that Dr Harry Wegeforth, hearing the roar of one of the caged lions, exclaimed, 'Wouldn't it be wonderful to have a zoo in San Diego? I believe I'll build one!' He soon formed the Zoological Society of San Diego. By pulling a few strings, Dr Wegeforth then ensured that quarantines made it almost impossible to remove exotic animals from the county, so the society acquired much of the menagerie left over from the exposition.

The city provided 100 canyon-filled, barren acres of Balboa Park for the zoo, but these seeming detriments became advantages: canyons helped separate different groups of animals to prevent the spread of disease, and they could be individually landscaped to simulate appropriate natural settings.

Locals loved it. They brought in various finds such as seals and rattlesnakes, which the zoo often profitably traded for animals from other zoos. In one exchange, the zoo provided fleas for a New York flea circus. The US Navy unofficially contributed an assortment of animals that had been adopted as mascots. US Marines landing in Nicaragua were offered prizes if they captured beasts for Dr Wegeforth. During the 1930s Wegeforth himself traveled the world, collecting jaguars from Venezuela, orangutans from Borneo and marsupials from Australia. On a trip to India, Wegeforth contracted pneumonia and malaria; he died in 1941. His final contributions to the zoo were three elephants, which arrived in San Diego two months after his death.

By the end of WWII the San Diego Zoo had a strong worldwide reputation, and helped to rebuild collections of European zoos that had been devastated by the war. The Zoological Society continued at the forefront of zoo management with the introduction of 'bioclimatic' habitats, which allowed a number of different types of animals to share a simulated natural environment. In the 1960s the society started work on a 2000-acre Wild Animal Park (p341), 32 miles north of the city, which now provides free-range areas for many large animals.

Orientation & Information

The **zoo** (Map pp290-1; ☎ 619-231-1515; www.sandiegozoo.org; adult/child $21/14, with 40-min guided bus tour & aerial tram ride $33/22; ☉ 9am-5pm, latest admission 4pm); ℗ ♿) is located in the northern part of Balboa Park. The parking lot and the zoo fill up on weekends. Bus 7 will get you there from Downtown. To leave the zoo and return the same day, get a hand stamp from the information booth near the entrance. Check the website for extended hours during the warmer months.

Discount admission coupons are widely available in local magazines, newspapers and hotels and information-center kiosks. Combination tickets cover unlimited admission for five days to the San Diego Wild Animal Park (p341) and SeaWorld (p320). They cost $59/39 per adult/child for the Zoo & Wild Animal Park, or $107/77 for all three. Parking is free.

Arrive early, as many of the animals are most active in the morning – though many perk up again in the afternoon. The guided double-decker bus tour gives a good overview of the zoo with informative commentary: sitting downstairs puts you closer to the animals. Once you've made the loop, your ticket remains good for an express bus service in the park, a big help if you're unable to walk far. The Skyfari cable car goes right across the park and can save you some walking time, though there may be a line to get on it. Either way, you're going to do a lot of walking: carry quarters for the electric foot-massagers located around the park.

Facilities are provided for disabled visitors; call the **zoo** (☎ 619-231-1515 ext 4318) for specifics.

GIVING BACK

The San Diego Zoo and Wild Animal Park share an active program of breeding endangered species in captivity for reintroduction into their natural habitats, including the Arabian oryx, the Bali starling and the California condor.

Sights

Pick up a map at the entrance to the zoo. Most visitors will have their own favorite exhibits. The **koalas** are so popular that Australians may be surprised to find them a sort of unofficial symbol of San Diego, and the **giant pandas** run a close second. The **Komodo dragon**, an Indonesian lizard that can grow up to 10ft long, looks fearsome and strides menacingly around the reptile house.

Bioclimatic environments include **Tiger River**, a re-created Asian rain forest; **Gorilla Tropics**, an African rain forest; and the **Sun Bear Forest**, where the Asian bears are famously playful.

Absolutely Apes is devoted to the apes of Indonesia, including orangutans and siamangs climbing in lush forests. The large, impressive **Scripps Aviary** and **Rainforest Aviary** have well-placed feeders to allow some close-up viewing. And you can walk right beneath 100 species of winged creatures inside the **Owens Aviary**. Finally, don't miss the **African Rock Kopje** (outcrop), where klipspringers (small antelopes) demonstrate their rock-climbing abilities.

The **zoo gardens** are renowned and some of the plants are used for the specialized food requirements of particular animals. Pick up a brochure for the self-guided botanical gardens tour.

And of course the zoo is made for kids, from **animal shows** in at least two venues, to a **children's zoo exhibit** (where youngsters can pet small critters). Both children and adults will enjoy the animal nursery, where you can see the zoo's newest arrivals. Babies are born every spring and summer.

CALIFORNIA QUADRANGLE & MUSEUM OF MAN

El Prado passes under an archway and into an area called the California Quadrangle, with the Classical Revival–style **Museum of Man** (Map pp290-1; ☎ 619-239-2001; www.museumofman.org; adult/child/senior $8/4/6; ⏱ 10am-4:30pm) to the north. Figures on either side of the arch represent the Atlantic and Pacific Oceans, while the arch itself symbolizes the Panama Canal. This was the main entrance for the 1915 exposition, and the building was one of Goodhue's most ornate Spanish Colonial Revival creations, said to be inspired by the churrigueresque church of Tepotzotlán near Mexico City. The **Tower of California**, richly decorated with blue and yellow tiles, is an architectural landmark.

Originally, the building displayed more than 5000 ethnographic artifacts, including some specially made for the exposition – cast concrete reproductions of Mayan carvings are still on display. The museum now specializes in Native American artifacts from the American Southwest and has an excellent display of local baskets and pottery. The museum shop sells handicrafts from Central America and elsewhere.

PLAZA DE PANAMA

In the middle of El Prado, Plaza de Panama was the center of the Panama–California Exposition. The equestrian statue on the southern side is **El Cid**, who led the Spanish revolt against the Moors in the 11th century. On the plaza's southwestern corner, next to a rare New Zealand kauri tree (a fragrant evergreen with flat leaves), is the **House of Charm**, the Indian Arts building for the Panama Exposition; it got its present name during the 1935 fair as a souvenir market. It now houses the **Mingei International Museum** (Map pp290-1; ☎ 619-239-0003; www.mingei.org; adult/student/senior $6/3/4; ⏱ 10am-4pm Tue-Sun) and its excellent permanent collection of folk art, costumes, toys, jewelry, utensils and other handmade objects from traditional cultures.

SAN DIEGO MUSEUM OF ART

Built in 1924, the **SDMA** (Map pp290-1; ☎ 619-232-7931; www.sdmart.org; adult/child/student/senior $10/4/7/8; ⏱ 10am-6pm Tue-Sun, to 9pm Thu) is the city's largest art museum. It was designed by San Diego architect William Templeton Johnson in the 16th-century Spanish plateresque style, so named because it features heavy ornamentation resembling silverwork. The facade is particularly ornate, with sculptures depicting Spanish artists, most of whom have pieces inside the museum. The permanent collection has works by a number of European masters from the renaissance to the modernists (though no renowned pieces), some worthwhile American landscape paintings and several fantastic pieces in the Asian galleries, and there are often important traveling exhibits. The **Sculpture Garden** has pieces by Alexander Calder and Henry Moore, and a great outdoor eatery – Waters Café (p309).

TIMKEN MUSEUM OF ART

Don't skip the Timken. Distinctive for *not* being in imitation Spanish style, this **museum** (Map pp290-1; ☎ 619-239-5548; www.timkenmuseum.org;

SAN DIEGO COUNTY

ı5uu ɛı Prado; admission free; ⏰ 10am-4:30pm Tue-Sat, from 1:30 Sun, closed Sep), built in 1965, houses the Putnam collection, a small but impressive group of paintings, including works by Rembrandt, Rubens, El Greco, Cézanne and Pissarro. There's also a wonderful selection of Russian icons.

BOTANICAL BUILDING

The **Botanical Building** (Map pp290-1; admission free; ⏰ Fri-Wed) looks lovely from El Prado, where you can see it reflected in the large lily pond that was used for hydrotherapy in WWII when the Navy took over the park. The building's central dome and two wings are covered with redwood lathes, which let filtered sunlight into the collection of tropical plants and ferns. The planting changes every season; in December there's a particularly beautiful poinsettia display.

CASA DEL PRADO

This is one of the most handsome buildings along El Prado. Rebuilt after an earthquake, it now stages theater and dance performances.

CASA DE BALBOA

Dating from the 1915 exhibition, this building house three museums.

The **Museum of Photographic Arts** (Map pp290-1; ☎ 619-238-7559; www.mopa.org; adult/student & senior/child $6/4/free; ⏰ 10am-5pm, to 9pm Thu) has some 7000 photos in its permanent collection, tracing the history of photography, and special exhibits from crowd-pleasing landscapes by Ansel Adams to avant-garde cell-phone photography.

The San Diego Historical Society operates the **Museum of San Diego History** (Map pp290-1; ☎ 619-232-6203; www.sandiegohistory.org; adult/child/student & senior $5/2/4), covering the American period of San Diego from about 1848.

Your (inner) four-year-old boy will love the **Model Railroad Museum** (Map pp290-1; ☎ 619-696-0199; www.sdmrm.org; adult/student/senior $6/3/5; ⏰ 11am-4pm Tue-Fri, 11am-5pm Sat & Sun; ♿), one of the largest in the world. It has some 40,000 sq ft of amazingly landscaped working models of actual Southern California railroads, both historical and contemporary.

REUBEN H FLEET SPACE THEATER & SCIENCE CENTER

One of Balboa Park's most publicized venues, this hands-on **science museum** (Map pp290-

1; ☎ 619-238-1233; www.rhfleet.org; adult/child & senior $7/6.25; ⏰ from 9:30am; ♿) features interactive displays (though with less flash and dazzle than at others you may have visited) and a toddler room. The big draw is the huge-screen **IMAX theater** (adult/child incl Science Center $11.75/9.75, Fri night $7, additional films $4; ⏰ 11am to close of museum; ♿), which screens several different films each day. The hemispherical, wraparound screen and 152-speaker state-of-the-art sound system create sensations ranging from pretty cool to mind-blowing. **Comet Impact** ($4) is a motion simulator ride through space.

NATURAL HISTORY MUSEUM

The original 1933 building by William Templeton Johnson has been renovated into a **museum** (Map pp290-1; ☎ 619-232-3821; www.sdnhm.org; adult/child/student/senior $9/4/6/7; ⏰ 10am-5pm; ♿) with beautiful spaces and a giant-screen cinema. Feature movies change but always focus on the natural world; kids love them. The museum houses 7.5 million specimens, including rocks, fossils and taxidermy animals, as well as an impressive dinosaur skeleton and a California fault-line exhibit. Children's programs are held most weekends. The museum also arranges field trips and nature walks in Balboa Park and further afield.

SPANISH VILLAGE ART CENTER

Behind the Natural History Museum is a grassy square with a magnificent Moreton Bay fig tree (sorry, no climbing). Opposite the square stand there's an enclave of small tiled cottages (billed by park authorities as 'an authentic reproduction of an ancient village in Spain') that are rented out as **artists' studios** (Map pp290-1; ☎ 619-233-9050; admission free; ⏰ 11am-4pm), where you can watch potters, jewelers, glass blowers, painters and sculptors churn out their crafts. North of the Spanish Village there's a 1924 **carousel** (Map pp290-1; ☎ 619-239-0512; admission $2; ⏰ 11am-5:30pm daily mid-Jun—early Sep, 11am-4:30pm Sat, Sun & school holidays rest of year; ♿) and a **miniature railroad** (Map pp290-1; ☎ 619-239-0512; admission $2; ⏰ 11am-6:30pm daily mid-Jun—early Sep, 11am-4:30pm Sat, Sun & school holidays rest of year; ♿) offering three-minute rides.

SPRECKELS ORGAN PAVILION

Going south from Plaza de Panama, you can't miss the circle of seating and the curved colonnade in front of the band shell housing the organ said to be the world's largest outdoor musical instrument. Donated by the Spreckels family of sugar fortune and fame, the pipe organ came with the stipulation that San Diego must always have an official organist. Make a point of attending the free **concerts** (Map pp290-1; ☎ 619-702-8138; www.sosorgan.com), held throughout the year from 2pm to 3pm Sunday and 7:30pm Monday from mid-June to August.

PAN-AMERICAN PLAZA

The plaza is now simply a large parking lot southwest of the Spreckels Organ. As you approach it from the organ, the **UN Building** is on your right. Its **Unicef International Gift Shop** (Map pp290-1; ☎ 619-233-5044; ☒ 10am-4:30pm) has a good selection of stationery, jewelry and candy, and donates its profits to world widechildren's causes. Nearby, the **House of Pacific Relations** (Map pp290-1; ☎ 619-234-0739; admission free; ☒ noon-4pm Sun) actually comprises 15 cottages from the 1915 exposition, inside which you will find furnishings and displays from various countries. When the cottages are open, they often have crafts and food for sale.

Nearby in the Palisades Building, the **Marie Hitchcock Puppet Theater** (Map pp290-1; ☎ 619-544-9203; www.balboaparkpuppets.com; adult/child $5/3; ☒) puts on terrific hand- and rod-puppet shows (11am, 1pm and 2:30pm Wednesday to Sunday in summer, shorter hours rest of year), and also has puppet-making workshops. The **San Diego Automotive Museum** (Map pp290-1; ☎ 619-231-2886; www.sdautomuseum.org; adult/child/senior $8/5/6; ☒ 10am-5pm) has a collection of more than 60 cars and motorcycles, perfectly restored and well displayed, with classics including a 1937 Cord and a collection of motorcycles manufactured by Indians. Special exhibits change quarterly.

The round building at the southern end of the plaza houses the excellent **Air & Space Museum** (Map pp290-1; ☎ 619-234-8291; www.aerospacemuseum .org; adult/child/student & senior $15/9/12; ☒ 10am-5:30pm Jun-Aug, to 4:30pm Sep-May; ☒), with an extensive display of aircrafts – originals, replicas, models and Charles Lindbergh memorabilia.

At the adjacent **Starlight Bowl**, the **Starlight Opera** (Map pp290-1; ☎ 619-544-7827; www.starlighttheatre.org) presents a summer season of musicals and light opera.

The Federal Building was built for the 1935 exposition and now holds the **San Diego Hall of Champions Sports Museum** (Map pp290-1; ☎ 619-234-2544; www.sdhoc.com; adult/senior/child $8/6/4; ☒ 10am-

4:30pm), a hall of fame for San Diego sports figures. Permanent and temporary exhibits cover themes as wide-ranging as Ted Williams, skateboarder Tony Hawk and the World Series of Poker. There's also a media center, in which kids can call the commentary on a game.

CENTRO CULTURAL DE LA RAZA

The **center** (Map pp290-1; ☎ 619-235-6135; www.centro raza.com; donation requested; ☒ noon-4pm Tue-Sun) hosts powerful exhibitions of Mexican and Native American art, including temporary exhibits of contemporary indigenous artwork. The round, steel building, which is actually a converted water tank, sits way out on the edge of the main museum area; easiest access is from Park Blvd.

MARSTON HOUSE

In the far northwestern corner of Balboa Park is the former home of George Marston, philanthropist and founder of the San Diego Historical Society. Built in 1904, **Marston House** (Map pp290-1; ☎ 619-298-3142; 3525 Seventh Ave; adult/ child/senior $5/2/4; ☒ 10am-4:30pm Fri-Sun by 45min tour) was designed by noted San Diego architects William Hebbard and Irving Gill, and is a fine example of the American Arts and Crafts style with furnishing and decorative objects.

BALBOA PARK GARDENS

Balboa Park includes a number of gardens, reflecting different horticultural styles and environments, including **Alcazar Garden**, a formal, Spanish-style garden; **Palm Canyon**, with more than 50 species of palms; **Japanese Friendship Garden** (Map pp290-1; ☎ 619-232-2721; www.niwa.org; adult/child/senior $3/2/2.50; ☒ 10am-5pm Mon-Fri, 10am-4pm Sat & Sun late May–early Sep, 10am-4pm Tue-Sun early Sep–late May); **Australian Garden**; **Rose Garden**; and **Desert Garden** (best in spring). **Florida Canyon** gives an idea of the San Diego landscape before Spanish settlement.

Free weekly **Offshoot tours** (Map pp290-1; www .balboapark.org/info/tours.php; 10am Sat Jan to Thanksgiving) depart the Balboa Park Visitor Center (p297).

Mission Valley

Although it would often dry up in late summer, the San Diego River was the most reliable source of fresh water for the crops and livestock of the early missions. The river valley, now called Mission Valley, flooded frequently until dams were completed upstream in the mid-1950s. The I-8 now runs its length. The restored Mission San Diego de Alcalá is worth visiting, but Mission Valley's most touted feature is its triad of shopping centers (p315).

The San Diego Trolley runs the length of the valley, from Downtown to the mission, with stops at Qualcomm Stadium and all the shopping centers. The trolley's route cuts through a scenic corridor of riparian land (and golf courses) not seen from the freeway.

MISSION SAN DIEGO DE ALCALÁ

Although the site of the first California mission was on Presidio Hill (opposite), in 1774 Padre Junípero Serra moved it about 7 miles upriver to its present location, closer to a water supply and more arable land. In 1784 the missionaries built a solid adobe and timber church, which was destroyed by an earthquake in 1803. The church was promptly rebuilt, and at least some of it still stands on a slope overlooking Mission Valley. With the end of the mission system in the 1830s, the buildings were turned over to the Mexican government and fell into disrepair. Some accounts say that they were reduced to a facade and a few crumbling walls by the 1920s.

Extensive restoration began in 1931, with financial support from local citizens and the Hearst Foundation, a philanthropic organization funded by one of California's most influential families. The pretty white church and buildings you see now are the fruits of that work.

The **visitors center** (Map p287; ☎ 619-281-8449; www.missionsandiego.com; 10818 San Diego Mission Rd, cnr Friars Rd; adult/child/senior $3/1/2; ☽ 9am-4:45pm) inside the mission has a friendly and informative staff. The mission sits north of I-8, off the Mission Gorge Rd exit; from the Mission trolley stop, walk two blocks north and turn right onto San Diego Mission Rd.

Old Town

Under the Mexican government, which took power in 1821, any settlement with a population of 500 or more was entitled to become a 'pueblo.' Since the Presidio's population was about 600, the land below became the first official civilian Spanish settlement in California – the *Pueblo de San Diego*. A plaza was laid out around Casa Estudillo, home of the pueblo's commandant, and within 10 years it was surrounded by about 40 huts

and several houses. This square mile of land (roughly 10 times what remains today) was also the center of American San Diego until the fire of 1872, after which the city's main body moved to the new Horton subdivision (now Downtown).

John Spreckels built a trolley line from Horton's New Town to Old Town in the 1920s and, to attract passengers, began restoring the old district. In 1968 the area was named **Old Town State Historic Park**, archaeological work began, and the few surviving original buildings were restored. Other structures were rebuilt, and the area is now a pedestrian district (with parking lots around the edges) of shade trees, a large open plaza, and a cluster of shops and restaurants.

Today's Old Town is primarily a shopping and eating destination, but interpretive rangers give tours and the **Old Town State Historic Park Visitor Center** (☎ 619-220-5422; www.parks .ca.gov; admission free; ☽ 10am-5pm) has an excellent American-period museum in the Robinson-Rose House at the southern end of the plaza. (Native-American pieces are in the Museum of Man at Balboa Park.) The center has memorabilia, a video of local history, and an educated staff. You'll also find good history books for sale and a diorama depicting the original pueblo. If you're particularly interested in history, pick up a copy of the *Old Town San Diego State Historic Park Tour Guide & Brief History* ($2), or take a guided tour, which leaves from the visitor center at 11am and 2pm daily.

Across from the center the restored **Casa de Estudillo** is filled with authentic period furniture. Pick up a self-guided tour map. Other buildings around the plaza include a blacksmith shop, print shop and a candle-dipping shop – call the visitors center for hours.

The **Plaza del Pasado**, just off the plaza's northwestern corner, is a colorful collection of import shops and restaurants – great for Mexican souvenirs without the trip to Tijuana. Along San Diego Ave, on the southern side of the plaza, small, historical-looking buildings (only one is authentic) house more souvenir and gift shops.

Two blocks from the Old Town perimeter sits **Whaley House** (Map pp290-1; ☎ 619-297-7511; www.whaleyhouse.org; 2476 San Diego Ave; adult/child $6/4; ☽ 10am-10pm daily Jun-Aug, 10am-5pm Mon & Tues, 10am-10pm Thu-Sun Sep-May; ☂), the city's oldest brick building, officially certified as haunted by the

US Department of Commerce. Check out the collection of period furniture and clothing from when the house served as a courthouse, theater and private residence.

Just north of Old Town, **Casa de Carillo** dates from about 1820 and is said to be the oldest house in San Diego. It is now the pro shop for the public 18-hole **Presidio Hills Golf Course** (Map pp290-1; ☎ 619-295-9476; www.golfsd.com; cnr Juan St & Wallace St; greens fee $10).

The Old Town transit center, on Taylor St at the northwestern edge of Old Town, is an important transit hub for the *Coaster* commuter train, the San Diego Trolley and buses. Old Town Trolley tours stop southeast of the plaza on Twiggs St.

PRESIDIO HILL

In 1769 Padre Junípero Serra and Gaspar de Portolá established the first Spanish settlement in California overlooking the valley of the San Diego River. You can walk up from Old Town along Mason St for excellent views of San Diego Bay and Mission Valley. Atop the hill, **Presidio Park** has several walking trails and shaded benches. A large cross, made with tiles from the original mission, commemorates Padre Serra. American forces occupied the hill in 1846, during the Mexican-American War, and named it Fort Stockton, for American commander Robert Stockton. A flagpole, a cannon, some plaques and earth walls now form the **Fort Stockton Memorial**. The nearby **El Charro Statue**, a bicentennial gift to the city from Mexico, depicts a Mexican cowboy on horseback. Nothing remains of the original Presidio structures.

The **Serra Museum** (Map pp290-1; ☎ 619-297-3258; 2727 Presidio Dr; adult/child/student & senior $5/2/4; ☷ 10am-4:30pm) has a small but interesting collection of artifacts and pictures from the Mission and rancho periods, and gives a good sense of the earliest days of European settlement up to 1929 when the museum was founded.

Uptown & Hillcrest

Uptown is roughly a triangle north of Downtown, east of Old Town and south of Mission Valley. In the late 19th century it was fashionable to live in the hills north of Downtown, since only those who owned a horse-drawn carriage could afford it. Called Bankers Hill after some of the wealthy residents – or Pill Hill, because of the many

doctors there – the upscale heights had unobstructed views of the bay and Point Loma before I-5 was built.

A few of the ornate Victorian mansions survive, most notably the 1889 **Long-Waterman House** (2408 1st Ave). Easily recognized by its towers, gables, bay windows and verandah, it was once the home of former California governor Robert Waterman. Also notable is the **Timken House**, one block to the north. The 375ft **Spruce St Footbridge** hangs over a deep canyon between Front and Brant Sts. The **Quince St Bridge**, between 3rd and 4th Aves, is a woodtrestle bridge built in 1905 and refurbished in 1988 after community activists protested its slated demolition.

In the 1970s, architect and artist Raoul Marquis designed a shingled complex on the west corner of this district, at the corner of Washington and India Sts. The art studios, import shops and theaters that originally occupied it are gone, since replaced by some first-rate, mostly inexpensive eateries – this area is sometimes referred to as **Mission Hills**.

The heart of Uptown is **Hillcrest**, the first suburban real-estate development in San Diego. If you drive around, you'll see the work of many of San Diego's best-known architects from the early 20th century, including Irving Gill and William Templeton Johnson. The Mediterranean, Spanish Mission and Arts and Crafts styles are much in evidence. But Hillcrest's chief attraction is its lively street life, due largely to its status as the center of San Diego's gay and lesbian community.

Begin at the **Hillcrest Gateway**, an illuminated electric sign that arches over University Ave at 5th Ave. East on University Ave at No 535, look for the 1928 **Kahn Building**, an original commercial building with architectural elements that border on kitsch. South of University Ave along 5th Ave, there's a variety of new and used bookstores, many with a good selection of nonmainstream publications.

Hillcrest's **farmers market** (Map pp290-1; 5th Ave, cnr Normal & Lincoln Sts; ☷ 9am-1pm Sun) is great for people-watching and fresh produce.

TOURS

Look for discounts in tourist literature or on line.

Not to be confused with the Metropolitan Transit System's trolleys, **Old Town Trolley Tours** (Map pp290-1; ☎ 619-298-8687, 800-868-7482; www.trolley tours.com; adult/child $30/15; ☷ 9am-7pm; ☷) operates

SAN DIEGO COUNTY

hop-on–hop-off open-air buses decorated like old-style streetcars, looping around the main attractions of Downtown and Coronado every 30 minutes or so. The official trolley stand is in Old Town (which is convenient for parking), but you can start or stop at any trolley-tour stop (they're well marked with orange and are usually next to regular transit bus stops). The tours are a great introduction to the city, and the commentary is entertaining. Kids like the Seal Tour (about 90 minutes, hourly from 10am to 6pm), which departs from Seaport Village and ventures in and around San Diego Bay in an amphibious vehicle.

San Diego Scenic Tours (☎ 858-273-8687; www.sandiegoscenictours.com; adult $29-57, child 3-11yr $14-28) leads half- and full-day bus tours around San Diego and Tijuana, some of which build in time to shop and dine. You can combine some tours with a harbor cruise.

Gray Line (☎ 800-331-5077, 619-236-7325; www.sandiegograyline.com; adult $29-57, child 3-11yr $15-27) is a larger outfit offering bus tours around the city and to Tijuana, in addition to more expensive excursions (up to $94/69 oper adult/child) to big-ticket attractions throughout SoCal: Wild Animal Park, SeaWorld, Legoland, Disneyland and Universal Studios Hollywood.

Original Bike Cab Co (☎ 888-245-3222, 619-245-3222; www.bikecab.com; 🕓 10am-midnight Mon-Fri, 10am-3am Sat & Sun) offers San Diego's version of a rickshaw: the pedicab, a bicycle pulling a carriage that seats up to four people. The drivers (pedalers?) often offer advice on what's going on around town. Flag an empty pedicab, or call and one will pick you up. Fares are negotiable, but figure on $5 to $10 per person depending on distance and demand. The same company offers Downtown pedicab tours and trips to other parts of San Diego (from $25 per half-hour).

San Diego Harbor Excursion (Map pp288-9; ☎ 800-442-7847, 619-234-4111; www.sdhe.com; adult/child from $17/8.50; ♿) and **Hornblower Cruises** (Map pp288-9; ☎ 619-725-8888; www.hornblower.com; adult/child from $18/9; ♿) run one- and two-hour sightseeing tours from the Embarcadero. Both also have nightly dinner-dance cruises for about $65 per person ($70 on Saturday) and whale-watching excursions in season.

FESTIVALS & EVENTS

March

Ocean Beach Kite Festival (☎ 858-274-2016) The first Saturday in March brings kite making, decorating, flying and competitions.

March/April

San Diego Crew Classic (☎ 619-225-0300; www.crewclassic.org) The national college rowing regatta takes places in late March/early April at Crown Point Shores Park in Mission Bay.

June

Rock 'n' Roll Marathon (☎ 858-450-6510; www.rnrmarathon.com) Live bands perform at each mile mark of this 26.2-mile race, with a big concert at the finish line. Early June.

San Diego County Fair (☎ 858-755-1161; www.sdfair.com) Mid-June to July 4; features headline acts and hundreds of carnival rides and shows at the Del Mar Fairgrounds.

July

Del Mar Horse Racing (☎ 858-755-1141; www.dmtc.com) The well-heeled bet on the horses, 'where the turf meets the sea,' at Del Mar Fairgrounds, from mid-July to early September.

US Open Sandcastle Competition (www.usopen-sandcastle.com) You won't believe what can be made out of sand at the amazing sandcastle-building competition held mid- or late July in Imperial Beach, south of Coronado.

San Diego LGBT Pride (☎ 619-297-7683; www.sdpride.org) The city's gay community celebrates in Hillcrest and Balboa Park at the month's end, with parades, parties, performances, art shows and more.

Comic-con International (☎ 619-491-2475; www.comic-con.org) America's largest event for collectors of comic, pop culture and movie memorabilia, at the San Diego Convention Center. Late July.

August

Summerfest Chamber Music Festival (☎ 858-459-3728; www.ljcms.org) La Jolla hosts this three-week series with international performers.

Old Globe Festival (☎ 619-239-2255; www.oldglobe.org) Renowned Shakespeare festival in Balboa Park, with both popular and lesser-known plays.

September

Thunderboat Regatta (☎ 619-225-9160; www.thunderboats.net) Some of the world's fastest boats compete on Mission Bay in mid-September.

Street Scene (www.street-scene.com) California's largest music festival features dozens of performers, outdoor stages and lots to eat. Late September.

San Diego Film Festival (☎ 619-582-2368; www.sdff.org) The silver screen takes center stage in the Gaslamp District, with screenings, panel discussions and parties. Past stars in attendance have included Joaquin Phoenix and James Woods. Late September.

Fleet Week (☎ 800-353-3893; www.fleetweeksandiego.org) Actually more like 'Fleet Month'. The US military shows its pride in events including a sea and air parade, special tours of ships, and the Miramar Air Show, the world's largest. Late September to late October.

October

Little Italy Festa (www.littleitalysd.com) Come for the tastes and aromas of old Italia, and stay for Gesso Italiano, chalk-art drawn directly onto the streets. Mid-month.

December

December Nights (☎ 619-239-0512; www.balboapark.org) Festival in Balboa Park includes crafts, carols and a candlelight parade.

Harbor Parade of Lights (www.sdparadeoflights.org) Dozens of decorated, illuminated boats float in procession on the harbor on two Sunday evenings in December.

Las Posadas and Luminaries (☎ 619-291-4903; www.oldtownsandiego.org) This traditional Latin Christmas celebration in Old Town re-enacts Mary and Joseph seeking shelter.

SLEEPING

High-season summer rates for double-occupancy rooms are listed here; suites cost more. Prices drop significantly between September and June. Whatever time of year, ask about specials and package deals.

The San Diego Convention & Visitor Bureau runs a **room-reservation line** (☎ 800-350-6205; www.sandiego.org).

Downtown & Little Italy

BUDGET

USA Hostels San Diego (Map pp288-9; ☎ 619-232-3100, 800-438-8622; www.usahostels.com; 726 5th Ave, Downtown; dm/d incl breakfast $25/61; 🖳 wi-fi) Housed in a former Victorian-era hotel, this convivial Gaslamp hostel has cheerful rooms, a full kitchen, a lounge for chilling and in-house parties and beach barbecues. The rate includes linen, lockers and tasty pancakes in the morning. It can be a bit noisy, but the crowd here doesn't seem to mind. No air-con.

our pick **500 West Hotel** (Map pp288-9; ☎ 619-234-5252, 866-500-7533; www.500westhotel.com; 500 W Broadway, Downtown; s/d/tw without bathroom $59/69/79; 🅿 🖳) Rooms are shoebox-sized and bathrooms are down the hallway in this 1920s YMCA building (renovated in 2004), but hipsters on a budget love the bright decor, flat-screen TVs, communal kitchen (or diner-style restaurant), fitness studio and easy access to trolleys and long-distance buses. No air-con.

La Pensione Hotel (Map pp288-9; ☎ 619-236-8000, 800-232-4683; www.lapensionehotel.com; 606 W Date St; r from $80; 🅿 wi-fi) Around a frescoed courtyard at the corner of busy India St in Little Italy, La Pensione has rooms with queen-size beds and private bathrooms, and is within walking distance to most Downtown attractions. There's an attractive café downstairs. Great bargain but no air-con.

J Street Inn (Map pp288-9; ☎ 619-696-6922; www.thejstreetinn.com; 222 J St; per night/week $90/300) All of the rooms have fridge, microwaves and private bathroom at this well-run single-room occupancy (it rents rooms to those who might otherwise be homeless) that also operates hotel style. The beds are way too soft, but the place is clean and safe, there are laundry and fitness facilities, and the price is right.

Hotel Occidental (Map pp288-9; ☎ 619-232-1336; www.hoteloccidental-sandiego.com; 410 Elm St; d incl breakfast $79-139; 🅿 wi-fi) Even if this one-time hospital is a tad antiseptic at first glance (eg industrial-style carpeting), it's got a lot to recommend it: kitchenettes, dual-pane windows to keep out street noise, free local calls, simple continental breakfast, bottled water and delivery from nearby restaurants. Rates are based on room size and en-suite facilities.

MIDRANGE

our pick **Hotel Solamar** (Map pp288-9; ☎ 619-531-8740, 877-230-0300; www.hotelsolamar.com; 435 6th Ave; r from $149; 🅿 🖳 🕸 wi-fi) A great compromise in the Gaslamp: hip style that needn't break the bank. Lounge beats provide the soundtrack to your view of skyscrapers from the pool deck. There's a fitness center and the 'Om away from home' yoga kit. Parking costs $30.

Bristol Hotel (Map pp288-9; ☎ 619-232-6141, 800-662-4477; www.thebristolsandiego.com; 1055 1st Ave; r $150-180; 🅿 🖳) A blah mid-century facade conceals a surprisingly stylish interior. Recently renovated rooms have bold black-and-white graphics, and there are antique-y wood moldings around the doorways. Expect extras such as bathrobes and minibars. Parking costs $22.

Sofia Hotel (Map pp288-9; ☎ 619-234-9200, 800-826-0009; www.thesofiahotel.com; 150 W Broadway; r from $175; 🅿 🖳 wi-fi) San Diego is in the midst of a boom of historic hotels receiving contemporary redos. Steps from Horton Plaza, the business district, the Sofia has 211 rooms, in-room spa services and a studio. Parking costs $25.

Horton Grand Hotel (Map pp288-9; ☎ 619-544-1886, 800-542-1886; www.hortongrand.com; 311 Island Ave; r $179; (P) (🖳) wi-fi) Some rooms in this 1886 brick hotel in the Gaslamp have wrought-iron balconies on the street, but the quietest face the inner courtyard. All are individually decorated in Victoriana and have gas fireplaces. Parking costs $24.

Westgate Hotel (Map pp288-9; ☎ 619-238-1818, 800-221-3802; www.westgatehotel.com; 1055 2nd Ave; r from $199; (P) (🖳) wi-fi) Despite the 1970s shell of its 233-room tower, the Westgate is pure white-glove luxury on the inside. Think handcrafted European furniture, high tea with harp music, staff with European accents and a coral, blue and yellow color scheme in rooms. There's a spa and fitness center. Parking costs $25.

Manchester Grand Hyatt (Map pp288-9; ☎ 619-232-1234; www.manchestergrand.hyatt.com; 1 Market Pl; r $209-399; (P) (🖳) (🏊) (👶) wi-fi) Adjacent to Seaport Village, the 1625-room Manchester is the largest waterfront hotel on the west coast. It fancies itself an 'urban resort', with multiple pools, an 'adventure cabana' offering excursions like kayaking and sailing, and forward-thinking kids' programs. Most of the well-maintained rooms have some sort of water view. Parking costs $20.

TOP END

W Hotel (Map pp288-9; ☎ 619-231-8220, 888-625-5144; www.whotels.com; 421 West B St; r from $230; (P) (🖳) (🏊) wi-fi) Sexy and stylin', the W is aggressively decked out in a sky-sand-and-sea theme, with deep blues and shades of grey and gold.

Every room features luxury amenities, and there's a spa, roof-top beach and a DJ spinning house music in the lobby on weekends. Parking costs $28.

our pick Ivy (Map pp288-9; ☎ 619-814-1000; www.ivyhotel.com; 600 F Street; r from $350; (🖳) wi-fi) The newest of the razzle-dazzle hotels to illuminate the Gaslamp district. It's ineffably chic and sexy (glass-enclosed shower with bed-views, anyone?), and guests get access to some of the city's most styling nightspots, on-site.

US Grant Hotel (Map pp288-9; ☎ 619-232-3121, 800-237-5029; www.starwood.com; 326 Broadway; r $329-529; (P) (🖳) wi-fi) Given a facelift in 2006, this 1910 hotel was built as the fancy city counterpart to the Hotel del Coronado (p318) and hosted everyone from Albert Einstein to Harry Truman. Today's quietly flashy lobby combines chocolate-brown and ocean-blue accents, and rooms boast original paintings on the headboards. Parking costs $28. See also p285.

Old Town

You almost don't need a car if you stay in Old Town. Most lodgings offer free airport shuttles, and there are convenient transit links.

Holiday Inn Express (Map pp290-1; ☎ 619-299-7400; www.hiexpress.com/ex-oldtown; 3900 Old Town Ave; r $140-160; (P) (🖳) (🏊) (👶) wi-fi) Hacienda-style building at the edge of Old Town. Rooms are clean, spacious and up-to-date with hardwood mission-style furniture and extras such as microwaves and refrigerators. Good value. Parking is $12.

Best Western Hacienda Hotel (Map pp290-1; ☎ 619-298-4707, 800-888-1991; www.haciendahotel-

---

MISSION VALLEY

Downtown rates got you down? Beach booked? The couple of dozen mostly chain hotels and motels along Hotel Circle Dr in Mission Valley offer in quantity and price what their neighborhood lacks in charm – they're popular for business gatherings, family vacations and shopping excursions. Particularly outside of summer peak, you can occasionally find weekday rates as low as $80. Here are some choices:

Handlery Hotel (Map pp290-1; ☎ 619-298-0511, 800-843-4343; www.handlery.com; 950 Hotel Circle N; r $120-160; (P) (🖳) (🏊) (👶) wi-fi) The Handlery has attractive furnishings (wooden armoires and writing desks) and a complimentary shuttle to area attractions. Parking costs $12.

Crowne Plaza San Diego (Map pp290-1; ☎ 619-297-1101; www.cp-sandiego.com; 2270 Hotel Circle N; r $129-229; (P) (🖳) (🏊) (👶) wi-fi) Convention-class hotel with a Polynesian theme (koi ponds and waterfall) and rooms with super-comfy mattresses. Parking costs $10.

Town & Country Hotel (Map pp290-1; ☎ 619-291-7131, 800-772-8527; www.towncountry.com; 500 Hotel Circle N; r from $195; (P) (🖳) (🏊) (👶) wi-fi) Four swimming pools, tropical landscaping and a 10-story tower make the Town & Country feel like Honolulu off the I-8. There's a trolley stop and bridge to Fashion Valley shopping center. Parking costs $14.

SAN DIEGO COUNTY

oldtown.com; 4041 Harney St; r $159-229; P 🖥 🚲 ♿ wi-fi) On four well-landscaped acres on the hillside above Old Town's restaurant row, the Hacienda has 199 rooms over eight buildings, neatly and conservatively decorated and some with pull-out sofas. Add in a workout room, Jacuzzi and nightly happy hour. Parking costs $12.

Hillcrest

Hillcrest Inn (Map pp290-1; ☎ 619-293-7078, 800-258-2280; www.hillcrestinn.com; 3754 5th Ave; r from $89; P wi-fi) Once a staple of the Hillcrest gay community, this courtyard-style inn now hosts a mixed clientele drawn by cheap rates, a Jacuzzi and the convenient location. Rooms are nothing special, with aging furniture and no air-con. Parking costs $12.

Sommerset Suites Hotel (Map pp290-1; ☎ 619-296-2101, 800-962-9665; www.sommersetsuites.com; 606 Washington St; r incl breakfast from $109; P 🖥 🚲 ♿) Originally built as condominiums in the 1980s, all rooms have full kitchens, many units are two-room suites, and there's a guest laundry. Clientele is split between visitors to Hillcrest's nightlife and the nearby hospital. It's on a busy street, so bring ear plugs if you're sensitive to noise.

Park Manor Suites (Map pp290-1; ☎ 619-291-0999, 800-874-2649; www.parkmanorsuites.com; 525 Spruce St; r incl breakfast $129-229; P wi-fi) This gay-friendly place, facing Balboa Park and a reasonable walk to central Hillcrest, used to be an apartment building, meaning mostly large rooms with kitchens and vast closets. Staff call the room decor 'old world,' though we'd say 'old' – take your pick. Breakfast is served on the top floor, with sweeping Downtown-to-ocean views. The roof becomes a gay party scene on Friday nights.

Britt Scripps Inn (Map pp290-1; ☎ 619-230-1991, 888-881-1991; www.brittscripps.com; 406 Maple St; r incl breakfast from $200; P 🖥 wi-fi) This nine-room Victorian belle just off Balboa Park offers a rare alchemy of high-tech and tradition. Vintage fixtures and furnishings seamlessly pair with flat-screen TVs and high-speed internet. Rates (which can rise steeply in peak season) include a wine-and-cheese reception in the cozy parlor.

Camping

KOA (Map p287; ☎ 619-427-3601, 800-562-9877; www.koa.com; 111 N 2nd Ave; campsites $41-53, RV sites $51-76, cabins $75-95; P 🖥 🚲 ♿ wi-fi) In Chula Vista, about 8 miles southeast of downtown San Diego, the KOA has good camping facilities for families like a pool and bike rental, plus a Jacuzzi for mom and dad.

EATING

Despite its border location, San Diego's food scene doesn't have the ethnic breadth of LA's. Still, you'll find some of America's top tables from Downtown to La Jolla and beyond. And some of the less expensive options are fun and satisfying. Make reservations whenever possible, especially on weekends.

Gaslamp Quarter

There are some 100 restaurants in the Gaslamp, many of them very good. Some have bar scenes that run well into the night.

BUDGET

Cafe Lulu (Map pp288-9; ☎ 619-238-0114; 419 F St; light meals $4-8; ⏰ 9am-1am Sun-Thu, to 2:30am Fri & Sat) Linger over lattes or muse over merlot at this hip café, and refuel on sandwiches, cheeseboards and cakes. Outside seating.

Cheese Shop (Map pp288-9; ☎ 619-232-2303; 627 4th Ave; mains breakfast $3-9, lunch $6-9; ⏰ breakfast & lunch; ♿) Less actual cheese shop than old-fashioned luncheonette, with long wooden counter, cozy booths and brick walls. Breakfasts are classics (have the corned-beef hash and you won't eat until dinner), or try the overstuffed sandwiches or house-roasted pork loin at lunch – never mind the apathetic service we received here.

our pick Café 222 (Map pp288-9; ☎ 619-236-9902; 222 Island Ave; mains $6-12; ⏰ 7am-1:45pm; ♿) Downtown's favorite breakfast place serves renowned pumpkin waffles, buttermilk, orange-pecan or granola pancakes, and eggs in scrambles or benedicts. They also sell lunchtime sandwiches and salads, but we always go for breakfast (available until closing).

Dick's Last Resort (Map pp288-9; ☎ 619-231-9100; 345 4th Ave; mains $7-16; ⏰ 11am-1:30am) At Dick's, a legendary indoor-outdoor place with a riotously fun atmosphere, you can carry on in full voice while guzzling beer and chowing down on pork ribs, fried chicken and fish. None of the other revelers will care a whit.

Ghirardelli Soda Fountain & Chocolate Shop (Map pp288-9; ☎ 619-234-2449; 643 5th Ave; ice cream $3-7; ⏰ 11am-11pm Sun-Thu, 11am-midnight Fri-Sun; ♿) Get jacked on sugar at this old-fashioned ice-cream parlor.

MIDRANGE & TOP END

Red Pearl Kitchen (Map pp288-9; ☎ 619-231-1100; 440 J St; small dishes $7-19; ☒ 5pm-2am) Orange County's restaurateurs of record, Tim and Liza Goodell, have opened this slick and chic Pan-Asian tapas bar, from dim sum to dessert: chicken-ginger pot stickers, miso-glazed salmon, shaking Kobe beef with papaya and mint... Late-night menu too.

Gaslamp Strip Club (Map pp288-9; ☎ 619-231-3140; 340 5th Ave; mains $14-24; ☒ dinner) Pull your own bottle from the wine vault, then char your own favorite cut of steak, chicken or fish on the open grills in the retro-Vegas dining room at Downtown's best bargain for steak. No bottle costs more than $36, no steak more than $24. Fab, creative martinis and 'pin-up' art by Alberto Vargas. Tons of fun. No one under 21 allowed.

Bandar (Map pp288-9; ☎ 619-238-0101; 825 4th Ave; mains lunch $8-14, dinner $14-26) Exotic spices and fragrant cooking make this white-tablecloth Persian–Middle Eastern a favorite for giant kebabs and salads that zing with flavor. Come hungry: portions are huge.

Bondi (Map pp288-9; ☎ 619-342-0212; 333 5th Ave; mains breakfast $4-12, lunch $10-16, dinner $14-34; ☒ 8am-2am) Iron ore, Australian rosewood and a steel baobab tree are your backdrop for inventive cooking inspired by Down Under. Try the ricotta hotcakes for breakfast (with grilled banana, honeycomb and more), or, later, barbecued jumbo prawns, chargrilled rack of lamb and Wagyu beef sliders, washed down with select Aussie beers.

Café Sevilla (Map pp288-9; ☎ 619-233-5979; 555 4th Ave; tapas $5-12, mains $16-28; ☒ dinner) The tapas and Spanish food are good, and the live tango and flamenco performances are sublime. They include a three-course meal for $40 per person, Friday to Sunday. Book in advance. There's music (and sangria) nightly in the tapas bar.

ourpick Oceanaire (Map pp288-9; ☎ 619-858-2277; 400 J St; most mains $20-35; ☒ dinner) The look is art deco ocean liner, and the service is just as elegant. Chef Brian Malarkey was named local chef of the year for the oyster bar and creations like Maryland-blue-crab cakes and horseradish-crusted Alaskan halibut. The 'stealing home' menu (5pm to 7pm) lives up to its name, $30 for three courses.

Croce's Restaurant & Jazz Bar (Map pp288-9; ☎ 619-233-4355; 802 5th Ave; mains breakfast & lunch $7-19, dinner $23-35; ☒ breakfast & lunch Sat & Sun, dinner daily) Empty tables are a rare sight at this sizzling restaurant, a pioneer of the Gaslamp and Ingrid Croce's (p238) tribute to her late husband, singer Jim Croce. Both the contemporary American cooking and the musicians who perform nightly hit the right notes. There's also an acclaimed wine list.

See also Karl Strauss Brewery & Grill (p312).

Little Italy

Little Italy is – surprise! – a happy hunting ground for cafes and trattorias, on India St and around Date St. Here are just some suggestions; you'll find plenty more with a little exploring.

Solunto Baking Co & Honey Bee (Map pp288-9; ☎ 619-233-0881; 1643 India St; mains $5-10; ☒ 8am-5pm Mon-Thu, 8am-8pm Fri & Sat, 8am-2pm Sun; ☒) Other establishments source their breads and Italian cookies and pastries from this workmanlike bakery. Pick up some for a housegift or picnic, or stop for sandwiches or simple breakfasts (pancakes $1.75).

Mimmo's Italian Village (Map pp288-9; ☎ 619-239-3710; 1743 India St; meals under $10; ☒ 8am-4pm Mon-Sat; ☒) In a tall-ceilinged space decorated like (wait for it) an Italian village complete with mini-Ponte Vecchio, Mimmo's deli serves salads, hot and cold sandwiches, and lunch specials, such as lasagna and eggplant parmigiana.

Filippi's Pizza Grotto (Map pp288-9; ☎ 619-232-5094; 1747 India St; dishes $5-20; lunch & dinner; ☒) There are often lines out the door for Filippi's old-school Italian cooking (pizza, spaghetti and ravioli) served on red-and-white-checked tablecloths in the dining room. The front of the shop is an excellent Italian deli.

Mona Lisa (Map pp288-9; ☎ 619-234-4893; 2061 India St; mains $10-17; ☒ lunch Mon-Sat, dinner daily; ☒) Aside from hearty meals (try the cannelloni), Mona Lisa also makes great sandwiches and

---

TOP FIVE CHEAP EATS

■ **Anthony's Fish Grotto & Fishette** (opposite) – fish, chips and harbor views

■ **Bread & Cie** (p310) – because inexpensive can also be gourmet

■ **Café 222** (p307) – ditto

■ **Porkyland** (p331) – burritos that may make you cry ¡Dios mio!

■ **Saffron Thai Grilled Chicken** (p311) – separate chicken and noodle shops

sells imported Italian specialty foods at its market and deli.

Buon Appetito (Map pp288-9; ☎ 619-238-9880; 1609 India St; mains lunch $11-16, dinner $10-19) Simple storefront trattoria with rustic walls and original art, serving equally simple pastas and salads.

Café Zucchero (Map pp288-9; ☎ 619-531-1731; 1731 India St; mains lunch $8-17, dinner $13-20; ☽ breakfast, lunch & dinner) Brass-rail and marble-floor kind of place for a bang-up Italian dinner. There's a phone-book's worth of pizzas, pastas and meat and seafood dishes, but save room (or make a special stop) for pastries by the dozen or a freezer-case's worth of gelati.

Indigo Grill (Map pp288-9; ☎ 619-234-6802; 1536 India St; mains lunch $6-14, dinner $19-32; ☽ lunch Mon-Fri, dinner daily) One Little Italy eatery that isn't Italian. Pacific Northwest totems and Mexican masks are the setting for chef Deborah Scott's stylized, bold and adventurous Oaxacan-Alaskan cooking (think fire and ice, spicy and sweet). The vibe is convivial and relaxed, and dinner portions are enormous (sharing encouraged). Make reservations.

Chi Chocolat (Map pp288-9; ☎ 619-501-9215; 2021 India St; per chocolate $2; ☽ 7:30am-7:30pm Tue-Fri, 8:30am-10pm Sat, 8:30am-6pm Sun) If you need a chichi housegift, this storefront café makes artisinal chocolates at sky-high prices.

Embarcadero & the Waterfront

Anthony's Fish Grotto & Fishette (Map pp288-9; ☎ 619-232-5105; 1360 N Harbor Dr; ☽) Fishette (mains $5-9; ☽ 8am-8:30pm) Grotto (mains lunch $7-14, dinner $10-33; ☽ 11am-10pm) Next to the Maritime Museum, this pair of restaurants serves seafood and chowders with views of the tall ships on the harbor. The sit-down Grotto has an old-style nautical theme (ahoy, mateys!), while the counter at the Fishette serves a more limited menu (think fish and chips or sandwiches) that you eat out on the deck.

Fish Market (Map pp288-9; ☎ 619-232-3474; 750 N Harbor Dr; most mains lunch $10-24, dinner $13-30) For a daily changing menu of sushi to smoked fish, chowder to the raw bar, steamers to cioppino and grilled fish, all with a harbor view in a snappy dining room, walk to Tuna Harbor, opposite the port side of the USS *Midway*. Snag a window table if you can.

Balboa Park

The kids will probably be happy with the park's street vendors or casual cafés. For something more sophisticated:

Waters Café (Map pp290-1; ☎ 619-237-0675; 1450 El Prado; mains $7-12; ☽ 11am-3pm Tue-Fri, 9am-3pm Sat & Sun) Savory homemade soups, grilled veggie salads, and baguette sandwiches and mango quesadilla are typical fare at the colonnaded, canopied café in the San Diego Museum of Art's courtyard. Save room for rich chocolate brownies and mouth-puckering lemon squares.

Prado (Map pp290-1; ☎ 619-557-9441; 1549 El Prado; mains lunch $14-18, dinner $17-24; ☽ lunch daily, dinner Tue-Sun) In one of San Diego's most beautiful dining rooms, feast on Cal-Latin cooking by one of San Diego's most renowned chefs: bakery sandwiches, chicken and *orecchiette* pasta, and pork prime rib. Go for a civilized lunch on the verandah or for afternoon cocktails and appetizers in the bar. Make reservations.

Old Town

Eateries all along San Diego Ave are known for good Mexican cooking. Choose your setting: touristy, raucous, local or sublime.

our pick Old Town Mexican Cafe (Map pp290-1; ☎ 619-297-4330; 2489 San Diego Ave; dishes $3-14; ☽ 7am-midnight; ☽) There's nothing like the flavor of freshly made tortillas, and this hometown favorite makes some of the best – watch the staff turn them out in the window while you wait to be seated. There's a big bar (try the Old Town ultimate margarita) and dining room serving famous *machacas* (shredded pork with onions and peppers). For breakfast: *chilaquiles* (fried or dried tortilla chips in green or red salsa or *mole*, broiled or grilled with a cheese topping).

Fred's (Map pp290-1; ☎ 619-858-8226; 2470 San Diego Ave; mains $8-11; ☽) Every night party people on a budget crowd into raucous Fred's, especially on 'Taco-licious Tuesday', when tacos sell for under $3. The straight-down-the-middle enchiladas, burritos and tacos won't set standards, but it's hard not to love the colorful interior and rangy patio.

Zócalo (Map pp290-1; ☎ 619-298-9840; 2444 San Diego Ave; mains lunch $9-17, dinner $12-24) Nuevo Latino cuisine in an upscale setting: think macadamia-crusted mahimahi, churrasco skirt steak and guava-glazed barbecue ribs. There's a great happy hour (4pm to 6:30pm Monday to Saturday, 3pm to 6:30pm Sunday) with deals on fish tacos, artichoke fritters and more.

El Agave (Map pp290-1; ☎ 619-220-0692; 2304 San Diego Ave; mains lunch $10-18, dinner $18-27; ☽ 11am-10pm) Candlelight flickers on the bottles adorning the walls of this romantic 2nd-floor, white-tablecloth, high-end Mexican place that serves real Mexican to the cognoscenti. The *mole* – a spicy sauce made with chilies and chocolate – is superb, and there are a whopping 1500 different tequilas to choose from. Reserve.

Hillcrest

Hillcrest offers a great diversity of cuisines, mostly at good prices (inquire about nightly specials). See also Gay & Lesbian San Diego (p312) for bar-restaurants.

BUDGET & MIDRANGE

Bread & Cie (Map pp290-1; ☎ 619-683-9322; 350 University Ave; pastries $2-4, sandwiches $5-8; ☺ 7am-7pm Mon-Fri, 7am-6pm Sat, 8am-6pm Sun; ♿) Aside from crafting some of San Diego's best bread (including anise and fig, kalamata and black olive, and three-raisin), this wide-open bakery-deli makes fabulous sandwiches with fillings such as curried-chicken salad and Black Forest ham. Boxed lunches cost $10. Great pastries, too.

Hash House a Go Go (Map pp290-1; ☎ 619-298-4646; 3628 5th Ave; mains $5-15; ☺ breakfast & lunch daily, dinner Tue-Sun) Serving possibly San Diego's best – and certainly the biggest – breakfasts, this busy, youthful place makes biscuits and gravy straight outta Carolina, towering benedicts, big-as-your-head pancakes, and, of course, hash seven different ways. Come hungry.

Corvette Diner (Map pp290-1; ☎ 619-542-1001; 3946 5th Ave; mains $7-14; ☺ 11am-10pm Sun-Thu, 11am-midnight Fri & Sat; ♿) Your kids will love you for bringing them to this over-the-top '50s-themed diner. A DJ spins rock-and-roll classics, waiters dance in the aisles, and kids wear drinking straws in their hair. See ya later, Chuck E Cheese. (Oh, and the food is good, too. Try the meatloaf.)

Crest Cafe (Map pp290-1; ☎ 619-295-2510; 425 Robinson Ave; dishes $7-14; ☺ 7am-midnight) Soulful preparations of down-to-earth cooking make this slick corner diner worth seeking. Try the Cuban sandwich, curry-chicken salad, garlic-butter 'burger' or chopped salad. At breakfast, the scramblers are delish.

ourpick Saigon on Fifth (Map pp290-1; ☎ 619-220-8828; 3900 5th Ave; mains $7-16; ☺ 11am-midnight; P) This Vietnamese place tries hard and succeeds, with dishes like fresh spring rolls, fish of Hue (with garlic, ginger and lemongrass) and rockin' 'spicy noodles.' Staff dress nicely

and the room is elegant but not overbearing. Entrance on University Ave.

Baja Betty's (Map pp290-1; ☎ 619-269-8510; 1421 University Ave; mains $10-14; ☺ lunch & dinner) Gay-owned and straight-friendly, this restaurant-bar is always a party with just-back-from Margaritaville vibe (and dozens of tequilas to take you back there) alongside dishes like Mexi Queen queso dip, You Go Grill swordfish tacos and Fire in the Hole fajitas. They also open for Sunday brunch.

Ono Sushi (Map pp290-1; ☎ 619-298-0616; 1236 University Ave; mains $9-18; ☺ lunch Fri-Sun, dinner daily) O yes. Ono bucks tradition with its specialty rolls (the PD roll has spicy crab, sprouts and seared albacore) and Pacific Rim–style appetizers and mains like macadamia-crusted chicken breast. Expect a wait at peak times.

Arrivederci (Map pp290-1; ☎ 619-299-6282; 3845 4th Ave; mains $10-20; ☺ lunch & dinner) This hole-in-the-wall is – *como se dice?* – *rustica*, with country-style dining room and cozy patio. It's much loved for its fresh-baked bread to start (and the tomato sauce that comes with it), mysteriously good salad dressing, and pastas prepared dozens of ways, by a chef who cares.

Khyber Pass (Map pp290-1; ☎ 619-294-7579; 523 University Ave; most mains $13-25; ☺ lunch & dinner; V) Afghan tapestries and moody photos set the atmosphere in this tall-ceilinged space, with adventuresome Afghan cooking. If you've never had it, it's kind of like Indian meets Middle-Eastern: yogurt curries, kabobs, stews and more.

TOP END

Kemo Sabe (Map pp290-1; ☎ 619-220-6802; 3958 5th Ave; mains $15-40; ☺ dinner) Prepare to send your tastebuds on a bold journey at this Hillcrest favorite where Asia meets the American Southwest, both in the decor and on the plate. The Thai jerk smoked-duck salad and 10-spice honey chicken are typical of chef Deborah Scott's audacious fusion fare.

Parallel 33 (Map pp290-1; ☎ 619-260-0033; 741 W Washington St; mains $19-32; ☺ dinner Mon-Sat) The invigorating flavors dance on the palette at this smart and casual neighborhood spot, where the chef skillfully fuses the cuisines of the globe's 33rd-north latitude. Expect savory and sweet combinations from Morocco, Lebanon, India, China, Japan – and San Diego, which also lies at this latitude. Seek this one out.

Mission Hills

Further north from Little Italy on India St, where it meets Washington St, there's a block of well-known casual eateries.

El Indio (Map pp290-1; ☎ 619-299-0333; 3695 India St; dishes $3-9; 🕙 8am-9pm) Counter-service shop famous since 1940 for its taquitos, tamales and excellent breakfast burritos. Eat in a rudimentary dining room or at picnic tables under metal umbrellas across the street.

Saffron Thai Grilled Chicken (Map pp290-1; ☎ 619-574-0177; 3731 India St; dishes $4-7; 🕙 lunch & dinner) This place and its sister restaurant Saffron Noodles & Saté (Map pp290–1; ☎ 619-574-7737; 3737 India St; mains $5 to $9; open lunch and dinner) serve their respective namesakes for under $10 and have been visited by culinary luminaries including Julia Child and Martha Stewart. Saffron Thai Grilled Chicken (takeout only) uses a charcoal-grill and comes with a choice of sauces, salad, jasmine rice and a menu of finger foods. Its neighbor, Noodles and Saté, serves big bowls of steaming noodle soup and stir-fried noodles by the plate.

Shakespeare Pub & Grille (Map pp290-1; ☎ 619-299-0230; 3701 India St; dishes $5-15; 🕙 10am-midnight Sun-Thu, 10am-1am Fri & Sat) One of San Diego's most authentic English ale houses, cedar-shake–shingled Shakespeare is the place for darts, soccer by satellite, beer on tap and pub grub, including fish and chips, and bangers and mash. It also has a great sundeck. On weekends, load up with a British breakfast: bacon, mushrooms, black and white pudding and more, served from 8am to noon.

Wine Vault & Bistro (Map pp290-1; ☎ 619-295-3939; www.winevaultbistro.com; 3731-A India St; prix-fixe dinner $45-55) Perched atop staircases, this spare yet homey white space with white chairs might recall Nantucket or Napa, and that's appropriate given that meals are meant to pair with wine. Menus change virtually nightly, so inquire when reserving. Hours vary so check the calendar on the website for details.

Gelato Vero Caffe (Map pp290-1; ☎ 619-295-9269; 3753 India St; gelato per oz $0.59; 🕙 6am-midnight Sun-Thu, 7am-1am Fri & Sat; wi-fi) This tiny, funky coffee shop sells 16 flavors of house-made ice cream, plus coffee, cake, raspberry bars and coffee.

DRINKING

San Diego may not have the swinging night scene of LA, but being in the Gaslamp Quarter it's hard to tell.

Coffeehouses

Coffeehouses in San Diego are popular hangouts as well as nighttime venues; often they have live music.

David's Coffeehouse (Map pp290-1; ☎ 619-296-4173; 3766 5th Ave; 🕙 7am-11pm Sun-Thu, 7am-midnight Fri & Sat) Hang out inside or out on the patio, check your email, and play chess or the baby grand piano at David's, the hub of social activity in Hillcrest, especially for the arty crowd and 12-steppers.

Living Room (Map pp290-1; ☎ 619-325-4445; 2541 San Diego Ave; 🕙 6am-midnight; wi-fi) In Old Town but tired of margaritas? Head here. Free wi-fi.

Also check out **Cafe Lulu** (Map pp288-9; ☎ 619-238-0114; 419 F St; 🕙 9am-1am Sun-Thu, 9am-2:30am Fri & Sat), or Little Italy's **Caffe Italia** (Map pp288-9; ☎ 619-234-6767; 1704 India St; 🕙 7am-10pm Mon-Fri, 8am-10pm Sat & Sun) with pastries, gelati and sidewalk seating.

Bars
GASLAMP QUARTER

The Gaslamp has the city's highest concentration of bars and nightclubs. Many establishments do double- (even triple-) duty as restaurants, bars and clubs.

Bitter End (Map pp288-9; ☎ 619-338-9300; 770 5th Ave) Wear khakis and quaff martinis at this former brothel, now an atmospheric watering hole. Always popular for its extensive selection of beers on tap. Dancing downstairs.

Moose McGillycuddy's (Map pp288-9; ☎ 619-702-5595; 535 5th Ave) The college crowd shoots pool and gets rowdy at this fun frat-boy bar.

Onyx Room & Thin (Map pp288-9; ☎ 619-235-6699; 852 5th Ave) The candlelit Onyx is a downstairs jazz lounge with a dance floor; Thin is an ultracool, industrial-look upstairs bar, great for cocktails and conversation. Wear nice shoes.

Red Circle Bar (Map pp288-9; ☎ 619-234-9211; 420 E St) Order a martini, raise your pinkie, and peruse the Soviet-era memorabilia and lissome crowd bathed in sexy red lighting at this Russian-themed boîte, with more than 100 varieties of vodka.

Star Bar (Map pp288-9; ☎ 619-234-5575; 423 E St) When you've had it with gentrified style and you're looking for a historic dive, head to this old-school bar decorated year-round with Christmas lights.

DOWNTOWN & LITTLE ITALY

Airport Lounge (Map pp288-9; ☎ 619-685-3881; 2400 India St) The clientele is cool, the DJs hot, the

GAY & LESBIAN SAN DIEGO

Ironically, historians trace the roots of San Diego's thriving gay community to the military. During WWII, amid the enforced intimacy of military life, gay men from around the country were suddenly able to create strong if clandestine social networks. After the war, many of these new friends stayed.

In the late 1960s, a newly politicized gay community began to make the Hillcrest neighborhood its unofficial headquarters, which still has the highest concentration of bars, restaurants, cafés and bookstores catering to lesbians and gays. The scene is generally more casual and friendly than in San Francisco or LA.

The following should give you a good start, or pick up the free, widely available, *Gay and Lesbian Times*. See also Hillcrest restaurant listings (p310):

Coffeehouses

David's Coffeehouse (Map pp290-1; ☎ 619-296-4173; 3766 5th Ave, Hillcrest; ⏰ 7am-11pm Sun-Thu, 7am-midnight Fri & Sat) Homey Hillcrest classic (see also p311).

Bookstores

Obelisk Bookstore (Map pp290-1; ☎ 619-297-4171; 1029 University Ave; ⏰ 10am-10pm Mon-Fri, 10am-11pm Fri & Sat, 11am-10pm Sun) Large gay, lesbian, bisexual and transgender selection.

Bars

Bourbon Street (Map pp290-1; ☎ 619-291-4043; www.bourbonstreetsd.com; 4612 Park Blvd) Away from Hillcrest's central strip, this gay bar's layout of rooms and courtyards, bar and dancefloor, makes for easy mingling during bingo nights, guest DJ appearances and martini happy hours.

Brass Rail (Map pp290-1; ☎ 619-298-2233; 3796 5th Ave) The city's oldest gay bar has a different music style nightly, from Latin to African to Top 40. It also gets its share of straight folk and has lots of games to play, including pinball, pool and darts.

Flicks (Map pp290-1; ☎ 619-297-2056; 1017 University Ave) Video bar dominated by big screens. Fun place to hang out and nurse a drink, sort of like Starbucks with booze.

The Hole (Map pp292-3; ☎ 619-225-9019; 2820 Lytton St) This gay dive near Point Loma is surrounded by auto repair shops, all the better for camo. Head down to the patio to find manly men enjoying Sunday beer bust, wet-underwear contests and more. It's near military housing, so you might ask, but please don't tell, OK?

Urban Mo's (Map pp290-1; ☎ 619-491-0400; 308 University Ave) Equal parts bar and restaurant, Mo's isn't particularly known for great food, service or prices, but it's popular nonetheless for its thumping club beats, casual vibe, dancefloor and happy hours.

See also Baja Betty's (p310).

Dance clubs

Club Montage (Map pp290-1; ☎ 619-294-9590; 2028 Hancock St; ⏰ Fri & Sat) One of San Diego's hippest cathedrals of dance, just southwest of Old Town. The crowd's young, trendy, good-looking and gay on Saturdays. Three floors, three bars, two dancefloors and a rooftop sushi bar.

Rich's (Map pp290-1; ☎ 619-295-2195; 1051 University Ave; ⏰ Tue-Sun) DJs shower the crowd with Latin, techno, pop and house at one of San Diego's biggest gay dance clubs, in Hillcrest.

design mod, the drinks strong and the servers dressed like flight attendants at this buzzy watering hole right in the flight path of San Diego Airport.

Karl Strauss Brewery & Grill (Map pp288-9; ☎ 619-234-2739; 1157 Columbia St) This brick-lined local microbrewery (with the beer tanks right inside) serves surprisingly decent pub grub (most mains $9 to $19). Hours vary, so phone ahead. Pitchers cost $10 during happy hour, which runs from 4pm to 6:30pm Monday to Friday.

W Hotel (Map pp288-9; ☎ 619-231-8220; 421 West B St) The silicone set twirls around in Louis Vuitton on the catwalk of the W Hotel on Thursday, Friday and Saturday nights, but the best night to go here is Thursday, when there's usually not a long line to get inside to stand around on the rooftop sand beach and poolside bar.

Waterfront (Map pp288-9; ☎ 619-232-9656; 2044 Kettner Blvd) San Diego's first liquor license was granted to this place in the 1930s (it was on the waterfront until the harbor was filled and the airport built), and it's still owned by the same family. A room full of historic bric-a-brac, big windows onto the street and the spirits of those who went before make this one of the best places to spend the afternoon or evening. It has a big window that opens onto the street, $5 bar food and live music on weekends.

OLD TOWN

Most of Old Town's nightlife revolves around the bars in its restaurants, but here are some other choices.

Harney Sushi (Map pp290-1; ☎ 619-295-3272; 3964 Harney St) Yes, it's a sushi bar (sushi $3 to $10, other dishes $7 to $15), but the *bar* bar takes over late at night as a rotation of DJs spins music from reggae to house to techno for a hip, younger crowd.

O'Hungry's (Map pp290-1; ☎ 619-298-0133; 2547 San Diego Ave) Despite its name, O'Hungry's is more for drinking than for eating. It serves beer by the yard glass, occasionally has live music and can sometimes be lots of fun.

Old Town Saloon (Map pp290-1; ☎ 619-298-2209; 2495 San Diego Ave) This one's for the locals, so be cool. Swill a Bud Light, and play pool at one of four tables.

HILLCREST

Most of the bars in Hillcrest are gay (see opposite), but here are some other choices:

Alibi (Map pp290-1; ☎ 619-295-0881; 1403 University Ave) All the straight people in Hillcrest who go out drinking – young, old, rich and poor – pass through the doors of Alibi, earning it the nickname the 'Star Wars Bar.'

Nunu's Cocktail Lounge (Map pp290-1; ☎ 619-295-2878; 3537 5th Ave) Dark and divey, this hipster haven started pouring when JFK was president and still looks the part with its curvy booths, big bar and lovably kitsch decor. Smoking patio.

ENTERTAINMENT

Check out the San Diego *Reader* or the Night and Day section in the Thursday edition of the San Diego *Union-Tribune* for the latest movies, theater, galleries and music gigs around town. **Arts Tix** (Map pp288-9; ☎ 619-497-5000; www .sandiegoperforms.com; cnr 3rd Ave & Broadway; ☑ 11am-6pm Tue-Thu, 10am-6pm Fri & Sat, 10am-5pm Sun), in a kiosk outside Horton Plaza, has half-price tickets for same-day evening or next-day matinee performances and offers discounted tickets to all types of other events – contact them for further details. **Ticketmaster** (☎ 619-220-8497; www.ticketmaster.com) and **House of Blues** (www .hob.com) sell tickets to other gigs around the city.

Nightclubs & Live Music

Anthology (Map pp288-9; ☎ 619-595-0300; www.an thologysd.com; 1337 India St; cover up to $60) Opened in 2007 just south of Little Italy, Anthology presents live jazz in a swank supper-club setting. It books both up-and-comers and big-name performers including Lee Ritenour, Beausoleil and Maria Muldaur.

Casbah (off Map pp288-9; ☎ 619-232-4355; www .casbahmusic.com; 2501 Kettner Blvd) Liz Phair, Alanis Morissette and the Smashing Pumpkins have all rocked the Casbah on their way up the charts and it's still a good place to catch tomorrow's headliners. Near Little Italy and the airport, it has couches, pinball machines and dimly lit alcoves if you don't feel like dancing.

4th & B (Map pp288-9; ☎ 619-231-4343; www.4thandB .com; 345 B St) This midsized venue has music lovers head-bobbing with performances from an eclectic mix of talent, from unsigned hopefuls to Macy Gray, Psychedelic Furs and the Last Comic Standing tour. Rest your feet – and eardrums – in the lounge. There's often a cover charge.

On Broadway (Map pp288-9; ☎ 619-231-0011; www .obec.tv; 615 Broadway; cover $20; ☑ Fri & Sat) Sprawling double-decker dance spot where DJs mix it up on – count them – five dancefloors. Dress to impress, or forget about making it past the velvet-rope goons.

Shout House (Map pp288-9; ☎ 619-231-6700; 655 4th Ave; cover up to $10) Good, clean fun at this cavernous Gaslamp bar with dueling pianos. Talented players have an amazing repertoire: standards, rock and more. We recently heard Justin Timberlake's 'D**k in a Box' (OK, maybe it's not so clean). Crowd: college-age to conventioneers.

Soma (Map pp292-3; ☎ 619-226-7662; www.somasd.com; 3350 Sports Arena Blvd; cover $8-23) This all-ages venue (no booze) puts the spotlight on up-and-coming local bands of the alterna-rock and punk persuasion. It's electric and edgy with fiercely loyal crowds.

Stingaree (Map pp288-9; ☎ 619-544-0867; www.stingsandiego.com; 454 Sixth Ave) Vegas in the Gaslamp. Super-slinky decor provides the backdrop for San Diego's most-likely-to-spot-a-celebrity club. Table service for your drinks and cabanas on the roof. The cover charge varies and can be expensive.

Also recommended:

Café Sevilla (p308) Live Latin and fusion performers and dancing most nights, and some dance lessons.

Croce's Restaurant & Jazz Bar (p308) Hosting great nightly jazz, blues and R&B performers.

House of Blues (Map pp288-9; ☎ 619-299-2583; www.hob.com; 1055 5th Ave) What you think it is.

Classical Music & Opera

The accomplished **San Diego Symphony** (Map pp288-9; ☎ 619-235-0804; www.sandiegosymphony.com; 750 B St; tickets $15-60) presents classical as well as family concerts in the **Copley Symphony Hall**. In summer, it moves to **Navy Pier** (Map pp288-9; 960 N Harbor Dr). There are summer and winter pop concerts and the Symphony Exposed series lets you explore classical favorites in depth.

High-caliber performances of small orchestral works are the hallmarks of the **San Diego Chamber Orchestra** (☎ 888-848-7326, 760-753-6402; www.sdco.org; tickets $20-35), whose season runs from October to April. Venues include **St Paul's Cathedral** (Map pp290-1; 2728 Sixth Ave) on the western edge of Balboa Park to the La Jolla branch of the Museum of Contemporary Art (p328).

San Diego Opera (Map pp288-9; ☎ 619-570-1100; www.sdopera.com; Civic Theatre, 3rd & B St; tickets $28-192) is ranked among America's top 10 opera companies. The SDO presents high-quality, eclectic programming under the direction of Maestro Karen Keltner. It occasionally draws international guest stars such as José Carreras and Cecilia Bartoli.

For light opera, musical theater, movies and musical extravaganzas, the reasonably priced **Lyric Opera San Diego** (☎ 619-239-8836; www.lyricoperasandiego.org; ticket prices vary), stages shows at the Birch North Park Theater (2891 University Ave) in the North Park section of town.

Cinemas

Check local papers or call theaters for show times. The main Downtown cinemas are the **Regal United Artists Horton Plaza 14** (Map pp288-9; ☎ 619-234-8602), at Horton Plaza, and **Pacific Gaslamp 15** (Map pp288-9; ☎ 619-232-0400; 701 5th St, cnr G St). Both show current-release movies.

In Hillcrest, **Hillcrest Cinemas** (Map pp290-1; ☎ 619-819-0236; 3965 5th Ave) is in the colorful, boxy postmodern **Village Hillcrest Center**. See also the shopping malls of Mission Valley (opposite) for multiplexes.

Cinema Under the Stars (Map pp290-1; ☎ 619-295-4221; www.topspresents.com; 4040 Goldfinch St) screens classic and contemporary American films on a heated patio in Mission Hills, a few nights a week from mid-May to October. See also the summer series **Movies before the Mast** at the Maritime Museum (p296).

Theater

Theater thrives in San Diego and is one of the city's greatest cultural attractions. Book tickets at the box office or with one of the agencies listed in the introduction to this section.

Worth a special mention are Balboa Park's **Old Globe Theaters** (Map pp290-1; ☎ 619-234-5623; www.theoldglobe.org; tickets $19-62), where visitors to the 1935–36 Pacific–California Exposition enjoyed 40-minute renditions of Shakespeare's greatest hits. Saved from demolition in 1937, the theaters became home to a popular summer Shakespeare festival, though nowadays it performs non-Shakespearean plays as well. In 1978 the complex was destroyed by arson, and then rebuilt in the style of the original 17th-century Old Globe in England and reopened in 1982, winning a Tony award in 1984 for its ongoing contribution to theater arts. Between the three venues here – Old Globe, Cassius Carter Stage and the outdoor Lowell Davies Festival Theater – there are performances most evenings and matinees on weekends.

Other venues:

Horton Grand Theatre (Map pp288-9; ☎ 619-234-9583; 444 4th Ave)

La Jolla Playhouse (Map p294; ☎ 619-550-1010; www.lajollaplayhouse.com; UCSD)

Lamb's Players Theater (Map p287; ☎ 619-437-0600; www.lambsplayers.org; 1142 Orange Ave, Coronado)

National Comedy Theatre (Map pp290-1; ☎ 619-295-4999; www.nationalcomedy.com; 3717 India St, Mission Hills)

A VERY FINE VINTAGE

From hipsters to drag queens, everyone shops for vintage and thrift-store clothing in Hillcrest. Shoe fetishists swear by **Mint** (Map pp290–1; ☎ 619-291-6468; 525 University Ave) for up-to-the-minute footwear. **Wear It Again Sam** (Map pp290–1; ☎ 619-299-0185; 3823 5th Ave) sells a well-organized selection of vintage togs. **Buffalo Exchange** (Map pp290–1; ☎ 858-273-6227; 3862 5th Ave) stocks both vintage and contemporary fashions including designer-name brands, while the bright colors at **Flashbacks** (Map pp290–1; ☎ 619-291-4200; 3849 5th Ave) are like a '60s dream come true.

Plus, vintage shopping is the gift that keeps on giving. If you run out of cash at one of these stores and want to sell the shirt off your back, ask. You just might find a buyer.

San Diego Junior Theatre (Map pp290–1; ☎ 619-239-8355; www.juniortheatre.com; Casa del Prado, Balboa Park)

San Diego Repertory Theatre (Map pp288–9; ☎ 619-231-3586; www.sandiegorep.com; Lyceum Theater, 79 Horton Plaza)

Spreckels Theater (Map pp288–9; ☎ 619-235-9500; www.spreckels.net; 121 Broadway)

Sports

The San Diego Padres Major League Baseball team began the 2004 season in the new **PETCO Park** (Map pp288–9; ☎ 619-795-5000, 888-697-2373, for tickets 877-374-2784; www.padres.com; 100 Park Blvd; tickets $7-67; ☼ season Apr–early Oct) stadium right in the middle of downtown San Diego. Tickets are usually available at the gate unless it's a game crucial to the standings or the LA Dodgers are in town.

The San Diego Chargers National Football League team share **Qualcomm Stadium** (Map p287; ☎ 619-280-2121; www.chargers.com; 9449 Friars Rd; tickets from $54; ☼ season Aug-Jan), in Mission Valley (there's a trolley stop right in front). It was originally named for sports journalist Jack Murphy, who worked to bring the Chargers to town in 1961, and the Padres in 1968.

SHOPPING

Souvenir hunters will find stuffed Shamus at SeaWorld, realistic-looking rubber snakes at the zoo, or reprinted historical photos at the Museum of San Diego History. The Spanish Village area of Balboa Park (p297) is a good place to find paintings (mostly watercolors) of local scenes.

For general shopping, **Westfield Horton Plaza Center** has the highest concentration of shops, most of them chain stores, a multi-screen cinema, two live theaters and a variety of eateries. The San Diego Trolley green line (or your car) takes you to each of three

large malls in Mission Valley, where shoppers can spend a day; all have movie theaters for nonshoppers and the usual array of restaurants. Premier shops at **Fashion Valley** (Map pp290–1; ☎ 619-688-9113; www.simon.com; 7007 Friars Rd; ☼ 10am-9pm Mon-Sat, 11am-7pm Sun) include Tiffany & Co, Burberry, James Perse and Restoration Hardware, and department stores Neiman Marcus, Saks Fifth Avenue, Macy's and Nordstrom. **Westfield Mission Valley** (Map pp290–1; ☎ 619-296-6375; www.westfield.com /missionvalley; 1640 Camino del Rio N; ☼ 10am-9pm Mon-Sat, 11am-6pm Sun) houses upscale discount outlets, including Nordstrom Rack, and the Inflatable World mini-amusement park for kids. **Hazard Center** (Map pp290–1; www.hazard center.com; 7510-7610 Hazard Center Dr; ☼ vary) is the smallest of the three but has a large Barnes & Noble bookstore.

Given that adventure-sports gods Tony Hawk and Shawn White are San Diegans, surf and skate clothing are natural purchases here. There's a strip of stores including Quicksilver, Volcom and Skatewear in the Gaslamp Quarter, on 5th Ave between J St and Island Ave.

Nearby are two respected art galleries, among a growing contingent in the Gaslamp. Check local listings or phone to see what's on at **Gallery 5+5** (Map pp288–9; ☎ 619-374-7119; 544 Sixth Ave) and **Michael J Wolf Fine Arts** (Map pp288–9; ☎ 619-702-5388; 363 5th Ave) and other venues around town.

Adams Avenue (Map p287; ☎ store directory 619-282-7329; www.adamsaveonline.com) is San Diego's main 'antique row,' and cuts across some of San Diego's less-visited neighborhoods. You'll find the greatest concentration of shops around Normal Heights between the I-805 and I-15. The area has dozens of shops selling furniture, art and antiques from around the world. For other antique shopping, check Newport Ave in the Ocean Beach neighborhood (p319).

The depth and breadth is awesome at the weekly flea market **Kobey's Swap Meet** (Map pp292-3; ☎ 619-226-0650; www.kobeyswap.com; 3500 Sports Arena Blvd; admission Fri 50¢, Sat & Sun $1; 7am-3pm Fri-Sun; P) in the parking lot of the San Diego Sports Arena, and often the bargains are too. Look for all sorts of new and used items including sunglasses, clothing, jewelry, produce, flowers and plants, tools and furniture.

GETTING THERE & AWAY
Air
Because of the limited length of runways, most flights to **San Diego International Airport-Lindbergh Field** (SAN; ☎ 619-231-2100; www.san.org) are domestic. The airfield sits just 3 miles west of Downtown; plane-spotters will thrill watching jets come in over Balboa Park for landing. Coming from overseas, you'll likely change flights – and clear US Customs – at one of the major US gateway airports, such as LA, San Francisco, Chicago, New York or Miami.

The standard one-way fare between LA and San Diego is about $100. The flight from LA takes only about 35 minutes – but by the time you drive to the airport, check in, clear security and board the flight, you could have made the two-hour drive (except during rush hour).

To/from other US cities, flights to San Diego are generally as cheap as to LA. All major US airlines serve San Diego, plus Aeromexico and Air Canada.

Bus
Greyhound (Map pp288-9; ☎ 619-239-3266, 800-231-2222; www.greyhound.com; 120 W Broadway) serves San Diego from cities across North America. Inquire about discounts and special fares.

Buses depart frequently for LA; the standard one-way/round-trip fare is $17/28 and takes 2½ to four hours, depending on the number of stops en route. There are six daily departures to Anaheim (p230; $16/27, about 2¼ hours).

There are also services to San Francisco (from $62/123; 12 hours; about eight daily), which require a transfer in Los Angeles; a round-trip airfare often costs about the same. If traveling to Las Vegas (one-way/round-trip $48/93; 7 to 12½ hours; about nine daily), most buses require you to transfer in LA or San Bernardino.

See p344 for information about getting to/from Tijuana, Mexico.

Car & Motorcycle
Car-rental prices are about the same in LA and San Diego, usually $35 to $40 per day. Allow two hours from LA with no traffic.

Train
Amtrak (☎ 800-872-7245; www.amtrak.com) runs the *Pacific Surfliner* several times daily to Anaheim ($24, two hours), Los Angeles ($34, three hours) and Santa Barbara ($37, 6½ hours) from the historic **Union Station** (Santa Fe Depot; Map pp288-9; 1055 Kettner Blvd).

GETTING AROUND
While most people get around by car, it's possible to have an entire San Diego vacation using municipal buses and trolleys run by the Metropolitan Transit System (MTS; ☎ 619-233-3004; www.sdcommute.com) and your own two feet. The **Transit Store** (Map pp288-9; www.transit.511sd.com; ☎ 619-234-1060; 102 Broadway; 9am-5pm Mon-Fri) is one-stop shopping for route maps, tickets and one/two/three/four-day Day Tripper passes (costing $5/9/12/15, also available at trolley stations).

To/From the Airport
Bus 992 (the Flyer, $2.25), operates at 10- to 15-minute intervals between the airport and Downtown, with stops along Broadway. Airport shuttle services (from about $10 to Downtown, more to other destinations) include **Cloud 9 Shuttle** (☎ 800-974-8885; www.cloud9shuttle.com) and **Xpress Shuttle** (☎ 800-900-7433; www.xpressshuttle.com). Call to reserve a day or two ahead. A taxi to Downtown from the airport costs between $8 and $13.

Boat
San Diego Harbor Excursion (Map pp288-9; ☎ 619-234-4111; per person $7; 3pm-10pm daily, plus 11am-11pm Sat & Sun Jun-Sep) operates a water taxi, serving Harbor Island, Shelter Island, Downtown and Coronado. It also operates the Coronado Ferry (p328).

Bus
The MTS covers most of the metropolitan area, North County, La Jolla and the beaches. It's most convenient if you're based in Downtown and not staying out late.

For route and fare information, call ☎ 619-233-3004 or 800-266-6883; operators are available 5:30am to 8:30pm Monday to Friday, 8am to 5pm Saturday and Sunday (note that the 800-number works only within San

Diego). For 24-hour automated information, call ☎ 619-685-4900. Online, visit www.sd commute.com.

Fares cost $2.25 for most trips, including a transfer good for up to two hours; express routes cost $2.50. Local buses with limited service cost $1.75. Exact fare is required on all buses.

Useful routes to/from Downtown include the following:

No 3 Balboa Park, Hillcrest, UCSD Medical Center.

No 7, 7A, 7B Balboa Park, Zoo, Hillcrest.

No 8/9 Old Town to Pacific Beach, SeaWorld.

No 11 Hillcrest, Adams Ave Antique Row.

No 30 Old Town, Pacific Beach, La Jolla, University Towne Centre.

No 35 Old Town to Ocean Beach.

No 901 Coronado.

Car

All the big-name car-rental companies have desks at the airport, and lesser-known ones may be cheaper. Shop around – prices vary widely, even from day to day within the same company. The airport has free direct-phones to a number of car-rental companies – you can call several and then get a courtesy bus to the agency. Rental rates tend to be comparable to LA.

Note that many car-rental companies do not allow you to take their vehicles into Mexico.

For contact information on the big-name companies, see p427. Smaller agencies include **California Rent a Car** (Map pp288-9; ☎ 619-238-9999, 800-995-5353; www.californiarent-a-car.com; 904 W Grape St) and **West Coast Rent a Car** (Map pp288-9; ☎ 619-544-0606; 834 W Grape St), both in Little Italy, and **Fox Rent a Car** (☎ 619-692-0300, 800-225-4369; www.foxrentacar.com; 2727 Kettner Blvd) near the airport.

Taxi

Taxi flag fall is $2.40, plus $2.60 for each additional mile. Established companies include the following:

American Cab (☎ 619-234-1111)

Orange Cab (☎ 619-291-3333; www.orangecabsan diego.com)

Yellow Cab (☎ 619-234-6161; www.driveu.com)

Train

Coaster commuter trains ($4 to $5.50) serve Santa Fe Depot downtown to North County, with stops including Old Town, Solana Beach, Encinitas, Carlsbad and Oceanside. Buy tick-

ets from vending machines at stations, and validate them before boarding; machines give change.

There are 11 daily trains in each direction Monday to Friday; the first trains leave Oceanside at 5:18am and the Santa Fe Depot downtown at 6:33am; the last ones depart at 5:30pm and 6:46pm, respectively. On Saturday, there are four trains only, and no Sunday service. Contact **North San Diego County Transit District** (☎ 619-233-3004, from North County 800-266-6883; www .gonctd.com) or www.sdcommute.com

Trolley

There are three main trolley lines. From the transit center across from the Santa Fe Depot, Blue Line trolleys go south to San Ysidro (Mexico border) and north to Old Town Transit Center, with peak period service through Mission Valley to Qualcomm Stadium. At other times the Green Line runs this section of the route from Old Town, including to Mission San Diego de Alcalá. The Orange Line connects the Convention Center and Seaport Village with Downtown, but otherwise it's more useful for commuters. Trolleys run between about 4:15am and 1am daily at 15-minute intervals during the day, and every 30 minutes in the evening. The Blue Line continues limited all-night service on Saturday. Fares vary with distance but peak at $3 each way. Tickets are dispensed from vending machines on the station platforms and are valid for three hours from the time of purchase. Machines give change.

Kid tip – on Saturdays and Sundays, up to two children can ride the trolley for free with each fare-paying adult.

CORONADO & THE BEACHES

Whoosh – here comes a skateboarder. And there goes a wet-suited surfer toting his board to the break, while a Chanel-clad lady lifts a coffee cup off a porcelain saucer. San Diego's coastal communities offer all that and more.

The city of Coronado, with its landmark 1888 Hotel del Coronado, sits across San Diego Bay from Downtown, accessible via a long bridge or a short ferry ride. At the entrance to the bay, Point Loma has sweeping views across sea and city from the Cabrillo National Monument. Mission Bay, northwest of downtown, has lagoons, parks and recreation from waterskiing to camping and the world-famous SeaWorld. The nearby coast – Ocean, Mission and Pacific Beaches – epitomizes the SoCal beach scene.

Other sections of this chapter cover La Jolla (p328) and San Diego's North Coast (p333). San Diego's Downtown sights are covered in the previous Downtown & Around section, as are tours, and festivals and events that encompass greater San Diego.

INFORMATION
Libraries & Internet Access
Coronado Public Library (☎ 619-522-7390; www.coronado.lib.ca.us; 640 Orange Ave; ❂ 10am-9pm Mon-Thu, 10am-6pm Fri & Sat, 1-5pm Sun; ☐ wi-fi) occupies a museumlike building and offers children's programs. For other library branches, visit www.sannet.gov/public-library.

Post
Coronado Post office (☎ 877-275-8777; www.usps.com; 1320 Ynez Pl; ❂ 8:30am-5pm Mon-Fri, 8:30am-noon Sat). Check the website or phone for other branches.

Tourist Information
San Diego Convention & Visitors Bureau's visitor centers (p283) serve other beach communities.
Coronado Visitors Center (☎ 619-437-8788; www.coronadovisitorcenter.com; 1100 Orange Ave; ❂ 9am-5pm Mon-Fri, 10am-5pm Sat & Sun)

SIGHTS
We've organized this section beginning with Coronado and heading north.

Coronado
Directly across the bay from downtown San Diego, Coronado is a civilized escape from the jumble of the city and the ordered quietness of the beaches. Follow the tree-lined, manicured median strip of Orange Ave toward the commercial center, Coronado Village, around the Hotel del Coronado. Then park your car; you won't need it again until you leave.

The story of Coronado is in many ways the story of the Hotel del Coronado (see following), opened in 1888. By 1900 John D Spreckels, the millionaire who bankrolled the first rail line to San Diego, took over Coronado and

turned the whole island into one of the most fashionable getaways on the West Coast.

The visitor center doubles as the **Coronado Museum of History and Art** and offers historical 90-minute **walking tours** (tour $12; ❂ 11am Tue, Thu & Sat), beginning at the Glorietta Bay Inn (p323). Inquire about other tours.

The spectacular 2.12-mile-long **Coronado Bay Bridge** opened in 1969 and joins Coronado to San Diego; Silver Strand, a long, narrow sand spit, runs south to Imperial Beach and connects Coronado to the mainland, though people still call it 'Coronado Island' in honor of its original status.

Use the electric Coronado Shuttle to get around (free). Alternatively, bus 901 from Downtown runs along Orange Ave to the Hotel del Coronado. The Old Town Trolley tour (p303) stops in front of Mc P's Irish Pub (p326). For information on ferries, water taxis and bike rentals, see p327.

Four-and-a-half miles south of Coronado Village, the white-sand **Silver Strand State Beach** (☎ 619-435-5184; www.parks.ca.gov; P ▲) has warm, calm water, perfect for swimming and good for families. Parking costs vary seasonally, from free up to $8.

HOTEL DEL CORONADO
Few hotels in the world are as easily recognized or as much loved as the **Hotel del Coronado** (☎ 619-435- 6611, 800-582-2595; www.hoteldel.com; 1500 Orange Ave; ▲). The world's largest resort when it was built, this all-timber, white-washed San Diego icon offers conical towers, cupolas, turrets, balconies, dormer windows and cavernous public spaces typical of their designers, railroad-depot architects James and Merritt Reed. Acres of polished wood give the interior a warm, old-fashioned feel that conjures daydreams of Panama hats and linen suits.

Guests have included 10 US presidents and world royalty – pictures and mementos are displayed in the hotel's history gallery. There's speculation that Edward (then Prince of Wales) first met Mrs Simpson (then Mrs Spenser) when he visited in 1920, though the two did not become an item until years later. The hotel achieved its widest exposure in the 1959 movie *Some Like It Hot,* which earned it a lasting association with Marilyn Monroe. There's an interesting resident ghost story, too, about a jilted woman who haunts the hotel; some claim she silently appears in hallways and on the TV screen in the room where she had her heart broken.

For a taste of the Del without a stay, enjoy breakfast or lunch at the beach-view **Sheerwater** restaurant or splurge on Sunday brunch under the grand dome of the spectacular **Crown Room** (adults cost $59 and children $23), designed by L Frank Baum, who wrote *The Wonderful Wizard of Oz*.

See p323 for details on staying here.

Point Loma

On maps Point Loma looks like an elephant's trunk guarding the entrance to San Diego Bay. At the very tip, atop a hill, the **Cabrillo National Monument** (☎ 619-557-5450; www.nps.gov /cabr; per car/person $5/3; ☷ 9am-5pm) is San Diego's finest locale for history and views. It's also the best place in town to see the gray-whale migration (January to March) from land. After a few minutes here you may forget you're in a major metropolitan area.

The **visitors center** (☎ 619-557-5450; ☷ 9am-5pm) has an excellent presentation on Portuguese explorer Juan Rodríguez Cabrillo's 1542 voyage up the California coast, plus good exhibits on the native inhabitants and the area's natural history. The 1854 **Old Point Loma Lighthouse**, atop the point, is furnished with typical pieces from the late 19th century, including lamps and picture frames hand-covered with hundreds of shells – testimony to the long, lonely nights endured by lighthouse keepers. On the ocean side, drive or walk down to the **tide pools** (at low tide) to look for anemones, starfish, crabs, limpets and dead man's fingers (thin, tubular seaweed). To reach the monument, take bus 28C from Old Town Transit Station.

San Diego's first fishing boats were based at Point Loma, and in the 19th century whalers dragged carcasses here to extract the whale oil. Chinese fishermen settled on the harbor side of the point in the 1860s but were forced off in 1888 when the US Congress passed the Scott Act, prohibiting anyone without citizenship papers from entering the area. Portuguese fishing families arrived about 50 years later and established a permanent community around the same time that Italian immigrants settled in present-day Little Italy (p285). Point Loma's **Portuguese Hall** remains a hub of activity for locals.

Charles Lindbergh tested his *Spirit of St Louis* airplane in 1927 on the tidal flats of **Loma**

Portal, where Point Loma joins the mainland (at the elephant's neck). The following year a functioning airport was established at his airstrip; it was named Lindbergh Field, now San Diego International Airport.

Ocean Beach

San Diego's most bohemian seaside community is a place of seriously scruffy haircuts, facial hair and body art. You can get tattooed, shop for antiques, and walk into a restaurant barefoot and shirtless without anyone batting an eye. **Newport Ave**, the main drag, runs perpendicular to the beach through a compact business district of bars, surf shops, music stores, used-clothing stores and antiques consignment stores.

The half-mile-long **Ocean Beach Pier** has all the architectural allure of a freeway ramp. Primarily a fishing pier, it's a good place to stroll; at its end, you'll have a great perspective on the coast. There's also the greasy-spoon **café** (OB Pier Café; ☎ 619-226-3474; ☷ 7am-9pm Mon-Fri, 7am-10pm Sat & Sun) where you can rent fishing-poles ($15 per day).

Just north of the pier, near the end of Newport Ave, is the beach scene's epicenter, with volleyball courts and sunset barbecues. Further north on **Dog Beach** (pp292–3), pups chase birds around the marshy area where the San Diego River meets the sea. Head a few blocks south of the pier to **Sunset Cliffs Park**, where surfing and sunsets are the main attractions.

There are good surf breaks at the cliffs and, to the south, off Point Loma. Under the pier, skillful surfers slalom the pilings, but the rips and currents can be deadly unless you know what you're doing.

If you're here on Wednesday afternoon, stop by the Ocean Beach **farmers market** (☎ 619-279-0032; 4900 Block of Newport Ave; ☷ 4-7pm Wed, 4-8pm Jun-Sep) to see street performers and sample fresh food.

Mission Beach & Pacific Beach

This is the SoCal of the movies: buffed surfers and bronzed bohemians pack the 3-mile-long stretch of beach from South Mission Jetty to Pacific Beach Point, to cheer the setting sun at these perfect sand beaches.

The beaches' kick-back scene is concentrated in a narrow strip of land between the ocean and Mission Bay. On Pacific Beach, to the north, activity extends inland, particularly along Garnet Ave, which is lined with bars, restaurants and used-clothing stores. At the ocean end of Garnet Ave, **Crystal Pier** is a mellow place to fish or gaze out to sea.

San Diego's best people-watching is on the **Ocean Front Walk**, a boardwalk that connects the two beaches. It's crowded with joggers, in-line skaters and cyclists anytime of the year. On warm summer weekends, oiled bodies, packed like sardines, cover the beach from end to end. A block off the beach, Mission Blvd (the main north–south road), is lined with surf, smoke and swimwear shops. At peak times it can get so crowded that the police simply close it down, and parking around noon is just not gonna happen.

Instead, consider biking or skating. **Cheap Rentals** (☎ 858-488-9070, 800-941-7761; 3689 Mission Blvd) rents bikes and skates ($5/15 per hour/day), plus surfboards ($15 per day) and wetsuits ($10 per day); it also accepts advance reservations, crucial if you sleep late. See opposite for info about surfing the beaches.

BELMONT PARK
This old-style family **amusement park** (☎ 858-228-9283; www.belmontpark.com; park admission free, ride $1-6, unlimited rides adult/child $23/16; ☒ from 11am; ☒) in the middle of Mission Beach has been here since 1925. When it was threatened with demolition in the mid-1990s, community action saved the large indoor pool, known as the **Plunge**, and the **Giant Dipper** (☎ 858-488-1549), a classic wooden roller coaster that'll shake the teeth right outta your mouth, plus bumper cars, a tilt-a-whirl, carousel and other classics. More modern attractions include Flowrider, a wave machine for simulated surfing.

MISSION BAY
In the 18th century, the mouth of the San Diego River formed a shallow bay when the river flowed and a marshy swamp when it didn't – the Spanish called it False Bay. After WWII an extraordinary combination of civic vision and coastal engineering turned the swamp into a 7-sq-mile playground, with 27 miles of shoreline and 90 acres of public parks on islands, coves and peninsulas. A quarter of that land has been leased to hotels, boatyards and other businesses.

Kite flying is popular in Mission Bay Park, beach volleyball is big on Fiesta Island, and there's delightful cycling and in-line skating on the miles of smooth bike paths. Sailing, windsurfing and kayaking dominate the waters in northwest Mission Bay, while waterskiers zip around Fiesta Island. For equipment rentals, see opposite.

For a lovely time without adrenaline overload, board the **Bahia Belle** (☎ 858-539-7779; 998 West Mission Bay Dr; adult/child $6/3), a floating bar disguised as a stern-wheeler paddleboat. It cruises between two resort hotels, the Catamaran (p324) and the Bahia, on Friday and Saturday evenings year-round, Wednesday to Saturday in June, and daily in July and August. Cruises start at 6:30pm; call for exact departure times.

SEAWORLD
One of San Diego's most popular attractions, **SeaWorld** (Map pp292-3; ☎ 800-257-4268, 619-226-3901; www.seaworld.com/seaworld/ca; 500 SeaWorld Dr; adult/child 3-9yr $57/47; ☒ 9am-11pm Jul–mid-Aug, shorter hr rest of year; ℗) opened here in 1964. Shamu, the park's killer whale, has become an unofficial symbol of the city. It's easy to spend a day here, shuttling among shows, rides and exhibits – pick up a map at the entry and plan your day around the scheduled events.

SeaWorld's highlights are live shows featuring trained dolphins, seals, sea lions and killer whales. *Believe* is the most visually spectacular, a 30-minute show in which the three star performers – Shamu, Baby Shamu and Namu – glide, leap, dive and flip through the water while interacting with each other, their trainers and the audience. Avoid marked 'soak zones' near the tanks or you *will* get wet (though of course that may be just what you want). Some of the showmanship may be a bit, well, *awww,* but the creatures inspire pure *awe* – we'll admit we got a little choked up when 12-year-old Caleb from Indiana got to hold Shamu's flipper.

There are numerous other installations where you can see and learn about underwater creatures, as well as petting pools where you can touch the slippery surface of a dolphin or manta ray. In **Penguin Encounter**, several penguin species share a habitat that faithfully simulates Antarctic living conditions. The temperature behind the glass-enclosed space is a constant 25°F, but light conditions change according to South Pole seasons. So, if you're visiting in July (winter in Antarctica), expect to catch them waddling and swimming in near-darkness in the middle of the day. You'll see dozens of sharks as you walk through a 57ft acrylic tube at **Shark Encounter**. Species include blacktip and whitetip, reef and sand tiger sharks, some of them impressively large.

Several amusement-park-style rides include **Journey to Atlantis**, a combination flume ride and roller coaster; and **Wild Arctic**, a simulated helicopter flight followed by a walk past beluga whales and polar bears. Expect long waits for rides, shows and exhibits during peak seasons.

The park is shamefully commercial – you'll be subjected to deafeningly loud advertisements (many designed to appeal to small eyes and ears) as you wait in lines, there's a corporate logo on everything in sight, and gift shops are unavoidable. Still, SeaWorld manages to do its share for animal conservation, rescue, rehabilitation, breeding and research.

At full price it's a rather expensive day out, especially if you're with kids to whom you can't say no, though discount coupons are often available at hotel kiosks or online. Two-day tickets often cost only marginally more than single-day tickets. Even the tiniest stuffed Shamu costs $8. Food is expensive ($3 for packaged ice-cream), and the park prohibits coolers and picnic lunches (keep a cooler in the car and picnic outside the gates – be sure to get a hand-stamp for re-entry).

Inquire also about discounted combination tickets which include the San Diego Zoo and Wild Animal Park, Universal Studios Hollywood and/or Disneyland.

By car, take SeaWorld Dr off I-5 less than a mile north of where it intersects with I-8. Parking costs $10. Check with the Metropolitan Transit System (p316) for public transit. Some hotels offer shuttles.

ACTIVITIES
Surfing
A good number of San Diegans moved here for the surfing, and boy is it good. Even beginners will understand why it's so popular.

Fall brings strong swells and offshore Santa Ana winds. In summer swells come from the south and southwest, and in winter from the west and northwest. Spring brings more frequent onshore winds, but the surfing can still be good. For the latest beach, weather and surf reports, call ☎ 619-221-8824.

Beginners should head to Mission or Pacific Beaches, where the waves are gentle. North of the Crystal Pier, Tourmaline Surf Beach is an especially good place to take your first strokes. **Pacific Beach Surf Shop** (Map pp292-3; ☎ 858-373-1138; www.pacificbeachsurfschool.com; 4150 Mission Blvd, Suite 161, Pacific Beach; lesson per person for 1/2/3-5 people $85/80/75) provides instruction through its Pacific Beach Surf School. It has friendly service, and also rents wetsuits and both soft (foam) and hard (fiberglass) boards. Call ahead for lessons. You can also try **Bob's Mission Surf** (Map pp292-3; ☎ 858-483-8837; www.missionsurf.com; 4320 Mission Blvd, Pacific Beach). Rental rates at both vary depending on the quality of the equipment, but generally soft boards cost from $10/15 per half/full day; wet suits cost $5. **Surfergirls** (Map pp292-3; ☎ 858-427-0644; www.alohasurfergirls.com; 736 Santa Clara Pl, Mission Beach; lessons from $55) is specially designed for, well, you get the idea, with private and group lessons and all the equipment. See also Cheap Rentals in Mission Beach (opposite).

The best **surf breaks**, from south to north, are at Imperial Beach (south of Coronado especially in winter); Point Loma (less accessible but less crowded; best in winter) and Sunset Cliffs in Ocean Beach (though it's somewhat 'owned' by locals, meaning that you can expect to be heckled unless you're an awesome surfer). The surf at Mission Beach is good for beginners and body boarders. In Pacific Beach, the waves are steep and fast around Crystal Pier, while Tourmaline Surfing Park is especially popular with long boarders.

Bodysurfing is good at Coronado and Mission and Pacific Beaches. See also the surfing sections in La Jolla (p330) and North County (p333). Oceanside and La Jolla both have great surf breaks.

Diving & Snorkeling
Off the coast of San Diego County, divers will find kelp beds, shipwrecks (including the *Yukon*, a WWII destroyer sunk off Mission Beach in 2000), and canyons deep enough to host bat rays, octopuses and squid. For current conditions, call ☎ 619-221-8824.

Fishing
The most popular public fishing piers are Imperial Beach Pier, Embarcadero Fishing Pier, Shelter Island Fishing Pier, Ocean Beach Pier and Crystal Pier at Pacific Beach. Generally the best pier fishing is from April to October, and no license is required. For offshore fishing, catches can include barracuda, bass and yellowtail and, in summer, albacore. A state

SAN DIEGO COUNTY

fishing license is required for people over 16 for offshore fishing – one/two/10 days costs $11.50/17.75/35.50, plus $4 if ocean fishing.

Many companies run daily fishing trips year-round. Prices start at about $40/30 per adult/child for a near-shore half-day trip and can be many times that for a full-day trip far offshore. These companies are reputable:

H&M Landing (Map p287; ☎ 619-222-1144; www .hmlanding.com; 2803 Emerson St) On Shelter Island.

Islandia Sportfishing (Map pp292-3; ☎ 619-222-1164; www.islandiasportfishing.com; 1551 West Mission Bay Dr)

Point Loma Sport Fishing (Map p287; ☎ 619-223-1627; www.pointlomasportfishing.com; 1403 Scott St)

Seaforth Sportfishing (Map pp292-3; ☎ 619-224-3383; www.seaforthlanding.com; 1717 Quivira Rd) In Quivira Basin on Mission Bay.

Boating

You can rent power- and sailboats, rowboats, kayaks and canoes on Mission Bay. Try either **Mission Bay Sportcenter** (Map pp292-3; ☎ 858-488-1004; www.missionbaysportcenter.com; 1010 Santa Clara Pl), or **Resort Watersports** (Map pp292-3; ☎ 858-488-2582; www.resortwatersports.com), which is located at the Bahia (p320) and Catamaran (p324) resort hotels.

Ocean kayaking is a good way to see sea life, and explore cliffs and caves inaccessible from land. **Family Kayak** (☎ 619-282-3520; www.familykayak .com; ♿) has guided tours (from $40 per adult and $15 per child for three hours) and lessons (from $65). Inquire about longer tours.

Experienced sailors can charter yachts and sailboats for trips on San Diego Bay and out into the Pacific. Charter operators around Shelter and Harbor Islands (on the west side of San Diego Bay near the airport) include the following:

Harbor Sailboats (Map p287; ☎ 619-291-9568, 800-854-6625; www.harborsailboats.com; 2040 Harbor Island Dr, Suite 104)

San Diego Yacht Charters (Map p287; ☎ 619-297-4555, 800-456-0222; www.sdyc.com; 1880 Harbor Island Dr)

Shelter Island Sailing (Map p287; ☎ 619-222-0351; www.shelterislandsailing.com; 2240 Shelter Island Dr)

Whale-Watching

Gray whales pass San Diego from mid-December to late February on their way south to Baja California, and again in mid-March on their way back up to Alaskan waters. Their 12,000-mile round-trip journey is the longest migration of any mammal on earth.

Cabrillo National Monument (p319) is the best place to see the whales from land, where you'll also find exhibits, whale-related ranger programs and a shelter from which to watch the whales breach (bring binoculars).

Half-day whale-watching boat trips are offered by all of the companies that run daily fishing trips (p321). The trips generally cost $20/15 per adult/child for a three-hour ex-cursion, and the companies will even give you a free pass to return again if you don't spot any whales. Look for coupons and spe-cial offers in the *Reader* (p284).

SLEEPING

High-season (summer) rates for double-occupancy rooms are listed here; suites cost more. Prices drop significantly between Sep-tember and June.

Coronado

A stay at the southern end of Coronado (around the Hotel del Coronado) puts you close to the beach, shops and restaurants. The northern end is an easy walk to the ferry to downtown San Diego. The lower the building number, the closer you are to the ferry.

BUDGET

Coronado Village Inn (Map p287; ☎ 619-435-9318; www .coronadovillageinn.com; 1017 Park Pl; r $85-95) The top budget choice in pricey downtown Coronado, this Spanish-style, 15-room 1928 hotel has a sense of history but no amenities such as air-conditioning or oversized bathrooms. Still, its tidy rooms and location – two blocks from the beach, half a block to shops and restaurants – more than compensate.

El Rancho Motel (Map p287; ☎ 619-435-2251; www .elranchocoronado.com; 370 Orange Ave; r $99-120; ❼) A wood-clapboard exterior and up-to-date rooms with marble tile and sparkling white bedding make the eight rooms here difficult to snag without luck or reservations.

MIDRANGE

Crown City Inn (Map p287; ☎ 619-435-3116, 800-422-1173; www.crowncityinn.com; 520 Orange Ave; r $129-209; ❼ ▣ ▣ ♿) This two-story motel with ex-terior corridors encircles a small parking area with a little pool. If its well-kept rooms were nearer the beach, they would start at $200 per night. The bistro on-site is a local fave.

Coronado Inn (Map p287; ☎ 619-435-4121, 800-598-6624; www.coronadoinn.com; 266 Orange Ave; r incl breakfast

$149-169, with kitchen $199-269; (P) (回) (圖) (圖) wi-fi) The friendly owner keeps this handsome motel near the ferry in tip-top shape, amid palms, little wooden gazebos, nautical-blue deck chairs around the pool, and afternoon snacks.

El Cordova Hotel (Map p287; ☎ 619-435-4131, 800-229-2032; www.elcordovahotel.com; 1351 Orange Ave; r $149-299; (P) (圖) (圖)) This is an exceedingly cozy Mediterranean-style former mansion from 1902, built around an outdoor courtyard of shops and restaurants. Rooms are charming in an antiquey sort of way, though nothing fancy. Internet connection by cable. Parking costs $6.

TOP END

Glorietta Bay Inn (Map p287; ☎ 619-435-3101, 800-283-9383; www.gloriettabayinn.com; 1630 Glorietta Blvd; r $195-280; (P) (回) (圖) (圖) wi-fi) Overshadowed by the neighboring Hotel Del, the Glorietta is built in and around the 1908 Spreckels Mansion – (11 rooms in the mansion, 89 in more standard two-story buildings). Rooms have handsome furnishings and extras such as triple-sheeted beds and high-end bath products. Mansion rooms start at $265 and have extra amenities, including 600-thread-count sheets and continental breakfast. Stop in and see the gorgeous music room, even if you're not staying here.

Loews Coronado Bay Resort (Map p287; ☎ 619-424-4000, 800-235-6397; www.loewshotels.com; 4000 Coronado Bay Rd; r $240-285; (P) (回) (圖) (圖)) Way down Silver Strand (there's a complimentary shuttle to downtown Coronado), the Loews is practically surrounded by water. Rooms are sea-hued, the lobby is all brass rails and ceiling fans, and there are plenty of kids' programs.

our pick Hotel del Coronado (Map p287; ☎ 619-435-6611, 800-468-3533; www.hoteldel.com; 1500 Orange Ave; r $300-500; (P) (回) (圖) (圖)) San Diego's iconic hotel provides the essential Coronado experience: over a century of history, tennis courts, a pool, full-service spa, shops, restaurants, manicured grounds and a white-sand beach. Even the basic rooms have luxurious marbled bathrooms. Note: half the accommodations are not in the main Victorian-era hotel but in an adjacent seven-story building constructed in the 1970s. For a sense of place, book a room in the original hotel.

Point Loma Area

HI San Diego Point Loma Hostel (Map pp292-3; ☎ 619-223-4778, 800-909-4776, ext 157; www.sandiegohostels.org;

3790 Udall St; dm incl breakfast $19; (P) (回)) minute walk from the heart of Oce to this hostel, in a largely residential area, and close to a market and library. There are free excursions around town and to Tijuana, movie nights and barbecues. Bus No 923 runs along nearby Voltaire St. No lock-out times. No air-con.

Humphrey's Half Moon Inn & Suites (Map p287; ☎ 619-224-3411, 800-345-9995; www.halfmooninn .com; 2303 Shelter Island Dr, Point Loma; r $150-210, ste $260-500; (P) (回) (圖) (圖)) Fans of boating, jazz and Polynesian style will feel at home in this waterfront resort. Its 182 newly spruced-up rooms, many with marina-view balconies, run the gamut of comforts. There's a good jazz club on-site.

Sheraton San Diego Hotel & Marina (Map p287; ☎ 619-291-2900, 800-325-3535; www.sheraton .com/sandiegomarina; 1380 Harbor Island Dr; r from $219; (P) (回) (圖) (圖) wi-fi) Designed for businesspeople traveling with spouses on leisure vacations, the nautical-themed Sheraton has spacious rooms with super-comfy beds, feather pillows, and crisp linens. Request a room overlooking the yacht harbor rather than the airport (airport shuttle available). Parking costs $26.

Best Western Island Palms Hotel (Map p287; ☎ 619-222-0561; www.islandpalms.com; 2051 Shelter Island Dr; r from $219; (P) (回) (圖) (圖) wi-fi) This Polynesian-themed, 174-room resort is laid out like an archipelago of little buildings. It fronts the yacht harbor and has comfortable, well-maintained upper-end-chain-motel-style rooms. Free bike rentals, too.

Ocean Beach

Ocean Beach (OB) is under the outbound flight path of San Diego airport, which won't be a problem if you rise at 6am. Light or late sleepers should stay elsewhere or bring earplugs.

Ocean Beach International Hostel (☎ 619-223-7873, 800-339-7263; www.californiahostels.com; 4961 Newport Ave; dm incl breakfast $24; (回) wi-fi) The cheapest option is only a couple of blocks from the ocean; it's a friendly, fun place that's reserved for international travelers and educators, with barbecues, bonfires and more. Free transfer from airport, bus or train station on arrival. No air-con.

Ocean Beach Hotel (☎ 619-223-7191; www.obhotel .com; 5080 Newport Ave; r without ocean view $99-149, with ocean view $149-199; (P) wi-fi) Walk everywhere in

OB from this three-story, 56-room motel on the beach – the courtyard overlooks the bike path. Rooms are small but have fridges and microwaves. The occasional crack in the paint or mushy mattress only makes it feel more authentic.

Inn at Sunset Cliffs (☎ 619-222-7901, 866-786-2543; www.innatsunsetcliffs.com; 1370 Sunset Cliffs Blvd; r from $149; P ⌨ ☺ wi-fi) At the south end of Ocean Beach, wake up to the sound of surf crashing onto the rocky shore. This charmer wraps around a flower-bedecked courtyard with small heated pool. Breezy rooms are compact, but some suites have full kitchens. Even with the occasional crack in the tiling, it's hard not to love this place.

Mission Beach & Pacific Beach

Pacific Beach (PB) has most of the beach-side accommodations. Motels provide better value in winter than summer, when rates are high and availability scarce (summer rates are listed here).

BUDGET

Banana Bungalow (Map pp292-3; ☎ 858-273-3060; www.bananabungalow.com; 707 Reed Ave; dm $25, d from $105; wi-fi) Right on Mission Beach, the Bungalow has a top location, a beach-party atmosphere and is reasonably clean, but it's very basic and gets crowded. The communal area is a patio, which fronts right on the boardwalk; it's a great place for people-watching and beer drinking. Breakfast included. No air-con.

Mission Bay Motel (Map pp292-3; ☎ 858-483-6440, 866-649-5828; www.missionbaymotel.com; 4221 Mission Blvd; r from $110; P ☺) The rooms are tiny, the overall feel is somewhat dumpy, there's no air-con and your view is of a parking lot and a busy street. But there are three reasons to stay here: location, location and location. Mission Beach and the nightspots and restaurants of Garnet Ave are nearby.

MIDRANGE & TOP END

ourpick Tower23 Hotel (Map pp292-3; ☎ 866-869-3723; www.t23hotel.com; 723 Felspar St, Pacific Beach; r from $199; P ⌨) If you like your beach stay with contemporary cool style, this is the place for you. This once-blah property has been transformed into a modernist show place, with minimalist decor, lots of teals and mint blues and a sense of humor. There's no pool, but you're right on the beach. See Jordan restaurant (p326).

Beach Cottages (Map pp292-3; ☎ 858-483-7440; 4255 Ocean Blvd; r $135-155, cottages from $285; P wi-fi) Family owned and operated, Beach Cottages bears the standard for service in PB and has everything from plain motel rooms to cozy 1940s beachfront cottages. It's hard not to love the throwback feel of clapboard construction, ping-pong, shuffleboard and rattan furniture. It can be a real bargain if you're traveling in a group and manage to secure one of the cottages. Book well in advance. No air-con.

Crystal Pier Hotel (Map pp292-3; ☎ 858-483-6983, 800-748-5894; www.crystalpier.com; 4500 Ocean Blvd; cottages $300-500; P ⚲) Charming, wonderful, and unlike anyplace else in San Diego, Crystal Pier has cottages built right on the pier above the water. All have full ocean views and kitchens, but the original 1936 clapboard units are the best. Newer, larger cottages sleep up to six. Book eight to 11 months in advance for summer reservations. Minimum-stay requirements vary by season. No air-con.

Pacific Terrace Hotel (Map pp292-3; ☎ 858-581-3500, 800-344-3370; www.pacificterrace.com; 610 Diamond St; r from $359; P ⌨ ☺) If your idea of a full-service hotel is old-world furnishings, ocean view and sky-high prices, the Pacific Terrace is your only choice in PB. There's a fitness center, spa and concierge services. Parking costs $18.

Mission Bay

Mission Bay has waterfront lodging and at lower prices than on the ocean.

Campland on the Bay (Map pp292-3; ☎ 858-581-4260, 800-422-9386; www.campland.com; 2211 Pacific Beach Dr; RV & campsites $65-140, beachfront from $150; P ☺ wi-fi) More than 40 acres fronting Mission Bay, reservable up to two years in advance. There's a restaurant, two pools, boating rentals and full RV hookups. Site costs vary depending on their proximity to the water. The location is great, but the tent area is not very attractive – too many RVs, not enough trees – and it gets crowded. Reservations are recommended.

ourpick Catamaran Resort Hotel (Map pp292-3; ☎ 858-488-1081, 800-422-8386; www.catamaranresort.com; 3999 Mission Blvd; r from $159; P ⚲ ⚲ wi-fi) Tropical landscaping and Polynesian decor fill this bayside resort, perfect for families (and there's a spa for mom and dad). Sail, kayak, play tennis, and rent a bike or skates and ride around Mission Bay, or board the Bahia Belle (p320) from here. Rooms are in low-rise buildings or in a 14-story tower; some have views and full kitchens. The resort hosts a luau on summer evenings. The staff are extremely helpful. Parking costs $12.

Paradise Point Resort (Map pp292-3; ☎ 858-274-4630, 800-344-2626; www.paradisepoint.com; 1404 Vacation Rd; r from $339; ☐ ☒ ☒ wi-fi) The grounds are so lush and dotted with so many palms that you'll feel like you're in Hawaii at this upperend resort, whose 462 rooms are in small ground-floor bungalows. Features for kids include a putting green and summer movies in one of the five swimming pools. Full-service spa. Parking costs $20.

EATING

In coastal San Diego, you're never very far from Downtown (Pacific Beach is furthest, only 20 minutes by car), so remember to also check out the restaurant listings for Downtown (p307).

Coronado

BUDGET & MIDRANGE

Villa Nueva (Map p287; ☎ 619-435-4191; 956 Orange Ave; mains $7-9; ☽ 6:30am-6pm) No breakfast at your inn? This bakery-café whips up awesome omelettes, pancakes and Mexican breakfasts (try the huevos rancheros) and bakes imaginative muffins – cappuccino cheesecake, pineapple coconut – plus dozens of pies, cakes and pastries (for later – that's not breakfast food).

1134 Cafe (Map p287; ☎ 619-437-1134; 1134 Orange Ave; mains $7-10; ☽ 6am-9pm) This local classic is bright and airy with tall ceilings and stained-glass accents, serving good scramblers, muffins and strong coffee at breakfast; at lunch and dinner there are soups, quiches and salads.

Coronado Brewing Co (Map p287; ☎ 619-437-4452; 170 Orange Ave; mains $10-19; ☽ lunch & dinner) The delicious house brew (the Pilsner-style Coronado Golden) goes well with the pizzas, pastas, sandwiches and fries at this good-for-your-soul, bad-for-your-diet bar and grill near the ferry. Happy hour 2pm to 6pm.

Mootime Creamery (Map p287; ☎ 619-435-2422; 1025 Orange Ave; ice cream from $3; ☽ 10am-11pm Mon-Fri, 11am-11pm Sat & Sun) All of Coronado screams for this wonderfully creative hometown ice-cream shop, decorated like a '50s diner: try peanut butter, Mexican chocolate or silly vanilly (you gotta see it). Sorbet flavors include kiwifruit and champagne.

TOP END

Primavera (☎ 619-435-0454; 932 Orange Ave; mains $18-34; ☽ dinner) Subdued, romantic setting for subdued, romantic Italian fare presented by black-tied waiters. It's known for steaks and seafood dishes like shrimp in mushroom and champagne sauce, plus an excellent wine list. Prices are high, but you get what you pay for.

Mistral (Map p287; ☎ 619-424-4000; Loews Coronado Bay Resort, 4000 Coronado Bay Rd; mains $16-38; ☽ dinner Tue-Sat) Grand for romantic, white-tablecloth Euro-Cal dining with views, and its to-die-for lobster risotto and bistecca fiorentina with spring greens and truffle pommes frites.

1500 Ocean (Map p287; ☎ 619-435-6611; Hotel del Coronado, 1500 Orange Ave; mains $30-42; ☽ dinner) It's hard to beat the romance of supping at the Hotel del Coronado, especially at a table overlooking the sea from the verandah of its 1st-class dining room, where silver service and coastal cuisine with local ingredients set the perfect tone for popping the question or fêting an important anniversary.

Point Loma Area

Point Loma Seafoods (Map p287; ☎ 619-223-1109; 2805 Emerson St; mains $7-13; ☽ 9am-6:30pm Mon-Sat, 11am-6:30pm Sun) Order at the counter at this fish-market-cum-deli and grab a seat at a picnic table for off-the-boat-fresh seafood and icy cold beer. Located in the Shelter Island Marina, it's a San Diego institution. Great sushi, too.

Brigantine (Map p287; ☎ 619-224-2871; 2725 Shelter Island Dr; mains lunch $8-17, dinner $12-45) Ships' wheels and captains' chairs decorate the original location of this respected local seafood chain. Sit on the balcony and you can peek through palm fronds to the harbor. Lunch is heavy on sandwiches (and famous fish tacos), while dinners are fancier with dishes like marinated swordfish. Awesome happy hours. Other locations in Coronado (☎ 619-435-4166; 1333 Orange Ave) and Del Mar (☎ 858-481-1166; 3263 Camino del Mar).

Ocean Beach

OB is great for dining on a shoestring. Most places are on Newport Ave.

OB People's Market (Map pp292-3; ☎ 619-224-1387; cnr Voltaire & Sunset Cliffs Blvd; ☽ 8am-9pm; Ⓥ) For vegetarian groceries, check out this organic cooperative with bulk foods, fresh soups, and excellent pre-made sandwiches, salads and wraps, most under $5. No meat.

SAN DIEGO COUNTY

our pick Hodad's (Map pp292-3; ☎ 619-224-4623; 5010 Newport Ave; burgers $4-9; ☽ lunch & dinner; 🏊) OB's legendary burger joint serves great shakes, massive baskets of onion rings and succulent hamburgers wrapped in paper. The walls are covered in license plates, grunge/surf-rock plays (loud!) and your bearded, tattooed server might sidle in to your booth to take your order. No shirt, no shoes, no problem.

Ortega's Cocina (Map pp292-3; ☎ 619-222-4205; 4888 Newport Ave; mains $3-13; ☽ breakfast, lunch & dinner) Tiny, family-run Ortega's is so popular that people often queue for a spot at the counter. Seafood, *moles* and *tortas* (sandwiches) are the specialties, but all its dishes are soulful and classic.

Rancho's Cocina (Map pp292-3; ☎ 619-226-7619; 1830 Sunset Cliffs Blvd; mains $4-12; ☽ 8am-10pm; **V**) Two blocks south of Newport Ave, Rancho's makes its own *mole* – a spicy sauce made with chilies and chocolate. In addition to Mexican standards, it also serves healthy and flavorful vegetarian and vegan dishes.

Portugalia (Map pp292-3; ☎ 619-222-7678; 4839 Newport Ave; mains lunch $6-12, dinner $17-20; ☽ lunch & dinner Tue-Sun) San Diego's only Portuguese restaurant slakes cravings for *bacalhau* (salt cod), *linguiça* sausage and Portuguese-style *bife* (steak). It caters to a growing local Brazilian community – try the *açaí* frozen drink. Entertainment (nightly) includes Brazilian, reggae and blues.

Mission Beach & Pacific Beach

Kono's (Map pp292-3; ☎ 858-483-1669; 704 Garnet Ave; dishes from $5; ☽ breakfast & lunch) This place makes $5 breakfast burritos that you eat out of a basket in view of Crystal Pier (patio seating available). It's always crowded but well worth the wait.

Mission Café (Map pp292-3; ☎ 858-488-9060; 3795 Mission Blvd; dishes $6-9; ☽ breakfast & lunch; **V** 🏊) Down in Mission Beach, you can have French toast or homemade cinnamon bread at breakfast, or Chino-Latino specialties at lunch, such as rosemary potatoes with black beans, salsa and eggs, or ginger sesame tofu. Famously good coffee, too.

Green Flash (Map pp292-3; ☎ 619-270-7715; 701 Thomas Ave; mains breakfast & lunch $4-13, dinner $8-30; ☽ 8am-10pm) A terrific breakfast or lunch spot for eggs, meaty burgers, big salads and triple-decker clubs, the Flash also has a weekday sunset specials (4:30pm to 6pm Sundya to Thursday). Score a table outside on the patio.

Dinners are OK, but you'll get more for your money inland.

our pick World Famous (Map pp292-3; ☎ 858-272-3100; 711 Pacific Beach Dr; mains breakfast & lunch $7-12, dinner $10-23; ☽ 7am-11pm) Watch the surf while enjoying 'California coastal cuisine,' an ever-changing menu of inventive dishes from the sea (banana rum mahimahi, bacon and spinach wrapped scallops), plus steaks, salads and lunchtime sandwiches and burgers and occasional specials like fish or lobster taco night. Popular at breakfast, too.

Gringo's Cocina y Cantina (Map pp292-3; ☎ 858-490-2877; 4474 Mission Blvd, Pacific Beach; mains lunch $8-14, dinner $12-20) Upbeat, contempo and vast, this kicky Mexican cantina serves up a roster of regional classics, from Oaxacan *mole* chicken to mango mustard-glazed salmon from Yucatán. The weekend brunch is popular too.

Jordan (Map pp292-3; ☎ 858-270-5736; 723 Felspar St; mains breakfast $8-14, lunch $9-23, dinner $20-43; ☽ breakfast, lunch & dinner) A big heaping dose of chic amid PB's congenital laid-backness. There's both an ocean view and a futuristic interior (and most excellent bar scene). Sustainably farmed meats and seafood join local veggies to create festivals on the plate. Try dry scallops with crabmeat risotto, miso halibut and green onion 'creamers' (aka mashed potatoes).

DRINKING & ENTERTAINMENT

For information about cinema, classical music, live theater, spectator sports and acquiring tickets to events, see p313.

Bars & Clubs

CORONADO

Mc P's Irish Pub (Map p287; ☎ 619-435-5280; www.mcpspub.com; 1107 Orange Ave) Dyed-in-the-wool Irish pub that's been there for a generation. Pints o' Guinness complement down-home Irish fare – corned beef, stew, meatloaf – as you listen to nightly live music from rock to Irish folk. Indoor and patio seating.

OCEAN BEACH

Winston's (Map pp292-3; ☎ 619-222-6822; www.winstonsob.com; 1921 Bacon St) Bands play most nights, and each night has a different happening: open mic, karaoke, poetry, Grateful Dead cover band, local artists, game day etc.

MISSION & PACIFIC BEACHES

In PB look for bars and clubs on and around Garnet Ave, as well as near the beach.

'Canes (Map pp292-3; ☎ 858-488-1780; www.canesbarandgrill.com; 3105 Ocean Front Walk, Mission Beach) Tropical, beachside bar that books live music and mixes punk with beach boys (both on stage and off).

710 Beach Club (☎ 858-483-7844; www.710beachclub.com; 710 Garnet Ave, Pacific Beach) The club books a solid lineup of blues musicians with the occasional rock act thrown in for good measure at PB's main venue for live music.

Club Tremors (☎ 858-272-7278; 860 Garnet Ave, Pacific Beach; cover up to $10; Wed-Sat) Popular with 20-somethings, Tremors has a well-dressed and coiffed crowd for dancing and a pickup scene. It's adjacent to Pacific Beach Bar & Grill.

Moondoggies (☎ 858-483-6550; 832 Garnet Ave, Pacific Beach) Next door to Club Tremors, Moondoggies has a large patio, big-screen TVs, pool tables, good food and an extensive tap selection.

Society Billiard Cafe (☎ 858-272-7665; 1051 Garnet Ave, Pacific Beach; 11am-2pm) Why settle for a beat-up pool table in the back of a dark bar when you can visit San Diego's plushest pool hall? The billiard room has 15 full-sized tables, snacks and a bar.

Coaster Saloon (Map pp292-3; ☎ 858-488-4438; 744 Ventura Pl, Mission Beach) This old-fashioned neighborhood dive bar has front-row views of the Belmont Park roller coaster and draws an unpretentious crowd. Good margaritas.

Coffeehouses

Jungle Java (Map pp292-3; ☎ 619-224-0249; 5047 Newport Ave, Ocean Beach; 7am-10pm summer, 7am-8pm winter) Funky-dunky, canopy-covered café and plant shop, also crammed with crafts and art treasures.

Newbreak Coffee Co & Café (Map pp292-3; ☎ 619-224-6666; 1959 Abbot St, Ocean Beach; 7am-6pm) A popular hangout for teetotalers and caffeine junkies in bar-crazy OB, the Newbreak also has internet kiosks and wi-fi.

Zanzibar (Map pp292-3; ☎ 858-272-4762; 976 Garnet Ave, Pacific Beach; 7am-11pm; wi-fi) Popular for its focaccia pizza and homemade soups.

Café 976 (Map pp292-3; ☎ 858-272-0976; 976 Felspar, Pacific Beach; 7am-11pm) Not everyone in PB spends the days surfing; some drink coffee and read books at this side-street café in a converted old house with green plants.

SHOPPING

Most of coastal San Diego's shopping is limited to surf shops and bikini boutiques. A notable exception: Newport Ave in Ocean Beach, where a dozen antiques consignment shops line the main drag; **Newport Avenue Antique Center** (Map pp292-3; ☎ 619-222-8686; 4864 Newport Ave) and **Mallory's** (Map pp292-3; ☎ 619-226-2068; 4916 Newport Ave) are good places to start. **Cow** (Map pp292-3; ☎ 619-523-0236; 5029 Newport Ave) gives the same treatment to music. Thrift shoppers should head to Garnet Ave in Pacific Beach for vintage and recycled drag. Most stores buy, sell and trade.

South Coast Wahines (Map pp292-3; ☎ 858-273-7600; 4500 Ocean Front Blvd, Pacific Beach) is at the foot of Garnet Ave at Crystal Pier in Pacific Beach, and South Coast carries spiffy surf apparel for women.

For swimwear, women should head to **Pilar's Beachwear** (Map pp292-3; ☎ 858-488-3056; 3745 Mission Blvd, Mission Beach), which has all the latest styles in all sizes.

If you don't find anything at Pilar's, head up the street to **Gone Bananas** (Map pp292-3; ☎ 858-488-4900; 3785 Mission Blvd, Mission Beach) for a large selection of mix-and-match bikinis and one-pieces. Look for Body Glove, Mossimo, Sauvage and three dozen other brands.

Apathetic surfer dudes staff the counter at **South Coast Longboards** (Map pp292-3; ☎ 619-223-7017; 5023 Newport Ave, Ocean Beach), a beach-apparel and surf-gear shop that carries a good selection of Quiksilver, Hurley, Billabong and O'Neill for men and women. Oh yes, you can buy a surfboard here too.

Buff (Map pp292-3; ☎ 858-581-2833; 1059 Garnet Ave) has a wide range of outrageous clothes, many of them suitable for Halloween costumes, at this super-fun shop. Hot accessories, too.

If you need something to wear to dinner, **Buffalo Exchange** (Map pp292-3; ☎ 858-273-6227; 1007 Garnet Ave) carries a good selection of contemporary and vintage fashions, including designer labels.

GETTING THERE & AROUND

For details on getting to and from the San Diego metropolitan area, as well as getting to and from the airport, riding MTS buses, and traveling by train, taxi and rental car, see p316.

Bicycle

Pacific Beach, Mission Beach, Mission Bay and Coronado are all great places to ride a bike. The **San Diego Bicycle Coalition** (☎ 858-487-6063; www.sdcbc.org) has maps and a wealth of information about biking in and around the city. Public buses are equipped with bike racks.

The following outfits all rent bicycles, from mountain and road bikes to kids' bikes and cruisers. In general, expect to pay about $7 per hour, $10 to $20 per half-day (four hours) and $20 to $25 per day.

Bikes & Beyond (Map p287; ☎ 619-435-7180; Coronado Ferry Landing, foot of Orange Ave)

Cheap Rentals (Map p292-3; ☎ 858-488-9070, 800-941-7761; www.cheap-rentals.com; 3689 Mission Blvd, Mission Beach)

Holland's Bicycles (Map p287; ☎ 619-435-3153; www.hollandsbicycles.com; 977 Orange Ave, Coronado)

Boat

San Diego Harbor Excursion operates the hourly **Coronado Ferry** (Map pp288-9; ☎ 619-234-4111; www.sdhe.com; one way/round-trip $3/6; ☉ 9am-9pm Mon-Fri, 9am-10pm Sat & Sun) shuttling between the Broadway Pier on the Embarcadero to the ferry landing at the foot of Orange Ave. Take your bike on the ferry for an additional $0.50. See also San Diego Water Taxi (p316).

LA JOLLA

Immaculately landscaped parks, white-sand coves, upscale boutiques and cliffs above deep, clear blue waters make it easy to understand why 'La Jolla' translates from Spanish as 'the jewel' – say la-*hoy*-yah, if you please. The name may actually date from Native Americans who inhabited the area from 10,000 years ago to the mid-19th century, who called the place 'mut la Hoya, la Hoya' – the place of many caves. Regardless of the name's origin, it's a lovely place to spend the day.

Today's La Jolla has its roots in 1897, when newspaper heiress Ellen Browning Scripps moved here, acquiring much of the land along Prospect St, which she subsequently donated to community uses. She hired Irving Gill to design local institutions, such as the **Bishop's School** (cnr Prospect St & La Jolla Blvd) and the **La Jolla Woman's Club** (715 Silverado St), setting the unadorned Mediterranean architectural tone of arches, colonnades, palm trees, red-tile roofs and pale stucco.

The surrounding area is home to the University of California San Diego (UCSD), several renowned research institutes and a new-money residential area called the Golden Triangle, bounded by I-5, I-805 and Hwy 52.

Bus 30 takes you from Downtown and La Jolla and stops at many sights en route.

INFORMATION
Bookstores

These bookstores have good selections and host readings and author events.

DG Wills (Map p294; ☎ 858-456-1800; 7461 Girard Ave)

Warwick's (Map p294; ☎ 858-454-0347; 7812 Girard Ave)

Money

Travelex (Map p287; ☎ 858-457-2412; University Towne Centre; ☉ 10am-6pm Mon-Fri, 10am-4pm Sat, 11am-4pm Sun) Foreign-currency exchange at inland shopping mall.

Tourist Information

La Jolla Visitor Center (Map p294; ☎ 619-236-1212; www.sandiego.org; 7966 Herschell; ☉ 9am-5pm Mon-Sat, 10am-5pm Sun) This outpost of the San Diego Convention & Visitors Bureau also promotes La Jolla.

SIGHTS
Downtown La Jolla

La Jolla Village sits atop cliffs with the ocean on three sides. The main crossroads, Girard Ave and Prospect St are the *x* and *y* axes of some of San Diego's best restaurants and certainly its best boutique shopping. For a bit of old La Jolla, head southwest from Girard Ave along Prospect St. Number 780 Prospect St was originally Ellen Browning Scripps guest cottage.

Around the corner from the cottage, **La Jolla Historical Society** (Map p294; ☎ 858-459-5335; 7846 Eads Ave; ☉ noon-4:30pm Tue & Thu) has vintage photos and beach memorabilia (think old bathing costumes and lifeguard buoys). Further southwest on Prospect St there's St James Episcopal Church, the La Jolla Recreation Center and the Bishop's School, all built in the early 20th century.

La Jolla's branch of the **Museum of Contemporary Art San Diego** (Map p294; ☎ 858-454-3541; www.mcasd.org; 700 Prospect St; adult/senior/25 & under $10/5/free; ☉ 11am-7pm Thu, 11am-5pm Fri-Tue) gets changing, world-class exhibitions. Originally designed by Irving Gill in 1916 as the home of Ellen Browning Scripps, the building was renovated by Philadelphia's postmodern architect Robert Venturi and has an Andy Goldsworthy sculpture out the front; tickets are good for one week at all three of the museum's locations (p285).

Read daily newspapers from around the globe at the quiet and civilized **Athenaeum Music & Arts Library** (Map p294; ☎ 858-454-5872; 1008 Wall St, cnr Girard Ave; ☼ 10am-5:30pm Tue-Sat, 10am-8:30pm Wed), which also displays small art exhibits. Lovely.

The Coast

A wonderful walking path skirts the shoreline for half a mile. At the west it begins at the **Children's Pool**, where a jetty protects the beach from big waves.

Originally intended to give La Jolla's youth a safe place to frolic, the beach is now given over to sea lions, which you can view up close as they lounge on the shore.

Atop Point La Jolla, at the path's eastern end, **Ellen Browning Scripps Park** is a tidy expanse of green lawns and palm trees, with **La Jolla Cove** to the north. The cove's gem of a beach provides access to some of the best snorkeling around; it's also popular with rough-water swimmers.

Look for the white buoys offshore from Point La Jolla to Scripps Pier (visible to the north) that mark the San Diego–La Jolla Underwater Park Ecological Reserve, a protected zone with a variety of marine life, kelp forests, reefs and canyons (see Diving & Surfing, p330). Waves have carved a series of caves into the sandstone cliffs east of the cove. The largest is called Sunny Jim Cave, which you can access via the **Cave Store** (Map p294; ☎ 858-459-0746; 1325 Cave St; adult/child $4/3; ☼ 10am-5pm); taller visitors, watch your head as you descend the 145 steps.

See p330 for info about surfing this area.

La Jolla Shores

Called simply 'the Shores,' the area northeast of La Jolla Cove is where La Jolla's cliffs meet the wide, sandy beaches north to Del Mar (p334). Primarily residential, the Shores is home to the members-only La Jolla Beach and Tennis Club (its orange-tile roof is visible from La Jolla Cove) and Kellogg City Park, whose beachside playground is good for families. Take La Jolla Shores Dr north from Torrey Pines Rd, and turn west onto Ave de la Playa. The waves here are gentle enough for beginner surfers, and kayakers can launch from the shore without much problem.

Some of the county's best **beaches** are north of the Shores in **Torrey Pines City Park**, which covers the coastline from the Salk Institute (right)

up to the Torrey Pines State Reserve (p330). At extreme low tides (about twice per year), you can walk from the Shores north to Del Mar along the beach. Hang-gliders and paragliders launch into the sea breezes rising over the cliffs at **Torrey Pines Gliderport**, at the end of Torrey Pines Scenic Dr. It's a beautiful sight – tandem flights are available if you can't resist trying it (p331). Down below, **Black's Beach** is one of America's most storied clothing-optional venues – though bathing suits are technically required, most folks here don't seem to know that; there's a gay section at the far (north) end.

Birch Aquarium at Scripps

Marine scientists were working at the Birch Aquarium at **Scripps Institution of Oceanography** (SIO) as early as 1910 and, helped by donations from the ever-generous Scripps family, the institute has grown to be one of the world's largest marine research institutions. It is now a part of UCSD, and its pier is a landmark.

Off N Torrey Pines Rd, SIO's **Birch Aquarium** (Map p294; ☎ 858-534-3474; www.aquarium.ucsd.edu; 2300 Expedition Way; adult/child/student/senior $11/7.50/8/9; ☼ 9am-5pm; **P**) has brilliant displays. The Hall of Fishes has more than 30 fish tanks, simulating marine environments from the Pacific Northwest to tropical seas. If you're interested in studying oceanography or seeing the campus, pick up the self-guided campus-tour brochure. Parking is free.

The SIO is not to be confused with the **Scripps Research Institute** (10550 Torrey Pines Rd), a private, nonprofit biomedical research organization.

Salk Institute

In 1960 Jonas Salk, the polio-prevention pioneer, founded the **Salk Institute** (Map p294; ☎ 858-453-4100 ext 1287; www.salk.edu; 10010 N Torrey Pines Rd; tours ☼ noon Mon & Wed-Fri by reservation) for biological and biomedical research. San Diego County donated 27 acres of land, the March of Dimes provided financial support and renowned architect Louis Kahn designed the building. Completed in 1965, it is regarded as a modern masterpiece, with its classically proportioned travertine marble plaza and cubist, mirror-glass laboratory blocks framing a perfect view of the Pacific, and the fountain in the courtyard symbolizing the River of Life. The Salk Institute attracts the best scientists to work in a research-only environment. The original buildings were expanded with new laboratories designed by Jack McAllister, a follower of Kahn's work.

Torrey Pines State Reserve

Between N Torrey Pines Rd and the ocean, and from the Torrey Pines Gliderport to Del Mar, this **reserve** (Map p294; ☎ 858-755-2063; www.torreypine.org; 12600 N Torrey Pines Rd; ☺ 8am-dusk; ℗) preserves the last mainland stands of the Torrey pine (Pinus torreyana), a species adapted to sparse rainfall and sandy, stony soils. Steep sandstone gullies are eroded into wonderfully textured surfaces, and the views over the ocean and north are superb.

The main access road, Torrey Pines Scenic Dr, off N Torrey Pines Rd (bues 41 and 301) at the reserve's northern end, leads to a simple adobe – built as a lodge in 1922 by – who else? – Ellen Browning Scripps. The lodge now serves as a **visitors center** with good displays on the local flora and fauna. Rangers lead **nature walks** from here at 10am and 2pm on weekends and holidays. Several walking trails wind through the reserve and down to the beach.

Torrey Pines State Reserve and La Jolla Cove are also good spots for whale-watching. Parking costs $8.

University of California, San Diego

UCSD (Map p294; ☎ 858-534-2230; www.ucsd.edu) was established in 1960, and now has more than 18,000 students and an excellent academic reputation, particularly for mathematics and science programs. It lies on rolling coastal hills in a parklike setting, surrounded by tall, fragrant eucalyptus trees. Its most distinctive structure is the **Geisel Library**, an upside-down pyramid of glass and concrete, whose namesake, children's author Theodor Geisel, is better known as Dr Seuss, creator of the Cat in the Hat. He and his wife contributed substantially to the library, which exhibits a collection of his drawings and books on the ground floor.

From the eastern side of the library's second level, an allegorical snake created by artist Alexis Smith winds down a native California plant garden past an enormous marble copy of John Milton's Paradise Lost. The piece is part of the **Stuart Collection** of outdoor sculptures spread around campus. Other works include Niki de Saint Phalle's Sun God, Bruce Nauman's Vices & Virtues (which spells out seven

of each in huge neon letters), Robert Irwin's very blue Fence and a forest of talking trees. Most installations are near the Geisel Library, and details are available from the Visual Arts Building or the Price Center, where the **UCSD bookstore** (Map p294; ☎ 858-534-7323) has excellent stock and helpful staff. Inside the Mandell Weiss Center for the Performing Arts, the **La Jolla Playhouse** (Map p294; ☎ 858-550-1010; www.lajollaplayhouse.com) is known for its high-quality productions.

ACTIVITIES
Diving & Surfing

Some of California's best and most accessible (no boat needed) diving is in the **San Diego–La Jolla Underwater Park Ecological Reserve**, accessible from La Jolla Cove. With an average depth of 20ft, the 6000 acres of look-but-don't-touch underwater real estate is great for snorkeling, too. Ever-present are the spectacular, bright orange Garibaldi fish – California's official state fish and a protected species (there's a $500 fine for poaching one). Further out, you'll see forests of giant California kelp (which can increase its length by up to 3ft per day) and the 100ft-deep La Jolla Canyon.

A number of commercial outfits conduct scuba-diving courses, sell or rent equipment, fill tanks, and conduct boat trips to nearby wrecks and islands. Snorkels and fins cost around $8 each per day, or rent all the equipment for $25; scuba-gear rental packages start at about $50. The Cave Store (p329) has them, or, by the water, **OEX** (☎ 858-454-6195; www.oeexpress.com; 2158 Avenida de la Playa) is a full-service PADI dive shop in La Jolla Shores that provides rentals and instruction. Dive tours start at $60.

Experienced surfers can head to **Windansea Beach**, 2 miles south of Downtown (take La Jolla Blvd south and turn west on Nautilus St); the surf's consistent peak (a powerful reef break that's not for beginners) works best at medium to low tide. However, some of the locals can be unfriendly toward outsiders. You'll find a more pleasant welcome immediately south, at the foot of Palomar Ave, **Big Rock**, California's version of Hawaii's Pipeline, which has steep, hollow, gnarly tubes. The name comes from the large chunk of reef protruding just offshore – a great spot for **tide-pooling** at low tide. La Jolla Shores and Black's Beach are also popular surfing spots.

The wonderful women at **Surf Diva** (Map p294; ☎ 858-454-8273; www.surfdiva.com; 2160 Avenida de la Playa) offer surf classes (some just for women), including two-day weekend workshops for $135.

Kayaking

OEX (opposite) rents kayaks for $28 for two hours and offers sightseeing instructions; two-hour kayak tours are $45 per person.

Hang Gliding

Glider riders hang at **Torrey Pines Gliderport** (Map p294; ☎ 858-452-9858; www.flytorrey.com; 2800 Torrey Pines Scenic Dr; 20min tandem flight per person $150), a world-famous gliding location. It's also one of the best gliding schools in the country.

Experienced pilots can join in if they have a USHGA Hang 4 rating and take out an associate membership of the Torrey Pines Hang Glider Association.

SLEEPING

Lodging in central La Jolla ain't cheap, but lower-priced chains are a quick drive outside the village. We've given high-season (summer) rack rates here. Inquire about specials and packages.

La Jolla Village Lodge (Map p294; ☎ 858-454-0791, 800-454-4361; www.lajollavillagelodge.com; 1141 Silverado St; r incl breakfast from $120; P wi-fi) At the edge of downtown La Jolla, this 1950s-era motel was recently restored in period style with custom-built tables and chairs, teak headboards and new mattresses. Flat-screen TVs (in some rooms) are a concession to the 21st century. A roof deck gives long-distance views.

Scripps Inn (Map p294; ☎ 858-454-3391; 555 Coast Blvd; r incl breakfast from $175; P) Tucked behind the Museum of Contemporary Art, across from the water, this cozy inn feels like a well-loved beach cottage, bedecked with climbing vines. Its airy, rather spacious rooms mix blond-wood and sandpiper motifs, and most have sleep-sofas. Its 13 units fill up quickly – book early. No air-con.

Estancia La Jolla Hotel & Spa (Map p294; ☎ 858-550-1000, 877-437-8262; www.estancialajolla.com; 9700 N Torrey Pines Rd; r $240-390; P 💻 🐾 wi-fi) Outside the town center, this rambling rancho-style resort with its pathways, patios and lush gardens is down-to-earth, romantic and cushy all at once. Unwind by the huge pool, during an expert massage at the spa, or while sipping killer margaritas by the outdoor fireplace. Rooms feature custom furniture, luxurious

linens and big bathrooms. Two restaurants. Parking costs $17.

Grande Colonial (Map p294; ☎ 858-454-2181, 800-826-1278; www.thegrandecolonial.com; 910 Prospect St; r $255-535; P 🐾 wi-fi) Demure stepsister to La Valencia, the smartly decorated 1927 Grande Colonial exudes conservative sophistication. Great beds with floral spreads, odd-shaped rooms with Victorian-style furniture, and sunny yellow walls add to the charm. New 'hillside' rooms start at $375.

ourpick La Valencia (Map p294; ☎ 858-454-0771, 800-451-0772; www.lavalencia.com; 1132 Prospect St; r $275-575; P 💻 🐾 wi-fi) Publicity stills of Lon Cheney, Lillian Gish and Greta Garbo line the hallways of La Jolla's iconic hotel from 1926: pink-walled, Mediterranean-style, and designed by William Templeton Johnson. Its 116 rooms are rather compact (befitting the era) and you'll find more modern amenities elsewhere, but La Valencia takes the cake for evoking old Hollywood romance. Parking costs $21.

Hotel Parisi (Map p294; ☎ 858-454-1511, 877-472-7474; www.hotelparisi.com; 1111 Prospect St; r $295-525; P 💻) So many hotels call themselves 'boutique' these days, but the Parisi is an original, with 20 sumptuous rooms, contemporary style (think sands, russets and chocolate browns) and in-room massage services at the crossroads of everything. There's a new-age vibe, but it's not beyond a little humor, like a plush pineapple on the bed.

Lodge at Torrey Pines (Map p294; ☎ 858-453-4420, 800-995-4507; www.lodgetorreypines.com; 11480 N Torrey Pines Rd; r from $350; P 💻 🐾) Inspired by the architecture of Greene & Greene, the turn-of-the-20th-century Arts and Crafts masters who designed the Gamble House in Pasadena (p148), the Lodge is built in Craftsman style down to the lap joints in the cherry-wood wainscoting and the column footings of random-set stone. Discretely luxurious rooms have Mission oak-and-leather furniture à la Stickley, Tiffany-style lamps, plein-air paintings and basket-weave bathroom-floor tiling of marble. There's a stellar full-service spa and even a croquet lawn. Parking costs $22.

EATING

Budget

ourpick Porkyland (Map p294; ☎ 858-459-1708; 1030 Torrey Pines Rd; dishes $3-8; 🕒 8am-8pm) This tiny Mexican joint on the edge of central La Jolla has no atmosphere, but the burritos and fish

BATTLE OF THE RESTAURANT HEAVYWEIGHTS

George started it.

Since the 1980s, **George's at the Cove** (Map p294; ☎ 858-454-4244; 1250 Prospect St; mains $15-44; ꙮ lunch & dinner) has been on just about every list of the best restaurants in San Diego, if not all of California. Casual diners at George's Ocean Terrace Bistro and George's Bar have marveled at chef Trey Foshee's California coastal menu as much as the coastal scenery, and folks have waxed rapturous about the Euro-Cal main dining room downstairs.

And then along came Jack. **Jack's La Jolla** (Map p294; ☎ 858-456-8111; 7863 Girard Av; mains $9-42) opened in 2006 and was instantly named one of the 10 best restaurants in America. Its seven venues offer something for everybody, each executed with panache: piano bar, sidewalk café selling pizza and croissants, wine bar, grill and more. It's overseen by chef Tony di Salvo, who cut his teeth at Jean-Georges in New York City.

George's responded by keeping the bar as it was but redoing the dining room in a style so futuristic it's called **George's California Modern**, and ramping up the imagination quotient in the seasonal menu.

Which is better? We ain't gonna go there. We were taught to keep to yourself when two guys bigger than you are dukin' it out. And besides, we think a little competition makes better players of everyone.

tacos have a devoted following. The habanero burrito ($4.50) will make your taste buds roar (in a good way) and still leave you money for beer.

Girard Gourmet (Map p294; ☎ 858-454-3321; 7837 Girard Ave; dishes under $8; ꙮ 7am-9pm Mon-Sat, 7am-7pm Sun) There's everything from chicken salad to chocolate cake at this Belgian delicatessen, which makes its own pastries and serves pre-plated hot foods you select from the glass case. La Jolla's best bargain.

Harry's Coffee Shop (Map p294; ☎ 858-454-7381; 7545 Girard Ave; dishes $4-11; ꙮ 6am-3pm; Ⓥ) This classic 1960 coffee shop has tufted brown-and-gold vinyl booths and a posse of regulars from blue-haired socialites to sports celebs. The cooking is standard-issue American – pancakes, tuna melts and iceberg-lettuce salads – but it's the aura of the place that makes it special.

Midrange

Cottage (Map p294; ☎ 858-454-8409; 7702 Fay Ave; mains breakfast $7-10, lunch $10-14, dinner $11-20; ꙮ breakfast & lunch daily, dinner in summer; Ⓥ) Shhh! Don't tell anybody that the buttermilk coffee cake, crab Benedict, fish tacos and granola-crusted mahimahi make this place a local favorite. It's crowded enough as it is, especially on weekends for brunch.

My Place (Map p294; ☎ 858-454-3535; 7777 Girard Ave; mains lunch $8-17, dinner $13-20; ꙮ lunch daily, dinner Tue-Sat) Francophiles love this casual sidewalk eatery that serves Cal-French café cuisine,

including *moules mariniére* (mussels in white wine) with hand-cut fries, grilled sardines with lemon-pesto, steak-frites, and blue-corn-battered calamari.

Trattoria Acqua (Map p294; ☎ 858-454-0709; 1298 Prospect St; mains lunch $10-18, dinner $17-35) Set into the hillside with a variety of spaces laid out like a treehouse, Acqua serves scrumptious Northern Italian cuisine.

Roppongi (Map p294; ☎ 858-551-5252; 875 Prospect St, La Jolla; tapas $10-25, mains $18-32; ꙮ 11:30am-9:30pm) Tapas-style Asian-fusion really shines at this gorgeous eatery with clever lighting that makes everyone look good. The Polynesian crab stack, piled high and tossed at table, is a killer choice, and the ahi (yellowfin) tuna with watermelon a surprising flavor bomb. Great wines and sakes, too.

Top End

Nine-Ten (Map p294; ☎ 858-964-5400; 910 Prospect St; mains lunch $9-14, dinner $21-34; ꙮ breakfast, lunch & dinner) Modern art adorns the walls at this sleek, understated downtowner that serves up-to-the-minute contemporary cuisine like striped bass and Hudson Valley duck. It's also the only morning-till-night restaurant in La Jolla. The $24 three-course lunch is a steal. Great burgers, too.

Marine Room (Map p294; ☎ 858-459-7222; 2000 Spindrift Dr; mains $27-42; ꙮ dinner daily) When money is no object and you want high-drama cooking and views, book a sunset table at this fancy dining room outside the town center. You'll feast on highly stylized contemporary-fusion meats and seafood, while waves splash against the window at high tide. Lounge menu too (from 4pm).

Tapénade (Map p294; ☎ 858-551-7500; 7612 Fay Ave; mains lunch $13-18, dinner $30-36; ⏱ lunch Mon-Fri, dinner daily) Foodies thrill for the brilliant, sunny flavors of Tapénade, San Diego's finest for Provençal French (think ratatouille and wine reductions, not potatoes and cream-based sauces). Consistently voted one of San Diego's top restaurants, Tapénade dazzles with its inspired seasonal French cuisine and diet-busting desserts. Gourmets on a budget should try the two-course lunch for $20 or the three-course sunset dinner for $30 (served 5:30pm to 6:30pm Sunday to Thursday).

DRINKING & ENTERTAINMENT
Bars & Clubs
The bulk of the bars in La Jolla are clustered around Prospect St and Girard Ave downtown.

La Jolla Brewhouse (Map p294; ☎ 858-456-6279; 7536 Fay Ave) Escape from the madding crowds of Downtown, and watch the game, down a pint and listen to live music at this off-the-beaten-path local hangout. Look for wood upon wood upon wood, and indoor-outdoor seating.

Comedy Store (Map p294; ☎ 858-454-9176; 916 Pearl St) One of the area's most established comedy venues, the Comedy Store also serves meals, drinks and barrels of laughs. Expect a cover charge ($15 to $20 on weekends with a two-drink minimum).

Cendio (Map p294; ☎ 858-454-9664; www.cendiolajolla .com; 909 Prospect St, 2nd fl) Skip the Hard Rock Cafe and head next door to this Latin-fusion restaurant and lounge, with DJs on weekends.

La Sala (Map p294; ☎ 858-454-0771; La Valencia Hotel, 1132 Prospect St) For civilized cocktails or Sunday afternoon Bloody Marys, visit the romantic, ocean-view lobby bar of La Valencia Hotel, which becomes a piano lounge on Friday and Saturday evenings.

Karl Strauss Brewery (Map p294; ☎ 858-551-2739; cnr Wall St & Herschel Ave) A branch of the downtown microbrewery (p312).

Coffeehouses
Pannikin (Map p294; ☎ 858-454-5453; 7467 Girard Ave, La Jolla; ⏱ 7am-8pm) A few blocks from the water, this beach-shack of a café with generous balcony is popular for its Italian espresso

and Mexican chocolate, and occasional live music.

Living Room Coffeehouse (Map p294; ☎ 858-459-1187; 1010 Prospect St, La Jolla; ⏱ 6am-midnight) Check your email and munch on sandwiches and pastries at the La Jolla branch of the popular Old Town café (p311).

Classical Music
La Jolla Symphony & Chorus (Map p294 ☎ 619-534-4637; www.lajollasymphony.com) holds quality concerts at UCSD's **Mandeville Auditorium** from October to June.

SHOPPING
La Jolla's skirt-and-sweater crowd pays retail for cashmere sweaters and expensive tchotchkes Downtown: paintings, sculpture and decorative items, and small boutiques fill the gaps between Talbot's, Banana Republic, Ralph Lauren, Jos A Bank and Armani Exchange.

The **Art & Design Building** (7661 Girard Ave) is one-stop shopping for art, furniture and adventurous textiles from a half-dozen galleries and studios.

Mall shoppers: make a bee line for **University Towne Centre** (UTC; Map p287; ☎ 858-546-8858; 4545 La Jolla Village Dr), east of I-5; anchor stores include Nordstrom, Macy's and Sears.

SAN DIEGO NORTH COAST

Like pearls on a strand, a handful of small beach towns extends northward from La Jolla. 'North County', as locals call it, begins with pretty Del Mar and continues through low-key Solana Beach, Encinitas and Carlsbad (home of Legoland), before hitting Oceanside, largely a bedroom community for Camp Pendleton Marine Base.

North County's coast evokes the San Diego of 40 years ago, even if inland development, especially east of I-5, has created giant bedroom communities for San Diego and Orange Counties. The beaches are terrific, and the small seaside towns are great for a few days' soaking up the laid-back SoCal scene, working on your tan and catching up on your reading while watching the sun glisten on the Pacific.

All that, and only about a half-hour's drive from downtown San Diego. Will wonders never cease?

SAN DIEGO COUNTY

Getting There & Around

N Torrey Pines Rd from La Jolla is the most scenic approach from the south. Heading north along the coast, S21 changes its name from Camino del Mar to Coast Hwy 101 to Old Hwy 101. If you're in a hurry or headed out of town, the faster I-5 parallels it to the east. Traffic can snarl everywhere during rush hour and race or fair season when heading toward Del Mar Racetrack.

Bus 101 departs from University Towne Centre and follows the coastal road to Oceanside, while bus 310 operates express service up I-5; for information call the **North County Transit District** (NCTD; ☎ 760-966-6500; www.gonctd.com). The NCTD also operates the *Coaster* commuter train, which originates in San Diego, and makes stops in Solana Beach, Encinitas, Carlsbad and Oceanside. All NCTD buses and trains have bike racks. Greyhound buses stop at Oceanside and San Diego, but nowhere in between.

DEL MAR

pop 4400

The ritziest of North County's seaside suburbs, with a Tudor aesthetic that somehow doesn't feel out of place, Del Mar boasts good (if pricey) restaurants, unique galleries, high-end boutiques and a horse-racing track, which is also the site of the annual county fair. Downtown Del Mar (sometimes called 'the village') extends for about a mile along Camino del Mar. At its hub, where 15th St crosses Camino del Mar, the tastefully designed Del Mar Plaza shopping center has restaurants, boutiques and upper-level terraces that look out to sea.

Sights & Activities

At the beach end of 15th St, **Seagrove Park** abuts the beach and overlooks the ocean. This little stretch of well-groomed beachfront lawn is a community hub and perfect for a picnic.

The **Del Mar Racetrack & Fairgrounds** (Map p295; ☎ 858-755-1141; www.delmarracing.com; admission from $5; ⊙ season mid-Jul–early Sep) was founded in 1937 by a prestigious group including Bing Crosby and Jimmy Durante. The lush gardens and pink, Mediterranean-style architecture are a visual delight.

Brightly colored hot-air balloons are a trademark of the skies above Del Mar, on the northern fringe of the metropolitan area. For flights, contact **California Dreamin'** (☎ 800-373-3359; www.californiadreamin.com; per person from $198), which also serves Temecula (p372).

Sleeping

Rooms in Del Mar in summer aren't cheap. For the best rates, stay a half-mile south of the town center at one of the first two properties listed here.

Clarion Del Mar (Map p295; ☎ 858-755-9765, 800-453-4411; www.delmarinn.com; 720 Camino Del Mar; r $135-190; P ☐ ☎ ❄ wi-fi) This well-kept, 81-room hotel tries hard to please with very helpful staff, new pool, large-ish rooms (many with balconies, kitchens or bathroom vanities with granite countertops), Victorian-style furniture, and continental breakfast delivered to your room. There's afternoon tea, too.

Best Western Stratford Inn (Map p295; ☎ 858-755-1501, 800-446-7229; www.pacificahost.com; 710 Camino Del Mar; r $150-244; P ☐ ☎ ❄ wi-fi) The sprawling Stratford has large, handsome rooms, many with new carpeting and bathroom fixtures, lots of wood in its construction, a spa for foot and body treatments, laundry facilities and two pools. Some units have kitchenettes and distant ocean views.

L'Auberge Del Mar Resort & Spa (Map p295; ☎ 858-259-1515, 800-553-1336; www.laubergedelmar.com; 1540 Camino Del Mar; r $350-540; P ☐ ☎ ❄ wi-fi) Rebuilt in the 1990s on the grounds of the historic Hotel del Mar, where 1920s Hollywood celebrities once frolicked, L'Auberge continues a tradition of European-style elegance with luxurious linens, a spa and lovely grounds. It feels so intimate and the service is so individual, you'd never know there are 120 rooms.

Eating

Café Del Mar (Map p295; ☎ 858-481-1133; 1247 Camino Del Mar; mains lunch $8-13, dinner $9-21; Ⓥ) Dine in the courtyard, beneath a coral tree, on main-sized salads (try the warm chicken salad with grilled onions and feta), pizza from the wood-fired oven, and classics like pan-seared scallops and steak-frites. Lots of veggie choices, too.

Bully's (Map p295; ☎ 858-755-1660; 1404 Camino del Mar; mains $9-28; ⊙ lunch & dinner) If you find Del Mar is just too…*too*, escape to this assiduously local steakhouse serving antibiotic- and hormone-free beef in a red-leatherette booth and stained-glass setting.

Americana Restaurant (Map p295; ☎ 858-794-6838; 1454 Camino del Mar; mains breakfast & lunch $7-12, dinner $15-26; ⊙ breakfast & lunch daily, dinner Tue-Sat) This quietly chichi and much-loved local landmark serves a diverse lineup of regional American cuisine, including some dishes you may not have thought of: cheese grits to chicken Reubens, sesame salmon on succotash to seared duck breast with Israeli couscous, all amid checkerboard linoleum floors, giant windows and homey wainscoting.

Jake's Del Mar (Map p295; ☎ 858-755-2002; 1660 Coast Blvd; mains lunch $9-14, dinner $18-32; ◷ lunch Tue-Sun, dinner daily) Head to Jake's for beachside drinks and half-price appetizers from 4pm to 6pm weekdays and 2:30pm to 4:30pm on Saturday. The view's great, the atmosphere chic and the food imaginative, like heart of palm salad, poke rolls and lemongrass beef tenderloin.

Sbicca (Map p295; ☎ 858-481-1001; 215 15th St; most mains lunch $11-17, dinner $20-37; ◷ lunch & dinner) Multiple-award-winning, family-owned contemporary California bistro cooks up flavorful combinations, such as banana-leaf-wrapped salmon paella or maple-roasted pork prime rib. At lunch, inventive salads and sandwiches take center stage. Make reservations for the mod dining room or patio.

Head to **Del Mar Plaza** (Map p295; 1555 Camino Del Mar) to pick up groceries and sandwiches for the beach at **Harvest Ranch Market** (☎ 858-847-0555; ◷ 8am-9pm). Or check out the rooftop patio and its upscale restaurants for North County's best vantage points, especially at sunset – **Il Fornaio** (☎ 858-755-8876; mains $11-20) for pizzas, pastas and salads; **Epazote** (☎ 858-259-9966; mains lunch $10-14, dinner $16-24) serving flavorful Southwestern-Asian fusion; **Pacifica Del Mar** (☎ 858-792-0476; mains lunch $10-18, dinner $23-34) with fresh seafood and inventive preparations (arrive by 6pm for two-course prix-fixe menu).

SOLANA BEACH
pop 13,500
Solana Beach is the next town north from Del Mar – it's not quite as posh, but it has good beaches and the **Cedros Design District** (Cedros Ave), which has unique home-furnishings stores, art and architecture studios, antiques shops and handcrafted-clothing boutiques. For camping and travel gear, stop by **Adventure 16** (Map p295; ☎ 858-755-7662; 143 S Cedros Ave, Suite M).

The **Belly Up Tavern** (Map p295; ☎ 858-481-8140; www.bellyup.com; 143 S Cedros Ave; cover charge $5-40) is a converted warehouse and bar that consistently books good bands from jazz to funk. Its

Wild Note Café (Map p295; ☎ 858-259-7310; 143 S Cedros Ave; mains lunch $6-12, dinner $12-20; ◷ lunch daily, dinner Tue-Sun) serves great pub food.

Order at the counter and sit outside at this all-veg **Zinc Café** (Map p295; ☎ 858-793-5436; 132 S Cedros Ave; mains $3-9; ◷ 7am-5pm; Ⓥ), which serves breakfasts, salads, vegetarian chili and pizza good enough to satisfy all but the most hardcore carnivores. Daily cake selections too.

Tony's Jacal (Map p295; ☎ 858-755-2274; 621 Valley Ave; mains $7-16; ◷ lunch Mon-Sat, dinner daily, closed Tue early Sep–mid-Jul) In business since 1946 (current building from the '60s), Tony's has rough-hewn wood beams, dark wood paneling, icy-delicious margaritas and some of North County's best traditional Mexican. Make reservations for dinner. (Valley Ave goes north of Via de la Valle, just west of I-5.)

CARDIFF-BY-THE-SEA
pop 12,000
Shortened to 'Cardiff' by most, this stretch of restaurants, surf shops and new age–style businesses along the Pacific Coast Hwy is good for surfing and is popular with a laid-back crowd, though it's losing ground to ever-growing shopping centers along the main drag, San Elijo Ave, one block east of the coast highway. The nearby **San Elijo Lagoon** (Map p295; ☎ 760-436-3944; www.sanelijo.org) is a 1000-acre ecological preserve popular with bird-watchers for its herons, coots, terns, ducks, egrets and more than 250 other species. A 7-mile network of trails leads through the area. At **Cardiff State Beach** (Map p295; www.parks.ca.gov; ◷ 7am-sunset; Ⓟ), just south of Cardiff-by-the-Sea, the surf break on the reef is mostly popular with long boarders, but it gets very good at low tide with a big north swell. Parking costs $6. A little further north, **San Elijo State Beach** has good winter waves.

Sleeping & Eating
San Elijo State Beach Campground (Map p295; ☎ 760-753-5091; reservations 800-444-7275; tent/RV sites in summer from $25/35) Overlooks the surf at the end of Birmingham Dr.

Ki's Restaurant (Map p295; ☎ 760-436-5236; 2591 S Coast Hwy 101; mains breakfast $5-8, lunch $7-11, dinner $9-21; ◷ 8am-9pm) A great indie café and a hub of activity, Ki's makes awesome smoothies, healthy burgers and salads; there's also a great 2nd-floor ocean view. Live music Friday nights.

Trattoria Positano (Map p295; ☎ 760-632-0111; 2171 San Elijo Ave; mains $14-29; ☺ lunch Mon-Sat, dinner daily) White-tablecloth Italian cooking and only partially obstructed ocean views in a mom-and-pop storefront. The garlicky tomato sauce for your bread is addictive, as is pasta with crabmeat and asparagus.

ENCINITAS
pop 58,500

Peaceful Encinitas has a decidedly down-to-earth vibe and a laid-back beach-town main street, perfect for a day trip or a weekend escape. Yogi Paramahansa Yoganada founded his **Self-Realization Fellowship Retreat & Hermitage** (Map p295) here in 1937, and the town has been a magnet for holistic healers and natural-lifestyle seekers ever since. The gold lotus domes of the hermitage – conspicuous on South Coast Hwy 101 – mark the southern end of Encinitas and the turn-out for **Swami's Beach**, a powerful reef break surfed by territorial locals. The fellowship's compact but lovely **Meditation Garden** (Map p295; 215 K St; ☺ 9am-5pm Tue-Sat, 11am-5pm Sun) has wonderful ocean vistas, a stream and koi pond.

The heart of Encinitas lies north of the hermitage between E and D Sts. Apart from outdoor cafés, bars, restaurants and surf shops, the town's main attraction is **La Paloma Theater** (Map p295; ☎ 760-436-7469; 471 S Coast Hwy 101), built in 1928. La Paloma shows current movies nightly.

Approximately 80% of all the poinsettias sold worldwide originate in commercial flower farms in the inland hills, most notably **Paul Ecke Poinsettia Ranch** (Map p295; ☎ 760-753-1134; www.ecke.com; P ☺), established in 1923. In December there's an enormous poinsettia display at the ranch, and later its 50 acres burst into bloom with flowers. Try to visit in early spring (March to early May), when ranunculuses create a rainbow of color (it's a great place to photograph kids). Call for directions.

The 30-acre **Quail Botanical Gardens** (Map p295; ☎ 760-436-3036; www.qbgardens.com; 230 Quail Gardens Drive; adult/child/senior $10/5/7; ☺ 9am-5pm; P ☺) has a large collection of California native plants and flora of regions of the world, including Australia and Central America. There are special activities in the children's garden (10am Tuesday to Thursday); check the website for a schedule. From I-5, go east on Encinitas Blvd to Quail Gardens Dr.

Sleeping & Eating

There's a strip of lodgings at the north end of the town center, along Encinitas Blvd and its continuation, B St (west of Coast Hwy 101).

Moonlight Beach Motel (Map p295; ☎ 760-753-0623, 800-323-1259; www.moonlightbeachmotel.com; 233 2nd St; r incl breakfast $115-150; P wi-fi) Upstairs rooms have private decks and partial ocean views at this mom-and-pop motel, 1½ blocks from the sea. Furnishings could use upgrading, but rooms are clean and quiet, and all have kitchens.

Best Western Encinitas Inn & Suites (Map p295; ☎ 760-942-7455, 866-326-4648; www.bwencinitas.com; 85 Encinitas Blvd; r incl breakfast $140-200; P ☐ ☺ wi-fi) If you wear nail polish and white pants, you'll be better off at this hotel, a few minutes on foot from the sand. It has all modern conveniences and recently renovated furniture, carpet and bathrooms. Some rooms have ocean or park views.

Swami's Café (Map p295; ☎ 760-944-0612; 1163 S Coast Hwy 101; mains $3-10; ☺ 7am-8pm; V ☺) For breakfast burritos, multigrain pancakes, stir-frys, salads, smoothies and three-egg *ohm*-lettes (sorry, we couldn't resist), you can't beat Swami's. Vegetarians will be happy too. Most seating is on an umbrella-covered patio.

El Callejon (Map p295; ☎ 760-634-2793; 345 S Coast Hwy 101; mains $5-23) Raucous, fun local favorite Mexican joint at the north end of the town center. The menu is as long as the phone book of a small village, and would take you over two years of trying a different tequila every day to go through their tequila list.

Jamroc 101 (Map p295; ☎ 760-436-3162; 101 N Coast Hwy 101; mains $8-16; ☺ lunch & dinner) It's little more than a roadside stand, but what a roadside stand! An island paint job and the obligatory reggae soundtrack make it as bright and sunny inside as out, the better to enjoy jerk chicken and crispy fried plantains. It's just north of the main drag through the town center.

Trattoria I Trulli (Map p295; ☎ 760-943-6800; 830 S Coast Hwy 101; mains $9-20) Country-style seating indoors and great people watching on the sidewalk. Just one taste of the homemade gnocchi, ravioli or lasagna, salmon in brandy mustard sauce or pollo 101 (chicken stuffed with cheese, spinach and artichokes in mushroom sauce), and you'll know why this mom-and-pop Italian trattoria is always packed. Reservations recommended.

Q'ero (Map p295; ☎ 760-753-9050; 540 S Coast Hwy 101; mains lunch $7-15, dinner $19-26; ⏰ lunch & dinner Tue-Sat) The flavors of Peru tempt from this atmospheric storefront. Try small plates like *ceviche* or *papa rellena* (potato inside ground beef), or mains like *lomo saltado* of Kobe beef or *aji gallina* (chicken in toasted walnut and chili sauce). Reservations recommended at dinner.

CARLSBAD
pop 78,500

Most visitors come to Carlsbad for Legoland and head right back out, and that's too bad because they've missed the charming, intimate downtown with shopping, dining and beaching. It's bordered by I-5 and Carlsbad Blvd, which run north–south and are connected by Carlsbad Village Dr running east–west. The **Visitor Information Center** (Map p295; ☎ 760-434-6093; www.carlsbadca.org; 400 Carlsbad Village Dr) is housed in the original 1887 Santa Fe train depot.

Carlsbad came into being with the railroad in the 1880s. John Frazier, an early homesteader, sank a well and found water that had a high mineral content, supposedly identical to that of spa water in Karlsbad, Bohemia (now the Czech Republic). He built a grand spa hotel, which prospered until the 1930s. That Queen Anne–style building is now **Neiman's Restaurant & Bar** (Map p295; ☎ 760-729-4131; 2978 Carlsbad Blvd), though there are better restaurants in town.

If you've come looking for Carlsbad Caverns, you're outta luck. Those are in New Mexico.

Sights & Activities
LEGOLAND CALIFORNIA

Modeled after the original Legoland in Denmark, **Legoland California** (Map p295; ☎ 760-918-5346; www.lego.com/legoland/california; 1 Legoland Dr; adult/child $57/44; ⏰ 10am-5pm; Ⓟ ♿) is an enchanting fantasy environment built entirely of those little colored plastic building blocks that many of us grew up with. Highlights include **Miniland**, in which the skylines of major metropolitan cities have been spectacularly recreated entirely of Lego. At **Water Works**, kids play with water and music. There's also face-painting, boat rides and several roller coasters scaled down for kids. Compared with some of the bigger, flashier parks, such as Disneyland and SeaWorld, it's all rather low-key and far

less commercial – though there are plenty of opportunities to buy Lego. At least it sparks creativity. The park is best for pre-adolescent kids. If you have toddlers, pick up the brochure '*What to do When You're Two*' for age-appropriate activities.

From I-5, take the Legoland/Cannon Rd exit. From downtown Carlsbad or downtown San Diego, take the *Coaster* to Carlsbad Village Station, from where bus 344 goes straight to the park.

Check the website for further details on extended hours in July and August, and closures from September to May; opening hours can vary hugely during these months. Parking costs $10.

CARLSBAD RANCH

The 50-acre flower fields of **Carlsbad Ranch** (Map p295; ☎ 760-431-0352; http://visit.theflowerfields .com; adult/child $9/5; ⏰ 9am-6pm early Mar–mid-May) are ablaze in a sea of carmine, saffron and the snow-white blossom of ranunculuses. The fields are two blocks east of I-5; take the Palomar Airport Rd exit.

BATIQUITOS LAGOON

One of the last remaining tidal wetlands in California, Batiquitos Lagoon separates Carlsbad from Encinitas. A self-guided tour lets you explore area plants, including the prickly pear cactus, coastal sage scrub and eucalyptus trees, as well as lagoon birds, such as the great heron and the snowy egret. One of the artificial islands in the lagoon is a nesting site for the California least tern and the western snowy plover, both endangered species. You can hike the reserve anytime, but stop by the **Nature Center** (☎ 931-0800; www .batiquitosfoundation.org; ⏰ noon-4pm Wed-Fri, 10am-2pm Sat & Sun) if it's open.

OTHER ATTRACTIONS

Take a thrilling open-cockpit ride in a 1920s biplane with **Barnstorming Adventures** (☎ 760-438-7680, 800-759-5667; www.barnstorming.com; 2016 Palomar Airport Rd; flights from $199).

On the ground, **K1 Speed** (Map p295; ☎ 760-929-2225; www.k1speed.com; 14-lap race $20; ⏰ 11am-7pm Sun, 11am-9pm Mon, 11am-10pm Tue-Thu, 11am-11pm Fri, 10am-11pm Sat) fills your need for speed with indoor karting (electric drag racing). They supply all equipment including helmet and 'head socks'. It's in an office park east of I-5; call for directions.

Slow down with alternative-health guru Deepak Chopra, who leads seminars on mind-body medicine, complemented by specialized spa treatments, at the **Chopra Center** (Map p295; ☎ 760-494-1600, 888-424-6772; www.chopra.com) at La Costa Resort & Spa (below).

The **Museum of Making Music** (Map p295; ☎ 760-438-5996, 877-551-9776; www.museumofmakingmusic.com; 5790 Armada Dr; adult/child $5/3; ☺ 10am-5pm Tue-Sun) has historical exhibits and listening stations of 450 instruments; call for directions.

Carlsbad's long, sandy **beaches** are great for walking and searching for seashells. Good access is from Carlsbad Blvd, two blocks south of Carlsbad Village Dr, where there's a boardwalk, rest rooms and free parking.

Carlsbad is an important center for golf; some major equipment manufacturers are based here including Titleist and Taylor Made. The Four Seasons Aviara and La Costa resorts (below) both have landmark golf courses. A new municipal course has also recently opened, the 6850-yard **Crossings at Carlsbad** (☎ 760-444-1800; www.thecrossingsatcarlsbad.com; 5800 the Crossings Dr).

Sleeping

South Carlsbad State Park Campground (Map p295; ☎ 760-438-3143, reservations 800-444-7275; RV & campsites $35; ℗) Three miles south of town, this campground has over 200 tent and RV sites.

Motel 6 (Map p295; ☎ 760-434-7135; www.motel6 .com; 1006 Carlsbad Village Dr; r $60; ☝) Cheap, no-frills lodging on the outer reaches of Carlsbad Village (a rarity). It's pet-friendly, and local calls are free.

Best Western Beach View Lodge (Map p295; ☎ 760-729-1151; www.beachviewlodge.com; 3180 Carlsbad Blvd; s/d incl breakfast $165/180; ℗ ⊠ wi-fi) Many of the 41 motel-style rooms at this U-shaped property around a small pool and hot-tub have balconies with partial ocean views. Spacious suites (from $210) have sleep sofas. Our favorite part, though, is the Craftsman-style, ocean-view breakfast room.

Carlsbad Inn Beach Resort (Map p295; ☎ 760-434-7020, 800-235-3939; www.carlsbadinn.com; 3075 Carlsbad Blvd; r $205-290; ℗ ⊠ ☝) A faux-Tudor upper-end-tourist-class hotel and time-share property on the beachfront, this inn has oodles of activities for kids, from ceramics to ping-pong tourneys.

La Costa Resort & Spa (☎ 760-438-9111, 800-729-4772; www.lacosta.com; Costa Del Mar Rd; r from $285; ℗ ⊠ ⊠ ☝ wi-fi) A splurge-worthy luxury resort, La Costa offers a sprawling, white-washed 800-room campus overlooking Batiquitos Lagoon. It's got two PGA golf courses, excellent children's programs including pools with multiple slides, nursery and educational programming, venues for grownups including the stunning spa and Chopra Center (left), lovely restaurants and a touch of Hollywood history. Check out their discounted packages.

Four Seasons Aviara Map p295; ☎ 760-603-6800, 800-332-3442; www.fourseasons.com/aviara; 7100 Four Seasons Point; r from $395; ℗ ⊠ ⊠ wi-fi) From the fresh-cut orchid in your bathroom to the attendant who brings around cups of water at the gym, this tippy-top resort offers superb service and top-flight amenities, golf, tennis and more. The Argyle steakhouse is worth a trip by itself. Aviara looks out over Batiquitos Lagoon and offers discounted packages. Parking costs $28.

Eating

Fidel's Norte (☎ 760-729-0903; 3003 Carlsbad Blvd; mains $6-15; ☺ lunch & dinner; ☝) Heavy wood booths inside and wrought-iron patio furniture are the backdrop for Carlsbad's Mexican restaurant of record. La Pachanga lets you sample Cal-Mex classic appetizers, or create your own *combinación*. Sure, it's touristy, but locals like it too.

Pizza Port (☎ 760-720-7007; 571 Carlsbad Village Dr; pizzas $7-20; ☺ 11am-11pm; ⓥ ☝) Head here for Carlsbad's best pies (the 'Carlsbad' has pesto, mesquite grilled chicken and artichoke hearts, and there's a list of 'anti-wimpy gourmet pizzas') and beer brewed on-site.

Le Passage (☎ 760-729-7097; 2961 State St; mains lunch $8-16, dinner $16-28; ☺ lunch Tue-Fri, dinner Tue-Sun) Escape from the beach fray at this country French bistro. There's a *rustique* interior and cozy back patio on which to enjoy baked brie or lavender-roasted chicken.

Also check out the restaurants at La Costa Resort & Spa (left) and Four Seasons Aviara (above).

Shopping

Big-name retailers, such as Donna Karan and Kenneth Cole, have outlets at the **Carlsbad Company Stores** (☎ 760-804-9000, 888-790-7467; Paseo del Norte; ☺ 10am-8pm). Take I-5 to Palomar Airport Rd; go east to Paseo del Norte and turn north.

OCEANSIDE

pop 175,000

Home for many of the employees who work at giant Camp Pendleton Marine Base on the town's northern border, Oceanside has a huge military presence. So despite its attractive natural setting, Oceanside feels more functional than its coastal neighbors. Amtrak, Greyhound, the *Coaster* and MTS buses all stop at the **Oceanside Transit Center** (Map p295; 235 S Tremont St).

Stop in at the **California Welcome Center** (Map p295; ☎ 760-721-1101, 800-350-7873; www.oceanside chamber.com, www.californiawelcomecenter.org; 928 N Coast Hwy; ☼ 9am-5pm), which has helpful staff, to get coupons for local attractions, as well as maps and information for the San Diego area and the entire state.

Sights & Activities

The wooden **Oceanside Pier** extends more than 1900ft out to sea. Bait-and-tackle shops rent poles. Two major surf competitions – the West Coast Pro-Am and the National Scholastic Surf Association (NSSA) – take place near the pier in June.

See a history of surf contests at the wonderful **California Surf Museum** (☎ 760-721-6876; www.surfmuseum.org; 223 N Coast Hwy; donations welcome; ☼ 10am-4pm). Displays change annually and have included topics from legendary surfers like Duke Kahanamoku and surfing's influence on pop culture. At the time of writing, the museum was due to move to its new location at 312 Pier View Way in summer 2008.

Little remains from the 1880s, when the new Santa Fe coastal railway came through Oceanside, but a few buildings designed by Irving Gill and Julia Morgan still stand. The Welcome Center has a pamphlet describing a self-guided history walk.

At the northern end of the waterfront, the extensive Oceanside Harbor provides slips for hundreds of boats. **Helgren's** (☎ 760-722-2133; www.helgrensportfishing.com; 315 Harbor Dr S) leads a variety of charter trips for sportfishing (from $42 per half day) and whale-watching (adult/child costs $25/15).

Founded in 1798, **Mission San Luis Rey de Francia** (☎ 760-757-3651; www.sanluisrey.org; 4050 Mission Ave, Hwy 76; admission $5; ☼ 10am-4pm) was the largest California mission and the most successful in recruiting Native American converts. At one point some 3000 neophytes lived and worked here. After the Mexican government secular-

ized the missions, San Luis fell into ruin; the adobe walls of the church, from 1811, are the only original parts left. Inside are displays on work and life in the mission, with some original religious art and artifacts. The mission is 4 miles inland.

Surfers can rent equipment at **Action Beach Board Shop** (Map p295; ☎ 760-722-7101; www.action beach.com; 310 Mission Ave; surfboards 2hr/full day $10/20, wet suits $5/10). **Team Wahine Surfing School** (☎ 760-439-5679; www.teamwahine.com; 260 Harbor Dr S;) gives year-round lessons (one/two persons costs $70/65 for the first hour, including gear) and has surf camps for kids.

Sleeping & Eating

Oceanside Marina Suites (Map p295; ☎ 760-722-1561, 800-252-2033; www.omihotel.com; 2008 Harbor Dr; r incl breakfast $135-200; P wi-fi) Inexpensive national chains abound in Oceanside, but this friendly property is locally owned. It sits on a peninsula with the harbor on one side and the ocean on the other. Huge variety of rooms, suites (more expensive) and furnishings, around a pool and courtyard. Look for internet specials.

Beach Break Café (Map p295; ☎ 760-439-6355; 1902 S Coast Hwy; mains under $8; ☼ breakfast & lunch; P) Fuel up on eggs, sandwiches, tacos and salads at this surfers' diner on the east side of the road in a small shopping center.

Kealani's (Map p295; ☎ 760-722-5642; 207 N Coast Hwy; mains $4-8; ☼ 11am-8pm Mon, Tue & Thu-Sat, 11am-6pm Wed;) Traditional Hawaiian plate lunches, such as kalua pig, teriyaki chicken and grilled mahimahi are the thing in this cheery storefront with booths like little grass shacks.

101 Café (Map p295; ☎ 760-722-5220; 631 S Coast Hwy; most mains $4-10; ☼ breakfast, lunch & dinner; P) This tiny 1928 streamline moderne diner serves the classics: omelettes, burgers etc. If you're lucky, you'll catch the owner and can quiz him about local history.

Ruby's Diner (☎ 760-433-7829; 1 Oceanside Pier; most mains $7-14; ☼ breakfast, lunch & dinner;) This mid-priced '50s-style diner has good burgers and milkshakes, big breakfasts and a full bar. Yes, it's a chain, but it's right at the end of the pier.

AROUND SAN DIEGO

JULIAN

pop 3000

This mountain hamlet (elevation 4450ft/1300m), with a three-block main street, is a favorite getaway for city folk for its 1870s streetscape, gold mining history and famous apple pies. Although it's near the geographical center of San Diego County, by the time you reach it from anywhere else it really feels like you've been on a journey.

Prospectors (many Confederate veterans) first arrived here after the Civil War (1861–1865), and the discovery of gold in 1869 led to a growth spurt (to a whopping 600); mining continued for over 60 years. Later, much of the land was given over to farming, and Julian-farmed apples won prizes at world fairs; today there are about 17,000 trees. Woe be it to the visitor who does not take home a pie, or at least do some taste-testing.

Autumn is prime time. Shops and stands sell fresh local apples (inquire locally about child-friendly 'pick-your-own' opportunities). It's especially busy during the Grape Stomp and Apple Days Festivals (early September and early October, respectively). Look for snow in winter.

Orientation

Central Julian (population 300) runs along Main St. Inside Town Hall, the friendly **Chamber of Commerce** (☎ 760-765-1857; www.julianca.com; 2129 Main St; ☺ 10am-4pm) offers info, maps and brochures.

Sights & Activities

Eagle and High Peak Mine (☎ 760-765-0036; end of C St; adult/child $10/5; ☺ from 10am; P ❧) offers instructive tours of Julian's now-defunct gold mines as you go through 1000ft (nearly 300m) of tunnels and learn to pan for gold. The **Julian Pioneer Museum** (☎ 760-765-0227; 2811 Washington St; suggested donation $3; ☺ 10am-4pm Fri-Sun Apr-Nov, Sat & Sun Dec-Mar) exhibits mining equipment, period clothing, photos and Native American artifacts, and a lace collection. Weather permitting, **Doves & Desperadoes** shows take place Sundays at 1pm, 2pm and 3pm on Main St; costumed, comedic recreations of late 1800s' mining days, minus the bloodshed, cursing and real bullets.

About 3 miles north of town, **Menghini Winery** (☎ 760-765-2072; 1150 Julian Orchards Dr; ☺ 10am-4pm Mon-Fri, 10am-5pm Sat & Sun) is one of several in the area; this one offers tastings and picnic grounds. Further afield, **Lake Cuyamaca** (☎ 760-765-0515; 15027 Hwy 79; ☺ 6am-sunset, check times in Dec & Jan) is well-stocked with trout, small-mouthed bass and more,

and has boats for rent. There's a dog-friendly 3.5 mile walk around the lake. **California Wolf Center** (☎ 760-765-0030; 18457 Hwy 79; admission $8; ☺ Sat by reservation) offers 1½-hour tours including a slide show and visit with wolf packs.

Sleeping

Julian Hotel (☎ 760-765-0201, 800-734-5854; www.julianhotel.com; 2032 Main St; r from $120, cottages from $160; P ❧) In the center of town, this 1897 hostelry boasts Victorian furnishings, friendly owners and a nice complimentary breakfast. Choose from the main house or cottages. The original owners were freed slaves.

our pick **Orchard Hill Country Inn** (☎ 760-765-0290, 800-716-7242; www.orchardhill.com; 2502 Washington St; r incl breakfast $195-325; P wi-fi) This romantic, immaculately maintained B&B features a Craftsman-style main lodge and a dozen cottages on 4 wooded acres. Each designer-furnished room is different but might include Jacuzzi tub, fireplace or balcony. Full, gourmet breakfasts include house-made jams such as plum, fig or pumpkin butter.

In addition to the inns above, Julian has many small B&B's. The **Bed & Breakfast Guild** (☎ 760-765-1555, 888-675-4333; www.julianbnbguild .com; ☺ 9am-9pm) can point you to available rooms.

Eating & Drinking

Rong Branch (☎ 760-765-2265; 2722 Washington St; most mains $8-27; ☺ lunch & dinner; ❧) Apart from buffalo burgers, it's familiar country cookin' (think barbecue, steaks and chili) amid country decor. The back-room **Boar's Head Saloon** is the town's only nightspot (closing hours vary, until 11pm or midnight).

Romano's Dodge House (☎ 760-765-1003; 2718 B St; mains $8-19; ☺ dinner Thu-Mon; ❧) Home-style Italian cooking in a gold-country setting, with wood paneled walls, Franklin stove, lace curtains and Johnny Mathis piped in. Hearty main dishes (pork chops in creamy garlic sauce, zucchini parmigiana) come with a side of pasta or veggies. Pizzas also available. Reservations recommended at peak times.

Among favorite local pie bakeries, **Julian Café & Bakery** (☎ 760-765-2712; 2112 Main St; ☺ 8am-7:30pm Mon-Fri, 8am-8:30pm Sat & Sun; ❧), serves breakfast, lunch and dinner, **Julian Pie Co** (☎ 760-765-2449; 2225 Main St; ☺ 9am-5pm; ❧) makes sandwiches to go (plus cider donuts), and **Mom's** (☎ 760-765-2472; 2119 Main St; ☺ 8am-5pm Sun-Fri, 8am-6pm Sat; ❧) has an open bake-

---

DETOUR: SAN DIEGO WILD ANIMAL PARK

Take a walk on the wild side at this 1800-acre **open-range zoo** (☎ 760-747-8͡ .org; 15500 San Pasqual Valley Rd, Escondido; adult/child $28.50/$17.50, incl tram $33/ Jun–early Sep, to 5pm early Sep–mid-Jun; **P** ☻), where giraffes graze, lions laze and ... more or less freely on the valley floor. The Journey to Africa tram ferries you around the world's second-largest continent in what feels like a half-hour safari. Elsewhere, animals are in enclosures so naturalistic it's as if the humans are guests, and there's a petting krall and animal shows; pick up a map and schedule. Combination tickets with the San Diego Zoo are $59/39 per adult/child.

The park is in Escondido, about 35 miles north of downtown San Diego. Take the I-15 Fwy to the Via Rancho Parkway exit, then follow the signs. Parking costs $8. For bus information contact **North San Diego County Transit District** (☎ 619-233-3004, from northern San Diego County 800-266-6883; www.gonctd.com).

---

shop and gourmet coffees. Pie: about $3/12 per slice/whole.

Getting There & Away

Julian sits at the junction of routes 78 and 79. It's about 1¼ hours from San Diego (via I-8 east to Rte 79 north), North County (via Rte 78) or Temecula (p372 I-15 south to Rte 78 east). Rte 78 also leads you toward Borrego Springs (p368 40 minutes).

TIJUANA, MEXICO

☎ country code 52, city code 664 / pop 2 million

Rita Hayworth was discovered here. Carlos Santana began his career here. And one of the world's great culinary inventions, the Caesar salad, hails from nowhere other than – drum roll please – yes, Tijuana, that grubby, noisy, frenzied, but oh-so-tantalizing city of two million souls, just a hop, skip and a jump from San Diego.

During Prohibition in the 1920s, Tijuana (pronounced 'tee-*hwah*-na', or TJ for short) was the darling of the Hollywood crowd. These days, tequila and beer exert their siren song over college students, sailors and other revelers who descend upon the rollicking bars and nightclubs of Av Revolución (La Revo), once notorious, now merely one of the wildest streets in North America. Its curio stores overflow with kitschy souvenirs, while touts bark at every passerby from liquor stores, low-priced pharmacies and strip clubs.

But Tijuana is no longer beholden exclusively to gringo tourists. In the wake of the North American Free Trade Agreement, the city has nearly doubled in population over the last decade as new businesses – particularly *maquiladoras* (assembly plants) – open every month. Tijuana – now Mexico's fourth-largest city and one of its richest – boasts an increasingly sophisticated cultural scene, from music to food to academia. Still, alongside this newfound wealth remains desperate poverty, as many of the rural poor arrive in the city daily, their numbers outpacing job creation and city services.

Orientation

Downtown Tijuana (Zona Centro) is a 15-minute walk southwest of the San Ysidro (California) border crossing. It's on a grid pattern of north–south *avenidas* (avenues) and east–west *calles* (streets). Av Revolución (La Revo), the city's main tourist artery, runs through Zona Centro.

Information
EMERGENCY & MEDICAL SERVICES

Dial ☎ 066 for crime, fire and medical emergencies. If you are the victim of a crime, you can call the state government's **tourist assistance number** (☎ 078).

Central police station (Av Constitución 1616) At the corner of Calle 8a (Hidalgo) in Zona Centro.

Hospital General (☎ 684-0922; Av Centenario 10851)

INTERNET RESOURCES

www.tijuanaonline.org – official website of the Tijuana Convention & Visitors Bureau, with sights, lodging and dining suggestions, and helpful tips.

MONEY

Although the currency here is Mexican pesos (written with a dollar sign locally) everyone accepts – even prefers – US dollars (written 'dlls'), and many establishments accept credit cards. Carry small US bills or you may end up receiving change in pesos (at a poor exchange

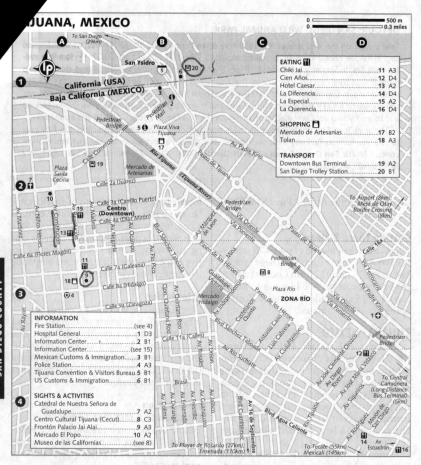

TIJUANA, MEXICO

EATING	
Chiki Jai	**11** A3
Cien Años	**12** D4
Hotel Caesar	**13** A2
La Diferencia	**14** D4
La Especial	**15** A2
La Querencía	**16** D4

SHOPPING	
Mercado de Artesanias	**17** B2
Tolan	**18** A3

TRANSPORT	
Downtown Bus Terminal	**19** A2
San Diego Trolley Station	**20** B1

INFORMATION
Fire Station.............................(see 4)
Hospital General.......................**1** D3
Information Center....................**2** B1
Information Center..................(see 15)
Mexican Customs & Immigration....**3** B1
Police Station...........................**4** A3
Tijuana Convention & Visitors Bureau.**5** B1
US Customs & Immigration..........**6** B1

SIGHTS & ACTIVITIES
Catedral de Nuestra Señora de
  Guadalupe...........................**7** A2
Centro Cultural Tijuana (Cecut)....**8** C3
Frontón Palacio Jai Alai..............**9** A3
Mercado El Popo......................**10** A2
Museo de las Californias...........(see 8)

rate). Numerous *casas de cambio* (currency-exchange houses) change money and travelers checks. Banks offer slightly better rates; most also have ATMs, generally the cheapest and most convenient solution.

TOURIST INFORMATION
Visit the following information centers:
Avenida Revolución (☎ 685-2210; ⏱ 10am-4pm Mon-Thu, 10am-7pm Fri-Sun) Between Calles 3a and 4a.
San Ysidro Border Crossing (☎ 607-3097; ⏱ 9am-6pm Mon-Thu, 9am-7pm Fri & Sat, 9am-3pm Sun) Just within Mexico.

VISAS & IMMIGRATION
US citizens or permanent residents not intending to go past the border zone (ie beyond Ensenada), or to stay in the border zone more than 72 hours, don't need a visa. All visitors, however, must bring their passport and US visa (if needed) for re-entry to the US.

Dangers & Annoyances
Officials are cracking down on petty crime, but theft, pickpocketing, short-changing, bill-padding and the 'gringo-tax' still happen. Bottom line when shopping: that $5 necklace probably isn't gold.

Driving in Tijuana can be an annoyance, car theft a danger. Don't leave anything valuable visible in your car, and park in a guarded garage or lot.

The Zona Norte, Tijuana's seedy red-light district west of Av Revolución and north of

HOT TOPIC: THE POROUS BORDER

In the 2004 satirical film *A Day without a Mexican*, a mysterious fog whisks away California's 14 million Latino residents, and chaos ensues.

The equation is simple: economic opportunity drives Mexican laborers north, and vocal opposition in the US is putting pressure on lawmakers to do something about those who have entered illegally. Decades of efforts to curb illegal immigration have led to hundreds of miles of border fence, vigilante 'Minutemen' patrolling the borders of Arizona, New Mexico and Texas, and measures in municipalities across the nation barring undocumented immigrants from obtaining drivers' licenses, educational funding and social services. And immigrants keep on coming, despite ever-greater risk to life and limb.

In 2006, attempts in the US Congress to impose tough new measures led to immigrants' rights marches in dozens of cities – the largest, in Los Angeles, topped out at an estimated 2 million; the bill failed. In 2007, Congress failed again in its attempt to tackle the problem (many say, in a more realistic manner) despite strong endorsement from President George W Bush and the national business lobby; opponents decried the measures as amnesty for illegal behavior.

Perhaps the only lasting solution will be for the Mexican economy to reach something like economic parity with the US economy, although one visit to Tijuana will tell you there's still a way to go.

Calle 1a (Artículo 123), is not recommended after dark for foreigners lacking street savvy.

Sights & Activities

Tijuana's historical sites and rowdy party scene are concentrated around Av Revolución. About half a mile southeast is Zona Río ('River District'), a more sophisticated cultural center.

LA REVO

Virtually every visitor to Tijuana has to experience at least a brief stroll up raucous **Av Revolución**, also known as 'La Revo,' between Calle 1a (Artículo 123) and Calle 8a (Hidalgo). It's a dizzying mishmash of nightclubs, street photographers with zebra-striped burros, tacky souvenir stores, restaurants from flashy to trashy, discount liquor stores and bellowing hawkers outside seedy strip bars.

If you find the sensory assault too overwhelming, the more conventional shopping street Av Constitución, parallels La Revo one block west. The colorful **Mercado El Popo** (Calle 2a & Av Constición) is a busy yet accessible market with locals selling daily needs from tamarind pods to candles and religious icons. Architecture fans may want to visit the **Catedral de Nuestra Señora de Guadalupe** (Cathedral of our Lady of Guadalupe; cnr Av Niños Héroes & Calle 2a), Tijuana's oldest church.

At the far end of La Revo, the oddly baroque art deco **Frontón Palacio Jai Alai** (Av Revolución btwn Calle 7a & Calle 8a) celebrated its 60th anniversary in 2007. For decades, this striking, block-long building hosted jai alai – kind of a hybrid between squash and lacrosse originating from Basque Country (in north Spain). The building now hosts cultural events including music and theater performances.

CENTRO CULTURAL TIJUANA (CECUT)

This aggressively modern **cultural center** (☎ 664-687-9695; www.cecut.gob.mx; Paseo de los Héroes at Av Independencia) is the city's showcase for highbrow events – concerts, theater, readings, conferences, dance recitals and more.

The **Museo de las Californias** (☎ 664-687-9641/42; admission US$2; ☽ 10am-6pm Tue-Fri, 10am-7pm Sat & Sun) provides an excellent history of Baja California from prehistoric times to the present, including the earliest Spanish expeditions, the Mission period, the Treaty of Guadalupe Hidalgo, the irrigation of the Colorado River delta and the advent of the railroad. Signage in English.

Eating

You won't have any problem finding tourist restaurants on Av Revolución; alternatively, take taxis to some of the city's best restaurants in the Zona Río and Zona Gastronómica (restaurant zone).

ZONA CENTRO

La Especial (☎ 664-685-6654; Av Revolucíon 18; mains breakfast US$5-12, lunch & dinner US$6-17; ☽ 9am-10pm Sun-Thu, 9am-11:30pm Fri & Sat) This woodsy, old-time dining room is a charming escape from the bustle of La Revo, in a shopping arcade below Hotel Lafayette. Enjoy vegetable soup (be sure to mix

> **HAIL, CAESAR!**
>
> To taste a Caesar salad at its birthplace, head to the restaurant at the venerable though shop-worn **Hotel Caesar** (☎ 685-1606; Av Revolución 827; ☯ 9am-midnight). The namesake salad will set you back $6, $8 with chicken. Wash it down with beer.

in the rice and squeeze in lime) and classics like *carne asada* and righteous tacos.

Chiki Jai (☎ 685-4955; Av Revolución 1388; mains US$9; ☯ 11am-9pm) Thanks to its Spanish/Basque seafood, the small, friendly Chiki Jai has been packed with patrons since 1947. Main courses (with soup or salad) include steak, salmon or lamb, or go for broke with seafood paella.

ZONA RIO & ZONA GASTRONOMICA

La Querencia (☎ 972-9935; Av Escuadrón 201 3110; mains US$6-16; ☯ 1pm-11pm Mon-Thu, 1pm-midnight Fri & Sat, 1-8pm Sun) The chef calls his cooking 'Baja-Med', and who are we to argue? Tacos might include oysters or marinated duck, there are sandwiches for lunchtime, and aged rib eye, duck or game main dishes. Stateside, this inventive cooking would command twice the price.

Cien Años (☎ 634-3039; Av José María Velasco 1407; mains US$12-18; ☯ 8am-11pm) One of Tijuana's temples of *alta cocina* (haute cuisine), Cien Años is worth the splurge. The chefs have dug deep into a box of ancient Mexican recipes, some going back to the Aztecs and Mayans, and have devised some unusual concoctions (how does 'spinal marrow soup' sound?). No shorts, jeans or T-shirts.

La Diferencia (☎ 634-3346; Blvd Sánchez Taboada 1061; mains US$15; ☯ noon-10:30pm Mon-Sat, noon-8pm Sun) Take a taxi to the Zona Rio for sumptuous dishes like out of *Like Water for Chocolate* (poblano pepper stuffed with beef and fruit; salmon with mango and habanero sauce) in the gracious dining room or covered patio. No tank tops or flip-flops.

Shopping

Many Americans make regular trips across the border to buy prescription drugs, which are much cheaper here. Other popular buys include leather goods, pottery, basketry, frocks, Mexican wrestler masks and, of course, tequila. Wise shoppers, especially for alcohol, will check prices at home first. Note that US Customs allows 1L per adult (over 21) to be imported duty-free. Each person returning to the USA is allowed to bring $800 worth of duty-free goods across the border.

Tolan (☎ 688-3637; Av Revolución 1471; ☯ 11am-5pm Mon-Sat) Founded by a prominent local artisan, this quirky collection of Mexican handicrafts is the most sophisticated in the town. Prices aren't cheap, but the quality's high.

Mercado de Artesanias (Plaza Viva Tijuana) This is the first big outdoor market you will encounter when coming over the border by foot. You'll find TJ's biggest concentration of souvenirs, crafts and curios, most of them mass-produced. If you see something you like, bargain for it.

Getting There & Away

Most sights in Tijuana are within an easy 20-minute walk from the border crossing. Just follow the blue and white signs reading 'Centro Downtown' through Plaza Viva Tijuana, take another pedestrian bridge across Río Tijuana and walk another couple of blocks to the northern end of Av Revolución. If you travel by taxi, be sure to take a white and green one (because these ones have meters).

BUS

Greyhound offers direct buses from San Diego to Tijuana. There are four buses daily to Tijuana; the trip takes an hour and costs $12/24 one-way/round-trip (see p316).

CAR

For day trips from the US to Tijuana, leave your car on the San Diego side. Traffic is frenetic, parking is competitive, there's likely to be a long wait to re-enter the US, and US rental car agencies don't allow their cars across the border anyway. Parking lots on the San Ysidro (USA) side of the border charge about $7.

If you do drive, Mexican law recognizes only Mexican *seguro* (car insurance). Driving in Mexico without this can land you in jail. On the US side of the border, there are many insurance offices at the Via de San Ysidro and Camino de la Plaza exits off I-5. Expect to pay a minimum of $10 to $15 per day for short stays.

TROLLEY

An easy way to reach Tijuana, the San Diego Trolley (p317) runs from downtown San Diego to San Ysidro ($3, about 30 minutes) every 15 minutes from about 5am to midnight. From the San Ysidro stop, take the pedestrian bridge over the road and go through the turnstile into Mexico.

Palm Springs & the Deserts

The desert is a land of contradictions: vast yet intimate, remote yet sophisticated, searing yet restorative. Over time you may find that what at first seemed barren and boring will transform into something of harrowing beauty: weathered peaks, subliminally erotic sand dunes, purple-tinged mountains, groves of cacti, tiny wildflowers pushing up from caramel-colored soil for their brief lives, lizards scurrying beneath colossal boulders, uncountable stars.

The Inland Empire, as locals call it, comprises Riverside County to the south and San Bernardino County to the north. The latter is the nation's largest county, at 20,105 sq miles (52,073 sq km). True, much of the drive from LA is through the sprawl-by-which-all-other-sprawl-is-measured, but once you've arrived you're really someplace special.

Palm Springs and the Coachella Valley, which stretches to the southeast, are the desert's chief draw for poolside lounging, golf, tennis and the 'it' factor. Nearby, Joshua Tree National Park is a favorite of hikers and rock climbers. Beyond the nearly two-mile-high San Jacinto Mountains, gigantic Anza-Borrego Desert State Park thrills with wide-open spaces and desolate hills. Back toward the coast, Temecula has developed a following for winemaking and a historic downtown.

Spend some time here, and you too may understand why so many find this land so magical, chic and irresistible.

HIGHLIGHTS

- Whisking 6000ft up the San Jacinto Mountains aboard the **Palm Springs Aerial Tramway** (p349)

- A nighttime mineral bath under infinite stars in **Desert Hot Springs** (p357)

- Checking out the trees and zipping up and down giant rocks at **Joshua Tree National Park** (p363)

- Marveling at Palm Springs **Modernist masterpieces** (p350)

- Watching for wildlife – and maybe even spotting a rare bighorn sheep – in **Indian** (p350) or **Tahquitz Canyons** (p352)

- Gazing at the vast expanse of desert that unfurls below you from Font's Point at **Anza-Borrego Desert State Park** (p368)

- Sipping chocolate port in **Temecula** (p372)

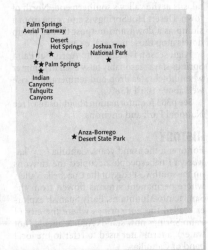

Palm Springs
Aerial Tramway
★
Desert
Hot Springs
★
Joshua Tree
National Park
★
★★ Palm Springs
★
Indian
Canyons;
Tahquitz
Canyons

★ Anza-Borrego
Desert State Park

PALM SPRINGS & COACHELLA VALLEY

The Rat Pack is back, baby, or at least its hangout is. In the 1950s and '60s, Palm Springs, some 100 miles east of LA, was the swinging getaway of Sinatra, Elvis, Liberace and dozens of other stars, partying the night away in futuristic homes built just for them. Once the Rat Pack packed it in, the 300-sq-mile Coachella Valley gave over to retirees in golf clothing and grew, well, *not* hip. That was until the mid-1990s, when a new generation latched onto the city's retro-chic charms: kidney-shaped pools, steel-and-glass bungalows, boutique hotels with vintage decor, and piano bars serving perfect martinis. In today's Palm Springs, retirees mix amiably with hipsters and a significant gay and lesbian contingent.

Around Palm Springs, hike palm-studded canyons or ski through silky snow (or both in the same day), play golf, explore museums, shop at massive malls or high-toned boutiques, sample a date milkshake, tour a windmill or straddle a fault line.

'Down Valley', as the Coachella Valley southeast of Palm Springs is called, boasts world-class golf resorts, ritzy shopping and expensive retirement homes in the cities of Rancho Mirage, Palm Desert, Indian Wells and La Quinta. Indio, America's date capital, sits at the valley's southern end. North of town, Desert Hot Springs is emerging from a slump as a down-and-outpost thanks to hip hotels atop those namesake springs.

High season is October to April, but Palm Springs stays reasonably busy even in summer when hotel rates drop and temperatures rise well above 100°F (38°C).

See p363 for information about Joshua Tree National Park and environs.

HISTORY

For over a thousand years, Cahuilla (say 'ka-wee-ya') tribespeople occupied the canyons on the southwest edge of the Coachella Valley, where permanent streams flowed from the San Jacinto Mountains. Early Spanish explorers called the hot springs where the city of Palm Springs now stands Agua Caliente (hot water), a term later used to refer to the local band of Cahuillas.

In 1876, the federal government divided the valley into a checkerboard pattern. The Southern Pacific Railroad received odd-numbered sections and the even-numbered sections were given to the Agua Caliente as their reservation. But boundaries were not established until the 1940s and by then much of the Native American land had been built on. (Tribes today are quite wealthy, though.)

Indio began as a railway construction camp and its artesian water was tapped to irrigate crops. Date palms were imported in 1890 and have become the major crop in the valley, along with citrus fruits and table grapes.

In the 1920s, Palm Springs became a winter playground for Hollywood celebrities, many of whom built mid-century modernist homes through the early 1960s. You can see many of their stars on Palm Springs' own Walk of Fame on Palm Canyon Dr. But as land grew scarce in town and golf became more of a pastime, construction of residences, hotels and resorts moved Down Valley, filling in the cities between Palm Springs and Indio, and Palm Springs went into an economic tailspin.

Thanks largely to the rediscovery of mid-century modern architecture in the mid-1990s, Palm Springs has boomed once again.

ORIENTATION

The compact downtown of Palm Springs fronts Palm Canyon Dr (Hwy 111). Here, traffic goes south on Palm Canyon Dr and north on the parallel Indian Canyon Dr. Tahquitz Canyon Way divides north from south (eg N Palm Canyon Dr and S Palm Canyon Dr) and heads east to the airport. South of the town center, Palm Canyon Dr splits: S Palm Canyon Drive continues straight on; the turnoff to the left becomes E Palm Canyon Dr, the continuation of Hwy 111. Other major thoroughfares include Sunrise Way (north–south) and Ramon Rd (east–west).

Around Palm Springs, Hwy 111 continues into the rather commercial Cathedral City and the tony Down Valley towns, where roads named for the likes of Frank Sinatra, Bob Hope, Gerald Ford and Dinah Shore take you through to upscale pleasures. From Palm Gene Autry Trail takes you no Desert Hot Springs.

INFORMATION
Bookstores
Look for large chain bookstores in the Down Valley malls and shopping centers.
Peppertree Bookstore (Map p351; ☎ 760-325-4821; www.peppertreebookstore.com; 155 S Palm Canyon Dr) Palm Springs' only in-town bookstore often hosts readings.

Internet Access
Palm Springs Public Library (Map p351; ☎ 760-322-7323; www.palmspringslibrary.org; 300 Sunrise Way; ⊙ 9am-8pm Mon & Tue, 9am-5:30pm Wed, Thu & Sat,

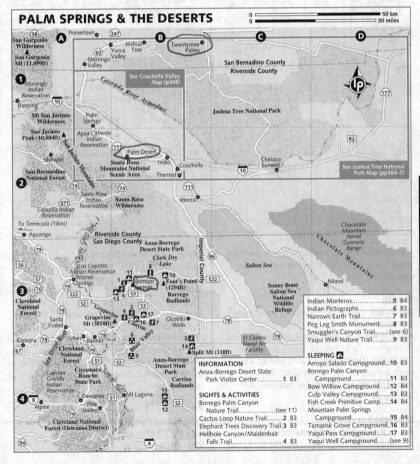

PALM SPRINGS & THE DESERTS

0 — 50 km
0 — 30 miles

San Gorgonio Wilderness
San Gorgonio Mt (11,499ft)
Pioneertown
Joshua Tree
Twentynine Palms
Yucca Valley
Morongo Valley
San Bernardino County
Riverside County
Morongo Indian Reservation
Banning
Colorado River Aqueduct
Palm Springs
See Coachella Valley Map (p348)
Joshua Tree National Park
Mt San Jacinto Wilderness
Agua Caliente Indian Reservation
San Jacinto Peak (10,804ft)
Idyllwild
Palm Desert
Santa Rosa Mountains National Scenic Area
Indio
Coachella
Thermal
Chiriaco Summit
See Joshua Tree National Park Map (pp364-5)
San Bernardino National Forest
Cahuilla Indian Reservation
Santa Rosa Indian Reservation
Santa Rosa Wilderness
Mecca
To Temecula (18mi)
Aguanga
Riverside County
San Diego County
Anza-Borrego Desert State Park
Clark Dry Lake
Imperial County
Salton Sea
Chocolate Mountain Aerial Gunnery Range
Los Coyotes Indian Reservation
Warner Springs
Borrego Springs
Font's Point (1294ft)
Borrego Badlands
Sonny Bono Salton Sea National Wildlife Refuge
Niland
Cleveland National Forest
Santa Ysabel
Grapevine Canyon
Grapevine Mt (3810ft)
Ocotillo Wells
Chocolate Mountains
Ramona
Julian
Banner
Cleveland National Forest
Cuyamaca Rancho State Park
Capitan Grande Indian Reservation
Blair Valley
Anza-Borrego Desert State Park
Carrizo Badlands
El Centro Naval Air Facility
Split Mt (110ft)
Descanso
Mt Laguna
Pine Valley
Alpine
Cleveland National Forest (Descanso District)

Indian Morteros...................5 B4
Indian Pictographs...............6 B3
Narrows Earth Trail..............7 B3
Peg Leg Smith Monument......8 B3
Smuggler's Canyon Trail......(see 6)
Yaqui Well Nature Trail..........9 B3

SLEEPING
Arroyo Salado Campground...10 B3
Borrego Palm Canyon
  Campground....................11 B3
Bow Willow Campground.......12 B4
Culp Valley Campground.......13 B3
Fish Creek Primitive Camp....14 B4
Mountain Palm Springs
  Campground....................15 B4
Tamarisk Grove Campground.16 B3
Yaqui Pass Campground.......17 B3
Yaqui Well Campground.......(see 9)

INFORMATION
Anza-Borrego Desert State
  Park Visitor Center.............1 B3

SIGHTS & ACTIVITIES
Borrego Palm Canyon
  Nature Trail....................(see 11)
Cactus Loop Nature Trail......2 B3
Elephant Trees Discovery Trail.3 B3
Hellhole Canyon/Maidenhair
  Falls Trail......................4 B3

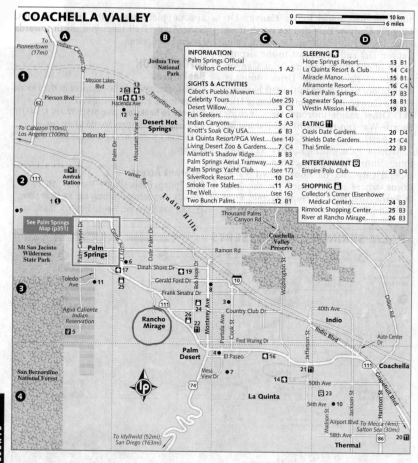

COACHELLA VALLEY

INFORMATION		
Palm Springs Official		
Visitors Center........................**1**	A2	
SIGHTS & ACTIVITIES		
Cabot's Pueblo Museum..........**2**	B1	
Celebrity Tours...................(see 25)		
Desert Willow........................**3**	C3	
Fun Seekers..........................**4**	C4	
Indian Canyons......................**5**	A3	
Knott's Soak City USA.............**6**	B3	
La Quinta Resort/PGA West....(see 14)		
Living Desert Zoo & Gardens....**7**	C4	
Marriott's Shadow Ridge...........**8**	B3	
Palm Springs Aerial Tramway.....**9**	A2	
Palm Springs Yacht Club......(see 17)		
SilverRock Resort..................**10**	D4	
Smoke Tree Stables................**11**	A3	
The Well.............................(see 16)		
Two Bunch Palms...................**12**	B1	

SLEEPING		
Hope Springs Resort................**13**	B1	
La Quinta Resort & Club..........**14**	C4	
Miracle Manor......................**15**	B1	
Miramonte Resort..................**16**	C4	
Parker Palm Springs...............**17**	B3	
Sagewater Spa......................**18**	B1	
Westin Mission Hills...............**19**	B1	
EATING		
Oasis Date Gardens.................**20**	D4	
Shields Date Gardens...............**21**	C4	
Thai Smile...........................**22**	B3	
ENTERTAINMENT		
Empire Polo Club...................**23**	D4	
SHOPPING		
Collector's Corner (Eisenhower		
Medical Center)...................**24**	B3	
Rimrock Shopping Center.........**25**	B3	
River at Rancho Mirage............**26**	B3	

10am-5:30pm Fri) Has 27 terminals with word-processing programs and free internet access. Free wi-fi with your own computer.

Media

Desert Sun Palm Springs' daily newspaper has mostly local news.

KWXY 1340AM, 98.5FM Campy Rat Pack cocktail music that matches Palm Springs' mid-century architecture.

Los Angeles Times The West Coast's most important newspaper gets delivered to Palm Springs daily.

Press-Enterprise Daily newspaper published out of Riverside, the county seat.

Medical Services

Desert Regional Medical Center (Map p351; ☎ 760-323-6511; 1150 N Indian Canyon Dr) Has 24-hour emergency care and nonemergency services during normal business hours (see inside front cover.

Money

There are ATMs scattered all over downtown Palm Springs. You'll also generally find them in supermarkets.

Anderson Travel (Map p351; ☎ 760-325-5556; 700 E Tahquitz Canyon Way; 9am-4:30pm Mon-Fri) Exchanges foreign currency and provides foreign-currency traveler's checks; call ahead if you want to exchange/purchase large sums.

Post

Palm Springs Post Office (Map p351; ☎ 760-322-4111, 800-275-8777; 333 E Amado Rd; 9am-5pm Mon-Fri, 9am-1pm Sat)

Tourist Information

Palm Springs Official Visitors Center (Map p348; ☎ 760-778-8418, 800-367-7746; www.palm-springs .org; 2901 N Palm Canyon Dr; ☙ 9am-5pm, seasonal variations possible) North of town, at the turnoff the Palm Springs Aerial Tramway, this information center occupies what was originally a 1965 Albert Frey–designed gas station. The center distributes the official visitors guide and specialty guides (mobility, impaired, gay and lesbian travelers, architecture, etc). The center can also book hotel reservations in Palm Springs.

SIGHTS
Palm Springs
PALM SPRINGS AERIAL TRAMWAY

A highlight of Palm springs, this **cable car** (Map p348; ☎ 888-515-8726, 760-325-1449; www.pstramway .com; 1 Tramway Rd; adult/child/senior $22/15/20, after 3pm $19/12/19; ☙ 10am-10:30pm Mon-Fri, 8am-10:30pm Sat & Sun) rotates ever so slightly as it climbs nearly 6000 vertical feet, from the desert floor up the San Jacinto Mountains, in about 14 minutes. You ascend through visibly different vegetation zones, from the Valley Station (2643ft)

SUM-SUM-SUMMERTIME

The Coachella Valley used to clear out between June and September, although recently it's become more of a year-round community. Still, many lodgings and restaurants lower their prices as the mercury rises.

Other sights, activities and restaurants operate on reduced hours or close altogether in warmer months, and these can vary from year to year. If traveling in summer, always phone ahead to avoid disappointment.

---

to the Mountain Station (8516ft). It's 30°F to 40°F cooler as you step out into pine forest at the top, so bring some warm clothing – the trip up is said to be the equivalent (in temperature) of driving from Mexico to Canada.

The **Mountain Station** at the top of the tramway has an observation area and a theater showing films on the tramway and the park, plus a lounge and restaurants.

Take time (a day or two if you're a backcountry enthusiast) at the top to enjoy the

---

PALM SPRINGS IN TWO DAYS

Day One

We always find it easier to get to know a place by starting with one piece of it, and Palm Springs is all about mid-century architecture. After breakfast in your **modernist hotel** (see p356 for suggestions), spend the morning with a **guided or self-guided tour** (p355) of the city's signature style . Soon you'll have figured your way around the city center. **Tyler's** (p357) makes a casual lunch break over burgers, or try **Spencer's** (p3580), which is more chichi. Either way, you're not far from the shops on **Palm Canyon Dr** (p361) and the **Palm Springs Art Museum** (p353). Return to the hotel to dip in the pool and take a rest before dinner at splashy **Wang's** (p358), followed by a show at the **Palm Springs Follies** or **Copykatz** (p360). Then stop at **Melvyn's** (p359) for old-style cocktails or **Citron** (p359) for new-style ones.

Day Two

After breakfast, drop by **Jensen's Finest Foods** (p358) or **Aspen Mills** (p357) to pick up a gourmet sandwich for your lunchtime excursion. If it's winter, grab that parka you thought you wouldn't have to use on your trip to California (don't worry: you won't need it in summer), and ascend 6000 feet via the **Palm Springs Aerial Tramway** (above), where snow-hiking and cross-country skiing are just some of the activities available. Depending on when you return to earth, commune with the flora and fauna of this arid climate at the **Living Desert Zoo & Gardens** (p353; about half an hour away in Palm Desert), or at the quaint **Moorten Botanical Gardens** (p352), which is closer to town. Again, it's back to the pool before dinner. Tonight make it Mexican, at **El Mirasol** (p358) - the margaritas will make you mellow as you spend the evening gazing at the stars over the hot tub at the inn.

To add a Day Three, pick up lunch and go explore **Joshua Tree National Park** (p363).

Mt San Jacinto Wilderness State Park. There are 54 miles of trails, including a nontechnical route up to the San Jacinto peak (10,804ft), for hiking in summer, and snowshoeing and cross-country skiing in winter. There are also several primitive campgrounds (free). Anyone heading into the backcountry (even for a few hours) must register for a wilderness permit at the ranger station just outside the Mountain Station; for information and advance permits, contact the **state park rangers** (☎ 909-659-2607, 909-659-2117). Pick up maps, books and gifts at the **State Park Visitor Information Center** at the Mountain Station. At the nearby **Adventure Center**, you can rent snowshoes ($15 per day) and cross-country skis (adult/child $18/10 per day). Staff members are knowledgeable about snow conditions and backcountry routes.

A **Ride 'n' Dine combination ticket** (adult/child $35.50/23) includes a simple dinner (think roast beef or turkey plus sides) at the **Pines cafeteria** in the Mountain Station, from 3pm. The restaurant, **Peaks** (☎ 760-325-4537; mains lunch $10-12, dinner $17-32; ☷ lunch & dinner), features a more upscale meat-and-seafood menu, local produce and brilliant views. Reservations are recommended. If you choose to dine up here, be sure to allow time for a leisurely look around at the top.

Allow three hours to park, ride the tram and take a leisurely stroll once at the top. It's also possible to hike to the mountain via the **Skyline Trail** (Map p351), which starts near the Palm Springs Art Museum (p353). This extremely challenging hike is recommended only for the very fit who have a whole day to spend; leave no later than 7am. The reward, besides stellar views and multiple climatic zones, is a free tram ride down.

INDIAN CANYONS

Streams flowing from the San Jacinto Mountains sustain a rich variety of plants in the canyons around Palm Springs. The **canyons** (Map p348; ☎ 760-325-3400, 800-790-3398; www.indian -canyons.com; adult/child $8/4; ☷ 8am-5pm daily Oct-Jun, Fri-Sun Jul-Sep) were home to Native American communities for hundreds of years and are now part of the Agua Caliente Indian Reservation. It's a delight to hike through these canyon oases, shaded by fan palms and surrounded by towering cliffs. From downtown, head south on Palm Canyon Dr (continue straight when the main road turns east) for about 2 miles to the reservation entrance. From here, it's 3 miles up to the Trading Post, which sells hats, maps, water and knickknacks. Trail posts at the entrance

---

PALM SPRINGS MODERN

Palm Springs has always been a party town. When snowbirds from Minneapolis, Pittsburgh or LA wanted a vacation home, they wanted it flashy. A generation of architects – William F Cody, Albert Frey, Richard Neutra, Donald Wexler, E Stewart Williams, the Alexander brothers and others – used the city as their testing ground for their innovative exuberant forms and techniques that are now commonplace: long overhangs and flying roofs to protect from the sun, rail-thin supports, clerestory windows and easy transitions between indoors and out.

Sinatra, Elvis, Liberace and their contemporaries strove to outdo each other with their homes, while enjoying long games of tennis on warm mornings before relaxing over cocktails by the pool. At one point in the 1950s, every real-estate ad in the Yellow Pages featured an illustration of a modernist building.

Starting after WWII and continuing through the 1960s, golf took over from tennis in prominence, and with little remaining real estate in Palm Springs, new construction moved Down Valley. The result: Palm Springs real estate withered.

But in the mid-1990s, fashion photographers began to rediscover these architectural treasures, which led to a second boom, this time in restoration. Take a guided or self-guided tour (p355) for an in-depth look, or here are some easily visible public buildings to get you started:

■ **Tramway Gas Station** – now Palm Springs' visitor center (p349)

■ **Del Marcos Hotel** (p356)

■ **Kaufmann House** (Map p351; 470 W Vista Chino)

■ **Washington Mutual Bank** (Map p351; 499 S Palm Canyon Dr)

■ **Palm Springs City Hall** (Map p351; 2300 E Tahquitz Canyon Way)

PALM SPRINGS

0 —————— 1 km
0 —————— 0.5 miles

INFORMATION
Anderson Travel.............................1 B5
Desert Regional Medical Center.........2 B3
Palm Springs Post Office..................3 B4
Palm Springs Public Library..............4 C5
Peppertree Bookstore...................(see 40)

SIGHTS & ACTIVITIES
Agua Caliente Cultural Museum....(see 16)
East Canyon Hotel & Spa.................5 B3
Estrella.....................................(see 33)
Kaufmann House............................6 A3
McCallum Adobe........................(see 16)
Moorten Botanical Gardens..............7 A6
Palm Springs Air Museum.................8 D3
Palm Springs Art Museum.................9 A4
Palm Springs City Hall...................10 D4
Revive......................................11 A5
Ruddy's General Store................(see 16)
Salon 119 - A Day Spa..................12 A4
Skyline Trail...............................13 A4
Spa Resort Casino........................14 B5
Tahquitz Canyon..........................15 A6

Village Green Heritage Center.........16 A5
Washington Mutual Bank...............17 A5

SLEEPING
7 Springs..................................18 B4
Alpine Gardens Hotel....................19 B6
Caliente Tropics Resort..................20 B6
Casa Cody Inn............................21 A5
Casitas Laquita...........................22 B6
Century....................................23 B6
Chase Hotel at Palm Springs........(see 21)
Del Marcos Hotel.........................24 A5
Hacienda at Warm Sands...............25 B5
Inndulge...................................26 B6
Korakia Pensione.........................27 A5
Orbit In....................................28 A5
Pepper Tree Inn..........................29 A4
Queen of Hearts Resort.................30 B6
Santiago...................................31 A5
Springs....................................32 A5
Viceroy....................................33 A5

EATING
Aspen Mills................................34 C5
Blame it on Midnight....................35 B5
Blue Coyote Grill.........................36 A4
Cactusberry...............................37 A5
Copley's on Palm Canyon..............38 B6
El Mirasol..................................39 A5
Falls..40 A5
Fisherman's Market
  & Grill....................................41 A5

Jensen's Finest Foods....................42 C5
Johannes...................................43 B5
Look..44 A4
Manhattan in the Desert................45 C6
Native Foods..............................46 C6
Rainbow...................................47 B5
Sherman's Deli............................48 B5
Spencer's..................................49 A5
Tyler's Burgers............................50 B5
Wang's in the Desert....................51 B5

DRINKING
Azul...52 A4
Citron....................................(see 33)
Hunter's...................................53 B5
Koffi.......................................54 A4
Streetbar..................................55 B5
Toucans...................................56 A3
Village Pub................................57 A5

ENTERTAINMENT
Blue Guitar.............................(see 61)
Copykatz..................................58 A5
Melvyn's...................................59 A5
Palm Canyon Theatre....................60 A5
Palm Springs Follies...................(see 61)
Plaza Theater.............................61 A5

SHOPPING
Angel View................................62 B4
Modern Way..............................63 A4
Trina Turk.................................64 A4

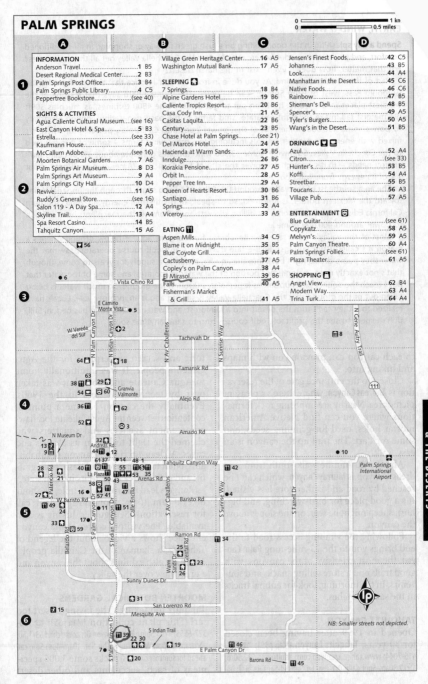

NB: Smaller streets not depicted.

PALM SPRINGS & THE DESERTS

& WATER

...shing in the pool, golfing on a lush green fairway or shopping in air-conditioned ...and you might wonder...where exactly does the Coachella Valley get all these resources? For that matter, how does it even exist in the harsh desert?

Part of that is thanks to wind. As you drive in from LA, you'll notice that the winds in the San Gorgonio Pass, west of Palm Springs, can be fierce. The tourist board says that it's one of the windiest places in the world. It's been put to good use. Some 4800 turbines, as much as 309ft (94 meters) tall, make up eight separate wind farms in the pass, generating enough electricity to power some 190,000 homes. All of that power goes into California's power grid, where it's mixed with energy from other sources including two other wind farms – some of it is returned to the Coachella Valley. Statewide, some 13,000 wind turbines generate about 3% of California's energy needs – that's enough to power the city of San Francisco (America overall gets about 1% of its energy from wind power).

The area southeast of the valley, around the Salton Sea and south through the Imperial Valley toward the Mexican border, is a hotbed, so to speak, of geothermal energy. In 2006, Southern California Edison purchased some 3.1 billion kilowatt-hours from geothermal plants here, enough to power around 400,000 homes.

Most of the valley's water, meanwhile, comes from a giant aquifer below ground (there's a reason it's called Palm Springs). Real-estate developers and golf-course operators say that the water they pump drains right back into the aquifer, ensuring a supply for years to come, though that's not exactly right. A significant portion of the water evaporates, and some of the water that does reach the aquifer picks up salt as it percolates through the ground. So much water is being taken out of the ground that the Coachella Valley is sinking about an inch per year. Locals have realized that they can't turn the desert into a rainforest, and water conservation has begun. Still, don't expect to see the profitable golf courses turn to sand anytime soon.

to each canyon can provide you with maps and hiking info.

Closest to the entrance gate of the reservation is **Andreas Canyon**, where there's a pleasant picnic area. Nearby are imposing rock formations where you can find Native American mortar holes, used for grinding seeds, and some rock art. The trail up the canyon is an easy walk.

About a 20-minute walk south from Andreas Canyon is **Murray Canyon**, which can't be reached by road and is therefore less visited. It's a good place for bird-watching, and big-horn sheep might be seen on the slopes above the canyon.

Following the winding access road to the end brings you to the 15-mile-long **Palm Canyon**, the most extensive of the canyons, with good trails and a store selling snacks and souvenirs. In the morning, look for animal tracks in the sandy patches.

TAHQUITZ CANYON

Opened in 1999 after having been closed for 30 years, **Tahquitz Canyon** (Map p351; ☎ 760-416-7044; www.tahquitzcanyon.com; adult/child $12.50/6; ⏱ 7:30am-5pm daily Oct-Jun, Fri-Sun Jul-Sep) is a his-

toric and sacred centerpiece for the Agua Caliente people. It was traditionally home to Agua Caliente ancestors, but was taken over by teenage squatters in the 1960s. Eventually the canyon became a point of contention between the Agua Caliente, local law-enforcement agencies and squatters who claimed the right to live in its alcoves and caves. A clean-up rid the canyon of inhabitants, but it took years to haul trash, erase graffiti and get the area back to its natural state.

Rangers lead informative 2-mile, 2½-hour hikes at 8am, 10am, noon and 2pm daily; call for reservations. Self-guided hiking is also available. The visitors center at the canyon entrance shows a video about the legend of Tahquitz, a shaman of the Cahuilla people. There are also exhibits about the canyon and a great view over the valley.

MOORTEN BOTANICAL GARDENS

Tahquitz too taxing? The Living Desert too far? This plant collection (Map p351; ☎ 760-327-6555; 1701 South Palm Canyon Dr; adult/child $3/1.50; ⏱ 9am-4:30pm Mon, Tue & Thu-Sat, 10am-4pm Sun, call ahead for summer closures) packs some 3,000 specimens of cacti, succulents and other desert flora into a small lot south of town. Founded in 1938, the garden became the life's passion of Slim Moorten, one of the original Keystone Cops, and his wife Patricia; today their son Clark is an expert on low-water vegetation.

PALM SPRINGS ART MUSEUM

Near the end of W Tahquitz Canyon Way, west of N Palm Canyon Dr, this **museum** (Map p351; ☎ 760-325-7186; www.psmuseum.org; 101 Museum Dr; adult/child/senior $12.50/5/10.50; ☼ 10am-5pm Tue, Wed & Fri-Sun, noon-8pm Thu) has a worthy modern-art collection, including an impressive piece by Seattle glass-artist Dale Chihuly, and a good selection of pre-Columbian and Native American art. The quality of temporary exhibits has greatly improved in recent years, with works of painting, glass, photography and design. The 433-seat Annenberg Theater presents frequent musical performances, films and lectures.

VILLAGE GREEN HERITAGE CENTER

This grassy little **square** (Map p351; 221 S Palm Canyon Dr) in the heart of downtown has some 'heritage' attractions, though most people use it as a place to sit and eat ice cream and fudge, which you can buy at the nearby sweets store. The true historic sites surrounding the square include the **Agua Caliente Cultural Museum** (Map p351; ☎ 760-323-0151; www.accmuseum.org; admission free; ☼ 10am-5pm Wed-Sat, noon-5pm Sun), which has pictures of and artifacts from the tribe's history; **Ruddy's General Store** (Map p351), a reproduction of a 1930s general store; and the 1884 **McCallum Adobe** (Map p351), said to be the oldest building in Palm Springs. The buildings are open from 10am to 4pm Thursday to Saturday, and noon to 3pm Sunday and

Wednesday; adult admission building (pay as you enter), a For more information, call **Historical Society** (☎ 760-323-829 historicalsociety.org).

PALM SPRINGS AIR MUSEUM

Adjacent to the Palm Springs International Airport, the **Air Museum** (Map p351; ☎ 760-778-6262; www.air-museum.org; 745 N Gene Autry Trail; adult/child/senior & student 13-17/ $10/5/8.50, senior Sat $10; ☼ 10am-5pm, call ahead in summer) has an exceptional collection of WWII aircraft, photos and flight memorabilia, as well as a large theater where movies are shown regularly for no additional charge.

KNOTT'S SOAK CITY USA

On a hot day, the kids will go nuts for this **water park** (Map p348; ☎ 760-327-0499; www.knotts .com/soakcity/ps; 1500 S Gene Autry Trail; adult/child $28/17, after 3pm all $17; ☼ hours vary, check website or phone), with activities including Pacific Spin 'river rafting', slides, tube rides and wave pools.

Around Palm Springs

LIVING DESERT ZOO & GARDENS

This excellent desert-species **zoo and botanical gardens** (Map p348; ☎ 760-346-5694; www.livingdesert .org; 47-900 Portola Ave, Palm Desert; adult/child $12/7.50 Sep–mid-June, $9/5 mid-Jun–Aug; ☼ 8am-1:30pm mid-Jun–Aug, 9am-5pm Sep–mid-Jun) presents a wide variety of desert plants and animals, plus exhibits on desert geology and Native American culture. Plan for 1½ to 3½ hours to explore the Living Desert, and check the website for additional nighttime and seasonal activities.

CABOT'S PUEBLO MUSEUM

Inside a rambling 1913 adobe house built by Cabot Yerxa of the legendary Boston Cabot

---

WHAT THE...?

You may do two double takes in Cabazon, a 17-mile drive west of Palm Springs: the first when you see a giant T-Rex and Apatosaurus north of the I-10 Freeway and the second when you see how they're being marketed. Claude K Bell, a sculptor for Knott's Berry Farm in Orange County (p249), spent 1964 to 1975 creating these concrete behemoths (55-feet and 45-feet tall, respectively). The **World's Biggest Dinosaurs** (☎ 951-922-8700; www.worldsbiggestdinosaurs.com; 50800 Seminole Dr, Cabazon; ☼ gift shop 10am-dusk, T-Rex hours vary) remained a temple of tourist kitsch until 2005, when they were purchased by a group of creation scientists, who contend that God created the original dinosaurs in one day, along with the other animals. In the gift shop in the Bronto belly, alongside the sort of dino-swag you might find at other science museums, you can read about the hoaxes and fallacies of evolution and Darwinism, biblical quotes purporting to refer to dinosaurs, and evidence that dinosaurs and man existed at the same time.

...an, a wealthy East Coaster who traded high society for the solitude of the desert, this quirky **museum** (Map p348; ☎ 760-329-7610; www .cabotsmuseum.org; 67-616 E Desert View Ave, Desert Hot Springs; adult/child $6/4; ⏰ 10am-3pm Sat Oct-May or by appointment) displays Native American basketry and pottery, as well as a photo collection from Cabot's turn-of-the-century travels to Alaska. It's also a great story told at an idiosyncratic venue.

ACTIVITIES
Cycling
Palm Springs and the valley have an excellent network of bike paths that are great for getting around. Check if your hotel has loaner bicycles to get around town. If not, **Fun Seekers** (☎ 760-340-3861; www.4funseekers.com; 73865 Hwy 111, Palm Desert) rents and sells bikes for city and mountain use, plus in-line skates, mopeds and even Segways. Bike rentals start at $7/28/75 per hour/day/week. They will deliver and pick up equipment.

Golf
The Coachella Valley boasts more than 100 public, semiprivate, private and resort golf courses. Top resorts include **Marriott's Shadow Ridge** (Map p348; ☎ 760-674-2700; www.golfshadowridge

.com) and **Desert Willow** (Map p348; ☎ 760-346-7060; www.desertwillow.com), both in Palm Desert, and **SilverRock** (Map p348; ☎ 888-600-7272; www.silverrock .com) in La Qunita. Greens fees run from $25 to $250 or more, depending on the course, season and day of the week; inquire directly or through your hotel. Alternatively, **Stand-by Golf** (☎ 760-321-2665; www.standbygolf.com) can book tee times at a discount for play at some 40 courses.

Golf spectators can check with tourist offices for upcoming large-purse big-name tournaments.

Some venues – particularly the Desert Willow resort – are making an effort to be more environmentally conscious and reduce the million gallons of water per day used to irrigate the courses (see p352).

Hiking
The best way to appreciate the subtlety of the desert is on foot, as long as you protect yourself from the heat (see p366).

For hiking in the immediate Palm Springs area check out the Indian (p350) and Tahquitz Canyons (p352), and the top of the aerial tramway (p349). See also Joshua Tree National Park (p363).

Trail Discovery Outdoor Guide Service (☎ 760-325-4453, 888-867-2327; www.palmspringshiking.com) offers

---

SPA ME

If the road has left you frazzled and achy, a spa day might be the cure. The valley has dozens of spas to choose from, from simple to sumptuous. A few favorites are listed here. Make reservations. Many hotels also provide in-room services, particularly in Desert Hot Springs.

East Canyon Hotel & Spa (Map p351; ☎ 760-320-1928; www.eastcanyonps.com; 288 E Camino Monte Vista) Palm Springs' only exclusively gay spa has facials, wraps (try the aloe wrap), massages and more.

Estrella (Map p351; ☎ 760-320-4117; www.viceroypalmsprings.com; 415 S Belardo Rd) Swanky full-service spa at the Viceroy, with salt scrubs, wraps, facials, botanical baths, a high-end salon and outdoor activities like hikes.

Palm Springs Yacht Club (Map p348; ☎ 760-770-5000; www.parkerpalmsprings.com; 4200 E Palm Canyon Dr) Ritzy, glitzy and fabulous, the spa at the Parker Palm Springs is a fave of society ladies and the occasional celeb.

Revive (Map p351; ☎ 760-325-4800; www.rosannas.com; 353 S Palm Canyon Dr) Massages, body treatments and a full-service hair salon. Internet specials.

Salon 119 – A Day Spa (Map p351; ☎ 760-327-4800; 119 N Indian Canyon Dr) Get a topflight manicure and cut-and-color, followed by a relaxing massage.

Spa Resort Casino (Map p351; ☎ 760-325-1461; www.sparesortcasino.com; 100 N Indian Canyon Dr) The valley's original hot springs are at this Native American casino hotel (p359). For $40 you can buy the 'taking of the waters' course through multiple baths, steam rooms and saunas.

Two Bunch Palms (Map p348; ☎ 760-329-8791; www.twobunchpalms.com; 67425 Two Bunch Palms Trail, Desert Hot Springs) Tim Robbins soaked in the mud baths here in *The Player*, but you needn't be a rainmaker to enjoy the mud, water and massage treatments or lush gardens.

The Well (Map p348; ☎ 760-341-2200; 40-500 Indian Wells Ln, Indian Wells) The renowned spa at the Miramonte Resort offers couples' massage, body-painting parties and chocolate treatments.

excellent and educational guided hiking trips locally and in Joshua Tree National Park. It operates fewer trips during summer. Call for availability and prices.

Horseback Riding

Smoke Tree Stables (Map p348; ☎ 760-327-1372; www.smoketreestables.com; 2500 Toledo Ave; ⏰ 8am-5pm in winter, 8am-noon summer, summer closures vary) arranges trail rides, from one-hour outings to all-day treks. The cost is from $40 per hour for both novice and experienced riders. Reserve ahead.

TOURS
Guided Tours

Celebrity Tours (Map p348; ☎ 760-770-2700; Rimrock Shopping Center, 4751 E Palm Canyon Dr; www.celebrity-tours.com; 1hr tour adult/child/senior $30/12/28, 2½hr tour $35/14/33) Offers gossip and glamour in a reservation-only bus tour of homes of bygone Hollywood stars, from Liberace to Lucy. You can do it yourself with a map from the visitors center, but you'll miss the insider commentary.

Desert Adventures (☎ 888-440-5337, 760-324-5337; www.red-jeep.com; 3/3½/4hr tours $129/139/149) Runs excellent guided jeep tours including the Indian Canyons, Santa Rosa Mountains, Bighorn Sheep Preserve and the shake-rattle-and-roll country of the San Andreas Fault. Driver-guides are full of information on the natural environment and Native-American lore.

Elite Land Tours (☎ 760-318-1200, 800-514-4866; www.elitelandtours.com; tours from $49) This outfit opened in 2003 and has built a huge range of respected tours throughout the region, including the windmills, Joshua Tree National Park, desert adventures, Pioneertown and the Integratron, all in vehicles from Hummers to helicopters. Prices vary by tour and number of guests.

Palm Springs Modern Tours (☎ 760-318-6118; psmoderntours@aol.com; $65) Three-hour van tours provide detailed descriptions of architecture from the 1920s to the '70s with special attention to the '50s and '60s. Reservation only.

Palm Springs Windmill Tours (☎ 760-320-1365; www. bestofthebesttours.com; 90-min tours adult/child/senior $23/10/20; ⏰ 9am, 11am & 2pm) Learn all about the groves of whirring turbines that are the gateway into town. Reservations required.

Self-Guided Tours

The Official Visitors Center (p349) has brochures for self-guided tours. The *Public Art and Historic Site Tour Map* (free) covers 37 sites throughout Palm Springs; most you can see on foot around downtown. It also

---

THE PS CELEBRITY CIRCUIT

Everyone knows about the dead celebs who used to spend time in Palm Springs, but who comes to the Coachella Valley today? Here's a short list of big-name homeowners:

- Michael Douglas and Catherine Zeta-Jones
- Bill Gates
- Monty Hall
- Barry Manilow
- Rita Rudner
- Suzanne Somers
- Michelle Wie

---

sells *A Map of Palm Springs Modern* ($5) for architecture fans. *Palm Springs Map of the Stars' Homes* ($5) lets you view from outside the abodes of the city's rich and famous, but you'll need a car and sometimes you'll only see the bougainvillea-covered wall of a compound.

FESTIVALS & EVENTS

Palm Springs International Film Festival (☎ 760-322-2930; www.psfilmfest.org) Early January brings a film festival with over 200 films from more than 60 countries.

Modernism Week (www.modernismweek.com) In mid-February, the week comprises a modernism art show, lectures, screenings and architecture tours, all centered on the Palm Springs Art Museum. Book well ahead.

Desert Swing 'N Dixie Jazz Festival (☎ 760-333-7932; www.desertjazz.org) This mid-March festival features three days of dancing and music, with a special jazz-gospel session on Sunday. The event is organized by the Dixieland Jazz Society of the Desert, which holds monthly jazz dances around Palm Springs. Call for details.

Dinah Weekend (☎ 888-923-4624; www.thedinah.com) Five days of lesbian comedy, pool parties, mixers, dances and more on the occasion of the Nabisco (formerly Dinah Shore) LPGA Golf Tournament. Early April.

White Party (☎ 888-777-8886; www.jeffreysanker.com) On Easter weekend, this four-day-long party is one of the biggest gay dance events in the US.

Coachella Valley Music & Arts Festival (www.coachella.com; 1-/3-day tickets $90/250) In late April or early May, 25 miles east of Palm Springs, Indio's Empire Polo Club (Map p348) hosts one of the hottest music festivals of its kind. Recent performers have ranged from hip indie no-names to Björk, Willie Nelson and somebody named Madonna.

Stagecoach Festival (www.stagecoachfestival.com) The weekend after Coachella, and in the same venue, appear new artists and a who's who of country and roots: Emmylou Harris, Kenny Chesney, Willie Nelson (again!), George Strait and Garrison Keillor.

Golf Cart Parade (☎ 760-346-6111; www.golfcart parade.com) Each October, dozens of elaborately decorated golf carts from around the region take to El Paseo in Palm Desert, reputed to be the world's only parade of its kind. And those folks in Pasadena thought their Rose Bowl Parade was so special.

Palm Springs Pride (www.pspride.org) The region's gay-pride festival takes place in early November, with a parade, dozens of entertainers including DJs, and dance and cultural events.

SLEEPING

Most inns serve continental breakfast, though some breakfasts are better than others. If it matters to you, inquire ahead.

Palm Springs

The Official Visitors Center (p349) operates a free **lodging-reservation service** (☎ 760-322-6368 or 800-325-6875; www.palm-springs.org). Shelling out a little more will put you within walking distance of downtown's major sights and nightlife.

BUDGET

Alpine Gardens Hotel (Map p351; ☎ 760-323-2231, 888-299-7455; www.alpinegardens.com; 1586 E Palm Canyon Dr; r $65-130; P ♨) All 10 rooms at this beautifully landscaped, impeccably kept motel, c 1954, have redwood beams in the ceilings, refrigerators, and slightly kitsch but extra-charming furnishings. Top in its class.

7 Springs (Map p351; ☎ 760-320-9110; www.7springs .info; 950 N Indian Canyon Dr; r from $80; P ♨ ⚓) Bargain-priced contempo cool. This former apartment complex has 48 rooms, all laid out differently but decorated with geometric carpeting and marble floors. Shared facilities include pool, Jacuzzis and barbecue grills. Breakfast not provided.

THURSDAY'S THE NIGHT, DOWNTOWN'S THE PLACE

Every Thursday evening, N Palm Canyon Dr is closed to traffic from Baristo Rd to Amado Rd for **Villagefest** (☎ 760-320-3781; ⏱ 6-10pm Oct-May, 7-10pm Jun-Sep) a certified farmers market with musicians, food vendors and purveyors of art and handicrafts.

Chase Hotel at Palm Springs (Map p351; ☎ 760-320-8866, 877-532-4273; www.chasehotelpalmsprings .com; 200 W Arenas Rd; r incl breakfast $109-139; P ♨) A classic mid-century motel complex with large open spaces, the Chase has immaculately kept oversized rooms decorated with contemporary furnishings. It's great value. Friendly service.

Campers can head to Joshua Tree National Park (p365) or Mount San Jacinto Wilderness State Park (p350).

MIDRANGE

Pepper Tree Inn (Map p351; ☎ 760-318-9850, 866-887-8733; www.peppertreepalmsprings.com; 622 N Palm Canyon Dr; r $129-229; P ♨) Spanish-style hotel with big, modern rooms, some with Jacuzzi and terrace.

Casa Cody (Map p351; ☎ 760-320-9346, 800-231-2639; www.casacody.com; 175 S Cahuilla Rd; r incl breakfast $99-179, ste $199-389; P ♨ wi-fi) This country inn with individual Spanish-style bungalows, tucked behind billowing bougainvillea once hosted Charlie Chaplin. Units have desert-themed decor, including some with full kitchens, wood-burning fireplaces and private patios.

Caliente Tropics Resort (Map p351; ☎ 760-327-1391, 866-468-9595; www.calientetropics.com; 411 E Palm Canyon Dr; r $125-240; P ♨ ♿ wi-fi) Impeccably kept 90-room Tiki-style motor lodge where Elvis Presley and Nancy Sinatra once splashed poolside. Children and pets are welcome (make reservations for pets).

our pick **Del Marcos Hotel** (Map p351; ☎ 760-325-6902, 800-676-1214; www.delmarcoshotel.com; 225 W Baristo Rd; r $150-260; P ♨ wi-fi) After suffering years of bad remodels, this 1947 gem finally looks like it should. Groovy tunes in the lobby usher you to a saltwater pool and ineffably chic rooms named for local architectural luminaries. Breakfast not provided, but you're one block from eateries on Palm Canyon Dr.

Korakia Pensione (Map p351; ☎ 760-864-6411; www .korakia.com; 257 S Patencio Rd; r $159-299; P ♨) Featured on *Boy Meets Boy*, this 1920s Moroccan-style compound is a romantic gem. Antique-filled rooms have sumptuous beds with luxurious linens, and bathrooms with custom-stone tile that echoes the masonry work of the inn's fountain courtyards and outdoor fire pits. Bring groceries – many units have kitchenettes – and you'll never have to leave. Cottages cost more.

Springs (Map p351; ☎ 760-327-5701; www .thespringsofps.com; 227 N. Indian Canyon Dr; r incl breakfast from $175; P ⊠ ♿ wi-fi) In the heart of everything, built in 1935 and renovated in 2004, this hotel and spa offers a courtyard setting, rooms with elegant accents like fireplaces and blinds, pillowtop mattresses, Jacuzzi tubs and an un-stuffy atmosphere.

TOP END

Orbit In (Map p351; ☎ 760-323-3585, 877-996-7248; www.orbitin.com; 562 W Arenas Rd; r incl breakfast $179-309; P ⌨ ⊠ wi-fi) It's back to the 1950s at Palm Springs' retro property of record, with high-end original mid-century furniture (think Eames, Noguchi and more) around a quiet pool.

Viceroy (Map p351; ☎ 760-320-4117, 800-237-3687; www.viceroypalmsprings.com; 415 S Belardo Rd; r from $199; ⊠) Wear a Pucci dress and blend right in at this 1960s-chic mini-resort done up in black, white and lemon-yellow (think Austin Powers meets Givenchy). There's also a full-service spa (p354), as well as a fab but pricey restaurant for a white-linen luncheon or swanky supper.

our pick **Parker Palm Springs** (Map p348; ☎ 760-770-5000, 888-450-9488; www.theparkerpalmsprings.com; 4200 E Palm Canyon Dr; r from $300; P ⌨ ⊠ wi-fi) Featured in the Bravo TV series *Welcome to the Parker*, this posh full-service resort boasts whimsical decor by designer-du-jour Jonathan Adler. Norma's and Mr Parker's restaurants are to die for and the grounds boast hammocks, lawn bowling and the Palm Springs Yacht Club spa (p354).

Around Palm Springs

Desert Hot Springs is known for small, Palm Springs–style inns with the advantage of being at the hot spring source. Your best bet Down Valley is large resorts catering to golfers and spa-goers; rack rates are pricey, but there are often discounts and package deals.

Miracle Manor (Map p348; ☎ 760-329-6641, 877-329-6641; www.miraclemanor.com; 12589 Reposo Rd, Desert Hot Springs; r from $175; P ⊠ wi-fi) Billed as a retreat, and by gum they're right. Absence of phones, faxes and children in its six rooms lends itself to sensory deprivation, and organic, insecticide-free cotton sheets help you enjoy the modernist surroundings.

Hope Springs Resort (Map p348; ☎ 760-329-4003; www.hopespringsresort.com; 68075 Club Circle Dr, Desert Hot Springs; r from $195; P ⊠) This modernist mecca put Desert Hot Springs on the map for stylish stays, and it continues to dazzle with 10 rooms featuring impeccable period furniture, artful public spaces, fantastic views and natural hot springs flowing through three pools.

Sagewater Spa (Map p348; ☎ 760-220-1554; www.sagewaterspa.com; 12689 Elisio Rd, Desert Hot Springs; r from $195-250; P ⌨ ⊠) It's minimalist to the max at this seven-room, adults-only inn with two spa pools (warm and warmer), on a hillside with views across the valley. Rooms have concrete floors and a white-on-white color scheme inflected with the occasional – wait for it – sage accent. Homemade coffee cake.

Miramonte Resort (Map p348; ☎ 760-341-2200, 800-237-2926; www.miramonteresort.com; 40-500 Indian Wells Ln, Indian Wells; r from $229; P ⌨ ⊠) Even if the publicity overplays the Tuscan theme of this resort, it's a great stay, not least for its spa, the Well (p354). Lots of nooks and crannies give you leisure to kick back and enjoy the views of the Santa Rosa Mountains.

La Quinta Resort & Club (Map p348; ☎ 760-564-4111, 800-598-3828; www.laquintaresort.com; 49499 Eisenhower Dr, La Quinta; r $229-439; P ⌨ ⊠) Opened in 1926, the sprawling La Quinta has a Spanish Colonial–style lobby, cushy ultraprivate bungalows, spectacular grounds, 41 pools, 53 hot tubs and 90 holes of golf.

Westin Mission Hills (Map p348; 760-328-5955, 800-937-8461; 71333 Dinah Shore Dr, Rancho Mirage; r from $295; P ⌨ ⊠ ♿) Classic Down Valley golf resort with two courses, numerous pools, tennis courts, an enormous spa and desert tones in its guest rooms (all with private balcony). Pet-friendly.

EATING

Because of its size, Palm Springs isn't a 'food town' on par with LA or San Diego, but there's plenty to keep foodies happy on short trips. Plus, you'll probably find that returning to restaurants makes you a steady customer, with the recognition that brings.

Budget

Tyler's Burgers (Map p351; ☎ 760-325-2990; 149 S Indian Canyon Dr; dishes $4-7; ⏱ 11am-4pm Mon-Sat, closed mid-Jul–Aug & some Mondays in warmer months) The city's favorite burger stand has a magazine rack stocked with the *Robb Report* and financial magazines. It's at La Plaza, a sort of drive-thru shopping street in the town center. Expect a wait.

Aspen Mills (Map p351; ☎ 760-323-3123; 555 S Sunrise Way; sandwiches $5-7; ⏱ 7am-6:30pm Mon-Sat; P) Although this bakery (located next to

Blockbuster Video) makes some of the best to-go sandwiches in town, you can also eat them here. Great homemade bread, muffins and brownies.

Thai Smile (Map p348; ☎ 760-320-5503; 651 N Palm Canyon Dr; mains lunch $6, dinner $6-14; ✦ lunch & dinner; P) Respected, casual eatery serving standards (pad Thai) and unusual dishes (grilled eggplant salad). There is a second branch at Palm Desert (☎ 760-341-6565; 42-467 Bob Hope Dr).

ourpick El Mirasol (Map p351; ☎ 760-323-0721; 140 E Palm Canyon Dr; mains $7-19; ✦ 11am-10pm) There are showier Mexican places in town, but everyone ends up back at El Marisol, with its informal decor, copious margaritas and snappy dishes from tacos to chicken mole. Indoor and outdoor seating available.

Native Foods (Map p351; ☎ 760-416-0070; 1775 E Palm Canyon Dr; mains $8-15; ✦ 11:30am-9:30pm Mon-Sat, closed Jul–mid-Aug; P V ✦) Vegan food so good it's seitan-ic (...seitan being a wheat-gluten-based dish). Soy and wheat proteins stand in for beef and chicken in tacos, burgers and bowls. It's tucked away in a rather pleasant outdoor mall, with giant masks on the wall.

Cactusberry (Map p351; ☎ 760-325-3228; 116 La Plaza; yogurt from $3; ✦ noon-8pm Sun-Wed, noon-10pm Thu-Sat) Palm Springs' contribution to SoCal's frozen-yogurt craze serves it with biodegradable bowls and spoons.

Jensen's Finest Foods (Map p351; ☎ 760-325-8282; 102 S Sunrise Way; sandwiches about $7; ✦ 7am-9pm) Local supermarket with fabulous specialty sandwiches for that desert hike, and homemade baked goods like Mexican wedding cookies and apple fritters.

Midrange

Look (Map p351; ☎ 760-778-3520; 139 E Andreas Rd; mains $8-23; ✦ lunch & dinner) There's a simple dining room with old Hollywood publicity stills but the real action is on the patio. Standard Cal-bistro cuisine (satay, quesadillas, Cobb salad, sandwiches and burgers) and larger mains go well with martinis. Has frequent drink specials and a substantial gay following.

Blue Coyote Grill (Map p351; ☎ 760-327-1196; 445 N Palm Canyon Dr; mains $9-25; ✦ lunch & dinner; ✦) The courtyard tables are the most coveted at this lively cantina serving Mexican and Southwestern standards plus options like *pollo naranja* (chicken with OJ and orange liqueur) or red snapper in cilantro sauce. The Wild Coyote margarita is legendary.

Wang's (Map p351; ☎ 760-325-9264; 424 S Indian Canyon Dr; mains $10-15; ✦ 5-9:30pm Sun-Thu, 5-10:30pm Fri & Sat, closed three weeks in Aug; P) The menu may sound like standard-issue upscale Chinese, but the atmosphere is anything but. This swank, mood-lit outpost, with indoor koi pond and giant cocktails, is the darling of the in-crowd. Come early or make reservations. Kiss, kiss.

Fisherman's Market & Grill (Map p351; ☎ 760-327-1766; 235 S Indian Canyon Dr; mains $13-24; ✦ lunch & dinner; ✦) From shrimp to cod to sea bass – the ocean fare at this counter-service shack is so fresh, you half-expect to feel waves lapping at your ankles. The fish-and-chips is a classic, as are combos with coleslaw and fries or rice.

Top End

Spencer's (Map p351; ☎ 760-327-3446; 701 W Baristo Rd; mains lunch $8-20, dinner $18-39; ✦ breakfast, lunch & dinner; P) Dramatically built into the mountainside and with big-city clean lines and sophistication (look for the piano player), Spencer's serves swanky cuisine like breakfast cocktails, lobster club sandwich, excellent burgers and steaks, and chicken with tarragon reduction.

ourpick Copley's on Palm Canyon (Map p351; ☎ 760-327-1196; 445 N Palm Canyon Dr; mains $25-35; ✦ dinner

---

THAT ONE, I NEVER GO TO!

Requirements to be a certified Old Hollywood hangout: retired stars, lots of sun, a pool, palm trees and a Jewish deli. Palm Springs has not one but two of the last, each with its passionate fans. As impartial journalists we see merits in both, so we're not going to say that one makes you *kvell,* while the other one...*feh!* **Sherman's** (Map p351; ☎ 760-329-1199; 401 E Tahquitz Canyon Way; mains $7-17; ✦ breakfast, lunch & dinner; P ✦) has been in business since 1995 in a strip-mall storefront with long terrace. It serves early-bird dinners and is festooned with headshots of aficionados no less than Don Rickles and Milton Berle. Newcomer **Manhattan in the Desert** (Map p351; ☎ 760-322-3354; 2665 E Palm Canyon Dr; most mains $6-18; ✦ breakfast, lunch & dinner; P ✦) has a more impressive deli counter, more polished surroundings and simply massive slices of cake, mirroring the enormity of its sandwiches.

THE PERFECT DATE

Coachella Valley is the ideal place to find the date of your dreams – the kind that grows on trees, that is. Some 90% of US date production happens here, with dozens of permutations of shape, size, juiciness, packaging and species, with exotic names like halawy, deglet, blonde and honey.

Dates grow around Indio, at the southeast end of the valley, atop some 4300 acres of date palms whose ancestries trace back to the Middle East and North Africa; they began to be imported about a century ago. The region's most famous variety, the medjool, arrived in the 1920s from Morocco. Some varieties will keep for years without refrigeration.

Date orchards let you sample different varieties for free, an act of shameless but delicious self-promotion. Another signature taste of the valley is the date shake: crushed dates mixed into a vanilla milkshake. Be careful – they're richer than they look! **Shields Date Gardens** (☎ 760-347-0996; www.shieldsdates.com; 80-225 Hwy 111, Indio; ⊙ 9am-5pm) is typical. You can watch the film *Romance & Sex Life of the Date*, with the chirpy 'Oh, you!' feel of a 1950s educational film. **Oasis Date Gardens** (Map p348; ☎ 800-827-8017; www.oasisdategardens.com; 59-111 Hwy 111, Thermal; ⊙ 9am-5pm) is on the way to the Salton Sea. Or for a quick grab-n-go on your way to or from LA, **Hadley Fruit Orchards** (off Map p348; ☎ 888-854-5655; www.hadleyfruitorchards.com; 48980 Seminole Dr, Cabazon; ⊙ 9am-7pm Mon-Thu, 8am-8pm Fri-Sun) claims to have invented trail mix.

---

nightly & 10am-2pm Sunday Jan–mid-May, dinner Tue-Sun mid-May–Dec, closed late Jul–late Aug) On the former Cary Grant estate, Andrew Manion Copley gets seriously inventive: think prosciutto-wrapped duck breast and 'Oh My Lobster Pot Pie'. Bring your sweetie and your credit card.

Johannes (Map p351; ☎ 760-778-0017; 196 S Indian Canyon Dr; mains $25-35; ⊙ dinner Tue-Sun) The chef-owner's Austrian roots shine through at this sedately decorated storefront. Diners rave over imaginative cooking without a lot of fuss: pan-seared ahi in Japanese spices to Wiener schnitzel with cranberry jelly.

Falls (Map p351; ☎ 760-322-6300; 155 S Palm Canyon Dr; mains $29-39; ⊙ dinner) Head upstairs for flaming martinis at this contempo-chic steakhouse with generous verandah. Steaks come with imaginative sauce choices (caramelized sugar and black raspberry, anyone?), or watch culinary prestidigitation as Caesar salad and bananas Foster are prepared tableside.

Please also see the restaurants at the Parker Palm Springs hotel (p357).

DRINKING
Bars
Village Pub (Map p351; ☎ 760-323-3265; 266 S Palm Canyon Dr; wi-fi) A casual place for kicking back with your buds, the pub has live music, darts and beer on tap.

Citron (Map p351; 760-320-4117; www.viceroypalm springs.com; 415 S Belardo Rd; P) Opinions waver about the food at the restaurant at the Vice-

roy (p357), but everyone agrees that the bar scene is supercool.

Azul (Map p351; ☎ 760-325-5533; 369 N Palm Canyon Dr; dishes $6-16) This tapas restaurant develops a fun bar scene at night with a mod lounge feel inside and, outside, a large patio with booths like covered porch-swings. Frequent happy hours.

See also Melvyn's (below).

Coffeehouses
Koffi (Map p351; ☎ 760-416-2244; 515 N Palm Canyon Dr; ⊙ 5:30am-8pm) Appropriately cool, minimalist café serves strong organic coffee.

ENTERTAINMENT
Casinos
Legal gambling is possible just a few blocks from Palm Canyon Dr.

Spa Resort Casino (Map p351; ☎ 760-883-2000, 800-258-2946; 401 E Amado Rd; ⊙ 24hr) Empty your pockets at Palm Springs' Native-American casino.

Live Music
Blue Guitar (Map p351; ☎ 760-327-1549; 120 S Palm Canyon Dr) Hear live jazz and blues upstairs Friday to Sunday nights at this venue next door to the Plaza Theater. Call for the current schedule. The venue's owned by Kal David, the celebrity guitarist.

Melvyn's (Map p351; ☎ 760-325-0046; 200 W Ramon Rd) The likes of Sinatra and McQueen were among the early customers at this swanky watering hole at the Ingleside Inn, and it still retains that feel. Listen to music from piano and vocals to jazz combos while quaffing martinis at the burnished bar. Sunday afternoon jazz is a long-standing tradition.

Theater

Palm Springs Follies (Map p3510; ☎ 760-327-0225; www.psfollies.com; 128 S Palm Canyon Dr; tickets $48-90; ⊗ evening shows & matinees from November to May) The historic Plaza Theater, dating from 1936, hosts this Ziegfeld Follies–style revue that includes music, dancing, showgirls and comedy. The twist? Many of the performers are as old as the theater – all are over 50, some are into their 80s. But this is no amateur hour; in their heyday, many of these old-timers hoofed it alongside Hollywood and Broadway's biggest,

who occasionally guest-star. The cast-from-the-past delivers high-energy shows with flash, splash, inspiration and patriotism.

Copykatz (Map p351; ☎ 760-864-9293, 800-834-2317; www.copykatzps.com; 200 S Palm Canyon Dr; tickets $29-49) The Osmond Hour this ain't. Skillful female impersonators ply their craft at this nightclub at the center of town. Energetic acts are inspired by Barbara Streisand, Carol Channing, Madonna, Tina Turner and, uh, Michael Jackson. Shows have more than just a gay following.

Palm Canyon Theatre (Map p351; ☎ 760-323-5123; www.palmcanyontheatre.org; 538 N Palm Canyon Dr; tickets $22-28, student $10) This theatre stages professional productions of plays and musicals from mid-September to mid-May.

GAY & LESBIAN PALM SPRINGS

Palm Springs is one of America's great gay destinations, a sort of Provincetown in the desert. Large annual events include the White Party, Dinah Weekend and Palm Springs Pride (p355), but just about any weekend of the year you're likely to find gay and lesbian Angelenos relaxing in their second homes or lounging at resorts.

LODGING

Gay lodging in Palm Springs, approximately 40 resorts in all, ranges from sleazy to sumptuous. Since they're small properties, many are conducive to finding companions for dinner, drinks, daytime activities or whatever. Some of the better ones are listed below.

Men's resorts tend to be concentrated in the Warm Sands neighborhood, just southeast of downtown Palm Springs, or on San Lorenzo Rd, about a mile away. Lesbian resorts (fewer in number) are throughout town. Most men's resorts are clothing-optional, and here we've assigned them a 'sexual temperature' between one and 10 (10 indicating that the joint may as well be a bathhouse).

Men's Resorts

Inndulge (Map p351; ☎ 760-327-1408, 800-833-5675; www.inndulge.com; 601 Grenfall Rd; r incl breakfast $129-199; P 💻 🐾 wi-fi) This midrange option gets plenty of repeat customers for its 1950s shell, variety of rooms and suites with mission furniture, fridges (some rooms also have kitchens), gay-themed photo posters, pool and hot tub that encourage mingling, and summer specials. Sexual temperature: 7.

Santiago (Map p351; ☎ 760-322-1300, 800-710-7729; www.santiagoresort.com; 650 San Lorenzo Rd; r incl breakfast & lunch $149-189; P 🐾 wi-fi) Smartly remodeled in 2006, this 24-room, two-story courtyard-style building features muted colors, frosted-glass showers, CD clock radios and original erotic artwork. There are excellent mountain views from the huge pool, and a hammock out back. Sexual temperature: 4.

Hacienda at Warm Sands (Map p351; ☎ 760-327-8111, 800-359-2007; www.thehacienda.com; 586 Warm Sands Dr; r incl breakfast & lunch $150-310; P 💻 🐾 wi-fi) The Hacienda raises the bar for service and luxury in gay lodging. Choose from nine different pillow types in its 10 generously proportioned rooms. The genial innkeepers are never intrusive, always available. Flawless landscaping. Bring your own lover. Sexual temperature: 2.

Century (Map p351; ☎ 760-323-9966, 800-475-5188; www.centurypalmsprings.com; 598 Grenfall Rd; r incl breakfast $159-259; P 💻 🐾 wi-fi) To stay gay and not give up the mid-century vibe, make a beeline.

SHOPPING

Browse the shops and galleries along Palm Canyon Dr downtown, but don't expect to find much more than expensive shops and galleries geared towards tourists. Major retailers that once had stores in Palm Springs have all moved to malls Down Valley.

Trina Turk (Map p351; ☎ 760-416-2856; 891 N Palm Canyon Dr) Find shagadelic resort-chic drag at Palm Springs' best – some say only – clothing boutique. If you love hip clothes, don't miss this place.

Modern Way (Map p351; ☎ 760-320-5455; 745 N Palm Canyon Dr) The largest, oldest and most stylin' consignment shop for collectors of modern furniture. Ask at the visitor center (p349) for directions to others.

El Paseo (Map p348; www.elpaseo.com) For serious shopping at midrange and high-end retailers, head to El Paseo, the main shopping street in Palm Desert, dubbed the Rodeo Dr of the desert. To get there, head 14 miles southeast of Palm Springs via Hwy 111. El Paseo runs parallel to Hwy 111, one block south of the highway.

River at Rancho Mirage (Map p348; ☎ 760-341-2711; 71-800 Hwy 111 at Bob Hope Dr, Rancho Mirage) Among the shopping centers en route to El Paseo, the River has about 20 upscale stores, restaurants and a big movie complex.

Desert Hills Premium Outlets (off Map p348; ☎ 951-849-6641; www.premiumoutlets.com; 48400 Seminole Dr, Cabazon) and **Cabazon Outlets** (off Map p348; ☎ 951-922-3000; www.cabazonoutlets.com; 48750

The small Century was designed by William Alexander in 1955 and was redesigned by architects with furnishings by Starck, Eames and Noguchi, plus plush bedding and cocktails. It's all around a minimalist pool deck. Sexual temperature: 5.

Women's Resorts

Queen of Hearts Resort (Map p351; ☎ 760-322-5793, 888-275-9903; www.queenofheartsps.com; 435 Avenida Olancha; r $105-160; P ⚥) This was Palm Springs' first gay-only resort, which opened as the Desert Knight in 1960. Now it's exclusively for women, with lovely rooms (most with kitchens) and robes, a sparkling pool and complimentary breakfast.

Casitas Laquita (Map p351; ☎ 760-416-9999; www.casitaslaquita.com; 450 E Palm Canyon Dr; r $135-145, ste from $185; P ⚥ wi-fi) All the rooms are individually decorated and have kitchens at this Spanish-style compound, which has a great pool and manicured grounds. If you can swing it, book the romantic cottage with its private backyard and barbecue.

EATING

Every restaurant in central Palm Springs has a significant gay clientele, but Look (p358) and **Blame it on Midnight** (Map p351; ☎ 760-323-1200; 777 E Tahquitz Canyon Way; most mains $13-22; ☽ dinner) market extensively to the gay community; the latter has grills, salads and eclectic mains, with live entertainment most nights in a Vegas-lounge setting. The crowd skews older and the piano bar can be quite lively at **Rainbow** (Map p351; ☎ 760-325-3868; cnr Arenas Rd & S Indian Canyon Dr; mains lunch $7-12, dinner $12-22; ☽ lunch & dinner). Weekend brunch.

NIGHTLIFE

Arenas Rd east of Indian Canyon Dr is gay-nightlife central. Park 'n' party. The following are a good start:

Hunter's (Map p351; ☎ 760-323-0700; 302 E Arenas Rd) Mostly male clientele, lots of TV screens, a fun dance scene and two pool tables.

Streetbar (Map p351; ☎ 760-320-1266; 244 E Arenas Rd) Congenial mix of locals, visitors and occasional drag performers. Streetside patio for watching the crowd go by.

Toucans (Map p351; ☎ 760-416-7584; 2100 N Palm Canyon Dr) A couple miles from Arenas, this locals' hangout has something for everyone: gay, lesbian, tropical froufrou, trivia network, smoking patio and dancefloor. Packed on weekends. Frequent drink specials.

See also **Copykatz** (opposite).

PALM SPRINGS & THE DESERTS

Seminole Dr, Cabazon) will appeal to discount shoppers: stop on your way to or from LA at these adjacent outlet malls with stores selling everything from Gap to Gucci, housewares to sunglasses. Some purchases are major bargains while others are mere great deals. For big purchases, scope out prices at home beforehand. The malls are just off I-10 in Cabazon, about 20 minutes northwest of central Palm Springs.

GETTING THERE & AWAY
Air
Palm Springs International Airport (Map p351; PSP; ☎ 760-318-3800; www.palmspringsairport.com; 3400 E Tahquitz Canyon Way) is served year-round by Alaska, American, Delta, Horizon, United and US Airways from gateways including Chicago, Dallas, Denver, Los Angeles, Phoenix, San Francisco and Seattle. There are additional seasonal services on Air Canada, Continental, Northwest and Sun Country. The airport is five minutes' drive to downtown.

Car & Motorcycle
From Los Angeles take I-10, the main route into and through the Coachella Valley; the journey to Palm Springs takes about two hours.

You can rent a Harley from **Eaglerider** (☎ 760-251-5990, 877-736-8243; www.eaglerider.com; Palm Springs International Airport) for around $130 per day; specials are often available. When motorcycling in the desert, pay extra attention to keeping yourself adequately hydrated. Hot, dry wind against your body causes rapid dehydration, so it's best to avoid riding with your skin exposed for any longer than a few minutes.

Train
Amtrak (☎ 800-872-7245; www.amtrak.com) serves the unstaffed and kinda creepy North Palm Springs Station, on a desolate stretch of desert 4 miles north of downtown Palm Springs, near where Indian Canyon Dr meets I-10. *Sunset Limited* trains (one way $34, 2½ hours) run to and from LA on Sundays, Wednesdays and Fridays (depart Los Angeles 2:30pm, depart Palm Springs around 6:35am). Trains continue, theoretically, to Orlando, Florida, though Hurricane Katrina wiped out service east of New Orleans and at the time of writing it was unclear whether it would resume.

GETTING AROUND
To/From the Airport
Unless your hotel provides airport transfers, plan to take a taxi; figure about $12 to downtown hotels.

Shuttle companies serve other valley towns; call for advance reservations:
At Your Service (☎ 760-343-0666, 888-700-7888)
Desert Valley Shuttle (☎ 760-251-4020, 800-413-3999)

Car
If you're staying in downtown Palm Springs and don't plan to leave, you won't need a car, but otherwise you'll probably want one for convenience and savings over taxis. Rent one at the airport, where all major agencies have counters.

Public Transportation
Readers have described **SunBus** (☎ 760-343-3451; www.sunline.org; ticket/day pass $1/3), the local bus service, as 'lethargic and unpredictable'. It does, however, serve most of the valley from about 6am to 10pm, and the air-conditioned buses are clean and comfortable. Line 111 follows Hwy 111 between Palm Springs and Palm Desert (one hour) and Indio (about 1½ hours). You can transfer to other lines that loop through the various communities. All buses have wheelchair lifts and a bicycle rack.

Taxi
Flag fall is $3.25, and each mile costs $3. It's best to reserve taxis in advance.
Ace Taxi (☎ 760-835-2445)
American Cab (☎ 760-775-1477)
Palm Springs Taxi (☎ 760-323-5100)

GO, DADDY-O!
The high percentage of well-heeled retirees living in the Coachella Valley, and their propensity to pass on to the next world, means there's a constant replenishment of retro threads at local thrift stores. Today's hipsters can buy clothes as cool as when they were first worn a generation or two ago. **Angel View** (Map p351; ☎ 760-373-8771; 462 N Indian Canyon Dr, Palm Springs) is the thrift-store chain of record, and at the Eisenhower Medical Center, **Collector's Corner** (Map p348; ☎ 760-346-1012; 39000 Bob Hope Dr, Rancho Mirage) draws enthusiastic bargain hunters from across the valley.

JOSHUA TREE NATIONAL PARK

Like a scene from a Dr Seuss book, the whimsical Joshua trees (actually tree-sized yuccas) welcome visitors to this 794,000 acre (321,000 hectare) park at the convergence of the Sonora and Mojave Deserts. Wonderfully shaped rocky outcroppings (mostly quartz monzonite) draw rock climbers while the flats and oases attract day-hikers, especially in spring when many trees send up a huge single cream-colored flower. The mystical quality of this stark, boulder-strewn landscape has inspired many artists, most famously the band U2, which named its 1987 album *The Joshua Tree.*

ORIENTATION

I-10 parallels the south side of the park. Twentynine Palms Hwy (Hwy 62) follows the north side, through the towns of Yucca Valley (population 20,330), Joshua Tree (population 4,200) and Twentynine Palms (population 30,500).

Unless you're day-tripping from Palm Springs, orient yourself in one of the latter two towns. Both are basically stretches along Twentynine Palms Hwy, but Joshua Tree has more soul and is favored by artists and writers. Twentynine Palms (named after the original 29 palm trees behind the visitor center) also serves the nearby Marine Corps Air Ground Combat Center (the world's largest marine facility at over 900 sq miles, or twice the footprint of the city of Los Angeles). Don't disparage US troops here, and don't freak out over the occasional kaboom.

INFORMATION

Pick up food and gasoline in the towns of Joshua Tree or Twentynine Palms. In Joshua Tree, **Coyote Corner** (Map pp364-5; ☎ 760-366-9683; 6535 Park Blvd; ✆ 9am-7pm) dispenses camping supplies, maps, books and helpful information.

Emergency

For emergency assistance, call either ☎ 911 or ☎ 909-383-5651 from any telephone in the park. You'll find emergency telephones at Hidden Valley Campground and the Indian Cove ranger station. For first aid, contact a ranger.

Internet Access

Beatnik Cafe See p368 for details and full review. Public use computers cost $2 per 15 minutes.

Internet Resources

National Park Service (www.nps.gov/jotr) The NPS website has extensive information on the park, from activities and accessibility to weather and wildflowers.

Tourist Information

The park has several official **visitor centers** (☎ 760-367-5500; www.nps.gov/jotr):

Black Rock Nature Center (Map pp364-5; ✆ 8am-4pm Sat-Thu, noon-8pm Fri, closed Jun-Sep) In the northwest corner of the park.

Cottonwood Visitor Center (Map pp364-5; ✆ 8am-4pm) A few miles inside the park's southern entrance.

Joshua Tree Visitor Center (Map pp364-5; Park Blvd, Joshua Tree; ✆ 8am-5pm)

Joshua Tree Chamber of Commerce (Map pp364-5; ☎ 760-366-3723; www.joshuatreechamber.org; 61325 Twentynine Palms Hwy; ✆ 10am-3pm Mon-Fri)

Oasis Visitor Center (Map pp364-5; National Monument Dr, Twentynine Palms; ✆ 8am-5pm) Stock up on books and maps, and talk to a ranger at park headquarters, just outside the park's northern boundary.

Twentynine Palms Chamber of Commerce (Map pp364-5; ☎ 760-367-3445; www.29chamber.com; 73660 Civic Center; ✆ 9am-5pm Mon-Fri, 9am-1pm Sat Sep-May, 9am-3pm Mon-Fri Jun-Aug)

SIGHTS

Park admission is $15 per vehicle, payable at any entry gate, good for seven days and including a map/brochure and the seasonal *Joshua Tree Guide.* There are no facilities besides restrooms, so gas up and bring food and plenty of water.

The most whimsically dramatic conglomeration of rocks is known locally as the **Wonderland of Rocks** area, while the biggest trees are near Covington Flats. To see the transition from the high Colorado Desert/Sonoran Desert to the low Mojave, drive along Pinto Basin Rd.

Those who enjoy history and local lore should take the 90-minute walking tour of the **Desert Queen Ranch** (Map pp364-5; reservations ☎ 760-367-5555; by tour only adult/child $5/2.50; ✆ tours 10am & 1pm daily Oct-May), around 2 miles northeast of Hidden Valley Campground up a dirt road. Russian immigrant William Keys built a homestead on 160 acres here in 1917 and over the following 60 years he set up a full working ranch, school, store and workshop,

PALM SPRINGS & THE DESERTS

which still stand pretty much as they did when Keys died in 1969. Reservations recommended – you can also make a reservation at the Oasis Visitor Center (p363).

ACTIVITIES
Cycling

Joshua Tree National Park is popular for biking, though bicycles must stay on the roads and trails. A mountain bike or, at minimum, a hybrid bike is necessary for the many unpaved roads.

Two favorite bicycle routes are the challenging **Pinkham Canyon Rd**, which begins at the Cottonwood Visitor Center, and the **Old Dale Rd**, which starts 6.5 miles north of there. The **Queen Valley** road network is a more gentle set of trails and has bike racks along the way so people can lock up their bikes and go hiking.

Bikes are a great means of transportation in this region: hop on your two-wheel steed to get from your campground to any destination and you'll have gorgeous scenery along the way. See p354 for information about bike hire.

Hiking

You should leave the car behind to appreciate Joshua Tree's trippy lunar landscapes. Visitor centers provide maps and advice about the 12 short nature walks (which range from 0.25 miles to 1.3 miles) and six hiking trails that focus on different features of the park (for the kids, pick up a Junior Ranger booklet and ask which trails are most kid-friendly). Trails include Fortynine Palms Oasis, Hidden Valley, Lost Horse Mine, Inspiration Point, Ryan Mountain, Cholla Cactus Garden and Lost Palm Oasis. If you don't have a lot of time, the 0.25-mile **Skull Rock Loop** is an easy walk, as is **Keys View Trail**, which provides views of the entire Coachella Valley.

Overnight backcountry hikers must register (to aid in census-taking, fire safety and rescue efforts) and deposit the stub at one of 12 backcountry boards in parking lots throughout the park. Unregistered vehicles left overnight may be cited or towed.

The well-traveled 16-mile **Boy Scout Trail**, on the western side of the park, starts from either the Indian Cove or Keys West backcountry board.

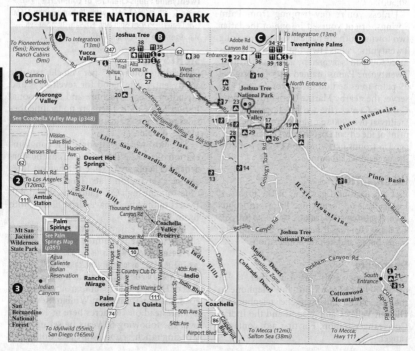
JOSHUA TREE NATIONAL PARK

A 35-mile-long stretch of the **California Riding & Hiking Trail**, administered by California State Parks, passes through Joshua Tree; plan two to three days to hike the trail through the park.

To protect fragile soil crusts (cryptobiotic soil), which allow plant life to grow and keep the desert from blowing away, stay on established trails.

Rock Climbing

From boulders to cracks to multipitch faces, there may be more routes here than anywhere else in the US. The longest climbs are not much more than 100ft or so, but there are many challenging technical routes, and most can be easily top-roped for training. Some of the most popular climbs are in the Hidden Valley area.

Pick up a specialized climbing book from the kind folks at Coyote Corner (p363). They also have route diaries that you can thumb through or buy.

For a day of instruction or for a guided climb, contact **Uprising Outdoor Adventure Guides** (☎ 760-366-3799, 888-254-6266; www.uprising.com; per person from $65). Also try Fun Seekers in Palm Springs (p354).

SLEEPING

There are no lodges in the park, only campgrounds. You can find motels, inns and B&Bs in the surrounding communities of Joshua Tree and Twentynine Palms.

Camping

There are nine **campgrounds** (☎ 877-444-6777; www.nps.gov/jotr, www.recreation.gov; campsites $10-15) in the park; see Map pp364–5 for locations. Some campgrounds will take reservations; check the websites for details. You can rent gear – from tents and bags to stoves and water jugs – from **Joshua Tree Outfitters** (Map pp364-5; ☎ 760-366-1848; 61707 Twentynine Palms Hwy, Joshua Tree; **P**)

Of the campgrounds, only Black Rock Canyon and Cottonwood have shared-use water, flush toilets and dump stations, and water is available at the ranger station near Indian Cove. All other campgrounds have pit toilets, picnic tables and fireplaces. None of the campgrounds have showers.

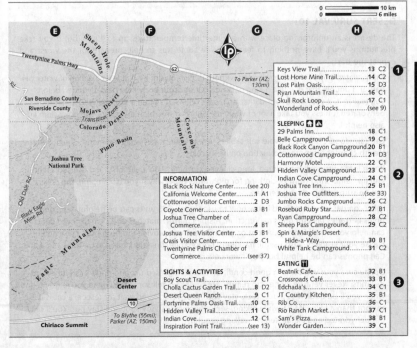

| 0 | 10 km |
| 0 | 6 miles |

Keys View Trail..................................13 C2
Lost Horse Mine Trail........................14 C2
Lost Palm Oasis................................15 D3
Ryan Mountain Trail..........................16 C1
Skull Rock Loop................................17 C1
Wonderland of Rocks.....................(see 9)

SLEEPING
29 Palms Inn.....................................18 C1
Belle Campground.............................19 C1
Black Rock Canyon Campground.20 B1
Cottonwood Campground................21 D3
Harmony Motel.................................22 B1
Hidden Valley Campground............23 C1
Indian Cove Campground................24 C1
Joshua Tree Inn.................................25 B1
Joshua Tree Outfitters...................(see 33)
Jumbo Rocks Campground..............26 C2
Rosebud Ruby Star...........................27 B1
Ryan Campground............................28 C2
Sheep Pass Campground..................29 C2
Spin & Margie's Desert
  Hide-a-Way....................................30 B1
White Tank Campground.................31 C2

EATING
Beatnik Cafe.....................................32 B1
Crossroads Café................................33 B1
Edchada's..34 C1
JT Country Kitchen...........................35 B1
Rib Co..36 C1
Rio Ranch Market.............................37 C1
Sam's Pizza..38 B1
Wonder Garden................................39 C1

INFORMATION
Black Rock Nature Center.........(see 20)
California Welcome Center.............1 A1
Cottonwood Visitor Center...........2 D3
Coyote Corner................................3 B1
Joshua Tree Chamber of
  Commerce....................................4 B1
Joshua Tree Visitor Center............5 B1
Oasis Visitor Center........................6 C1
Twentynine Palms Chamber of
  Commerce..............................(see 37)

SIGHTS & ACTIVITIES
Boy Scout Trail................................7 C1
Cholla Cactus Garden Trail............8 D2
Desert Queen Ranch........................9 C1
Fortynine Palms Oasis Trail..........10 C1
Hidden Valley Trail........................11 C1
Indian Cove...................................12 C1
Inspiration Point Trail................(see 13)

Twentynine Palms Hwy

Sheep Hole Mountains

San Bernardino County
Riverside County

Mojave Desert
Transition Zone
Colorado Desert

Pinto Basin

Coxcomb Mountains

Joshua Tree
National Park

Old Dale Rd

Black Eagle Mine Rd

Eagle Mountains

Desert Center

Chiriaco Summit

To Parker (AZ; 130mi)

To Blythe (55mi);
Parker (AZ; 150mi)

PALM SPRINGS & THE DESERTS

Black Rock Canyon, **Indian Cove** and the six group sites at **Sheep Pass** may be reserved; check online for dates and details on individual sites. Campsites at **Belle**, **Cottonwood**, **Hidden Valley**, **Jumbo Rocks**, **Ryan** and **White Tank** are available on a first-come, first-served basis. Jumbo Rocks is especially attractive for its sheltered rock alcoves that provide great sunset- and sunrise-viewing platforms. At busy times, during spring and fall, find a site before noon to stake your claim.

Backcountry camping is permitted as long as it's 1 mile from the road and 500ft from any trail; registration is required at one of the 12 backcountry boards throughout the park. Fires are strictly forbidden.

Motels, Inns & Cabins

Twentynine Palms has the biggest selection of accommodations, but many are grotty no-tell motels (some geared more toward hourly than nightly rentals). As in other desert communities, we're giving high season (winter/spring) rates. Look for national chain lodgings via their websites. See also Pioneertown (opposite).

TWENTYNINE PALMS

Harmony Motel (Map pp364-5; ☎ 760-367-3351; www .harmonymotel.com; 71161 Twentynine Palms Hwy; r $60-85; P 🖳 🞉 👶 wi-fi) U2 wrote and recorded the *Joshua Tree* album here, and that's only one reason it's top pick for its class. The eight-room Harmony is a little designy (corrugated metal fencing around the pool and hot tub) and a little hippy-dippy (rooms decorated in a jumble of styles). There are large rooms (several with kitchens), gorgeous views and nooks for reading or meditating, a favorite pastime of the owner. Breakfast is not included, but there's a communal kitchen and library.

29 Palms Inn (Map pp364-5; ☎ 760-367-3505; www.29palmsinn.com; 73950 Inn Ave, Twentynine Palms; most rooms & suites incl breakfast $85-225; P 🖳 🞉 👶) Built on and around the 'Oasis of Mara', this charming collection of old adobe-and-wood cabins is Twentynine Palms' inn of record. Some cabins have decks and fireplaces, perfect for relaxing on cool desert evenings. The continental breakfast includes scratch muffins. There's also a great restaurant on the premises.

DESERT SURVIVAL 101

The desert is an unforgiving place with summertime temperatures up to 120°F, but if you take precautions you'll have nothing to fear. Here are some tips to help prepare for the worst and expect the best:

▪ Drink: water. Don't risk being stranded without it. Plan on drinking at least a gallon of water per day, and double that if you're hiking or boozing it up. Your body may be dehydrated before you realize it. If your urine runs darker than pale yellow, it's often a sign that you're getting dehydrated (unless you take a lot of vitamins). Sports drinks high in sodium and potassium are also helpful.

▪ Eat: salty foods. However, avoid salt tablets unless your physician recommends them. See the Health chapter for more information on heatstroke.

▪ Wear: loose-fitting, light-colored, long-sleeved clothing. Also wear a hat and use sunscreen and lip balm. Bring warmer clothing for nighttime, especially if you're camping; the desert can be surprisingly chilly after dark.

▪ Take: compass and map (and know how to use them). GPS units can be helpful, but sometimes batteries fail and units malfunction. A small mirror, matches and perhaps even flares can help you signal for help. A tent or groundsheet can provide vital sun protection and increase your visibility. Also useful: flashlight, pocketknife, first-aid kit and extra food and water. Cell phones can be helpful but don't work everywhere.

▪ Do: be sure your vehicle is in good condition and well gassed up, and don't push it beyond its limits. Never venture alone into remote areas. Always tell someone where you're going and when you'll be back. If you get stuck, stay with your vehicle and wait for rescue; a car is easier to spot than a hiker. If lost while hiking, seek the closest shady spot and stay put. You'll only get dehydrated and exhausted by walking around.

DETOUR: PIONEERTOWN

From Hwy 62 (Twentynine Palms Hwy) in the town of Yucca Valley, head 5 miles north up Pioneer Town Rd, and you'll drive straight up a hill and into the past. **Pioneertown** (off Map pp364-5; www .pioneertown.com) was built as a movie backdrop in 1946, developed by Roy Rogers, Dale Evans, Gene Autry and other Western stars, and has hardly changed since. The idea was that actors would have homes here, become part of the set and really live the Wild West life they acted out. The main street (Mane St) is lined with buildings that were used in countless Western movies and TV shows, including *Gunfight at the OK Corral*. You can witness a 'real' **gunfight** (☎ 760-228-0494; www.pioneertown-posse.org) in the street here from April to October at 2:30pm on Saturdays. It's a little cheesy but highly kitschy, and kids love it.

Pioneer Bowl (☎ 760-366-3025; 56313 Mane St; ☼ 11am-7pm Sat & Sun, Apr-Oct) is an old-fashioned bowling alley built for Roy Rogers in 1947. It's still in use, with original equipment and an amazing collection of vintage arcade games for which any good antique hound would pay big bucks. Its saloon sells beer and burgers.

Pappy & Harriet's Pioneertown Palace (☎ 760-365-5956; www.pappyandharriets.com; mains lunch $5-11, dinner $9-25; ☼ opens 11am Thu-Sun, 5pm Mon, closing varies with shows) is an Old West honky-tonk bar that defines nightlife in the Joshua Tree area. Expect cowboy hats, cheap beer, and big-as-Texas Tex-Mex grub. Make reservations. Best of all, there's free live music every night it's open. Sometimes it has big names, from Leon Russell to Shelby Lynne, and you'll need tickets.

Nearby are the marvelous **Rimrock Ranch Cabins** (☎ 760-228-1297; www.rimrockranchcabins.com; 50857 Burns Canyon Rd; cabins $103-157; **P** 🐾), built in the 1940s as the area's first homestead. They reopened in autumn 2007 after a fire that ravaged outer Pioneertown. The four lovingly decorated cabins each come with a kitchen and a private patio, perfect for stargazing. Or try the more basic **Pioneertown Motel** (☎ 760-365-4879; www.pioneertownmotel.com; 5040 Curtis Rd; r $70-85) and board your horse in its corral ($15).

JOSHUA TREE

Joshua Tree Inn (Map pp364-5; ☎ 760-366-1188; www .joshuatreeinn.com; 61259 Twentynine Palms Hwy; r incl breakfast from $85; **P** 🐾) Gram Parsons overdosed at this large U-shaped motel (and his fans still flock here to stay in Room 8). Rooms have beamed ceilings and country-style furniture, the dining room has paintings by local artists and there's a nice pool.

ourpick **Spin & Margie's Desert Hide-a-Way** (Map pp364-5; ☎ 760-366-9124; www.deserthideaway.com; 64491 Twentynine Palms Hwy; ste $125-160; **P**) Every boldly colorful, snappy-looking suite has its own kitchen at this delightful and homey four-room inn on three fenced-in acres. Design motifs include corrugated tin, old license plates and cartoon art. Charming, knowledgeable owners ensure a relaxed visit. It's down the dirt Sunkist Rd, about 3.5 miles east of central Joshua Tree.

Rosebud Ruby Star (Map pp364-5; ☎ 760-366-4676, 877-887-7370; www.rosebudrubystar.com; s/d $140/155, cabins from $155, houses from $235; **P** 🖥) Just south of Joshua Tree, near the western entrance of the park, this out-of-the-way Western-style charmer has two guest rooms, a cabin that sleeps up to five people, and two houses that sleep from four to six people. There's a two-night minimum stay at peak times. No phones or TVs in rooms.

EATING
Twentynine Palms

Wonder Garden (Map pp364-5; ☎ 760-367-2429; 73511 Twentynine Palms Hwy; mains breakfast $3-6, lunch $5-10; ☼ 7:45am-3pm Mon-Sat; 🚫) Southwestern colors and a weathervane usher you into this café. Look for turkey and melted brie or Reuben sandwiches, veggie wraps and all-important ice cream and smoothies.

Edchada's (Map pp364-5; ☎ 760-367-2131; 73502 Twentynine Palms Hwy; meals $6-12; ☼ lunch & dinner; **P** 🚫) Opinions vary on the food at this standard-issue Mexican eatery, but the margaritas are huge and you won't leave hungry. Look for lunch specials.

Rib Co (Map pp364-5; ☎ 760-367-1663; 72183 Twentynine Palms Hwy; mains $9-29; ☼ lunch Fri-Sun, dinner nightly; **P** 🚫) The fun atmosphere makes this roadside BBQ place worth a look. Expect sandwiches, burgers, chicken and ribs (some in Jack Daniels glaze), plus salads and sides.

Also worth visiting is the 29 Palms Inn (opposite), which makes it's own bread, grills great steaks and serves a variety of nightly specials (lunch mains $6 to $14, dinner mains $15 to $23). Make reservations.

Rio Ranch Market (Map pp364-5; ☎ 760-367-7216; cnr Twentynine Palms Hwy & Tamarisk Rd; ☼ 7am-10pm; ℗) Shop here for groceries and produce.

Joshua Tree

JT Country Kitchen (Map pp364-5; ☎ 760-366-8988; 61768 Twentynine Palms Hwy; most mains $4-8; ☼ breakfast & lunch) This roadside shack serves down home cookin': eggs, pancakes, biscuits with gravy, sandwiches and…what's this? Cambodian noodles and salads? Try the crispy chicken or peanut chicken salad.

Beatnik Cafe (Map pp364-5; ☎ 760-366-2090; www.jtbeat.com; 61597 Twentynine Palms Hwy; mains $4-9; ☼ 11am-11pm most nights; ℗ 🖳 Ⓥ ♿) This funky strip-mall coffeehouse with beat-up furniture serves breakfasts, sandwiches and light meals, like the Beatnik pizza with pesto and artichoke hearts. There's something doing almost every night: films, live music, open mic etc. Young crowd.

our pick **Crossroads Café** (Map pp364-5; ☎ 760-366-5414; 61715 Twentynine Palms Hwy; dishes $6-10; ☼ 7am-8pm Thu-Tue; ℗ Ⓥ ♿) The much-loved Crossroads serves healthy breakfasts, huge sandwiches, big salads and tasty dinner specials. Earth-goddess atmosphere.

Sam's Pizza (Map pp364-5; ☎ 760-366-9511; 61380 Twentynine Palms Hwy; mains $8-11; ☼ lunch & dinner Mon-Sat, dinner Sun; ℗ Ⓥ) Pizza? Yeah, but *cognoscenti* come here for Indian dishes like chicken tikka masala and *aloo gobhi*. Atmosphere: nil. Solution: takeout.

GETTING THERE & AWAY

The only way to reach Joshua Tree is by car. Rent one in Palm Springs or Los Angeles. From LA the trip takes two to three hours via I-10;

from Palm Springs it takes about an hour, depending on where you enter the park.

ANZA-BORREGO DESERT STATE PARK

Encompassing some of SoCal's most spectacular and accessible desert scenery, the little-developed Anza-Borrego comprises almost a fifth of San Diego County and extends almost all the way to Mexico, making it the largest state park in the USA outside Alaska: 640,000 acres, or 51% of the land in the California state-park system.

Human history here goes back 10,000 years, evidenced by the site's Native American pictographs. The park is named for Spanish explorer Juan Bautista de Anza, who in 1774 led some 240 soldiers and colonists through the area, and the *borregos* (Spanish for 'bighorn sheep') they no doubt saw. These are viewable even today, along with jackrabbits, roadrunners, kit fox and mule deer. In the 1850s, Borrego Springs became a stop along the Butterfield stagecoach line, which delivered mail between St Louis and San Francisco.

Winter and spring are high season here. In spring, wildflowers bloom in brilliant displays of bright color, a striking contrast to the subtle earth tones you'll see here all year long. Summers are extremely hot, hotter than in Joshua Tree. The average daily maximum temperature in July is 107°F, but it can reach 125°F.

ORIENTATION

The park's main town, **Borrego Springs** (Map p347, population 2989, elevation 590ft) has

---

DETOUR: INTEGRATRON

In the late 1940s, former aerospace engineer George van Tassel moved to the desert and began meditating near giant rocks on a desolate stretch some 10 miles north-west of Joshua Tree. The story is that visitors from Venus arrived in a flying saucer and told him of a process for cell rejuvenation involving a dome based on principles of sacred geometry. He began work on it in 1953. Van Tassel called the dome at once a time machine, a rejuvenation machine and an anti-gravity device. There's no documentation of its actually achieving any of that, but the **Integratron** (off Map pp364-5; ☎ 760-364-3126; www.integratron.com; 2477 Belfield Boulevard, Landers; depending on number of people, sound baths $25-50 ; ☼ check website) is still worth a visit. The draw today is 30-minute 'sound baths', in which docents stroke crystal bowls under the acoustically perfect dome; many visitors report an out-of-body experience, so maybe van Tassel realized his goal after all.

a handful of restaurants and lodgings. It's about 40 miles from Palm Springs as the crow flies, but it's about double that if you're driving. Just outside the town, the park's great visitor center and the easily accessible sights, including Font's Point and Borrego Palm Canyon, are fairly representative of the park as a whole.

The desert's southernmost region is the least visited and – aside from Blair Valley – has few developed trails and facilities. Attractions include Goat Trestle and the Carrizo Badlands, which has an overlook affording great views. The Split Mountain area, in the desert's southeast, is popular with 4WD vehicles, but also contains interesting geology and spectacular wind caves.

INFORMATION

The park's excellent **visitor center** (Map p347; ☎ 760-767-4205; www.anzaborrego.statepark.org; 200 Palm Canyon Dr; ◐ 9am-5pm Oct-May, Sat & Sun only Jun-Sep), 2 miles west of Borrego Springs township, is built partly underground. From the parking lot, it looks like a low scrubby hill. Its stone walls blend beautifully with the mountain backdrop, while the interior has award-winning displays and audiovisual presentations. Staff are helpful and informative. The park newspaper has a trail guide and notes which roads are accessible and by what type of vehicle.

Depending on winter rains, spring wildflowers in Anza-Borrego can be absolutely stunning. Flowers blossom in late February at lower elevations and progress over subsequent months at higher levels. Call the **Wildflower Hotline** (☎ 760-767-4684) for updates.

Permits ($6 per day) are required only for visitors entering campgrounds like Borrego Palm Canyon, Tamarisk Grove and Horse Camp to access trails, camp overnight or go picnicking. Fires are permitted in metal containers only; wood gathering is strictly prohibited.

WHERE ARE THE SPRINGS?

Early visitors to the area came across the springs along with the *borregos* (bighorn sheep), lending the town its name. But the springs stopped flowing due to earthquakes. Wait around, though; the next earthquake may yet bring another spring...

In an emergency, dial ☎ don't work everywhere in sary, climb to the highest

SIGHTS

Northeast of Borrego Springs, where S22 takes a 90-degree turn to the east, there's a pile of rocks just north of the road. This, the **Peg Leg Smith Monument** (Map p347), is a monument to Thomas Long 'Peg Leg' Smith: mountain man, fur trapper, Native American fighter, horse thief, liar and Wild West legend. Around 1829, Peg Leg passed through Borrego Springs on his way to LA and supposedly picked up some rocks that were later found to be pure gold. Strangely, he didn't return to the area until the 1850s, when he was unable to find the lode. Nevertheless, he told lots of people about it (often in exchange for a few drinks), and many came to search for the gold and add to the myths.

On the first Saturday of April, the **Peg Leg Smith Liars Contest** is an hilarious event in which amateur liars compete in the Western tradition of telling tall tales. Anyone can enter, so long as the story is about gold and mining in the Southwest, is less than five minutes long and is anything but the truth.

East of Borrego, a 4-mile dirt road, sometimes passable without a 4WD (check with the visitor center), goes south of S22 to **Font's Point** (Map p347, 1249ft), which offers a spectacular panorama over the Borrego Valley to the west and the Borrego Badlands to the south. Walking the 4 miles to the point is a good way to *really* be amazed when the desert seemingly drops from beneath your feet.

South of Hwy 78 at Ocotillo Wells there's a **ranger station** (☎ 760-767-5391). From here, paved Split Mountain Rd takes you past the **Elephant Trees Discovery Trail** (Map p347), one of the few places to see a 'herd' of the unusual elephant, trees named for their resemblance to an elephant's leg. Related to myrrh, the trees have a wonderful fragrance not unlike department stores around the holidays. The trees were thought not to exist in the Colorado Desert until a full-fledged hunt was launched in 1937. Expect to see (and hear) 4WD off-road vehicles around Ocotillo Wells.

About 4 miles south along Split Mountain Rd is a dirt-road turnoff for the primitive Fish Creek campground (p370); another 4 miles brings you to **Split Mountain** (Map p347). The road – popular with 4WD enthusiasts

...s right through Split Mountain between ...0ft-high walls created by earthquakes and erosion. The gorge is about 2 miles long from north to south. At the southern end, several steep trails lead up to delicate caves that have been carved into the sandstone outcroppings by the wind.

In the west of the park, around 5 miles southeast of Scissors Crossing (where S2 crosses Hwy 78), is **Blair Valley** (Map p347), known for its Native American pictographs and *morteros* (hollows in rocks used for grinding seeds). The area also offers nice campgrounds and hiking trails.

A monument at Foot and Walker Pass marks a difficult spot on the Butterfield Overland Stage Route, and in **Box Canyon** you can still see the marks of wagons on the Emigrant Trail. A steep 1-mile climb leads to **Ghost Mountain** and the remains of a house occupied by the family of desert recluse Marshall South.

ACTIVITIES
Hiking
There is a wide variety of hiking trails (Map p347) on offer. **Borrego Palm Canyon Nature Trail**, a popular self-guided loop trail that goes northeast from the Borrego Palm Canyon Campground (day fee $6 per vehicle), climbs 350ft in 3 miles past a palm grove and waterfall, a delightful oasis in the dry, rocky countryside.

Hellhole Canyon/Maidenhair Falls Trail starts from the Hellhole Canyon Trailhead, 2 miles west of the visitor center on S22, and climbs past several palm oases to a seasonal waterfall that supports bird life and a variety of plants.

In a 3-mile round-trip you can see pictographs and a view of the Vallecito Valley from **Pictograph/Smuggler's Canyon Trail**, which starts 3.5 miles from S2 in Blair Valley.

A variety of other short trails have interpretive signs or self-guiding brochures. The 1-mile **Cactus Loop Nature Trail** shows a variety of cacti. Nearby, the 2-mile **Yaqui Well Nature Trail** has many labeled desert plants and passes a natural water hole that attracts a rich variety of birdlife as well as the occasional bighorn sheep in winter. The short **Narrows Earth Trail**, 2 miles east of Tamarisk Grove, highlights the local geology; look for the unusual chuparosa shrubs, which attract hummingbirds.

For last-minute equipment, stop by **Borrego Outfitters** (☎ 760-767-3502; 519 The Mall).

Mountain Biking
Both primitive roads and paved roads are open to bikes. Popular routes are Grapevine Canyon, Oriflamme Canyon and Canyon Sin Nombre. The visitor center (p369) has a free mountain-bike guide. **Carrizo Bikes** (☎ 760-767-3872; 648 Palm Canyon Dr; bike hire per first hr/additional hrs/24hr $7/5/30), in Borrego Springs, rents bikes and also leads guided rides (inquire ahead).

Organized Tours
The **Anza Borrego Foundation** (☎ 760-767-0446; www.theabf.org; 587 Palm Canyon Dr) has an impressive lineup of interpretive programs from stargazing to three-day hikes for the fittest outdoors folk. Phone or check online for upcoming events.

SLEEPING
Camping
Camping is permitted anywhere in the park as long as you're not within 200 yards of any road or water source. You can't light a fire on the ground, and gathering vegetation (dead or alive) is prohibited.

Bow Willow Campground (Map p347; campsites $7; P) Off S2 in the southern part of the park, Bow Willow has only 16 campsites available, with water, pit toilets, tables and fire pits. No reservations.

Tamarisk Grove Campground (Map p347; reservations ☎ 800-444-7275; www.reserveamerica.com; campsites $29; mid-Sep–mid-May; P) Twelve miles south of Borrego Springs, near Hwy 78 and at 1400ft of elevation, Tamarisk is smaller than Borrego Palm Canyon but has more shelter. It also has flush toilets.

Borrego Palm Canyon Campground (Map p347; reservations ☎ 800-444-7275; www.reserveamerica.com; tent/RV sites Oct–mid-May $20/29, mid-May–Sep $15/24; P) This campground has award-winning toilets (rebuilt after a devastating 2003 flash flood), close-together campsites and a amphitheater with lectures on topics like astronomy and local bats.

There are several other primitive campgrounds in the park – **Culp Valley**, **Arroyo Salado**, **Yaqui Well**, **Yaqui Pass**, **Fish Creek** and **Mountain Palm Springs** – which are free and have pit toilets but no water and only minimal facilities. Information about all campgrounds can be obtained from any ranger station or visitor center in the park, or online at www.parks.ca.gov.

Motels & Resorts

The following are in Borrego Springs. In summer temperatures soar and rates drop; prices following are for winter.

HaciendadelSol (☎ 760-767-5442; www.haciendadelsol-borrego.com; 610 Palm Canyon Dr; r $75, units with kitchen $120-160; P ⊠ ☒ wi-fi) This 6-acre property has rooms from motel-size to cottages, all pretty Spartan with desert-plant landscaping. It's good for groups of mates seeking to socialize around the pool, and has a picnic area with horseshoes and shuffleboard.

Stanlund's Inn & Suites (☎ 760-767-5501; www.stanlunds.com; 2771 Borrego Springs Rd; incl breakfast r $85-115; P ⊡ ☒ ☒) Stanlund's, outside the town center, is a standard-issue motel, though clean and well kept with concrete block walls. Some rooms have kitchens, but all have coffeemaker, microwave and fridge.

Palm Canyon Resort (☎ 760-767-5341, 800-242-0044; www.palmcanyonresort.com; 221 Palm Canyon Dr; r $109-189; P ☒ ☒) A quarter of a mile from the park's visitor center, you'll get a comfy motel-style room at this Old West village-style inn (though built in the 1980s). There are two pools, a restaurant and saloon, laundry, store and RV parking.

Palms at Indian Head (☎ 760-767-7788, 800-519-2624; www.thepalmsatindianhead.com; 2220 Hoberg Rd; r incl breakfast $159-229; P ☒) One mile north from Palm Canyon Dr and on 240 acres abutting the state park, the 12-room Palms is a real retreat in a 1950s shell with mostly Southwestern-style rooms, no in-room phones or internet. There's a 25-yard-long pool and suites have wood-burning fireplaces. No children under 13.

Borrego Valley Inn (☎ 760-767-0311, 800-333-5810; www.borregovalleyinn.com; 405 Palm Canyon Dr; r incl breakfast $200-230; P ☒ wi-fi) This small, immaculately kept inn (15 rooms on 9-plus acres), filled with Southwestern artifacts and Native American weavings, is an intimate spa-resort, perfect for adults. One pool is clothing-optional. Rates include a healthy breakfast and all-day soft drinks. Most rooms have kitchenettes.

La Casa del Zorro (☎ 760-767-5323, 800-824-1884; www.lacasadelzorro.com; 3845 Yaqui Pass Rd; r from $365, casitas from $395; P ⊡ ☒ ☒ wi-fi) The area's top luxury resort has manicured grounds, glorious swimming pools, croquet, a putting green and excellent tennis and fitness facilities. Southwestern architecture boasts spacious rooms with marble everything and folk-craft–inspired design, wood-burning fireplaces, private pools.

EATING

All of the following are in Borrego Springs.

Center Market (☎ 760-767-3311; 590 Palm Canyon Dr; ☻ 8:30am-6:30pm Mon-Sat, 8:30am-5pm Sun; P) The better of the town's two supermarkets is across from the mall.

Kendall's Cafe (☎ 760-767-3491; the Mall; mains breakfast & lunch $5-11, dinner $11-15; ☻ 6am-8pm; P ☒) This coffee shop is a hometown favorite for blueberry pancakes at breakfast and a combination of Mexican (enchiladas, fajitas etc) and straight-down-the-middle American standards the rest of the day.

Jilberto's Taco Shop (☎ 760-767-1008; 655 Palm Canyon Dr; most dishes under $6; P) Jilberto's makes up with flavor and price what it lacks in atmosphere. Outdoor tables.

Carlee's Place (☎ 760-767-3262; 660 Palm Canyon Dr; mains lunch $6-12, dinner $12-21; ☻ lunch & dinner; P) Even if the decor feels like it hasn't been updated since the '70s, locals pick Carlee's, near Christmas Circle, for its burgers, pastas and steak dinners – the pool table is a big draw too. There's live music on Friday and karaoke on Thursday and Saturday.

Red Ocotillo (☎ 760-767-7400; 818 Palm Canyon Dr; mains breakfast $6-13, lunch & dinner $6-15; ☻ breakfast, lunch & dinner; P ☒ wi-fi) This rather stylish Quonset hut (no, really) serves breakfast all day (think Benedicts and skillet omelettes) as well as hulking sandwiches and cold beer. Pet-friendly.

Krazy Coyote Saloon & Grill (☎ 760-767-7788; 2220 Hoberg Rd; mains $10-36; ☻ dinner Wed-Sun; P) The bar and grill at the Palms at Indian Head serves famous martinis and classics like chicken cordon bleu, alongside newer fare like sesame-garlic pork tenderloin. The atmosphere is fun and the views terrific.

our pick Butterfield Room (☎ 760-767-5323; 3845 Yaqui Pass Rd; mains lunch $10-16, dinner $14-28; ☻ breakfast, lunch & dinner; P ☒) The fine-dining restaurant at La Casa del Zorro is very fine indeed. A changing menu provides fresh takes on standards, plus plenty of local ingredients (the kit fox salad combines lettuce, citrus, walnuts and dates), and there's an enviable if pricey wine list. Desserts are off the wall. Dress code is collared shirt, dress pants and shoes for men, 'appropriate attire' for women.

HOT TOPIC: SALTON SEA

It's a most unexpected sight: California's largest lake in the middle of its largest desert. The Salton Sea has a fascinating past, complicated present and uncertain future.

Geologists say that the Gulf of California once extended about 150 miles north of its present shore to the present-day Coachella Valley, but millions of years' worth of silt flowing through the Colorado River gradually sealed the valley off, leaving a sink behind. Occasional overflows from the river came to rest in the sink, eventually evaporating. By the mid-1800s the sink was the site of salt mines, and geologists realized that the mineral-rich soil would make excellent farmland. Colorado River water was diverted into irrigation canals.

In 1905 the Colorado breached its banks once again, and thus the Salton Sea, today about 35 miles long, 15 miles wide and with nearly a third higher salt content than in the gulf, was born. It took 18 months, 1500 workers and half-a-million tons of rock to put the river back on its course.

By mid-century, the Salton Sea was stocked with fish including tilapia and corvina, and marketed as the California Riviera, with vacation homes along its shores. The fish, in turn, attracted birds, and the sea remains a prime spot for bird-watching, including migratory and endangered species such as snow geese, mallards, ruddy ducks, white and brown pelicans, bald eagles and peregrine falcons.

These days, if you've heard of the Salton Sea at all it's probably due to annual fish die-offs. These, along with the sea's distinctive odor and poor publicity from 1980s environmental studies, have significantly diminished it as a tourist destination (though recent environmental studies have refuted some of the 1980s results). The die-offs are due to phosphorous and nitrogen in runoff from surrounding farmland. The minerals cause algae blooms, and when the algae die they deprive the water – and fish – of oxygen. Even if farming were to stop tomorrow, there are still generations' worth of minerals in the soil, waiting to reach the sink.

One obvious solution would seem to be to cut off the water to the sea and let it die, but that carries its own dilemma. A dry Salton Sea would leave a dust bowl, with projections of a permanent dust cloud devastating air quality valley-wide. The debate rages.

To see the sea for yourself, try the **Salton Sea State Recreation Area** (☎ 760-393-3052; www .parks.ca.gov; Hwy 111, North Shore), or **Sonny Bono Salton Sea National Wildlife Refuge** (☎ 760-348-5278; 906 W Sinclair Rd; ⏰ 7am-3:30pm Mon-Fri year-round, 8am-4:30pm Sat & Sun Nov-Mar) is off Hwy 11,1 between Niland and Calipatria.

GETTING THERE & AWAY

You'll need a car to get to Anza-Borrego Desert State Park. From San Diego (approximately 2½ hours), I-8 to S2 is easiest because it mostly follows freeway. Alternatively, take the scenic and twisty Hwy 79 from I-8 north through Cuyamaca Rancho State Park and into Julian, then head east on Hwy 78.

From Orange County (via Temecula), take Hwy 79 to CA 2 and CA 22; the descent into Borrego Springs is breathtaking. From Palm Springs (1½ hours), take I-10 to Indio, then Hwy 86 south along the Salton Sea. Turn west on S22.

TEMECULA

Temecula has become a popular short-break destination for its Old West Americana main street, nearly two dozen wineries, and California's largest casino, Pechanga.

Temecula means 'Place of the Sun' in the language of the native Luiseño people, who were present when Fr Fermín Lasuen became the first Spanish missionary to visit in 1797. In the 1820s, the area became a ranching outpost for the Mission San Luis Rey (p339), in present-day Oceanside. Later, Temecula became a stop on the Butterfield stagecoach line (1858–1861) and the California Southern railroad.

But it's Temecula's late-20th-century growth that's been most astonishing, from 2700 people in 1970 – the city didn't get its first traffic light until 1984 – to some 91,000 residents today. Between Old Town and the wineries is a buffer zone of off-putting suburban sprawl. Ignore that and you'll do fine.

ORIENTATION

Temecula is in the southeast corner of Riverside County, near San Diego and Orange Counties. The five-block Old Town Front St, heart of Old Town Temecula, is a minute's drive from the I-15 Freeway. From here, Rancho California Rd is the main route into wine country.

INFORMATION

Temecula Valley Convention & Visitors Bureau operates a cheery **visitor center** (☎ 951-506-0056; www.temeculacvb.com; 42031 Main St, Suite C; ◷ 9am-6pm Sun-Thu, 9am-7pm Fri & Sat). In an emergency, dial ☎ 911.

SIGHTS & ACTIVITIES

Old Town Front St's turn-of-the-last-century storefronts make for an attractive stroll – pick up the *Historic Old Town Temecula* leaflet with building descriptions. En route, sample local products at shops like **Temecula Olive Oil Company** (☎ 951-693-0607, 866-653-8396; www.temeculaoliveoil.com; 28653 Old Town Front St) and **Temecula House of Jerky** (☎ 951-308-9232, 28655 Old Town Front St). The latter offers ostrich, buffalo, venison and more traditional beasties. Hundreds of **antique dealers** populate the neighborhood, most agglomerated into large antique halls.

Wine tasting is big in the rolling hills east of Old Town, about 10 minutes' drive. Pick up the *Wineries of Temecula Valley* map and guide at the visitor center. The newness of the wineries and the preponderance of large gift shops make them less quaint than elsewhere in California, but you can find award-winning and creative wines.

Wilson Creek (☎ 951-699-9463; www.wilsoncreekwinery.com; 35960 Rancho California Rd; tasting $10; ◷ 10am-5pm) makes almond champagne (infused with almond oil in the fermentation process) and a chocolate-infused port. A nice stop if you've got children in tow is **Longshadow Ranch** (☎ 951-687-6221; www.longshadowranchwinery.com; 39847 Calle Contento; tasting $7-10; ◷ noon-5pm Mon-Fri, 10am-5pm Sat & Sun; ⊛); the kids can look at Clydesdales and goats while mommy and daddy sip. Further afield, **Leonesse Cellars** (☎ 951-302-7601; www.leonessecellars.com; 38311 De Portola Rd; tasting $10; ◷ 10am-5pm) offers award-winning Viognier and Melange des Reves, plus sweeping views from its sort-of-Teutonic tower.

To leave the driving to someone else, **Grapeline Temecula** (☎ 888-894-6379; www.gogrape.com) offers day-long wine tours by minivan

with pickup at many of the area's lodgings. Rates start at $38 per person; tastings and lunch are extra.

To see the region from the air, contact **California Dreamin'** (☎ 800-373-3359; www.californiadreamin.com; per person from $198), which operates balloon rides in Temecula.

SLEEPING

Palomar Inn Hotel (☎ 951-676-6503; www.palomarinnhotel.com; 28522 Old Town Front St; r weekday/weekend from $48/75; P wi-fi) This 1927 10-room hostelry is Old Town's cheapest, with mismatched furniture and no private bathrooms or air-con. At the time of writing it was in the midst of a renovation, although it had a ways to go. Still, the price is right and the location is primo.

Loma Vista B&B (☎ 951-676-7047, 877-676-7047; www.lomavistabb.com; 33350 La Serena Way; r incl breakfast $130-220; P) Welcoming hilltop B&B with 10 rooms (four with vineyard-view balconies) and a hot tub. Rooms are individually furnished from country to art-deco styles. Known for delicious full breakfasts.

South Coast Winery (☎ 951-587-9463; www.wineresort.com; 34843 Rancho California Rd; r from $209; P ⊛ wi-fi) A very Temecula way to stay. Rooms in a few dozen villas dot the edge of the vineyards, around a spa and a well-maintained fitness facility. Your room key comes with a wine glossary and rates include a bottle of wine and tastings.

EATING & DRINKING

Bank of Mexican Food (☎ 951-676-6160; 28645 Old Town Front St; mains $7-12; ◷ lunch & dinner daily, breakfast Sat & Sun; ⊛) In this handsome former bank (c 1913), try mahi tacos, huevos rancheros or anything with the righteous Mexican rice.

Swing Inn Cafe (☎ 951-676-2321; 28676 Old Town Front St; mains $5-14; ◷ breakfast, lunch & dinner; ⊛) A proud local institution since 1927, with red leatherette seating and lots of windows to watch the world go by. The Swing Inn serves three square meals, but everyone goes for breakfast – luckily it's served all day. The biscuits and gravy are renowned.

Sweet Lumpy's Barbeque (☎ 951-506-3747; 28464 Old Town Front St; mains lunch $6-23; ◷ 11am-8pm Tue-Sat, 11am-4:30pm Sun; P ⊛) Tops in town for barbecue-pulled pork (get yours on a sandwich with coleslaw) alongside burgers, chicken and garlic fries. Eat in the dining room or on the terrace at picnic tables next to hay bales.

Vineyard Rose (☎ 951-587-9463; 34843 Rancho California Rd; lunch mains $12-25, dinner mains $18-34; ♥ breakfast, lunch & dinner; ℗) South Coast Winery's gracious cavernous restaurant has a Craftsman-style barn feel and vineyard views from the balcony. Penne with seafood and petite filet mignon are big hits. At breakfast, the banana pancake with vanilla-bean sauce and coconut may make your head spin.

Wine & Beer Garden (☎ 951-506-4474; 28464 Old Town Front St) Rough 'n' ready outdoor bar with frequent nighttime entertainment like guitar soloists and singers. It's right by Sweet Lumpy's.

ENTERTAINMENT

Many wineries offer entertainment, from guitar soloists to chamber concerts. Check at the visitor center or www.temeculacvb.com for upcoming events. **Pechanga Resort & Casino** (☎ 877-711-2946; www.pechanga.com; 45000 Pechanga Pkwy) books stand-up in its Improv comedy club, and the 1200-seat Pechanga Theater hosts the likes of Aretha Franklin, Jonny Lang and the Shanghai Acrobats.

GETTING THERE & AWAY

Temecula is just off the I-15 freeway. Either of the Rancho California Rd or Rte 79 exits will take you to Old Town Front St. Allow 45 minutes from San Diego, 55 from Anaheim, 75 from Palm Springs or 80 from LA.

Temecula's **Greyhound stop** (☎ 951-676-9768; 28464 Old Town Front Street) sells tickets for twice-daily buses heading to San Diego ($17) and Los Angeles ($23).

Santa Barbara County

Santa Barbara's gotten a bit frisky in the new millennium. Tucked between the majestic Santa Ynez Mountains and the shimmering Pacific, the city's red-tile roofs, white stucco buildings, Spanish mission and sleepy Mediterranean vibe have long given credence to Santa Barbara's claim to the title of the 'American Riviera.' It's a gorgeous place to loll on the beach, eat well, shop a bit and push your cares off to another day. But the city's waking up, jump-starting the nation's nascent 'green movement' in an outside-the-box, upbeat style highlighting electric shuttles, accessible urban bike trails, ecofocused attractions and earth-friendly wine tours.

This energy has trickled into the agricultural heart of Santa Barbara County. With the success of Oscar-winning movie *Sideways* (2004), winemaking is booming in the bucolic Santa Ynez Valley, where a hundred or so wineries now vie for your attention. Many of the newest winemakers are implementing their passion for the vine in earth-conscious ways, using organic practices and biodynamic farming techniques while enthusiastically sharing their knowledge in the tasting room. And they're producing top-notch pinots, Syrahs and Chardonnays in the meantime.

Mother Nature returns the love with hiking, biking, surfing, kayaking, scuba diving and camping opportunities galore. There's even an Outdoor Visitor Center to help you plan your adventure. But if all you want to do is relax, sunny beaches still await your arrival.

HIGHLIGHTS

- Enjoying panoramic views of the city from the 85ft tower of the **Santa Barbara County Courthouse** (p378) in downtown Santa Barbara
- Pedaling past vineyards, farms and rolling countryside in the scenic **Santa Rita Hills** (p395)
- Window shopping, wine tasting and patio dining in **Los Olivos** (p399)
- Hiking Rattlesnake Canyon Trail in the southern foothills of the **Santa Ynez Mountains (p384)**
- Pretending to understand Einstein's written description of the theory of relativity at the **Karpeles Museum** (p382) in Santa Barbara
- Exploring the **Foxen Canyon Wine Trail** (p396) and tasting California's best pinot noirs and Syrahs
- Watching for migrating whales from Cavern Point on Santa Cruz Island in **Channel Islands National Park** (p405)

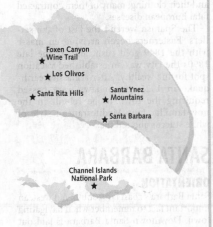

★ Foxen Canyon Wine Trail

★ Los Olivos

★ Santa Rita Hills

★ Santa Ynez Mountains

★ Santa Barbara

★ Channel Islands National Park

FAST FACTS

■ **Population Santa Barbara County** 399,347

■ **Average temps** Jan 45/64°F, Jul 59/75°F

■ **Santa Barbara to LA** 95 miles

■ **Santa Barbara to Solvang** 35 miles (via Hwy 154)

■ **Santa Barbara to Ojai** 30 miles

■ **Santa Barbara to Ventura** 27 miles

HISTORY

The Chumash people thrived in the Santa Barbara area for thousands of years before the arrival of the Spanish, setting up elaborate trade routes between the mainland and the Channel Islands, which they reached via sturdily constructed canoes known as *tomols*. In 1542 explorer Juan Rodríguez Cabrillo sailed into the channel, claimed the area for Spain then sailed off to winter – and eventually die – on one of the nearby islands.

The Chumash had little reason for concern until the permanent return of the Spanish in the mid-1700s, when missionaries and padres arrived to establish missions and to convert the Chumash to Christianity – a systematic process that was occurring up and down the coast. The Spaniards used the converted Chumash to construct the missions and presidios and provide subsequent labor. Conversion saw these Native Americans change their diet and their clothing; many of them contracted fatal European diseases.

The Spanish weren't the last of the settlers. Easterners began arriving en masse with the 1849 gold rush, and by the late 1890s the city was an established vacation spot for the wealthy. After a massive earthquake in 1925, tough laws were passed requiring the town to be rebuilt in the now-familiar faux-Mediterranean style of white stuccos and red tile.

SANTA BARBARA

ORIENTATION

Santa Barbara's coast faces south, not west, an important fact to remember when navigating town. Downtown Santa Barbara is laid out in a square grid – its main artery is State St, which runs north–south. State St divides the east side from the west side. Lower State St (south of Ortega St) has a large concentration of bars, while Upper State St (north of Ortega St) has most of the pretty shops and museums. Cabrillo Blvd hugs the coastline and turns into Coast Village Rd as it enters the eastern suburb of Montecito. Just south of Hwy 101, east of State St, the burgeoning Funk Zone lures the curious with its eclectic mix of rough-and-tumble indie shops – a refreshing poke in the eye to the conformist Spanish Mission–style designs prominent downtown. The southern foothills of the Santa Ynez mountains, just north of the city, are known locally as the Front Country.

Santa Barbara is surrounded by small affluent communities: Hope Ranch to the west, and Montecito and Summerland to the east. UCSB is just west of Hope Ranch in Isla Vista.

Interstate 101 and the railroad tracks – which run parallel – cut east to west across State St, just north of the coast. Be prepared to wait for the train about once every hour or so if you're traveling on State St. Access to and from Interstate 101 can be found at Garden St.

The Santa Barbara Visitor Center (p378) has free maps.

INFORMATION
Bookstores

Book Den (Map p380; ☎ 805-962-3321; 15 E Anapamu St) The oldest used bookstore in California specializes in history, art, architecture and academic-press titles. It has an excellent tracking system for locating used books. Bibliophiles and perpetual students, beware: you may never get out of here.

Chaucer's Books (Map pp378-9; ☎ 805-682-6787; 3321 State St, Loreto Plaza) Best selection in town – 150,000 plus – for any new book you could ever want.

Pacific Travelers Supply (Map p380; ☎ 805-963-4438, 800-546-8060; 12 W Anapamu St) The best spot in town to buy guidebooks and maps, as well as miscellaneous travelers' accessories including hats, Crocs, tents, GPS systems and surfing guides.

Internet Access

FedEx Kinko's (Map p380; ☎ 805-966-1114; 1030 State St; per min 25¢; 🕑 7am-10pm Mon-Thu, 7am-9pm Fri, 9am-7pm Sat, 10am-8pm Sun)

Grayphics (Map p380; ☎ 805-899-2387; 1114 State St, #7 La Arcada, La Arcada; per 15min/hr $2/8; 🕑 8:30am-5pm Mon-Fri) Five stations available.

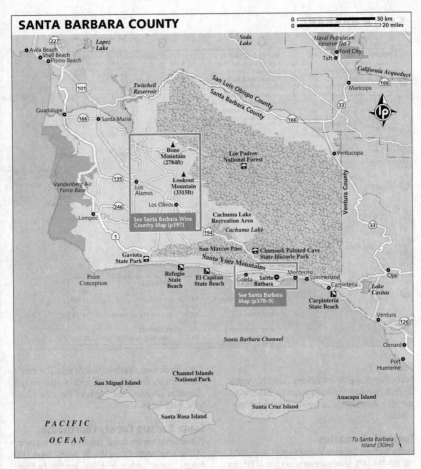

SANTA BARBARA COUNTY

Muddy Waters (Map p380; ☎ 805-966-9328; 508 E Haley St; per 30min/hr $3/5; ☼ 6am-6pm, later if there's a show, closed Sun)

Santa Barbara Public Library (Map p380; ☎ 805-962-7653; www.sbplibrary.org; 40 E Anapamu St; ☼ 10am-9pm Mon-Thu, to 5:30pm Fri & Sat, 1-5pm Sun)

Libraries

Santa Barbara Public Library (Map p380; ☎ 805-962-7653; www.sbplibrary.org; 40 E Anapamu St; ☼ 10am-9pm Mon-Thu, to 5:30pm Fri & Sat, 1-5pm Sun) The main branch of the public library also has computers with free internet for public use.

Media

Independent (www.independent.com) Published on Thursday, it has thorough events listings and reviews.

Santa Barbara News-Press (www.newspress.com) Santa Barbara's daily newspaper also has an events calendar and a special Friday supplement called 'Scene', helpful for learning what's going on.

Medical Services

Santa Barbara Cottage Hospital (Map pp378-9; ☎ 805-682-7111; cnr Pueblo & Bath Sts; ☼ 24hr) Emergency room operating 24/7.

Money

Bank of America (Map pp378-9; ☎ 805-564-2064; 834 State St)

Paul A Brombal Coin & Jewelry (Map pp378-9; ☎ 805-687-3641; 3601a State St; ☼ 10am-5pm Mon-Fri, 10am-2pm Sat) Exchanges currency; call ahead. It's on the corner of Ontare.

SANTA BARBARA

INFORMATION
Chaucer's Books.................1 E2
Los Padres National Forest
  Headquarters..................2 A2
Paul A Brombal Coin & Jewelry..3 E2
Santa Barbara Cottage Hospital..4 F2

SIGHTS & ACTIVITIES
Cold Spring Ridge Trail...........5 H1
Inspiration Point..................6 F1
Mission Santa Barbara...........7 F2
Museum of Natural History &
  Gladwin Planetarium............8 F2
Rattlesnake Canyon Trail.........9 G1
Santa Barbara Botanic Garden....10 F1
Santa Barbara Zoological Garden..11 G2

SLEEPING
Cabrillo Inn.....................12 G3
Four Seasons Biltmore Hotel..13 H2
Hacienda Motel.................14 E2
Montecito Inn..................15 H2
Motel 6 Santa Barbara.......16 G2
Secret Garden Inn &
  Cottages....................17 F2

EATING
Lazy Acres.....................18 F3
Los Arroyos....................19 H2
Lucky's........................20 H2
McConnell's Ice Cream..........21 F2

TRANSPORT
Santa Barbara Airbus Stop.......22 G3

Post

Post office (Map p380; ☎ 805-564-2226; 836 Anacapa St; ☺ 8:30am-6pm Mon-Fri, 9am-2pm Sat) Full-service post office. Automated Postal Center and stamp machine in lobby.

Tourist Information

Santa Barbara Outdoor Visitor Center (Map p380; ☎ 805-884-1475; www.outdoorsb.noaa.gov; 113 Harbor Way, 4th fl, Waterfront Center Bldg) Lots of info on Channel Islands National Park and Los Padres National Forest. Great harbor view from deck. Volunteer-based, so hours depend on availability. Generally open for around four hours a day – call for precise times.

Santa Barbara Visitor Center (Map p380; ☎ 805-965-3021; www.santabarbaraca.com; 1 Garden St; ☺ 9am-5pm Mon-Sat, 10am-5pm Sun) Pick up maps and brochures, and consult with the helpful, but busy, staff.

SIGHTS

Grab a free map from the visitors center for the self-guided 12-block **Red Tile walking tour**. This tour is a convenient and easy introduction to downtown's historical highlights, including the Santa Barbara County Courthouse and El Presidio de Santa Barbara State Park. The tour's name comes from the half-moon-shaped red clay tiles covering the roofs of the city's historic buildings.

Santa Barbara County Courthouse

Panoramic views from the 85ft clock tower of the **courthouse** (Map p380; ☎ 805-962-6464; 1100 Anacapa St; admission free; ☺ 8:30am-5pm Mon-Fri, 10am-5pm Sat & Sun) are not to be missed. Built in Spanish-Moorish Revival style in 1929, the courthouse features hand-painted ceilings, wrought-iron chandeliers, and tiles from Tunisia and Spain. Check out the mural room on the 2nd floor. You're free to explore it on your own, but you'll get a lot more out of the free docent-led tour offered at 2pm Monday through Saturday, and at 10:30am Monday, Tuesday and Friday.

Santa Barbara Museum of Art

With a collection containing 26,500 works of art, this well-regarded **art museum** (Map p380; ☎ 805-963-4364; www.sbma.net; 1130 State St; adult $9, student, senior & child 6-17 $6, Sun free; ☺ 11am-5pm Tue-Sun) displays European and American celebs –

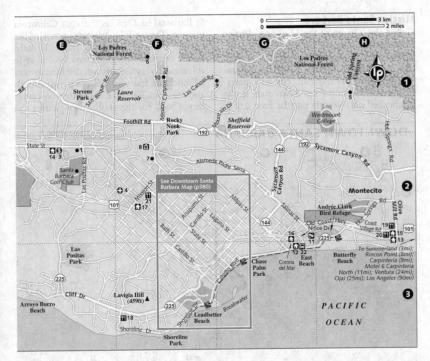

Monet, Matisse, Hopper and O'Keeffe – as well as photography and classical sculpture. Spend a few minutes exploring the Asian exhibit on the 2nd floor where displays include an intricate, colorful Tibetan sand mandala and the iron-chainmail armor of a Japanese warrior. There's also an interactive children's gallery, a museum shop and a café that makes good sandwiches.

Waterfront

The southern end of State St gives way to **Stearns Wharf** (Map p380; P), a rough wooden pier with a few snack and souvenir shops. Built in 1872 by John Peck Stearn, it's the oldest continuously operating wharf on the West Coast. During the 1940s it was owned by Jimmy Cagney and his two brothers. Partly destroyed by a 1998 fire, it has now been restored. Parking is available for $2 per hour, with the first 90 minutes free with validation. Also on the wharf, look for the **Ty Warner Sea Center** (Map p380; ☎ 805-962-2526; www.sbnature.org; 211 Stearns Wharf; adult/child 2-12/teen 13-17 & senior $7/4/6; ☼ 10am-5pm; ☼), part of the Santa Barbara Museum of Natural History (p381).

This is a great place for kids: the staff here is so darn engaging and enthusiastic, your child will be contemplating a career in marine biology in no time. From touch-a-shark water tanks and crawl-through aquariums to whale sing-alongs, it's interactive, educational and plain old fun. The Sea Center also has opportunities for volunteers – from a few days to a week – so if oceanography's your thing, give 'em a ring before you arrive.

Kids will also get a kick out of the small but worth-a-stop **Santa Barbara Maritime Museum** (Map p380; ☎ 805-962-8404; www.sbmm.org; 113 Harbor Way; adult/child 1-5/youth 6-17 & senior $7/2/4; ☼ 10am-6pm Jun-Aug, 10am-5pm Sep-May, closed Wed; ☼), located southwest of the wharf on the harbor. The two-level museum celebrates the town's briny history with memorabilia and hands-on exhibits, including a big-game fishing chair from which you can 'reel in' a trophy marlin – who knew a fake fish could tug so hard? Elsewhere you can take a virtual trip through the Santa Barbara Channel and peek through a 45ft-tall US Navy periscope, the latter no longer trained on people's homes. Admission is free the third Thursday of the month.

Mission Santa Barbara

Called the 'Queen of the Missions,' **Mission Santa Barbara** (Map pp378-9; ☎ 805-682-4713, tour info 805-682-4149; www.sbmission.org; 2201 Laguna St; adult/senior/child 6-15/child under 6 $5/4/1/free; 🕒 9am-5pm; Ⓟ) shimmers above the city on a majestic perch half a mile from downtown. It was established on December 4 (the feast day of St Barbara) in 1786, as the 10th California mission. Three adobe structures preceded the current stone version from 1820, the main facade of which integrates neoclassical-style columns. Today the mission still functions as a Franciscan friary as well as a parish church and museum. Behind it is an extensive cemetery – look for the skull carvings over the

DOWNTOWN SANTA BARBARA

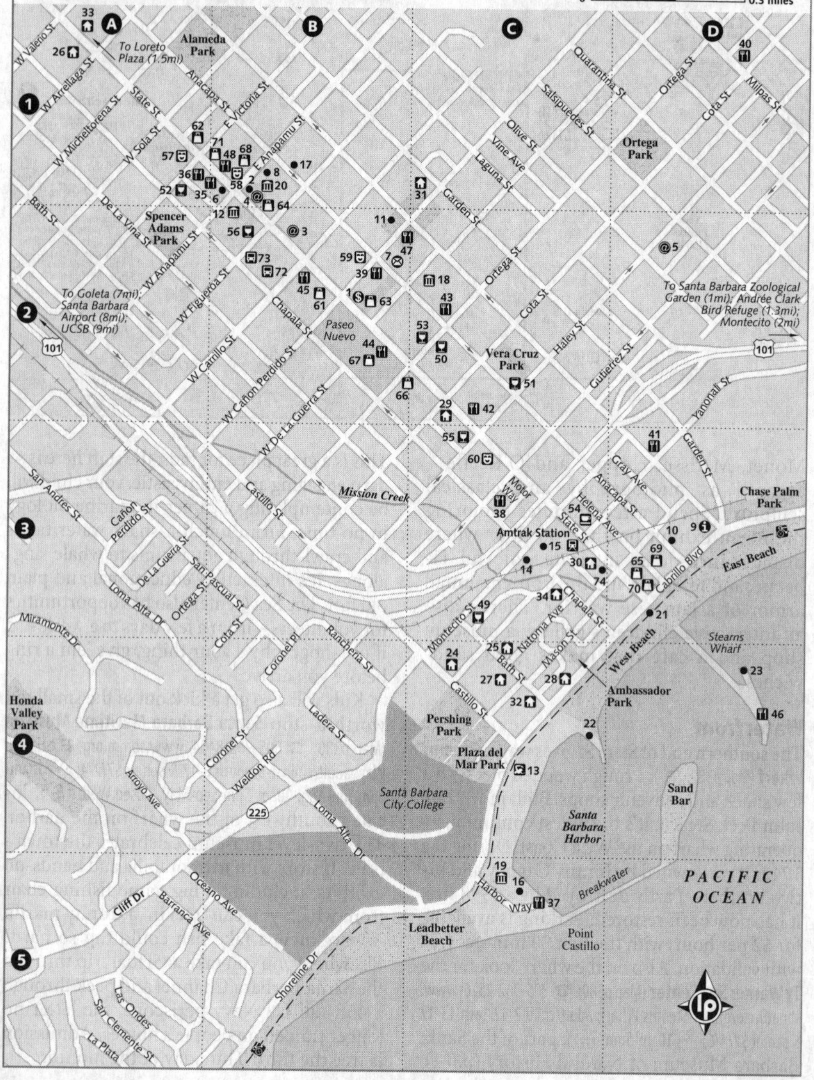

doorway – with 4000 Chumash graves and the elaborate mausoleums of early California settlers. As you walk through the mission's exhibits – which include Chumash baskets, a missionary's bedroom, and fascinating black-and-white mission photos dating from the 1980s – keep in mind that doors lock behind you, so make sure you're finished before moving on. Closed Thanksgiving Day, Christmas Day and Easter.

Santa Barbara Botanic Garden

Want the perfect place to stop and smell the redwoods? After visiting the mission, take a soul-satisfying jaunt to the 65-acre **botanic garden** (Map pp378-9; ☎ 805-682-4726; www.sbbg.org; 1212 Mission Canyon Rd; adult/child 2-12yr/teen 13-17yr & senior $8/4/6; ⏱ 9am-6pm Mar-Oct, to 5pm Nov-Feb; **P**), devoted to California's native flora. About 5.5 miles of trails meander through cacti, redwoods and wildflowers past the old mission dam, built by the Chumash to irrigate the mission's fields. Grab a map from the staffed info kiosk at the entrance. Leashed dogs welcome.

Museum of Natural History & Gladwin Planetarium

The permanent exhibits may lack the 'hands-on' sparkle *de rigueur* of some children's discovery centers, but this **museum** (Map pp378-9; ☎ 805-682-4711; www.sbnature.org; 2559 Puesta del Sol Rd; adult/child 2-12yr /teen 13-17yr & senior $8/5/7; ⏱ 10am-5pm) boasts a few noteworthy gems and also stages excellent special exhibits. Bug buffs should check out the glass wall holding 4000 Santa Barbara insects – all mounted – as well as the replica of a pygmy-mammoth skeleton unearthed on Santa Rosa Island in 1994. Outside you'll find the complete skeleton of a 72ft blue whale. Kids especially like the **planetarium** (admission $4), which has intro-to-astronomy shows for children as well as adult programs that explore current scientific theory; call for show times. The museum is two blocks north of the mission and 1 mile south of the botanic garden.

Santa Barbara Zoological Garden

Big cats, monkeys, elephants and giraffes await at the 500-animal **zoo** (Map pp378-9; ☎ 805-962-5339; www.sbzoo.org; 500 Ninos Dr; adult/child under

INFORMATION		
Bank of America	1	B2
Book Den	2	B1
FedEx Kinko's	3	B2
Grayphics	4	B1
Muddy Waters	5	D2
Pacific Travelers Supply	6	B1
Post Office	7	B2
Santa Barbara Outdoor Visitor Center	(see 19)	
Santa Barbara Public Library	8	B1
Santa Barbara Visitor Center	9	D3

SIGHTS & ACTIVITIES		
Anacapa Dive Center	10	D3
El Presidio State Historic Park	11	B2
Karpeles Museum	12	B2
Los Baños del Mar	13	C4
Moreton Bay Fig Tree	14	C4
Open Air Bikes	15	C3
Paddle Sports	16	C5
Santa Barbara County Courthouse	17	B1
Santa Barbara Historical Museum	18	C2
Santa Barbara Maritime Museum	19	C5
Santa Barbara Museum of Art	20	B1
Santa Barbara Old Town Trolley Main Stop	21	D3
Santa Barbara Sailing Center	(see 22)	
Sea Landing	(see 22)	
Sunset Kidd's Sailing Cruises	(see 16)	
Truth Aquatics	22	C4
Ty Warner Sea Center	23	D4
Wheel Fun	(see 70)	

SLEEPING		
Colonial Beach Inn	24	C4
Eagle Inn	25	C4
El Prado Inn	26	A1
Franciscan Inn	27	C4
Hotel Oceana	28	C4
Hotel Santa Barbara	29	C2
Hotel State Street	30	C3
Inn of the Spanish Garden	31	C1
Marina Beach Motel	32	C4
Presidio Motel	33	A1
Santa Barbara Tourist Hostel	34	C3

EATING		
Arigato	35	B1
Bouchon	36	A1
Brophy Brothers	37	C5
Chuck's Waterfront Grill & Endless Summer Café	(see 37)	
D'Angelo Pastry & Bread	38	C3
Intermezzo	39	B2
La Super Rica	40	D1
Metropulos	41	D3
Natural Café	42	C2
Paradise Café	43	C2
Pascucci	44	B2
Roy	45	B2
Santa Barbara Shellfish Company	46	D4
Sojourner Café	47	B2
Tupelo Junction	48	B1
Wine Cask	(see 39)	

DRINKING		
Brew House	49	C3
Dargan's	50	C2

EOS Lounge	51	C2
Epiphany	52	A1
Press Room	53	C2
Red's Espresso Bar and Gallery	54	C3
Santa Barbara Brewing Company	55	C3
SB Roasting Co	(see 38)	
Sportsman Lounge	56	B2

ENTERTAINMENT		
Arlington Center for the Performing Arts	57	A1
Granada Theatre	58	B1
Lobero Theatre	59	B2
Soho	(see 35)	
Velvet Jones	60	C3

SHOPPING		
Blue Bee & Blue Beetle	61	B2
Diani	62	A1
El Paseo	63	B2
La Arcada	64	B1
Mountain Air Sports	65	D3
Particle	66	B2
Paseo Nuevo	67	B2
Santa Barbara Outfitters	68	B1
Santa Barbara Skate Shop	69	D3
Surf-n-Wear's Beach House	70	D3
Victorian Vogue & The Costume Shop	71	B1

TRANSPORT		
Greyhound	72	B2
MTD Transit Center	73	B2
Wheel Fun	74	C3

12yr & senior $10/8; ⏰ 10am-5pm; Ⓟ), where you'll also find beautiful gardens. The Humboldt penguins, housed in the Crawford Family Penguin House, are the current stars, and these tuxedoed show-offs seem to know it. If you're in need of a giggle, hit the 'Eeeww!' insect exhibit. Its hissing cockroaches and giant African millipedes will leave you giggling at the grossed-out kids. Or deeply disturbed. Parking costs $3.

El Presidio de Santa Barbara State Historic Park

Built to protect the missions between Monterey and San Diego, this 18th-century former Spanish **fort** (Map p380; ☎ 805-965-0093; www.sbthp.org; 123 E Cañon Perdido St; adult $3, child 16 & under free; ⏰ 10:30am-4:30pm), was protected by adobe walls nearly 4ft thick and more than 9ft high. But its purpose wasn't solely to protect – the presidio, which recently celebrated the 225th anniversary of its founding, also served as a social and political hub, and as a stopping point for traveling Spanish military. Today, the small urban park, between Anacapa and Santa Barbara Sts, harbors some of the city's oldest structures, which seem to be in constant need of propping up and restoring. Be sure to stop by the chapel: its interior is radiant with kaleidoscopic color.

Karpeles Manuscript Library Museum

This free **museum** (Map pp84-5; ☎ 805-962-5322; www .rain.org/~karpeles; 21 W Anapamu St; ⏰ 10am-4pm) is an embarrassment of riches for history nerds, science geeks and music lovers. Filled with historical written artifacts from the private

---

MORETON BAY FIG TREE & PORTOLA CAMPSITE

Approaching the corner of Montecito and Chapala Sts, you can't miss the massive Moreton Bay fig tree, imported from Brisbane, Australia, and planted in 1877. The tree is believed to be the largest of its kind in North America. Not only is it a whopping 78ft tall (almost eight stories!), but it has a 171ft canopy. Just east, you'll see the historic plaque marking the site of Captain Portolá's campsite in August 1769 during his exploratory trip up the coast to establish California as a Spanish colony.

TOP FIVE FREEBIES

- Climb to the top of the **courthouse tower** (p378)or 360° views.
- Window-shop along **State St** (p391), ending up at the beach and Stearns Wharf.
- Scan the harbor from the 4th-floor deck at the **Outdoor Visitors Center** (p378).
- Hike **Rattlesnake Canyon Trail** (p384) just north of town in the Santa Ynez foothills.
- Study a draft of the Bill of Rights at the **Karpeles Museum** (left).

---

collection of David Karpeles, a Santa Barbara real-estate investor, it's a true SoCal treasure. One of just eight Karpeles manuscript museums in the country, this branch houses the original proposed draft of the Bill of Rights, an Emancipation Proclamation Amendment signed by Abraham Lincoln, and Einstein's description of the theory of relativity. A recent special exhibit highlighting historic women contained writings from Lucretia Borgia, Catherine the Great and Harriet Beecher Stowe. Lots of helpful explanatory brochures are available.

Beaches

The long sandy stretch between Stearns Wharf and Montecito is **East Beach** (Map p380); it's Santa Barbara's largest and most popular beach, and has a dozen volleyball nets for pick-up games. At its eastern end Armani swimsuits and Gucci sunglasses abound at the narrow but chic **Butterfly Beach** (Map pp378–9), in front of the Biltmore Hotel.

Between Stearns Wharf and the harbor, **West Beach** (Map p380) has calm water. It's popular with families and tourists staying in nearby motels. On the other side of the harbor, **Leadbetter Beach** (Map pp378–9) is a good spot for surfing and windsurfing, with access to a grassy picnic area atop the cliffs.

West of Santa Barbara near the junction of Cliff Dr and Las Positas Rd, **Arroyo Burro Beach** (Map pp378–9; also called Hendry's) has a parking lot, a picnic area and a restaurant. It's flat, wide, away from tourists and great for families with kids.

ACTIVITIES
Cycling & Skating

For info on biking in Santa Barbara, contact the **Santa Barbara Bicycle Coalition** (www.sbbike.org), which also has online printable self-biking tours.

The Cabrillo Blvd **beachfront bike path** runs for 3 miles along the water, between the Andrée Clark Bird Refuge and Leadbetter Beach. The **Goleta Bikeway** continues west to UCSB – see www.sbbike.org for route details. **Wheel Fun Rentals** (Map p380; www.wheelfunrentals .com); Cabrillo Blvd (☎ 805-966-2282; 23 E Cabrillo Blvd; 8am-8pm) State St (☎ 805-962-2585; 101 State St; 10am-5pm) rents bikes at two locations near the beach. Beach cruisers cost about $7 per hour for the first two hours and $16 per half day; single surreys, which seat two people, cost $34 per hour for the first two hours and $72 per half day.

Road cyclists should check out **Open Air Bikes** (Map p380; ☎ 805-962-7000; www.openairbicycles.com; 209 State St) for rentals, sales and accessories. The helpful staff has loads of information on local rides. Road bikes rent for about $75 per day, with costs decreasing the longer the rental. It's about $210 per week.

Boating & Whale-Watching

The whale-watching season runs from February 15 to May 15. The following companies offer trips to see the whales, but this list is not comprehensive; you can also wander the harbor, talk to captains and pick a boat based on whom you like best. Always make sure the vessel is Coast Guard certified – and that you dig the captain.

Sea Landing (Map p380; ☎ 805-882-0088, 888-779-4253; www.condorcruises.com; 301 W Cabrillo Blvd), on the beach at the foot of Bath St, rents kayaks, jet skis and jet boats and also operates whale-watching excursions to the Channel Islands aboard the *Condor Express*, a state-of-the-art high-speed catamaran that is stable enough for most stomachs. Trips last about 4½ hours and cost $88 per adult and $45 per child. Whale sightings are guaranteed, so if you miss out you can come back for a free trip. It also runs half-day fishing excursions for $42 per adult and $34 per child.

Santa Barbara Sailing Center (Map p380; ☎ 805-962-2826, 800-350-9090; www.sbsail.com; 133 Harbor Way), next to Sea Landing in the harbor, will take you sailing on the *Double Dolphin*, a 50ft sailing catamaran, for $35. One child, age 12 and under, is free with each paid adult. If you want to pilot your own craft, the center also rents paddleboats, motorboats, fishing boats and sailboats. In season they offer whale-watching too.

Sunset Kidd's Sailing Cruises (Map p380; ☎ 805-962-8222; www.sunsetkidd.com; 125 Harbor Way) will take

---

SANTA BARBARA IN FOUR DAYS

Spend your first morning soaking up rays at convenient **East Beach** (opposite) then savor the indie lifestyle with a vegetarian lunch at **Soujourner Café** (p388) or **Nature's Grill** (p403). Explore the museums, landmarks and shops downtown, using the Red Tile tour map as your guide. Conclude with a stop by the **courthouse** (p378) for views from its 85ft tower. Head to Julia Child's favorite Mexican restaurant, **La Super Rica** (p388), for a casual but delicious authentic Mexican dinner. Finish with ice cream at **McConnell's** (p389) or a cold one at the **Brewhouse** (p390).

Start Day Two with a diet-busting breakfast at **Tupelo Junction** (p389). Stop by the Funk Zone for a sandwich to go from **Metropulos** (p388) then bike along the coast or hike in the Santa Ynez foothills. Visit **Montecito** (p392) or **Summerland** (p405) for afternoon shopping and people-watching. Return to State St for a Cal-Mediterranean feast. End with a low-key show at **Soho** (p391) or a rowdier set at **Velvet Jones** (p391).

Day Three is set aside for wine country. Pick a wine trail, then enjoy a do-it-yourself tasting day via car, bike or motorcycle. **Guided tours** (p400) are an option for those who prefer not to navigate. Pack a picnic lunch or eat in charming **Los Olivos** (p399). End with a hearty steak dinner at the **Hitching Post II** (p393).

Start your last day in **Solvang** (p393). Grab abelskiver, pancakes or pastries for your breakfast then ogle the gorgeous scenery with a scenic drive to the trails off Paradise Rd in **Los Padres National Forest** (p401) or bike along one of the scenic wine trails – **Foxen Canyon Rd** (p396) and the **Santa Rita Hills loop** (p399) are exceptionally beautiful. Cap it off with fine, but not stuffy, Italian cuisine at **Grappolo** (p400).

you on a two-hour whale-watching trip in an 18-passenger sailboat for $35 per person. It also operates pleasure trips – try the sunset cocktail cruise – for the same price.

Truth Aquatics (Map p380; ☎ 805-962-1127; www .truthaquatics.com; 301 W Cabrillo Blvd) runs scuba-diving trips, kayaking excursions and an occasional hikers shuttle to the Channel Islands (p405).

Kayaking

Paddle the coves of Gaviota, the coast of Carpinteria and the calm waters of the harbor, or hitch a ride to the Channel Islands for caves, bluffs and solitude.

Santa Barbara Adventure Co (☎ 805-898-0671, 888-773-3239; www.sbadventureco.com) leads guided kayaking trips that focus on marine ecology; ask about stargazing floats.

Paddle Sports (Map p380; ☎ 805-899-4925, 888-254-2094; www.kayaksb.com; 117b Harbor Way) leads kayaking trips and offers instruction. Kayak rentals cost $20 for two hours or $30 for four hours.

Surfing

Santa Barbara's south-facing coast and proximity to the wind-breaking Channel Islands make it a good spot for plying the waves on a surfboard. **Rincon Point** has long, glassy, point-break waves; **Leadbetter Point** and **Goleta Beach** are best for beginners. Unless you're a novice, conditions are too mellow in summer – head to Orange County's beaches (p252), then come back in winter when swells kick back up.

Learn to surf with **Santa Barbara Adventure Co** (☎ 805-452-0671, 888-773-3239; www.sbadventureco .com) – four-hour classes cost $110 per person, including necessary accoutrements and lunch. **Surf Happens** (☎ 805-966-3613; www.surfhappens.com) offers lessons incorporating the zen of surfing; begin your spiritual journey for $60 per hour (two-hour minimum). Across the street from Stearns Wharf you can rent soft (foam) boards from the **Surf-n-Wear's Beach House** (Map p380; ☎ 805-963-1281; 10 State St; per hr/half-/full-day $7/21/35). It also rents boogie boards ($4/10/16 per hour/half-/full-day).

Hiking

Gorgeous day hikes await in the Santa Ynez foothills (part of Los Padres National Forest, p401), which are part of the mountain chain that towers over the city. By car, it's about 2 miles from downtown Santa Barbara to Foothill Rd, also known as Rt 192, which travels east–west along the foot of the Santa Ynez, and another 2 to 3 miles to various trailheads from Foothill Rd. The hills are full of hiking trails, most of which cut through rugged chaparral and steep canyons. Savor the jaw-dropping coastal views. **Rattlesnake Canyon** is a popular, 3-mile round-trip hike offering shade and waterfalls as you ascend into the canyon. Take Mission Canyon Rd north from Foothill Rd, turn right on Las Canoas Rd and follow it to the trailhead. You can extend this hike using the Rattlesnake Canyon connector trail to the Tunnel Trail. Also popular is the hike along Tunnel Trail to **Inspiration Point**. Just east off Mountain Dr is **Cold Spring Canyon** where the Cold Spring Ridge Trail woos hikers with cascading waterfalls and refreshing pools.

In town, the best place for gathering info and maps is Pacific Travelers Supply (p376). At the harbor, check the Santa Barbara Outdoor Visitor Center (p378), a helpful, volunteer-staffed resource for information on the entire Los Padres National Forest. If you're here in winter, inquire about the best places to see the monarch butterflies roosting in the trees, an extraordinary sight. *A Hiker's Guide to the Santa Barbara Front Country and Paradise Road* by Raymond Ford is a user-friendly map with brief trail descriptions. It's available from the Santa Barbara Maritime Museum (p379; $8) and from Los Padres National Forest Headquarters (p401). See also Raymond Ford's website www.sb -outdoors.org. and www.santabarbarahikes .com for trail summaries.

In summer, when the city is shrouded in cool coastal fog, the inland hills will likely be sunny and hot; wear layers and carry plenty of water, sunscreen and a hat. In winter, the coast may be only slightly chilly, while the hills are downright cold. It's also worth noting that weather conditions inland may be different from conditions at the coast.

Swimming

Beyond the beaches previously listed (p382), mile-long, family-friendly **Carpinteria State Beach** (☎ 805-968-1033, camping info 805-684-2811; www.parks .ca.gov; P ⓔ), about 12 miles south, is great for swimming, wading and tide-pooling. It's often referred to as the world's safest beach for its calm waters. Parking is available for $8.

You can also swim in **Los Baños del Mar** (Map p380; ☎ 805-966-6110; 401 Shoreline Dr; admission $5; ⏰ 7:30-9am, noon-2pm & 7:15-8:15pm Mon-Fri, noon-2pm Sat & Sun; ♿), a municipal outdoor pool near West Beach that is good for recreational and lap swimming. For little ones under eight years old, there's a wonderful wading pool.

TOURS

For tours exclusively on the water, see Boating (p383).

Maximize your time in Santa Barbara's stunning outdoors with **Santa Barbara Adventure Company** (☎ 805-898-0671, 888-773-3239; www .sbadventureco.com). This outdoor outfitter leads surfing, kayaking, rock-climbing, mountain-biking and wine-tasting tours (by van or by bike). Prices range from $60 to $179 per person. Trips require a minimum of two to four people.

Santa Barbara Old Town Trolley (Map p380; ☎ 805-965-0353; www.sbtrolley.com; adult/child $18/9; ⏰ 10am-5pm) operates 90-minute guided tours in an open-sided, San Francisco–style, motorized cable car. It gives a great overview of the city's sights, and allows you to get on and off at 14 different stops. Start the tour at Stearns Wharf, or call for other pickup points. Pay the driver directly; check online for discounts.

If you dig James Bond–style gadgets and vehicles, take a guided tour of the city on the *Land Shark* with **Land & Sea Tours** (☎ 805-683-7600; www.out2seesb.com; adult/child $25/10), then drive right into the water for a tour in this amphibious vehicle.

Cloud Climbers Jeep Tours (☎ 805-646-3200; www .ccjeeps.com) runs guided jeep tours of the mountains and forest above the town, including hiking/driving tours, horseback-riding/driving tours, family outings, wine-country jaunts, and sunset-chasing journeys for adults. Tours of three to 6½ hours cost $89 to $150 per person. The charge per child for the Family Discovery Mountain Tour is $69.

FESTIVALS & EVENTS

Santa Barbara throws a good party. For the current calendar of events, contact the Santa Barbara Visitor Center (p378).

FEATURE: IT'S SO EASY BEING GREEN

It's clear Kermit never visited Santa Barbara. This ecofriendly community makes 'being green' not only easy but downright entertaining. And all you disengaged, green-weary cynics? Keep reading – turns out the tree huggers are having the most fun.

One of the city's best-promoted initiatives is Santa Barbara Car Free. Visit www.santabarbara carfree.org or pick up their pamphlet at the visitors center for tips on seeing the city without your car. From LA, for example, you can hop on the *Pacific Surfliner* for a three-hour coastal chug to the Amtrak station (p392) – two blocks from the beach and three from downtown. From there, hoof it or catch the electric shuttle that arrives every 15 minutes or so. It zips downtown along State St or east–west along the coast. If you ride the shuttle to the zoo, you'll save the $3 parking fee. To get to the mission, grab MTD Bus Line 22. For a self-guided tour of the city, amble over to Wheel Fun Rentals (p383), just south of the train station on State St, and rent a bike.

Check out www.greensantabarbara.com for a list of ecofriendly attractions, activities and lodging. (Admittedly, some listed green-hotel employees don't seem to have gotten the memo – when asked for green-hotel policies, one confused desk clerk said she thought she, um, recycled?)

The nearby Wine Country's getting into it too. Many newer vineyards are implementing biodynamic farming techniques and following organic guidelines. Not sure about the quality of organic wines? Wonder no more. Many vintners and purchasers are starting to think that the more natural the growing process, the better the wine. Flip through *Destination Wine Country* magazine, available at most wineries and around town, for info on vineyards going green, or try the new Sustainable Vine Wine Tour (p400), which uses a biodiesel van to whisk you to ecofriendly vineyards.

Beyond that, hiking, cycling, kayaking and surfing remain environmentally friendly – just pay attention to posted guidelines and rules about outdoor activities. For specific info, cyclists can check out www.sbbike.org while hikers should visit the Los Padres National Forest website at www.r5.fs.fed.us/lospadres. Surfers can check out the usually up-to-date www.santabarbara surfing.com for local info.

Santa Barbara International Film Festival
(☎ 805-963-0023; www.sbfilmfestival.org) Film buffs arrive in droves for this always-wonderful fest, that takes place in mid-January to early February and presents new independent US and foreign films.

Summer Solstice Parade (☎ 805-965-3396; www.solsticeparade.com) Kicking off the summer, this wacky parade up State St in late June feels like something out of Marin County in Northern California or a Burning Man processional, not a staid Santa Barbara event. Draws a crowd of 100,000.

Santa Barbara County Fair (☎ 805-925-8824; www.santamariafairpark.com) In mid-July, this old-fashioned county fair has agriculture booths, rides, and lots of food and wine. The fairgrounds are in Santa Maria, about an hour north of Santa Barbara.

Old Spanish Fiesta Days (☎ 805-962-8101; www.oldspanishdays-fiesta.org) The town gets packed in early August for this long-running – if slightly overrated – festival celebrating Santa Barbara's multicultural heritage.

SLEEPING

Finding a cheap room at the last minute is not so easy in Santa Barbara, especially on weekends. A bottom-of-the-heap dive motel that's $60 on weekdays can triple in price on a Saturday night. Tariffs quoted here are high-season published weekend rates. Book in advance and you can almost always do better. Because nights are generally cool, most places don't have air-conditioning. Unless

---

KEEPING THE KIDS ENTERTAINED

Santa Barbara is made for kids.

■ **Arroyo Burro Beach** (aka Hendry's, p382) – wide sandy beach, away from the tourists, popular with local families.

■ **Maritime Museum** (p379) – peer through a periscope, reel in a virtual fish, or check out the gorgeous model ships.

■ **Museum of Natural History** (p381) – giant skeletons and a pitch-dark planetarium captivate kids' imaginations.

■ **Santa Barbara Zoological Garden** (p381) – preening penguins, creepy insects and lumbering elephants are the big draw at this 30-acre zoo. Lush gardens overlook the sea.

■ **Ty Warner Sea Center** (p379) – see a 70ft whale, play with hands-on exhibits and feel the sea critters that live in the touch pool.

---

otherwise noted, the lodgings listed here are without air-con. Although the midrange listings might seem high, you can save money by booking the ones that have kitchens (it's pricey to eat in Santa Barbara, but not if you cook for yourself). Rates fluctuate depending on demand, so use the rates listed below only as a guide.

Budget
CAMPING

You won't find a campground anywhere near downtown, but about 17 miles and 20 miles west of town, respectively, right on the beach off Hwy 101, are **El Capitan State Beach** and **Refugio State Beach** (both ☎ 805-968-1033, reservations 800-444-7275; www.parks.ca.gov, www.reserveamerica.com; campsites Mar-Nov/Dec-Feb $25/20; ⓟ). Refugio is a popular surf spot and student hangout, while El Capitan, perched on low bluffs, is more popular with families. Amenities include flush toilets, hot showers, picnic tables and barbecues. There's also camping in the Los Padres National Forest and at Cachuma Lake(p402). Parking costs $8.

HOSTELS

Santa Barbara Tourist Hostel (Map p380; ☎ 805-963-0154; www.sbhostel.com; 134 Chapala St; dm $29, r $89-95; reception ⏰ 8:15am-12:30pm & 3:45pm-midnight; ⓟ □ wi-fi) Traveling strangers, evening trains and a rowdy brewhouse only steps from your door – it's either the perfect country song or the Santa Barbara Tourist Hostel, a low-slung bungalow right next to the train station (bring earplugs). This raucous little hostel skews young but with a kitchen, a pool table, lockers, a laundry and a book exchange, the price is right for anyone looking for inclusive lodging and the chance to make new friends. You can rent in-line skates, bikes and boogie boards. You need proof that you're a traveler to stay here.

MOTELS & HOTELS

For a cheap room on a busy weekend, you may have to drive north on Hwy 101 toward Santa Maria or south to Carpinteria, where you'll find properly low rates for plain motel rooms.

Hotel State Street (Map p380; ☎ 805-966-6586; 121 State St; r $85-135; □ wi-fi) This off-beat hotel is the cheapest place in downtown, excluding the hostel. Pros: friendly staff, clean rooms, and the beach is two blocks away. Cons: noise from trains (Amtrak station is next door) and shared bathrooms. If earplugs and walking to the shower are no biggie to you, then you'll be perfectly fine. Note that bathroom sharing here isn't college dorm–style; it's European-style – you have privacy, just shut the door and lock it.

El Prado Inn (Map p380; ☎ 805-966-0807, 800-669-8979; www.elprado.com; 1601 State St; r $100-210; P ⌨) Just north of downtown, about a mile from the beach, El Prado has better-than-average, clean motel rooms with attractive furnishings, and landscaping surrounding the large heated pool. Cool oversized aerial photo of Santa Barbara in the lobby. Good value; ask about specials.

The very first Motel 6 to 'leave the light on for you,' **Motel 6 Santa Barbara** (Map pp378-9; ☎ 805-564-1392, 800-466-8356; www.motel6.com; 443 Corona del Mar; s $110-140, d $116-146; P ⌨) no longer offers $6 rooms. Considering its proximity to the beach, it remains a bargain. Book as far in advance as possible; it fills up nightly. For better rates and a higher likelihood of availability try **Motel 6 Carpinteria North** (☎ 805-684-6921, 800-466-8356; 4200 Via Real; P ⌨), 10 miles south just off Interstate 101. Recorded wake-up calls are from the chain's folksy founder, Tom Burdett.

Midrange

Secret Garden Inn & Cottages (Map pp378-9; ☎ 805-687-2300; www.secretgarden.com; 1908 Bath St; r $135-255; P) Tucked behind a high hedgerow in a residential neighborhood, the Secret Garden Inn has cottage rooms decorated with a down-to-earth mishmash of folksy, country-style furnishings. The cheapest rooms are in the main house; all others have private entrances. Look out for the commemorative Charles-and-Diana tea tin in the dining room. One of a few B&Bs good for kids and dogs. Full breakfast is included. Most rooms have an air-con unit.

ourpick Franciscan Inn (Map p380; ☎ 805-963-8845; www.franciscaninn.com; 109 Bath St; r $140-185, with kitchen $185-295; P ⌨ wi-fi) Bees will flee your bonnet as you settle into the relaxing, French-country charms of the Franciscan, a 53-room motel that's about one block from the beach. Rooms differ in shape and decor but all boast a charming pastoral, floral motif – one that could prove annoying to curmudgeons and ultimate street fighters. Everyone else will embrace the friendly vibe, the afternoon cookies, the big TV sets, the on-site laundry and the

Jacuzzi. Some rooms have kitchenettes and some have air-con.

Hacienda Motel (Map pp378-9; ☎ 805-687-6461; www.haciendamotel.com; 3643 State St; r $149-199; P ⌨ wi-fi) There once was a motel named Hacienda, with standard rooms and HBO on the agenda, summer rates are crazy high, I'm not sure why, but optional kitchenettes and laundry are nice addenda. Two miles from beach.

Presidio Motel (Map p380; ☎ 805-963-1355; 1620 State St; www.thepresidiomotel.com; r $150-210; P) The Presidio is the H&M of Santa Barbara motels, a budget option flaunting what its got with sassy, irresistible style. From mod lounge chairs on the sundeck and artsy photos on the walls to origami dangling from the ceiling, the owners make the most of an older, standard-issue building. Located just north of downtown, the motel attracts a slightly younger crowd. Wi-fi available in some rooms.

Colonial Beach Inn (Map p380; ☎ 805-963-4317, 800-649-2669; www.sbhotels.com; 206 Castillo St; r $208-248; P ⌨ wi-fi) Every guest looks happy at this two-story motel where bright window boxes and a welcoming magnolia tree complement the clean, slightly formal Southern-style furnishings. Rooms are slightly bigger than average, though showing a bit of wear. Wine and cheese are served in the afternoon.

Hotel Santa Barbara (Map p380; ☎ 805-957-9300, 888-259-7770; www.hotelsantabarbara.com; 533 State St; r $219-269; P ⌨ wi-fi) As unpretentiously sophisticated as its namesake city, the 1925 Hotel Santa Barbara has rooms done up with rattan and blond-wood furnishings and sunny Mediterranean colors – Provence meets the beach. A continental breakfast is included. Top choice downtown for upper-middle budgets. Parking costs $5 per day. Best of all, you can walk everywhere.

Cabrillo Inn (Map pp378-9; ☎ 805-966-1641, 800-648-6708; www.cabrilloinn.com; 931 E Cabrillo Blvd; r $209-289, ste $369; P ⌨) Prices have jumped here in recent years, but the Cabrillo, with its two pools, two sundecks and beach access just across the street, is still a pretty good deal for pricey Santa Barbara. Most rooms have partial ocean views; for a full ocean view, add another $40. Score a good rate, and this place is excellent for value and location.

Eagle Inn (Map p380; ☎ 805-965-3586; www.theeagleinn.com; 232 Natoma Ave; r $275-350; P ⌨ wi-fi) You'll feel like Spanish royalty strolling underneath the colorful tile-lined archway into this white, two-story inn. Average-sized rooms are brightened with crisp floral motifs. For more space, try one of the four new cottages in back. This tranquil, family-owned property is popular with business travelers.

Marina Beach Motel (Map p380; ☎ 805-963-9311, 877-627-4621; www.marinabeachmotel.com; 21 Bath St; r $239-294; (P) (R) (□) wi-fi) Family-owned since 1942, this flower-festooned, one-story motel that wraps around a central courtyard is also worth a visit.

Top End

El Capitan Canyon (off Map p378-9; ☎ 805-685-3887, 866-352-2729; www.elcapitancanyon.com; 11560 Calle Real; safari tents $145, cabins $225-345; (P) (△) (ॐ) wi-fi) This upscale woodsy retreat is a current media darling, garnering magazine and morning-show kudos as a premier 'glamping' (glamorous camping) resort. At El Capitan you can sleep in a tent or a cabin on a top-quality mattress with high-thread-count sheets. Each site has its own picnic table and fire pit. No cars are allowed tent-side, so it feels like a walk-in campground – but oh! that bed. Die-hard campers shouldn't despair – communal bathrooms and un-Disney-like critter sightings keep things real. It's sandwiched between the Santa Ynez mountains and a state beach, 17 miles west of Santa Barbara, off Hwy 101 northbound (30 minutes' drive). There's on-site massage, a café and a yurt for yoga. Ask about family cabins if you're with kids.

Hotel Oceana (Map p380; ☎ 805-965-4577, 800-965-9776; www.hoteloceana.com; 202 W Cabrillo Blvd; r $219-410; (P) (R)) Just when you think you've driven past your hotel, it pops up again, and again… and again. Nope, you're not losing it – the Hotel Oceana is an assemblage of four once-independent motels across the street from West Beach. The Oceana is being entirely re-styled and updated from 1950s kitsch to new-millennium chic, with aggressive color schemes, crisp cotton sheets, down comforters and aromatherapy bath products. Ask for a restyled room. Parking is available for $9 per day.

our pick **Inn of the Spanish Garden** (Map p380; 805-564-4700, 866-564-4700; www.spanishgardeninn.com; 915 Garden St; r $269-399, ste $379-515; (P) (□) (R)) You'll feel 'to the manor born' at this Spanish-style inn where casual elegance, top-notch service and an impossibly charismatic central courtyard will have you lording about like the royal overseer of your own private villa. Beds have luxurious linens; bathrooms have oversize soaking tubs. Lush palms surround the pool, and the outdoor courtyard gets lit with candles every evening – the perfect spot to enjoy the evening wine bar. Breakfast included.

Four Seasons Biltmore Hotel (Map pp378-9; ☎ 805-969-2261, 888-424-5866; www.fourseasons.com/santabarbara; 1260 Channel Dr; r $600-950; (P) (□) (R)) Don white linen and live like the Great Gatsby at the oh-so-cushy 1927 Biltmore, Santa Barbara's iconic beachfront resort and spa where rooms are decorated in retro '20s chic and every detail is perfect. Bathrooms have custom Mediterranean-style tiles, huge soaking tubs, French-milled soaps and 300-jet waterfall showers; bedrooms are decked out with ultra-high-thread-count sheets and 40in flat-screen TVs. Perfect for a honeymoon or a great big splurge. Wi-fi in the lobby.

EATING
Budget

Sojourner Café (Map p380; ☎ 805-965-7922; 134 E Cañon Perdido; dishes $6-13; 🕙 11am-11pm Mon-Sat, to 10pm Sun; (V)) Vegetarians rejoice – the food is fab and the menu extensive at this upbeat, mostly veggie café that gets creative with vegetables, tofu, tempeh, chicken, fish, rice, seeds and other healthy ingredients. Outdoor seating, too. The tempeh taco salad is delish.

Santa Barbara Shellfish Company (Map p380; ☎ 805-966-6676; 230 Stearns Wharf; dishes $5-16 🕙 11am-9pm, to 9:30pm summer) 'From sea to skillet to plate' best describes the process at Santa Barbara Shellfish, an end-of-the-wharf crab shack that's more of a counter joint than a sit-down restaurant. The food and atmosphere go best with beer, not chardonnay. Decent prices; awesome crab bisque; great water views; same owners for 25 years.

La Super Rica (Map p380; ☎ 805-963-4940; 622 N Milpas St; dishes under $7; 🕙 11am-9:30pm, closed Wed) This low-slung, unmarked shack – the one with the happy hordes spilling out the door – was culinary guru Julia Child's favorite Mexican restaurant. Who are we to argue? Make your choice from the 20 meals written on the board overhead, order from the window, then join local families at the picnic-style tables for authentic south-of-the-border cooking. Avoid peak meal times, when the place gets packed and searching for a seat is an Olympic sport.

our pick **Metropulos** (Map p380); ☎ 805-899-2300; 216 E Yanonali St; mains under $10; 🕙 8:30am-6pm Mon-Fri, 10am-4pm Sat) Before a hike in the front country, order up some picnic-perfect gourmet salads and sandwiches at this new-ish, super-nice deli east of the tracks in the Funk Zone. Try the smoked turkey and brie with cranberry-fig confit on honey whole wheat. Mmmm. They've got wine and cheese too.

Natural Café (Map p380; ☎ 805-962-9494; 508 State St; mains under $10; ☾ 11am-9pm) The lunch line – stretching 10 deep from the counter – can look daunting at this beachy, mostly vegetarian bistro in the thick of things on State St. But no worries, the line moves fast. Options range from spinach salads to tempeh veggie burgers to black-bean enchiladas. Grilled chicken pitas and turkey sandwiches available for carnivores.

D'Angelo Pastry & Bread (Map p380; ☎ 805-962-5466; 25 W Gutierrez St; dishes under $12; ☾ 7am-1:30pm) Come in the morning for a fresh-from-the-oven flaky croissant, poached eggs and big cups of strong coffee at this sidewalk café and bakery off Lower State St. The best pastries go quick, so get here early; the bakery closes at 2pm.

Stock up on fresh produce, nuts and honey at the **farmers market** (Map p380; ☎ 805-962-5354; www.sbfarmersmarket.org) held late afternoon Tuesday on the 500 and 600 blocks of State St between E Haley and E Ortega Sts, and Saturday morning at the corner of Santa Barbara and Cota Sts. For the best in healthy groceries, head to **Lazy Acres** (Map pp378-9; ☎ 805-564-4410; 302 Meigs Rd; ☾ 7am-10pm), which is reached most easily by car. The best place for homemade ice cream is **McConnell's Ice Cream** (Map pp378-9; ☎ 805-569-2323; 201 W Mission St; ☾ 10:30am-11:30pm).

Midrange

Arigato (Map p380; ☎ 805-965-6074; 1225 State St; maki $5-12, mains $14-18; ☾ dinner) Out-of-towners drive an hour and a half for the swoon-inducing sushi at this bustling but breezy State St hotspot. Settle in on the sidewalk patio or grab a seat inside at the L-shaped sushi bar where friendly sushi chefs will steer you right. One can't-miss is the jalapeño yellowtail nigiri. Hot dishes are also available. No reservations, so expect a wait.

Tupelo Junction (Map p380; ☎ 805-899-3100; 1218 State St; mains breakfast $5-16, lunch $13-17, dinner $13-19; ☾ 8am-2pm daily, 5:30pm-8:30pm Sun-Thu, to 9pm Fri & Sat) Marinated in upscale Southern charm, Tupelo Junction stirs up a gourmet menu that can only be described as a masterpiece: every dish sounds delectable. From the smoked bacon, spinach and Gouda cheese scramble at breakfast to the Southern shrimp and scallops with cheddar-jalapeno grits at dinner – it's enough to make a foodie lose her mind. Cyclists heading out for a long ride can fuel up on a heaping bowl of homemade granola with fresh berries and yogurt.

Pascucci (Map p380; ☎ 805-963-8123; 729 State St; mains lunch $7-10, mains dinner $8-13) Don't let the sight of tourists deter you from palazzo-style Pascucci. Despite occasionally spotty service, locals love the filling pastas, pizzas and *paninis* here, not to mention the bargain prices. For a taste of Italian heaven, try the Bellagio: smoked chicken, mushroom, red onions and sun-dried tomatoes in a roasted garlic-parmesan cream sauce over bowtie pasta. Sit at the bar for the quickest service.

Intermezzo (Map p380; ☎ 805-966-9463, 800-436-9463; 813 Anacapa St; mains $10-18; ☾ 3pm-10pm Mon-Fri, 11am-11pm Sat & Sun) Foodies take note: the swank and stylin' little sister of the Wine Cask (p390) serves a less formal menu – cheese plates, lamb kibbes, club sandwiches – that's every bit as gratifying. Same chef, same kitchen, *way lower* prices. Great for cocktails too.

Paradise Café (Map p380; ☎ 805-962-4416; 702 Anacapa St; lunch $6-16, dinner $10-30; ☾ 11am-11pm Mon-Sat, 9am-11pm Sun) Everything you'd hope for in a hometown corner café – fantastic oak-grilled burgers (the best in Santa Barbara), great salads, and a respectable brunch. Sit outside on the big patio (no smoking). Great wine list that's reasonably priced.

Roy (Map p380; ☎ 805-966-5636; 7 W Carrillo St; 3-course dinner $20-30; ☾ 6pm-midnight) Roy serves later than anyplace else in town, and 30 bucks or less buys you a damn good three-course meal with soup, salad and choice of main, from handmade pasta with prawns to grilled lamb chops. It's dark, hip, happening and popular with scenesters on weeknights; on weekends it gets packed with 20- and 30-something bacchanalian revelers. Call ahead or wait. Major bar scene.

There are two spots for seafood by the harbor (as opposed to the wharf); both are exclusively tourist restaurants and serve pretty good, but pricey meals. **Brophy Brothers** (Map p380; ☎ 805-966-4418; 119 Harbor Way; mains $10-20; ☾ 10am-10pm Sun-Thu, to 11pm Sat & Sun) is a longtime favorite for its fresh-off-the-dock fish and seafood, its party atmosphere and its salty harborside setting. People love the clam chowder and *cioppino* (seafood stew), which is chock-full of fish, mussels and shrimp, and served with chewy sourdough. Tables on the upstairs deck are worth the long wait – they're quieter and have the best views. Try **Chuck's Waterfront Grill & Endless Summer Bar Café** (Map p380; ☎ 805-564-1200; 113 Harbor Way) Endless Summer (mains $7-17; ⏰ 11:30am-9pm); Waterfront (mains $12-30; ⏰ dinner) for someplace dressier than Brophy Brothers, and reserve a table in the nautical-theme dining room or outside overlooking the sailboats. Come between 5pm and 6:30pm for $15 to $17 sunset dinner specials, such as an 8oz steak or grilled salmon. Upstairs at the publike Endless Summer, the scene is Jack Johnson–casual (and cheaper), with fish-and-chips, burgers, billiards and beer.

Top End

Wine Cask (Map p380; ☎ 805-966-9463, 800-436-9463; 813 Anacapa St; lunch mains $14-18, dinner mains $28-40; ⏰ lunch Mon-Fri, dinner daily) Let your sexy shine through at the Wine Cask, where 19th-century Spanish-style adobe, two-story-high gold-leaf-stenciled ceilings, and elegant fish, beef and pasta dishes make every guest feel chic. It's Santa Barbara's hottest table for serious eating. On balmy evenings (or at lunch), feast on the invigorating New California menu outdoors in the romantic garden courtyard. The wine list brags 2500 labels, with vintages dating back to 1900. One detail: verify the price of the bottle before you let the sommelier pick a wine for you.

Bouchon (Map p380; ☎ 805-730-1160; 9 W Victoria St; mains $24-34; ⏰ dinner) The perfect, unhurried, follow-up dinner to a day in Wine Country, convivial Bouchon's bright, flavorful California cooking uses only locally grown small-scale-farm produce and meats, which marry beautifully with the more than 50 local wines available by the glass. For romance, book a table on the cozy candlelit patio.

DRINKING
Cafés

Muddy Waters (Map p380; ☎ 805-966-6328; 508 E Haley St; ⏰ 6am-6pm, later if there's a show) A yard sale's mix of cosy furniture? Check. Pool table? Check. Internet access? Check. Live music on the weekends and a kick-ass backyard patio? You got it. Seems Muddy Waters has everything required for the quintessential indie coffeehouse. And the coffee's darn good too. Great place to escape the State St hordes.

Red's Espresso Bar and Gallery (Map p380; ☎ 805-966-5906; 211 Helena Ave; ⏰ 6:30am-6pm Mon-Wed, to 8pm Thu & Fri, to 5pm Sat) With *Ring of Fire* on the stereo, a concrete floor underfoot and scruffy barflies at the counter, Red's is just your typical small-town bar. 'Cept this is Santa Barbara, so make that your typical small-town *coffee* bar with local art hanging on the very red walls. In the heart of the Funk Zone, east of the tracks, the vibe is cool and the java cheap. Live music on the weekends.

SB Roasting Co (Map pp84-5; ☎ 805-962-0320; 321 Motor Way; ⏰ 5:30am-9pm Mon-Fri, 6am-9pm Sat, 6:30am-9am Sun; wi-fi) Lads with laptops fill the tables in this exposed-brick, industrial space. Poets? Day traders? Hackers? Who knows. All come for the potent java – this place roasts its own coffee – and casual vibe. Try a 'flattened' bagel for 75¢. One block off State St.

Bars

Santa Barbara's after-dark scene centers on lower State and Ortega Sts. Most places have happy hour and college nights, when the booze is cheap and the atmosphere rowdy. Check the *Independent* and the *Santa Barbara News-Press* (see p377) for up-to-date listings.

Sportsman Lounge (Map p380; ☎ 805-564-4411; 20 W Figueroa) Tucked on a low-traffic corner just west of tourist-heavy State St, this dark and cozy watering hole is a plain-old dive bar with no higher pretensions. Great jukebox.

Dargan's (Map p380; ☎ 805-568-0702; 18 E Ortega St) Settle in for the craic at welcoming Dargan's Irish pub, where appreciative crowds listen to lively Irish bands in the back room on Thursday nights. Up front, shoot pool and sip Guinness just past the big green leprechaun waiting by the door.

our pick Brewhouse (Map p380; ☎ 805-884-4664; 229 W Montecito St) Perfect for a rowdy reunion or a night on the town, ever-popular Brew House crafts its own beer, serves wines by the glass and has cool art and awesome fries. It's raucous good fun, with live music Wednesday to Saturday from 9pm to close. On Wednesday it serves all-you-can-eat ribs; arrive early.

Press Room (Map p380; ☎ 805-936-8121; 15 E Ortega St) Tiny but raucous Press Room can barely contain the locals, Brooks photography students and European travelers that cram the place to its seams. But there's no better place to catch the game or quaff some views with your tastebuds.

Santa Barbara Brewing Co (Map pp84-5; ☎ 805-730-1040; 501 State St) Home to half a dozen microbrews plus a couple of seasonal specialties, this bustling brewery draws a consistent State St dinner crowd as well as the beer connoisseurs. Santa Barbara Blonde, Gold Coast Wheat and State Street Stout are a few permanent attractions.

EOS Lounge (Map pp84-5; ☎ 805-564-2410; 500 Anacapa St) Ladies love the lighting at this trendy nightclub currently hot with SB's martini-sipping scenesters. The sexy decor – rippling waterfall, glimmering fireplace, twinkling patio – is on par with the hippest of Hollywood lounges. Small dancefloor for those wanting to get their groove on.

Epiphany (Map pp84-5; ☎ 805-564-7100; 21 W Victoria St) Ideal for a glass of bubbly if you're wearing heels and a dress (or if you want to impress someone who is); it's also a chic little restaurant.

ENTERTAINMENT

Santa Barbara's appreciation of the arts is evidenced not only in the wide variety of performances available on any given night but also in its gorgeous, often historic, venues.

Soho (Map pp378-9; ☎ 805-962-7776; www.sohosb.com; 1221 State St, #205) Never mind the office-complex setting: once inside the casually intimate brick walls of stylin' Soho – where the focus is on the performer – you'll be transported to a whole new place. There's jazz on Monday night, blues several times per month, plus rock, bluegrass, funk, soul, salsa and folk on other nights at this 2nd-floor club. Cover is $7 to $15.

Velvet Jones (Map p380; ☎ 805-965-8676; www.velvet-jones.com; 423 State St) The place to hear rock, hip-hop and comedy. Many bands stop here between gigs in LA and San Francisco.

Lobero Theatre (Map pp84-5; ☎ 805-963-0761; 33 E Cañon Perdido St) The oldest California theater in continuous operation – since 1873 – presents ballet, modern dance, opera, chamber music and special events, often featuring internationally renowned top talent.

Granada Theatre (Map pp84-5; ☎ 805-899-3000; 1216 State St) Set to reopen in March 2008 following a complete restoration, this 1930s Spanish-Moorish-style theater will become the new home of several arts institutions, including the ballet, the opera and the symphony.

Santa Barbara supports a variety of theater companies and beautiful historic venues. For a current list of performing-arts events, pick up the *Santa Barbara Performing Arts Guide*, a fold-out brochure available at the Santa Barbara Visitor Center (p378); you can also check with the **Santa Barbara Performing Arts League** (☎ 805-563-8068; www.sbperformingartsleague.org). Aside from being home to the Santa Barbara Symphony, **Arlington Center for the Performing Arts** (Map p380; ☎ 805-963-4408; 1317 State St) is a drop-dead-gorgeous, old-fashioned movie palace when the orchestra isn't playing. Great place to catch a flick.

SHOPPING

Shops along State St carry clothing, knick-knacks, antiques and books. There are chain stores here, but all conform to the Spanish-style architectural mandate. You'll find plenty of terrific boutiques and gung-ho outdoor stores in Santa Barbara, but very few used-clothing stores.

Paseo Nuevo (Map p380; btwn Cañon Perdido & Ortega Sts) This attractive outdoor mall is anchored by Nordstrom and Macy's department stores, with retail chains such as Gap and Victoria's Secret.

La Arcada (Map p380; 1114 State St) Near Figueroa St, this historical red-tile passageway was designed by Myron Hunt (builder of the Rose Bowl in LA) in 1926. It's filled with boutiques, restaurants and whimsical public art – check out the back pocket of the window washer to see what's on his reading list.

El Paseo (Map p380; State St) Locally owned shops and restaurants fill this tiny, flower-festooned courtyard opposite Paseo Nuevo.

Surf-n-Wear's Beach House (Map p380; ☎ 805-963-1281; 10 State St) Surfboards dangle from the ceiling at this beach-minded emporium where bikinis, beachbags and flip-flops jostle for your attention.

Blue Bee & Blue Beetle (Map p380; ☎ 805-897-1137; 923-925 State St) Find eclectic, stylin' clothes at one of the best indie boutiques in town; there's a denim shop and a men's section tucked in back. In fact, wander downtown and you'll start seeing Blue Bee specialty shops everywhere you look. Their ever-expanding local empire includes shops for kids, luxury and shoes. Also has its own line of hip jeans.

Diani (Map p380; ☎ 805-966-3114; 1324 State St, Arlington Plaza) Carries more high-fashion-oriented, Euro-inspired designs, with a touch of funky soul thrown in for good measure.

DETOUR: MONTECITO

The unincorporated community of Montecito (Map pp378–9) hovers just east of Santa Barbara like a bashful cousin – a bashful cousin who's just inherited the family fortune, that is. This leafy village in the Santa Ynez foothills is not just home to the rich and famous but to the obscenely rich and the uberfamous; the type of guarded enclave that would incite revolutions in eras past, but today, well, we all think we're just one smart investment away from living there ourselves. And really, residents Oprah Winfrey, Ellen DeGeneres and Steven Spielberg can't be all bad, right?

Though many homes hide behind manicured hedges, a taste of the Montecito lifestyle can be savored on the main drag, Coast Village Rd (follow Cabrillo Blvd east, turn right). For lunch, nab a spot on the red-tile patio at **Los Arroyos** (☎ 805-969-9059; 1280 Coast Village Rd; mains $8-14; ◷ 9am-11pm) and enjoy neatly prepared Mexican dishes (alas, chips and salsa are $3) and watch the ritzy stroll past. To nibble fancy chops in a high-end steakhouse frequented by local celebs, make a reservation at the chic, sometimes-too-hip-for-its-own-good **Lucky's** (☎ 805-565-7540; 1279 Coast Village Rd; mains $14-69; ◷ dinner, lunch Sat & Sun).

For lodging, the three-story **Montecito Inn** (☎ 805-969-7854, 800-843-2017; www.montecitoinn.com; 1295 Coast Village Rd; r $245-345, ste 375-725; P ⌨ ☟ wi-fi) is a friendly Mediterranean-style retreat founded in 1928 by a group of investors headed by Charlie Chaplin. The upscale décor is lightened by fun (but not overdone) Charlie Chaplin movie posters. Some rooms are on the small side, but plush. For groups ask about the Chaplin suite that sleeps six.

Mountain Air Sports (Map p380; ☎ 805-962-0049; 14 State St) Great place to load up on gear before a trip into the backcountry.

Santa Barbara Outfitters (Map p380; ☎ 805-564-1007; 1200 State St) Located downtown, it sells similar outdoor clothing and gear.

Particle (Map p380; ☎ 805-899-4245; 1 W Ortega St) Men should check out this place for hip and trendy styles.

Victorian Vogue & the Costume Shop (Map p380; ☎ 805-962-8824; 1224 State St) For vintage and drag, from fabulous to outrageous, stop by this shop, which also rents costumes and has fun kids' stuff too.

Skaterats will dig small, in-your-face **Santa Barbara Skate Shop** (Map p380; ☎ 805-899-8669; 16C Helena Ave), while divers will love the **Anacapa Dive Center** (Map p380; ☎ 805-963-8917; 22 Anacapa St). For more shops, pick up a Funk Zone map at the Visitors Center (see p378).

GETTING THERE & AWAY

If you don't drive your car to Santa Barbara, you're eligible for discounts at select hotels, plus a bag of coupons for local restaurants and activities, courtesy of **Santa Barbara Car Free** (www.santabarbaracarfree.com).

The small **Santa Barbara Airport** (Map pp378-9; ☎ 805-967-7111; www.flysba.com; 500 Fowler Rd) in Goleta, about 8 miles west of downtown via Hwy 101, has scheduled flights to and from LA, San Francisco, Las Vegas, Denver, Phoenix and other western US cities. The following agencies have car-rental desks at the airport:

Budget (☎ 800-527-0700; www.budget.com)

Enterprise (☎ 800-261-7331; www.enterprise.com)

Hertz (☎ 800-654-3131; www.hertz.com)

National (☎ 800-227-7368; www.nationalcar.com)

Santa Barbara Airbus (☎ 805-964-7759, 800-423-1618; www.santabarbaraairbus.com) shuttles between LAX International Airport (LAX) and Santa Barbara ($46/86 one way/round-trip, 14 departures per day). The more people in your party, the cheaper the fare. Also consider buying discounted tickets online.

Greyhound (Map p380; ☎ 805-965-7551; www.greyhound.com; 34 W Carrillo St) operates six buses daily to LA ($12, two to three hours) and up to six to San Francisco ($39, 7¾ to 9½ hours).

Amtrak (Map p380; ☎ 800-872-7245; www.amtrak.com; 209 State St) has direct train services to LA ($25, 2¾ hours) and San Diego ($37, 5¾ hours) via the *Pacific Surfliner* and *Coast Starlight*.

Santa Barbara is bisected by Hwy 101. For downtown, take the Garden St or Cabrillo Blvd exits. Parking on the street and in any of the 10 municipal lots is free for the first 75 minutes. Each hour or part of an hour after that costs $1.50.

GETTING AROUND

A taxi from the airport costs about $30 to $35 plus tip. **Super Ride** (☎ 800-977-1123; www.superride.net) provides a door-to-door shuttle service from the airport to downtown for about $20 for one person, $25 for two.

Buses operated by **Santa Barbara Metropolitan Transit District** (MTD; ☎ 805-683-3702; www.sbmtd.gov) cost $1.25 (exact change) per ride and travel all over town and to adjacent communities, including Goleta and Montecito; request a free transfer when you pay your fare. The **MTD Transit Center** (1020 Chapala St) has details on routes and schedules.

The Downtown–Waterfront shuttle bus (operated by MTD) runs every 10 minutes from 10am to 6pm along State St to Stearns Wharf. A second route travels from the zoo to the yacht harbor at 15-to-30-minute intervals. The fare is 25¢ per ride; transfers between routes are free.

Taxis are metered and cost about $1.90 for the drop rate (initial fare), plus $2.70 to $3.20 per mile. Try one of the following taxi companies:

Blue Dolphin (☎ 805-962-6886)
Gold Cab (☎ 805-685-9797)
Rose Cab (☎ 805-564-2600, 866-767-3222)
Yellow Cab (☎ 805-965-5111, 800-549-8294)

For an ecofriendly water-taxi ride between Stearns Wharf and points of interest on Harbor Dr, hop aboard yellow, biodiesel-powered **Lil' Toot** (☎ 805-896-6900; adult/child $3/1; 1:30-6pm Mon, Tue, Thu & Fri, noon-6pm Sat & Sun Sept-May, noon-6pm daily Jun-Aug; ♿). Look for the Lil' Toot booth beside the water; trips run every half-hour.

AROUND SANTA BARBARA

Can't quit your day job to follow your bliss? Don't despair, a long weekend in the mountains, valleys, beaches and parks surrounding Santa Barbara will help keep you inspired 'til you can. In this gorgeous land of daydreams, perfect waves beckon off Ventura's coast, shady trails wind skyward in the Los Padres mountains, spiritual zen awaits within Ojai valley, and flirtatious pinots beckon from the Santa Rosa Hills. Surf, stroll, seek, sip – if sunny, outdoor rejuvenation is your goal, this is the place to reach it.

And then there's Channel Islands National Park, a stunning chain of islands shimmering just off the coast where you can kayak into majestic sea caves, scuba dive near lan-

guorous kelp forests, wander fields of yellow coreopsis blooms or simply disappear from the 'cultural apparatus' at a remote but soul-enriching campsite.

BUELLTON
pop 3900

Often described as the gateway to the Wine Country, tiny Buellton is perhaps best known for the restaurant towering over the intersection of Hwy 101 and Hwy 246: Anderson's Pea Soup Restaurant, where you can indeed get heaping bowls of the green stuff.

Ever since the release of *Sideways* in 2004, the **Hitching Post II** (☎ 805-688-0676; 406 E Hwy 246; mains $18-40; ☻ 5pm-9:30pm) has been giving Andersen's some competition as the town's most recognizable landmark. Seen in the movie as the restaurant where Miles meets waitress Maya, this legendary, dark-paneled chophouse offers oak-grilled steaks as well as baby back ribs, California quail and ostrich meat. Every meal comes with a veggie tray, shrimp cocktail or soup, salad and a starch. If you like pinot noir, the Hitching Post II makes its own, and its pretty darn good. The bar opens at 4pm.

In the strip mall behind the Burger King, the cooks at **Pattibakes Bakery & Café** (☎ 805-686-9582; 240 E Highway 246, shop 109; mains under $8; ☻ breakfast & lunch) whip up delicious homemade muffin, tarts and scones for breakfast, as well as a wide selection of sandwiches great for a picnic lunch.

In keeping with the green-soup theme, the rooms at the two-story **Pea Soup Andersen's Best Western Inn** (☎ 805-688-3216, 800-732-7687; www .peasoupandersens.com; 51 E Hwy 246; r $121; Ⓟ ♿) are accessed by pea-green doors. Some of Solvang's Scandinavian flair spills into the 'quaint village' decor but the big draw is the central courtyard where kids go nuts for the miniputting green and pool. First-floor rooms with patio doors onto the courtyard are fun for families; upstairs rooms are quieter. Rooms are a bit on the older side but clean with comfy beds. Cheaper than most lodging in Solvang, 3 miles east.

SOLVANG
pop 5400

My God, captain, we've hit a windmill. Which can only mean one thing in central California Wine Country: Solvang, a kitschy faux-Danish village about 35 miles north of

SANTA BARBARA COUNTY

Santa Barbara, where windmills are part of the skyline. Founded in 1911 by Danish-American settlers from the Midwest, the town holds tight to its Danish heritage – or at least its stereotypical images. In fact, with its knickknack stores, cutesy motels and Danish-style bakeries, the town is almost as sticky-sweet as the syrupy pastries foisted upon the wandering hordes looking for a point to it all. And what is the point to it all? Solvang's kitschy charms are so utterly unique that they make the town worth visiting – at least once.

Beyond pastries, Solvang is a good jumping-off point for oenophiles exploring the Wine Country and outdoor enthusiasts seeking adventure in Los Padres National Forest. The town is well known in bicycling circles for the Solvang Century, a 100-mile race through surrounding countryside in March.

From Santa Barbara, follow Hwy 154 north to Hwy 246 west, continuing west to the windmills. You can reserve rooms through the **visitors bureau** (☎ 805-688-6144; 800-468-6765; www.solvangusa.com; 1511a Mission Dr). For local guides and trail maps, stop by the **Book Loft** (☎ 805-688-6010; 1680 Mission Dr), a fabulous indie bookstore where the helpful staff can point you toward the right trail guide, latest best-seller or one-of-a-kind used book. Enjoy wi-fi with your java at the **Bulldog Café** (☎ 805-686-9770) next door. There's a satellite **visitors center** (1639 Copenhagen Dr) in the center of town.

Sights & Activities

Half the fun of Solvang is wandering among the kitschy shops and bakeries downtown, which cover about three square blocks south of Mission Dr between Atterdag Rd and Alisal Rd. If you remember childhood fairy tales with fondness, stop by the tiny **Hans Christian Andersen Museum** (☎ 805-688-2052; 1680 Mission Dr), above the Book Loft, where original letters and 1st-edition copies of the Danish storyteller's books are on display. The **Elverhoj Museum of History & Art** (☎ 805-686-1211; www.elverhoj.org; 1624 Elverhoj Way; requested donation $3; ☿ 1-4pm Wed & Thu, noon-4pm Fri-Sun) has exhibits on Danes in America and Solvang's Danish history.

Unwind with a Pure Indulgence massage and reflexology treatment ($69) at **De-stress Café** (☎ 805-693-8776; 1636 Copenhagen Dr), a day spa across the street from the visitors bureau.

Newly remodeled Hadsten House Inn & Spa (see below) opened a day spa in late 2007.

Sleeping

Hadsten House Inn & Spa (☎ 805-688-3210, 800-457-5373; www.hadstenhouse.com; 1450 Mission Dr; r $237-336) Why does my luxury inn and spa look like a dumpy two-story motel? Because brand new Hadsten House revamped a former motel property, updating just about everything except the uninspiring exterior. But once inside your room? Ahhh. The decor is surprisingly plush. Flatscreen TVs, triple sheets, comfy duvets, L'Occitane bath products – it's all quite refined. At the time of writing, the day spa was about to open. The minivineyard on the front lawn is a nice touch.

Eating

Paula's Pancake House (☎ 805-688-2867; 1531 Mission Dr; mains $6-9; ☿ breakfast & lunch) This thatched-roofed, breakfast-focused restaurant is where the crowds congregate for Danish pancakes, Danish sausages and the not-so-Danish California omelette with avocado.

Solvang Restaurant (☎ 805-688-4645; 1672 Copenhagen Dr; mains $6-10; ☿ 6am-3pm Mon-Fri, to 4pm Jun-Aug, 6am-5pm Sat & Sun) Film buffs may recognize the Danish-inscribed beams and decorative borders from *Sideways*. The other reason to visit is for the restaurant's infamous abelskiver – round pancake balls covered in raspberry-jam sauce and powdered sugar.

Food-wise, Solvang is best known for Danish inspired bakeries. Tubs of Danish butter cookies are popular takeaways at the **Solvang Bakery** (☎ 805-688-4939; 460 Alisal Rd), but for a more decadent treat, try their custard butter ring or the crispy Florentine lace cookie (the latter's Danish heritage slightly unclear). Also popular is **Olsen's Bakery** (☎ 805-688-6314; 1529 Mission Dr) with its varied assortment of Danish butter cookies, lace cookies and rich almond custard kringles – dough layers folded over butter then twisted. And as Hans Christian Andersen once wrote, never dingle with anyone's kringle.

Drinking & Entertainment

Anywhere but here. Sorry, but true. After dinner this place is deader than a Danish boneyard. In fact, if you're just one abelskiver from sugar-and-kitsch-induced insanity, drive east 3 miles on Hwy 246 'til you reach **Chumash Casino Resort** (☎ 800-248-6274; www.chumashcasino.com;

3400 E Hwy 246; ⏱ 24hr), Solvang's vice-minded doppelganger, where the coffee is bad, the slots are plenty and the cigarette smoke so thick you could cut it with a Danish butter knife.

Shopping

If colorful quilts, miniclog magnets, and decorative Danish plates top your shopping list, you'll be crossing off items like mad. Crowded **Rasmussen's** (☎ 805-688-6636; 1697 Copenhagen Dr) displays a primo mix of Scandinavian wares – from Hummel figurines and Lindt chocolates to corny 'Sour Kraut' tiles, it's all here. For handcrafted quilts, pillows and bedroom decor try the **Nodding Place** (☎ 805-693-0251; 1662 Copenhagen Dr), a homespun shop where hubbies slip out the door without telling their wives. If Solvang's got you feeling vaguely out of sync, have your aura photographed and analyzed at the **Mystic Merchant** (☎ 805-693-1424; 1640 Copenhagen Dr).

SANTA BARBARA WINE COUNTRY

Oak-dotted hillsides, charming country lanes, gorgeous mountain views, tidy rows of grape vines stretching as far as the eye can see – it's hard not to gush when describing Santa Barbara's Wine Country, a primo spot for roadtripping. From fancy convertibles and ecofriendly touring vans to sleek road bikes and sputtering Harleys, it's an eclectic, friendly mix of visitors sharing these bucolic roads.

The citizens here are typically friendly too, from longtime landowners and farmers displaying small-town graciousness to the vineyard owners who've fled big cities to follow their passion. Many of them are happy to share their local knowledge and fascinating histories as well as their love of this beautiful land. A love you should prepare to share with travelers inspired by Oscar-winning *Sideways*, an ode to the joys – and hazards – of wine-tasting as seen through the adventures of road-tripping middle-aged buddies Miles and Jack.

The area is perfect for do-it-yourself exploring. With more than 100 wineries dotting the landscape, it can seem daunting to organize a tour. But don't worry about sticking to a regimented plan or following overly detailed wine guides. Soak in the scenery, pull over where the sign seems welcoming or where the vibe feels right. Serendipity may lead you to a new favorite wine or even new friends of the road.

Orientation & Information

The Wine Country is north of Santa Barbara; you can get there in just under an hour, via Hwys 154 (San Marcos Pass Rd) and 101. The Santa Ynez Valley, where you'll find most of the wineries, lies south of the Santa Maria Valley. Hwy 246 runs east–west, via Solvang, across the bottom of the Santa Ynez Valley, and connects Hwy 101 and Hwy 154. North–south secondary roads where you'll find good

---

A WINE COUNTRY PRIMER

Though large-scale winemaking has only been happening in Santa Barbara since the 1980s, its climate has always been perfect for growing grapes. Two parallel, east–west–trending mountain ranges (the Santa Ynez and the San Rafael) cradle the region and funnel coastal fog eastward off the Pacific into the valleys between. The further inland you go, the warmer it gets. At the shore, fog and low clouds can hover all day, keeping the weather downright chilly, even in July, while only a few miles inland, temperatures can soar a full 30°F hotter, sometimes approaching 100°F in mid-July. These delicately balanced microclimates support two major varieties of grape.

Near the coast in the Santa Maria Valley, pinot noir – a particularly fragile grape – and other Burgundy-style varieties thrive in the fog. Inland in the warmer Santa Ynez Valley, where there can be as much as a 50°F variance in temperatures from day to night, Rhône-style grapes do best. These include Syrah, Mourvèdre and viognier.

As you work your way through Wine Country you'll see vineyards and you'll see wineries. They are not the same thing. The term 'vineyard' refers only to the place where grapes are grown. A winery, on the other hand, is the place where the grapes are actually fermented into wine. Wineries buy grapes from vineyards. If a winery makes wine using grapes from its own vineyards, it's properly called an estate, as in 'estate grown' or 'estate bottled.' But estates, too, ferment grapes from other vineyards as well as their own. When you see 'vineyard-designated' wines, this means that a winery buys grapes from a particular vineyard known for its superior quality.

wineries include Alamo Pintado Rd from Hwy 246 to the town of Los Olivos, and Refugio Rd into neighboring Ballard.

Five small towns in the Santa Ynez Valley – Buellton, Solvang, Santa Ynez, Ballard and Los Olivos – are scattered within 8 miles of each other, making it easy to stop, shop and eat during your travels. The cute, centrally located town of Los Olivos is a particularly good place to recharge since it's essentially on the line between the Santa Ynez Valley and the Santa Maria Valley.

For a half-day trip, expect to spend no less than four hours, which will allow you to see one winery or tasting room, have lunch and return to Santa Barbara. Otherwise make it a full day and plan to have lunch and possibly dinner before returning to the city. There are numerous tours (see p400) offering guided Wine Country trips from Santa Barbara or Solvang.

The three appellations for the area are Santa Ynez Valley, Santa Maria Valley and Santa Rita Hills (the newest), but local wine guides typically organize the wineries and tasting rooms into three primary wine trails: the Santa Ynez, Foxen Canyon and Santa Rita Hills. Tasting rooms dot Solvang and Los Olivos – town-based wine trails perfect for those with limited time.

The **Santa Barbara Vintners' Association** (☎ 805-668-0881, 800-218-0881; www.sbcountywines.com) publishes a touring map of all the wineries in the area and has some useful information about the area, including lodgings, on its website. You can pick up its map in the Santa Barbara Visitor Center (p378).

Santa Ynez Valley Trail

Most of the wineries on this route cluster along Alamo Pintado Rd and Refugio Rd south of Roblar Ave and just west of Hwy 154.

SUNSTONE VINEYARDS & WINERY

After a short jaunt on a dirt road, you'll find this Provence-style destination **winery** (☎ 805-688-9463, 800-313-9463; www.sunstonewinery.com; 125 Refugio Rd; tastings $10; ☽ 10am-4pm), which looks like an 18th-century stone farmhouse. Inside, wander past the main tasting area into dimly lit hillside caves housing the barrel room and a library of vintage Sunstone wines. Sunstone crafts great Bordeaux-style wines and blends of cabernet franc and cabernet sauvignon –

made from 100% organically grown grapes. Bring a picnic to eat in the courtyard beneath the gnarled oaks.

BUTTONWOOD FARM WINERY & VINEYARD

Bordeaux and Rhône varieties do well in the sun-dappled limestone soil at this friendly 39-acre **winery** (☎ 805-688-3032; www.buttonwoodwinery.com; 100 Alamo Pintado Rd; tastings $7.50; ☽ 11am-5pm) that's fronted by a cozy, shacklike tasting room bordering Buttonwood Farms – look for the peach trees. Matriarch and founder Betty Williams is another earth-conscious wine grower; her family has implemented sustainable and environmentally sound growing practices. The trellised back patio, bordering the orchard, is a nice spot to relax with a bottle of their sauvignon blanc.

RIDEAU VINEYARD

The owner of this festive **winery** (☎ 805-688-0717; www.rideauvineyard.com; 1562 Alamo Pintado Rd; tastings $10; ☽ 11am-5pm), is Iris Rideau, a transplanted New Orleans native who brings Mardi Gras beads and Creole conviviality to her tasting room. The winery is located inside a restored 1884 adobe house that was the site of the first stagecoach stop in Los Olivos. See the fringed surry out front. Today people come for the Rhône varietals, good Chardonnay and great Syrah.

BECKMEN VINEYARDS

Bring a picnic to the pondside gazebo at tranquil **Beckmen Vineyards** (☎ 805-688-8664; www.beckmenvineyards.com; 2670 Ontiveros Rd; tastings $8; ☽ 11am-5pm), where Rhône varieties are grown according to biodynamic farming principles. This means that natural, not chemical, means are used to prevent pests, and that planting and harvesting schedules are based on lunar calendars. To sample their stellar Syrahs, follow Roblar Ave west to Ontoveros Rd, bearing left at the sign for Demetri's Arabians.

Foxen Canyon Wine Trail

The scenic Foxen Canyon Wine Trail runs north from Hwy 154, just west of Los Olivos' main drag, and into the Santa Maria Valley, a more rural area with fewer visitors. It's a must-see for oenophiles or those wanting to get off the beaten path. For the most part, the trail follows Foxen Canyon Rd.

SANTA BARBARA WINE COUNTRY

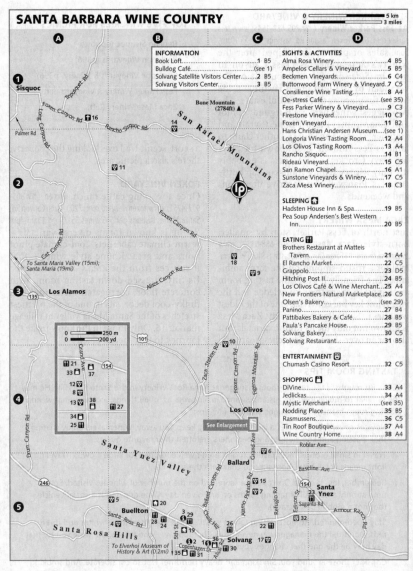

INFORMATION	
Book Loft	1 B5
Bulldog Café	(see 1)
Solvang Satellite Visitors Center	2 B5
Solvang Visitors Center	3 B5

SIGHTS & ACTIVITIES	
Alma Rosa Winery	4 B5
Ampelos Cellars & Vineyard	5 B5
Beckmen Vineyards	6 C4
Buttonwood Farm Winery & Vineyard	7 C5
Consilience Wine Tasting	8 A4
De-stress Café	(see 35)
Fess Parker Winery & Vineyard	9 C3
Firestone Vineyard	10 C3
Foxen Vineyard	11 B2
Hans Christian Andersen Museum	(see 1)
Longoria Wines Tasting Room	12 A4
Los Olivos Tasting Room	13 A4
Rancho Sisquoc	14 C5
Rideau Vineyard	15 C5
San Ramon Chapel	16 A1
Sunstone Vineyards & Winery	17 C5
Zaca Mesa Winery	18 C3

SLEEPING	
Hadsten House Inn & Spa	19 B5
Pea Soup Andersen's Best Western Inn	20 B5

EATING	
Brothers Restaurant at Matteis Tavern	21 A4
El Rancho Market	22 C5
Grappolo	23 D5
Hitching Post II	24 B5
Los Olivos Café & Wine Merchant	25 A4
New Frontiers Natural Marketplace	26 C5
Olsen's Bakery	(see 29)
Panino	27 B4
Pattibakes Bakery & Café	28 B5
Paula's Pancake House	29 B5
Solvang Bakery	30 C5
Solvang Restaurant	31 B5

ENTERTAINMENT	
Chumash Casino Resort	32 C5

SHOPPING	
DiVine	33 A4
Jedlickas	34 A4
Mystic Merchant	(see 35)
Nodding Place	35 B5
Rasmussens	36 C5
Tin Roof Boutique	37 A4
Wine Country Home	38 A4

FIRESTONE VINEYARD

Located just east of Hwy 101 and three miles south of Zaca Canyon Rd, **Firestone Vineyard** (☎ 805-688-3940; www.firestonewine.com; 5000 Zaca Station Rd; tastings $10; ☼ 10am-5pm) is Santa Barbara's oldest estate winery, founded in 1972. Sweeping views of the vineyard from the sleek, wood-paneled tasting room are as impressive as the sauvignon blanc, Syrah, merlot and Bordeaux-style wines. True oenophiles should arrive in time for a winery tour, offered at 11:15am, 1:15pm, and 3:15pm daily. And ladies, who knows, there's always the chance the former *Bachelor* himself, Andrew Firestone, will amble past.

FESS PARKER WINERY & VINEYARD

At **Fess Parker Winery** (☎ 805-688-1545; www.fess parker.com; 6200 Foxen Canyon Rd; tastings $8; ⏰ 10am-5pm) sales of pinot noir jumped after the winery's appearance as Frass Canyon in the film *Sideways*. Sip wine outside on the verandah by the lush green lawn or inside by the fireplace at this beautiful estate. The two biggest wines here are Burgundy (pinot and Chardonnay) and Rhône (Syrah and viognier) styles. The winery's other claim to fame is Fess himself, best known for playing Davy Crockett on TV. This is probably the only winery selling coonskin-cap bottle stoppers. Plan well – buses arrive afternoons and weekends.

ZACA MESA WINERY

Just north of Fess Parker, stop by smaller, barn-style **Zaca Mesa** (☎ 805-688-9339; www .zacamesa.com; 6905 Foxen Canyon Rd; tastings $10; ⏰ 10am-4pm) for a rustic, sipping-on-the-farm ambiance. The friendly hosts at the tasting room are happy to share their knowledge and the vibe is low key but convivial. One of the oldest wineries in Santa Barbara County, Zaca Mesa is known not only for its Rhône varietals, but also for an over-sized outdoor chessboard and

---

TOP FIVE WINERIES FOR PICNICS

- Rancho Sisquoc (opposite)
- Beckmen Vineyards (p396)
- Sunstone Vineyards & Winery (p396)
- Fess Parker Winery & Vineyard (left)
- Zaca Mesa Winery (left)

---

a short, scenic trail overlooking the property; there's also a picnic area.

FOXEN VINEYARD

Once a working cattle ranch, **Foxen** (☎ 805-937-4251; www.foxenvineyard.com; 7200 Foxen Canyon Rd, Santa Maria; tastings per 5-6 wines $5-7; ⏰ 11am-4pm Mon-Fri) is known for its diverse varietals – warm-climate cabernets, cool-climate pinot noirs and great Rhône-style wines – that it sources from the area's best vineyards. Its tiny, dressed-down tasting room, with concrete floor, corrugated-metal roof and funky-cool decor, sits in one of the prettiest stretches of the Santa Maria Valley at mileage marker 16. Only those in the know make the journey to this special place.

TASTING ROOM TIPS

Chris Burroughs is the tasting-room manager at Alma Rosa Winery in the Santa Rita Hills. He may be familiar to moviegoers for his appearance in *Sideways* as, of all things, a cowboy-hat-wearing tasting-room manager. Burroughs shares a few tips:

- Novices never fear. Don't let a lack of wine savvy keep you away. Winemakers enjoy sharing their passion and knowledge, and beginners are often their favorite guests.

- Travel in small groups. Most tasting rooms aren't well equipped for large crowds. Traveling light means you'll have more time to chat with the staff.

- Remember, less is more. Don't keep a scorecard on the number of wineries visited. Spend time at only a handful of tasting rooms on any given day. Wine drinking is a social vehicle (but not a mobile party crawl).

- Stay open-minded. At most tasting rooms you'll sample six wines: three whites and three reds. Don't tell the manager you never drink Chardonnay – who knows, the wine you try that day may be the one that changes your mind.

- Consider those around you. Smoking and heavy perfume? Not so considerate. And smoking dulls your wine-tasting senses.

- Picnics and purchases welcome. It's very cool to purchase a bottle from the winery before spreading out the picnic blanket.

- Be kind to your tasting-room manager. Managers tend to be social creatures. Be friendly, but that doesn't mean acting like Miles and Jack – Miles dumped a spit cup over himself, remember? Burroughs sums up the wine-sipping philosophy best: 'I'd rather drink a mediocre bottle of wine with a cool person than special wine with a jerk.'

RANCHO SISQUOC

For a malbec and surprisingly good cabernet, head northeast to **Rancho Sisquoc** (☎ 805-934-4332; www.ranchosisquoc.com; 6600 Foxen Canyon Rd; ☻ 10am-4pm Mon-Thu, to 5pm Fri-Sun). This tranquil gem is worth the extra mileage. The charmingly rustic tasting room is surrounded by shade-covered decks, sun-dappled lawns and gorgeous pastoral views, making this the perfect spot for a picnic. In fact, *sisquoc* is the Chumash term for 'gathering place', befitting considering your typical Sunday afternoon crowd – picnicking quartets, mom-and-son duos and friendly, leather-clad Harley riders. Turn off Foxen Canyon Rd when you spot the **San Ramon Chapel**, a drafty little church built in 1875, where you can attend Mass at 10:30am on Sunday; it's on the east side of the road and worth a visit for those curious about local history and architecture.

Santa Rita Hills Wine Trail

Santa Rita Hills may be the new kid on the block, but when it comes to country-road scenery, ecoconscious farming practices and top-notch pinots, Santa Rita holds its own. A half-dozen tasting rooms line this scenic loop. Be prepared to share the road with cyclists and the occasional John Deere tractor.

One of the most-talked-about new ventures is **Alma Rosa Winery** (☎ 805-688-9090; www.almarosawinery.com; 7250 Santa Rosa Rd; tastings $5; ☻ 11am-5pm), opened by Richard Sanford, founder of nearby Sanford Wineries. He left the powerhouse bearing his name in 2005 to start this new winery with his wife, Thekla, using sustainable, California-certified organic farming techniques. Cacti and cobblestones welcome visitors to the stick-built shack where tasting-room manager Chris Burroughs (opposite) will happily explain what you're tasting. The reserve pinot is a favorite of Patagonia's Yvon Chouinard, a friend of Sanford's.

Danish grower Peter Work, a former LA businessman, and wife Rebecca display their passion for the vine at **Ampelos Cellars & Vineyard** (☎ 805-736-9957; www.ampeloscellars.com; tastings ☻ 10am-3pm Tue-Sat by appointment), through rigorous adherence to biodynamic farming techniques, encyclopedic knowledge of their lots and a willingness to try innovative, ecofriendly approaches to wine-growing. This passion shines through in their pinot and grenache. Tastings are by appointment,

although Ampelos – Greek for 'vine' – is often a stop on the Sustainable Vine Wine Tour (p400). It's on Rte 246 slightly east of Drum Canyon Rd.

Also just east of Hwy 246 is the Hitching Post II restaurant (p393), which offers tastings of its own well-regarded pinots at the bar from 4pm to 6pm nightly. It's $8 for a taste of seven wines.

Los Olivos Wine Trail

The four-block main street in charming Los Olivos is lined with tasting rooms and shops, as well as several restaurants, a luxurious inn and a full-service spa. If you're short on time, the three tasting rooms listed below will give you a good idea of what the Wine Country has to offer. Ask about shipping wine back to other US states before you assume that you can; not all states allow alcohol to be sent across their borders (ask wineries how some people have gotten around this).

Consilience Wine Tasting (☎ 805-691-1020; www.consiliencewines.com; 2933 Grand Ave; ☻ 11am-5pm) This Spanish-style tasting room specializes in vineyard-designated Syrah and Rhône varietals, with some pinot noir and zinfandel as well.

Longoria Wines Tasting Room (☎ 805-688-0305, 866-759-4637; www.longoriawine.com; 2935 Grand Ave; ☻ noon-4:30pm Mon, Wed & Thu, 11am-4:30pm Fri-Sun) Sip your favorite red on the garden patio where flowers burst from wine barrels. Run by one of the county's most experienced vintners, Longoria's tasting room specializes in pinot, cabernet-franc blends and Syrah.

Los Olivos Tasting Room (☎ 805-688-7406, 800-209-8103; www.losolivostastingroom.com; 2905 Grand Ave; ☻ 11am-5:30pm) Open since 1987, the first independent tasting room in California sits right on the main drag and specializes in high-end pinot noir from the region's smaller vineyards. When you phone dial 2934 at the prompt.

TOP FIVE PLACES FOR PICNIC FIXINGS

- El Rancho Market, Solvang (p400)
- New Frontiers Natural Marketplace, Solvang (p400)
- Panino, Los Olivos (p400)
- Pattibakes, Buellton (p393)
- Metropulos, Santa Barbara (p388)

Eating

You won't have any problem finding picnic fare in Santa Barbara County; the region is chock-full of groceries, delis and bakeries serving up portable sandwiches and salads. When picnicking at a winery, it's polite to buy a bottle of wine before spreading out your blanket on the lawn.

El Rancho Market (☎ 805-688-4300; 2886 Mission Dr, Solvang; sandwiches from $7; ☻ 6am-10pm; P) The place to stop if you want to fill a picnic basket, not to mention reintegrate into society after a day of windmills, clogs and abelskiver. An easy pull-off east of downtown Solvang, this grocery is known for its fantastic deli and wine selection. The gumbo is scrumptious.

New Frontiers Natural Marketplace (☎ 805-693-1746; 1984 Old Mission Dr; sandwiches $7-8; ☻ 8am-8pm Mon-Sat, to 7pm Sun; P V) If you're trying to keep things organic, stop here for a tasty variety of deli sandwiches; especially nice selection for those wanting a veggie picnic – though carnivores have plenty of options too.

Panino (☎ 805-688-9304; 2900 Alamo Pintado Ave, downtown Los Olivos; sandwiches under $9; ☻ 9am-4pm Mon-Fri, to 5pm Sat & Sun; V) This tiny shop also packs a vegetarian punch, offering nine meat-free sandwiches as well as a healthy selection of gourmet sandwiches such as curried chicken salad and roast turkey with brie. Order at the counter and eat outside at an umbrella-covered table or pack a vineyard-worthy picnic.

Grappolo (☎ 805-688-6899; 3687 Sagunto St, Santa Ynez; mains lunch $12-17, dinner $13-30; ☻ lunch Tue-Sun, dinner daily; P) Serving up crispy pizza, pasta, wonderful salads, rotisserie chicken and grilled meats, Grappolo's is a local Italian favorite whose chef hails from Tuscany. The crowd is convivial and lovin' this little

restaurant. Don't be surprised to hear a local tell you it's the best Italian restaurant on the West Coast.

Los Olivos Café & Wine Merchant (☎ 805-688-7265; 2879 Grand Ave, Los Olivos; mains lunch $10-15, dinner $10-24) *Sideways* promoted Los Olivos Café, and now Los Olivos Café promotes *Sideways* – buy a copy of the book here. With white canopies, a concrete floor and a wisteria-covered trellis, this happenin' wine bistro swirls up a casual-chic ambience that adds a nice finish to a long day of touring. Menu includes tasty sandwiches and lush salads.

Brothers Restaurant at Mattei's Tavern (☎ 805-688-4820; 2350 Railway Ave, Los Olivos; mains $18-40; ☻ 5-9pm; P) Relaxing on the terrace at fashionably rustic Mattei's (pronounced 'Matty's'), you half expect a stagecoach to come thundering up in time for dinner. Which would've been the norm 120 years ago at this one-time stagecoach stop and tavern first opened in 1886. The menu lists American-country comfort food, such as prime rib, roasted chicken breast and rack of lamb. Make reservations and get gussied up.

Tours

There are numerous wine tours. Check area visitor centers for brochures. Prices for the tours below hover just above $100 per person. Some may require a minimum number of participants.

Cloud Climbers Jeep Tours (☎ 805-965-6654; www .ccjeeps.com) Offers wine tours in canopied jeeps. Trip includes four wineries and picnic lunch.

Sustainable Vine Wine Tours (☎ 805-698-3911; www.sustainablevine.com). Owner Bryan Hope escorts guests in his biodiesel shuttle to wineries implementing organic and sustainable agricultural practices. Don't fear, the wines are top notch. Price includes lunch from an organic-minded deli.

SHOPPING & SPA SERVICES

Boutiques and specialty shops cluster along Grand Ave in Los Olivos – they can be covered in half day.

The roof's not rusted at bright-red, brand-new **Tin Roof Boutique** (☎ 805-688-7844; 2982 Grand Ave), where fashionistas will find cute tees, sassy shoes and stylin' belts. For authentic cowboy couture, wranglers and prairie babes should mosey over to **Jedlicka's** (☎ 805-688-2626; 2883 Grand Ave) for name-brand boots – Lucchese, Justin – as well as hats and model horses. Decorate your cottage with vineyard-inspired style with furnishings from **Wine Country Home** (☻ 805-686-9100; 2900 Grand Ave). For postwine pampering, stop by **DiVine** (☎ 805-686-9000; 2971 Grand Ave), a cozy cottage of relaxation where a 50-minute Vino Therapy treatment – grapeseed-oil moisturizer and therapeutic massage – is $98.

Wine EdVentures (☎ 805-965-9463; www.we lovewines.com) Serves up a fun-lovin' side dish of local history & wine education with its shuttle-driven tasting tours.

Getting There & Away

From Santa Barbara, you can follow Hwy 101 or Hwy 154 north to the wine country (see p395). Via Hwy 101, it's 45 miles from Santa Barbara to Buellton, located at the intersection of Hwy 246. Hwy 246 runs east–west from Buellton to Solvang and then across the bottom of the Santa Ynez Valley to Hwy 154. You can also follow Hwy 154 north from Santa Barbara. This is the more scenic route (and shorter at 35 miles), but the road is often only two lanes wide. Once past Hwy 246, Hwy 154 leads to Los Olivos.

Amtrak (☎ 800-872-7245; www.amtrak.com) provides a daily bus service from the Santa Barbara station to Solvang.

Super Ride (☎ 800-977-1123; www.superide.net) offers rides from the Santa Barbara Airport to Solvang, one way, for $75. **Central Coast Shuttle** (☎ 800-470-8818; www.centralcoastshuttle.com) will carry you from LAX to Buellton for $69, one way, slightly less if you pre-pay 24 hours in advance.

On weekdays, **MTD Santa Barbara** (☎ 805-683-3702; www.sbmtd.gov) runs express buses between Santa Barbara and Buellton on the Valley Express. Tickets are $4 one way. In the Valley, the **Santa Ynez Valley Transit** (☎ 805-688-5452; www .cityofsolvang.com/syvtroutes.html) runs buses Monday through Saturday on a loop between Buellton, Solvang and Los Olivos for $1.50 one-way.

Many tour operators offer wine tasting and adventure trips to the area. See Tours (opposite) for examples, check www.sbcounty wines or pick up brochures at one of the visitors centers.

ALONG HIGHWAY 154

Highway 154 (San Marcos Pass Rd) heads north of Santa Barbara through the Los Padres National Forest. It bisects the Santa Barbara Wine Country and the Santa Ynez Valley before joining up with Hwy 101 north of Los Olivos.

Chumash Painted Cave State Historic Park

This tiny **historic site** (☎ 805-733-3713; www.parks .ca.gov; ☉ dawn-dusk) shelters vivid pictographs painted by the Chumash over 400 years ago.

The sandstone cave is protected by a metal screen, so a flashlight helps for getting a good view. Look for the turnoff to Painted Cave Rd, about 8 miles north of Santa Barbara. Follow the road for 2 miles; the last stretch is very narrow and steep and not suited for RVs. There's a small pull-off on the left.

Los Padres National Forest

Customize your own outdoor adventure in Los Padres National Forest, which stretches 220 miles from the Carmel Valley to the western edge of Los Angeles County. It's great for hiking, camping, horseback riding and mountain biking. For information, check with the **Santa Barbara Outdoor Visitor Center** (Map p380; ☎ 805-884-1475; www.outdoorssb.noaa.gov; 113 Harbor Way, 4th fl, Waterfront Center Bldg) or with the **Los Padres National Forest Headquarters** (Map pp378-9; ☎ 805-968-6640; www.r5.fs.fed.us/lospadres; 6755 Hollister Ave, Suite 150; ☉ 8am-4:30pm Mon-Fri) in Goleta, located at the back of a nondescript office park.

Call headquarters or check the national forest website to determine which sections are fee areas requiring the purchase of a National Forest Adventure Pass, which must be displayed on your vehicle. The fee areas are extensive. To avoid a ticket, check before parking. Passes cost $5 per day, and you can purchase them at the Forest Headquarters, the Paradise Rd ranger station (both open Monday to Friday), some campgrounds and others outlets noted on the website.

There are several good trails off Paradise Rd, which crosses Hwy 154 north of San Marcos Pass. Try the **Red Rock Trail** (clearly marked from the ranger station), where the Santa Ynez River deeply pools among rocks and waterfalls, creating a great swimming and sunning spot. Many hiking trails radiate out from here. You will need an Adventure Pass. The **Snyder Trail** leads to great views and the remains of Knapp's Castle off East Camino Cielo. It can be done round-trip or one-way using two cars. See *A Hiker's Guide to Santa Barbara Front Country and Paradise Road* by Raymond Ford.

Paradise Rd also provides the best access to developed facilities in the forest. About 4 miles up the road there's a **ranger station** (☎ 805-967-3481) with posted maps and information. There are **campgrounds** nearby: Fremont, Paradise and Los Prietos (campsites $15), with a mix of first-come-first-serve sites and reserved sites, are all before the ranger station while another, Sage Hill (group campsites $75 to $100), is just past it. Check the Los Padres website for more campground information then visit the Fed's new recreation 'portal' at www.recreation.gov to reserve a spot. Eight miles north of Ojai, you can pick up information on weekends at **Wheeler Gorge Visitor Center** off Hwy 33. During the week, pick up information at the Ojai Ranger Station (p404).

Paradise Rd also gives access to a great slice of Americana: **Cold Spring Tavern** (☎ 805-967-0066; 5995 Stagecoach Rd), a legendary stagecoach stop that's still a popular watering hole and restaurant. A rough-hewn plank floor connects a warren of dimly lit rooms decorated with an odd assortment of Western memorabilia. The food, alas, is mediocre and overpriced. The turnoff to Stagecoach Rd – and great scenic drive – is about 0.3 miles north of the junction of Paradise Rd and Hwy 154. Follow it for about 3 miles to the tavern, passing underneath the fabulous San Marcos Bridge. Continue on and you'll hook back up to Hwy 154.

Cachuma Lake Recreation Area

Cachuma Lake, an SB county park, is a haven for anglers and boaters and also has a large **campground** (☎ 805-686-5055, recorded info 805-686-5054; www.cachuma.com; campsites/RV sites $18/25) with picnic tables, barbecue pits, flush toilets and hot showers. Sites are on a first-come, first-served basis and fill quickly on weekends. You can also rent a **yurt** (☎ 805-686-5050; per night $45-65), essentially a round tent cabin on a redwood deck. Park admission is $6 per vehicle.

VENTURA

pop 101,000

Ventura, an agricultural center and the primary departure point for Channel Island trips, may not be the most enchanting coastal city, but this town has its charms, especially in its ungentrified historic downtown along Main St, north of Hwy 101 via Seaward Ave. Here, you'll find a terrific assortment of antique and thrift shops, as well as the town's **visitor center** (☎ 805-483-6214, 800-333-2989; www.ventura-usa.com; 89 S California St, near E Santa Clara, Suite C; ☺ 8:30am-5pm Mon-Fri, 9am-5pm Sat, 10am-4pm Sun).

Sights

Ventura's roots go back to the 1782 **Mission San Buenaventura** (☎ 805-643-4318; 211 E Main St; admission $2; ☺ 10am-5pm Mon-Fri, 9am-5pm Sat, 10am-4pm Sun), the ninth and last mission founded by

Padre Junipero Serra. The restored church is still home to an active congregation. A stroll around the complex leads you through a courtyard and a small museum, past statues of saints and 250-year-old paintings of the stations of the cross. On Sundays, the best time to visit is from 10am to noon, which is the time between services.

Archaeology fans and history buffs will enjoy the free **Albinger Archaeological Museum** (☎ 805-648-5823; 113 E Main St; ☺ 10am-4pm Wed-Sun Jun-Aug, to 2pm Sep-May) just west of the mission. The museum displays an astounding array of artifacts culled from within the surrounding one-block area. The artifacts date from 3500 years ago and include Chumash, Spanish, Mexican American and Chinese relics – all reflective of the various communities inhabiting the block over the years. Outside, you can see the mission's original foundations.

Across the street, the **Museum of Ventura County** (☎ 805-653-0323; www.venturamuseum.org; 100 E Main St; adult/child/senior $4/1/3; ☺ 10am-5pm Tue-Sun; P) has an eclectic mix of exhibits. Highlights include quarter-life-sized historical figures, dressed in period costumes (by George Stuart), and an exhibit tracing Ventura's history complete with Chumash baskets, 1920s-era wooden surfboards, and a brief description of the now-endangered California condor that's accompanied by a massive stuffed specimen, wings outspread. A chihuahua wouldn't stand a chance.

Ventura Harbor (southwest of Hwy 101 via Harbor Blvd) is the departure point for boats to the Channel Islands (p407). Even if you don't embark on an island adventure, the **Channel Islands National Park Visitor Center** (☎ 805-658-5730; 1901 Spinnaker Dr; ☺ 8:30am-5pm) has a smart natural-history display, a touch tank with sharks and a three-story lookout perfect for viewing the islands (on a clear day, at least). On Saturday and Sunday, at 11am and 3pm, rangers lead interpretive programs on tide pools, a terrific primer on California marine ecology.

Sleeping

Bella Magiore Inn (☎ 805-652-0277, 800-523-8479; 67 S California St; r $75-180; P) The downtown location of this 1921 hotel – just off Main St – is great: within walking distance of the harbor and many shops and restaurants. The simple rooms aren't fancy but have good character; quieter rooms are in the back.

THRIFTING IN VENTURA

There's kick-ass thrifting in downtown Ventura. Just take note that the stores are named after the charities benefited – and often presented in blunt terms. Most cluster on Main St west of California St.

CAAN – Child Abuse & Neglect (☎ 805-643-5956; 340 E Main) You'll find rack and racks of pants, shirts and dresses inside this massive space, plus plenty of pots and pans.

Coalition Thrift Store – Battered Women (☎ 805-643-4411; 270 E Main St) Loads of clothes to sift through – without the heavy crowds.

Retarded Children's Thrift Shop (☎ 805-485-6690, 800-228-1413; 265 E Main St). The best and most well known. The hordes flipping through the racks can be daunting, but there are some great deals, especially three-for-one Wednesdays.

Clocktower Inn (☎ 805-652-0141, 800-727-1027; www.clocktowerinn.com; 181 E Santa Clara St; r $129-159; Ⓟ) For quick access to the Mission and museum as well as the beach, this small modern (c 1985) hotel is an option. The rooms, with Navaho-style rustic furnishings, are a bit worn but clean.

Eating

Despite its dowdy appearance, Ventura has some good restaurants.

Nature's Grill (☎ 805-643-7855; 566 E Main St; mains $6-10; Ⓨ 11am-9pm; Ⓟ Ⓥ) Nosh on green cuisine at this breezy but busy grill and juice bar, where the menu is mostly vegetarian. Choices include salads, chicken and fish dishes, and a few hot veggie mains. Vegan options too. Order at the counter.

Cafe Fiore (☎ 805-653-1266; 66 S California St; lunch mains $9-13, dinner mains $9-29) With exposed wooden crossbeams, a concrete floor and lots of fancy throw pillows, Fiore's is the most stylish place in town, packing in Ventura's bon vivants, who sip cold gin while savoring contemporary Italian cooking, from pizza to osso bucco. Make reservations.

Jonathan's at Peirano's (☎ 805-648-4853; 204 E Main St; mains $9-32; Ⓨ dinner Tue-Sun) Jonathan's serves Euro-Mediterranean cooking, from *cioppino* to paella; make reservations. Smaller plates from the same kitchen are available at the bar (dishes $6 to $16), which also has many wines by the glass.

Drinking & Entertainment

Anacapa Brew Pub (☎ 805-643-2337; 472 E Main St Ⓨ closed lunch Mon) Crafts its own microbrews and makes a mean pulled-pork sandwich.

Margarita Villa (☎ 805-654-7906; 1567 Spinnaker Dr) Seeking sunset views and tasty margaritas after a hard day's hike on the Chan-

nel Islands? For an upbeat *olé*!, follow the señorita murals to this 2nd-floor cantina just east of Island Packers (p407) in the Harbor Village.

Weaver Wines (☎ 805-653-9463; 14 S California St) At this upbeat wine shop you can sidle up to the wine bar for a $10 tasting, loiter over a tasty cheese plate, or shop for a gourmet gift. In other words, follow the Weaver Wines credo: 'Taste, lounge, shop'.

Zoey's Café (☎ 805-652-1137; www.zoeyscafe.com; 451 E Main St) Tucked at the end of a brick-lined passageway, Zoey's is a cosy indie bistro showcasing a wide range of live acts almost nightly – folk, soul, acoustic surf rock and comedy to name a few. If you dig fiddle and banjos, stop by for Thursday-night bluegrass jams. During the day, it's a low-key café and coffeehouse serving salads and sandwiches. Try a chocolate-chip cookie – one of the best on the coastal California trail.

Century Theater Downtown 10 (☎ 800-326-3264; 555 E Main St) For movies and popcorn on Main St, stop here.

Shopping

Antique shopping along Main St is good too, especially for used-book lovers. Shopping maps are available at the visitors center. Here's a sampling:

Bank of Books (☎ 805-643-3154; 748 E Main St) This bibliophile's gem recently moved a few blocks east. In addition to the huge selection of used books on the 1st floor, there's a basement filled with maps, magazines and vinyl.

Calico Cat Book Shop (☎ 805-643-7849; 495 E Main St) On the corner of California St and Main St, there's a little of everything crammed into this tiny store. Includes sections on the Civil War, film and poetry.

Times Remembered Antiques Mall (☎ 805-643-3137; 467 E Main St) Civil War relics, wooden tennis racquets, Coca-Cola signs, Star Wars figurines, vintage cameras. As one hipster shopper remarked, 'Dude, I seriously love this place.'

Getting There & Away

Greyhound (☎ 805-653-0164; 291 E Thompson Blvd) runs four buses daily from LA ($12, two to 2½ hours) to Ventura, and four from Ventura to Santa Barbara ($9, 40 minutes). **Amtrak** (☎ 800-872-7245; www.amtrak.com; cnr Harbor Blvd & Figueroa) operates five daily trains to Santa Barbara ($13, 40 minutes) and five to LA ($20, two hours).

OJAI

pop 8000

Tucked in a tiny valley only 10 miles long and 3 miles wide, scenic Ojai (pronounced '*oh*-hi', meaning 'moon' to the Chumash) attracts artists, spiritual seekers and those ready to indulge in a little spa-style pampering. Ojai is also famous for the rosy glow that emanates from its mountains at sunset, the so-called Pink Moment. In fact, the scenery here is so stunning that Frank Capra chose the Ojai Valley to represent the mythical Shangri-La in his 1937 movie *Lost Horizon*. Bring shorts: Shangri-La gets hot in the summer.

For information, head to the **Ojai Chamber of Commerce** (☎ 805-646-8126; www.ojaichamber.org; 201 S Signal St; ☼ 9am-4pm Mon-Fri). The **Ojai Library** (☎ 805-646-1634; 111 E Ojai Ave; ☼ 10am-8pm Mon-Thu, noon-5pm Fri-Sun) will give you a temporary pass for internet access at one of its computers. During the week, pick up information on camping and hiking in the Los Padres National Forest at the **Ojai Ranger Station** (☎ 805-646-4348; 1190 E Ojai Ave; ☼ 8am-4:30pm Mon-Fri) On weekends, stop by the Wheeler Gorge Visitor Center (p402).

Sights & Activities

The 9-mile **Ojai Valley Trail**, converted from old railway tracks, is popular with walkers, joggers, cyclists and equestrians. It links with Ventura's Foster Park.

Ojai is famous for its annual **Ojai Music Festival** (☎ 805-646-2053; www.ojaifestival.org), a longstanding classical-music fest held in early June.

SPAS

For the ultimate in relaxation, spend a day – or a week – enjoying the services of **Spa Ojai** (☎ 888-772-6524; www.ojairesort.com; 905 Country Club Rd) at Ojai Valley Inn & Spa (right). A relaxation

massage costs $140, a mother-of-pearl facial costs $170, and a sounds-like-you-should-eat-it Moroccan Mint Sugar Scrub costs $75. Day-spa services are available to those not overnighting at the inn. Pampering is a little less frou-frou at the easy-going **Oaks at Ojai** (☎ 805-646-5573, 800-753-6257; www.oaksspa.com; 122 E Ojai Ave) – just be sure to turn off your cell phone. The rates at this destination spa include accommodations, low-fat meals and use of the sauna, pool and other facilities. À la carte fees apply for certain additional spa treatments. Weekend rates range from $190 per person per night for a lodge room to $330 per person per night for a minispa suite. Day-trippers can unwind in a hobbitlike cottage at the **Day Spa of Ojai** (☎ 805-640-1100; www.thedayspa.com; 1434 E Ojai Ave), where massages start at $80 for one hour. The signature body wrap is $190 for a two-hour treatment.

Sleeping

Blue Iguana Inn (☎ 805-646-5277; www.blueiguanainn.com; 11794 N Ventura Ave; r $149, ste $189-249; P ☼) If you wanna tie-one-onna with a bright-blue iguana, then this funky, southwestern inn is the place to start. Artsy iguanas lurk everywhere – on the motel's adobe walls, in the parking lot, and anywhere else that hip amphibian style might prompt a smile. The staff is helpful, the rooms are unique, and the pool is a friendly central gathering place. For a more romantic atmosphere, try sister property Emerald Iguana Inn (☎ 805-646-5277; 11794 N Ventura Ave), just north of downtown.

Ojai Valley Inn & Spa (☎ 805-646-5511, 800-422-6524; www.ojairesort.com; 905 Country Club Rd; P ☼ ☼) At the extreme other end of the spectrum, this luxury resort on the western end of town has manicured gardens, golf courses and a fabulous spa. Golfers and spa-goers should check online for money-saving packages.

The knotty-pine-paneled rooms and cottages at the **Ojai Rancho Inn** (☎ 805-646-1434, 800-799-1881; www.ojairanchoinn.com; 615 West Ojai Ave; r $125-140, cottages $165-205; ☼), formerly the Rose Garden Inn, are sturdy with a relaxing country-style vibe, while the **Best Western Casa Ojai** (☎ 805-646-8175, 800-255-8175; www.ojaiinn.com; 1302 E Ojai Ave; r $140-180; ☼) has better-than-average motel rooms. Free cookies at check-in.

Eating

Boccali's (☎ 805-646-6116; 3277 Ojai Ave (Santa Paula Rd); mains $9-18; ☼ lunch Wed-Sun, dinner daily) Beloved

Boccali's is a mom-and-pop, homestyle-Italian roadside café where patio picnic tables are backed by rural mountain views worthy of a Renaissance master. The warm-off-the-vine tomato salad – from the restaurant's gardens – is fantastic; pair it with hot garlic bread for a great meal. There's homemade lemonade and towering strawberry shortcake too. No credit cards. East of town.

Ranch House (☎ 805-646-2360; S Lomita Ave; brunch $22; dinner mains $21-33; ☽ dinner Tue-Sun, brunch Sun) Hold hands by candlelight in the lush gardens of Ojai's top choice for white-tablecloth contemporary Euro-Cal cooking. There's Sunday brunch too.

Seafresh Seafood (☎ 805-646-7747; 533 E Ojai Ave; mains $8-26; ☽ 11am-9pm) Right on the main drag, this is the local spot for seafood.

Shopping

Shoppers amble through **Arcade Plaza**, a maze of Mission-Revival-style buildings on Ojai Ave (the main thoroughfare), filled with cutesy boutiques and galleries. **Human Arts Gallery** (☎ 805-646-1525; 310 E Ojai Ave) and **Human Arts Home** (☎ 805-646-8245; 246 E Ojai Ave) sell unique, art-minded jewelry and furnishings respectively. **Two Sisters** (☎ 805-640-9719; 318 E Ojai Ave) sports the latest casual chic clothing lines perfect for a postspa outing.

Bart's Books (☎ 805-646-3755; 302 W Matilija St), is one block north of Ojai Ave. This inviting indoor-outdoor bookstore, selling new and used books, demands at least a half-hour browse. Just don't step on the lurking but nimble gray cat. **Cowboy Babies** (☎ 805-646-6950; 423 E Ojai Ave) carries ever-so-precious rodeo-to-go packs and hobby horses – not to mention Paul Frank – for tots ready to crawl the open range.

Mingle with residents at the **farmers market** (300 E Matilija St; ☽ 9am-1pm Sun), where you'll find eggs, oils, jams, nuts and candles, in addition to locally grown fruit and vegetables.

Getting There & Away

Ojai is 35 miles east of Santa Barbara via Hwy 150, and 14 miles inland from Ventura off Hwy 33. Hwy 150 is the prettier route. The only direct bus service is from the city of Ventura. Take the Greyhound bus or Amtrak train to Ventura, then board bus 16 ($1.25, one hour, once hourly) at Main and Figueroa Sts, which goes straight to downtown Ojai. The bus company, formerly known as SCAT, is now called **Gold Coast Transit** (☎ 805-487-4222; www.goldcoast transit.org).

SUMMERLAND

pop 1545

This drowsy seaside community is locally famous for its supernatural-minded origins. The town was founded by Henry Lafayette Williams, a former Treasury agent, in 1885. Williams was a Spiritualist, a religion in vogue at the time, whose followers believed in the power of mediums to connect the living with the dead. Rumor had it that the spiritualists kept hidden rooms in their homes to welcome the dearly departed – a practice earning the town the indelicate nickname of 'Spookville.' Today, those wanting to connect to the past wander the town's antique shops, where you won't find any bargains, but you can ooh and ahh over beautiful furniture from centuries gone by. There are some hidden shops on the hill just up from the interstate. Head south on Hwy 101 to exit 91 at Evans Ave. Park on Lillie Ave and walk around town – you'll never feel far from the hum of the freeway or the racket of the trains.

For the beach, turn right off exit 91, cross the railroad tracks and park at Lookout Park, where you'll find grills, picnic tables, a playground, and access to a wide, relatively quiet beach.

Stop for lunch at **Stacky's** (☎ 805-969-9908; 2315 Lillie Ave; mains $4-6; ☽ 6:30am-7:30pm Mon-Fri, 7am-7:30pm Sat & Sun), a pine-paneled, eat-out-of-a-basket diner where the waitress will tell you if something's not good. If you want a plate and a waiter, walk across the street to the Victorian-style **Summerland Beach Café** (☎ 805-969-1019; 2294 Lillie Ave; mains $8-10; ☽ 7am-3pm), which is known for its fluffy omelettes. For drinking, tip back a draft or two under the watchful eye of a mounted jackalope at the **Nugget** (☎ 805-969-6135; 2318 Lillie Ave; ☽ 11am-9pm), a scruffy, wood-darkened locals' lair where Bill and Hillary were kickin' it on the 1992 campaign trail – see the photos.

CHANNEL ISLANDS NATIONAL PARK

Don't let this stunning five-island park loiter too long on your lifetime to-do list. It's easier to access than you might think, and the payoff is immense. Hiking, kayaking, scuba diving, camping, whale-watching – you'd have to try hard to get bored.

Geographically, the Channel Islands are an eight-island chain off the Southern

California coast, stretching from Santa Barbara to San Diego. Five of them – San Miguel, Santa Rosa, Santa Cruz, Anacapa and tiny Santa Barbara – comprise Channel Islands National Park. Rich with unique species of flora and fauna, extensive tide pools and kelp forests, the islands are home to over 100 plant and animal species found nowhere else in the entire world, earning them the nickname 'California's Galapagos.'

Originally inhabited by the Chumash and Gabrieleño peoples (who were taken to the mainland missions in the early 1800s), the islands were subsequently taken over by sheep ranchers and the US Navy until the mid-1970s, when conservation efforts began. San Miguel, Santa Rosa, Anacapa and Santa Barbara Islands are now owned by the **National Park Service** (NPS; ☎ 805-658-5730; www.nps.gov/chis), which also owns about a quarter of Santa Cruz Island.

Human beings have left a heavy footprint. Livestock overgrazed, causing erosion, and rabbits fed on native plants. The US military even practiced bombing techniques on San Miguel. Deep-sea fishing has caused the destruction of three-quarters of the islands' kelp forests, which play a key part in the marine ecosystem.

Despite past abuses, the future isn't all bleak. Brown pelicans – decimated by the effects of DDT and reduced to one surviving chick on Anacapa in 1970 – have rebounded. On San Miguel Island vegetation returned – albeit 50 years later – after overgrazing sheep were removed. On Santa Cruz Island, the Park Service and the Nature Conservancy have implemented plans to restore natural vegetation and hope the recovery efforts will have the same success as those on Santa Miguel.

By boat, Anacapa and Santa Cruz are within an hour of Ventura and two hours off Santa Barbara. Both have stellar hiking and make do-able day trips:

Ventura to Anacapa 12 miles
Santa Barbara to Anacapa 40 miles
Ventura to Santa Cruz 22 miles
Santa Barbara to Santa Cruz 30 miles

Park information is available at the Channel Islands National Park Visitors Center (p402).

Sights & Activities

Anacapa, which is actually three separate islets, gives a memorable introduction to the islands' ecology and is the best option for those short on time. Boats dock on the East Island

and after a short climb you'll find 2 miles of trails offering fantastic views of island flora, a historic lighthouse, and the rocky Middle and West Islands. Kayaking, diving, tidepooling and seal-watching are popular activities here. After checking out the small museum, ask about ranger-led programs; occasionally park rangers scuba dive with a video camera, broadcasting images on a monitor you can watch on the dock.

Santa Cruz, the largest island at 96 sq miles, has two mountain ranges with peaks reaching 2450ft (Mt Diablo). The western side of Santa Cruz is owned and managed by the Nature Conservancy – 76% of the island – and can only be accessed with a permit. But the remaining eastern section, managed by the NPS, packs a wallop – ideal for those wanting an action-packed day trip or a slightly more relaxing overnight trip. You can swim, snorkel, scuba dive and kayak. There are excellent hikes too, including the 1-mile climb to captivating **Cavern Point**. Views don't get much better than from this lovely spot. For a longer jaunt, continue another couple of easy miles – mostly along scenic bluffs – to **Potato Harbor**. The **Scorpion Canyon–Island Jay** hike is also good. Starting in the upper campground, scramble across the old stream bed, then head steeply uphill to the old oil well for fantastic views. Connect with Smugglers Rd atop the hill and loop back to Scorpion Anchorage. The strenuous middle section of this trail is best not attempted at midday – there's little shade on the uphill.

The Chumash called Santa Rosa 'Wima' (Driftwood) because of the logs that often came ashore here. They built plank canoes called *tomols* from the logs. This island has rare Torrey pines, sandy beaches and nearly 200 bird species. There's beach and canyon hiking but high winds can make swimming, diving and kayaking tough for any but the most experienced.

San Miguel, the most remote of the four northern islands, guarantees solitude and a wilderness experience, but it's often windy and shrouded in fog. Some sections are off-limits to prevent disruption of the fragile ecosystem.

Santa Barbara, only 1 sq mile in size and the smallest of the islands, is a treasure trove of riches for nature lovers. Big, blooming coreopis, cream cups and chicory are just a few of the island's memorable plant species. You'll also find the humongous northern elephant seal here as well as Xantus' murrelets, a bird that nests in cliff crevices. You can get more information from the visitors center here.

Most visitors come to the park from June through August; however, the prettiest times to visit are during the spring wildflower season (April and May) and in September and October, when the fog clears. If you have any budding botanists or biologists in your brood – or kids who love the outdoors – the Channel Islands are a great family getaway. The boat trip can be a bit rough, but it's relatively short and Island Packers boats (below) brake for leaping dolphins and breaching whales – always a nice distraction.

Tours

Island Packers (☎ 805-642-1393; www.islandpackers.com; 1691 Spinnaker Dr), located near the **Channel Island National Park Visitor Center** (☎ 805-658-5730; 1901 Spinnaker Dr; ⏰ 8:30am-5pm), leads trips year-round and offers packages to all the islands; from December to March it operates terrific one-day whale-watching excursions. Rates start at $42 per adult and $25 per child for the East Anacapa trip; going to the other islands costs more and campers pay extra for their gear. Staff provide excellent interpretations of the history and ecology of the islands. Ask about guided hikes.

Take note, seas can feel choppy to some landlubbers. To avoid seasickness, sit outside on the second level – not too close to the diesel fumes in back. The ride to the island is typically against the wind and a bit bumpier than the return. Staring at the horizon is a myth but ginger chews may help some people.

Truth Aquatics (Map p380; ☎ 805-962-1127; www.truthaquatics.com; 301 Cabrillo Blvd), the park's Santa Barbara–based concessionaire, leads comparable excursions, also with excellent interpretation.

Most trips require a minimum number of participants, and may be canceled due to surf and weather conditions. If you camp overnight and the seas are rough the next day, you could get stuck. In short, landing is never guaranteed. Reservations are recommended, especially on weekends and in summer.

Island Packers offers **whale-watching** tours starting at $27 ($18 for kids) for a 3½-hour trip to watch gray whales.

For diving trips from Ventura, **Raptor Dive Charters** (☎ 805-650-7700; www.raptordive.com; 1559 Spinnaker Dr) runs trips to Anacapa Island starting at $100. Equipment rentals available.

If kayaking is on your agenda, **Paddle Sports of Santa Barbara** (☎ 805-899-4925, 888-254-2094; www.kayaksb.com; 117b Harbor Way, Santa Barbara) offers trips from Ventura, through Island Packers, to Anacapa and Santa Cruz, starting at $180. Kayaks, paddles, wet suits and life vests are included, as is van transportation from Santa Barbara. Also try **Aquasports** (☎ 805-968-7231, 800-773-2309; www.islandkayaking.com; 111 Verona Ave, Goleta) and **Channel Islands Kayak Center** (☎ 805-644-9699; www.cikayak.com; 1691 Spinnaker Dr, Ventura).

Sleeping

All of the islands have primitive **campgrounds** (☎ reservations 800-365-2267; www.nps.gov; campsites $15), which are open year-round. Each has pit toilets and picnic tables, but you must pack everything in and out, including trash. Water is only available on Santa Rosa and Santa Cruz Islands. Due to fire danger, campfires aren't allowed, but you can use a camp stove. Be prepared to trek up to 1.5 miles to the campground from the landing areas.

The campground on Santa Barbara is large, grassy and surrounded by hiking trails; the one on Anacapa is high, rocky and isolated. Camping on San Miguel, with its unceasing wind, fog and volatile weather, is not for the faint of heart. Santa Rosa's campground has wonderful views of Santa Cruz. It's situated in a eucalyptus grove in a canyon (it can get very windy). Del Norte, a backcountry campground on Santa Cruz, lies in a shaded oak grove, 3.5 miles from the landing.

Getting There & Away

Access to the Channel Islands is via Ventura or Santa Barbara. See opposite for information on boat travel to the islands and tour options.

To get to the Channel Islands National Park Visitors Center (p402) and the boat docks in Ventura from Hwy 101 northbound, exit at Victoria Ave, turn left on Victoria and right on Olivas Park Dr to Harbor Blvd; Olivas Park Dr runs straight into Spinnaker Dr. From Hwy 101 southbound, exit at Seaward Ave onto Harbor Blvd, then turn right on Spinnaker Dr.

Boating to the islands can be rough; those prone to seasickness should consider taking a 25-minute flight to Santa Rosa Island, from either Santa Barbara or Camarillo, with **Channel Islands Aviation** (☎ 805-987-1301; www.flycia.com; 305 Durley Ave, Camarillo; day trips adult/child $160/135, campers round-trip $250).

Directory

CONTENTS

Accommodations	408
Activities	411
Business Hours	411
Climate Charts	411
Dangers & Annoyances	411
Discount Cards	412
Festivals & Events	413
Food	414
Gay & Lesbian Travelers	414
Holidays	414
Insurance	415
International Visitors	415
Internet Access	417
Legal Matters	417
Maps	418
Shopping	418
Solo Travelers	419
Tipping	419
Tourist Information	419
Tours	419
Travelers with Disabilities	419
Women Travelers	420

ACCOMMODATIONS

Southern California has all types of places to unpack your suitcase, from hostels, campgrounds and B&Bs to chain motels, hotels and luxury resorts. Reservations are a good idea for weekend travel year-round and all the time during peak season, that is, June to September everywhere except the desert and the ski areas where November to February are the busiest periods. Demand and prices also spike around major holidays (p414) and big local festivals (mentioned throughout this book; see also p413) when some properties may impose two- or three-day minimum stays.

This book lists accommodations as budget (less than $130), midrange ($130 to $280) and top end (more than $280) in ascending order starting with the cheapest property. Unless noted, rates do not include taxes. We have marked our top picks within the lists, but just because a place isn't a top pick doesn't mean it's not good. Each property we

recommend has been inspected and meets a certain baseline quality standard within its category.

Prices listed in this book do not – and in fact cannot – take into account seasonal variations or promotional discounts. Always check the property's website for specials and compare it to what's offered by the big players such as www.orbitz.com, www.expedia.com, www.travelocity.com and www.hotel.com. For comparison, also feed your travel dates through www.onetime.com, which searches multiple websites.

Generally, midweek rates are lower except in city hotels geared to the suit brigade, which often also lure leisure travelers with weekend deals. Membership in AARP or AAA lops 10% off standard rates at participating properties.

Our budget recommendations comprise campgrounds, hostels and motels, but since midrange properties generally offer better value for money, most of our listings fall into this category. Expect clean, comfortable and decent-sized double rooms with at least a modicum of style, a private bathroom and such standard amenities as cable TV, direct-dial telephone, a coffeemaker, perhaps a microwave and a small refrigerator. Pools and shared Jacuzzi tubs are quite common as well.

Top-end lodgings offer top-notch amenities and perhaps a scenic location, edgy decor or historical ambience. Pools, fitness rooms, business centers and other upscale facilities are pretty standard, but unless you're going to use them, it's rarely worth spending the extra money.

Smoking rooms are becoming increasingly rare in health-conscious California. Where they exist, they are often in less desirable locations or are the last to be renovated. Be careful: some properties levy a hefty 'clean-up fee' if you light up in your nonsmoking room. Bed-and-breakfasts especially are often entirely smokefree, meaning you're not allowed to smoke anywhere on the property, not even outside.

By law, all hotels must have at least one room compliant with the American Disabilities Act. Air-conditioning is a standard amenity except in some beachfront properties.

Properties offering free or fee-based broadband internet access for guests not traveling with their own equipment are designated with the internet icon (🖳). Listings also mention whether wireless internet access (wi-fi) is offered.

B&Bs

Bed-and-breakfast lodgings are usually high-end accommodations in converted private homes, typically lovely old Victorians or other heritage buildings. Owners take great pride in decorating the guest rooms and common areas and have a personal interest in ensuring that you enjoy your stay. People in need of lots of privacy may find B&Bs a bit too intimate. Rates typically include a lavish, home-cooked breakfast. Amenities vary widely, but rooms with TV and telephone are the exception; the cheapest units share bathroom facilities. Most B&Bs require advance reservations, though some will accommodate the occasional drop-in guest. Smoking is generally prohibited and minimum stays are common in peak season and on weekends.

Standards are highest at places certified by the California Association of Bed & Breakfast Inns (www.cabbi.com).

Camping

Camping in Southern California can be a lot more than just a cheap way to spend the night. The nicest sites have you waking up to ocean views, splendid rock formations or a canopy of pines. Most campgrounds are open year-round, and popular ones get jammed in summer, so make reservations as early as possible.

Basic campsites with fire pits, picnic benches and access to drinking water and pit toilets are most common in national forests and on Bureau of Land Management (BLM) land. Campgrounds in state and national parks tend to have flush toilets, sometimes hot showers and RV (recreational vehicle) hookups. Private campgrounds are usually located close to cities and cater more to the RV crowd.

Most campgrounds accept reservations for all or some of their sites through one or both of the following agencies.

National Recreation Reservation Service (NRSS; ☎ 877-444-6777, outside the US 518-885-3639; www .recreation.gov; per reservation $9) Reservations in national parks (up to 180 days in advance); national forests and BLM land (up to 240 days in advance).

Reserve America (☎ 800-444-7275, outside the US 916-638-5883; www.reserveamerica.com; per reservation $7.50) Reservations for camping in California state parks and some private sites; you can book up to seven months in advance.

Hostels

Southern California has five hostels affiliated with **Hostelling International USA** (HI-USA; ☎ 301-495-1249, 800-909-4776; www.hiusa.org). Two are in each of San Diego and LA, and there's one in Fullerton, near Disneyland; see those chapters for details. Dorms in HI hostels are gender-segregated and alcohol and smoking are prohibited.

Indie hostels are most common in Hollywood, Venice and San Diego. They're generally more convivial with regular guest parties and other events. Some include a light breakfast in their rates, arrange local tours or pick

DIRECTORY

up guests at transportation hubs. No two hostels are alike but typical facilities include communal kitchens, lockers, internet access, laundry and TV lounges.

Besides dorms (usually mixed) of varying sizes, many hostels have pricier private rooms, although bathrooms are usually shared. Some hostels say they accept only international visitors (basically to keep out destitute locals), but Americans who look like they are travelers are usually admitted, especially during the slower months.

Rates range from $14 to $28, including tax. Most hostels take bookings online and by phone, fax, mail or email. Many independent hostels belong to reservation services such as www.hostels.com, www.hostelworld.com and www.backpackers.com, which sometimes offer lower rates than the hostels directly, so check these out too.

Hotels & Motels

Hotels differ from motels in that they don't surround a parking lot and usually have some sort of a lobby. Hotels may provide extra services such as laundry, but such conveniences usually come at a price. If you walk in without reservations, always ask to see a room before paying for it, especially at motels.

Rooms are often priced by the size and number of beds in a room, rather than the number of occupants. A room with one double or queen-size bed usually costs the same for one or two people, while a room with a king-size bed or two double beds costs more. Rooms with two doubles can accommodate up to four people, making them a cost-saving choice for families and small groups. A small surcharge often applies to the third and fourth person, but children under a certain age (this varies) often stay free. Cribs or rollaway beds usually incur an extra charge.

The room location may also affect the price; recently renovated or larger rooms, or those with a view, are likely to cost more. Hotels facing a noisy street may charge more for quieter rooms.

Many hotels offer suites for people in need of more elbow room. While this should technically get you at least two rooms, one of them a bedroom, this is not always the case as some properties simply call their larger rooms 'suites' or 'junior suites.' Always ask about a suite's size and layout before booking it.

Rates increasingly include breakfast, which may be just a stale donut and wimpy coffee, an all-out gourmet affair with fresh croissants and homemade jam, or anything in between.

Make reservations at chain hotels by calling their central reservation lines, but to learn about specific amenities and possible local promotions, call the property directly. Every listing in this book includes local direct numbers.

Resorts

One type of accommodation Southern California has plenty of is full-service luxury resorts, usually with integrated spas offering the latest in pampering techniques. For busy urbanites they serve as quick getaways, places that offer a respite from the rat race and restore balance to the body and soul. Luxury resorts are normally so attractive that they're often destinations in themselves.

Expect very comfortable, attractively designed rooms with quality furnishings and beds dressed up with pillow-top mattresses, high-thread-count linens and both down and foam pillows. Higher-end properties offer such additional services as in-room massages, shoeshining, and evening turndown; some of these cost extra. On-site restaurants serving three meals a day are commonplace, as are bars.

ACTIVITIES

For outdoor enthusiasts Southern California offers the mother lode of possibilities. No matter what kind of activity gets you off that couch, you'll be able to pursue it in this land of oceans and mountains, deserts and forests. Everywhere you go, you'll find outfitters and local operators eager to gear you up. Go to the Southern California Outdoors chapter (p63) for an overview of the main types of active pursuits that await you in the region.

BUSINESS HOURS

Standard business hours, including most government offices, are 9am to 5pm Monday to Friday. Bank hours are usually from 9am or 10am to 5pm or 6pm weekdays; some branches have Saturday hours from 9am to 1pm or 2pm. Bigger post-office branches do business from 8am to 5:30pm weekdays and 8am to 2pm on Saturday.

Most shops open doors around 10am, although noon is common for boutiques and art galleries. Closing time is anytime from 6pm to 9pm in shopping malls, except on Sunday when hours are noon to 5pm (malls to 6pm).

Convenience stores and supermarkets often stay open until 10pm or midnight; in cities, some stay open around the clock.

Restaurants don't follow standard hours, although typical opening hours are 7am to 11am (breakfast), 11:30am to 2:30pm (lunch) and 5:30pm to 10pm (dinner). Bars usually open around 5pm or 6pm and keep pouring until 1am or 2am. Pubs are sometimes open during the daytime. Always confirm precise hours if you've got your eye on a particular place.

CLIMATE CHARTS

For general advice on Southern California's climate and the best times to travel here, see p14.

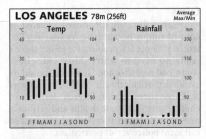

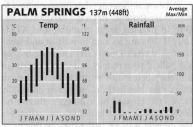

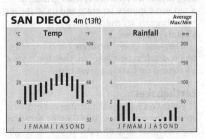

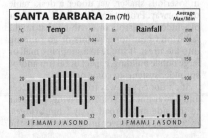

DIRECTORY

DANGERS & ANNOYANCES

By and large, Southern California is not a dangerous place. The most publicized problem is violent crime, but incidents are mostly confined to areas that few travelers would visit. Wildlife may pose some danger, and of course there is the dramatic, albeit unlikely, possibility of a natural disaster, such as an earthquake. Prepare for the worst, but expect the best.

Crime

Travelers will rarely get tricked, cheated or conned simply because they're tourists. Potential violence is a problem for all but there's really no need to worry. Most cities have some 'bad neighborhoods,' which should be avoided, particularly after dark. The Dangers & Annoyances section in each destination chapter provides some details and seriously nervous nellies can always quiz hotel staff or call local police about particulars.

Here are some general pointers on how to minimize trouble. Exercise particular caution in parking areas at night. Use ATMs only if they are located in well-lit and well-trafficked areas. Don't carry lots of cash; keep the bulk of your money and your passport in a money belt inside your clothes and stash other valuables in the room safe or hotel safe. If you're accosted by a mugger, there's no fail-safe policy but handing over whatever the mugger wants is better than getting hurt. Keep some money separate and hand it over fast. Muggers are not too happy to find their victims penniless.

That said, don't meditate on crime. Protect yourself as best you can, then focus your awareness on having a great trip.

Earthquakes

Earthquakes happen all the time but most are so tiny they are detectable only by sensitive seismological instruments. If you're caught in a serious shaker, get under a desk, table or doorway. Protect your head and stay clear of windows, mirrors or anything that might fall. Don't head for elevators or go running into the street. If you're in a shopping mall or large public building, expect the alarm and/or sprinkler systems to come on.

If outdoors, get away from buildings, trees and power lines. If you are driving, pull over to the side of the road away from bridges, overpasses and power lines. Stay inside the car until the shaking stops. If you are on a sidewalk near buildings, duck into a doorway to protect yourself from falling bricks, glass and debris. Prepare for aftershocks. Use the telephone only if it's absolutely necessary. Turn on the radio and listen for bulletins.

Riptides

The biggest hazard lurking in the ocean is the dangerous ocean current called a riptide. If you find yourself being carried offshore by a rip, the important thing is to just keep afloat; don't panic or try to swim against the current, as this will quickly exhaust you. Swim parallel to the shoreline and once the current stops, swim back to shore.

Scams

There are no scams unique to Southern California. A healthy skepticism is your best defense. In restaurants it pays to study your final bill as some servers have been observed slipping in an extra drink or adding their tip to the final tally without telling you (thereby hoping for a double tip). European visitors, who are perceived as cheap tippers, are especially prone to being victims of this annoying practice.

Wildlife

Mountain lions – also called cougars or pumas – inhabit forests and mountains throughout Southern California, especially in areas teeming with deer. This includes some areas near the coast. Attacks on humans are rare. If you encounter a cougar, face the animal and retreat slowly, trying to appear large by raising your arms or grabbing a stick. If attacked, you'll need to fight back, shouting and throwing objects at it.

Although an estimated 16,000 to 24,000 black bears roam around California, the chances of bear encounters in the southern part of the state are exceedingly unlikely and limited to the San Gabriel Mountains and the San Bernardino Mountains east of LA. Look for instructions posted at trailheads and campgrounds.

Watch your step when hiking, especially on hot summer afternoons when rattlesnakes like to bask in the middle of the trail. Also beware of scorpions and black widow spiders, which hide under rocks and wood piles (see p432 for more information).

DISCOUNT CARDS

Cutting costs while exploring Southern California is as easy as locating the Hollywood Sign. If you're a full-time student, the **International Student Identity Card** (ISIC; www.isic .org) is your ticket to savings on airline fares, travel insurance and many local attractions. For nonstudents under 26 years of age, the International Youth Travel Card (IYTC) grants similar savings and benefits. All these cards are issued by student unions, hostelling organizations and youth-oriented travel agencies. Check the website for the one nearest you. Cards cost $22 and are valid for a year.

International and US students can also buy the **Student Advantage Card** (☎ 877-256-4672; www .studentadvantage.com) for 15% savings on Amtrak and Greyhound plus discounts of up to 50% at participating hotels, shops and airlines. It's sold online and costs $20 for the first year and $10 for each additional year.

People over the age of 65 (although sometimes it's 55, 60 or 62) often qualify for the same discounts as students; any identification showing your birth date should suffice as proof of age. Members of the **American Association of Retired Persons** (AARP; ☎ 800-687-2277; www.aarp.org; annual membership fee $12.50), an advocacy group for Americans 50 years and older, and of the **American Automobile Association** (AAA; ☎ 800-874-7532; www.aaa.com; per yr from $47) or its foreign affiliates qualify for small discounts (usually 10%) in many places. Just make it a habit to ask every time you book a room, reserve a car, order a meal or pay an entrance fee, especially since these discounts are not usually advertised.

Also look for discount coupons in tourist offices, hotels, gas stations and newspapers. Be aware that discounts may have restrictions and conditions or may not be valid at peak times, so always read the fine print. Online hotel discount coupons are available through **Roomsaver** (www.roomsaver.com).

If Southern California's theme parks are the focus of your trip, a **Southern California CityPass** (www.citypass.com) may be a wise investment. Passes cost $235 for adults and $189 for children aged three to nine, and buy a three-day admission to Disneyland and Disney's California Adventure, a one-day admission each to Universal Studios and SeaWorld and another day at either the San Diego Zoo or the San Diego Wild Animal Park. Passes are valid for 14 days from the day of the first use and may be purchased online or at any of the attractions. The total savings are $94 for adults and $79 for children.

The Hollywood CityPass (p109) offers a similar deal but is limited to attractions within LA.

FESTIVALS & EVENTS

Southern California has a wonderful and packed schedule of festivals and special events taking place throughout the year. The following list is an overview of some of the major festivities, each of which is detailed in the relevant destination chapter.

January & February
Rose Parade (Los Angeles, p160) January 1
Chinese New Year (Los Angeles, p160) Late January/early February

March
LA Marathon (Los Angeles, p160) First Sunday in March

April & May
Los Angeles Times Festival of Books (Los Angeles, p160) Third weekend in April
Fiesta Broadway (Los Angeles, p160) Last Sunday in April
Coachella Valley Music & Arts Festival (Indio, Palm Springs, p355) Late April/early May
Cinco de Mayo (most cities, especially Los Angeles, p160) Early May

June
LA Pride (Los Angeles, p160) Mid-June
Summer Solstice Parade (Santa Barbara, p386) Late June

July
Central Avenue Jazz Festival (Los Angeles, p160) Late July
Festival of the Arts & Pageant of the Masters (Laguna Beach, p274) July to August
US Open Sandcastle Competition (San Diego, p304) Mid-July
San Diego LGBT Pride (San Diego, p304) Late July

August
Nisei Week Japanese Festival (Los Angeles, p161) Early to mid-August
Sunset Junction Street Fair (Los Angeles, p161) Mid-August
African Marketplace & Cultural Faire (Los Angeles, p161) Late August/early September

September
Fleet Week (San Diego, p305) Mid- to late September
Los Angeles County Fair (Los Angeles, p161) Mid- to late September
Abbot Kinney Festival (Los Angeles, p161) Late September

October
West Hollywood Halloween Carnival (Los Angeles, p161) October 31

November
Día de los Muertos (Los Angeles, p161) November 1
Pasadena Doo Dah Parade (Los Angeles, p161) Sunday before Thanksgiving
Hollywood Christmas Parade (Los Angeles, p161) Sunday after Thanksgiving
December
Christmas Boat Parade (Newport Beach, p266) Week before Christmas
Las Posadas and Luminaries (Los Angeles, p162; San Diego, p162) Late December

FOOD

Restaurant listings in this guide run the gamut from plain and simple to fabulous and stunning. Budget eateries include takeouts, delis, cafés, snack bars, markets and basic restaurants where you can fill up for $12 or less. At mid-range establishments, you usually get table-cloths, full menus, beer and wine lists and main courses from $12 to $25. Top-end places tend to be full gourmet affairs with fussy service, creative and freshly prepared food and matching wine lists; expect mains to start at $25. As with accommodations, we identify our top picks, but simply because a restaurant isn't our top pick doesn't mean it's not good. Remember that your final tally will be swelled by the 8.25% sales tax and a tip of 15% to 20%.

Most restaurants serve lunch and dinner daily; consult individual listings for specifics.

There is no smoking inside restaurants, although some have patios or sidewalk tables where lighting up may still be tolerated. The one exception is Santa Monica where smoking in or within 20ft of any business is now *verboten*.

For the full run-down of cuisine, customs and table manners in Southern California, see p55.

GAY & LESBIAN TRAVELERS

Southern California is a magnet for gay travelers, with the major hot spots being West Hollywood (WeHo), Silver Lake and Long Beach in the LA area, the Hillcrest quarter of San Diego and the desert resort of Palm Springs. Laguna Beach in Orange County also has a small gay scene. All of these hubs have humming nightlife scenes, magazines, associations and support groups, and major Gay Pride celebrations. As elsewhere, the scene is predominantly male-oriented, although lesbians won't feel left out. See p112 for an overview of the LA scene, p312 for San Diego and p360 for Palm Springs.

California offers gays and lesbians extensive domestic rights but stops short of the legalization of gay marriage and civil unions. Californians tend to be tolerant but bigotry has not been completed rooted out and there have been cases of bashings even in metropolitan areas. In small towns 'tolerance' sometimes comes down to a don't-ask-don't-tell policy.

Damron (www.damron.com) publishes the classic gay travel guides, including *Men's Travel Guide* and *Women's Traveler*, but they're advertiser-driven and sometimes out of date. *Damron's Accommodations* lists gay-owned and gay-friendly hotels, B&Bs and guesthouses nationwide. On the web check out www.gay.com for loads of information, including downloadable Out & About travel guides. If you're looking for a gay mechanic or florist, see the **Gay & Lesbian Yellow Pages** (www .glyp.com).

If you find yourself in need of counseling or referrals of any kind, contact the **Gay & Lesbian National Hotline** (☎ 888-843-4564; www.glnh.org; ☯ 4pm-midnight Mon-Fri, noon-5pm Sat).

Other good resources:
Gay Travelocity (www.travelocity.com/gaytravel) Gay-specific articles, listings and hotels.
Out Traveler (www.outtraveler.com) Bimonthly magazine; free subscription to e-newsletter.
Purple Roofs (www.purpleroofs.com) Online directory of gay and lesbian accommodations.

HOLIDAYS

On the following national holidays banks, schools and government offices (including post offices) all close, and transportation, museums and other services operate on a Sunday schedule. Holidays falling on a weekend are usually observed the following Monday.
New Year's Day January 1
Martin Luther King Jr Day Third Monday in January
Presidents' Day Third Monday in February
Memorial Day Last Monday in May

Independence Day July 4 (aka the Fourth of July)
Labor Day First Monday in September
Columbus Day Second Monday in October
Veterans' Day November 11
Thanksgiving Day Fourth Thursday in November
Christmas Day December 25

School Holidays

Colleges take a one- or two-week 'spring break' around Easter, sometime in March or April. Although SoCal is currently not among the sizzling-hot destinations for libidinous students to let loose, some hotels may hike up prices during this time. School summer vacations run from late June to early September, making July and August the busiest travel months.

INSURANCE

No matter how long or short your trip, make sure you have adequate travel insurance. At a minimum you need coverage for medical emergencies and treatment, including hospital stays and an emergency flight home. Medical treatment in the USA is of the highest caliber, but the expense could kill you.

While you may find a policy that pays doctors or hospitals directly, many health-care professionals still demand payment at the time of service, especially from out-of-towners. Except in emergencies, call around for a doctor willing to accept your insurance. Be sure to keep all receipts and documentation. Some policies ask you to call (reverse charges) a center in your home country for an immediate assessment of your problem. For further details, see p430.

You should also consider coverage for luggage theft or loss. If you already have health insurance or a home-owners or renters policy, check what they will cover and only get supplemental insurance. If you have prepaid a large portion of your vacation, trip cancellation insurance is a worthwhile expense.

For information about what insurance you need while driving in Southern California, see p428.

Worldwide travel insurance is available at www.lonelyplanet.com/travel_services. You can buy, extend and claim online anytime – even if you're already on the road.

INTERNATIONAL VISITORS
Entering the USA

Depending on your country of origin, getting into the USA can be a bureaucratic nightmare, as the rules keep changing. For up-to-date information about entry requirements and eligibility, we highly recommend checking with a US consulate in your home country.

In 2004, the US Department of Homeland Security introduced a new set of security measures called US-VISIT. Upon arrival in the US, all visitors will be photographed and have their index fingers scanned. Eventually, this biometric data will be matched when you leave the US. The goal is to ensure that the person who entered the US is the same as the one leaving it and to catch people who've overstayed the terms of their admission. For full details about US-VISIT, check with a US consulate or www.dhs.gov/us-visit.

PASSPORTS & VISAS

For full background information, check the visa website of the **US Department of State** (www.unitedstatesvisas.gov). You can even sign up for emailed newsletters to keep abreast of developments.

Currently, under the US Visa Waiver Program, visas are not required for citizens of 39 countries for stays up to 90 days (no extensions) as long as they travel with a machine-readable passport (MRP). If you don't have an MRP, you will need to get a visa to enter the USA.

MRP passports issued or renewed after October 26, 2006 require an integrated chip with biometric information from the data page. MRP issued or renewed between October 26, 2005 and October 25, 2006 must have a digital photograph or integrated chip on the data page. If your passport was issued before October 26, 2005 it will still be accepted as long as it's an MRP. In other words, there is *no* need to get a new passport until your current one expires.

Since January 2007, under the Western Hemisphere Travel Initiative, citizens from the US, Canada, Mexico and Bermuda must also have a valid passport when entering the US by air and, most likely starting in the middle of 2008, by land or sea.

Citizens from all other countries need to apply for a visa in their home country. The process costs a nonrefundable $100, involves a personal interview and can take several weeks, so you should apply as early as possible.

Again, we'd like to stress that this information, while accurate at press time, may change. Always get the latest scoop from your nearest US consulate.

Customs

Non-US citizens and permanent residents over the age of 21 may bring 1L of alcohol, 200 cigarettes or 50 cigars or 3lbs (1.35kg) of smoking tobacco, and $100 worth of gifts into the US. Amounts higher than $10,000 in cash, traveler's checks, money orders and other cash equivalents must be declared. Unless you're curious about the US jail lifestyle, don't even think about bringing in illegal drugs.

California is an important agricultural state. To prevent the spread of pests and diseases there are certain food items (including meats, fresh fruit and vegetables) that may not be brought into the state. Bakery items, chocolates and hard-cured cheeses are admissible.

If you drive into California across the border from Mexico or the neighboring states of Oregon, Nevada and Arizona, you may have to stop for a quick inspection and questioning by officials of the California Department of Food and Agriculture.

For complete information, visit the US Customs and Border Protection website at www.cbp.gov.

Embassies & Consulates

Most foreign embassies are in Washington, DC, but many countries, including the following, have consular offices in LA. For additional countries, visit www.ss.ca.gov/business/ibrp/fgncons.htm.

Australia (Map pp90-1; ☎ 310-229-4800; 2049 Century Park E, 19th fl) Near Beverly Hills.

Canada (Map pp84-5; ☎ 213-346-2700; 550 S Hope St, 9th fl) Downtown.

France (Map pp90-1 ☎ 310-235-3200; 10990 Wilshire Blvd, Suite 300) Westwood.

Germany (Map pp88-9; ☎ 323-930-2703; 6222 Wilshire Blvd, Suite 500) Mid-City.

Japan (Map pp84-5; ☎ 213-617-6700; 350 S Grand Ave, Suite 1700) Downtown.

Netherlands (off Map pp90-1; ☎ 310-268-1598; 11766 Wilshire Blvd, Suite 1150) Near Westwood.

New Zealand (off Map pp90-1; ☎ 310-566-6555; 2425 Olympic Blvd, Suite 600E) Santa Monica.

UK (off Map pp90-1; ☎ 310-481-0031; 11766 Wilshire Blvd, Suite 1200) Near Westwood.

Money

For exchange rates, see the inside cover of this book. For an overview of how much things cost in Southern California, see p15.

You can exchange money at airports, some banks and currency-exchange offices such as American Express and Travelex. Always enquire about rates and fees. In rural areas, exchanging money may be a problem, so make sure you have plenty of cash, a credit card or US-dollar traveler's checks on hand.

Usually the best and quickest way to obtain cash is by using ATMs, which are ubiquitous and accessible around the clock. Most are linked to international networks such as Cirrus, Plus, Star and Maestro. Most charge a small transaction fee and your own bank may impose additional charges.

Credit cards are almost universally accepted and, in fact, you'll find it hard or impossible to rent a car, book a room or order tickets over the phone without one. A credit card may also be vital in emergencies. Most ATMs also spit out cash if you use your credit card, but it's expensive because, in addition to a steep service fee, you'll be charged interest immediately on the entire statement-period's balance (ie there's no grace period as with purchases).

For exact fees, check with your bank or credit-card company.

Traveler's checks have pretty much fallen out of use. Big-city restaurants, hotels and large stores generally accept US-dollar traveler's check, same as cash, but clerks at small businesses, markets and fast-food chains may be unfamiliar with them and refuse to honor them.

Post

The **US Postal Service** (USPS; www.usps.com) is inexpensive and reliable. Postcards and standard letters up to 1oz (about 30g) cost 41¢ within the US, 69¢ to Canada and Mexico and 90¢ to all other countries. Postal rates increase by a couple of pennies every few years. For other rates, zip (postal) codes and general information, stop by any post office, call the **USPS toll-free helpline** (☎ 800-275-8777) or visit the website.

Mail can be sent general delivery (poste restante) to any post office that has its own zip code. There is no charge, but you must show photo identification when picking up mail. Post offices will hold mail for 10 days.

Telephone

PAY PHONES

Public pay phones are a dying breed and are usually coin-operated, although some accept credit cards and the fanciest ones (usually found at airports) have data ports for accessing the internet using your laptop. Local calls usually cost 35¢ minimum and increase with the distance and length of call. In most cases you'll be better off using a prepaid phonecard, sold in convenience stores, supermarkets, newsstands and electronics stores. Be sure to read the fine print for hidden fees; a surcharge of about 30¢ for calls made from pay phones is normal.

PHONE CODES

US phone numbers consist of a three-letter area code followed by a seven-digit local number. When dialing a number within the same area code, just punch in the seven-digit number. Long-distance calls must be preceded by ☎ 1. For direct international calls, dial ☎ 011 plus the country code plus the area code plus the local phone number. If you're calling from abroad the country code for the US is ☎ 1.

For local directory assistance, dial ☎ 800-373-3411. For directory assistance outside your area code, dial ☎ 1 plus the area code plus ☎ 555-1212; this is charged as a long-distance call. For international assistance, dial ☎ 00.

Toll-free numbers begin with ☎ 800, ☎ 866, ☎ 877 or ☎ 888 and must be preceded by ☎ 1. Most can only be used within the USA, some only within the state, and some only outside the state. To find any toll-free number, call ☎ 800-555-1212 (no charge).

CELL PHONES

Cell (mobile) phones operate on GSM 1900. If your home country uses a different standard, you'll need a multiband GSM phone in order to make calls in SoCal. If you have an unlocked multiband phone, a prepaid rechargeable SIM chip is usually cheaper than using your own network and available at any major telecommunications or electronics store. If your phone doesn't work in the US, these places also sell inexpensive prepaid phones, including some airtime. For short stays, you could also rent such a phone, eg from **Trip-Tel** (☎ 310-645-3500; www.triptel.com), at the Los Angeles International Airport (outside the customs gate in the Tom Bradley International terminal). Rentals cost $5 per day ($25 per week) plus $1.50 per minute for incoming and outgoing calls within the US ($3 for international calls), including taxes.

Time

California is in the Pacific time zone, which is Greenwich Mean Time minus eight hours. When it's noon in LA, it's 3pm in New York, 8pm in London and 6am (the next day) in Sydney or Auckland. Daylight-saving time comes into effect on the second Sunday in March, when clocks are put forward one hour, and ends on the first Sunday in November.

See p454-55 for a map of time zones.

INTERNET ACCESS

California leads the world in technology, so it's generally pretty easy to check your email. Public libraries offer free terminals and wifi access, internet cafés (listed throughout) and **FedEx Kinko's branches** (☎ 800-254-6567; www.fedexkinkos.com) exist in most towns, free public wi-fi hot spots are proliferating and even some state parks are now wi-fi enabled (see www.parks.ca.gov/wifi for a list). Lodging properties, cafés and restaurants providing guest terminals for going online are identified with the internet icon ▣ . The availability of wi-fi is also indicated with each review. There may be a fee for either service.

If you're traveling with your own laptop, you'll find that most hotels have the technology that lets you get online from your room, although again there may be a charge. Both high-speed access and wi-fi are common and only in older properties may you have to resort to dial-up. Depending on where you bought your laptop, you may need to buy adapters for US electrical outlets and telephone sockets at larger electronics stores.

Check www.wififreespot.com/ca.html or www.jiwire.com to locate wi-fi hot spots anywhere. For useful trip-planning websites, see p15.

LEGAL MATTERS

If you are stopped by the police, remain courteous at all times and, if driving, keep your hands where the cop can see them, ie atop the steering wheel. Don't get out of the car unless asked. There is no system of paying fines on the spot. Attempting to pay the fine to the officer may lead to a charge of attempted bribery. There is usually a 30-day period to pay a fine. For traffic offenses, the police officer

DIRECTORY

will explain the options to you. Most matters can be handled by mail.

If you are arrested for more serious offenses, you have the right to remain silent and are presumed innocent until proven guilty. There is no legal reason to speak to a police officer if you don't wish. Everyone arrested has the right to make one phone call. If you don't have a lawyer, friend or family member to help you, call your embassy. The police will give you the number upon request. If you don't have a lawyer, one will be appointed to you free of charge.

When driving in California, you need to carry your driver's license and obey road rules carefully (p428). The highest permissible blood-alcohol limit is 0.08%. Driving under the influence (DUI) is a serious offense that entails stiff fines, a suspended license, higher insurance premiums and other nasty consequences. Police can give roadside sobriety checks to assess if you've been drinking or using drugs. If you fail, they'll require you to take a breath, urine or blood test to determine the level of alcohol in your body. Refusing to be tested is treated the same as if you had taken and failed the test. Penalties for DUI range from license suspension and fines to jail time. If you're in a group, choose a 'designated driver' who agrees not to consume alcohol or drugs.

Consuming alcohol anywhere other than at a residence or licensed premises is also a no-no, which puts parks, beaches and the rest of the great outdoors off limits. It is also illegal to carry open containers of alcohol inside a vehicle, even in the passenger section, even if they are empty. Containers that are full and sealed may be carried, but if they have ever been opened they must be stored in the trunk.

Possession of under 1oz of marijuana is a misdemeanor in California, and though it is punishable by up to one year in jail, a fine is more likely for first-time offenders. Possession of any other drug, including cocaine, ecstasy, LSD, heroin, hashish or more than an ounce of weed, is a felony punishable by lengthy jail sentences, depending on the circumstances. For foreigners, conviction of any drug offense is grounds for deportation.

MAPS

Visitors centers distribute free (but often very basic) maps, but if you're doing a lot of driv-

---

MAY I SEE YOUR ID, PLEASE?
The legal minimum age in California to…
■ Drink alcohol: 21
■ Drive a car: 16
■ Fly a plane: 17
■ Buy a shotgun: 18
■ Go to war: 17
■ Have sex: 18
■ Smoke tobacco: 18
■ Vote in an election: 18

---

ing, you'll need a detailed road map or a map atlas, such as the *California Road & Recreation Atlas* ($25), by Benchmark Maps (www .benchmarkmaps.com), which includes *every* road in the state, as well as topographic details, campgrounds and land features.

Members of the **American Automobile Association** (AAA; ☎ 800-874-7532; www.aaa.com) or one of its international affiliates, can get AAA's high-quality maps for free from any local office. Bookshops and tourist offices usually stock a good assortment of maps, while newsagents and gas stations have a more limited selection. For downloadable maps and driving directions try **Google Maps** (www.maps.google.com), **Mapquest** (www.mapquest.com) or **Yahoo! Maps** (http:// maps.yahoo.com).

SHOPPING

Southern Californians spend a lot of time spending their money and there's certainly no shortage of big malls, department stores, outlet centers, boutiques and markets to help them do it. To many visitors the sheer variety and quantity of consumer goods can be as staggering as it is tempting. There's really nothing you can't buy here, be it computers or couture, flip-flops or funky designer outfits, anime DVDs or sex toys, surf gear or antiques. Orange County has the biggest concentration of malls, while LA is best for tomorrow's fashions and accessories and unique items such as clothing worn by the stars. Palm Springs has the region's best outlet mall, while places with local artist communities in LA, Laguna Beach and Santa Barbara are good for picking up originals. Rural towns, especially in the desert or mountain areas, are usually best for digging up Americana and Old West paraphernalia.

If you're keen on Native American items, like rugs, jewelry or artwork, be aware that much of the stuff sold in stores and trading posts is mass-produced. Genuine products usually have a tag or stamps identifying them as 'Indian handmade' while imitations will say something like 'Indian style.' Be conscious of who's doing the selling and ask a lot of questions. Who made the item? What tribe is the artist from? What kinds of materials were used? A reputable dealer will know the answers and happily talk about their origin.

SOLO TRAVELERS

There are no particular problems or difficulties traveling alone in Southern California. Although it is not for everybody, the obvious advantage is the freedom to do whatever, whenever you want.

Americans are generally friendly and easy to talk to. Women don't need to be afraid of initiating conversation, even with men. Unless you're overtly coquettish, it most likely won't be interpreted as a sexual advance. Hostels are great places for meeting up with other people, as are guided tours, major tourist attractions and internet cafés.

In general, don't advertise where you're staying or that you're traveling alone. When going for a long hike, let someone else know about your intended whereabouts in case something should happen to you. Carrying a cell phone can be a lifesaver in this situation and other emergencies.

Some issues of safety are slightly different for women than they are for men – for more, see p420.

TIPPING

Most people in service industries receive minimum wage and rely on tips as their primary source of income. However, if service is truly appalling, don't tip. Here are some customary tipping amounts:

Bartenders 15% of the bill.
Bellhops, skycaps in airports $1 to $2 per bag.
Concierges nothing for simple information (like directions); $2 to $20 for securing restaurant reservations, concert tickets or providing services outside usual duties.
Housekeeping staff $1 to $2 daily, left on the pillow each day; more if you're messy.
Parking valets $1 to $2 unless rates are stated.
Restaurant servers 15% to 20% of the pretax bill.
Taxi drivers 10% to 15% of metered fare.

TOURIST INFORMATION

Almost every city and town has a local visitors center or chamber of commerce. For pretrip planning, consult the information-packed website maintained by the **California Travel & Tourism Commission** (www.visitcalifornia.com). This state-run agency also operates several **California Welcome Centers** (www.visitcwc.com) where staff dispense maps and brochures and can help find accommodations. The following branches are in Southern California:

Barstow (☎ 760-253-4782; 2796 Tanger Way, Suite 106) Off the I-15 at the Tanger Outlet Mall, en route to Death Valley and Las Vegas.
Oceanside (☎ 760-721-1101; 928 N Coast Hwy) In northern San Diego County.
Oxnard (☎ 805-988-0717; 1000 Town Center Dr, Suite 135) Exit Hwy 101 at Oxnard Blvd.
San Bernardino (☎ 909-891-1874; 1955 Hunts Ln, Suite 102) Exit Waterman Ave off I-10 Fwy en route to Palm Springs.
Santa Ana (☎ 714-667-0400; 2800 N Main St, Suite 112) In the Westfield Main Place shopping mall in Orange County.
Yucca Valley (☎ 760-365-5464; 56711 Twentynine Palms Hwy) Near Joshua Tree National Park.

TOURS

Backpacker Bus (☎ 888-464-6460; www.backpacker bus.com) A hop-on hop-off service operating various loops, including one between LA, San Diego and Big Bear Lake ($55, all three legs).
California Motorcycle Tours (☎ 858-677-9892, 888-408-7631; www.ca-motorcycletours.com) San Diego–based outfit offering various trips, including a seven-day 'Beach & Mountain Tour' that takes in all of Southern California's hot spots ($2300, including Harley Sportster rental, lodging and food).
Elderhostel (☎ 877-426-8056; www.elderhostel.org) Nonprofit organization that offers learning trips throughout the world, including Southern California, for active people over 55. Includes bus and walking tours.

TRAVELERS WITH DISABILITIES

If you have a physical disability, you'll find that Southern California is a fairly accessible place compared to other parts of the world. The Americans with Disabilities Act (ADA) requires that public buildings be wheelchair accessible and have accessible restrooms; most do. However, when it comes to nonpublic buildings, such as hotels, restaurants, museums and theaters, there are no guarantees. In theory, properties built after 1992 must be ADA compliant, but sadly violations are commonplace. When making lodging reservations, always discuss your particular needs. For other venues, call ahead to find out what access issues to expect.

Buses and trains must have wheelchair lifts and telephone companies are required to provide relay operators (available via TTY numbers) for the hearing impaired. Many banks provide ATM instructions in Braille, and you'll find dropped curbs at most intersections and sometimes audible crossing signals as well.

Major car-rental agencies offer hand-controlled vehicles and vans with wheelchair lifts at no extra charge, but you must reserve them well in advance.

All major airlines, Greyhound buses and Amtrak trains can accommodate people with disabilities, although they usually need at least a day or two advance notice. Just describe your specific needs when making reservations. Seeing-eye dogs are permitted to accompany passengers.

Most national and state parks and recreation areas have paved or boardwalk-style nature trails. For free admission to national parks and federal recreation lands, US citizens and permanent residents with a permanent disability should obtain the **America the Beautiful Access Pass** (www.nps.gov/fees_passes .htm).

Various regional access brochures are available for download from the internet.

A Wheelchair Rider's Guide: Los Angeles and Orange County Coast (www.scc.ca.gov/Wheel/index .html) Free download.

Access-Able Travel Source (www.access-able.com) This excellent website has many useful links.

Access Guide: In San Diego (www.accessangdiego.org) Order booklet for $5.

Society for Accessible Travel & Hospitality (SATH;

☎ 212-447-7284; www.sath.org) Lots of useful links and information for disabled travelers.

Theme Park Access Guide (www.mouseplanet .com/tag/dlintro.htm) An insider's view of Disneyland and other parks 'on wheels.'

WOMEN TRAVELERS

Southern California is generally a safe place to travel, even for solo women. Use the same common sense as you would at home.

Going alone to cafés and restaurants is perfectly acceptable, although how comfortable you feel depends entirely on you. In bars and nightclubs, solo women are likely to attract attention from men, but if you don't want company, most will respect a firm 'no thank you.' If you feel threatened, protesting loudly will often make the offender slink away with embarrassment – or will at least spur other people to come to your defense.

The website www.journeywoman.com facilitates women exchanging travel tips and includes links to other sites. Another good source is **Her Own Way** (www.voyage.gc.ca/main/pubs /PDF/her_own_way-en.pdf), an online booklet published by the Canadian government but filled with lots of good general travel advice useful for any woman.

Although physical attack is unlikely, it does, of course, happen. If you are assaulted, you could call the **police** (☎ 911), although you do not need to do so in order to get help. Many women prefer first to contact a women's or rape crisis center whose staff can help you deal with emotional and physical issues surrounding an assault. They can make referrals to medical, legal and social service providers as well as give information about useful organizations and support groups. To find one near you, call the 24-hour **National Sexual Assault Hotline** (☎ 800-656-4673; www.rainn.org).

Transportation

CONTENTS

Getting There & Away	**421**
Air	421
Land	423
Getting Around	**424**
Air	424
Bicycle	424
Bus	425
Car & Motorcycle	426
Hitchhiking	428
Local Transportation	428
Train	429

GETTING THERE & AWAY

Flights, tours and rail tickets can be booked online at www.lonelyplanet.com/travel_services.

AIR
Airports & Airlines

If you're traveling to Southern California, you'll most likely touch down at **Los Angeles International Airport** (code LAX; ☎ 310-646-5252; www.lawa.org/lax), which is huge, bewildering and super-busy. You'll likely experience a lot less hassle arriving at one of the regional airports, which may even be more convenient to your final destination. With few exceptions, they handle only domestic departures. Also see the regional chapters for details.

Bob Hope Airport (code BUR; ☎ 818-840-8840, 800-835-9287; www.burbankairport.com) Also known as Burbank Airport, in northern LA county close to Universal Studios Hollywood.

John Wayne Airport (code SNA; ☎ 949-252-5200; www.ocair.com) In Santa Ana, Orange County, convenient for Disneyland.

Long Beach Airport (code LGB; ☎ 562-570-2600; www.longbeach.gov/airport) Cute art deco terminal, free wi-fi in the restaurant and easy access to both LA and Orange County.

Ontario International Airport (code ONT; ☎ 909-937-2700, 866-456-3900; www.lawa.org/ont) In Riverside County, east of LA, close to the desert destinations.

Palm Springs International Airport (code PSP; ☎ 760-318-3800; www.palmspringsairport.com) Easy in, easy out.

San Diego International Airport (code SAN; ☎ 619-231-2100; www.san.org) Some international flights to Mexico, Canada and the UK.

Santa Barbara Airport (code SBA; ☎ 805-967-7111; www.flysba.com) Tiny and hassle-free.

Major domestic and international carriers serving Southern California are listed below.

DOMESTIC AIRLINES

AirTran (code FL; ☎ 800-247-8726; www.airtran.com)

Alaska Air (code AS; ☎ 800-426-0333; www.alaskaair.com)

American Airlines (code AA; ☎ 800-433-7300; www.aa.com)

Continental (code CO; ☎ 800-525-0280; www.continental.com)

Delta (code DL; ☎ 800-221-1212; www.delta.com)

Frontier Air (code F9; ☎ 800-432-1359; www.frontierairlines.com)

Jet Blue (code B6; ☎ 800-538-2583; www.jetblue.com)

Northwest Airlines (code NW; ☎ 800-225-2525; www.nwa.com)

Southwest (code WN; ☎ 800-435-9792; www.southwest.com)

United Airlines (code UA; ☎ 800-241-6522, 800-538-2929; www.united.com)

US Airways (code US; ☎ 800-428-4322; www.usairways.com)

INTERNATIONAL AIRLINES

Aer Lingus (code EI; ☎ 800-474-7424; www.aerlingus.com)

THINGS CHANGE...

The information in this chapter is particularly vulnerable to change. Check directly with the airline or a travel agent to make sure you understand how a fare (and ticket you may buy) works and be aware of the security requirements for international travel. Shop carefully. The details given in this chapter should be regarded as pointers and are not a substitute for your own careful, up-to-date research.

TRANSPORTATION

Aeromexico (code AM; ☎ 800-237-6639; www
.aeromexico.com)
Air Canada (code AC; ☎ 888-247-2262; www.air
canada.com)
Air France (code AF; ☎ 800-237-2747; www.air
france.com)
Air New Zealand (code NZ; ☎ 800-262-1234; www
.airnewzealand.com)
Alitalia (code AZ; ☎ 800-223-5730; www.alitalia.com)
British Airways (code BA; ☎ 800-247-9297; www
.britishairways.com)
Cathay Pacific (code CX; ☎ 800-233-2742; www
.cathaypacific.com)
Iberia (code IB; ☎ 800-772-4642; www.iberia.com)
Japan Airlines (code JL; ☎ 800-525-3663; www
.japanair.com)
KLM (code KL; ☎ 800-374-7747; www.klm.com)
Lufthansa (code LH; ☎ 800-645-3880; www.lufthansa
.com)
Mexicana (code MX; ☎ 800-531-7921; www.mexicana
.com)
Qantas (code QF; ☎ 800-227-4500; www.qantas.com)
Singapore Airlines (code SQ; ☎ 800-742-3333; www
.singaporeair.com)
Virgin Atlantic (code VS; ☎ 800-862-8621; www
.virgin-atlantic.com)
WestJet (code WS; ☎ 888-538-5696; www.west
jet.com)

Tickets

Everybody loves a bargain and timing is key
when it comes to snapping up cheap airfares.
You can generally save a bundle by booking early, traveling midweek (Tuesday to
Thursday) or flying in the late evening or
early morning.

Your best friend in ferreting out deals is
the internet. Start by checking fares at www
.expedia.com, www.travelocity.com and www
.orbitz.com, then run the same flight request
through meta-search engines such as www
.sidestep.com or www.kayak.com, which
comb the websites of major airlines, consoli-
dators and online travel agencies. If you're
not tied to particular travel dates, use the flex-
ible-dates search tool to find the best fares
or consult www.itasoftware.com, which not
only finds the cheapest fare within a 30-day
period but also alerts you to potential down-
sides such as long layovers, tight connections
or overnight travel.

If you're based in North America and not
loyal to a particular air carrier, you might be
able to save a bundle through www.priceline
.com or www.hotwire.com, where you name
the fare you're willing to pay, then wait and
see if an airline bites.

CLIMATE CHANGE & TRAVEL

Climate change is a serious threat to the ecosystems that humans rely upon, and air travel
is the fastest-growing contributor to the problem. Lonely Planet regards travel, overall, as a
global benefit, but believes we all have a responsibility to limit our personal impact on global
warming.

Flying & climate change

Pretty much every form of motorized travel generates CO2 (the main cause of human-induced
climate change) but planes are far and away the worst offenders, not just because of the sheer
distances they allow us to travel, but because they release greenhouse gases high into the atmosphere. The statistics are frightening: two people taking a return flight between Europe and
the US will contribute as much to climate change as an average household's gas and electricity
consumption over a whole year.

Carbon offset schemes

Climatecare.org and other websites use 'carbon calculators' that allow travellers to offset the
level of greenhouse gases they are responsible for with financial contributions to sustainable
travel schemes that reduce global warming – including projects in India, Honduras, Kazakhstan
and Uganda.

Lonely Planet, together with Rough Guides and other concerned partners in the travel industry, support the carbon offset scheme run by climatecare.org. Lonely Planet offsets all of its
staff and author travel.

For more information check out our website: www.lonelyplanet.com.

Many airlines now guarantee that you'll find the lowest fare on their own websites, so check these out as well, especially since such discount carriers as Southwest and JetBlue are not included in online-agency searches.

To find out about late-breaking special fares, sign up for free email newsletters with the airlines or such websites as www.smartertravel.com and www.airfarewatchdog.com. Use www.seatguru.com to determine which seat you'd like to request when making a booking.

And don't forget about travel agents, who can be especially helpful when planning extensive trips or complicated routes. STA Travel and Flight Centre, both with worldwide branches, are recommended.

Asia

Tokyo, Seoul, Bangkok and Hong Kong are among the Asian cities that have good flight connections to LA. Many flights go via Honolulu, but stopovers usually cost extra.

Australia & New Zealand

The dominant carriers from Down Under are Air New Zealand and Qantas, although United Airlines, US Airways and American Airlines also fly across the Pacific. Prices are higher if you stop over in Honolulu.

Canada

Air Canada, American Airlines, United Airlines and WestJet all offer regular nonstop services to LAX from most major Canadian cities. WestJet also flies to Palm Springs from Calgary and Vancouver.

Continental Europe

Many airlines, including Air France, Lufthansa, Alitalia, Iberia, Delta, United Airlines and US Airways, have direct flights to LA from major European cities. Many other international and US airlines fly to a gateway city (usually Chicago or Miami) and continue to LA on domestic flights.

Mexico

Aeromexico and Mexicana are among the airlines with frequent flights to LA from most major Mexican cities. Aeromexico has flights to Ontario and San Diego as well. Also look into flights to Tijuana, just across the border from San Diego, which may actually be cheaper.

UK & Ireland

One of the busiest and most competitive air sectors in the world is between the UK and the USA. American Airlines, British Airways, Continental, United Airlines and Virgin Atlantic all operate direct flights from London to Los Angeles. All but American also fly nonstop to San Francisco. Aer Lingus and American Airlines fly nonstop from Dublin to LA, although you'll find more choices and probably cheaper fares by going via London.

USA

Domestic airfares fluctuate hugely depending on the season, day of the week, length of stay and flexibility of the tickets for changes and refunds. Still, nothing determines fares more than demand, and when business is slow, airlines lower fares to fill seats. Discount carriers such as AirTran, Frontier Air, Jet Blue and Southwest have been giving the big guys, including United Airlines, American Airlines and US Airways, a run for their money.

LAND
Border Crossings

San Ysidro on the US–Mexico border between San Diego and Tijuana is the world's busiest border crossing. Traveling into Mexico is usually not a problem but coming back into the US almost always entails a long wait, especially if you're driving. The US Department of Homeland Security maintains a handy website at http://apps.cbp.gov/bwt showing the current border wait times. US citizens and residents do not require a visa for stays of 72 hours or less within the border zone (ie as far south as Ensenada). Starting as early as January 1, 2008, US citizens need to present a valid US passport to get back into the USA. Citizens from other countries can be subject to a full immigration interrogation upon returning to the US, so bring your passport and US visa if you need one (see p415). For details on traveling between San Diego and Tijuana, see p344.

Bus

Greyhound (☎ 800-231-2222; www.greyhound.com) is the king of the bus world in the US, plowing along a nationwide route system serving some 2200 destinations, including dozens in Southern California. See p424 for some sample fares, and p425 for information on tickets, reservations and fares.

TRANSPORTATION

TRANSPORTATION

If SoCal is part of a wider US itinerary or you are planning on making the bus your main method of travel to, from and around the region, you might save money by purchasing Greyhound's **Discovery Pass** (www.discoverypass.com). It's good for unlimited travel throughout the entire US and Canada for the periods of seven days ($283), 15 days ($415), 30 days ($522) and 60 days ($645). Passes may be bought at Greyhound terminals and online up to two hours before start of travel (to be picked up at the terminal) and at ticket agents worldwide. For people starting their trip in Canada, online purchases must be made at least three weeks in advance (two weeks for Canadians) to receive the pass by mail.

SAMPLE BUS FARES

Route	Adult Fare	Duration	Frequency
Las Vegas-San Diego	$51	8¼hr	2 direct buses daily
Phoenix-LA	$46	6½-10½hr	up to 8 direct buses daily
San Francisco -LA	$46	7½-13hr	up to 16 direct buses daily

Car & Motorcycle

If you're driving to the USA from Canada or Mexico, bring your vehicle's registration papers, liability insurance and driver's license. Some car-rental agencies allow their vehicles to be taken into Mexico for a hefty insurance surcharge (about $25 per day).

Another alternative is sharing your ride with others headed for the same destination. This way you split the cost of gasoline, have company during your ride and do your bit for the environment. Websites such as www.erideshare.com, www.rideboard.com and www.digihitch.com let you advertise a ride yourself or make arrangements with drivers.

Train

Amtrak (☎ 800-872-7245; www.amtrak.com) operates a fairly extensive rail system throughout the US. The trains are comfortable, if slow, and are equipped with dining and lounge cars on long-distance routes. See p429 for details about services within California. There are three interstate trains that serve Southern California:

Coast Starlight Travels along the West Coast daily from Seattle to LA via Portland, Sacramento and Oakland.

Southwest Chief Daily departures between Chicago and LA via Kansas City, Albuquerque and Flagstaff.
Sunset Limited Thrice-weekly service between Orlando and LA via Tucson, El Paso and New Orleans.

TRAIN PASSES

Amtrak also offers passes for exploring other parts of the US. The USA Rail Pass is available to non-US-or-Canadian citizens only and is sold online and by travel agents outside North America. The pass offers unlimited coach-class travel within a specific US region for either 15 or 30 consecutive days; price depends on the region, number of days, peak or off-peak travel and the season. Prices for the West Rail Pass (valid for travel anywhere west of Chicago and New Orleans) are $369/459 for 15-/30-day periods between June and early September (and around Christmas) and $329/359 the rest of the year. Children aged two to 15 pay half-price.

Amtrak's North America Rail Pass, available to anyone, offers unlimited travel on Amtrak and Canada's **VIA Rail** (www.viarail.ca) for 30 consecutive days. Prices are $999 for travel between June and mid-October and $709 at other times of the year. Seniors, students and children get a 10% discount.

GETTING AROUND

AIR

Although it is possible to fly, say, from LA to San Diego or Palm Springs, the time and cost involved don't make air travel a sensible way to get around Southern California.

BICYCLE

Cycling around Southern California is a great, nonpolluting way to travel but is really only a feasible option if you're in fairly good shape and able to cope with high temperatures, especially in summer. Cycling in the desert is brutal and not recommended during that period. Some cities have designated bicycle lanes, but you really want to have your wits about you when venturing out into heavy traffic.

Cyclists must follow the same rules of the road as vehicles, but don't expect drivers to always respect your right of way. Helmets may give you a bad hair day but using one is the smart thing to do and is mandatory for anyone under 18. Cycling is allowed on all roads and highways – even along freeways if there's no suitable alternative like a smaller parallel road; all mandatory exits are marked.

You can rent bikes by the hour, day, week or month or buy them new, at sporting-goods stores and discount-warehouse stores, or used, at flea markets and from notice boards at hostels. Also check the newspaper classified ads or online bulletin boards such as www .craigslist.org. The **Adventure Cycling Association** (www.adv-cycling.org) is an excellent source for maps, bike routes and gadgets.

Emergency roadside assistance is available from the **Better World Club** (☎ 866-238-1137; www .betterworldclub.com). Membership costs $40 per year, plus $10 enrollment fee, and entitles you to two free pickups and transportation to the nearest repair shop within a 30-mile radius. The company donates 1% of its revenue to environmental causes.

If you tire of pedaling, some local bus companies operate buses equipped with bike racks. Greyhound transports bicycles as luggage for about $15 to $25, provided the bicycle is disassembled and placed in a box (available at terminals for $10). Most of Amtrak's *Pacific Surfliner* trains feature special racks where you can secure your bike unboxed, but be sure to reserve a spot when making your ticket reservation. There's a fee of $5 to $10, depending on the destination. On trains without racks, bikes must be put in a box and checked as luggage ($5 fee, box $10).

Bicycle theft is fairly common, so protect yours with a heavy-duty bicycle lock and park in well-lit, busy areas. Some parking garages have special bike parking areas. If possible, bring your bike inside your hotel room at night.

BUS

Southern California cities served by **Greyhound** (☎ 800-231-2222; www.greyhound.com) include Los Angeles, Santa Barbara, San Diego, Anaheim, Oceanside, San Bernardino, Temecula and Ventura. Buses are a cheap and environmentally friendly way to travel between these major cities, but they won't get you off the beaten path or into parks and forests. Frequency of service varies, but main routes operate every hour or so, sometimes around the clock. Stopovers are allowed on full-fare tickets only.

The cheapest method of getting around, Greyhound generally serves the less-affluent strata of society, but by international standards the service is not bad. There is only one

class, but buses are usually clean, comfortable and reliable; the best seats are near the front away from the bathroom. Other amenities include air-conditioning (bring a sweater) and slightly reclining seats. Smoking is prohibited.

Bus stations are dreary places and often in sketchy areas. This is especially true of LA.

Greyhound can accommodate disabled travelers, but you should make your needs known either at the time of booking or by calling ☎ 800-752-4841 at least 48 hours in advance of travel.

Costs

Tickets are sold online, by phone, at bus terminals and through ticket agents. Fares are quite competitive but you can knock off a few dollars by purchasing round-trips and traveling between Monday and Thursday. Discounts are also available – on unrestricted fares only – for seniors over 62 (5% discount), students with a Student Advantage Card (p413; 15%) and children under 12 (40%). Also check the website for fare specials. Other promotions, including advance purchase and companion fares, become available all the time, although they may come with restrictions or blackout periods. Simply ask or check the website for the latest deals. For specific route and fare information, see the Getting There & Away section of the destination chapters. For bus passes, see p423.

SAMPLE BUS FARES

Route	Adult Fare	Duration	Frequency
LA-San Diego	$17	2-3hr	up to 19 per day
San Diego - Anaheim (Disneyland)	$17	2-2¼hr	up to 7 per day
Santa Barbara -LA	$12.50	2-3hr	up to 7 per day

Reservations

Greyhound does not take reservations and all boarding is done on a first-come, first-served basis. Even buying tickets in advance does not guarantee you a seat on any particular bus. Show up one hour prior to the scheduled departure and chances are pretty good you'll get on. Allow more time on Friday and Sunday afternoons and around holidays.

ROAD DISTANCES (MILES)

	Anaheim	Big Bear Lake	Death Valley	Las Vegas	Los Angeles	Newport Beach	Palm Springs	San Diego	San Francisco	Santa Barbara
Big Bear Lake	84									
Death Valley	283	236								
Las Vegas	263	216	141							
Los Angeles	26	96	289	270						
Newport Beach	19	96	297	276	44					
Palm Springs	91	83	300	280	110	104				
San Diego	96	144	350	331	120	90	140			
San Francisco	405	474	528	568	379	426	486	498		
Santa Barbara	123	189	377	357	95	138	200	220	334	
Tijuana	110	157	363	345	135	104	155	17	831	229

CAR & MOTORCYCLE

Automobile Associations

For long road trips, an auto-club membership is an excellent thing to have. The **American Automobile Association** (AAA; ☎ 800-874-7532; www .aaa.com), with offices throughout the country, is the main auto club in the US. Many AAA services, including 24-hour **emergency roadside assistance** (☎ 800-222-4357), are also available to members of its international affiliates such as CAA in Canada, AA in the UK and ADAC in Germany. The club also offers free trip-planning advice and maps, plus a range of discounts on hotels, car rentals, Amtrak tickets, admissions etc. An alternative is the **Better World Club** (www.betterworldclub.com), which offers similar coverage and donates 1% of revenue to environmental causes.

Bring Your Own Vehicle

Requirements for bringing your car to the USA from Canada or Mexico are briefly discussed on p424. Forget about shipping your car from overseas unless you're actually moving to the US. Otherwise, it simply doesn't make economic sense; you'll be better off renting one.

Driver's License

Visitors can legally drive in California for up to 12 months with their home driver's license. If you're from overseas, an International Driving Permit (IDP) is not compulsory but may give you greater credibility with traffic police. It may also be required for renting a vehicle, especially if your home license is not in English or doesn't have a photograph. IDPs are easy to obtain. Just grab a passport photo and your home license and stop by your local automobile association, which will make you one for a small fee. Always carry your home license along with the IDP.

Fuel & Spare Parts

Gas stations in California, nearly all of which are self-service, are ubiquitous except in sparsely populated desert areas, where you should carry a filled gas canister as a backup, if possible. Gas is sold in gallons (one gallon equals 3.78L). At the time of writing, the cost for mid-grade fuel ranged from $3 to $3.50. Prices are generally a few dimes higher in national parks and remote mountain and desert areas. Find out where gas is cheapest at the daily updated www.gasbuddy.com.

Finding spare parts should not be a problem, especially in the cities, although actual availability depends on the age and model of your car. Always bring some tools and a spare tire and be sure to have an emergency roadside-assistance number (see opposite) in case your car breaks down.

Rental

CARS

As anywhere, rates for car rentals vary considerably by model and pickup location, but, with advance reservations especially, you should be able to get an economy-size vehicle from about $25 per day, plus insurance and taxes. If you belong to an auto club, ask about discounts. It's also worth asking whether car rentals are eligible for frequent-flyer miles. Rates usually include unlimited mileage, but expect surcharges for rentals originating at airports and train stations, as well as for additional drivers and one-way rentals. Child or infant safety seats are compulsory (reserve at the time of booking) and cost about $10 per day or $50 per week.

To rent your own wheels you generally need to be at least 25 years old and hold a valid driver's license and a major credit card. Some companies may rent to drivers between 21 and 24 for an additional charge (between $10 and $25 per day). If you don't have a credit card, you may be able to make a large cash deposit.

Super Cheap Cars (☎ 310-645-3993; www.supercheap-car.com; 10212 La Cienega Blvd; ☼ 9am-4:30pm Mon-Sat) has no surcharge for anyone over 21, but you must buy full insurance from them. This is also one of the few companies renting to 20-year-olds, albeit with a $10 per day surcharge.

The following major international car-rental companies have dozens of branches throughout California:

Alamo (☎ 800-327-9633; www.alamo.com)

Avis (☎ 800-331-1212; www.avis.com)

Budget (☎ 800-527-0700; www.budget.com)

Dollar (☎ 800-800-4000; www.dollar.com)

Enterprise (☎ 800-325-8007; www.enterprise.com)

Hertz (☎ 800-654-3131; www.hertz.com)

National (☎ 800-227-7368; www.nationalcar.com)

Thrifty (☎ 800-367-2277; www.thrifty.com)

Overseas travelers should look into prepaid deals or fly-drive packages arranged in your home country, which often work out cheaper than on-the-spot rentals. Search the rental and airline companies' websites as well as online travel agencies for deals.

MOTORCYCLES

With a heritage that predates *Easy Rider* and *The Wild One*, motorcycling in America is an iconic experience. You need a valid motorcycle license and preferably also an International Driving Permit, endorsed for motorcycles, to simplify the rental process. To drive on freeways, you must have at least a 150cc engine.

Motorcycle rentals and insurance are not cheap, especially if you've got your eye on a Harley-Davidson or BMW. **Eagle Rider** (☎ 310-536-6777, 888-900-9901; www.eaglerider.com) has rental outlets in San Francisco, Los Angeles, San Diego, San Jose, Palm Springs and Las Vegas. Depending on the model, it costs $60 to $150 per day, including helmets, unlimited miles and liability insurance. Collision insurance (CDW) costs extra. You can rent in one city and return in another for an extra $100.

RECREATIONAL VEHICLES

Traveling by RV is a popular way of exploring Southern California. It's easy to find campgrounds with hookups for electricity and water, but in big cities RVs are a nuisance, since there are few places to park or plug it in. They're cumbersome to navigate and burn fuel at an alarming rate, but they

---

ECO CARS

If you'd like to minimize your contribution to SoCal's polluted air, consider renting a biodiesel-powered car from **Bio-Beetle** (☎ 877-876-6121, 808-873-6121; www.bio-beetle.com), based at LA International Airport (LAX). With rates starting at $50 a day and $200 a week, these cars are a bit more expensive, but with 30 to 45 miles per gallon you'll get a major break at the pump. Besides VW Beetles, their fleet also includes the larger Golf, Jetta and Passat.

Fox Rent-a-Car (☎ 800-225-4369, ext 1; www.foxrentacar.com) rents Prius, Honda Civic and Escape hybrids from $50 a day and $270 per week. The company has offices at LAX, John Wayne, Palm Springs and San Diego airports.

TRANSPORTATION

solve transportation, accommodation and cooking needs in one fell swoop.

Costs vary by size and model, but you can generally expect to pay from $100 per day for a small campervan sleeping two or three adults to as much as $300 for a mansion on wheels. Your local travel agency may have the best deals, or contact **Cruise America** (☎ 800-327-7799; www.cruiseamerica.com) or LA-based **Happy Travel Campers** (☎ 310-675-1335, 800-370-1262; www.camperusa.com).

Insurance

California law requires liability insurance for all vehicles, but it's not automatically included in rental contracts because many Americans are covered for rental cars under their personal car-insurance policies. Check your own policy carefully and don't pay extra if you're already covered. If you're not, expect to pay about $15 per day. Foreign visitors should check their travel-insurance policies to see if they cover rental cars.

Insurance against damage to the car itself, called Collision Damage Waiver (CDW) or Loss Damage Waiver (LDW), costs about $15 per day; it may require that you pay the first $100 to $500 for any repairs. Some credit cards, especially the gold and platinum versions, cover CDW/LDW for a certain rental period provided you charge the entire cost of the rental to the card. Check with your card issuer to determine the extent of coverage.

Personal Accident Insurance (PAI) covers you and any passengers for medical costs incurred as a result of an accident. If your travel insurance or your health-insurance policy at home does this as well – and most do, but check – then this is one expense (about $5 per day) you can do without.

Road Rules

For full details consult the *California Driver Handbook* or the *California Motorcycle Handbook,* which may be picked up for free at any Department of Motor Vehicles office or downloaded from www.dmv.ca.gov.

Californians drive on the right-hand side of the road. The use of seat belts and infant and child safety seats is required at all times, while motorcyclists must wear a helmet. Distances and speed limits are shown in miles. Unless otherwise posted, the speed limit is 65mph on freeways, 55mph on two-lane undivided highways, 35mph on major city

streets and 25mph in business and residential districts and near schools. It's forbidden to pass a school bus when its rear red lights are flashing.

Except where indicated, turning right at red lights after coming to a full stop is permitted so long as you don't impede intersecting traffic, which has the right of way. Talking on a cell phone while driving is still legal in California. At four-way stop signs, cars proceed in the order in which they arrived. If two cars arrive simultaneously, the one on the right has the right of way. When emergency vehicles (ie police, fire or ambulance) approach from either direction, pull over to get out of their way.

On freeways, slower cars may be passed on either the left or the right lane. If two cars are trying to get into the same central lane, the one on the right has priority. Lanes marked with a diamond symbol are reserved for cars with multiple occupants. California has strict anti-littering laws, and throwing trash from a vehicle can incur a fine up to $1000. For penalties for drinking and driving, see p417.

HITCHHIKING

Hitchhiking is never entirely safe anywhere in the world and we don't recommend it. Quite frankly, it's also fairly uncommon in modern-day America where hitchers are generally viewed with suspicion. In urbanized areas you'll find few motorists willing to stop for a thumb, although the practice may be more accepted in remote, rural areas where public transport is sporadic or nonexistent. Generally speaking, you can hitchhike on roads and highways; on freeways you must stand at the on-ramp. Use extreme caution, both when hitchhiking and picking up hitchhikers.

If you're undeterred by the potential risks, you may at least want to familiarize yourself with conditions in California by checking out **digihitch** (www.digihitch.com), a community website and portal that posts safety tips, specific road advice, links and stories.

LOCAL TRANSPORTATION

Buses are the most ubiquitous form of public transportation and practically all towns have their own system. Most are commuter-oriented and offer only limited or no service at all in the evenings and on weekends. Los

Angeles also has a combination subway/ light-rail network and San Diego operates a trolley to the Mexican border. Check the Getting Around sections of the destination chapters for local transportation options. Among Southland cities, Santa Barbara is the most bicycle-friendly. Cycling is not recommended in traffic-dense LA and San Diego.

Taxis are metered, with charges from $1.80 to $2.65 at flag-fall, plus $1.50 to $2.50 per mile. It isn't customary to hail a cruising cab: you normally phone ahead for one. Numbers of local companies are listed throughout this book or look under 'Taxi' in the Yellow Pages. Cabbies expect a 10% to 15% tip.

TRAIN

Amtrak (☎ 800-872-7245; www.amtrak.com) operates train services throughout California. At some stations, trains are met by motorcoaches (called Amtrak Thruways) for onward connections to smaller destinations. Travel on these buses is only permitted in conjunction with a train ticket.

The *Pacific Surfliner* is the main rail service within Southern California. The sleek, double-decker cars have comfortable seats, and there's a café car as well. Business-class seats feature nifty little video screens, slightly more legroom and outlets for plugging in laptops or other electrical devices. Smoking is prohibited.

Up to 11 trains daily ply the LA–San Diego route, making stops in Solana Beach, Oceanside (for Legoland), San Juan Capistrano and Anaheim (for Disneyland), among others. As many as five trains continue north to Santa Barbara via Oxnard and Ventura. The trip itself, which hugs the coastline for much of the route, is a visual treat.

Of Amtrak's long-distance trains, the *Coast Starlight* stops in Santa Barbara and LA, while the *Sunset Limited* travels to LA and northern Palm Springs.

Costs

Tickets can be purchased at train stations, by phone and online. Fares depend on the day of travel, the route, the type of seating and other factors. Fares are slightly higher between late May and early September. Round-trip tickets cost the same as two one-way tickets. If you're flexible with your travel dates, use the Fare Finder tool online to find the best deal.

Seniors over 62 and students with an ISIC or Student Advantage Card (p413) receive a 15% discount, while up to two children, aged two to 15 and accompanied by an adult, get 50% off. Children under two years of age travel for free. AAA members (p426) enjoy 10% off regular fares. Special promotions can become available at any time, so be sure to ask when booking tickets or check the website.

SAMPLE TRAIN FARES (at peak travel times)

Route	Coach	Business Class	Duration
LA–Santa Barbara	$25	$38	2½hr
San Diego–LA	$34	$48	2¾hr
San Diego –Santa Barbara	$37	$54	5½hr

Metrolink

Southern California's major population centers are linked to LA by a commuter-train network called **Metrolink** (☎ 800-371-5465; www.metrolinktrains.com). Seven lines connect Downtown LA's Union Station with the surrounding counties – Orange, Riverside, San Bernardino and Ventura – as well as northern San Diego County. Most trains depart between 6am and 9am and 3pm and 6pm Monday to Friday, with only one or two services operating during the day. Some lines also offer limited services on weekends. The most useful line for visitors is the Orange County Line, which stops in Anaheim, Santa Ana, San Juan Capistrano and Oceanside. The Ventura County Line stops at Bob Hope Airport in Burbank. Tickets are available from vending machines at the stations and fares are zone-based.

Reservations

Reservations can be made up to 11 months prior to departure. In summer and around holidays, trains sell out quickly, so book seats as early as possible.

Train Passes

Amtrak's California Rail Pass costs $159 ($80 for children aged two to 15) and is valid on all trains and Amtrak Thruway buses for seven days of travel within a 21-day period. This pass may be worth your while if you're planning a lot of travel within California.

Health Dr David Goldberg

CONTENTS

Before You Go   **430**
Insurance   430
Recommended Vaccinations   430
Internet Resources   430
In Southern California   **430**
Availability & Cost of Health Care   430
Infectious Diseases   430
Environmental Hazards   431

BEFORE YOU GO

INSURANCE

The USA, and Los Angeles in particular, offers possibly the finest health care in the world. The problem is that, unless you have good insurance, it can be prohibitively expensive. It's essential to purchase travel health insurance if your regular policy doesn't cover you when you're abroad.

Bring any medications you may need in their original containers, clearly labeled. A signed, dated letter from your physician that describes all medical conditions and medications, including generic names, is also a good idea.

If your health insurance does not cover you for medical expenses abroad, consider supplemental insurance. Find out in advance if your insurance plan will make payments directly to providers or reimburse you later for overseas health expenditures.

RECOMMENDED VACCINATIONS

No special vaccinations are required or recommended for travel to the USA. All travelers should be up to date on routine immunizations: tetanus-diphtheria, measles, chicken pox and influenza.

INTERNET RESOURCES

There is a wealth of travel health advice on the internet. The World Health Organization publishes a superb book, *International Travel and Health,* which is revised annually and is available online at no cost at www.who

.int/ith. Another website of general interest is MD Travel Health at www.mdtravelhealth .com, which provides complete travel-health recommendations for every country, updated daily, also at no cost.

It's usually a good idea to consult your government's travel-health website before departure, if one is available:
Australia (www.smartraveller.gov.au)
Canada (www.hc-sc.gc.ca/index_e.html)
UK (www.doh.gov.uk/traveladvice/index.htm)
US (www.cdc.gov/travel/)

IN SOUTHERN CALIFORNIA

AVAILABILITY & COST OF HEALTH CARE

In general, if you have a medical emergency, the best bet is to find the nearest hospital and go to its emergency room. If the problem isn't urgent, you can call a nearby hospital and ask for a referral to a local physician, which is usually cheaper than a trip to the emergency room. You should avoid stand-alone, for-profit urgent-care centers, which tend to perform large numbers of expensive tests, even for minor illnesses.

Pharmacies are abundantly supplied, but you may find that some medications that are available over the counter in your home country require a prescription in the USA, and, as always, if you don't have insurance to cover the cost of prescriptions, they can be shockingly expensive.

INFECTIOUS DISEASES

In addition to more common ailments, there are several infectious diseases that may be acquired by mosquito or tick bites.

Giardiasis

This parasitic infection of the small intestine occurs throughout North America and the world. Symptoms may include nausea, bloating, cramps, and diarrhea, and may last for weeks. To protect yourself from *Giardia,* you should avoid drinking directly from lakes, ponds, streams and rivers, which may be contaminated by animal or human feces. The infection can also be transmitted from person to person if proper hand-washing is not performed. Giardiasis is easily diagnosed by a stool test and readily treated with antibiotics.

HIV/AIDS
As with most parts of the world, HIV infection occurs throughout the USA. You should never assume, on the basis of their background or appearance, that someone is free of this or any other sexually transmitted disease. Be sure to use a condom for all sexual encounters.

West Nile Virus
This virus was unknown in the USA until a few years ago, but has now been reported in almost all 50 states. The virus is transmitted by culex mosquitoes, which are active in late summer and early fall and generally bite after dusk. Most infections are mild or asymptomatic, but the virus may infect the central nervous system, leading to fever, headache, confusion, lethargy, coma and sometimes death. There is no treatment for West Nile virus. For the latest update on the areas affected by West Nile, go to the **US Geological Survey website** (http://diseasemaps.usgs.gov/wnv_us_human.html).

ENVIRONMENTAL HAZARDS
Bites & Stings
The most effective ways to avoid bites and stings are common-sense approaches: wear boots when hiking to protect from snakes, wear long sleeves and pants to protect from ticks and mosquitoes. If you're bitten, don't overreact. Stay calm and follow the recommended treatment.

ANIMAL BITES
Do not attempt to pet, handle or feed any animal, with the exception of domestic animals known to be free of any infectious disease. Most animal injuries are directly related to a person's attempt to touch or feed the animal.

Any bite or scratch by a mammal, including bats, should be promptly and thoroughly cleansed with large amounts of soap and water, followed by application of an antiseptic such as iodine or alcohol. The local health authorities should be contacted immediately for possible postexposure rabies treatment, whether or not you've been immunized against rabies. It may also be advisable to start an antibiotic, since wounds caused by animal bites and scratches frequently become infected.

MOSQUITO BITES
When traveling in areas where West Nile or other mosquito-borne illnesses have been reported, keep yourself covered (wear long sleeves, long pants, a hat, and shoes rather than sandals) and apply a good insect repellent, preferably one containing DEET, to exposed skin and clothing. In general, adults and children over 12 should use preparations containing 25% to 35% DEET, which will usually last about six hours. Children between two and 12 years of age should use preparations containing no more than 10% DEET, applied sparingly, which will usually last about three hours. Neurological toxicity has been reported as a result of using DEET, especially in children, but appears to be extremely uncommon and generally related to overuse. DEET-containing compounds should not be used on children under age two.

Insect repellents containing certain botanical products, including oil of eucalyptus and soybean oil, are effective but last only 1½ to two hours. Products based on citronella are not effective.

Visit the **Center for Disease Control's website** (CDC; www.cdc.gov/ncidod/dvbid/westnile/prevention_info.htm) for further prevention information.

SNAKE BITES
There are several varieties of venomous snakes in the USA, but unlike those in other countries they do not cause instantaneous death, and antivenins are available. The rattlesnake is the most common; most have triangular-shaped heads, diamond patterns along their backs and vary in length from 2ft to 6ft.

If you're bitten, place a light constricting bandage over the bite, keep the wounded part below the level of the heart and move it as little as possible. Stay calm and get to a medical facility as soon as possible. Bring the dead snake for identification if you can, but don't risk being bitten again. Do not use the mythical 'cut an X and suck out the venom' trick; this causes more damage to snakebite victims than the bites themselves.

HEALTH

SPIDER & SCORPION BITES

Although there are many species of spiders in the USA, the only ones that cause significant human illness are the black widow and brown recluse (or hobo) spiders. The black widow is black or brown in color, measuring about 15mm in body length, with a shiny top, fat body, and distinctive red or orange hourglass figure on its underside. It's found throughout the USA, usually in barns, woodpiles, sheds, harvested crops and the bowls of outdoor toilets. The brown recluse spider is brown in color, usually 10mm in body length, with a dark violin-shaped mark on the top of the upper section of the body. It's usually found in the south and southern Midwest, but has spread to other parts of the country in recent years. The brown recluse is active mostly at night, lives in dark sheltered areas such as under porches and in woodpiles, and typically bites when trapped.

If bitten by a black widow, you should apply ice or cold packs and go immediately to the nearest emergency room. Complications of a black widow bite may include muscle spasms, breathing difficulties and high blood pressure. The bite of a brown recluse spider typically causes a large, inflamed wound, sometimes associated with fever and chills. If bitten, apply ice and see a physician.

The large (up to 6in in diameter) and hairy tarantula looks much worse than it actually is; it very rarely bites and then usually only when it is roughly handled. The bite is not very serious, although it is temporarily quite painful.

The only dangerous species of scorpion in the USA is the bark scorpion, which is found in the southwestern part of the country, chiefly Arizona. If stung, you should immediately apply ice or cold packs, immobilize the affected body part, and go to the nearest emergency room. To prevent scorpion stings, be sure to inspect and shake out clothing, shoes and sleeping bags before use, and wear gloves and protective clothing when working around piles of wood or leaves.

Sun

To protect yourself from excessive sun exposure, you should stay out of the midday

sun, wear sunglasses and a wide-brimmed hat, and apply sunscreen with SPF 15 or higher, providing both UVA and UVB protection. Sunscreen should be generously applied to all exposed parts of the body approximately 30 minutes before sun exposure and be reapplied after swimming or vigorous activity. Drink plenty of fluids and avoid strenuous exercise when the temperature is high.

Heatstroke

Heatstroke may occur in those who are exposed to excessively high temperatures for a number of days. The elderly are at greatest risk, especially those with chronic medical problems. Heatstroke often occurs during physical exertion but, particularly in the elderly, may also occur at rest. The first sign may be an abrupt collapse, but there may be early, subtle warnings, including dizziness, weakness, nausea, headache, confusion, drowsiness, rapid pulse and unreasonable behavior. If early symptoms of heat illness are observed, remove the victim from direct sunlight, loosen their clothing, give cold fluids and make sure the victim rests for at least 24 hours. In the event of heatstroke, the victim should be taken immediately to the nearest medical facility. To prevent heatstroke, drink plenty of fluids, eat salty foods, protect yourself from sun exposure and avoid alcohol and strenuous exercise when the temperature is high.

The Authors

ANDREA SCHULTE-PEEVERS
Coordinating Author

Andrea fell in love with Southern California – its pizzazz, people and near-perpetual sunshine – almost the instant she first landed in the Golden State in the late '80s. She'd grown up in Germany, lived in London and traveled the world, but it was in Los Angeles where she settled in the late '80s, got a degree from UCLA and embarked on a career in travel writing. A veteran Lonely Planet author, Andrea has written or contributed to about three dozen books, including several earlier editions of this one and the guide to California.

AMY BALFOUR
Orange County, Santa Barbara

Amy arrived in Los Angeles by way of Virginia where she'd been a deskbound attorney living her life in six-minute billable increments. Hearing the call of Hollywood, she ditched her stable salary to break in as a screenwriter. After a stint reviewing legal documents in Downtown LA, she accepted a writer's assistant gig with Law & Order. She's lived in Manhattan Beach and Mid-City, hiked the Santa Monica mountains, biked the Santa Barbara wine country, navigated the coast's diviest dives, led renegade tours of the Universal Studios backlot, and sampled margaritas all over SoCal. Amy recently jumped from TV into fulltime freelancing and has written for the *Los Angeles Times*, *Women's Health*, *Every Day with Rachael Ray*, *Backpacker*, and *Travelers Tales*.

ANDREW BENDER
The Culture, SoCal for Children, San Diego, Palm Springs & the Deserts

After writing LP titles as far away as Japan, Amsterdam and Nantucket, Andy is thrilled to finally be writing about Southern California, his home since the early 1990s. Yet another LP author with an MBA, this native New Englander first came to LA to work in film production, but he ended up leaving to do what every MBA secretly dreams of: travel the world and write about it. You can see his writing and photography in the *Los Angeles Times*, *Forbes*, *SilverKris* (Singapore Airlines in-flight magazine) and at www.andrewbender .com, among many others. When not on the road, he can be seen biking the beach in Santa Monica, discovering the next greatest ethnic dive and scheming over ways to spoil his nieces and nephews.

THE AUTHORS

LONELY PLANET AUTHORS

Why is our travel information the best in the world? It's simple: our authors are independent, dedicated travelers. They don't research using just the internet or phone, and they don't take freebies in exchange for positive coverage. They travel widely, to all the popular spots and off the beaten track. They personally visit thousands of hotels, restaurants, cafés, bars, galleries, palaces, museums and more – and they take pride in getting all the details right, and telling it how it is. For more, see the authors section on www.lonelyplanet.com.

Behind the Scenes

THIS BOOK

This guidebook was commissioned in Lonely Planet's Oakland office, and produced by the following:

Commissioning Editor Suki Gear
Coordinating Editor Averil Robertson
Coordinating Cartographer Corey Hutchison
Coordinating Layout Designer Sin Choo
Managing Editor Geoff Howard
Managing Cartographer Alison Lyall
Managing Layout Designer Celia Wood
Assisting Editors Daniel Corbett, Barbara Delissen, Brigitte Ellemor, Penelope Goodes, Helen Koehne, Kirsten Rawlings, Erin Richards
Assisting Cartographers Karen Grant, Tadhgh Knaggs, Anthony Phelan
Assisting Layout Designers Barry Cooke, Jim Hsu, Wibowo Rusli
Cover Designer Suki Gear
Color Designer Jacqui Saunders
Project Manager Fabrice Rocher
Thanks to Gabrielle Clark, Owen Eszeki, Ryan Evans, Jennifer Garrett, James Hardy, Liz Heynes, Lisa Knights, Chris Lee Ack, Adriana Mammarella, Wayne Murphy, Darren O'Connell, Naomi Parker, Laura Stansfeld, Andrew Tudor, Glenn van der Knijff, Wendy Wright

THANKS

ANDREA SCHULTE-PEEVERS

Lots of good folks to thank on this one, including Kim Cooper and Richard Schave for telling me about even wackier places than even I knew, Carol Martinez for letting me hobnob at the Daytime Emmies, Bob Maguglin and Megan Rodriguez for reacquainting me with Long Beach, and Kenny G for showing me a side of Hollywood nightlife. A big round of applause also to my brilliant coauthors Amy Balfour and Andy Bender, to my superpatient and understanding editors Suki Gear and Averil Robertson and to Corey Hutchison for making some fantastic maps. And David, as always, I couldn't do life without you.

AMY C BALFOUR

I'd like to thank the Academy…oh wait, I mean, I'd like to thank Suki Gear for entrusting me with another awesome assignment and for kindly not mocking my thrift store neuroses. Big thanks to coordinating author Andrea Schulte-Peevers for her guidance, enthusiasm, and great cookouts with husband David. Thanks also to co-author Andy Bender for first giving me the Lonely Planet scoop. I also had the best OC and Santa Barbara guides ever – thanks to Allan, Megan, Mike, Eli, David, and Kelly. And a tip of the wineglass to my favorite road-tripping Memphis mama, Melissa, who's always up for an adventure and game of slots. If mama ain't happy, ain't nobody happy. And of course, the Apocalypse Gang for suffering through all my boring stories with nothing but love and encouragement.

ANDREW BENDER

Thanks go to Joe Timko, Kate Buska and Junvi Ola at the San Diego Convention & Visitors Bureau, Mark Graves of Palm Springs Desert Resorts,

---

LONELY PLANET: TRAVEL WIDELY, TREAD LIGHTLY, GIVE SUSTAINABLY

The Lonely Planet Story

The story begins with a classic travel adventure: Tony and Maureen Wheeler's 1972 journey across Europe and Asia to Australia. There was no useful information about the overland trail then, so Tony and Maureen published the first Lonely Planet guidebook to meet a growing need.

From a kitchen table, Lonely Planet has grown to become the largest independent travel publisher in the world, with offices in Melbourne (Australia), Oakland (USA) and London (UK). Today Lonely Planet guidebooks cover the globe. There is an ever-growing list of books and information in a variety of media. Some things haven't changed. The main aim is still to make it possible for adventurous individuals to get out there – to explore and better understand the world.

Carol Martinez, Mike McDowell, Robin McClain and Rebekah Kim at LA Inc, John Brice, Juan Saldaña, Vanessa McGrady, Rachel Panush and all those local voices who volunteered to be interviewed.

In house, thanks to Suki Gear for the opportunity, Andrea Schulte-Peevers for friendship and stick-to-it-ness, Daniel Corbett, and Averil Robertson for her professionalism and good cheer.

OUR READERS

Many thanks to the travelers who used the last edition and wrote to us with helpful hints, useful advice and interesting anecdotes:

Dana Bean, Scott Godwin, Angie Mizeur, Heather Monell, David Pappas, David Rizzo, Alessandra van Otterlo

ACKNOWLEDGMENTS

Many thanks to the following for the use of their content:

Globe on title page ©Mountain High Maps 1993 Digital Wisdom, Inc.

SEND US YOUR FEEDBACK

We love to hear from travelers – your comments keep us on our toes and help make our books better. Our well-traveled team reads every word on what you loved or loathed about this book. Although we cannot reply individually to postal submissions, we always guarantee that your feedback goes straight to the appropriate authors, in time for the next edition. Each person who sends us information is thanked in the next edition – and the most useful submissions are rewarded with a free book.

To send us your updates – and find out about Lonely Planet events, newsletters and travel news – visit our award-winning website: **www.lonelyplanet.com/contact**.

Note: we may edit, reproduce and incorporate your comments in Lonely Planet products such as guidebooks, websites and digital products, so let us know if you don't want your comments reproduced or your name acknowledged. For a copy of our privacy policy visit www.lonelyplanet.com/privacy.

Index

Index

A

A+D Museum 111
Abalone Cove 78, 128
Abbot Kinney Blvd 126
Abbot Kinney Festival 161, 414
Academy Awards 160, 234
accommodations 18, 408-11
Adamson House 121
Adventureplex 158
AFI Fest 196
African American Firefighter Museum 142
African Marketplace & Cultural Faire 161, 413
agriculture 30-1
Agua Caliente Cultural Museum 353
Agua Caliente Indian Reservation 350
Ahmanson Theatre 50, 135, 203
Air & Space Museum 301
air travel 421-4
Alexandria Hotel 156
Alias Apartment Building 149
Aliso & Woods Canyons Wildnerness Park 273
amusement parks
  Belmont Park 320
  Disney's California Adventure 230, 242-4
  Disneyland 19, 23, 230-49, 231
  food 74
  Knott's Berry Farm 23, 249
  Knott's Soak City USA (Palm Springs) 353
  Legoland California 20, 337
  Pacific Park 124
  SeaWorld 23, 320-2
  Six Flags Magic Mountain 221
Anacapa Island 405-7
Anaheim 230-49, 231
  accommodations 244-5
  drinking 247
  entertainment 247
  food 245-7
  history 230

shopping 247
travel to/from 248
travel within 248-9
Anderton Court 114
Andreas Canyon 352
Angeles Crest Highway 25
Angeles National Forest 150
Angels Flights 135
Aniston, Jennifer 116
Annenberg Theater 47, 353
Anza-Borrego Desert State Park 19, 345, 368-72, 347
Arabian oryx 298
Aratani/Japan America Theater 138
archaeological sites 110-11
architecture 50-1, 239
  Art Deco 51
  Arts & Crafts 301
  Craftsman 51, 132, 148
  Mission Revival 133
  modernism 51, 345, 350, 355
  postmodernism 51
  Southern California Institute of Architecture 139
  Spanish Colonial 50, 297
  Spanish Mission 50-1
  Spanish-Moorish revival 378
  Victorian 50-1
Aroma Wilshire Center 140
Arquette, David 116
Art Center College of Design 149
art galleries 50
  A+D Museum 111
  Barnsdall Art Park 108
  Blum & Poe 119
  Brewery Art Complex 139, 206-7
  Broad Art Center 118
  Centro Cultural de la Raza 301
  Craft & Folk Art Museum 111
  Fashion Institute of Design & Merchandising 139
  Frederick R Weisman Museum of Art 122
  Gallery Row 206-7
  Geffen Contemporary at MOCA 135, 138, 157
  Getty Center 24, 50, 51, 78, 117
  Hammer Museum 50, 118
  Laguna Art Museum 272
  Long Beach Museum of Art 132

Los Angeles County Museum of Art (LACMA) 110
MAK Center for Art & Architecture 110
MOCA Pacific Design Center 109
Municipal Art Gallery 108
Museum of Contemporary Art (MOCA) Grand Ave 135, 155
Museum of Contemporary Art San Diego (La Jolla) 328
Museum of Contemporary Art San Diego 285
Museum of Design Art & Architecture 119
Museum of Latin American Art 132
Norton Simon Museum 148
Orange County Museum Art 264
Pacific Design Center 109-10
Palm Springs Art Museum 353
Pasadena Museum of California Art 148
Pharmaka Gallery 156
Red Dot Gallery 156
San Diego Museum of Art 299
Santa Barbara Museum of Art 378
Santa Monica Museum of Art 125
Self-Help Graphics & Art 141
Southern California Institute of Architecture 139
Timken Museum of Art 299-300
USC Fisher Gallery 120
Watts Towers Art Center 142
Williamson Gallery 149
art tours 147, 159
arts district (Culver City) 119
Arts District (Downtown Los Angeles) 138-9
Athenaeum Music & Arts Library 328
Av Revolución, see La Revo
aviation 32-3, 79
Avila Adobe 133

B

B&Bs 409
Bailey House 123-4
Balboa Fun Zone 263
Balboa Island 263-4
Balboa Park 20, 51, 281, 297-301, 309, 290-1
Balboa Park Gardens 301-2

000 Map pages
000 Photograph pages

Balboa Pavilion 263
Balboa Peninsula 263-4
bald eagles 59
Ballerina Clown 126
Ballona Wetlands 127
ballooning 71, 334
Bankers Hill, *see* Uptown (San Diego)
Banning Residence Museum 130
Barstow 419
baseball 40, 205, 285, 315
basketball 40, 205-6
Batiquitos Lagoon 59, 337
beach volleyball 41, 66, 127
beaches 37-8, 5, *see also* surf beaches
　Aliso Beach 272
　Arroyo Burro Beach 382
　Black's Beach 329
　Bolsa Chica State Beach 258
　Butterfly Beach 382
　Cardiff State Beach 335
　Carlsbad State Beach 338
　Corona del Mar State Beach 268-9
　Crystal Cove State Park 69, 264
　Descanso Beach 220
　Dog Beach 258
　Doheny State Beach 227, 279
　East Beach 382
　El Matador 154
　Hermosa Beach 127-8, 154
　Huntington Beach 256-61
　Leadbetter Beach 382
　Leo Carrillo 154
　Malaga Cove 154
　Malibu Lagoon State Beach 25,
　　59, 121
　Manhattan Beach 20, 127, 154
　Mission Beach 319-2
　Mother's Beach 126
　Newport Beach 20, 261-8
　Ocean Beach 319
　Orange County Beaches 270-7
　Pacific Beach 319-21
　Paradise Cove 149, 154
　Redondo Beach 20, 128
　Salt Creek Beach 279
　San Elijo State Beach 335
　Santa Monica 124-5, 154, **236**
　Seal Beach 252-5
　Silver Strand State Beach 318
　Solana Beach 335
　Sunset Beach 255-6
　Surfrider Beach 78, 121
　Swami's Beach 336
　Venice Beach 154
　Victoria Beach 272

　West Beach 382
　Will Rogers 154
　Windansea Beach 330
　Zuma Beach 78, 154
Beckham, David 206
Beckmen Vineyards 396
Bel Air 166-7, 115-8, 178-9, **90-1**
Bell, Claude K 353
Belmont Park 320
Belmont Shore 131, 132, **82-3**
Berry, Halle 116
Bert Green Fine Art 156
Beverly Hills 40, **90-1**
　accommodation 165-6
　attractions 111-18
　Beverly Hills Hotel 47, 114, 166
　drinking 190
　farmers market 209
　food 177-8
　Greystone Park 115
　Museum of Tolerance 115
　Paley Center for Media 114
　Rodeo Drive 21, 114
　shopping 207
　tourist information 101
　Virginia Robinson Gardens 114
Big Bear Lake 19, 25, 26, 221-3
Big Rock 330
Birch Aquarium 329
birds 59
bird-watching 59
Black's Beach 329
Blair Valley 370
Blessing of the Animals 160
Blessing of the Cars 161
boating 71, 265, 322
Bob Baker Marionette Theater 158
Bob Hope/Burbank Airport 217, 218
bodysurfing & bodyboarding,
　see boogie boarding
Bolsa Chica State Beach 258
Bolsa Chica State Ecological Reserve
　59, 258
boogie boarding 65, 321
bookstores
　Los Angeles 100
　Palm Springs 347
　San Diego 283
　Santa Barbara 376
border crossings 343, 423
borrego 59
Borrego Palm Canyon Nature Trail
　370
Borrego Springs 368-72
Botanical Building 300

Bowers Museum of Cultural Art
　50, 250
Box Canyon 370
Boyle, TC 49
Bradbury Building 137, 157
Brady Bunch House 149
Brentwood
　accommodations 166-7
　attractions 115-18
　food 178-9
　Getty Center 24, 117
Brewery Art Complex 139, 206-7
Broadway (Los Angeles) 136-8
Bronson Caves 144-5, 149
Brookside Park 151
Buellton 393
Bukowski, Charles 48, 129, 134
Bullocks Wilshire 140
Bunker Hill Steps 136, 156
bus travel 423-4, 425
business hours 411
butterflies 57, 384
Buttonwood Farm Winery & Vineyard
　396

C
Cabazon 353
Cabot's Pueblo Museum 353-6
Cabrillo Marine Aquarium 129
Cabrillo Marine Museum 130
Cabrillo National Monument 28,
　319, 322
Cabrillo, Juan Rodríguez 28, 282, 376
Cachuma Lake Recreation Area 402
cacti 60
Cahuilla 346
California African American Museum
　120
California Heritage Museum 125
California Institute of Arts (Cal
　Arts) 50
California Institute of Technology
　(Caltech) 150
California Plaza, *see* Angels Flights
California Quadrangle 299
California Riding & Hiking Trail 365
California Science Center 120
California Surf Museum 339
Caltrans District 7 Headquarters
　24, 157
camping *see individual regions*
canyons, *see individual canyons*
Capitol Records Tower 108
car travel 14, 424, 426-8, **426**
Cardiff-By-The-Sea 335-6

Carlos III, King 133
Carlsbad 337-8
Casa de Carillo 303
Casa de Estudillo 302
Casa del Balboa 300
Casa del Prado 300
Casino Point Marine Park 25
Catalina Island 161, 220-1, 280
Catalina Island Museum 220
catclaw 60
Catedral de Nuestra Señora de
    Guadalupe 343
Cathedral of Our Lady of the Angels
    24, 135, 155
celebrities 116, 355, 178
Central Ave 142, 160-1
Centro Cultural de la Raza 301
Centro Cultural Tijuana (Cecut) 343
Chandler, Raymond 48
Channel Islands National Park 19, 25,
    60, 69, 375, 405-7
Chaplin, Charlie 136, 138, 392
Cher 116
children, travel with 23, 72-7, 157-8,
    214-15, 386
Chinatown (Los Angeles) 40, 134,
    84-5
Chinese American Museum 133
Chinese New Year 160, 413
Chopra Center 24, 338
Christmas Boat Parade 266, 414
Chumash Native Americans 79, 376,
    406
Chumash Painted Cave State Historic
    Park 27, 401
Cinco de Mayo 54, 160, 413
cinema 43-6, 195-201
City Hall (Los Angeles) 51, 134,
    149, 157
city planning 59, 61
Clifton's Cafeteria 156
climate 14, 73, 384, 411-12
climbing 365
clothes shopping 209-12, 6
Coachella Valley 346-362, 348
Coca-Cola Bottling Plant 51, 140
Cody, William F 350
Colburn School of Performing Arts
    135, 155
Cold Spring Canyon 384
Cold Spring Tavern 402

Colorado St Bridge 151
Comic-con International 304
condors 61, 298
consulates 416
cooking courses 56
Copley Symphony Hall 47
Corona del Mar 268-9
Coronado 317-28
Coronado Bay Bridge 318
Coronado Museum of History & Art
    318
Costa Mesa 269-70
costs 14-15
Coupland, Douglas 49
courses 56, 157
Cox, Chris 37
Cox, Courteney 116
Craft & Folk Art Museum 111
Craftsman 148
Crescent Bay 272
crime 412
Cronk, Rip 126
Crossroads of the World 51, 108
Cruise, Tom 116
Crystal Cathedral 24, 250
Crystal Cove State Park 69, 264
culture 36-51
Culver City 118-19, 97
    accommodations 167
    art galleries 208
    arts district 119
    attractions 118-19
    drinking 193
    farmers market 209
    food 179-80
    Hayden Tract 119
    Helms Bakery Complex 119
    Museum of Design Art &
        Architecture 119
    Museum of Jurassic Technology
        26, 119
    Under the Sea 158
customs regulations 416
cycling 70, 152, 424-5, see
    also mountain biking and
    individual locations

D
Dana Point 227, 278-80, 279
dates 54, 359
Davis, Mike 37, 38
Davis, William Heath 282
Days Inn 23
Death Valley National Park 22, 69,
    223-4

December Nights 305
Del Mar 25, 281, 334-5
Del Mar Horse Racing 304
Del Marcos Hotel 350
Descanso Gardens 148-9
desert bighorn sheep see borrego
Desert Hills Premium Outlets 22
Desert Hot Springs 345, 348
Desert Queen Ranch 363
desert safety 366
Día de los Muertos 141, 161, 414
DiCaprio, Leonardo 59, 116
Didion, Joan 36, 48
disabled travelers 419-20
discounts 109, 413
discovery centers 23, 119, 143, 227,
    250
Disney's California Adventure 230,
    242-4
Disneyland 19, 23, 230-49, 231
    accommodation 244-5
    entertainment 247
    food 245-7
    history 230
    opening hours 231-2
    planning 232
    shopping 247
    tickets 231-2
    travel within 248-9
Disneyland Parade of Dreams 227
Diver's Cove 272, 273
diving & snorkeling 67
    Channel Islands National Park 407
    Crescent Bay 272
    rentals 67
    La Jolla 330
    Laguna Beach 273
    Newport Beach 265
    San Diego County 321
    Santa Barbara 384
    tours 67
Dodger Stadium 40, 134
Doheny State Beach 227, 279
Doheny, Ned 115
dolphins 58, 279
Dorothy Chandler Pavilion 47, 135,
    161
Downtown (San Diego) 305-6
Downtown Los Angeles 84-5
    accommodations 172-3
    Alexandria Hotel 156
    Angels Flights 135
    art galleries 206-8
    Arts District 138-9
    attractions 132-40

Avila Adobe 133
Bert Green Fine Art 156
Bradbury Building 137, 157
Broadway 136-8
Bunker Hill steps 136, 156
California Plaza 135
Caltrans District 7 Headquarters 24, 157
Cathedral of Our Lady of the Angels 24, 135, 155
City Hall 51, 134, 149, 157
Clifton's Cafeteria 156
Colburn School of Performing Arts 155
Dodger Stadium 134
drinking 194
El Pueblo de Los Angeles 50, 132-3, 150-1, 155
Fashion District 139, 213
food 185-6
Geffen Contemporary at MOCA 135, 138, 157
Go for Broke monument 157
Grand Avenue Cultural Corridor 134
Grand Central Market 137, 157, 185
Japanese American National Museum 138, 157
Jewelry District 136, 156
Little Tokyo 40, 138, 161
Los Angeles Theater 137,156
Los Angeles Times 42, 134, 157
Metropolitan Detention Center 157
Millennium Biltmore Hotel 136, 156, 172-3
Museum of Contemporary Art (MOCA) Grand Ave 135, 155
Music Center 135, 155
Olvera St 133, 162, **235**
Pershing Square 136, 156
Pete's Café & Bar 157
Pharmaka Gallery 156
Red Dot Gallery 156
Richard Riordan Central Library 136, 156
St Vincent Court 136, 156
San Antonio Winery 139
shopping 207
South Park 139
Staples Center 40, 139, 197
tourist information 101
Union Station 21, 133-4, 155, 217
US Bank Tower 136, 156
walking tours 155-7, **156**

Walt Disney Concert Hall 24, 47, 51, 134-5, 155, **6**
Wells Fargo History Museum 136, 156
Dr Phil 116
drinks 53-4, *see also* wine
road distance chart **426**
Drum Barracks Civil War Museum 130

E
Eagle & High Peak Mine 340
Eames House & Studio 123-4
earthquakes 58, 376, 412
East Los Angeles 141, 187, 235
Eastern Columbia Building 51, 138
economy 40
Edgemar Center for the Arts 125
Egyptian Theatre 105
El Capitan Theatre104-5
El Charro Statue 303
El Matador 154
El Mercado 141
El Molino Viejo 148
El Presidio de Santa Barbara State Historic Park 382
El Pueblo de la Reina de Los Angeles 79
El Pueblo de Los Angeles 50, 132-3, 150-1, 155
elephant trees 369
Ellen Browning Scripps Park 329
Ellis, Bret Easton 48
Embarcadero 309
Embarcadero Marina Park 297
embassies 416
emergencies 100
Emmy Awards 115
Encinitas 336-7
energy 35, 62, *see also* wind farms, sustainable planning
Ennis-Brown House 108
Enron 35
Entenza House 123
environment 57-62
environmental issues 61-2, 372, *see also* wind farms, sustainable planning
events, *see* festivals & events
Exposition Park 119-20, **97**
California African American Museum 120
California Science Center 120
food 187-8
Natural History Museum of LA County 119-20

Rose Garden 119
University of Southern California (USC) 120
extreme sports 41

F
Farmer John Pig Mural 142
farmers market 54, 209, 303
Fashion District 139, 213
Fashion Institute of Design & Merchandising 139
Fashion Island 268
Fashion Valley 315
Faulkner, William 48
Fess Parker Winery & Vineyard 23, 398
Festival of the Arts 50, 274
festivals & events 159-62, 413-14, *see also* music festivals, film festivals
Abbot Kinney Festival 161, 414
African Marketplace & Cultural Faire 161
Blessing of the Animals 160
Blessing of the Cars 161
Boardfest 259
Chinese New Year 160, 413
Christmas Boat Parade 266, 414
Cinco de Mayo 54, 160, 413
Comic-con International 304
December Nights 305
Día de los Muertos 141, 161, 414
Dinah Weekend 355
Festival of the Arts 274
Festival of the Arts & Pageant of the Masters 413
Festival of the Swallows 278
Fiesta Broadway 160, 413
Fiesta Hermosa 128, 160
Fleet Week 305, 414
Golf Cart Parade 356
Harbor Parade of Lights 305
Hollywood Christmas Parade 161, 414
Independence Day 160
Japan America Kite Festival 254
LA County Holiday Celebration 161
LA Greek Fest 161
LA Pride 160, 413
LADWP Light Festival 161
Las Posadas (LA) 162
Las Posadas & Luminaries (San Diego) 305, 414
Little Italy Festa 305
Los Angeles County Fair 161, 414

Los Angeles Times Festival of
Books 160, 413
Lotus Festival 160
Mariachi USA Festival 160
Marina del Rey Holiday Boat
Parade 161
festivals & events *continued*
Mexican Independence Festival
161
Modernism Week 355
Nisei Week Japanese Festival
161, 413
Ocean Beach Kite Festival 304
Oktoberfest 161
Old Spanish Fiesta Days 386
Pageant of the Masters 50, 274
Palm Springs Pride 356
Pasadena Doo Dah Parade 161, 414
Rose Parade 151, 160, 413
San Diego County Fair 304
San Diego LGBT Pride 304, 413
Santa Barbara County Fair 386
Santa Clarita Cowboy Festival 160
Sawdust Festival 274
Summer Solstice Parade 386, 413
Sunset Junction Street Fair 161,
413
US Open Sandcastle Competition
304, 413
West Hollywood Halloween
Carnival 161, 414
White Party 355
Feuchtwanger, Lion 122
Fiesta Broadway 160, 413
Fiesta Hermosa 128, 160
Filipinotown 40
film 31-2, 41, 57, 196
film festivals 196, 304, 355, 386
film studios 108, 110, 145-6
Warner Bros 146
Firehouse Museum 296
Firestone Vineyard 23, 397
Fisherman's Village 127
fishing 53, 71, 265, 297, 321-2, 340
Fitzgerald, F Scott 48
flea markets 209
Fleet Week 305, 414
Flower Market 140
Font's Point 369
food 18, 52-6, 74
football 41, 206

Ford Amphitheatre 105, 197
Ford, Raymond 384
Forest Lawn Memorial Park (Glendale)
146
Forest Lawn Memorial Park
(Hollywood Hills) 144
Fort MacArthur Military Museum 130
Fort Stockton Memorial 303
Fowler Museum at UCLA 117
Foxen Canyon Wine Trail 375, 396
Foxen Vineyard 23, 398
foxes 59
Freeth, George 256
Frey, Albert 24, 51, 350

G
Gabrieleño Native Americans 79, 406
Gamble House 24, 51, 148
Gaslamp Quarter 50, 281, 307-11, 238
gay & lesbian travelers 38, 414
Black's Beach 329
festivals 38, 355, 356, 413
LA Pride 160
Los Angeles 112-13
Palm Springs 360-1
San Diego 304, 312
resorts 360-1
Geffen Contemporary at MOCA 135,
138, 157
Gehry House 125
Gehry, Frank 24, 51, 125, 126, 134,
138, 159
Geisel Library 330
geography 57-8
geology 58
Getty Center 24, 50, 51, 78, 117
Getty Villa 50, 122, 123
Ghost Mountain 370
giardiasis 430-1
Gibson Amphitheatre 146
Gill, Irving 51, 301, 328
Gladwin Planetarium 381
Glen Ivy Hot Springs 26
Globe Theater 137
Go for Broke monument 157
Go Los Angeles Card 109
gold rush 282
Gold, Jonathan 52
Goleta Beach 384
Goleta Bikeway 383
golf 70-1, 220, 303, 354, 356
Golf Cart Parade 356
Goodhue, Bertram 136
Grafton, Sue 49
Granada Theatre 47

Grand Avenue Cultural Corridor 134
Grand Central Market 137, 157, 185
Grand Hope Park 139
Grauman's Chinese Theatre 103, 196
Greek Theatre 145, 197
Green Hills Memorial Park 129
Greene, Charles 51, 148
Greene, Henry 51, 148
Greystone Park 115
Grier Musser Museum 140
Griffith Observatory 143
Griffith Park 69, 143-5, 152, **95**
attractions 143-5
Bronson Caves 144-5
Forest Lawn Memorial Park
(Hollywood Hills) 144
Greek Theatre 145, 197
Griffith Observatory 143
Los Angeles Zoo & Botanical
Gardens 143
Museum of the American West
143-4
Travel Town Museum 144
Groundlings 205
grunions 130
Guinness World of Records Museum
106
gyms 152

H
Haggerty's 128
Halprin, Lawrence 139
Hammer Museum 50, 118
Hancock Park 111
hang gliding 329, 331
Hannah Carter Japanese Garden 118
Harbor Parade of Lights 305
Harman, Jane 36
health 430-2
heatstroke 432
Heisler Park 227, 272
Hellhole Canyon 370
Helms Bakery Complex 119
Heritage Square Museum 147
Hermosa Beach 20, 127-8, 154, **94**
Highland Park 146-7, 187
Highway 154 401-7
hiking 68-69, 153, 222, 375
Anza-Borrego Desert State Park 370
books & maps 68
Channel Islands National Park 69
Crystal Cove State Park 69
Death Valley National Park 69
fees 69
Griffith Park 69

000 Map pages
000 Photograph pages

Joshua Tree National Park 69, 364
Laguna Beach 272-3
Los Angeles 153
Los Padres National Forest 69, 401-2
Malibu Creek State Park 153, 349-50
Mt San Jacinto Wilderness State Park 69
Orange County 69
Pacific Crest Trail 69
Palm Springs 69
Runyon Canyon 153
safety 68
San Diego 69
Santa Barbara 69, 384
Santa Monica Mountains 69
Santa Ynez Mountains 69
Skyline Trail 350
Tahquitz Canyon 69
Torrey Pines State Reserve 69
West Ridge Trail 69
Hillcrest 281, 303-5, 307, 310, **290-1**
Hilton, Paris 116
history 27-35
    immigration 31
    Los Angeles 79
    race retaliations 34
    Santa Barbara 376
    Spanish exploration 79, 282, 346, 372, 376, 382
hitchhiking 428
Hitching Post II 23, 393
HIV/AIDS 431
Hoffman, Dustin 124
holidays 54, 414-15
Hollenbeck Youth Center 141
Hollyhock House 24, 51, 108
Hollywood **86-7**
    accommodation 162-3
    attractions 102-9
    Crossroads of the World 108
    drinking 78, 191-2
    Egyptian Theatre 105
    El Capitan Theatre 104-5, 195-6
    farmers market 209
    food 174-7
    Grauman's Chinese Theatre 103, 196
    Guinness World of Records Museum 106
    Hollywood & Highland 103-4
    Hollywood Boulevard 21

Hollywood Bowl 47, 105-6, 197
Hollywood Christmas Parade 161, 414
Hollywood CityPass 109, 413
Hollywood Museum 105
Hollywood Roosevelt Hotel 104, 163
Hollywood Sign 103
Hollywood Walk of Fame 103
Hollywood Wax Museum 106-7
Mulholland Drive 106
Musso & Frank Grill 106
Ripley's Believe It or Not! 106
shopping 207
Sunset Strip 109
tourist information 101
Holmes, Katie 116
Hope Ranch 376
horse racing 41, 151, 206
horseback riding 71, 152-3, 355
Horton, Alonzo E 282, 284, 297
hostels 409-10
Hotel del Coronado 50, 281, 318-20, 323
hotels 410
House of Pacific Relations 301
Hughes, Howard 114
Huntington Beach 20, 227, 256-61, **257**
Huntington Central Park 259
Huntington Library, Art Collections & Botanical Gardens 147-8
Huntington, Henry 127
Huxley, Aldous 48

I
ice hockey 206
immigration 31
Independence Day 160
Indian Canyons 69, 345, 350-2
Inspiration Point 123, 268-9, 384
insurance 415, 428, 430
Integratron 26, 368
International Surfing Museum 258
internet access 417
internet resources 15-16, 430
Isla Vista 376
Italian Hall 133
itineraries 19-26, **19-26**, see also individual regions

J
Jackie Robinson Memorial 148
jackrabbits 59
James Irvine Garden 138

Japanese American Cultural & Community Center 138
Japanese American National Museum 138, 157
Japanese Village Plaza 138
Japanese-American War 151
Jet Propulsion Laboratory 150
jewelry 214
Jewelry District 136, 156
Jewish Federation Center 157
Johnson, William Templeton 51
Joshua Tree National Park 19, 22, 25, 60, 69, 345, 363-8, **364-5, 8**
Joshua trees 60
Julian 26, 339-41
Julian Pioneer Museum 340

K
Kahn Building 303
kangaroo rats 59
Karpeles Manuscript Library Museum 375, 382
Kaufmann House 350
kayaking 66, 67, 322, see also individual regions
Kennedy, John F & Robert F 114
Kidspace Children's Museum 151, 157
King Harbor 128
King, Larry 116
King, Rodney 34
Kinney, Abbot 125, 126, 161
Kirk Douglas Theatre 203
kitesurfing 253
kiteboarding 65-6
Knott's Berry Farm 23, 249
Knott's Soak City USA (Palm Springs) 353
Kodak Theatre 103-4, 160
Korean American Museum 140-1
Korean Friendship Bell 130
Koreatown 40, 140-1, 194-5, 186-7
Koyasan Buddhist Temple 138
KROQ Acoustic Christmas 48
KROQ Weenie Roast 48

L
La Brea Tar Pits 27, 110-11
La Cañada-Flintridge 149
La Jolla 281, 328-33, **294**
La Jolla Cove 329
La Jolla Playhouse 50
La Jolla Shores 329
La Jolla Underwater Park Ecological Reserve 25
LA Live 139
La Placita 133

LA Pride 160, 413
La Revo 343
LADWP Light Festival 161
Laguna Art Museum 272
Laguna Beach 19, 20, 227, 270, 270-7, **271**
Larchmont Village 111
Las Posadas (LA) 162
Las Posadas & Luminaries 305, 414
Las Vegas 26, 224-6
latinos 39-40, **7**
laurel 59
Leadbetter Point 384
Lefcourt, Peter 49
legal matters 417-18
Legoland California 20, 337
Leimert Park 142, 187-8, **97**
Leo Carrillo 154
Leonard, Elmore 49
lesbian travelers, see gay travelers
Lindbergh, Charles 319
Lipkis, Andy 59
literature 15, 17, 48-9
Little Corona Beach 268
Little Ethiopia 40
Little Italy 285-96, 305-6, 308-9
Little Saigon 40, 251-2
Little Tokyo 40, 138, 161, **84-5**
Living Desert Zoo & Gardens 353
lizards 59
Lockheed brothers 79
Lohan, Lindsay 116
Long Beach 20, 130, **82-3**
    accommodation 171-2
    Aquarium of the Pacific 131
    attractions 130-2
    Belmont Shore 131, 132
    drinking 194
    food 184-5
    Long Beach Museum of Art 132
    Long Beach Outdoor Antique &
        Collectible Market 209
    Museum of Latin American Art 132
    Naples 132
    Queen Mary 131
    tourist information 101
    Toyota Grand Prix of Long Beach 160
Long Beach Airport 217, 218
Longshadow Ranch 373
Long-Waterman House 303
Lookout Point 268

Los Angeles 22, 39, 78-226, **80-99,**
    see also individual suburbs
    accommodations 162-74
    activities 152
    airports 216-17, 217-18
    art galleries 206-8
    attractions 102-51, 119-20
    Bel Air 115-18, **90-1**
    Belmont Shore 132, **82-3**
    Beverly Hills 111-18, **90-1**
    bookstores 100
    Brentwood 115-18
    bus terminals 217
    children 75, 157-8
    Chinatown 134, **84-5**
    cinema 195-201
    classical music 202-3
    climate **411**
    comedy 204-5
    courses 157
    Culver City 118-19, **97**
    Downtown Los Angeles 132-40,
        84-5
    drinking 190-5
    emergencies 100
    entertainment 195-206
    Exposition Park 119-120, **97**
    festivals 159-62
    food 174-90, 190
    freeways 218, **98**
    Griffith Park 143-5, 152, **95**
    Hermosa Beach 127-8, **94**
    Highland Park 146-7
    hiking 69
    Hollywood 78, 102-9, **86-7**
    internet 100
    Leimert Park 142, **97**
    Little Tokyo 138, **84-5**
    live music 197-8
    Long Beach 130-2, **82-3**
    Los Feliz 108-9, **86-7**
    Malibu 120-2, **80-1**
    Manhattan Beach 127, **94**
    Marina del Rey 126-7, **92**
    medical services 101
    Metro Rail System **99**
    Mid-City 109-11, **88-9**
    Mt Washington 146-7
    nightclubs 201-2
    opera 202-3
    Pacific Palisades 122-4, **80-1**
    Palos Verdes Dr 78
    Palos Verdes Peninsula 128, **82-3**
    Pasadena 147-52, **96**
    public transportation 218-19, **99**

Redondo Beach 128, **94**
San Fernando Valley 145-6
San Gabriel Valley 147-52
San Pedro 129, **82-3**
Santa Monica 124-5, **92**
Santa Monica mountains 152
shopping 206-16
Silver Lake 108-9, **86-7**
South Bay 127-8, **94**
sports 205-8
theaters 203-4
tourist information 101
tours 158
train stations 217
travel to/from 216-17
travel within 217-20
Venice 78, 125, **92**
walking tours 155-7, **156**
West Hollywood 109-11, **88-9**
Westwood 115-18, **90-1**
Los Angeles Aqueduct 61
Los Angeles Conservancy 78
Los Angeles County Arboretum &
    Botanic Garden 151
Los Angeles County Fair 161, 414
Los Angeles County Holiday
    Celebration 161
Los Angeles County Museum of Art
    (LACMA) 50, 110
Los Angeles Film Festival 196
Los Angeles Greek Fest 161
Los Angeles International Airport
    (LAX) 171, 216-17, 217-18, **82-3**
Los Angeles Live Steamers 144
Los Angeles Marathon 161, 213
Los Angeles Maritime Museum 129
Los Angeles Memorial Coliseum 119
Los Angeles Memorial Sports Arena 119
Los Angeles River 58
Los Angeles Theater 137, 156
Los Angeles Times 42, 134, 157, 413
Los Angeles Times Festival of Books
    160, 413
Los Angeles Triathlon 161
Los Angeles Zoo & Botanical Gardens
    143, 144
Los Feliz 174-7, 191-2, **86-7**
Los Olivos 375
Los Olivos Café 23
Los Olivos Wine Trail 399-400
Los Padres National Forest 26, 69, 401
Los Rios Historic District 278
Lotus Festival 160
Love, Courtney 116
Lovell House 108, 263

Lucy Florence's Coffeehouse & Cultural Center 142
Luiseño 372
Lummis House 147

M

Madison Performing Arts Center 124
Madonna 116
Magicopolis 158
Maguire, Tobey 40, 116
mail services 416
Malaga Cove 128, 154
Malibu 20, 120-2, **80-1**
    accommodation 167-8
    attractions 120-2
    beaches 122
    food 180
    Pepperdine University 121
    Serra Retreat 121
    Surfrider Beach 121
Malibu Bluffs Park 121
Malibu Creek State Park 149, 153
Malibu Hindu Temple 122
Malibu Lagoon Museum 121
Malibu Lagoon State Beach 25, 59, 121
Malibu Pier 121
Manhattan Beach 20, 127, 154, **94**
maps 63, 418
Mariachi Plaza 141
Marie Hitchcock Puppet Theater 301
Marina del Rey 101, 126-7, 169-70, **92**
Marina del Rey Holiday Boat Parade 161
Mark Taper Forum 50, 135
Marston House 301
Maritime Museum (San Diego) 296
massages 153-4, 265
Mayne, Thom 24, 51
McCallum Adobe 353
meat 53
medical services 284, 430
    Anaheim 230
    Los Angeles 101
    Palm Springs 348
    San Diego 284
    Santa Barbara 376
Medieval Times Dinner & Tournament 26, 249
Meier, Richard 24, 51, 114, 117, 118
Melrose Trading Post 209
Mercado de Artesanias 344
Mercado El Popo 343
Mercado La Paloma 119
Metlox Plaza 127

Metro Rail System **99**
Metropolitan Detention Center 157
Mexican Independence Festival 161
Mexican-American War 79
Mexico border 343
Mid-City (Los Angeles) **88-9**
    A+D Museum 111
    accommodations 163-5
    art galleries 208
    attractions 109-11
    Craft & Folk Art Museum 111
    drinking 192
    farmers market 110
    food 176-7
    La Brea Tar Pits 110-11
    Los Angeles County Museum of Art (LACMA) 110
    Page Museum 110-11
    Petersen Automotive Museum 111
    shopping 207
Mildred E Mathias Botanical Garden 118
military 32-3
Millennium Biltmore Hotel 136, 156, 172-3
Million Dollar Theater 137
Mingei International Museum 299
Mission Bay 320, 324-5, **292-3**
Mission Beach 319-21, 324, **292-3**
Mission Hills 311
Mission Valley 301-2, 306
missions
    history 28-9
    Mission San Buenaventura 24
    Mission San Diego de Alcalá 24, 302-3
    Mission San Fernando Rey de España 24, 151
    Mission San Juan Capistrano 20, 24, 277-8
    Mission San Luis Rey de Francia 339
    Mission Santa Barbara 24, 380-1
    San Gabriel Mission 24, 150-1
Museum of Contemporary Art (MOCA) Grand Ave 155
Model Railroad Museum 300
Modernism Week 355
Mojave Desert 22, 363
monarch butterflies, see butterfiles
Moneo, Rafael 24
money 14-15, 416, see also inside front cover
monorail 248
Monroe, Marilyn 114, 118
Montecito 376, 392

Moorten Botanical Gardens 352-3
Morgan, Julia 51
Mosley, Walter 49
mosquito bites 431
motels 410
motorcycle travel 424, 426-8
Mt San Antonio 150
Mt San Jacinto Wilderness State Park 69, 349-50
Mt Washington 146-7
Mt Wilson Observatory 150
mountain biking 70, 152, 222, 370, see also cycling
movies, see film
Mulholland Drive 25, 106
Mulholland, William 62
Mullally, Megan 116
Murphy Sculpture Garden 117
Murray Canyon 352
Muscle Beach Body Building Competition 160
Muscle Beach Venice 152, see also Original Muscle Beach
Museo de las Californias 343
Museum of Design Art & Architecture 119
museums 50, see also art galleries
    African American Firefighter Museum 142
    Agua Caliente Cultural Museum 353
    Air & Space Museum 301
    Banning Residence Museum 130
    Bowers Museum of Cultural Art 250
    Cabot's Pueblo Museum 353-6
    Cabrillo Marine Museum 130
    California African American Museum 120
    California Heritage Museum 125
    California Science Center 120
    California Surf Museum 339
    Casa del Balboa 300
    Catalina Island Museum 220
    Chinese American Museum 133
    Coronado Museum of History & Art 318
    Craft & Folk Art Museum 111
    Drum Barracks Civil War Museum 130
    Firehouse Museum 296
    Fort MacArthur Military Museum 130
    Fowler Museum at UCLA 117
    Getty Villa 122

museums *continued*
Grier Musser Museum 140
Guinness World of Records
Museum 106
Hammer Museum 118
Heritage Square Museum 147
Hollywood Bowl Museum 105
Hollywood Heritage Museum 105
Hollywood Museum 105
Hollywood Wax Museum 106-7
House of Pacific Relations 301
International Surfing Museum 258
Japanese American National
Museum 138
Julian Pioneer Museum 340
Karpeles Manuscript Library
Museum 382
Kidspace Children's Museum 157
Korean American Museum 140-1
Los Angeles Maritime Museum 129
Malibu Lagoon Museum 121
Mingei International Museum 299
Model Railroad Museum 300
Museo de las Californias 343
Museum of Contemporary Art
(MOCA) Grand Ave 135, 155
Museum of Contemporary Art San
Diego (La Jolla) 328
Museum of Contemporary Art San
Diego 285
Museum of Jurassic Technology 119
Museum of Latin American Art 132
Museum of Making Music 338
Museum of Man 299
Museum of Natural History, *see* Ty
Warner Sea Center
Museum of Photographic Arts 300
Museum of San Diego History 300
Museum of the American West
143-4
Museum of Tolerance 115
Natural History Museum (San
Diego) 300
Natural History Museum of LA
County 119-20
Newport Harbor Nautical Museum
264
Norton Simon Museum 148
O'Neill Museum 278
Old Plaza Firehouse 133
Pacific Asia Museum 148

Page Museum 110-11
Palm Springs Air Museum 353
Pasadena Museum of History 151
Petersen Automotive Museum 111
Ripley's Believe It or Not! 106
Ronald Reagan Library & Museum
147
San Diego Aircraft Carrier 296-7
San Diego Automotive Museum
301
San Diego Children's Museum 285
San Diego Chinese Historical
Museum 285
San Diego Hall of Champions
Sports Museum 301
Santa Barbara Maritime Museum
379
Santa Barbara Museum of Natural
History 381
Serra Museum 303
Southwest Museum of the
American Indian 147
Travel Town Museum 144
Wells Fargo History Museum 136
William Heath Davis House 284
Zimmer Children's Museum 157
music 17, 46-8
Music Center 47, 50, 135, 155
music festivals 48
Catalina Island JazzTrax Festival
161
Central Avenue Jazz Festival 142,
160-1, 413
Coachella Valley Music & Arts
Festival 48, 355, 413
Desert Swing 'N Dixie Jazz Festival
355
Long Beach Bayou Festival 160
Long Beach Jazz Festival 161
Mariachi USA Festival 160
Rock 'n' Roll Marathon 304
Stagecoach Festival 356
Street Scene 304
Summerfest Chamber Music
Festival 304
Topanga Banjo Fiddle Contest &
Folk Festival 160
Watts Towers Day of the Drum &
Jazz Festival 142, 161
Musso & Frank Grill 106
Muth Interpretive Center 264

N
Naples 132, 158-9
Nate 'n Al's 21

National Forest Adventure Pass 69-70
national forests 69-70, 150, 401-2
national parks 60-2, *see also* parks &
reserves
biking 70
Channel Islands National Park
60, 405-7
Death Valley National Park 223-4
fees 69
Joshua Tree National Park 60,
363-8, **364-5, 8**
Native Americans 27-8, 406
Natural History Museum (San Diego) 300
Natural History Museum of LA County
119-20
Navy Pier 47
NBC 146
Neutra, Richard 24, 51, 108, 123, 350
Neve, Felipe de 133
Newport Bay Ecological Reserve 25,
59, 264
Newport Beach 20, 261-8, **262**
Newport Beach Film Festival 196
Newport Harbor Nautical Museum 264
Nicholson, Jack 40
Nisei Week Japanese Festival 161, 413
Nixon, Richard 250
Noah's Ark 157-8
Norton Simon Museum 148

O
oak trees 59
Ocean Beach 319, 323-4, 325-6, **292-3**
Ocean Beach Kite Festival 304
Ocean Front Walk 320, *see* Venice
Boardwalk
Oceanside 339, 419
ocotillo 60
Ojai 24, 26, 404
Oktoberfest 161
Old Baldy 150
Old Globe Festival 304
Old Plaza Firehouse 133
Old Point Loma Lighthouse 319
Old Town (San Diego) 50, 281, 302-3,
306-7, 309-11, **290-1**
Old Town State Historic Park 302
Old Town Trolley Tours 303
Olvera St 133, 162, 235
O'Neill House 114
O'Neill Museum 278
Ontario International Airport 217
Orange 250-2
Orange County 69, 227-80, **228**
beaches 252-80

000 Map pages
000 Photograph pages

children 75-6
  history 228-9
  travel within 229
Orange County Museum of Art 264
Orange County Performing Arts
  Center 47
Original Muscle Beach 124, 160
Orpheum Theater 137
Our Lady of the Rosary Catholic
  Church 296
outdoors 63-71
outdoor activities 70-1
  ballooning 71
  beach volleyball 66
  boating 71
  boogie boarding 65
  cycling & mountain biking 70
  diving & snorkeling 67
  equipment 216
  fishing 71
  hiking 68
  horse riding 71
  rock climbing 71
  surfing 63-6
  swimming 63
  whale-watching 67-70
  windsurfing & kiteboarding 65-6
Outfest 196
Owens Valley 62
Oxnard 419

P

Pacific Asia Museum 148
Pacific Beach 281, 319-21, 324, **292-3**
Pacific Coast Highway 25
Pacific Crest Trail 69
Pacific Design Center 109-10
Pacific Flyway 59, 61, 264
Pacific Marine Mammal Center 272
Pacific Palisades 122-4, **80-1**
  attractions 122-4
  Eames House & Studio 123-4
  Getty Villa 50, 122, 123
  Self-Realization Fellowship Lake
    Shrine 123
  Villa Aurora 122
  Will Rogers State Historic Park
    122-3
Pacific Park 124
Pacific-California Exposition 297
Padgett, Abigail 49
Page Museum 110-11
Pageant of the Masters 50, 274
Palace Theater 137
Paley Center for Media 114

Palm Canyon 352
Palm Springs 19, 22, 25, 345-74, **347,
  351, 411, 8, 239**
  accommodation 356-7
  activities 354-5
  attractions 349-53
  children 76-7
  Death Valley National Park 69
  drinking 359
  entertainment 359-60
  festivals 355-6
  food 357-9
  hiking 350, 354-5
  history 346
  Indian Canyons 69
  information 347
  internet access 347-8
  itineraries 349
  Joshua Tree National Park 69
  medical services 348
  shopping 361-2
  Tahquitz Canyon 69
  tourist information 349
  tours 355
  travel to/from 362
  travel within 362
Palm Springs Aerial Tramway 69, 345,
  349-50
Palm Springs Air Museum 353
Palm Springs Art Museum 47, 353
Palm Springs City Hall 350
Palm Springs Follies 26
Palm Springs International Airport 362
Palm Springs International Film
  Festival 196, 355
Palm Springs Pride 356
palm trees 59
Palms to Pines Highway 25
Palos Verdes Dr 20, 25, 78
Palos Verdes Peninsula 128-30,
  82-3
Panama-California Exposition 282,
  297, 298, 299
Pan-American Pavilion 301
Pantages Theatre 50, 107, 136
Paradise Cove 149, 154
Paramount Studios 108, 146
Paramount Ranch 153, 160
parks & reserves
  Abalone Cove Shoreline Park
    78, 128
  Aliso & Woods Canyons
    Wilderness Park 273
  Anza-Borrego Desert State Park
    368-72

biking 70
  Brookside Park 151
  Cachuma Lake Recreation Area 402
  Casino Point Marine Park 25
  Crystal Cove State Park 69, 264
  El Presidio de Santa Barbara State
    Historic Park 382
  Ellen Browning Scripps Park 329
  Forest Lawn Memorial Park
    (Glendale) 146
  Forest Lawn Memorial Park
    (Hollywood Hills) 144
  Grand Hope Park 139
  Green Hills Memorial Park 129
  Greystone Park 115
  Hollywood Park 206
  Los Angeles County Arboretum &
    Botanic Garden 151
  Malibu Bluffs Park 121
  Malibu Creek State Park 153
  Mt San Jacinto Wilderness State
    Park 69, 349-50
  Pierce Bros Westwood Memorial
    Park 118
  Point Fermin Park 129-30
  Presidio Park 303
  San Diego-La Jolla Underwater
    Park Ecological Reserve, 330
  Sand Dune Park 158
  Santa Anita Park 151, 206
  Santa Monica Mountains National
    Recreation Area 26, 153
  Torrey Pines State Reserve 330
  Will Rogers State Historic Park
    122-3
Pasadena 147-52, **96**
  accommodation 173-4
  Art Center College of Design 149
  attractions 147-52
  California Institute of Technology
    (Caltech) 150
  food 188-90
  Gamble House 24, 148
  Norton Simon Museum 148
  Pasadena Civic Center 148
  Pasadena Museum of History 151
  tourist information 101
  Tournament House 151
  Wrigley Gardens 151
Pasadena Doo Dah Parade 161, 414
Pasadena Playhouse 50
passports 415
Paul Ecke Poinsettia Ranch 336
pay phones 416-17
Pearl Harbor 282

Peg Leg Smith Liars Contest 369
Peg Leg Smith Monument 369
pelicans 59, 406
Pepperdine University 121
Perry, Matthew 116
Pershing Square 136, 156
PETCO Park 40, 285, 315
Pete's Café & Bar 157
Petersen Automotive Museum 111
phone codes 417
Pico House 133
Pico, General Andrés 79
Pierce Bros Westwood Memorial
    Park 118
Pioneertown 367
Pirate's Cove 268
planetariums 381
planning 14-18, 37
plants 59-60, see also individual plants
Plaza de Panama 299
Plaza del Pasado 302
Point Fermin Park 129-30
Point Loma 319, 323, 325
Point Vicente Lighthouse 128
politics 36-7
pollution 61, 63
porpoises 58
Portolá, Gaspar de 282, 382
Ports O'Call Village 129
postal services 416
Powell Library 117
Presidio 50
Presidio Hill 303-5
Presidio Hills Golf Course 303
Presidio Park 303
prickly pears 60
prohibition 341
public art 272
public transportation 21, 218-19, 99
Puppet & Magic Center 158
puppets 301

Q
Quail Botanical Gardens 336
Qualcomm Stadium 315
Queen Mary 20, 131
Quince St Bridge 303

R
race riots 39
Raleigh Studios 127

000 Map pages
000 Photograph pages

rancheros 29-31
Rancho Sisquoc 399
Rattlesnake Canyon 384
Rayner, Richard 48
Reagan, Ronald 114
recreational vehicles 427-9
Redondo Beach 20, 128, 94
Reeves, Keanu 116
resorts 411-12
Reuben H Fleet Space Theater &
    Science Center 300
Richard Nixon Presidential Library 250
Richard Riordan Central Library 51,
    136, 156
Rideau Vineyard 396
Rim of the World Drive 25
Rincon Point 384
Ripley's Believe It or Not! 106, 249
riptides 412
Riviera Village 128
road rules 424, 428
roadrunners 59
Robertson Blvd 78
rock art 27
rock climbing 71, see also climbing
Rodeo Drive 21, 114
Rogers, Will 114, 122-3
Rohrabacher, Dana 37
Ronald Reagan Library & Museum
    147
Rose Bowl Stadium 151
Rose Garden 119
Rose Parade 151, 160, 413
Roundhouse Marine Studies Lab &
    Aquarium 127
Ruddy's General Store 353
Runyon Canyon 78, 153
Ryder, Winona 116

S
safe travel 366, 412
St Sophia Cathedral 141, 161
St Vincent Court 136, 156
Salk Institute 24, 329-30
Salton Sea State Recreation Area
    19, 372
San Antonio Winery 139
San Bernardino 419
San Diego 19, 281-344, 286-95,
    286-93, 411
    accommodations 305-7
    attractions 284-303
    Balboa Park 281, 297-301, 309,
        290-1
    ballooning 71

bars 311-13, 312
camping 307
children 76
cinemas 314-15
classical music 314
coffeehouses 311
Del Mar 281
Downtown 284-5, 305-6, 288-9
drinking 311-13
Embarcadero 296-7, 309
entertainment 313-15
festivals 304-5
food 307-11
Gaslamp Quarter 50, 281, 307-11,
    240-1, 238
gay travelers 312
hiking 69
Hillcrest 281, 303-5, 307, 310,
    290-1
history 282
Horton, Alonzo E 284
internet access 283
La Jolla 281
Little Italy 285-96, 305-6, 308-9
live music 313-14
medical services 284
Mission Hills 311
Mission Valley 301-2, 306
nightclubs 312, 313-14
Old Town 281, 302-3, 306-7,
    309-11, 290-1
opera 314
Pacific Beach 281
San Diego Zoo 281, 298-9
Seaport village 297
shopping 315-16
sports 315
surfing 66
theater 314-15
tourist information 284-303
tours 303-4
travel to/from 316
travel within 316-18
Uptown 303-5
Waterfront 296-7, 309
San Diego Aircraft Carrier 296-7
San Diego Automotive Museum 301
San Diego Children's Museum 285
San Diego Chinese Historical Museum
    285
San Diego Convention Center 297
San Diego County Fair 304
San Diego Crew Classic 304
San Diego Film Festival 304
San Diego LGBT Pride 304, 413

San Diego Hall of Champions Sports
Museum 301
San Diego Museum of Art 299
San Diego Trolley 302, 317, 344
San Diego Wild Animal Park 341
San Diego Zoo 23, 281, 298, 298-9, 7
San Diego's Old Globe Theaters 50
San Diego-La Jolla Underwater Park
Ecological Reserve 329, 330
San Elijo Lagoon 335
San Fernando Valley 145-6
accommodations 173
attractions 145-6
food 188
Forest Lawn Memorial Park
(Glendale) 146
Gibson Amphitheatre 146
Universal City Walk 145-6
Universal Studios Hollywood
145-6
San Gabriel Mission 24, 150-1
San Gabriel Valley 40, 147-52
San Jacinto Mountains 345
San Juan Capistrano 51, 277-8
San Marcos Pass Road 25
San Miguel Island 405-7
San Pedro 129, **82-3**
attractions 129
Cabrillo Marine Aquarium 129
Cabrillo Marine Museum 130
food 184-5
Los Angeles Maritime Museum 129
Point Fermin Park 129-30
Sunken City 131
Wilmington 130
San Pedro Fish Market & Restaurant
184
Sanchez, Loretta 37
Sand Dune Park 158
Santa Ana 50, 419
Santa Anita Park 151
Santa Barbara 19, 20, 376-93, **377,
378-9, 380,** 240
activities 383
attractions 378-85
beaches 382
boating 383-4
bookstores 376
children 77
cycling 383
drinking 390-1
entertainment 391
festivals 385
food 388-90
hiking 69

history 376
internet access 376
itineraries 383
medical services 377
shopping 391-2
sleeping 386
surfing 66
tourist information 378
tours 385
travel to/from 392
travel within 392
whale-watching 383-4
Santa Barbara Botanic Garden 381
Santa Barbara County Courthouse 375,
378, 240
Santa Barbara Island 405-7
Santa Barbara Maritime Museum 379
Santa Barbara Museum of Art 378
Santa Barbara Museum of Natural
History 381
Santa Barbara Old Town Trolley 385
Santa Barbara Wine County 19, 23,
395-401, **397, 7**
Santa Clarita Cowboy Festival 160
Santa Cruz 405-7
Santa Fe Railroad 228
Santa Monica 20, 21, 124-5, 154,
92, 236
accommodations 168-9
art galleries 208
attractions 124-5
drinking 192-3
farmers market 125, 209
food 180-2
Gehry House 125
Main Street 125
Original Muscle Beach 124
Santa Monica Museum of Art 125
Santa Monica Outdoor Antique &
Collectible Market 209
Santa Monica Pier 124
Santa Monica Pier Aquarium 124
shopping 207
Third Street Promenade 125
tourist information 101
Santa Monica Mountains 26, 69,
152, 153
Santa Rita Hills 375
Santa Rita Hills Wine Trail 399
Santa Rosa Island 381, 405-7
Santa Ynez Mountains 69, 375
Santa Ynez Valley Trail 396
Sawdust Festival 274
Sawtelle Blvd 40
Schindler House 24, 110

Schindler, Rudolph 24, 51, 110, 263
Schlesinger, Christina 126
school holidays 415
Schwarzenegger, Arnold 35, 62, 125
science centers 120, 227, 250, 300
scientology 43
scorpion bites 432
Scripps Institution of Oceanography
329
Scripps Research Institute 329
Scripps, Ellen Browning 328, 329
Seal Beach 252-5, **253**
Seaside Lagoon 128
SeaWorld 20, 23, 320-2
See, Carolyn 49
Segal, Fred 78, 157
Self-Help Graphics & Art 141
Self-Realization Fellowship Lake
Shrine 123
Self-Realization Fellowship Retreat &
Hermitage 24, 336
Serra Museum 303
Serra Retreat 121
Serra, Junípero 28, 282, 302, 303
Sessions, Kate 297
Seuss, Dr 48
Shakespeare festivals 304
Sherman Library & Gardens 269
Shooters 149
shopping 55, 216, 418-19, 6
Sideways 23, 393, 395
Silver Lake 108-9, 191-2, 174-7, **86-7**
Simpson, OJ 117
Sinclair, Upton 48
Siqueiros, David Alfaro 133
Six Flags Hurricane Harbor 221
Six Flags Magic Mountain 23, 221
skateboarding 153
skating 152, 259, 265
skiing 222
Skirball Cultural Center 118, 157-8
Skyline Trail 350
smoke tree 60
smoking 55
Smuggler's Canyon 370
snakes 59
snake bites 431
Snoop Dogg 40
soccer 41, 206
Social & Public Art Resource Center 126
Solana Beach 335
solar energy 62
Solvang 23, 393-5
Sonny Bono Salton Sea National
Wildlife Refuge 372

Sontag, Susan 49
Sony 146
South Bay 127-8, **94**
   accommodations 170-1
   attractions 127-8
   drinking 193-4
   farmers markets 209
South Bay *continued*
   food 183-4
   Hermosa Beach 127-8
   Manhattan Beach 127
   Redondo Beach 128
   Sand Dune Park 158
South Bay Bicycle Trail 124
South Central (Los Angeles)
   attractions 141-3
   Central Ave 142
   Leimert Park 142
   Watts Labor Community Action
      Committee 142
   Watts Towers 141-2
South Coast Botanic Garden 129
South Park 139
Southern California CityPass 413
Southern California Institute of
   Architecture 139
Southern Pacific Railroad 228
Southwest Museum of the American
   Indian 147
Spanish conquest 28-9
Spanish Village Art Center 300
spas 26, 71, 153-4, 251, 265, 273,
   338, 354, 400, 404
spiders 59, 432
Split Mountain 369
Spoke(n) Art Tour 147
sporting events 160, 161, 304, 413
sports 40-1, 301, 315, *see also*
   outdoor activities
Spreckels Organ Pavilion 300-1
Spreckels, John 302
Spruce St Footbridge 303
SS Lane Victory 129
Staples Center 40, 139, 197
Starlight Bowl 301
Starr, Ken 121
State Theater 137
Sterling, Christine 133
Storyopolis 158
Streamline Moderne 51
Student Advantage Card 413

Summer Solstice Parade 413
Summerland 376, 405
Sunken City 131
Sunset Beach 255-6, **255**
Sunset Cliffs Park 319
Sunset Junction 48
Sunset Junction Street Fair 161, 413
Sunset Strip 109
Sunset Tower Hotel 51
Sunstone Vineyards & Winery 396
surf beaches **64**
   Aliso Beach 272
   Big Rock 330
   Crystal Pier 321
   Goleta Beach 384
   Haggerty's 128
   Imperial Beach 321
   Leadbetter Point 384
   Mission Beach 321
   Newport Pier 265
   Pacific Beach 321
   Point Loma 319, 321
   Rincon Point 384
   Sunset Cliffs 321
   Sunset Cliffs Park 319
   Surfrider Beach 78, 121
   the Wedge 264
   Tourmaline Surf Beach 321
   Trestles 279
   Zuma Beach 78
surfing 41, 63-6, 154-5, 257-9, 273-6,
   339, 384, 412, *see also* surf beaches
Surfrider Beach 78, 121
Surfrider Foundation 61
sustainable planning 298, 352
   alternative energy 62
   environmental issues 61-2
   Los Angeles 59
   Million Trees Initiative 59
   Santa Barbara 385
   solar energy 62
   Sonny Bono Salton Sea National
      Wildlife Refuge 372
   Surfrider Foundation 61
   Tree People 59
   trees 59
   water 62
   windmills 62
sustainable travel 16-18, 21, 26, 422
   accommodations 18
   carbon offset schemes 422
   food 18
   hybrid cars 62
   organizations & programs 18
   slow travel 16

Sustainable Vine Wine Tours 400
   transport 16, 71
swimming 63, 154-5, 384-5, 412

T
Tahquitz Canyon 69, 345, 352
taxis 429
Taylor, Elizabeth 114
telephone services 416-17
television 43-6
Temecula 345, 372-4
Terranea 128
Thai Town 40
theater 50
theaters 195-201
Third Street Promenade 125
Thunderboat Regatta 304
tidepooling 78, 128
Tijuana, (Mexico) 341-4, **342**
time 417
Timken House 303
Timken Museum of Art 299-300
tipping 55, 419
Torrance 161
Torrance High School 149
Torrey pine 59
Torrey Pines City Park 329-330
Torrey Pines State Reserve 330
tourist information 419, *see also*
   individual regional chapters
Tournament House 151
tours 419, *see also individual regional*
   chapters
Tower of California 299
Tower Theater 137
Toyota Grand Prix of Long Beach 160
train travel 424, 429
Tramway Gas Station 350
transportation 421-9, *see*
   also individual transport types
travel equipment 216
travel literature 15
Travel Town Museum 144
Tree People 59
trees 59
Trestles 279
TV studios 104, 146
Twentynine Palms 363, 364-8
Two-buck Chuck 55
Ty Warner Sea Center 379

U
U2 60
UCLA Film & Television Archive 117
UN Building 301

Under the Sea 158
Union Station 21, 133-4, 155, 217
United Artists Theater 138
Universal City Walk 145-6
Universal Studios Hollywood 145-6
University of California, Santa Barbara (UCSB) 376
University of California, Los Angeles (UCLA) 117-18
University of California, San Diego 282, 328, 329, 330
University of Southern California (USC) 120
Uptown (San Diego) 303-5
US Bank Tower 136, 156
US Grant Hotel 285
US Open Sandcastle Competition 304, 413
USS Midway 296-7

V
vaccinations 430
Vasquez, Richard 48
vegan travelers 55
Las Vegas 22
vegetarian travelers 55, 180
Venice 20, 125, **92**
    Abbot Kinney Blvd 126
    accommodations 169-70
    art galleries 208
    art walk 126
    attractions 125
    drinking 192-3
    food 182-3
    Original Muscle Beach 160
    shopping 207
    Venice canals 126
Venice Beach 154
Venice Blvd 40
Venice Boardwalk 26, 78, 125-6
Venice Muscle Beach 160
Ventura 19, 20, 402-4
Villa Aurora 122
Village Green Heritage Center 353
Villaraigosa, Anthony 59, 234, 234
Virginia Robinson Gardens 114
visas 415
Vista del Arroyo Hotel 151
visual arts 49-50
Vizcaíno, Sebastián 28

W
Walker Café 130
walking tours 155-7, 378
Walt Disney 230

Walt Disney Concert Hall 24, 47, 51, 134-5, 155, 6
Wambaugh, Joseph 49
Warner Bros 146, 237
Washington Mutual Bank 350
water supply 62, 352
Waterfront (San Diego) 309
Watts 39
Watts Riots 34
Watts Towers 141-2
Wayfarers Chapel 128-9
Wegeforth, Dr Harry 298
Wells Fargo History Museum 136, 156
West Hollywood 21, 40, 109-11, **88-9**
    accommodation 163-5
    art galleries 208
    attractions 109-11
    drinking 192
    farmers markets 176, 209
    food 176-7, 178
    Pacific Design Center 109-10
    Schindler House 24, 110
    shopping 207
    tourist information 101
West Hollywood Halloween Carnival 161, 414
West Nile Virus 431
West Ridge Trail 69
West, Nathanael 48
Westfield Horton Plaza Center 285, 315
Westlake 140-1, 186-7
Westwood 115-18, 166-7, 209, **90-1**
Wetlands 127
Wexler, Donald 350
whales 58, 67-8
whale-watching 67-70, see also individual regions
Whaley House 302
Wild Animal Park 23, 298
wildflowers 60, 369
wildlife 58-60, 412, see also individual animals
Will Rogers 154
Will Rogers Polo Club 123
Will Rogers State Beach 149
William Heath Davis House 284
Williams, E Stewart 350
Wilmington 130
Wiltern Theater 141, 197
wind farms 62, 352
windsurfing 65-6
wine 53, 55
wine tasting 375, 398
wineries

Alma Rosa Winery 399
Ampelos Cellars & Vineyard 399
Beckmen Vineyards 396
Buttonwood Farm Winery & Vineyeard 396
Fess Parker Winery & Vineyard 398
Firestone Vineyard 397
Foxen Vineyard 23, 398
Rancho Sisquoc 399-404
Rideau Vineyard 396
San Antonio Winery 139
Sunstone Vineyards & Winery 396
Temecula 373
tours 400
Zaca Mesa Winery 398
women travelers 420
Wonderland of Rocks 363
Woodruff, Dennis 233
World's Biggest Dinosaurs 26, 353
Wright, Frank Lloyd 24, 51, 108, 114, 159
Wrigley Gardens 151
Wrigley Memorial & Botanical Gardens 60, 220
Wrigley, William 151

Y
Yerxa, Cabot 353
yoga 71, 123, 155, 336
Yogananda, Paramahansa 123
Yucca Valley 419

Z
Zaca Mesa Winery 398
Zimmer Children's Museum 157
zoos
    Living Desert Zoo & Gardens 353
    Los Angeles Zoo & Botanical Gardens 143
    San Diego Wild Animal Park 341
    San Diego Zoo 298-9, 7
    Santa Barbara Zoological Garden 381-2
Zuma Beach 78, 154

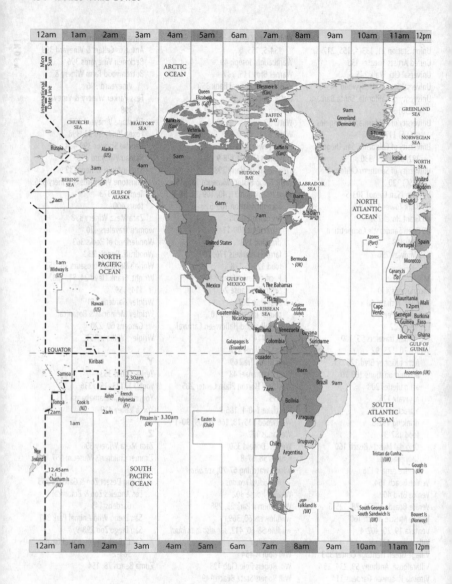

Top scale (left to right): 12pm | 1pm | 2pm | 3pm | 4pm | 5pm | 6pm | 7pm | 8pm | 9pm | 10pm | 11pm | 12am

Bottom scale (left to right): 12pm | 1pm | 2pm | 3pm | 4pm | 5pm | 6pm | 7pm | 8pm | 9pm | 10pm | 11pm | 12am

Mon / Sun
International Date Line

Svalbård (Norway)

Zemlya Frantsa-Iosifa (Russia)

Severnaya Zemlya (Russia)

Novaya Zemlya (Russia)

KARA SEA

LAPTEV SEA

Novosibirskie Ostrova (Russia)

EAST SIBERIAN SEA

BARENTS SEA

Sweden 1pm
Norway
Finland 2pm
3pm
Latvia
Denmark
Germany
Poland
Belarus
France
Austria
Ukraine
Romania
Italy
4pm
Greece
Turkey
Tunisia
MEDITERRANEAN SEA
Syria
Iraq
Algeria
Libya
Egypt
Niger
1pm
Chad
Sudan
Nigeria
Central African Republic
Congo
Gabon 1pm
Congo (Zaire)
Angola
Zambia
Malawi
Namibia
Zimbabwe
Botswana
Mozambique
South Africa

Russia 3pm | 4pm | 5pm | 6pm | 7pm | 9pm | 10pm | 11pm | 12am

Kazakhstan
Uzbekistan
Turkmenistan 4pm
Kyrgyzstan
Mongolia
Iran 3.30pm
Afghanistan 4.30pm
Pakistan 5pm
China 8pm
North Korea
South Korea
Japan
Saudi Arabia
Oman
4pm
Nepal 5.45pm
Tibet (China)
India 5.30pm
Eritrea
Yemen
Ethiopia 3pm
Somalia
Kenya
Tanzania

Myanmar 6.30pm
BAY OF BENGAL
Sri Lanka 5.30pm
Thailand
Vietnam
Taiwan
EAST CHINA SEA

SEA OF OKHOTSK

BERING SEA
3am
2am

NORTH PACIFIC OCEAN

Northern Mariana Is (US)

Marshall Is (US)
12am

Philippines 9pm
Palau

Federated States of Micronesia 11am

Kiribati

Nauru EQUATOR

Maldives

ARABIAN SEA

Malaysia
Indonesia

Papua New Guinea
Solomon Is

SOUTH PACIFIC OCEAN

Seychelles 4pm

Cocos (Keeling) Is (Aust) 6.30pm

East Timor

Vanuatu

New Caledonia (Fr)

Fiji

Madagascar
Mauritius
Reunion (Fr)

INDIAN OCEAN

Australia 9.30pm

10.30pm
Lord Howe Is (Aust)
11.30pm
Norfolk Is (Aust)

Prince Edward Is (S. Africa)

French Southern & Antarctic Territories (Fr)

New Zealand

TASMAN SEA

Heard & McDonald Is (Aust)

SOUTHERN OCEAN

MAP LEGEND

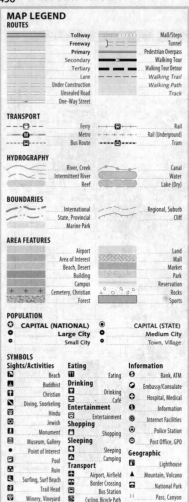

ROUTES

Tollway	Mall/Steps
Freeway	Tunnel
Primary	Pedestrian Overpass
Secondary	Walking Tour
Tertiary	Walking Tour Detour
Lane	Walking Trail
Under Construction	Walking Path
Unsealed Road	Track
One-Way Street	

TRANSPORT

Ferry	Rail
Metro	Rail (Underground)
Bus Route	Tram

HYDROGRAPHY

River, Creek	Canal
Intermittent River	Water
Reef	Lake (Dry)

BOUNDARIES

International	Regional, Suburb
State, Provincial	Cliff
Marine Park	

AREA FEATURES

Airport	Land
Area of Interest	Mall
Beach, Desert	Market
Building	Park
Campus	Reservation
Cemetery, Christian	Rocks
Forest	Sports

POPULATION

CAPITAL (NATIONAL)	CAPITAL (STATE)
Large City	Medium City
Small City	Town, Village

SYMBOLS

Sights/Activities
- Beach
- Buddhist
- Christian
- Diving, Snorkeling
- Hindu
- Jewish
- Monument
- Museum, Gallery
- Point of Interest
- Pool
- Ruin
- Surfing, Surf Beach
- Trail Head
- Winery, Vineyard
- Zoo, Bird Sanctuary

Eating
- Eating

Drinking
- Drinking
- Café

Entertainment
- Entertainment

Shopping
- Shopping

Sleeping
- Sleeping
- Camping

Transport
- Airport, Airfield
- Border Crossing
- Bus Station
- Cycling, Bicycle Path
- Parking Area

Information
- Bank, ATM
- Embassy/Consulate
- Hospital, Medical
- Information
- Internet Facilities
- Police Station
- Post Office, GPO

Geographic
- Lighthouse
- Mountain, Volcano
- National Park
- Pass, Canyon
- Picnic Area

LONELY PLANET OFFICES

Australia
Head Office
Locked Bag 1, Footscray, Victoria 3011
☎ 03 8379 8000, fax 03 8379 8111
talk2us@lonelyplanet.com.au

USA
150 Linden St, Oakland, CA 94607
☎ 510 893 8555, toll free 800 275 8555
fax 510 893 8572
info@lonelyplanet.com

UK
2nd Floor, 186 City Road,
London EC1V 2NT
☎ 020 7106 2100, fax 020 7106 2101
go@lonelyplanet.co.uk

Published by Lonely Planet Publications Pty Ltd
ABN 36 005 607 983

© Lonely Planet Publications Pty Ltd 2008

© photographers as indicated 2008

Cover photograph: Surfers gather next to a 1958 Ford wagon at Huntington Beach, Catherine Karnow/Corbis. Many of the images in this guide are available for licensing from Lonely Planet Images: www.lonelyplanetimages.com.